TORT LAW:
CASES, PERSPECTIVES, AND PROBLEMS

Fourth Edition

LexisNexis Law School Publishing Advisory Board

TORT LAW:
Cases, Perspectives, and Problems

Fourth Edition

THOMAS C. GALLIGAN, JR.
President and Professor of Humanities
Colby-Sawyer College

PHOEBE A. HADDON
Professor of Law
Temple University Beasley School of Law

FRANK L. MARAIST
Nolan J. Edwards and Holt B.
Harrison Professor of Law
Louisiana State University

FRANK M. MCCLELLAN
Professor of law
Temple University Beasley School of Law

MICHAEL L. RUSTAD
Thomas F. Lambert Jr. Professor of Law
and Co-Director of Intellectual Property Law Concentration
Suffolk University Law School

NICOLAS P. TERRY
Chester A. Myers Professor of Law
Co-Director, Center for Health Law Studies
Saint Louis University School of Law

STEPHANIE M. WILDMAN
Professor of Law and Director, Center
for Social Justice and Public Service
Santa Clara University School of Law

Library of Congress Cataloging-in-Publication Data

Tort law : cases, perspectives, problems / Thomas C. Galligan . . . [et al.]. — 4th ed.
    p. cm.
Includes bibliographical references and index.
ISBN 0-8205-7040-0 (hardbound)
1. Torts — United States — Cases. I. Galligan, Thomas C.
KF1249.T656 2007
346.7303 — dc22

2007025970

Editorial Offices
744 Broad Street, Newark, NJ 07102 (973) 820-2000
201 Mission St., San Francisco, CA 94105-1831 (415) 908-3200
701 East Water Street, Charlottesville, VA 22902-7587 (434) 972-7600
www.lexis.com

(Pub. 3103)

ACKNOWLEDGMENTS

Tom Galligan would like to thank and acknowledge his former friend, colleague and co-author, Jerry Phillips; Tom thinks of him often. Tom Galligan would also like to thank his colleagues, Lisa Tedeschi and Linda Varnum, whose support enables him to continue to think about torts.

Phoebe A. Haddon and Frank M. McClellan are deeply grateful for the patience and the excellent research, editing, and proofreading of Joshua Garbarino, a 2007 graduate of Syracuse University College of Law, who spent his last year of law school at Temple University Beasley School of Law. Phoebe Haddon also thanks John B. Lough, Jr., Trina Grillo Research Associate and Assistant to the Director, Center for Public Service and Social Justice at Santa Clara University, for his proofreading and editing assistance. Both Frank and Phoebe thank the library staff at Temple Law School, in particular, John Necci and Leopoldo Carino, for their diligence. They thank Andrew Seaberg, Rachel Kaplan, Avi Cohen, Tyler Graden and Ahmed Riaz for additional research support.

Michael L. Rustad thanks Daryl Abbas, Matthew Bowie, John Gillis, Michelle Dhanda, Molly Hartman, Nicole Nelson, and Jo-Na Williams for their research assistance and tireless efforts in editing the manuscript. He would also like to thank Chryss J. Knowles, Tom Koenig, John Teeter and Martha Chamallas for their insights and ideas. He greatly appreciates the research assistance and editorial work of his daughter, Erica Knowles Rustad, a law student at Fordham University Law School.

Nicolas P. Terry thanks his research assistant, Natalie Kean.

Stephanie Wildman thanks Jennifer Alesio, Brad Jacklin, and John B. Lough, Jr. for diligent research help in completing the manuscript. Special thanks to Ivy Flores and Dorice Kunis for their administrative contributions. She would like to acknowledge Robert Rabin, her first torts teacher, and John Adler, Marc Franklin, Tom Grey, Trina Grillo, Jeremy Harrison, and Jack Pemberton for being wonderful torts colleagues. Special thanks also go to Jack Pemberton for the evolution of the prima facie case of negligence scenarios (Chapter 4).

PREFACE

In this fourth edition we place increased emphasis on problems and perspectives as a means of promoting dialogue and thought about the critical issues in tort law which courts, legislatures, practitioners, and other participants in the legal system face today. This edition presents cases, statutes, relevant sections of Restatements (including proposed drafts), empirical data, and competing tort theories in a problem-oriented format that is designed to help students acquire a sophisticated understanding of tort law through active learning. Each of the substantive chapters contains informative notes and at least four problems in order to teach tort law doctrine and procedural issues through applied examples. Many chapters contain more than this minimum number of practice problems to help students hone their skill at applying legal principles to concrete fact patterns.

Chapter One sets the stage for the substantive chapters by introducing the basic concepts and methods of torts. The first chapter is unique among American torts casebooks in its examination of how the dominant twenty-first century tort theories influence judicial decision-making and scholarship. Being introduced to multiple perspectives helps students to understand the larger public policies underlying tort verdicts. Tort law is "a battleground of social theory." W. PAGE KEETON, ET AL., PROSSER AND KEETON ON THE LAW OF TORTS § 3, p.15 (5th ed. 1984). In order to be effective advocates, attorneys must understand the broader societal context such as the role of culture, economic efficiency, corrective justice, race, gender, and political conflict in order to be effective advocates.

The first chapter helps first-year students understand the complexities of tort doctrine by introducing the concepts and methods of tort law and provides examples and explanations of the key procedural steps in the life of a tort case from the complaint stage to the appellate level. The chapter includes basic information on how to read and brief appellate cases. This introductory chapter also describes legal and equitable remedies, the social functions of tort law, and explains how tort law interacts with civil procedure.

First year law students should not be studying tort cases in isolation. Students need to understand the broad public policies and tort politics underlying civil liability, not just the black-letter law. The seven editors of this casebook have diverse backgrounds and views that represent varying jurisprudential traditions. Judges, legislators, administrators, and juries face value conflicts when resolving tort claims. Case law analysis often draws upon concepts from other fields. Law and economics topics such as loss spreading, risk attitude, moral hazard, transactions costs, and cost minimization or social efficiency are useful tools in examining tort law. Race, class, gender, pragmatism, social justice, and other sociological factors play a role in many tort cases.

The cases, problems, and questions in this text present an opportunity to learn about the broader jurisprudential theories underlying all of tort law. The six tort perspectives addressed in Chapter One are: (1) *Law and Economics*; (2) *Corrective Justice*; (3) *Critical Race Theory*; (4) *Critical Feminism*; (5) *Pragmatism*; and (6) *Social Justice*. These competing perspectives shed light on many of the appellate cases and issues raised in the text. Chapter One, for example, explains how the competing perspectives illuminate different views of the McDonald's hot coffee case, perhaps the most famous tort story in the past decade. The McDonald's case helps students understand the difference between the three bases of tort liability: intentional torts, negligence, and strict liability. The six tort perspectives also illuminate the appellate decision presented in the chapter, *Perez v. Wyeth Laboratories, Inc.*, 734 A.2d 1245 (N.J. 1999). Each of the subsequent chapters features cases, problems, and perspectives that can be easily adapted to either a traditional case-method or problem approach. The updated edition includes teachable cases both classic and new.

The overarching goal of this book is to provide students with the tools to go beyond passive memorization of case holdings and to feel empowered to be active participants in the discussion of the important issues raised in torts. This edition emphasizes the development of critical inquiry skills by offering students opportunities to utilize what they have learned in response to the problems and contemporary tort law debates raised in the notes in each chapter. The book builds upon the belief that students are best served by being exposed to more than the distilled view of law which often comes from reading appellate cases in a vacuum and without an understanding of the legal system and social environment that informs the legal context of decided cases.

Chapter One provides law students with an overview of the torts system and how this subject fits into the larger picture. It will help students understand the differences between tort law and their other first year subjects. Subsequent chapters invite the students to return to the competing perspectives and policy discussion offered in the first chapter while they are acquiring increased understanding of the substantive law and attaining competence in problem-solving.

The authors dedicate this book to the memory of Jerry J. Phillips, whose dynamic classroom and thoughtful writings took the broad perspective reflected in this edition. Jerry was one of the greatest tort teachers and scholars of his generation and the senior editor on the first three editions of this casebook. He encouraged his students and colleagues to see the interrelationship between concepts. Professor Phillips found ideas fascinating and he lived life with a smile on his face and in his heart.

TABLE OF CONTENTS

Chapter 1

PERSPECTIVES ON TORT LAW

A. INTRODUCTION

> "Certainty generally is illusion, and repose is not the destiny of man" [sic]

Oliver Wendell Holmes, *The Path of the Law*, 10 HARV. L. REV. 457, 466 (1897).

Tort law provides monetary compensation to redress a plaintiff's claim that the defendant injured her, interfered with her property, invaded her privacy, or invaded another legally protected interest. In some circumstances, where future harm is threatened, equitable relief, usually in the form of an injunction, may be available. While the circumstances that led to the harm might also support a criminal prosecution, claim for breach of contract, or other civil law complaint, the law of torts focuses on non-contractual rights and liabilities arising where no one promised to pay for the damages and without regard to whether the government could prosecute the actor for a crime. DAN B. DOBBS, THE LAW OF TORTS § 1, p. 1 (2001) ("A tort is conduct that amounts to a legal wrong and that causes harm for which courts will impose civil liability."). *See also* Thomas C. Galligan Jr., *Deterrence: The Legitimate Function of the Public Tort*, 58 WASH. & LEE L. REV. 1019, 1022 (2001) (torts is about redress or equitable relief to prevent or restrain injury).

Major technological advances create new forms of injury that require updating the law of torts. *See, e.g.*, Nicolas P. Terry, *When the "Machine That Goes 'Ping'" Causes Harm: Default Torts Rules and Technologically-Mediated Health Care Injuries*, 46 ST. LOUIS U. L.J. 37 (2002). In the 1960s, products liability evolved to address the social problems caused by marketing dangerously defective products. Today, tort law is evolving to address new injuries from the vulnerabilities of Internet networks. Society faces new threats related to cybersecurity, software, and the mutual vulnerabilities of the networked world. Software vulnerabilities negligently enable cybercrimes such as the misappropriation of trade secrets, computer crimes and abuse, and economic espionage. Creative lawyers apply ancient personal property torts, such as trespass to chattels, to counter threats such as computer viruses and the disruption of massive amounts of e-mail spam. Old torts counter new Internet-related threats such as the enablement of cybercrime, inadequate cybersecurity, online privacy, and identity theft. *See* Michael L. Rustad & Thomas H. Koenig, *Rebooting Cybertort Law*, 80 WASH. L. REV. 335 (2005); Nicolas P. Terry, *A Medical Ghost in the E-Health Machine*, 14 HEALTH MATRIX 225 (2004); *Cyber-Malpractice: Legal Exposure for Cybermedicine*, 25 AM. J. L. & MED. 327 (1999); *Legal Pitfalls of Cybermedicine*, MED. ETHICS 4, LAHEY CLINIC, (Winter 2000).

Tort law offers a unique opportunity for insight into the legal system far beyond the comprehension of a set of legal rules that define the various torts. The new law student will gain an appreciation of the fundamental value conflicts faced by judges, legislators, administrators, and juries who must resolve tort claims. The tort system is a site for struggles between the societal need for containment of risks and freedom to take action. The student should reflect on the process by which the legal system attempts to resolve these disputes and the ethical dilemmas that arise out of the litigation process. A true appreciation of the public policy implications of tort law requires reflection on the immediate and long-range impact of the tort system. As Justice Mathew O. Tobriner observed, while commenting on "this risk-infested society:" "Our current crowded and computerized society compels the interdependence of its members." *Tarasoff v. Regents of the University of California*, 551 P.2d 334, 347 (Cal. 1976).

Over the past few decades, tort law has been at the center stage of public policy debates. William L. Prosser, in his classic tort treatise, described tort law as a "battleground of social theory." W. PAGE KEETON, ET AL., PROSSER AND KEETON ON THE LAW OF TORTS § 3, p. 15 (5th ed. 1984). Today competing perspectives characterize the field of tort law. While some law professors may view the subject as value-free and neutral, tort law remains inevitably contested and contestable socio-legal terrain. Consider how: (1) plaintiffs state a claim and defendants respond to those causes of action; (2) the tort litigation process determines the facts (the events that produced the injuries) and the law (the rules determining who should bear the loss); (3) different perspectives reflect value preferences supporting the plaintiff's claim for legal redress and the defendant's response; (4) identity categories, such as race, gender, and economic wealth, reverberate throughout the torts processes addressed by this casebook. To be a successful tort lawyer in the twenty-first century, litigators need to understand a case from different and often competing perspectives.

In every historical era, tort perspectives reflect the dominant ideologies. The jurisprudence of legal formalism dominated early tort law. At early common law, a tort plaintiff would need to "show that he had sustained a physical contact on his person or property, due to the activity of another." Charles O. Gregory, *Trespass to Negligence to Absolute Liability*, 37 VA. L. REV. 359, 361–62 (1951). Legal formalism constrained early tort law; a plaintiff would be denied a cause of action simply because his or her injury could not fit into an "existing and recognized writ." WILLIAM L. PROSSER, HANDBOOK OF THE LAW OF TORTS § 4, p. 19 (4th ed. 1971); *see also* W. PAGE KEETON, ET AL., PROSSER AND KEETON ON THE LAW OF TORTS § 4 at 20 (5th ed. 1984). Writs were formalistic forms of action used to vindicate rights and remedies. For an excellent history of tort law, exposing underlying value choices, see MORTON J. HORWITZ, THE TRANSFORMATION OF AMERICAN LAW, 1780–1860, at 85–99 (1977).

The legal realists of the 1920s and 1930s challenged formalistic assumptions by conducting empirical research and applying the social sciences to the law. WILLIAM TWINING, KARL LLEWELLYN AND THE REALIST MOVEMENT 54–55 (1973). Today all good lawyers are realists who examine cases within their existing social context. Contemporary tort law is a pluralistic field with diverse perspectives on how to resolve an evolving and varied set of legal dilemmas.

WALTER H. BECKHAM, JR., ET AL., REPORT TO THE AMERICAN BAR ASSOCIATION: TOWARDS A JURISPRUDENCE OF INJURY: THE CONTINUING CREATION OF A SYSTEM OF SUBSTANTIVE JUSTICE IN AMERICAN TORT LAW 2–10 (1984). The purpose of this chapter is to introduce tort law, its background, social functions, and relationship to other first year subjects.

Tort law is a common law subject, but it is also private law with a public purpose at the center of political controversy. President George W. Bush called for limitations on tort liability for medical malpractice and an end to frivolous lawsuits in his 2007 State of the Union Address. President George W. Bush, State of the Union Address (Jan. 23, 2007). Indeed, President Bush called for tort reform in nearly every State of the Union Address of his administration and he believes introducing limitations on tort law is a high domestic priority. *See, e.g.,* President George W. Bush, State of the Union Address (Jan. 28, 2003); (Feb. 2, 2005); (Jan 31, 2006). Tort critics claim the overuse of tort remedies is responsible for declining U.S. competitiveness, excessive delays in developing new products, the withdrawal of useful pharmaceuticals and medical devices from the market, and high insurance rates. These "tort reformers" claim that defensive practices to avoid groundless litigation create a tort tax on all goods and services. In contrast, plaintiff's lawyers believe they are protecting the public from careless or dangerous actors.

B.   COMPETING PERSPECTIVES ON TORT LAW

For almost thirty years now, a poor beleaguered torts professor, who once could rest comfortably on the mastery of Prosser and the latest case law developments, has been assaulted from any number of directions. . . . [I]t was the economists, championed by the path-breaking work of Guido Calabresi and Richard Posner, who recast analysis of the tort system in economic efficiency terms. Strong medicine for the uninitiated. But at least the adherents of optimal resource allocation and their antagonists from other "law and" perspectives labored within the same vineyards — namely, academia.

Robert L. Rabin, *Book Review, Law for Law's Sake,* 105 YALE L. J. 2261, 2261 (1996).

The torts casebook as traditionally conceived does not devote much attention to competing perspectives and academic commentary. Traditional casebooks, for example, do not address the way tort doctrines such as the reasonable man theory reflects patriarchal assumptions. All casebooks discuss legal remedies but few examine the gender injustice that results from caps on noneconomic damages. Every torts casebook examines risk/utility as a method of setting the standard of care in negligence, but few critically examine this doctrine from a law and economics perspective. While law students need to understand the black letter law contained in torts treatises, law students, like their law professors and practitioners, must also master the competing perspectives that shed light on tort rules. Tort law represents more than a collection of causes of action; it also embodies ways of seeing the world.

Two competing perspectives in tort law are law and economics and corrective justice, which are "unfriendly camps." Law and economics focuses on deterrence, paying little attention to justice, fairness, or distribution. In contrast, corrective justice focuses on justice issues avoiding questions of allocative efficiency, externalities, or the economic welfare of society. Gary T. Schwartz, *Mixed Theories of Tort Law: Affirming Both Deterrence and Corrective Justice*, 75 TEX. L. REV. 1801, 1801 (1997) (discussing two opposing camps in tort law). Scholars widely acknowledge the impact that the law and economics movement has had on the study of tort law. *See, e.g.,* STEVEN SHAVELL, ECONOMIC ANALYSIS OF ACCIDENTS LAW (1987); DONALD WITTMAN, ECONOMIC FOUNDATIONS OF LAW AND ORGANIZATION (2006), and Keith N. Hylton, *The Influence of Litigation Costs on Deterrence Under Strict Liability and Under Negligence*, 10 INT'L. REV. L. & ECON. 161 (1990). Though controversial, economics provides a useful heuristic framework to approach nearly every tort doctrine and defense.

Beginning in the 1970s, corrective justice theorists such as Jules Coleman, George Fletcher, and Ernest Weinrib began to examine liability rules from the perspective of fairness, allocation, or distribution of resources. Gary T. Schwartz, *Mixed Theories of Tort Law: Affirming Both Deterrence & Corrective Justice*, 75 TEX. L. REV. 1801, 1802–03 (1997). While many scholars, lawyers, and judges employ the law and economics or corrective justice views, critical race theory, feminist jurisprudence, pragmatism, and social justice also offer useful insights challenging the more dominant views. *See* John C. P. Goldberg, *Twentieth-Century Tort Theory*, 91 GEO. L.J. 513, 514 (2003) (explaining the interpretative, prescriptive, and critique of five dominant tort theories: "compensation-deterrence theory, enterprise liability theory, economic deterrence theory, social justice theory, and individual justice theory"). The next section introduces some of these theories and provides examples of how the multiple perspectives may promote a better understanding of the policies underlying tort cases and theories.

For one professor's description of a torts course infused with perspectives, see Anita Bernstein, *Perspectives on a Torts Course*, 43 J. LEGAL EDUC. 289 (1993). *See also* SAUL LEVMORE, FOUNDATIONS OF TORT LAW vi (1994) (explaining how law and economics, feminist theory, statistics, sociology and political theory can provide the modern lawyer with "tools with which to understand the materials at hand"); ROBERT L. RABIN, PERSPECTIVES ON TORT LAW 184–303 (4th ed. 1995).

C. SIX PERSPECTIVES AND A WELL-KNOWN TORT STORY

At least a thousand media accounts reported that a clumsy elderly woman spilled coffee on her lap, sued McDonald's because the hot coffee she ordered was too hot, and recovered almost three million dollars. *See, e.g., Big Jury Award for Coffee Burn*, N.Y. TIMES, Aug. 19 1994, at D5; *McDonald's Cup of Scalding Coffee: 2.9 Million Award*, CHI. TRIB., Aug, 18 1994, at 1; Andrea Gerlin, *A Matter of Degree*, WALL ST. J., Sept. 1 1994, at A1. The mischaracterization of McDonald's hot coffee case has done more than any other tort horror story to create a climate of distrust about America's civil justice system. The vast majority of law students entering the first year law school throughout the United States believe that the McDonald's hot coffee case is a tort story about frivolous lawsuits. Each semester, Professor Michael Rustad has polled his first year law students about their attitudes toward the McDonald's hot coffee case. THOMAS H. KOENIG & MICHAEL L. RUSTAD, IN DEFENSE OF TORT LAW 7 (2001). Over the past ten years, he has found that an average of three out of four law students viewed the McDonald's hot coffee case as a frivolous lawsuit. When he distributed a trial exhibit demonstrating the severity of third degree burns caused by coffee, one student remarked, with the compassion of a buzz saw: "the old lady must have spilled the coffee on herself for a quick buck."

Although the case is unusually well-known, few entering law students actually know the facts of the case. Learning how to see a case from both the plaintiff's perspective and the defense perspective is a critically important lawyering skill. The better lawyer will evaluate a case employing diverse perspectives, not just the defense or plaintiff's side. Inaccurate truths about the McDonald's hot coffee case have misled the public. Significantly, the case, as widely reported, lacked any contextualization of the plaintiff's life experience or the corporation's choices. Few journalists reported that McDonald's served its coffee at 180 to 190 degree temperatures. *Id.* at 7. In contrast, the temperature of home-brewed coffee generally ranges from 130 to 140 degrees. McDonald's own records demonstrated that it had received more than 700 prior complaints about burns suffered from its super-heated coffee. *Id.* at 8. Coffee served at that higher temperature has the potential to produce napalm-like injuries, as was the case in the factual account of the McDonald's hot coffee case. As the temperature of coffee decreases to 155 degrees and below, the risk of serious burns goes down exponentially. *Id.* at 7. Mrs. Liebeck (the injured plaintiff) underwent excruciatingly painful debridement procedures to remove layers of dead skin and underwent several skin graft operations. *Id.*

Mrs. Liebeck initially sought out a lawyer to help her recover reimbursement for her medical bills. She filed a strict products liability lawsuit (discussed in chapter 8 of the casebook) after McDonald's flatly refused to pay her medical bills. She introduced past medical bills for $9,900, but made no claim for future medical costs. Mrs. Liebeck, who worked as a sales clerk at the time of her injury, did not make a claim for lost earnings. The New Mexico jury awarded the plaintiff $200,000 in compensatory damages, reduced to $160,000 because the jury found Mrs. Liebeck partially at fault. Notably, however, the jury awarded the plaintiff $2.7 million in punitive damages. The trial judge reduced the punitive damages award to $480,000. (See chapter 15 for a discussion of damages.) The parties reached a confidential, post-trial settlement.

Judge Robert H. Scott presided over the McDonald's hot coffee case in an Albuquerque, New Mexico state court. Judge Scott entered a final judgment in an unpublished opinion in which he stated that it "was appropriate to punish and deter" McDonald's corporate coffee policy. Judge Robert Scott, a self-described conservative Republican, said the case "was not a runaway. I was there." Robert Cooter & Thomas Ulen, *The McDonald's Hot Coffee Case*, (2000), *available at* http://www.cooter-ulen.com/tort_liability.htm.

Rather than focusing on the woman who spent more than a week in the hospital because of severe burns from needlessly overheated coffee, the mass media extended sympathy to a Fortune 500 company, ignoring the fact that it had received hundreds of reported burn claims related to its hot coffee prior to this case. In order to become a knowledgeable critic of the tort system, it is important to see tort cases like the McDonald's case from multiple perspectives. The next section explores how the plaintiff's attorney as well as defense counsel would use competing tort law perspectives.

[1] Law and Economics

[a] Concepts & Methods

"The Law and Economics movement has established a strong beachhead in law and legal education because it provides a powerful tool for assessing the costs and benefits of a given legal rule or case outcome." BAILEY KULIN & JEFFREY W. STEMPEL, FOUNDATION OF THE LAW: AN INTERDISCIPLINARY AND JURISPRUDENTIAL PRIMER 29 (1994). Tort law is largely about reducing the cost of accidents in the most efficient manner possible. "Standard textbooks in economics define the field as the study of resource allocation in the presence of scarcity. Laws affect resource allocation and help to determine what, how, and for whom." DONALD WITTMAN, ECONOMIC FOUNDATIONS OF LAW AND ORGANIZATION 2 (2006).

Tort law determines who bears the burden of an injury and what forms of injury are compensable. TORT LAW IN AMERICAN HISTORY xi (Kermit L. Hall ed. 1987) (stating that the critical question of tort law is, "who would pay for the damages and on what basis — what legal standard — would their responsibility be based"). The twenty-first century tort lawyer needs to be able to make policy-based arguments considering competing perspectives. If you are making an argument before a judge with a law and economics perspective, you may need to consider concepts you studied in your economics class such as Pareto Optimality or Kaldor-Hicks Efficiency. Pareto efficiency is an allocative decision that makes at least one individual better without making any other individual worse off. In contrast, the Kaldor-Hicks compensation principle would define an outcome as efficient if those made better off would compensate those made worse by a given allocative decision. Many economically based models have unrealistic assumptions such as "the parties have perfect information" and "there are no transaction costs." Another criticism is that efficiency leaves considerations of consumer protection, fairness, and distributive justice unaddressed or unduly minimized.

Economics provides an analytical framework to approach many tort law issues. "Tort reformers" use law and economics arguments such as specific cost-containment and efficiency to argue for caps on damages. For an analysis of the role these arguments play in contemporary tort reform battles, see Frank McClellan, *Medical Malpractice Law, Morality and the Cultural Wars, A Critical Assessment of the Tort Reform Movement*, 27 J. LEGAL MED. 33, 42 (2006).

Law and economics, an interdisciplinary field, applies economic theory to examine the formation as well as impact of tort law and tort damages. Public choice, neoclassical, and game theory are, in turn, competing approaches within law and economics. However, the two most important forms for the study of tort law are *positive* (descriptive or "what is") economics or *normative* (prescriptive or "what should be") economics. Positivistic economics employs the vocabulary of the scientific method. A judge employing a positive economics perspective will ask what rule of tort law will induce the industry to undertake efficient precautions. Positive economics describes how legal rules influence behavior whereas normative economics prescribes changes that will increase the efficiency of legal rules or institutions. *See* WILLIAM M. LANDES & RICHARD POSNER, THE ECONOMIC STRUCTURE OF TORT LAW (1987); *see generally* MITCHELL A. POLINSKY, AN INTRODUCTION TO LAW AND ECONOMICS (3d ed. 2003); *see also* MITCHELL A. POLINSKY AND STEVEN SHAVELL (EDS.), HANDBOOK OF LAW AND ECONOMICS (2006) (discussing basic economic principles and applying the economic principles to legal problems).

"For law-and-economics scholars, deterrence is the primary rationale for torts, easily outstripping corrective justice and compensation." Michelle M. Mello & Troyen Brennan, *Deterrence of Medical Errors: Theory and Evidence for Malpractice Reform*, 80 TEX. L. REV. 1595, 1603 (1995). Guido Calabresi's THE COST OF ACCIDENTS: A LEGAL AND ECONOMIC ANALYSIS (1970) applied economic analysis to explain the functioning of specific and general deterrence to tort remedies. It is "axiomatic that the principal function of accident law is to reduce the sum of the costs of accidents and the costs of avoiding accidents." *Id.* at 26. Specific deterrence assesses a price to a particular wrongful act whereas general deterrence fulfills the larger function of vindicating the broader societal interest by making wrongful acts more expensive and less attractive to potential wrongdoers. *Id.* at 26–27. "The idea of punishment or retribution is that it is just for the defendant to suffer for his misconduct. The idea of deterrence is quite different. It is that a sufficient sum should be exacted from the defendant to make repetition of the misconduct unlikely." DAN B. DOBBS, THE LAW OF TORTS § 381, p. 1063 (2000). Personal injury verdicts send the deterrent signal "tort does not pay." *Rookes v. Barnard*, [1964] L.R. 28 at 66 (H.L.).

Judge Guido Calabresi, formerly Yale Law School's Dean and currently a judge on the U.S. Court of Appeals for the Second Circuit, has been a prominent figure in law and economics. He broke new ground with *Some Thoughts on Risk Distribution and the Law of Torts*, 70 YALE L. J. 499 (1961), by applying economic principles to tort law. Law and economics has become the most influential paradigm of torts scholarship. Judge Calabresi would later expand on his 1961 article's economic approach to torts in THE COST OF ACCIDENTS: A LEGAL AND ECONOMIC ANALYSIS (1970), developing a framework for analyzing market deterrence on achieving accident law's primary function of reducing the cost of accidents. Calabresi argued that accident law can best be viewed as a social problem to be cured in the most efficient and optimum way. *Id.* at 26. Calabresi argues that primary accident losses may be reduced where primary accident costs exceed prevention costs. *Id.* Furthermore, loss-spreading arrangements reduce secondary losses. *Id.* at 39–40. Calabresi and Hirschoff propose a search for the cheapest cost-avoider as the *sine qua non* of strict products liability.

Guido Calabresi & Jon T. Hirschoff, *Toward a Test for Strict Liability in Torts*, 81 YALE L. J. 1055, 1060 (1972). For example, the manufacturer is usually in the best position to avoid losses in the research laboratory as opposed to the consumer marketplace. Law and economic scholars often view judge-made common law as an attempt to "bring about (economically) efficient results." Richard S. Markovitz, *On the Economic Inefficiencies of Liberal-Corrective-Justice-Securing Law of Torts,* 2006 U. ILL. L. REV. 525, 538. Law and economics scholars who determine efficiency on the grounds of wealth maximization have influenced American tort teachers who now focus upon efficiencies, transactions costs, redistributive motives, and indeterminacies.

The more liberal law and economics scholars go far beyond wealth maximization and economic efficiency in their analysis. Judge Calabresi incorporates his economic analysis in his judicial decision-making. *See Ciraolo v. City of New York*, 216 F.3d 236, 242 (2d Cir. 2000) (Calabresi, J., concurring). Tort law's capacity to efficiently punish and deter conduct through socially compensatory damages is another economics-based observation central to Calabresi's theory of punitive damages. He reasoned that in many cases, "compensatory damages are . . . an inaccurate measure of the true harm caused by an activity." *Ciralo*, 216 F.3d at 244. Judge Calabresi contends that punitive damages in tort law play multiple roles including the enforcement of social norms through private attorney's general, deterrence. Guido Calabresi, *The Complexity of Torts — The Case of Punitive Damages*, in EXPLORING TORT LAW 333, 337 (M. Stuart Madden ed. 2005). Judge Calabresi takes issues with law and economics proponents who reduce complex tort rights and remedies to economic efficiency. *Id.* at 334.

Economists quickly embraced Ronald Coase's theorem that the choice of a specific legal rule did not affect allocative efficiency. Ronald Coase, *The Problem of Social Cost*, 3 J.L. & ECON. 1 (1960). In order to carry out a market transaction it is necessary to discover who it is that one wishes to deal with, to inform people that one wishes to deal and on what terms, to conduct negotiations leading up to a bargain, to draw up the contract, to undertake the inspection needed to make sure that the terms of the contract are being observed, and so on. These operations are often extremely costly, sufficiently so to prevent many transactions that would be carried out in a world in which the pricing system worked without costs. *Id.* at 7.

Professor Coase received the Sveriges Riksbank Prize in Economic Sciences in Memory of Alfred Nobel (commonly referred to as the Nobel Prize in Economics) in 1991 "for his discovery and clarification of the significance of transaction costs and property rights for the institutional structure and functioning of the economy." Nobel Foundation, http://nobelprize.org/nobel_prizes/economics/laureates/1991/index.html (last visited February 4, 2006). *See also* MICHAEL G. GAURE & GORAN SKOGH, THE ECONOMIC ANALYSIS OF ENVIRONMENT POLICY AND LAW: AN INTRODUCTION (2003). "The Coase Theorem is based on exchange. Exchange is a bargain. Bargaining is a game." JULES L. COLEMAN & JEFFRIE G. MURPHY, PHILOSOPHY OF LAW: AN INTRODUCTION TO JURISPRUDENCE 216 (1990).

For more on the law and economics perspective, see RICHARD A. POSNER, ECONOMIC ANALYSIS OF LAW (5th ed. 1998); RICHARD POSNER, PRINCIPLES AND

METHODS OF LAW AND ECONOMICS ENHANCING NORMATIVE ANALYSIS (2005);
MARGARET OPPENHEIMER & NICHOLAS MERCURIO, LAW AND ECONOMICS:
ALTERNATIVE ECONOMIC APPROACHES TO LEGAL AND REGULATORY ISSUES (2004);
CASS R. SUNSTEIN, BEHAVIOR LAW AND ECONOMICS (2000); HANS-BERND SCHÄFER
AND CLAUS OTT, THE ECONOMIC ANALYSIS OF CIVIL LAW (2004).

[b] Applying Law & Economics to the Hot Coffee Case

Tort lawyers for both sides can apply economic analysis to the McDonald's
hot coffee case. Defense counsel for McDonald's Corporation could apply neoclassical economic theory to argue that the company was not engaged in excessive risk-creation. After all, McDonald's sold billions of cups of coffee and
registered only 700 or so complaints that resulted in settlements. Legal norms
that improve the safety of consumers are not cost-free and are borne by the
consuming public in the form of higher prices. Increased tort verdicts will
increase the price of coffee and perhaps even change the preferences of consumers. Do consumers prefer lower prices or slightly safer products? HANS-
BERND SCHÄFER & CLAUS OTT, THE ECONOMIC ANALYSIS OF CIVIL LAWS 9 (2004).
The task of law and economics is to develop tort rules "with respect to their
effect on the well-being of individuals in society." LOUIS KAPLOW & STEVEN
SHAVELL, FAIRNESS VERSUS WELFARE 3–4 (2002).

Where the probability of injury is low, a punitive damages award against
McDonald's may "over deter" socially beneficial activities. *TVT Records v.
Island Def Jam Music Group*, 279 F. Supp. 2d 413, 430 (S.D.N.Y. 2003). The
deterrent message sent by a large punitive damages award will result in inefficiency. Consumers prefer superheated coffee, judging from the billions of cups
sold. Punitive damages will encourage the company to serve tepid coffee causing consumers to change their preferences and perhaps drink more beer, tea,
or other beverages. The company could argue that punitive damages will create a disincentive for marketing coffee in a way that reflects consumer preferences. A cost-benefit analysis might balance the benefits of selling 2.5 billion
cups of McDonald's coffee against only approximately 700 consumer injuries.
McDonald's could argue that if it lowered the temperature of its coffee, there
will not be a net benefit. McDonald's best neoclassical economics argument is
that the efficiency rule dictates that it should be able to continue selling its hot
coffee since the cost of lowering the coffee is greater than the benefit of eliminating 700 burn injuries.

A plaintiff will argue that McDonald's should be assessed a large punitive
damages to deter the company from failing to take prompt remedial steps in
the wake of hundreds of prior reported injuries. The social cost of under deterrence is that "actor[s] will have an incentive to undertake activities whose
social costs exceed their social benefits." *Ciraolo, supra*, 216 F.3d at 243
(Calabresi, J., concurring). *See also* LOUIS KAPLOW & STEVEN SHAVELL, FAIRNESS
VERSUS WELFARE 318–31 (2002) (arguing that proportional sanctions on the
criminal side of the law, based solely on the factor of the gravity of the offense,
will result in under deterrence and will increase social costs). The plaintiff will

argue that McDonald's can spread the loss paying the judgment across millions of sales. The giant corporation is in the best position to pass costs along to its customers.

A law and economics oriented court might ask whether McDonald's burden of precaution exceeds the costs of injury avoidance. If the burden of precaution exceeds the probability of the injury factored with the severity of the injury should it occur, then this precaution is not cost-justified. The defense would contend that minimizing a mere 700 injuries might not be worth the overall costs of lowering the temperature on 2.5 billion cups of coffee. The plaintiff might counter that the 700 prior reported injuries underestimates the magnitude of the risk, because many unreported injuries due to the superheated coffee may have likely occurred.

Plaintiff's counsel would argue that a large punitive damages award is essential to economic deterrence. Punitive damages, according to Judge Calabresi, may be viewed as "socially compensatory damages," because they are "designed to make society whole" as compared with compensatory damages, which are "assessed to make an individual victim whole." *Ciraolo*, 216 F.3d at 245 (Calabresi, J., concurring). Actors are continually engaging in cost-benefit analyses to determine whether a given activity is worth the price. Punitive damages serve as a mechanism for ensuring that the wrongdoer "bears all the costs of its actions, and is thus appropriately deterred from causing harm, in those categories of cases in which compensatory damages alone result in systematic underassessment of costs, and hence in systematic under-deterrence." *Id.* at 243.

Since McDonald's is a multi-billion dollar corporation, it could be argued that punitive damages should even be larger than the amount the New Mexico jury awarded to achieve deterrence. The net effect of the punitive damages award was that McDonald's only lost two days worth of coffee revenue. Stan Diel, *Activist Nader Raps Suit-Limit Supporters*, BIRMINGHAM NEWS, March 10, 1995, at 1. Social justice theorists and other commentators urge that punitive damage awards should bear some relevance to the wealth of the defendant. Michael Rustad & Thomas Koenig, *The Historical Continuity of Punitive Damages Awards: Reforming the Tort Reformers*, 42 AM. U. L. REV. 1269, 1317–18 (1993) (supporting rule that punitive damages be calibrated to the wealth of the defendant to maximize deterrence).

[2]   Corrective Justice

[a]   Concepts & Methods

Corrective justice views the goal of tort law to be providing victims with the legal weapons necessary to right wrongs. Of course, tort remedies will seldom be able to restore the plaintiff to the pre-injury situation in the literal sense. While the circumstances that led to the harm might also support a criminal charge, a claim for breach of contract, or other complaint, the torts case focuses on rights and liabilities that arise although no one promised to pay for the damages and without regard to whether the government could prosecute the actor for a crime.

Corrective justice theory is based on the simple and elegant idea that an injurer who wrongfully injures another must make the injured party whole. This idea of justice presupposes the Aristotelian idea of normative equilibrium. One party wrongfully injuring another disturbs this equilibrium. Corrective justice restores it. Benjamin C. Zipursky, *Civil Recourse, Not Corrective Justice*, 91 GEO. L.J. 695, 695 (2003).

Aristotle's distinction between voluntary and involuntary harm anticipates modern concepts of negligence. M. Stuart Madden, *Tort Law Through Time and Culture: Themes of Economic Efficiency*, in EXPLORING TORT LAW 11, 32–33. (M. Stuart Madden ed. 2005). Corrective justice is central to the jurisprudence underlying negligence. *See* Ernest Weinreb, *Corrective Justice in a Nutshell*, 52 U. TORONTO L.J. 349, 349 (2002). "For the defendant to be held liable, it is not enough that the defendant's negligent act resulted in harm to the plaintiff. The harm has to be to an interest that has the status of a right, and the defendant's action has to be wrongful with respect to that right." *Id.* at 352. Corrective justice posits a correlative relationship between the doer and sufferer of harm. The reason that the plaintiff is entitled to win a torts lawsuit is the same as the reason why the defendant should lose it. *Id.* Vindicating the moral basis of society through a just verdict is important, not increasing overall societal wealth through promoting economic efficiency.

For more reading on corrective justice, see Jules L. Coleman, *Tort Liability and the Limits of Corrective Justice*, in IN HARM'S WAY: ESSAYS IN HONOR OF JOEL FEINBERG 139 (Jules L. Coleman & Allen Buchanan eds., 1994). Christopher Schroeder, *Corrective Justice, Liability for Risks, and Tort Law*, 38 U.C.L.A. L. REV. 143 (1990).

[b] Applying Corrective Justice to the Hot Coffee Case

Corrective justice requires that the party at fault make the victim whole. Proving fault in this case is problematic as often happens in complicated torts cases where the plaintiff and the defendant may be both at fault or where there may be multiple causes of a given injury. The defense view would be that Mrs. Liebeck was the primary cause of her own injuries and therefore should not be able to recover. The real life McDonald's hot coffee case was based upon strict liability and breach of the implied warranty of merchantability. Mrs. Liebeck's attorney could also have filed a negligence claim.

The plaintiff would counter that McDonald's was negligent in serving super-heated coffee and was in the best position to avoid the peril by turning down the heat, strengthening warnings, or redesigning cups so they would not easily collapse. The jury's finding of contributory negligence is entirely consistent with corrective justice in that McDonald's should be liable for the portion of damages reflecting its share of responsibility. Corrective justice would dictate that McDonald's disgorge its illicit gains from not paying the price for marketing superheated coffee. "Injustice occurs when, relative to this baseline, one party realizes a gain and the other a corresponding loss. The law corrects this injustice when it re-establishes the initial equality by depriving one party of the gain and restoring it to the other party. Aristotle likens the parties' initial positions to two equal lines." *Weinrib, supra,* at 349. *See generally* JULES COLEMAN, RISKS AND WRONGS (1992).

The purpose of corrective justice is "to make repair, to make good the victim's loss." Jules I. Coleman, *The Practice of Corrective Justice,* 37 ARIZ. L. REV. 15, 18 (1995). "[O]nly wrongful losses can give rise to a duty of repair in corrective justice; and. . . an individual has a duty to make good another's wrongful loss only if he is responsible for having brought the loss about." *Id.* A corrective justice theorist would consider evidence that McDonald's corporation failed to take prompt remedial steps in the face of a developing profile of danger that emerged from reported injuries. The defendant should be accountable for bearing "the cost of the harm for which it is legally responsible." *U.S. v. B.P. Amoco Oil PLC,* 277 F.3d 1012, 1020 (8th Cir. 2002). Mrs. Stella Liebeck sought redress for an injury caused by this conduct.

> In tort cases, the first person (the plaintiff) seeks redress for some wrong caused or threatened by the second person (the defendant). The litigation focuses on those two people and their actions. That focus allows for an application of the law — i.e., fault, cause, damages, and defenses — to the particular facts and equities of a specific case. Thus, the system achieves a result that is fair or just to the parties before the court.

Thomas C. Galligan Jr., *Deterrence: The Legitimate Function of the Public Tort,* 58 WASH. & LEE L. REV. 1019, 1029 (2001). Justifying recovery in terms of some broader societal good, however, may sacrifice justice or fairness between the parties. An optimal system must be both moral as well as efficient. Madden, *supra,* at 47 (2005).

[3] Critical Race Theory

[a] Concepts & Methods

A growing body of scholarship confirms that race matters when it comes to tort rights and remedies. Critical race theorists argue that the legal system cannot ignore the racial dynamics underlying many cases. Theorists ask practitioners and scholars to acknowledge that, even though national ideals aspire to equality, not all Americans receive equal treatment and opportunities. Furthermore, treating those situated differently in merely an equal manner can produce systematic injustice.

Intersectionality, an analytical tool used by some critical race theorists and others concerned about equality, examines the ways that race, ethnic, economic, and educational factors interact to create and perpetuate oppression and postulates that that more than one axis of oppression may be operating in a given situation. *See* STEPHANIE M. WILDMAN WITH CONTRIBUTIONS BY MARGALYNNE ARMSTRONG, ADRIENNE D. DAVIS & TRINA GRILLO, PRIVILEGE

REVEALED: HOW INVISIBLE PREFERENCE UNDERMINES AMERICA 22–24 (1996) (describing the multidimensional intersection as a koosh ball).

The late Jerome Culp, a Black law professor, always introduced himself to his students as the "son of a poor coal miner." Jerome McCristal Culp, Jr., *Autobiography and Legal Scholarship and Teaching: Finding the Me in the Legal Academy*, 77 VA. L. REV. 539, 539 (1991). Culp tells of his visit when in college to a white suburb where an elderly white woman "turn[ed] her back and assumed a 'pseudo-fetal posture'" as Culp and his companion approached. *Id.* at 552. "She saw us not as the well-dressed black college students that we were, but as mythic black revolutionaries." *Id.* Culp asks his class if it would have been as assault if he leaned over and whispered, "Boo." *Id.* at 553. He adds that he thought about doing so, but did not. *Id.* Some students are angry to learn that Culp considered that path. *Id.* Culp "posed the hypothetical to alter the assumptions that we make about the relationships between people and the tradeoffs imposed by the law." The story illustrates "how race influences the construction of law and legal doctrine" and that other rules limit Culp and require his self-censorship. *Id.*

Tort law remedies against the perpetrators of hate crimes illustrate how the civil justice system can serve to supplement the criminal law. Morris Dees, Director of the Southern Poverty Law Center, and others have utilized civil lawsuits as a weapon against organizations that championed racial violence. In 1988, racist thugs in Portland, Oregon beat an Ethiopian man to death with their fists, a baseball bat, and steel-toed boots. The victim, an Avis shuttle bus driver, was inadvertently dropped off in front of his home just as a White Pride gathering was breaking up. Michael L. Rustad, *Nationalizing Tort Law: The Republican Attack on Women, Blue Collar Workers, and Consumers*, 48 RUTGERS L. REV. 673, 687 (1996). "A skinhead named Kenneth Mieske came up behind [the victim] with a baseball bat," striking him repeatedly so violently that his skull was split wide open. James Willwerth Portland, *Making War on WAR: An Alabama Civil Rights Advocate Invokes Liability Doctrine in a Bid to Drive a California Race-Hatred Monger Out of Business*, TIME, October 22, 1990, at 60. Morris Dees represented the victim's family and won a $12,475,000 verdict against Tom and John Metzger, the organizers and leaders of the White Aryan Resistance (WAR). WAR was assessed a multi-million dollar punitive damage award because it sent violent racists into the city for the explicit purpose of fomenting racial strife." *Plaintiff Verdict for $12,475,000*, NORTHWEST PERSONAL INJURY LITIGATION REPORTS (Dec. 1990) at 1.

The Public Broadcasting Service documentary, *Forgotten Fires*, depicts the Klan as aiding and abetting a series of arson fires through inflammatory rhetoric, which falsely claimed that black churches were teaching their members how to be welfare cheats. *Forgotten Fires, Gripping ITVS Documentary About Black Church Burnings*, PR NEWSWIRE (April 26, 1999) at 1. In one of the church fire cases, a South Carolina jury ordered the Klan to pay $37.8 million for conspiring to burn down the Macedonia Baptist Church. The assets of the Klan and some of its leaders were seized and used, in part, to help rebuild the black church. Brad Knickerbocker, *Latest Tactic Against Hate Groups: Bankruptcy*, CHRISTIAN SCIENCE MONITOR (Aug. 25, 2000) at 1. Criminal law can effectively target the direct perpetrator of violent racist acts but the organization that promotes racial hatred and encourages violent acts against minorities generally runs little risk of government prosecution.

Tort victims and their lawyers play the role of "private attorneys general" by financing civil lawsuits that uncover and publicize patterns of systematic wrongdoing. Punitive damages are the classic remedy for the private attorney general because the claimant receives a bounty beyond the amount necessary for compensation as a reward for serving the public interest. The private attorney general plays a vital societal role when government enforcement agencies lack the will, expertise, or financial resources to police new social dangers.

Tort law has long been a means of social control against oppressors. In the cases discussed above, the individual racists committing crimes were dealt with on the criminal side of law, but tort damages struck at the organizational roots of evil. Although tort law can be a weapon that can be mobilized to protect racial and cultural minorities, tort law has often fallen short of fulfilling this promise. The modern torts scholar and litigator need to consider the realities of race, class, and gender on tort recovery. Caps on non-economic damages, for example, will typically have a disparate impact on elderly black women who will find it difficult to find representation because they have low imputed earnings. *See* Frank M. McClellan, *The Dark Side of Tort Reform: Searching for Racial Justice*, 48 RUTGERS L. REV. 761(1996).

Few torts classrooms tackle the intersection of gender, class, and race in teaching the topic of intentional torts. Professor Camille Nelson employs traditional intentional tort doctrines such as assault, battery, and negligence-based concepts such as the infliction of nervous shock to construct tort remedies for the mental and physical harms caused by racial abuse. She reconceptualizes the victim of racial hatred as a "thin-skulled" or "egg-shell" claimant. The English case, *Dulieu v. White & Sons*, [1901] 2 K.B. 669, first articulated the eggshell plaintiff doctrine. In *Dulieu*, the court observed:

> If a man is negligently run over or otherwise negligently injured in his body, it is no answer to the sufferer's claim for damages that he would have suffered less injury or no injury at all, if he had not had an unusually thin skull or an unusually weak heart.

Dulieu 2 K.B. at 679. The traditional "eggshell plaintiff" rule requires the defendant to take the plaintiff as he finds him.

In racial abuse cases, the hateful defendants must compensate the plaintiff for harm an ordinary person would not have suffered. The victims of racial hatred are especially vulnerable claimants because of the long history of racial violence in this country. Camille A. Nelson, *Considering Tortious Racism*, 9 DEPAUL J. HEALTH CARE L. 905, 907–09 (2005). Professor Nelson connects the "racial dots" in traditional tort law, extending the eggshell doctrine to the victims of racism. She reconceptualizes the "leveler of a racial abuse and the orchestrator of racial conduct" as an intentional tortfeasor because they "intentionally inflict harm based upon race — this is usually calculated and premeditated behavior." *Id.* at 933. She contends that tort remedies for cross burnings and other racial abuse may be predicated upon the special vulnerability of [intended] victims. *Id.* at 918–919.

Critical race theory offers a great deal of promise to explain the differential injuries experienced by people of color and the often frustrating experiences they have trying to redress their injuries in the civil justice system. Race, as well as social class and gender, matters when it comes to jury selection as well as case selection. Juries undervalue tort claims if people of color are the victims. Insurance companies reduce their settlement offer if a person of color is the tort victim, according to the research and litigator's experience of Frank McClellan:

> People of color usually exercise vigilance to detect and control the impact of racism when they know that white people will participate in decision-making that will affect their lives. Personal experience has demonstrated that race-based assumptions will conspicuously infect decision-making. Tort cases involving "personal" injuries or large money damages present significant risks to clients who are people of color. A substantial risk is that race will trump other considerations affecting the resolution of the dispute in jurisdictions where people of color represent a minority among the judicial decision makers. I believe that we underestimate the extent to which race impacts on the case resolution; most tort cases are resolved through negotiations that occur outside of formal proceedings. In addition, tort principles and rules are value-packed. When we examine the informal process, we must conclude that DuBois's description of the great American challenge of the twentieth century remains the great American challenge of the twenty-first century. That challenge is reflected in our own tort system as "the problem of the colorline."

Frank M. McClellan, *The Dark Side of Tort Reform: Searching for Racial Justice,* 48 RUTGERS L. REV. 761, 768–69 (1996). Modern tort lawyers must consider race because juries undervalue tort claims if people of color are the victims. McClellan calls for empirical research to study the role of race in deflating the value of tort verdicts and settlements for persons of color. *Id.* at 773. The best available empirical data supports the proposition that race impacts tort awards and settlements. *See* Jennifer B. Wriggins, *Torts, Race, and the Value of Injury, 1900–1949*, 49 HOW. L.J. 99 (2005).

For an in-depth exploration of the ramifications of addressing or ignoring race issues in the development and application of the law, see generally JUAN PEREA, RICHARD DELGADO, ANGELA HARRIS & STEPHANIE WILDMAN, RACE AND RACES: CASES AND MATERIALS FOR A DIVERSE AMERICA 2d ed. (2007).

[b] Applying Critical Race Theory to the Hot Coffee Case

A critical race theorist would be skeptical of the media's portrayal of a tort system out of control. The narrative that a hapless grandmother caused her own injury and blamed a deep-pocket corporation reflects the pervasive ageism and sexism of American society. This portrayal of an unworthy plaintiff shares much common ground with the false stereotype of the black welfare mother driving a Cadillac. Similarly, critical race theorists would see parallels between the concept of Stella Liebeck as an irresponsible claimant and the false stereotype that black juries are overly sympathetic to plaintiffs.

> For people of color, the role of juries has peculiar equivocal signifi-cance. People of color are aware of the democratic symbolism of the jury as "preserv[ing] liberty by wresting "the law" from the experts." People of color are also conscious, however, that the "firm rootings" of the jury in the American past did not include representation of women, blacks, or Indians, and that unrepresentative jury decisions have fre-quently underscored their marginalized status. Indeed the reprieve of no jury has been seen as an advantage for people of color: jury deci-sion-making on more than one occasion, after all, has confirmed that the political majority devalues the worth of the lives and dignity of outsiders.

Phoebe A. Haddon, *Rethinking the Jury,* 3 WM. & MARY BILL RTS J. 29, 31 (1994).

In fact, Stella Liebeck was a staunch Republican and the New Mexico jury was composed largely of white jurors. The jurors in Albuquerque, New Mexico tend to be more "conservative" and juries in southern New Mexico are "real, real hard." Winthrop Quiqley, *N.M. Juries Are Often Generous,* ALBUQUERQUE (N.M.) JOURNAL (Feb. 21, 2001) at A1. A critical race theorist would ask the question of whether the hot coffee case would have ever been brought, and whether the white jury would have reached the same verdict, if the plaintiff had been an elderly black woman. An empirically based torts scholar would do further study on jury attitudes and composition in New Mexico.

Race remains an important factor guiding an attorney's decision to file a suit. Frank McClellan, *The Dark Side of Tort Reform: Searching for Racial Justice,* 48 RUTGERS L. REV. 761 (1996). A race-conscious tort pedagogy might center on why black plaintiffs are less likely to find representation or per-ceived to be more anti-corporate. *See generally* Kimberlé W. Crenshaw, *Foreword: Toward a Race-Conscious Pedagogy in Legal Education,* 11 NAT'L BLACK L.J. 1, 9–10 (1989) (arguing for a race-conscious pedagogy to increase participation of minority students in the law school classroom); Mari J. Matsuda, *When the First Quail Calls: Multiple Consciousness as Jurisprudential Method,* 14 WOMEN'S RTS. L. REP. 297 (1992) (urging consciousness of race and other identity categories). Perhaps the most important insight of a critical race perspective questions the continuing exclusion of blacks and other minorities from juries deciding tort cases.

The "tort reformer's" concept of a "hell hole jurisdiction" reflects a race-based view since each of these supposed plaintiff-friendly jurisdictions have a large minority population. Perhaps it is not a coincidence that the McDonald's ver-dict occurred in New Mexico. An empirical study found that that a mere increase of the Hispanic county poverty rate of 1 percentage point could raise tort awards as much as 7 percent. Erik Helland & Alexander Tabarrok, *Race, Poverty, and American Tort Awards: Evidence from Three Data Sets,* 32 J. LEGAL STUDIES 27, 27 (2003). If the hypothesis of Helland and Tabarrok is correct, the McDonald's hot coffee case could have resulted in a larger verdict if more poor Hispanics were included on the jury. The intersectionality of race and class play a role in plaintiff's choice of venue. Significantly, a growing number of states place restrictions on plaintiffs' choice of venue because of the perception that poor, minority juries are more generous in their judgments.

The centrality of race in tort litigation and jury selection, as well as the tendency of conventional tort teachers to overlook this variable would be another critical race theory observation. Angela P. Harris, *Foreword: The Jurisprudence of Reconstruction*, 82 CAL. L. REV. 741 (1994); Kimberlé W. Crenshaw, *Race, Reform and Retrenchment: Transformation and Legitimation in Antidiscrimination Law*, 101 HARV. L. REV. 1331 (1988).

[4] Critical Feminism

[a] Concepts & Methods

Feminist theory criticizes the misogynistic view of women that characterizes society and advocates the "radical notion" that women are people. Critical feminism makes gender a central focus of inquiry, asking "the woman question." The "woman question" identifies and challenges the omission of women and their needs from the analysis of any societal issue. Critical feminism examines power relationships, making the political visible. The notion that "the personal is political" challenges the public and private dichotomy that characterizes liberal thought.

Tort casebooks traditionally have not viewed tortious harms through a female lens. *See,* Lucinda M. Finley, *A Break in the Silence: Including Women's Issues in a Torts Course*, 1 YALE J.L. & FEMINISM 41, 52 (1989). Traditional tort law has been openly patriarchal. Ronald K.L. Collins, *Language, History and the Legal Process: A Profile of the "Reasonable Man,"* 8 RUTGERS-CAM. L.J. 311, 312 (1977). Thomas Koenig and Michael Rustad observe that courts and legal academics have traditionally overlooked the degree to which tort law is gender-linked:

> Social scientists have documented the ways that gender discrimination and sex role socialization track women and men into separate, although overlapping, social and occupational spheres. . .

> Many scholars argue that by not taking full account of the manifold differences between males and females, law and the courts are deeply biased against women. . . .

Thomas Koenig & Michael Rustad, *His and Her Tort Reform: Gender Injustice in Disguise,* 70 WASH. L. REV. 1, 8 (1995). The "perspectivelessness" of the dominant views of tort law also overlooks the role of gender in tort rights and remedies. Martha Chamallas, *Civil Rights in Ordinary Torts Cases: Race, Gender and the Calculation of Economic Loss*, 38 LOY. L.A. L. REV. 1435 (2005). "This tendency in tort law to overlook or diminish a woman's pecuniary loss is connected to the fact that the injuries from reproductive loss, sexual harassment, or assault seem more emotional than physical." Lucinda M. Finley, *Female Trouble: The Implications of Tort Reform for Women,* 64 TENN. L. REV. 847, 858 (1997). *See also* Leslie Bender, *A Lawyer's Primer on Feminist Theory and Tort*, 38 J. LEGAL EDUC. 3, 31–32 (1988) (Proposing a feminist "standard of caring" as an alternative to the "masculine voice of rights and autonomy").

Contemporary women rely primarily upon tort remedies rather than government regulators to ensure the safety of medical products. Females benefit disproportionately from the liberalization of recovery for reproductive injury in the fields of medical malpractice and products liability. Lucinda Finley found "[r]eproductive or sexual harm caused by drugs and medical devices [have] a disproportionate impact on women because far more drugs and devices have been devised to control women's fertility or bodily functions associated with sex and childbearing than have been devised for men." Finley, *supra*, 64 TENN. L. REV. at 855. Over the past few decades, punitive damages have expanded from punishing intentional torts committed maliciously to controlling reckless product manufacturers and health care providers.

Should it be relevant to a decision maker that only women use the product? For an introduction to feminist legal theory and methodology, see Katharine Bartlett, *Cracking Foundations as Feminist Method*, 8 AM. U. J. GENDER SOC. POL'Y & L. 31 (1999); Lorena Fries and Veronica Matus, *Why Does the Method Matter?* 7 AM. U. J. GENDER SOC. POL'Y & L. 291 (1999). For a discussion of gender issues in the specific context of tort law, see Leslie Bender, *A Lawyer's Primer on Feminist Theory and Tort,* 38 J. LEGAL EDUC. 3 (1998); Martha Chamallas, *Civil Rights in Ordinary Torts Cases: Race, Gender and the Calculation of Economic Loss*, 38 LOY. L.A. L. REV. 1435 (2005). Would it be relevant if most of the women using the product were poor and women of color? *See* DOROTHY ROBERTS, KILLING THE BLACK BODY: RACE, REPRODUCTION, AND THE MEANING OF LIBERTY (1997). In recent years, some scholars have argued that assessing issues from a feminist perspective must be refined in some contexts to acknowledge differences in the experiences of women as a consequence of race and class. One author observes:

> The notion that there is a monolithic "women's experience" that can be described independent of other facets of experience like race, class, and sexual orientation . . . [may be called] "gender essentialism.". . . The result of essentialism is to reduce the lives of people who experience multiple forms of oppression to addition problems: "racism + sexism = straight black women's experience," or "racism + sexism + homophobia = black lesbian experience." Thus, in an essentialist world, black women's experience will always be forcibly fragmented before being subjected to analysis, as those who are "only interested in race" and those who are "only interested in gender" take their separate slices of our lives.

Angela P. Harris, *Race and Essentialism in Feminist Legal Theory*, 42 STAN. L. REV. 581, 588–89 (1990).

In the twenty-first century, torts scholars are beginning to understand and take into account the role of gender in tort litigation. Empirical research confirms that women as tort claimants receive smaller economic awards for similar injuries because they earn less than men do and spend fewer years in the workplace. *See* Thomas Koenig & Michael Rustad, *His and Her Tort Reform: Gender Injustice in Disguise*, 70 WASH. L. REV. 1, 78–79 (1995).

Tort reform's capping of non-economic damages and punitive damages have a disparate negative impact on women's recovery. Lucinda M. Finley, *The Hidden Victims of Tort Reform: Women, Children, and the Elderly*, 53 EMORY L.J. 1263, 1263 (2004). Without the prospect of non-economic and punitive damages, many grievously injured women will be unable to convince an attorney to take their case. Consequently, from the perspective of critical feminists and critical race theorists, tort reforms that propose limitations on punitive damages are gender and race injustice in disguise.

A proposed federal tort reform capping non-economic damages at $250,000 imposes a regressive tort tax on judgments recovered by women, children, and the elderly. Professor Finley's study also illustrates the importance of non-economic damages for the elderly, who usually have no imputed earnings and relatively insignificant out-of-pocket expenses. *Id.* at 1283. Torts students who will be representing or defending clients in tort litigation need to consider the impact of societal gender roles.

Think about the different views of work and family roles in the cases in this text. Many cases will involve the hidden injuries of race, class gender, and age. Consider whether a legislature adopting a given tort reform is devaluing an identity category by not considering the social reality of that category. For further reading on critical feminism, see Lucinda M. Finley, *A Break in the Silence: Including Women's Issues in a Torts Course*, 1 YALE J. L. & FEMINISM 41, 65–66 (1989); Martha Minow, *Feminist Reason: Getting It and Losing It*, 38 J. LEGAL EDUC. 47 (1990).

[b] Applying Critical Feminism to the Hot Coffee Case

A tort theorist evaluating the hot coffee case from a critical feminist perspective might focus upon the intersectionality of the plaintiff's age and gender. Others might ignore the situated lives of the elderly. An outraged reader wrote a letter about the hot coffee case to columnist, Ann Landers:

> The plaintiff was 81 years old. I say she was a malingering old biddy who pumped up her alleged injuries to get more money. Spending eight days in the hospital was her lawyer's way of creating a situation to make her case appear legit. Third degree burns my eye! There are plenty of unethical doctors who will testify to anything as long as they get a fat fee.
>
> Nothing was said about the woman riding in her grandson's sports car or how fast he was going. In the accounts of the case I read, it said there was no place to put the coffee cup, so she placed it between her legs. What kind of an idiot does that in a sports car? Where is the common sense here?

Marc Galanter, *An Oil Strike in Hell: Contemporary Legends About the Civil Justice System*, 40 ARIZ. L. REV. 717, 733 (1998).

Feminist tort scholars, in contrast, focus on the unequal status of women as outsiders and the existence of bias in tort awards. Mrs. Liebeck was the age of a typical plaintiff in a nursing home neglect case. The victims of nursing home neglect or abuse will often receive awards composed entirely upon non-economic damages. Because women constitute a significantly larger proportion of the elderly demographic segment, caps on damages will ultimately hurt elderly female plaintiffs more than other plaintiff categories. While elderly men as well as women were unlikely to have lost wages, the women nursing home residents "received a notably larger share of their compensatory damage awards in noneconomic loss categories than elderly men." Lucinda M. Finley, *The Hidden Victims of Tort Reform: Women, Children, and the Elderly*, 53 EMORY L.J. 1263, 1283 (2004). The media marginalization of Stella Liebeck reveals a narrative reflecting bias and oppression.

A substantial contribution of feminist scholarship has been the acknowledgment that law making by courts has contributed to the oppressed and unequal status of outsiders — groups, like women, whose experiences of exclusion confirm the bias of existing legal doctrine. Feminists utilize the social fact of difference and identify the social and political consequences of group membership in their critique of law. "Feminist theory challenges the notion that missing perspectives in law can be accounted for by generalizing from the experiences of others, particularly those who have been socially or economically privileged: those who have not experienced oppression have difficulty recognizing it." Phoebe A. Haddon, *Rethinking the Jury*, 3 WM. & MARY BILL RTS. J. 29, 77 (1994).

Gender, reproductive, and occupational roles determine whether a plaintiff may find representation in the contingency fee system. Mrs. Liebeck suffered severe burns to her genitals requiring skin grafts. Most of Mrs. Liebeck's damages were non-economic harm, dependent upon her attorney's ability to commodify her pain and suffering. Attorneys have traditionally regarded injuries to elderly claimants as "no damages" cases because the claimants have no imputed earnings. While Mrs. Liebeck suffered both second and third degree burns requiring debridement and skin grafting, her medical bills were less than $10,000 and she made no claim for future medical costs. Mrs. Liebeck worked in a modest position in a store, so her economic damages were slight compared to a typical employed, middle-class, white, male breadwinner. The critical race and critical feminist perspectives focus upon the intersectional impact of age, race, and gender to the non-economic and punitive damages reduced by the trial court in the hot coffee case. Without the possibility of non-economic damages and punitive damages, Mrs. Liebeck would not have been able to find representation. Tort reforms proposing to cap these damages will make it unlikely that similar cases will be brought in the future.

[5] Pragmatism

[a] Concepts and Methods

Pragmatism is a philosophical tradition based on the idea that every concept should be understood in terms of its practical effects. This idea means that every theory should be seen as relating to some particular practice and, more specifically, as a theory that generates implications for the reform of that practice. For example, as Catharine Wells explains:

[A] pragmatic theory of bridge building should begin by looking at actual practices of bridge construction. The examination of these practices is both descriptive and normative; it is not aimed simply at enumerating the methods of construction, but at determining which methods produce the "best" bridges. And the question — What is the best bridge? — cannot be answered in the abstract; we cannot give the same answer on the first day as we might give after a thousand years of bridge building. Theory and practice evolve together within a context of human purpose and activity; the practice informs the theory while the theory, in turn, informs the practice. Thus, the hallmark of a pragmatic method is its continual reevaluation of practices in the light of the norms that govern them and of the norms in the light of the practices they generate.

Catharine P. Wells, *Improving One's Situation: Some Pragmatic Reflections on the Art of Judging*, 49 WASH. & LEE L. REV. 323, 331 (1992).

From a pragmatic perspective, one of the difficulties with traditional legal theory is that it makes an absolute distinction between fact and value. "Thus, for example, it pits the realist 'is' against the formalist 'ought.' The pragmatist rejects this division and urges instead that every abstract conception should be understood in relation to its consequences for human activity." *Id.*

Applying this theory to judicial decision making, Wells contrasts "the notion of impersonal decisionmaking — the kind that a computer might do — and situated decisionmaking — the kind that requires a real human agency. . . . [J]udges are not computers [and] they are not entirely free from legal constraint." *Id.* at 334. Thus, legal judgments occupy a middle ground.

In concluding that legal decisionmaking is inherently situated, Wells urges judges to attend to their situation, recognizing the impossibility of being an impersonal agent in the decisionmaking process, while striving to be fair minded. "Fairness requires that we consider all points of view and this, in turn, requires that we open our minds and our hearts to the viewpoints of others." *Id.* at 338.

Jean Love, a well-known torts scholar, sums up the promise of pragmatism as follows: "pragmatism offers both the hope of a constructive way of thinking about society's problems and the hope of a common language." Jean C. Love, *Afterword: Symposium on the Renaissance of Pragmatism in American Legal Thought*, 63 S. CAL. L. REV. 1911, 1925 (1990). She explains:

By "common" language I mean two things. First, I mean "common" in the sense of "ordinary." Pragmatism encourages us to speak in the language of common ordinary people, rather than in the language of metaphysical philosophers. Second, I mean "common" in the sense of "shared." Pragmatism helps us to talk across our differences by encouraging us to pay attention to context. In one situation, I may play the role of the oppressed — a woman among men, for example. In another situation, I may play the role of the oppressor — a white woman in a predominantly white society, for example.

Id. at 1927.

For further reading on pragmatism, see WILLIAM JAMES, PRAGMATISM AND OTHER ESSAYS (1965); HILARY PUTNAM, REASON, TRUTH AND HISTORY (1981); RICHARD RORTY, CONSEQUENCES OF PRAGMATISM (1982); Margaret Radin, *The Pragmatist and the Feminist,* 63 S. CAL. L. REV. 1699 (1990); Catharine Wells, *Tort Law as Corrective Justice: A Pragmatic Justification for Jury Adjudication,* 88 MICH. L. REV. 2348 (1990); Thomas C. Grey, *Holmes and Legal Pragmatism,* 41 STAN. L. REV. 787 (1989); RICHARD POSNER, LAW, PRAGMATISM, AND DEMOCRACY (2003); Stanley Fish, *Almost Pragmatism: Richard Posner's Jurisprudence,* 57 U. CHI. L. REV. 1447 (1990); Daniel A. Farber, *Legal Pragmatism and the Constitution,* 72 MINN. L. REV. 1331 (1988).

[b]   Applying Pragmatism to the Hot Coffee Case

Pragmatism would inform the judicial role in the McDonald's case by instructing the judge to "attend to his situation." Even though the judge was neither an elderly woman nor a multinational corporation, pragmatism would lead the judge to consider the perspectives of the parties before him. Many judges are pragmatists in practice without naming their behavior as such, because they seek a resolution of the problem the parties, themselves, face. The jury, too, would seek a verdict that reflects the particular situation giving rise to the injury as well as the extent of Mrs. Liebeck's injuries. Margaret Radin, *The Pragmatist and The Feminist,* 63 S. CAL. L. REV. 1699, 1704 (1990) (explaining how the definition of the situation affects legal decision-making). A pragmatist might argue that Mrs. Liebeck's personhood has been threatened by McDonald's externalization of excessive risk that injured her. The process of casting Mrs. Liebeck's injuries in the form of a verdict commodifies her as an object. *Id.* at 1700. The theory of pragmatism also focuses on the everyday experience of the warring perspectives of the plaintiff and the defendant. Pragmatism could also inform the advocates' roles, urging them to seek a practical resolution to the dispute separating their clients. Pragmatism counsels the trial and error of negotiation that might bring parties closer together, talking across their differences.

[6]   Social Justice

[a]   Concepts and Methods

Social justice theorists start from the proposition that tort law remains contested terrain precisely because it is public policy in disguise. Leon Green, *Tort Law, Public Law in Disguise,* 38 TEX L. REV. 257, 269 (1959–60). Tort law not only alleviates "the plight of the injured" but it also furthers the "the cause of social justice." THOMAS H. KOENIG & MICHAEL L. RUSTAD, IN DEFENSE OF TORT LAW 2 (2001) (quoting JOHN G. FLEMING, AN INTRODUCTION TO THE LAW OF TORTS 1 (1967)). John C. P. Goldberg coined the term "social justice theory" to refer to the work of theorists who view torts as a means of social control over powerful corporate interests.

Goldberg states:

> Social justice theorists conceive of tort law as a device for rectifying imbalances in political power. Specifically, they posit that tort concepts

correct for pathologies of interest-group politics. Moneyed interests, particularly corporations, block or distort legislation and capture regulatory agencies designed to monitor and control them. As a result, these interests are able to pursue the self-interest of their executives and shareholders at the expense of the public by producing dangerous products and hiding critical information about their dangerousness. By arming citizens with the power to sue corporations for misconduct outside of the legislative and regulatory process, tort law serves to correct this imbalance of power. In particular, it permits independent judges and especially juries to hold corporate America and other powerful actors accountable. Thus, negligence actions by gunshot victims and public nuisance actions by cities that bear the cost of treating those victims make up for the absence of effective gun control. Likewise, product liability suits restrain pharmaceutical companies from profiteering on dangerous and ineffective drugs. The social justice conception of torts is most closely associated in practice with Ralph Nader. Scholars who have developed this conception further include Richard Abel, Anita Bernstein, Carl Bogus, Thomas Koenig, and Michael Rustad.

John C.P. Goldberg, *Twentieth-Century Tort Theories*, 91 GEO. L. J. 513, 561 (2003).

The social justice school, as its name suggests, treats torts as a form of social control. It seeks to control corporate misconduct by generating penalties that send a message of deterrence to corporate America. In tort, the citizen can both vindicate his or her own claim to rights against the powerful and act as a private attorney general policing the conduct of these actors. *See* THOMAS H. KOENIG & MICHAEL L. RUSTAD, IN DEFENSE OF TORT LAW (2001). "[S]ocial justice theory emphasizes the pivotal role played by damage awards — particularly punitive damage awards — in restraining self-interested corporate conduct. Only punitive damages, social justice theory supposes, can establish that 'tort does not pay' by hitting the rich and powerful in the bank account." Goldberg, *supra*, at 561. The theory of social justice may be seen in tort litigation where private plaintiffs uncovered "smoking gun" documents that revealed that there was an industry-wide conspiracy of asbestos manufacturers to conceal the deadly consequences of unprotected exposure to asbestos dust that destroyed the health of hundreds of thousands of American workers. Social justice theorists stress the importance of private attorney generals because a private citizen "can both vindicate his or her own claim to rights against the powerful and act as a private attorney general policing the conduct of these actors." *Id*.

Another insight of the social justice theorists is that torts may be instrumental in bringing about social justice because of the "evolving and open-ended nature of tort causes of action, a quality that permits tort plaintiffs to bring to light, and seek remedies for, new forms of domination and exploitation as they emerge." *Id*. Johns-Manville Corporation, for example, suppressed publications that would have warned the medical community of the risks of asbestosis. *Janssens v. Johns-Manville Co.*, 463 So. 2d 242, 249 (Fla. 1984). The company had a policy of not informing employees that x-rays taken by company doctors revealed clear evidence of asbestosis. *Id*. at 263. Johns-Manville executives claimed that their failure to warn workers was motivated by concern for employees so they "can live and work in peace and the company benefit by their many years of experience." *Id*. at 250. Private attorneys general litigating their claims, rather than public regulators, brought the asbestos problem to light.

[b]   Applying Social Justice to the Hot Coffee Case

A social justice theorist would view Mrs. Liebeck and her lawyer as "private attorneys general" whose lawsuit resulted in a public safety victory for all Americans. Law school classes, court decisions, and even tort litigants rarely recognize the public justice role of tort law. Tort law not only performs the manifest function of alleviating the plight of the injured, but it also fulfills the cause of social justice. In the wake of the McDonald's verdict, McDonald's and most major fast food companies placed warning labels on their cups and turned down the heat on their coffee, reducing the radius of the risk of injury. Peter Carlson, *Hey Don't Say They Didn't Warn You*, WASH. POST (Sept. 1, 2006) at C01 (noting that "McDonald's and other coffee vendors to put labels on coffee cups warning that hot coffee is hot").

"[S]ocial justice theory notes the value of the discovery process in tort litigation, through which plaintiffs' lawyers can uncover paper trails documenting instances of corporate misinformation and malfeasance." John C.P. Goldberg, *Twentieth-Century Tort Theory*, 91 GEO. L.J. 513, 561 (2003). This theory "emphasizes the pivotal role played by damage awards — particularly punitive damage awards — in restraining self-interested corporate conduct. Only punitive damages, social justice theorists argue, can establish that "'tort does not pay' by hitting the rich and powerful in the bank account." *Id*. The punitive damages imposed by the New Mexico jury in the McDonald's case sent a similar message to McDonald's and to other products manufacturers that they must not sacrifice safety for the bottom line.

Another theme of the social justice theorists is that the corporate funded "tort reformers" frequently use untrue tort horror stories and hyperbole to buttress their case for tort reform. The majority opinion, striking down Illinois' 1995 tort reform statute, noted the "tort reformer's" distorted use of the McDonald's hot coffee case:

> An example, . . . cited frequently in the legislative debates, is the infamous McDonald's spilled coffee case. As one author has noted, the facts of this case were presented to the public in a skewed fashion. M. Rustad, *Nationalizing Tort Law: The Republican Attack on Women, Blue Collar Workers and Consumers*, 48 RUTGERS L. REV. 673, 720–21 (1996). [The court describes the serious burns plaintiff suffered and prior knowledge of McDonald's as the these effects of its super-heated coffee.] . . .[T]he excessive award was for punitive, not compensatory, damages.

Best v. Taylor Mach. Works, 689 N.E.2d 1057, 1067 n. 1 (Ill. 1997).

Consider whether policy arguments based upon any of the six perspectives will aid analysis of the cases and problems in this text. Think about how a judge or law professor might approach the case from a law and economics, corrective justice, critical race theory, critical feminist, pragmatist, or social justice perspective. In every torts case there are at least two perspectives: the appellant (petitioner) and the appellees (respondents). Consider how an appellant or appellee could use insights from the multiple perspectives to win his or her case.

In a recent article, *Can There Be a Unified Theory of Torts? A Pluralist Suggestion from History and Doctrine*, 43 BRANDEIS L.J. 369, 369–70 (2005), Professor Christopher Robinette recounts the parable of three blind men. Each encounters a different part of an elephant and attempts to describe how the elephant looks and feels based on the part of the elephant that he has touched. Professor Robinette uses the parable to illustrate why he doubts torts scholars will succeed in developing a unified theory to explain and justify torts doctrine. He observes:

> Much of contemporary torts scholarship reflects the problem of the blind men in the parable: an exclusive focus on one aspect of the object of study and a concomitant failure to acknowledge the validity of competing perspectives. There are currently two major camps of torts scholars. One camp regards the consequentialist goal of deterring accidents as the rationale for tort liability. The other camp regards tort law as a way to vindicate individual moral rights or to achieve "corrective justice" between the parties. Corrective justice theories are not based upon their effects or consequences, but rather upon an assertion that an act or rule of law is right or wrong "in itself." The scholars in these camps frequently ignore or attack scholars in the "opposing" camp. Furthermore, both deterrence and corrective justice scholars frequently deride the importance of compensation, a third goal many scholars deem crucial to tort law.

D. INTRODUCTION TO BASES OF LIABILITY IN TORT LAW

Alice and Blanche are neighbors in a farmland community. They have a history of disputes about boundary lines; some disputes have included threats. Alice's crop-dusting airplane crashed onto Blanche's land, destroying her barn. Blanche comes to you for advice. She wants to know if she can recover for the destruction of her barn.

A lawyer must evaluate what tort causes of action are available to Blanche. Does the history of animosity between these neighbors suggest an intentional act by Alice? Chapters 2–3 explore intentional torts. Might a lack of reasonable care have led to the crash, suggesting negligence by Alice? Chapter 4 addresses the standard of care and other issues related to negligence. Should operators of crop dusting airplanes always be responsible for harm that they cause? Chapter 8 examines strict liability for abnormally dangerous activities. The tort lawyer must determine which tort causes of action apply to her client's case:

The first inquiry in the traditional tort approach is identifying the general type of risk that may apply — is there a general principle of tort law which condemns the actor's conduct? If there is, then the other question is whether that general risk protects against the specific risk that caused the damage, i.e., should this actor be liable to this victim for these damages occurring in this particular manner. There are six general risks: 1) was the actor's conduct intentional, (2) was the actor's conduct willful or wanton (sometimes termed reckless or gross negligence), 3) was the actor negligent, 4) does the actor's relationship to a person make the actor liable for the wrongful conduct of that person (vicarious liability), 5) does the actor's relationship to a thing make the actor liable for the damage-causing condition of the thing (strict liability), and 6) does the actor's participation in an activity subject him or her to liability for the damages caused by that activity (absolute liability)? When the actor's conduct does not fit within one of these six general risks, traditional tort law dictates that the loss should stay where it is, i.e., with the victim. At this point one may say there is "no tort" or that the injury-causing event was "an accident," although the latter term is too legally imprecise to be helpful.

Frank L. Maraist, *Of Envelopes and Legends: Reflections on Tort Law*, 61 LA. L. REV. 153, 156 (2000).

Courts and tort scholars broadly categorize the general principles of tort law into intentional torts, negligence, and strict liability. Nicolas P. Terry, *Collapsing Torts*, 25 CONN. L. REV. 717, 718 (1993) (contending that common law courts collapse and uncollapse tort doctrines as a standard way of adjusting the degree of loss allocation and deterrence). Each of these paradigmatic branches of tort law poses different conceptual problems as well as problems of proof. Professor Nicolas Terry explains how good lawyers as well as judges make conscious choices about which allocational models fit a given fact pattern:

> The placement of any fact pattern within a particular allocation model has been essentially heuristic, involving rule-of-thumb labeling of fact patterns in a process informed by historical, conceptual, and even anecdotal or accidental rationales. . . .
>
> Assume that a plaintiff is injured when a rail car transporting natural gas explodes. There are two possible scenarios, depending upon whether the supreme court of Xanadu previously decided that the transportation of natural gas is an 'abnormally dangerous activity.'. . . What determines the allocation model to which the gas transportation attaches? If this was a product liability cause of action, complex meta-legal considerations would determine whether the general fact pattern attracted strict liability, followed by a fact-sensitive inquiry into whether this particular fact pattern was included (i.e., a categorization decision followed by a characterization stage).

Id. at 719, 730.

Another characterization of bases of liability would be fault (intent and negligence) and no-fault (strict liability). The categorization of a particular fact pattern is a strategic decision that is often outcome-determinative. The job of a lawyer is not to *make* the categories, but rather to be able to argue *why* a certain category should be selected. Lawyers who become judges can decide cases and make categories. The job of the law student is not to discover the law, but rather to learn how to argue what the law should be as applied to the facts. Tort law assigns responsibility for injuries to the wrongdoer by requiring the payment of compensation. Tort liability is predicated upon evidence that the defendant's conduct (a) was intentional; or (b) was negligent; or (c) engaged in an abnormally dangerous activity that poses excessive risks to others. A tort plaintiff must prove every element of the case. The burden of proof as well as persuasion is typically on the plaintiff. In contrast, defendant has the burden of proof and persuasion for defenses to tort actions.

In the McDonald's hot coffee case, Reed Morgan, the plaintiff's attorney, chose to approach the case as one of strict liability rather than negligence. Chapters 8 and 10 address strict liability and liability for product-related injuries, respectively. Negligence or fault-based tort theory remains the dominant meta-legal theory. Tort law utilizes negligence as the model for the redistribution of accident costs. Chapter 4 introduces the topic of negligence in depth. Negligence is an act or omission by which one fails to exercise the due care of a reasonable person in the circumstances. Alternatively, phrased another way, negligence is conduct that falls below the standard of care established by the law for the protection of others against unreasonable risks of harm.

As a preview of negligence doctrine, consider how negligence might have affected the McDonald's hot coffee case. If Mr. Morgan had filed a negligence claim, his burden would have been to demonstrate that McDonald's act or omission in selling coffee to Mrs. Liebeck violated a standard of care owed to her. New Mexico, like all other jurisdictions, measures the standard of care by objective rather than subjective standards, asking how a reasonable corporation would have behaved. Mrs. Liebeck's attorney would need to prove: duty, breach of duty, causation, and damages in order to establish that McDonald's negligently marketed the hot coffee that injured the plaintiff. The issue of duty would not have been problematic because McDonald's owes a duty of care to all consumers or anyone likely to consume coffee or even a bystander injured by spilled coffee. The controversy would likely have turned on the reasonableness of the company's conduct. The McDonald's hot coffee case is typical in that the parties settled the case prior to an appeal. Many cases never reach a jury because the trial judge has entered a motion of summary judgment in favor of the defendant or dismissed a complaint for failure to state a claim. The next section in this chapter examines the procedural stages in the life of a tort case. In the true-life McDonald's hot coffee case, few reporters uncovered what happened at the post-verdict stage when the trial judge slashed the punitive damages. McDonald's illustrates the role of the trial judge as an umpire. Pay attention to how procedural rules affect the outcome in each case.

E.   THE PROCEDURAL STAGES OF A TORT CASE

Civil procedure is the first year course, which addresses "procedural law" or the rules for presenting a case. Evidence, usually a second year course, focuses on admissible testimony, exhibits, and other information relevant to conducting a trial. The law of torts works in concert with the laws of evidence and civil procedure. The Federal Rules of Civil Procedure and the Federal Rules of Evidence, for example, give federal district judges broad discretion to orchestrate the conduct of a trial. State courts similarly afford authority for the judge to move the case to final disposition — dismissal, trial, settlement, or other resolution. The trial judge shapes the nature and scope of admissible evidence and procedural posture of a case, serving as a gatekeeper to the conduct of the litigation. This section focuses on how the civil procedural course interrelates with the study of substantive tort law.

1. Finding Legal Representation

A contingency fee is a contract through which the plaintiff pays a fixed percentage of any collected judgment award to her attorneys. If personal injury practice required victims to pay an hourly rate or retainer, only those wealthy enough to pay a retainer fee could redress their claims, no matter how worthy the case. Contingency fee lawyers will not bring a case unless it is cost-justified. Consequently, the financial realities of this practice provide a screen against frivolous lawsuits. "Tort reformers" would counter that nuisance lawsuits are filed to extract settlements because it is cheaper to settle unworthy claims than to defend them. Ultimately, this issue depends upon the definition of frivolousness. The elderly plaintiff in the McDonald's hot coffee case had no imputed earnings and was partially responsible for her own injury. Even though Mrs. Liebeck had only modest general damages, she was able to secure legal representation because of the possibility of receiving non-economic damages and punitive damages. Mrs. Liebeck paid her attorney out of the settlement she received from McDonald's. Counsel deducts all litigation expenses from the settlement as well as the attorney's contingency fee before Mrs. Liebeck receives a single dollar. The meaning of "contingency" is that the lawyer's fee is contingent upon the success of the case. A plaintiff's counsel will typically receive one-third to forty percent of the judgment or settlement, though in some jurisdictions, fees are capped or subject to a fixed schedule. A few jurisdictions have capped the percentage depending upon what is recovered or the complexity of the case. *Contingent-Fee Caps Don't Achieve 'Reform' Goals, Study Finds*, Trial (Dec. 2005) at 67, 67.

2. Pre-Trial Settlement

Following an accident or tort injury, several important steps precede the litigation process. The plaintiff's attorney may engage in letter writing, negotiation, and other efforts to settle the matter short of suit. When liability is clear, parties tend to settle cases without any record of litigation or appeal. Ninety-eight percent of personal injury cases filed in federal district court for 2002–03 were resolved by mediation, settled out of court, or handled in some non-trial disposition. Only 2 percent of all tort cases filed resulted in a trial in federal cases. U.S. DEPT. OF JUSTICE, BUREAU OF JUSTICE STATISTICS, FEDERAL TORT TRIALS AND VERDICTS 1 (2002–03). The appellate cases in casebooks are exceptional in the sense that they are among the handful of cases that did *not* end with a pre-trial settlement. Tort trials are increasingly rare events. The popular culture glorifies groundbreaking trials, but in a sense, a client has lost if the litigation goes to trial and appeal. A brilliant lawyer might get a spectacular result for the client without trial.

3.   Pre-Litigation Case Preparation

The first step in a torts lawsuit is the decision of the injured party to take legal action. The second stage in the life of a tort claim is the initial interview with the client. At some point Reed Morgan, the Dallas attorney who took Mrs. Liebeck's case interviewed her and then made the decision to take her case. A plaintiff must file her complaint within the jurisdiction's statute of limitations. Torts statutes of limitation vary from state to state but are generally two or three years from the time when the plaintiff sustained the alleged injuries. In a complex toxic torts case, the plaintiff's attorney may need to obtain a soil report to measure contamination. In Mrs. Liebeck's case, the discovery focused on what McDonald's knew about prior hot coffee cases and when she knew it. The plaintiff needed to retain experts such as scientists who could testify as to the impact of superheated beverages on human tissue.

4.   Filing a Complaint

The pleadings consist of claims, answers, and counter-claims. In addition, the federal rules of civil procedure as well as state procedural rules permit litigants to add parties, claims, or amendments. If the parties do not settle, the litigation begins with the *complaint,* which states the facts of harm. In the complaint, the plaintiff tells what happened to entitle the plaintiff to relief. The federal rules, for example, provide that plaintiff's pleading should set forth "a short and plain statement of the claim showing that the pleader is entitled to relief." FED. R. CIV. P. 8(a). New Mexico's state civil procedure rules are functionally equivalent to those of the federal rules as to liberal pleading and filing a complaint. Mrs. Liebeck served a complaint on McDonald's Corporation with one count for strict products liability and another for the implied warranty of merchantability under New Mexico's Article 2 of the Uniform Commercial Code.

5.   Jury or Bench Trial

Mrs. Liebeck, like all plaintiffs, had a Seventh Amendment right under the U.S. Constitution to have her civil action decided by a jury. A plaintiff may waive that right to a jury and have the case decided by a trial judge, a proceeding known as a bench trial. Mrs. Liebeck's counsel made a strategic decision to try her case before a jury instead of a "bench" or judge trial. In complex business cases, in contrast, a plaintiff may prefer that a judge decide a case. In fact, contrary to public perception, empirical research demonstrates that a plaintiff is likely to fare better before a judge than a jury. Theodore Eisenberg, *Juries, Judges, and Punitive Damages: An Empirical Study*, 87 CORNELL L. REV. 743 (2002). This empirical study found that plaintiff prevailed at a higher rate in judge trials as compared to jury proceedings. Apparently, the "tort reformers" campaign to impugn the motives of injured plaintiffs has poisoned the jury pool. The "tort reformers" would counter that their campaign educates the public that we all pay for expanded liability with higher prices and insurance premiums.

6. Motion to Dismiss or Demurrer

In many jurisdictions, including federal jurisdiction, the contention that plaintiff is not entitled to relief despite the truth of her allegations is urged by a motion to dismiss for "failure to state a claim upon which relief can be granted." FED. R. CIV. P. 12(b)(6). It is likely that McDonald's filed a number of motions challenging the sufficiency of the evidence in the hot coffee case. Rule 12(b)(6) of the Federal Rules uses the concept of the motion to dismiss rather than the *demurrer*. A *demurrer* or motion to dismiss assumes that the facts alleged by plaintiff are true and contends that there is no legal theory supported by those facts that grants relief. For example, suppose Paula Plaintiff files a tort claim against Dan Defendant for failing to invite her to a social event. While this social slight may be humiliating to Paula, it does not constitute a tort action. If the court decides to grant the *demurrer*, the case is terminated at an early stage. The granting of a *demurrer* could be the end of the case, or plaintiff could appeal or seek to amend the complaint to address the shortcoming.

7. Defendant's Answer

An answer is the formal written statement by a defendant responding to a civil complaint and setting forth the grounds for her defense. If the court denies the *demurrer*, the defendant can file an appeal, admit facts, or file an *answer* that admits or denies the plaintiff's allegations of fact and contentions of law and pleads affirmative defenses. The defense counsel has to make strategic decisions whether to admit or deny facts, plead defenses, or make counterclaims (against the plaintiff) or cross claims (against a co-defendant).

8. Preliminary Objections

Prior to, or in addition to, answering the plaintiff's complaint, the defendant may file preliminary objections. *See* FED. R. CIV. P. 12(b). Defendants will frequently make preliminary objections as to jurisdiction. The course in civil procedure will highlight the problems of obtaining personal jurisdiction over a defendant located outside the forum. At this stage in the litigation, the defendant will challenge the sufficiency of evidence for punitive damages, where this remedy has been pleaded. The defendant's goal will be to dismiss the plaintiff's causes of action as well. In an employment torts case, the defendant will seek dismissal of the plaintiff's wrongful discharge claim. A defendant may for example, successfully argue that a federal statute such as an auto safety standard preempted a products liability action.

9. Pretrial Discovery

Mrs. Liebeck's attorney learned through discovery that McDonald's files contained more than 700 reports of prior similar injuries caused by its super-heated coffee, yet the company had taken no steps to turn down the heat. *See* Andrea Gerlin, *A Matter of Degree: How a Jury Decided That One Coffee Spill Is Worth $ 2.9 Million*, WALL ST. J., Sept. 1 1994, at A1. The plaintiff was able to obtain these documents through requests for production and depositions of key corporate witnesses. A trial court has wide discretion to manage pre-trial discovery that requests evidence from the other side. The Federal Rules of Civil Procedure grant a district court judge a number of devices to control discovery such as the ability to set the time limits as well as what is discoverable. The trial court's decisions will be upheld unless the appellate court finds that there has been an abuse of discretion. It is rare for an appellate court to overturn a trial court's decision as to the quantity, scope, and the sequencing of discovery. Both parties can use discovery to obtain documents, exhibits, records or other evidence in the possession of the other side. The Federal Rules of Civil Procedure, first adopted in 1938, as well as state civil procedure laws provide for a number of devices to facilitate discovery, including depositions or oral questions, written interrogatories, and request for documents.

Civil discovery is based on a philosophy of openness and access to information rather than surprises or dramatic courtroom disclosures. Indeed attorneys may be penalized for failing to disclose requested information. A deposition is an oral statement made by a person before an officer authorized by law to administer oaths. During discovery, a plaintiff will frequently seek to depose key corporate officials. In the McDonald's case, plaintiff's attorney, Reed Morgan, sent interrogatories to McDonald's counsel. Interrogatories are questions asked by one party of an opposing party, who must answer them in writing under oath. The plaintiff's counsel also deposed a high-level McDonald's manager who admitted that he had not evaluated the safety ramifications of serving coffee at superheated temperatures. This evidence was damaging because other establishments sold coffee at substantially lower temperatures, and coffee served at home is generally 135 to 140 degrees. This evidence, relevant to the issue of McDonald's compliance with industry custom, provided insight into the company's conduct.

10. Summary Judgment

The purpose of summary judgment is to eliminate nonmeritorious claims. In a products liability case, for example, summary judgment is proper when the plaintiff is unable to show that a product is defective at the time of sale. Summary judgment is also properly entered against the plaintiff when she cannot show that the defendant had a duty to warn an end-user of a particular use of a product. A trial court grants summary judgment only where the evidence is such that no reasonable jury could return a verdict for the non-moving party. There is a triable issue of material fact if, and only if, the evidence would allow a reasonable trier of fact to find the underlying fact in favor of the party opposing the motion. *See Anderson v. Liberty Lobby, Inc.*, 477 U.S. 242, 250 (1986). If the judge grants the motion, the defense saves the time and money of a trial whereas the plaintiff loses the opportunity to have her case heard by a jury. Summary judgment is appropriate when there is no dispute as to the facts of the case and one party is entitled to judgment as a matter of law. Summary judgment is appropriate only if there is no genuine issue as to a material fact. Either side may file a motion for summary judgment in the appropriate case. The court makes its determination based upon the pleadings, depositions, answers to interrogatories, and admissions on file, together with the affidavits. *See* FED. R. CIV. P. 56(C). Summary judgment is an example of a judicial control device that courts utilize to screen out questionable claims.

11. Choosing a Jury: Voir Dire

A growing number of states have devised model instructions to a jury before *voir dire*. In the McDonald's hot coffee case, counsel for the plaintiff and the defense used the *voir dire* to question jurors and get some sense of whether a prospective juror has a predisposition toward a side of the controversy. Each side of a case will typically be able to challenge potential jurors for cause and may also be able to use a limited number of *peremptory challenges* to strike potential jurors for no reason. The judge in any torts action will typically explain this process to the potential jury pool. New Jersey's model instructions explain how peremptory challenges work:

> After I have asked you a number of questions, which relate to your ability to hear and decide this case with an open mind and with complete impartiality, the attorneys who represent the parties in this lawsuit can exercise the right to excuse one or more of the jurors without giving any explanation or reason. If you are excused in that manner, please do not take it personally. No offense is intended. The law traditionally gives each attorney the right to have a limited number of jurors excused for no expressed reason.

New Jersey Model Civil Jury Charges 1.10 Instruction to Jurors Before Voir Dire 5. Counsel's Right to Preemptory Challenges (11/98).

The first stage in selecting a jury is when potential jurors receive a letter that they have been selected for jury service. The jurors will be given the time and place for reporting for service. "*Voir dire*" is a Latin phrase meaning "to speak the truth." The *voir dire* is the system, which permits attorneys or judges to question potential jurors to determine if they can decide the case in a fair and impair manner. "The *voir dire* examination of jurors. . .[is] to enable counsel to exercise intelligently the peremptory challenges allowed by law." *State v. Brown*, 280 S.E.2d 31, 32 (N.C. App. 1981). The purpose of the *voir dire* is to devise questions for potential jurors to determine whether they will be fair and impartial.

"To assume that a person, simply by virtue of *voir dire* and a judge's instructions, can set aside [his or her biases] is naïve." David A. Logan, *Tort Law and the Central Meaning of the First Amendment*, 51 U. PITT. L. REV. 493, 545 (1990). Commentators observe that "[o]ld assumptions that an injured plaintiff can rely upon jurors' . . . empathy for the underdog, or skepticism toward large corporate defendants, are no longer viable in preparing for trials or making decisions about *voir dire* and jury selection." Lois Heaney, *Jury Selection in the Era of Tort Reform*, 31 TRIAL 72, 72 (Nov. 1995).

Voir dire questions probe whether the potential juror can see past the notion of the tort system as a lottery. Cognitive dissonance is a psychological phenomenon that refers to the discomfort we feel when there is a discrepancy between our prior values or beliefs and new information. The danger for the plaintiff is that potential jurors will selectively perceive and distort evidence by relying on their "values" and "beliefs" on how the tort system works. To be receptive to the plaintiff, the potential juror must be favorably predisposed to the public policy underlying the tort system to make defendants accountable for recklessly endangering the public as opposed to giving the plaintiffs something for nothing as a windfall.

Plaintiffs' attorneys seek jurors who are open to the argument that tort law benefits society and not just the individual claimant. Tort issues are often complex with conflicting evidence, not black and white. Every potential juror knows about frivolous lawsuits and the anti-tort message of the McDonald's hot coffee case. A Texas trial judge constructed the following *voir dire* questions drawing upon the McDonald's coffee case:

> THE COURT: Now, talking about bias or prejudice. It's real important. Now, a lot of times we have opinions. Who has heard about the McDonald's coffee case where the lady spilled coffee, got burned and got all kinds of money? Who's heard about that? Raise your hand. Mr. _____.
>
> PROSPECTIVE JUROR: Yes.
>
> THE COURT: Did you have any strong opinions about that case based upon what you read in the newspaper?
>
> PROSPECTIVE JUROR: Yes, sir.
>
> THE COURT: What kind of opinion did you have?
>
> PROSPECTIVE JUROR: I thought it was kind of outlandish.
>
> THE COURT: Sounded ludicrous, didn't it? Just — you have some strong opinions. But those opinions they gave you, should those guide you in this case between these parties?
>
> PROSPECTIVE JUROR: Would they what?
>
> THE COURT: Should they guide you in this case?
>
> PROSPECTIVE JUROR: Could have.
>
> THE COURT: They could, but should they?
>
> PROSPECTIVE JUROR: No.
>
> THE COURT: No, not at all, because that's completely different. These folks aren't from McDonald's, are they? So does that case have anything to do with this lawsuit?

Lisa Blue and Robert Hirschhorn, *Example of Judge's Voir Dire*, 2 BLUE'S GUIDE TO JURY SELECTION app. E-1 (2006) (quoting Texas Judge Ken Curry's *Voir Dire*). *See also* Phoebe A. Haddon, *Rethinking the Jury*, 3 WM. & MARY BILL RTS. J. 29 (1994) (ability of attorneys to "deselect" potential jurors through the voir dire process and exercise of peremptory challenges).

Lawyers for both sides probe potential jurors to determine whether they are predisposed to favor the plaintiff or the defense. Critical theorists have researched the impact of race, class, and gender in striking or choosing jurors. A prominent jury consultant has stated, however: "[I]t's clear that [juror decisions are] in part shaped by being of a particular race or gender. . . . But that's only part of one's life experiences, which is why focus groups are so important, because otherwise you're relying on stereotypes." Leonard Post, *A Loaded Box of Stereotypes: Despite 'Batson,' Race, Gender Play Big Roles in Jury Selection*, NAT'L L. J., April 25, 2005, at 18 (quoting Jim Dobson, Vice President of DOAR Litigation Consulting).

12. Trial

If there is no resolution of the case at the summary judgment stage, then the case will proceed to *trial*. Plaintiff presents her case first. The burden of proof in a civil case is "preponderance of the evidence." Trial judges will sometimes hold brief informal conferences with attorneys from both sides out of earshot of the jury and spectators. In these sidebar conferences, the judge will remind counsel about introducing highly prejudicial matters that might compromise jury decisonmaking. The burden of proof is significant because if facts stand in equipoise — the 50-50 case — then the party with the burden of proof loses.

13. Opening Statement

The plaintiff's attorney is generally the first to give an *opening statement*. The purpose of the opening statement is to give the judge or jury an outline of the case. In the McDonald's hot coffee case, Stella Liebeck's attorney gave an opening statement which previewed the plaintiff's position that the extreme heat of the coffee led to her injury. McDonald's defense counsel explained why the company was not liable for Mrs. Liebeck's tragic accident. The theme of the defense was that, while Mrs. Liebeck suffered a tragic accident, the company was not liable for paying her damages.

14. Plaintiff's Case in Chief

In the McDonald's hot coffee case, Reed Morgan, attorney for the plaintiff, painted a picture of McDonald's conduct using "smoking gun" evidence that the restaurant chain was aware of the risk of injury posed by serving coffee at such high temperatures for more than ten years through numerous substantially similar claims and lawsuits. Mrs. Liebeck's counsel produced documents demonstrating that McDonald's knew of hundreds of similar claims settled from 1982 to 1992. Documents he obtained in discovery revealed hundreds of prior hot coffee cases where claimants suffered burn injuries to the genital area, perineum, inner thighs, and buttocks. The plaintiff elicited an admission from McDonald's quality control manager acknowledging that most consumers would be unaware of the risk of serious burn injuries from coffee served at 180 degrees or greater.

15.   Rulings on Admissibility of Evidence

In state courts as well as federal courts, the rules of civil procedure and the rules of evidence give judges a great deal of control over the nature and scope of admissible evidence to be considered at trial. In *Daubert v. Merrell Dow Pharmaceuticals*, 509 U.S. 579, 592–93 (1993), the U.S. Supreme Court established a new gate-keeping role for federal district judges in evaluating whether scientific evidence is admissible. *See* Margaret A. Berger, *Upsetting the Balance Between Adverse Interests: Expert Testimony in Toxic Tort Litigation*, 64 L. & CONTEMP. PROBS. 289, 325 (2001) (contending that *Daubert* has shifted the balance to defendants in toxic torts by . . . "converting rulings on the admissibility of evidence into rulings on the sufficiency of evidence. The result is that the critical issue of causation in toxic tort is being decided by federal judges, not . . . jurors, and in pretrial proceedings, rather than at trial.").

In addition to ruling on the qualification of experts and the admissibility of expert testimony, trial judges rule on the admissibility of evidence challenged under the hearsay rule or challenged for lack of relevance. These rulings may be the subject of appeals.

Evidence is relevant if it merely has "any tendency to make the existence of any fact that is of consequence to the determination of the action more probable or less probable than it would be without the evidence." Fed. R. Evid. 401. However, in Mrs. Liebeck's case, Judge Robert Scott excluded a number of graphic photographs of burn injuries from other McDonald's hot coffee cases on the grounds that they were more prejudicial than probative. Fed. R. Evid. 401.

16.   Closing Arguments

Closing arguments, like the opening statements, give each side's take on the evidence, causes of action, and defenses. Closing arguments are generally 15–30 minutes long and are the last attempt to communicate directly with the jurors. The trial court sets time limits and is the umpire that settles disputes about the content of closing arguments. Either counsel may challenge unfair arguments. The defense counsel, for example, may challenge arguments that inflame the jury in order to inflate damage awards. The plaintiff's counsel will remind the jury that the burden of proof and persuasion is only more probable than not or slightly more than 50/50 (reflecting a preponderance of the evidence). Closing arguments give both sides a chance to summarize their take on the evidence presented at trial. Plaintiff's counsel will typically summarize her view of the witnesses, exhibits and other evidence that was presented at trial.

In some states, counsel may not request a specific sum of money to compensate for pain and suffering. Many defense counsel will acknowledge that the plaintiff has been injured in a tort case but remind the jury that his client owed no duty to the plaintiff. Defense counsel will frequently emphasize that the plaintiff did not prove the elements of the case. If the plaintiff was contributorily negligent as in the McDonald's case, defense counsel may use a theme of "personal responsibility." Plaintiff's counsel in the hot coffee case also could have used the "personal responsibility" theme to ask the jury to make McDonald's accountable for its failure to protect the consuming public.

After the closing arguments, either side may file directed verdict motions, arguing that no reasonable jury could rule otherwise than conclude that the party should prevail.

17. Jury Instructions

The judge explains to the jury the law that applies to the set of facts that has given rise to the tort. The judge instructs the jury before it begins deliberations. These *jury instructions*, sometimes called the *charge to the jury,* explain the law that governs the case and enumerates questions the jury must answer. Judge Scott instructed the New Mexico jury to consider whether Mrs. Liebeck contributed to her own injury and, if so, to what degree.

> Jury instructions must . . . *communicate* the law to jurors. Bear in mind that communicating is different from merely *speaking* or *reading* to someone. You can speak to someone without that person understanding what you said, as happens when the hearer does not share the speaker's language. Communication, in contrast, requires not just that you speak or read to someone but also that the audience actually understand what you intended to communicate. Otherwise, your attempt to communicate has failed. Simply reading instructions to jurors cannot, by itself, be considered communication.

Peter M. Tiersma, *Communicating with Juries: How to Draft More Understandable Instructions,* 10 Scribes J. Legal Writing 1, 1–2 (2005/2006) (emphasis added). *See generally* Ronald W. Eades, Jury Instructions on Damages in Tort Actions (5th ed. 2003).

18. Directed Verdict and Judgment Notwithstanding the Verdict (J.N.O.V.)

After the close of the plaintiff's case, the defendant may file a motion for a *directed verdict*, which alleges, even if everything plaintiff says is true, defendant still has to win. A directed verdict motion argues that an essential fact is missing and the plaintiff has not proven the case. This directed verdict motion may also be renewed after the verdict. The Federal Rules of Civil Procedure and the equivalent procedures in state courts treat the directed verdict and the *judgment non obstante veredicto* (J.N.O.V.) in the post-verdict period as functional equivalents.

Each state has a procedure for entering judgment that parallels the federal rules of civil procedure. *See* Fed. R.Civ. P. 58. After the jury verdict, it is typical for the losing party to file a motion for judgment not withstanding the verdict. The Federal Rules of Civil Procedure permit the losing party to renew its motions for judgment as a matter of law, which is equivalent to the J.N.O.V. motion in many states. *See* Fed. R. Civ. P. 50(b). Under the Federal Rules of Civil Procedure, the losing party combines the renewed motion for judgment as a matter of law and the motion for a new trial. The standard for either motion is the same and a judge will grant the motion if the jury could not have reasonably reached the verdict on evidence in case. The losing party will frequently argue that it is entitled to a new title because the jury's verdict is against the weight of the evidence. In the McDonald's case, the trial judge ruled against McDonald's on its post-verdict motions for a directed verdict and a new trial.

19.   Motion for Remittitur or Additur

In many jurisdictions, a trial court has the discretion to enter either a remittitur or additur, reducing or enlarging the damages. After the jury's decision in the McDonald's hot coffee case, counsel for McDonald's filed a Motion for J.N.O.V. and in the alternative, a motion of remittitur. The trial judge reduced (remitted) the punitive damages awarded to Mrs. Liebeck from $2.7 million to $480,000. Eventually, the parties reached a confidential post-verdict settlement, presumably for a substantially reduced dollar amount. The $2.7 million award represented only about two days' profit from the nationwide sales of McDonald's coffee — not two days' total earnings.

Punitive damages were reduced or overturned on appeal in fifty percent of the cases decided between the years 1965–90. No additurs were entered. Michael Rustad, *In Defense of Punitive Damages in Product Liability: Testing Tort Anecdotes with Empirical Data*, 78 IOWA L. REV. 1, 30 (1992). *See also* Thomas Koenig & Michael Rustad, *The Quiet Revolution Revisited: An Empirical Study of the Impact of State Tort Reform of Punitive Damages in Products Liability*, 16 JUST. SYS. J. 21 (1993).

Consider the following case in light of the perspectives, procedures, and other information that has been discussed in this chapter. Approach a torts case or problem by first considering the potential basis or bases of liability. Which of the three tort bases of liability is at issue? Think about the procedural history of the case, as well as the issue before the court. Reflect upon the multiple perspectives and what light they shed upon this appellate case.

F.   A CASE TO STUDY

PEREZ v. WYETH LABORATORIES INC.
161 N.J. 1, 734 A.2d 1245 (1999)

O'HERN, JUSTICE.

Our medical-legal jurisprudence is based on images of health care that no longer exist. At an earlier time, medical advice was received in the doctor's office from a physician who most likely made house calls if needed. The patient usually paid a small sum of money to the doctor. Neighborhood pharmacists compounded prescribed medicines.

Pharmaceutical manufacturers never advertised their products to patients, but rather directed all sales efforts at physicians. In this comforting setting, the law created an exception to the traditional duty of manufacturers to warn consumers directly of risks associated with the product as long as they warned health-care providers of those risks.

For good or ill, that has all changed. Medical services are in large measure provided by managed care organizations. Medicines are purchased in the pharmacy department of supermarkets and often paid for by third-party providers. Drug manufacturers now directly advertise products to consumers on the radio, television, the Internet, billboards on public transportation, and in magazines. . . .

The question in this case, broadly stated, is whether our law should follow these changes in the marketplace or reflect the images of the past. We believe that when mass marketing of prescription drugs seeks to influence a patient's choice of a drug, a pharmaceutical manufacturer that makes direct claims to consumers for the efficacy of its product should not be unqualifiedly relieved of a duty to provide proper warnings of the dangers or side effects of the product.

This appeal concerns Norplant, a Food and Drug Administration (FDA)-approved, reversible contraceptive that prevents pregnancy for up to five years. The Norplant contraceptive employs six thin, flexible, closed capsules that contain a synthetic hormone, levonorgestrel. The capsules are implanted under the skin of a woman's upper arm during an in-office surgical procedure characterized by the manufacturer as minor. A low, continuous dosage of the hormone diffuses through the capsule walls and into the bloodstream. Although the capsules are not usually visible under the skin, the outline of the fan- like pattern can be felt under the skin. Removal occurs during an in-office procedure, similar to the insertion process.

. . . According to plaintiffs, Wyeth began a massive advertising campaign for Norplant in 1991, which it directed at women rather than at their doctors. Wyeth advertised on television and in women's magazines such as Glamour, Mademoiselle and Cosmopolitan. According to plaintiffs, none of the advertisements warned of any inherent danger posed by Norplant; rather, all praised its simplicity and convenience. None warned of side effects including pain and permanent scarring attendant to removal of the implants. Wyeth also sent a letter to physicians advising them that it was about to launch a national advertising program in magazines that the physicians' patients may read.

Plaintiffs cite several studies published in medical journals that have found Norplant removal to be difficult and painful. One study found that thirty-three percent of women had removal difficulty and forty percent experienced pain. Another study found that fifty-two percent of physicians reported complications during removal. Medical journals have catalogued the need for advanced medical technicians in addition to general surgeons for Norplant removal. Plaintiffs assert that none of this information was provided to consumers.

In 1995, plaintiffs began to file lawsuits in several New Jersey counties claiming injuries that resulted from their use of Norplant. Plaintiffs' principal claim alleged that Wyeth, distributors of Norplant in the United States, failed to warn adequately about side effects associated with the contraceptive. Side effects complained of by plaintiffs included weight gain, headaches, dizziness, nausea, diarrhea, acne, vomiting, fatigue, facial hair growth, numbness in the arms and legs, irregular menstruation, hair loss, leg cramps, anxiety and nervousness, vision problems, anemia, mood swings and depression, high blood pressure, and removal complications that resulted in scarring. . . .

After a case management conference, plaintiffs' counsel sought a determination of whether the learned intermediary doctrine applied. . . .

In New Jersey, as elsewhere, we accept the proposition that a pharmaceutical manufacturer generally discharges its duty to warn the ultimate user of prescription drugs by supplying physicians with information about the drug's dangerous propensities. This concept is known as the "learned intermediary" rule because the physician acts as the intermediary between the manufacturer and the consumer. . . .

It is paradoxical that so pedestrian a concern as male-pattern baldness should have signaled the beginning of direct-to-consumer marketing of prescription drugs. Upjohn Company became the first drug manufacturer to advertise directly to consumers when it advertised for Rogaine, a hair-loss treatment. The ad targeted male consumers by posing the question, "Can an emerging bald spot . . . damage your ability to get along with others, influence your chance of obtaining a job or date or even interfere with your job performance?" A related ad featured an attractive woman asserting suggestively, "I know that a man who can afford Rogaine is a man who can afford me."

Advertising for Rogaine was the tip of the iceberg. Since drug manufacturers began marketing directly to consumers for products such as prescription drugs in the 1980s, almost all pharmaceutical companies have engaged in this direct marketing practice.

. . . Among the most controversial of the new marketing techniques employed by pharmaceutical manufacturers is direct-to-consumer prescription advertising in a variety of formats and media. Pharmaceutical remedies for varied problems such as allergies, nail fungus, hypertension, hair loss, and depression are placed directly before the consumer in magazines, television, and via the Internet. The utilization of direct consumer marketing raises questions and issues addressing manufacturer liability for failure to adequately warn of risks possibly associated with pharmaceutical use.

The American Medical Association (AMA) has long maintained a policy in opposition to product-specific prescription ads aimed at consumers. A 1992 study by the Annals of Internal Medicine reports that a peer review of 109 prescription ads found 92 per cent of the advertisements lacking in some manner. . . .

The difficulties that accompany this [type of advertising] practice are manifest. "The marketing gimmick used by the drug manufacturer often provides the consumer with a diluted variation of the risks associated with the drug product." Even without such manipulation, "[t]elevision spots lasting 30 or 60 seconds are not conducive to 'fair balance' [in presentation of risks]." Given such constraints, pharmaceutical ads often contain warnings of a general nature. However, "[r]esearch indicates that general warnings (for example, see your doctor) in [direct-to-consumer] advertisements do not give the consumer a sufficient understanding of the risks inherent in product use." Consumers often interpret such warnings as a "general reassurance" that their condition can be treated, rather than as a requirement that "specific vigilance" is needed to protect them from product risks.

. . . [T]he New Jersey Products Liability Act provides:

An adequate product warning or instruction is one that a reasonably prudent person in the same or similar circumstances would have provided with respect to the danger and that communicates adequate information on the dangers and safe use of the product, taking into account the characteristics of, and the ordinary knowledge common to, the persons by whom the product is intended to be used, or in the case of prescription drugs, taking into account the characteristics of, and the ordinary knowledge common to, the prescribing physician. If the warning or instruction given in connection with a drug or device or food or food additive has been approved or prescribed by the federal Food and Drug Administration under the "Federal Food, Drug, and Cosmetic Act," 52 Stat. 1040, 21 U.S.C. § 301 *et seq.*, . . . a rebuttable presumption shall arise that the warning or instruction is adequate. . . .

[N.J.S.A. 2A:58C-4.]

Although the statute provides a physician-based standard for determining the adequacy of the warning due to a physician, the statute does not legislate the boundaries of the doctrine. . . . Rather, the statute governs the content of an "adequate product warning," when required. As noted, direct-to-consumer marketing of prescription drugs was in its beginning stages. . . .

Our dissenting member suggests that we should await legislative action before deciding that issue. . . . We are satisfied that our decision today is well within the competence of the judiciary. Defining the scope of tort liability has traditionally been accepted as the responsibility of the courts. If we decline to resolve the question, we are making the substantive determination that the learned intermediary doctrine applies to the direct marketing of drugs, an issue recently debated but left unanswered by the drafters of the Restatement. Either course, then, requires us to adopt a principle of law. The question is which is the better principle.

A more recent review summarized the theoretical bases for the doctrine as based on four considerations:

First, courts do not wish to intrude upon the doctor-patient relationship. From this perspective, warnings that contradict information supplied by the physician will undermine the patient's trust in the physician's judgment. Second, physicians may be in a superior position to convey meaningful information to their patients, as they must do to satisfy their duty to secure informed consent. Third, drug manufacturers lack effective means to communicate directly with patients, making it necessary to rely on physicians to convey the relevant information. Unlike [over the counter products], pharmacists usually dispense prescription drugs from bulk containers rather than as unit-of-use packages in which the manufacturer may have enclosed labeling. Finally, because of the complexity of risk information about prescription drugs, comprehension problems would complicate any effort by manufacturers to translate physician labeling for lay patients.

Lars Noah, *Advertising Prescription Drugs to Consumers: Assessing the Regulatory and Liability Issues*, 32 GA. L. REV. 141, 157–59 (1997). These premises: (1) reluctance to undermine the doctor patient-relationship; (2) absence in the era of "doctor knows best" of need for the patient's informed consent; (3) inability of drug manufacturer to communicate with patients; and (4) complexity of the subject, are all (with the possible exception of the last) absent in the direct-to-consumer advertising of prescription drugs.

First, with rare and wonderful exceptions, the "'Norman Rockwell' image of the family doctor no longer exists." Informed consent requires a patient-based decision rather than the paternalistic approach of the 1970s.

Second, because managed care has reduced the time allotted per patient, physicians have considerably less time to inform patients of the risks and benefits of a drug.

Third, having spent $1.3 billion on advertising in 1998, drug manufacturers can hardly be said to "lack effective means to communicate directly with patients," Noah, *supra*, 32 GA. L. REV. at 158, when their advertising campaigns can pay off in close to billions in dividends.

Consumer-directed advertising of pharmaceuticals thus belies each of the premises on which the learned intermediary doctrine rests:

> First, the fact that manufacturers are advertising their drugs and devices to consumers suggests that consumers are active participants in their health care decisions, invalidating the concept that it is the doctor, not the patient, who decides whether a drug or device should be used. Second, it is illogical that requiring manufacturers to provide direct warnings to a consumer will undermine the patient-physician relationship, when, by its very nature, consumer-directed advertising encroaches on that relationship by encouraging consumers to ask for advertised products by name. Finally, consumer-directed advertising rebuts the notion that prescription drugs and devices and their potential adverse effects are too complex to be effectively communicated to lay consumers. Because the FDA requires that prescription drug and device advertising carry warnings, the consumer may reasonably presume that the advertiser guarantees the adequacy of its warnings. Thus, the common law duty to warm the ultimate consumer should apply.

Susan A. Casey, Comment, *Laying an Old Doctrine to Rest: Challenging the Wisdom of the Learned Intermediary Doctrine*, 19 WM. MITCHELL L. REV. 931, 956 (1993).

When all of its premises are absent, as when direct warnings to consumers are mandatory, the learned intermediary doctrine, "itself an exception to the manufacturer's traditional duty to warn consumers directly of the risk associated with any product, simply drops out of the calculus, leaving the duty of the manufacturer to be determined in accordance with general principles of tort law." *Edwards v. Basel Pharms.*, 116 F.3d 1341, 1343 (10th Cir. 1997) . . . .

Concerns regarding patients' communication with and access to physicians are magnified in the context of medicines and medical devices furnished to women for reproductive decisions. *In MacDonald Ortho Pharmaceutical Corp.*, 475 N.E.2d 65, *cert. denied*, 474 U.S. 920 (1985), the plaintiff's use of oral contraceptives allegedly resulted in a stroke. The Massachusetts Supreme Court explained several reasons why contraceptives differ from other prescription drugs and thus "warrant the imposition of a common law duty on the manufacturer to warn users directly of associated risks." For example, after the patient receives the prescription, she consults with the physician to receive a prescription annually, leaving her an infrequent opportunity to "explore her questions and concerns about the medication with the prescribing physician." Consequently, the limited participation of the physician leads to a real possibility that their communication during the annual checkup is insufficient. The court also explained that because oral contraceptives are drugs personally selected by the patient, a prescription is often not the result of a physician's skilled balancing of individual benefits and risks but originates, instead, as a product of patient choice. Thus, "the physician is relegated to a . . . passive role."

Patient choice is an increasingly important part of our medical-legal jurisprudence. New Jersey has long since abandoned the "professional standard" in favor of the objectively-prudent-patient rule, recognizing the informed role of the patient in health-care decisions. When a patient is the target of direct marketing, one would think, at a minimum, that the law would require that the patient not be misinformed about the product. It is one thing not to inform a patient about the potential side effects of a product; it is another thing to misinform the patient by deliberately withholding potential side effects while marketing the product as an efficacious solution to a serious health problem. Further, when one considers that many of these "life-style" drugs or elective treatments cause significant side effects without any curative effect, increased consumer protection becomes imperative, because these drugs are, by definition, not medically necessary.

. . . Obviously, the learned intermediary doctrine applies when its predicates are present. "In New Jersey, as elsewhere, we accept the proposition that a pharmaceutical manufacturer generally discharges its duty to warn the ultimate users of prescription drugs by supplying physicians with information about the drug's dangerous propensities." *Niemiera v. Schneider*, 114 N.J. 550, 559 (1989). Had Wyeth done just that, simply supplied the physician with information about the product, and not advertised directly to the patients, plaintiffs would have no claim against Wyeth based on an independent duty to warn patients. The question is whether the absence of an independent duty to warn patients gives the manufacturer the right to misrepresent to the public the product's safety.

In reaching the conclusion that the learned intermediary doctrine does not apply to the direct marketing of drugs to consumers, we must necessarily consider that when prescription drugs are marketed and labeled in accordance with FDA specifications, the pharmaceutical manufacturers should not have to confront "state tort liability premised on theories of design defect or warning inadequacy.". . .

We believe that in the area of direct-to-consumer advertising of pharmaceuticals, the same rebuttable presumption should apply when a manufacturer complies with FDA advertising, labeling and warning requirements. That approach harmonizes the manufacturer's duty to doctors and to the public when it chooses to directly advertise its products, and simultaneously recognizes the public interest in informing patients about new pharmaceutical developments. Moreover, a rebuttable presumption that the duty to consumers is met by compliance with FDA regulations helps to ensure that manufacturers are not made guarantors against remotely possible, but not scientifically-verifiable, side-effects of prescription drugs, a result that could have a "significant anti-utilitarian effect."

We believe that this standard is fair and balanced. For all practical purposes, absent deliberate concealment or nondisclosure of after-acquired knowledge of harmful effects, compliance with FDA standards should be virtually dispositive of such claims. By definition, the advertising will have been "fairly balanced."

. . . On balance, we believe that the patient's interest in reliable information predominates over a policy interest that would insulate manufacturers.

. . . [T]he dramatic shift in pharmaceutical marketing to consumers is based in large part on significant changes in the health-care system from fee- for-service to managed care. Managed care companies negotiate directly with pharmaceutical companies and then inform prescribers which medications are covered by the respective plans. Because managed care has made it more difficult for pharmaceutical companies to communicate with prescribers the manufacturers have developed a different strategy, marketing to consumers. . . .

The direct marketing of drugs to consumers generates a corresponding duty requiring manufacturers to warn of defects in the product. The FDA has established a comprehensive regulatory scheme for direct-to-consumer marketing of pharmaceutical products. Given the presumptive defense that is afforded to pharmaceutical manufacturers that comply with FDA requirements, we believe that it is fair to reinforce the regulatory scheme by allowing, in the case of direct-to-consumer marketing of drugs, patients deprived of reliable medical information to establish that the misinformation was a substantial factor contributing to their use of a defective pharmaceutical product.

[The court notes that because of the procedural posture of the case, Wyeth has not had a chance to offer evidence in defense of Norplant and thus the product may be presently cast in an unfair light.]

Finally, we return briefly to the main theme of the dissent, that our decision is inconsistent with legislative mandate. We are certain that legislative codification of the learned intermediary doctrine — which generally relieves a pharmaceutical manufacturer of an independent duty to warn the ultimate user of prescription drugs, as long as it has supplied the physician with information about a drug's dangerous propensities — does not confer on pharmaceutical manufacturers a license to mislead or deceive consumers when those manufacturers elect to exercise their right to advertise their product directly to such consumers.

The judgment of the Appellate Division is reversed and the matter is remanded to the Law Division for further proceedings.

POLLOCK, J., dissenting.

With disarming understatement, the majority opinion raises profound questions about the purpose of judicial opinions, the role of courts, and the separation of powers. . . .

Judges, although they may disagree with a legislative policy, are bound to respect it. In adapting the common law to society's needs, this Court may not have favored manufacturers, including pharmaceutical companies, as enthusiastically as has the Legislature. The issue, however, is not whether the Court shares the Legislature's enthusiasm or even whether the majority would prefer to amend the common-law learned intermediary doctrine. Because of the enactment of the NJPLA, the issue is whether the majority should respect the learned intermediary doctrine as declared by the Legislature. . . .

NOTES

1. *Judicial and Legislative Roles in Establishing Liability Rules. Perez* held that when pharmaceutical companies market directly to consumers, they owe a duty to adequately warn those consumers. This ruling marked a major shift in existing tort doctrine. The majority in *Perez* explains the decision to adopt a new rule extending liability of drug companies to consumers, notwithstanding the "learned intermediary" rule, on the basis that methods of practicing medicine and selling prescription drugs have changed dramatically since the learned intermediary rule was adopted. Is this decision, as the dissent suggests, better made by elected legislatures or an example of how the common law system remains viable?

Does the court have the power, and should it exercise the power, to change a tort rule if the legislature has enacted a new law on the same subject in recent years? Is the reasoning of the majority in *Perez* persuasive on the question of whether the recently enacted New Jersey statute should govern the result in this case? For broad discussion of the impact of modern technologies and business models on tort rules, see Nicolas P. Terry, *Cyber-Malpractice: Legal Exposure for Cybermedicine*, 25 AM. J.L. & MED. 327 (1999); *Structural and Legal Implications of e-Health*, 33 J. HEALTH L. 605 (2000).

Assume that there had been no statute relevant to the issue of whether a drug company could be liable to a consumer for failing to directly warn the consumer about the dangers of its product. Would it be proper for the court to decide the issue in the first instance and create a precedent? Once the precedent has been set, would the court lack the power to change it? If it is proper for a court to create a precedent for liability, is it nevertheless proper for the state legislature to change the rules set by the court for allocating the risks? *Cf. Ives v. South Buffalo Ry. Co.*, 94 N.E. 431, 448 (N.Y.1911) (holding that the state legislature violated the due process rights of employers when it enacted a Worker's Compensation statute making employers in certain industries liable for workers injured on the job, regardless of fault); and *New York Cent. R. Co. v. White*, 243 U.S.188, 198 (1917) (declaring that no man has a vested interest in the common law, and holding that it was not a violation of due process for the state to provide for employer liability without fault.) What is the distinction between a court's role and the legislature's role in creating new systems and standards for resolving tort disputes? What limitations exist, or ought to exist, in the American legal system on the power of the state legislature to adopt new approaches to compensating persons who are victims of accidents?

2. *Impact of Legal Rules.* While the resolution of a dispute in a tort case immediately affects only the parties to the lawsuit, in the long run the rules adopted and applied will affect other persons with similar disputes and, sometimes, identifiable classes of persons. The values at stake in the controversy influence decision-makers. How decision-makers regard the class of people who will benefit from or be hurt by a particular law also impact decision-making. What classes are most affected by the controversy in *Perez?*

3. *Race, Gender, Economic Wealth, and Other Identity Categories.* The United States legal system aspires to treat all parties equally, regardless of race, gender, economic wealth or other identity categories. This ideal is not yet fully realized. If evidence shows that a product such as Norplant has a disproportionately damaging impact on individuals of a particular race, gender, or economic background should the court or jury take race, gender, or economic class issues into conscious consideration in a tort action brought against the seller of the product? What are the dangers of consciously considering or ignoring such issues? With respect to the Norplant controversy, one author who studied in great detail the marketing of the birth control device observes:

> At a time when legislatures nationwide are slashing social programs for the poor, public aid for Norplant became a popular budget item. Without financial assistance, the cost of Norplant would be prohibitive. The capsules cost $365 and the implantation procedure can run from $150 to $500. Removal costs another $150 to $500, or more if there are complications. The government sprang into action. Every state and the District of Columbia almost immediately made Norplant available to poor women through Medicaid. Tennessee passed a law in 1993 requiring that anyone who receives AFDC or other forms of public assistance be notified in writing about the state's offer of free Norplant. Women in Washington State who receive maternity care assistance also get information about Norplant. By 1994, states had already spent $34 million on Norplant-related benefits. As a result, at least half of the women in the United State who have used Norplant are Medicaid recipients.

DOROTHY ROBERTS, KILLING THE BLACK BODY: RACE, REPRODUCTION, AND THE MEANING OF LIBERTY 108 (1997).

Reflecting critical race and critical feminist theorist's perspectives, Professor Roberts sees a link between the actions of the states and race:

> Although we should not underestimate this class dimension of programs that regulate welfare mothers, it is crucial to see that race equally determines the programs' features and popularity. Because class distinctions are racialized, race and class are inextricably linked in the development of welfare policy. When Americans debate welfare reform, most have single Black mothers in mind.

Id. at 110.

AmericanWarner, parent company of Wyeth Labs, recalled all Norplant issued after 2000 in the wake of multiple lawsuits and discontinued production in July, 2002. *See* Leslie Berger, *After Long Hiatus, New Contraceptives Emerge*, N.Y. TIMES, Dec. 10, 2002, at F5.

Should it be relevant to a decision maker that only women use the product? For an introduction to feminist legal theory and methodology, see Katharine T. Bartlett, *Cracking Foundations as Feminist Method*, 8 AM. U. J. GENDER SOC. POL'Y & L. 31 (2000); Lorena Fries and Verónica Matus, *Why Does the Method Matter?*, 7 AM. U. J. GENDER SOC. POL'Y & L. 291 (1999). For a discussion of gender issues in the specific context of tort law, see Leslie Bender, *A Primer on Feminist Tort Theory*, 38 J. LEGAL EDUC. 3 (1988); Martha Chamallas, *Civil Rights in Ordinary Torts Cases: Race, Gender and the Calculation of Economic Loss*, 38 LOY. L.A. L. REV. 1435 (2005). Would it be relevant if most of the women using the product were poor and women of color?

Should attorneys representing the plaintiffs attempt to marshal evidence related to identity categories and bring it to the court's attention? For different perspectives on these questions, see Martha Chamallas, *Questioning the Use of Race-Specific and Gender-Specific Economic Data in Tort Litigation: A Constitutional Argument*, 63 FORDHAM L. REV. 73 (1994); Frank M. McClellan, *The Dark Side of Tort Reform: Searching for Racial Justice*, 48 RUTGERS L. REV. 761 (1996); JODY D. ARMOUR, NEGROPHOBIA AND REASONABLE RACISM (1997). For an in-depth exploration of the ramifications of addressing or ignoring race and gender issues in the development and application of the law, see JUAN PEREA, RICHARD DELGADO, ANGELA HARRIS & STEPHANIE WILDMAN, RACE AND RACES: CASES AND MATERIALS FOR A DIVERSE AMERICA 2d. ed. (2007).

4. *Teaching and Learning.* For an article exploring the relevance of race, gender, class, and culture to the teaching of torts, see Taunya Lovell Banks, *Teaching Laws With Flaws: Adopting a Pluralist Approach to Torts,* 57 MO. L. REV. 443 (1992); *see also* Lucinda M. Finley, *A Break in the Silence: Including Women's Issues in a Torts Course*, 1 YALE J. L. & FEMINISM 41 (1989) (exploring gender issues).

5. *The Goal of Accident Cost Avoidance.* In a book that has had considerable influence on the trends of modern tort law, Guido Calabresi described the goals of tort law as including deterrence, cost spreading, and justice. GUIDO

CALABRESI, THE COSTS OF ACCIDENTS. A LEGAL AND ECONOMIC ANALYSIS 24–33 (1970). He explores in depth the meaning and application of each of these goals except "justice." While acknowledging that justice is an important goal, he doubts whether one can say much about it independent of the other goals, except to acknowledge that it exists as an ultimate goal. *Id.* at 24–26. In light of the introductory discussion of perspectives, is it possible to define justice without referring to deterrence and cost spreading? Employing Calabresi's list of goals, which goal should dominate the resolution of the controversy in *Perez*, and why? Is it possible to adopt an approach that would promote all of these goals in this fact situation?

6. *Sources for Further Study of Tort Law.* For a good review of the basic elements of tort law and the public policies supporting that law, see Frank L. Maraist, *Of Envelopes and Legends: Reflections on Tort Law*, 61 LA. L. REV. 153 (2000); WILLIAM L. PROSSER ET AL., PROSSER AND KEETON ON TORTS (5th ed. 1984); ROBERT L. RABIN, PERSPECTIVES ON TORT LAW (4th ed. 2003); A TORTS ANTHOLOGY (Lawrence C. Levine et al. eds. 1998); THOMAS H. KOENIG & MICHAEL L. RUSTAD, IN DEFENSE OF TORT LAW (2003); ALAN CALNAN, REVISIONIST HISTORY OF TORT LAW FROM HOLMESIAN REALISM TO NEOCLASSICAL RATIONALISM (2005); G. EDWARD WHITE, TORT LAW IN AMERICA: AN INTELLECTUAL HISTORY (2003); TORT STORIES (Robert L. Rabin & Stephen D. Sugarman eds., 2003); and EXPLORING TORT LAW (M. Stuart Madden ed. 2005). For additional problems, see JOSEPH W. GLANNON, LAW OF TORTS: EXAMPLES AND EXPLANATIONS (3d ed. 2005).

Chapter 2

INTENTIONAL TORTS

A. INTRODUCTION

This chapter addresses the elements of intentional torts directed to individual persons and property. At common law, civil wrongs were largely about intentional injuries to the person and invasions of personal and real property. Today, tort law primarily focuses on negligently caused accidents. A National Center for State Courts study concluded that intentional torts accounted only for 2.9% (or 10,879) of the approximately 378,000 torts decided by courts in 1992. The largest number of state tort law were tried in negligence, with automobile accident cases alone accounting for 60% of the cases. U.S. Dep't of Justice, Bureau of Justice Statistics, *Tort Cases in Large Counties, Civil Justice Survey of State Courts* 1992 (1995) at 2. While small in number, intentional torts have evolved to address modern problems such as new Internet-related threats. Torts once used to defend against the dispossession of cows are now used to redress social problems such as online stalking, spam e-mail, and computer viruses.

Intentional torts redress legally protected interests arising out of interference with the person, intentional infliction of emotional distress, interference with the use of land, interferences with chattels, malicious prosecution, abuse of process, intentional interference with an interest in personal dignity, and the invasion of privacy. Chapter 14 also covers intentional economic torts such as fraud, misappropriation, and interference with contract.

This chapter introduces the *prima facie* case for intentional torts. For a plaintiff to survive a motion for summary judgment, there must be some evidentiary basis to support each element of the tort. If the plaintiff is able to present such evidence to the factfinder, she has established a *prima facie* case. For each intentional tort, the trial judge instructs the jury that it is the Plaintiff's burden of proof and persuasion to prove each element of the *prima facie* case for an intentional tort by a preponderance of the evidence. A *prima facie* case is the minimum sufficient proof for each element of a tort cause of action if the court disregards evidence to the contrary. The defendant may avoid tort liability by asserting and proving affirmative defenses. Chapter 3 covers the classic affirmative defenses to, and justification for, intentional torts including consent, self defense, the defense of others, the defense of property, parental discipline, protection of public interests, and necessity.

B. INTENT

An injury is intentional only if the defendant did some volitional act and intended the consequences. For example, in a 1647 case, the court ruled that a man carried onto the plaintiff's land against his will by third parties was not liable for trespass. *Smith v. Stone*, 82 Eng. Rep. 533 (1647). The plaintiff has the burden of demonstrating intent as well as an act in order to establish a *prima facie* case. In tort law, as in criminal law, an act is defined as an "external manifestation of the actor's will." REST. 2D TORTS § 2.

The *Bazley v. Tortorich* case, that follows below, explains the tort concept of intent. As you read *Bazley*, determine how the plaintiff attempted to prove the defendant's intent and act. Intent means "that the actor desires to cause consequences of his act or that he believes that the consequences are substantially certain to result from it. REST. 2D TORTS § 8A. "General awareness — an understanding that harm is resulting or will result from the illegal use and possession of handguns — is not enough to satisfy the requirement that a defendant know[s] interference with a public right is resulting or will be substantially certain to result from its conduct." *NAACP v. AcuSport, Inc.*, 271 F. Supp. 2d 435, 488 (E.D. N.Y. 2003). "Intent may be proven by circumstantial evidence, that is, by inferences reasonably drawn from the facts established." *Id.*

Must the plaintiff prove that the defendant intended harmful or offensive consequences as well as the resultant injuries in a case? Or, must the plaintiff only prove that the defendant intended the physical contact? Counsel must make strategic decisions about how to characterize a given fact pattern in contemplation of the substantive requirements of the tort. As you read the case, consider why the plaintiff's counsel structured the case as an intentional tort action rather than an ordinary negligence case. What role did Louisiana's Workers' Compensation Act play in this decision? What was the flaw in the plaintiff's unorthodox definition of intent?

BAZLEY v. TORTORICH
397 So. 2d 475 (La. 1981)

DENNIS, JUSTICE.

This case presents the question of whether the worker's compensation statute. . . . constitutionally makes compensation an employee's exclusive remedy for a work-related injury caused by a co-worker, except for a suit based on an intentional tort. The trial court sustained an exception of no cause of action to plaintiff's suit against his fellow employee because he alleged that the co-worker was guilty of negligence and not an intentional tort. The court of appeal reversed, holding that, to afford due process and equal protection of the laws, the worker's compensation statute, as amended, must be interpreted to permit an employee the same remedy in tort against co-employees for negligently caused work-related injuries as he would have if injured by any other tortfeasor. We reverse the judgment of the court of appeal. The worker's compensation statute was amended . . . to preclude suits by an employee to recover for work-related injuries from certain designated persons, including a fellow employee engaged at the time of injury in the normal course and scope of employment, unless his injury resulted from the co-worker's intentional tortious act. The 1976 amendment does not deprive the plaintiff of due process of law, equal protection of law or access to the judicial process. It was duly adopted in accordance with the Louisiana constitution.

Recovery in worker's compensation does not include an allowance for pain and suffering, punitive damages, property damages, and many other elements of full damages. In a worker's compensation case, defenses such as contributory negligence or the assumption of risk may not be asserted. The tradeoff is that workers receive a smaller, certain remedy foregoing the possibility of fuller recovery under the tort system). . . .

Plaintiff, Sidney Bazley, a garbage worker, filed suit against an unidentified co-employee truck driver, the co-employee's insurer, Sardo Tortorich and Tortorich's insurer as result of work-related injuries Bazley received when he was struck by Tortorich's car while he was mounting the back of a parish garbage truck. In his petition . . . Bazley alleged that the accident was caused by his co-employee's intentional acts in operating a garbage truck without a working horn, disregarding mechanical and electrical maintenance standards, failing to keep a lookout, failing to stop in a safe place and failing to warn plaintiff of danger. Bazley did not allege, however, that the co-employee desired the consequences of his acts or believed that they were substantially certain to follow his acts . . .

We are called upon to decide . . . whether [our worker's compensation statute] prevents an injured employee from seeking recovery in tort for a work-related injury negligently caused by his co-employee. . . .

In drawing a line between intentional and unintentional acts, we believe the legislative aim was to make use of the well-established division between intentional torts and negligence in common law. *See* W. PROSSER, LAW OF TORTS, § 7, et seq. (4th ed. 1971). Universally, harmful conduct is considered more reprehensible if intentional. As Holmes said, "Even a dog distinguishes between being stumbled over and being kicked." HOLMES, THE COMMON LAW 3 (1881). There is a definite tendency to impose greater responsibility upon a defendant whose conduct has been intended to do harm, or morally wrong. W. PROSSER, LAW OF TORTS, § 7 (4th ed. 1971). . . .

Plaintiff ingeniously has proposed . . . that the concept "intentional act" should be equated with "voluntary act." He interprets "intentional" to mean merely that before the actor acted he directed his mind on his own physical movement and not on the consequences of his act. Under his interpretation, an injured employee may sue in tort on any voluntary act setting in motion events leading to his injury regardless of whether the harm appeared likely or was even apparent at all to the actor. For example, in the present case, plaintiff contends he alleged an intentional act triggering his escape from the compensation system when he averred that the defendant garbage truck driver intentionally did not blow his horn to warn plaintiff of an oncoming motorist, although plaintiff concedes that the driver did not intend for harm to come to him. Plaintiff's interpretation is incongruous, not only because it departs from the almost universal practice of differentiating between intentional and unintentional harms, prevalent in most workers' compensation programs, but also because it ignores the accepted usage of the statutory terms in this state and generally, and his construction would thwart the legislative purpose. . . .

The word act is used to denote external manifestations of the actor's will which produces consequences. There cannot be an act subjecting a person to civil or criminal liability without volition. Therefore, a contraction of a person's muscles which is purely a reaction to some outside force, such as a knee jerk or the blinking of the eyelids in defense against an approaching missile, or the convulsive movements of an epileptic, are not acts of that person. REST. 2D TORTS § 2 (1965). . . . The meaning of "intent" is that the person who acts either (1) consciously desires the physical result of his act, whatever the likelihood of that result happening from his conduct; or (2) knows that that result is substantially certain to follow from his conduct, whatever his desire. . . .

Our jurisprudence likewise reflects approval of the general notions of act and intent. This Court as early as 1936 approvingly recited the following: "It seems clear that, in the absence of language expressing a contrary meaning, an 'act' involves an exercise of the will. It signifies something done voluntarily." *Heiman v. Pan American Life Ins. Co.* 183 La. 1045, (1936). Only where the actor entertained a desire to bring about the consequences that followed or where the actor believed that the result was substantially certain to follow has an act been characterized as intentional . . . Plaintiff's suggested interpretation of "intentional act," equates the term with "voluntary act" and robs it of any reference to the actor's state of mind concerning the consequences of his act. It is most unlikely the legislature intended the words as plaintiff suggests, rather than in their most usual signification and in the sense in which the lawmakers have used them in other legislation.

For these reasons, we construe the legislation under review as providing that the exclusive remedy rule shall be inapplicable to intentional torts or offenses. The meaning of intent in this context is that the defendant either desired to bring about the physical results of his act or believed they were substantially certain to follow from what he did. Several courts of appeal have stated the two prongs of the definition in the conjunctive, thus requiring a plaintiff to prove, in order to recover, that the defendant desired the physical results of his act in every case. Intent is not, however, limited to consequences, which are desired. If the actor knows that the consequences are certain, or substantially certain, to result from his act, and still goes ahead, he is treated by the law as if had in fact desired to produce the result. REST. 2D TORTS § 8A. [REVERSED AND REMANDED].

NOTES

1. *Volition or Intent?* How did the plaintiff try to establish "intent?" How did the court respond? In order to satisfy the intent requirement, the defendant's act must be voluntary, which is a bodily movement performed consciously as an "external manifestation of the actor's will." REST. 2D TORTS § 2. Involuntary movements do not qualify as intent. In most cases the intention need not be malicious nor need it be an intention to inflict actual damage. For example, in the tort of battery it is sufficient if the actor intends to inflict either a harmful or an offensive contact without the other's consent. The intent requirement closely parallels the concepts of the *mens rea* element of a crime in that "the actor desires to cause consequences of his act, or that he believes that the consequences are substantially certain to result from it." REST. 2D TORTS §8A. Where the parallel breaks down, however, is that for most intentional torts the necessary intent is the intent to make contact, not an intent to cause harm.

2. *Intent to Do What?* "Intent is not . . . limited to consequences which are desired. If the actor knows that the consequences are certain, or substantially certain, to result from his act, and still goes ahead, he is treated by the law as if he had in fact desired to produce the result. As the probability that the consequences will follow decreases, and becomes less than substantial certainty, the actor's conduct loses the character of intent, and becomes mere recklessness." . . . REST. 2D TORTS §8A, cmt. *b.* Is Justice Dennis' test for intent subjective or objective? That is, does it turn on whether the individual defendant subjectively desired or was substantially certain a harmful or offensive contact would result? Alternatively, does intent turn upon what the ordinary, normal, or reasonable person would intend? Even if it is subjective, are objective factors relevant?

In *Garratt v. Dailey,* 279 P.2d 1091 (Wash. 1955), Brian Dailey (five years, nine months) was visiting with Naomi Garratt, an adult and a sister of Ruth Garratt, the plaintiff. It is plaintiff's contention that she was coming into the back yard to talk to her sister when she started to sit down in a wood and canvas lawn chair. Brian deliberately pulled it out from under her, causing her to fall and suffer "a fractured hip and other painful and serious injuries." The trial court accepted the boy's version of the facts — that, although he had moved the chair away, when he saw Ruth about to sit down, he tried to move the chair back and under her. The Washington Supreme Court remanded the case with instructions to make definite findings on the issue of whether defendant knew with substantial certainty that plaintiff would attempt to sit down at the location from which he had moved the chair, noting:

> A battery would be established if, in addition to plaintiff's fall, it was proved that, when Brian moved the chair, he knew with substantial certainty that the plaintiff would attempt to sit down where the chair had been. . . . The mere absence of any intent to injure the plaintiff or to play a prank on her or to embarrass her, or to commit an assault and battery on her would not absolve him from liability if in fact he had such knowledge.

3. *Comparing Intent to Lesser States of Mind:* Chief Justice Lemuel Shaw was the first American jurist to recognize a negligence-based cause of action in *Brown v. Kendall*, 60 Mass. 292, 295-96 (1850) when he stated that "the plaintiff must come prepared with evidence to show either that the intention was unlawful or that the defendant was in fault." What is the relationship between intent and negligence? Are there "degrees" of intent? Of fault? The *prima facie* case for negligence requires the plaintiff to prove that the defendant failed to exercise the due care of a reasonable person in the circumstances. The gist of negligence is the failure to use reasonable care to avoid an unreasonable risk of harm. In *Bazley,* the Louisiana Supreme Court found that the plaintiff's complaint failed to state a cause of action in intentional tort or offense because "the pleadings do not express or imply that the co-employee garbage truck driver desired the consequences of his acts or omissions or that he believed that the consequences were substantially certain to result from them." How does the mental attitude for negligence differ from that required for intentional torts? What is the aim of the rule that the exclusivity bar of worker's compensation subsumes negligence but not intentional torts?

4. *Dual Criminal Intent and Civil Actions:* Many of the intentional torts against the person or property have functionally equivalent criminal law analogues: (1) Intentional homicide, for example supports a civil action for wrongful death; (2) Assault and battery can be both crimes and torts; (3) The torts of conversion or trespass to chattels have parallels in crimes punishing theft; (4) Nuisance is both a crime and a tort; (5) The torts of false imprisonment and false arrest are also crimes; (6) Trespass is both a tort and a crime. The *prima facie* case for crimes; may differ for torts. Criminal assault, for example, does not have an imminence requirement, unlike the tort of assault.

McGUIRE v. ALMY
297 Mass. 323, 8 N.E.2d 760 (1937)

QUA, JUSTICE.

This is an action of tort for assault and battery. The only question of law reported is whether the judge should have directed a verdict for the defendant.

The following facts are established by the plaintiff's own evidence: In August, 1930, the plaintiff was employed to take care of the defendant. The plaintiff was a registered nurse and was a graduate of a training school for nurses. The defendant was an insane person. Before the plaintiff was hired she learned that the defendant was a "mental case and was in good physical condition," and that for some time two nurses had been taking care of her. The plaintiff was on "twenty-four hour duty." The plaintiff slept in the room next to the defendant's room. Except when the plaintiff was with the defendant, the plaintiff kept the defendant locked in the defendant's room. There was a wire grating over the outside of the window of that room. During the period of "fourteen months or so" while the plaintiff cared for the defendant, the defendant "had a few odd spells," when she showed some hostility to the plaintiff and said that "she would like to try and do something to her." The defendant had been violent at times and had broken dishes "and things like that," and on one or two occasions the plaintiff had to have help to subdue the defendant.

On April 19, 1932, the defendant, while locked in her room, had a violent attack. The plaintiff heard a crashing of furniture and then knew that the defendant was ugly, violent, and dangerous. The defendant told the plaintiff and a Miss Maroney, "the maid," who was with the plaintiff in the adjoining room, that if they came into the defendant's room, she would kill them. The plaintiff and Miss Maroney looked into the defendant's room, "saw what the defendant had done," and "thought it best to take the broken stuff away before she did any harm to herself with it." They sent for one Emerton, the defendant's brother-in-law. When he arrived the defendant was in the middle of her room about ten feet from the door, holding upraised the leg of a lowboy as if she were going to strike. The plaintiff stepped into the room and walked toward the defendant, while Emerton and Miss Maroney remained in the doorway. As the plaintiff approached the defendant and tried to take hold of the defendant's hand which held the leg, the defendant struck the plaintiff's head with it, causing the injuries for which the action was brought.

The extent to which an insane person is liable for torts has not been fully defined in this Commonwealth. . . . In *Morain v. Devlin,* 132 Mass. 87, this court said, through Chief Justice Gray, "By the common law, as generally stated in the books, a lunatic is civilly liable to make compensation in damages to persons injured by his acts, although, being incapable of criminal intent, he is not liable to indictment and punishment," citing numerous cases (page 88). But the actual decision went no further than to hold the lunatic, as a landowner receiving the benefits of ownership, liable for the defective condition of his premises. . . .

Turning to authorities elsewhere, we find that courts in this country almost invariably say in the broadest terms that an insane person is liable for his torts. As a rule no distinction is made between those torts which would ordinarily be classed as negligent, nor do the courts discuss the effect of different kinds of insanity or of varying degrees of capacity as bearing upon the ability of the defendant to understand the particular act in question or to make a reasoned decision with respect to it, although it is sometimes said that an insane person is not liable for torts requiring malice of which he is incapable. Defamation and malicious prosecution are the torts more commonly mentioned in this connection. . . . These decisions are rested more upon grounds of public policy and upon what might be called a popular view of the requirements of essential justice than upon any attempt to apply logically the underlying principles of civil liability to the special instance of the mentally deranged. Thus it is said that a rule imposing liability tends to make more watchful those persons who have charge of the defendant and who may be supposed to have some interest in preserving his property; that as an insane person must pay for his support, if he is financially able, so he ought also to pay for the damage which he does; that an insane person with abundant wealth ought not to continue in unimpaired enjoyment of the comfort which it brings while his victim bears the burden unaided; and there is also a suggestion that courts are loath to introduce into the great body of civil litigation the difficulties in determining mental capacity which it has been found impossible to avoid in the criminal field.

The rule established in these cases has been criticized severely by certain eminent text writers both in this country and in England, principally on the ground that it is an archaic survival of the rigid and formal medieval conception of liability for acts done, without regard to fault, as opposed to what is said to be the general modern theory that liability in tort should rest upon fault. Notwithstanding these criticisms, we think that as a practical matter there is strong force in the reasons underlying these decisions. They are consistent with the general statements found in the cases dealing with the liability of infants for torts, including a few cases in which the child was so young as to render his capacity for fault comparable to that of many insane persons. Fault is by no means at the present day a universal prerequisite to liability, and the theory that it should be such has been obliged very recently to yield at several points to what have been thought to be paramount considerations of public good. Finally, it would be difficult not to recognize the persuasive weight of so much authority so widely extended.

But the present occasion does not require us either to accept or to reject the prevailing doctrine in its entirety. For this case it is enough to say that where an insane person by his act does intentional damage to the person or property of another he is liable for that damage in the same circumstances in which a normal person would be liable. This means that insofar as a particular intent would be necessary in order to render a normal person liable, the insane person, in order to be liable, must have been capable of entertaining that same intent and must have entertained it in fact. But the law will not inquire further into his peculiar mental condition with a view to excusing him if it should appear that delusion or other consequence of his affliction has caused him to entertain that intent or that a normal person would not have entertained it.

We do not suggest that this is necessarily a logical stopping point. If public policy demands that a mentally affected person be subjected to the external standard for intentional wrongs, it may well be that public policy also demands that he should be subjected to the external standard for wrongs which are commonly classified as negligent, in accordance with what now seems to be the prevailing view. We stop here for the present, because we are not required to go further in order to decide this case, because of deference to the difficulty of the subject, because full and adequate discussion is lacking in most of the cases decided up to the present time, and because by far the greater number of those cases, however broad their statement of the principle, are in fact cases of intentional rather than of negligent injury. Coming now to the application of the rule to the facts of this case, it is apparent that the jury could find that the defendant was capable of entertaining and that she did entertain an intent to strike and to injure the plaintiff and that she acted upon that intent. We think this was enough. [AFFIRMED].

NOTES

1. *Psychiatric Characteristics and Intent.* Insanity and diminished capacity may generally not be invoked as defensive arguments in intentional tort cases. "This rule, which holds the mentally disabled liable for their torts, emerged from *Weaver v. Ward,* 80 Eng. Rep. 284 (K.B. 1616), a seventeenth-century trespass case sounding in the theory of strict liability." *Jankee v. Clark County*, 612 N.W.2d 297, 312 (Wis. 2000). Courts are reluctant to adjust the intentional torts formula because of the mental state of the defendant. Oliver Wendell Holmes contended that the mentally disabled must be held accountable for their torts: "The law takes no account of the infinite varieties of temperament, intellect, and education which make the internal character of a given act so different in different men." OLIVER WENDELL. HOLMES, JR., THE COMMON LAW 108 (1881).

What does the result in *McGuire v. Almy* disclose as to the form *and* function of a simple intentional tort such as battery? The majority of courts recognize that an insane person cannot have the requisite intent for certain torts such as defamation. In contrast, what is the "particular intent" which, according to *McGuire v. Almy,* is required in some other intentional torts? Justice Qua notes that malice is not required for the tort of battery but is an element of malicious prosecution. To prevail on a claim of malicious prosecution a plaintiff must establish, among other things, that the defendant lacked probable cause for instituting the underlying proceeding.

2. *Children.* "Infancy is, as a general rule, no defense against a tort, just as it is, as a general rule, no defense against a crime." *Thomas v. State*, 69 So. 908, 909 (1915). "What has been said about mistake is largely true with infancy and mental disability as well. The general rule is that children . . . are liable for their intentional torts." DAN B. DOBBS, THE LAW OF TORTS 158 (2000). Infancy goes to the question of whether a child of tender years can manifest the requisite intent. *Id.* at 158.

In *Fromenthal v. Clark,* 442 So. 2d 608 (La. App. 1983), *cert. denied,* 444 So. 2d 1242 (La. 1984), plaintiff, a two-week-old infant, was severely bitten by the defendant Clark, age two, while plaintiff was sleeping on a bed. The trial court held that "the child, Shawn Clark, was below the age of discernment and reason and, therefore, cannot be held liable for his delictual acts, negligent or intentional, because he lacks the ability to be legally at fault." Compare *Garratt v. Dailey,* 279 P.2d 1091 (Wash. 1955), discussed above, where the court held that children were generally liable for intentional torts and noted the "conceded volitional act of Brian." Is there an age at which you believe a court should rule as a matter of law that a child is incapable of meeting the legal definition of intent? What would that age be?

3. *Insane Drunks? Intent Redux.* Voluntary intoxication is not a defense to any intentional torts. Courts are particularly unwilling to consider the diminished capacity due to voluntary alcohol consumption. In *Janelsins v. Button,* 648 A.2d 1039 (Md. App. 1994), plaintiff Button, a bar employee, was injured while attempting to escort defendant Janelsins, a drunk bar patron, to the latter's car:

> Although Janelsins admittedly had no memory of the events, it is apparent that he did not want anyone to force him into his car. Nor did he want anyone to drive it for him. When Button and the customers tried to push Janelsins into the back seat of his car, Janelsins resisted, shouting obscenities and threats. As Button attempted to put Janelsins's legs in the car, Janelsins kicked Button in the face. As a result, Button lost a tooth, and suit followed.

The court rejected defendant's argument that there was insufficient evidence to support a battery claim:

> A battery is the "unpermitted application of trauma by one person upon the body of another person." *McGuiggan v. Boy Scouts of America,* 714, 536 A.2d 137 (Md. App. 1988). Accidental or inadvertent contact does not constitute battery. Rather, the tort of battery requires *intent* by the actor "to bring about a harmful or offensive contact. . . . [It is] confined

to intentional invasions of the interests in freedom from harmful or offensive contact." FOWLER V. HARPER, ET AL., 1 THE LAW OF TORTS § 3.3, at 272–73, 276 (2d ed. 1986).

Janelsins's insufficiency of the evidence argument must fail. The evidence, including Janelsins's threats and his flailing about, adequately supports a finding that he intended to strike Button. Although Janelsins apparently was inebriated at the time of the incident, his voluntary intoxication does not vitiate the intent element of battery.

In *McEachern v. Muldovan*, 505 S.E.2d 495 (Ga. 1998), decedent was killed as he and a minor friend, both of whom were under the influence of alcohol, took turns pointing a handgun at each other and pulling the trigger. The *McEachern* court observed that:

> For more than a century, Georgia has followed the rule that one who becomes voluntarily intoxicated is held thereafter to the same standard as if he were a sober person. That school of jurists who consider torts as akin to crimes apply to the case of a drunk man, as to his capacity both for negligence and for contributory negligence, the ancient maxim that drunkenness is no excuse for crime. The other school, although they do not base their theories of tort on the criminal law, just as uniformly hold the drunk man responsible for his conduct under a given state of circumstances as if he were sober. Irrespective of the various reasons given, all courts now hold that the drunk man, so far as his own conduct is concerned, is to be considered, in all matters of volition, judgment, caution, and general mental state, just as if he were sober. The state of mind produced by intoxication will be disregarded in viewing his actions, and he will be judged as if he possessed his normal capacities.

4. *Mistake.* Typically, mistake of fact is not a defense to an intentional tort. In *Seigel v. Long,* 169 Ala. 79 (1910), the defendant mistakenly believed the plaintiff was the person who had frightened his team of horses the day before. He angrily accosted the plaintiff, pushing back the plaintiff's hat in order to get a better look at his face. This touching was held to be a battery:

> It is true that defendant's testimony tended to show that defendant made a mistake as to the identity of the party whom he assaulted, and he told plaintiff that, if he was not the person who frightened his team, he owed him an apology; but this did not prevent what he did from being an assault and battery.

In *Ranson v. Kitner,* 31 Ill. App. 241 (1889), the plaintiff sued defendants for the value of his dog, which defendants killed. "The defense was that [defendants] were hunting for wolves, that [plaintiff's] dog had a striking resemblance to a wolf, that they in good faith believed it to be one, and killed it as such." The court affirmed a jury finding of liability. The defendants, the court said, "are clearly liable for the damages caused by their mistake, notwithstanding they were acting in good faith."

Neither is mistake of law a defense. "'Persons deal with the property in chattels or exercise acts of ownership over them at their peril, and must take the risk that there is no lawful justification for their acts." W. KEETON, ET. AL. PROSSER AND KEETON ON THE LAW OF TORTS § 15 at 93 (5th ed. 1985).

5. *An Insurance Perspective.* The issue of whether the insane defendant can have the requisite state of mind for an intentional tort is of practical importance when it comes to insurance coverage. If an act is deemed to be intentional, it may be subject to the exclusionary provisions of liability policies. *Rajspic v. Nationwide Mut. Ins. Co.*, 718 P.2d 1167 (1986). Courts, however, distinguish between liability for intentional torts and the intentional torts exclusions: "An insane person may be liable for an intentional tort, yet may still not have intentionally caused an injury within the meaning of the insurance exclusion. In fact, many courts have held that, *as a matter of law,* an insane person *cannot* intentionally cause injury as excluded in insurance policies." *Id.* at 1170. What perspective would a court bring to its decision to have "two meanings" for intentional?

6. *Insanity & Tort Accountability.* The court in *Jankee v. Clark County*, 612 N.W.2d 697, 734 (Wis. 2000) employs law and economics reasoning in explaining the rule that mental deficit may not be taken into account:

> This court's policy rationales for embracing the rule trace their origins to the 1930s, when we observed that the imposition of liability on the mentally disabled: (1) better apportions loss between two innocent persons to the one who caused the loss, (2) encourages restraint of the disabled, and (3) prevents tortfeasors from feigning incapacity to avoid liability . . .
>
> . . . . Nonetheless, observers today find more contemporary justifications for the general rule. For instance, in an era in which society is less inclined to institutionalize the mentally disabled, the reasonable person standard of care obligates the mentally disabled to conform their behavior to the expectations of the communities in which they live. More practically, the reasonable person standard of care allows courts and juries to bypass the imprecise task of distinguishing among variations in character, emotional equilibrium, and intellect.

A law and economics oriented scholar would find an allocative efficiency rationale for the rule that the insane are liable for their intentional torts. The black letter law is that insane persons are liable for their torts "for the reason that where one of two innocent persons must suffer a loss, it should be borne by the one who occasioned it; to induce those interested in the estates of insane persons to restrain and control them; and, because of the fear that permitting an insanity defense in actions for tort would lead to false claims of insanity." Michele M. Hughes, Mentally Impaired Persons, 53 AM. JUR. 2d § 167 (2006). Does the *McGuire v. Almy* decision promote economic efficiency? Suppose the insane were not held liable for their intentional torts? What are the consequences of such a rule?

C.   BATTERY

The tort of battery is an unpermitted, unprivileged, and offensive or harmful touching of the person of another by a defendant whose act is intended to result and results in such contact. According to REST. 2D TORTS §§ 13 and 18: "An actor is subject to liability to another for battery if (a) he acts intending to cause a harmful or offensive contact with the person of the other or a third person, or an imminent apprehension of such a contact" and "(b) a harmful contact with the person of the other directly or indirectly results," *id.* § 13, or, "(b) an offensive contact with the person of the other directly or indirectly results," *id.* § 18.

The defendant's touching need not result in a physical harm if it is offensive measured by the reasonable person standard. If A spits in B's face, the offensive contact is enough for a battery. Touching for purposes of battery is not limited to "tactile" contact because it is possible to commit a battery by poisoning food or drink or, for example, by placing a tripwire that causes the plaintiff to fall to the ground. An act may qualify as a battery where the contact is with something closely connected to the plaintiff such as clothing. If a defendant knocks the plaintiff's hat off, that also meets the contact requirement.

As you read the *Brzoska* case that follows, try to answer the following questions: (1) What was the plaintiff's cause of action? (2) What was the plaintiffs' best evidence that the dentist intended to do an act causing harm? (3) What was the lower court's holding? (4) What is the holding of the Delaware Supreme Court in the case?

BRZOSKA v. OLSON
668 A.2d 1355 (Del. 1995)

WALSH, JUSTICE.

In this appeal from the Superior Court, we confront the question of whether a patient may recover damages for treatment by a health care provider afflicted with Acquired Immunodeficiency Syndrome ("AIDS") absent a showing of a resultant physical injury or exposure to disease. The appellants, plaintiffs below, are 38 former patients of Dr. Raymond P. Owens, a Wilmington dentist who died of AIDS on March 1, 1991. In an action brought against Edward P. Olson, the administrator of Dr. Owens' estate, the plaintiffs sought recovery under theories of negligence, battery, and misrepresentation. After limited discovery, the Superior Court granted summary judgment in favor of Dr. Owens' estate, ruling that, in the absence of a showing of physical harm, absence of a showing that any of the plaintiffs had suffered physical harm. Specifically, plaintiffs cannot recover under battery *as a matter of law* because they could not show that their alleged offense was reasonable in the absence of being actually exposed to a disease-causing agent. We further conclude, however, that, as to those plaintiffs to whom Dr. Owens made a direct representation that he did not suffer from AIDS and thereafter rendered treatment, the facts of record, when viewed from the plaintiffs' perspective, preclude the grant of summary judgment, if recovery is limited to economic damages. . . . [Plaintiffs are] not entitled to recover under any theory advanced. Plaintiffs have appealed only the rulings disallowing recovery on the claims of battery and misrepresentation.

We conclude that the Superior Court correctly ruled that, under the circumstances of Dr. Owens' treatment, there can be no recovery for fear of contracting a disease in the absence of a showing that any of the plaintiffs had suffered physical harm. Specifically, plaintiffs cannot recover under battery *as a matter of law* because they could not show that their alleged offense was reasonable in the absence of being actually exposed to a disease-causing agent. We further conclude, however, that, as to those plaintiffs to whom Dr. Owens made a direct representation that he did not suffer from AIDS and thereafter rendered treatment, the facts of record, when viewed from the plaintiffs' perspective, preclude the grant of summary judgment, if recovery is limited to economic damages.

Prior to his death, Dr. Owens had been engaged in the general practice of dentistry in the Wilmington area for almost 30 years. Although plaintiffs have alleged that Dr. Owens was aware that he had AIDS for at least ten years, it is clear from the record that it was in March, 1989, that Dr. Owens was advised by his physician that he was HIV-positive. Dr. Owens continued to practice, but his condition had deteriorated by the summer of 1990. Toward the end of 1990, he exhibited open lesions, weakness, and memory loss. In February, 1991, his physician recommended that Dr. Owens discontinue his practice because of deteriorating health. Shortly thereafter, on February 23, Dr. Owens was hospitalized. He remained hospitalized until his death on March 1, 1991.

Shortly after Dr. Owens' death, the Delaware Division of Public Health (the "Division") undertook an evaluation of Dr. Owens' practice and records, in part to determine if his patients had been placed at risk through exposure to HIV. The Division determined that Dr. Owens' equipment, sterilization procedures, and precautionary methods were better than average and that he had ceased doing surgery since being diagnosed as HIV-positive in 1989. Although the Division determined that the risk of patient exposure was "very small," it notified all patients treated by Dr. Owens from the time of his 1989 diagnosis until his death that their dentist had died from AIDS and that there was a possibility that they were exposed to HIV. The Division also advised the former patients that they could participate in a free program of HIV testing and counseling. Some patients availed themselves of the Division's testing while others secured independent testing. Of the 630 former patients of Dr. Owens who have been tested, none have tested positive for HIV.

In their Superior Court action, the plaintiffs alleged that each of them had been patients of Dr. Owens in 1990 or 1991. Each claimed to have received treatment, including teeth extraction, reconstruction and cleaning, during which their gums bled. The plaintiffs alleged that Dr. Owens was HIV-positive and that he exhibited open lesions and memory loss at the time of such treatment. The plaintiffs did not allege the contraction of any physical ailment or injury as a result of their treatment, but claimed to have suffered "mental anguish" from past and future fear of contracting AIDS. They also alleged embarrassment in going for medical testing to a State clinic which they found to be "an uncomfortable environment." Plaintiffs sought compensation and punitive damages for mental anguish, the cost of medical testing and monitoring, and reimbursement for monies paid to Dr. Owens for dental treatment. . . .

After brief discovery, the Owens defendants ("Owens") moved for summary judgment . . . [T]he Superior Court ruled that plaintiffs had no basis for recovery for "fear of AIDS" in the absence of an underlying physical injury.

Accordingly, the court dismissed all counts of the complaint. Plaintiffs have appealed only the Superior Court ruling with regard to the battery and misrepresentation claims. . . .

Under the REST. 2D TORTS, "[a]n actor is subject to liability to another for battery if (a) he acts intending to cause a harmful or offensive contact with the person . . . and (b) a harmful contact with the person of the other directly or indirectly results." REST. 2D. TORTS § 18 (1965); *see also* W. PAGE KEETON, ET. AL., PROSSER AND KEETON ON TORTS, § 9 at 39 (5th ed. 1984) (hereafter "Prosser and Keeton") ("A harmful or offensive contact with a person, resulting from an act intended to cause the plaintiff or third person to suffer such a contact, or apprehension that such contact is imminent, is a battery.") This Court has recognized that, under appropriate factual circumstances, a patient may have a cause of action against a medical practitioner for the tort of battery for acts arising from the practitioner's professional conduct. . . .

In essence, the tort of battery is the intentional, unpermitted contact upon the person of another which is harmful or offensive. Lack of consent is thus an essential element of battery. . . . The intent necessary for battery is the intent to make contact with the person, not the intent to cause harm. . . . In addition, the contact need not be harmful, it is sufficient if the contact offends the person's integrity. . . . "Proof of the technical invasion of the integrity of the plaintiff's person by even an entirely harmless, yet offensive, contact entitles the plaintiff to vindication of the legal right by the award of nominal damages." *Id.* The fact that a person does not discover the offensive nature of the contact until after the event does not, ipso facto, preclude recovery. *See* REST. 2D TORTS § 18 cmt. d.

Although a battery may consist of any unauthorized touching of the person which causes offense or alarm, the test for whether a contact is "offensive" is not wholly subjective. The law does not permit recovery for the extremely sensitive who become offended at the slightest contact. Rather, for a bodily contact to be offensive, it must offend a reasonable sense of personal dignity. REST. 2D TORTS § 19.

In order for a contact to be offensive to a reasonable sense of personal dignity, it must be one which would offend the ordinary person and as such one not unduly sensitive as to his personal dignity. It must, therefore, be a contact which is unwarranted by the social usages prevalent at the time and place at which it is inflicted. REST. 2D TORTS § 19 cmt. a.; PROSSER AND KEETON, § 9, at 42. The propriety of the contact is therefore assessed by an objective "reasonableness" standard.

Plaintiffs contend that the "touching" implicit in the dental procedures performed by Dr. Owens was offensive because he was HIV-positive. We must therefore determine whether the performance of dental procedures by an HIV-infected dentist, standing alone, may constitute offensive bodily contact for purposes of battery, i.e., would such touching offend a reasonable sense of personal dignity?

As noted, HIV is transmitted primarily through direct blood-to-blood contact or by the exchange of bodily fluids with an infected individual. In a dental setting, the most probable means of transmission is through the exchange of bodily fluids between the dentist and patient by percutaneous (through the skin) contact, by way of an open wound, non-intact skin, or mucous membrane, with infected blood or blood-contaminated bodily fluids. During invasive dental procedures, such as teeth extraction, root canal and periodontal treatments, there is a risk that the dentist may suffer a percutaneous injury to the hands, such as a puncture wound caused by a sharp instrument or object during treatment, and expose the dentist and patient to an exchange of blood or other fluids. . . . Although the use of gloves as a protective barrier during invasive dental procedures reduces the risk of exposure of HIV, their use cannot prevent piercing injuries to the hands caused by needles, sharp instruments or patient biting. . . .

The risk of HIV transmission from a health care worker to a patient during an invasive medical procedure is very remote. In fact, even a person who is exposed to HIV holds a slim chance of infection. The CDC has estimated that the theoretical risk of HIV transmission from an HIV-infected health care worker to patient following actual percutaneous exposure to HIV-infected blood is, by any measure, less than one percent.

Instead, plaintiff's alleged "injuries" arise solely out of their fear that they have been exposed to HIV. In essence, they claim mental anguish damages for their "fear of AIDS." As noted in *Mergenthaler v. Asbestos Corp. of Am.*, 480 A.2d 647 (Del. Super. Ct. 1984), however, damages for claims of emotional distress or mental anguish (which would include fear of contracting a disease) are recoverable only if the underlying physical injury is shown. *Id.*, 480 A.2d at 651. In this case, plaintiffs have sustained no physical injury, and therefore, they could not recover under a negligence theory. *Id.* We recognize, however, that where an intentional tort is the basis for a claim of emotional distress an accompanying physical injury is not required "if such conduct is viewed as outrageous." *Cummings v. Pinder*, Del. Supr. 574 A.2d 843, 845 (1990).

As earlier noted, the offensive character of a contact in a battery case is assessed by a "reasonableness" standard. In a "fear of AIDS" case in which battery is alleged, therefore, we examine the overall reasonableness of the plaintiffs' fear in contracting the disease to determine whether the contact or touching was offensive. Since HIV causes AIDS, any assessment of the fear of contracting AIDS must, *ipso facto*, relate to the exposure to HIV. Moreover, because HIV is transmitted only through fluid-to-fluid contact or exposure, the reasonableness of a plaintiff's fear of AIDS should be measured by whether or not there was a channel of infection or actual exposure of the plaintiff to the virus.

It is unreasonable for a person to fear infection when that person has not been exposed to a disease. In the case of AIDS, actual exposure to HIV may escalate the threat of infection from a theoretical, remote risk to a real and grave possibility if the person exposed is motivated by speculation unrelated to the objective setting. Such fear is based on uninformed apprehension, not reality. In such circumstances, the fear of contracting AIDS is per se unreasonable without proof of actual exposure to HIV. In our view, the mere fear of contracting AIDS, in the absence of actual exposure to HIV, is not sufficient to impose liability on a health care provider. AIDS phobia, standing alone, cannot form the basis for recovery of damages, even under a battery theory because the underlying causation/harm nexus is not medically supportable.

AIDS is a disease that spawns widespread public misperception based upon the dearth of knowledge concerning HIV transmission. Indeed, plaintiffs rely upon the degree of public misconception about AIDS to support their claim that their fear was reasonable. To accept this argument is to contribute to the phobia. Were we to recognize a claim for the fear of contracting AIDS based upon a mere allegation that one may have been exposed to HIV, totally unsupported by any medical evidence or factual proof, we would open a Pandora's Box of "AIDS-phobia" claims by individuals whose ignorance, unreasonable suspicion or general paranoia cause them apprehension over the slightest of contact with HIV-infected individuals or objects. Such plaintiffs would recover for their fear of AIDS, no matter how irrational. . . . We believe the better approach is to assess the reasonableness of a plaintiff's fear of AIDS according to the plaintiff's actual — not potential — exposure to HIV. . . .

In sum, we find that without actual exposure to HIV, the risk of its transmission is so minute that any fear of contracting AIDS is per se unreasonable. We therefore hold, as a matter of law, that the incidental touching of a patient by an HIV-infected dentist while performing ordinary, consented-to dental procedure is insufficient to sustain a battery claim in the absence of a channel for HIV infection. In other words, such contact is "offensive" only if it results in actual exposure to the HIV virus. We therefore adopt an "actual exposure" test, which requires a plaintiff to show "actual exposure" to a disease-causing agent as a prerequisite to prevail on a claim based upon fear of contracting disease. Attenuated and speculative allegations of exposure to HIV do not give rise to a legally cognizable claim in Delaware. [AFFIRMED IN PART, REVERSED IN PART, AND REMANDED].

NOTES

1. *The Requirement of "Harmful or Offensive Contact."* An actor is subject to liability to another for battery if "[S]he acts intending to cause a harmful or offensive contact with the person of the other or a third person, or an imminent apprehension of such a contact," and a harmful or offensive contact with the person of the other directly or indirectly results. REST. 2D TORTS, §§ 13, 18. The necessary intent can be inferred if the act is done "with knowledge on the part of the actor that such contact or apprehension is substantially certain to be produced."

The plaintiff must prove *either* harm or offensive contact was the net result. The offensiveness prong of battery is a normative evaluation. Contact is offensive if it would offend a reasonable person. The key question is whether the defendant's act offends a reasonable sense of personal dignity. A subway rider slightly jostled while entering a crowded car has no battery action because a reasonable person would not find this contact to be offensive. As noted above, the intent necessary to constitute a battery is not necessarily the intent to cause harm, only the intent to do the act. *Lopez v. Surchia* 112 Cal. App. 2d 314, 318 (1952). The harmful prong of battery does not require an assessment of whether norms have been broken. If X punches Y, there is no doubt that a battery has been committed. An offensive act, in contrast, means that the act would offend a reasonable person's sense of personal dignity. "The element of personal indignity involved always has been given considerable weight. Consequently, the defendant is liable not only for contacts that do actual physical harm, but also for those relatively trivial ones which are merely offensive and insulting." *Swope v. Columbian Chems. Co.*, 281 F.3d 185, 195 (5th Cir. 2002).

2. *Single or Dual Concept of Intent*: The intent concept creates problems for courts as well as first-year law students. Jurisdictions are split on whether they require the plaintiff to prove intent to cause a harmful or offensive contact or only the intent to make contact. Professor Kenneth Simon summarizes this conceptual problem as follows:

> Must the defendant intend only to cause the contact? Or must she also intend that the contact be harmful or offensive? The courts are split on the issue: a substantial group follows the so-called dual-intent approach, requiring both an intent to contact and an intent either to harm or offend; another substantial group follows the single-intent approach, requiring only an intent to contact. (The REST. 2D gives muddled guidance here: some language appears to endorse the dual-intent view, but there is also some language that supports the single-intent view.) My own view is that the single-intent approach is much more defensible and indeed is the only plausible interpretation of the case law in this area.

Kenneth W. Simon, *A Restatement (Third) of Intentional Torts?* 48 ARIZ. L. REV. 1061, 1066–67 (2006).

The Colorado Supreme Court apparently disagrees. In *White v. Muniz*, 999 P.2d 814 (Colo. 2000), an eighty-three year-old grandmother was placed in an assisted living facility where she was diagnosed as suffering from Alzheimer's and degenerative dementia. She became agitated easily, and occasionally acted aggressively toward others. When a caregiver attempted to change her adult diaper she punched the caregiver in the jaw. Affirming a defense verdict the court stated:

> [S]ome courts around the nation have abandoned this dual intent requirement in an intentional tort setting, that being an intent to contact and an intent that the contact be harmful or offensive, and have required only that the tortfeasor intend a contact with another that results in a harmful or offensive touching. Under this view, a victim need only prove that a voluntary movement by the tortfeasor resulted in a contact which a reasonable person would find offensive or to which the victim did not consent . . . The actor thus could be held liable for battery because a reasonable person would find an injury offensive or harmful, irrespective of the intent of the actor to harm or offend.
>
> Colorado law requires a dual intent . . . A jury can, of course, find a mentally deficient person liable for an intentional tort, but in order to do so, the jury must find that the actor intended offensive or harmful consequences. As a result, insanity is not a defense to an intentional

tort according to the ordinary use of that term, but is a characteristic, like infancy, that may make it more difficult to prove the intent element of battery. Our decision today does not create a special rule for the elderly, but applies Colorado's intent requirement in the context of a woman suffering the effects of Alzheimer's.

Contrary to [plaintiff's] arguments, policy reasons do not compel a different result. Injured parties consistently have argued that even if the tortfeasor intended no harm or offense, "where one of two innocent persons must suffer a loss, it should be borne by the one who occasioned it." Our decision may appear to erode that principle. Yet, our decision does not bar future injured persons from seeking compensation. Victims may still bring intentional tort actions against mentally disabled adults, but to prevail, they must prove all the elements of the alleged tort. Furthermore, because the mentally disabled are held to the reasonable person standard in negligence actions, victims may find relief more easily under a negligence cause of action.

Id. at 818.

The dual intent test requires proof by a preponderance of the evidence that the defendant both intended the contact and intended the contact to be either harmful or offensive. In a single intent jurisdiction followed by most jurisdictions, it is enough to show that a person intentionally contacted another resulting in either harm or offense.

3. *Context?* In *White v. University of Idaho,* 768 P.2d 827 (Idaho 1989), the defendant professor was a social guest in plaintiff's house and plaintiff was writing at a counter when "unanticipated by Mrs. White, Professor Neher walked up behind her and touched her back with both of his hands in a movement later described as one a pianist would make in striking and lifting the fingers from a keyboard." The contact caused the plaintiff to suffer unanticipated injuries. The court, in holding that a claim for battery was stated, defined the necessary mental state of the defendant as the intent to make bodily contact that is harmful or offensive. Does this "intent" differ from that required in *Brzoska*? How? Would it make a difference if the professor and Mrs. White were having an affair? Is the single or double-pronged test for intent more favorable to the plaintiff in proving intent?

4. *Consent a Negative Element?* Is lack of consent an essential element of battery, as stated by the *Brozska* court, or is it an affirmative defense? According to Prosser "[c]onsent ordinarily bars recovery," not because it is a defense, but because it "goes to negative the existence of any tort in the first place." W. PAGE KEETON, PROSSER & KEETON ON TORTS 112 (5th ed. 1984). However, as explained in Chapter 3, consent is a classic affirmative defense asserted in intentional tort cases.

5. *No Harm, No Foul?* The Delaware court granted summary judgment in *Brozska* because the plaintiffs could not produce evidence that the contact with the dentist was either harmful or offensive. In the offensive prong of battery, nominal damages are awarded because actual damages are often difficult to prove. Nominal damages such as a token $1 are awarded to plaintiff where law recognizes technical intentional tort, but where plaintiff has failed to prove actual personal, property, or other damages. When a cause of action for a battery exists but no harm has been proven by the tort or the amount of harm is so insignificant as to be *de minimus*, the plaintiff will be given *nominal damages*. The American Law Institute (ALI) Reporters state:

> When a cause of action for a tort exists but no harm has been caused by the tort or the amount of harm is not significant . . . , judgment will be given for nominal damages, consisting of a trivial award against a wrongdoer who has caused no harm or an insignificant harm.

REST. 2D TORTS § 907, cmt. *a.*

6. *Tortfeasor Takes His Victim as He Finds Her.* The fact that a tort victim, because of a preexisting weakness, suffers a worse injury than a typical person would suffer is not in itself a ground for reducing tort damages. Under the "thin skull," or the "eggshell skull," rule, the defendant is fully liable for the consequences of his intentional torts. The public policy rationale for making the intentional wrongdoer liable for all the consequences is based upon the simple law and economics concept of deterrence. Courts typically require the intentional tortfeasor to pay the full price of wrongdoing. The leading "thin skull" case is an oft-cited Wisconsin case arising out of a student kicking a classmate. *Vosburg v. Putney*, 50 N.W. 403, 404 (Wis. 1891). In *Vosburg*, the defendant, George Putney (age 12), playfully kicked Andrew Vosburg, his 14-year-old classmate. The incident occurred on February 20, 1889 in a Waukesha, Wisconsin classroom. The classmates had returned to their desks and the class convened. Andrew was part way in his seat with his right leg "angling out in the aisle." George "made a sudden move and (to put it cautiously) deliberately caused the shoe on one of his feet to come in contact with Andrew's angling leg. Andrew turned around, looked at George, and said nothing. However, a couple of minutes later, Andrew burst out crying, whereupon More (teacher) sent him out into the hall. . . . The mark, at first dim red in appearance, was about one and one half inches wide and lay towards the inside of the bone's crown." Zigurds L. Zile, *Vosburg v. Putney: A Centennial Story*, 1992 WIS. L. REV. 883, 885. What began as a slight kick led to decayed bone and an unsuccessful surgery to repair the crippled leg. *Id.* at 891.

Andrew filed suit against George for the twin torts of assault and battery. On appeal, the court reversed the judgment. The trial court found that the injury was inflicted in school after the regular exercises of the school had commenced. Thus, the court ruled that no implied license to kick the older child existed. The court also found that the trial court properly refused to submit to the jury questions founded upon the theory that only such damages could be recovered as the younger child might reasonably be supposed to have contemplated as likely to result from his kicking the older child. In the passage below, The *Vosburg* court explains that there would have been no battery if the injury occurred upon the playground:

> Had the parties been upon the play-grounds of the school, engaged in the usual boyish sports, the defendant being free from malice, wantonness,

or negligence, and intending no harm to plaintiff in what he did, we should hesitate to hold the act of the defendant unlawful, or that he could be held liable in this action. Some consideration is due to the implied license of the play-grounds. But it appears that the injury was inflicted in the school, after it had been called to order by the teacher, and after the regular exercises of the school had commenced. Under these circumstances, no implied license to do the act complained of existed, and such act was a violation of the order and decorum of the school, and necessarily unlawful.

Vosburg v. Putney, 50 N.W. 403, 404 (Wis. 1891).

7. *Racial Injustice & Battery.* Battery fact patterns may involve insult rather than physical injury. The least touching of "anything connected" with the Plaintiff's person may be sufficient to constitute a battery "when done in an offensive manner." In *Fisher v. Carrousel Motor Hotel, Inc.*, 424 S.W.2d 627 (Tex. 1967), a motor hotel was found liable for battery when a manager intentionally snatched a plate from an African-American patron in an offensive matter. The court described the allegedly tortious encounter:

> After the morning session, the group of 25 or 30 guests adjourned to the Brass Ring Club for lunch. The luncheon was buffet style, and Fisher stood in line with others and just ahead of a graduate student of Rice University who testified at the trial. As Fisher was about to be served, he was approached by Flynn, who snatched the plate from Fisher's hand and shouted that he, a Negro, could not be served in the club. Fisher testified that he was not actually touched, and did not testify that he suffered fear or apprehension of physical injury; but he did testify that he was highly embarrassed and hurt by Flynn's conduct in the presence of his associates.

> The jury found that Flynn 'forcibly dispossessed plaintiff of his dinner plate and 'shouted in a loud and offensive manner' that Fisher could not be served there, thus subjecting Fisher to humiliation and indignity. It was stipulated that Flynn was an employee of the Carrousel Hotel and, as such, managed the Brass Ring Club. The jury also found that Flynn acted maliciously and awarded Fisher $400 actual damages for his humiliation and indignity and $500 exemplary damages for Flynn's malicious conduct.

Id. at 629.

The trial court entered a JNOV motion in favor of the defendants affirmed by the Court of Civil Appeals. The Texas Supreme Court reversed the Court of Appeals decision affirming the JNOV and finding no assault since there was no physical contact and Fisher had no fear or apprehension of physical contact. The Texas Supreme Court concluded that Flynn's conduct was offensive because it embarrassed the plaintiff in front of his professional colleagues. The Texas Supreme Court therefore reversed, reinstating the jury award:

> Under the facts of this case, we have no difficulty in holding that the intentional grabbing of plaintiff's plate constituted a battery. The

intentional snatching of an object from one's hand is as clearly an offensive invasion of his person as would be an actual contact with the body. 'To constitute an assault and battery, it is not necessary to touch the plaintiff's body or even his clothing; knocking or snatching anything from plaintiff's hand or touching anything connected with his person, when, done in an offensive manner, is sufficient.

Id.

How would the concept of intersectionality explain the status differences between the white restaurant manager and the African American professional in *Fisher?* The essence of the injury in *Fisher* was a racially offensive tort committed in a Southern state on the eve of the Civil Rights era. RODNEY A. SMOLLA, LAW OF DEFAMATION § 11.20 (2d ed. 2006). How do the status disparities of race, class and education converge in this case? Should the intersectional factors of race, class and education be considered in determining the offensiveness of an action? Race and class went to the essence of this action for battery. What are the problems of ratcheting up tort awards because of past injustice? Is the problem one of enhanced damages or ensuring that African American plaintiffs receive comparable compensation for similar injuries? What are the special vulnerabilities of African-Americans living in the apartheid-like conditions in the South during the 1960s? Consider after you study the tort of outrage, whether that tort would be cognizable on these facts. While *Fisher* compensated the African American scientist for the indignity he suffered in front of his colleagues while in the buffet line, what public purpose was served by his lawsuit? How has tort law evolved to take into account new forms of racial offensiveness? Professor Nelson writes:

> Thus, conceptually there might exist a zone of proximity beyond the physical body, yet deserving of tort law protection. This zone is important to those subjected to racial terrorism as the techniques of racial abuse are often more subtle than in yesteryear. Indeed, it is not uncommon for the manifestation of racial microaggressions to take the form of snatching items or utensils from the hand of a racialized persons, or the dropping or throwing of currency at the person etc. Indignities *du jour* often involves such contact which is humiliating and offensive.

How should courts ensure that racism does not infect tort awards? How would a law and economics oriented scholar examine the punitive damages awarded in *Fisher?* Would a $500 punitive damages award result in either specific deterrence of a motel's management or send a message of general deterrence to other establishments in the South? What social message does the jury send in awarding punitive damages against racial injustice? Did the context of racism make the court more willing to call the "snatching of the plate" a battery?

D. ASSAULT

An assault is the intentional creation of a reasonable apprehension of an imminent battery. At common law, the action for assault was an action of trespass for assault. A fourteenth century drunk desperate for more wine was the defendant in the first common law case to recognize assault as a form of trespass to the person. JAMES BARR AMES & JEREMIAH SMITH, A SELECTION OF CASES ON THE LAW OF TORTS 1 (1917 ed.) (noting that *I De S Et Ux. V. W De S* was the first trespass action reported in Year Book, At the Assizes, Coram, Thorpe, C.J. in 1348 or 1349). In *I De S Et UX. V. W De S.*, the plaintiffs were tavern owners who also lived in the building. W, the defendant, attempted to rouse them by knocking on the door of the tavern with a hatchet. The wife of the plaintiff stuck her head out the window commanding him to stop. When W saw the woman's head, he threw the hatchet at her but did not hit her. Justice Thorpe, for the first time in Anglo-American jurisprudence recognized an action for assault for a "failed battery" and assessed damages.

CASTIGLIONE v. GALPIN
325 So. 2d 725 (La. App. 1976)

GULOTTA, JUDGE.

This is a suit for damages resulting from an alleged assault based on plaintiffs,' Sewerage & Water Board employees, claims that they were placed in reasonable apprehension of receiving a battery when defendant pointed a shotgun at them. This incident occurred after plaintiffs informed defendant that the water would be turned off because of defendant's nonpayment of a water bill. The trial judge rendered judgment in favor of each plaintiff in the sum of $750.00. Defendant appeals. We affirm.

According to plaintiffs' versions of the incident, upon arrival at defendant's residence and after informing him that they were under instructions to turn the water off if the bill was not paid, Galpin stated, "I'll get a gun and shoot you if you dare to close that water." Whereupon, after reiterating the threat, defendant obtained a shotgun from inside the premises and returned to the front porch, where he pointed the gun at plaintiffs while they were preparing to turn the water off at the water main located in the front yard.

Defendant's version of the incident is that he objected to plaintiffs' stated intention to turn off the water and obtained a shotgun. However, he denied that he at any time pointed the weapon at plaintiffs. According to his version, he merely laid the gun across his knee while in a squatting position.

In the absence of trial court reasons, we are unable to ascertain whether the judge made a factual determination that the gun was either in defendant's lap, or pointed at plaintiffs. Nevertheless, we are convinced from the circumstances surrounding the incident that defendant's action (whether the gun remained on the defendant's lap or was pointed at plaintiffs) resulted in plaintiffs being placed in reasonable apprehension of receiving a battery and was sufficient to constitute an assault.

Words alone may not be sufficient to constitute an assault; however, threats coupled with the present ability to carry out the threats are sufficient when one is placed in reasonable apprehension of receiving an injury. It is clear that defendant threatened plaintiffs with bodily harm in the event they turned the water off and that defendant did possess the ability to carry out those threats. Under the circumstances, it is plausible that plaintiffs were in reasonable apprehension of receiving a battery. Accordingly, we find no error on the part of the trial judge finding defendant liable. . . . [AFFIRMED].

NOTES

1. *Unpacking the Elements of Assault.* According to REST. 2D TORTS § 21(1):

An actor is subject to liability to another for assault if

(a) he acts intending to cause a harmful or offensive contact with the person of the other or a third person, or an imminent apprehension of such a contact, and

(b) the other is thereby put in such imminent apprehension.

The legally protectible interest protected by this tort is the interest in freedom from apprehension of a harmful or offensive contact. The plaintiff must produce evidence by a preponderance of the evidence to answer three questions: (1) Did the defendant engage in some volitional (voluntary) act? (2) Did the defendant act with a purpose or knowledge that the results were substantially certain to occur, placing the plaintiff in apprehension of an imminent battery? (3) Did the plaintiff have a reasonable apprehension of an imminent battery?

2. *Apprehension is the Key.* A plaintiff must have a well-founded apprehension of an imminent battery in order to recover for assault. The test is whether one is placed in reasonable apprehension of receiving an injury. In *Castiglione,* the shotgun on the defendant's lap satisfied the imminence requirement.

A reasonable apprehension means that a reasonable person would have believed a battery was imminent. If A points an unloaded gun at B and pulls the trigger, A has committed a battery because a reasonable person would have believed the battery to be imminent. Apprehension is not fear, but awareness. Thus, it is possible for a 97-pound nerd to assault a 350-pound lineman for the World Champion football team. Apprehension is the injury and therefore a defendant cannot assault an unconscious person. Words alone do not constitute an assault but words accompanied by a show of force may constitute an assault caused from the distress of being threatened with immediate bodily harm. REST. 2D TORTS § 7.

3. *Impossibility.* Suppose that in *Castiglione* the defendant had unloaded the gun before the incident? The plaintiff nevertheless would be in apprehension, but would the defendant have the necessary intent? Suppose the plaintiff knows the gun is unloaded, but the defendant thinks it is loaded? The defendant would have the necessary intent, but would plaintiff be put in apprehension of a harmful contact? Is it sufficient that there is apprehension of an offensive contact?

4. *Battered Women & Words & Acts That Wound.* Words alone may not be sufficient to constitute an assault; however, threats coupled with the present ability to carry out the threats are sufficient when one is placed in reasonable apprehension of receiving an injury. *Castiglione.* Assume that an abusive husband frequently "became enraged while intoxicated, raised his hand and threatened to strike his wife and beat on the door in the middle of the night?" Would his wife be placed in a reasonable apprehension of a battery? *See Harper v. Harper,* 537 So. 2d 282 (La. App. 1988) (finding that these acts constituted assault and domestic abuse). Intentional torts are rarely employed in spousal abuse cases. *See* Douglas D. Scherer, *Tort Remedies for Victims of Domestic Abuse,* 43 S.C. L. REV. 543 (1992) (reporting empirical study confirming that only fifty-three victims of domestic abuse were plaintiffs in battery or assault lawsuits against their abusive partners in state cases decided between 1981 to 1990). How does a feminist framework shed light on domestic abuse?

HOLCOMBE v. WHITAKER
294 Ala. 430 (1975)

SHORES, JUSTICE.

Suit was brought seeking damages for fraudulently inducing plaintiff into an illegal or void marriage, and for assault. This is an appeal from a judgment which was rendered on a jury verdict in favor of the plaintiff in the amount of $35,000. . . .

The plaintiff, Joan Whitaker, met the defendant, M. C. Holcombe, Jr., a medical doctor, in March or April 1970. Shortly thereafter the two began seeing each other socially; and about a month later the defendant moved into the Plaintiff's apartment, where they lived together for some time. It was the Plaintiff's testimony that the defendant told her he was a divorced man. Sometime after the defendant moved into the Plaintiff's apartment, he invited her to accompany him to a medical convention in San Francisco. She did so, and testified that she was asked by the defendant to pose as Mrs. Holcombe at that meeting. Following the convention, the two flew to Las Vegas, Nevada, and were married there. They left Las Vegas and went to New Orleans for a "honeymoon" and finally returned to Birmingham, where they lived together as husband and wife for approximately a month. At about that time, Dr. Holcombe began seeing a woman he had been dating prior to his marriage to the plaintiff. He had previously told Miss Whitaker that he wanted to tell this woman personally about his having married. When the plaintiff objected to his resuming his relationship with this woman, he then told her that he was still married to his first wife. She then asked him to either have the marriage with her annulled or get a divorce from his first wife and marry her legally. Her testimony was that the defendant said "he wasn't going to do either one."

To say the least, the relationship between Miss Whitaker and Dr. Holcombe began to disintegrate from this point forward. He moved out of the apartment, but came back from time to time, staying for as long as a week on at least one occasion. The plaintiff continued to ask him to get an annulment or to get a divorce from his wife and legally marry her. She went to the apartment occupied by the woman the defendant was then seeing again and found him there. Again, she had a conversation with him about getting an annulment. On that occasion he said, "If you take me to court, I will kill you."

From that point on, the plaintiff testified that she began receiving telephone calls from Dr. Holcombe and from his lady friend at all hours of the night. She also received anonymous calls.

There was other evidence to the effect that, after Dr. Holcombe threatened the plaintiff the first time, she moved to another apartment and got an unlisted telephone number. For a period of time the calls from Dr. Holcombe and his friend stopped. Then her apartment was broken into and some of her clothes were soaked with what later appeared to be iodine. Thereafter, the calls resumed. After the break-in, she had new locks put on the door and the windows were nailed closed. She also had friends spend the night with her thereafter.

. . . . The plaintiff claimed that the defendant committed an assault when in June of 1971, she went to see him and tried to get him to get an annulment and he said, "If you take me to court, I will kill you;" and again in October, 1971, after she had filed the instant suit on September 29, 1971, when he went to her apartment and beat on the door, tried to pry it open, and said again, "If you take me to court, I will kill you." The defendant claims this in no way can constitute an assault, because it was merely a conditional threat of violence and because no overt act was involved. In order to safeguard freedom from apprehension of harm or offensive conduct, the law provides an individual with a remedy at law.

An assault consists of "an intentional, unlawful offer to touch the person of another in a rude or angry manner under such circumstances as to create in the mind of the party alleging the assault a well-founded fear of an imminent battery, coupled with the apparent present ability to effectuate the attempt, if not prevented." *Western Union Telegraph Co. v. Hill,* 150 So. 709, 710 (Ala. 1933).

While words standing alone cannot constitute an assault, they may give meaning to an act and both, taken together, may constitute an assault. In addition, words may negative an act in a manner that apprehension in such a case would be unreasonable. "On the other hand, a show of force accompanied by an unlawful or unjustifiable demand, compliance with which will avert the threatened battery, is an assault." 1 HARPER & JAMES, THE LAW OF TORTS, page 223 (1956). "[T]he defendant is not free to compel the plaintiff to buy his safety by compliance with a condition which there is no legal right to impose." PROSSER, LAW OF TORTS, 40 (4th ed. 1971). It is obvious that the defendant in the instant case had no right to impose the condition he did on the plaintiff; and we cannot say that this condition explained away his threat to harm her.

The defendant says his conduct cannot constitute an assault because there was no overt action taken by him. The evidence from the plaintiff was that the defendant was pounding on her door making every effort to get into the apartment, and threatening to kill her if she persisted in "taking him to court." We cannot say, as a matter of law, that this was not sufficient to arouse an apprehension of harm or offensive conduct. We think it was a jury question, as was the question of whether the defendant had the apparent ability to effectuate the threatened act. . . . [AFFIRMED].

NOTES

1. *Present Apprehension.* Recall that REST. 2D TORTS § 21 states that the apprehension must be of an "imminent" harmful or offensive contact. Thus, a threat to harm in the future typically is not an assault. Similarly, there is no assault if the plaintiff learns of the threatened contact after the peril has ended. REST. 2D TORTS § 22, cmt. *b,* illus. 1 (no assault where A learns of B's threat to shoot him only after the threat has passed). What explains these restrictions?

In *Tuberville v. Savage,* [1669] 86 Eng. Rep. 684, the defendant, arguing with plaintiff, put his hand on his sword and said, "If it were not *assize*-time, I would not take such language from you." The court said there was no assault, since it *was assize*-time. Is this explicable on the basis that the threat was conditional (the condition being that the touring justices *not* be in town). How can the arguably conditional threats in *Holcombe* be distinguished?

2. *The Physical Act.* It frequently is stated that there is no assault unless the defendant makes some gesture or movement, indicating an intent to carry out the threat, i.e., mere words do not make an assault. REST. 2D TORTS § 31 provides: "Words do not make the actor liable for assault unless together with other acts or circumstances they put the other in reasonable apprehension of an imminent harmful or offensive contact with his person." The imminence requirement is that there be a close proximity between carrying out the possibility of the threat and some action. Should that be a doctrinal element, or merely good evidence of intent or imminent apprehension? What if a heavyweight champion, whom you know tells you as the elevator in which the two of you are riding begins a 50-story descent, that he is going to "beat you up now." Are these merely words? Are they substantially certain to place you in apprehension of an immediate offensive touching?

HALL v. McBRYDE
919 P.2d 910 (Colo. App.1996)

HUME, JUDGE.

Plaintiff, Eric Hall, appeals from a judgment entered in favor of defendant, Marcus McBryde (Marcus), on a claim of battery, and in favor of Marcus' parents, defendants, James McBryde and Kathleen McBryde, on claims of negligent maintenance of a weapon and negligent supervision. We affirm in part, reverse in part, and remand with directions.

On January 14, 1993, Marcus was at his parents' home with another youth after school. Although Marcus was, pursuant to his parents' wishes, actually living in a different neighborhood with a relative and attending a different high school in the hope of avoiding gang-related problems, he had sought and received permission from his father to come to the McBryde house that day to retrieve some clothing. Prior to that date, Marcus had discovered a loaded gun hidden under the mattress of his parents' bed. James McBryde had purchased the gun sometime earlier.

Soon after midday, Marcus noticed some other youths in a car approaching the McBryde house, and he retrieved the gun from its hiding place. After one of the other youths began shooting towards the McBryde house, Marcus fired four shots toward the car containing the other youths.

During the exchange of gunfire one bullet struck plaintiff, who lived next to the McBryde residence, causing an injury to his abdomen that required extensive medical treatment. Although plaintiff testified that it was Marcus who shot him, the trial court made no finding as to whether plaintiff was struck by a bullet fired by Marcus. . . . Plaintiff . . . contends that the trial court erred in entering judgment for James and Kathleen McBryde on the claim of negligent supervision. Again, we disagree.

A parent is not liable for the torts committed by his or her child merely because of the parent-child relationship. However, when a child has a known propensity to commit a potentially harmful act, the parent has a duty to use reasonable care to prevent the child from causing such harm if the parent knows or should know of the propensity and has the ability and opportunity to control the child. . . .

Here, the trial court found no evidence that Marcus had been a member of a gang, that he had ever been arrested prior to the shooting incident, or that he otherwise had any history of violent or improper behavior. The trial court also determined that allowing Marcus to return to the McBryde home unsupervised during the afternoon of the shooting to pickup clothing "was not a breach of [the parents'] duty of supervision that any reasonable person would recognize."

Once again, because more than one inference or conclusion may be drawn from the facts and because the trial court's determination is supported by evidence in the record, it will not be disturbed. . . . Finally, plaintiff contends that the trial court erred in entering judgment for Marcus on the claim of battery. We agree. An actor is subject to liability to another for battery if he or she acts intending to cause a harmful or offensive contact with the person of the other or a third person, or an imminent apprehension of such a contact, and a harmful or offensive contact with the person of the other directly or indirectly results. REST. 2D TORTS §§ 13,18 (1965); W. KEETON ET AL., PROSSER & KEETON ON THE LAW OF TORTS § 9 (5th ed. 1985). . . .

Here, the trial court found that there was no evidence indicating that Marcus intended to shoot at plaintiff. Furthermore, based upon statements by Marcus that he was not purposely trying to hit the other youths but, instead, was shooting at their car, the trial court also determined that plaintiff had failed to prove Marcus intended to make contact with any person other than plaintiff. Based upon this second finding . . . the trial court concluded that, in reaching its determination that no battery occurred, the trial court did not properly analyze the intent required for battery or the transferability of such intent.

As set forth above, the intent element for battery is satisfied if the actor either intends to cause a harmful or offensive contact or if the actor intends to cause an imminent apprehension of such contact. Moreover, with respect to the level of intent necessary for a battery and the transferability of such intent, REST. 2D TORTS § 16 provides as follows:

(1) If an act is done with the intention of inflicting upon another an offensive but not a harmful bodily contact, or of putting another in apprehension of either a harmful or offensive bodily contact, and such act causes a bodily contact to the other, the actor is liable to the other for a battery although the act was not done with the intention of bringing about the resulting bodily harm.

(2) If an act is done with the intention of affecting a third person in the manner stated in Subsection (1), but causes a harmful bodily contact to another, the actor is liable to such other as fully as though he intended so to affect him.

See also REST. 2D TORTS § 20 (1965); *Alteiri v. Colasso*, 362 A.2d 798 (Conn. 1975) (when one intends an assault, then, if bodily injury results to someone other than the person whom the actor intended to put in apprehension of harm, it is a battery actionable by the injured person); *Brown v. Martinez*, 361 P.2d 152 (N.M. 1961).

Here, the trial court considered only whether Marcus intended to inflict a contact upon the other youths. It did not consider whether Marcus intended to put the other youths in apprehension of a harmful or offensive bodily contact.

However, we conclude, as a matter of law, that by aiming and firing a loaded weapon at the automobile for the stated purpose of protecting his house, Marcus did intend to put the youths who occupied the vehicle in apprehension of a harmful or offensive bodily contact. Hence, pursuant to the rule set forth in REST. 2D TORTS § 16(2) (1965), Marcus' intent to place other persons in apprehension of a harmful or offensive contact was sufficient to satisfy the intent requirement for battery against plaintiff.

[AFFIRMED IN PART, REVERSED AND REMANDED IN PART].

NOTES

1. *Transferred Intent to Different Torts.* "If A shoots B intending to shoot C, A is liable to C for battery, just as if he had intended to hurt C." *United States v. Martinez*, 16 F.3d 202, 207 (7th Cir. 1994). Courts use the legal fiction of transferred intent to make the defendant accountable for the consequences of his tortious act. If Al takes a swing at Bill but strikes Carl, a bystander, Al is liable to Carl, the bystander, for battery.

The transferred intent doctrine may apply only when the torts involved are one or more of the following: battery, assault, false imprisonment, trespass to land, or trespass to chattel. William Prosser, *Transferred Intent,* 45 TEX. L. REV. 650 (1967). Should intent transfer between torts that protect the same or similar interests? In these examples, the intent to batter one person transfers to the battery committed upon another person, albeit not an "intended" victim. Here the intent transfers between people. Additionally, if A shoots to frighten B but instead hits C, A has committed a battery on C. The intent to assault B transfers to a battery against C. Here the intent transfers between people and torts (assault and battery) *Brown v. Martinez,* 361 P.2d 152 (N.M. 1961). Or if A shoots at a dog and hits C, then A is liable to C for battery. *Corn v. Sheppard,* 229 N.W. 869 (Minn. 1930).

Is there any doctrinal reason for not extending transferred intent to all intentional torts? No court has recognized transferred intent for the intentional infliction of emotional distress. There is no apparent reason why transferred intent could not apply to other intentional torts, such as conversion, invasion of privacy, and the like. The concept of transferred intent is well established in the criminal law. A defendant, for example who planned to murder one person and, in so attempting, killed another is guilty of the murder of the unintended victim. The felony-murder doctrine roughly parallels transferred intent in tort law. What are the aims and problems of transferred intent in tort law? Why do these policies not apply equally well to criminal law?

2. *Perspectives on Transferred Intent.* What insights would a pragmatist have on the use of the transferred intent in *McBryde?* How would a critical race theorist and a social justice theorist approach this case? How do larger social problems such as race, class, and urban violence impact tort rules such as transferred intent? How would a law and economics oriented judge evaluate the doctrine of transferred intent? Is there a deterrent aspect of the doctrine of transferred intent? How likely is it that intentional tortfeasors will react to the disincentive of transferred intent?

E. FALSE IMPRISONMENT AND FALSE ARREST

False imprisonment is a nonconsensual, intentional confinement of a person, without lawful privilege, for an appreciable length of time. In order to be liable for false imprisonment, the defendant must do an act which is substantially certain to confine another within fixed boundaries for a period of time. The methods of confinement may be by force, threat of force, or duress. The tort of false imprisonment concerns the violation of someone's liberty of movement without the authority of legal process. The elements of false imprisonment are: "1) the nonconsensual, intentional confinement of a person, 2) without lawful privilege, and 3) for an appreciable period of time, however brief." *Blaxland v. Commonwealth Director of Public Prosecutions,* 323 F.3d 1198 (9th Cir. 2000) (applying California law). Notably, the tort of false imprisonment is functionally equivalent to the crime of false imprisonment.

The defendant must intend to confine the plaintiff within boundaries set by the defendant and the plaintiff must be conscious of the confinement or harmed by it. The awareness of confinement is the gist of the injury. In *Herring v. Boyle,* 149 Eng. Rep. 1126 (1834), a ten-year-old boy was attending an English boarding school. When his mother came to take the boy home over the Christmas holidays, the schoolmaster refused permission unless the term bill was paid. The boy knew nothing of either the request or refusal. The Court of Exchequer held there was no false imprisonment since the boy was unaware that he was confined. An infant, however, may be falsely imprisoned even though it has no awareness of confinement. *Cf. Sager v. Rochester General Hosp.,* 647 N.Y.S.2d 408 (N.Y. Sup. 1996) (finding no false imprisonment of five month infant held in a hospital from parents after medical staff found a suspicious fracture of the femur). If a person is severely injured due to confinement, he may recover despite his lack of awareness of his confinement. What is the confinement and the injury in the *Dupler* case that follows?

DUPLER v. SEUBERT
69 Wis. 2d 373, 230 N.W.2d 626 (1975)

WILKIE, CIRCUIT JUDGE.

This is a false imprisonment action. On April 23, 1971, plaintiff-appellant Ethel M. Dupler was fired from her job with the defendant-respondent Wisconsin Telephone Company. She was informed of her discharge during an hour-and-a-half session with her two superiors, defendants-respondents Keith Peterson and Helen Seubert, who, Dupler claims, falsely imprisoned her during a portion of this time period. A jury found that Peterson and Seubert did falsely imprison Dupler. [Plaintiff appealed an order of the trial court reducing the amount of the jury verdict. That order was affirmed.]

Dupler had worked for the telephone company as a customer service representative since 1960. At approximately 4:30 on April 23rd, Seubert asked Dupler to come to Peterson's office. When all three were inside, sitting down, with the door closed, Seubert told Dupler the telephone company would no longer employ her and that she could choose either to resign or be fired. Dupler testified that she refused to resign and that in the conversation that followed, Peterson discussed several alternatives short of dismissal, all of which had been considered but rejected.

At approximately 5 o'clock, Dupler testified, she began to feel sick to her stomach and said "You have already fired me. Why don't you just let me go?" She made a motion to get up but Peterson told her to sit down in "a very loud harsh voice." Then, Dupler testified, she began to feel violently ill and stated "I got to go. I can't take this any more. I'm sick to my stomach. I know I'm going to throw up." She got up and started for the door but Seubert also arose and stood in front of the door. After Dupler repeated that she was sick, Seubert allowed her to exit, but followed her to the men's washroom, where Dupler did throw up.

Following this, at approximately 5:25, Seubert asked Dupler to return to Peterson's office where she had left her purse to discuss the situation further. Dupler testified that she went back to the office and reached for her purse; Seubert again closed the door and Peterson said "[in] a loud voice 'Sit down. I'm still your boss. I'm not through with you.'" At approximately 5:40 Dupler told Peterson her husband was waiting for her outside in a car and Peterson told her to go outside and ask her husband to come inside.

Dupler then went outside and explained the situation to her husband who said, "You get back in there and get your coat and if you aren't right out I'll call the police." Dupler returned to Peterson's office and was again told in a loud tone of voice to sit down. She said Seubert and Peterson were trying to convince her to resign rather than be fired and again reviewed the alternatives that had been considered. Dupler then said: "What's the sense of all this? Why keep torturing me? Let me go. Let me go." She stated that Peterson replied "No, we still aren't finished. We have a lot of things to discuss, your retirement pay, your vacation, other things." Finally, at approximately 6 o'clock Peterson told Dupler they could talk further on the phone or at her house, and Dupler left. When asked why she had stayed in Peterson's office for such a long time, Dupler replied:

> Well, for one thing, Helen, Mrs. Seubert, had blocked the door, and tempers had been raised with all the shouting and screaming, I was just plain scared to make an effort. There were two against one.

Peterson and Seubert did not dispute that Dupler had been fired on April 23rd, or that the conference lasted from 4:30 to 6 p.m., or that Dupler became very upset and sick to her stomach and had to leave to throw up. Peterson admitted that Dupler had asked to leave and that he requested that she stay and continue talking so she could indicate whether she wished to resign or be fired. Seubert said Dupler did not so indicate until "within three minutes of her leaving." Both denied that any loud or threatening language had been used, or that Dupler was detained against her will. Peterson said neither he nor Seubert even raised their voices. He said the session was so lengthy because Dupler continued to plead for another chance, and to request reasons for the dismissal.

. . . The essence of false imprisonment is the intentional, unlawful, and unconsented restraint by one person of the physical liberty of another. In *Maniaci v. Marquette University,* 50 Wis. 2d 287, 184 N.W.2d 168 (1971), the court adopted the definition of false imprisonment contained in sec. 35 of the REST. 2D TORTS, which provides in part:

> (1) An actor is subject to liability to another for false imprisonment if
>
> > (a) he acts intending to confine the other or a third person within boundaries fixed by the actor, and
> >
> > (b) his act directly or indirectly results in such a confinement of the other, and
> >
> > (c) the other is conscious of the confinement or is harmed by it.

Sections 39 and 40 provide that the confinement may be caused by physical force or the threat of physical force, and the comment to sec. 40 indicates the threat may either be express, or inferred from the person's conduct. As Prosser comments:

> The restraint may be by means of physical barriers, or by threats of force which intimidate the plaintiff into compliance with orders. It is

sufficient that he submits to an apprehension of force reasonably to be understood from the conduct of the defendant, although no force is used or even expressly threatened. . . . This gives rise, in borderline cases, to questions of fact, turning upon the details of the testimony, as to what was reasonably to be understood and implied from the defendant's conduct, tone of voice and the like, which seldom can be reflected accurately in an appellate record, and normally are for the jury.

This is precisely such a case and we conclude that the record contains sufficient evidence from which the jury could have concluded that Mrs. Dupler was intentionally confined, against her will, by an implied threat of actual physical restraint. She testified that defendant Peterson ordered her in a loud voice to remain seated several times, after she expressed the desire to leave. She reported being "berated, screamed and hollered at," and said the reason she did not just walk out of the room was that "Mrs. Seubert had blocked the door, and tempers had been raised with all the shouting and screaming, I was just plain scared to make an effort. There were two against one." The jury obviously believed Mrs. Dupler's rather than the defendants' account of what transpired, as it had the right to do, and we conclude her testimony was sufficient to support the jury's verdict.

Defendants rely upon the 1926 case of *Weiler v. Herzfeld-Phillipson Co.* [208 N.W. 599], where this court held that an employer, who had detained an employee in his office for several hours upon suspicion of theft and then discharged her, was not liable for false imprisonment. This case is distinguishable, however, principally upon the ground that in *Weiler* the court emphasized several times that during the entire session the plaintiff was still employed by defendant and "was compensated for every minute of the time spent by her in the office." In the instant case, Dupler was compensated only through 5 p.m., and according to her testimony, she was not ordered to remain in the office, after she requested to leave, until after 5 p.m.

We conclude that *Weiler* is not controlling here and that the jury could properly find that defendants falsely imprisoned Dupler by compelling her to remain in Peterson's office against her will after 5 p.m. We conclude the imprisonment ceased when Dupler left the building to visit her husband, but resumed when she re-entered Peterson's office to get her coat in order to leave, but was commanded to stay. . . .

NOTES

1. *Imprisonment by Exclusion?* The legally protectible interest underlying false imprisonment is the freedom "to choose one's own location and, therefore, in freedom from the realization that one's will to choose one's location is subordinated to the will of another." REST. 2D TORTS § 35, cmt. *h.*

In *Bird v. Jones*, 115 Eng. Rep. 668 (1845), plaintiff was prohibited from traversing a portion of the highway which was enclosed for spectators of a boat race. The court, finding no false imprisonment, observed that "the plaintiff was at liberty to move his person and go in any other direction, at his free will and pleasure." Thus "there was no imprisonment. To call it so appears to confound partial obstruction and disturbance with total obstruction and detention." Can there be false imprisonment in an entire city? REST. 2D TORTS § 36, illus. 6. *See Allen v. Fromme,* 126 N.Y.S. 520 (N.Y. App. Div. 1910) (refusal to vacate a void execution holding forbidding plaintiff to leave city after being released from custody of sheriff). If so, could there not also be false imprisonment in an entire state, or in a country? If all the world except the United States were totalitarian, and a totalitarian person was unlawfully barred from entering the United States, would that person be falsely imprisoned in the totalitarian portion of the world? "

In *Morris v. Faulkner,* 361 N.E.2d 112 (Ill. App. 1977), the court said that "cases have stated that false imprisonment consists of any unlawful exercise or show of force by which a person is compelled to remain where he does not wish to remain or to go where he does not wish to go, or is prevented from doing what he desires." The court found the plaintiffs did not state a claim for false imprisonment based on exclusion from a tavern, since the tavern owner had the right to exclude them. The court also said, "It would be absurd to consider plaintiffs as having been confined to all the world but the tavern." Why is that "absurd"?

2. *Transferred Intent in False Imprisonment Cases.* Transferred intent is a doctrine that provides that "the intention to confine any person is sufficient intent to render one liable to the person actually confined, and it is immaterial that the defendant did not know the identity of the person he or she intended to confine, nor does it matter that the defendant intended to affect some person other than the one actually confined." DOUGLAS DANNER & LARRY VARN, 3 PATTERN DISCOVERY TORT ACTIONS § 34:2 (2006).

3. *Shoplifting Statutes.* Some states have enacted statutes granting shopkeepers the right to retain a suspected shoplifter for a reasonable time to permit a reasonable investigation. The terms of these statutes vary from jurisdiction to jurisdiction. They affect such matters as the amount of force that can be used, what constitutes probable cause, and whether the privilege extends beyond the premises. The right to detain a suspected shoplifter usually is asserted as an affirmative defense to a false arrest or imprisonment claim brought against the shopkeeper.

4. *Restraint Through Property.* Threats to property may suffice as force to confine. *See* REST. 2D TORTS § 40A. In *Marcano v. Northwestern Chrysler-Plymouth Sales, Inc.,* 550 F. Supp. 595 (N.D. Ill. 1982), defendant sold a car to plaintiff Marcano. Some months thereafter, while plaintiff and her friend, also a plaintiff, were renegotiating the overdue payments on the car at defendant's place of business, defendant's employee Greene asked Marcano for the keys to the car, allegedly so that he could inspect it for damage. Plaintiff acquiesced, but on receiving the keys, Greene promptly locked the car and kept the keys. The contents of the car included the plaintiff's purse, house keys and medicine for her child. The plaintiffs remained at the dealership from 2:30 P.M. to 7:30 P.M., at which time a Northwestern employee drove them to their homes. The court commented as follows:

While it is clear that the modern concept of false imprisonment does not require that the confinement be by iron bars and stone walls, PROSSER, HANDBOOK OF THE LAW OF TORTS § 11 at 42 (4th ed. 1971), it does require the "unlawful restraint of individual liberty of freedom of locomotion against a person's will." *Marcus v. Liebman*, 375 N.E.2d 486 (Ill. App. 1978). In order for a false imprisonment to be present, there must be an actual or legal intent to restrain. Additionally, while actual force is not a requisite to an action for false imprisonment . . . not every inducement to remain can rise to the level of false imprisonment.

In the view of this Court, the tort of false imprisonment contemplates an actual or perceived restraint on the freedom of the individual allegedly confined. Such a confinement must be "involuntary." *Fort v. Smith*, 407 N.E.2d 117 (Ill. App. 1980). While the facts as alleged in the instant case appear to show that plaintiff Marcano may have been justified in choosing to remain with the automobile and the personal belongings allegedly contained therein, such a choice does not raise the conduct of defendant to the level of a false imprisonment. Indeed, when plaintiffs Marcano and Provencio chose to leave the premises, they were clearly allowed to do so without interference.

Which defendant's conduct do you find more egregious? Is there another adequate remedy for the plaintiff in the *Marcano* case? Should that influence the outcome of her claim for false imprisonment?

5. *Religious Restraint.* The plaintiffs in *Molko v. Holy Spirit Ass'n*, 762 P.2d 46 (Cal. 1988), brought an action for fraud and deceit, intentional infliction of emotional distress and false imprisonment against the Holy Spirit Association for the Unification of World Christianity, headed by the Rev. Sun Myung Moon. Plaintiffs claimed they were fraudulently induced to join the association, then "brainwashed" and forced to remain in the association by psychological pressures. They "escaped" only after they were kidnapped by relatives and "deprogrammed." REST. 2D TORTS § 40A provides that "[t]he confinement may be by submission to duress other than threats of physical force, where such duress is sufficient to make the consent given ineffective to bar the action."

The *Molko* court found that plaintiffs stated a claim for fraud and deceit because they were induced to join the association by misrepresentations as to its true nature. They also stated a claim for intentional infliction of emotional distress based on enforced fasting, poverty, silence, cloistered living, and long hours of work. This claim, however, could not rest on alleged threats of divine retribution, since these threats "were protected religious speech." For the same reason the claim of false imprisonment, arising from psychological coercion based on divine threats of retribution, would not lie.

Misrepresentation and fraud are also independent torts. Fraud is the intentional tort where a defendant intentionally makes false statements that causes the plaintiff to suffer harm. The tort of fraud has five elements: (1) a false representation by a defendant; (2) scienter; (3) intention to induce the plaintiff to act or refrain from acting; (4) justifiable reliance by plaintiff; and (5) damage to plaintiff. *Insight Technology Inc. v. Freight Check LLC*, 633 S.E.2d (Ga. 2006).

6. *Employee Status & Gender Injustice: Dupler* implies that detaining an employee during working hours for questioning does not constitute false imprisonment. Compare *Fermino v. Fedco,* 7 Cal. 4th 701 (1994). In *Fermino,* an employer questioned an employee during working hours about an alleged appropriation of $4.95 from the sale of a ring to a customer. Defendant falsely stated that the customer and a co-employee were outside the interrogation room ready to confirm the appropriation. Plaintiff was repeatedly asked to confess and prevented from leaving the room, profanities were "hurled" at her, and she was retained until she became "hysterical, and broke down into tears."

The *Fermino* court said that although an employer has a right to investigate alleged employee theft, the investigation must be for a reasonable time and in a reasonable manner. Here a jury could find that the investigation was unreasonable. The court rejected defendant's contention that there was "no false imprisonment . . . because the employee had received her normal compensation for the time during which she was held in interrogation." The right of an employer to require an employee to follow directions, the court said, does "not authorize the employer to forcibly detain the person of an employee for the purpose of compelling a confession of a theft." What role does the intersectionality of Ethel Dupler's gender and age play in determining whether the telephone company falsely imprisoned her? Did differences in size and strength play a role in determining whether there was an act of obstruction?

WRIGHT v. STATE
752 P.2d 748 (Mont. 1988)

HUNT, JUSTICE.

. . . On January 20, 1984, plaintiff John Wright was arrested for . . . disorderly conduct, and . . . criminal trespass, while attempting to renew his expired Montana driver's license at the Licensing Bureau offices in Bozeman. Wright entered the Bureau offices in midmorning with the intention of renewing his expired license. He was first waited upon by examiner Rena Knapp, who informed him that because his license was past 90 days expired, he was required to pass a complete driving examination before being issued a new license. Wright took and successfully passed the written exam and then was required by Knapp to fill out the standard application form called a DL-40. The form he filled out contained a clause that required the disclosure of his Social Security number. Although Montana law no longer mandates the use of a Social Security number, many of the old forms are still being used. Either Knapp or examiner Ray Houghton asked him what his number was. He indicated he did not wish to disclose his Social Security number and there is testimony that he replied by saying, "Hell, no." Additional testimony indicates he was given a random number.

At this point, examiner Houghton took over the application of Wright. After apparently completing the rest of the form, Wright left the office and returned with the vehicle he wished to use for the driving portion of the exam. Before he left he was advised by Houghton to be sure to bring back adequate proof of insurance.

Wright returned but with what Houghton thought to be inadequate proof of insurance, and he refused to allow Wright to finish the exam because an examiner is prohibited from getting into a vehicle without adequate proof of insurance. A loud argument ensued and ended when Wright called Houghton a "horse's ass." Houghton then told Wright not to come back that day as he would not be waited upon further. Wright left, attempting to slam the office door as he went. Wright did return later that day and tried to use an office phone restricted to office business only. Having several customers and not wanting a disturbance, Houghton called the police and Wright was arrested after refusing the police officer's request to leave. He was taken to the detention center, booked, and released on bail. The next Monday, Wright returned to the Bureau office, showed adequate proof of insurance and was given the driving portion of the exam by Houghton. He passed and was given a new driver's license. All charges were later dismissed. It should be noted that Wright's renewed license does not contain his Social Security number.

Wright brought suit for false arrest and other claims against the State of Montana, Houghton, City of Bozeman and the arresting officer, Ed Malone. All defendants filed a motion for summary judgment which was granted July 29, 1987. In its order, the District Court noted the lack of any evidence submitted in opposition to the motion and found no material issue of fact existed. Plaintiff appeals. . . .

The relevant depositions in the District Court file are all consistent on the point of Wright's Social Security number. Both Knapp and Houghton testified that Wright was not required to use his Social Security number and was in fact assigned a random number. There is no opposing evidence that shows he was forced to use his Social Security number. That number is not on his driver's license. Knapp's, Houghton's and Malone's depositions are consistent in showing that the conflict arose over Wright's lack of proof of insurance. Even if Wright's deposition showed an inconsistency it was not before the court and cannot be considered. The appellant failed to carry his burden and the District Court made its decision accordingly.

Appellant also argues that whether officer Malone had probable cause to arrest Wright is a question of fact which the appellant is entitled to present to a jury. The general rule is that where the facts are undisputed the question of whether an arrest was legal or illegal becomes a question of law for the court. Since no material fact exists the respondents were entitled to summary judgment as a matter of law. [AFFIRMED DISTRICT COURT'S ORDER FOR SUMMARY JUDGMENT].

SHEEHY, JUSTICE, DISSENTING.

In Hamlet's soliloquy, one of the "whips and scorns" which led the great Dane to consider whether death was better than life was "the insolence of office." In those few words, the Bard managed to express the aggravations and futilities pressed on any of us when public officials vent their sour stomachs in performing their duties. The authority to wear a badge or to wield a pen in power over others seems to fuel in us a sense of mastery, and not of service. It is a common failing, and all of us public servants succumb to it at some point.

. . . This Court assumes without question that the version of incidents propounded by the public officers in this case is the only version. It ignores the opposite version posed by the plaintiff, that he went to a public building to renew his driver's license; that his Social Security number was demanded; that he later produced proof of insurance but that the examiner refused to issue him a license that day, and told him to return on the following Monday; and that the examiner called the police and had him arrested; that the charges against him were disorderly conduct and criminal trespass; and that both of these charges were later dismissed. In short, he went to a public building for a driver's license and wound up handcuffed and led off to the police station.

The real question in this case is whether there was probable cause for Wright's arrest. If his arrest was groundless, he has a cause of action against the perpetrators. Neither the District Court nor this Court addresses that question. The deposition testimony of Rena Knapp is strong evidence that his arrest was groundless. She describes how the examiner (without any authority to do so) told Wright not to return for his license that day.

When Wright returned, with his proof of insurance, the examiner immediately, without exchanging a word with Wright, telephoned for the police. Rena Knapp describes the interval until the policeman came as no shouting and no threatening by Wright. When the policeman came and asked what the problem was, the examiner said that Wright had been asked to leave, and would not, and that the examiner wanted Wright out of the office; "that he would no longer be helped that day." There appears no justification for refusal to help Wright on that day, since he had paid for his license, successfully taken the written exam, and had insurance papers which entitled him to a test drive. For reasons of his own, it appears the patrolman was punishing Wright. Without any struggle or tumult, Wright was handcuffed and taken out of a public building where he had a right to be, and groundlessly charged with crimes. . . . [AFFIRMED].

NOTES

1. *More "Whips and Scorns:" A Dissent Vindicated?* Police officers may not exercise their authority to vindicate perceived slights or personal motives. Whether a police officer is privileged to make an arrest depends upon state law. In general, a police officer may arrest without a warrant for a misdemeanor committed in his presence. In *Enright v. Groves,* 560 P.2d 851 (Colo. App. 1977) a police officer observed a dog running at large in violation of the city's dog leash ordinance. He observed the dog approaching the house of Mrs. Enright and ask her eleven-year-old son if the dog belonged to him. The boy acknowledged it was his dog and told the officer that his mother was in the car parked at the curb by the house. The officer ordered that the dog and boy go into the house and began walking toward the Enright vehicle. The officer demanded that the plaintiff produce her driver's license and she declined to produce it. He told her to produce the license or he would take her to jail. Mrs. Enright's response was that this was a ridiculous demand. The office then grabbled her arms stating, "Let's Go!" Mrs. Enright cried out, telling the officer that he was hurting her. When he refused to release her arm, she struck him in the stomach. He seized both of her arms throwing her to the ground. Groves then took Enright to the patrol car and advised her that she was under arrest for violation of the leash law. She was convicted of the ordinance. The defendant contends that he had probable cause to arrest Mrs. Enright, and that she was in fact arrested for and convicted of violation of the dog-at-large ordinance. The court disagreed, finding that the officer arrested Mrs. Enright, not for violation of the dog leash ordinance, but for failing to produce her driver's license. The court found no Colorado statute or case law in this jurisdiction which required Mrs. Enright to show her driver's license upon demand.

What accounts for the different results in *Wright* and *Enright*? Is there a "procedural" explanation; that the plaintiff in Wright was unrepresented and therefore at a disadvantage because he did know about how to file a motion in response to summary judgment?

2. *False Arrest and Probable Cause.* In *Leonard v. Robinson*, 2007 U.S. App. LEXIS 2275 (6th Cir. Feb. 2, 2007), the Sixth Circuit reversed a trial court's entry of summary judgment in favor of a police officer in a false arrest case. In *Leonard*, the plaintiff's wife operated a towing company. The police chief sought to increase police jurisdiction. The wife's mother was a member of the township council who opposed expanded jurisdiction. The police chief asked the wife to persuade her mother to change her opposition. When the wife refused, the police chief stopped using the towing company. The plaintiff and other family members attended a council meeting to address why the police were no longer using the towing company. The police chief sent an officer to attend the meeting. During the town meeting the plaintiff used mild obscenity in arguing with a council member. The police officer arrested the plaintiff, who filed a civil rights claim predicated upon false arrest. The Sixth Circuit reversed, finding that no reasonable police officer could believe that the plaintiff's mild profanity while peacefully advocating a political position could constitute a criminal act. The court also found a *prima facie* case that the false arrest was motivated by First Amendment retaliation. What role does arrogance and abuse of power play in the outcome of false arrest cases?

In *Leonard*, the plaintiff's complaint raised three state law torts: battery, false arrest, and false imprisonment as well as 42 U.S.C. § 1983, a statutory claim that allows a plaintiff to go to federal court for redress of violations of statutory or constitutional rights committed by tortfeasors acting "under color of state law." The plaintiff claimed the police violated his First and Fourth Amendment rights. Recall the 1991 Rodney King case that set off the tragic race riot in which 55 people were killed and thousands injured in Los Angeles. The riot was incited by police officers caught on videotape beating an African American man with metal batons following a car chase. If probable cause is not a defense, for example, to false imprisonment, battery, or a civil rights violation, then why should it be a defense to false arrest? See REST. 2D TORTS § 119, providing that a private person can lawfully arrest a misdemeanant for breach of the peace only if the breach is, or is about to be, committed in her presence. An arrest is not privileged if excessive force is used. *Id.* § 131. In *City of Miami v. Sanders*, 672 So. 2d 46 (Fla. 1996), the Florida Supreme Court stated:

> Traditionally, a presumption of good faith attaches to an officer's use of force in making a lawful arrest and an officer is liable for damages only

where the force used is clearly excessive. . . . REST. 2D TORTS § 132 cmt. *a* (1965). If excessive force is used in an arrest, the ordinarily protected use of force by a police officer is transformed into a battery . . .

A battery claim for excessive force is analyzed by focusing upon whether the amount of force used was reasonable under the circumstances. . . . Law enforcement officers are provided a complete defense to an excessive use of force claim where an officer 'reasonably believes [the force] to be necessary to defend himself or another from bodily harm while making the arrest.'[citations omitted]

Id. at 47.

F. INTENTIONAL INFLICTION OF EMOTIONAL DISTRESS

The intentional infliction of emotional distress, sometimes called the tort of outrage, is the newest of the intentional torts. The tort of outrage evolved in the 1950s and 1960s in part at least, to fill the gap left in assault when a defendant's threats of harmful or offensive contact were not imminent threats. Justice Roger Traynor's magisterial opinion in *State Rubbish Collectors Ass'n v. Siliznoff*, 240 P.2d 282 (Cal. 1952) permitted the plaintiff to recover for the extreme outrageous acts of an association of rubbish collectors who threaten to beat him up, trash his truck, and drive him out of business. This was the first judicial recognition that extreme emotional distress intentionally inflicted must be redressed. The tort of assault was not available in that case because the threats were "future threats" thus not meeting the imminent harm requirement.

In order for the defendant to be liable for the intentional infliction of emotional distress, the misconduct must be outrageous and the distress extreme. The distress suffered must be such that no reasonable person could be expected to endure it. Liability arises only where the mental suffering or anguish is extreme. REST. 2D OF TORTS § 46, cmt. *j*. The requirement that the distress be extreme is to limit the possibility of numerous questionable claims. Jurisdictions following the REST. 2D TORTS § 46 permit the plaintiff to recover for mere recklessness, though some jurisdictions require the stiffer burden of intent. According to the Restatement:

One who by extreme and outrageous conduct intentionally or recklessly causes severe emotional distress to another is subject to liability for such emotional distress, and if bodily harm to the other results from it, for such bodily harm.

Id. § 46(1).

In a jurisdiction adopting Section 46, some of the strictures of the doctrine of assault (e.g., imminent apprehension, words plus threatening act) may be avoided. However, the requirement that the defendant's conduct be extreme and outrageous is probably more demanding than the assault requirement (*see* REST. 2D TORTS, § 23) that one merely be put "in apprehension" of an immediate and harmful or offensive conduct. The tort of outrage requires extreme emotional distress. In contrast, assault has no requirement for the severity of apprehension. In considering *Todd v. Byrd* below, consider the role that the outrage tort has in giving guidelines to potential tortfeasors about what conduct is acceptable and what is not.

TODD v. BYRD
640 S.E.2d 652 (Ga. Ct. App. 2006)

BARNES, JUDGE.

Fred's Stores of Tennessee and its employees Joyce Todd and Phyllis Purcell appeal the trial court's denial of their motion for summary judgment on the claims of the plaintiff, Sylvia Byrd, as next friend of her nine-year-old daughter Tynesha, arising from Tynesha's visit to Fred's Store. For the reasons that follow, we affirm in part and reverse in part the trial court's order denying summary judgment to the defendant. . . . Viewed in the light most favorable to Byrd, as the nonmovant, the record shows that Byrd and her daughter Tynesha were shopping at a Goodwill store around 5:00 p.m. when Tynesha needed to use a bathroom. Because the Goodwill store's bathroom was out of service, Byrd told her daughter to go next door to Fred's, where Purcell and Todd were working, and use its bathroom.

Tynesha went into Fred's for the sole purpose of using its bathroom, which Purcell had cleaned earlier in the day, and which Todd (the manager) had checked at noon. Tynesha testified that they only planned to shop at Goodwill. Tynesha testified that when she entered the bathroom, she noticed feces on the toilet seat and saw blood, bloody underwear, and an empty underwear package in the trash can. Purcell, who was working next to the bathroom, noticed a strong smell of feces coming from it, even though its door was shut. When Tynesha left the bathroom, Purcell saw her, and concluded that she had been in the bathroom throughout the time during which Purcell had smelled the foul odor.

When Purcell checked the bathroom, she found fresh feces on the wall, toilet seat, and floor as well as bloody underwear and an empty underwear wrapper in the trash can. Because Fred's carried that brand of underwear, Purcell formed the suspicion that Tynesha might have taken some new underwear into the bathroom and then discarded both her own soiled underwear and the underwear wrapper in its trash can.

Purcell found Tynesha just outside the store, accused her of stealing underwear, and asked her to return to the store to speak to Todd. In a manner that Tynesha agreed was motherly, Purcell took her hand and led her back into the store. Tynesha felt that she had to hold Purcell's hand. Todd joined them, and the two women led Tynesha by the hand back to the bathroom and showed her the filthy scene. Purcell told Todd that Tynesha had stolen some underwear and pads, and Purcell asked her if she was on her period before she pulled the used underwear from the trash and showed it to her. At the time, the child did not understand what "pads" were and had not yet begun to have her period. Todd then asked Tynesha if she could see her underwear. When the girl said nothing, Todd lifted her shirt and said she saw that she was wearing a brand matching the discarded package. Tynesha, however, claims that Purcell said the brands were not the same. Todd then told Tynesha to leave the store and not to return without an adult. Tynesha left and began crying outside the store.

Byrd soon entered the store with her daughter and began yelling, cursing, and throwing merchandise. Byrd testified that Tynesha was crying outside the store, fainted in the car afterward, has woken up crying about the incident, and has had nightmares. Tynesha confirmed she had dreamed of being at Fred's when "bad people" came after here, and it now "bothers her" to go into a store or a different part of the store by herself for fear of a similar incident.

Byrd brought suit on her daughter's behalf alleging torts of tortious misconduct, invasion of privacy, intentional infliction of emotional distress, false imprisonment, and false arrest . . .

The complaint sought general and exemplary damages and expenses of litigation and attorneys fees. The Fred's Store defendants answered denying liability and after discovery, they filed motions for summary judgment. Byrd responded to the motion, and the trial court denied the defendants' motion for partial or entire summary judgment without explaining its reasoning. After our grant of an interlocutory appeal, this appeal followed.

The Fred's Store defendants . . . assert that the trial court erred by denying their motion for summary judgment on Byrd's claim for intentional infliction of emotional distress. They argue that their conduct did not rise to the level of outrageousness and egregiousness required to maintain an action for this tort, and whether that standard is met is a question of law for the court. . . .

The elements of a cause of action for intentional infliction of emotional distress are: (1) intentional or reckless conduct; (2) that is extreme and outrageous; (3) a causal connection between the wrongful conduct and the emotional distress; and (4) severe emotional distress. . . . Liability for this tort has been found only where the conduct has been so outrageous in character, and so extreme in degree, as to go beyond all possible bounds of decency, and to be regarded as atrocious, and utterly intolerable in a civilized community. Generally, the case is one in which the recitation of the facts to an average member of the community would arouse his resentment against the actor, and lead him to exclaim, "Outrageous!". . . . "If a reasonable person might find the conduct extreme and outrageous, causing severe emotional distress, the jury then must find the facts and make its own determination." *Mableton Parkway CVS v. Salter, supra*, 273 Ga. App. at 482, 615 S.E.2d 558.

Given the Fred's Store defendants' conduct toward Tynesha discussed above, the trial court did not err by denying their motion for summary judgment on this claim. Notwithstanding Tynesha's testimony that she felt they were "nice and sweet" to her, they led her by the hand back in the store even though she did not want to go, accused her of theft, caused her to reveal her underwear, and put dirty, bloody, smelly underwear in her face for her to see. Further, Tynesha also testified that she has had nightmares and is afraid to shop by herself. Under this evidence, the jury should make the determination of liability. [AFFIRM IN PART AND REVERSE IN PART]

ANDREWS, PRESIDING JUDGE, concurring in part and dissenting in part. . . . .[T]he defendants' conduct did not meet the threshold necessary to sustain a claim for intentional infliction of emotional distress, the trial court erred by denying summary judgment on this claim. Construed in favor of Byrd's claims brought on behalf of her minor child, the evidence fails to establish all of the elements which must be present to support a claim for intentional infliction of emotional distress: "(1) the conduct must be intentional or reckless; (2) the conduct must be extreme and outrageous; (3) there must be a causal connection between the wrongful conduct and the plaintiff's emotional distress; and (4) the emotional distress must be severe." *MARTA v. Mosley*, 280 Ga. App. 486, 490–491 (2006). . . . Although Byrd produced evidence that the defendants acted intentionally or recklessly toward her child (element 1), and evidence showing a causal connection between the defendants' conduct and some degree of emotional distress suffered by the child (element 3), she failed to produce evidence sufficient to show that the defendants' conduct was extreme and outrageous (element 2), or that the emotional distress suffered by the child as a result of the defendants' conduct was severe (element 4).

The female child at issue was nine years old at the time of the incident, but she was large for her age weighing between 200 and 230 pounds according to Byrd. The child testified by deposition that she walked into Fred's store to use the restroom, and that, after entering the restroom, she left without using it because she saw "dookey" on the toilet seat, saw blood, bloody underwear, and package wrappers in the trash can, and smelled a "real bad" odor of "dookey." A store employee, Ms. Purcell, stated by affidavit that she was near the door of the restroom when the child left, and that, because of the strong smell of feces emanating from the restroom, she went inside to check the restroom. Purcell stated that she saw fresh feces on the toilet, wall, and floor, saw fresh blood on the toilet, floor, and trash can, and saw bloody underwear and an empty merchandise wrapper in the trash can. Based on these observations, Purcell thought the child probably had some sort of problem in the restroom and was responsible for the feces and blood, and she suspected that, because of the problem, the child may have taken some Fred's merchandise and left the empty wrapper in the trash can. According to Purcell and the store manager, Ms. Joyce, Purcell notified Joyce of the situation, and Joyce approached the child and asked her to walk back to the restroom.

The child testified that, as she walked out of the store immediately after leaving the restroom, Purcell approached her, said she stole some underwear and some pads, then took her by the hand, led her back into the store, and told Joyce that she had stolen some underwear and pads. She said Joyce held her hand and took her into the restroom accompanied by Purcell. According to the child, Joyce said she stole something, "asked her if she had done the poop that was on the seat," asked her if she was "on her period," then used a glove to pick up the bloody underwear from the trash can and asked her if the underwear belonged to her. The child said she told Joyce and Purcell that she did not steal anything, that she did not mess up the seat, and that it was not her underwear. The child further testified that, while they were in the restroom, Purcell asked if she could see her underwear, and then lifted up her shirt enough to look at the top band of her underwear which was visible above the waistband of her pants. According to the child, Purcell said that her underwear was not the same kind as the underwear in the trash can. At that point, the child said

Joyce told her that she could go and told her not to come back to the store unless she was accompanied by an adult.

The child testified that she left the store and immediately told her mother, Byrd, who was shopping in an adjacent store, that she had been accused of stealing from Fred's store and messing up the restroom, and that the people at Fred's wanted to talk to her. The child said she was crying at that point because she had been accused of stealing and might get in trouble with her mother. The child testified that, when they got to the store, her mother started "yelling real loud," cursing and throwing shoes. Byrd recalled at her deposition that she called Joyce a bitch and a whore, and that she knocked paperwork by the store cash register onto the floor and threw shoes and other store merchandise. According to the child, her mother's "crazy" conduct in the store scared her worse than being brought back in the store by Joyce and Purcell, and that when she fainted later in the day it was because her mother had gotten her upset. When asked if the incident at Fred's store bothered her after that day, the child said she had dreams about "people coming to get me," but she said her dreams were no worse after the Fred's incident than they were before the incident. In fact, the child repeatedly testified at her deposition that Purcell and Joyce spoke to her sweetly and were nice to her during the entire incident. Defense counsel questioned the child at length about any emotional distress she may have suffered as a result of the incident. . . .

Whether the conduct at issue was sufficiently extreme or outrageous to support a claim for intention infliction of emotion distress is a question of law for the court. *Kaiser v. Tara Ford, Inc.,* 546 S.E.2d 861 (Ga. App. 2001). As the majority opinion states, to meet this stringent burden of proof, the conduct "must be so extreme in degree, as to go beyond all possible bounds of decency, and to be regarded as atrocious, and utterly intolerable in a civilized society." . . . . It is not enough to prevail on a claim for intentional infliction of emotional distress to show "that the defendant has acted with an intent which is tortious or even criminal, or that he has intended to inflict emotional distress, or even that his conduct has been characterized by malice, or a degree of aggravation that would entitle the plaintiff to punitive damages for another tort." *Odem v. Pace Academy,* 235 Ga. App. 648, 654–655 (1998). . . .

Moreover, there is no recovery for intentional infliction of emotional distress for insults, threats, indignities, or the like, which cause commonly inflicted emotional distress "includ[ing] all highly unpleasant mental reactions such as fright, horror, grief, shame, humiliation, embarrassment, anger, chagrin, disappointment, worry, and nausea.". . . . Rather, there must be major outrage in the conduct complained of, so beyond the bounds of decency and so atrocious and intolerable in civilized society, that it inflicts emotional distress "so severe that no reasonable [person] could be expected to endure it." . . . .Construing the record in favor of Byrd on summary judgment, there is evidence that the conduct at issue was harsh, inappropriate, insulting, and embarrassing, and that it could be sufficient to support the award of damages (including possible punitive damages) for the commission of other torts. But the conduct was not sufficient to satisfy the stringent standards for a claim of intentional infliction of emotional distress. Moreover, the record is devoid of any evidence that, as a result of the conduct at issue, Byrd's child suffered severe emotional distress.

NOTES

1. *Extreme and Outrageous Conduct.* Intentional infliction of emotional distress is an independent tort that should be distinguished from emotional injuries arising out of a traditional tort such as battery, assault, or false imprisonment. The term "parasitic damages" is sometimes used to refer to emotional injuries when they arise out of the commission of a tort. In contrast, the independent tort of outrage requires the plaintiff to demonstrate four elements:

> 1) that the actor either intended to cause emotional distress or knew or should have known that actions taken would result in serious emotional distress to the plaintiff; 2) that the actor's conduct was so extreme and outrageous as to go beyond all possible bounds of decency and was such that it can be considered as utterly intolerable in a civilized community; (3) that the actor's actions were the proximate cause of the plaintiff's psychic injury; and (4) that the mental anguish suffered by plaintiff is serious and of a nature that no reasonable man could be expected to endure it.

Wilson v. Wilson, No. 21443, 2007 WL 127657 *5 (Ohio App. 2 Dist. Jan. 19, 2007).

"Before the infliction tort was created judges stretched the torts of battery, assault, and trespass to provide redress for outrageous conduct that inflicted severe mental anguish." Mark P. Gergen, *The Jury's Role in Deciding Normative Issues in the American Common Law*, 68 FORDHAM L. REV. 407, 440 (1999). Extreme and outrageous conduct is conduct that "has been so outrageous in character, and so extreme in degree, as to go beyond all possible bounds of decency, and to be regarded as atrocious, and utterly intolerable in a civilized community." REST. 2D TORTS § 46 cmt. *d*. The plaintiff must demonstrate that she suffered psychic injury or that her mental anguish was of a nature that no reasonable person could be expected to endure it. The tort of outrage does not require the plaintiff to demonstrate physical illness or other injurious physical consequences, unlike the tort of negligent infliction of emotional distress. Jurisdictions are split in whether recovery may be permitted for mere recklessness.

2. *Cases Prefiguring the Modern Tort of Outrage.* It generally is held that a threat of future injury does not constitute an assault, because the tort requires that the actor "put the other in apprehension of an *imminent* contact." *Dickens v. Puryear,* 302 N.C. 437, 276 S.E.2d 325 (1981). However, intentional infliction of emotional distress can result from a threat of future harm. *See Wilson v. Wilkins,* 25 S.W.2d 428 (Ark. 1930) (actionable claim stated where defendants threatened to harm plaintiff if he were not out of town by nightfall). A false imprisonment can also presumably occur from a threat of future harm. (*E.g.,* A says to B by long distance telephone call: "If you leave your room today, I will kill you the next time we meet." B would be falsely imprisoned if she remains in her room because of A's threat.) Why should a threat of present harm be necessary for assault, but not for intentional infliction of emotional distress or false imprisonment, since all three torts may be characterized as involving the infliction of emotional distress? Prior to the early 1950s, the common law permitted recovery for emotional distress in cases involving the mishandling of dead bodies and where the defendant had knowledge of a plaintiff's eccentricities or susceptibility to emotional illnesses. Under modern tort law, no recovery is available unless a plaintiff proves extreme distress and conduct by the defendant that would be viewed as outrageous in the larger community. REST. 2D TORTS § 46.

3. *The History of Outrage.* Traditionally, emotional injuries could be recovered only if attached to another independent tort such as assault, battery or false imprisonment. Justice Roger Traynor's landmark opinion in *State Rubbish Collectors Ass'n v. Siliznoff*, 240 P.2d 282 (Cal. 1952), was the first Anglo-American case to carve out an independent, non-parasitic cause of action for the intentional infliction of emotional distress. The new tort was predicated upon the right to be free from "serious, intentional, and unprivileged invasions of emotional and mental tranquility." *Id.* at 286. The *Siliznoff* case was the first U.S. appellate case to permit recovery for severe emotional distress even if there were no physical manifestations. Section 46 of the Restatement (Second) of Torts cited *Siliznoff* with approval in recognizing a cause of action for the tort of outrage. REST. 2D TORTS § 46, cmt. *d* requires that the defendant's actions be extreme and outrageous.

GOMEZ v. HUG
7 Kan. App. 2d 603 (1982)

WAHL, DISTRICT JUDGE.

. . . On April 21, 1978, Silvino Gomez was employed as a supervisor at the Shawnee County fairgrounds. His immediate supervisor was the fairgrounds administrator, Robert Kanatzer. During the evening hours of April 21, 1978, Gomez and Kanatzer were engaged in preparing an area of the fairgrounds for a horse show. They learned of a waterline break and, after determining the problem, proceeded to the administrator's office to phone a piping contractor.

Appellee Roland Hug, a member of the Board of County Commissioners of Shawnee County, and a companion, Robert Corbett, were in Kanatzer's office when Gomez and Kanatzer arrived. As they entered the office, Hug asked Kanatzer, "What is that fucking spic doing in the office?" Hug then repeated the question, again referring to Gomez as a "fucking spic." Hug then ordered Gomez over to where he was, again referring to Gomez as a "fucking spic." Gomez complied with Hug's order to approach him and inquired of Hug as to what he meant by that name. Gomez testified in his deposition that the following exchange took place between him and Hug:

A. . . . 'Commissioner, you have repeatedly stated that remark throughout the day and in the past day or two. Can you give me your interpretation of a fucking spic?' He said, 'You are a fucking spic.' I said, 'What does it mean?' He said, 'A fucking Mexican greaser like you, that is all you are. You are nothing but a fucking Mexican greaser, nothing but a pile of shit.' And he repeated it over and over and he raised his fist and he said, 'Now what are you going to do about it?' He got that close to me (indicating) and said, 'What are you going to do about it?' He kept hollering it out and hollering it out. He said, 'Go ahead and do something about it, you fucking Mexican greaser. I have told you what you are. You are nothing but a fucking spic.' And he repeated it over and he kept shaking his fists in front of my eyes and pounding on the desk and he would come up to me and say, 'Are you going to do something, you coward, you greaser, you fucking spic? What are you going to do? Don't stand there like a damn fool because that is all you are is a pile of shit.'

" . . . He kept threatening me. What was I going to do about it? He kept putting his fist in front of my face and pounding on that table, 'What are you going to do about it?' and repeating it over and over that I was nothing but a fucking spic. 'Now, you said you know what the definition of a spic is. You are nothing but a fucking spic and a Mexican greaser,' and he kept repeating it over and over, and he kept shaking his fist in front of me. I was froze because I was afraid of the man. For the first time in my life, I was terrified of one man calling me that. I was afraid for my job. I was afraid for my family.

It is variously estimated that this tirade lasted from five to fifteen minutes. After the exchange between Gomez and Hug, Kanatzer escorted Gomez out of the office and took him home. Gomez appeared to be upset.

Gomez began having serious medical problems. He sought medical advice and treatment from Dr. D. J. Weber, his family physician, Dr. Vinod Patel, a neurologist, and Dr. James N. Nelson, a psychiatrist. Both Dr. Nelson and Dr. Patel stated in their reports that Gomez' medical problems were related to the complained-of incident. Gomez was hospitalized from July 5, 1978, through July 18, 1978. He was unable to work due to his health-related problems and finally resigned his job with the county in November, 1979.

Appellees moved for summary judgment and the motion was sustained and judgment entered for the appellees. Gomez appealed. . . . The Kansas Supreme Court considered a comparable wrong in *Whitsel v. Watts,* 159 P. 401 (Kan. 1916). There, the plaintiff suffered a miscarriage after being frightened when the defendant jumped from his buggy, ran towards the plaintiff in an angry, threatening manner, swearing, shaking his fist and saying, "You are fooling with the wrong person this time." The Court . . . held:

> Defendant insists that he inflicted no bodily injury upon her, that no physical injury was in fact threatened, that there was no assault upon her and that proof of a mere fright furnishes no basis for a recovery. It has long been the rule here that there can be no recovery for fright or mental anguish unless it results in or is accompanied by physical injury to the person. The plaintiff, however, is not asking a recovery for fright alone, but for the personal injuries directly resulting from fright caused by the willful tort of the defendant. It is argued that as the acts of the defendant did not amount to an assault she had no right to recover; but the defendant's liability does not depend upon whether his wrongful onset constituted an assault.

In *Dawson v. Associates Financial Services Co.,* 529 P.2d 104 (Kan. 1974), the plaintiff, a former employee of Associates, was delinquent on a car loan from Associates due to having lost her job when she developed multiple sclerosis. She received four phone calls from Associates about the account similar in content to calls she had had to make to delinquent debtors when she worked there. She referred them to her insurance carrier on the first call. On the second call Associates threatened to repossess the car, sell it and hold her responsible for any deficiency. On the third call plaintiff was told when the car would be repossessed, that it would ruin her credit rating, and would somehow involve her parents' business. On the fourth call, plaintiff got emotional and told Associates to call her attorney. After receiving these calls, plaintiff suffered physical distress and had to go under a doctor's care. In *Dawson,* the Court adopted the rule from REST. 2D TORTS, § 46(1), which provides:

> One who by extreme and outrageous conduct intentionally or recklessly causes severe emotional distress to another is subject to liability for such emotional distress, and if bodily harm to the other results from it, for such bodily harm.

The Court further held:

> [T]hat it is for the court to determine, in the first instance, whether the defendant's conduct may reasonably be regarded as so extreme and outrageous as to permit recovery, or whether it is necessarily so, and where reasonable men may differ, the question is for the jury to determine. 215 Kan. at 824, 529 P.2d 104.

In *Dawson,* the trial court excluded evidence of telephone calls by Associates to Plaintiff's parents about the delinquency of Plaintiff's loan as being irrelevant. The Supreme Court held the evidence should have been admitted. . . . The Supreme Court . . . concluded:

> Certainly creditors must be permitted to pursue reasonable methods of collecting debts, and debtors are protected only from extreme and outrageous conduct. Nonetheless, methods of collecting debts which might be reasonable in some circumstances, might also be regarded as outrageous in others where it is known that the debtor is particularly susceptible to emotional distress due to a disease such as multiple sclerosis. Here the appellant made claim for payments on an insurance policy which Associates had sold her.

> The cases thus far decided have found liability only where the defendant's conduct has been extreme and outrageous. . . . Liability has been found only where the conduct has been so outrageous in character, and so extreme in degree, as to go beyond all possible bounds of decency, and to be regarded as atrocious, and utterly intolerable in a civilized community. Generally, the case is one in which the recitation of the facts to an average member of the community would arouse his resentment against the actor, and lead him to exclaim "outrageous!"

> . . . .The liability clearly does not extend to mere insults, indignities, threats, annoyances, petty oppressions, or other trivialities. The rough edges of our society are still in need of a good deal of filing down, and in the meantime plaintiffs must necessarily be expected and required to be hardened to a certain amount of rough language, and to occasional acts that are definitely inconsiderate and unkind. There is no occasion for the law to intervene in every case where someone's feelings are hurt. There must still be freedom to express an unflattering opinion,

and some safety valve must be left through which irascible tempers may blow off relatively harmless steam. . . . No abusive language was employed. The mere fact of frequent phone calls from Dotson to McLaughlin to state that SBA loans would be foreclosed if McLaughlin did not cooperate was not sufficiently extreme or outrageous to give rise to liability.

Bradshaw v. Swagerty, 1 Kan. App. 2d 213 (1977), was an action for slander and outrage. The epithets in question were "nigger," "bastard" and possibly "knot-headed boy." Plaintiff's legitimacy was conceded. The trial court granted summary judgment to the defendant on both counts. The appellate court agreed that these words were "mere insults' of the kind which must be tolerated in our rough-edged society." 1 Kan. App. 2d at 216. . . . The relative positions of Gomez and Hug are important here. Hug was the employer. Gomez was the employee. Hug spoke from the position of a county commissioner. These remarks had been made to Gomez by Hug over a period of several days. The tirade unleashed upon Gomez on April 21, 1978, was terrifying to him. He was afraid of Hug, afraid for his job, afraid for his family. Each party argues a different meaning from these statements of Gomez' fear. It is an issue for the trier of fact.

Contreras v. Crown Zellerbach Corp., 88 Wash. 2d 735 (1977), concerned the allegations of a Mexican-American that he had been the object of racial insults, humiliation and embarrassment during the course of his employment. The Washington Court found that liability for infliction of mental distress could attach under the facts alleged. The Court held, 88 Wash. 2d at 741:

> When one in a position of authority, actual or apparent, over another has allegedly made racial slurs and jokes and comments, this abusive conduct gives added impetus to the claim of outrageous behavior. REST. 2D TORTS, § 46, cmt. e. The relationship between the parties is a significant factor in determining whether liability should be imposed.

We can agree with the comment from Restatement of Torts quoted above. We cannot agree that it was for the trial court to rule that what was said to Gomez was a mere insult, a petty oppression or other triviality. This was a matter for the jury. Certainly there is no occasion for the law to intervene in every case where someone's feelings are hurt. Certainly the rough edges of our society still need smoothing down and there must still be freedom to blow off harmless steam. But this vituperation was well beyond the bounds of freedom to blow off harmless steam. It is not a burden of American citizenship in the State of Kansas that such vitriolic bullying as was turned by Hug against Gomez, and its emotional and physical consequences, must be accepted without possibility of redress and accepted as often as it amuses the speaker to utter it. Kansas courts are not so impotent. At the very least the victim of such an attack has the right to have his grievance heard by a jury of average members of the community to know whether they would exclaim, "Outrageous!"

It cannot be said that reasonable persons could reach but one conclusion from the evidence in this case. The trial court erred in sustaining the motion for summary judgment as to the allegation of intentional infliction of emotional distress by the defendant Hug. . . . The acts of the defendant, Hug, were personal to him. He was exceeding all statutory authority granted to him. His acts were not the acts of Shawnee County. The trial court properly entered judgment for the defendant Board of County Commissioners. [THE JUDGMENT OF THE TRIAL COURT IS AFFIRMED IN PART AND REVERSED IN PART AND REMANDED FOR FURTHER PROCEEDINGS . . . AS TO THE DEFENDANT ROLAND].

NOTES

1. *Outrages or Mere Insults.* As noted in *Gomez,* REST. 2D TORTS, § 46(1), cmt. *d* states "liability clearly does not extend to mere insults, indignities, threats, annoyances, petty oppressions, or other trivialities." In *Slocum v. Food Fair Stores of Fla., Inc.,* 100 So. 2d 396 (Fla. 1958), the court affirmed dismissal of a claim for intentional infliction of emotional distress in the absence of any allegation that the defendant's words were calculated to cause severe emotional distress — even though plaintiff alleged she suffered a heart attack as a result. Plaintiff, a customer in defendant's store, asked an employee of defendant the price of an item. In reply, the employee allegedly said: "If you want to know the price, you'll have to find out the best way you can. . . . You stink to me." In denying recovery, the court said: "There is no inclination to include all instances of mere vulgarities, obviously intended as meaningless abusive expressions." *Id.* at 398. The *Slocum* court also noted:

> A broader rule has been developed in a particular class of cases, usually treated as a distinct and separate area of liability originally applied to common carriers. REST. 2D TORTS, § 48. The courts have from an early date granted relief for offense reasonably suffered by a patron from insult by a servant or employee of a carrier, hotel, theater, and most recently, a telegraph office. The existence of a special relationship, arising either from contract or from the inherent nature of a non-competitive public utility, supports a right and correlative duty of courtesy beyond that legally required in general mercantile or personal relationships.

Id. However, the court found "no impelling reason" to extend the rule of such cases to "the area of business invitees generally."

2. *Pet Cemetery.* In *Corso v. Crawford Dog & Cat Hosp.,* 415 N.Y.S.2d 182 (1979), plaintiff was allowed actions for intentional and negligent infliction of emotional distress suffered when defendant animal hospital erroneously sent plaintiff the remains of a cat for burial, instead of the remains of plaintiff's pet dog. In *Richardson v. Fairbanks North Star Borough*, 705 P.2d 454 (Alaska 1985), the court denied recovery under REST. § 46(1) to plaintiffs who sought damages against the borough for emotional distress they sustained when their dog was killed by an employee of the borough animal shelter in violation of the shelter's policy. Can these cases be reconciled? Should a pet owner be able to recover for the intentional infliction of emotional distress associated with the tortious killing of a pet? Or should the owner be limited to recovery of the fair market value of the pet? Is that remedy adequate?

3. *Gender, Race & Tort Law's Public Face.* Social scientists frequently criticize the law's assumption of formal equality because large corporations have innumerable advantages over an individual in any transaction. *See, e.g.*, JAMES S. COLEMAN, THE ASYMMETRIC SOCIETY 22 (1982) (arguing that "two parties beginning with nominally equal rights in a relation, but coming to it with vastly different resources, end with very different actual rights in the relation"). As the perspectives discussion in Chapter 1 reflects, tort law impacts men and women in different ways, reflecting the different social roles men and women play in American society. In a number of outrage cases, women suffer extreme distress arising out of their care-taking role. For example, in *Johnson v. Woman's Hospital*, 527 S.W.2d 133 (Tenn. Ct. App. 1975), the plaintiff miscarried and gave birth to an infant who lived for only an hour. In a subsequent visit to the hospital, the mother inquired about the burial of her baby's remains. When the distraught mother returned to the hospital for a checkup six weeks later, she read a pathologist's report which indicated that the infant's body had not been buried or otherwise decently disposed of. Her inquiries led her to a hospital employee who said that she had the infant's body and that the body had been preserved. The employee then took from a refrigerator and handed to plaintiff a jar of formaldehyde containing the floating, shriveled body of her infant. Plaintiff subsequently suffered nightmares, insomnia and depression when around children. She also suffered from pseudo-pregnancy which caused pelvic pain and nausea and led to exploratory surgery and psychiatric treatment. The court held that the plaintiff had a cause of action for intentional or reckless infliction of emotional distress; the facts "could be considered to cause the exclamation of 'outrage' from the general community." *Id.* at 140. How would the average member of the community respond to the nurse's actions? What role did gender roles play in determining extreme outrage in these circumstances?

The sociological term "degradation ceremony" has been used to describe the rituals through which low-status individuals are humiliated by the powerful in order to manipulate and reinforce social position or hierarchy. *See* Harold Garfinkel, *Conditions of Successful Degradation Ceremonies*, 61 AM. J. SOC. 420, 420 (1956). Critical race theorists have observed that African Americans and other people of color experience "micro-aggressions" that confirm their unequal social status in their daily work and social interactions with whites. Peggy Cooper Davis, *Law as Microaggression*, 98 YALE L. REV. 1559 (1989). *See also* STEPHANIE WILDMAN, WITH CONTRIBUTIONS FROM MARGALYNNE ARMSTRONG, ADRIENNE DAVIS & TRINA GRILLO, PRIVILEGE REVEALED: HOW INVISIBLE PREFERENCE UNDERMINES AMERICA 126-127 (1996).

4. *What Harm in Asking?* In *Samms v. Eccles*, 11 Utah 2d 289 (1961), the court held that plaintiff stated a claim for emotional distress based on the following allegations:

> Plaintiff alleged that she is a respectable married woman; that she has never encouraged the defendant's attentions in any way but has repulsed them; that all during the time from May to December, 1957, the defendant repeatedly and persistently called her by phone at various hours including late at night, soliciting her to have illicit sexual relations with him; and that on one occasion came to her residence in connection with such a solicitation and made an indecent exposure of his person. She charges that she regarded his proposals as insulting,

indecent and obscene; that her feelings were deeply wounded; and that as a result thereof she suffered great anxiety and fear for her personal safety and severe emotional distress for which she asks $1500 as actual, and a like amount as punitive, damages.

Would the result be the same if he only asked her once? If he did not know she was married? What impact do changing gender roles have on the definition of the defendant's conduct as a tort? In his 1964, third edition, Prosser stated: "There's no harm in asking." Is that legal aphorism still accurate in 2007? Does this doctrine reflect male dominant values? Have "male norms" distorted doctrinal concepts such as consent? *See* Leslie Bender, *A Lawyer's Primer on Feminist Theory and Tort*, 38 J. LEGAL ED. 3 (1988) (contending that feminist theory can help us reevaluate traditional tort rules); Martha Chamallas, *Discrimination and Outrage: The Migration From Civil Rights to Tort Law*, 48 WM. & MARY L. REV. 1 (2007) (exploring question of whether discriminatory and harassing conduct in the workplace may qualify as a tort for intentional infliction of emotional distress). Professor Chamallas contends that the tort of outrage "was created in part to provide protection for vulnerable persons — often women — [since] older causes of action, notably assault and slander, failed to capture and respond to their injuries." *Id.* at 7.

Leon Green argues that tort law doctrines: "can be stretched or contracted to meet the needs of the moment and is always colored by the desires of the user. Doctrine for doctrine's sake may become an obsession with lawyers as it does with preachers and politicians. It feeds on itself; hardens into clichés and blocks the arteries of thought." Leon Green, *Tort Law: Public Law in Disguise*, 38 TEX. L. REV. 257, 266 (1960). How did the court stretch the tort of battery in *Gomez* to address racial injustice? What public purpose would a social justice theorist attach to the tort judgment assessed in the *Gomez* case? Is this a "private case with a public face"? THOMAS H. KOENIG & MICHAEL L. RUSTAD, IN DEFENSE OF TORT LAW 1-3 (2001) (describing tort law as a "protector of core American values"). How would a critical race theorist view the same facts?

In *Vietnamese Fishermen's Ass'n v. Knights of the Ku Klux Klan*, 518 F. Supp. 993 (C. D. Tex. 1981), a racist organization intimidated Vietnamese fishermen by wearing robes and hoods, brandishing weapons, and burning crosses as well as several shrimp boats owned by Vietnamese refugees used in Galveston Bay. The district court found a pattern of racketeering but rejected a claim for the intentional infliction of emotional distress on these facts. In *Contreras v. Crown Zellerbach Corp.*, 565 P.2d 1173 (Wash. 1977) an employer was found liable for hurling racist epithets at an employee causing him to suffer extreme emotional distress. Punitive damages have been awarded to punish and deter racist acts. *See Berhanu v. Metzger*, 850 P.2d 373 (Or. Ct. App. 1993) (upholding punitive damages against hate group for inciting skinhead gang to commit the murder of black bus driver).

G. REAL PROPERTY TORTS

Real property consists of land and some buildings and improvements on it. A plaintiff must prove two elements in order to prevail in a trespass to land case: (1) the plaintiff was in possession of the land; and (2) the defendant entered the land without right. A physical entry on the land without permission is the gist of the tort of trespass. Section 158 makes it clear that a trespasser is liable "irrespective of whether harm is thereby caused to [the plaintiff's] legally protected interests." *Id.* at § 158. A trespasser need not have knowledge that he has entered the land of another. The intent is simply the intent to enter an area possessed by another. "The trespasser must intend an act which constitutes unwarranted entry on another's land, even though trespasser need not intend or expect damaging consequences." *Snow v. City of Columbia*, 409 S.E.2d 797 (S.C. 1991). A number of states have enacted statutory trespass causes of action that closely track the elements of the common law as the *Fondren* case below. As you read the case, think about the following questions: (1) What does it mean to enter the land? (2) What is the meaning of intrusion? (3) What is the meaning of the intent to trespass?

FONDREN v. REDWINE
905 S.W.2d 156 (Mo. App. 1995)

AHRENS, JUSTICE.

In this jury-tried case for statutory trespass and damage to a tree pursuant to a [Missouri statute]. . . . plaintiff appeals and defendant cross appeals the judgment on a verdict in favor of plaintiff. We reverse.

On November 26, 1991, defendant, Brad Redwine, was driving his father's automobile northbound on Partridge Run in St. Louis County. While apparently attempting to pass another car, defendant lost control of the automobile. Defendant's automobile then entered plaintiffs Kyle and Hildegard Fondren's property, and struck a large pin oak tree growing in the front yard. There was no dispute that defendant did not have plaintiffs' permission to enter the property.

Defendant testified at trial, however, that he did not intentionally enter plaintiffs' property, nor did he intentionally injure the tree.

As a result of the accident plaintiffs' tree was permanently injured and scarred. The tree, however, was not fatally injured, and was living at the time of trial . . . Plaintiffs' petition alleged that defendant negligently drove his vehicle and that defendant's negligence proximately caused plaintiffs' damages. Plaintiffs sought treble damages for statutory trespass pursuant to § 537.340 . . . [that] states, in pertinent part:

> If any person shall cut down, injure or destroy or carry away any tree placed or growing for use, shade or ornament, . . . being or growing on the land of any other person, . . . the person so offending shall pay to the party injured treble the value of the things so injured, broken, destroyed or carried away, with costs.

. . . At trial, plaintiffs' verdict director submitted the issue of whether defendant "entered unauthorized on the land of the plaintiffs." The trial court refused plaintiffs' tendered damage instruction under § 537.340 and [instructed on negligence damage pursuant to a Missouri pattern instruction]. The jury returned a verdict in favor of plaintiffs for $375.00. In their appeal, plaintiffs allege that the trial court erred in submitting a negligence damage instruction . . . and refusing plaintiffs' damage instruction based on § 537.340 . . .

Defendant cross appeals, alleging the trial court erred in denying his motion for a directed verdict because plaintiffs failed to make a submissible case under § 537.340.

As we find the issue on defendant's cross appeal dispositive, we will address this point first. Defendant contends that the trial court erred in denying defendant's motion for a directed verdict because plaintiffs failed to make a submissible case under RSMo § 537.340, in that there was no evidence that defendant intentionally entered plaintiffs' property and injured plaintiffs' tree.

In an action for damages, the claimant has the burden of proving a submissible case . . . To make a submissible case . . . plaintiffs must provide evidence that defendant trespassed on their property. This court, in *McNamee v. Garner,* 624 S.W.2d 867 (Mo. App. 1981), held that the "statute does not require specifically that the offending party enter the land wrongfully; however, the statute does require that the tortfeasor trespass on the land." *Id.* at 868. The court explained that "both entering land wrongfully and entering land with consent or license and exceeding the scope of that consent or license constitute a trespass." Therefore, to determine whether a directed verdict would have been proper, we must determine if there was evidence from which a jury could determine that defendant trespassed on plaintiffs' property.

To constitute a trespass there generally must be an intent to do that which causes the trespass. Although it is not necessary that the trespasser intend to commit a trespass, or even know that the act will constitute a trespass, it is required for trespass that there be an intentional act; i.e. an intent to enter the land which results in the trespass. Although the language of the statute does not specifically require an intentional act, for the reasons previously noted, we find this element to be required in an action . . . and that such was the intent of the legislature. We, therefore, hold that, under the facts of this case, § 537.340 requires an intent to enter the property. Plaintiffs' pleadings alleged and plaintiffs introduced evidence which showed that defendant did not have permission to enter upon plaintiffs' property. Plaintiffs chose not to pursue negligence claims, but instead submitted their claims under § 537.340. However, plaintiffs neither pleaded nor proved that defendant intentionally entered upon plaintiffs' property. Accordingly, plaintiffs failed to make a submissible case of statutory trespass under § 537.340. The trial court therefore erred in not directing a verdict in favor of defendant. [REVERSED]

NOTES

1. *Tangible Invasions of Land Possessed by Another. Fondren* was a statutory trespass action that featured elements functionally equivalent to the common law of trespass. Increasingly, torts is becoming a statutory subject as state legislatures displace common law courts' jurisprudence. Trespass to land is an unprivileged invasion of the boundaries of land belonging to another. Trespass had a broader meaning at early common law and applied to a broad range of wrongs. In what we think of as trespass to land cases, the plaintiff filed a writ of *trespass quare clausum fregit* if the defendant "broke the close" or entered past the boundaries of land possessed by a plaintiff without a privilege to do so. *Trespass de bonis asportatis*, in contrast, was the writ that applied if the defendant carried away personal property of another, and today that claim is redressed by the tort of conversion. The rigid common law trespass writ divided civil wrongs into *direct* injuries redressed by *trespass vi armis* (acted with force and arms) and indirect injures vindicated by *trespass upon the action*. If a defendant ran the plaintiff through with a sword, the writ filed would be *trespass vi armis*. In contrast, if the defendant laid a trap to injure the plaintiff, the *trespass upon the action* would be appropriate. The writ of trespass was classified as a criminal fine as late as 1694. Thomas H. Koenig & Michael L. Rustad, In Defense of Tort Law 17 (2001). W. Page Keeton et. al., Prosser & Keeton on the Law of Torts § 6, at 28 (5th ed. 1984) (observing that the action of trespass was primarily concerned with punishment of a crime and "damages first came to be awarded incidentally to the injured plaintiff"). At early common law, the boundary between tort law and criminal law was not distinct:

> The rigid doctrinal distinction between tort and criminal law is an example of the disease of "hardening of the categories." The separation between criminal law and tort law occurred over centuries. At early common law, tort injuries did not give rise to a distinct cause of action. The criminal law encompassed what we know as torts today. At early common law, torts such as trespass "had a basic criminal character." However, tort law was so firmly split off from criminal law that it was viewed as an entirely different branch of the law by the middle of the nineteenth century. The result was that criminal law patrolled conduct inimical to the public order, while tort law was primarily concerned with rectifying the wrongs done to private individuals.

Thomas H. Koenig & Michael L. Rustad, *'Crimtorts,' as Corporate Just Deserts*, 31 U. Mich. J.L. Reform 289, 299 (1998) (footnotes omitted).

2. *Timing of a Trespass.* The real property torts vindicate the exclusive rights to possess real property. A defendant who exceeds their license is treated as a trespasser from the time of entry. Even if the defendant has a right initially to remain on the land, it is a trespass for failing to leave after the right to remain has terminated. The doctrine of trespass *ab initio* treats a defendant as a trespasser from the beginning even though they once had a license to enter the close of another. A trespass may result from the failure to remove oneself or one's property from the land of another after a permission to enter or remain ends. The ALI Reporters note:

> a) trespass may be committed by the continued presence on the land of a structure, chattel, or other thing which the actor or his predecessor in legal interest has placed on the land (a) with the consent of the person then in possession of the land, if the actor fails to remove it after the consent has been effectively terminated, or (b) pursuant to a

privilege conferred on the actor irrespective of the possessor's consent, if the actor fails to remove it after the privilege has been terminated, by the accomplishment of its purpose or otherwise.

REST. 2D TORTS § 160.

3. *Trespass Fact Patterns.* Trespass protects the legally protected interest of exclusive possession of land. A trespass is an intentional and wrongful entry onto land possessed by another. A wall, fence, or other encroachment that breaks the close is a trespass. A defendant may be liable in trespass for causing a third person or a thing to enter the land of another. Trespass occurs when the defendant causes a third person to wrongfully enter the land of another. If A, against B's will, forcibly carries B upon the land of C, A is a trespasser but B is not. *See* REST. 2D TORTS § 158, illus. 1. The Latin phrase, *quase clausum fregit* signifies that the defendant has broken the close of another or unlawfully invaded the boundaries of land possessed by the plaintiff. Mistake is no defense to trespass as a defendant need not have knowledge that he has entered the plaintiff's "close." The intent necessary to prove trespass is simply the intent to enter onto the land. A trespass action is available even where the entry on the lands of another is the result of a reasonable mistake. *See also* REST. 2D TORTS § 164. As a consequence, one may argue that the law is imposing absolute liability. However, the entry must be deliberate or intentional. *See, e.g.,* REST. 2D TORTS § 166 (non-liability for accidental intrusion). A prevailing plaintiff need not show actual damages or physical injury from the entry because nominal damages are recoverable where no actual damages are proven. The Restatement gives the following illustrations to help determine trespass actions:

[1]. A, against B's will, forcibly carries B upon the land of C. A is a trespasser; B is not.

[2]. A tornado lifts A's properly constructed house from A's land and deposits it on B's land. This is not a trespass.

[3]. A intentionally throws a pail of water against a wall of B's house. A is a trespasser.

[4]. A intentionally drives a stray horse from his pasture into the pasture of his neighbor, B. A is a trespasser.

[5]. A erects a dam across a stream, thereby intentionally causing the water to back up and flood the land of B, an upper riparian proprietor. A is a trespasser.

[6]. A, on a public lake, intentionally discharges his shotgun over a point of land in B's possession, near the surface. The shot falls into the water on the other side. A is a trespasser.

REST. 2D TORTS § 158, illustrations.

H. PERSONAL PROPERTY TORTS

Trespass to chattels and conversion are the two personal property torts. The term chattels is a medieval expression for personal property. A trespass to chattels occurs when the defendant either dispossesses the plaintiff of personal property or uses or intermeddles with chattels without permission. REST. 2D TORTS § 217. "Intermeddling" is "bringing about a physical contact with the chattel." *Id.*, illus. e. The Restatement gives the following examples of intermeddling:

> The actor may commit a trespass by an act which brings him into an intended physical contact with a chattel in the possession of another, as when he beats another's horse or dog, or by intentionally directing an object or missile against it, as when the actor throws a stone at another's automobile or intentionally drives his own car against it. So too, a trespass may be committed by causing a third person through duress or fraud to intermeddle with another's chattel. *Id.*

The only difference between trespass to chattels and conversion is the remedy. When the intermeddling becomes so significant, it is classified as a conversion demanding a remedy of a forced sale at market value. To establish a conversion claim, a plaintiff must prove that it had a possessory interest in the property, that the defendants intentionally interfered with the plaintiff's possession, and that the defendants' acts were the legal cause of the plaintiff's loss of property. Conversion is an intentional exercise of dominion or control over a chattel which so seriously interferes with the right of another to control it that the actor may justly be required to pay the other the full value of the chattel. REST. 2D TORTS § 222a. The amount of damages for the conversion of a chattel is diminished by its recovery or acceptance by a person entitled to its possession. REST. 2D TORTS § 922(1). Can you imagine why the law may provide more protection from minor disturbances to real property? Why does the law permit greater self-help in protecting personal property than real property? How should traditional personal property torts apply in the information age? In the next section, we discuss the extent to which personal property torts may be imported to cyberspace.

KREMEN v. ONLINE CLASSIFIEDS, INC.
337 F.3d 1024 (9th Cir. 2003)

KOZINSKI, CIRCUIT JUDGE.

We decide whether Network Solutions may be liable for giving away a registrant's domain name on the basis of a forged letter. "Sex on the Internet?," they all said. "*That'll* never make any money." But computer-geek-turned-entrepreneur Gary Kremen knew an opportunity when he saw it. The year was 1994; domain names were free for the asking, and it would be several years yet before Henry Blodget and hordes of eager NASDAQ day traders would turn the Internet into the Dutch tulip craze of our times. With a quick e-mail to the domain name registrar Network Solutions, Kremen became the proud owner of sex.com. He registered the name to his business, Online Classifieds, and listed himself as the contact.

Con man Stephen Cohen, meanwhile, was doing time for impersonating a bankruptcy lawyer. He, too, saw the potential of the domain name. Kremen had gotten it first, but that was only a minor impediment for a man of Cohen's boundless resource and bounded integrity. Once out of prison, he sent Network Solutions what purported to be a letter he had received from Online Classifieds. It claimed the company had been "forced to dismiss Mr. Kremen," but "never got around to changing our administrative contact with the internet registration [sic] and now our Board of directors has decided to *abandon* the domain name sex.com." Why was this unusual letter being sent via Cohen rather than to Network Solutions directly? It explained:

> Because we do not have a direct connection to the internet, we request that you notify the internet registration on our behalf, to delete our domain name sex.com. Further, we have no objections to your use of the domain name sex.com and this letter shall serve as our authorization to the internet registration to transfer sex.com to your corporation.

Despite the letter's transparent claim that a company called *"Online Classifieds"* had no Internet connection, Network Solutions made no effort to contact Kremen. Instead, it accepted the letter at face value and transferred the domain name to Cohen. When Kremen contacted Network Solutions some time later, he was told it was too late to undo the transfer. Cohen went on to turn sex.com into a lucrative online porn empire. And so began Kremen's quest to recover the domain name that was rightfully his. He sued Cohen and several affiliated companies in federal court, seeking return of the domain name and disgorgement of Cohen's profits. The district court found that the letter was indeed a forgery and ordered the domain name returned to Kremen. It also told Cohen to hand over his profits, invoking the constructive trust doctrine and California's "unfair competition" statute, Cal. Bus. & Prof. Code § 17200 *et seq.* It awarded $40 million in compensatory damages and another $25 million in punitive damages. We dismissed Cohen's appeal in an unpublished memorandum disposition. . . . Kremen, unfortunately, has not had much luck collecting his judgment. The district court froze Cohen's assets, but Cohen ignored the order and wired large sums of money to offshore accounts.

His real estate property, under the protection of a federal receiver, was stripped of all its fixtures — even cabinet doors and toilets — in violation of another order. The court commanded Cohen to appear and show cause why he shouldn't be held in contempt, but he ignored that order, too. The district judge finally took off the gloves — he declared Cohen a fugitive from justice. . . .

Then things started getting *really* bizarre. Kremen put up a "wanted" poster on the sex.com site with a mug shot of Cohen, offering a $50,000 reward to anyone who brought him to justice. Cohen's lawyers responded with a motion to vacate the arrest warrant. They reported that Cohen was under house arrest in Mexico and that gunfights between Mexican authorities and would-be bounty hunters seeking Kremen's reward money posed a threat to human life. The district court rejected this story as "implausible" and denied the motion. Cohen, so far as the record shows, remains at large. Given his limited success with the bounty hunter approach, it should come as no surprise that Kremen seeks to hold someone else responsible for his losses. That someone is Network Solutions, the exclusive domain name registrar at the time of Cohen's antics.

Kremen sued it for mishandling his domain name, invoking four theories at issue here. He argues that he had an implied contract with Network Solutions, which it breached by giving the domain name to Cohen. He also claims the transfer violated Network Solutions's cooperative agreement with the National Science Foundation — the government contract that made Network Solutions, the .com registrar. His third theory is that he has a property right in the domain name sex.com, and Network Solutions committed the tort of conversion by giving it away to Cohen. Finally, he argues that Network Solutions was a "bailee" of his domain name and seeks to hold it liable for "conversion by bailee."

The district court granted summary judgment in favor of Network Solutions on all claims. *Kremen v. Cohen,* 99 F. Supp. 2d 1168 (N.D. Cal. 2000). It held that Kremen had no implied contract with Network Solutions because there was no consideration: Kremen had registered the domain name for free. *Id.* at 1171–72. It rejected the third-party contract claim on the ground that the cooperative agreement did not indicate a clear intent to grant enforceable contract rights to registrants. . . . The conversion claims fared no better. The court agreed that sex.com was Kremen's property. It concluded, though, that it was intangible property to which the tort of conversion does not apply. . . . The conversion by bailee claim failed for the additional reason that Network Solutions was not a bailee. . . . Kremen appeals, and we consider each of his four theories in turn. . . .

. . . [To establish the conversion claim] a plaintiff must show "ownership or right to possession of property, wrongful disposition of the property right and damages." *G.S. Rasmussen & Assocs., Inc. v. Kalitta Flying Serv., Inc.,* 958 F.2d 896, 906 (9th Cir. 1992). The preliminary question, then, is whether registrants have property rights in their domain names. Network Solutions all but concedes that they do. This is no surprise, given its positions in prior litigation. . . . Network Solutions acknowledged during oral argument before this Court that the right to use a domain name is a form of intangible personal property."); *Network Solutions, Inc. v. Clue Computing, Inc.,* 946 F. Supp. 858, 860 (D. Colo. 1996) (same). The district court agreed with the parties on this issue, as do we.

Network Solutions does suggest in passing that we should distinguish domain names supported by contracts from those (like Kremen's) that are not. It also stresses that Kremen didn't develop the sex.com site before Cohen stole it. But this focus on the particular domain name at issue is misguided. The question is not whether Kremen's domain name in isolation is property, but whether domain names as a class are a species of property.

Property is a broad concept that includes "every intangible benefit and prerogative susceptible of possession or disposition." *Downing v. Mun. Court,* 88 Cal. App. 2d 345, 350, 198 P.2d 923 (1948) (internal quotation marks omitted). We apply a three-part test to determine whether a property right exists: "First, there must be an interest capable of precise definition; second, it must be capable of exclusive possession or control; and third, the putative owner must have established a legitimate claim to exclusivity." *G.S. Rasmussen,* 958 F.2d at 903 (footnote omitted). Domain names satisfy each criterion.

Like a share of corporate stock or a plot of land, a domain name is a well-defined interest. Someone who registers a domain name decides where on the Internet those who invoke that particular name — whether by typing it into their web browsers, by following a hyperlink, or by other means — are sent. Ownership is exclusive in that the registrant alone makes that decision. Moreover, like other forms of property, domain names are valued, bought and sold, often for millions of dollars, see Greg Johnson, *The Costly Game for Net Names,* L.A. Times, Apr. 10, 2000, at A1, and they are now even subject to *in rem* jurisdiction, see 15 U.S.C. § 1125(d)(2).

Finally, registrants have a legitimate claim to exclusivity. Registering a domain name is like staking a claim to a plot of land at the title office. It informs others that the domain name is the registrant's and no one else's. Many registrants also invest substantial time and money to develop and promote websites that depend on their domain names. Ensuring that they reap the benefits of their investments reduces uncertainty and thus encourages investment in the first place, promoting the growth of the Internet overall. *See G.S. Rasmussen*, 958 F.2d at 900. Kremen therefore had an intangible property right in his domain name, and a jury could find that Network Solutions "wrongful[ly] dispos[ed] of" that right to his detriment by handing the domain name over to Cohen. *Id.* at 906. The district court nevertheless rejected Kremen's conversion claim. It held that domain names, although a form of property, are intangibles not subject to conversion. This rationale derives from a distinction tort law once drew between tangible and intangible property: Conversion was originally a remedy for the wrongful taking of another's lost goods, so it applied only to tangible property. *See Prosser and Keeton on the Law of Torts* § 15, at 89, 91 (W. Page Keeton ed., 5th ed. 1984). Virtually every jurisdiction, however, has discarded this rigid limitation to some degree. *See id.* at 91.

Many courts ignore or expressly reject it. . . . Others reject it for some intangibles but not others. The *Restatement,* for example, recommends the following test: Where there is conversion of a document in which intangible rights are merged, the damages include the value of such rights. 1. One who effectively prevents the exercise of intangible rights of the kind customarily *merged in a document* is subject to a liability similar to that for conversion, even though the document is not itself converted. REST. 2D TORTS § 242 (emphasis added).

An intangible is "merged" in a document when, "by the appropriate rule of law, the right to the immediate possession of a chattel and the power to acquire such possession is *represented by* [the] document," or when "an intangible obligation [is] *represented by* [the] document, which is regarded as equivalent to the obligation." *Id.* cmt. a (emphasis added). The district court applied this test and found no evidence that Kremen's domain name was merged in a document.

The court assumed that California follows the *Restatement* on this issue. Our review, however, revealed that "there do not appear to be any California cases squarely addressing whether the 'merged with' requirement is a part of California law." *Kremen,* 325 F.3d at 1042. We invoked the California Supreme Court's certification procedure to offer it the opportunity to address the issue. . . . We conclude that California does not follow the *Restatement*'s strict merger requirement. Indeed, the leading California Supreme Court case rejects the tangibility requirement altogether. In *Payne v. Elliot,* 54 Cal. 339, 1880 WL 1907 (1880), the Court considered whether shares in a corporation (as opposed to the share certificates themselves) could be converted. It held that they could. . . .

California courts ignored the *Restatement* again in *A & M Records, Inc. v. Heilman,* 75 Cal. App. 3d 554, 142 Cal. Rptr. 390 (1977), which applied the tort to a defendant who sold bootlegged copies of musical recordings. The court held broadly that "such misappropriation and sale of the intangible property of another without authority from the owner is conversion." *Id.* at 570, 142 Cal. Rptr. 390. It gave no hint that its holding depended on whether the owner's intellectual property rights were merged in some document. One might imagine physical things with which the intangible was associated — for example, the medium on which the song was recorded. But an intangible intellectual property right in a song is not merged in a phonograph record in the sense that the record *represents* the composer's intellectual property right. The record is not like a certificate of ownership; it is only a medium for one instantiation of the artistic work. . . .

In rejecting the tangibility requirement, *FMC* echoes *Payne*'s holding that personal property of any species may be converted. And it flouts the *Restatement* because the intangible property right in confidential information is not represented by the documents on which the information happens to be recorded. Our own recent decision in *Bancroft & Masters, Inc. v. Augusta National Inc.,* 223 F.3d 1082 (9th Cir. 2000), is especially relevant. That case involved a domain name — precisely the type of property at issue here. The primary question was personal jurisdiction, but a majority of the panel joined the judgment only on the understanding that the defendant had committed conversion of a domain name, which it characterized as "tortious conduct." *Id.* at 1089 (Sneed & Trott, JJ., concurring); *cf. Astroworks, Inc.,* 257 F. Supp. 2d at 618 (holding that the plaintiff could maintain a claim for conversion of his website).

In short, California does not follow the *Restatement*'s strict requirement that some document must actually represent the owner's intangible property right. On the contrary, courts routinely apply the tort to intangibles without inquiring whether they are merged in a document and, while it's often possible to dream up *some* document the intangible is connected to in some fashion, it's seldom one that represents the owner's property interest. To the extent *Olschewski* endorses the strict merger rule, it is against the weight of authority. That rule cannot be squared with a jurisprudence that recognizes conversion of music recordings, radio shows, customer lists, regulatory filings, confidential information and even domain names. . . .

Kremen's domain name falls easily within this class of property. He argues that the relevant document is the Domain Name System, or "DNS" — the distributed electronic database that associates domain names like sex.com with particular computers connected to the Internet. We agree that the DNS is a document (or perhaps more accurately a collection of documents). That it is stored in electronic form rather than on ink and paper is immaterial. . . . Torching a company's file room would then be conversion while hacking into its mainframe and deleting its data would not. That is not the law, at least not in California. . . .

Kremen's domain name is protected by California conversion law, even on the grudging reading we have given it. Exposing Network Solutions to liability when it gives away a registrant's domain name on the basis of a forged letter is no different from holding a corporation liable when it gives away someone's shares under the same circumstances. . . . .We apply the common law until the legislature tells us otherwise. And the common law does not stand idle while people give away the property of others. The evidence supported a claim for conversion, and the district court should not have rejected it. [We need not decide the issue [of whether Network Solutions was a converter by a bailee] . . . As we read California law, "conversion by bailee" is not a distinct tort, but merely the tort of conversion committed by one who is a bailee. . . . To prove "conversion by bailee," Kremen must establish all the elements of conversion but, having done so, he gains nothing by also showing that Network Solutions is a bailee. Kremen had a viable claim for conversion. [REVERSED AND REMANDED FOR FURTHER PROCEEDINGS]

NOTES

1. *From Rover to Trover, Cows to Computers.* Eighteenth century tort law vindicated the rights of property-owners to possess and enjoy chattels. Professors Rustad and Koenig explain the distinction between different writs that prefigure today's personal property torts:

> Personal property consisted of all moveable chattels. Actions for dispossessed chattels were divided into actions for taking personal property away and for "*detaining* them, though the original taking might be lawful. The rights of personal property owners were vindicated in an action for the deprivation of, or damage to, chattels. Originally, trespass covered the wrongful taking of a chattel, in contrast to *detinue*, which covered the wrongful detention of personal property. *Trover* was a common law action for the recovery of personal property. *Trover* was a far more flexible writ than *detinue* because it permitted an action against a defendant who unlawfully exercised dominion or control over the personal property of another by any means. If, for example, a neighbor borrowed a horse and did not return it, the owner could bring a writ for any damage done to the horse and to compensate for the loss of the horse's services.

> With increased urbanization, tort remedies expanded to encompass more complex forms of property deprivation. The more modern tort of conversion has been extended to a wide variety of situations such as the misdelivery of goods, mortgages, gifts, and even to a finder who made an innocent mistake in possessing chattels. The difference between conversion and trespass to chattels is only in remedy. The remedy for conversion is a forced sale versus compensation for mere diminished value due to intermeddling with personal property.

Michael L. Rustad & Thomas H. Koenig, *Taming the Tort Monster: The American Civil Justice System as a Battleground of Social Theory*, 68 BROOKLYN L. REV. 1, 24 (2002).

The modern tort of conversion shares much common ground with the writs. Modern conversion always involves a factual analysis to determine whether there has been sufficient exercise of dominion or control over chattels, as REST. 2D TORTS § 222A recognizes:

> (1) Conversion is an intentional exercise of dominion or control over a chattel which so seriously interferes with the right of another to control it that the actor may justly be required to pay the other the full value of the chattel.
>
> (2) In determining the seriousness of the interference and the justice of requiring the actor to pay the full value, the following factors are important:
>
>> (a) the extent and duration of the actor's exercise of dominion or control;
>>
>> (b) the actor's intent to assert a right in fact inconsistent with the other's right of control;
>>
>> (c) the actor's good faith;
>>
>> (d) the extent and duration of the resulting interference with the other's right of control;
>>
>> (e) the harm done to the chattel;
>>
>> (f) the inconvenience and expense caused to the other.

Comment *d* to Section 222A states: "No one factor is always predominant in determining the seriousness of the interference, or the justice of requiring the forced purchase at full value. *Id.* § 222A, cmt. *d*. Section 217 provides that a trespass to chattel may be committed "by intentionally (a) dispossessing another of the chattel, or (b) using or intermeddling with a chattel in the possession of another." *Id.* § 217. Thus a police officer by writ of execution levies on a car, by notifying the owner that the car has been taken into possession of the law, "but does not remove it or otherwise interfere with it." An hour later the officer discovers that she has levied on the wrong person's car, and promptly so informs the owner. The officer is liable to the owner "for at least nominal damages." *Id.* § 218, cmt. *d*, illus. 1.

The tort of conversion was first recognized at early common law when neighbors filed actions for converted cows, dogs, or horses. This flexible tort has been stretched to cybertorts. The Internet is not a physical or tangible entity, but rather a network of networks based upon intangible property interests. Can it be the subject of trespass to chattels or conversion? "Trespass to chattels has evolved from its original common law application, concerning primarily the asportation of another's tangible property, to include the unauthorized use of personal property." *CompuServe v. CyberPromotions, Inc.*, 962 F. Supp. 1015 (D. Ohio 1997). Conversion is a personal property tort that applied to identifiable corporeal property such as cows and horses. Michael L. Rustad & Thomas H.

Koenig, *Cybertorts and Legal Lag: An Empirical Analysis*, 13 S. CAL. INTERDISC. L.J. 77 (2004) (describing how personal property torts have been imported to cyberspace cases). The district court held that a domain name was an intangible that could not be converted. Judge Kozinski cited a number of Internet-related cases where intangible interests were subject to a trespass to chattels. *Thrifty-Tel, Inc. v. Bezenek*, 54 Cal. Rptr. 2d 468, 473 (Cal. App. Ct. 4th Dist. 1996); *eBay, Inc. v. Bidder's Edge, Inc.,* 100 F. Supp. 2d 1058, 1069 (N.D. Ca. 2000). What makes this case different from intermeddling with eBay's computer system or the telephone system in *Bezenek*? Why did the plaintiff file suit against Network Solutions for conversion rather than the trespass to chattels?

2. *The Requisite Intent for Property-Based Torts.* In *Mountain States Tel. & Tel. Co. v. Horn Tower Constr. Co.,* 363 P.2d 175 (Colo. 1961), the trial court dismissed the trespass claim against a construction company which severed a buried cable while grading a street and installing a curb because the defendant lacked intent. In *Mountain States Tel. & Tel. Co. v. Vowell Constr. Co.,* 341 S.W.2d 148 (Tex. 1960), the Texas Supreme Court held the defendant liable on similar facts in a case where the city's road scraper severed the telephone cable. Was the intent to make a cut in the designated subgrade or another intent? Would the defendant be liable in *Vowell* even if the city was not negligent in making the cut? Can these cases be reconciled? What *did* the defendant intend to do in both cases?

3. *Stolen Goods v. Purloined Ideas.* The general rule is that one cannot take good title to stolen goods, regardless of the acquirer's good faith. REST. 2D TORTS § 229. But one can acquire good title from another who has obtained the goods by fraud or deceit, if the acquirer acquires the goods in good faith for value. *See* UCC § 2-403. Can one "convert" an idea? In *Pearson v. Dodd*, 410 F.2d 701 (D.C. Cir. 1969), columnists Drew Pearson and Jack Anderson published a column based upon documents stolen by an aide to Senator Edwin Dodd of Connecticut. The D.C. Appeals Court held that newspaper columnists were not liable for conversion even though they relied upon information surreptitiously removed from office files by Senator Dodd's aides, photocopied at night, and returned to files undamaged before Senate office operations resumed in the morning.

INTEL CORP. v. HAMIDI
71 P.3d 296 (Cal. 2003).

WERDEGAR, JUSTICE.

Intel Corporation (Intel) maintains an electronic mail system, connected to the Internet through which messages between employees and those outside the company can be sent and received, and permits its employees to make reasonable nonbusiness use of this system. On six occasions over almost two years, Kourosh Kenneth Hamidi, a former Intel employee, sent e-mails criticizing Intel's employment practices to numerous current employees on Intel's electronic mail system. Hamidi breached no computer security barriers in order to communicate with Intel employees. He offered to, and did, remove from his mailing list any recipient who so wished. Hamidi's communications to individual Intel employees caused neither physical damage nor functional disruption to the company's computers, nor did they at any time deprive Intel of the use of its computers. The contents of the messages, however, caused discussion among employees and managers.

On these facts, Intel brought suit, claiming that by communicating with its employees over the company's e-mail system Hamidi committed the tort of trespass to chattels. The trial court granted Intel's motion for summary judgment and enjoined Hamidi from any further mailings. A divided Court of Appeal affirmed. After reviewing the decisions analyzing unauthorized electronic contact with computer systems as potential trespasses to chattels, we conclude that under California law the tort does not encompass, and should not be extended to encompass, an electronic communication that neither damages the recipient computer system nor impairs its functioning. Such an electronic communication does not constitute an actionable trespass to personal property, i.e., the computer system, because it does not interfere with the possessor's use or possession of, or any other legally protected interest in, the personal property itself. . . . The consequential economic damage Intel claims to have suffered, i.e., loss of productivity caused by employees reading and reacting to Hamidi's messages and company efforts to block the messages, is not an injury to the company's interest in its computers — which worked as intended and were unharmed by the communications — any more than the personal distress caused by reading an unpleasant letter would be an injury to the recipient's mailbox, or the loss of privacy caused by an intrusive telephone call would be an injury to the recipient's telephone equipment.

Our conclusion does not rest on any special immunity for communications by electronic mail; we do not hold that messages transmitted through the Internet are exempt from the ordinary rules of tort liability. To the contrary, e-mail, like other forms of communication, may in some circumstances cause legally cognizable injury to the recipient or to third parties and may be actionable under various common law or statutory theories. Indeed, on facts somewhat similar to those here, a company or its employees might be able to plead causes of action for interference with prospective economic relations. . . . Intel's claim fails not because e-mail transmitted through the Internet enjoys unique immunity, but because the trespass to chattels tort — unlike the causes of action just mentioned — may not, in California, be proved without evidence of an injury to the plaintiff's personal property or legal interest therein . . .

The pertinent undisputed facts are as follows. Hamidi, a former Intel engineer, together with others, formed an organization named Former and Current Employees of Intel (FACE-Intel) to disseminate information and views critical of Intel's employment and personnel policies and practices. FACE-Intel maintained a Web site (which identified Hamidi as Webmaster and as the organization's spokesperson) containing such material. In addition, over a 21-month period Hamidi, on behalf of FACE-Intel, sent six mass e-mails to employee addresses on Intel's electronic mail system. The messages criticized Intel's employment practices, warned employees of the dangers those practices posed to their careers, suggested employees consider moving to other companies, solicited employees' participation in FACE-Intel, and urged employees to inform themselves further by visiting FACE-Intel's Web site.

The messages stated that recipients could, by notifying the sender of their wishes, be removed from FACE-Intel's mailing list; Hamidi did not subsequently send messages to anyone who requested removal. Each message was sent to thousands of addresses (as many as 35,000 according to FACE-Intel's Web site), though some messages were blocked by Intel before reaching employees. Intel's attempt to block internal transmission of the messages succeeded only in part; Hamidi later admitted he evaded blocking efforts by using different sending computers. When Intel, in March 1998, demanded in writing that Hamidi and FACE-Intel stop sending e-mails to Intel's computer system, Hamidi asserted the organization had a right to communicate with willing Intel employees; he sent a new mass mailing in September 1998.

The summary judgment record contains no evidence Hamidi breached Intel's computer security in order to obtain the recipient addresses for his messages; indeed, internal Intel memoranda show the company's management concluded no security breach had occurred. Hamidi stated he created the recipient address list using an Intel directory on a floppy disk anonymously sent to him. Nor is there any evidence that the receipt or internal distribution of Hamidi's electronic messages damaged Intel's computer system or slowed or impaired its functioning. Intel did present uncontradicted evidence, however, that many employee recipients asked a company official to stop the messages and that staff time was consumed in attempts to block further messages from FACE-Intel. According to the FACE-Intel Web site, moreover, the messages had prompted discussions between "[e]xcited and nervous managers" and the company's human resources department.

Intel sued Hamidi and FACE-Intel, pleading causes of action for trespass to chattels and nuisance, and seeking both actual damages and an injunction against further e-mail messages. Intel later voluntarily dismissed its nuisance claim and waived its demand for damages. The trial court entered default against FACE-Intel upon that organization's failure to answer. The court then granted Intel's motion for summary judgment, permanently enjoining Hamidi, FACE-Intel, and their agents "from sending unsolicited e-mail to addresses on Intel's computer systems." Hamidi appealed; FACE-Intel did not.

The Court of Appeal, with one justice dissenting, affirmed the grant of injunctive relief. The majority took the view that the use of or intermeddling with another's personal property is actionable as a trespass to chattels without proof of any actual injury to the personal property; even if Intel could not show any damages resulting from Hamidi's sending of messages, "it showed he was disrupting its business by using its property and therefore is entitled to injunctive relief based on a theory of trespass to chattels." The dissenting justice warned that the majority's application of the trespass to chattels tort to "unsolicited electronic mail that causes no harm to the private computer system that receives it" would "expand the tort of trespass to chattel in untold ways and to unanticipated circumstances." We granted Hamidi's petition for review.

Dubbed by Prosser the "little brother of conversion," the tort of trespass to chattels allows recovery for interferences with possession of personal property "not sufficiently important to be classed as conversion, and so to compel the defendant to pay the full value of the thing with which he has interfered." (PROSSER & KEETON, TORTS (5th ed.1984) § 14, pp. 85–86.). Though not amounting to conversion, the defendant's interference must, to be actionable, have caused some injury to the chattel or to the plaintiff's rights in it. Under California law, trespass to chattels "lies where an intentional interference with the possession of personal property *has proximately caused injury.*" (*Thrifty-Tel, Inc. v. Bezenek* (1996) 46 Cal. App. 4th 1559, 1566, italics added.) In cases of interference with possession of personal property not amounting to conversion, "the owner has a cause of action for trespass or case, *and may recover only the actual damages suffered by reason of the impairment of the property or the loss of its use.*" . . . In modern American law generally, "[t]respass remains as an occasional remedy for minor interferences, *resulting in some damage,* but not sufficiently serious or sufficiently important to amount to the greater tort" [of conversion] . . .

The Restatement, too, makes clear that some actual injury must have occurred in order for a trespass to chattels to be actionable. Under section 218 of the Restatement Second of Torts, dispossession alone, without further damages, is actionable . . . . but other forms of interference require some additional harm to the personal property or the possessor's interests in it. (*Id.,* pars. (b)–(d).) "The interest of a possessor of a chattel in its inviolability, unlike the similar interest of a possessor of land, is not given legal protection by an action for nominal damages for harmless intermeddlings with the chattel. In order that an actor who interferes with another's chattel may be liable, his conduct must affect some other and more important interest of the possessor.

Therefore, one who intentionally intermeddles with another's chattel is subject to liability only if his intermeddling is harmful to the possessor's materially valuable interest in the physical condition, quality, or value of the chattel, or if the possessor is deprived of the use of the chattel for a substantial time, or some other legally protected interest of the possessor is affected as stated in Clause (c). Sufficient legal protection of the possessor's interest in the mere inviolability of his chattel is afforded by his privilege to use reasonable force to protect his possession against even harmless interference. . . . But while a harmless use or touching of personal property may be a technical trespass (*see* REST. 2D TORTS, § 217), an interference (not amounting to dispossession) is not *actionable,* under modern California and broader American law, without a showing of harm. . . . In this respect, as Prosser explains, modern day trespass to chattels differs both from the original English writ and from the action for trespass to land: "Another departure from the original rule of the old writ of trespass concerns the necessity of some actual damage to the chattel before the action can be maintained."

Where the defendant merely interferes without doing any harm — as where, for example, he merely lays hands upon the Plaintiff's horse, or sits in his car — there has been a division of opinion among the writers, and a surprising dearth of authority. By analogy to trespass to land there might be a technical tort in such a case . . . Intel suggests that the requirement of actual harm does not apply here because it sought only injunctive relief, as protection from future injuries . . . Even in an action for trespass to real property, in which damage to the property is not an element of the cause of action, "the extraordinary remedy of injunction" cannot be invoked without showing the likelihood of irreparable harm . . .

The dispositive issue in this case, therefore, is whether the undisputed facts demonstrate Hamidi's actions caused or threatened to cause damage to Intel's computer system, or injury to its rights in that personal property, such as to entitle Intel to judgment as a matter of law. To review, the undisputed evidence revealed no actual or threatened damage to Intel's computer hardware or software and no interference with its ordinary and intended operation . . .

Relying on a line of decisions, most from federal district courts, applying the tort of trespass to chattels to various types of unwanted electronic contact between computers, Intel contends that, while its computers were not damaged by receiving Hamidi's messages, its interest in the "physical condition, quality or value" (REST. 2D TORTS, §218, cmt. e, p. 422) of the computers was harmed. We disagree. The cited line of decisions does not persuade us that the mere sending of electronic communications that assertedly cause injury only because of their contents constitutes an actionable trespass to a computer system through which the messages are transmitted. Rather, the decisions finding electronic contact to be a trespass to computer systems have generally involved some actual or threatened interference with the computers' functioning. . . . In each of these spamming cases, the plaintiff showed, or was prepared to show, some interference with the efficient functioning of its computer system . . .

A basic element of trespass to chattels must be physical harm to the chattel (not present here) or some obstruction of its basic function (in the court's opinion not sufficiently shown here). . . . Reading an e-mail transmitted to equipment designed to receive it, in and of itself, does not affect the possessory interest in the equipment . . . Indeed, if a chattel's receipt of an electronic communication constitutes a trespass to that chattel, then not only are unsolicited telephone calls and faxes trespasses to chattel, but unwelcome radio waves and television signals also constitute a trespass to chattel every time the viewer inadvertently sees or hears the unwanted program." We agree. While unwelcome communications, electronic or otherwise, can cause a variety of injuries to economic relations, reputation and emotions, those interests are protected by other branches of tort law; in order to address them, we need not create a fiction of injury to the communication system.

Nor may Intel appropriately assert a *property* interest in its employees' time. "The Restatement test clearly speaks in the first instance to the impairment of the chattel . . . But employees are not chattels (at least not in the legal sense of the term)." . . . Intel connected its e-mail system to the Internet and permitted its employees to make use of this connection both for business and, to a reasonable extent, for their own purposes. In doing so, the company necessarily contemplated the employees' receipt of unsolicited as well as solicited communications from other companies and individuals. That some communications would, because of their contents, be unwelcome to Intel management was virtually inevitable. Hamidi did nothing but use the e-mail system for its intended purpose — to communicate with employees. The system worked as designed, delivering the messages without any physical or functional harm or disruption. These occasional transmissions cannot reasonably be viewed as impairing the quality or value of Intel's computer system. We conclude, therefore, that Intel has not presented undisputed facts demonstrating an injury to its personal property, or to its legal interest in that property, that support, under California tort law, an action for trespass to chattels.

We next consider whether California common law should be *extended* to cover, as a trespass to chattels, an otherwise harmless electronic communication whose contents are objectionable. We decline to so expand California law. Intel, of course, was not the recipient of Hamidi's messages, but rather the owner and possessor of computer servers used to relay the messages, and it bases this tort action on that ownership and possession. The property rule proposed is a rigid one, under which the sender of an electronic message would be strictly liable to the owner of equipment through which the communication passes — here, Intel — for any consequential injury flowing from the *contents* of the communication . . .

It may see fit in the future also to regulate noncommercial e-mail, such as that sent by Hamidi, or other kinds of unwanted contact between computers on the Internet, such as that alleged in *eBay, supra,* 100 F. Supp. 2d 1058. But we are not persuaded that these perceived problems call at present for judicial creation of a rigid property rule of computer server inviolability. We therefore decline to create an exception, covering Hamidi's unwanted electronic messages to Intel employees, to the general rule that a trespass to chattels is not actionable if it does not involve actual or threatened injury to the personal property or to the possessor's legally protected interest in the personal property. No such injury having been shown on the undisputed facts, Intel was not entitled to summary judgment in its favor. Because we conclude no trespass to chattels was shown on the summary judgment record, making the injunction improper on common law grounds, we need not address at length the dissenters' constitutional arguments. [REVERSED]

NOTES

1. *Trespass to Chattels: Conversion's Little Brother.* 'Trespass to chattels' is a tort where the "interferences with the possession of chattels which are not sufficiently important to be classed as conversion, and so to compel the defendant to pay the full value of the thing with which he has interfered." Trespass to chattels survives today, in other words, largely as a little brother of conversion. PAGE KEETON, PROSSER & KEETON, PROSSER AND KEETON ON TORTS, § 14, 85–86 (1984). If the trespass constitutes a mere use of or intermeddling with the chattel, however, as opposed to a dispossession, then the trespasser is liable only if "the chattel is impaired as to its condition, quality, or value," the possessor is "deprived of the use of the chattel for a substantial time," or harm is caused to the possessor or to some person or thing in which the possessor has a legally protected interest. REST. 2D TORTS § 218 & cmt. *e.* Thus if a child climbs onto the back of a person's dog and pulls the dog's ears, but does not hurt the dog, there is no trespass. If A moves B's car four feet doing no harm to it, there is no trespass; but if A moves the car around the corner so that B on looking for the car is unable to find it for an hour, there is a trespass. *Id.,* cmt. *e,* illus. 2, cmt. *I,* illus. 3 & 4. Comment *c* to § 217 states that the intent necessary to make one liable for trespass to chattel "is similar to that necessary to make one liable for an invasion of another's interest in bodily security, in freedom from an offensive contact, or confinement." *Id.* § 217, cmt. *c.* It is unclear whether there can be a trespass to intangible rights, within the terms of the Restatement.

2. *Mistake of Fact & Personal Property Torts:* Section 244 of the Restatement (Second) states that an actor is not relieved from liability to another for trespass to chattel or for conversion "because of a mistake of law or fact not induced by the other" regarding the actor's right of possession of the goods, or of the existence of consent or other privilege to use the goods. REST. 2D TORTS § 244. Where defendants were hunting for wolves and plaintiff's dog had a striking resemblance to a wolf, and they believed it to be one and killed it as such, they were liable for damages caused by their mistake. *Ranson v. Kitner,* 31 Ill. App. 241 (1889). The court affirmed a $50 judgment for the value of the dog, even though the defendants killed the dog with a good faith belief that it was a wolf. Mistake is not a good defense in intentional torts against the person. A person is liable for damages caused by a mistake of identity, even if it is made in good faith. Why is this so?

3. *Property, Promises or Mere Paper?* According to one commentator, the "traditional common law rule" was that "intangible properties such as paper which merely represented a right to get gold or silver" were not subject to conversion. DAN D. DOBBS, TORTS AND COMPENSATION 59 (1985). The Restatement declares, however, that there can be conversion of "a document in which intangible rights are merged," and that one who "effectively prevents the exercise" of the rights in those documents is also guilty of conversion. REST. 2D TORTS § 242. Section 242 applies to "promissory notes, bonds, bills of exchange, share certificates, and warehouse receipts, whether negotiable or non-negotiable." *Id.*, cmt. *b.* Comment *f* to section 242 extends the tort of conversion to intangible assets. *Id., cmt. f.* However, the Restatement takes no position on whether other kinds of intangible rights should be subject to conversion. The court in *Kremen, supra,* extended conversion to cyberspace in its ruling that domain names can be converted.

I.   MISUSE OF THE JUDICIAL PROCESS

Three distinct tort actions also protect against the misuse of judicial process: (1) Malicious prosecution; (2) Malicious Civil Proceedings; and (3) Abuse of Process. To prevail on a claim of malicious prosecution, a plaintiff must establish, among other things, that the defendant lacked probable cause for instituting an underlying criminal proceeding. Probable cause, in turn, is defined as that quantum of evidence which would lead a reasonable layman in the same circumstances to honestly suspect that another person had committed a crime. A plaintiff must prove four elements for a malicious prosecution based upon a prior criminal judicial proceeding: (1) Existence of a criminal proceeding instituted against her; (2) Proof that the defendant was responsible for causing proceedings to be instituted; (3) Establish that the criminal proceeding terminated favorable to her (i.e., voluntary withdrawal, failure to indict, or abandonment) or (4) Demonstrate lack of reasonable or probable cause for the criminal prosecution. *See* NEW JERSEY JURY INSTRUCTION, 3.12. A defendant's use of either civil or criminal proceedings for an ulterior purpose is tortious. Many jurisdictions recognize an action for malicious civil proceedings as well as malicious criminal prosecution. The Restatement defines abuse of process as:

> One who uses a legal process, whether criminal or civil, against another primarily to accomplish a purpose for which it is not designed, is subject to liability to the other for harm caused by the abuse of process.

REST. 2D TORTS § 672.

The plaintiff must prove three elements to prevail in a malicious civil prosecution lawsuit: (1) Proof that the defendant instituted or caused to be instituted a civil lawsuit; (2) Proof that the civil suit terminated favorably to her in a manner not adverse; (3) Lack of reasonable or probable cause for the civil suit. *See* NEW JERSEY JURY INSTRUCTION 3.13.

The tort of abuse of process is intended to limit wrongful adversarial conduct by clients and their attorneys. This limit is consistent with the public policy favoring open access to courts and zealous representation. Nonetheless, the purview of the tort, which is restricted to cases involving misuse of valid judicial processes, is too narrow to encompass the broad range of injuries caused by malicious actions by defendants. Jonathan Van Patten & Robert E. Willard, *The Limits of Advocacy: A Proposal for the Tort of Malicious Defense in Civil Litigation*, 35 HASTINGS L.J. 891, 909 (1984).

Abuse of process generally involves improper leverage "to compel the victim to yield on some matter not involved in the suit." 2 DAN B. DOBBS, THE LAW OF TORTS § 439 (2001). The abuse of process is for an improper use of legal process while the malicious prosecution tort is for instigating process to issue without probable cause. The abuse of process is about the improper use of process without legal justification whereas the tort of malicious prosecution concerns prosecuting a groundless cause of action. The elements of an abuse of process are the misuse of process for an irregular purpose coupled with an ulterior motive or purpose. The gist of the malicious prosecution claim is to have an improper or ulterior motive in getting a prosecution to issue. Lisa A. Zakolski, *Abuse of Process*, 1 AM. JUR. 2D ABUSE OF PROCESS § 3 (2006). Most states have extended the malicious prosecution tort to include the filing of frivolous civil lawsuits as in *Cult Awareness Network* below. As you read this case, consider how the plaintiff proves each element of the *prima facie* case. In particular, how does the plaintiff prove damages?

CULT AWARENESS NETWORK v. CHURCH OF SCIENTOLOGY INTERNATIONAL, INC.
177 Ill.2d 267, 226 Ill. Dec. 604 (1997).

FREEMAN, CHIEF JUSTICE.

Plaintiff, Cult Awareness Network, filed suit in the circuit court of Cook County against defendants, Church of Scientology International and Church of Scientology of Illinois (collectively, the Church of Scientology), as well as the law firm of Bowles & Moxon. In the complaint, as amended, plaintiff alleged that defendants had engaged in a conspiracy to maliciously prosecute numerous civil actions against plaintiff. The circuit court dismissed the suit for failure to state a cause of action. The court ruled that (i) plaintiff had failed to allege a favorable termination of the underlying actions and (ii) plaintiff had not satisfied the special damage requirement for actions sounding in malicious prosecution. The appellate court affirmed the order of dismissal . . . and we allowed Plaintiff's petition for leave to appeal . . . For the reasons that follow, we reverse the judgments of the appellate and circuit courts and remand the matter to the circuit court for further proceedings.

Plaintiff is a not-for-profit corporation engaged in, among other things, educating the public with respect to religious rights, freedoms, and responsibilities. Defendants are two religious corporations and their attorneys. Plaintiff claimed that defendants conspired with each other to carry on a campaign of malicious prosecution for the express purpose of causing Plaintiff's bankruptcy and eventual disbandment. Specifically, plaintiff alleged that, between January 24, 1992, and July 1, 1993, various members of the Church of Scientology filed 21 lawsuits which named plaintiff as the defendant. Plaintiff further alleged that the lawsuits were filed in several jurisdictions around the country, including Illinois, California, Massachusetts, Minnesota, New York, and Washington, D.C. All but one of the suits alleged that plaintiff had violated various state and federal civil rights laws by denying each complainant membership in Plaintiff's organization and/or access to its meetings.

The lone cause of action that did not contain such allegations was filed by a church member who claimed that plaintiff had fraudulently induced him to do volunteer work. Each of the underlying suits was alleged to have terminated in Plaintiff's favor, either by summary judgment or by voluntary and involuntary dismissals. In particular, plaintiff claimed that the Church of Scientology "suggested, instigated, encouraged, and assisted the named plaintiffs in the [underlying] lawsuits and complaints." Plaintiff also alleged that Bowles & Moxon [law firm] provided assistance and support to the Church of Scientology in each of the underlying lawsuits.

According to plaintiff, each of those actions was filed without probable cause. Finally, plaintiff claimed that it had suffered damages as a result of the "multiplicity of actions brought by, at the behest of, or with the assistance of defendants." For example, plaintiff alleged that it had incurred substantial attorney fees and increased costs for liability insurance, among other things. Defendants thereafter filed a motion to dismiss the complaint with prejudice for failure to state a cause of action. In support of their motion, defendants argued that none of the underlying suits had ended in a judicial termination that dealt with the factual issues of the case, and thus plaintiff had failed to allege that the actions had terminated in its favor as required under Illinois law. Moreover, defendants claimed that plaintiff had failed to satisfy Illinois' special injury requirement. In their view, the damages alleged by plaintiff constituted nothing more than the usual costs and anxiety associated with defending against an ordinary civil action. The circuit court agreed with both points and granted the motion to dismiss.

As previously noted, the appellate court affirmed the judgment of the circuit court. Although the court acknowledged that plaintiff had alleged that each of the underlying suits was terminated in its favor, either by summary judgment or by dismissal (both voluntary and involuntary), the court nevertheless held that such allegations were insufficient to satisfy the favorable termination requirement as that term had been defined in previous appellate court opinions. The court noted that, under Illinois law, "[a] favorable termination for purposes of a malicious prosecution claim is one which deals with the *factual* issue or issues of a case" . . . The dispositive issue for our review is whether plaintiff has alleged sufficient facts to support a cause of action for civil conspiracy. However, because such an action necessarily depends upon the commission of some underlying tort. . . . the viability of plaintiff's complaint in this case turns upon whether plaintiff has alleged enough facts to satisfy the elements of malicious prosecution. Therefore, it is appropriate that we examine those elements in determining the adequacy of plaintiff's charge. In Illinois, the elements of malicious prosecution are well established. The plaintiff must show that the defendant brought the underlying suit maliciously and without probable cause. Moreover, the plaintiff must establish that the former action was terminated in his or her favor. Finally, the plaintiff must plead and prove some "special injury" or special damage beyond the usual expense, time or annoyance in defending a lawsuit.

The necessity of alleging a favorable termination in actions for malicious prosecution is a long-standing and deeply rooted principle in this court's jurisprudence. Indeed, as early as 1832, this court concluded that the former proceeding must have been legally determined in favor of the malicious prosecution plaintiff before the malicious prosecution action will lie. . . . As a result, the contours of the requirement have been shaped by our appellate court, which, in 1970, announced that the favorable termination requirement could be satisfied only by "a judgment which deals with the *factual* issue of the case, whether the judgment is rendered after a trial or upon motion for summary judgment."

In *Siegel,* the owners of certain property filed a multicount complaint for declaratory relief against the City of Chicago. In the complaint, plaintiffs sought to nullify a zoning amendment that would have permitted another defendant, Stein, to erect a high-rise apartment building near plaintiffs' properties. Stein filed a counterclaim, alleging that one of the counts in plaintiffs' complaint was filed without probable cause and with malice, thereby constituting malicious prosecution. The circuit court, however, had previously dismissed the count which had given rise to Stein's counterclaim, and, as a result, dismissed Stein's counterclaim as well. The court ruled that the dismissal of plaintiffs' count could not be viewed as a favorable termination for purposes of Stein's malicious prosecution action. Stein appealed the ruling.

The appellate court affirmed the judgment of the circuit court, holding that a dismissal of the former action could not qualify as a favorable termination in the context of a malicious prosecution suit. The court predicated its holding on the fact that the favorable termination requirement "goes to the question of probable cause." . . . As a result, the court reasoned that:

> The legal termination requirement necessitate[d] a judgment which deals with the *factual issue of the case,* whether the judgment is rendered after a trial or upon motion for summary judgment. However, it is not sufficient to simply obtain a dismissal of the opponents' complaint, for such dismissal need bear no logical relationship to the legitimacy of the assertions contained therein; therefore, such dismissal lends no credence to the claim that the assertions were baseless. . . .

Consonant with this conclusion, the appellate court affirmed the dismissal of Stein's counterclaim. As noted above, the *Siegel* analysis has, throughout the years, been relied upon by different panels of our appellate court, including the one which affirmed the circuit court's judgment in this case. We note that several of these later appellate court opinions state that voluntary dismissals do not satisfy the favorable termination requirement. . . . We begin our review of this issue with a discussion of the REST. 2D TORTS, which suggests looking beyond the type of disposition that was obtained in the previous action when determining if that termination is, indeed, "favorable" for purposes of a malicious prosecution action. Specifically, the Restatement provides as follows:

> *Termination in favor of the person against whom civil proceedings are brought.* Civil proceedings may be terminated in favor of the person against whom they are brought . . . by (1) the favorable adjudication of the claim by a competent tribunal, or (2) the withdrawal of the proceedings by the person bringing them, or (3) the dismissal of the proceedings because of his failure to prosecute them.

A favorable adjudication may be by a judgment rendered by a court after trial, or upon demurrer or its equivalent. In either case the adjudication is a sufficient termination of the proceedings, unless an appeal is taken . . .

Whether a withdrawal or an abandonment constitutes a final termination of the case in favor of the person against whom the proceedings are brought and whether the withdrawal is evidence of a lack of probable cause for their initiation, *depends upon the circumstances under which the proceedings are withdrawn."* REST. 2D TORTS § 674. cmt. *j.* Unlike the holding in *Siegel,* . . . [under the Restatement approach] whether or not the requirement is met is to be determined not by the *form* or *title* given to the disposition of the prior proceeding, but by the *circumstances* under which that disposition is obtained . . . As a result, terminations which do not rise to the level of adjudications on the merits may satisfy the favorable termination requirement. [I]f the dismissal was merely a formal means of securing a negotiated settlement, it cannot serve as the basis for a malicious prosecution action . . . Likewise, a malicious prosecution claim cannot be premised on a dismissal that was entered in order to enable the plaintiff to file the claim in another forum . . . We agree with the reasoning espoused by the courts of our sister states. We regard the Restatement's treatment of the favorable termination requirement as more balanced than our appellate court's interpretation as set forth in *Siegel* Nevertheless, defendants criticize the Restatement approach as being too sweeping in its scope. We disagree. Contrary to defendants' arguments, we do not necessarily view the Restatement's position, as expressed in the case law, as more expansive than our appellate As the case law demonstrates, a favorable termination is limited to only those legal dispositions that can give rise to an inference of lack of probable cause. *See also* 54 C.J.S. Malicious Prosecution § 54 (1987) (dismissal cannot serve as favorable termination if based solely on technical or procedural grounds) . . . Under this approach, a disingenuous plaintiff can merely nonsuit his or her frivolous lawsuit in order to guard against a future malicious prosecution action . . . Having adopted the Restatement approach, we find that plaintiff's complaint in this case, which alleges that each of the underlying actions was terminated in its favor either by the entry of summary judgment or by dismissal (voluntary and involuntary), satisfies the favorable termination requirement, at least for purposes of defendant's motion to dismiss . . . Whether or not these dispositions ultimately *are proved by plaintiff* to be indicative of a lack of probable cause remains a question of fact which cannot be answered at this stage of the litigation . . . Accordingly, the circuit court erred in ruling that plaintiff had failed to sufficiently allege the favorable termination of the underlying actions at issue.

We must next determine whether plaintiff's complaint adequately pleaded special injury or damage. Like the favorable termination requirement, the necessity of pleading some special injury or damage is firmly rooted in our jurisprudence. . . . Notwithstanding the above, defendants submit that if this court were to conclude that the special injury requirement has been met in this case, we would be infringing upon defendants' exercise of their first amendment rights. Specifically, defendants rely upon several United States Supreme Court decisions which have held that the litigation activities of a national membership organization, including encouraging, financing, and coordinating a series of lawsuits challenging discriminatory practices, are protected by the first amendment . . .

While we do not dispute the correctness of these Supreme Court decisions, we do dispute the defendants' reliance upon them. The Constitution affords protection to the *honest* litigator in search of resolutions to *true* legal disputes; however, it does not provide the right to any individual to assist another, with money or otherwise, in the prosecution of a suit which has been filed with malice and without probable cause . . . Therefore, defendants' constitutional argument, which is a fact-dependent defense to the action grounded in probable cause, cannot be considered in the context of the present motion to dismiss. Nothing in our opinion prevents defendants from raising the first amendment's protections at the appropriate juncture in this case.

As a final matter, we wish to stress that our holding with respect to the special injury requirement should not be viewed as a rejection of the rule as set forth in our earlier opinions. We further emphasize that today's decision should not be read to mitigate the strict requirement that a malicious prosecution plaintiff show not only that the action complained of has been terminated, but that it was commenced maliciously and without probable cause. These latter two required elements are no easy hurdle for a plaintiff, as many courts and commentators have noted . . .

In the view of the foregoing analysis, we hold that plaintiff has sufficiently alleged the elements of the tort of malicious prosecution and, for purposes of this case, the tort of civil conspiracy to commit malicious prosecution. The circuit court, therefore, erred in dismissing the amended complaint. Accordingly, we reverse the judgments of the appellate and circuit courts, and remand the matter to the circuit court for further proceedings.

NOTES

1. *Malicious Prosecution and Probable Cause.* According to REST. 2D TORTS § 653, a private citizen is subject to a claim for malicious persecution if "(a) he initiates or procures the proceedings without probable cause and primarily for a purpose other than that of bringing an offender to justice, and (b) the proceedings have terminated in favor of the accused." For this purpose probable cause is defined as a correct or reasonable belief:

> (a) that the person whom he accuses has acted or failed to act in a particular manner, and

> (b) that those acts or omissions constitute the offense that he charges against the accused, and

> (c) that he is sufficiently informed as to the law and facts to justify him in initiating or continuing the prosecution.

REST. 2D TORTS § 662.

2. *Damages & Special Injury Elements.* Where a malicious prosecution action is based upon the prior institution of a civil — as opposed to a criminal — action, some courts have required that the plaintiff in the malicious prosecution suit show "special damages" resulting from the prior civil prosecution. *Nagy v. McBurney,* 392 A.2d 365 (R.I. 1978). Special damages may exist if the prior civil proceeding results in arrest or deprivation of property, involves allegations of insanity or insolvency, or results in repetitious civil proceedings. *See* REST. 2D TORTS §§ 677–679. The Restatement and some courts do not require proof of special damages in this context. REST. 2D TORTS § 674; *id.* § 679, cmt. *a*; *Shaffer v. Stewart,* 473 A.2d 1017 (Pa. Super. 1984). Many courts refer to an action for malicious prosecution based upon a prior civil proceeding as a "wrongful civil proceeding." *See generally* Kimberly A. Frost & Michael J. Frost, *Malicious Prosecution No Longer Risk-Free in Illinois,* ILL. BAR ASSOC. J. 6 (1999) (discussing *Cult Awareness* above).

3. *Hard-Ball Tactics as Abuse of Process?* The common-law tort of "abuse of process" is a remedy for the abuse of legal process, whether criminal or civil. The tort action is available where legal process is used for an ulterior purpose for which it was not designed. In *Board of Educ. v. Farmingdale Classroom Teachers Ass'n,* 343 N.E.2d 278 (N.Y.1975), the school board and the teachers were embroiled in a bitter labor dispute. In that case, the teachers association was charged with violating the civil service law. A hearing was scheduled beginning on October 5, 1972. The attorney for the association then subpoenaed 87 teachers to appear on that day. As a result the school board was forced to hire 77 substitute teachers to keep its schools open. The court held that a cause of action for abuse of process had been stated against the association:

> While it is true that public policy mandates free access to the courts for redress of wrongs and our adversarial system cannot function without

zealous advocacy, it is also true that legal procedure must be utilized in a manner consonant with the purpose for which that procedure was designed. Where process is manipulated to achieve some collateral advantage, whether it be denominated extortion, blackmail or retribution, the tort of abuse of process will be available to the injured party.

The appellants raise several arguments against the sufficiency of this complaint. The most troublesome contention raised is that it is standard, appropriate and proper practice to subpoena all witnesses for the first day of any judicial proceeding. While we acknowledge this an appropriate procedure and in no way intend this decision to proscribe it, we are obligated to determine appeals in the context in which they are presented. Here we consider solely whether the complaint states a valid cause of action. If the proof at trial establishes that defendants attempted to reach a reasonable accommodation at a time when the accommodation would have been effectual, the cause of action will be defeated. However, on its face an allegation that defendants subpoenaed 87 persons with full knowledge that they all could not and would not testify and that this was done maliciously with the intent to injure and to harass plaintiff spells out an abuse of process. Another factor to be weighed at trial is whether the testimony of so many witnesses was material and necessary. As this complaint is framed, it may be inferred that defendants were effecting a not too subtle threat which should be actionable. . . .

Id. at 283.

PROBLEMS

2.1

Wife (W) developed a slight sore throat while at work. During the course of the day she kissed Friend (F), hoping that she would not contaminate him thereby. At the end of the day, W's sore throat was much worse. On arriving home she kissed Husband (H), hoping thereby to give him whatever illness she herself had. After having several alcoholic drinks that evening, she put her Child (C) to bed and kissed him as she tucked him in, hoping thereby to immunize the child from any cold-related disease. Unknown to W, she then had a cut in her mouth which caused her to bleed slightly. F and H developed influenza, and C contracted hepatitis, as the result of kissing W. Does F, H, or C have a valid battery action against W?

2.2

Principal McVicker called Beavis a ten-year-old to his office for hurling hamburgers onto the ceiling fan in the library causing a mess. Beavis pulled McVicker's chair out from under him causing him to hit the ground. While McVicker was not seriously injured, he was so exasperated that he suffered a heart attack and died. Beavis felt terrible about McVicker's death and began to ramble incoherently from grief. Beavis intended his prank only as a joke and did not mean to hurt McVicker. Does McVicker's estate have a valid battery action against Beavis? How would you prove intent? What questions would you ask Beavis to prove intent? Suppose Beavis moved McVicker's chair because he spotted a thumb tack on it and did not want him to get hurt? Would there be intent to commit a battery? Assuming there is a battery, will the age of Beavis protect him from liability?

2.3

Mrs. Reaves placed her five-week-old daughter upon a bed, encompassed by pillows and blankets to prevent the baby from falling off the bed. Mrs. Reaves then left the child unattended for two and one-half hours while she visited a next-door neighbor, Mrs. Horton. As Mrs. Reaves was returning to her home, Johnny and Keith Horton, four and three-year-old children of Mrs. Horton, were seen jumping from the porch of the Reaves home and running across the yard to their home. Johnny said something to his mother which indicated that the Reaves baby might need attention. In response to the severe questioning of his mother, Johnny admitted that he had dropped the Reaves baby. Mrs. Horton immediately called to Mrs. Reaves to check on her child. Mrs. Reaves found the infant on the bedroom floor with a crushed skull. Through her legal guardian, the infant filed suit against Johnny and Keith Horton for battery and their parents for negligent supervision. Prior to trial, the district court dismissed the simple negligence claim against Mrs. Reaves on grounds of parental immunity. At the close of the plaintiff's case, the court dismissed the claim against Mrs. Horton and the remaining claim against Mrs. Reaves by reason of insufficiency of evidence. What jury instruction should be given the jury concerning the intent requirement of an infant charged with an intentional tort? What result?

2.4

A is playing golf. B, his caddie, is inattentive and A becomes angry. Intending to frighten but not to harm B, A aims a blow at him with a golf club which he stops some eight inches from B's head. Owing to the negligence of the club maker from whom A has just bought the club, the rivet which should have secured the head is defective, though A could not have discovered the defect without removing the head. The head of the club flies off and strikes B in the eye, putting it out. Is A subject to liability to B for the loss of his eye?

2.5

Wife sees standing in a crowd a man who she in good faith believes is her husband. She walks up behind him and playfully pats him on the derriere. In fact the man is a stranger, who suffers a heart attack as a result of the unexpected physical contact. What claims might the stranger have against wife? Would it be different if this occurred in their home, and the beneficiary of the "pat" was a late-arriving overnight guest about whose presence in the home the wife was unaware?

2.6

On September 16, 2006 there was a professional baseball game at Fenway Park in Boston between the Red Sox and their rival, The New York Yankees. The Yankee pitcher overreacted to Red Sox hecklers and hurled a ball at more than 80 miles per hour in their direction to frighten them. Unfortunately, the ball passed through the wire mesh fence and hit the plaintiff fracturing his skull. The injured patron sued the Yankees and their pitcher for battery, but the trial judge entered a verdict in favor of the defendants. You have been hired as a clerk for the appellate court and have been asked for your opinion about whether the trial court's order should be upheld.

2.7

Al and Ben are trespassers upon Carl's land. Carl sees Al but does not see Ben, nor does he know that Ben is in the neighborhood. Carl throws a stone at Al. Immediately after Carl has done so, Ben raises his head above a wall behind which he has been hiding. The stone misses Al but strikes Ben, putting out his eye. Is Carl liable to Ben?

2.8

Just before closing time, Allan, a shopkeeper, sends Bella into a cold storage vault to take inventory of the articles therein. Forgetting that he has done so, he locks the door of the vault on leaving the premises. If Allan, who has mild Alzheimer's, realizes within in a few moments that he sent Bella into the storage vault, he will be able to go back and release her. However, Allan does not remember immediately and makes it home before realizing his mistake. Although he promptly returns to the shop to open the storage vault to release Bella, she has suffered serious frost bite. Is Allan liable to Bella for false imprisonment? Would it make a difference if Allan remember only after a few minutes and returned to release Bella. Please explain.

2.9

The New Town Police Officers observe Sam Smear, a 55-year-old male whom they know to be a chronic alcoholic, staggering down a street at 2 a.m. The officers arrested him on several occasions and had him dry out in jail. Instead of arresting him, they took him to an abandoned golf course to "sleep it off." Sam was assaulted and beaten into a semi-comatose state. Sam has no present memory of being taken to the golf course. You represent Sam Smear and need to decide what causes of action that you may file against the New Town police department.

2.10

Checkers is a former aide to Senator Foghorn of Big State. He was recently appointed as an associate professor of law at Big City Law School. His special interests lie in condominium law and government ethics. Soon after Professor Checkers joined the law faculty at Big City Law School,, Jessica Butler's

"Senateienne" Web log splashed onto the Internet with racy tidbits about the personal habits of her various lovers in Washington D.C. Jessica identified Professor Checkers as one of her paramours with a taste for bondage and a reluctance to wear condoms. Checkers has come to your law firm seeking legal representation to pursue an intentional infliction of emotional distress claim. He admits having an affair with Butler so the statement is not defamatory since truth is a defense. You are a new associate in a large law firm who has been asked to research whether Checkers has a claim for the intentional infliction of emotional distress. Consider only the potential liability of the poster for the intentional infliction of emotional distress.

2.11

In the following hypotheticals determine whether there is liability for trespass to land:

(a) Beavis throws an egg at McVicker's house. Is Beavis a trespasser? Please explain.

(b) Beavis intentionally drives Alvin the Beefalo onto a pasture owned by McVicker.

(c) Beavis erects a dam across a ditch causing water to flood the land of McVicker.

(d) Beavis carries Butthead (against his will) onto McVicker's land.

2.12

A ships goods to B. During the transit, A discovers that B has induced the shipment by fraud, and thereupon notifies the carrier not to deliver the goods to B. B presents a straight bill of lading and demands the goods, whereupon the carrier delivers them. May the carrier sue A for conversion?

2.13

Laura, a first year law student, at Big Law School, was studying torts in the law library when Tom Thief stole her *Black's Law Dictionary*. Laura had placed a decal from the Montreux Jazz festival on the cover of her book. A few days later she spotted Andrew Unaware with what she thought was her casebook. Further investigation revealed that this was in fact her casebook. Andrew had purchased it as a used book from the Campus Bookstore. Tom Thief had presented a forged identification card when he sold the casebook to the Campus Bookstore. Laura files a conversion action against Andrew and Campus Bookstore? What result?

2.14

Client came to Attorney complaining about what Client believed was medical malpractice committed on her by her Doctor. Attorney did not have any information about what occurred other than Client's statement, but since the statute of limitations would run on the claim the same day that Client came to see Attorney, Attorney hastily filed a claim against Doctor on that day. The following day Doctor's Lawyer called Attorney stating that Client's claim was groundless. Attorney said he was authorized to settle the claim for $10,000, but Lawyer refused to settle the claim. Assuming the evidence shows that the claim is merit less, discuss Doctor's claims against Attorney.

2.15

A group of Big University Students were videotaped without their permission in various states of undress by hidden cameras in restrooms, locker rooms, or showers. The videotapes were sold on a number of websites that transmitted still images of nude or partially clothed young male athletes on the Internet. What causes of action do the athletes have? What problems will the plaintiffs likely have in pursuing this lawsuit?

2.16

Z-Bay, a leading Internet-based auction trading site learned that Ez-Bay its online rival was using web spiders, or automated querying software programs to copy data from its website. Z-Bay has a user's agreement specifically prohibiting data mining which encompasses Ez-Bay's use of spiders to access and copy data. Did Ez-Bay trespass on Z-Bay's web site given that it violated the terms of Z-Bay's service agreement? What problems will Z-Bay have in obtaining a torts remedy on these facts?

Chapter 3

DEFENSES TO INTENTIONAL TORTS

A. INTRODUCTION

Chapter 2 discussed the elements of the intentional torts. Chapter 3 considers the affirmative defenses that typically are raised in connection with intentional torts. Whereas the plaintiff has the burden of proving the *prima facie* case, the defendant has the burden of asserting and proving any affirmative defense that may negate the plaintiff's claims. The practical import of an affirmative defense is that even if the defendant has invaded a legally protected interest, the defendant will not be liable for her conduct if she establishes all the elements of an applicable affirmative defense. Affirmative defenses to intentional torts are often called privileges.

The list of affirmative defenses covered in this chapter is not exhaustive. There can be other defenses such as statutes of limitations, immunities, or lack of jurisdiction that bar recovery for the plaintiff. *See* Chapter 14, *infra*. The defenses considered here are also limited to intentional tort claims. Yet some of the defenses discussed are functionally equivalent to defenses available in response to negligence claims; notably, asserting consent to negate an intentional tort is akin to asserting assumption of the risk as a defense to a negligence claim. Some defenses available in negligence or strict liability actions are not applicable to intentional torts. For example, contributory negligence has no relevance to an intentional tort action.

The defenses discussed in this chapter shed light on the nature of intentional tort liability and, for that matter, on the nature of tort liability in general. Why is contributory negligence a valid defense to a negligence claims but not to an intentional tort claim? When should a person be permitted to harm others with impunity? What are the policy reasons for allowing injurious conduct to go uncompensated? Self defense and defense of others must be recognized as valid justifications for invading the interest of others under some circumstances, but how imminent or serious must the threat be in order to justify those defenses? What is the relationship between self-defense and necessity? Should mistake be a defense? Should one be permitted to consent to the commission of a tort? The cases and materials in this chapter provide bases for answering most of the preceding questions. However, after answering those fundamental questions the reader will confront n other challenging and complicated questions arising out of both the doctrine and policies applicable to intentional torts.

We begin with the threshold question of consent. A person may expressly consent to conduct that invades a legally protected interest or he may impliedly consent based on customs in the community or his particular action or inaction in a specific situation. Are there some activities in which a person's voluntary participation impliedly says to others that there are not limits to what you may do to me?

B. CONSENT

HACKBART v. CINCINNATI BENGALS, INC.
601 F.2d 516 (10th Cir. 1979)

DOYLE, CIRCUIT JUDGE.

The question in this case is whether in a regular season professional football game an injury which is inflicted by one professional football player on an opposing player can give rise to liability in tort where the injury was inflicted by the intentional striking of a blow during the game.

The injury occurred in the course of a game between the Denver Broncos and the Cincinnati Bengals, which game was being played in Denver in 1973. The Broncos' defensive back, Dale Hackbart, was the recipient of the injury and the Bengals' offensive back, Charles "Booby" Clark, inflicted the blow . . .

By agreement the liability question was determined by the United States District Court for the District of Colorado without a jury. The judge resolved the liability issue in favor of the Cincinnati team and Charles Clark. Consistent with this result, final judgment was entered for Cincinnati and the appeal challenges this judgment. In essence the trial court's reasons for rejecting plaintiff's claim were that professional football is a species of warfare and that so much physical force is tolerated and the magnitude of the force exerted is so great that it renders injuries not actionable in court; that even intentional batteries are beyond the scope of the judicial process. Clark was an offensive back and just before the injury he had run a pass pattern to the right side of the Denver Broncos' end zone.

The injury flowed indirectly from this play. The pass was intercepted by Billy Thompson, a Denver free safety, who returned it to mid-field. The subject injury occurred as an aftermath of the pass play. As a consequence of the interception, the roles of Hackbart and Clark suddenly changed. Hackbart, who had been defending, instantaneously became an offensive player. Clark, on the other hand, became a defensive player. Acting as an offensive player, Hackbart attempted to block Clark by throwing his body in front of him. He thereafter remained on the ground. He turned, and with one knee on the ground, watched the play following the interception.

The trial court's finding was that Charles Clark, "acting out of anger and frustration, but without a specific intent to injure stepped forward and struck a blow with his right forearm to the back of the kneeling plaintiff's head and neck with sufficient force to cause both players to fall forward to the ground." Both players, without complaining to the officials or to one another, returned to their respective sidelines since the ball had changed hands and the offensive and defensive teams of each had been substituted. Clark testified at trial that his frustration was brought about by the fact that his team was losing the game. Due to the failure of the officials to view the incident, a foul was not called.

However, the game film showed very clearly what had occurred. Plaintiff did not at the time report the happening to his coaches or to anyone else during the game. However, because of the pain which he experienced he was unable to play golf the next day. He did not seek medical attention, but the continued pain caused him to report this fact and the incident to the Bronco trainer who gave him treatment. Apparently he played on the specialty teams for two successive Sundays, but after that the Broncos released him on waivers. (He was in his thirteenth year as a player.) He sought medical help and it was then that it was discovered by the physician that he had a serious neck fracture injury.

Despite the fact that the defendant Charles Clark admitted that the blow which had been struck was not accidental, that it was intentionally administered, the trial court ruled as a matter of law that the game of professional football is basically a business which is violent in nature, and that the available sanctions are imposition of penalties and expulsion from the game. Notice was taken of the fact that many fouls are overlooked; that the game is played in an emotional and noisy environment; and that incidents such as that here complained of are not unusual.

The trial court spoke as well of the unreasonableness of applying the laws and rules which are a part of injury law to the game of professional football, noting the unreasonableness of holding that one player has a duty of care for the safety of others. He also talked about the concept of assumption of risk and contributory fault as applying and concluded that Hackbart had to recognize that he accepted the risk that he would be injured by such an act.

The evidence at the trial uniformly supported the proposition that the intentional striking of a player in the head from the rear is not an accepted part of either the playing rules or the general customs of the game of professional football. The trial court, however, believed that the unusual nature of the case called for the consideration of underlying policy which it defined as common law principles which have evolved as a result of the case to case process and which necessarily affect behavior in various contexts. From these considerations the belief was expressed that even Intentional injuries incurred in football games should be outside the framework of the law. The court recognized that the potential threat of legal liability has a significant deterrent effect, and further said that private civil actions constitute an important mechanism for societal control of human conduct.

Due to the increase in severity of human conflicts, a need existed to expand the body of governing law more rapidly and with more certainty, but that this had to be accomplished by legislation and administrative regulation. The judge compared football to coal mining and railroading insofar as all are inherently hazardous. Judge Matsch said that in the case of football it was questionable whether social values would be improved by limiting the violence. Thus the district court's assumption was that Clark had inflicted an intentional blow which would ordinarily generate civil liability and which might bring about a criminal sanction as well, but that since it had occurred in the course of a football game, it should not be subject to the restraints of the law; that if it were it would place unreasonable impediments and restraints on the activity. The judge also pointed out that courts are ill-suited to decide the different social questions and to administer conflicts on what is much like a battlefield where the restraints of civilization have been left on the sidelines. We are forced to conclude that the result reached is not supported by evidence.

Plaintiff, of course, maintains that tort law applicable to the injury in this case applies on the football field as well as in other places. On the other hand, plaintiff does not rely on the theory of negligence being applicable. This is in recognition of the fact that subjecting another to unreasonable risk of harm, the essence of negligence, is inherent in the game of football, for admittedly it is violent. Plaintiff maintains that in the area of contributory fault, a vacuum exists in relationship to intentional infliction of injury. Since negligence does not apply, contributory negligence is inapplicable. Intentional or reckless contributory fault could theoretically at least apply to infliction of injuries in reckless disregard of the rights of others. This has some similarity to contributory negligence and undoubtedly it would apply if the evidence would justify it. But it is highly questionable whether a professional football player consents or submits to injuries caused by conduct not within the rules, and there is no evidence which we have seen which shows this. However, the trial court did not consider this question and we are not deciding it.

Contrary to the position of the court then, there are no principles of law which allow a court to rule out certain tortious conduct by reason of general roughness of the game or difficulty of administering it. Indeed, the evidence shows that there are rules of the game which prohibit the intentional striking of blows. Thus, Article 1, Item 1, Subsection C, provides that:

> All players are prohibited from striking on the head, face or neck with the heel, back or side of the hand, wrist, forearm, elbow or clasped hands. . . . The general customs of football do not approve the intentional punching or striking of others. That this is prohibited was supported by the testimony of all of the witnesses. They testified that the intentional striking of a player in the face or from the rear is prohibited by the playing rules as well as the general customs of the game. Punching or hitting with the arms is prohibited. Undoubtedly these restraints are intended to establish reasonable boundaries so that one football player cannot intentionally inflict a serious injury on another. Therefore, the notion is not correct that all reason has been abandoned, whereby the only possible remedy for the person who has been the victim of an unlawful blow is retaliation. . . .

Reckless misconduct differs from negligence, according to the authors, in that negligence consists of mere inadvertence, lack of skillfulness or failure to take precautions; reckless misconduct, on the other hand, involves a choice or adoption of a course of action either with knowledge of the danger or with knowledge of facts which would disclose this danger to a reasonable man. Recklessness also differs in that it consists of intentionally doing an act with knowledge not only that it contains a risk of harm to others as does negligence, but that it actually involves a risk substantially greater in magnitude than is necessary in the case of negligence . . . saying that the difference is so significant as to amount to a difference in kind.

Subsection (f) also distinguishes between reckless misconduct and intentional wrongdoing. To be reckless the Act must have been intended by the actor. At the same time, the actor does not intend to cause the harm which results from it. It is enough that he realized, or from the facts should have realized, that there was a strong probability that harm would result even though he may hope or expect that this conduct will prove harmless. Nevertheless, existence of probability is different from substantial certainty which is an ingredient of intent to cause the harm which results from the act. Therefore, recklessness exists where a person knows that the act is harmful but fails to realize that it will produce the extreme harm which it did produce. It is in this respect that recklessness and intentional conduct differ in degree. . . .

There was a film of the actual injury suffered by plaintiff. It showed the sequence of events and also depicted the manner of infliction. Obviously we need not consider the relevancy of this. There were incidents that were designed to show that the plaintiff Hackbart was a dirty player. . . . Unless the game of football is on trial, and it appeared to be in the case at bar, the acts of violence which occurred in other games and between other teams and players were without relevance. The view we take is that the game of football is not on trial, but, rather, the trial involves a particular act in one game. Therefore, this evidence would appear to be questionable if not irrelevant. . . .

On retrial the admissibility of prior unrelated acts should be very carefully considered and should not be received merely for the purpose of showing that the defendant himself had violated rules in times past since this is not *per se* relevant. Indeed it would be necessary for an issue to exist as to whether Hackbart was the aggressor in order for such evidence to be relevant. In sum, having concluded that the trial court did not limit the case to a trial of the evidence bearing on defendant's liability but rather determined that as a matter of social policy the game was so violent and unlawful that valid lines could not be drawn, we take the view that this was not a proper issue for determination and that plaintiff was entitled to have the case tried on an assessment of his rights and whether they had been violated. The trial court has heard the evidence and has made findings. . . .

[REVERSED AND REMANDED]

NOTES

1. *Consent.* As defined by REST. 2D OF TORTS § 892, consent is "willingness in fact for conduct to occur." One who "effectively consents to conduct of another intended to invade his interests cannot recover in an action of tort . . . " *Id.* § 892A. The Restatement also recognizes that a plaintiff's consent to an illegal act should not be effective to bar a civil action for damages if the conduct has been criminalized to protect persons like the plaintiff from harm irrespective of their consent. *Id.* § 892(c). This provision eliminates consent as a complete defense to a civil action for damages. "Consent turns a trespass into a dinner party, a battery into a handshake, a theft into a gift, [and] an invasion of privacy into an intimate moment." Steven L. Wilborn, *Consenting Employees, Workplace Privacy, and the Role of Consent*, 66 LA. L. REV. 975, 1008 (2006), quoting Heide Hurd, *The Moral Magic of Consent*, 2 LEGAL THEORY 12, 123 (1996).

2. *Scope of Consent.* According to REST. 2D OF TORTS § 892A:

(1) One who effectively consents to conduct of another intended to invade his interests cannot recover in an action of tort for the conduct or for harm resulting from it.

(2) To be effective, consent must be

(a) by the one who has the capacity to consent or by a person empowered to consent for him, and

(b) to the particular conduct, or to substantially the same conduct.

(3) Conditional consent or consent restricted as to time, area or in other respects is effective only within the limits of the condition or restriction.

(4) If the actor exceeds the consent, it is not effective for the excess.

(5) Upon termination of consent its effectiveness is terminated, except as it may have become irrevocable by contract or otherwise, or except as its terms may include, expressly or by implication, a privilege to continue to act.

In Hellriegel v. Tholl, 417 P.2d 362 (Wash. 1966), a teenager named Dicka was injured when three of his friends attempted to throw him into a lake "during an afternoon spent in water-skiing, sunbathing, and engaging in horseplay." The court concluded that the scope of consent had not been exceeded:

[W]e have Dicka's own statement that he had joined in the pillow throwing and the grass throwing. Dicka also stated that he and the boy who fell on him . . . were used to wrestling together prior to this accident. Dicka was very athletic and this activity was regarded by all of the boys as "fun." Under the circumstances shown by the evidence, it would be a strained and unreasonable interpretation of Dicka's statement [Oh, you couldn't throw me in even if you tried] to the boys to construe it as a warning not to try to throw him into the lake, because he did not want to be thrown in, even in fun, and that he would resist such an attempt.

3. *Illegality & Consent.* In *Lee v. Nationwide Insurance Co.*, 497 S.E.2d 328 (Va. 1998), the court affirmed the trial court's holding as a matter of law that the defense of illegality barred the claim for damages of a 13-year-old boy injured in an accident involving a stolen automobile. The doctrine of illegality barring tort claims is indeterminate and difficult to apply. Should it depend upon whether the illegality is a serious crime? The defense of illegality of the plaintiff has an ancient lineage. The Latin phrase *ex turpi causa non oritur actio* can be translated as a cause of action may not be founded on an immoral or illegal act. The maxim was first used in contract cases and extended to tort claims. The Law Commission authored a Consultation Paper that reviewed cases utilizing the defense of illegality in England and Wales. THE LAW COMMISSION (CONSULTATION PAPER NO. 160), THE ILLEGALITY DEFENSE IN TORT: A CONSULTATION PAPER (2001) at 5. The Commission concluded that reform was "necessary, or at least advantageous to remedy . . . problems with the current operation of the law, as well as for purposes of clarity and consistency." *Id.* at 4–5. Should the illegality defense be extended to reach immoral behavior? The Commission concluded that the "operation of the illegality doctrine in tort cases is not confined to criminal illegality, but in principle can include other reprehensible or grossly immoral conduct." *Id.* What problems will a court have in applying a rule that would deny recovery for a tort claimant engaged in some immoral activity?

Should a burglar be able to recover if he is bitten by the burglarized householder's dog? *Id.* at 85. What about a safe cracker who blows himself up in a failed bank robbery? *Id.* What about a mere trespasser who is mauled by the householder's dog? *Id.* at 86. The Commission proposes a "policy-based structured discretion" to assist the court in deciding when illegality can be a defense. *Id.* at 8. It proposes that in a catastrophic injury case, a personal injury claimant's medical expenses will be borne by the taxpayer, family, or society rather than the wrongdoer. *Id.* at 10. How appropriate is the illegality doctrine in personal injury cases? The countervailing policy is that claimants should not "profit or benefit from their own wrongdoing." *Id.* at 84.

Is there a need for the doctrine of illegality in tort law? If the doctrine should not be abolished, is there any particular aspect of the law that is in need of reform? Jurisdictions adopting the illegality defense will exclude recovery to illegal conduct that tends to be serious:

> In recent decades, courts employed *ex turpi causa* to exclude recovery by plaintiffs whose conduct was perceived to be extremely grievous. For example, in *Barker v. Kallash*, 468 N.E.2d 39 (1984), a teenager was injured when a pipe-bomb that he was constructing using material supplied by the defendants exploded. The Court of Appeals of New York reasoned that, when the plaintiff's injury is a direct result of his knowing and intentional participation in a criminal act, he cannot seek compensation for the loss when the criminal act is judged to be so serious an offense as to warrant denial of recovery. Justice Jasen opined that the court would bar recovery only if the plaintiff's violation of the law was either gravely immoral or grievously injurious to the public interests, as is the case with rape or arson.

Ronen Perry, *The Role of Retributive Justice in the Common Law of Torts: A Descriptive Theory*, 73 TENN. L. REV. 177, 212 (2006).

A few states have created a statutory illegality defense that applies the doctrine only if a tort injury occurred during the commission of a felony. ALASKA STAT. § 09.65.210 (Michie Supp. 1989), for example, provides that:

> A person who suffers personal injury or death may not recover damages for the personal injury or death if the injuries or death occurred while the person was engaged in the commission of a felony, the person has been convicted of the felony, including conviction based on a guilty

plea or plea of *nolo contendere*, and the felony substantially contributed to the injury or death. . . .

See also FLA. ANN. STAT. 776.085 (providing defense to civil action for personal injury for participant in a felony). *Cf.* REST. 2D TORTS § 892C(2): "[C]onsent is effective to bar recovery in a tort action although the conduct consented to is a crime." Section 889 provides: "One is not barred from recovery . . . merely because at the time of the [defendant's interference] he was committing a tort or a crime. . . ." How do these positions differ? Suppose that the criminal conduct complained of exceeds the consent granted by the victim? Consider comment *c*, illustration 5: After an altercation, A and B agree to a fight with fists. In the course of the fight A draws a knife and stabs B. B's consent does not bar his recovery for the knife wound. *Id.* § 892C, cmt. *c*.

Is the issue in these cases really the narrow one of whether "consent" bars recovery, or is it a broader determination that tort consequences should not follow certain types of conduct? *See, e.g., Bowlan v. Lunsford,* 54 P.2d 666 (Okla.1936) (adult woman precluded on public policy grounds from pursuing battery action against sexual partner for inducing her to have pregnancy terminated).

4. *Failure of Consent as Battery or Negligence.* Treatment by a physician in a non-emergency that is rendered without the patient's informed consent is treated as a battery. In *Mohr v. Williams,* 104 N.W. 12 (Minn. 1905), a Minnesota jury awarded the plaintiff $14,322 for assault and battery consisting of an alleged unauthorized surgical operation performed by defendant upon plaintiff's ear. In *Mohr,* the patient consented to an operation on her right ear to remove a polyp and diseased tissue. She was not informed that her left ear was in any way diseased. During the operation to repair the left ear, the physician examined the left ear and discovered an even more serious condition. He then performed the operation of the plaintiff's left ear and removed a portion of the drum membrane, scraping away the diseased portion of the inner wall of the ear. The operation was skillfully performed but plaintiff claimed that the operation greatly impaired her hearing. The Minnesota Supreme Court affirmed the validity of her battery action, but remanded to determine whether there was a medical emergency justifying the physician's actions.

In *Doe v. High-Tech Institute, Inc.,* 972 P.2d 1060 (Colo. App. 1998), the plaintiff, a student in defendant's medical assistant training program, consented to a blood test by the defendant to test for rubella. Without plaintiff's knowledge, the defendant also tested the blood for HIV and found that plaintiff was HIV positive. The plaintiff sued the defendant alleging invasion of privacy, and the court held the plaintiff stated a cause of action.

5. *Fraud Vitiated Consent.* Consent obtained through the defendant's misrepresentation does not constitute a defense; the fraud "vitiates" the consent. REST. 2D OF TORTS § 892B states: if "the person consenting . . . is induced to consent by a substantial mistake concerning the nature of the invasion of his interests or the extent of the harm to be expected from it and the mistake is known to the other or is induced by the other's misrepresentation, the consent is not effective for the unexpected invasion or harm." Section 892B also provides that consent given under duress is not effective. The classic example of vitiated consent is supplied by § 892B cmt. *d*, illus. 7:

> A, believing B to be a physician, removes her clothing and permits B to lay hands on her person for the purpose of a medical examination. B is not a physician and knows that A believes him to be one. B is subject to liability to A for battery.

In *Hogan v. Tavzel*, 660 So. 2d 350 (Fla. 1996), the court imposed liability for battery against a husband who infected his wife with genital warts. He knew of his condition and failed to warn her. The court cited the Restatement which also took the view that consent to sexual intercourse was not consent to be infected with a venereal disease. *See also Kathleen K. v. Robert B.*, 198 Cal. Rptr. 273 (1984) (reversing judgment on pleadings in favor of defendant in case where plaintiff sought damages for contracting genital herpes during intercourse induced by false representations).

Incapacity to give consent also may vitiate consent. *See, e.g., Cardwell v. Bechtol*, 724 S.W.2d 739, 746 (Tenn. 1987) (age); *State v. Johnson*, 661 S.W.2d 854, 859 (Tenn. 1983) (intoxication); *Knight v. Lancaster*, 988 S.W.2d 172, 180 Tenn. Ct. App. 1998) (mental incompetency). Tennessee applies the rule of sevens as a yardstick in determining whether infants may consent. Under this approach a child under the age of seven has no capacity to consent; for a child between seven and fourteen there is a rebuttable presumption of no capacity; and for a youth between fourteen and twenty-one, there is a rebuttable presumption of capacity." *John Doe v. Mamo Taori's Premium Pizza*, No. M1998-00992-COA-R9-CV, 2001 WL 327906 (Tenn. Ct. App. Apr. 5, 2001).

6. *Substituted Consent.* The law generally protects a person's right to do what she wishes with her own body. Where the person is incapacitated the court's attempt to protect the person's right to autonomy by either recognizing a substitute decisionmaker or carrying out the person's previously expressed preferences. For example, the elderly hospital patient in *In re Westchester County Med. Center on Behalf of O'Connor*, 72 N.Y.2d 517 (1988), was mentally incompetent and unable to obtain food or drink without medical assistance. Her daughters objected to the insertion of a nasogastric tube to provide her with sustenance. The court ruled that a person has the right to decline medical treatment, even lifesaving treatment, unless there is an overriding state interest and therefore the plaintiffs asserted a valid tort claim.

7. *Consent & Gender Justice.* Professor Ellen Bublick describes how coercive conditions may negate consent in rape cases:

> The case of consent provides a useful example of the shared difficulties in criminal and civil case law. Like the troubling criminal law cases in which courts ignore coercive conditions surrounding consent to sex, in tort law too, courts have at times disregarded even the most coercive of circumstances. The recent Indiana Supreme Court opinion, *Robins v. Harris*, 769 N.E. 2d 586 (Ind. 2002) is illustrative. In *Robins*, a female county jail inmate charged that she had been sexually assaulted by a deputy at the jail. In a criminal action against him, the deputy admitted to sexual contact and pleaded guilty to misdemeanor official misconduct. In a tort suit stemming from the same conduct, the deputy

argued that the inmate consented to sex. The state appellate court ruled that the consent defense should have been barred. Although the case was settled before review, the Indiana Supreme Court nevertheless chose to affirm the appellate court's decision, 'except as to the availability of consent as a defense to the claim of battery,' leaving open the possibility that a jailer might raise the inmate's consent to sex as a defense in future cases.

In dissent, Justice Sullivan argued that the appellate court had been correct — consent should not furnish a defense where a detainee is involved. Ellen M. Bublick, *Tort Suits Filed by Rape and Sexual Assault Victim in Civil Courts: Lessons for Courts, Classrooms, and Constituencies*, 59 S.M.U. L. REV. 55, 81 (2006). Why does consent present such a challenge for sexual assault victims? In what ways do gender or age differences play a role in consent?

C. SELF-DEFENSE AND DEFENSE OF OTHERS

BRADLEY v. HUNTER
413 So. 2d 674 (La. Ct. App. 1982)

CUTRER, JUDGE.

The shooting death of J.W. Bradley (J.W.) took place at approximately 9.00 P.M., on May 14, 1980, in Campti, Louisiana. J.W. was shot by defendant, Aurila F. Hunter (Aurila), in front of the "Honeydripper Cafe" which is operated by Aurila and her mother, Ora Edwards (Ora), also named as a defendant in this suit.

Plaintiff, Susie Mae Bradley, "wife" of decedent, filed this suit on her own behalf and that of her four children seeking damages for the death of her "husband," and the loss of the children's father. J.W. is survived by four children, the last of which was born posthumously. . . . Aurila testified that J.W., a twenty-eight-year-old man, came into the "Honeydripper" around 9:00 to 9:30 P.M., May 14, 1980, wanting to purchase a soft drink ("coke"). Aurila is sixty-five years old, not in particularly good health, unmarried and lives with her eighty-two-year-old mother, Ora, who owns the cafe. Ora, a widow, also in poor health and under a doctor's care, works in the cafe with Aurila. No one else is employed in the restaurant. The cafe sells food, a little beer and no hard liquor.

Aurila testified at trial that she has had trouble with J.W. on at least two prior occasions and told him not to come into the cafe. That night J.W. entered wanting his "coke" but Aurila refused to serve him. Ora offered J.W. the "coke" but he refused. J.W. began to threaten and curse Aurila who restrained herself despite his cursing the two old women. She told him to go home. He did not leave until he had finished cursing and threatening Aurila.

A Smith & Wesson Model 10.38 caliber revolver was kept under the counter near the cash register. While J.W. remained in the store Aurila did not pick up the gun but she did so after he had left. J.W. walked out of the cafe cursing and threatening the women. After he had left, Ora went outside to see if J.W. had gone. Aurila went out onto the porch to see about her mother. As she stood on the porch, Aurila saw J.W. coming toward her, walking rapidly, as she said he had a tendency to do, with his arms flailing away, fists clenched, and cursing and threatening her. She then pulled the gun from her blouse pocket and told J.W. not to come to the cafe. She fired one warning shot (probably two, as three shots were fired but only one hit J.W.), and fired again whenever J.W. kept coming, walking fast, cursing and threatening Aurila. She fired from about thirty feet away; the bullet struck J.W. in the head, killing him.

Aurila testified that J.W. had threatened her two weeks before the incident in question, after she had refused to sell him some beer. She stated that he threatened to "get her" should she go outside to the mailbox. From that time until the incident in question, Aurila stated that she did not go to the mailbox for fear of J.W. She stated that she had known J.W. since he was a small child and knew of his reputation in the community. Aurila stated that she knew J.W. had previously shot a man in the back with a shotgun. Also, she saw him strike another person across the back with a crutch for refusing him a drink of wine. J.W.'s "wife" and aunt both stated that he had spent considerable periods of time in jail. Plaintiff stated that since they began living together in 1972 or 1973, he had spent over one-half of the time in prison. Deputy Dowden, an investigating officer, stated that he had known the decedent due to having received calls about him and his prior arrests. He further testified that J.W. was very belligerent toward the law enforcement officers; he had made threats to them and felt he was capable of carrying them out.

. . . As can be _____tiff, J.W. was considered to be less than a model citizen. He was known to have a quick temper and violent propensities. He was a young man of twenty-eight who had threatened, cursed and intimidated two old women aged sixty-five and eighty-two. At the time of the shooting J.W. was walking rapidly toward the two women, who were standing on their porch. He was cursing and throwing his arms about in a threatening manner. A warning both verbally and by a discharge of the gun failed to dissuade J.W. from his continued harassment of Aurila and Ora. Aurila fired again in fear of her and her mother's safety, killing J.W. Aurila stated that she was really fearful for her and her mother's safety at the time of the incident.

. . . The law applicable to a case of this kind is clear and well settled. In the case of *Roberts v. American Employers Ins. Co.,* 221 So. 2d 550 (La. Ct. App. 1969), this court stated as follows:

> The privilege of self-defense in tort actions is now well recognized by our jurisprudence. Where a person reasonably believes he is threatened with bodily harm, he may use whatever force appears to be reasonably necessary to protect against the threatened injury. . . . Of course, each case depends on its own facts, such as, for instance, the relative size, age and strength of the parties, their reputations for violence, who was the aggressor, the degree of physical harm reasonably feared and the presence or absence of weapons.

In summary, the trial judge found decedent, J.W. Bradley, to be a man *"of a pugnacious and aggressive nature, with a long record, ever since he had been an adult, and perhaps even before, a long record of violence, which brought him into contact with the law."* The trial judge pointed out that J.W. had spent about four of the last nine years in prison. J.W. had been warned on prior occasions to stay out of the "Honeydripper Cafe," yet he refused; he entered the cafe that fateful night cursing and threatening the two elderly women who operated it. He refused to leave, despite their request, until he had sufficiently cursed them. Aurila took the gun with her when she went onto the porch to see about her mother who had gone out to see if J.W. had left:

> Then, with the passage of some period of time, here he comes back again, rushing at her with his fists balled up and walking at her and threatening her, while she stood on her own porch. She warned him. Her testimony was that she told him, 'Go away.' She fired a warning shot. Even Mr. Kirkendoll, who was cold sober, according to his testimony, testified that the first shot did not hit Bradley. And his testimony was that Bradley was not hit and said something to her, or something of that nature. But, this didn't slow him down. He kept on coming at her. The evidence, as a whole, indicates to me that the decedent made Mrs. Hunter shoot him. And the finding of the Court is that this was a case of justifiable self-defense and the motion for the directed verdict is granted in favor of the defendant. The case is dismissed.

From our perusal of the record, we conclude that the trial court was correct in finding that Aurila acted in self-defense.

Plaintiff cites the case of *Brasseaux v. Girouard,* 269 So. 2d 590 (La. Ct. App. 1972), *writ denied,* 271 So. 2d 262 (La. 1973), as a basis for the contention that Aurila did not shoot in self-defense. We disagree. In *Brasseaux,* self-defense was disallowed. It is, however, clearly distinguishable from the case at hand.

In *Brasseaux,* the plaintiff and defendant were involved in a boundary dispute. On the day in question, during daylight hours, plaintiff and defendant each drove their vehicles to an open pasture. A fence separated the parties. Accompanying defendant in his pickup truck were four men: defendant's brother-in-law, a son-in-law and two nephews. Brasseaux was accompanied by one person who remained in the vehicle during the incident. Defendant got out of his truck with a shotgun and stood behind his truck as Brasseaux walked from his vehicle toward the fence. When Brasseaux was near the fence, defendant shot him while he was thirty-five feet away and had made no effort to cross the fence. The court observed as follows:

> . . . Girouard's position behind the truck near four relatives and armed with an automatic shotgun was ample protection from Brasseaux who was at least 35 feet away, alone and not making an attempt to cross the fence. To the argument that Girouard feared that Brasseaux's hidden hand concealed a weapon, we state that Girouard had the drop on Brasseaux and could have readily ascertained that Brasseaux was unarmed. . . . The court concluded . . . We do not feel that under the circumstances presented here a reasonable person would or could have believed in good faith that it was necessary for him to shoot plaintiff in self defense.

In the case at hand, Aurila and her mother did not have the protection of four men, the fence or truck. Under the circumstances of this case, Aurila, as a reasonable person, could have believed in good faith that it was necessary for her to shoot J.W. to prevent bodily harm to her and/or her mother.

[AFFIRMED.]

NOTES

1. *Reasonableness in Self-Defense.* The concept of reasonableness is key to understanding self-defense, defense of others, and defense of property. REST. 2D TORTS §613 states:

> (1) An actor is privileged to use reasonable force, not intended or likely to cause death or serious bodily harm, to defend himself against unprivileged harmful or offensive contact or other bodily harm which he reasonably believes that another is about to inflict intentionally upon him.

> (2) Self-defense is privileged under the conditions stated in Subsection (1) although the actor correctly or reasonably believes that he can avoid the necessity of so defending himself,

>> (a) by retreating or otherwise giving up a right or privilege, or

>> (b) by complying with a command with which the actor is under no duty to comply or which the other is not privileged to enforce by the means threatened.

A person may use reasonable force in self-defense even if she could have avoided the need to use force by retreating or taking some other action. Self defense, as in the criminal law, gives everyone a privilege to take reasonable steps to defend herself. In *Hunter* above, Aurila was permitted to use deadly force. Did Aurila have a duty to retreat? Force intended to inflict death or serious bodily injury is only available if the individual reasonably believes she would suffer serious bodily injury or death if she did not repel the attack. Did Aurila fear for her own safety? REST. 2D TORTS §65(1). Alaska's model jury instruction on deadly force states:

> A person may not, even in self-defense, use that amount of force likely to inflict death or serious bodily harm on another person unless (he/she) reasonably believes that (he/she) is in danger of death or serious bodily harm and there is no other reasonable means of defense. A person may not use force likely to inflict death or serious bodily harm if there is a reasonable way for (him/her) to escape the danger by retreating. [However, a person need not retreat from (his/her) own home if (he/she) is not the initial aggressor.] Alaska Jury Instruction, §12.08, Assault or Battery — Self Defense, Deadly Force.

2. *Limitations on the Right of Self-Defense.* The privilege to use force to defend one's self is narrowly circumscribed. When the assault or battery is no longer threatened, the privilege ends. One may use only reasonable force, i.e., the force that reasonably appears necessary to protect against the threatened harm. A person may not use force likely to cause death or great bodily harm unless he has a reasonable apprehension of suffering the same kind of harm from the threatened conduct.

In *Courvoisier v. Raymond,* 47 P. 284 (Colo. 1896), the defendant repelled some rioters, who broke into his house at night, by firing a pistol at them. The firing attracted the plaintiff, a police officer, whom the defendant shot as the plaintiff was proceeding toward him, the defendant mistaking the plaintiff for one of the rioters. The trial judge instructed the jury that if they believed that at the time the defendant shot the plaintiff, the plaintiff was not assaulting the defendant, then their verdict should be for the plaintiff. The appellate court held this instruction was erroneous because there was riot in progress, and the circumstances were such that a reasonable man could believe that his life was in danger, or that he was in danger of receiving great bodily harm.

Assume that defendant did make a reasonable mistake as to the identity of the assailant, but then opened fire from his premises with a semi-automatic weapon, spraying the crowd outside. What issues arise in the actions brought by those injured?

Self-defense does not extend to retaliation. "A, a small boy, throws a snowball at B, hitting B in the eye and causing him severe pain. B is not privileged to inflict a beating upon A either as a punishment or as a warning against similar misconduct in the future." REST. 2D TORTS § 63, illus. 4. Reasonableness must be proportional to the peril:

> The contact or other bodily harm which the actor is privileged to inflict in self-defense must be reasonable; that is, it must not be dispropor-tionate in extent to the harm from which the actor is seeking to protect himself. A degree of force may be privileged to ward off a blow which threatens substantial harm, where the same degree of force would not be privileged merely to prevent touching in an insulting manner. REST. 2D TORTS § 63, cmt. *j*. Self-defense is privileged only if there is a necessity.

As the Restatement notes, in order for self-defense to be assertable:

> [T]he actor [must] reasonably believe that the apprehended offensive contact or bodily harm can be safely prevented only by the immediate infliction of such offensive contact or bodily harm upon the other. . . . [T]he actor is privileged to use force in his own defense only as a last resort. He is not privileged to use such force so long as there is a reasonable likelihood that the other will abandon his aggressive purpose or that the actor will have a later opportunity to protect himself. Therefore, he is privileged to defend himself only when the other actually or apparently threatens an immediate attack upon him, unless the other's conduct puts the actor in reasonable apprehension of an attack in the near future and the circumstances are such that it reasonably appears to the actor that the other's purpose is fixed and that there will be no later opportunity of preventing the attack. Save in this situation, there is no privilege to disarm another who threatens a future attack upon the actor or otherwise to disable him from carrying his purpose into

effect, since there is always the chance that the other may abandon his purpose, and if he does not, that the actor will have an opportunity of repelling the attack when it becomes imminent.

REST. 2D TORTS § 63, cmt. *k*.

In general, the law of torts imposes no general duty of retreat. A person may stand her ground and repel attacks with reasonable force, even if the attack does not threaten serious harm or death. Fifteen states have enacted tort reforms expanding the right of self-defense since 2005. These state statutes permit crime victims to use deadly force "in situations that might formerly have subjected them to prosecution for murder." Adam Liptak, *15 States Expand Right to Shoot in Self-Defense*, THE N.Y. TIMES (Aug. 7, 2006) at 1. Should these laws be labeled "stand your ground laws" or "shoot first laws."

3. *Defense of Others.* REST. 2D TORTS § 76 provides:

The actor is privileged to defend a third person from a harmful or offensive contact or other invasion of his interests of personality under the same conditions and by the same means as those under and by which he is privileged to defend himself if the actor correctly or reasonably believes that:

(a) the circumstances are such as to give the third person a privilege of self-defense, and

(b) his intervention is necessary for the protection of the third person.

The Restatement represents the majority rule. Under the minority rule, the actor takes the risk of whether the person on whose behalf he interferes is actually privileged to defend himself. The court in *Wardlaw v. Pickett,* 1 F.3d 1297 (D.C. Cir. 1993), held that justifiable defense of another was a defense to a tort action brought against the intervening defender, but that the defender could not use the justified intervention as a basis for suing the attacker for injuries received in the intervention. This holding is contrary to cases that allow justified intervention as a basis for the intervenor to sue in tort for resulting injuries. *See Dixon v. Richer*, 922 F.2d 1456 (10th Cir. 1991) (explaining that the plaintiff's characterization of a kick could be reconceptualized as a "reasonable act" intended to prepare arrestee for a pat down); *Gortarez v. Smitty's Super Valu, Inc.*, 680 P.2d 807 (Ariz. 1984) (reversing the trial court's directed verdict for the defendants and holding that the jury should determine whether a shopkeeper's detention had been undertaken for a proper purpose and in a reasonable manner).

4. *Mistake as a Tort Defense.* The majority of jurisdictions give the defendant a privilege to use reasonable force to protect a third party whenever the actor reasonably believes a third party is entitled to exercise self-defense. REST. 2D TORTS § 76. A reasonable mistake does not excuse force that is directed against an innocent party to protect property. REST. 2D TORTS § 77. Suppose a person mistakenly trespasses on A's land, and then mistakenly undertakes to defend herself against A — both mistakes being reasonably made? *See* REST. 2D TORTS § 72. (An actor is not privileged to defend against force which another is privileged to use, unless the other's privilege is based on a reasonable mistake of fact not caused by the actors fault).

D. DEFENSE OF PROPERTY

KATKO v. BRINEY
183 N.W. 2d 657 (Iowa 1971)

MOORE, CHIEF JUSTICE.

. . . Most of the facts are not disputed. In 1957 defendant Bertha L. Briney inherited her parents' farm land in Mahaska and Monroe Counties. Included was an 80-acre tract in southwest Mahaska County where her grandparents and parents had lived. No one occupied the house thereafter. Her husband, Edward, attempted to care for the land. He kept no farm machinery thereon. The outbuildings became dilapidated.

For about 10 years, 1957 to 1967, there occurred a series of trespassing and housebreaking events with loss of some household items, the breaking of windows and "messing up of the property in general." The latest occurred June 8, 1967, prior to the event on July 16, 1967 herein involved.

Defendants through the years boarded up the windows and doors in an attempt to stop the intrusions. They had posted "no trespass" signs on the land several years before 1967. The nearest one was 35 feet from the house. On June 11, 1967 defendants set "a shotgun trap" in the north bedroom. After Mr. Briney cleaned and oiled his 20-gauge shotgun, the power of which he was well aware, defendants took it to the old house where they secured it to an iron bed with the barrel pointed at the bedroom door. It was rigged with wire from the doorknob to the gun's trigger so it would fire when the door was opened. Briney first pointed the gun so an intruder would be hit in the stomach but at Mrs. Briney's suggestion it was lowered to hit the legs. He admitted he did so "because I was mad and tired of being tormented" but "he did not intend to injure anyone." He gave no explanation of why he used a loaded shell and set it to hit a person already in the house. Tin was nailed over the bedroom window. The spring gun could not be seen from the outside. No warning of its presence was posted.

. . . Prior to July 16, 1967 plaintiff and McDonough had been to the premises and found several old bottles and fruit jars which they took and added to their collection of antiques. On the latter date about 9.30 p.m. they made a second trip to the Briney property. They entered the old house by removing a board from a porch window which was without glass. While McDonough was looking around the kitchen area plaintiff went to another part of the house. As he started to open the north bedroom door the shotgun went off striking him in the right leg above the ankle bone. Much of his leg, including part of the tibia, was blown away. Only by McDonough's assistance was plaintiff able to get out of the house and after crawling some distance was put in his vehicle and rushed to a doctor and then to a hospital. He remained in the hospital 40 days.

. . . There was undenied medical testimony plaintiff had a permanent deformity, a loss of tissue, and a shortening of the leg. . . . Plaintiff testified he knew he had no right to break into and enter the house with intent to steal bottles and fruit jars therefrom. He further testified he had entered a plea of guilty to larceny in the nighttime of property of less than $20 value from a private building. He stated he had been fined $50 and costs and paroled during good behavior from a 60-day jail sentence. Other than minor traffic charges, this was plaintiff's first brush with the law. . . . The main thrust of defendants' defense in the trial court and on this appeal is that "the law permits use of a spring gun in a dwelling or warehouse for the purpose of preventing the unlawful entry of a burglar or thief. . . ."

In the statement of issues the trial court stated plaintiff and his companion committed a felony when they broke into and entered defendants' house. In instruction 2 the court referred to the early case history of the use of spring guns and stated under the law their use was prohibited except to prevent the commission of felonies of violence and where human life is in danger. The instruction included a statement that breaking and entering is not a felony of violence.

Instruction 5 stated: "You are hereby instructed that one may use reasonable force in the protection of his property, but such right is subject to the qualification that one may not use such means of force as will take human life or inflict great bodily injury. Such is the rule even though the injured party is a trespasser and is in violation of the law himself."

Instruction 6 stated: "An owner of premises is prohibited from willfully or intentionally injuring a trespasser by means of force that either takes life or inflicts great bodily injury; and therefore a person owning a premise is prohibited from setting out 'spring guns' and like dangerous devices which will likely take life or inflict great bodily injury, for the purpose of harming trespassers. The fact that the trespasser may be acting in violation of the law does not change the rule. The only time when such conduct of setting a 'spring gun' or a like dangerous device is justified would be when the trespasser was committing a felony of violence or a felony punishable by death, or where the trespasser was endangering human life by his act."

Instruction 7, to which defendants made no objection or exception, stated: "To entitle the plaintiff to recover for compensatory damages, the burden of proof is upon him to establish by a preponderance of the evidence each and all of the following propositions:

1. That defendants erected a shotgun trap in a vacant house on land owned by defendant, Bertha L. Briney, on or about June 11, 1967, which fact was known only by them, to protect household goods from trespassers and thieves.

2. That the force used by defendants was in excess of that force reasonably necessary and which persons are entitled to use in the protection of their property.

3. That plaintiff was injured and damaged and the amount thereof.

4. That plaintiff's injuries and damages resulted directly from the discharge of the shotgun trap which was set and used by defendants.

The overwhelming weight of authority, both textbook and case law, supports the trial court's statement of the applicable principles of law.

PROSSER ON TORTS, Third Edition, pages 116–118, states:

> . . . the law has always placed a higher value upon human safety than upon mere rights in property, it is the accepted rule that there is no privilege to use any force calculated to cause death or serious bodily injury to repel the threat to land or chattels, unless there is also such a threat to the defendant's personal safety as to justify self-defense. . . . [S]pring guns and other man-killing devices are not justifiable against a mere trespasser, or even a petty thief. They are privileged only upon those whom the landowner, if he were present in person would be free to inflict injury of the same kind."

REST. 2D TORTS § 85 states:

> "The value of human life and limb, not only to the individual concerned but also to society, so outweighs the interest of a possessor of land in excluding from it those whom he is not willing to admit thereto that a possessor of land has, as is stated in § 79, no privilege to use force intended or likely to cause death or serious harm against another whom the possessor sees about to enter his premises or meddle with his chattel, unless the intrusion threatens death or serious bodily harm to the occupiers or users of the premises. . . . A possessor of land cannot do indirectly and by a mechanical device that which, were he present, he could not do immediately and in person. Therefore, he cannot gain a privilege to install, for the purpose of protecting his land from intrusions harmless to the lives and limbs of the occupiers or users of it, a mechanical device whose only purpose is to inflict death or serious harm upon such as may intrude, by giving notice of his intention to inflict, by mechanical means and indirectly, harm which he could not, even after request, inflict directly were he present."

In Volume 2, HARPER AND JAMES, THE LAW OF TORTS, section 27.3, pages 1440, 1441, this is found: "The possessor of land may not arrange his premises intentionally so as to cause death or serious bodily harm to a trespasser. The possessor may of course take some steps to repel a trespass. If he is present he may use force to do so, but only that amount which is reasonably necessary to effect the repulse. Moreover if the trespass threatens harm to property only — even a theft of property — the possessor would not be privileged to use deadly force, he may not arrange his premises so that such force will be inflicted by mechanical means. If he does, he will be liable even to a thief who is injured by such device."

. . . The facts in *Allison v. Fiscus,* 156 Ohio St. 120, 100 N.E.2d 237, decided in 1951, are very similar to the case at bar. There plaintiff's right to damages was recognized for injuries received when he feloniously broke a door latch and started to enter defendant's warehouse with intent to steal. As he entered a trap of two sticks of dynamite buried under the doorway by defendant owner was set off and plaintiff [was] seriously injured. The court held the question whether a particular trap was justified as a use of reasonable and necessary force against a trespasser engaged in the commission of a felony should have been submitted to the jury. The Ohio Supreme Court recognized plaintiff's right to recover punitive or exemplary damages in addition to compensatory damages.

. . . In addition to civil liability many jurisdictions hold a landowner criminally liable for serious injuries or homicide caused by spring guns or other set devices. . . .The legal principles stated by the trial court in instructions 2, 5 and 6 are well established and supported by the authorities cited and quoted *supra*. There is no merit in defendants' objections and exceptions thereto. Defendants' various motions based on the same reasons stated in exceptions to instructions were properly overruled. . . . This opinion is not to be taken or construed as authority that the allowance of punitive damages is or is not proper under circumstances such as exist here. We hold only that question of law not having been properly raised cannot in this case be resolved. . . . [AFFIRMED].

NOTES

1. *Sequels.* Subsequent to the decision in *Katko*, 183 N.W. 2d 657, the Nebraska legislature passed a law providing in part that "no person . . . shall be placed in jeopardy . . . for protecting, by any means necessary, himself, his family, or his real or personal property." However, the statute was held unconstitutional in *State v. Goodseal*, 186 Neb. 359, 183 N.W.2d 258, *cert. den.*, 404 U.S. 845 (1971). The court held the statute unconstitutionally delegated to the defender the power to determine the amount and extent of force to be used in self-defense, this power being placed exclusively in the legislature by the state constitution. For an enlightening commentary on *Katko v. Briney*, see Rt. Hon. Sir Geoffrey Palmer, *The Iowa Spring Gun Case: A Study in American Gothic*, 56 IOWA L. REV. 1219 (1971).

Assume that a landlord boarded up her disused property and set spring guns because she was concerned that criminals might use the property to commit violent crimes. Would defendant be liable if the spring gun went off and shot a rapist and murderer who was dragging a potential victim into the room to rape and murder? Should she?

Does the existence of a criminal penalty provide a sufficient deterrence in cases such as this? *See People v. Ceballos*, 526 P.2d 241 (Ca. 1974) (assault with deadly weapon conviction appropriate against property owner who set trap gun to prevent burglarizing of garage where he sometimes slept but was not sleeping when his victim attempted to burglarize premises; the "if he were present" exception was inappropriate for criminal law, the court said, and there was no threat of death or serious bodily harm).

How would a case such as *Katko v. Briney* be decided in a state with a statute such as the Alaska provision discussed in note 3 following *Colby v. McClendon* above?

2. *Defense of Property Cum Defense of Person.* This defense rests on an actor's reasonable belief of imminent and immediate danger and justifiable self-defense, defense of others or defense of property. However, deadly force or force likely to cause bodily harm is ordinarily not justified merely in defense of property, as in ejecting a trespasser or recovering a chattel. *Calvillo-Silva v. Home Grocery,* 48 Cal. App. 4th 889, 909 (App. Ct. 1996). Recall that in *Courvoisier v. Raymond,* 23 Colo. 113 (1896), discussed in the notes following *Bradley v. Hunter, supra,* the defendant opened fire from his premises upon someone he thought was a trespasser. Why was he permitted to use such deadly force?

3. *Less-Threatening Mechanical Devices.* The result in *Katko v. Briney* is endorsed by REST. 2D TORTS § 85. Note, however, REST. 2D TORTS § 84:

> The actor is so far privileged to employ, for the purpose of protecting his possession of land or chattels from intrusion, a device not intended or likely to cause death or serious bodily harm that he is not liable for bodily harm done thereby to a deliberate intruder, if:
>
> > (a) the use of such a device is reasonably necessary to protect the land or chattels from intrusion, and
> >
> > (b) the use of the particular device is reasonable under the circumstances, and
> >
> > (c) the device is one customarily used for such a purpose, or reasonable care is taken to make its use known to probable intruders.

What mechanical devices are contemplated by this provision? What criteria will you apply to determine reasonableness in subsections (a)-(c)? What judicial value preferences may be reflected in the application of "reasonable" in this situation? Should a "balancing" approach such as that used in § 84 be extended to the classic spring gun case? *See generally* Richard A. Posner, *Killing or Wounding to Protect a Property Interest,* 14 J.L. & ECON. 201, 214–17 (1971).

4. *Repelling Trespassers.* A person cannot repel a mere trespass on his land by the taking of life, or proceed beyond what necessity requires. "The law, out of tenderness for human life and the frailties of human nature, will not permit the taking of it to repel a mere trespass." *Beard v. United States,* 158 U.S. 550, 561 (1895). The criminal law has a similar rule for repelling trespassers. If a deadly weapon is used in repelling trespassers, the property possessor will be liable for murder or manslaughter depending upon the circumstances According to REST. 2D TORTS § 77:

> An actor is privileged to use reasonable force, not intended or likely to cause death or serious bodily harm, to prevent or terminate another's intrusion upon the actor's land or chattels, if :
>
> (a) the intrusion is not privileged or the other intentionally or negligently causes the actor to believe that it is not privileged, and
>
> (b) the actor reasonably believes that the intrusion can be prevented or terminated only by the force used, and

(c) the actor has first requested the other to desist and the other has disregarded the request, or the actor reasonably believes that a request will be useless or that substantial harm will be done before it can be made.

5. *Defense of Personal Property.* The majority rule is that one can only use what reasonable force may be necessary to effectively prevent the unlawful taking or detention of property." *Donnell v. Great Atlantic & Pacific Tea Co.,* 156 So. 844 (Ala. 1934). The retaking of previously dispossessed chattels ("recaption") is governed by REST. 2D TORTS §§ 101–106. The defense is dependent upon tortious taking of the chattel by the plaintiff, typically without "claim of right," REST. 2D TORTS § 101, the immediate right to possession of the chattel by the defendant, § 102, and the defendant's attempted retaking occurring promptly after the dispossession, § 103. Consistent with other "self-help" activities associated with the protection of property, the Restatement encourages a pre-action demand, § 104, and prohibits force likely to cause death or serious injury, § 106. For example, in *Godwin v. Stanely,* 331 S.W.2d 341, 342 (Tex. Civ. App. 1959), an altercation began when defendant sought to repossess an accordion he had sold to plaintiffs. In affirming plaintiffs' judgment based upon battery, the court wrote that:

> We think this record clearly shows that the appellant [defendant] went to the home of appellees [plaintiff] with the idea of taking the accordion regardless of any protests on the part of the appellees . . . [W]hen [defendant] insisted on looking for the accordion, and Mrs. Stanley ordered him from her home, he refused to leave, but started into the bedroom and then she stepped into the door and refused to permit him to proceed — this is what provoked the difficulty. We think she had this right . . . If appellees were delinquent in their payments the appellant had a legal remedy to get possession of the accordion. The taking of such possession, however, must be by legal action or must be effected peaceably; that is, the exercise of force or violence will not be permitted.

Id. at 342.

E.   NECESSITY

HARRISON v. WISDOM
54 Tenn. 99 (1872)

SNEED, JUSTICE.

The defendants were, on the 17th of February, 1862, citizens of the city of Clarksville, and were present and participated in the proceedings of a public meeting of the citizens of said city, convened at the Mayor's office on that day. The meeting was called to concert measures for the protection of the people of said city in anticipation of an immediate invasion by the Federal forces, to whom Fort Donelson, which seems to have been regarded as the military key to Clarksville, had surrendered on the day preceding. The city of Clarksville was about thirty miles distant from Fort Donelson, and the occupation of the city was expected as the immediate result of the capitulation of the fort. There was at the time in the hands of merchants and dealers in the city a large quantity of whiskey and other spirituous liquors, which it was supposed would imperil the lives and property of the inhabitants if it should fall into the hands of the Federal soldiery, then flushed with victory and inflamed with the evil passions of civil war.

It was therefore resolved by the citizens, convened as aforesaid, to destroy said spirituous liquors, as a measure of safety, and to recommend to the common council of said city, and to the county authorities, to levy a special tax upon the people in order to raise a fund for the reimbursement of those whose property should be thus destroyed. To this end agents were appointed to advise the owners of the resolution aforesaid, to invoke their acquiescence and to carry out the objects of the meeting. The plaintiff was the owner of a considerable quantity of whiskey, brandy, and wine stored in said city, and he was called upon by one of the agents, who advised him of the action of the meeting, and he thereupon delivered his key to his salesman, with instructions to deliver the liquors to the agent, by whom it was destroyed.

This action was brought by the plaintiff . . . to recover of defendants, who were among the citizens composing said meeting, the value of the liquors so destroyed. The cause was submitted to a jury on the general issue and the defendants' special plea of public necessity, and resulted in a verdict and judgment for the defendants, from which the plaintiff has appealed in error. . . .

We come now to consider the last and most important question involved in this case, and that is, whether the law of the case was correctly expounded to the jury. The defendants insist that at the time of the alleged trespass upon the plaintiff's property there existed an absolute public necessity for its destruction. The right of defense and self-preservation is a right inherent in communities as well as individuals. Whether an imminent and absolute necessity exists to destroy private property for the common good, is a question to be determined by a jury upon the facts of each particular case. An individual may take life to preserve his own, if he be in danger of death or great bodily harm, or think himself so upon reasonable grounds. But the grounds of his apprehension must be founded upon such facts as will acquit him of acting upon a mere fancied peril or with reckless incaution.

The law is jealous in the protection it throws around human life and property, and the right to take either as a measure of self-preservation is to be exercised in a moment of extraordinary exigency when the private or public necessity absolutely demands it. The right to destroy property in cases of extreme emergency, as to prevent the spread of a conflagration, or as in the case now under consideration, is not the exercise of the right of eminent domain, nor the taking of property for public use, but a right existing at common law, founded on necessity, and it may be exercised by individuals in any proper case, free from all liability for the value of the property destroyed. . . .

[F]amiliar examples are cited in the English books, as where the plaintiff's dog was killed in the act of pursuing the defendant's deer in his park, or rabbits in his warren, or poultry within his own grounds, this will justify the killing without the proof of any higher necessity. 2 Greenl. Ev., s. 630; 3 Lev., 28; Cro. Jac., 45; 1 Campb., 41; 11 East, 568. We have cited these general principles in the language of the books, to illustrate as nearly as possible the nature and character of that necessity which will justify the destruction of private property in like cases. It is difficult to define it except in general terms and each case must depend upon its own facts. An unsubstantial panic is not such a necessity, but such a state of facts must be shown as to leave no doubt of an impending and imminent peril, or that a reasonable ground existed for the apprehension of such a peril, to justify the act; or in the language of Mr. Greenleaf already cited, if the defendant justifies the destruction of the plaintiff's property by the defense of his own he must show he could not otherwise preserve his own property. 2 Greenl. Ev., 630. The advance of the hostile army is cited as among the exigencies when such a necessity might exist to justify the destruction of private property. But what kind of private property may be thus destroyed would depend much upon the character of the warfare waged at the time, and upon the circumstances existing in the community.

Thus the destruction of a bridge or a boat, to check the advance of an army, or the explosion of a magazine of powder, or the destruction of munitions of war or military supplies, or any articles contraband or war, would be but the exercise of a recognized belligerent right, and the rapid advance of a hostile army known to be undisciplined and licentious, and whose occupation of captured places in the line of march was known to be accompanied by acts of besotted vandalism, imperiling the lives and property of the people, would upon the ground of public necessity justify the destruction of such property as is calculated to increase the public peril. But all these facts must enter into the consideration of the question whether the public peril did exist, or whether there were reasonable and substantial grounds to believe so. Necessity, says Lord Coke, makes that lawful which would be otherwise unlawful. 8 Coke, 69. It is the law of a particular time and place. Hale P.C., 54. It overcomes the law. Hob., 144; and it defends what it compels. Hale P.C., 54. In these brief maxims is written the whole reason of the law that justifies the destruction of private property for the public good. We are unable to discover wherein his honor the Circuit Judge has made any material departure from the principles herein announced, either in his general or supplemental charge. [REVERSED]

VINCENT v. LAKE ERIE TRANSPORTATION CO.
109 Minn. 456 (1910)

O'BRIEN, JUSTICE.

The steamship Reynolds, owned by the defendant, was for the purpose of discharging her cargo on November 27, 1905, moored to plaintiffs' dock in Duluth. While the unloading of the boat was taking place a storm from the northeast developed, which at about ten o'clock p.m., when the unloading was completed, had so grown in violence that the wind was then moving at fifty miles per hour and continued to increase during the night. There is some evidence that one, and perhaps two, boats were able to enter the harbor that night, but it is plain that navigation was practically suspended from the hour mentioned until the morning of the twenty ninth, when the storm abated, and during that time no master would have been justified in attempting to navigate his vessel, if he could avoid doing so. After the discharge of the cargo the Reynolds signaled for a tug to tow her from the dock, but none could be obtained because of the severity of the storm. If the lines holding the ship to the dock had been cast off, she would doubtless have drifted away; but, instead, the lines were kept fast, and as soon as one parted or chafed it was replaced, sometimes with a larger one. The vessel lay upon the outside of the dock, her bow to the east, the wind and waves striking her starboard quarter with such force that she was constantly being lifted and thrown against the dock, resulting in its damage, as found by the jury, to the amount of $500.

We are satisfied that the character of the storm was such that it would have been highly imprudent for the master of the Reynolds to have attempted to leave the dock or to have permitted his vessel to drift away from it. One witness testified upon the trial that the vessel could have been warped into a slip, and that, if the attempt to bring the ship into the slip had failed, the worst that could have happened would be that the vessel would have been blown ashore upon a soft and muddy bank. The witness was not present in Duluth at the time of the storm, and, while he may have been right in his conclusions, those in charge of the dock and the vessel at the time of the storm were not required to use the highest human intelligence, nor were they required to resort to every possible experiment which could be suggested for the preservation of their property. Nothing more was demanded of them than ordinary prudence and care, and the record in this case fully sustains the contention of the appellant that, in holding the vessel fast to the dock, those in charge of her exercised good judgment and prudent seamanship.

It is claimed by the respondent that it was negligence to moor the boat at an exposed part of the wharf, and to continue in that position after it became apparent that the storm was to be more than usually severe. We do not agree with this position. The part of the wharf where the vessel was moored appears to have been commonly used for that purpose. It was situated within the harbor at Duluth, and must, we think, be considered a proper and safe place, and would undoubtedly have been such during what would be considered a very severe storm. The storm which made it unsafe was one which surpassed in violence any which might have reasonably been anticipated.

The appellant contends . . . that, because its conduct during the storm was rendered necessary by prudence and good seamanship under conditions over which it had no control, it cannot be held liable for any injury resulting to the property of others, and claims that the jury should have been so instructed. An analysis of the charge given by the trial court is not necessary, as in our opinion the only question for the jury was the amount of damages which the plaintiffs were entitled to recover, and no complaint is made upon that score.

The situation was one in which the ordinary rules regulating property rights were suspended by forces beyond human control, and if, without the direct intervention of some act by the one sought to be held liable, the property of another was injured, such injury must be attributed to the act of God, and not to the wrongful act of the person sought to be charged. If during the storm the Reynolds had entered the harbor, and while there had become disabled and been thrown against the plaintiffs' dock, the plaintiffs could not have recovered. Again, if while attempting to hold fast to the dock the lines had parted, without any negligence, and the vessel carried against some other boat or dock in the harbor, there would be no liability upon her owner. But here those in charge of the vessel deliberately and by their direct efforts held her in such a position that the damage to the dock resulted, and, having thus preserved the ship at the expense of the dock, it seems to us that her owners are responsible to the dock owners to the extent of the injury inflicted.

In *Depue v. Flateau,* 100 Minn. 299 (1907), this court held that where the plaintiff, while lawfully in the defendants' house, became so ill that he was incapable of traveling with safety, the defendants were responsible to him in damages for compelling him to leave the premises. If, however, the owner of the premises had furnished the traveler with proper accommodations and medical attendance, would he have been able to defeat an action brought against him for their reasonable worth?

In *Ploof v. Putnam,* 81 Vt. 471 (1908), the Vermont Supreme Court held that where, under stress of weather, a vessel was without permission moored to a private dock at an island in Lake Champlain owned by the defendant, the plaintiff was not guilty of trespass, and that the defendant was responsible in damages because his representative upon the island unmoored the vessel, permitting it to drift upon the shore, with resultant injuries to it. If, in that case, the vessel had been permitted to remain, and the dock had suffered an injury, we believe the shipowner would have been held liable for the injury done.

Theologians hold that a starving man may, without moral guilt, take what is necessary to sustain life; but it could hardly be said that the obligation would not be upon such person to pay the value of the property so taken when he became able to do so. And so public necessity, in times of war or peace, may require the taking of private property for public purposes; but under our system of jurisprudence compensation must be made.

Let us imagine in this case that for the better mooring of the vessel those in charge of her had appropriated a valuable cable lying upon the dock. No matter how justifiable such appropriation might have been, it would not be claimed that, because of the overwhelming necessity of the situation, the owner of the cable could not recover its value.

This is not a case where life or property was menaced by any object or thing belonging to the plaintiffs, the destruction of which became necessary to prevent the threatened disaster. Nor is it a case where, because of the act of God, or unavoidable accident, the infliction of the injury was beyond the control of the defendant, but is one where the defendant prudently and advisedly availed itself of the plaintiffs' property for the purpose of preserving its own more valuable property, and the plaintiffs are entitled to compensation for the injury done. Order Affirmed.

LEWIS, JUSTICE, dissenting.

I dissent. It was assumed on the trial before the lower court that appellant's liability depended on whether the master of the ship might, in the exercise of reasonable care, have sought a place of safety before the storm made it impossible to leave the dock. The majority opinion assumes that the evidence is conclusive that appellant moored its boat at respondents' dock pursuant to contract, and that the vessel was lawfully in position at the time the additional cables were fastened to the dock, and the reasoning of the opinion is that, because appellant made use of the stronger cables to hold the boat in position, it became liable under the rule that it had voluntarily made use of the property of another for the purpose of saving its own.

In my judgment, if the boat was lawfully in position at the time the storm broke, and the master could not, in the exercise of due care, have left that position without subjecting his vessel to the hazards of the storm, then the damage to the dock, caused by the pounding of the boat, was the result of an inevitable accident. If the master was in the exercise of due care, he was not at fault. The reasoning of the opinion admits that if the ropes, or cables, first attached to the dock had not parted, or if, in the first instance, the master had used the stronger cables, there would be no liability. If the master could not, in the exercise of reasonable care, have anticipated the severity of the storm and sought a place of safety before it became impossible, why should he be required to anticipate the severity of the storm, and, in the first instance, use the stronger cables?

I am of the opinion that one who constructs a dock to the navigable line of waters, and enters into contractual relations with the owner of a vessel to moor the same, takes the risk of damage to his dock by a boat caught there by a storm, which event could not have been avoided in the exercise of due care, and further, that the legal status of the parties in such a case is not changed by renewal of cables to keep the boat from being cast adrift at the mercy of the tempest.

NOTES

1. *Public vs. Private Necessity.* Public necessity is entry onto the land of another for the public purposes whereas private necessity is entry to protect one's own property or personal safety. "Entry of property in emergencies, for reasons of public necessity, or to avert disaster such as fire or flood, is privileged and does not constitute a trespass." *Galarza v. Pettit*, 2003 Cal. App. (Unpub. LEXIS) 11454 (Ct. of App. 2003). Public necessity is an emergency exception to property rights. The emergency exception arises when damage to private property is inflicted by government out of public necessity to avert impending peril. *Thousand Trails, Inc. v. California Reclamation Dist.*,124 Cal. App. 4th 450 (2004) (affirming no liability in flood emergency where government made a cut in levee to divert raging water, thereby causing further flooding of plaintiff's campground). The doctrine of public necessity allows the government to take or damage private property without compensation if such action is necessary to address an immediate danger to public health, safety or morals. Courts narrowly construe the type of emergency since the plaintiff receives no compensation. The concern is that public necessity shields government entities from inverse condemnation liability. The Restatement provides:

(1) Except as stated in Subsection (2), the liability of a possessor of land to one who enters the land only in the exercise of a privilege, for either a public or a private purpose, and irrespective of the possessor's consent, is the same as the liability to a licensee.

(2) The liability of a possessor of land to a public officer or employee who enters the land in the performance of his public duty, and suffers harm because of a condition of a part of the land held open to the public, is the same as the liability to an invitee.

REST. 2D TORTS § 345.

Private and public necessity require an emergency that is not of the defendant's own making. The common law rule is that a landowner owes a trespasser no duty. If private or public necessity are available defenses, the land entrant's status is raised from a mere trespasser to that of a licensee. REST. 2D § 345(1) requires the possessor to warn the visitor of dangerous conditions they may not discover or appreciate. The doctrine of necessity is an exception to that general rule. Where a trespasser enters the property of another pursuant to the privilege of private necessity, that is, for the purpose of advancing or protecting his own interests, the property owner owes a duty of reasonable care under the circumstances. *Lange v. Fisher Real Estate Dev. Corp.*, 832 N.E.2d 274 (Ill. App. 2005). The private necessity defense may be invoked "only where in an emergency the actor enters land for the purpose of protecting himself or the possessor of the land or a third person or the land or chattels of any such persons." REST. 2D § 197, cmt. *a*.

Assuming that there is an emergency, REST. 2D TORTS, § 196 states the "public necessity" justification for unauthorized entry onto the land of another:

One is privileged to enter land in the possession of another if it is, or if the actor reasonably believes it to be, necessary for the purpose of averting an imminent public disaster.

Professor Christie questions the Restatement's view that property may be destroyed to save another's person, land, or chattels:

For example, sections 197 of both the original *Restatement* and the *Restatement (Second)* take the position that one is privileged to enter the land of another in order to prevent serious harm to oneself, to one's land, to one's chattels, or to the person, land, or chattels of another. A person who enters under this privilege, however, must pay compensation for any harm done to the possessor's interest in the land. A similar provision, section 263, covers what amounts to trespass to chattels and the conversion of chattels. Section 263 of the *Restatement* limited the privilege to situations in which chattels were destroyed or used to save life or to avoid serious bodily harm and took no position as to whether one was authorized to take a chattel over the objection of its owner. Section 263 of the *Restatement (Second)* not only extends the privilege to cover the destruction or use of chattels to save property, but also permits the taking of property even if its possessor objects. The person destroying or using the property is, however, liable for any harm done. The reason given by the drafters of both the *Restatement* and the *Restatement (Second)* for recognizing a "privilege" to destroy or use others' chattels to save one's property was the same: to take from the possessor of the chattel "the privilege . . . to use reasonable force to defend his exclusive possession." The Reporter's notes to the *Restatement (Second)* are at least candid enough to admit that "[t]here is scarcely any authority to support the principle stated in this Section, and it must rest largely upon the analogy to the corresponding privilege to interfere with the exclusive possession of land, stated in § 197.

George Christie, *The Defense of Necessity Considered from Legal & Moral Points of View*, 48 DUKE L. J. 975, 989–90 (1999).

If the law requires a person acting under a private necessity to pay for the damage done to the possessor's property is such liability based in trespass? Then what practical effect does the privilege of private necessity serve? Does it allow the defendant to say I am not a tortfeasor? Is liability based in negligence? But wasn't the defendant behaving reasonably in staying at the dock? Is liability strict? Is it tortious or quasi-contractual?

2. *Necessity, Fault and Scope of the Risk.* The privilege of necessity does not apply if the peril which the actor seeks to avoid is one caused by his own fault. It then may be said that the damage he sought to avoid, and resulting damage to the plaintiff's property, were within the scope of the risk of his original faulty conduct. Thus, in *Southport Corp. v. Esso Petrol. Co.*, [1954] 2 Q.B. 182 (C.A.), *rev'd in part*, [1953] 3 All E.R. 864 (H.L.), defendants' tanker developed a steering fault and stranded on a revetment wall. To save the vessel and crew from grave danger, the master jettisoned 400 tons of oil which damaged plaintiff's shore. The court held defendants liable to plaintiffs for this damage because it was caused by defendants' fault. *See also Protectus Alpha Navigation Co. v. North Pacific Grain Growers, Inc.*, 767 F.2d 1379 (9th Cir. 1985) (grain terminal owner, who cast off from dock a burning vessel on which firefighters had gathered, held liable on negligence *per se* theory for breach of criminal statute prohibiting interference with operations of Fire Department).

3. *Bodily Safety.* In *Eilers v. Coy*, 582 F. Supp. 1093 (D.C. Minn. 1984), the plaintiff was a member of a religious group, "Disciples of the Lord Jesus Christ." There was evidence that the leader of the group directed it with an iron hand. The plaintiff's personality and appearance changed substantially after he became a member of the group. Fearing for the plaintiff's health, his parents hired defendants to kidnap the plaintiff and to subject him to a deprogramming regimen which they did. The plaintiff was grabbed by two security guards and taken to a center where he was handcuffed to a bed for the first two days. He was allowed out of the room only to use the bathroom, and was heavily guarded whenever allowed outside of the room. Plaintiff brought an action for false imprisonment and the court rejected the defense of necessity and found the defendants liable for false imprisonment as a matter of law. The court reasoned that even if the defendants acted under a reasonable belief that plaintiff was in danger of imminent physical injury, once they had him under their control they were justified in holding only so long as necessary to turn him over to lawful authority, seek civil commitment or obtain professional psychological help for him.

How would you characterize "deprogramming?" As a process designed to provide a church or cult member with "an opportunity in a neutral setting to sleep, to eat, to evaluate the manner in which he wishes to live his life and then, well-rested and well-fed, to make an independent decision about whether to remain involved in the group?" Or as "a process involving kidnapping and forcing an individual to renounce his religious beliefs?" *See Colombrito v. Kelly,* 764 F.2d 122, 125 (2d Cir. 1985) (reversing district court's order that the parents of a Unification Church member pay attorneys fees to church and member arising out of the defendants kidnapping and forcibly deprogramming of member).

What torts are committed when a parent or other close relative abducts a church member? What problems would a court have in carving out a defense for parents or close relatives who use mental or physical duress on family members who have joined sects?

4. *Perspectives on Necessity.* The Restatement (Second) provides that, "[w]here the entry is for the benefit of the actor or a third person, he is subject to liability for any harm done in the exercise of the privilege . . . to any legally protected interest of the possessor in the land or connected with it. . . " REST. 2D TORTS § 197(2).

This rule is described as creating an incomplete privilege because while the actor is not technically liable for trespassing on the land of another he is still required to pay for any actual harm caused by his entry or presence on the land. Is it consistent with principles of economic efficiency, corrective justice or social justice to make an actor pay for harm caused to another's property if it was reasonable for the actor to expose the other's property to the risk posed by the intrusion in order to protect a more valuable interest than that which is possessed by the other?

Would it be consistent with principles of economic efficiency, corrective justice or social justice to hold that the actor did not have a privilege at all to invade the property interest of another, no matter how valuable the property he may be protecting is, and no matter how minimal the risk of harm to the other's property may be as a result of the invasion? *Cf. Vincent v. Lake Erie, supra,* and *Ploof v. Putnam, supra.* Both cases involve a boat-owner and a dock-owner. The *Vincent* court held that a boat owner was privileged to tie his boat to another person's dock in order to avoid the risk of harm posed by an imminent storm. However, the court ruled further that the boat owner would be held liable for any harm his boat caused to the other's dock. In *Ploof,* the court ruled that the boat owner had a right to moor to the dock and that the dock owner is liable for interfering with that right under the exigent circumstances posed by the storm. Two scholars, in a highly influential article, presented the following conceptualization of the competing values at stake when property is taken without negotiation and agreement. *See generally* Guido Calabresi & A. Douglas Melamed, *Property Rules, Liability Rules, and Inalienability*: One *View of the Cathedral,* 85 HARV. L. REV. 1089, 1090–1105 (1972).

The authors posit that legal rules are usefully categorized as property rules designating entitlements, liability rules designating responsibility for taking or damaging entitlements without negotiation and agreement, and inalienability rules designating matters that cannot be taken or voluntarily transferred for public policy reasons. Taking this perspective, an analysis of *Vincent* and *Ploof is* that the legal system designates the boat-owner's interest in the boat as an "entitlement," and the dock-owner's interest in the dock as an "entitlement." At issue is how the legal system will protect and nurture those entitlements against non-negotiated takings. Entitlements to boats (personalty) and docks (realty) usually are protected by a "property" rule. A property rule makes use of an official state bargaining mechanism (the law of contract) so that boat-owners can negotiate with dock-owners for a place to tie up. A property rule protection for an entitlement also brings with it certain exclusionary mechanisms to stop boat-owners from tying up without payment, i.e., rules designed to force people to use the market. These mechanisms include criminal sanctions, the tort of trespass, and an affirmative defense to battery available property owners vis-à-vis trespassers whom they "gently" remove.

Ploof may not interfere with any basic entitlement decision, but in the narrow range of fact-patterns that are characterized as occasions of "necessity," *Ploof* suspends the operation of the enforcement mechanisms, *i.e.,* the boat-owner *in extremis* is not considered a trespasser. However, a property rule is not the only method that can be used to protect an entitlement.

An entitlement may also be protected using a "liability" rule. A liability rule functions so as to permit non-bargainers who value entitlements more than those to whom they have been allocated to use the entitlements for a "fee" (damages) later assessed by a court. *See generally* Jules L. Coleman & Jody Kraus, *Rethinking the Theory of Legal Rights*, 95 YALE L.J. 1335 (1986). Clearly, *Vincent v. Lake Erie*, while endorsing *Ploof's* suspension of the property rule enforcement mechanism, nevertheless enforced the dock-owner's entitlement with a liability rule. But why?

The perspective offered by Calabresi and Melamed is that the answer lies in the theoretical preference for property rules over liability rules. In broad terms, forced transfers (no negotiations, followed by court-determined compensation) only roughly approximate what a negotiated transaction would have achieved in overall efficiency terms, and are transactionally inefficient. Thus, forced transfers, and hence liability rules, are used only when, with all their deficiencies, they operate more efficiently than property rules. One of the clearest ways in which a property rule can operate inefficiently is when bargaining is impossible or extremely difficult (high "transaction costs"). Coleman & Kraus, *supra* at 1336–37. And clearly a boat-owner caught in a life-threatening storm will find it difficult to identify, let alone bargain with, a dock-owner. Faced with such a market imperfection, *Vincent* correctly adopted a liability rule.

However (even if you are able to follow the complex reasoning so far), some questions do remain. First, if a liability rule is appropriate, why should it apply only to the damage caused to the dock? Should the court also assess a rent for the use of the dock during the storm? Second, what type of liability rule is appropriate? *Vincent* appears to use a strict liability rule, because the court found that the boat-owner acted reasonably in how, when and where he tied up his boat. Yet he was still liable. That means all boat-dock-storm-necessity costs will be allocated to boat-owners. But don't dock-owners have the cheapest information as to the number and severity of storms in their area? Or do boat-owners on a lake have similarly low information costs?

F. JUSTIFICATION

SINDLE v. NEW YORK CITY TRANSIT AUTHORITY
33 N.Y.2d 293 (1973)

JASEN, JUSTICE.

At about noon on June 20, 1967, the plaintiff, then 14 years of age, boarded a school bus owned by the defendant, New York City Transit Authority, and driven by its employee, the defendant Mooney. It was the last day of the term at the Elias Bernstein Junior High School in Staten Island and the 65 to 70 students on board the bus were in a boisterous and exuberant mood. Some of this spirit expressed itself in vandalism, a number of students breaking dome lights, windows, ceiling panels and advertising poster frames. There is no evidence that the plaintiff partook in this destruction.

The bus made several stops at appointed stations. On at least one occasion, the driver admonished the students about excessive noise and damage to the bus. When he reached the Annadale station, the driver discharged several more passengers, went to the rear of the bus, inspected the damage and advised the students that he was taking them to the St. George police station.

The driver closed the doors of the bus and proceeded, bypassing several normal stops. As the bus slowed to turn on to Woodrow Road, several students jumped without apparent injury from a side window at the rear of the bus. Several more followed, again without apparent harm, when the bus turned onto Arden Avenue.

At the corner of Arden Avenue and Arthur Kill Road, departing from its normal route, the bus turned right in the general direction of the St. George police station. The plaintiff, intending to jump from the bus, had positioned himself in a window on the right-rear side. Grasping the bottom of the window sill with his hands, the plaintiff extended his legs (to mid-thigh), head and shoulders out of the window. As the bus turned right, the right rear wheels hit the curb and the plaintiff either jumped or fell to the street. The right rear wheels then rolled over the midsection of his body, causing serious personal injuries.

The plaintiff, joined with his father, then commenced an action to recover damages for negligence and false imprisonment. At the outset of the trial, the negligence cause was waived and plaintiffs proceeded on the theory of false imprisonment. At the close of the plaintiffs' case, the court denied defendants' motion to amend their answers to plead the defense of justification. The court also excluded all evidence bearing on the justification issue.

We believe that it was an abuse of discretion for the trial court to deny the motion to amend and to exclude the evidence of justification. It was the defendants' burden to prove justification — a defense that a plaintiff in an action for false imprisonment should be prepared to meet — and the plaintiffs could not have been prejudiced by the granting of the motion to amend. The trial court's rulings precluded the defendants from introducing any evidence in this regard and were manifestly unfair. Accordingly, the order of the Appellate Division must be reversed and a new trial granted.

In view of our determination, it would be well to outline some of the considerations relevant to the issue of justification. In this regard, we note that, generally, restraint or detention, reasonable under the circumstances and in time and manner, imposed for the purpose of preventing another from inflicting personal injuries or interfering with or damaging real or personal property in one's lawful possession or custody is not unlawful. (*Cf.* Penal Law, §§ 35.20, 35.25; *see also*, General Business Law, § 218, which affords a retail merchant a defense to an action for false arrest and false imprisonment where a suspected shoplifter is reasonably detained for investigation or questioning.) Also, a parent, guardian or teacher entrusted with the care or supervision of a child may use physical force reasonably necessary to maintain discipline or promote the welfare of the child.

Similarly, a bus driver, entrusted with the care of his student-passengers and the custody of public property, has the duty to take reasonable measures for the safety and protection of both — the passengers and the property. In this regard, the reasonableness of his actions — as bearing on the defense of justification — is to be determined from a consideration of all the circumstances. At a minimum, this would seem to import a consideration of the need to protect the persons and property in his charge, the duty to aid the investigation and apprehension of those inflicting damage, the manner and place of the occurrence, and the feasibility and practicality of other alternative courses of action.

. . . .

Order reversed, without costs, and a new trial granted.

NOTES

1. *Policies Underlying Justification.* Does the defense of justification apply in any case in which the defendant intentionally harms the plaintiff or his property, and the societal value of the defendant's conduct outweighs society's interest in protecting the invasion of the plaintiff's interests? If so, why not a generic defense of "justification" which would encompass consent, self-defense and all of the "pigeonhole" defenses which have been considered in this chapter? Why not a "generic" intentional tort, i.e., if one does an act which is substantially certain to cause harm to a protected interest, he has committed an intentional tort? How do you determine what is "reasonable" force? The issue of reasonable force is context-specific. What is the purpose of adopting a "generic" defense such as justification? Is it the beginning of a general trend towards doctrinal simplification, or is it designed to provide courts with an "escape valve" defense where the other defenses are not available?

2. *Discipline?* Some courts have held that the physical discipline by a teacher is actionable only where it is maliciously motivated or willfully and wantonly inflicted. *See, e.g., Gordon v. Oak Park School Dist.*, 24 Ill. App. 3d 131 (1974); *Baikie v. Luther High School South,* 51 Ill. App. 3d 405 (1977). Note also that some state statutes specifically permit teachers to administer corporal punishment, as long as it is not "excessive or unduly severe." *See, e.g., Maddox v. Boutwell*, 176 Ga. App. 492 (1985).

PROBLEMS

3.1

Plaintiff consulted defendant, an ear specialist, about trouble she was having with her right ear. On examining the ear the defendant discovered a diseased condition, and plaintiff consented to defendant's operating on the ear. During the operation on the sedated plaintiff, defendant discovered a more serious condition in the left ear. Because the condition with the left ear would soon require surgery, defendant proceeded to operate on it also. Does the operation on the left ear constitute a battery? Did the defendant have the plaintiff's implied consent to operate? Should this depend on how serious the condition in the left ear was? On whether the condition in the left ear was related to that in the right ear? On whether there were relatives of the plaintiff close at hand whom the defendant could consult? On whether the operation was a success, or had untoward consequences?

3.2

A 14-year-old boy, aided by another youngster, tilted a soft-drink machine forward at night outside a business establishment, in order to dislodge cans of drink which they could then steal. They were unable to steady the machine and it fell forward, killing the boy. The boy's estate sued the machine manufacturer for wrongful death, alleging the machine was defectively designed because it had no anti-theft device to prevent cans from falling out when the machine was tipped forward, and because there were no brackets to anchor the machine to the ground. Is a jury question presented? Suppose the defendant was aware of other such accidents that had occurred as a result of similar theft attempts?

3.3

Eric Pitfall owns a convenience store at the corner of Regent and Oxford. Recently, there have been several robberies at night at the store. Particularly popular amongst the criminal fraternity has been the cash left in the vending machines located in the entrance to the store. Eric, determined to abort this local crime wave, removed all the candy bars from one of the vending machines, and replaced them with several sticks of dynamite, wired to explode if the lock was forced. Seven-year-old Nigel, who was trying burglary for the first time, broke into the convenience store and was severely maimed when the machine exploded. Would Eric succeed with a plea of defense of property?

Assume in the alternative that Eric was a frail 90-year-old who had been severely beaten by 24-year-old Thug during a robbery at the convenience store the previous week. Eric has set a remote control trigger for the vending machine booby-trap. Eric triggers the trap when he sees Saul, Thug's twin brother, break into the convenience store late at night. Could Eric successfully urge defense of property?

3.4

Defendant owns a field that is fenced. Plaintiff, because of a grudge he held against Defendant, enters the field and begins to systematically pull down Defendant's fence. Defendant observes this conduct for a few minutes and then shoots and wounds Plaintiff. At trial Plaintiff argues that Defendant should have requested him to leave before shooting him. Defendant argues that Plaintiff was a violent trespasser to whom a warning need not have been given. Is either correct?

3.5

Oldy Olson, 86, was asleep in his brick shed when he was awoken by the sound of Lance Interloper trying to break in to his shed. Oldy took his shotgun, loaded it, poked the barrel through a small hole in the door, and fired. He did not give a word of warning nor a warning shot. The shotgun blast blew a large hole in Interloper's favorite arm. Interloper was subsequently prosecuted for the various offences which he had committed that night and pleaded guilty. Interloper sued Olson for assault.

To these claims Olson raises the defenses of no cause of action (because of Olson's immoral and illegal act), self-defense and defense of property. What result?

3.6

Defendant was driving a bus containing 20 elderly persons down a steep narrow mountain road, en route to a senior citizens' function, when the bus brakes suddenly gave way. The bus quickly reached a high rate of speed. There was no safe place to pull off the road; on one side was a steep rock wall, and on the other, a deep canyon.

Ahead of the bus was the entrance to a private subdivision, which provided the driver with the only chance to save the lives of her passengers and herself. Five school children were awaiting a school van pickup at the entrance to the subdivision, and the driver could not enter it without hitting the children. The driver's horn failed to function when she attempted to use it. Prior to the accident, the driver had no reason to know that the brakes or horn on the bus would fail. If the driver hits the children, will she be liable in tort to them? If she does not attempt to use the subdivision entrance, will she be liable in tort to her passengers? Is she liable for entry into, or any damage to the subdivision?

3.7

A wrongful death lawsuit was brought by the administrator of the estate of Hamilton I. Cartwright, deceased, who died as the result of a blow received in a Strong Man prize fight. The complaint stated that plaintiff's decedent and defendant engaged in a prize fight and that plaintiff died as a result of the encounter. A state statute made Strong Man competitions illegal. What result? The promoters hosted the Strong Man competition as one of the concessions, for which a separate admission fee was charged. What about the liability of the promoter of the Strong Man competition?

3.8

One night after work Pietlo a policeman, decided to celebrate his birthday by getting drunk with two fellow off duty officers under the banyan tree in front of the police station. He got obnoxiously drunk. Dan, plaintiff's long suffering senior officer, was on duty. Dan told Pietlo not to bring beer into the station. He did and was evicted. Dan told Pietlo to go home. He didn't. Finally Dan went on patrol. Somehow Pietlo got on the police radio and broadcast: "I'm waiting for you at the police department. Come back and I'll put you down." Dan returned to the station. Pietlo grabbed him by his shirt and said, "Go ahead. Hit me." He repeated this statement two or three times. By this time Dan was out of patience with Pietlo. He didn't want to arrest him because it would cost Pietlo his job. So, he acceded to Pietlo's request and gave him a good old-fashioned thrashing. Unfortunately, when Pietlo hit the ground after Dan "clocked him," he suffered head injuries for which he sued defendant. Pietlo filed a civil rights action for this alleged battery against Dan, the Commissioner of Public Safety and the city. What result?

3.9

Jill was hiking in the White Mountain of New Hampshire when she lost her bearings due to a sudden snow storm. Jill was suffering from the beginning stages of frost bite when she spotted a deer camp. She broke a window and found a deer camp with an ingenious layout including cook stops, a gas refrigerator, and shelves with canned goods. Jill started a fire in the camp fireplace and ate some of the food. What torts? What defenses? *See* Joel Feinberg, Voluntary Euthanasia and the Inalienable Right to Life, 7 PHIL & PUB AFF. 93, 102 (1978) (posing hypothetical where hiker must break into an unoccupied cabin to save himself).

Chapter 4

THE STANDARD OF CARE IN NEGLIGENCE

A. INTRODUCTION

For many, the defining concept of the tort of negligence is the standard of care. Phrases like reasonable, prudent, or due care all refer to the standard of care. The issues presented in determining the appropriate standard of care for actors in a negligence case represent a microcosm of modern accident law. Thus, this chapter reflects the tensions inherent in the torts system as a whole. To what extent should standards be objective rather than subjective? Are liability rules driven by compensation rather than culpability concerns? To what extent should decisionmakers tailor liability to particular fact patterns rather than apply broad rules? What is the appropriate degree of control that the judiciary should exercise over the jury in the determination of fault?

This chapter begins with an introduction to negligence and an overview of the *prima facie* case for the tort. It then canvasses the primary tools used by the courts to set the standard of care for negligence. Beginning with the standard of care, emphasizing risk-utility analysis and the reasonable prudent person, the chapter moves to custom and professional practices, followed by judicial and statutory standards of care. The chapter concludes with issues involved in proving negligence, including an examination of the doctrine of *res ipsa loquitur*.

As chapter 2 highlighted, modern tort law emerged out of the English common law system that was based on pleading by writs. The two writs available, the writ of *trespass* and the writ of *trespass on the case*, represented actions for direct harm and indirect harm. For example, if "a man throws a log into the highway" and in that act hits a person, that harm was direct and actionable in trespass. *Reynolds v. Clarke*, (1726) 92 Eng. Rep. 410 (K.B.). If the person "tumbles over" the log, then trespass on the case was the correct action.

Because of the existence of this writ system distinction between trespass and case, many scholars believed that pre-industrial tort law imposed a kind of strict liability for all harm that could be categorized as trespass. The writ of trespass led to the notion that one who acts pays or that a direct harm equaled liability. *See, e.g.*, Charles O. Gregory, *Trespass to Negligence to Absolute Liability*, 37 Va. L. Rev. 359 (1951). More recent scholarship challenged the notion that all trespass actions were based on strict liability. Gary T. Schwartz, *Tort Law and the Economy in Nineteenth Century America: A Reinterpretation*, 90 Yale L.J. 1717 (1981) (arguing that negligence existed in pre-industrial English law). Robert Rabin has asserted that pre-industrial law was "no-liability" oriented because of the existence of doctrines involving immunities and limited duties. Robert L. Rabin, *The Historical Development of the Fault Principle: A Reinterpretation*, 15 Ga. L. Rev. 925 (1981). Rabin's view, that one could only sue if a relationship existed, meant that many kinds of suits were just not brought. According to Rabin, this "no liability" thinking, the idea of letting the parties harm stay as it fell, has continued to influence the development of negligence law.

Brown v. Kendall, 60 Mass. 292 (1850), ushered in the modern era of tort law, stating "the plaintiff must come prepared with evidence to show either that the intention was unlawful, or that the defendant was in fault." *Id.* at 295–96. The case concerned a trespass action for harm that occurred during a dogfight between animals owned by the plaintiff and defendant. Defendant, in using a stick to try to separate the dogs, raised the stick over his shoulder and accidentally hit plaintiff in the eye. This action would have been a classic direct harm, under the theory of trespass, yet the court spoke in terms of intent and fault, signaling a significant change in legal doctrine.

Charles Gregory, *supra*, speculated that the motive underlying *Brown* may have been "to make risk-creating enterprise less hazardous to investors and entrepreneurs." *Id.* at 368. Oliver W. Holmes opposed strict liability or "one who acts, pays" as a theoretical basis of liability. He believed that people must act, and strict liability penalized people for doing what they must do anyway as part of daily life: "A man need not, it is true, do this or that act, — the term *act* implies a choice, — but he must act somehow. OLIVER WENDALL HOLMES, THE COMMON LAW 94–96 (1881).

Is it more desirable, as a policy matter, for the injured party to bear the burden of proving fault by the defendant actor? Or should the injured party always recover? Why might a court deny recovery to an injured party? Consider this example: A state decides to build a bridge over a bay, connecting two cities. Studies show that the risk this project entails will be death or serious injury to construction workers, even if the work proceeds carefully. Should the state build the bridge that will benefit many in the community? Will they build it under a liability theory that says "one who acts, pays?" Would their view be different, if the injured party had to prove fault on their part?

B. AN OVERVIEW OF THE PRIMA FACIE CASE OF NEGLIGENCE

Chapters 4–7, 9, 12 and 15 examine issues related to the *prima facie* case of negligence and defenses to negligence. This section presents a roadmap to follow about the *prima facie* case. Do not worry about understanding this roadmap perfectly. The text will explore these issues in depth. This section aims to familiarize the reader with the negligence vocabulary because students learn much of law by assimilation, plunging in, using the vocabulary, and developing a sense of meaning through that use.

Early negligence cases involved actual acts, not failures or omissions to act. These acts often involved outrageous behavior or misbehavior. Later cases developed the idea there might be liability for nonfeasance or failure to take an affirmative action. This action/non-action distinction has been important historically. *See infra* chapter 7, discussing duty.

Negligence is a kind of behavior or conduct of the defendant, who is essentially not being as careful as she or he should be. But the cause of action for negligence requires more than simply careless conduct by the defendant. The five elements of the negligence *prima facie* case are Duty, Breach, Actual Cause or Cause in Fact, Proximate Cause or Legal Cause, and Actual Loss or Damages.

Here are some examples to illustrate each of these elements.

Duty (*see infra* Chapter 7)

> Agnes is sailing in her sailboat. Bertha is sailing in a separate sailboat. Bertha does not know Agnes; she has never heard of her. Agnes capsizes. Bertha is sailing so carelessly that she does not notice that Agnes has capsized. Agnes drowns.

Did Bertha have a duty toward Agnes to conform her conduct to a standard of care to avoid unreasonable risks or to protect others against unreasonable risks?

Generally, a person owes a duty when (1) the defendant engages in conduct which creates *a foreseeable risk of harm to a class of persons of which plaintiff is a member* or (2) the defendant has some relationship with plaintiff that imposes a duty. So foreseeability of risk or the existence of relationship are keys to finding duty. Exceptions and special duty issues are considered in detail, *infra* Chapter 6–7, including the foreseeable plaintiff; prenatal injuries; duty to rescue; negligent infliction of emotional distress; negligent infliction of economic harm; and owners and occupiers of land.

In most negligence cases, duty is not an issue; one must act in a way that avoids unreasonable risks to others. The concept of duty is one way to set a limit on the defendant's liability for harm caused, because if the defendant owes no duty, then there can be no liability.

Breach of Duty (*see infra* Chapter 4)

> Agnes and Bertha, again, are sailing on a collision course, right at each other. A rule of sailing, similar to rules of the road, mandates "port tack yields to starboard tack." But Bertha does not know the rule and though she is on the port tack and *should* yield, she does not yield. A collision occurs in which Agnes is injured.

Has there been a breach of the duty? Breach of duty is the failure to conform one's conduct to the standard required. Here, under the customary rule of sailing, port tack yields. If no breach by the defendant has occurred, then the defendant is not responsible. This element, "breach," is common parlance negligence. Technically that usage, equating negligence to breach, is incorrect because there can be no negligence without some preexisting duty. So the first two elements, duty and breach together, are more correctly considered as negligence. So the term *negligence* may be used to refer to solely the element of breach (as in "breach of a duty") or to the entire cause of action for negligence.

Cause in Fact or Actual Cause (*see infra* Chapter 5).

> The sailboats suffer the same collision because Bertha failed to yield. The ambulance takes Agnes to the hospital where she dies of cancer. Her heirs sue Bertha for Agnes' death from cancer.

Did the defendant's act (the failure by Bertha to yield) actually cause the injury to Agnes (the death from cancer)? If defendant's conduct did not cause the harm, then defendant should not be responsible for it.

Proximate Cause or Legal Cause (*see infra* Chapter 6)

> The two sailors, again, are on a collision course. Bertha *could* avoid the collision, but Bertha sees two nude sunbathers. (Consider these nude sunbathers. Do the sunbathers share identity characteristics with the reader or with the dominant cultural images of beauty? Imagine the sunbathers in a non-sexist, non-heterosexist way.) Bertha sees one male and one female nude sunbather and she is distracted. Perhaps one of them distracts her or maybe both of them command her attention. Nude sunbathing violates a state penal code section.

> Being distracted by the sunbathers, Bertha collides with Agnes injuring her. Agnes sues Bertha and the sunbathers.

The sunbathers owed a duty not to violate state law. The breach of that law was negligence and actually caused the harm. The issue raised by this suit against the sunbathers is proximate cause or legal cause. Should sunbathers pay for the injury to Agnes when the consequence of their conduct, a sailboat accident from nude sunbathing, is remote from the original harm anticipated by the statutory violation?

Proximate cause is a policy question, asking "Is it fair?" to make this defendant pay for the harm plaintiff suffered? The policy question examines the relation between defendant's negligent act (here nude sunbathing in violation of statute) and plaintiff's harm (the sail boating injury).

This doctrine provides another way of limiting the defendant's liability. When the unexpected happens, it is usually a question of proximate cause.

Actual Loss or Damages (*see infra* Chapter 15)

> Returning to the sailboats on a collision course, Bertha continues refusing to yield. At the last minute Agnes avoids Bertha, so no collision results. Agnes sues Bertha for Bertha's negligent conduct in almost causing this collision.

Tort law does not provide a remedy for mere inconvenience. Actual loss or damage must occur. In each of these scenarios, an actor created a risk of harm, yet liability only results when each element of the cause of action is met.

For further discussion of the elements of the negligence *prima facie* case, see Thomas C. Galligan, Jr., *A Primer on the Patterns of Negligence*, 53 LA. L. REV. 1509 (1993) (discussing the analysis in negligence cases and common patterns).

C. THE STANDARD OF CARE

It is the confluence of the elements of duty and breach that this text turns to first. This chapter focuses on breach, but remember there can be no breach without duty. Duty is not, however, an issue in these cases. The text will return to cases in which duty is an issue, *infra* Chapter 7.

The heart of the negligence system concerns the standard of care. Two ideas vie for primacy in standard of care discussions: (1) reasonable care and (2) the reasonable prudent person. These ideas reflect a tension between economic evaluation and morality as yardsticks for measuring human behavior. This text first considers reasonable care and then the reasonable prudent person.

Evaluation of an actor's conduct, whether that actor is the plaintiff or defendant, occurs in the interplay between the judge and the jury. As Fleming James noted: "The jury system plays an important part in the administration of accident law. . . . [P]rocedural rules and devices which allocate power between court and jury may have great bearing on the way accident law actually works." Fleming James, Jr., *Functions of Judge and Jury in Negligence Cases*, 58 YALE L. J. 667, 667 (1949).

James notes that the common observation "questions of law are for the court and questions of fact for the jury" has never been "fully true." *Id.* The court decides questions as to the admissibility of evidence, which may raise questions of relevancy or exclusionary rules. *Id.* at 669. While the jury determines facts when faced with conflicting testimony, e.g. the light was red; the light was green, the court "determines the sufficiency of the evidence to show the existence of a fact." *Id.* at 672. Thus, while the jury has a central role in evaluating what the parties should have done, the court sets outer limits.

> Thus, for example, the jury may not require a train to stop before passing over each grade crossing in the country. . . . [A] pedestrian may not be excused from looking at some point when he is about to cross a busy thoroughfare. Since it is the courts which determine what is clearly or undoubtedly reasonable under this rule of limitation, they could so administer it as to leave little or nothing for the jury to decide in this sphere.

Id. at 677. Compare the roles of judge and jury in the following two cases.

Bernardi v. Roedel, 168 A.2d 886 (Md. 1961), involved a rear-end collision. Plaintiff was driving a three-quarter ton truck, towing heavy equipment that extended eight to ten feet to the rear with no lights. The day was hazy and snow patches remained on the two-lane highway. Plaintiff saw a snowdrift blocking his lane and a car coming from the opposite direction. He slowed down to a stop to let the opposing car pass, anticipating he would then pass the obstacle. When the plaintiff stopped, the defendant rear-ended the equipment being towed. Defendant testified that he had been following the plaintiff for one to one and a half miles at a distance of two car lengths when the plaintiff suddenly stopped. The trial court rendered judgment for the defendant following driver and the plaintiff appealed. Plaintiff argued that the trial court committed reversible error by refusing to instruct the jury that defendant "was negligent as a matter of law, that such negligence was the sole cause of the accident, and that the [plaintiff] was not chargeable with any contributory negligence." 168 A.2d. at 886.

The appellate court held that since the parties presented conflicting facts about which reasonable people could differ, the jury should resolve the dispute as to the weight and value of the evidence. The court stated that "unless facts are undisputed and lead to conclusions from which reasonable minds could not differ, negligence as a matter of law cannot be a basis for an instruction to a jury." *Id.* at 887. The court stated that "[o]nly in exceptional cases will questions of negligence and contributory negligence pass from the realm of fact to that of law." *Id.*

In *Adams v. Bullock*, 125 N.E. 93 (N.Y. 1919), the defendant's trolley wire ran under the bridge of a railroad company. Pedestrians, including children, frequently used the railroad bridge as a shortcut, carrying them over the trolley wires. A pedestrian standing on the bridge and leaning over its eighteen-inch parapet could not reach the trolley wires. Plaintiff, a twelve year old boy, crossed the bridge swinging an eight foot long wire. The boy's wire came into contact with the trolley wire, shocking and burning the child. No similar accident had ever occurred. The trial court rendered a verdict for the plaintiff and the appellate division affirmed. Justice Cardozo, writing for New York's highest court found no negligence as a matter of law.

The court reasoned: "There was, of course, a duty to adopt all reasonable precautions to minimize the resulting perils. We think there is no evidence that this duty was ignored. The trolley wire was so placed that no one standing on the bridge or even bending over the parapet could reach it. Only some extraordinary casualty, not fairly within the area of ordinary prevision, could make it a thing of danger." *Adams,* 125 N.E. at 93.

The *Bernardi* court found a jury question. The *Adams* court overturned a jury decision, replacing it by a judicial decision of "no negligence as a matter of law." Should these cases have been treated differently? What implications for the tort system does this example of different treatment suggest?

In *Adams* a jury found the defendant was negligent and an appellate court agreed. Why should a higher court intervene in that decision? Wasn't the accident very foreseeable under the law of gravity that objects will fall down? Wouldn't a warning have been simple and of little burden to the defendant? Couldn't defendant have placed a wider side-guard in the areas where people would be above the wires — umbrella like?

On the other hand, how could the defendant have possibly foreseen this kind of accident, especially when no similar accident had previously occurred? Wasn't the plaintiff the careless actor here, thoughtless and mischievous? What could defendants have possibly done to prevent this accident; didn't they act reasonably?

Do these arguments suggest that *Adams* should necessarily have been a jury decision? These cases show three potential situations involving the interplay between judge and jury: (1) the jury *must* find negligence; (2) the jury *may* find negligence (the jury could find either way); (3) the jury *cannot* find negligence. The final responsibility for determining what category a case falls into belongs to the judge and the appellate courts. A judge's own ideas about judging will influence that judicial decision. *See* Catharine Pierce Wells, *Improving One's Situation: Some Pragmatic Reflections on the Art of Judging*, 49 WASH. & LEE L. REV. 323 (1992) and the discussion of pragmatism, *supra* Chapter 1. Another tort law theme, limiting liability, plays a role here; some judges fear that too much jury discretion always means an injured plaintiff will win.

1. Reasonable Care

UNITED STATES v. CARROLL TOWING CO.
159 F.2d 169 (2d Cir. 1947)

[This case arose under admiralty jurisdiction; admiralty rules were a precursor of comparative negligence. The United States owned cargo aboard the barge Anna C. Harbor workers on the tug Carroll readjusted lines holding the Anna C. to the pier. They secured these lines negligently resulting in the Anna C. breaking loose as part of a several boat collision. Another boat's propeller caused a hole near the bottom of the barge. Although another tug had come to help the flotilla and could have kept the Anna C. afloat had it known of the hole, the bargee "had left her on the evening before, and nobody was on board to observe that she was leaking." The Anna C. sank, resulting in the loss of both the cargo and the ship. Defendant's negligence was clear; the defendant had been negligent in retying the barge. Thus the case raises the negligence issue in the context of plaintiff's conduct: the custodian was absent from the barge. The court considered whether damages should be divided under admiralty rules, under which plaintiff's negligence, if present, would not serve as a complete bar to recovery.]

L. HAND, CIRCUIT JUDGE.

. . . It appears from the foregoing review that there is no general rule to determine when the absence of a bargee or other attendant will make the owner of the barge liable for injuries to other vessels if she breaks away from her moorings. . . . It becomes apparent why there can be no such general rule, when we consider the grounds for such a liability. Since there are occasions when every vessel will break from her moorings, and since, if she does, she becomes a menace to those about her; the owner's duty, as in other similar situations, to provide against resulting injuries is a function of three variables: (1) The probability that she will break away; (2) the gravity of the resulting injury, if she does; (3) the burden of adequate precautions. Possibly it serves to bring this notion into relief to state it in algebraic terms: if the probability be called P; the injury, L; and the burden, B; liability depends upon whether B is less than L multiplied by P: i.e., whether B less than PL. Applied to the situation at bar, the likelihood that a barge will break from her fasts and the damage she will do, vary with the place and time; for example, if a storm threatens, the danger is greater; so it is, if she is in a crowded harbor where moored barges are constantly being shifted about. On the other hand, the barge must not be the bargee's prison, even though he lives aboard; he must go ashore at times. We need not say whether, even in such crowded waters as New York

Harbor, a bargee must be aboard at night at all; it may be that the custom is otherwise . . . and that, if so, the situation is one where custom should control. We leave that question open; but we hold that it is not in all cases a sufficient answer to a bargee's absence without excuse, during working hours, that he has properly made fast his barge to a pier, when he leaves her. In the case at bar the bargee left at five o'clock in the afternoon of January 3rd, and the flotilla broke away at about two o'clock in the afternoon of the following day, twenty-one hours afterwards. The bargee had been away all the time, and we hold that his fabricated story was affirmative evidence that he had no excuse for his absence. At the locus in quo — especially during the short January days and in the full tide of war activity — barges were being constantly 'drilled' in and out. Certainly it was not beyond reasonable expectation that, with the inevitable haste and bustle, the work might not be done with adequate care. In such circumstances we hold — and it is all that we do hold — that it was a fair requirement that the Conners Company [charterers of the Anna C.] should have a bargee aboard (unless he had some excuse for his absence), during the working hours of daylight. . . .

[REDUCTION OF DAMAGES AFFIRMED.]

NOTES

1. *Assessing Risk.* The negligence determination requires an assessment of risk. Should an actor be financially responsible for any and all conduct that results in harm? How can courts evaluate risk? Hand suggests that the court measure the barge custodian's conduct by the relation of three variables: (1) the *probability* (P) that the risks will occur; (2) the *gravity* of resulting injury or *loss* (L); and (3) the *burden* (B) of adequate precaution to prevent the harm. Liability results for negligence if the burden of adequate precaution is less than the probability of harm times the gravity of harm (B < LP). So where a recognizable danger of injury exists, the formula asks whether the defendant had a responsibility to conduct herself differently and the evaluation of these variables yields an answer. Compare Hand's formulation with the Restatement (Second) of Torts § 291, which provides:

> Where an act is one which a reasonable man would recognize as involving a risk of harm to another, the risk is unreasonable and the act is negligent if the risk is of such magnitude as to outweigh what the law regards as the utility of the act or of the particular manner in which it is done.

REST. 2D TORTS § 291 (1965). The Restatement (Second) then supplies the following details:

§ 292. FACTORS CONSIDERED IN DETERMINING UTILITY OF ACTOR'S CONDUCT

> In determining what the law regards as the utility of the actor's conduct for the purpose of determining whether the actor is negligent, the following factors are important:
>
> > (a) the social value which the law attaches to the interest which is to be advanced or protected by the conduct;

(b) the extent of the chance that this interest will be advanced or protected by the particular course of conduct;

(c) the extent of the chance that such interest can be adequately advanced or protected by another and less dangerous course of conduct.

§ 293. FACTORS CONSIDERED IN DETERMINING MAGNITUDE OF RISK

In determining the magnitude of the risk for the purpose of determining whether the actor is negligent, the following factors are important:

(a) the social value which the law attaches to the interests which are imperiled;

(b) the extent of the chance that the actor's conduct will cause an invasion of any interest of the other or of one of a class of which the other is a member;

(c) the extent of the harm likely to be caused to the interests imperiled;

(d) the number of persons whose interests are likely to be invaded if the risk takes effect in harm.

REST. 2D TORTS §§ 292-293 (1965).

The Restatement (Third) (in draft as this book goes to press) revised and shortened The Restatement (Second) above as follows:

A person acts negligently if the person does not exercise reasonable care under all the circumstances. Primary factors to consider in ascertaining whether the person's conduct lacks reasonable care are the foreseeable likelihood that the person's conduct will result in harm, the foreseeable severity of any harm that may ensue, and the burden of precautions to eliminate or reduce the risk of harm.

REST. 3D TORTS § 3 (P.F.D. No. 1, 2005). Does this change in language from the Restatement (Second) to Restatement (Third) clarify the notion of standard of care?

2. *Practical Utility.* Does the "Hand formula" operate at a decisional level, or only at a theoretical one? Can the formula operate on an individual decisional basis, or only with regard to broad categories of fact patterns, that is to say, is it more useful when resolving "standard of care" or "duty" issues? Does this type of analysis operate so as to determine the issue of negligence or nonnegligence in a given case, or is this style of analysis better suited, not to mention more efficiently executed, in a more abstract determination of redistribution in general types of fact patterns? *See, e.g., Union Oil Co. v. Oppen,* 501 F.2d 558 (9th Cir. 1974). *See generally* George P. Fletcher, *Fairness and Utility in Tort Theory,* 85 HARV. L. REV. 537 (1972).

In *Johnson v. Thompson,* 143 S.E.2d 51 (Ga. 1965), the plaintiff was injured in defendant's drive-in theatre as he walked between parked automobiles to the snack bar. The defendant did not provide a safe walk way to the snack bar from the parking rows behind the snack bar, where the plaintiff was parked, and, as the plaintiff raised the wire leading from a post between parked cars to the speaker box placed in one of the cars, to pass under the wire, a person seated in the car opened the door and the door struck the plaintiff in his left eye and caused him to be seriously injured.

> In view of the uses for which the defendant invited patrons to the premises, reasonable men could disagree and it is a question of fact whether the risk of a patron walking to the snack bar being struck by a car door, was foreseeable. The next question is more difficult. If the risk was foreseeable, was it an unreasonable risk — was it a risk of such magnitude as to outweigh what the law regards as the utility of the defendant's alleged negligent conduct (not providing a walkway to the snack bar where this risk would not be present)? American Law Institute, Restatement, Torts 785 *et seq.*, §§ 291-293. This standard is complex but affords an opportunity for reaching substantial justice. The magnitude of a risk involves the social value of the interests imperiled (in this case the plaintiff's interest in bodily safety), the probability of harm to those to whom a duty is owed, and the extent of harm likely to be caused to them by exposure to the risk. *Id.* 791, § 293. Factors relating to the utility of particular conduct are the social usefulness of the enterprise (in this case the drive-in theatre), the value to the defendant of the particular way of conducting the enterprise (the alleged acts and omissions of negligence), and the extent to which the defendant's interest can be adequately advanced by another and less dangerous course of conduct (such as providing a special walk way to the snack bar). *Id.*, 788, § 292. We again believe that reasonable men could disagree whether, if the risk to the plaintiff was foreseeable, it was reasonable or unreasonable, considering the magnitude of the risk and the utility of the defendant's alleged negligent conduct.

Johnson, 143 S.E.2d at 53–54.

3. *Competing dangers.* Consider *Cooley v. Public Serv. Co.,* 10 A.2d 673 (N.H. 1940). There, a storm caused the defendant power company's cable to fall onto a telephone line, injuring the plaintiff telephone user's ear with a loud noise. Plaintiff argued that the power cable should have been insulated. Evidence suggested, however, that insulation could produce the result that the cable would not ground if it fell. The court noted,

> In the case before us, there was danger of electrocution in the street. As long as the Telephone Company's safety devices are properly installed and maintained, there is no danger of electrocution in the house. The only foreseeable danger to the telephone subscriber is from noise — fright and neurosis. Balancing the two, the danger to those such as the plaintiff is remote, that to those on the ground near the broken wire is obvious and immediate. The balance would not be improved by taking a chance to avoid traumatic neurosis of the plaintiff at the expense of greater risk to the lives of others. To the extent that the duty to use care depends upon relationship, the defendant's duty of care towards the plaintiff is obviously weaker than that towards the man in the street.

The defendant's duty cannot, in the circumstances, be to both. If that were so, performance of one duty would mean nonperformance of the other. . . . The law could tolerate no such theory of "be liable if you do and liable if you don't. . . ."

Cooley, 10 A.2d at 676–77. Might a defendant breach a duty to more than one party? Did the court properly apply a risk utility calculus in this case? Was the court's reasoning sound?

4. *The Hand Formula as the Criteria for the Negligence Determination.* According to then Professor, now Judge Richard A. Posner:

> Hand was adumbrating, perhaps unwittingly, an economic meaning of negligence. Discounting (multiplying) the cost of an accident if it occurs by the probability of occurrence yields a measure of the economic benefit to be anticipated from incurring the costs necessary to prevent the accident.

Richard A. Posner, *A Theory Of Negligence*, 1 J. LEGAL STUD. 29, 32 (1972).

Do you agree that Hand's formula is purely a mathematical formulation as Judge Posner suggests? Note that Hand observes the bargee must go ashore at times. Judge Hand's formula remains a central part of torts lore. It is the underpinning of much of today's economic analysis of the torts system. For more on Hand, see Benjamin C. Zipursky, Sleight of Hand, 48 WM. & MARY L. REV. 1999 (2007); RICHARD A. POSNER, ECONOMIC ANALYSIS OF LAW 147–51 (3d ed. 1986); GUIDO CALABRESI, THE COST OF ACCIDENTS: A LEGAL AND ECONOMIC ANALYSIS (1970); Frank J. Vandall, *Judge Posner's Negligence-Efficiency Theory: A Critique*, 35 EMORY L.J. 383 (1986); Izhak England, *The System Builders: A Critical Appraisal of Modern American Tort Theory*, 9 J. LEGAL STUD. 27 (1980); Ernest J. Weinrib, *Toward a Moral Theory of Negligence Law*, 2 LAW & PHIL. 37 (1983).

In *McCarty v. Pheasant Run, Inc.,* 826 F.2d 1554 (7th Cir. 1987), a case involving innkeeper liability under Illinois law, Judge Posner remarked:

> There are various ways in which courts formulate the negligence standard. The analytically (not necessarily the operationally) most precise is that it involves determining whether the burden of precaution is less than the magnitude of the accident, if it occurs, multiplied by the probability of occurrence. (The product of this multiplication, or "discounting," is what economists call an expected accident cost.) If the burden is less, the precaution should be taken. This is the famous "Hand Formula." . . .
>
> We are not authorized to change the common law of Illinois, however, and Illinois courts do not cite the Hand Formula but instead define negligence as failure to use reasonable care, a term left undefined. But as this is a distinction without a substantive difference, we have not hesitated to use the Hand Formula in cases governed by Illinois law. The formula translates into economic terms the conventional legal test for negligence. This can be seen by considering the factors that the

Illinois courts take into account in negligence cases: the same factors, and in the same relation, as in the Hand Formula. Unreasonable conduct is merely the failure to take precautions that would generate greater benefits in avoiding accidents than the precautions would cost.

McCarty, 826 F.2d at 1556–57.

Do you agree that the distinction between "reasonable care" and the Hand formula is one "without a substantive difference?"

5. *Life, Death, and Dollars* (1). Can B, P, and L satisfactorily be quantified? In *McCarty, supra*, Judge Posner observed:

> Ordinarily . . . the parties do not give the jury the information required to quantify the variables that the Hand Formula picks out as relevant. That is why the formula has greater analytic than operation significance. Conceptual as well as practical difficulties in monetizing personal injuries may continue to frustrate efforts to measure expected accident costs with the precision that is possible, in principle at least, in measuring the other side of the equation — the cost of burden of precaution. For many years to come juries may be forced to make rough judgments of reasonableness, intuiting rather than measuring the factors in the Hand Formula. . . .

826 F.2d at 1557.

Recall that in *Cooley v. Public Serv. Co.*, 10 A.2d 673 (N.H. 1940), one of the costs associated with the safety device suggested by plaintiff was an increased risk of electrocution to a different class of potential plaintiffs.

6. *Life, Death, and Dollars* (2). After a series of injuries and deaths allegedly caused by Ford Pinto and Mercury Bobcat fuel tanks rupturing in rear-end collisions, reports showed that the manufacturer had known of a defect but, on the basis of a cost-benefit analysis, had decided not to remedy the defect by installing $11 rubber bladders in the fuel tanks. An internal Ford memorandum entitled *Fatalities Associated with Crash-Induced Fuel Leakage and Fires*, known as the "Grush-Saunby Report," hypothesized a savings of $49.5 million for preventing an estimated 180 burn deaths, 180 serious burn injuries, and 2100 burned vehicles. The report further predicted a cost of $137 million for installing the $11.00 device in 11 million cars and 1.5 million light trucks. Mark Dowie, *Pinto Madness*, MOTHER JONES, Sept.-Oct. 1977, at 18, 24.

The court excluded this evidence from the most famous Ford Pinto trial, *Grimshaw v. Ford Motor Co.*, 174 Cal. Rptr. 348, 376 (Cal. Ct. App. 1981), dealing with damages from a rear-end collision. *See* Gary Schwartz, *The Ford Pinto Case*, 43 RUTGERS L. REV. 1013 (1991).

In a Pinto rear-end case involving a fire from fuel leakage, would you accept any of the following conclusions?

(1) In a situation such as this, where B > PL, it would be a misallocation of resources to redistribute accident costs through the torts system.

(2) Whatever the merits of the Hand formula as a judicial tool, its strategic use by potential defendants will not be tolerated.

(3) If the automobile market had operated properly (e.g., if consumers had known of the contents of the memorandum), the manufacturer would have been forced to correct the defect and governmental or judicial intervention would have been unnecessary.

(4) The whole point of the torts system is to intervene and deter when the market creates intolerable results.

(5) The memorandum involves retrofit costs and does not provide the data necessary for the application of the Hand formula.

(6) The automobile manufacturer should have been prosecuted for reckless homicide.

7. *The Maritime History of the Hand Formula.* Federal courts, and particularly those dealing with maritime issues, have shown the greatest interest in the literal application of the Hand formula. For example, in *United States Fidelity & Guaranty Co. v. Jadranska Slobodna,* 683 F.2d 1022 (7th Cir. 1982), Judge Posner noted:

> Though mathematical in form, the Hand formula does not yield mathematically precise results in practice; that would require that B, P, and L all be quantified, which so far as we know has never been done in an actual lawsuit. Nevertheless, the formula is a valuable aid to clear thinking about the factors that are relevant to a judgment of negligence and about the relationship among those factors. It gives federal district courts in maritime cases, where the liability standard is a matter of federal rather than state law, a useful framework for evaluating proposed jury instructions, for deciding motions for directed verdict and for judgment notwithstanding the verdict. . . . We do not want to force the district courts into a straitjacket, so we do not hold that they must use the Hand formula in all maritime negligence cases. We merely commend it to them as a useful tool — one we have found helpful in this case in evaluating the plaintiff's challenge to the jury instructions and its contention that negligence was shown as a matter of law.

Jadranska Slobodna, 683 F.2d at 1026. Why does it make sense to apply the Hand Formula to maritime cases? Should the formula be restricted to maritime cases?

8. *The "Market" Placed in Evidence.* What is the relationship between custom and risk-utility analysis? In *Jadranska Slobodna,* Judge Posner stated:

> The fact that the practice of leaving the hatches open in darkened holds was customary (or so the jury could find) and not just an idiosyncrasy of this Yugoslavian ship or ship owner has additional relevance to this case. Although custom is not a defense to a charge of negligence, *The T. J. Hooper,* 60 F.2d 737, 740 (2d Cir. 1932), it is a material consideration in evaluating the charge, especially where the victim and the alleged tortfeasor are linked, even if indirectly, in a voluntary relation-

ship, as they were here. If a ship owner were to follow a practice that flunked the Hand formula — that in other words was not cost-justified, because the expected accident costs associated with the practice exceeded the costs of abandoning the practice and so preventing any accident from happening — then he would have to pay his stevedores higher rates, to compensate them for the additional risk to their employees, the longshoremen, whom the stevedores must compensate under 33 U.S.C. § 904, regardless of fault, for any injury the longshoremen sustain in the course of their employment. And since by hypothesis the cost to the stevedores of the additional compensation — the expected accident cost, in other words — would exceed the cost of abandoning the practice (for otherwise the practice would be cost-justified), it would pay the ship owner to abandon it. Hence if the ship owner persists in a dangerous practice — if the whole trade persists in the practice — that is some evidence, though not conclusive, that the practice is cost-justified, and not negligent.

Jadranska Slobodna, 683 F.2d at 1028–1029.

9. *Jury Instruction for Negligence.* Consider this example of a jury instruction on the standard of care:

> Negligence is the doing of something which a reasonably prudent person would not do, or the failure to do something which a reasonably prudent person would do, under circumstances similar to those shown by the evidence.

> It is the failure to use ordinary or reasonable care.

> Ordinary or reasonable care is that care which persons of ordinary prudence would use in order to avoid injury to themselves or others under circumstances similar to those shown by the evidence.

> [You will note that the person whose conduct we set up as a standard is not the extraordinarily cautious individual, nor the exceptionally skillful one, but a person of reasonable and ordinary prudence.]

California Jury Instructions — Civil (BAJI) § 3.10 (2006). Would this instruction help you, if you were a juror, to decide if an actor had complied with the standard of care? What questions might it raise for you? As this instruction illustrates, a determination of reasonable care is incomplete without a consideration of the reasonable prudent person.

2. The Reasonable Person

The notion of negligence (that one should act to avoid unreasonable risks) assumes a uniformity of behavior or the idea of a standard of conduct. To what extent is this uniformity possible? The judge articulates the standard of care in a negligence case to the jury in terms of the hypothetical person who would act reasonably under the circumstances. *See, e.g.,* note 9 *supra.* Should individual attributes of the actor be taken into account by the jury, in determining whether the person acted reasonably? Consider this hypothetical fact pattern:

Defendant farmer Bill had stored hay near his neighbor's property. It was widely known that the method of storing hay that he used created a high risk of fire. The hay did catch fire and the fire spread, damaging the neighbor's property. The neighbor sued and defendant testified, "I exercised my best judgment; I did the best I could, but this terrible accident happened anyway." Should Bill be held liable?

In *Vaughan v. Menlove*, (1837) 132 Eng. Rep. 490 (C.P.), based on similar facts, the court rejected the notion that an actor's best judgment should be the measure of liability.

If the standard is not measured by an actor's best judgment, what should be used to inform the applicable standard? What are the characteristics of a reasonable person? The Restatement (Second) of Torts § 283 provides: "Unless the actor is a child, the standard of conduct to which [s]he must conform to avoid being negligent is that of a reasonable [person] under like circumstances." REST. 2D TORTS § 283 (1965). Is this standard objective or subjective? Are some aspects of the general standard contained in § 283 less objective than others? What are the practical advantages and disadvantages of using either a subjective or an objective standard?

The comments to Section 283 state that the real person is "required to do what this ideal[, hypothetical] individual would do in his place. The reasonable man is a fictitious person, who is never negligent, and whose conduct is always up to the standard." *Id.*, cmt. *c*. This fictitious person is "not to be identified with any real person"; in fact, it would be "error to instruct the jury that the conduct of a reasonable man is to be determined by what they would themselves have done." *Id.* Is it realistic to expect real people to meet the standard of the reasonable person? By the comments saying that the ideal individual is not to be identified with a real person, are the commentators suggesting that a real person, having caused a personal injury, will always be negligent? How should real people act? *See* REST. 2D TORTS § 285, cmt. *a* (1965).

Does the reasonable person have a race or gender? Should she or he? Consider this view recognizing the need for a gendered perspective in the context of a hostile environment sexual harassment case:

> We adopt the perspective of a reasonable woman primarily because we believe that a sex-blind reasonable person standard tends to be male-biased and tends to systematically ignore the experiences of women. The reasonable woman standard does not establish a higher level of protection for women than men. Instead, a gender-conscious examination of sexual harassment enables women to participate in the workplace on an equal footing with men. By acknowledging and not trivializing the effects of sexual harassment on reasonable women, courts can work towards ensuring that neither men nor women will have to "run a gauntlet of sexual abuse in return for the privilege of being allowed to work and make a living."

Ellison v. Brady, 924 F.2d 872, 879–80 (9th Cir. 1991). Should this reasoning apply in the personal injury context?

Although objective in nature, the decision-making process for the standard of care continually exhibits subjective characteristics; it might be termed subjective objectivism. The ability to fine-tune the standard for a particular defendant is institutionalized in the commonly found language in the jury charge, "in all the circumstances." The "in all the circumstances" tag found in the typical objective negligence instruction permits the consideration of specific, detailed factors, and thus deviates from a totally objective model, captured in "the reasonable person." What does this apparent ambivalence in the instruction suggest about the competing goals of accident law and the tension likely to be encountered? Which "circumstances" are relevant to the negligence inquiry? Which are, or should be, irrelevant? Of all the specific elements that courts have recognized as having continued relevance in the determination of objectively tested negligence, none has been as perplexing as the actor's personal characteristics.

Courts have imbued the reasonable person with subjective characteristics in the case of children, physical disability or other-abledness, and superior attributes, such as professionals in the context of alleged malpractice.

a.   Children

ROBINSON v. LINDSAY
598 P.2d 392 (Wash. 1979)

UTTER, C.J.

[Kelly Robinson, age 11, lost full use of a thumb in a snowmobile accident. The defendant, Billy Anderson, 13 years of age at the time of the accident, was the driver of the snowmobile. The jury rendered a verdict for defendant.]

The single issue on appeal is whether a minor operating a snowmobile is to be held to an adult standard of care. The trial court failed to instruct the jury as to that standard and ordered a new trial because it believed the jury should have been so instructed. We agree and affirm the order granting a new trial.

The trial court instructed the jury under WPI 10.05 that:

> In considering the claimed negligence of a child, you are instructed that it is the duty of a child to exercise the same care that a reasonably careful child of the same age, intelligence, maturity, training and experience would exercise under the same or similar circumstances.

> Respondent [plaintiff] properly excepted to the giving of this instruction and to the court's failure to give an adult standard of care.

The question of what standard of care should apply to acts of children has a long historical background. Traditionally, a flexible standard of care has been used to determine if children's actions were negligent. Under some circumstances, however, courts have developed a rationale for applying an adult standard.

In the courts' search for a uniform standard of behavior to use in determining whether or not a person's conduct has fallen below minimal acceptable standards, the law has developed a fictitious person, the "reasonable man of ordinary prudence." That term was first used in *Vaughan v. Menlove*, 132 Eng. Rep. 490 (1837).

Exceptions to the reasonable person standard developed when the individual whose conduct was alleged to have been negligent suffered from some physical impairment, such as blindness, deafness, or lameness. Courts also found it necessary, as a practical matter, to depart considerably from the objective standard when dealing with children's behavior. Children are traditionally encouraged to pursue childhood activities without the same burdens and responsibilities with which adults must contend As a result, courts evolved a special standard of care to measure a child's negligence in a particular situation.

. . . The current law in this state is fairly reflected in WPI 10.05, given in this case. In the past we have always compared a child's conduct to that expected of a reasonably careful child of the same age, intelligence, maturity, training and experience. This case is the first to consider the question of a child's liability for injuries sustained as a result of his or her operation of a motorized vehicle or participation in an inherently dangerous activity.

Courts in other jurisdictions have created an exception to the special child standard because of the apparent injustice that would occur if a child who caused injury while engaged in certain dangerous activities were permitted to defend himself by saying that other children similarly situated would not have exercised a degree of care higher than his, and he is, therefore, not liable for his tort. Some courts have couched the exception in terms of children engaging in an activity which is normally one for adults only. *See, e.g., Dellwo v. Pearson*, 107 N.W.2d 859 (Minn.1961) (operation of a motorboat). We believe a better rationale is that when the activity a child engages in is inherently dangerous, as is the operation of powerful mechanized vehicles, the child should be held to an adult standard of care.

Such a rule protects the need of children to be children but at the same time discourages immature individuals from engaging in inherently dangerous activities. Children will still be free to enjoy traditional childhood activities without being held to an adult standard of care. Although accidents sometimes occur as the result of such activities, they are not activities generally considered capable of resulting in "grave danger to others and to the minor himself if the care used in the course of the activity drops below that care which the reasonable and prudent adult would use. . . ." *Daniels v. Evans*, 107 N.H. 407, 408 (1966).

Other courts adopting the adult standard of care for children engaged in adult activities have emphasized the hazards to the public if the rule is otherwise. We agree with the Minnesota Supreme Court's language in its decision in *Dellwo v. Pearson*:

> Certainly in the circumstances of modern life, where vehicles moved by powerful motors are readily available and frequently operated by immature individuals, we should be skeptical of a rule that would

allow motor vehicles to be operated to the hazard of the public with less than the normal minimum degree of care and competence.

Dellwo applied the adult standard to a 12-year-old defendant operating a motorboat. Other jurisdictions have applied the adult standard to minors engaged in analogous activities. *Goodfellow v. Coggburn*, 98 Idaho 202, 203–04, (1977) (minor operating tractor); *Williams v. Esaw*, 214 Kan. 658, 668, (1974) (minor operating motorcycle); *Perricone v. DiBartolo*, 14 Ill. App. 3d 514, 520 (1973) (minor operating gasoline-powered minibike); *Krahn v. LaMeres*, 483 P.2d 522, 525–26 (Wyo. 1971) (minor operating automobile). The holding of minors to an adult standard of care when they operate motorized vehicles is gaining approval from an increasing number of courts and commentators.

The operation of a snowmobile likewise requires adult care and competence. Currently 2.2 million snowmobiles are in operation in the United States. 9 BNA Envir. Rptr. 876 [1978 Current Developments]. Studies show that collisions and other snowmobile accidents claim hundreds of casualties each year and that the incidence of accidents is particularly high among inexperienced operators.

At the time of the accident, the 13-year-old petitioner had operated snowmobiles for about 2 years. When the injury occurred, petitioner was operating a 30-horsepower snowmobile at speeds of 10 to 20 miles per hour. The record indicates that the machine itself was capable of 65 miles per hour. Because petitioner was operating a powerful motorized vehicle, he should be held to the standard of care and conduct expected of an adult.

The order granting a new trial is affirmed.

NOTES

1. *Setting the Standard of Care.* This case articulates the standard of care applied to children. The child actor's conduct will be compared to a child of like age, intelligence, maturity, training, and experience. Courts have created an exception to this standard for children engaged in adult activities.

Compare this expression of the standard of care for children to the adult standard, articulated in REST. 2D TORTS § 283 (1965) *supra*. Does it make sense to measure children's behavior by a separate standard? Does it make sense to create an exception to that differential treatment?

2. *Rationales for Exceptions to the Child Standard.* Judicial approaches to the reasoning in cases like *Robinson* vary. Some courts apply the adult standard to children using "dangerous instrumentalities." Others apply the adult standard to "adult activities" or "adult *and* dangerous activities." Still others are specific as to the activities covered, for example, driving an automobile. What considerations underlie such different formulations? Can one expect that different jurisdictions will reach differing conclusions on what activities are appropriate for adults or children? Why?

Should imposition of an adult standard of care upon a child depend upon who is the best accident avoider? *See, e.g., Dellwo v. Pearson,* 107 N.W.2d 859 (Minn. 1961), where the issue was the negligence of a 12-year-old driver of a powerboat. The court concluded:

> While minors are entitled to be judged by standards commensurate with age, experience, and wisdom when engaged in activities appropriate to their age, experience, and wisdom, it would be unfair to the public to permit a minor in the operation of a motor vehicle to observe any other standards of care and conduct than those expected of all others. A person observing children at play with toys, throwing balls, operating tricycles or velocipedes, or engaged in other childhood activities may anticipate conduct that does not reach an adult standard of care or prudence. However, one cannot know whether the operator of an approaching automobile, airplane, or powerboat is a minor or an adult, and usually cannot protect himself against youthful imprudence even if warned. Accordingly, we hold that in the operation of an automobile, airplane, or powerboat, a minor is to be held to the same standard of care as an adult.

Dellwo, 107 N.W.2d at 863. Is this view consistent with a statement that the age of a potential child victim may impose upon the adult actor a "higher standard of care?" *See Kilpack v. Wignall,* 604 P.2d 462 (Utah 1979); *Buckley v. Exxon Corp.,* 390 So. 2d 512 (La. 1980) (motorist who sees a child on or near the road is under a high degree of care and must anticipate that the child, possessed of limited judgment, might be unable to appreciate impending danger, is likely to be inattentive, and might suddenly place himself in a position of peril). Compare *Vitale v. Belmont Springs,* 916 P.2d 359 (Utah App. 1996) (standard of care required by a defendant to a plaintiff over the age of 14 is the same as that required for an adult).

How do children shift the risk of their alleged negligence? Are they worth suing? Do your answers affect the choice of the responsibility rule for which you would argue?

3. *Judge and Jury.* Should the court or the jury make the determination as to whether an activity is "potentially hazardous" or "adult" in nature? What are the effects of the decision on this issue?

4. *Children of "Tender Years."* A few courts have grappled with the question as to whether some children simply are too immature to be responsible in negligence. For example, in *DeLuca v. Bowden,* 329 N.E.2d 109 (Ohio 1975), the court held a seven-year-old child was incapable of negligence, remarking that:

> The basic dilemma of all these cases is that a child of tender years has only some dim and imponderable responsibility for his acts — and yet those acts, as those of an adult, may cause injury to others. . . . Our laws and our moral concepts assume actors capable of legal and moral choices, of which a young child is incapable. For that reason, a child under seven years of age was at common law considered incapable of criminal responsibility. For the same reason, we cannot accept those rules which hold a child strictly liable, or which permit a jury to find liability, in cases of intentional tort. Our choice is between rules which permit the imposition of a legal judgment upon a young child for his

intentional acts, and a rule which holds that members of society must accept the damage done by very young children to be no more subject to legal action than some force of nature or act of God. Our choice is the latter rule. . . .

DeLuca, 329 N.E.2d at 111. *Compare Camerlinck v. Thomas*, 312 N.W.2d 260 (Neb. 1981) (minor's responsibility was not to be subject to arbitrary line drawing, but should be determined on a case-by-case basis).

In *Dunn v. Teti*, 421 A.2d 782 (Pa. Super. Ct.1980), the court took a different approach, recognizing:

The application of this (child of like age, experience, capacity and development) standard is clarified by the use of several presumptions delineating convenient points to aid in drawing the uncertain line between capacity to appreciate and guard against danger and incapacity: (1) minors under the age of seven years are conclusively presumed incapable of negligence; (2) minors between the ages of seven and fourteen years are presumed incapable of negligence, but the presumption is a rebuttable one that weakens as the fourteenth year is approached; (3) minors over the age of fourteen years are presumptively capable of negligence, with the burden placed on the minor to prove incapacity. . . .

Dunn, 421 A.2d at 784. How do the *DeLuca, Dunn* and *Camerlinck* approaches differ in practical terms and in their distributional effects?

5. *The Double-Standard Debate*. Does it matter whether the child to be measured by an adult standard is the plaintiff (facing an affirmative defense of contributory or comparative fault) or the defendant? What if both plaintiff and defendant are minors?

In *Daniels v. Evans*, 224 A.2d 63, 66 (N.H. 1966), the court stated, "[W]hen a minor is operating a motor vehicle there is no reason for making a distinction based on whether he is charged with primary negligence, [or] contributory negligence."

However, in *Dellwo v. Pearson*, 107 N.W.2d 859, 863 (Minn. 1961), the court stated, "[T]his court has previously recognized that there may be a difference between the standard of care that is required of a child in protecting himself against hazards and the standard that may be applicable when these activities expose others to hazards."

What are the reasons for this "double standard" debate? What tensions in the system does it highlight? How should the debate be resolved? Might the answer depend on which perspective, discussed in Chapter 1, *supra*, a court adopts?

b. Physical and Mental Characteristics

The REST. 2D TORTS § 283C (1965) provides: "If the actor is ill or otherwise physically disabled, the standard of conduct to which he must conform to avoid being negligent is that of a reasonable [person] under like disability." Okianer Christian Dark explains: "One cannot ask a person with a physical disability to conduct him or herself as though the physical disability does not exist. . . . Therefore, a blind person is not judged by the standard of a seeing person nor is the conduct of a person in a wheelchair evaluated by that of a person able to walk." Okianer Christian Dark, *Tort Liability and the "Unquiet Mind": A Proposal to Incorporate Mental Disabilities into the Standard of Care*, 30 T. MARSHALL L. REV. 169, 175 (2004).

What is a physical disability? Which disabilities should or should not be taken into account in evaluating reasonable, prudent conduct? Suppose the defendant was an alcoholic. Would the court then permit an instruction phrased in terms of a reasonably prudent inebriate? How should that standard compare to the conduct expected of a hyperglycemic diabetic?

Note that consideration of a physical disability does not automatically mean that the actor will not be liable. "[T]he person with such a disability is expected to conduct him or herself in a manner that takes this limitation into account. If the person with a physical disability fails to take his or her limitation into account, as a reasonable person would be expected to do, then he or she will nonetheless be liable." Dark, *supra*, at 175.

Why should the court concern itself with any such personalization of the standard of care before imposing liability? Does such a concern unjustifiably focus our attention on the wrongdoer at the expense of the victim?

Should mental disabilities receive different treatment from physical ones? Does this physical/mental distinction even make sense? Consider this case that arises in the context of a mental disability.

CREASY v. RUSK
730 N.E.2d 659 (Ind. 2000)

SULLIVAN, JUSTICE.

. . . In July, 1992, Lloyd Rusk's wife admitted Rusk to the Brethren Healthcare Center ("BHC") because he suffered from memory loss and confusion and Rusk's wife was unable to care for him. Rusk's primary diagnosis was Alzheimer's disease. Over the course of three years at BHC, Rusk experienced periods of anxiousness, confusion, depression, disorientation, and agitation. Rusk often resisted when staff members attempted to remove him from pro-hibited areas of the facility. On several occasions, Rusk was belligerent with both staff and other residents. In particular, Rusk was often combative, agitated, and aggressive and would hit staff members when they tried to care for him.

BHC had employed Creasy as a certified nursing assistant for nearly 20 months when the incident at issue occurred. Creasy's responsibilities included caring for Rusk and other patients with Alzheimer's disease. Creasy did not have specialized training on how to care for people with Alzheimer's disease, but she did attend a short BHC presentation on the pathological effects of Alzheimer's. Residents with Alzheimer's had bruised Creasy during the course of her work for BHC, and Creasy knew that Rusk had Alzheimer's disease.

On May 16, 1995, Creasy and another certified nursing assistant, Linda Davis, were working through their routine of putting Rusk and other residents to bed. Creasy knew that Rusk had been "very agitated and combative that evening." By Creasy's account:

> [Davis] was helping me put Mr. Rusk to bed. She was holding his wrists to keep him from hitting us and I was trying to get his legs to put him to bed. He was hitting and kicking wildly. During this time, he kicked me several times in my left knee and hip area. My lower back popped and I yelled out with pain from my lower back and left knee.

Creasy filed a civil negligence suit against Rusk, seeking monetary damages for the injuries she suffered as a result of Rusk's conduct. Rusk moved for summary judgment and the trial court granted his motion. . . .

In many, if not most, jurisdictions, the general duty of care imposed on adults with mental disabilities is the same as that for adults without mental disabilities. *See* Restatement (Second) of Torts § 283B (1965). Adults with mental disabilities are held to the same standard of care as that of a reasonable person under the same circumstances without regard to the alleged tortfeasor's capacity to control or understand the consequences of his or her actions.

. . . The Court of Appeals held "that [under Indiana law, not following the Restatement] a person's mental capacity, whether that person is a child or an adult, must be factored [into] the determination of whether a legal duty exists." *Creasy v. Rusk*, 696 N.E.2d 442, 446 (Ind. Ct. App. 1998). We believe that the Court of Appeals accurately stated Indiana law but that the law is in need of revision.

* * *

. . . [T]he generally accepted rule in jurisdictions other than Indiana is that mental disability does not excuse a person from liability for "conduct which does not conform to the standard of a reasonable man under like circumstances." Restatement (Second) of Torts § 283B; accord Restatement (Third) of Torts § 9 (Discussion Draft Apr. 5, 1999) ("Unless the actor is a child, the actor's mental or emotional disability is not considered in determining whether conduct is negligent."). People with mental disabilities are commonly held liable for their intentional and negligent torts. No allowance is made for lack of intelligence, ignorance, excitability, or proneness to accident.

Legal scholars and authorities recognize that it is "impossible to ascribe either the volition implicit in an intentional tort, the departure from the standard of a 'reasonable' person which defines an act of ordinary negligence, or indeed any concept of 'fault' at all to one who . . . is by definition unable to control his [or her] own actions through any exercise of reason." *Anicet v. Gant*, 580 So. 2d 273, 275 (Fla. Dist. Ct. App. 1991) (citations omitted). Rather, the Restatement rule holding people with mental disabilities liable for their torts was founded upon public policy considerations.

The public policy reasons most often cited for holding individuals with mental disabilities to a standard of reasonable care in negligence claims include the following.

(1) Allocates losses between two innocent parties to the one who caused or occasioned the loss. *See, e.g., Gould v. American Family Mut. Ins.*, 198 Wis. 2d 450, 543 N.W.2d 282, 286 (Wis. 1996). Under this rationale, the one who experienced the loss or injury as a result of the conduct of a person with a mental disability is presumed not to have assumed risks or to have been contributorily negligent with respect to the cause of the injury. This policy is also intended to protect even negligent third parties from bearing excessive liabilities.

(2) Provides incentive to those responsible for people with disabilities and interested in their estates to prevent harm and "restrain" those who are potentially dangerous.

(3) Removes inducements for alleged tortfeasors to fake a mental disability in order to escape liability. The Restatement mentions the ease with which mental disability can be feigned as one possible basis for this policy concern.

(4) Avoids administrative problems involved in courts and juries attempting to identify and assess the significance of an actor's disability. As a practical matter, it is arguably too difficult to account for or draw any "satisfactory line between mental deficiency and those variations of temperament, intellect, and emotional balance."

(5) Forces persons with disabilities to pay for the damage they do if they "are to live in the world." The Restatement adds that it is better that the assets, if any, of the one with the mental deficiency be used "to compensate innocent victims than that [the assets] remain in their hands." A discussion draft for the Restatement (Third) of Torts rephrases this policy rationale and concludes: "If a person is suffering from a mental disorder so serious as to make it likely that the person will engage in substandard conduct that threatens the safety of others, there can be doubts as to whether this person should be allowed to engage in the normal range of society's activities; given these doubts, there is nothing especially harsh in at least holding the person responsible for the harms the person may cause by substandard conduct."

To assist in deciding whether Indiana should adopt the generally accepted rule, we turn to an examination of contemporary public policy in Indiana as embodied in enactments of our state legislature.

Since the 1970s, Indiana law has strongly reflected policies to deinstitutionalize people with disabilities and integrate them into the least restrictive environment. National policy changes have led the way for some of Indiana's enactments in that several federal acts either guarantee the civil rights of people with disabilities or condition state aid upon state compliance with desegregation and integrationist practices. . . .

These legislative developments reflect policies consistent with those supporting the Restatement rule generally accepted outside Indiana in that they reflect a determination that people with disabilities should be treated in the same way as non-disabled persons.

We pause for a moment to consider in greater detail the [argument] that the Restatement rule may very well have been grounded in a policy determination that persons with mental disabilities should be institutionalized or otherwise confined rather than "live in the world." It is clear from our recitation of state and federal legislative and regulatory developments that contemporary public policy has rejected institutionalization and confinement for a "strong professional consensus in favor of . . . community treatment . . . and integration into the least restrictive . . . environment." Indeed, scholarly commentary has noted that "new statutes and case law . . . have transformed the areas of commitment, guardianship, confidentiality, consent to treatment, and institutional conditions." We observe that it is a matter of some irony that public policies favoring the opposite ends of institutionalization and confinement on the one hand and community treatment and integration into the least restrictive environment on the other should nevertheless yield the same common law rule: that the general duty of care imposed on adults with mental disabilities is the same as that for adults without mental disabilities.

In balancing the considerations presented in the foregoing analysis, we reject the Court of Appeals' approach and adopt the Restatement rule. We hold that a person with mental disabilities is generally held to the same standard of care as that of a reasonable person under the same circumstances without regard to the alleged tortfeasor's capacity to control or understand the consequences of his or her actions . . .

We turn now to the question of whether the circumstances of Rusk's case are such that the general duty of care imposed upon adults with mental disabilities should be found to run from him to Creasy.

In asking this question, we recognize that exceptions to the general rule will arise where the factual circumstances negate the factors supporting imposition of a duty particularly with respect to the nature of the parties' relationship and public policy considerations. For example, courts in jurisdictions that apply the reasonable person standard to individuals with mental disabilities have uniformly held that Alzheimer's patients who have no capacity to control their conduct do not owe a duty to their caregivers to refrain from violent conduct because the factual circumstances negate the policy rationales behind the presumption of liability. *See Colman v. Notre Dame Convalescent Home, Inc.*, 968 F. Supp. 809 (D. Conn. 1997) (holding that while an adult with mental disabilities is ordinarily responsible for injuries resulting from negligence, no duty arises between an institutionalized patient and his or her caregiver); *Gould v. American Family Mut. Ins. Co.*, 198 Wis. 2d 450, 543 N.W.2d 282 (Wis. 1996) (carving out an exception to the presumption of liability for institutionalized mentally disabled people who are unable to control or appreciate the consequences of their conduct when they injure paid caregivers and noting that these circumstances negate the rationale behind the presumption and that application of the presumption would place an unreasonable burden on people with mental disabilities who are institutionalized); *Herrle v. Estate of Marshall*, 45 Cal. App. 4th 1761, 53 Cal. Rptr. 2d 713 (Ct. App. 1996) (concluding that public policy precluded imposition of liability because the healthcare provider, not the patient, is in the best position to protect against risk of injury to the service provider where the risk is rooted in the reason for the treatment), review denied; *Mujica v. Turner*, 582 So.2d 24 (Fla. Dist. Ct. App. 1991) (holding nursing home patient with Alzheimer's was not liable for injury to a physical therapist), review denied; *Anicet v. Gant*, 580 So.2d 273 (Fla. Dist. Ct. App. 1991) (concluding that a person who has no capacity to control his or her conduct does not owe a duty to refrain from violent conduct toward a person who is specifically employed to treat or control the patient), review denied.

We find that the relationship between Rusk and Creasy and public policy concerns dictate that Rusk owed no duty of care to Creasy. . . .

Unlike the typical victim supporting the Restatement rationale, Creasy was not a member of the public at large, unable to anticipate or safeguard against the harm she encountered. Creasy knew of Rusk's violent history. She could have changed her course of action or requested additional assistance when she recognized Rusk's state of mind on the evening when she received the alleged injury. Rusk's inability to comprehend the circumstances of his relationship with Creasy and others was the very reason Creasy was employed to support Rusk. The nursing home and Creasy, through the nursing home, were "employed to encounter, and knowingly did encounter, just the dangers which injured" Creasy. In fact, caregivers and their employers under these circumstances are better positioned to prevent caregiver injury and to protect against risks faced as a result of job responsibilities. In Indiana, the workers' compensation system, not the tort system, exists to cover such employment-related losses. To the extent that the workers' compensation system is inadequate as Creasy asserts, the inadequacy reflects defects in the workers' compensation system and is not a ground for alternative recovery under tort law.

. . . The first rationale behind the Restatement rule justifies imposing a duty on a defendant with a mental disability where it seems unfair to force a plaintiff who did not contribute to the cause of his or her injury to bear the cost of that injury. This policy concern overlaps with the relationship analysis set forth *supra*. The nature of Creasy and Rusk's relationship was such that Creasy cannot be "presumed not to have assumed risks . . . with respect to the cause of the injury." *See* Rationale (1), *supra*. Therefore, imposing a duty on Rusk in this circumstance is not justified by the first Restatement policy rationale.

The second Restatement policy rationale creates an inducement for those responsible for a person with a mental disability to prevent harm to others. By placing Rusk in a nursing home, we presume Rusk's wife made a difficult decision based on her desire to prevent Rusk from being violent and harming himself, herself, or others. Without endorsing the incentives for confinement arguably fostered by the Restatement rationale, we agree with the conclusion set forth by the Wisconsin Supreme Court in *Gould* that a family member who places a relative in a long-term care facility, institution, nursing home, or similarly restrictive environment is unlikely to need further inducement to restrain the one for whom they are responsible. *See Gould*, 543 N.W.2d at 287. Mrs. Rusk entrusted her husband's care, including prevention of the harm he might bring to others, to the nursing home staff and the nursing home. And as a business enterprise, the nursing home received compensation for its services.

With respect to the third policy rationale, "it is virtually impossible to imagine circumstances under which a person would feign the symptoms of mental disability and subject themselves to commitment to an institution in order to avoid some future civil liability." *Id. See also* Rationale (3), *supra.* To the extent that such circumstances exist, there is no evidence whatsoever that they are present under the facts in this case.

Finally, there are no administrative difficulties in this case with respect to determining the degree and existence of Rusk's mental disability.[11] Under the relationship analysis set forth above and the present policy analysis, it is unnecessary to determine the degree of Rusk's mental disability. We need only conclude that Rusk had a mental disability which served as the reason for his presence in the nursing home and the foundation of his relationship with Creasy.

. . . [T]here was no material question of fact as to the existence, let alone the advanced stage, of Rusk's Alzheimer's disease and his inability to appreciate or control his violent behavior. Rusk was admitted to the nursing home because he was confused and suffering from memory loss such that his wife could not care for him. By May 1995, when Creasy was injured by Rusk, Rusk had been a resident of the nursing home for three years and his condition had deteriorated. He regularly displayed behaviors characteristic of a person with advanced Alzheimer's disease such as aggression, belligerence, and violence. As evidence of Rusk's state of mind, Rusk presented an affidavit from Sharon Ayres [a licensed practical nurse employed by the nursing home] stating that Rusk was in the advanced stage of Alzheimer's and was therefore unable to appreciate the consequences of his actions . . .

In addition to the public policy concerns behind the Restatement rule, we find that it would be contrary to public policy to hold Rusk to a duty to Creasy when it would place "too great a burden on him because his disorientation and potential for violence is the very reason he was institutionalized and needed the aid of employed caretakers." *Gould*, 543 N.W.2d at 286.

Rusk was entitled to summary judgment because public policy and the nature of the relationship between Rusk, Creasy, and the nursing home preclude holding that Rusk owed a duty of care to Creasy under these factual circumstances.

. . . [W]e now affirm the trial court, finding that Rusk did not owe a duty to Creasy, and grant Rusk's motion for summary judgment.

NOTES

1. *Psychological Characteristics.* REST. 2D TORTS § 283B (1965) provides:

---

[11] Many legal scholars have questioned the significance of the "administrative difficulties and judicial efficiency" policy rationale behind the Restatement rule. They argue that our legal system regularly entrusts judges and juries as fact-finders to make difficult determinations about mental competence for a range of legal issues (e.g., guardianship, contract and testamentary capacity, criminal proceedings, contributory negligence allocations in tort claims, and commitment hearings) because fact-finders are uniquely positioned to weigh evidence, judge credibility, assess witness testimony, and apply the law thereto.

Unless the actor is a child, his insanity or other mental deficiency does not relieve the actor from liability for conduct which does not conform to the standard of a reasonable man under like circumstances.

Why should physical, but not mental, characteristics be taken into account when setting the standard of care? Which is the more *efficient* approach: *Creasy* or that followed in the Restatement (Second)? Does the Restatement contemplate liability only in the case of a more or less permanent mental disability, as opposed to a sudden seizure? Why should any such distinction be drawn between sudden mental incapacitation and an ongoing disorder?

In *Goff v. Taylor,* 708 S.W.2d 113 (Ky. App. 1986), involving an unprovoked killing by a defendant who was apparently mentally unstable, the court made these comments about the criticisms of the Restatement approach:

> [T]hat a subjective standard would afford fairer treatment of a defendant afflicted with a mental disability cannot be disputed. The question the commentators do not attempt to reach is the fairness to the victim of the wrongful conduct. Is a victim any less entitled to compensation for his loss because of the mental deficiencies of his tortfeasor? We believe that the answer is no, and the tort law as it stands has long served to accommodate that principle. This view does not penalize the mentally incompetent, it merely places them on a par with the rest of society in terms of responsibility for their wrongful acts. The mentally deficient are insulated from punitive damages, reinforcing our belief that tort law has kept faith with its duty to balance the protection of society at large with compassion for those unable to conform their conduct to the expected standard.

Goff, 708 S.W.2d at 115. Does *Goff* stop at placing such a defendant "on a par with the rest of society," or is the risk of the mentally ill defendant's conduct being shifted elsewhere?

Okianer Christian Dark urges courts to treat mental and physical disabilities in the same way. She explains that the traditional rule has been based on the notion "that mental disabilities are somehow unconnected to and unrelated to physical disabilities or limitations." Dark, *supra* at 200. In contrast, the medical community concurs "that nearly all psychiatric and developmental problems which might prevent one from conforming his conduct to [the] standard required of 'healthy people' are manifestations of physiological abnormalities." *Id.*

> [A]n examination of the scientific research on the causes of mental illness reveals clear organic or physiological connections. Thus, distinguishing between physical and mental disabilities by promulgating two different rules that govern the standard of care in negligence cases based on this distinction makes less sense . . .
>
> [T]he courts could easily adopt an approach that modifies the Restatement (Third) of Torts in the following way: "Unless the actor is a child, the actor's mental or emotional disability which is not signifi-

cantly physical in origin, is not considered in determining whether conduct is negligent. Those mental or emotional disabilities that have significant physical causality will be evaluated under [the Restatement section for physical differences]." This proposal is based on the current scientific research on mental disabilities. It takes advantage of what we know and allows the courts to access that information in making the assessment as to whether to allow a defendant with mental disabilities to proceed under one rule or the other. One advantage of allowing the courts to receive and review this kind of information is that it will permit courts to develop a better understanding of the range and types of disorders under the category of mental disabilities or mental illness. Under the traditional rule, this information is irrelevant and therefore not included in the record since the "actor's mental or emotional disability is not considered in determining whether conduct is negligent."

Id. at 200, 207. Is Dark's proposal an improvement on the Restatement approach?

2. *Voluntary and Involuntary Intoxication.* REST. 2D TORTS § 283C, cmt. *d*, (1965), provides in part:

The rule [of nonliability] stated in this Section applies to involuntary intoxication, as in the highly unusual case in which one who believes he is drinking tea is plied with liquor, and so becomes disabled. . . . Where, however, the intoxication is voluntary, or where it results from deliberate drinking with knowledge of what is being consumed, so that the result is deliberately risked, the policy of the law has refused to make any allowance for the resulting disability, and the rule stated in this Section is not applied.

What standard of care is expected of a voluntarily intoxicated pedestrian? Of a voluntarily intoxicated automobile driver?

3. *Other Standard of Care Issues.* Sudden emergencies and distracting circumstances raise additional standard of care issues.

a. *Sudden Emergencies.* In *Myhaver v. Knutson*, 942 P.2d 445 (Ariz. 1997), the defendant accelerated and swerved left, avoiding what he perceived to be an impending head-on collision with another driver. In doing this, he crossed the double-yellow line into oncoming traffic and collided with plaintiff's pickup. The trial judge ruled that the "sudden emergency" instruction was appropriate under the facts and instructed the jury as follows:

In determining whether a person acted with reasonable care under the circumstances, you may consider whether such conduct was affected by an emergency. . . .

An "emergency" is defined as a sudden and unexpected encounter with a danger which is either real or reasonably seems to be real. If a person, without negligence on his or her part, encountered such an emergency and acted reasonably to avoid harm to self or others, you may find that the person was not negligent. This is so even though, in hindsight, you find that under normal conditions some other or better course of conduct could and should have been followed.

Myhaver, 942 P.2d at 446. On appeal, the Arizona Supreme Court affirmed, noting:

> [W]e join those courts that have discouraged use of the instruction and urge our trial judges to give it only in the rare case. The instruction should be confined to the case in which the emergency is not of the routine sort produced by the impending accident but arises from events the driver could not be expected to anticipate.
>
> We do not, however, join those courts that absolutely forbid use of the instruction. There are cases in which the instruction may be useful or may help to explain the need to consider a sudden emergency and the consequent reflexive actions of a party when determining reasonable care. We believe, however, that in those few cases in which the instruction is given, it would be important to explain that the existence of a sudden emergency and reaction to it are only some of the factors to be considered in determining what is reasonable conduct under the circumstances. Even though a judge may exercise his discretion and give a sudden emergency instruction in a particular case, it will rarely, if ever, be error to refuse to give it.
>
> Applying these principles to the case at bench, we conclude that the trial judge did not abuse his discretion in giving the instruction. This is a case in which there was no evidence of antecedent negligence by [the defendant], in whose favor the instruction was given. In light of the testimony of the various witnesses, there was no question about the existence of an emergency. [The defendant] was faced with a situation not ordinarily to be anticipated and one of imminent peril when [another driver] pulled out of the shopping center and suddenly turned toward him in the wrong lane of traffic. Finally, [defendant's] reaction — swerving across the center line into the path of [plaintiff's] oncoming vehicle — was probably both reflexive in nature and the type of conduct that absent a sudden emergency would almost automatically be found as negligence, if not negligence *per se*. Given these facts, the real and only issue was whether [defendant's] conduct was reasonable under the circumstances of the emergency. We believe, therefore, the trial judge had discretion to instruct on the sudden emergency as a factor in the determination of negligence.

Id. at 450. Compare the view of the Alaska Supreme Court in *Lyons v. Midnight Sun Transportation Services, Inc.*, 928 P.2d 1202 (Alaska 1996):

> We believe that the sudden emergency instruction is a generally useless appendage to the law of negligence. With or without an emergency, the standard of care a person must exercise is still that of a reasonable person under the circumstances. With or without the instruction, parties are still entitled to present evidence at trial which will establish what the circumstances were, and are also entitled to argue to the jury that they acted as a reasonable person would have in light of those

circumstances. Thus, barring circumstances that we cannot at the moment hypothesize, a sudden emergency instruction serves no positive function. Further, the instruction may cause confusion by appearing to imply that one party is less blameworthy than the other. Therefore, we hold that it should not be used unless a court finds that the particular and peculiar facts of a case warrant more explanation of the standard of care than is generally required.

Lyons, 928 P.2d at 1206.

b. *Distracting Circumstances*. In *Harfield v. Tate*, 598 N.W.2d 840 (N.D. 1999), the court examined the related doctrines of "distracting circumstances" and "momentary forgetfulness," concluding:

The "distracting circumstances" doctrine does not lower or minimize one's expected standard of care. Under such circumstances the person invoking the doctrine is required to exercise that degree of care which an ordinarily prudent person would exercise under similar circumstances. A person invoking the doctrine is not exonerated merely because of the presence of distracting circumstances. As we have stated with regard to the sudden emergency doctrine, "the doctrine is simply a principle of law to be utilized in determining the issue of negligence where the actor is suddenly confronted with [distracting circumstances] not of his own making or fault."

Harfield, 598 N.W.2d at 845.

D. CUSTOM AND PROFESSIONAL PRACTICES

Many behaviors are customary and taken for granted. For example, airlines warn travelers to beware of objects shifting in overhead bins during flight; landlords provide door locks for residences. How relevant are these customs, if injury occurs? Professional training provides the doctor, lawyer, or other professional with expertise beyond that of the average person. How should that professional knowledge be measured in assessing the standard of care?

1. Custom

How should a jury, in measuring the standard of care, evaluate evidence that an actor complied with or failed to comply with customary practice? In a case involving barges and tugs that were lost in a gale, the tugs did not have radio receiving sets that would have allowed them to receive warning of the impending storm in time to seek shelter. Justice Learned Hand wrote:

It is not fair to say that there was a general custom among coastwise carriers so as to equip their tugs. One line alone did it. . . . An adequate receiving set suitable for a coastwise tug can now be got at small cost and is reasonably reliable if kept up; obviously it is a source of great protection to their tows. Twice every day they can receive these predictions, based upon the widest possible information, available to every vessel within two or three hundred miles and more. Such a set is the ears of the tug to catch the spoken word, just as the master's binoculars are her eyes to see a storm signal ashore. Whatever may be said as to other vessels, tugs towing heavy coal-laden barges, strung out for half a mile, have little power to maneuver, and do not, as this case proves, expose themselves to weather which would not turn back stauncher craft. They can have at hand protection against dangers of which they can learn in no other way.

Is it then a final answer that the business had not yet generally adopted receiving sets? There are yet, no doubt, cases where courts seem to make the general practice of the calling the standard of proper diligence; we have indeed given some currency to the notion ourselves. Indeed in most cases reasonable prudence is in fact common prudence; but strictly it is never its measure; a whole calling may have unduly lagged in the adoption of new and available devices. It may never set its own tests, however persuasive be its usages. Courts must in the end say what is required; there are precautions so imperative that even their universal disregard will not excuse their omission. But here there was no custom at all as to receiving sets; some had them, some did not; the most that can be urged is that they had not yet become general. Certainly in such a case we need not pause; when some have thought a device necessary, at least we may say that they were right, and the others too slack. . . .

The T.J. Hooper, 60 F.2d 737, 739–40 (2d Cir. 1932).

The RESTATEMENT (SECOND) OF TORTS § 295A (1965) comments *b* and *c* provide:

b. Relevance of custom. Any such custom of the community in general, or of other persons under like circumstances, is always a factor to be taken into account in determining whether the actor has been negligent. Evidence of the custom is admissible, and is relevant, as indicating a composite judgment as to the risks of the situation and the precautions required to meet them, as well as the feasibility of such precautions, the difficulty of any change in accepted methods, the actor's opportunity to learn what is called for, and the justifiable expectation of others that he will do what is usual, as well as the justifiable expectation of the actor that others will do the same. If the actor does what others do under like circumstances, there is at least a possible inference that he is conforming to the community standard of reasonable conduct; and if he does not do what others do, there is a possible inference that he is not so conforming. . . .

c. When custom not controlling. Any such custom is, however, not necessarily conclusive as to whether the actor, by conforming to it, has exercised the care of a reasonable man under the circumstances, or by departing from it has failed to exercise such care. Customs which are entirely reasonable under the ordinary circumstances which give rise to them may become quite unreasonable in the light of a single fact in the particular case. It may be negligence to drive on the right side of the road, and it may not be negligence to drive on the left side when the right side is blocked by a dangerous ditch. Beyond this, customs and usages themselves are many and various. Some of them are the result of careful thought and decision, while others arise from the kind of inadvertence, neglect, or deliberate disregard of a known risk which is associated with negligence. No group of individuals and no industry or trade can be permitted, by adopting careless and slipshod methods to save time, effort, or money, to set its own uncontrolled standard at the expense of the rest of the community. If the only test is to be what has always been done, no one will ever have any great incentive to make any progress in the direction of safety. It follows, therefore, that whenever the particular circumstances, the risk, or other elements in the case are such that a reasonable man would not conform to the custom, the actor may be found negligent in conforming to it; and whenever a reasonable man would depart from the custom, the actor may be found not to be negligent in so departing.

Suppose there was evidence that radio forecasts were needed by tugs only once or twice a year, and traditional methods of forecasting were otherwise perfectly safe. Suppose further that, at this stage of the development of the telecommunications industry, the amortized installed cost of suitable equipment would be approximately one-third to one-half of the net annual profit generated by a tug. How should the standard of care be assessed? Is the evidence of custom relevant?

With his famous words, "courts must in the end say what is required," Judge Learned Hand ushered in a period of explicit judicial intervention. In addition to the general costs associated with litigation which *T.J. Hooper* imposes, does the opinion allocate to industry the information costs for future judicial decision-making? Contrast the opportunity for consultation by industry and others affected by the proposed regulation provided by traditional governmental regulatory agencies prior to the promulgation of safety regulations.

According to one torts scholar, "There are many competitors for this questionable honor, but Hand's famous bon mot is perhaps the most influential, and mischievous, sentence in the history of the law of torts." Richard A. Epstein, *The Path to the T.J. Hooper: The Theory and History of Custom in the Law of Torts*, 21 J. LEGAL STUD. 1, 38 (1992). Does T.J. Hooper mark the beginning of the so-called "torts crisis?"

Can it be argued that the use of a custom standard is a good approximation of the most efficient method of accident avoidance in a given fact pattern? According to W.M. LANDES & R.A. POSNER, THE ECONOMIC STRUCTURE OF TORT LAW 131 (1987), "the adoption of a safety practice by most members of the industry shows that its cost is less than its expected benefit in accident avoidance; there is no reason for the industry to adopt the practice otherwise."

2. Custom and Professional Liability

In *Osborn v. Irwin Memorial Blood Bank*, 7 Cal. Rptr. 2d 101 (Cal. Ct. App. 1992), the question arose whether a blood bank could be held liable for failing to run anti-HBc tests for AIDS in early 1983, a time when there had been some discussion of such testing but no such testing was being used. The court stated:

> Plaintiffs contend that custom and practice are relevant, but not conclusive, on the standard of care. This is the general rule in cases of ordinary negligence. . . .
>
> This is a case of professional negligence, however, and we must assess the role of custom and practice in that context. The question presented here is whether California law permits an expert to second-guess an entire profession. We have found no definitive precedent on this issue and it is not one that is likely to arise.
>
> Custom and practice are not controlling in cases, unlike ours, where a layperson can infer negligence by a professional without any expert testimony. In *Leonard v. Watsonville Community Hosp.* (1956) [305 P.2d 36], for example, where a clamp was left in the plaintiff's body after surgery, the lack of an "established practice" of counting clamps did not preclude a finding of negligence: "Defendants seek to avoid liability on the theory that they were required to exercise only that degree of skill employed by other hospitals and nurses in the community. It is a matter of common knowledge, however, that no special skill is required in counting instruments. Although *under such circumstances* proof of practice or custom is some evidence of what should be done and may assist in the determination of what constitutes due care, it does not conclusively establish the standard of care." (*Id.*, at 519 [italics added].)
>
> On the other hand, in cases like ours where experts are needed to show negligence, their testimony sets the standard of care and is said to be "conclusive." . . . Qualified expert opinion will thus generally preclude a directed verdict in a professional negligence case.
>
> . . . This case, however, is distinguishable. Experts' testimony ordinarily cannot be "disregarded" because it cannot be said that their opinions about what should have been done do not reflect the custom and practice of the profession. When an expert describes the "standard technique" for a knee operation, or what a reasonable attorney would do to settle a wrongful death action, or how long an architect should take to approve change orders on a construction, it is impossible to say that no surgeon, lawyer or architect was doing what the expert said was required. Here it is undisputed that no blood bank in the country was doing what the plaintiffs' experts' standard of care would require of Irwin, and we have an unusual situation where we are called upon to address the significance of a universal practice.
>
> . . . While it may be true that "an increasing number of courts are rejecting the customary practice standard in favor of a reasonable care or reasonably prudent doctor standard" (Prosser & Keeton, The Law of Torts (5th ed., 1988 pocket supp) (p. 30, fn. 53), numerous commentaries have noted that custom generally sets the standard of care.

Most commentators have urged that a customary or accepted practice standard is preferable to one that allows for the disregard of professional judgment. Indeed, the more recent commentaries are not concerned with whether customary practices should be the maximum expected of medical practitioners, but rather with whether those practices should continue to set a minimum standard in a time of increasing economic constraints.

The basic reason why professionals are usually held only to a standard of custom and practice is that their informed approach to matters outside common knowledge should not be "evaluated by the ad hoc judgments of a lay judge or lay jurors aided by hindsight." . . .

. . . It follows that Irwin cannot be found negligent for failing to perform tests that no other blood bank in the nation was using. Judgment notwithstanding the verdict was properly granted to Irwin on the issue of anti-HBc testing because there was no substantial evidence that failure to conduct the tests was not accepted *practice* for blood banks in January and February of 1983.

Osborn, 7 Cal. Rptr. 2d. at 124–125,128.

If custom is not controlling, what is the role of custom? What other evidence will the parties rely upon? Why does the court say that expert testimony is not necessary in a case where a surgical clamp is left in the patient's body? How does the *Osborn* case differ?

The following case addresses standard of care issues in the context of medical malpractice, including the role of expert testimony. For a fuller discussion of medical malpractice, see Chapter 9, *infra*.

HALL v. HILBUN
466 So. 2d 856 (Miss. 1985)

ROBERTSON, JUSTICE, for the Court:

. . . Terry O. Hall was admitted to the Singing River Hospital in Jackson County, Mississippi, in the early morning hours of May 18, 1978, complaining of abdominal discomfort. Because he was of the opinion his patient had a surgical problem, Dr. R.D. Ward, her physician, requested Dr. Glyn R. Hilbun, a general surgeon, to enter the case for consultation. Examination suggested that the discomfort and illness were probably caused by an obstruction of the small bowel. Dr. Hilbun recommended an exploratory laporatomy. Consent being given, Dr. Hilbun performed the surgery about noon on May 20, 1978, with apparent success.

Following surgery Mrs. Hall was moved to a recovery room at 1:35 p.m., where Dr. Hilbun remained in attendance with her until about 2:50 p.m. At that time Mrs. Hall was alert and communicating with him. All vital signs were stable. Mrs. Hall was then moved to a private room where she expired some 14 hours later.

[Prior to trial, all of Plaintiff's claims, except those against Dr. Hilbun, were dismissed on grounds of sovereign immunity and failure of service.]

. . . At trial Glenn Hall, plaintiff below and appellant here, described the fact of the surgery. He then testified that he remained with his wife in her hospital room from the time of her arrival from the recovery room at approximately 3:00 p.m. on May 20, 1978, until she ultimately expired at approximately 5:00 a.m. on the morning of May 21. Hall stated that his wife complained of pain at about 9:00 p.m. and was given morphine for relief, after which she fell asleep. Thereafter, Hall observed that his wife had difficulty in breathing which he reported to the nurses. He inquired if something was wrong and was told his wife was all right and that such breathing was not unusual following surgery. The labored breathing then subsided for an hour or more. Later, Mrs. Hall awakened and again complained of pain in her abdomen and requested a sedative, which was administered following which she fell asleep. Mrs. Hall experienced further difficulty in breathing, and her husband reported this, too. Again, a nurse told Hall that such was normal, that patients sometimes make a lot of noise after surgery.

After the nurse left the following occurred, according to Hall.

[A]t this time I followed her [the nurse] into the hall and walked in the hall a minute. Then I walked back into the room, and walked back out in the hall. Then I walked into the room again and I walked over to my wife and put my hand on her arm because she had stopped making that noise. Then I bent over and flipped the light on and got closer to her where I could see her, and it looked like she was having a real hard problem breathing and she was turning pale or a bluish color. And I went to screaming.

Dr. Hilbun was called and came to the hospital immediately only to find his patient had expired. The cause of the death of Terry O. Hall was subsequently determined to be adult respiratory distress syndrome (cardio-respiratory failure).

Dr. Hilbun was called as an adverse witness . . . He stated Dr. Ward requested consultation concerning Mrs. Hall's illness. He related that his diagnosis of a blocked intestine was correct, as revealed by the surgery, and that the surgery was a success . . .

. . . When questioned at trial, Dr. Hilbun first stated that he had practiced for 16 years in the Singing River Hospital and was familiar with the routine of making surgical notes, i.e., a history of the surgery. He explained that the post-operative orders were noted on the record out of courtesy by Dr. Judy Fabian, the anesthesiologist on the case. He stated such orders were customarily approved by his signature or he would add or subtract from the record to reflect the exact situation.

[At trial Dr. Hilbun testified that he had remained with Mrs. Hall in the recovery room "listened to her chest, took her vital signs, stayed there with her and discharged her to the floor." He further testified that he would follow a patient like Mrs. Hall "[u]ntil she leaves the hospital."]

... However, Dr. Hilbun had no contact with Mrs. Hall after 3:00 p.m. on May 20. Fourteen hours later she was dead.

The plaintiff called Dr. S.O. Hoerr, a retired surgeon of Cleveland, Ohio, as an expert witness. The record reflects that Dr. Hoerr is a *cum laude* graduate of the Harvard Medical School, enjoys the respect of his peers, and has had many years of surgical practice. Through him the plaintiff sought to establish that there is a national standard of surgical practice and surgical care of patients in the United States to which all surgeons, including Dr. Hilbun, are obligated to adhere. Dr. Hoerr conceded that he did not know for a fact the standard of professional skill, including surgical skills and post-operative care, practiced by general surgeons in Pascagoula, Mississippi, but that he did know what the standard should have been.

Relying on *Dazet v. Bass*, 254 So.2d 183 (Miss.1971), which at the time [July 13, 1981] was this Court's latest utterance on the subject of who may testify as an expert witness in a medical malpractice action, the trial court ruled that Dr. Hoerr was not qualified to give an opinion as to whether Dr. Hilbun's post-operative regimen departed from the obligatory standard of care. In his ruling the trial judge made the following statement:

> I think the local rule [the locality rule] has been applied too restrictively in this state, and my basic belief is that it has got to be enlarged. But I don't believe our Supreme Court has gone that far and I personally don't think it can be applied nationally. Anyway, that is left up to the Supreme Court and *I hope this case will help verify that.*

... Dr. David Peter Lango Sachs, also of Cleveland, Ohio, was offered by the plaintiff as a witness, and it appears that he was eminently qualified in his specialty of pulmonary diseases. He also was unfamiliar with the standard of care in Pascagoula, Mississippi, although well versed in the national standards. Dr. Sachs was not permitted to testify because of this court's ruling in *Dazet v. Bass*. ...

... Dr. Donald Dohn, of expertise unquestioned by plaintiff and with years of practical experience, gave testimony for the defendant. He had practiced on the staff at the Cleveland Clinic Foundation in Cleveland, Ohio, beginning in 1958. Fortuitously, he had moved to Pascagoula, Mississippi, about one month before the trial. Dr. Dohn stated he had practiced in the Singing River Hospital for a short time and there was a great difference in the standard of care in medical procedures in Cleveland, Ohio, and those in Pascagoula, Mississippi. Although he had practiced three weeks in Pascagoula, he was still in the process of acquainting himself with the local conditions. He explained the differences as follows:

> Well, there are personnel differences. There are equipment differences. There are diagnostic differences. There are differences in staff responsibility and so on. For example, at the Cleveland Clinic on our service we had ten residents that we were training. They worked with us as our right hands. Here we have no staff. So it is up to us to do the things that our residents would have done there. There we had a team of five or six nurses and other personnel in the operating room to help us. Here we have nurses in the operating room, but there is no assigned

team. You get the luck of the draw that day. I am finding out these things myself. Up there it is a big center; a thousand beds, and it is a regional center. We have tremendous advantages with technical systems, various types of x-ray equipment that is [sic] sophisticated. Also in terms of the intensive care unit, we had a Neurosurgical Intensive Care with people who were specially trained as a team to work there. From my standpoint personally, I seldom had to do much paperwork there as compared to what I have to do now. I have to dictate everything and take all my notes. So, as you can see, there is a difference.

Finally, he again stated the standard of care in Ohio and the standard of care in the Singing River Hospital are very different, although it is obvious to the careful reader of Dr. Dohn's testimony that in so doing he had reference to the differences in equipment, personnel and resources and not differences in the standards of skill, medical knowledge and general medical competence a physician could be expected to bring to bear upon the treatment of a patient.

At the conclusion of the plaintiff's case, defendant moved for a directed verdict on the obvious grounds that, the testimony of Drs. Hoerr and Sachs having been excluded, the Plaintiff had failed to present a legally sufficient quantum of evidence to establish a *prima facie* case. . . .

[Plaintiff appealed.]

. . . . Medical malpractice is legal fault by a physician or surgeon. It arises from the failure of a physician to provide the quality of care required by law. When a physician undertakes to treat a patient, he takes on an obligation enforceable at law to use minimally sound medical judgment and render minimally competent care in the course of the services he provides. A physician does not guarantee recovery. If a patient sustains injury because of the physician's failure to perform the duty he has assumed under our law, the physician may be liable in damages. A competent physician is not liable *per se* for a mere error of judgment, mistaken diagnosis or the occurrence of an undesirable result.

The twin principles undergirding our stewardship of the law regulating professional liability of physicians have always been reason and fairness. For years in medical malpractice litigation we regarded as reasonable and fair what came to be known as the "locality rule" (but which has always consisted of at least two separate rules, one a rule of substantive law, the other a rule of evidence).

First, under the locality rule, we have heretofore recognized as a rule of substantive law that a physician is bound to bestow to each patient such reasonable and ordinary care, skill, and diligence and to exercise such good medical judgment as physicians and surgeons in good standing in the same neighborhood or locality, in the same general line of practice, ordinarily have and exercise in like cases.

Second, as a rule of evidence, we have heretofore held that, in addition to possessing all of the other qualities requisite for judicial acceptance as an expert witness generally, a medical expert would not be allowed to testify in a medical malpractice case unless he practiced in the neighborhood or locality and was familiar with the local standard of care.

Both "prongs" of the locality rule have fallen under attack in recent years. It is urged that the circumstances which have given rise to the rules have passed out of existence. The practice of medicine in general and medical malpractice litigation in particular are said to have achieved a level sophistication that require a modernization of our law. There is merit in the attack. Suffice it to say that the rules we have heretofore employed do not seem nearly so consonant with reason and fairness as they once did.

Just over two years ago we recognized that all was not well in this troubled area of the law. In *King v. Murphy,* 424 So.2d 547 (Miss. 1982), we greatly expanded the concept of the "neighborhood or locality," within the contemplation of the substantive rule regulating the standard of care, to include geographically at least the entire state of Mississippi plus "a reasonable distance adjacent to state boundaries." 424 So.2d at 550. (emphasis added).

King also removed the geographical restrictions on the pool from which expert witnesses might be drawn by either adversary. *King* held that

> an expert witness who is knowledgeable of, and familiar with, the statewide standard of care *shall not have his testimony excluded on the ground that he does not practice in this state.*

424 So.2d at 550 (emphasis added).

Under *King* an otherwise competent medical expert, say, from New York, would be eligible to testify if he had, prior to taking the witness stand, substantially familiarized himself with the standard of care in the (greatly enlarged) "locality or neighborhood."

Since *King,* the docket of this Court has continued to be supplied with medical malpractice cases, a number of which are pending at this time. In the light of these cases, and the excellent briefs and arguments we have received from counsel, several things are apparent:

First, *King* recognizes that the locality rule is not and has never been just one rule. *King* draws a distinction between the substantive rule of law governing the liability *vel non* of physicians and the rule of evidence regulating the appearance of expert witnesses. In this sense *King* establishes a satisfactory general framework within which to handle these cases in the future.

Second, regarding the substantive standard, reflection suggests that further refinement and clarification are necessary. More sharpness needs to be brought to the distinction between the level of care a physician may be expected to render by reference to his skill, knowledge, judgment and general competence, on the one hand, and that which may reasonably be expected by reference to the facilities, equipment, personnel and resources reasonably available to him in the course of treatment. On the point of reasonable availability of resources, there are great variances from rural to urban areas *within* the *King*-defined "locality or neighborhood." These need be taken into account. Further, for the sake of intellectual honesty, we should go ahead and state forthrightly what everyone who has read *King* surely knows: that the "locality or neighborhood" concept as we have heretofore known it has been obliterated.

Third, ... [the court affirms *King*'s evidentiary rule regulating expert witnesses that where a proffered medical expert lives or practices has no relevance to whether he may give expert testimony.]

[The court discusses the operation of the locality rule in other states, imposing a uniform standard of care, noting that "a physician [needs to] possess and exercise that degree of skill and care which a physician of ordinary prudence and skill, practicing in the same or a similar community, would have exercised in the same or similar circumstances."]

. . . Liability turns on a failure to provide the required level of care. It matters not whether this failure results from incompetence or negligence. Some of our cases have misleadingly stated that liability may result from either of two causes: "lack of skill or neglect to apply it if possessed." The matter is properly seen from the patient's point of view. Liability results from the physician's failure to provide requisite care under the circumstances, and nothing turns on whether this failure resulted from incompetence or neglect.

. . . The locality rule was superimposed upon this obviously valid general premise [that a physician must possess that reasonable degree of learning, skill and experience which is ordinarily possessed by others in his profession.]. We perceived physicians as more or less isolated in their local communities and held the level of care they were obligated to render was that generally prevailing in the community. By custom, physicians in each community were empowered to set the standards by which their professional conduct would be judged.

. . . We would have to put our heads in the sand to ignore the "nationalization" of medical education and training. Medical school admission standards are similar across the country. Curricula are substantially the same. Internship and residency programs for those entering medical specialties have substantially common components. Nationally uniform standards are enforced in the case of certification of specialists. Differences and changes in these areas occur temporally, not geographically.

Physicians are far more mobile than they once were. They frequently attend medical school in one state, do a residency in another, establish a practice in a third and after a period of time relocate to a fourth. All the while they have ready access to professional and scientific journals and seminars for continuing medical education from across the country. Common sense and experience inform us that the laws of medicine do not vary from state to state in anything like the manner our public law does.

. . . That a patient's temperature is 105 degrees means the same in New York as in Mississippi. Bones break and heal in Washington the same as in Florida, in Minnesota the same as in Texas . . . Bacteria, physiology and the life process itself know little of geography and nothing of political boundaries.

It is absurd to think that a physician examining a patient in his or her office would, by reference to the genuine health care needs of the patient, say: Because I practice in Mississippi (or the Deep South), I will make this diagnosis and prescribe this medication and course of treatment, but if I were in Iowa, I would do otherwise. We are confident (as the medical community of this state is no doubt confident) that Mississippi's physicians are capable of rendering and do in fact render a quality of care on a par with that in other parts of the country.

All of the above informs our understanding and articulation of the competence-based duty of care. Each physician may with reason and fairness be expected to possess or have reasonable access to such medical knowledge as is commonly possessed or reasonably available to minimally competent physicians in the same specialty or general field of practice throughout the United States, to have a realistic understanding of the limitations on his or her knowledge or competence, and, in general, to exercise minimally adequate medical judgment. Beyond that, each physician has a duty to have a practical working knowledge of the facilities, equipment, resources (including personnel in health related fields and their general level of knowledge and competence), and options (including what specialized services or facilities may be available in larger communities, e.g., Memphis, Birmingham, Jackson, New Orleans, etc.) reasonably available to him or her as well as the practical limitations on same.

In the care and treatment of each patient, each physician has a non-delegable duty to render professional services consistent with that objectively ascertained minimally acceptable level of competence he may be expected to apply given the qualifications and level of expertise he holds himself out as possessing and given the circumstances of the particular case. The professional services contemplated within this duty concern the entire caring process, including but not limited to examination, history, testing, diagnosis, course of treatment, medication, surgery, follow-up, after-care and the like.

[The court notes that jury instructions should avoid use of the term "average," which might mislead the jury by suggesting "the lower 50 percent of our physicians regularly engage in medical malpractice."]

. . . We must be vigilant that liability never be imposed upon a physician for the mere exercise of a bona fide medical judgment which turns out, with the benefit of 20-20 hindsight, (a) to have been mistaken, and (b) to be contrary to what a qualified medical expert witness *in the exercise of his good medical judgment* would have done. We repeat: a physician may incur civil liability only when the quality of care he renders (including his judgment calls) falls below minimally acceptable levels.

Different medical judgments are made by physicians whose offices are across the street from one another. Comparable differences in medical judgment or opinion exist among physicians geographically separated by much greater distances, and in this sense local custom does and must continue to play a role within our law, albeit a limited one.

We recognize that customs vary within given medical communities and from one medical community to another. Conformity with established medical custom practiced by minimally competent physicians in a given area, while evidence of performance of the duty of care, may never be conclusive of such compliance. The content of the duty of care must be objectively determined by reference to the availability of medical and practical knowledge which would be brought to bear in the treatment of like or similar patients under like or similar circumstances by minimally competent physicians in the same field, given the facilities, resources and options available. The content of the duty of care may be informed by local medical custom but never subsumed by it.

Conformity with a local medical custom may be one factor suggesting that a physician has fulfilled his obligation of care. On the other hand, failure to conform to an established medical custom regarding care will generally lead inescapably to the conclusion that the duty of care has been breached.

. . . For reasons well known to all, the facilities, equipment, health care personnel, and other such resources reasonably available to Mississippi's physicians vary from community to community. Major differences exist between the tools the physician has to work within rural Mississippi as contrasted with our more urban areas. Generally speaking, the most comprehensive availability of sophisticated medical facilities and equipment in this state may be found in Jackson.

Because of these differences in facilities, equipment, etc., what a physician may reasonably be expected to do in the treatment of a patient in rural Humphreys County or Greene County may vary from what a physician in Jackson may be able to do. A physician practicing in Noxubee County, for example, may hardly be faulted for failure to perform a CAT scan when the necessary facilities and equipment are not reasonably available. In contradistinction, objectively reasonable expectations regarding the physician's knowledge, skill, capacity for sound medical judgment and general competence are, consistent with his field of practice and the facts and circumstances in which the patient may be found, *the same everywhere.*

. . . As a result of its resources-based component, the physician's non-delegable duty of care is this: given the circumstances of each patient, each physician has a duty to use his or her knowledge and therewith treat through maximum reasonable medical recovery, each patient, with such reasonable diligence, skill, competence, and prudence as are practiced by minimally competent physicians in the same specialty or general field of practice throughout the United States, who have available to them the same general facilities, services, equipment and options.

[The court holds the trial court judge erred in excluding the testimony of Drs. Hoerr and Sachs because they lived and practiced in Cleveland.]

NOTES

1. *Locality Rule versus Nationalized Standard of Care.* Why did the trial court bar plaintiff's experts from testifying? Does a locality rule, measuring medical professionals by others in the same locality make sense? Why do you suppose such a rule originated? Is the court correct that times have changed and that a doctor's performance should be measured against a national standard of reasonable care?

2. *Expert Testimony and the Standard of Care.* What will plaintiff have to prove at a new trial? Will expert testimony be necessary for that proof? Why, doesn't the reasonable prudent person set the standard of care in a negligence case?

Are there situations where expert testimony should be held *inadmissible*? *See, e.g., Board of Supervisors v. Lake Services, Inc.,* 440 S.E.2d 600 (Va. 1994):

> Expert testimony is inadmissible regarding "matters of common knowledge" or subjects "such that [persons] of ordinary intelligence are capable of comprehending them, forming an intelligent opinion about them, and drawing their own conclusions therefrom." Thus, when the question presented can be resolved by determining what precautions a reasonably prudent person would have taken under like circumstances, no expert testimony is required or permitted.
>
> Further, expert testimony is admissible only when specialized skill and knowledge are required to evaluate the merits of a claim. Issues of this type generally arise in cases involving the practice of professions requiring advanced, specialized education, such as engineering, medicine, and law, or those involving trades that focus upon scientific matters, such as electricity and blasting, which a jury cannot understand without expert assistance.

Bd. of Supervisors, 440 S.E.2d at 602.

3. *Custom and Medical Malpractice.* National, state, or local standards implicate customs among doctors. How does the role of custom in a medical malpractice case differ from the role of custom in a conventional negligence case?

4. *Professional Malpractice and Lawyers.* Would it be malpractice for an attorney to fail to research using electronic library services like Westlaw and Lexis? How should the standard of care for attorneys be measured?

The *ABA Model Rules for Professional Conduct* provide: "A lawyer shall provide competent representation to a client. Competent representation requires the legal knowledge, skill, thoroughness and preparation reasonably necessary for the representation." MODEL RULES OF PROF'L CONDUCT R. 1.1(2002). While the breach of a rule or statute regulating the conduct of lawyers does not give rise to civil liability, such rules or statutes are relevant in determining the standard of conduct expected from a lawyer. REST.3D LAW GOVERNING LAWYERS § 52(2) (2000). What does it mean for a lawyer to be "competent"? Does this mean that the lawyer should always have the "right" answer? What if the legal question is really complicated with no clear answer? Does a lawyer have to always comprehend the rule against perpetuities from the law of estates? "Of the California law on perpetuities and restraints it has been said that few, if any, areas of law have been fraught with more confusion or concealed more traps for the unwary draftsman. . . ." *Lucas v. Hamm,* 364 P.2d 685, 690 (1961). *Lucas* states:

> The general rule with respect to the liability of an attorney for failure to properly perform his duties to his client is that the attorney, by

accepting employment to give legal advice or to render other legal services, impliedly agrees to use such skill, prudence, and diligence as
lawyers of ordinary skill and capacity commonly possess and exercise
in the performance of the tasks which they undertake. The attorney is
not liable for every mistake he may make in his practice; he is not, in
the absence of an express agreement, an insurer of the soundness of
his opinions or of the validity of an instrument that he is engaged to
draft; and he is not liable for being in error as to a question of law on
which reasonable doubt may be entertained by well-informed
lawyers.

Lucas, 364 P.2d at 689.

After *Lucas*, does this mean that any area of law "fraught with more confusion or concealed more traps for the unwary draftsman" will immunize the
lawyer from malpractice liability? *See Smith v. Lewis*, 530 P.2d 589, 596 (Cal.
1975) (holding that had the attorney "conducted minimal research into either
hornbook or case law, [the attorney] would have discovered with modest effort
that the [husband]'s state retirement benefits were likely to be treated as community property and that his federal benefits at least arguably belonged to the
community as well").

E. JUDICIAL AND LEGISLATIVE STANDARDS OF CARE

Rules of law present another alternative for setting the standard of care and
for evaluating if an actor's conduct has been negligent. The notion of *stare
decisis*, a cornerstone of common law jurisprudence, suggests that a decision of
an appellate court establishes a precedent to be followed in that jurisdiction
when a similar fact situation arises again. Thus a decision on a fact pattern
about the required standard of care dictates it should be followed. For example,
in *Baltimore & Ohio Railroad v. Goodman*, 275 U.S. 66 (1927), the defendant's
train killed plaintiff as he attempted to drive across the defendant's track.
Justice Holmes wrote:

[N]othing is suggested by the evidence to relieve Goodman from
responsibility for his own death. When a man goes upon a railroad
track he knows that he goes to a place where he will be killed if a train
comes upon him before he is clear of the track. He knows that he must
stop for the train, not the train stop for him. In such circumstances it
seems to us that if a driver cannot be sure otherwise whether a train
is dangerously near he must stop and get out of his vehicle, although
obviously he will not often be required to do more than to stop and
look.

Goodman, 275 U.S. at 69–70. The court established a rule of law setting the
standard of care for railroad crossing cases. Several years later in *Pokora v.
Wabash Railway Co.*, 292 U.S. 98 (1934), another train crossing case, Justice
Cardozo explained:

Standards of prudent conduct are declared at times by courts, but they are taken over from the facts of life. To get out of a vehicle and reconnoiter is an uncommon precaution, as everyday experience informs us. Besides being uncommon, it is very likely to be futile, and sometimes even dangerous. If the driver leaves his vehicle when he nears a cut or curve, he will learn nothing by getting out about the perils that lurk beyond. By the time he regains his seat and sets his car in motion, the hidden train may be upon him.

Pokora, 292 U.S. at 104. As Cardozo suggested, the rule of law regulating behavior at train crossings almost invariably breaks down in face of the necessity of basing the standard on the particular circumstances in a given case. The apparent risk and the actors opportunity to handle it remain central to the notion of standard of care, making it difficult to frame standards of conduct that amount to a rule of law. This approach is not favored but courts do set the standard of care from time to time. For a modern example, see *Helling v. Carey*, 519 P.2d 981 (Wash. 1974), *infra* in Chapter 9.

Does the difficulty in establishing a standard of conduct by judicial rule confirm criticisms about the lack of predictability in tort law?

Legislative standards of care or statutes potentially present another measure of the standard of care. A statute, for example, requiring a driver to use lights at night or a pedestrian to walk facing traffic, establishes a rule of behavior. How should a court handle evidence of a statutory violation?

O'GUIN v. BINGHAM COUNTY
122 P.3d 308 (Idaho 2005)

TROUT, JUSTICE.

. . . On July 7, 1999, Shaun and Alex O'Guin were killed while playing at the Bingham County landfill. Apparently, a section of the pit wall collapsed and crushed the children. Their older brother, Frank Jr., initially discovered their bodies at the bottom of the pit. Earlier that day, the children had been eating lunch at Ridgecrest Elementary School as part of a summer lunch program. As they started walking home, the children went through an unlocked gate at the back of the schoolyard and through a privately owned empty field. The empty field is situated between the landfill and the schoolyard. The border between the empty field and the landfill was unobstructed. At the time of the children's death, the landfill was open to the public one day a week. It was closed on the day the children were killed and no landfill employees were present on the site.

. . . [The Court granted the defendant county's motion for summary judgment on the negligence *per se* claim. This appeal followed.]

. . . Negligence *per se,* which results from the violation of a specific requirement of law or ordinance, is a question of law, over which this Court exercises free review. *Ahles v. Tabor,* 34 P.3d 1076, 1078 (2001).

. . . The dispute in this case focuses on the duty or standard of care the County owed to the O'Guin children. . . . The O'Guins argue that once the district court determined the regulations established a duty and the County had breached that duty, there was no need to apply the common law . . . standard. . . . The County . . . argues that negligence *per se* does not apply here.

"The elements of a common law negligence action are (1) a duty, recognized by law, requiring the defendant to conform to a certain standard of conduct; (2) a breach of that duty; (3) a causal connection between the defendant's conduct and the resulting injury; and (4) actual loss or damage." *Black Canyon Racquetball Club, Inc. v. Idaho First Nat'l Bank, N.A.*, 804 P.2d 900, 904–05 (1991). . . .

"[I]n Idaho, it is well established that statutes and administrative regulations may define the applicable standard of care owed, and that violations of such statutes and regulations may constitute negligence *per se*." *Sanchez v. Galey*, 112 Idaho 609, 617, 733 P.2d 1234, 1242 (1986). "A court may adopt 'as the standard of conduct of a reasonable man the requirements of a legislative enactment or an administrative regulation. . . .'" *Brizendine v. Nampa Meridian Irr. District*, 548 P.2d 80, 86 (1976) (quoting Restatement (Second) of Torts § 286 (1965)). "The effect of establishing negligence *per se* through violation of a statute is to conclusively establish the first two elements of a cause of action in negligence. . . ." *Slade v. Smith's Management Corp.*, 808 P.2d 401, 408 (1991). "Negligence *per se* lessens the plaintiff's burden only on the issue of the 'actor's departure from the standard of conduct required of a reasonable man.'" *Ahles v. Tabor*, 34 P.3d 1076, 1078 (2001) (quoting Restatement (Second) of Torts § 288B cmt. B (1965)). "Thus, the elements of duty and breach are 'taken away from the jury.'" *Ahles*, 34 P.3d at 1078 (quoting *Prosser and Keeton on Torts* 230 (5th ed.1984)).

In order to replace a common law duty of care with a duty of care from a statute or regulation, the following elements must be met: (1) the statute or regulation must clearly define the required standard of conduct; (2) the statute or regulation must have been intended to prevent the type of harm the defendant's act or omission caused; (3) the plaintiff must be a member of the class of persons the statute or regulation was designed to protect; and (4) the violation must have been the proximate cause of the injury. *Ahles*, 34 P.3d at 1078 (citing *Sanchez v. Galey*, 733 P.2d 1234, 1242 (1986)).

As to the first element, the district court found, and we agree, that the statute and regulations in this case clearly define the County's standard of conduct. Idaho Code Title 39, Chapters 1 and 74 grant authority to the Board of Environmental Quality to adopt solid waste management rules and standards. Those rules require municipal solid waste landfill units to block access by unauthorized persons. The rule in effect at the time of the boys' deaths provided in pertinent part:

Solid waste management sites shall comply with the following:

e. Access to the site shall be limited to those times when an attendant is on duty.

i. Hours of operation and other limitations shall be prominently displayed at the entrance.

ii. The site shall be fenced or otherwise blocked to access when an attendant is not on duty.

iii. Unauthorized vehicles and persons shall be prohibited access to the site.

IDAPA 58.01.06.005.02. In addition, Idaho Code § 39-7412(6) states that owners or operators of all municipal solid waste landfill units shall "[p]rovide and control access as provided in 40 CFR 258.25." That section of the Code of Federal Regulations states:

> Owners or operators of all municipal solid waste landfill units must control public access and prevent unauthorized vehicular traffic and illegal dumping of wastes by using artificial barriers, natural barriers, or both, as appropriate to protect human health and the environment.

40 C.F.R. § 258.25. These regulations require the County to fence or otherwise block access to the landfill when an attendant is not on duty. The Legislature has specifically declared it to be "unlawful" to fail to comply with the landfill rules. I.C. § 39-7402(1). In this case, the record reveals that on July 7, 1999, some of the landfill boundaries were not fenced or blocked. There is also evidence that the landfill was closed and no attendant was on duty on July 7, 1999. Therefore, the district court was correct that the regulations clearly define the County's required standard of conduct, and the County failed to meet that standard.

The second element asks whether the death of the O'Guin children is the type of harm the statute and regulations were intended to prevent. Idaho Code Section 39-7401(2) states:

> [I]t is the intent of the legislature to establish a program of solid waste management which complies with 40 CFR 258 and facilitates the incorporation of flexible standards in facility design and operation. The legislature hereby establishes the solid waste disposal standards and procedures outlined herein and a facility approval process for the state of Idaho, the political subdivisions thereof, and any private solid waste disposal site owner in order to facilitate the development and operation of solid waste disposal sites, to effect timely and responsible completion of statutory duties and to ensure protection of human health and the environment, to protect the air, land and waters of the state of Idaho.

I.C. § 39-7401(2). This section demonstrates the legislature's desire to ensure the "protection of human health" in the "development and operation of solid waste disposal sites." It also makes specific reference to 40 C.F.R. § 258. As quoted previously, Section 258.25 of the Code of Federal Regulations states "[o]wners or operators of all municipal solid waste landfill units must control public access . . . by using artificial barriers, natural barriers, or both, as appropriate to protect human health. . . ." Further indication of the intent of this section can be found in the Technical Manual on Solid Waste Disposal Facility Criteria (Manual) promulgated by the United States Environmental Protection Agency. The Manual contains a disclaimer that the policies set forth in the

Manual are not intended to create any enforceable rights in litigation and are simply for guidance. However, the Manual can serve to give further insight into the interpretation of the provisions in the CFR. Specifically, Section 3.7.3 entitled "Technical Considerations" relates to the access requirements of 40 CFR § 258.25 and provides in part

> Frequently, unauthorized persons are unfamiliar with the hazards associated with landfill facilities, and consequences of uncontrolled access may include injury and even death. Potential hazards are related to inability of equipment operators to see unauthorized individuals during operation of equipment and haul vehicles; direct exposure to waste (e.g., sharp objects and pathogens); inadvertent or deliberate fires; and earth-moving activities.

This provision indicates a broad definition of what is intended by "protection of human health" and certainly includes possible injury or death to people on the facility grounds. Operators of a landfill have a duty not only to prevent illegal dumping and unauthorized vehicular traffic, but to control public access as well.

The County argues that the intent of these provisions is merely to prevent unauthorized vehicular traffic and illegal dumping. However, the inclusion of physical injury to "unauthorized individuals" by equipment or earth-moving activities, as potential landfill hazards, would indicate otherwise. A similar hazard is presented by a dangerously sloping wall in the landfill. The O'Guin's expert testified that the angle of the slope where the accident occurred "was extremely dangerous" and violative of EPA and OSHA regulations. These statutes and rules demonstrate that the Legislature intended to safeguard both human health and safety. The injury to the safety of the O'Guin children is the type of harm the Idaho statute and regulations were intended to prevent because the children's deaths relate directly to control of public access and protection of human health and safety.

As to the third element, the O'Guin children are members of the class of persons the regulations were designed to protect. The regulations state "[u]nauthorized vehicles and persons shall be prohibited access to the site." IDAPA 58.01.06.005.02. As trespassers, the O'Guin children were certainly "unauthorized persons" and the regulations do not differentiate between the unauthorized person who comes to the landfill to dump improper materials and the unauthorized person who comes to the landfill to play. Furthermore, the regulations require the landfill "be fenced or otherwise blocked to access when an attendant is not on duty." IDAPA 58.01.06.005.02. This regulation demonstrates the connection between the requirement that the landfill perimeter be fenced or blocked and the protection of persons whose access is unauthorized. Therefore, the regulations controlling access were designed to protect the human health and safety of the unauthorized person who comes to a landfill when an attendant is not on duty and the O'Guin children fit within that category.

Finally, as to the fourth element, there is at least a disputed issue of fact created by an affidavit in the record, as to whether the County's violation of the statute and regulations resulted in the O'Guin children's deaths.

. . .

The district court erred in determining that the County's violations here were not negligence *per se*. . . . The district court's grant of summary judgment is vacated and the case remanded for further proceedings. We award costs on appeal to the O'Guins.

JUSTICE EISMANN, Dissenting.

I cannot concur in the majority opinion because the regulations cited therein as supporting a claim of negligence *per se* were clearly not intended to prevent the type of harm involved in this case.

. . .

The majority opinion relies upon IDAPA 58.01.06.005.02 and 40 C.F.R. 258.25 as providing the applicable standard of care. Neither of those regulations is intended to prevent trespassers from injuring themselves through an accident at a landfill. They are intended to prevent trespassers from dumping or salvaging materials that may be harmful to health or the environment.

. . .

The regulations are intended to protect against health hazards from pollution and disease. They are not intended to protect against injury from accidents. The same holds for 40 C.F.R. 258.25, which states:

> Owners or operators of all MSWLF [municipal solid waste landfill] units must control public access and prevent unauthorized vehicular traffic and illegal dumping of wastes by using artificial barriers, natural barriers, or both, as appropriate to protect human health and the environment.

The concern is illegal dumping of wastes that are dangerous to human health and the environment. The word "health" is not normally construed to include freedom from accidents. Rather, it simply means "freedom from disease or abnormality." The majority can reach its conclusion only by redefining the word "health" to include "safety." Such redefinition is not supported either by Idaho law or by the federal regulations.

The majority quotes a portion of §3.7.3 from the Solid Waste Disposal Facility Criteria technical manual for its construction of 40 C.F.R. §258.25 in order to arrive at the conclusion that Bingham County was required to fence out trespassing pedestrians from its landfill. Reading that entire subsection of the technical manual shows that the majority's interpretation is wrong. The last paragraph of that subsection states:

> Acceptable measures to limit access of unauthorized persons to the disposal facility include gates and fences, trees, hedges, berms, ditches, and embankments. Chain link, barbed wire added to chain link, and open farm-type fencing are examples of fencing that may be used. Access to facilities should be controlled through gates that can be locked when the site is unsupervised. Gates may be the only additional measure needed at remote facilities.

Obviously, barriers consisting of "trees, hedges, berms, ditches, and embankments" or "open farm-type fencing" are not designed to keep out trespassing pedestrians. They are only designed to keep out vehicles that may be transporting waste into the facility when it is closed. The fact that these types of barriers are expressly stated as being acceptable shows that the regulation was not intended to require municipal solid waste disposal facilities to fence out trespassing pedestrians.

NOTES

1. *Violation of Statute as a Breach of Duty.* REST. 2D TORTS § 286 (1965) provides:

> The court may adopt as the standard of conduct of a reasonable man the requirements of a legislative enactment or an administrative regulation whose purpose is found to be exclusively or in part
>
> (a) to protect a class of persons which includes the one whose interest is invaded, and
>
> (b) to protect the particular interest which is invaded, and
>
> (c) to protect that interest against the kind of harm which has resulted, and
>
> (d) to protect that interest against the particular hazard from which the harm results.

Section 288A of the Restatement (Second) states that unless a statute or administrative regulation "is construed not to permit such excuse," a violator of the statute or regulation may be excused, *inter alia*, if he shows that "he neither knows or should know of the occasion for compliance, or that he is "unable after reasonable diligence or care to comply." REST. 2D. TORTS § 288A (1965). Thus the effect of proof of negligence *per se* in most situations is to shift the burden of proof to the defendant to prove due care on her part. Will the issue normally be one of fact, no matter what proof the defendant offers?

2. *Adopting a Statute to Measure Breach of Duty.* In *Newport v. Moran*, 721 P.2d 465 (Or. Ct. App. 1985), plaintiff and her husband took in a stray dog wandering the neighborhood. They tried to find a home for the dog, because they could not keep it confined. They offered it to their neighbors, the defendants, who first declined but later accepted it. One day when plaintiff left her house to get her mail Rowdy was roaming unattended in the yard. Plaintiff tried to "shoo" him home, but he responded by sitting down at the street end of plaintiff's driveway. Subsequently the plaintiff heard a noise, turned around, and was struck on her right knee by Rowdy's shoulder, causing her to fall and suffer a broken leg. She relied, *inter alia*, on a claimed violation of County Code § 5.255(1), which provides:

> (1) No dog owner shall permit a dog to be at large.
>
> (2) A dog owner, whose dog runs at large, commits a Class B infraction.

The Lane County ordinance defines a dog being at large as,

> (5) A dog off the premises of the owner and not under the owner's immediate control.

Newport, 721 P.2d at 467. The court held that:

> Violation of an ordinance may be negligence *per se* if the violation is the cause of the injury, the plaintiff is within the class of persons intended to be protected by the legislation and the injury is within the area of risk intended to be avoided by the ordinance.

> The Lane County ordinance is substantively equivalent to the Washington County ordinance considered in *Kathren v. Olenik,* [613 P.2d 69 (1980)] which involved a dog bite. We held that the Washington County ordinance operated against a dog's owners only if they knew or should have known that the dog had a propensity to bite, saying:

>> This evinces concurrence with the general knowledge that dogs as a class of animal do not normally attack human beings. Because it is not reasonably foreseeable that dogs will attack persons, injury from dog bites is not within the area of risk the running at large provision was designed to avoid.

The trial judge ruled that, although *Kathren* held that dog bites were not within the area of risk that the dog-at-large ordinance was designed to avoid, that decision did not explain what risks were contemplated by the ordinance. Therefore, the trial judge submitted the issue to the jury on the basis that dogs knocking people down could be one of the anticipated risks covered by the statute.

> . . . Plaintiff claimed that Rowdy charged her with his shoulder in an unprovoked assault. That kind of animal behavior is less likely than biting and, correspondingly, even less likely to be the kind of harm that is within the area of risk contemplated by the ordinance. Therefore, we conclude that the evidence did not warrant submission of the case to the jury on the theory of negligence *per se* for violation of the dog control ordinance.

Id. Judge Newman, dissenting, stated:

> Even if dog bites are not within the area of risk contemplated by the ordinance, *Kathren v. Olenik*, 46 Or. App. 713, 724, 613 P.2d 69 (1980), I do not believe that it necessarily follows that dog knock-downs are similarly outside the scope of the ordinance. Although, as we stated in *Kathren*, dogs as a class are not vicious and do not attack people, they do tend to roam at large along streets and in yards and get under foot. The ordinance was intended to protect the public from harm caused by this type of dog behavior.

Id. at 468. Why didn't the plaintiff in *Newport* rely upon a theory of strict liability? *See infra* Chapter 8.

3. *Defective Electrical Wiring.* The plaintiff tenants, parents and a child, sued the defendant landlord in *Smith v. Owen*, 841 S.W.2d 828 (Tenn. Ct. App. 1992), for electrical shock received by the child while playing near a clothes dryer. The shock occurred because the back of the dryer was energized owing to faulty wiring which had been done before the defendant acquired the premises. At the time the plaintiffs leased the premises, an applicable city ordinance required that every owner or lessor of a dwelling shall install and maintain the electrical outlets therein in good and safe working condition. The appellate court said:

> The trial court found that the defendant's violation of the ordinance was the proximate cause of the injury. As we have stated, the ordinance imposed a duty on defendant to inspect the wiring before turning the premises over to plaintiffs. In the instant case, the electrician discovered the faulty wiring using a meter with which any electrician would be familiar. The trial court specifically found that "an inspection of the premises prior to the lease would have revealed the defective condition." The preponderance of the evidence supports the trial court's finding of proximate cause.

Smith, 841 S.W.2d at 833. A dissent argued:

> The record reflects that the defective wiring was installed without the knowledge or consent of the defendant-landlord before the enactment of the city code which, according to the majority, made the landlord an insurer of the safety of the premises. This is contrary to the long established law of landlord and tenant in this State.

Id.

4. *Risk Identification.* In *Larrimore v. American National Ins. Co.*, 89 P.2d 340 (Okla.1939), the plaintiff, a coffee shop employee, was injured in an explosion while attempting to light the burner on a steam table. Her match ignited a can of "Rat Doom" under the table. She sued the lessor of the premises who had provided the rat poison to her employer. She relied on a statute providing, "Whoever shall, except in a safe place on his own premises, lay out strychnine or other poison, is guilty of a misdemeanor." *Larrimore*, 89 P.2d at 343. The court concluded:

> It is clear enough that the substance laid out was poison. It may further be said that if the owner had not furnished the lessee with the rat poison the plaintiff would not have been injured; and still it does not follow that the statute makes defendant liable for plaintiff's injury. It is clear that the purpose of the above statute is to protect persons and animals from injury by being poisoned. The injury here was not the class of injury intended to be prevented by the statute. There was no connection between the poisonous nature of the substance and plaintiff's injury.
>
> It is not enough for a plaintiff to show that the defendant neglected a duty imposed by statute. He must go further and show that his injury was caused by his exposure to a hazard from which it was the purpose of the statute to protect him. Negligence is a breach of duty. Those only to whom that duty is due and who have sustained injuries of the character its discharge was designed to prevent can maintain actions for its breach.

The rule in this jurisdiction is that one who does an unlawful act is not thereby placed outside of the protection of the law, but that to have this effect the unlawful act must have some causal connection with the injury complained of. Plaintiff having in no way become poisoned by the "Rat Doom" furnished by defendant, the above section of our statute does not, of itself, render the defendant negligent as to plaintiff's injury.

It may be observed that there is still another reason why our conclusion in this respect is correct. The statute forbids the laying out of strychnine or other poison "except in a safe place." The "safe place" contemplated by the statute obviously means that place which would be safe in regard to the substance's character as poison. What would be a safe place for poison might not be a safe place for gasoline, and vice versa. The evidence reveals that the can was placed by Mrs. Schultz on the floor, under the lower metal shelf of the steam table, which shelf was about six inches above the floor, and said poison was pushed back under the shelf some eight or ten inches. It might also be said that it was hidden. At any rate, it could not correctly be said that the can was placed other than in a safe place for poison, in view of the particular circumstances of the case. . . .

Id. at 343–344. Was *Larrimore* concerned with legal or factual causation? Was not the defendant in *Larrimore* put on notice of the danger of explosion by the label which referred to the phosphorous content of the poison, although not the percentage of that content, as follows: "Rat Doom, Poison, This phosphorus paste is guaranteed to rid any premise of rats and mice. In case of poisoning take an emetic to cause vomiting, after which take a stimulant and consult a physician at once." *Id.* at 342.

Would the plaintiff have been more likely to recover had there been no statutory provision?

5. *Sanitation Versus Safety.* In *Gorris v. Scott,* (1874) 9 Ex. 125 (Ex. Ct.), defendant violated a statute requiring transporters of animals by water to provide separate pens for the animals while being transported. Because the sheep were not separated, they were washed overboard during a storm. The court found the statutory violation did not provide the plaintiff with a cause of action, since the statute was intended as a sanitation rather than a safety measure. Suppose, because of the absence of pens, the sheep became diseased, and then washed overboard during a storm because of their weakness from the disease?

6. *Keys-in-Cars.* In *Ross v. Hartman,* 139 F.2d 14 (D.C. Cir. 1943), plaintiff was struck by defendant's stolen truck. Defendant had left his keys in the truck. A traffic ordinance provided:

Locks on Motor Vehicles. Every motor vehicle shall be equipped with a lock suitable to lock the starting lever, throttle, or switch, or gear-shift lever, by which the vehicle is set in motion, and no person shall allow any motor vehicle operated by him to stand or remain unattended on any street or in any public place without first having locked the lever, throttle, or switch by which said motor vehicle may be set in motion.

Ross, 139 F.2d at 14 n.1. Noting authority suggesting that there would be no liability at common law, the court continued:

> But the existence of an ordinance changes the situation. If a driver causes an accident by exceeding the speed limit, for example, we do not inquire whether his prohibited conduct was unreasonably dangerous. It is enough that it was prohibited. Violation of an ordinance intended to promote safety is negligence. If by creating the hazard which the ordinance was intended to avoid it brings about the harm which the ordinance was intended to prevent, it is a legal cause of the harm. . . .
>
> . . . The particular ordinance involved here is one of a series which require, among other things, that motor vehicles be equipped with horns and lamps. Ordinary bicycles are required to have bells and lamps, but they are not required to be locked. The evident purpose of requiring motor vehicles to be locked is not to prevent theft for the sake of owners or the police, but to promote the safety of the public in the streets. . . .

Id. at 15–16.

7. *The Class to be Protected.* Statutes in Oklahoma prohibited selling or giving alcoholic beverages to anyone under 21, and prohibited anyone under 21 from consuming such beverages. In *Busby v. Quail Creek Golf & Country Club*, 885 P.2d 1326 (Okla. 1994), the court held the defendant could be liable for injuries received by a minor as a result of consuming alcoholic beverages furnished to her by the defendant. "Following the reasoning of the majority of states," the court had previously "refused to extend the duty of the tavern owner to the adult customer who voluntarily consumed intoxicants and injured himself." *Busby*, 885 P.2d at 1330. But this case was different:

> We agree with jurisdictions which allow a cause of action against a commercial vendor on behalf of a minor who voluntarily drinks to the point of intoxication and is thereby injured, regardless of whether the minor violated statutes in attempting to purchase or to consume beer. The Legislature, recognizing the foreseeable danger to both third parties and to minors who injure themselves, has taken specific steps to treat minors differently from adults by preventing minors from consuming and possessing alcohol. We believe that 37 O.S. 1991 §241, which prohibits selling beer to a minor, and 37 O.S. 1991 §246, which prohibits minors from consuming and possessing beer, constitute legislative recognition of the foreseeable danger to both third parties and to minors who injure themselves. As a matter of public policy, minors as a class are incompetent by reason of their youth and inexperience to deal responsibly with the effects of alcohol.

Id. 1331–1332.

F.   CIRCUMSTANTIAL EVIDENCE OF NEGLIGENCE

The course in evidence will explore proof and evidentiary issues. This section considers only those aspects of proof particular to tort law. Recall that no real issue exists as to duty in these cases. The issue here is how will plaintiff prove that the duty has been breached. This question of breach has two parts: (1) What happened; what are the facts? and (2) Did the defendant act reasonably in relation to the risk of harm?

This section concerns the nature of the evidence from which the factfinder can infer negligence. The system seeks to avoid speculation and conjecture. The jury verdict must be grounded in some evidence. Plaintiff must prove his or her case by a preponderance of evidence, that is, evidence more likely than not, favoring the plaintiff.

WIDMYER v. SOUTHEAST SKYWAYS, INC.
584 P.2d 1 (Alaska 1978)

BOOCHEVER, CHIEF JUSTICE.

On November 15, 1974, a DeHavilland Beaver airplane, owned by Southeast Skyways, Inc., and piloted by Richard Norvell, crashed in the waters of False Bay, Chichagof Island, Alaska. The pilot and three passengers . . . were killed in the crash. . . . [P]ersonal representatives of the estates of the deceased passengers brought this action for wrongful death against appellees, Southeast Skyways, Inc., and James Norvell, personal representative of the estate of Richard Norvell.

A jury returned a verdict for Skyways. Numerous issues have been raised on this appeal including the refusal of the trial court to instruct regarding . . . the doctrine of *res ipsa loquitur.* . . .

. . . The airplane left Juneau on November 15, 1974 bound for Tenakee Springs. William Bernhardt, who piloted another plane from Juneau on the 15th bound for Basket Bay, testified that the weather at Juneau International Airport was generally "good" on that day. Both planes proceeded toward their destinations and, in so doing, traveled in a southerly direction down Chatham Strait which separates Admiralty and Chichagof Islands. Bernhardt observed Skyways' airplane in a parallel flight pattern near Hawk Inlet on Admiralty Island. A heavy snow squall was encountered by both airplanes. Bernhardt overtook Skyways' craft near Point Marsden on Admiralty Island; and, at that time, both airplanes were flying at an altitude of 50 to 100 feet. Bernhardt lost sight of the Skyways' craft when it executed a turn to the right, away from the Admiralty Island beach, and disappeared from view.

The Skyways' craft was next sighted on the Chichagof side of the Chatham Strait by Charles and Esther Kaze. The airplane was flying at low altitude near their cabin, and it crashed a few seconds after they observed it. There was no change in the audible pitch of the motor prior to impact. It was snowing very hard, and visibility was poor. They found the craft wreckage in a vertical, nosedown position in rough tidal water; there were no survivors.

James Nielson, a witness for the plaintiffs and an expert on accident reconstruction, testified that, in his opinion, the crash was due to a "stall/spin" that he attributed to pilot error. He stated that the pilot also was in violation of Visual Flight Rules (VFR) of the Federal Aviation Administration.

William Bernhardt, who had observed the craft on the Admiralty side of the Strait, testified to his opinion that the pilot had crossed the Chatham Strait, looking for the Chichagof beach, which was not visible from Point Marsden; and that when he encountered the trees, he was forced to pull up and make a sharp turn, which stalled the aircraft.

Skyways' evidence focused on inclement weather as a cause of the accident. Harold Searby, a defense witness and an expert in meteorology, testified that the weather in Southeast Alaska on the day of the crash was unstable; and that, in his opinion, strong and severe turbulence existed in False Bay at the time of the crash.

Ray Renshaw, a defense witness and an expert on aviation in Southeast Alaska, testified to his opinion that Richard Norvell, whom he had supervised and trained, was an experienced pilot with approximately 3000 hours of flight. He then testi-fied to his opinion that, after completing his turn from the Admiralty side of the Chatham Strait, Norvell was in clear air; that he crossed the Strait and proceeded down a corridor on the Chichagof side in clear air; that he encountered a snow squall and attempted to land in False Bay when the craft was struck by an unex-pected gust of wind; and that the crash was not due to pilot error.

Renshaw further stated that one of his assumptions was that Norvell did not commit pilot error. Plaintiffs' objections to expert testimony based on such an assumption were overruled.

. . . Plaintiffs allege error in the superior court's denial of their proposed instruction on the doctrine of *res ipsa loquitur.*

The doctrine of *res ipsa loquitur,* meaning "the thing or transaction speaks for itself," permits a finding of negligence from the circumstances surrounding the injury. It does not allow negligence to be established from the mere fact of injury itself. The doctrine, where applicable, is a bridge, dispensing with the requirement that a plaintiff specifically prove breach of duty, once that duty and proximate cause have been established.[6]

---

[6] Sec. 328 D of the RESTATEMENT OF TORTS (SECOND) (1965) provides:

(1) It may be inferred that harm suffered by the plaintiff is caused by negligence of the defendant when;

(a) the event is of a kind which ordinarily does not occur in the absence of negligence;

(b) other responsible causes, including the conduct of the plaintiff and third persons, are sufficiently eliminated by the evidence; and

(c) the indicated negligence is within the scope of the defendant's duty to the plaintiff.

(2) It is the function of the court to determine whether the inference may reasonably be drawn by the jury, or whether it must necessarily be drawn.

(3) It is the function of the jury to determine whether the inference is to be drawn in any case where different conclusions may reasonably be reached.

The Restatement comment pertaining to § 328 D(1)(b) reads:

Eliminating other responsible causes. It is never enough for the plaintiff to prove that he was injured by the negligence of some person unidentified. It is still necessary to make the negligence point to the defendant. On this too the plaintiff has the burden of proof by a preponderance of the evidence; and in any case where there is no doubt that it is at least equally probable that the negligence was that of a third person, the court must direct the jury that the plaintiff has not proved his case. Again, however, the plaintiff is not required to exclude all other possible conclu-sions beyond a reasonable doubt, and it is enough that he makes out a case from which the jury may reasonably conclude that the negligence was, more probably than not, that of the defendant. *Id.* at 160.

Plaintiffs requested an instruction stating in part:

> From the happening of the accident involved in this case, you may draw an inference that a proximate cause of the occurrence was some negligent conduct on the part of the defendant.

> However, you shall not find that a proximate cause of the occurrence was some negligent conduct on the part of the defendant unless you believe, after weighing all the evidence in the case and drawing such inferences therefrom as you believe are warranted, that it is more probable than not that the occurrence was caused by some negligent conduct on the part of the defendant. . . .

The instruction was rejected, and the following instruction was given:

> The mere fact that an accident happened, standing alone, does not permit the jury to draw the inference that the accident was caused by anyone's negligence.

The doctrine of *res ipsa loquitur* is recognized law in Alaska and in nearly all jurisdictions in the United States. Traditionally, the doctrine has been applied when the following requirements are met:

> 1) the accident is one which ordinarily does not occur in the absence of someone's negligence;

> 2) the agency or instrumentality is within the exclusive control of the defendant;

> 3) the injurious condition or occurrence was not due to any voluntary action or contribution on the part of the plaintiff.

Before these requirements are examined, however, two preliminary issues will be discussed.

The first concerns the applicability of *res ipsa loquitur* when specific acts of negligence are alleged. Although there is a split of authority on whether the doctrine is applicable to cases in which the plaintiff introduces specific evidence of negligence, Alaska does not preclude use of the doctrine unless the specific acts furnish a "complete explanation" of the accident. We have declined to apply *res ipsa loquitur* in an air crash case when the injured plaintiff, the only passenger, testified to specific acts of the pilot prior to the crash. We stated:

> . . . if the evidence discloses the circumstances of the accident to the extent that there is nothing left to infer, then the doctrine of *res ipsa loquitur*, which is founded upon inference, is no longer needed.

Crawford v. Rogers, 406 P.2d 189, 193 (Alaska 1965).

Skyways argues that plaintiffs proffered a "complete explanation" here:

> . . . plaintiffs' evidence, if believed, was that Norvell flew blindly into a snow squall at low altitude, stalled his aircraft in an attempt to avoid some trees, and crashed. . . . There was accordingly nothing left to infer.

We do not agree. It would follow from Skyways' argument that, whenever an expert gives an opinion as to the cause of a crash and is corroborated in part by witnesses, no *res ipsa loquitur* instruction is permitted. Of note is the fact that in the Alaska cases which have applied this "complete explanation" standard regarding evidence of specific acts of negligence, there has been direct, rather than circumstantial evidence: in each case, a witness directly involved at the time of the occurrence had been available to testify.

We have previously referred to the applicability of *res ipsa loquitur* only in cases with "incomplete *factual* descriptions." We do not find that in the present case in which heavy reliance was placed by both parties on inferences of expert witnesses, that a complete *factual* explanation was offered. There were matters of considerable uncertainty, including the exact path of the plane from the Admiralty to the Chichagof side of the Chatham Strait and the precise sequence of events which occurred immediately prior to the crash. In an accident in which there are no survivors to testify and no other direct evidence of the cause, we do not believe that plaintiffs should be precluded from utilizing the doctrine of *res ipsa loquitur* because they have offered a possible explanation to the jury.

The second preliminary issue involves the question of superior knowledge. The superior court specifically noted Skyways' lack of superior knowledge as to the cause of the crash in denying a *res ipsa loquitur* instruction. In this case, neither party possessed superior knowledge: both were equally ignorant of the facts which occurred immediately prior to the crash.

. . . Skyways cites no Alaska case specifically requiring superior knowledge on a defendant's part as to the immediate cause of a crash before *res ipsa loquitur* may be invoked. There are no compelling reasons to apply such a rule to an aircraft accident in which there are no survivors and in which the parties place heavy reliance upon expert testimony. Moreover, while the carrier may not have superior knowledge as to the specific circumstances at the time of the crash, it has superior knowledge as to the characteristics of the particular airplane involved, its maintenance, the training and instruction of its pilots and its general operating procedure under varying conditions.

We now return to analysis of the three traditional prerequisites to the applicability of *res ipsa loquitur:* an accident that normally does not happen without negligence; exclusive control of the instrumentality by the defendant; and absence of voluntary action or contribution by the plaintiff.

The requirements are, in essence, "foundation facts," which must be established before invoking the doctrine.

. . . Skyways relies primarily on the weather conditions incident to the crash to refute plaintiffs' argument that the requirements have been met. Weather conditions, however, are not material to the issue of plaintiff contribution. Accordingly, we shall first address this prerequisite.

Plaintiff contribution is not the equivalent of contributory negligence. Instead, the former term refers to the question of control: the doctrine of *res ipsa loquitur* will not apply if the plaintiff had control of the instrumentality. Skyways argues that plaintiffs have not established lack of plaintiff contribution, since the passengers could have interfered with the controls. Reliance is placed on *Crawford v. Rogers,* 406 P.2d 189 (Alaska 1965), a case in which there was evidence of passenger interference before the court. Here, however, there was no evidence regarding passenger interference presented by any of the parties.

If the requirement of no plaintiff contribution is strictly applied, no *res ipsa loquitur* instruction could be given where the plaintiff lacks sufficient evidence, or any evidence, upon which to prove a negative. . . . We believe that there must be some evidence upon which a jury could find plaintiff contribution before a *res ipsa loquitur* instruction can be denied for this reason. In the face of a silent record, the conclusion that a passenger did not interfere with the operation of an aircraft is much more compelling than the conclusion that he did interfere.

While it is clear that *res ipsa loquitur* is applicable in general to aviation cases, it is not necessarily applicable to every such case since the specific circumstances will vary. Weather may impinge upon the first prerequisite for *res ipsa loquitur* in that it may contribute to a set of circumstances in which it is not more likely than not that the crash was caused by the defendant's negligence. Again, the totality of the circumstances must be considered in each factual setting.

Cases involving in-flight injuries to passengers as a result of bumps, lurches or jerks of an aircraft in turbulence do not give rise to the application of the doctrine. In cases involving crashes, some courts, in applying *res ipsa loquitur,* have specifically noted the absence of evidence of weather as a causative factor.

To require a plaintiff to show that a crash was not caused by weather, as a prerequisite to the application of *res ipsa loquitur,* presents the problems inherent in proving a negative. Again, a strict application of this requirement would have disallowed the *res ipsa loquitur* instruction in *Haasman,* [100 F. Supp. 1 (D. Alaska 1951)], where the plane disappeared without a trace. We will not require plaintiff to negate the possibility of weather as a cause of an airplane crash in order to obtain the benefit of a *res ipsa loquitur* instruction.

The general safety record of air travel and the present state of air technology compel us to conclude that air crashes do not normally occur absent negligence, even in inclement weather. In *Alaska Airlines, Inc. v. Sweat,* 568 P.2d 916, 925 (Alaska 1977), we stated:

> [Air] travel may no longer be regarded as inherently dangerous and . . . flights aboard certified carriers do not involve an unreasonable risk of harm.

Thus, under the circumstances of this case, we find no reason to preclude the applicability of the doctrine of *res ipsa loquitur.* We find the lack of an instruction on the doctrine to be error.

NOTES

1. *Circumstantial Evidence.* The *res ipsa loquitur* doctrine resonates as a common sense application of rules governing the strength of circumstantial evidence. If (1) the accident ordinarily would not occur in the absence of some negligence; (2) if the defendant was in control of the harm-causing instrumentality; and (3) plaintiff did not cause the harm, reasonable minds could conclude that more probably than not defendant was negligent. Adding a Latin title and giving the evidence stronger weight (such as requiring an inference of negligence unless the defendant provides rebuttal evidence) have given *res ipsa* a life of its own. However, not every circumstantial evidence case involves *res ipsa*.

Negri v. Stop & Shop, Inc., 480 N.E.2d 740 (N.Y. 1985), concerned a negligence action against a supermarket by a shopper who allegedly slipped and fell on some broken jars of baby food. There was evidence that the baby food was "dirty and messy" and a witness had not heard any jars falling from the shelves prior to the accident. There was further evidence that the aisle had not been inspected for about an hour. The court concluded:

> Viewing the evidence in a light most favorable to the plaintiffs and according plaintiffs the benefit of every reasonable inference, it cannot be said, as a matter of law, that the circumstantial evidence was insufficient to permit the jury to draw the necessary inference that a slippery condition was created by jars of baby food which had fallen and broken a sufficient length of time prior to the accident to permit defendant's employees to discover and remedy the condition.

Negri, 480 N.E.2d at 741. How does this fact pattern differ from a *res ipsa* case?

2. *Genesis of Res Ipsa Loquitur.* The doctrine of *res ipsa loquitur* had its origin in *Byrne v. Boadle,* (1863)159 Eng. Rep. 299 (Ex. Ct.). A barrel of flour rolled out of a window of defendant's warehouse, striking plaintiff passerby on the head. Plaintiff could not prove how the barrel escaped. Holding for plaintiff, Baron Pollock remarked: "There are certain cases of which it may be said *res ipsa loquitur* [the thing speaks for itself], and this seems one of them." *Id.*

3. *Characterizing the Conduct.* The core of the inference of negligence, via the *res ipsa* principle, is the characterization of the occurrence as one that ordinarily does not happen absent negligence.

In *Coury v. Safe Auto Sales, Inc.*, 297 N.E.2d 88 (N.Y. 1973), the trial court had charged the jury that they could not infer negligent driving solely from the fact that the defendant had crossed the center line into opposing traffic. The appellate court reversed and remanded, stating:

> The jury should have been instructed that the crossing over was a circumstance for their consideration in determining whether the driver had exercised reasonable care in the operation of his vehicle, even though that fact, standing alone, did not necessarily require a finding that he was negligent.

Coury, 297 N.E.2d at 90.

In *Pinecrest Stables, Inc. v. Hill*, 487 So. 2d 82 (Fla. Dist. App. 1986), the owner of a horse claimed that the horse had suffered a rib injury while at defendant's stables. The injury had not been noticed until the owner had removed the horse from the stables. The owner admitted that horses might have been injured during transport or during training, by running into other horses, fences or trees. The court held that a *res ipsa* instruction was inappropriate. The injury was one which could have occurred other than from negligence.

4. *An Inference of Negligence.* Generally a *res ipsa* instruction creates an inference of negligence "which the jury is free to accept or reject." *Lambrecht v. Estate of Kaczmarczyk*, 623 N.W.2d 751, 761 (Wis. 2001). This inference protects plaintiff from a directed verdict in favor of defendant. *See, e.g., Sullivan v. Snyder*, 374 A.2d 866 (D.C. App. 1977). A subsequent failure by the defendant to meet the explanatory burden is sufficient to support a jury verdict in *plaintiff's* favor. In some states a *res ipsa* instruction creates a presumption of negligence on the part of defendant. *See, e.g., Fields v. Yusuf*, 51 Cal. Rptr. 3d 277, 282 (Cal. App. 2006) (the doctrine of *res ipsa loquitur* establishes a presumption of negligence requiring the defendant to come forward with evidence to disprove it). How does an inference of negligence differ from a presumption of negligence?

5. *Res Ipsa and Expert Testimony.* In *Morgan v. Children's Hosp.*, 480 N.E.2d 464 (Ohio 1985), the court held that the doctrine of *res ipsa* applied to a medical malpractice action, even though expert testimony was required to establish the cause of the injury. "Much as the courts have implemented the malpractice standard of care through expert testimony, the court can adapt *res ipsa loquitur* to malpractice by requiring expert testimony that the injury bespeaks negligence." *Morgan*, 480 N.E.2d at 467. *See also Scott v. James*, 731 A.2d 399 (D.C. 1999), in which the plaintiff was alleging negligence by a hair stylist in the application of a hair relaxer. The court affirmed a directed a verdict in favor of the defendant because the plaintiff had failed to present expert testimony to show the standard of care in applying the hair relaxer.

Does the application of the *res ipsa* doctrine turn on the occurrence of an accident which "ordinarily" does not happen in the absence of negligence? If so, in cases where the ordinariness of an event must be determined by expert testimony, does the doctrine lose its moorings?

6. *Identifying the Risk-Taker (1): Exclusive Control by Defendant.* The *res ipsa* doctrine is premised both upon circumstantial evidence of negligence and evidence, circumstantial or direct, linking that conduct to the defendant. In *American Elevator Co. v. Briscoe*, 572 P.2d 534 (Nev. 1977), the defendant held the maintenance contract on an elevator for several years. The plaintiff was injured during a "speeding" episode. There was evidence of other anomalies in the elevator's operation, and there was no evidence of maintenance by others, or of design defects. The court concluded:

> To require a plaintiff to establish exclusive control in the defendant with respect to *any possible cause* of the accident before permitting the application of *res ipsa loquitur* would emasculate the doctrine. He was required, *as was done,* only to produce sufficient evidence from which it could be said that it was more likely than not that it was negligence on the part of his adversary. There was a reasonable showing by respondent of variances from the recognized standards of maintenance and that the same could have possibly proximately caused his injuries.

Had appellants established a possible design defect, a contrary verdict may have been rendered. However, there was no evidence of design defect, and the jury found that appellants failed to discharge their burden of explanation.

Brisco, 572 P.2d at 537.

Suppose the evidence suggested that the accident in question may have been the result of concurrent causes. Should *res ipsa* be permitted? Consider *Tompkins v. Northwestern Union Trust Co.,* 645 P.2d 402 (Mont. 1982) (doctrine applicable when pilot error may have combined with equipment failure caused by negligent maintenance of a third party, resulting in airplane crash).

7. *Identifying the Risk-Taker (2): Exclusive Control, But of What?* In *Victory Park Apts., Inc. v. Axelson,* 367 N.W.2d 155 (N.D. 1985), plaintiff brought an action against one of its tenants following a fire in her apartment. Plaintiff's theory was that the tenant had negligently dropped a smoked cigarette between the cushions of the couch. Plaintiff requested a *res ipsa* instruction on the basis that the defendant had exclusive control of the couch and the apartment. The court disagreed because it characterized the instrumentality in question as the cigarette, and there was insufficient evidence that the tenant, rather than other smokers who had been in the apartment earlier, had exclusive control of the cigarette. *Cf. Olswanger v. Funk,* 470 S.W.2d 13 (Tenn. Ct. App. 1970) (only tenants had been in the apartment shortly before fire).

8. *Identifying the Risk-Taker (3): Eliminating the Plaintiff.* In the aircraft crash case of *Newing v. Cheatham,* 540 P.2d 33 (Cal. 1975), the court noted:

> The purpose of [the innocence of the plaintiff] requirement, like that of control by the defendant is to establish that the defendant is the one probably responsible for the accident. The plaintiff need not show that he was entirely inactive at the time of the accident in order to satisfy this requirement, so long as the evidence is such as to eliminate his conduct as a factor contributing to the occurrence.

Newing, 540 P.2d at 41. The court concluded that the foundational fact was established in part because

> the body of plaintiffs' decedent was found by the rescue party in one of the rear seats of the four-seater aircraft. From that position, it is difficult to imagine how he could have interfered physically with the operation of the aircraft in any way.

Id. at 42.

9. *Res Ipsa Loquitur and Comparative Fault.* Most jurisdictions that have considered the issue have held that when the contributory negligence bar has been replaced with comparative negligence, the third foundational fact (eliminating the plaintiff's contribution) in the *res ipsa* doctrine no longer is required. *See, e.g., Montgomery Elevator Co. v. Gordon,* 619 P.2d 66 (Colo. 1980). Why? Consider this scenario: defendant's car leaves the street, jumps the curb and strikes plaintiff, who, intoxicated, is lying on the sidewalk. Should *res ipsa* apply, although plaintiff plainly is contributorily negligent? Why?

10. *Res Ipsa and Information Costs.* To what extent is the *res ipsa* doctrine designed to identify the party who must expend the cheapest information costs in order to identify the risk-taker? Is that requirement of disparate information *all* that the traditional doctrinal elements are seeking to approximate? Consider the following statement by the Supreme Court of Alabama:

> The function of the doctrine is to supply a fact which must have existed in the causal chain stretching from the act or omission of the defendant to the injury suffered by the plaintiff, but which the plaintiff, because of circumstances surrounding the causal chain, cannot know and cannot prove to have actually existed. The missing fact is that the defendant was negligent. The rationale of the theory, in part, is that [the] defendant in charge of the instrumentality which caused the injury is possessed of superior knowledge and by reason thereof is better advantaged than plaintiff to know the true cause and therefore, negligence is presumed and the burden is upon the defendant to adduce proof to overcome the presumption.

Alabama Power Co. v. Berry, 48 So.2d 231, 238 (Ala. 1950).

The majority of cases, however, hold that application of *res ipsa* does not turn on superior knowledge of the defendant. *See, e.g., Johnson v. Foster,* 202 So.2d 520 (Miss. 1967) (car unaccountably leaves highway — driver and passenger both dead). If the doctrine does not depend on superior knowledge, then what is the basis for its application?

11. *Direct Evidence of Negligence.* Should direct evidence of negligence preclude the application of the *res ipsa loquitur* doctrine? A Colorado appellate court observed that:

> *Res ipsa loquitur* is a rule which presumes evidence which applies when it is judicially determined that a particular unexplained occurrence creates a *prima facie* case of negligence without proof of specific misfeasance. . . .

> A corollary requirement is that no direct evidence exists establishing that a specific act of negligence was the only likely cause for the harm. . . . The mere introduction of evidence as to how an accident could have occurred and its *possible* causes does not necessarily preclude application of *res ipsa loquitur* so long as that evidence does not clearly resolve the issue of culpability.

Kitto v. Gilbert, 570 P.2d 544, 548 (Colo. Ct. App. 1977). *See also Swann v. Prudential Insurance Company of America*, 620 A.2d 989 (Md. App. 1993) ("[T]he majority of American jurisdictions . . . hold that 'an unsuccessful attempt to prove specific negligence on the defendant's part, or the introduction of evidence of specific negligence not clearly establishing the precise cause of injury, will not deprive the plaintiff of the benefits otherwise available under the doctrine. . . .'").

PROBLEMS

4.1

Dana Derby was driving through downtown Filly, heading south. While Dana was stopped at an intersection for a red light, two strangers walked toward Dana's car with rags and window cleaner in hand. Dana, who lived in the suburbs, was frightened and stepped on the accelerator, speeding into the intersection just as Bo Burt's car was entering the intersection from the west. In the ensuing collision, Bo's car was damaged, and Bo sued Dana.

The speed limit for driving in the city was 35 miles per hour. Both parties stipulated that Bo entered the intersection at approximately 45 miles per hour.

> 1. Should the judge merely instruct the jury that Dana's conduct must be evaluated in light of what the ordinary prudent person would do in similar circumstances? What instruction should Dana's attorney request to evaluate whether Dana's conduct was negligent?

> 2. Should the judge permit evidence that people customarily drove at 45 miles per hour at the intersection?

4.2

A criminal statute requires bicyclists to ride on right side of road along *with traffic* or face criminal sanction. No statute regulates pedestrians. Because of unusually heavy car and pedestrian traffic on right side, Deborah defendant rides her bike on the left side of the road, so she is riding into traffic. She could be cited, criminally.

While she is riding on the left side, Deborah's bike goes out of control and injures Paul pedestrian, who is walking on that side of the road, also into traffic. What issues arise in Paul's effort to prove negligence and what responses might Deborah make?

4.3

The Old Ferry Creek bed in northern Anystate has become the regular Saturday afternoon haunt of the Suzonda All-Terrain Vehicle Club. The club, which is run by Fred, has a membership of approximately 20 children, all less than eighteen years of age. The club rents the powerful all-terrain vehicles (ATVs) from local motorcycle dealers and provides them to the children as a community service. One Saturday, Fred was supervising a group of riders, including Jason, his 15-year-old son, and six-year-old Chris.

The session progressed well, albeit noisily, until Chris and Jason decided upon an impromptu race and left the other riders. Attempting to turn at high speed, both riders lost control of their machines. Chris headed back toward the main group at high speed. Fred saw him coming and rushed to head him off, but succeeded only in colliding with Chris. Fred suffered serious injuries in the collision.

Meanwhile, Jason exited the creek bed at high speed and proceeded onto the street. He was beginning to regain control of his machine when he swerved onto the sidewalk. There, he struck Timmy, who had been skateboarding down the sidewalk at high speed. Timmy and Jason were seriously injured.

Timmy and Jason were in the same grade at school and had been involved in numerous scuffles. A primary cause of the scuffles was Jason's jealousy over Timmy's victory in the state skateboarding championship.

After the accident, Fred was found to have a minute quantity of alcohol in his blood system. In Anystate, the minimum age for an operator's permit for a motorcycle is 15 years. It is illegal for any person to operate an ATV on a public road. Fred brings an action in negligence against Chris, and Timmy brings an action in negligence against Jason. Both Chris and Jason counter with allegations of contributory negligence.

> 1. Assume that the cases go to trial. What jury instructions will be sought by Chris, Jason, Fred and Timmy? What arguments will they employ, and how should the court resolve the issues?

> 2. Should Timmy consider bringing anything other than a negligence action against Jason?

> 3. Should Fred or Timmy consider joining any other parties as defendants? What allegations could they make, and what difficulties would they face?

4.4

Sammy was enrolled as an undergraduate student at Anystate College in Anystate Springs. A number of incidents including thefts and assaults had occurred on the campus. Sammy had not been a victim herself, although she had been outraged by the College's apparent failure to tighten up security. Sammy had written to the school newspaper complaining that the attacks had led many students to confine themselves to their dorms. In partial response the University President issued a press release stating that the College's current financial condition made it impossible to hire more security personnel.

However, Anystate College arranged a self-defense class at a nearby gym. The college employed Barry to conduct the classes. For five years Barry had been an Anystate Springs police officer. However, he had suffered a back injury in a high-speed chase of a fleeing felon, and had been forced to retire. Barry frequently has disturbing flashbacks to the chase and the accident. During the first class the students worked in pairs. After having received instruction from Barry, they practiced on one another. Sammy's partner was Geordie, her classmate. The first exercise was a hip throw. The person executing the hip throw grasps the partner by the shoulders and turns quickly. By throwing the person grasped over the hip it causes her (or him) to lose balance. Sammy threw the 200-pound Geordie six feet down the mat. Geordie landed where two of the gym's floor mats had come apart. Sammy was heard by other students to have muttered, "That'll teach him!".

Barry decided to carry the seriously injured Geordie to the college's Emergency Health Center (EMC) located near the University's main administrative building in the middle of the campus. Barry soon found Geordie to be something of a "dead weight." He saw Sammy's Honda outside the gym with the keys left in it; he quickly put Geordie on the back seat and drove the car towards the EMC. Unfortunately, the tension caused Barry to temporarily black out and lose his way. By the time he recovered and reached the administrative building he was so flustered that he rammed the University president's illegally parked Mercedes. Both the Mercedes and the Honda were badly damaged.

Before Barry left the gym he asked Daisy, one of the more advanced students to "take the mat," and substitute for him for the rest of the class. Daisy was a "first-degree black belt," a rank or status certifying to and requiring weekly school attendance, knowledge as to lower ranks, understanding of judo training and instructional methods, and qualifying as able to conduct classes with the approval of the ranking "yudansha" or black belt instructor. Daisy had assisted in instructing judo classes at the local YMCA and she scrupulously followed the training conventions used there.

Daisy now asked Sammy to assist her in demonstrating the next move. This move was the "osotogari," a leg throw in which one leg is used to sweep the opponent's leg out from under her. Sammy fell on her arm, breaking it.

Following an emergency call, an ambulance rushed Sammy to the EMC. She arrived just after Barry came in with the unconscious Geordie. Unfortunately, the EMC was unable to locate an emergency care physician. In the interim Sammy and Geordie were wheeled into a treatment room. In serious pain and concerned that her treatment would be further delayed, Sammy reached over to Geordie's gurney and switched charts with him. As soon as the doctor arrived, Sammy was the first patient to be treated. Medical reports suggested that if Geordie had been treated earlier he would have been less likely to suffer from the permanent disability with which he is now afflicted.

What issues of tort law arise? How are they likely to be resolved?

4.5

Fun, Inc. runs a hamburger and other fast foods restaurant in downtown Bannan. To promote business from shoppers with children, Fun, Inc. has a video-game area in the restaurant, near the rear, where the bathroom, storage closet, and kitchen doors are located. They also give away a toy clown with every child's meal that is ordered. The clown give-away and video games are widely advertised on television and on signs in the front window of the restaurant.

Orlando Orloff, aged 15, was shopping downtown with his first cousin Pico, who was 6 years old.

As they passed Fun, Inc. and looked in the windows, Orlando asked Pico if he was thirsty. Pico said, "No, but I need to go to the bathroom." They entered the restaurant and asked where the bathroom was. "Keep walking back, through the video arcade," they were told by the host.

At the video arcade, they could see no marked bathroom doors. The bathroom doors, which were marked MEN and WOMEN, were located down a hall in the corner of the arcade, but the sign over the hall entrance said, "EXIT."

Still searching, Orlando and Pico tried an unmarked door at the rear of the video arcade, but it turned out to be a storage closet. They closed that door, and tried the next door, which opened into the restaurant kitchen. As they entered the kitchen, holding hands, a loud angry voice yelled, "Hey, you can't come in here."

Pico jumped and turned to run, pushing Orlando into a hot pot of soup boiling on the stove, which was about three feet to the right of the door. Orlando was burned severely by the hot soup.

A Bannan state statute says: "All restaurant kitchens must place stoves at least 10 feet away from doors, for the safety of employees." Fun, Inc. had placed the stove in the location near the door because otherwise the stove could not be safely vented.

Your law firm represents Fun, Inc. in the lawsuit brought by Orlando. Your senior partner has asked you to draft a memo detailing and analyzing the legal issues that might arise in this litigation.

Chapter 5

CAUSE IN FACT

A. INTRODUCTION

Courts have divided the issue of *"causation"* into *cause in fact* and *legal (or proximate) cause*. This chapter will focus principally on cause in fact; Chapter 6 will be concerned primarily with legal (or proximate) cause. According to orthodox tort theory, cause in fact is concerned with whether one person's conduct caused another person's injury. It is an inquiry into the legal response to factual, scientific or forensic evidence that relates to the relationship between the defendant's conduct and the plaintiff's damage (literally, *did* X cause Y?). Supposedly, cause in fact is a factual question and, almost always, a jury issue.

Legal cause is a normative issue; it is a question of fairness or policy: given that A has caused B's injury in a factual sense (cause in fact), should A be liable for B's damages (legal cause)? Like "duty," legal cause asks whether A should be liable as a matter of policy for B's injuries. One key question, which we begin to address in the next chapter, is: (1) what policies are relevant to this legal cause determination, and (2) whether the judge or the jury should apply those policies in a particular case. In essence, then, legal cause has little to do with causation in any factual or scientific sense and may well invite a consideration of duty. Chapters 6 and 7 will explore the concept of duty.

While cause in fact is supposedly a factual issue and legal cause is a policy issue, courts, predictably, have experienced difficulty in distinguishing between the issues. This is one of the problems you will face as you work through the next few important chapters. This chapter deals with "cause in fact" and the following chapter discusses the concept usually termed "proximate cause" or "legal cause."

B. "BUT-FOR" CAUSATION

EAST TEXAS THEATRES, INC. v. RUTLEDGE
453 S.W.2d 466 (Tex. 1970)

SMITH, JUSTICE.

This is a damage suit alleging personal injuries were sustained by Sheila Rutledge, on or about September 25, 1966, while attending a midnight movie in a theatre owned and operated by East Texas Theatres, Inc. . . . [S]uit was brought by Sheila . . . alleging that certain acts of negligence on the part of the theatre were a proximate cause of the injuries Sheila sustained while a patron of the theatre. . . . The jury found the defendant guilty of negligence in failing to remove certain unidentified 'rowdy persons' from the theatre and that such negligence was a proximate cause of Sheila's injuries. . . .

The defendant presents two major questions for our decision: (1) the error of the Court of Civil Appeals in holding that there was any probative evidence of record to support the jury finding on proximate cause, and (2) the error of the Court of Civil Appeals in holding that the testimony was sufficient to prove a causal connection between the injuries alleged to have been sustained by Sheila and her subsequent complaints of chronic headache, etc. In view of our holding on the first question, it is unnecessary to pass upon the second. . . .

On September 24 and the early morning of September 25, 1966, Sheila, a paying guest, was attending a special 'midnight show' at the Paramount Theatre, one of the several theatres owned by the defendant. The interior of the theatre was arranged with a lower floor and a balcony for the seating of patrons. Sheila and her friends took seats on the lower floor in the left section close to an aisle which ran parallel with the left wall and out beyond the overhang of the balcony. When the picture came to an end, Sheila started making her exit, after the lights were turned on, using the aisle between the left section and the wall. As she proceeded up the aisle toward the front of the building for the purpose of leaving the theatre and just before she walked under the balcony overhang, some unidentified person in the balcony threw a bottle which struck her on the side of her head just above her left ear.

Conduct of the Theatre Patrons

Since the jury found that the patrons in the balcony were acting in a 'rowdy' manner and that the defendant, its agents, servants and employees, negligently failed to remove such rowdy persons from the premises and that such negligence proximately caused the injuries sustained by Sheila, we deem it important to particularly point out the evidence bearing on the conduct of the patrons during the evening. The evidence favorable to the verdict is that during the progress of the show, the patrons in the theatre, both on the lower floor and in the balcony, were engaged in 'hollering.' . . . This 'hollering' was intermittent; it occurred 'off and on' during parts of the movie. . . . [A witness] testified that he saw paper or cold drink cups either 'drafting down' or being thrown down toward the front of the theatre. . . . In regard to the duration of the commotion in the theatre, the evidence shows that there was more commotion on the lower floor than in the balcony. . . . [b]efore the accident, all commotion in the theatre had ceased. The last disturbance of any kind before the show was over was not throwing but 'hollering.' . . .

The Balcony Patrons and Their Conduct

The balcony, which would seat 263 people, was 'just about full.' [One] witness . . . estimated that about 175 of the balcony seats were occupied. The disturbance in the balcony seemed to come from the balcony generally, 'just all over it.' The evidence does not identify any particular person as being a 'rowdy person.' No witness could state which persons in the balcony were rowdy and which were not. No witness could identify the person who threw the bottle. Incidentally, there is no evidence that a hard substance of any character was thrown, other than the bottle which struck Sheila. . . . . [A] witness . . . testified that he could not identify the person who threw the bottle, but that out of the corner of his eye, he saw a 'movement, a jerking motion' by someone in the balcony and then saw the bottle hit Sheila. No witness testified that the bottle thrower had been engaged in 'hollering' or throwing paper cups. The jury found that Sheila's injuries were not solely caused by the action of 'some unknown person who threw a bottle. . . .'

Assuming without deciding that the finding of negligence is supported by evidence of probative force, we go direct to the question of whether there is in the record evidence or probative force to support the finding of proximate cause. We hold that there is no evidence to support the finding of the jury that the failure of the defendant to remove 'rowdy persons' from its premises was a proximate cause of Sheila's injuries. . . .

[I]t is well settled that proximate cause includes two essential elements: (1) there must be cause in fact — a cause which produces an event and without which the event would not have occurred; and (2) foreseeability. . . . 'An essential element of the plaintiff's cause of action for negligence is that there be some reasonable connection between the act or omission of the defendant and the damage which the plaintiff has suffered.' PROSSER, LAW OF TORTS (3rd Ed.) 240–241. We base our decision here on the ground that the plaintiffs have failed to offer evidence of probative force to establish the cause-in-fact element of proximate cause. In particular, the plaintiffs contend that the act of omission in failing to remove 'rowdy persons' from the theatre was a proximate cause of the injuries resulting from the throwing of the bottle by an unknown patron of the theatre. We recognize that cause-in-fact covers the defendant's omissions as well as its acts. However, it cannot be said from this record that had the defendant removed the 'rowdy persons' from the premises, the bottle thrower would not have thrown the bottle. The record in this case clearly shows a complete lack of proof that the bottle would not have been thrown 'but for' the failure of the defendant to remove 'rowdy persons' from the premises. There is no evidence that the bottle thrower was one of the 'rowdy persons' engaged in 'hollering' and throwing paper cups from the balcony. We cannot say from this evidence what persons would have been removed. We agree with the defendant's contention . . . that the judgment of the trial court cannot be sustained in that there is no evidence that the alleged injuries were proximately caused by any act of commission or omission of the defendant. As said by this Court in *Enloe v. Barfield*, 422 S.W.2d 905 (1967), 'a finding of 'proximate cause' cannot be sustained unless there is proof of cause in fact and foreseeability. . . .'

The plaintiffs further contend that cause-in-fact was proved on the theory that 'it would be considerably more probable that had even minimum supervision, such as a request by theatre employees to cease such rowdy behavior, or for the policeman to even go to the balcony and stand so that he might be seen by the patrons in the balcony, would have prevented the person who did throw the bottle from doing so because of his fear of being apprehended. That the theatre, by and through its employees, in failing to give this minimum supervision or yet, the more burdensome elements submitted upon the part of the plaintiff, failure to oust persons engaging in rowdy behavior, encouraged the wrongdoer by guaranteeing his anonymity in a crowd to the point that he felt he could and did in fact, get away with throwing the bottle.' This theory is related in no way to the single act of throwing the bottle. It is purely speculative as to what would have happened had the defendant attempted to remove the 'rowdy persons' from the theatre. The bottle thrower may not have been present at a time when the 'rowdy persons' were being ejected. If present at the time of removal of the persons who were 'hollering' and throwing paper cups, it would be just a guess as to what subjective effect such action may have had upon the bottle thrower . . .

We recognize that the theatre was under a duty to exercise reasonable care for the safety of its patrons. However, operators of theatres are not insurers of their patrons' safety.

The judgments of the Court of Civil Appeals and the trial court are reversed and judgment is here rendered that plaintiffs take nothing.

NOTES

1. *Cause in Fact or Legal Cause?* The *East Texas Theaters* case alludes to the outdated view that cause in fact is a part of proximate or legal cause. The distinction between the two, which now is well established in the jurisprudence and scholarly writings, was expressed by one court in these terms:

> Defining legal or proximate cause has proved to be a Herculean task for the judiciary in all places and all times. The very term "proximate cause" is fraught with confusion, as it has nothing to do either with cause or proximity. Moreover, it is not to be mistaken for cause-in-fact, as the two elements satisfy entirely different functions in the negligence analysis. To meet the cause-in-fact element, a plaintiff must prove only that the conduct was a necessary antecedent of the accident, that is, but for the defendant's conduct, the incident probably would not have occurred. Once it is determined the conduct is a cause-in-fact of the injury, all causation inquiries are complete.

> "The problem [of proximate cause is] not one of causation for which it has been so often mistaken, but one of defining the boundaries of the rule invoked." Because substandard conduct does not render the actor liable for all consequences spiraling outward until the end of time, the concept of proximate cause, or one of its functional equivalents, such as scope of the duty in duty-risk analysis, is necessary to truncate liability at some point. The primary inquiry, then, in a proximate cause determination is: "whether plaintiff will be granted the legal system's protection — that is, will the defendant be required to have met a specified standard of conduct in the case at issue or be subject to liability."

Roberts v. Benoit, 605 So. 2d 1032, 1052 (La. 1992) (citations omitted).

2. *The "But For" Test.* The court applies a "but for" test for cause in fact. Can one say that "but for" the defendant's negligence, the plaintiff's injuries would not have occurred? *See generally* REST. 3D TORTS: LIABILITY FOR PHYSICAL HARM PROPOSED FINAL DRAFT § 26 (2005), which provides that "[a]n actor's tortious conduct must be a factual cause of another's physical harm for liability to be imposed. Conduct is a factual cause of harm when the harm would not have occurred absent the conduct."

What is the particular alleged act of negligence in *East Texas Theatres, Inc.*? What are the plaintiff's injuries? Is the "but for" test effective in establishing cause in fact?

3. *A Counterfactual Inquiry.* Note how the "but for" test sets up a counterfactual inquiry. It asks the factfinder to decide if what happened would have happened anyway if the defendant had not done whatever it is that the plaintiff said defendant did wrong. Counterfactual inquiries can be troublesome because they ask us to make decisions about a world that did not come to pass.

Suppose that A makes a left hand turn without signaling and runs over a pedestrian who is blind. Is the failure to signal a cause in fact of the pedestrian's injuries? Suppose that A drives off a canyon road and his car falls two hundred feet before bursting into flames, killing A. Even though the passenger section of the car is severely burned as is A's body, an expert establishes that the car's air bag did not open. Would the failure of the air bag to open be a cause in fact of A's death under the "but for" test?

4. *Careful and Precise Analysis and Articulation.* Before applying the "but for" test, it is critical to carefully and precisely identify the particular alleged act of negligence and the particular injuries allegedly caused by the alleged negligent act. *See* David W. Robertson, *The Common Sense of Cause-In-Fact*, 75 TEX. L. REV. 1765 (1997).

> Properly framing the but-for issue in a lawsuit is a significantly complex mental operation involving four essential steps. First, one must identify the injury or injuries for which redress is sought. This step rarely presents any difficulty. However . . . when it does present difficulties they can be substantial.
>
> Second, one must identify the defendant's wrongful conduct. Care is required here. It is not enough for the plaintiff to show that her injuries would not have occurred if the defendant had never been born; the plaintiff must show that her injuries probably would not have occurred if the defendant had not engaged in the particular conduct alleged (and ultimately proved) in the lawsuit to have been wrongful. As Professor Malone put it: "The determination of cause-in-fact is launched by fixing as precisely as possible the piece of conduct — the exact act or omission — with which the defendant is charged."
>
> The third step is the trickiest. It involves using the imagination to create a counterfactual hypothesis. One creates a mental picture of a situation identical to the actual facts of the case in all respects save one: the defendant's wrongful conduct is now "corrected" to the minimal extent necessary to make it conform to the law's requirements. It is important to stress that the mental operation performed at this third step must be careful, conservative, and modest; the hypothesis must be counterfactual only to the extent necessary to ask the but-for question. Only the defendant's wrongful conduct must be "changed,"

and that only to the extent necessary to make it conform to the requirements of law. The mental precision required here is a corollary of the step two requirement of "fixing as precisely as possible the piece of conduct — the exact act or omission — with which the defendant is charged." At step three, one mentally alters only that piece of conduct.

The fourth step asks the key question whether the injuries that the plaintiff suffered would probably still have occurred had the defendant behaved correctly in the sense indicated.

The fifth and final step is answering the question. When we say that "lay opinion" is as good as the "learning, literature, and lore of the law" on the matter of factual causation, we are referring only to this fifth step, that is, to the common sense and intuition used in answering the question posed at the fourth step. The first four steps, necessary for properly framing that question, require precision of thought and call for legal expertise.

Id. at 1770–71 (footnotes omitted).

5. *This or That.* In *Dillon v. Twin State Gas & Electric Co.*, 85 N.H. 449, 163 A. 111 (1932), the decedent was electrocuted when he fell from a bridge girder and grasped a wire, charged with a high voltage current and strung below the girder. The court observed that:

The circumstances of the decedent's death give rise to an unusual issue of its cause. In leaning over from the girder and losing his balance he was entitled to no protection from the defendant to keep from falling. Its only liability was in exposing him to the danger of charged wires. If but for the current in the wires he would have fallen down on the floor of the bridge or into the river, he would without doubt have been either killed or seriously injured. Although he died from electrocution, yet, if by reason of his preceding loss of balance he was bound to fall except for the intervention of the current, he either did not have long to live or was to be maimed. In such an outcome of his loss of balance, the defendant deprived him, not of a life of normal expectancy, but of one too short to be given pecuniary allowance, in one alternative, and not of normal, but of limited, earning capacity, in the other.

If it were found that he would have thus fallen with death probably resulting, the defendant would not be liable, unless for conscious suffering found to have been sustained from the shock. In that situation his life or earning capacity had no value. To constitute actionable negligence there must be damage, and damage is limited to those elements the statute prescribes.

If it should be found that but for the current he would have fallen with serious injury, then the loss of life or earning capacity resulting from the electrocution would be measured by its value in such injured condition. Evidence that he would be crippled would be taken into account in the same manner as though he had already been crippled.

His probable future but for the current thus bears on liability as well as damages. Whether the shock from the current threw him back on the girder or whether he would have recovered his balance, with or without the aid of the wire he took hold of, if it had not been charged, are issues of fact, as to which the evidence as it stands may lead to different conclusions.

Id. at

6. *Burden of Persuasion.* Where the evidence is doubtful, who should have the burden of proof? According to REST. 2D TORTS §433B(1), "the burden of proof that the tortious conduct of the defendant has caused the harm to the plaintiff is upon the plaintiff."

In causation cases how should this burden of persuasion (typically referred to as the *balance of probabilities*) best be characterized? In *Bell v. United States*, 854 F.2d 881 (6th Cir. Mich. 1988), the plaintiff claimed that decedent's death was caused by the failure of physicians at the veterans administration medical center to diagnose timely decedent's abdominal aortic aneurysm. The trial court found that plaintiff had failed to prove that decedent had a better than 50 percent chance of surviving an operation to correct the aneurysm on and after the date that the duty of care was breached. On appeal, the Court of Appeals for the Sixth Circuit stated that the trial court had been in error in interpreting Michigan state law as requiring proof of a probability of recovery that was greater than 50 percent.

> [T]he Michigan Supreme Court long ago rejected the notion that a plaintiff must prove with mathematical certainty that had a physician diagnosed and treated a medical condition within the time period that a doctor exercising a reasonable standard of care would have done so, the probability that the patient would have recovered was better than 50%. Rather, under Michigan law, a "reasonable probability" is proven if a finder of fact legally could conclude from the evidence presented that the patient had . . . a "fairly good" chance of surviving the operation. Although we acknowledge the imprecision which nearly always is the necessary companion of any legal standard that rejects quantitative analysis, Michigan law leaves no doubt that it has rejected such analysis in favor of a qualitative one.

> We recognize that when making a choice between a "bright line" cut-off of 50%, and a more amorphous standard of "reasonable probability," we only have shifted the problem slightly, not eliminated it. In either case, a plaintiff falling below the threshold will obtain no recovery, even though something of value has certainly been lost. On the other hand, recovery for the full loss, when only some lesser chance for it has been taken away, may appear unjust as well.

Id. at 889.

Does this judicial skepticism inevitably set the stage for the "loss of chance" and "market share" liability cases that follow later in this chapter?

SHARPE v. PETER PAN BUS LINES
401 Mass. 788 (1988)

WILKINS, JUSTICE.

On Sunday morning, February 22, 1981, Sharon Lee Glynn, a sixteen-year-old who had purchased a bus ticket to go home after visiting a friend in Westfield, was waiting in the Springfield bus terminal to board a Peter Pan bus. Without warning and without provocation, one Patrick Werner, a stranger to Sharon, walked up behind her while she was talking with two young friends seated with her in the terminal, and stabbed her three times in the back, killing her. The circumstances of the crime and Werner's appeal from his conviction of murder in the second degree appear in *Commonwealth v. Werner*, 16 Mass. App. Ct. 686 (1983).

In this action the jury found by a special verdict that each defendant was negligent and that its negligence was a proximate cause of Sharon's death. They awarded damages for wrongful death and for conscious suffering. We transferred the appeals of the defendant bus company (Peter Pan) and the defendant bus terminal (Springfield) to this court. We affirm the judgment.

. . . We turn then to the issue whether the evidence presented a case for the jury. Our inquiry first concerns the question whether either defendant failed to act reasonably in the circumstances to provide the utmost care and diligence to protect patrons of the terminal. The second issue, by far the harder question of the two to answer, is whether any breach of duty may have been a reasonably foreseeable cause of the attack on Sharon.

We have little hesitancy in ruling that the evidence warranted a finding that each defendant failed to fulfill its high duty of care concerning security in the terminal. The jury would have been warranted in finding that the terminal was in a rundown section of the city. Homeless people and drunks frequented the area. The terminal was in an active area for crimes against the person, one characterized by a Springfield police captain as an area of high criminal activity. There had been robberies in the terminal's restrooms and assaults in the terminal. Evidence concerning the neighborhood of a bus terminal and the people who frequent it is relevant to a case of this type. The terminal management called the police every week because of a security or other problem. The terminal had no uniformed security person working for it. The defendants were aware of a need to have security present in some form but had no security plan. Because of security problems, the management of the terminal had asked the local police to make periodic patrols. Sunday morning was a time of substantial activity in the terminal; as many as fifteen buses would arrive at or leave the terminal each hour.

There was evidence warranting a finding that the stabbing of Sharon was within the reasonably foreseeable risks created by each defendant's breach of duty. The jury could have reasonably found that the defendants were negligent in failing to provide a uniformed security force in the terminal. It is likely that a uniformed security officer in the terminal could not have prevented Werner's attack on Sharon. The fact that a physical attack could not have been prevented, once a person had decided to undertake it, however, does not fully answer the causation question.

The presence of uniformed police or security personnel provides a deterrent effect. Lay people would have a sense that this is true. In this case, an expert on security procedures testified that uniformed police or security officers are the best deterrent to crime that one could have and that a security officer could have been placed effectively in the terminal. The jury could reasonably have concluded that as a deterrent to crime the defendants had a duty to provide uniformed security personnel in the terminal at the time of the attack.

The question, of course, is not simply whether crime in general might have been deterred by a police presence, but whether the jury would have been warranted in finding that it was more probable than not that sudden, unprovoked attacks, such as Werner's attack on Sharon, could have been prevented. The jury could have found that Werner was concerned about not being caught. He fled the scene, hid the knife, tried to elude the police, and was found hiding in the vicinity. The evidence warranted a finding that Werner probably would have been deterred from attacking Sharon if a uniformed security guard had been present. The plaintiff's expert answered responsively to a question on cross-examination that, if a uniformed security guard had been there, the attack probably could have been prevented. On the evidence, it was within the jury's province to reach the same conclusion, as they did . . .

LYNCH, JUSTICE, dissenting. . . .

Moreover, the negligent act of failing to provide *uniformed* security personnel did not create the opportunity for the criminal act inflicted upon the plaintiff's decedent. The attack on Sharon occurred in broad daylight in a terminal full of people. Sharon sat with two friends, one of whom was a two-hundred-pound, six-foot-tall young man. In such circumstances, the presence or absence of a uniformed security guard could have had little effect on whether the attack would or would not have occurred. One could speculate over such a question. Perhaps a security guard would have intervened successfully in the attack, or perhaps he would have been at the other end of the waiting room. Possibly a uniformed security guard would have deterred the killer from entering the station. In all likelihood, since the killer was an ordinary traveler on his way through Massachusetts from Colorado, the presence of a security guard would have had no effect at all. The jury are entitled to draw reasonable inferences from the evidence. They are not entitled to base a verdict on conjecture. The question whether the defendants' failure to employ a uniformed guard was the proximate cause of Sharon's death may be resolved only through the exercise of conjecture. Therefore, it is a question not properly for the jury . . .

NOTES

1. *Proving a Causal Positive.* The distinction between misfeasance and non-feasance is frequently accorded more importance than it warrants. Nevertheless, it raises some interesting issues in the case of factual causation. The paradigmatic cause in fact issue concerns a jury inquiry into whether X's negligent *act* caused Y's injuries. Theoretically at least, and notwithstanding the standard of proof required in any particular jurisdiction, it should be *possible* to answer that question with scientific certainty. However, can the same be said with regard to the question of whether X's failure to provide a safety device or procedure *caused* injuries suffered by Y from a non-X source? The prevalent view ignores any such distinction.

For example, in *Jackson v. Ray Kruse Constr. Co.,* 708 S.W.2d 664, 667–68 (Mo. 1986), the court affirmed a jury verdict in favor of a four-year-old against the owner of the apartment complex where she lived, following injuries she suffered when she was struck by a speeding bicycle rider in the parking lot. Her theory of liability was that the bicycle would not have been traveling so fast if there had been "speed bumps" installed in the parking lot. The court concluded:

> The defendants argue vigorously . . . that the plaintiff has not established the element of causation. The accident was precipitated, of course, by the bicycle rider, who no doubt could be faulted for excessive speed and inattention. There may, however, be more than one proximate cause of an accident. . . . [T]he subject of causation has been the subject of much discussion among legal scholars, often because of bizarre hypotheticals such as the one in which two persons fire at a third at the same time, with each inflicting a wound which would have been fatal without regard to the other shot. Another favorite has a person furnishing to another a car with brakes he knows to be defective, with the driver making no effort to apply the brakes. A recent article summarizing the views of the several distinguished commentators is that of Professor Richard W. Wright, *Causation in Tort Law,* 73 CAL. L. REV. 1737 (1985).

> This case would be characterized by Professor Wright as one of "doubtful" causation, akin to a case involving a public swimming pool in which a child drowns while the lifeguard is absent. It is extremely difficult to prove that the drowning would not have occurred if the lifeguard had been present, but it would certainly be reasonable for a jury to conclude that the presence of a lifeguard would make the chances of rescue "more likely than not." Professor Wright argues that no more should be required and his view has substantial support. There are obvious difficulties in this case in setting up a counterfactual situation which definitively projects the sequence of events under the assumption that a safety bump had been in place. Striving for certainty is a *tour de force.* The jury must deal in terms of probabilities.

> . . . [T]he jury could have believed a speed bump at the place [the plaintiff's expert] suggested could have greatly reduced the chance of an accident, either by slowing down the bicycle or shifting its direction. No more should be required. The law deals with probabilities. . . .

Id. at

Would it help to analyze the question in *Jackson* as one of duty? How did the court in *Sharpe* characterize the issue? Did the dissent characterize it differently? Consider your response to this question of characterization in light of the Perspectives that are included in Chapter 1.

2. *Clearer Cases?* In *Ford v. Trident Fisheries Co.,* 232 Mass. 400 (1919), a seaman on defendant's steam trawler fell overboard when the ship suddenly rolled. The seaman disappeared immediately. The lifeboat was lashed to the deck and only had one oar. The fact that defendant negligently maintained its lifeboat was held immaterial. Similarly, in *McWilliams v. Sir William Arrol & Co.,* [1962] W.L.R. 295 (H.L.), plaintiff alleged the defendant was at fault in failing to provide a safety belt to a steel erector; it was argued that, as a consequence of the lack of a safety belt, decedent plunged 70 feet to his death. The court affirmed a verdict for the defendant because the facts established an "irresistible inference" that the decedent would not have worn a safety belt if it had been provided.

3. *When "But-For" Cause is an Unsatisfactory Test.* The "but for" test will provide the answer to the cause in fact question in many cases, but not always. The rest of this chapter is concerned with cases where the "but for" test does not provide a clear answer. In such a case, is the court deciding a factual question, or is it making a decision based on policy? If it is making a policy decision, is it deciding cause in fact or is it also deciding legal cause?

C. THE SUBSTANTIAL FACTOR TEST

ANDERSON v. MINNEAPOLIS, ST. P. & S.S.M. RY.
146 Minn. 430 (1920)

LEES, CHIEF JUSTICE.

[This] appeal is from an order denying [defendant's] motion in the alternative for judgment notwithstanding the verdict or for a new trial.

The complaint alleged, that early in August, 1918, sparks from one of defendant's locomotive engines set a fire on or near the right of way, and that this fire spread until it finally reached plaintiff's land, where it destroyed some of his property. The answer was a general denial followed by an allegation that, if plaintiff was damaged by fire, the fire was not due to any act of defendant, was of unknown origin, and, by reason of extraordinary weather conditions, became a huge conflagration. The reply put these allegations in issue.

Plaintiff's case in chief was directed to proving that in August, 1918, one of defendant's engines started a fire in a bog near the west side of plaintiff's land; that it smoldered there until October 12, 1918, when it flared up and burned his property, shortly before it was reached by one of the great fires which swept through Northeastern Minnesota at the close of that day. Defendant introduced evidence to show that on and prior to October 12th fires were burning west and northwest of, and were swept by the wind towards, plaintiff's premises. It did not show how such fires originated, neither did it clearly and certainly trace the destruction of plaintiff's property to them. By cross-examination of defendant's witnesses and by his rebuttal evidence, plaintiff made a showing which would have justified the jury in finding that the fires proved by defendant were started by its locomotive on or near its right of way in the vicinity of Kettle river. . . .

The following proposition is stated in defendant's brief and relied on for a reversal:

"If plaintiff's property was damaged by a number of fires combining, one being the fire pleaded, the others being of no responsible origin, but of such sufficient or such superior force that they would have produced the damage to plaintiff's property regardless of the fire pleaded, then defendant was not liable."

This proposition is based upon *Cook v. Minneapolis, S. P. & S.S.M. R. Co.,* 98 Wis. 624 (1898). In *Farrell v. Minneapolis & R.R. Ry.,* 121 Minn. 357 (1913), this court considered the case, but refrained from expressing approval or disapproval of its doctrine. The Supreme Court of Michigan has referred to it as good law. The Supreme Court of Idaho says the opinion is logical and well reasoned, but the discussion is in a large measure theoretical and academic. Judge Thompson in his work on NEGLIGENCE (Vol. 1, § 739), says that the conclusion reached is so clearly wrong as not to deserve discussion. If the *Cook* case merely decides that one who negligently sets a fire is not liable if another's property is damaged, unless it is made to appear that the fire was a material element in the destruction of the property, there can be no question about the soundness of the decision. But if it decides that if such fire combines with another of no responsible origin, and after the union of the two fires they destroy the property, and either fire independently of the other would have destroyed it, then, irrespective of whether the first fire was or was not a material factor in the destruction of the property, there is no liability, we are not prepared to adopt the doctrine as the law of this state. If a fire set by the engine of one railroad company unites with a fire set by the engine of another company, there is joint and several liability, even though either fire would have destroyed plaintiff's property. . . . We, therefore, hold that the trial court did not err in refusing to instruct the jury in accordance with the rule laid down in the *Cook* case. In the foregoing discussion we have assumed, although it is doubtful, that the evidence was such that a foundation was laid for the application of the rule if it was otherwise applicable.

. . . We find no error requiring a reversal, and hence the order appealed from is affirmed.

NOTES

1. *Two Forces Actively Operating.* Section 432 of Restatement (Second) of Torts provides that:

(1) Except as stated in Subsection (2), the actor's negligent conduct is not a substantial factor in bringing about harm to another if the harm would have been sustained even if the actor had not been negligent.

(2) If two forces are actively operating, one because of the actor's negligence, the other not because of any misconduct on his part, and each of itself is sufficient to bring about harm to another, the actor's negligence may be found to be a substantial factor in bringing it about.

REST. 2D TORTS § 432.

As an example of this proposition, the Second Restatement gives the "two-fires" situation of *Anderson*. Compare REST. 3D TORTS, PROPOSED FINAL DRAFT 1, §28 (2000), which provides:

> (a) Subject to Subsection (b), the plaintiff has the burden to prove that the defendant's tortuous conduct was a factual cause of the plaintiff's physical harm.

> (b) When the plaintiff sues all of the multiple actors and proves that each engaged in tortuous conduct that exposed the plaintiff to a risk of physical harm and that the tortuous conduct of one or more of them caused the plaintiff's harm but the plaintiff cannot reasonably be expected to prove which actor caused the harm, the burden of proof, including both production and persuasion, on factual causation is shifted to the defendants.

2. *"Substantial Factor."* Section 430 of the Restatement (Second) of Torts states that an actor is not liable for his negligent conduct unless that conduct is a "legal cause" of another's harm. REST. 2D TORTS §430. Legal cause is defined as conduct which is a "substantial factor" in bringing about the harm. *Id.* §431. Section 433 states:

> The following considerations are in themselves or in combination with one another important in determining whether the actor's conduct is a substantial factor in bringing about harm to another:

> (a) the number of other factors which contribute in producing the harm and the extent of the effect which they have in producing it;

> (b) whether the actor's conduct has created a force or series of forces which are in continuous and active operation up to the time of the harm, or has created a situation harmless unless acted upon by other forces for which the actor is not responsible;

> (c) lapse of time.

REST. 2d TORTS §433.

Section 431, comment *a* recognizes that "substantial cause" is not content-neutral, stating:

> The word "substantial" is used to denote the fact the defendant's conduct has such an effect in producing the harm as to lead reasonable men to regard it as a cause, using that word in the popular sense, in which there always lurks the idea of responsibility, rather than in the so-called "philosophic sense," which includes every one of the great number of events without which any happening would not have occurred.

Id. § 431.

3. *Coming to Terms with Substantial Factor.* According to Professor Robertson:

> The term "substantial factor" has come to have a number of different meanings in the jurisprudence. By using the term in three different

senses, the RESTATEMENT (SECOND) OF TORTS has contributed to a nationwide confusion on the matter. In the narrowest and only fully legitimate usage, the term describes a cause-in-fact test that is useful as a substitute for the but-for test in a limited category of cases in which "two causes concur to bring about an event, and either cause, operating alone, would have brought about the event absent the other cause . . . " In a looser and potentially confusing usage, the substantial factor test is treated as more or less interchangeable with the but-for test; in this usage courts seem to feel that it is appropriate to shift to the substantial factor vocabulary whenever the but-for test is proving difficult to work with for whatever reason. In a third usage, "substantial factor" describes an approach to the issue of legal causation or ambit of duty, a matter that should be kept entirely distinct from the cause-in-fact issue.

. . . [O]nly the first usage adds anything useful to the vocabulary of causation. The second — roughly equating substantial factor and but for — and third — treating substantial factor as part of an approach to legal cause — should both be discouraged.

David W. Robertson, *The Common Sense of Cause-In-Fact*, 75 TEX. L. REV. 1765, 1776–77 (1997).

4. *Substantial Factor and Concurrent Tortfeasors. See Daugert v. Pappas,* 104 Wash. 2d 254, 704 P.2d 600, 605–06 (1985) (refusal to apply substantial factor test to legal malpractice case):

Such a change in the test for cause in fact is normally justified only when a plaintiff is unable to show that one event alone was the cause of the injury. As noted by Dean Prosser, the substantial factor test aids in the disposition of three types of cases. First, the test is used where either one of two causes would have produced the identical harm, thus making it impossible for plaintiff to prove the but for test. In such cases, it is quite clear that each cause has played so important a part in producing the result that responsibility should be imposed on it. Second, the test is used where a similar, but not identical, result would have followed without the defendant's act. Third, the test is used where one defendant has made a clearly proven but quite insignificant contribution to the result, as where he throws a lighted match into a forest fire. W. PROSSER & W. KEETON, TORTS § 41 (5th ed. 1984).

See also In re Bendectin Litigation, 857 F.2d 290, 311 (6th Cir. 1988):

The substantial factor standard applies only to initial negligent actors in determining their liability in the face of action by a subsequent actor, or in determining causation between simultaneous actors, both of whose acts could have been "but for" causes of plaintiffs' injuries.

Compare REST 3D TORTS, PROPOSED FINAL DRAFT § 27 (2000), which provides that "If multiple acts exist, each of which alone would have been a factual cause under § 26 of the physical harm at the same time, each act is regarded as a factual cause of the harm."

5. *Reciprocity of Cause and the Economics of Causation.* The discussion in *Anderson* poses the question of whether fire A or fire B caused the damage to the plaintiff's property? Was the fire or the weather that helped the fires spread responsible for the damage? However, was not the presence of the plaintiff's property near the railroad as much a cause of the damage? For an economist, the only question is which distribution of responsibility will promote the most efficient allocation of resources. Thus, causation has no meaningful role, other than to signify a conclusion as to the most efficient allocation (that is, the wealth maximizer). *See, e.g.,* Ronald Coase, *The Problem of Social Cost,* 3 J. LAW & ECON. 1 (1960); W.M. LANDES & R.A. POSNER, THE ECONOMIC STRUCTURE OF TORT LAW 228–30 (1987). As a result, those holding such views have attracted the label "causal minimalists," although "causal nihilists" might be more appropriate. *See generally* David Howarth, *"O Madness of Discourse, That Cause Sets Up With and Against Itself!,"* 96 YALE L.J. 1389, 1392 (1987) (an excellent primer). Hart & Honoré disagree not only with the causal nihilists, but also those who (more appropriately) attract the title of "causal minimalists" — those who relegate the causal question to "but for," and proceed to label all other "causal" issues as normative, and thus matters of duty, legal cause or the like. H.L.A. HART & T. HONORÉ, CAUSATION IN THE LAW (2d ed. 1985). For Hart & Honoré, such a minimalist approach robs causation of much of its "common sense" or "ordinary usage." *See* Howarth, *supra,* at 1394–98.

# D.	LOST OR DIMINISHED CHANCE

SMITH v. STATE DEPARTMENT OF HEALTH AND HOSPITALS
676 So. 2d 543 (La. 1996)

LEMMON, JUSTICE.

. . . In August 1987, Benjamin Smith went to E.A. Conway Memorial Hospital, complaining of a sore on top of his right foot. The attending physician diagnosed cellulitis with lymphangitis, and Smith underwent minor surgery to drain the fluid from his foot.

Smith's five-day hospitalization included a routine chest x-ray which the staff radiologist reported as showing "a mediastinal mass projected to the right of the trachea." The doctor stated that "lymphoma must be considered in the differential diagnosis" and recommended a CT scan of the thoracic area. The hospital staff failed to inform Smith or his family of the x-ray results or to recommend further testing. Smith was simply discharged from the hospital without any information about the mass in his chest.

Almost fifteen months later, Smith returned to E.A. Conway, complaining of a three-week history of "left pleuritic chest pain, fever, and chills." A second chest x-ray on October 31, 1988, compared with the August 1987 x-ray, revealed that the mass had doubled in size. Smith and his family then learned for the first time of the August 1987 x-ray report.

Further testing confirmed the diagnosis of small cell carcinoma of the lungs, a fast-acting and lethal cancer. By this time, Smith's cancer had progressed to the "extensive" stage, in that the cancer was present in both lungs and was non-operable. Despite aggressive drug treatment and chemotherapy, Smith died on March 16, 1989, nineteen months after the initial x-ray. He was forty-five years old at his death.

. . . At trial, the parties presented evidence by several doctors relating to the percentage chance of survival for certain periods of time after discovery of small cell carcinoma of the lung at various stages of progression of the disease. The trial court ruled that plaintiffs had not met their burden of proving that the fifteen-month delay in treatment resulting from the State's admitted negligence had caused Smith to die or to lose a chance of survival. . . .

The court of appeal reversed, concluding that the trial court was plainly wrong in failing to find the loss of a chance of survival. . . .

As to the method of measuring those damages, the intermediate court rejected plaintiffs' contention that they were entitled to full damages for the death, noting that plaintiffs failed to prove, more probably than not, that Smith would have survived but for the Department's malpractice. Drawing heavily on Joseph H. King, Jr., *Causation, Valuation and Chance in Personal Injury Torts Involving Preexisting Conditions and Future Consequences*, 90 YALE L.J. 1353 (1981), the court reasoned that granting recovery upon lesser proof than the more-probable-than-not rule should be balanced by a concomitant reduction of the potential damages for a case where the tort victim's death probably would not have occurred but for the defendant's fault. However, the court pointed out that the plaintiff in a loss of a chance of survival case still retains the burden of proving by a preponderance of the evidence that the defendant's negligence caused the loss of a chance.

Accordingly, the court held that "the percentage probability of loss, if less than 50%, is the proper measure of the plaintiff's damages in a case of wrongful death due to medical malpractice. . . ." Referring to expert evidence that recurrence of cancer after five years is rare, the court then reviewed other expert testimony as to the chance of survival for five years. Four doctors testified that the chance of survival, at the stage of the disease when the initial x-ray was taken, was one to twelve percent, ten to fifteen percent, five percent, and seven to twenty- five percent respectively.[3] The experts further agreed that Smith's chance of survival at the time of the October 1988 x-ray was less than one percent. Analyzing this evidence de novo, the court concluded that the evidence preponderated to show that the Department's negligence was a substantial factor in depriving Smith of a ten percent chance of surviving for five years. Fixing the total damages at $764,347,[4] the court reduced this

---

[3] From this testimony, the court concluded that a range of seven to twelve percent encompasses most of the experts' estimates.

[4] The court fixed the total damages as follows:

Wrongful death damages (one-third each)	$450,000
Funeral expenses	4,004
Future lost earnings and value of household services	250,343
Survival action damages	60,000
	$764,347

amount proportionate to the lost ten percent chance of survival and awarded a total of $76,434 to Mrs. Smith and her two minor children.

. . . The issues in loss of a chance of survival cases are whether the tort victim lost any chance of survival because of the defendant's negligence[5] and the value of that loss. The question of degree may be pertinent to the issue of whether the defendant's negligence caused or contributed to the loss, but such a tort-caused loss in any degree is compensable in damages.

Allowing recovery for the loss of a chance of survival is not, as the court of appeal suggested, a change or a relaxation of the usual burden of proof by a preponderance of the evidence. Rather, allowing such recovery is a recognition of the loss of a chance of survival as a distinct compensable injury caused by the defendant's negligence, to be distinguished from the loss of life in wrongful death cases, and there is no variance from the usual burden in proving that distinct loss.

Thus, in a medical malpractice case seeking damages for the loss of a less-than-even chance of survival because of negligent treatment of a pre-existing condition, the plaintiff must prove by a preponderance of the evidence that the tort victim had a chance of survival at the time of the professional negligence and that the tortfeasor's action or inaction deprived the victim of all or part of that chance, and must further prove the value of the lost chance, which is the only item of damages at issue in such a case.

All experts testified that Smith had some chance of survival if he had been treated immediately after the August 1987 x-ray, and that he had virtually no chance of survival in October 1988 after he went almost fifteen months without treatment because of the Department's negligence. Smith's chance of survival in August 1987, though not better than even, was still a chance that was denied him as a result of the Department's failure to meet its standard of care. That chance had some value when viewed from the standpoint of the tort victim and his heirs, and that value is the appropriate focus of the analysis in this case.

Courts and commentators have recognized three possible methods of valuation of the loss of a chance of survival in professional malpractice cases.

The first, and the method we adopt today in this decision, is for the fact-finder — judge or jury — to focus on the chance of survival lost on account of malpractice as a distinct compensable injury and to value the lost chance as a lump sum award based on all the evidence in the record, as is done for any other item of general damages.

The second method, as advocated by plaintiffs, is to allow full survival and wrongful death damages for the loss of life partially caused by malpractice, without regard to the chance of survival. We reject this argument, agreeing with the court of appeal that full recovery is not available for deprivation of a chance of survival of less than fifty percent. To allow full recovery would ignore

---

[5] The pre-existing condition causes the conceptual problem. The jury should focus on the damages that the defendant caused — the loss of a chance of avoiding a death that might not have occurred if the health care provider had performed properly. The court should instruct the jury to determine the amount of damages for this specific loss on the basis of all the evidence.

the claimants' inability to prove by a preponderance of the evidence that the malpractice victim would have survived but for the malpractice, which is a requirement for full recovery.

The third method, and the method adopted by the court of appeal in this case, is to compute the compensable chance as "the percentage probability by which the defendant's tortious conduct diminished the likelihood of achieving some more favorable outcome." Joseph H. King, Jr., *Causation, Valuation and Chance in Personal Injury Torts Involving Preexisting Conditions and Future Consequences*, 90 YALE L.J. 1353, 1382 (1981). Professor King's percentage-probability-of-loss theory estimates "the compensable value of the victim's life if he survived" and reduces that estimate according to the percentage chance of survival at the time of the malpractice. *Id*. This method has gained acceptance by the courts and commentators because of its pragmatic appeal, providing concrete guidelines for calculating damages and alleviating the perceived "pulling out of the hat problem" allegedly associated with the method that we adopt today.

Our point of disagreement with the court of appeal's method of computing damages for the loss of a chance of survival is its rigid use of a precise mathematical formula, based on imprecise percentage chance estimates applied to estimates of general damages that never occurred, to arrive at a figure for an item of general damages that this court has long recognized cannot be calculated with mathematical precision. When these total hypothetical damages are reduced by a numerical factor determined from evidence of percentage rates of survival for certain periods after discovery of the disease at various stages of the disease, the uncertainty progresses geometrically.

The starting point of our analysis is to recognize that the loss of a less-than-even chance of survival is a distinct injury compensable as general damages which cannot be calculated with mathematical certainty. Next, we recognize that the factfinder should make a subjective determination of the value of that loss, fixing the amount of money that would adequately compensate the claimants for that particular cognizable loss. On the other hand, the approach of the court of appeal requires the factfinder first to make a hypothetical determination of the value of survival and wrongful death claims that are not really at issue and then to discount that value mathematically. This mathematical discounting of the subjective valuation of inapplicable claims does not magically make that approach more precise or more accurate than simply allowing the factfinder to value directly the loss of a chance of survival that is the sole item of damages at issue in the case.

The lost chance of survival in professional malpractice cases has a value in and of itself that is different from the value of a wrongful death or survival claim.[9] The jury can calculate the lost chance of survival without going through

---

[9] Valuation of the loss of a chance of survival in this medical malpractice case is similar to the valuation of the loss of a chance of recovery by judgment or settlement in a legal malpractice action in which a lawyer lets a case prescribe and the tort victim sues the lawyer for malpractice. In the early cases, a plaintiff could only recover by trying a "case-within-a-case" — that is, by proving that he or she would have prevailed on the underlying cause of action. If not, the plaintiff could not recover. (The parallel in the medical malpractice area is the jurisprudence that rejects entirely the loss of a chance of survival doctrine.) Recognizing the unfairness to tort victims who had a

the illusory exercise of setting a value for the wrongful death or survival claims and then mechanically reducing that amount by some consensus of the expert estimates of the percentage chance of survival. The methodology for fixing damages attributable to the loss of a chance of survival should not be so mechanistic as to require the jury merely to fill in the blanks on a verdict sheet with a consensus number for the percentage chance of survival and the total amount of damages, and then have the judge perform the multiplication task.

The calculation of damages for the loss of a chance of survival is not like the calculation of comparative fault damages. In the comparative fault context, the jury determines the entire amount of general and special damages actually sustained by the tort victim, which is an amount that would be awarded in the absence of contributory negligence. The percentage reduction merely implements the law of comparative fault in fixing the tortfeasor's total obligation. But in the loss of a chance of survival context, the award of damages for this particular loss is the "bottom line" figure. Any theoretical figure representing the amount the claimants would have been awarded if they had been successful in proving the defendant's fault more probably than not caused the loss of the tort victim's life is not a concrete figure that can properly be subjected to a reduction because of plaintiffs' failure of proof. Rather, the jury in a loss of a chance of survival case merely considers the same evidence considered by a jury in a survival and wrongful death action, and the loss-of-chance jury then reaches its general damages award for that loss on that evidence as well as other relevant evidence in the record.[10]

This approach for valuation of the loss of a chance of survival is more appropriate than the method used by the court of appeal in that it allows the jury to render a verdict in the lump sum amount of damages attributable only to the lost chance of survival. This is a valuation of the only damages at issue — the lost chance — which is based on all of the relevant evidence in the record, as is done for any other measurement of general damages. Allowing the jury to consider all the evidence, including expert medical testimony regarding the percentage chances of survival, and to value directly the lost chance is more logical than requiring the jury to calculate damages for wrongful death when the physician's negligence was not the more probable cause of the death. The method we adopt today will not leave the jury without any guidance or any factors to consider. The jury will be allowed to consider an abundance of evidence and factors, including evidence of percentages of chance of survival

---

chance of recovery and lost it because of legal malpractice, the courts, including this one, modified the case-within-a-case doctrine somewhat by shifting the burden of proof to the negligent attorney. Even under this approach, however, the jury must engage in a pretend exercise of measuring damages based on events that never in reality occurred or can occur. The preferable approach in legal malpractice cases (although not yet adopted by a holding of this court) is to let the jury value the lost chance of recovery based on the value of the claim before prescription [i.e., time-bar] . . .

[10] Evidence of loss of support, loss of love and affection and other wrongful death damages is relevant, but not mathematically determinative, in loss of a chance of survival cases, as is evidence of the percentage chance of survival at the time of the malpractice. The plaintiff may also present evidence of, and argue, other factors to the jury, such as that a ten percent chance of survival may be more significant when reduced from ten percent to zero than when reduced from forty to thirty percent. The jury may also consider such factors as that the victim, although not likely to survive, would have lived longer but for the malpractice.

along with evidence such as loss of support and loss of love and affection, and any other evidence bearing on the value of the lost chance. The jury's verdict of a lump sum amount of damages can be tested on appeal for support in the record by reviewing the percentage chances and the losses incurred by the tort victim and his or her heirs, and any other relevant evidence, thus providing assurance against speculative verdicts.

. . . For these reasons, the judgment of the court of appeal is set aside, and the case is remanded to the district court for further proceedings in accordance with this opinion.

VICTORY, JUSTICE, dissenting.

. . . My disagreement with the Court's adoption of the lost chance of survival doctrine is both pragmatic and theoretical. From a pragmatic standpoint, the doctrine yields unfair results. How the doctrine of lost chance results in erroneous and inequitable outcomes is illustrated by the Court of Appeals of Maryland:

> Because loss of chance of recovery is based on statistical probabilities, it might be appropriate to examine the statistical probabilities of achieving a "just" result with loss of chance damages . . . To compare the two rules, assume a hypothetical group of 99 cancer patients, each of whom would have had a 33 1/3% chance of survival. Each received negligent medical care, and all 99 die. Traditional tort law would deny recovery in all 99 cases because each patient had less than a 50% chance of recovery and the probable cause of death was the preexisting cancer not the negligence. Statistically, had all 99 received proper treatment, 33 would have lived and 66 would have died; so the traditional rule would have statistically produced 33 errors by denying recovery to all 99. The lost chance rule would allow all 99 patients to recover, but each would recover 33 1/3% of the normal value of the case. Again, with proper care 33 patients would have survived. Thus, the 33 patients who statistically would have survived with proper care would receive only one-third of the appropriate recovery, while the 66 patients who dies as a result of the preexisting condition, not the negligence, would be overcompensated by one-third. The loss of chance rule would have produced errors in all 99 cases.

Fennell v. Southern Maryland Hospital, 320 Md. 776, 580 A.2d 206, 212–13 (1990) (declining to adopt the doctrine of loss of chance of survival [in Maryland]). . . .

. . . The majority's approach ignores this trend and allows the jury to simply arrive at a damage figure without properly explaining the basis of the figure. This "rabbit-out-of-the-hat" approach will be virtually impossible to review on appeal under the manifest error standard. The reviewing court will have little idea of what chance of survival the jury determined was lost, thus little basis to determine if the jury was manifestly erroneous.

The "percentage probability test" proposed by Professor King is a much fairer and much more precise test than that adopted by the majority. . . .

NOTES

1. *Chance Adopted.* In *Perez v. Las Vegas Medical Center*, 805 P.2d 589 (Nev. 1990), the court, after finding that the plaintiff could not prove that the alleged negligence of the health care provider caused the ultimate injury (death) because the decedent probably would have died anyway because of his serious preexisting medical condition, adopted the "loss of chance" doctrine for a medical malpractice case. According to the court:

> Applying the traditional preponderance requirement strictly, some courts have held that plaintiffs with fifty-fifty or lower chances of survival due to their original ailment cannot demonstrate that medical malpractice was the actual cause of the death. Several other courts have relaxed the traditional preponderance requirement for causation to allow limited recovery under these circumstances.

> . . . Of the various arguments against the position urged by respondents, the following is most fundamental: the respondents' position would bar any recovery in tort on behalf of the survivors of many potentially terminal patients, no matter how blatant the health care provider's negligence. Through negligence, a physician or other health care provider could reduce a patient's chances of survival from as high as fifty percent to, for example, ten percent, and yet remain unanswerable in the law of tort. This position is simply untenable. . . .

> The disadvantages of the position urged by respondents are both more certain and more severe than any disadvantages of the position we adopt today. Additionally, it is important to recall that no cause of action will lie absent some instance of negligence by the health care provider. . . .

> [C]ourts have adopted various rationales in order to avoid the harsh and unjustified result just discussed. We conclude that the best rationale supporting recovery in these circumstances is the "loss of chance" doctrine. Under this doctrine, the injury to be redressed by the law is not defined as the death itself, but, rather, as the decreased chance of survival caused by the medical malpractice. . . .

> By defining the injury as the loss of chance of survival, the traditional rule of preponderance is fully satisfied. In cases in which the plaintiff prevails, it can be said that the medical malpractice more probably than not decreased a substantial chance of survival and that the injured person ultimately died or was severely debilitated. Specifically, in order to create a question of fact regarding causation in these cases, the plaintiff must present evidence tending to show, to a reasonable medical probability, that some negligent act or omission by health care providers reduced a substantial chance of survival given appropriate medical care. In accord with other courts adopting this view, we need not now state exactly how high the chances of survival must be in order to be "substantial." We will address this in the future on a case by case basis. There are limits, however, and we doubt that a ten percent chance of survival as referred to in the example in the dissenting

opinion would be actionable. Survivors of a person who had a truly negligible chance of survival should not be allowed to bring a case fully through trial. Perhaps more importantly, in cases where the chances of survival were modest, plaintiffs will have little monetary incentive to bring a case to trial because damages would be drastically reduced to account for the preexisting condition.

If one recovers 10% of one's damages for loss of a 10% chance of survival, then why not recover only 60% of one's damages in a situation of the loss of a 60% chance of survival?

2. *No Chance.* In *Kilpatrick v. Bryant*, 868 S.W.2d 594 (Tenn. 1993), the court held that there can be no liability in a medical malpractice case for negligent diagnosis or treatment that decreases a patient's chances of avoiding death or other adverse medical condition where the death or adverse medical condition probably would have occurred anyway. The court explained:

> We decline to relax traditional cause in fact requirements and recognize a new cause of action for loss of chance. . . . Plaintiffs in this case are not entitled to recover damages for the impaired opportunity for obtaining a more favorable medical result, the increase in the risk of harm, or the loss of a better chance of recovery or survival. Plaintiffs also seek damages for additional medical treatment, pain and suffering, loss of earning capacity, etc., directly attributable to the negligence of the Defendant. We conclude that these items of damages are recoverable because the Plaintiffs have shown that such damages would not have been incurred but for the Defendant's negligence.

Justice Daughtrey, concurring and dissenting, stated in part:

> The courts in the 30 or more jurisdictions that have recognized the "loss of chance" doctrine or permitted recovery for "increased risk of harm" certainly cannot be accused of doing so with the intent to dismantle the law of proximate cause in medical malpractice cases. They have, instead, recognized the reality of medical practice and the difficulty of predicting with any scientific certainty which patients with a life-threatening disease will survive and which will not. Without a crystal ball to guide them, medical experts must fall back on statistics, on percentages, and on five-year and ten-year survival rates.

Was *Dillon* a loss of chance case? Did not the electric wire deprive young Dillon of a chance of regaining his balance? *See Dillon, supra,* p. 238, note 5.

3. *Be Careful What You Ask For.* The *Perez* court noted, "[o]f course, the plaintiff or injured person cannot recover merely on the basis of a decreased chance of survival or of avoiding a debilitating illness or injury; the plaintiff must in fact suffer death or debilitating injury before there can be an award of damages. Additionally, the damages are to be discounted to the extent that a preexisting condition likely contributed to the death or serious debilitation. . . ."

4. *Burden of Proof Revisited.* Even with extensive expert medical testimony, it may be difficult to prove causation as to certain injuries. In *Kramer Serv., Inc. v. Wilkins,* 184 Miss. 483 (1939), plaintiff was hit in the forehead by a piece of glass that fell from a broken transom as he opened a door in defendant's hotel. Plaintiff established negligence by showing that the transom had been in a broken condition long enough to charge defendant with notice of it. The forehead wound did not heal, and two years after the injury a skin specialist found that skin cancer had developed at the point of the wound. Plaintiff could not recover from defendant for this skin cancer, however, since the medical testimony did not establish a causal connection between the injury and the cancer, and that while such a connection was possible, the chances of causation were only one out of a hundred.

5. *The Non-Medical Loss of Chance*. In a footnote, the *Smith* court limited its holding to medical malpractice cases, leaving to "another day" the application of that doctrine "against other types of tortfeasors," and citing *Hardy v. SW. Bell Tel. Co.*, 910 P.2d 1024 (Okla. 1996). There, the court wrote that,

> [t]he public policy concerns of medical practice which have been held to justify a reduced burden of causation in lost chance cases do not transfer over to ordinary negligence cases. Public policy is not served by extending the causation exception to the "but for" rule to other tort-feasors. . . . [T]he physician had the opportunity to perform properly under the terms of the physician-patient special relationship but was alleged to have failed to do so.

> The essence of the doctrine is the special relationship of the physician and the patient. In these cases the duty is clear, the negligence is unquestioned and the resulting harm, the destruction of a chance for a better outcome, has obvious value and is not so speculative as to be beyond being reasonably considered a result of defendant's negligence.

Id. at

In *Daugert v. Pappas*, previously noted, the Supreme Court of Washington rejected an attempt to apply principles of loss of chance to an action for legal malpractice based on failure to file an appeal. The court found that while the loss of chance to recover from misdiagnosis of cancer such as was present in *Herskovits v. Group Health Coop of Puget Sound*, 664 P.2d 474 (Wash.1983), resulted in a very real injury with definite value which would require compensation, there is no commensurate harm, no lost chance, in a legal malpractice case as the matter may eventually be reviewed. Neither, held the court, is there in a legal malpractice action a separate and distinguishable harm, a diminished chance.

Would it be more accurate to read the *Hardy* court holding not as saying that loss of chance is inapplicable outside medical malpractice, but that the plaintiff in *Hardy* failed to prove that loss of chance by a preponderance of the evidence? The court in *Smith* said the lower court was "correct in holding that plaintiff proved by a preponderance of the evidence" that defendant deprived Smith of a less-than-50% chance of survival.

In a legal malpractice action arising out of mishandled litigation, the plaintiff traditionally must prove not only that the defendant lawyer committed malpractice but also that the malpractice prevented the plaintiff from winning the earlier suit. Predictably, a negligent attorney would be happy to tell the court in the malpractice case that the first suit was a loser! Even if the plaintiff had less than a fifty percent chance of prevailing in the earlier suit, didn't the attorney's malpractice deprive the plaintiff of a chance of prevailing? Alternatively, wouldn't the settlement value of the earlier suit be an appropriate measure of damages? Expert testimony easily could establish a range of settlement values.

E.   "ALTERNATIVE" AND "MARKET SHARE" CAUSATION

HYMOWITZ v. ELI LILLY & CO.
73 N.Y.2d 487 (1989)

WACHTLER, JUSTICE.

Plaintiffs in these appeals allege that they were injured by the drug diethylstilbestrol (DES) ingested by their mothers during pregnancy. They seek relief against defendant DES manufacturers. While not class actions, these cases are representative of nearly 500 similar actions pending in the courts in this State; the rules articulated by the court here, therefore, must do justice and be administratively feasible in the context of this mass litigation. With this in mind, we now resolve the issue twice expressly left open by this court, and adopt a market share theory, using a national market, for determining liability and apportioning damages in DES cases in which identification of the manufacturer of the drug that injured the plaintiff is impossible . . .

DES is a synthetic substance that mimics the effect of estrogen, the naturally formed female hormone. It was invented in 1937 by British researchers, but never patented.

In 1941, the Food and Drug Administration (FDA) approved the new drug applications (NDA) of 12 manufacturers to market DES for the treatment of various maladies, not directly involving pregnancy. In 1947, the FDA began approving the NDAs of manufacturers to market DES for the purpose of preventing human miscarriages; by 1951, the FDA had concluded that DES was generally safe for pregnancy use, and stopped requiring the filing of NDAs when new manufacturers sought to produce the drug for this purpose. In 1971, however, the FDA banned the use of DES as a miscarriage preventative, when studies established the harmful latent effects of DES upon the offspring of mothers who took the drug. Specifically, tests indicated that DES caused vaginal adenocarcinoma, a form of cancer, and adenosis, a precancerous vaginal or cervical growth.

Although strong evidence links prenatal DES exposure to later development of serious medical problems, plaintiffs seeking relief in court for their injuries faced two formidable and fundamental barriers to recovery in this State; not only is identification of the manufacturer of the DES ingested in a particular case generally impossible, but, due to the latent nature of DES injuries, many claims were barred by the Statute of Limitations before the injury was discovered.

The identification problem has many causes. All DES was of identical chemical composition. Druggists usually filled prescriptions from whatever was on hand. Approximately 300 manufacturers produced the drug, with companies entering and leaving the market continuously during the 24 years that DES was sold for pregnancy use. The long latency period of a DES injury compounds the identification problem; memories fade, records are lost or destroyed, and witnesses die. Thus the pregnant women who took DES generally never knew who produced the drug they took, and there was no reason to attempt to discover this fact until many years after ingestion, at which time the information is not available . . .

The present appeals are before the court in the context of summary judgment motions. In all of the appeals defendants moved for summary judgment dismissing the complaints because plaintiffs could not identify the manufacturer of the drug that allegedly injured them . . . The trial court denied all of these motions . . . The Appellate Division affirmed in all respects and certified to this court the questions of whether the orders of the trial court were properly made. We answer these questions in the affirmative.

In a products liability action, identification of the exact defendant whose product injured the plaintiff is, of course, generally required. In DES cases in which such identification is possible, actions may proceed under established principles of products liability. The record now before us, however, presents the question of whether a DES plaintiff may recover against a DES manufacturer when identification of the producer of the specific drug that caused the injury is impossible.

As we noted in *Bichler v Lilly & Co.*, 55 NY2d 571, 580, n.5 (1982), the accepted tort doctrines of alternative liability and concerted action are available in some personal injury cases to permit recovery where the precise identification of a wrongdoer is impossible. However, we agree with the near unanimous views of the high State courts that have considered the matter that these doctrines in their unaltered common-law forms do not permit recovery in DES cases.

The paradigm of alternative liability is found in the case of *Summers v Tice*, 33 Cal.2d 80 (1948). In *Summers*, plaintiff and the two defendants were hunting, and defendants carried identical shotguns and ammunition. During the hunt, defendants shot simultaneously at the same bird, and plaintiff was struck by bird shot from one of the defendants' guns. The court held that where two defendants breach a duty to the plaintiff, but there is uncertainty regarding which one caused the injury, "the burden is upon each such actor to prove that he has not caused the harm." RESTATEMENT [SECOND] OF TORTS § 433B(3). The central rationale for shifting the burden of proof in such a situation is that without this device both defendants will be silent, and plaintiff will not recover; with alternative liability, however, defendants will be forced to speak, and reveal the culpable party, or else be held jointly and severally liable themselves. Consequently, use of the alternative liability doctrine generally requires that the defendants have better access to information than does the plaintiff, and that all possible tortfeasors be before the court. It is also recognized that alternative liability rests on the notion that where there is a small number of possible wrongdoers, all of whom breached a duty to the plaintiff, the likelihood that any one of them injured the plaintiff is relatively high, so that forcing them to exonerate themselves, or be held liable, is not unfair.

In DES cases, however, there is a great number of possible wrongdoers, who entered and left the market at different times, and some of whom no longer exist. Additionally, in DES cases many years elapse between the ingestion of the drug and injury. Consequently, DES defendants are not in any better position than are plaintiffs to identify the manufacturer of the DES ingested in any given case, nor is there any real prospect of having all the possible producers before the court. Finally, while it may be fair to employ alternative liability in cases involving only a small number of potential wrongdoers, that fairness disappears with the decreasing probability that any one of the defendants actually caused the injury. This is particularly true when applied to DES where the chance that a particular producer caused the injury is often very remote. Alternative liability, therefore, provides DES plaintiffs no relief.

Nor does the theory of concerted action, in its pure form, supply a basis for recovery. This doctrine, seen in drag racing cases, provides for joint and several liability on the part of all defendants having an understanding, express or tacit, to participate in "a common plan or design to commit a tortious act" (PROSSER AND KEETON, TORTS § 46, at 323 [5th ed]). As we noted in *Bichler v. Lilly & Co.*, and as the present record reflects, drug companies were engaged in extensive parallel conduct in developing and marketing DES. There is nothing in the record, however, beyond this similar conduct to show any agreement, tacit or otherwise, to market DES for pregnancy use without taking proper steps to ensure the drug's safety. Parallel activity, without more, is insufficient to establish the agreement element necessary to maintain a concerted action claim. Thus this theory also fails in supporting an action by DES plaintiffs.

In short, extant common-law doctrines, unmodified, provide no relief for the DES plaintiff unable to identify the manufacturer of the drug that injured her. This is not a novel conclusion; in the last decade a number of courts in other jurisdictions also have concluded that present theories do not support a cause of action in DES cases. Some courts, upon reaching this conclusion, have declined to find any judicial remedy for the DES plaintiffs who cannot identify the particular manufacturer of the DES ingested by their mothers (*see, Zafft v. Lilly & Co.*, 676 S.W.2d 241 (1984); *Mulcahy v. Lilly & Co.*, 386 N.W.2d 67 (Iowa 1986) (stating that any change in the law to allow for recovery in nonidentification DES cases should come from the Legislature)). Other courts, however, have found that some modification of existing doctrine is appropriate to allow for relief for those injured by DES of unknown manufacture.

We conclude that the present circumstances call for recognition of a realistic avenue of relief for plaintiffs injured by DES. These appeals present many of the same considerations that have prompted this court in the past to modify the rules of personal injury liability, in order "to achieve the ends of justice in a more modern context" (*see, People v Hobson*, 39 N.Y.2d 479, 489 (1976)), and we perceive that here judicial action is again required to overcome the "'inordinately difficult problems of proof'" caused by contemporary products and marketing techniques (*see, Bichler v. Lilly & Co., supra*, at 579–580).

Indeed, it would be inconsistent with the reasonable expectations of a modern society to say to these plaintiffs that because of the insidious nature of an injury that long remains dormant, and because so many manufacturers, each behind a curtain, contributed to the devastation, the cost of injury should be borne by the innocent and not the wrongdoers. This is particularly so where the Legislature consciously created these expectations by reviving hundreds of DES cases. Consequently, the ever-evolving dictates of justice and fairness, which are the heart of our common-law system, require formation of a remedy for injuries caused by DES.

We stress, however, that the DES situation is a singular case, with manufacturers acting in a parallel manner to produce an identical, generically marketed product, which causes injury many years later, and which has evoked a legislative response reviving previously barred actions. Given this unusual scenario, it is more appropriate that the loss be borne by those that produced the drug for use during pregnancy, rather than by those who were injured by the use, even where the precise manufacturer of the drug cannot be identified in a particular action. We turn then to the question of how to fairly and equitably apportion the loss occasioned by DES, in a case where the exact manufacturer of the drug that caused the injury is unknown.

The past decade of DES litigation has produced a number of alternative approaches to resolve this question. Thus, in a sense, we are now in an enviable position; the efforts of other courts provided examples for contending with this difficult issue, and enough time has passed so that the actual administration and real effects of these solutions now can be observed. With these useful guides in hand, a path may be struck for our own conclusion.

First, this court's opinion in *Bichler v. Lilly & Co.* must be considered. There the jury was instructed on a modified. version of concerted action, which, in effect, substituted the fact of conscious parallel activity by manufacturers for the usual common-law requirement that there be proof of an actual agreement between actors to jointly act tortiously. The defendant in *Bichler* did not object to this instruction, and the modified concerted action theory became the law applicable to that particular case.

Now given the opportunity to assess the merits of this theory, we decline to adopt it as the law of this State. Parallel behavior, the major justification for visiting liability caused by the product of one manufacturer upon the head of another under this analysis, is a common occurrence in industry generally. We believe, therefore, that inferring agreement from the fact of parallel activity alone improperly expands the concept of concerted action beyond a rational or fair limit; among other things, it potentially renders small manufacturers, in the case of DES and in countless other industries, jointly liable for all damages stemming from the defective products of an entire industry.

A narrower basis for liability, tailored more closely to the varying culpableness of individual DES producers, is the market share concept. First judicially articulated by the California Supreme Court in *Sindell v. Abbott Laboratories*, 26 Cal. 3d 588 (1980), variations upon this theme have been adopted by other courts. In *Sindell v. Abbott Labs*, the court synthesized the market share concept by modifying the *Summers v. Tice* alternative liability rationale in two ways. It first loosened the requirement that all possible wrongdoers be before the court, and instead made a "substantial share" sufficient. The court then held that each defendant who could not prove that it did not actually injure plaintiff would be liable according to that manufacturer's market share. The court's central justification for adopting this approach was its belief that limiting a defendant's liability to its market share will result, over the run of cases, in liability on the part of a defendant roughly equal to the injuries the defendant actually caused.

In the recent case of *Brown v. Superior Ct.*, 44 Cal.3d 1049 (1988), the California Supreme Court resolved some apparent ambiguity in *Sindell v. Abbott Labs.*, and held that a manufacturer's liability is several only, and, in cases in which all manufacturers in the market are not joined for any reason, liability will still be limited to market share, resulting in a less than 100% recovery for a plaintiff. Finally, it is noteworthy that determining market shares under *Sindell v. Abbott Labs.*, proved difficult and engendered years of litigation. After attempts at using smaller geographical units, it was eventually determined that the national market provided the most feasible and fair solution, and this national market information was compiled (*see, In re Complex DES Litig.*, No. 830/109, Cal. Super. Ct.).

Four years after *Sindell v Abbott Labs.*, the Wisconsin Supreme Court followed with *Collins v. Lilly & Co.*, 116 Wis. 2d 166 (1984). Deciding the identification issue without the benefit of the extensive California litigation over market shares, the Wisconsin court held that it was prevented from following *Sindell* due to "the practical difficulty of defining and proving market share" (*id.* at 189). Instead of focusing on tying liability closely to the odds of actual causation, as the *Sindell* court attempted, the *Collins* court took a broader perspective, and held that each defendant is liable in proportion to the amount of risk it created that the plaintiff would be injured by DES. Under the *Collins* structure, the "risk" each defendant is liable for is a question of fact in each case, with market shares being relevant to this determination (*id.* at 191). Defendants are allowed, however, to exculpate themselves by showing that their product could not have caused the injury to the particular plaintiff (*id.* at 198).

The Washington Supreme Court, writing soon after *Collins v. Lilly & Co.*, took yet another approach (*see, Martin v. Abbott Labs.*, 102 Wash. 2d 581 (1984). The *Martin* court first rejected the *Sindell* market share theory due to the belief (which later proved to be erroneous in *Brown v. Superior Ct.*) that California's approach distorted liability by inflating market shares to ensure plaintiffs of full recovery. The *Martin* court instead adopted what it termed "market share alternative liability," justified, it concluded, because "[each] defendant contributed to the *risk* of injury to the public, and, consequently, the risk of injury to individual plaintiffs" (*id.* at 604).

Under the Washington scheme, defendants are first allowed to exculpate themselves by proving by the preponderance of the evidence that they were not the manufacturer of the DES that injured plaintiff. Unexculpated defendants are presumed to have equal market shares, totaling 100%. Each defendant then has the opportunity to rebut this presumption by showing that its actual market share was less than presumed. If any defendants succeed in rebutting this presumption, the liability shares of the remaining defendants who could not prove their actual market share are inflated, so that the plaintiff received a 100% recovery. The market shares of defendants is a question of fact in each case, and the relevant market can be a particular pharmacy, or county, or State, or even the country, depending upon the circumstances the case presents.

Turning to the structure to be adopted in New York, we heed both the lessons learned through experience in other jurisdictions and the realities of the mass litigation of DES claims in this State. Balancing these considerations, we are led to the conclusion that a market share theory, based upon a national market, provides the best solution. As California discovered, the reliable determination of any market smaller than the national one likely is not practicable. Moreover, even if it were possible, of the hundreds of cases in the New York courts, without a doubt there are many in which the DES that allegedly caused injury was ingested in another State. Among the thorny issues this could present, perhaps the most daunting is the specter that the particular case could require the establishment of a separate market share matrix. We feel that this is an unfair, and perhaps impossible burden to routinely place upon the litigants in individual cases.

Nor do we believe that the Wisconsin approach of assessing the "risk" each defendant caused a particular plaintiff, to be litigated anew as a question of fact in each case, is the best solution for this State. Applied on a limited scale this theory may be feasible, and certainly is the most refined approach by allowing a more thorough consideration of how each defendant's actions threatened the plaintiff. We are wary, however, of setting loose, for application in the hundreds of cases pending in this State, a theory which requires the fact finder's individualized and open-ended assessment of the relative liabilities of scores of defendants in every case. Instead, it is our perception that the injustices arising from delayed recoveries and inconsistent results which this theory may produce in this State outweigh arguments calling for its adoption.

Consequently, for essentially practical reasons, we adopt a market share theory using a national market. We are aware that the adoption of a national market will likely result in a disproportion between the liability of individual manufacturers and the actual injuries each manufacturer caused in this State. Thus our market share theory cannot be founded upon the belief that, over the run of cases, liability will approximate causation in this State. Nor does the use of a national market provide a reasonable link between liability and the risk created by a defendant to a particular plaintiff. Instead, we choose to apportion liability so as to correspond to the over-all culpability of each defendant, measured by the amount of risk of injury each defendant created to the public-at-large. Use of a national market is a fair method, we believe, of apportioning defendants' liabilities according to their total culpability in marketing DES for use during pregnancy. Under the circumstances, this is an equitable way to provide plaintiffs with the relief they deserve, while also rationally distributing the responsibility for plaintiffs' injuries among defendants.

To be sure, a defendant cannot be held liable if it did not participate in the marketing of DES for pregnancy use; if a DES producer satisfies its burden of proof of showing that it was not a member of the market of DES sold for pregnancy use, disallowing exculpation would be unfair and unjust. Nevertheless, because liability here is based on the over-all risk produced, and not causation in a single case, there should be no exculpation of a defendant who, although a member of the market producing DES for pregnancy use, appears not to have caused a particular plaintiff's injury. It is merely a windfall for a producer to escape liability solely because it manufactured a more identifiable pill, or sold only to certain drugstores. These fortuities in no way diminish the culpability of a defendant for marketing the product, which is the basis of liability here.

Finally, we hold that the liability of DES producers is several only, and should not be inflated when all participants in the market are not before the court in a particular case. We understand that, as a practical matter, this will prevent some plaintiffs from recovering 100% of their damages. However, we eschewed exculpation to prevent the fortuitous avoidance of liability, and thus, equitably, we decline to unleash the same forces to increase a defendant's liability beyond its fair share of responsibility.

We are confronted here with an unprecedented identification problem, and have provided a solution that rationally apportions liability. We have heeded the practical lessons learned by other jurisdictions, resulting in our adoption of a national market theory with full knowledge that it concedes the lack of a logical link between liability and causation in a single case. [Affirmed].

NOTES

1. *The Market Share Theory.* As noted in *Hymowitz,* the seminal cases on the defendant identification issue are *Summers v. Tice*, 33 Cal.2d 80 (1948) and *Sindell v. Abbott Labs.,* 26 Cal. 3d 588 (1980). Exactly how does market share liability differ from alternative liability? Are the differences conceptual, operational or both?

How do the issues discussed in *Hymowitz* — alternative liability and market share liability — differ from those issues discussed in other cases in this chapter, specifically, the concurrent causation issue in *Anderson v. Minneapolis, St. P. & S.S.M. Ry., supra*, and the apportionment issue in *Piner v. Superior Court, infra*?

2. *Horses for Courses. Hymowitz* and *Sindell* were both products liability claims brought on strict liability theories (*see* Chapter 10). Is that sufficient justification for the expansion of liability beyond the alternative liability theory used in the negligence case of *Summers v. Tice*? Do you agree with that expansion? Consider how your response is affected by the different perspectives discussed in Chapter 1.

3. *The Mechanics of Market Share Liability.* In *Zafft v. Eli Lilly & Co.,* 676 S.W.2d 241, 248–49 (Mo. 1984), Judge Gunn, in dissent, addressed some of the practical issues involved in using a market share approach:

It would seem that there are actually two different concepts of "relevant market" applicable to this situation. The first is a component of the threshold requirement that the named defendants together account for a substantial share of the relevant market, i.e., a substantial likelihood that their products were actually purchased and consumed by the DES mother. Since this threshold need not be a stringent one to meet, this likelihood could be demonstrated by fairly general proof regarding defendants' shares of the total amount of DES marketed. No great degree of specificity should be required of plaintiffs prior to discovery.

The second "relevant market" concept comes into being once plaintiff has survived a motion to dismiss. At that point the precise issue becomes the relative likelihood that the plaintiff's mother actually purchased the product manufactured by the individual defendant. The relevant market is the area of her residence, her drugstore, her pharmacist. While proof of this issue may be fraught with difficulty, it is a difficulty which is more appropriately borne by the manufacturers than by the plaintiffs — a legitimate concept in products liability. In either sense of the term, the "relevant market" is defined by the DES mother herself, the only real distinction being the means of proof used to describe that market.

676 S.W.2d at 248–49.

4. *Other Approaches to Generic Defendants.* In *Martin v. Abbott Labs*, 102 Wash. 2d 581 (1984), Washington adopted a complex version of market share liability in which defendants were allowed to exculpate themselves from liability but un-exculpated defendants were presumed to have equal market shares, totaling 100%. Thereafter, un-exculpated defendants could rebut the presumption that their market shares were equal. In contrast, the Wisconsin Supreme Court, in *Collins v. Eli Lilly Co.,* 116 Wis. 2d 166 (1984), discussed in the next case, did not tie liability to market share but held that each DES defendant would be liable in proportion to the amount of risk that it created.

THOMAS v. MALLETT
285 Wis. 2d 236 (2005)

BUTLER, JUSTICE.

Steven Thomas, by his guardian *ad litem*, seeks review of a published court of appeals decision that declined to extend the risk-contribution theory announced in *Collins v. Eli Lilly Co.*, 116 Wis. 2d 166 (1984), to the defendant-respondent lead pigment manufacturers . . .

Thomas was born on June 23, 1990. He claims that he sustained lead poisoning by ingesting lead paint from accessible painted surfaces, paint chips, and paint flakes and dust at two different houses he lived in during the early 1990s . . .

According to Dr. John F. Rosen, a professor of pediatrics and head of the Division of Environmental Sciences at the Children's Hospital at Montefiore of the Albert Einstein College of Medicine, Thomas's cognitive deficits are a "signature or constellation of cognitive effects" that are typical of lead poisoning.

In Thomas's case, Rosen states that these deficits are permanent. In addition, due to Thomas's elevated BPb over the extended period of time, Thomas will require lifetime medical monitoring-surveillance for physical disorders, as he is now at a high risk for developing future medical complications, including kidney disease, peripheral neuropathy, hypertension, and cardiovascular disease. Rosen opines that Thomas's high lead levels are exclusively derived from ingesting lead based pigments in paint . . .

As noted, the houses where Thomas alleges he ingested lead paint were built in 1900 and 1905. During that period, use of lead paint for residences was common. Lead paint contained up to 50 percent lead pigment and maintained widespread use through the 1940s. The use and manufacturing of interior lead-based paints declined during the 1950s, and, in 1955, the lead industry voluntarily adopted a standard of the American National Standards Institute that limited lead content to a maximum of one percent in paints intended for children's toys, furniture, and interior surfaces. However, lead paint for interiors continued to be available until the 1970s.

As of December 31, 1972, lead paint for interior and exterior household use containing more than 0.5 percent lead of its total weight was banned from interstate commerce. In 1978, the ban was expanded to residential use of paint containing more than 0.06 percent lead by weight. In 1980, Wisconsin banned the use of lead paint.

Although all of the Pigment Manufacturers or their predecessors-in-interests manufactured white lead carbonate at various times during the existence of Thomas's prior residences, Thomas conceded that he cannot identify the specific pigment manufacturer that produced the white lead carbonate he ingested. The Pigment Manufacturers moved for summary judgment, arguing, as relevant here, that Thomas could not prove causation in fact or proximate cause . . . The Milwaukee County Circuit Court, Honorable Timothy G. Dugan, granted the motion.

The circuit court concluded that the DES fact situation in *Collins* was too different from the circumstances of Thomas's lead paint claims . . .

Thomas appealed, and the court of appeals affirmed.

Thomas seeks review . . .

A problem facing Thomas, who alleges that he was injured by white lead carbonate pigment, is that he is unable to identify the precise producer of the white lead carbonate pigment he ingested at his prior residences due to the generic nature of the pigment, the number of producers, the lack of pertinent records, and the passage of time . . .

The consequences of child lead poisoning are well documented. According to the Center for Disease Control (CDC):

> Very severe lead exposure in children (blood lead levels >80 g/dL) can cause coma, convulsions, and even death. Lower levels cause adverse effects on the central nervous system, kidney, and hematopoietic system. Blood lead levels as low as 10g/dL, which do not cause distinctive

symptoms, are associated with decreased intelligence and impaired neurobehavioral developments.

Id. [at] 9. The CDC also states that "the weight of the evidence clearly supports the hypothesis that decrements in children's cognition are evident at blood lead levels well below 25 g/dL." *Id.*

Although lead can originate from many different materials, such as food, soil, water, or air, lead paint is the primary culprit . . .

Lead poisoning disproportionately affects lower-income, inner-city populations. The National Health and Nutrition Examination Survey (conducted from October 1991 to September 1994) indicated that BPb levels among children aged 1–5 years "were more likely to be elevated among those who were poor, non-Hispanic, black, living in large metropolitan areas, or living in older housing (with potential exposure to lead from lead-based paint)." *Id.* The differences in housing conditions and exposures to lead-containing house dust "appear to contribute to the racial differences in urban children's [BPb] levels." *Id.* [at] 417.

Approximately 3 million tons of lead remain in an estimated 57 million occupied private housing units built before 1980. Of those units, 3.8 million contain children and deteriorated lead paint. *Id.* Although lead paint is typically found on kitchen and bathroom walls, it is also commonly found on doors, windows, and wood trim in pre-1950s homes . . .

The predominant lead pigment that was manufactured and integrated into paint was white lead carbonate. White lead carbonate was the first chemical produced commercially in this country. That pigment was initially favored because when used alone it was the most durable and easy to apply. It was also believed to be a mildewcide. All of the Pigment Manufacturers, or their predecessors-in-interests, produced this pigment at varying times since the houses in which Thomas resided were constructed in 1900 and 1905.

In addition to having different chemical compositions, the physical properties of white lead carbonate varied. These variances included different specific gravity, bulking values, oil absorption, hiding power, and particle size and shape. Pigment Manufacturers also distinguished between grades of lead carbonate and apparently promoted each for different purposes.

Thomas's toxicologist expert, Mushak, opines that the toxicological effects of white lead carbonate remain the same notwithstanding the formulary differences between the white lead carbonate pigments. Mushak states that there is little relationship between chemical diversity and the "bioavailability" of the lead, which refers to the lead uptake or lead absorption into the human body. Mushak explains that "the reasons why one cannot automatically equate differences in chemical composition with differences in bioavailability is because bioavailability operates via a set of biological, biochemical and physico-chemical processes that will often render starting forms of lead in pigments indistinguishable in toxicokinetic terms." Based on observational evidence (which Mushak characterizes as "the huge body of toxicological literature showing that lead paint poisoning is pervasive and rather uniformly intense as to the severity of exposures") and laboratory evidence,

Mushak concludes that there is no basis to conclude that formulary changes among white lead carbonates affect the bioavailability of the lead . . .

By the turn of the 20th century, it was well-recognized that controlling lead dust could significantly reduce lead poisoning, although the recognition was initially limited to industrial settings. European countries had acknowledged the harm of lead dust, and by 1910, Germany, England, and France were already regulating lead industries to protect their workers from lead dust and fumes . . .

The appreciation of the dangers lead paint posed inside the home to the residents was also emerging during this time. In July 1904, in its monthly publication The S.W.P., Sherwin-Williams publicized the hazards of white lead paint. Under the bold headline, "DANGERS OF WHITE LEAD," Sherwin-Williams reported that a committee in France had been appointed to investigate the use of white lead and other lead mixtures for painting houses. Sherwin-Williams noted that one of the committee's experts indicated that lead paints were "poisonous in a large degree, both for the workmen and for the inhabitants of a house painted with lead colors." Sherwin-Williams also noted that the expert was of the opinion "that the absolute disuse of white lead has become an imperative necessity." Nevertheless, six years later, in 1910, Sherwin-Williams began manufacturing white lead carbonate after it acquired a white lead processing plant. Moreover, in 1917, during the First World War, Sherwin-Williams advised the War Department that government specifications for 50 percent white lead carbonate paint for war helmets should be replaced with its lead-free lithopone pigment. Sherwin-Williams stated that the advantage of switching to its lithopone pigment was that the danger from lead poisoning was entirely eliminated . . .

In 1939, the National Paint Varnish and Lacquer Association (NPVLA) confidentially warned its members — which included National Lead, Sherwin Williams, Glidden, and W.P. Fuller — that white lead pigments were toxic . . .

Nevertheless, the NPVLA fought to weaken states' proposals that required paint to contain warning labels and particularly objected to the American Medical Association's proposal that would have required lead paint to be labeled as "poisonous."

By 1942, the National Safety Council determined that "the most obvious method of preventing lead poisoning is to substitute for lead and its compounds other materials that are non-toxic." By the early 1920s, there were safe alternatives to white lead paint . . .

Parallel with the emerging knowledge of the dangers caused by lead in industrial and residential settings grew the awareness of childhood lead poisoning. During the mid-1800s, child lead poisoning was already linked to mouthing lead-painted toys. Australia was at the forefront of identifying and examining childhood lead poisoning. Following the first well-documented study of childhood lead poisoning from paint in 1908, Australian researchers went so far as to call for prohibiting the use of lead paint within the reach of children . . .

In the early 1900s, children's particular susceptibility to lead poisoning was also gaining recognition. In Great Britain, the dangers of lead exposure to fetuses were identified, and women were later removed from working in the lead industries. In the United States, in 1908, Dr. Hamilton noted that "lead is a most potent producer of abortion, and it is very rare that a woman lead worker bears a healthy child at term." And, in 1912, researchers in the United States acknowledged that young people were more vulnerable to lead poisoning than adults. In its 1912 annual report, National Lead noted that it did not employ women in its factories, except as occasional messengers or other similar jobs, or boys . . .

During the mid to late 1920s, the view that children were more susceptible to lead poisoning was almost universal . . .

Thomas's public health historians, Gerald E. Markowitz, Ph.D., and David Rosner, Ph.D. (hereinafter "Markowitz and Rosner"), opine that by the mid-1920s there was "strong and ample convergent evidence of the toxicity of lead paint" in general, and the dangers it posed to children in particular. Markowitz and Rosner conclude that given the increasing evidence, "the manufacturers of lead pigments should have ceased producing it, at the very least for interior use, before the mid-1920s."

. . . In 1928, the rising alarms regarding the hazards of lead and the need for coordination among lead producers and manufacturers led to the formation of the Lead Industries Association (LIA). Although comprised of many lead industries, the white lead industry was the most important of the lead manufacturing industries in the LIA . . .

According to Markowitz and Rosner, the LIA's campaign was multi-pronged: it sought to rebut any research findings or other news of lead's toxicity; it sponsored its own research to demonstrate that lead was harmless; and it refused to warn the public of lead's dangers, even in the face of overwhelming evidence from research and clinical findings that many children were dying. All the while, Markowitz and Rosner submit, the LIA promoted the use of lead paint and successfully lobbied against laws and regulations that would curb its use . . .

. . . According to Markowitz and Rosner, "The LIA did not advocate the use of warning labels, nor did it encourage the elimination of interior use of white lead. Only these measures could have served to diminish or eliminate the problem. To the contrary, . . . the LIA and its members continued to promote lead paint for interior use." Sherwin-Williams and Glidden actually still promoted lead paint for use on toys at this time.

Also in December 1945, the LIA launched "The Safety and Hygiene Program" to undercut the growing medical literature regarding the toxicity of lead that it characterized as faulty. Recognizing that the lead industry "must be losing a vast amount of business each year because of the fact that lead has such unpleasant connections in the minds of so many Americans," the LIA persisted in complaining about how the lead industry "continues to be plagued unfairly by attacks made upon lead products because of their toxicity" and indicated it would "meet attacks on lead due to its toxic qualities by correcting published erroneous statements."

. . . In 1955, the LIA characterized the problem of childhood lead poisoning as "a major 'headache' and a source of much adverse publicity." The LIA wrote:

> With us, childhood lead poisoning is common enough to constitute perhaps my major "headache," this being in part due to the very poor prognosis in many such cases, and also to the fact that the only real remedy lies in educating a relatively ineducable category of parents. It is mainly a slum problem with us, estimated . . . to run into four figures annually, and . . . we have no monopoly on either substandard housing or substandard mentalities in the USA . . .

Two years later, in 1957, the LIA finally recognized what the literature had supported for nearly half a century: lead paint was the major source of childhood lead poisoning . . . This time, the LIA suggested the blame fell on the children's parents' shoulders, as it stated:

> As the major source of trouble is the flaking of lead paint in the ancient slum dwellings of our older cities, the problem of lead poisoning in children will be with us for as long as there are slums, and because of the high death rate, the frequency of permanent brain damage in the survivors, and the intelligence level of the slum parents, it seems destined to remain as important and as difficult as any with which we have to deal.

. . . The LIA still saw the problem as a "headache" and a public relations issue, not a public health disaster. In 1959, in its annual report, the LIA wrote:

> The toxicity of lead poses a problem that other nonferrous industries generally do not have to face. Lead poisoning, or the threat of it, hurts our business in several different ways. While it is difficult to count exactly in dollars and cents, it is taking money out of your pockets every day.

> [I]t means thousands of items of unfavorable publicity every year. This is particularly true since most cases of lead poisoning today are in children, and anything sad that happens to a child is meat for newspaper editors and is gobbled up by the public. It makes no difference that it is essentially a problem of slums, a public welfare problem. Just the same the publicity hits us where it hurts.

. . . With approximately 85 percent of all sales, National Lead dominated the white lead pigment market in 1900. Through its advertisements and promotions, National Lead promoted and reinforced the perception that no paint was as good, or as safe, as white leaded paint. Despite numerous articles showing that lead was a potent poison by the 1920s, in 1923, one of National Lead's ads declared that lead paint helps guard health by preventing a resting place for germs. Although there were warnings from the medical communities about the dangers of white lead paints in schools and hospitals, National Lead also specifically targeted those institutions from the 1920s into the 1930s. National

Lead repeatedly claimed that its lead paint protected public health, as it was a deadly enemy of tuberculosis and other germs. In 1931, National Lead contended that its lead paint helped "speed patients' recovery."

Between 1910 and 1925, three new major pigment manufacturers entered the market: Sherwin-Williams, Anaconda, and Glidden. National Lead's market share fell to between 60 and 70 percent during this time. Sherwin-Williams did not manufacture white lead until 1910, when it began operating a newly constructed white lead manufacturing plant in Chicago. Although Sherwin-Williams recognized the dangers of lead paint in a 1904 publication, and cautioned the War Department about the dangers of lead poisoning from lead paint in 1917, in 1922 it advocated using lead-based paint on children's toys.

During the mid-1920s, Sherwin-Williams continued to recommend using white-lead based paint (paint which contained upwards of 75 percent white lead) on interior surfaces, including walls, woodwork, doors, and ceilings. From 1936 until the 1940s, Sherwin-Williams promoted use of its lead based paints on toys.

. . . In 1938, after recognizing the declining sales of white lead, the LIA began its "White Lead Promotion Campaign." The LIA characterized the campaign as follows: "This campaign by showing the importance of white lead to industry would help offset the constant threat of anti-lead legislation and propaganda." The campaign carried on until 1952 . . .

According to Markowitz and Rosner, the Pigment Manufacturers' marketing and ad campaigns created an enduring belief among consumers that the best paint was lead paint — as National Lead stated, "Remember, also, that the more white-lead you use, the better the paint." They further opine that "notwithstanding repeated statements over the years that it no longer produced white lead paint for interior use, the industry continued to sell white lead paints that were applied on interiors."

We begin our analysis with a discussion of *Collins*. In that case, the plaintiff developed adenocarcinoma of the vagina and benign adenosis of the vagina in 1975 . . .

After the discovery of the cancer, the plaintiff had much of her reproductive system surgically removed and developed other complications. She sued 12 drug companies, all of which produced or marketed DES.

The plaintiff was "unable to identify the precise producer or marketer of the DES taken by her mother due to the generic status of some DES, the number of producers or marketers, the lack of pertinent records, and the passage of time." *Id.* at 177 . . .

. . . [T]his court adopted the risk-contribution theory, which relaxed the plaintiff's burden of proof in establishing causation in her negligence and product liability claims, for three reasons . . .

Under the risk-contribution theory as stated in *Collins*, a plaintiff need commence an action against only one defendant, but the plaintiff will have to allege the following elements and prove each to the satisfaction of the trier of fact:

That the plaintiff's mother took DES; that DES caused the plaintiff's subsequent injuries; that the defendant produced or marketed the type of DES taken by the plaintiff's mother; and that the defendant's conduct in producing or marketing the DES constituted a breach of a legally recognized duty to the plaintiff.

Id. at 193. It was not fatal to a plaintiff's claim if he or she could not identify the type of DES taken by the mother. The *Collins* court held that "in the situation where the plaintiff cannot allege and prove what type of DES the mother took, as to the third element the plaintiff need only allege and prove that the defendant drug company produced or marketed the drug DES for use in preventing miscarriages during pregnancy." *Id.* at 194. If these elements could be proven, the plaintiff could recover all damages from the named defendant.

However, this court was concerned that only those defendant drug companies that "*reasonably could have* contributed *in some way* to the actual injury" be held accountable. *Id.* at 191 n.10 (emphasis added). Thus, after the plaintiff made a *prima facie* case under either negligence or strict products liability theory, a defendant could escape liability if it proved by a preponderance of evidence that the DES it produced or marketed could not have reached the plaintiff's mother. A defendant could accomplish this by establishing "that it did not produce or market the subject DES either during the time period the plaintiff was exposed to DES or in the relevant geographical market area in which the plaintiff's mother acquired the DES." *Id.* at 198.

Providing defendants the ability to prove their way out of liability "will result in a pool of defendants which it can reasonably be assumed could have caused the plaintiff's injuries." *Id.* This procedure, however, was imprecise, as it could mean that some of the remaining defendants may still be innocent. Nevertheless, this court accepted that possibility "as the price the defendants, and perhaps ultimately society, must pay to provide the plaintiff an adequate remedy under the law." *Id.* at 198.

For those defendants that could not exculpate themselves, this court concluded that the application of comparative negligence "provided the most equitable means to assign liability and apportion damages among the liable defendants." *Id.* at 199. In assigning liability among the defendants, this court determined that the jury may consider the following nonexhaustive list of factors:

> Whether the drug company conducted tests on DES for safety and efficacy in use for pregnancies; to what degree the company took a role in gaining FDA approval of DES for use in pregnancies; whether the company had a small or large market share in the relevant area; whether the company took the lead or merely followed the lead of others in producing or marketing DES; whether the company issued warnings about the dangers of DES; whether the company produced or marketed DES after it knew or should have known of the possible hazards DES presented to the public; and whether the company took any affirmative steps to reduce the risk of injury to the public. *Id.* at 200 . . .

There is no dispute that Thomas is an innocent plaintiff who is probably not at fault and will be forced to bear a significant cost of his injuries if he is not allowed to sue the possibly negligent Pigment Manufacturers. Further, given the disturbing numbers of victims of lead poisoning from ingesting lead paint, and given that white lead carbonate was the overwhelming pigment added to that paint, it is clear from the summary judgment record that we are not dealing with an isolated or unique set of circumstances. As far as the summary judgment record reveals, the problem of lead poisoning from white lead carbonate is real; it is widespread; and it is a public health catastrophe that is poised to linger for quite some time.

The main policy reasons identified by *Collins* warrant extension of the risk-contribution theory here.

First, the record makes clear that the Pigment Manufacturers "contributed to the risk of injury to the public and, consequently, the risk of injury to individual plaintiffs such as" Thomas. *See id.* at 191. Many of the individual defendants or their predecessors-in-interest did more than simply contribute to a risk; they knew of the harm white lead carbonate pigments caused and continued production and promotion of the pigment notwithstanding that knowledge. Some manufacturers, paradoxically, even promoted their nonleaded based pigments as alternatives that were safe in that they did not pose the risk of lead poisoning. For those that did not have explicit knowledge of the harm they were engendering, given the growing medical literature in the early part of the century, Thomas's historical experts, Markowitz and Rosner, submit that by the 1920s the entire industry knew or should have known of the dangers of its products and should have ceased producing the lead pigments, including white lead carbonate. In short, we agree with Thomas that the record easily establishes the Pigment Manufacturers' culpability for, at a minimum, contributing to creating a risk of injury to the public.

Second, as compared to Thomas, the Pigment Manufacturers are in a better position to absorb the cost of the injury. They can insure themselves against liability, absorb the damage award, or pass the cost along to the consuming public as a cost of doing business. *See id.* As we concluded in *Collins*, it is better to have the Pigment Manufacturers or consumers share the cost of the injury rather than place the burden on the innocent plaintiff.

Thomas is also unable to identify the precise manufacturer of the white lead carbonate that caused his injuries due to the number of manufacturers, the passage of time, and the loss or records. Additionally, he cannot identify which of the three types of white lead carbonate he ingested. On this failure of proof, the Pigment Manufacturers contend, Thomas's claim must fall. They argue that because white lead carbonate was not "fungible" or manufactured from a chemically identical formula, *Collins*' risk-contribution cannot be applied here. We disagree.

One of the proof problems the *Collins* court recognized the plaintiff had was that she was unable to identify the precise producer or marketer of the DES her mother took due to, among other things, "the generic status of some DES." *Id.* at 177. In different terms, this court stated that the plaintiff could not identify the drug company that caused her injury because "DES was, for the most part, produced in a 'generic' form which did not contain any clearly identifiable shape, color, or markings." *Id.* at 180. This court also observed that "DES was a fungible drug produced with a chemically identical formula, and often pharmacists would fill DES prescriptions from whatever stock they had on hand, whether or not a particular brand was specified in the prescription." *Id.*

There is no denying that *Collins* involved a situation where a chemically identical formula allegedly caused harm. It is also true that white lead carbonate was made from three different chemical formulas. However, *Collins* did not address whether DES was fungible because of its chemical identity, because of its interchangeability due to its generic status, or because of both. The question is, does fungibility require chemical identity? We conclude that it does not.

Chemical identity was a feature that DES apparently shared, and it was that chemical formula that created a possibility of causing harm. Here, although the chemical formulas for white lead carbonate are not the same, Thomas's toxicologist, Mushak, opines that it is the common denominator in the formulas that counts lead. According to Mushak, the formulary differences between white lead carbonates do not affect the bioavailability of, and hence the consequences caused by, the lead pigment. Thus, the formulas for both DES and the white lead carbonate are in a sense on the same footing as being inherently hazardous. Therefore, it would be imprudent to conclude that chemical identity is a touchstone for fungibility and, in turn, for the risk-contribution theory. To prevent the triumph of form over substance, we conclude that chemical identity is not required.

But the question still remains: what does fungibility mean? It has been noted that "while 'fungibility' [has] become an obsession for courts discussing market share liability, no court has ever explained thoroughly what 'fungibility' means or why it is important." Allen Rostron, *Beyond Market Share Liability: A Theory of Proportional Share Liability for Nonfungible Products*, 52 UCLA L. REV. 151, 163 (2004). Rostron writes that a product can be fungible in at least three different senses.

First, a product can be "functionally interchangeable." Under this meaning, whether a product is fungible is a matter of degree and heavily dependent on the context of whatever "function" is at issue. For example, "'for signaling New Year's Eve, a blast from an auto horn and one from a saxophone may be equivalent as noise, but few would want to dance to the former.'" *Id.* at 163–64 (quoting *Hamilton v. Accu-Tek*, 32 F. Supp. 2d 47, 51 (E.D.N.Y. 1998)). This type of fungibility is significant "because it is a reason why a product may pose unusually severe identification problems." *Id.* at 164.

Second, a product can be fungible in the sense that it is "physically indistinguishable." *Id.* at 164. Because appearances can be deceiving, the degree of physical similarity required, as with functional interchangeability, depends heavily on context: "For example, the difference between two brands of a cola drink in their original packaging will be obvious. After being poured from the can or bottle, they might be completely indistinguishable in appearance, distinguishable by taste for some consumers and not others, and easily distinguishable to chemists analyzing them in a laboratory." *Id.* at 164. As with functional interchangeability, fungibility in the sense that a product is physically indistinguishable is significant because it is also a reason why a product may pose identification problems. *Id.* at 165.

Third, a product can be fungible as it presents a "uniformity of risk." *Id.* at 165. Under this meaning, "as a result of sharing an identical or virtually identical chemical formula, each manufacturer's product posed the same amount of risk as every other manufacturer's product. The products therefore were 'identically defective,' with none being more or less defective than the rest." *Id.* However, "whether a product poses a uniform risk can depend on the choice of the unit for which risk is measured. While each milligram of DES presented the same amount of risk, each DES pill did not, because the pills came in different dosages." *Id.* at 166. Thus, as products may contain different concentrations of the hazardous substance, there is leeway to conclude that strict chemical uniformity does not render all substances fungible . . .

Fungibility, therefore, is not a term that is capable of being defined with categorical precision. Its character will depend on the context of the injury, its cause, and the particular obstacles encountered in linking the causation to the possibly negligent defendants. The facts presented in this case, when construed in the light most favorable to Thomas, however, establish that white lead carbonate is fungible under any of the above meanings.

First, white lead carbonate was functionally interchangeable. All forms of white lead carbonate were lead pigments, which constituted one of the two necessary components of paint (the other being the "vehicle"). The pigment is what provided the hiding power of the paint. Although there may be varying grades of hiding powers based on differing physical properties and concentrations of the particular pigments, those are differences of degree, not function.

Second, based on the summary judgment record, white lead carbonates are physically indistinguishable. As far as Thomas has been able to tell, the pigment at issue is white lead carbonate pigment. And as far as Thomas has been able to tell, there appears to be no difference between the various white lead carbonates. Although the Pigment Manufacturers contend that white lead carbonates were manufactured according to different processes, which resulted in white lead carbonates of different physical properties, these physical differences are available only on the microscopic scale. Our concern here is whether the white lead carbonates are physically indistinguishable in the context in which it is used (in paint) and to whom is using it (the consumer or injured party). We acknowledge that the physical identity in this case is markedly different from that in *Collins*. Whereas in *Collins*, the plaintiff's mother could identify certain characteristics about the particular DES pill she ingested, that type of analysis is not possible here, as pigment in paint by its nature and concentration defy more specific identification. Nevertheless, we conclude the factual circumstances of physical interchangeability that are present are still sufficiently similar to remain within *Collins'* confines.

Third, we have already noted that white lead carbonates were produced utilizing "virtually identical chemical formulas" such that all white lead carbonates were "identically defective." *See id.* at 165 . . . It is the common denominator in the various white lead carbonate formulas that matters; namely, lead.

Therefore, based on the factors identified in *Collins*, we conclude that Thomas's case is factually similar to warrant extension of the risk-contribution theory.

The Pigment Manufacturers, however, contend that there are a number of factual dissimilarities between this case and *Collins* that should preclude recognizing the risk-contribution theory here. While there are dissimilarities between the two, we do not agree that these defeat the extension of *Collins* in this case.

First, the Pigment Manufacturers note that the paint Thomas allegedly ingested could have been applied at any time between construction of the two houses in 1900 and 1905 and the ban on lead paint in 1978. This significant time span greatly exceeds the nine-month window during which a plaintiff's mother would have taken DES, the Pigment Manufacturers note . . .

We recognize that the window during which the possible injury causing white lead carbonate was placed in a house that eventually harmed Thomas is drastically larger than a nine-month window for pregnancy. However, the window will not always be potentially as large as appears in this case. Even if it routinely will be, the Pigment Manufacturers' argument must be put into perspective: they are essentially arguing that their negligent conduct should be excused because they got away with it for too long. As Thomas says, the Pigment Manufacturers "are arguing that they should not be held liable under the risk contribution doctrine because of the magnitude of their wrongful conduct."

Collins was concerned with providing possibly innocent defendants a means to exculpate themselves by establishing their product could not have caused the injury. If they could not do so, this court stated that the equities "favor placing the consequences on the defendants." *Id.* at 198. Equity does not support reversing that balance simply because the Pigment Manufacturers benefited from manufacturing and marketing white lead carbonate for a significant period of time.

Next, the Pigment Manufacturers contend that the risk-contribution theory should not be extended because Thomas's lead poisoning could have been caused from many different sources. We agree that the record indicates that lead poisoning can stem from the ambient air, many foods, drinking water, soil, and dust.

Further, the Pigment Manufacturers argue that the risk-contribution theory should not be extended because lead poisoning does not produce a "signature injury." As alternate explanations for Thomas's cognitive deficits, the Pigment Manufacturers have brought forth evidence that genetics, birth complications causing damage to the central nervous system, severe environmental deprivation, inadequate parenting, parental emotional disorders, and child abuse could all, in varying ways, cause such impairments.

These arguments have no bearing on whether the risk-contribution theory should be extended to white lead carbonate claims. Harm is harm, whether it be "signature" or otherwise. Even under the risk-contribution theory, the plaintiff still retains a burden of establishing causation. To establish a negligence claim under the risk-contribution theory, this court concluded that the plaintiff nonetheless needed to prove that "DES caused the plaintiff's subsequent injuries." *Collins*, 116 Wis. 2d at 193. Similarly, on a products liability claim, the *Collins* court held that the plaintiff has to prove "that the defect was a cause of the plaintiff's injuries or damages." *Id.* at 196. On whatever theory the plaintiff chooses to proceed, this causation showing must be made by a preponderance of the evidence, and ultimately "to the satisfaction of the trier of fact." *Id.* at 194. The plaintiff's burden is relaxed only with respect to establishing the specific type of DES the plaintiff's mother took, which, in this case, translates into the specific type of white lead carbonate Thomas ingested.

While *Collins* concerned a plaintiff who had injuries of a "signature" nature, that merely means that Thomas may have a harder case to make to his jury. Further, while the Pigment Manufacturers are correct to argue that Thomas's lead poisoning could have come from any number of sources that is an argument to be made before the jury.

Finally, the Pigment Manufacturers argue that because they were not in exclusive control of the risk their product created, the risk-contribution model should not apply to them. We again disagree.

This was again not a distinction relevant in *Collins*. Further, we see no reason why it should be for at least two reasons. First, as doctors were the ones who prescribed the dosage of DES, so too were the paint manufacturers that mixed the amount of white lead carbonate in the paint. However, the paint did not alter the toxicity of the white lead carbonate anymore than the pharmacist did by filling a prescription. To the contrary, at best, the paint manufacturers actually diluted the white lead carbonate's toxicity. In other words, the inherent dangerousness of the white lead carbonate pigment existed the moment the Pigment Manufacturers created it.

Second, the record is replete with evidence that shows the Pigment Manufacturers actually magnified the risk through their aggressive promotion of white lead carbonate, even despite the awareness of the toxicity of lead. In either case, whoever had "exclusive" control over the white lead carbonate is immaterial . . .

Once Thomas makes a *prima facie* [products liability] case . . . , the burden of proof shifts to each defendant to prove by a preponderance of the evidence that it did not produce or market white lead carbonate either during the relevant time period or in the geographical market where the house is located. However, if relevant records do not exist that can substantiate either defense, "we believe that the equities of [white lead carbonate] cases favor placing the consequences on the [Pigment Manufacturers]." *Id.* at 198. In addition to these specific defenses, and unlike in the DES cases, the Pigment Manufacturers here may have ample grounds to attack and eviscerate Thomas's *prima facie* case, with some of those grounds including that lead poisoning could stem from any number of substances (since lead itself is ubiquitous) and that it is difficult to know whether Thomas's injuries stem from lead poisoning as they are not signature injuries.

We continue to believe that this procedure will result in a pool of defendants which can reasonably be assumed "could have caused the plaintiff's injuries."

See *id.* at 198 . . . [O]ur application of *Collins* here achieves *Collins'* requirement that it be shown that the defendant pigment manufacturer "reasonably
could have contributed . . . to the actual injury." *Id.* at 191 n.10 (emphasis
added). The procedure is not perfect and could result in drawing in some defendants who are actually innocent, particularly given the significantly larger
time span at issue in this particular case. However, *Collins* declared that "we
accept this as the price the defendants, and perhaps ultimately society, must
pay to provide the plaintiff an adequate remedy under the law." *Id.*

. . . In sum, we conclude . . . that the risk-contribution theory applies to white
lead carbonate cases . . .

[AFFIRMED IN PART AND REVERSED IN PART.]

WILCOX, JUSTICE, dissenting.

It is often said that bad facts make bad law. Today's decision epitomizes that
ancient legal axiom. The end result of the majority opinion is that the defendants, lead pigment manufacturers, can be held liable for a product they may
or may not have produced, which may or may not have caused the plaintiff's
injuries, based on conduct that may have occurred over 100 years ago when
some of the defendants were not even part of the relevant market. Even
though the injury in this case is tragic, the plaintiff cannot demonstrate that
he was lead poisoned as a result of white lead carbonate, much less the type of
white lead carbonate produced by any of the respective defendants. More
importantly, he cannot prove when the supposed white lead carbonate that
allegedly poisoned him was manufactured or applied to the houses in which he
was supposedly lead poisoned. However, none of these facts seem to matter to
the majority.

Subjecting the defendants in this case to liability under these circumstances
amounts to an unwarranted and unprecedented relaxation of the traditional
rules governing tort liability, and raises serious concerns of fundamental fairness, as the defendants will be unable to realistically exculpate themselves.
The majority opinion not only creates the risk that liability may be wholly out
of proportion with the culpability of each individual defendant; it raises a distinct possibility that some defendants may be held liable for an injury they did
not and could not have caused. The majority seems content to run roughshod
over established principles of causation and the rights of each defendant to
present a defense and be judged based on its own actions. The majority's decision renders Wisconsin the only state to apply some form of collective liability
in lead paint suits under similar facts.

While I recognize the validity of the risk-contribution theory of recovery
articulated by this court in *Collins*, under the unique facts of that case, I
wholly disagree with the majority's expansion of that theory to cover the present case . . .

NOTES

1. *Beyond Prescription Drugs.* The *Thomas* case stands alone in applying an
extended causation theory to lead pigments. *Compare Santiago v. Sherwin*

Williams Co., 3 F.3d 546, 550–51 (1st Cir. 1993) (plaintiff unable to prove pigment manufacturers were in the market during the relevant time or portion of damages represented by the pigment manufacturers); *Brenner v. American Cyanamid Co.*, 699 N.Y.S.2d 848, 852–53 (N.Y. App. Div. 1999) ("The inability to identify a narrow time period in which to apply the market share theory, the absence of a fungible product, and the absence of a signature injury are among the reasons that other courts have refused to apply the market share theory in lead poisoning cases.")

Courts have also shown no enthusiasm for extending market-share like theories to other products that lacked fungibility or created different degrees of risk. *See, e.g., In re New York State Silicone Breast Implant Litig.*, 631 N.Y.S.2d 491 (N.Y. Sup. Ct. 1995) (silicone breast implants; *DaSilva v. American Tobacco Co.*, 667 N.Y.S.2d 653 (N.Y. Sup. Ct. 1997) (cigarettes); *Black v. Abex Corp.*, 603 N.W.2d 182 (N.D. 1999) (asbestos).

In *Hamilton v. Beretta U.S.A. Corp.*, 96 N.Y.2d 222 (2001), relatives of gunshot victims unsuccessfully sued 49 handgun manufacturers. The court stated:

> We recognize the difficulty in proving precisely which manufacturer caused any particular plaintiff's injuries since crime guns are often not recovered. Inability to locate evidence, however, does not alone justify the extraordinary step of applying market share liability. Rather, a more compelling policy reason — as was shown in the DES cases — is required for the imposition of market share liability.
>
> Notably, courts in New York and other jurisdictions have refused to extend the market share theory where products were not fungible and differing degrees of risk were created. Similarly, plaintiffs here have not shown a set of compelling circumstances akin to those in *Hymowitz* justifying a departure from traditional common-law principles of causation.

Id. at 241–242. Liability for gun manufacturers is also discussed in Chapters 7 and 8.

2. *From Generic to Fungible.* In *Black v. Abex Corp.*, 603 N.W.2d 182 (N.D. 1999), the plaintiff's decedent had worked in the Air Force as an auto mechanic for 15 years before dying of lung cancer. She sued forty-eight asbestos manufacturers, alleging her husband's death had been caused by his occupational exposure to asbestos-containing products. The trial court granted the defendants' motion for summary judgment on her market share claim. The court noted that "Black essentially concedes market share liability is inappropriate in a "shotgun" asbestos case, where the plaintiff is alleging injury from exposure to many different types of asbestos products," but asserts that "market share liability may be appropriate when the plaintiff seeks to hold liable only manufacturers of one type of asbestos-containing product" and that "she should be allowed to proceed in her market share claims against the manufacturers of asbestos-containing 'friction products,' including brake and clutch products." *Black*, 603 N.W. 2d at 186. According to the court:

The dispositive question presented is whether Black has raised a genuine issue of material fact on the issue of fungibility. Market share liability is premised upon the fact that the defendants have produced identical (or virtually identical) defective products which carry equivalent risks of harm. Accordingly, under the market share theory, it is considered equitable to apportion liability based upon the percentage of products each defendant contributed to the entire relevant market.

This reasoning hinges, however, upon each defendant's product carrying an equal degree of risk . . .

Unless the plaintiff can demonstrate that the defendants' products created a "singular risk factor," the balance between the rights of plaintiffs and defendants evaporates and it is no longer fair or equitable to base liability upon each defendant's share of the relevant market. The rationale underlying market share liability, as developed in *Sindell*, is that it did not matter which manufacturer's product the plaintiff's mother actually ingested; because all DES was chemically identical, the same harm would have occurred. Thus, any individual manufacturer's product would have caused the identical injury, and it was through mere fortuity that any one manufacturer did not produce the actual product ingested. Under these circumstances, viewing the overall DES market and all injuries caused thereby, it may be presumed each manufacturer's products will produce a percentage of those injuries roughly equivalent to its percentage of the total DES market . . .

Black failed to present competent, admissible evidence from which a fact finder could determine the "friction products" her husband was exposed to carried equivalent risks of harm and were fungible under *Sindell*. Accordingly, summary judgment was appropriate.

Id. at 189–91.

3. *Unapportionable Fault.* The above cases illustrate the complexities arising when there is a field of potential tortfeasors engaged in similar conduct, such as asbestos manufacturers. If the potential tortfeasors are engaged in dissimilar conduct, however, the problem of apportionment becomes arguably even more difficult, since the plaintiff must first prove which type of conduct caused the harm. In *Martin v. Owens-Corning Fiberglass Corp.*, 528 A.2d 947 (Pa. 1987), the court refused to apportion damages between defendant's asbestos product and plaintiff's smoking, because the evidence did not support such an apportionment. But such an apportionment was made in *Davler v. Raymark Indus., Inc.*, 611 A.2d 136 (N.J. App. Div. 1992), *aff'd* 622 A.2d 1305 (N.J. 1993):

We conclude that there was ample basis in the record of this trial to submit the issue of apportionment to the jury. The extant legal precedent supports rational efforts to apportion responsibility in such circumstances rather than require one party to absorb the entire burden. The jury obviously accepted the epidemiological testimony based on relative risk factors, the smoking history over 45 years, and the substantial occupational exposure over six years. The synergistically resultant disease, lung cancer, was produced by a relative risk factor of 10:1 contributed by plaintiff and 5:1 contributed by defendant. The jury probably shaded the apportionment slightly in defendant's favor, 70% instead of two-thirds, because of the strong emphasis on cigarette smoking as the greatly predominant overall cause of lung cancer in the country.

Id. at 145–46.

4. *"Medical Monitoring" Damages.* In addition to claims for medical expenses, lost wages or earning capacity, pain and suffering, mental anguish, and loss of enjoyment of life, plaintiffs in toxic tort cases may seek other types of damages or make other claims, including fear of developing a disease in the future, increased risk of developing some adverse health condition, and medical monitoring.

Many plaintiffs who are exposed to a toxic substance that might cause some future adverse health consequences seek to recover "medical monitoring" damages — the costs of medical testing and monitoring to determine if the disease has developed. The purpose of medical monitoring is to encourage early detection of the relevant disease, treatment, and minimization of the health risks associated with the disease. Several courts have recognized the claim. *See, e.g., Ayers v. Township of Jackson*, 106 N.J. 557 (1987). There the court said:

> . . . The claim for medical surveillance expenses stands on a different footing from the claim based on enhanced risk. It seeks to recover the cost of periodic medical examinations intended to monitor plaintiffs' health and facilitate early diagnosis and treatment of disease caused by plaintiffs' exposure to toxic chemicals. At trial, competent medical testimony was offered to prove that a program of regular medical testing and evaluation was reasonably necessary and consistent with contemporary scientific principles applied by physicians experienced in the diagnosis and treatment of chemically-induced injuries.

> . . . Recognition of pre-symptom claims for medical surveillance serves other important public interests. The difficulty of proving causation, where the disease is manifested years after exposure, has caused many commentators to suggest that tort law has no capacity to deter polluters, because the costs of proper disposal are often viewed by polluters as exceeding the risk of tort liability. However, permitting recovery for reasonable pre-symptom, medical-surveillance expenses subjects polluters to significant liability when proof of the causal connection between the tortious conduct and the plaintiffs' exposure to chemicals is likely to be most readily available. The availability of a substantial remedy before the consequences of the plaintiffs' exposure are manifest may also have the beneficial effect of preventing or mitigating serious future illnesses and thus reduce the overall costs to the responsible parties.

Other considerations compel recognition of a pre-symptom medical surveillance claim. It is inequitable for an individual, wrongfully exposed to dangerous toxic chemicals but unable to prove that disease is likely, to have to pay his own expenses when medical intervention is

clearly reasonable and necessary. In other contexts, we have intervened to provide compensation for medical expenses even where the
underlying disease was not compensable. In *Procanik v. Cillo,* 97 N.J.
339, 478 A.2d 755 (1984), an action for "wrongful birth," we allowed
compensation for medical expenses but disallowed the claims for pain
and suffering and for a diminished childhood attributable to birth
defects. In *Schroeder v. Perkel,* 87 N.J. 53, 432 A.2d 834 (1981), we
upheld the claim of parents for incremental medical costs associated
with raising a child who suffered from cystic fibrosis, without recognizing a "wrongful birth" cause of action based on that condition.

. . . In our view, the use of a court-supervised fund to administer medi-
cal-surveillance payments in mass exposure cases, particularly for
claims under the Tort Claims Act, is a highly appropriate exercise of
the Court's equitable powers. *Cf. In re "Agent Orange" Prod. Liab.
Litig.,* 611 F. Supp. 1396 (E.D. N.Y. 1985) at 1402–03 (since "implementation of any distribution plan based on traditional tort principles is
impossible because of a virtual absence of proof of causation," it was
appropriate to consider "alternate methods of distributing [the] settlement fund [that] may be premised on a rationale similar to the cy pres
doctrine of testamentary interpretation.") Such a mechanism offers
significant advantages over a lump-sum verdict. . . . For Tort Claims
Act cases, it provides a method for offsetting a defendant's liability by
payments from collateral sources. Although the parties in this case
sharply dispute the availability of insurance coverage for surveillance-
type costs, a fund could provide a convenient method for establishing
credits in the event insurance benefits were available for some, if not
all, of the plaintiffs.

In addition, a fund would serve to limit the liability of defendants to
the amount of expenses actually incurred. A lump-sum verdict
attempts to estimate future expenses, but cannot predict the amounts
that actually will be expended for medical purposes. Although conventional damage awards do not restrict plaintiffs in the use of money
paid as compensatory damages, mass-exposure toxic-tort cases involve
public interests not present in conventional tort litigation. The public
health interest is served by a fund mechanism that encourages regular
medical monitoring for victims of toxic exposure. Where public entities
are defendants, a limitation of liability to amounts actually expended
for medical surveillance tends to reduce insurance costs and taxes,
objectives consistent with the legislature's admonition to avoid recognition of novel causes of action.

Id. at 591–611.

5. *Causal Perspective.* In Chapter 4 we identified cause-in-fact (which
includes the plaintiff's obligation to identify the responsible defendant) as one
of the key elements of plaintiff's *prima facie* case. Dissenting in *Thomas v.
Mallett,* Justice Wilcox noted:

Our common law used to require a plaintiff to prove four elements in
order to recover under a theory of negligence: duty, breach, causation,

and damages. Throughout the years, this court has essentially eliminated the requirement that a plaintiff prove the second element by
holding that in Wisconsin, everyone owes a duty of reasonable care to
the entire world. Today, the majority proclaims that if a plaintiff is
sympathetic enough and the "industry" of which a defendant was a
part is culpable enough, a plaintiff may dispense with proof of the
third element and recover against a party even though it has not been
shown that the party reasonably could have contributed in some way
to the plaintiff's actual injury. Simply put, the majority opinion
amounts to little more than this court dictating social policy to achieve
a desired result. . . .

285 Wis. 2d at 329–30. Of the Perspectives you encountered in Chapter 1,
which would provide the most support for the decision in *Thomas*? Which
would suggest that the decision was in error?

F. INDIVISIBLE INJURY

PINER v. SUPERIOR COURT
192 Ariz. 182 (1999)

FELDMAN, JUSTICE.

On his way to work on Friday, October 12, 1990, William Piner stopped his
truck to let a pedestrian cross the street. While he was stopped, a car driven
by Billy Jones hit Piner's truck from behind. Police were called to investigate
the incident. Piner waited for the police to finish their investigation before
calling his physician to complain of pain in his neck, upper back, left arm, and
head. The doctor's staff told Piner that the doctor was unavailable but would
call him back later that day. Piner then fixed the broken tail lights on his truck
and went to work.

Later that day, Piner was driving to lunch when the car ahead of him
stopped to let some pedestrians cross the street. Piner stopped and was again
hit from the rear, this time by a vehicle driven by Cynthia Richardson. Feeling
similar pain symptoms after this accident, Piner called his doctor's office and
was again told that the doctor was occupied and would contact him later.

Piner was unable to see his physician until Monday. After examination, the
doctor concluded that Piner suffered a number of injuries as a result of the
collisions. Due to the nature of the injuries, however, neither she nor any other
physician has been able to attribute any particular part of Piner's total injuries to one accident or the other.

Piner filed an action against Jones and Richardson (together "Defendants")
alleging indivisible injuries resulting from the successive impacts. Neither
defendant has asserted that he or she could apportion the particular physical
harm Piner suffered between the separate accidents. Apparently, all parties
agree that both collisions contributed to Piner's total physical injuries.

Piner moved for partial summary judgment, arguing that because his injuries are indivisible, Defendants should be held jointly and severally liable. *See Holtz v. Holder*, 101 Ariz. 247 (1966). According to Piner, in a successive accident, indivisible injury case, defendants have the burden of proving apportionment; if neither defendant can demonstrate what portion of the total damage he or she caused, they should be held jointly and severally liable for the entire amount.

Richardson responded that A.R.S. § 12-2506 abolished the system of joint and several liability, leaving only two exceptions in which the doctrine can still be invoked. *See* A.R.S. § 12-2506(D) and (F). Richardson concluded that because neither exception applied to Piner's claim, "the trier of fact must be directed to either apportion, or deny damages in this case." After hearing oral argument on the motion, the trial judge, in a June 4, 1996 order, denied Piner's motion for "the reasons stated [by] Defendant Richardson. . . ."

We granted review to determine which rule of liability applies to cases in which successive acts of negligence combine to produce separate but indivisible injuries.

Black-letter tort law tells us that as an essential element of the action, the plaintiff must provide evidence that the defendant's conduct caused plaintiff's damage. W. PAGE KEETON ET AL., PROSSER & KEETON ON THE LAW OF TORTS § 41, at 263 (5th ed.1984). A plaintiff's case failed if that plaintiff was unable to establish the damage attributable to a defendant's conduct. *See id.* The law eventually recognized an exception for multiple, culpable actors if the plaintiff, through no fault of his own, was unable to apportion causation for a single injury. In such instances, many courts placed the "burden of proof on the issue of causation [apportionment] upon the . . . defendants. . . . [This] seems a very desirable solution where negligence on the part of both defendants is clear, and it is only the issue of causation which is in doubt, so that the choice must be made between letting a loss due to failure of proof fall upon the innocent plaintiff or the culpable defendants." *Id.* at 271.

The present case involves a somewhat different problem. Instead of producing a single injurious event, Defendants' successive acts of negligence resulted in two injuries yielding an indivisible result. The question nevertheless is causation, a concept that presents a "series of distinct problems, more or less unrelated" but includes "apportionment of damages among causes." *Id.* § 42, at 279.

Differentiating between doctrines involving joint tortfeasors acting in concert and joinder of defendants, Prosser's treatise approaches apportionment of damages as a separate topic. *See id.* §§ 46 and 47, at 322–30. The apportionment question arises not only in successive injury cases but every time the total damage results from multiple causes:

Once it is determined that defendant's conduct has been a cause of some damage suffered by the plaintiff, a further question may arise as to the portion of the total damage sustained which may properly be assigned to the defendant, as distinguished from other causes. The question is primarily not one of the fact of causation, but of the feasibility and practical convenience of splitting up the total harm into separate parts which may be attributed to each of two or more causes. Where a factual basis can be found for some rough practical apportionment, which limits the defendant's liability to that part of the harm of which that defendant's conduct has been a cause in fact, it is likely that the apportionment will be made. Where no such basis can be found, the courts generally hold the defendant for the entire loss, notwithstanding the fact that other causes have contributed to it.

The distinction is one between injuries which are reasonably capable of being separated and injuries which are not.

Id. § 52, at 345; *see also Summers v. Tice*, 199 P.2d 1, 3–4 (1948) (defendants jointly and severally liable for entire damage resulting from independent acts, even though plaintiff could not prove which defendant caused the injury).

The evolution of Arizona law on the subject reflects these common-law principles. In 1928, Arizona recognized joint and several liability as a well-settled rule but one that applied only in cases involving tortious injury brought about by concerted action of two or more tortfeasors. . . .

In *Salt River Valley Water Users' Ass'n v. Cornum*, 49 Ariz. 1, 8 (1937), the negligent conduct of the two defendants was neither concerted nor related in character or time. Thus, the court held that the defendants could not be joined in one action,[1] they were not jointly liable, and the verdict for the plaintiff against one of the defendants for the entire amount of damages was reversed. *Id.* at 9–10. However, if proximate cause had been established, the plaintiff would have been "given the option of deciding against which defendant he would proceed." *Id.* at 10. The effect was to require the plaintiff, on pain of dismissal, to apportion damages caused by separate and independent acts of negligence, even when those acts caused an indivisible injury. The same rule was applied in a successive accident case, *Sweet Milk Co. v. Stanfield*, 353 F.2d 811, 813 (9th Cir. 1965) (applying Arizona law).

White v. Arizona Eastern R. Co., 26 Ariz. 590, 594 (1924), and *Cornum* recognized one exception: when the negligence of different tortfeasors "coincided in time, place, and character," such as "cases involving the negligent operation of colliding instrumentalities," joint and several liability could be applied even though the defendants' actions were not concerted. *Cornum*, 49 Ariz. at 9. When the plaintiff's case fell outside the exception, the plaintiff would have to apportion damage by causation or prove that one of the tortfeasors was the proximate cause of the entire injury. *Id.* at 11. If the plaintiff was unable to do so, the case failed. *Id.*

In 1966, *Holtz* recognized another circumstance in which a plaintiff could be excused from apportioning damages. The facts in *Holtz* are similar to those in both *Sweet Milk* and the present case. Holtz, like Piner, suffered an indivisible injury from separate accidents. We held that the tortfeasors were jointly and severally liable for Holtz's entire damage. Such a result was "desirable as a matter of policy" even though it extended the exception recognized in *White* and *Cornum* to include incidents of successive injury. *Id.*

---

[1] This problem was cured by modern rules of pleading.

To reach this result, *Holtz* actually applied two different rules. First, when the injury was indivisible, even though caused by successive accidents, the plaintiff could assert a claim against all wrongdoers without having the burden of "proving the extent of damage or injury caused by each. . . ." *Id.* at 250. We described this as the "'single indivisible injury' rule." *Id. Holtz* shifted the burden of apportionment to the defendants and gave them incentive to apportion cause by holding each liable for the entire amount of unapportioned damages. Successive tortfeasors are responsible for the entire amount of damages if "their acts occur closely in time and place" and the plaintiff receives successive injuries that "the trier of fact determines to be unapportionable between or among the several tortfeasors." *Id.* at 251. Thus, as in *Summers*, if the plaintiff could not apportion fault between negligent, potential tortfeasors, the burden of apportionment shifted to the tortfeasors.

Holtz's rule on indivisibility of damages necessarily incorporated another: damages were not to be apportioned on the basis of fault. Thus, all defendants were jointly and severally liable for the whole amount of damage. At common law, degrees of fault were never assigned to the parties involved and were unnecessary because they were unrelated to the damages assessed. This rule applied to both contributory negligence and apportionment between tortfeasors. This, of course, was the common law in Arizona — each tortious actor was jointly and severally liable for all of the damage caused by his conduct, even if one was much more at fault than another.

Defendants claim the *Uniform Contribution Among Tortfeasors Act* (UCATA) (§§ 12-2501 to 12-2509) effectively overruled *Holtz* and its progeny, thus requiring the factfinder to apportion damages between multiple actors and making each tortfeasor severally liable only for the portion of damages caused by his conduct. If the plaintiff is unable to provide enough evidence to form a basis for apportionment of damages, then, Defendants argue, the claim must be dismissed. We disagree with this view because UCATA does not require limiting liability by apportioning damages but by apportioning fault.

The Arizona Legislature enacted its first version of UCATA in 1984 . . . These provisions replaced contributory negligence with comparative fault and abolished the rule forbidding contribution between joint tortfeasors. Under this new regime, the factfinder allocated a percentage of fault to each culpable actor. Even though the culpable defendants were still jointly and severally liable for all damages, the legislature established a right of contribution that allowed a defendant held liable for more than his share of fault to recover from the other tortfeasors in proportion to their several contributions of fault. . . . This change was intended to bring about a system in which each tortfeasor would eventually contribute only a portion of damage equal to the percentage of fault attributed to that tortfeasor by the factfinder. But Arizona's negligence law still produced harsh results when one defendant was insolvent, thus leaving the others unable to obtain contribution. *See, e.g., Gehres v. City of Phoenix*, 156 Ariz. 484, 487 (App. 1987). (defendants assigned five percent of fault held jointly and severally liable for one hundred percent of damages).

In response, the Arizona Legislature amended UCATA, abolishing joint liability and replacing it with a system that requires the court to allocate responsibility among all parties who caused the injury, whether or not they are present in the action. . . . Under the present version of UCATA, "the liability of each defendant is several only and not joint." § 12-2506(D). Taken in isolation, this wording tends to support Defendants' argument, but several factors militate against such an interpretation. First, the legislative intent was to cure the *Gehres* "deep pocket" problem of a defendant only minimally at fault yet liable for the full amount of damages. . . .

A second factor is that the old rule conditioned the plaintiff's recovery on the impossible: if unable to divide the indivisible, the plaintiff was denied relief and the culpable parties were relieved of all responsibility. The injustice inherent in this policy has been repeatedly recognized by our courts. . . . We do not believe that when the legislature attempted to eliminate the injustice it perceived in the deep pocket problem, it also intended to reestablish an unfair regime under which an innocent victim is denied any relief because the damages caused by independent wrongdoers result in an indivisible, unapportionable injury.

Most important, the clear text of UCATA does not require that a defendant's liability be limited by apportioning damages, but only by apportioning fault:

> A. In an action for personal injury, property damage or wrongful death, the liability of each defendant for damages is several only and is not joint. . . . Each defendant is liable only for the amount of damages allocated to that defendant in direct proportion to that defendant's percentage of fault. . . . [T]he trier of fact shall multiply the total amount of damages recoverable by the plaintiff by the percentage of each defendant's fault, and that amount is the maximum recoverable against the defendant . . .

> B. In assessing percentages of fault the trier of fact shall consider the fault of all persons who contributed to the alleged injury . . .

> F. (2) "Fault" means an actionable breach of legal duty, act or omission proximately causing or contributing to injury or damages sustained by a person seeking recovery, including negligence in all of its degrees, contributory negligence, assumption of risk, strict liability, breach of express or implied warranty of a product, products liability and misuse, modification or abuse of a product.

§ 12-2506(A), (B), & (F)(2).

Thus, while UCATA requires the plaintiff to prove that a defendant's conduct was a cause of injury, it does not instruct us to limit liability by apportioning damages. Instead, each tortfeasor whose conduct caused injury is severally liable only for a percentage of the total damages recoverable by the plaintiff, the percentage based on each actor's allocated share of fault. § 12-2506(B) & (F)(2).

We conclude, therefore, that the present version of UCATA has left intact the rule of indivisible injury, relieving the plaintiff of apportioning damage according to causal contribution. When the tortious conduct of more than one defendant contributes to one indivisible injury, the entire amount of damage resulting from all contributing causes is the total amount "of damages recoverable by the plaintiff," as that term is used in § 12- 2506(A). The second part of the *Holtz* rule, however, was abrogated by § 12-2506(A). Contrary to the common law and cases such as *Gehres*, the fault of all actors is compared and each defendant is severally liable for damages allocated "in direct proportion to that defendant's percentage of fault." § 12-2506(A). To determine each defendant's liability "the trier of fact shall multiply the total amount of damages recoverable by the plaintiff by the percentage of each defendant's fault, and that amount is the maximum recoverable against the defendant." *Id.*

Thus in an indivisible injury case, the factfinder is to compute the total amount of damage sustained by the plaintiff and the percentage of fault of each tortfeasor. Multiplying the first figure by the second gives the maximum recoverable against each tortfeasor. This result conforms not only with the intent of the legislature and the text of the statute but also with common sense. When damages cannot be apportioned between multiple tortfeasors, there is no reason why those whose conduct produced successive but indivisible injuries should be treated differently from those whose independent conduct caused injury in a single accident. Like our predecessors in *Holtz*, we see no reason to employ a different rule if the injuries occur at once, five minutes apart or, as in the present case, several hours apart. The operative fact is simply that the conduct of each defendant was a cause and the result is indivisible damage.

The interpretation we give the statute also accords with the principles of fairness espoused by modern common law. The RESTATEMENT (SECOND) OF TORTS, for example, requires damages for harm to be apportioned among the various actors whose conduct contributed to the result if the harm is "distinct" or if "there is a reasonable basis for determining the contribution of each cause to a single harm." RESTATEMENT (SECOND) OF TORTS § 433A. The Restatement goes on to provide that the plaintiff has the burden of proving that the conduct of each defendant was a cause of the injury, but when a defendant "seeks to limit his liability on the ground that the harm is capable of apportionment. . . . the burden of proof as to the apportionment is upon each such actor." *Id.* § 433B.

. . . [T]he appropriate method is to have the jurors apportion one hundred percent of the fault for each accident separately. The trial judge would then combine the findings and divide by the number of accidents. Using a case involving two accidents as an example, suppose for the first accident the jurors apportion twenty percent fault to the plaintiff, forty percent to non-party #1, and forty percent to defendant X; for the second accident the jurors apportion fifteen percent fault to the plaintiff, ten percent to non-party #2, seventy percent to defendant Y, and five percent to defendant Z. In calculating the amount for which each party is responsible, the trial judge would simply divide each allocation by two and multiply the figure so obtained by the total, indivisible damage sustained by the plaintiff.

In the hypothetical given, therefore, the plaintiff would be allocated seventeen and one-half percent fault for the two accidents combined, non-party #1 twenty percent, defendant X twenty percent, defendant Y thirty-five percent, non-party #2 five percent, and defendant Z two and one-half percent. Each percentage would then be multiplied by the total of the indivisible damage sustained by plaintiff to produce the amount for which each defendant was liable under § 12-2506(A).[3]

NOTES

1. *Unapportionable Cause.* According to Section 433B(2) of the Second Restatement:

> Where the tortious conduct of two or more actors has combined to bring about harm to the plaintiff, and one or more of the actors seeks to limit his liability on the ground that the harm is capable of apportionment among them, the burden of apportionment is upon each such actor.

Are the principal case and Section 433B(2) different from the two fires problem at issue in *Anderson*? One difference is that we know who the two tortfeasors are in *Piner*. Is that the only difference? If *Anderson* had identified the parties responsible for both fires and sued both, would the case be essentially the same as *Piner*?

2. *Divisible Injuries, Indivisible Injuries, and Joint & Several Liability.* If the cause of the injury is divisible, the plaintiff may recover from each wrongdoer the damages which that wrongdoer caused. Thus if B caused A to suffer a broken leg and C caused A to suffer a broken arm, B would be liable for the leg and C would be liable for the arm. The injuries would be divisible. Unfortunately, as the principal case illustrates, life is not always that simple. What if the jury had found that the second accident did not cause any injury at all, that is, no new injury and no aggravation of an earlier injury flowed from the second tortiuous conduct? Then, the second tortfeasor would not be liable. Alternatively, what if the jury concluded that the second tortfeasor did cause some injury but it cannot apportion the injury between the first tortfeasor and the second tortfeasor. Then the injury is indivisible, and application of the general rule (plaintiff must prove, more probably than not, the damages which he sustained was caused by the particular defendant's wrongful conduct) would have the effect of denying plaintiff recovery from either of the wrongdoers.

Shifting the burden of proving cause in fact from the plaintiff to each defendant has the effect of making each defendant liable for all of the plaintiff's

---

[3] Expressed in numbers, the computation would look like this:

Accident	Plaintiff	Defendant X	Defendant Y	Defendant Z	Non-party #1 & #2	Total
First	20.0	40.0	NA	NA	40.0	100.0
Second	15.0	NA	70.0	5.0	10.0	100.0
Totals for both accidents	35.0	40.0	70.0	5.0	50.0	200.0
Percentage allocation per accident	17.5	20.0	35.0	2.5	25.0	100.0

Thus, if plaintiff's total damages were found to be $10,000, defendant X would be liable for $2,000, defendant Y for $3,500, and defendant Z for $250.

damages. It has the effect of making the defendants jointly and severally liable, which means that the plaintiff can recover 100% of her damages from either faulty defendant. For example, if B and C negligently cause A to suffer a broken back, an indivisible injury, B and C might be jointly and severally liable. A could recover 100% of his damages from B or C (or part from one and the rest from the other).

This hypothetical can be taken a step further, to a jurisdiction that allocates fault between tortfeasors. Assume A is blameless, B is 60% at fault and C is 40% at fault (note that the allocated fault must add up to 100%). Further, assume that A has suffered $100,000 in damages. If the jurisdiction still holds joint tortfeasors jointly and severally liable, A could recover $100,000 from either B or C. If A chose to recover $100,000 from C, most jurisdictions would give C a right of contribution against B to recover the amount C paid in excess of C's allocated share. Here C would be able to recover 60% or $60,000 from B. However, if B is insolvent, C is left "holding the liability bag."

In a jurisdiction that has eliminated joint and several liability, like Arizona, B would be liable for $60,000 and C would be liable for $40,000. If B was insolvent, A would recover $40,000 from C, and A would be denied full compensation.

Is responsibility apportioned between two causal agents on the basis of both causation and fault? If apportionment is made separately for cause and fault, which apportionment comes first — the one based on cause, or the one based on fault? *See, e.g., Watson v. State Farm Fire and Cas. Ins. Co.*, 469 So. 2d 967 (La. 1985), applying the Uniform Comparative Fault Act which provides that a factfinder allocating fault should consider: (1) the causal relationship between a person's conduct and the plaintiff's resulting injuries, and (2) the nature of the conduct. *See also Whitehead v. Toyota Motor Corp.*, 897 S.W.2d 684 (Tenn. 1995).

3. *Crashworthiness and Second Collisions.* In the so called second-collision, or crashworthiness, cases, where one agent causes an accident but a second agent — the defendant's defective product — exacerbates the injury, some courts require the plaintiff to apportion damages between the first and second agent, while others shift the burden of proof of apportionment to the defendant. *See Polston v. Boomershine Pontiac-GMC Truck, Inc.*, 262 Ga. 616 (1992). These cases frequently arise in the automobile collision context, but they may arise in other contexts as well. *See, e.g., Cartell Capital Corp. v. Fireco of New Jersey*, 81 N.J. 548 (1980) (defective fire extinguisher).

If one agent is viewed as exacerbating an injury caused by a prior agent, the prior agent may be liable for the subsequent exacerbation if that exacerbation is proximately caused by the prior agent. *See Futch v. Commercial Union Ins. Co.*, 64 So. 2d 766 (La. App. 1995) ("the duty to refrain from negligent automobile operation encompasses the risk that an accident victim's medical treatment may cause him further damage"). If B negligently causes A to suffer a back injury in an automobile accident and Dr. C, in the course of treating A, commits malpractice that aggravates the injury, traditional legal cause rules held B responsible for Dr. C's malpractice, unless the professional misconduct was unforeseeably reckless. In a several-liability jurisdiction, what would be the result today? Does it matter if the injury is divisible or indivisible?

PROBLEMS

5.1

Mary Martin's 10-year-old son was injured in a "hit and run" accident in which the negligent driver was speeding through a school zone. The next week, Mary observed Jim Jones driving through the same school zone at a speed far in excess of the speed limit. She reported this observation to the local police, who monitored the scene for the next week with radar guns and caught 50 people, including Jim Jones, speeding through the zone. Each person caught speeding was subjected to a monetary fine that was collected by the state. Should they also have to pay for all or part of the injuries sustained by Mary or her son?

Suppose the evidence shows that Jim Jones was in fact the person who hit Mary's son and that, at the time of the accident, Jim was driving 30 mph in a 15 mph zone. However, the accident occurred when Mary's son unexpectedly ran into the path of the car after running from the sidewalk between two parked cars. Should Jim be required to pay for any or all of the damages sustained by Mary or her son?

5.2

A state statute requires that any house constructed after 1985 must be built to withstand winds of up to 100 mph. Defendant built and sold to plaintiff in 1989 a new house that was capable of withstanding winds of up to 75 mph. Two months after plaintiff moved into the house, an extraordinary wind of 125 mph raged through the town, blowing the roof off plaintiff's house. Assuming that defendant was negligent in constructing the house in a manner that failed to meet the requirements of the statute and plaintiff was unaware of this negligence when he purchased the house, was the defendant's negligence the cause in fact of the plaintiff's damages?

5.3

Farmer Brown owns a prize bull that stands a fair chance of winning the first, second, or third prize in the annual state fair competition. The first prize carries a $100,000 cash award, the second $75,000, and the third $50,000. In addition, the first-place winner will receive commercial publicity that will redound to his owner's benefit. Brown's bull, and 19 other bulls were slated to enter the contest.

Brown contracts with Railroad to transport his bull to the state fair. Because of negligent maintenance, Railroad's train is disabled en route to the fair, and as a result Brown's bull misses the competition. Can Brown recover from Railroad? How would he prove his damages?

5.4

XYZ, Inc. is in the business of residential and commercial weed control. XYZ bought almost identical chemical formulations of a certain herbicide from various manufacturers, mixed the herbicides in large vats, and then distributed the mixture to its employees who applied it at XYZ's customers' homes and places of business.

Various XYZ employees and customers have filed suit against all American herbicide manufacturers alleging that as a result of their exposure to herbicide they have developed lung cancer, colon cancer, fear of developing cancer, increased risk of developing cancer, and the need to seek medical monitoring. What issues arise?

5.5

A negligently leaves his car keys in the ignition of his car. B steals the car, using the keys, and flees the scene. Eight blocks away B's hurried driving forces motorist C to leave the roadway and strike a telephone pole which D has negligently located only three feet from the traveled portion of the road. Is D's negligence a cause in fact of C's ensuing injury? Suppose, instead, that B makes his escape but causes a similar injury to E several weeks after, and a thousand miles away from, the scene of the theft. Would A's negligence be a cause in fact of E's injury? If it would be, are you likely as a juror to impose liability upon A for the injury to E? Why?

Chapter 6

LEGAL CAUSE

A. INTRODUCTION

A defendant may have engaged in conduct that falls beneath the requisite standard of care, and that conduct may have been a cause-in-fact of the plaintiff's damage. However, in tort law (and particularly in the case of the tort of negligence) there is another frequently vital consideration: should the defendant be liable to the particular plaintiff for a particular injury that occurred in a particular manner? The question of whether the defendant is liable often turns on the existence of a duty of care, which is a question of law. "The duty element of negligence focuses on whether the defendant's conduct foreseeably created a broader 'zone of risk' that poses a general threat of harm to others." *Goldberg v. Florida Power & Light Co.,* 899 So. 2d 1105, 1110 (Fla. 2005). This chapter examines the ways courts place limitations on liability for fortuitously inflicted damage even when there is no doubt that the defendant's conduct factually caused the damages.

The question of whether a defendant is liable for remote damages is based upon the application of judicial policies to particular factual circumstances. Courts use the concept of the scope of risk as an analytical tool to cut off the defendant's liability in remote damages cases. If the damage suffered bears no relation to the risk created, why should the defendant be liable? MARK LUNNEY & KEN OLIPHANT, TORT LAW: TEXT AND MATERIALS 236 (2003). Thus liability may involve difficult decisions about the closeness of connection between what the defendant did and the injury suffered. One may be liable for the negligence of third parties if such negligence is reasonably foreseeable. If a utility company permits a pole adjacent to the highway to rot away, the company may be liable when a car negligently driven by B strikes the pole and causes injury to B. Third party rescuers may have intervened in some manner and their foreseeable presence can affect defendant's liability. In general, however, defendants are not liable for failing to guard against intentional acts of third parties.

The legal issue may be phrased in terms of whether the defendant owed the particular plaintiff a duty to guard against the particular risk, or it may be conceptualized in terms of the scope of the defendant's duty. Where a defendant's conduct creates a foreseeable risk, within a reasonably foreseeable zone of danger the law generally will recognize a duty placed upon defendant to either lessen the risk or see that sufficient precautions are taken to protect others from the harm. *See Borda v. East Coast Entertainment, Inc.* 2007 WL 601476 (Fla. App. 2007) (reinstating jury verdict in favor of patron injured in a bar fight where there were prior similar melees). The related concept of "limited duty," defining additional policy-related boundaries on liability, is explored in Chapter 7.

An important consideration in the decision to impose liability is fairness to the actor. If he could not have foreseen the particular harm from his conduct, should he be relieved of liability? Suppose X negligently injures Y, a potential NBA draft pick. X is not liable for Y's death if he becomes depressed because the injury deprives him of chance of going pro. A second significant consideration is whether the victim's pre-injury condition or the subsequent action of others that contributed to the victim's harm should "break the chain of causation" and relieve the initial wrongful actor of liability for the damages. The issue is often phrased in terms of whether the subsequent action was a "superseding cause" which relieves the original actor, or is merely an "intervening cause" which does not do so. A defendant is not liable for not foreseeing an unprecedented frost. A defendant is liable if an unusual event is foreseeable. These two considerations highlighted in this paragraph are approached under the rubric of "proximate cause" or "legal cause." "Proximate cause is an act or omission that in a natural and continuous sequence, unbroken by any new independent causes, produces the injury and without which the injury would not have occurred." *Thetford v. City of Clanton,* 605 So. 2d 835, 840 (Ala. 1992). Proximate cause is just as policy-driven as duty but, typically, the jury rather then judge does the line-drawing. The use of duty and proximate cause to limit the defendant's liability will be the focus of this chapter. As the following cases will reflect, these concepts are overlapping and controversial.

B. DIRECT CAUSE OR FORESEEABILITY

IN RE POLEMIS
[1921] 3 K.B. 560 (C.A.)

. . . By a charter party dated February 21, 1917, Messrs. Polemis and Boyazides, the owners of the Greek steamship *Thrasyvoulos* (hereinafter called the owners), chartered the steamship to Furness, Withy & Co., Ltd. (hereinafter called the charterers), for the period of the duration of the war and at charterers' option up to six months afterwards. . . .

The vessel . . . arrived at Casablanca on July 17, and there discharged a portion of her cargo . . . The cargo in No. 1 hold included a considerable quantity of cases of benzine or petrol which had suffered somewhat by handling and/or by rough weather on the voyage, so that there had been some leakage from the tins in the cases into the hold. On July 21 it had become necessary to shift from No. 1 lower hold a number of cases of benzene . . . , and for this purpose the . . . stevedores had placed heavy planks across the forward end of the hatchway in the'tween decks, using it as a platform in the process of transferring the cases from the lower hold to the'tween decks. There were four or five of the . . . shore laborers in the lower hold filling the slings which, when filled, were hove up by means of the winch situated on the upper deck to the'tween decks level of the platform on which some [men] . . . were working. In consequence of the breakage of the case there was a considerable amount of petrol vapor in the hold. In the course of heaving a sling of the cases from the hold the rope by which the sling was being raised or the sling itself came into contact with the boards placed across the forward end of the hatch, causing one of the boards to fall into the lower hold, and the fall was instantaneously followed by a rush of flames from the lower hold, and this resulted eventually in the total destruction of the ship.

The owners contended (so far as material) that the charterers were liable for the loss of the ship; that fire caused by negligence was not an excepted peril; and that the ship was in fact lost by the negligence of the stevedores, who were the charterers' servants, in letting the sling strike the board, knocking it into the hold, and thereby causing a spark which set fire to the petrol vapor and destroyed the ship.

The charterers contended . . . that the danger and/or damage were too remote — i.e., no reasonable man would have foreseen danger and/or damage of this kind resulting from the fall of the board.

The three arbitrators made the following findings of fact . . .

(d) That the fall of the board was caused by the negligence of [those] (other than the winchman) engaged in the work of discharging. . . .

(f) That the causing of the spark could not reasonably have been anticipated from the falling of the board, though some damage to the ship might reasonably have been anticipated. . . .

Subject to the opinion of the Court on any questions of law arising the arbitrators awarded that the owners were entitled to recover from the charterers the before-mentioned sum [of £196,165].

If the Court should be of opinion that the above award was wrong, then the arbitrators awarded that the owners should recover nothing from the charterers. . . .

BANKS, L.J.

. . . In the present case the arbitrators have found as a fact that the falling of the plank was due to the negligence of the defendants' servants. The fire appears to me to have been directly caused by the falling of the plank. Under these circumstances I consider that it is immaterial that the causing of the spark by the falling of the plank could not have been reasonably anticipated. The appellant's junior counsel sought to draw a distinction between the anticipation of the extent of damage resulting from a negligent act, and the anticipation of the type of damage resulting from such an act. He admitted that it could not lie in the mouth of a person whose negligent act had caused damage to say that he could not reasonably have foreseen the extent of the damage, but he contended that the negligent person was entitled to rely upon the fact that he could not reasonably have anticipated the type of damage which resulted from his negligent act. I do not think that the distinction can be admitted. Given the breach of duty which constitutes the negligence, and given the damage as a direct result of that negligence, the anticipations of the person whose negligent act has produced the damage appear to me to be irrelevant. I consider that the damages claimed are not too remote. . . .

For these reasons I think that the appeal fails, and must be dismissed with costs.

NOTES

1. *"Directness."* How does one tell if the defendant directly caused the plaintiff's injuries? Is it directness in terms of time? Space? Is it defined by the absence of any or many intervening causes? Note that Justice Banks in the principal case says "the claimed damages are not too remote. . . ." Remote damages are the opposite of direct damages; thus direct cause equates with liability, and remote cause means no liability. But "direct" and "remote" are merely conclusions. Do those words help one to decide what are sufficient grounds for determining there is no liability?

2. *Doctrinal Simplification.* Does *Polemis* actually espouse a rule of legal cause or does it simplify the negligence tort by collapsing cause in fact and legal cause rules into one? Was this an appropriate "opportunity to cull redundant operational rules"? Nicolas P. Terry, *Collapsing Torts*, 25 CONN. L. REV. 717, 775 (1993).

3. *Directness vs. Foreseeability.* Does *some* risk have to be foreseeable for there to be liability? Isn't foreseeable risk essential to finding the defendant negligent to begin with? The *Polemis* court apparently imposes liability even though the risk that the plank would fall and cause a spark and resulting fire was not foreseeable. Does foreseeability matter at all to the court?

Does *In re Polemis* stand for the proposition that once there is some foreseeable risk of harm that the defendant fails to exercise reasonable care to avoid, then the defendant is liable for any risk or injury that directly results, even though those risks are not foreseeable? Is that good policy? Is it fair to make someone liable for injuries she could not foresee? Will such a rule cause people to be too careful? On the other hand, is it fair to deny an injured plaintiff recovery from a defendant whose negligence was a cause-in-fact of the plaintiff's injuries?

4. *Arguendo.* As the *Polemis* court noted: "The appellant's junior counsel sought to draw a distinction between the anticipation of the extent of damage resulting from a negligent act, and the anticipation of the type of damage resulting from such an act." Can you provide an example of the point counsel was attempting to make?

5. *Legal Cause.* There have been many attempts to explain the intricacies of legal cause. Some approaches have only served to render the subject more opaque. Thus, according to one court:

> The area within which liability is imposed is that which is within the circle of reasonable foreseeability using the original point at which the negligent act was committed or became operative, and hence looking in every direction as the semidiameter of the circle, and those injuries which from this point could or should have been reasonably foreseen as something likely to happen, are within the field of liability, while

those which, although foreseeable, were foreseeable only as remote possibilities, those only slightly probable, are beyond and not within the circle — in all of which time, place and circumstance play their respective and important parts.

The difficulty is not in the rule, but in applying the facts of a particular case, and in determining whether the facts bring the case within the circle, which limits the rule, or whether they fall beyond it . . . [*Mauney v. Gulf Ref. Co.,* 9 So. 2d 780, 781 (Miss. 1942)].

6. *Corrective Justice?* According to Professor (and Judge) Robert E. Keeton, in his book LEGAL CAUSE IN THE LAW OF TORTS 9 (1963): "[a] negligent actor is legally responsible for that harm, and only that harm, of which the negligent aspect of his conduct is a cause in fact." Thus, if one carelessly stores an unlabeled can of poison near a hot stove in a restaurant, the risk is that someone will be poisoned, but not that someone will be injured by an explosion of the can. *Id.* at 3. If the defendant negligently transports dynamite in an unmarked truck, the risk is one of injury by explosion on collision, but not of injury on impact with someone who suddenly darts in front of the truck. *Id.* at 21. To hold the store liable for injury by explosion in the first instance, and the trucker liable for personal injury in the second, would be "unfair" because these injuries were not within the scope of the respective risks created by the actors' negligent conduct.

Do you agree? Are these not foreseeable risks? Why does the question of "fairness" even enter into the picture, since the negligent or careless defendant probably did not think about the risk she was creating in the first place? Alternatively, if she thought about the risk and consciously decided to expose others to it, what is unfair about holding such a callous risk-creator liable for risks that she did not foresee?

OVERSEAS TANKSHIP (U.K.) LTD. v. MORTS DOCK & ENGINEERING CO. (THE WAGON MOUND)
[1961] A.C. 388 (P.C)

. . . The respondents at the relevant time carried on the business of ship-building, ship-repairing and general engineering at Morts Bay, Balmain, in the Port of Sydney. They owned and used for their business the Sheerlegs Wharf, a timber wharf about four hundred feet in length and forty feet wide, where there was a quantity of tools and equipment. In October and November, 1951, a vessel known as the *Corrimal* was moored alongside the wharf and was being refitted by the respondents. Her mast was lying on the wharf and a number of the respondents' employees were working both on it and on the vessel itself, using for this purpose electric and oxy-acetylene welding equipment.

At the same time, the appellants were charterers by demise of *The S.S. Wagon Mound,* an oil-burning vessel which was moored at the Caltex Wharf on the northern shore of the harbour at a distance of about six hundred feet from the Sheerlegs Wharf. She was there from about 9 a.m. on Oct. 29, until

11 a.m. on Oct. 30, 1951, for the purpose of discharging gasoline products and taking in bunkering oil.

During the early hours of Oct. 30, 1951, a large quantity of bunkering oil was, through the carelessness of the appellants' servants, allowed to spill into the bay, and, by 10:30 on the morning of that day, it had spread over a considerable part of the bay, being thickly concentrated in some places and particularly along the foreshore near the respondents' property. The appellants made no attempt to disperse the oil. The *Wagon Mound* unberthed and set sail very shortly after.

When the respondents' works manager became aware of the condition of things in the vicinity of the wharf, he instructed their workmen that no welding or burning was to be carried on until further orders. He inquired of the manager of the Caltex Oil Co., at whose wharf the *Wagon Mound* was then still berthed, whether they could safely continue their operations on the wharf or on the *Corrimal*. The results of this inquiry, coupled with his own belief as to the inflammability of furnace oil in the open, led him to think that the respondents could safely carry on their operations. He gave instructions accordingly, but directed that all safety precautions should be taken to prevent inflammable material falling off the wharf into the oil.

For the remainder of Oct. 30 and until about 2 p.m. on Nov. 1, work was carried on as usual, the condition and congestion of the oil remaining substantially unaltered. But at about that time the oil under or near the wharf was ignited and a fire, fed initially by the oil, spread rapidly and burned with great intensity. The wharf and the *Corrimal* caught fire and considerable damage was done to the wharf and the equipment on it.

The outbreak of fire was due, as the learned judge found, to the fact that there was floating in the oil underneath the wharf a piece of debris on which lay some smoldering cotton waste or rag which had been set on fire by molten metal falling from the wharf; that the cotton waste or rag burst into flames; that the flames from the cotton waste set the floating oil afire either directly or by first setting fire to a wooden pile coated with oil and that, after the floating oil became ignited, the flames spread rapidly over the surface of the oil and quickly developed into a conflagration which severely damaged the wharf. . . .

Viscount Simonds

. . . The trial judge also made the all-important finding, which must be set out in his own words: "The raison d'être of furnace oil is, of course, that it shall burn, but I find the [appellants] did not know and could not reasonably be expected to have known that it was capable of being set afire when spread on water." This finding was reached after a wealth of evidence. . . .

One other finding must be mentioned. The judge held that, apart from damage by fire, the respondents had suffered some damage from the spillage of oil in that it had got on their slipways and congealed on them and interfered with their use of the slips. He said: "The evidence of this damage is slight and no claim for compensation is made in respect of it. Nevertheless it does establish some damage, which may be insignificant in comparison with the magnitude of the damage by fire, but which nevertheless is damage which beyond question was a direct result of the escape of the oil." It is on this footing that their Lordships will consider the question whether the appellants are liable for the fire damage. . . .

It is inevitable that first consideration should be given to the case of *In Re Polemis and Furness, Withy & Co., Ltd* . . . (f)or it was avowedly in deference to that decision and to decisions of the Court of Appeal that followed it that the full court was constrained to decide the present case in favor of the respondents. In doing so, MANNING, J., after a full examination of that case, said:

> To say that the problems, doubts and difficulties which I have expressed above render it difficult for me to apply the decision *In Re Polemis* with any degree of confidence to a particular set of facts would be a grave understatement. I can only express the hope that, if not in this case, then in some other case in the near future, the subject will be pronounced upon by the House of Lords or the Privy Council in terms which, even if beyond my capacity fully to understand, will facilitate for those placed as I am, its everyday application to current problems.

This *cri de coeur* would, in any case, be irresistible, but in the years that have passed since its decision, *Polemis* has been so much discussed and qualified that it cannot claim, as counsel for the respondents urged for it, the status of a decision of such long standing that it should not be reviewed.

. . . There can be no doubt that the decision of the Court of Appeal in *Polemis* plainly asserts that, if the defendant is guilty of negligence, he is responsible for all the consequences, whether reasonably foreseeable or not. The generality of the proposition is, perhaps, qualified by the fact that each of the lords justices refers to the outbreak of fire as the direct result of the negligent act. There is thus introduced the conception that the negligent actor is not responsible for consequences which are not "direct," whatever that may mean. It has to be asked, then, why this conclusion should have been reached. The answer appears to be that it was reached on a consideration of certain authorities, comparatively few in number, that were cited to the court.

. . . The impression that may well be left on the reader of the scores of cases in which liability for negligence has been discussed is that the courts were feeling their way to a coherent body of doctrine, and were at times in grave danger of being led astray by scholastic theories of causation and their ugly and barely intelligible jargon. . . .

Enough has been said to show that the authority of *Polemis* has been severely shaken, though lip-service has from time to time been paid to it. In their Lordships' opinion, it should no longer be regarded as good law. It is not probable that many cases will for that reason have a different result, though it is hoped that the law will be thereby simplified, and that, in some cases at least, palpable injustice will be avoided. For it does not seem consonant with current ideas of justice or morality that, for an act of negligence, however slight or venial, which results in some trivial foreseeable damage, the actor should be liable for all consequences, however unforeseeable and however grave, so long as they can be said to be "direct." It is a principle of civil liability, subject only to qualifications which have no present relevance, that a man must be considered to be responsible for the probable consequences of his act. To demand more of him is too harsh a rule, to demand less is to ignore that civilized order requires the observance of a minimum standard of behavior.

This concept applied to the slowly developing law of negligence has led to a great variety of expressions which can, as it appears to their Lordships, be harmonized with little difficulty with the single exception of the so-called rule in *Polemis*. For, if it is asked why a man should be responsible for the natural or necessary or probable consequences of his act (or any other similar description of them), the answer is that it is not because they are natural or necessary or probable, but because, since they have this quality, it is judged, by the standard of the reasonable man, that he ought to have foreseen them. Thus it is that, over and over again, it has happened that, in different judgments in the same case and sometimes in a single judgment, liability for a consequence has been imposed on the ground that it was reasonably foreseeable, or alternatively on the ground that it was natural or necessary or probable. The two grounds have been treated as conterminous, and so they largely are. But, where they are not, the question arises to which the wrong answer was given in *Polemis*. For, if some limitation must be imposed on the consequences for which the negligent actor is to be held responsible — and all are agreed that some limitation there must be — why should that test (reasonable foreseeability) be rejected which, since he is judged by what the reasonable man ought to foresee, corresponds with the common conscience of mankind, and a test (the "direct" consequence) be substituted which leads to nowhere but the never ending and insoluble problems of causation. "The lawyer," said Sir Frederick Pollock, "cannot afford to adventure himself with philosophers in the logical and metaphysical controversies that beset the idea of cause." Yet this is just what he has most unfortunately done and must continue to do if the rule in *Polemis* is to prevail. A conspicuous example occurs when the actor seeks to escape liability on the ground that the "chain of causation" is broken by a "*nova causa*" or "*novus actus interveniens. . . .*"

In the same connection may be mentioned the conclusion to which the full court finally came in the present case. Applying the rule in *Polemis* and holding, therefore, that the unforeseeability of the damage by fire afforded no defence, they went on to consider the remaining question. Was it a "direct" consequence? On this, MANNING, J., said:

> Notwithstanding that, if regard is had separately to each individual occurrence in the chain of events that led to this fire, each occurrence was improbable and, in one sense, improbability was heaped upon improbability, I cannot escape from the conclusion that if the ordinary man in the street had been asked, as a matter of common sense, without any detailed analysis of the circumstances, to state the cause of the fire at Morts Dock, he would unhesitatingly have assigned such cause to spillage of oil by the appellants' employees.

Perhaps he would, and probably he would have added, "I never should have thought it possible." But, with great respect to the full court, this is surely irrelevant, or, if it is relevant, only serves to show that the *Polemis* rule works in a very strange way. After the event even a fool is wise. Yet it is not the hindsight of a fool, but it is the foresight of the reasonable man which alone can determine responsibility. The *Polemis* rule, by substituting "direct" for "reasonably foreseeable" consequence, leads to a conclusion equally illogical and unjust.

. . . It is, no doubt, proper when considering tortious liability for negligence to analyze its elements and to say that the plaintiff must prove a duty owed to him by the defendant, a breach of that duty by the defendant, and consequent damage. But there can be no liability until the damage has been done. It is not the act but the consequences on which tortious liability is founded. Just as (as it has been said) there is no such thing as negligence in the air, so there is no such thing as liability in the air. Suppose an action brought by A for damage caused by the carelessness (a neutral word) of B, for example a fire caused by the careless spillage of oil. It may, of course, become relevant to know what duty B owed to A, but the only liability that is in question is the liability for damage by fire. It is vain to isolate the liability from its context and to say that B is or is not liable, and then to ask for what damage he is liable. For his liability is in respect of that damage and no other. If, as admittedly it is, B's liability (culpability) depends on the reasonable foreseeability of the consequent damage, how is that to be determined except by the foreseeability of the damage which in fact happened — the damage in suit? And, if that damage is unforeseeable so as to displace liability at large, how can the liability be restored so as to make compensation payable?

But, it is said, a different position arises if B's careless act has been shown to be negligent and has caused some foreseeable damage to A. Their Lordships have already observed that to hold B liable for consequences, however unforeseeable, of a careless act, if, but only if, he is at the same time liable for some other damage, however trivial, appears to be neither logical nor just. This becomes more clear if it is supposed that similar unforeseeable damage is suffered by A and C, but other foreseeable damage, for which B is liable, by A only. A system of law which would hold B liable to A but not to C for the similar damage *suffered by each* of them could not easily be defended. Fortunately, the attempt is not necessary. For the same fallacy is at the root of the proposition. It is irrelevant to the question whether B is liable for unforeseeable damage that he is liable for foreseeable damage, as irrelevant as would the fact that he had trespassed on Whiteacre be to the question whether he had trespassed on Blackacre. Again, suppose a claim by A for damage by fire by the careless act of B. Of what relevance is it to that claim that he has another claim arising out of the same careless act? It would surely not prejudice his claim if that other claim failed; it cannot assist it if it succeeds. Each of them rests on its own bottom and will fail if it can be established that the damage could not reasonably be foreseen. . . .

Their Lordships conclude this part of the case with some general observations. They have been concerned primarily to displace the proposition that unforeseeability is irrelevant if damage is "direct." In doing so, they have inevitably insisted that the essential factor in determining liability is whether the damage is of such a kind as the reasonable man should have foreseen. This accords with the general view thus stated by Lord Atkin in *Donoghue v. Stevenson:* "The liability for negligence, whether you style it such or treat it as in other systems as a species of 'culpa,' is no doubt based upon a general public sentiment of moral wrongdoing for which the offender must pay." [1932] A.C. 562, 580. It is a departure from this sovereign principle if liability is made to depend solely on the damage being the "direct" or "natural" consequence of the precedent act. Who knows or can be assumed to know all the processes of nature? But if it would be wrong that a man should be held liable for damage unpredictable by a reasonable man because it was "direct" or "natural," equally it would be wrong that he should escape liability, however "indirect" the damage, if he foresaw or could reasonably foresee the intervening events which led to its being done.

NOTES

1. *Directness Discounted?* Does the "direct cause" test of *In re Polemis* play any role in the test that is adopted in *Wagon Mound (No. 1)*? If not, is the concept of the intervening cause irrelevant? Note that even though the *Wagon Mound (No. 1)* court purports to overrule *Polemis*, the direct cause test retains its vitality in many jurisdictions, and should be kept it in mind as an analytical tool. The prevailing rule by the end of the Twentieth Century in this country is the "foreseeability" test.

2. *Breach and Remoteness of Damage.* REST. 2D TORTS § 284 (1965) defines negligent conduct as "an act which the actor as a reasonable [person] should recognize as involving an unreasonable risk of causing an invasion of an interest of another." What is the relationship between the doctrinal requirement of an unreasonable risk and the *Wagon Mound's* approach to limiting the potential exposure of a defendant?

3. *Foresight and Hindsight.* How does one tell if a risk is foreseeable? After the fact, even a fool is wise. Does that fact mean that the decision-maker must decide what is foreseeable by putting itself in the reasonable person's shoes before the injury, that is, at the time the defendant did whatever it was that the plaintiff alleges was negligent? How does that inquiry relate to the Learned Hand formula for negligence that was discussed in Chapter 4? Does the *Wagon Mound* court hold that the defendant was not negligent? It does not seem to so hold; recall that spilling the oil posed the risk of and caused greasy spillways on plaintiff's dock.

Does the court hold defendant was not negligent vis-à-vis the risk of fire? In saying that the defendant's conduct was not the proximate cause of the fire, isn't the court essentially saying that in relation to fire, the defendant was not negligent? Is that a breach issue?

4. *Decision Maker?* Who decides whether the injuries are direct, remote, foreseeable, or unforeseeable? Is that allocation of decision-making power at issue in *Polemis?* In *Wagon Mound (No. 1)?* Traditionally, proximate cause has been viewed as a decision for the jury in jury trials. However, proximate cause is decided by the trial court by a summary judgment if "there is a total lack of evidence from which the fact-finder may reasonably infer a direct causal relation between the culpable conduct and the resulting injury." *Green v. Alabama Power, Co.,* 597 So. 2d 1325, 1328 (Ala. 1992).

5. *The Importance of Facts and of Strategy.* In a later case, *Overseas Tankship (U.K.) Ltd. v. Miller S.S. Co. Pty., The Wagon Mound (No. 2),* [1967] A.C. 617 (P.C.), involving the same accident, the plaintiffs, owners of neighboring wharves damaged by the fire, *were* permitted to recover. The trial judge made the finding that reasonable persons in the position of the officers of the *Wagon Mound* "would regard furnace oil as very difficult to ignite on water," but that if they had "given attention to the risk of fire from the spillage, they would have regarded it as a possibility, but one which could become an actuality only in very exceptional circumstances."

The court held that the trial judge was in error in finding on these facts that the fire was not reasonably foreseeable. "In *Wagon Mound (No.1)* the [court was] not concerned with degrees of foreseeability because the finding was that the fire was not foreseeable at all." *Miller SS Co. Pty., The Wagon Mound (No. 2),* at 717. Here, the court concluded that the risk was small, but there was no counterbalancing utility in taking the risk:

> In the present case there was no justification whatever for discharging the oil into Sydney Harbour. Not only was it an offence to do so, but also it involved considerable loss financially. If the ship's engineer had thought about the matter, there could have been no question of balancing the advantages and disadvantages. From every point of view, it was both his duty and his interest to stop the discharge immediately.

Id. at 718.

Why do you suppose the plaintiff in *Wagon Mound (No. 1)* failed to adduce evidence of risk? Is this an example of poor preparation of the case? Counsel's strategy? Notably, the plaintiff in the first *Wagon Mound* case was the one who was using the fire-producing welder. In *Wagon Mound (No. 1),* if the plaintiff had emphasized foreseeability, the fact finder may have found plaintiff negligent, which would have barred recovery through contributory negligence. *See generally* Dias, *Trouble on Oiled Waters: Problems of The Wagon Mound (No. 2),* [1967] CAMBRIDGE. L.J. 62.

Even if a court applies the *Wagon Mound (No.1)* foreseeable risk test, there is respectable authority that if a foreseeable risk arises in an unforeseeable manner, there will be liability. For instance, in *Hughes v. Lord Advocate,* [1963] A.C. 837, 845 (H.L.), workers left a hole in the street unguarded, but covered with a tent and surrounded by paraffin-burning lights. An 8-year-old boy entered the tent and knocked over one of the lamps, which fell into the hole causing a freak, violent explosion. The court held that the damage was foreseeable on the basis that there *was* a foreseeable risk of fire, albeit one from contact with a lamp, rather than a fiery explosion. Lord Reid stated: "[A defendant] is liable, although the damage may be a good deal greater in extent than was foreseeable. He can only escape liability if the damage can be regarded as differing in kind from what was foreseeable."

6. *Collapsing "Breach" and "Legal Cause."* Does the "within the risk" approach of *Wagon Mound (No. 1)* simply collapse together the determination whether the defendant acted unreasonably in the face of a foreseeable risk and the legal cause question whether the damage (results) were foreseeable? *See* note 2 following *In Re Polemis, supra.* Recall in that case that Viscount

Simonds thought that it was not "consonant with current ideas of justice or morality that, for an act of negligence, however slight or venial, which results in some trivial foreseeable damage, the actor should be liable for all consequences . . ." and that "a man must be considered to be responsible for the probable consequences of his act. To demand more of him is too harsh a rule . . ." What perspective do you think Viscount Simonds was bringing to the case? Corrective justice, in the sense that requiring compensation for "beyond the risk" harms would exceed the obligation of an actor to make the victim whole for reasonably foreseeable and thus preventable risks that result in injury? Alternatively, did he deny corrective justice by refusing to find liability in a case where the negligent defendant had caused (as a matter of fact) the plaintiff's injuries? Is it easier to explain the case by reference to law and economics, i.e., that imposing liability for such low probability risks would inefficiently over-deter the defendant's conduct? Or that the commercial entities doing business in this locale were in no worse position than the defendant, either regarding the information costs of potential accidents or the cost or availability of insurance? Are there other perspectives that lead to conflicting conclusions about liability?

C.   LEGAL CAUSE, DUTY OR BREACH?

PALSGRAF v. LONG ISLAND RAILROAD CO.
248 N.Y. 339 (1928)

CARDOZO, CHIEF JUSTICE.

Plaintiff was standing on a platform of defendant's railroad after buying a ticket to go to Rockaway Beach. A train stopped at the station, bound for another place. Two men ran forward to catch it. One of the men reached the platform of the car without mishap, though the train was already moving. The other man, carrying a package, jumped aboard the car, but seemed unsteady as if about to fall. A guard on the car, who had held the door open, reached forward to help him in, and another guard on the platform pushed him from behind. In this act, the package was dislodged, and fell upon the rails. It was a package of small size, about fifteen inches long, and was covered by a newspaper. In fact it contained fireworks, but there was nothing in its appearance to give notice of its contents. The fireworks when they fell exploded. The shock of the explosion threw down some scales at the other end of the platform, many feet away. The scales struck the plaintiff, causing injuries for which she sues.

The conduct of the defendant's guard, if a wrong in its relation to the holder of the package, was not a wrong in its relation to the plaintiff, standing far away. Relative to her it was not negligence at all. Nothing in the situation gave notice that the falling package had in it the potency of peril to persons thus removed. Negligence is not actionable unless it involves the invasion of a legally protected interest, the violation of a right. "Proof of negligence in the air, so to speak, will not do. . . ." The plaintiff as she stood upon the platform of the station might claim to be protected against intentional invasion of her bodily security. Such invasion is not charged. She might claim to be protected against unintentional invasion by conduct involving in the thought of reasonable men an unreasonable hazard that such invasion would ensue. These, from the point of view of the law, were the bounds of her immunity, with perhaps some rare exceptions, survivals for the most part of ancient forms of liability, where conduct is held to be at the peril of the actor. If no hazard was apparent to the eye of ordinary vigilance, an act innocent and harmless, at least to outward seeming, with reference to her, did not take to itself the quality of a tort because it happened to be a wrong, though apparently not one involving the risk of bodily insecurity, with reference to someone else. "In every instance, before negligence can be predicated on a given act, back of the act must be sought and found a duty to the individual complaining, the observance of which would have averted or avoided the injury. . . ." The plaintiff sues in her own right for a wrong personal to her, and not as the vicarious beneficiary of a breach of duty to another.

A different conclusion will involve us, and swiftly too, in a maze of contradictions. A guard stumbles over a package which has been left upon a platform. It seems to be a bundle of newspapers. It turns out to be a can of dynamite. To the eye of ordinary vigilance, the bundle is abandoned waste, which may be kicked or trod on with impunity. Is a passenger at the other end of the platform protected by the law against the unsuspected hazard concealed beneath the waste? If not, is the result to be any different, so far as the distant passenger is concerned, when the guard stumbles over a valise which a truckman or a porter has left upon the walk? The passenger far away, if the victim of a wrong at all, has a cause of action, not derivative, but original and primary. His claim to be protected against invasion of his bodily security is neither greater nor less because the act resulting in the invasion is a wrong to another far removed. In this case, the rights that are said to have been violated, the interests said to have been invaded, are not even of the same order. The man was not injured in his person nor even put in danger. The purpose of the act, as well as its effect, was to make his person safe. If there was a wrong to him at all, which may very well be doubted, it was a wrong to a property interest only, the safety of his package. Out of this wrong to property, which threatened injury to nothing else, there has passed, we are told, to the plaintiff by derivation or succession a right of action for the invasion of an interest of another order, the right to bodily security. The diversity of interests emphasizes the futility of the effort to build the plaintiff's right upon the basis of a wrong to some one else. The gain is one of emphasis, for a like result would follow if the interests were the same. Even then, the orbit of the danger as disclosed to the eye of reasonable vigilance would be the orbit of the duty. One who jostles one's neighbor in a crowd does not invade the rights of others standing at the outer fringe when the unintended contact casts a bomb upon the ground. The wrongdoer as to them is the man who carries the bomb, not the one who explodes it without suspicion of the danger. Life will have to be made over, and human nature transformed, before prevision so extravagant can be accepted as the norm of conduct, the customary standard to which behavior must conform.

The argument for the plaintiff is built upon the shifting meanings of such words as "wrong" and "wrongful," and shares their instability. What the plaintiff must show is "a wrong" to herself, *i.e.*, a violation of her own right, and not merely a wrong to some one else, nor conduct "wrongful" because unsocial, but not "a wrong" to any one. We are told that one who drives at reckless speed through a crowded city street is guilty of a negligent act and, therefore, of a wrongful one irrespective of the consequences. Negligent the act is, and wrongful in the sense that it is unsocial, but wrongful and unsocial in relation to other travelers, only because the eye of vigilance perceives the risk of damage. If the same act were to be committed on a speedway or a race course, it would lose its wrongful quality. The risk reasonably to be perceived defines the duty to be obeyed, and risk imports relation; it is risk to another or to others within the range of apprehension. This does not mean, of course, that one who launches a destructive force is always relieved of liability if the force, though known to be destructive, pursues an unexpected path. "It was not necessary that the defendant should have had notice of the particular method in which an accident would occur, if the possibility of an accident was clear to the ordinarily prudent eye. . . ." Some acts, such as shooting, are so imminently dangerous to any one who may come within reach of the missile, however unexpectedly, as to impose a duty of prevision not far from that of an insurer. Even to-day, and much oftener in earlier stages of the law, one acts sometimes at one's peril. Under this head, it may be, fall certain cases of what is known as transferred intent, an act willfully dangerous to A resulting by misadventure in injury to B. These cases aside, wrong is defined in terms of the natural or probable, at least when unintentional. The range of reasonable apprehension is at times a question for the court, and at times, if varying inferences are possible, a question for the jury. Here, by concession, there was nothing in the situation to suggest to the most cautious mind that the parcel wrapped in newspaper would spread wreckage through the station. If the guard had thrown it down knowingly and willfully, he would not have threatened the plaintiff's safety, so far as appearances could warn him. His conduct would not have involved, even then, an unreasonable probability of invasion of her bodily security. Liability can be no greater where the act is inadvertent.

Negligence, like risk, is thus a term of relation. Negligence in the abstract, apart from things related, is surely not a tort, if indeed it is understandable at all. Negligence is not a tort unless it results in the commission of a wrong, and the commission of a wrong imports the violation of a right, in this case, we are told, the right to be protected against interference with one's bodily security. But bodily security is protected, not against all forms of interference or aggression, but only against some. One who seeks redress at law does not make out a cause of action by showing without more that there has been damage to his person. If the harm was not willful, he must show that the act as to him had possibilities of danger so many and apparent as to entitle him to be protected against the doing of it though the harm was unintended. Affront to personality is still the keynote of the wrong. . . .

The law of causation, remote or proximate, is thus foreign to the case before us. The question of liability is always anterior to the question of the measure of the consequences that go with liability. If there is no tort to be redressed, there is no occasion to consider what damage might be recovered if there were a finding of a tort. We may assume, without deciding, that negligence, not at large or in the abstract, but in relation to the plaintiff, would entail liability for any and all consequences, however novel or extraordinary. There is room for argument that a distinction is to be drawn according to the diversity of interests invaded by the act, as where conduct negligent in that it threatens an insignificant invasion of an interest in property results in an unforeseeable invasion of an interest of another order, as, *e.g.*, one of bodily security. Perhaps other distinctions may be necessary. We do not go into the question now. The consequences to be followed must first be rooted in a wrong.

The judgment of the Appellate Division and that of the Trial Term should be reversed, and the complaint dismissed, with costs in all courts.

ANDREWS, JUSTICE, dissenting.

Assisting a passenger to board a train, the defendant's servant negligently knocked a package from his arms. It fell between the platform and the cars. Of its contents the servant knew and could know nothing. A violent explosion followed. The concussion broke some scales standing a considerable distance away. In falling they injured the plaintiff, an intending passenger.

Upon these facts may she recover the damages she has suffered in an action brought against the master? The result we shall reach depends upon our theory as to the nature of negligence. Is it a relative concept — the breach of some duty owing to a particular person or to particular persons? Or where there is an act which unreasonably threatens the safety of others, is the doer liable for all its proximate consequences, even where they result in injury to one who would generally be thought to be outside the radius of danger? This is not a mere dispute as to words. We might not believe that to the average mind the dropping of the bundle would seem to involve the probability of harm to the plaintiff standing many feet away whatever might be the case as to the owner or to one so near as to be likely to be struck by its fall. If, however, we adopt the second hypothesis we have to inquire only as to the relation between cause and effect. We deal in terms of proximate cause, not of negligence. . . .

(W)e are told that "there is no negligence unless there is in the particular case a legal duty to take care, and this duty must be one which is owed to the plaintiff himself and not merely to others." (SALMOND, TORTS [6th ed.], 24.) This, I think is too narrow a conception. Where there is the unreasonable act, and some right that may be affected there is negligence whether damage does or does not result. That is immaterial. Should we drive down Broadway at a reckless speed, we are negligent whether we strike an approaching car or miss it by an inch. The act itself is wrongful. It is a wrong not only to those who happen to be within the radius of danger but to all who might have been there — a wrong to the public at large. Such is the language of the street. Such the language of the courts when speaking of contributory negligence. Such again and again their language in speaking of the duty of some defendant and discussing proximate cause in cases where such a discussion is wholly irrelevant on any other theory. As was said by Mr. Justice Holmes many years ago, "[T]he measure of the defendant's duty in determining whether a wrong has been committed is one thing, the measure of liability when a wrong has been committed is another." (*Spade v. Lynn & B. R.R. Co.,* 172 Mass. 488 (1899)). Due care is a duty imposed on each one of us to protect society from unnecessary danger, not to protect A, B or C alone. It may well be that there is no such thing as negligence in the abstract. "Proof of negligence in the air, so to speak, will not do." In an empty world negligence would not exist. It does involve a relationship between man and his fellows. But not merely a relationship between man and those whom he might reasonably expect his act would injure. Rather, a relationship between him and those whom he does in fact injure. If his act has a tendency to harm some one, it harms him a mile away as surely as it does those on the scene. We now permit children to recover for the negligent killing of the father. It was never prevented on the theory that no duty was owing to them. A husband may be compensated for the loss of his wife's services. To say that the wrongdoer was negligent as to the husband as well as to the wife is merely an attempt to fit facts to theory. An insurance company paying a fire loss recovers its payment of the negligent incendiary. We speak of subrogation — of suing in the right of the insured. Behind the cloud of words is the fact they hide, that the act, wrongful as to the insured, has also injured the company. Even if it be true that the fault of father, wife or insured will prevent recovery, it is because we consider the original negligence not the proximate cause of the injury.

In the well-known *Polemis* case [1921] 3 K.B. 560, SCRUTTON, L. J., said that the dropping of a plank was negligent for it might injure "workman or cargo or ship." Because of this possibility the owner of the vessel was to be made good for his loss. The act being wrongful the doer was liable for its proximate results. Criticized and explained as this statement may have been, I think it states the law as it should be and as it is.

The proposition is this. Every one owes to the world at large the duty of refraining from those acts that may unreasonably threaten the safety of others. Such an act occurs. Not only is he wronged to whom harm might reasonably be expected to result, but he also who is in fact injured, even if he be outside what would generally be thought the danger zone. There needs be duty due the one complaining but this is not a duty to a particular individual because as to him harm might be expected. Harm to some one being the natural result of the act, not only that one alone, but all those in fact injured may complain. We have never, I think, held otherwise. . . . Unreasonable risk being taken, its consequences are not confined to those who might probably be hurt. . . .

The right to recover damages rests on additional considerations. The plaintiff's rights must be injured, and this injury must be caused by the negligence. We build a dam, but are negligent as to its foundations. Breaking, it injures property downstream. We are not liable if all this happened because of some reason other than the insecure foundation. But when injuries do result from our unlawful act we are liable for the consequences. It does not matter that they are unusual, unexpected, unforeseen and unforeseeable. But there is one limitation. The damages must be so connected with the negligence that the latter may be said to be the proximate cause of the former.

These two words have never been given an inclusive definition. What is a cause in a legal sense, still more what is a proximate cause, depends in each case upon many considerations, as does the existence of negligence itself. Any philosophical doctrine of causation does not help us. A boy throws a stone into a pond. The ripples spread. The water level rises. The history of that pond is altered to all eternity. It will be altered by other causes also. Yet it will be forever the resultant of all causes combined. Each one will have an influence. How great only omniscience can say. You may speak of a chain, or if you please, a net. An analogy is of little aid. Each cause brings about future events. Without each the future would not be the same. Each is proximate in the sense it is essential. But that is not what we mean by the word. Nor on the other hand do we mean sole cause. There is no such thing.

Should analogy be thought helpful, however, I prefer that of a stream. The spring, starting on its journey, is joined by tributary after tributary. The river, reaching the ocean, comes from a hundred sources. No man may say whence any drop of water is derived. Yet for a time distinction may be possible. Into the clear creek, brown swamp water flows from the left. Later, from the right comes water stained by its clay bed. The three may remain for a space, sharply divided. But at last, inevitably no trace of separation remains. They are so commingled that all distinction is lost.

As we have said, we cannot trace the effect of an act to the end, if end there is. Again, however, we may trace it part of the way. . . . An overturned lantern may burn all Chicago. We may follow the fire from the shed to the last building. We rightly say the fire started by the lantern caused its destruction.

A cause, but not the proximate cause. What we do mean by the word "proximate" is, that because of convenience, of public policy, of a rough sense of justice, the law arbitrarily declines to trace a series of events beyond a certain point. This is not logic. It is practical politics. Take our rule as to fires. Sparks from my burning haystack set on fire my house and my neighbor's. I may recover from a negligent railroad. He may not. Yet the wrongful act as directly harmed the one as the other. We may regret that the line was drawn just where it was, but drawn somewhere it had to be. We said the act of the railroad was not the proximate cause of our neighbor's fire. Cause it surely was. The words we used were simply indicative of our notions of public policy. Other courts think differently. But somewhere they reach the point where they cannot say the stream comes from any one source.

Take the illustration given in an unpublished manuscript by a distinguished and helpful writer on the law of torts. A chauffeur negligently collides with another car which is filled with dynamite, although he could not know it. An explosion follows. A, walking on the sidewalk nearby, is killed. B, sitting in a window of a building opposite, is cut by flying glass. C, likewise sitting in a window a block away, is similarly injured. And a further illustration. A nursemaid, ten blocks away, startled by the noise, involuntarily drops a baby from her arms to the walk. We are told that C may not recover while A may. As to B it is a question for court or jury. We will all agree that the baby might not. Because, we are again told, the chauffeur had no reason to believe his conduct involved any risk of injuring either C or the baby. As to them he was not negligent.

But the chauffeur, being negligent in risking the collision, his belief that the scope of the harm he might do would be limited is immaterial. His act unreasonably jeopardized the safety of any one who might be affected by it. C's injury and that of the baby were directly traceable to the collision. Without that, the injury would not have happened. C had the right to sit in his office, secure from such dangers. The baby was entitled to use the sidewalk with reasonable safety.

The true theory is, it seems to me, that the injury to C, if in truth he is to be denied recovery, and the injury to the baby is that their several injuries were not the proximate result of the negligence. And here not what the chauffeur had reason to believe would be the result of his conduct, but what the prudent would foresee, may have a bearing. May have some bearing, for the problem of proximate cause is not to be solved by any one consideration. It is all a question of expediency. There are no fixed rules to govern our judgment. There are simply matters of which we may take account. We have in a somewhat different connection spoken of "the stream of events." We have asked whether that stream was deflected — whether it was forced into new and unexpected channels. This is rather rhetoric than law. There is in truth little to guide us other than common sense.

There are some hints that may help us. The proximate cause, involved as it may be with many other causes, must be, at the least, something without which the event would not happen. The court must ask itself whether there was a natural and continuous sequence between cause and effect. Was the one a substantial factor in producing the other? Was there a direct connection between them, without too many intervening causes? Is the effect of cause on result not too attenuated? Is the cause likely, in the usual judgment of mankind, to produce the result? Or by the exercise of prudent foresight could the result be foreseen? Is the result too remote from the cause, and here we consider remoteness in time and space. Clearly we must so consider, for the greater the distance either in time or space, the more surely do other causes intervene to affect the result. When a lantern is overturned the firing of a shed is a fairly direct consequence. Many things contribute to the spread of the conflagration — the force of the wind, the direction and width of streets, the character of intervening structures, other factors. We draw an uncertain and wavering line, but draw it we must as best we can.

Once again, it is all a question of fair judgment, always keeping in mind the fact that we endeavor to make a rule in each case that will be practical and in keeping with the general understanding of mankind.

Here another question must be answered. In the case supposed it is said, and said correctly, that the chauffeur is liable for the direct effect of the explosion although he had no reason to suppose it would follow a collision. "The fact that the injury occurred in a different manner than that which might have been expected does not prevent the chauffeur's negligence from being in law the cause of the injury." But the natural results of a negligent act — the results which a prudent man would or should foresee — do have a bearing upon the decision as to proximate cause. We have said so repeatedly. What should be foreseen? No human foresight would suggest that a collision itself might injure one a block away. On the contrary, given an explosion, such a possibility might be reasonably expected. I think the direct connection, the foresight of which the courts speak, assumes prevision of the explosion, for the immediate results of which, at least, the chauffeur is responsible.

It may be said this is unjust. Why? In fairness he should make good every injury flowing from his negligence. Not because of tenderness toward him we say he need not answer for all that follows his wrong. We look back to the catastrophe, the fire kindled by the spark, or the explosion. We trace the consequences — not indefinitely, but to a certain point. And to aid us in fixing that point we ask what might ordinarily be expected to follow the fire or the explosion.

This last suggestion is the factor which must determine the case before us. The act upon which defendant's liability rests is knocking an apparently harmless package onto the platform. The act was negligent. For its proximate consequences the defendant is liable. If its contents were broken, to the owner; if it fell upon and crushed a passenger's foot, then to him. If it exploded and injured one in the immediate vicinity, to him also as to A in the illustration. Mrs. Palsgraf was standing some distance away. How far cannot be told from the record — apparently twenty-five or thirty feet. Perhaps less. Except for the explosion, she would not have been injured. We are told by the appellant in his brief "it cannot be denied that the explosion was the direct cause of the plaintiff's injuries." So it was a substantial factor in producing the result — there was here a natural and continuous sequence — direct connection. The only intervening cause was that instead of blowing her to the ground the concussion smashed the weighing machine which in turn fell upon her. There was no remoteness in time, little in space. And surely, given such an explosion as here it needed no great foresight to predict that the natural result would be to injure one on the platform at no greater distance from its scene than was the plaintiff. Just how no one might be able to predict. Whether by flying fragments, by broken glass, by wreckage of machines or structures no one could say. But injury in some form was most probable.

Under these circumstances I cannot say as a matter of law that the plaintiff's injuries were not the proximate result of the negligence. That is all we have before us. The court refused to so charge. No request was made to submit the matter to the jury as a question of fact, even would that have been proper upon the record before us.

The judgment appealed from should be affirmed, with costs.

NOTES

1. *Duty or Proximate Cause?* Justice Cardozo decided that the defendant railroad did not owe a duty to Mrs. Palsgraf to protect her from the risk that caused her injuries. Why did he decide this case on the issue of duty? If the case had been decided on grounds of proximate cause, using *In re Polemis supra,* (which the dissent says was the controlling rule in New York at that time) what result? What result if the case had been decided on the basis of foreseeability? *See The Wagon Mound (No. 1), supra.* Justice Andrews thought the critical element was proximate cause, not duty. What was Justice Andrews' test for duty?

It is important to note the significance of the decision whether legal responsibility is resolved on the basis of duty or proximate cause: the judge decides duty as a matter of law and traditionally, at least, the jury decides proximate cause. What guidelines does Cardozo provide us about when the judge should decide the case as a matter of duty and when the jury should decide it? For further insights into the social history as well as an in-depth analysis of the case, see WILLIAM H. MANZ, THE PALSGRAF CASE: COURTS, LAW AND SOCIETY IN 1920s NEW YORK (2005). This decision's analysis of duty and proximate cause is a law school classic. As Manz observes:

> The most immediate question that arises when considering the case from an historical perspective is its apparently bizarre fact pattern, one that has been described as 'the supreme illustration of a freak accident,' 'a law professor's dream,' and 'as improbable as a Rube Goldberg cartoon'. . . . Cardozo's impossible version of the event has proved remarkably resistant to criticism or correction. . . . It might seem that Palsgraf was an unequal struggle between a large and wealthy corporation and a poor working class woman. However, the Long Island Railroad was hardly an invincible, corporate empire. In reality, it was beleaguered on many fronts and highly vulnerable to lawsuits by sympathetic plaintiffs with able legal assistance. Such was the case with Mrs. Palsgraf, who had an experienced attorney with a more impressive legal education than most of the railroad's legal department or outside counsel.

Id. at ix, x.

2. *Cardozo's Opinion.* Under Justice Cardozo's test for determining whether the railroad is responsible for Mrs. Palsgraf's injuries, what must be foreseeable? The plaintiff or the risk or both? The plaintiff and some risk to the plaintiff? If some risk must be foreseeable to the plaintiff, then would Cardozo hold the defendant responsible for all the injuries suffered? If so, how different is his approach from *In re Polemis, supra*? Alternatively, must the particular risk that causes the injury be foreseeable? If so, how different is Cardozo's approach from *Wagon Mound (No. 1, supra)*? Can you answer these questions from his opinion?

3. *How Close Is Near?* Cardozo's majority opinion in *Palsgraf* suggests that a factor in denying recovery was that the plaintiff was a significant distance from the explosion. On petition for rehearing, counsel pointed out that Mrs. Palsgraf was much closer to the explosion than the majority opinion appeared to indicate. In denying the petition, the court said:

> If we assume that the plaintiff was nearer the scene of the explosion than the prevailing opinion would suggest, she was not so near that the injury from a falling package, not known to contain explosives, would be within the range of reasonable prevision. 249 N.Y. at 511.

Under this reasoning she was "not so near" as to permit recovery. Could she have recovered, under the majority opinion, if she had been standing next to the person carrying the fireworks and had been injured by the explosion?

4. *Andrews' Opinion.* What is Justice Andrews' test for responsibility? Or, would it be better to say, what are his *tests* for responsibility? Is this an "everything but kitchen sink" approach, that is, throw in all the tests and make a decision based on "practical politics," not "logic." In particular, focus on his application of the "foreseeable risk" test. Is it the same as the "foreseeable risk" test in *Wagon Mound (No.1)*? Is it the same "foreseeable risk" test Cardozo applies? Is Justice Andrews' "foreseeable risk" test a foresight inquiry? Or is it a hindsight test?

5. *Duty Function.* "[L]egal duties are not discoverable facts of nature, but merely conclusory expressions that, in cases of a particular type, liability should be imposed for damage done." *Tarasoff v. Regents of University of Cal.*, 551 P.2d 334, 342 (Cal. 1976).

The function of the duty concept is to provide a basic filtering device at an early stage in the litigation process. The "duty-no duty" determination arguably applies to whole classes of cases. As such, it should be the least fact-sensitive aspect of the tort of negligence. But that is not true of Justice Cardozo's opinion in *Palsgraf*, is it? His "no duty" determination is rather fact specific.

6. *Judicial Perspectives.* Generations of law students have puzzled over what was or was not proximate or foreseeable after the package of fireworks exploded and why a railroad company should not be responsible for the placing of scales that could not withstand an apparently minor shock. Was the dispute between Justices Cardozo and Andrews less about the particular facts in *Palsgraf* and more about judicial control of the negligence determination? Was Cardozo promoting a new categorical rule — "duty": that judges should decide as a matter of law the threshold question whether a particular class of cases (or fact-pattern) should be processed by the negligence system, while Andrews was content with a less doctrinally structured, more fact-intensive approach, leaving to the jury the liability determination in most cases? Consider whether the same argument about whether to assess liability in terms of a categorical or fact-intensive inquiry resurfaces in the *Bigbee* case that follows, *infra*. How would you assess the categorical approach from a corrective justice or critical race perspective? Would a law and economics theorist embrace a fact-intensive or categorical approach?

LINDSEY v. BELL SOUTH TELECOMMUNICATIONS, INC.
943 So. 2d 963 (Fla. App. 2006)

LEWIS, TERRY P., ASSOCIATE JUDGE.

This is an appeal of a final summary judgment entered in favor of the Appellee Hennessy Industries, Inc. ("Hennessy"), the manufacturer of a tire changing machine. The appellants claim that the machine was defective and that the defect was a legal cause of injury to appellant Mark Lindsey. Because there were disputed issues of material fact, we hold that the trial court erred in entering summary judgment.

In his work as a vehicle mechanic, Mark Lindsey used a tire changing machine manufactured by the appellee. The machine worked by using a rim clamp to dismount the tire from the rim as the machine rotated the tire. It was supposed to be able to handle tires with a rim diameter of up to 20 inches.

However, Lindsey had problems using the machine on 19 inch or 19.5 inch tires. Specifically, the machine did not have the power to break the bead on those tires and roll the tire off the rim. The machine would just turn the wheel a few inches and stop. The appellant discovered that by inserting a tire iron in the spoke of the tire to help it along, he could get the machine to rotate and remove the tire from the rim. Lindsey's employer had received complaints from other employees about the difficulty of changing 19 and 19.5 inch tires with the machine, and had received reports that some assistance was needed to help the machine along. The employer did not know of any other employees using a tire iron for this purpose, but he was aware of a vendor doing so.

On May 7, 2001, Lindsey was using the bar to help the tire along when the bar slipped and he almost fell over. He felt a stabbing pain in his low back, filled out a report with his employer and then went to the hospital. He was diagnosed with a herniated disk at L4-5 and L5-S1 and required a laminectomy at two levels. The appellants assert that it was a jury question as to whether this injury was caused by the negligent design or manufacture of the machine. We agree. A trial court order granting summary judgment is reviewed *de novo*. . . .

Hennessy argues that summary judgment was proper for two reasons: (1) appellants presented no record evidence that the product was defective when it was sold; (2) assuming the product was defective, the record evidence established that the injury was not caused by the defect, but was solely attributable to Lindsey's misuse or modification of the machine via the tire iron. As to the first point, there was clearly record evidence to support a conclusion that the machine was defective, i.e., that it would not perform as represented. Hennessy argues, however, that such malfunction could be attributable to a number of factors other than negligent design or manufacture of the product, including improper use of the machine, improper maintenance, or simply worn out parts. That is true, but it misses the point. It was Hennessy's burden, in moving for summary judgment, to conclusively show from the record evidence that the product was not defective. The record evidence did not show conclusively that the defect in the product at the time of injury, as described by the appellant, was not present when it left the control of the manufacturer, and was attributable to some other factor.

Nor can we agree that the record evidence shows conclusively that any negligence on the part of the appellant, i.e., misuse or modification of the product, was the sole legal cause of his injury. Proximate causation consists of both cause in fact and foreseeability. As the Florida Supreme Court has explained:

> The issue of proximate cause is generally a question of fact concerned with "whether and to what extent the defendant's conduct foreseeably and substantially caused the specific injury that actually occurred." This Court has stated that "harm is 'proximate' in a legal sense if prudent human foresight would lead one to expect that similar harm is likely to be substantially caused by the specific act or omission in question.". . .

Goldberg v. Fla. Power & Light Co., 899 So.2d 1105, 1116 (Fla.2005). "[O]ne who is negligent is not absolved of liability when his conduct 'sets in motion' a chain of events resulting in injury to the plaintiff."

. . . .Hennessy argues that Lindsey's action in using the metal bar to help the tire along was an intervening cause of the injury. "A negligent actor . . . is not liable for damages suffered by an injured party 'when some separate force or action is the active and efficient intervening cause' of the injury." *Goldberg*, 899 So. 2d at 1116. It is only when an intervening cause is completely independent of, and not in any way set in motion by, the tortfeasor's negligence, however, that the intervening cause will relieve a tortfeasor from liability. . . .

The key question is one of foreseeability. As the Florida Supreme Court in *Goldberg* stated:

> The proper question is whether the individual's conduct is "so unusual, extraordinary or bizarre (i.e., so 'unforeseeable') that the policy of the law will relieve the [defendant] of any liability for negligently creating this dangerous situation." 899 So. 2d at 1116.

The circumstances under which a court may resolve proximate cause as a matter of law are extremely limited. If reasonable people could differ as to whether the facts establish proximate causation (i.e., whether the specific injury was genuinely foreseeable or an improbable freak occurrence), the issue must be left to the fact finder. . . . This is not one of those rare cases where only one reasonable inference is possible. A jury could easily find that Lindsey's actions were set in motion by Hennessy's negligence and were not any sort of bizarre or freakish reaction to the stalling of the machine. Accordingly, the final summary judgment is reversed and the case remanded for further proceedings consistent with this opinion. [REVERSED AND REMANDED].

NOTES

1. *Proximate Cause is Policy-Driven.* Proximate cause, like duty, is often a rule of exclusion that cuts off the defendant's liability where the injury inflicted is "so unusual, extraordinary or bizarre (i.e., so 'unforeseeable') that the policy of the law will relieve the [defendant] of any liability for negligently creating this dangerous situation." *Goldberg v. Florida Power & Light Co,* 899 So. 2d 1105, 1116 (Fla. 2005).

Courts require that a plaintiff prove that the defendant's negligence is both the direct and proximate cause of their injury. The proximity in the concept of proximate cause refers to the degree of closeness between the defendant's negligence and the plaintiff's injury. The concept of proximate cause gives the jury the power to exclude liability by placing limits on the defendant's liability even where the cause in fact is clear.

2. *Recurrent Proximate Cause Fact Patterns.* Certain fact patterns recur so frequently that the courts have forged specific proximate cause rules. The "thin skull" rule, discussed *infra,* makes a defendant liable for even unusual physical injuries. Courts will not cut off liability because a "defendant takes his victim as he finds him." Similarly, courts will hold a defendant accountable for injuries suffered when a plaintiff is attempting to escape from danger caused by the defendant. Courts will extend the duty to include rescuers under the doctrine of danger invites rescue. Another common proximate cause scenario is if X leaves the key in the ignition of a car and a teenager steals it running down Y. Y is liable to Y in this key in the ignition scenario in the majority of jurisdictions.

3. *The Tension Between Judge and Jury in Cutting Off Liability.* "Should the judge decide whether there is a duty in the particular case before the court (Cardozo's position), or should the jury decide the scope of liability in a particular case when it decides proximate cause (Andrews's position)?" Thomas C. Galligan, *U.S. Supreme Court Tort Reform: Limiting State Power to Articulate and Develop Tort Law — Defamation, Preemption, and Punitive Damages,* 74 U. Cin. L. Rev. 1189, 1199 (2006). Should the judge or the jury make the decision to cut off the defendant's liability? Is there a tension between the role of judge and jury in determining duty and proximate cause? Consider the effects of this allocation of decision-making power in light of the Perspectives found in Chapter 1.

BIGBEE v. PACIFIC TELEPHONE & TELEGRAPH CO.
34 Cal. 3d 49 (1983)

Bird, Chief Justice.

On November 2, 1974 . . . at approximately 12:20 a.m., plaintiff was standing in a public telephone booth located in the parking lot of a liquor store on Century Boulevard in Inglewood, California. Roberts, who was intoxicated, was driving east along Century Boulevard. She lost control of her car and veered off the street into the parking lot, crashing into the booth in which plaintiff was standing.

Plaintiff saw Roberts' car coming toward him and realized that it would hit the telephone booth. He attempted to flee but was unable to do so. According to the allegations of the complaint, the telephone booth was so defective in design and/or manufacture, or so negligently installed or maintained that the door to the booth "jammed and stuck, trapping" plaintiff inside. Had the door operated freely, [plaintiff] averred, he would have been able to escape and would not have suffered injury.

Additionally, plaintiff alleged that the telephone booth was negligently located in that it was placed too close to Century Boulevard, where "traffic . . . traveling easterly, generally and habitually speeded in excess of the posted speed limit," thereby creating an unreasonable risk of harm to anyone who used the telephone booth.

. . . [D]efendants argued that they had no duty to protect phone booth users from the risk encountered by plaintiff — a car veering off the street and crashing into the phone booth — since that risk was unforeseeable as a matter of law. For the same reason, they maintained that Roberts' intervening negligent driving constituted a "superseding cause" of plaintiff's injuries. Therefore, no act or omission of [defendants] could be found to be a proximate cause of those injuries.

[Defendants established that] the phone booth in which plaintiff was standing when injured was one of two booths located in the parking lot of the

Fortune Liquor Store. The booths were situated close to the front wall of the store, between the front door and the sidewalk bordering Century Boulevard, near an entrance to the parking lot. Plaintiff occupied the booth nearest the street, 15 feet to the south of the curb line of Century Boulevard, . . . [and also] Roberts may have been speeding when she lost control of her car. In the opinion of defendants' expert witness, her car was traveling at a speed of 30 to 35 miles per hour when it struck the phone booth. . . .

. . . [P]laintiff introduced declarations which established that this accident was not the first one involving a phone booth at this particular location. On February 13, 1973, some 20 months prior to plaintiff's accident, another car struck a phone booth in this same location. Following this previous accident, defendants placed three steel "bumper posts" between the phone booths and the parking lot. No such posts were placed between the booths and Century Boulevard.

In addition, plaintiff introduced a telephone company manual which states that telephone booth doors, when operating normally, "should open with a slight pull on the handle. . . ."

At the hearing on the motion [to dismiss] . . . the court granted the motion and entered a judgment of dismissal. This appeal by the plaintiff followed.

Defendants contend that their duty to use due care in the location, installation, and maintenance of telephone booths does not extend to the risk encountered by plaintiff and that neither their alleged negligence in carrying out these activities nor any defect in the booth was a proximate cause of plaintiff's injuries. These contentions present the same issue in different guises. Each involves this question — was the risk that a car might crash into the phone booth and injure plaintiff reasonably foreseeable in this case? . . .

Ordinarily, foreseeability is a question of fact for the jury. (*Weirum v. RKO General, Inc.,* 15 Cal. 3d 40, 46 (1975)).

. . . Turning to the merits of this case, the question presented is a relatively simple one. Is there room for a reasonable difference of opinion as to whether the risk that a car might crash into the phone booth and injure an individual inside was reasonably foreseeable under the circumstances set forth above?

In pursuing this inquiry, it is well to remember that "foreseeability is not to be measured by what is more probable than not, but includes whatever is likely enough in the setting of modern life that a reasonably thoughtful (person) would take account of it in guiding practical conduct." . . . One may be held accountable for creating even "the risk of a slight possibility of injury if a reasonably prudent (person) would not do so." . . . Moreover, it is settled that what is required to be foreseeable is the general character of the event or harm — *e.g.,* being struck by a car while standing in a phone booth — not its precise nature or manner of occurrence.

Here, defendants placed a telephone booth, which was difficult to exit, in a parking lot 15 feet from the side of a major thoroughfare and near a driveway. Under these circumstances, this court cannot conclude as a matter of law that it was unforeseeable that the booth might be struck by a car and cause serious injury to a person trapped within. A jury could reasonably conclude that this risk was foreseeable. . . . This is particularly true where, as here, there is evidence that a booth at this same location had previously been struck.

Indeed, in light of the circumstances of modern life, it seems evident that a jury could reasonably find that defendants should have foreseen the possibility of the very accident which actually occurred here. Swift traffic on a major thoroughfare late at night is to be expected. Regrettably, so too are intoxicated drivers. . . . Moreover, it is not uncommon for speeding and/or intoxicated drivers to lose control of their cars and crash into poles, buildings or whatever else may be standing alongside the road they travel — no matter how straight and level that road may be.

Where a telephone booth, which is difficult to exit, is placed 15 feet from such a thoroughfare, the risk that it might be struck by a car veering off the street, thereby causing injury to a person trapped within, cannot be said to be unforeseeable as a matter of law.

It is of no consequence that the harm to plaintiff came about through the negligent or reckless acts of Roberts. "If the likelihood that a third person may act in a particular manner is the hazard or one of the hazards which makes the actor negligent, such an act whether innocent, negligent, intentionally tortious, or criminal does not prevent the actor from being liable for harm caused thereby." (RESTATEMENT (SECOND) OF TORTS, § 449.) Here, the risk that a car might hit the telephone booth could be found to constitute one of the hazards to which plaintiff was exposed.

. . . Considering the case law and the circumstances of this case, this court cannot conclude as a matter of law that injury to plaintiff, inflicted by negligent or reckless third party drivers, was unforeseeable. . . .

This is not to say, of course, that defendants are liable for plaintiff's injury. This court decides only that this question is one that should be reserved for a jury.

Reversed and remanded.

KRONINGER, JUSTICE, concurring in part and dissenting in part.

. . . Whether a duty of care is owed in any particular instance is a question of law and "is the court's 'expression of the sum total of those considerations of policy which lead the law to say that the particular plaintiff is entitled to protection.'" (*Weirum v. RKO General, Inc.* 15 Cal. 3d 40, 46 (1975)) There are a number of such considerations; "the major ones are the foreseeability of harm to plaintiff, the degree of certainty that the plaintiff suffered injury, the closeness of the connection between the defendant's conduct and the injury suffered, the moral blame attached to the defendant's conduct, the policy of preventing future harm, the extent of the burden to the defendant and consequences to the community of imposing a duty to exercise care with resulting liability for breach, and the availability, cost, and prevalence of insurance for the risk involved." (*Rowland v. Christian* 69 Cal. 2d 108, 113 (1968)) Thus, foreseeability is but one of many considerations in weighing the question of whether a duty should be found to exist. . . .

The location of the telephone booth here, 15 feet from the curb, beside a straight and level roadway, and adjacent to a building, provided, if anything, more protection from the risk of curb-jumping automobiles than the adjacent sidewalk itself. To hold that defendants could be found liable for locating the booth where they did is tantamount to holding that one may be found negligent whenever he conducts everyday activities on or adjacent to the public sidewalk. It will go far toward making all roadside businesses insurers of safety from wayward travelers.

There is no suggestion of anything defendants might reasonably have done differently with respect to siting except simply not to maintain a telephone booth in the vicinity at all. Public telephones have, in fact, long been maintained adjacent to streets and highways for the convenience of the public, despite the obvious but remote risks. But "virtually every act involves some conceivable danger. Liability is imposed only if the risk of harm resulting from the act is deemed unreasonable — *i.e.*, if the gravity and likelihood of the danger outweigh the utility of the conduct involved." (*Weirum v. RKO General, Inc., supra,* at 47). Balancing the gravity and likelihood of danger against the usefulness of conveniently located public telephones, and applying each of the other "considerations" enumerated in *Rowland, supra,* I would opt for encouraging their continued maintenance adjacent to streets and highways, and would hold that on the present facts there arose no duty which could impose liability based on location of the booth.

. . . It does not follow, however, that defendants might not be found liable for injury resulting from defective maintenance. The sticky door, if it existed, increased plaintiff's danger by frustrating effective use of his own self-protective faculties. Needlessly to increase the usual risks could be found negligent by the jury. The risk of a sidewalk-jumping car is a risk a pedestrian might seek to avoid by getting out of the way. Such an occurrence could be deemed not to supersede but to concur with negligently impeding plaintiff's freedom to take protective action. The judgment is properly reversed on that question.

NOTES

1. *Duty, Duty/Risk, and Foreseeability.* Although the concept of duty was not part of the early English common law of torts, it has become an essential element in all negligence cases. Properly defined, duty is the legal obligation owed by defendant to plaintiff to conform to a "reasonable person" standard of care for the protection against unreasonable risks of harm. A risk is unreasonable and gives rise to a duty to act with due care if the foreseeable probability and gravity of harm posed by defendant's conduct outweigh the burden upon defendant to engage in alternative conduct that would have prevented the harm. REST. 2D TORTS § 291 (1964) states: "Where an act is one which a reasonable [person] would recognize as involving a risk of harm to another, the risk is unreasonable and the act is negligent if the risk is of such magnitude as to outweigh what the law regards as the utility of the act or of the particular manner in which it is done."

Factors that should be considered in determining whether a risk is an unreasonable one include the foreseeable probability of the harm or injury occurring; the possible magnitude of the potential harm or injury; the importance or social value of the activity engaged in by defendant; the usefulness of the conduct to defendant; the feasibility of alternative, safer conduct and the relative costs and burdens associated with that conduct; the relative usefulness of the safer conduct; and the relative safety of alternative conduct. Stated succinctly, a duty of reasonable care exists if defendant's conduct poses an unreasonable and foreseeable risk of harm to persons or property.

Once it is determined that defendant owed plaintiff a legal obligation to conform to a reasonable person standard of conduct — owed a duty, the question becomes whether defendant failed to exercise reasonable care under the circumstances — or breached that duty. "What the defendant must do, or must not do, is a question of the standard of conduct required to satisfy the duty." PROSSER AND KEETON ON THE LAW OF TORTS, *supra*, at § 356.

Note that some of the factors are very similar to the Learned Hand negligence formula. Is that formula a test for the existence of a duty? Breach? Both?

2. *Duty and Foreseeability.* One of the most confusing aspects of the duty issue involves its apparent reliance on foreseeability as a vital ingredient. In the proximate cause area, foresight is used primarily as a limitation on recoverable damages. However, in the duty context foreseeability is a manipulable cover for a legion of different judicial concerns, including many of the same ones that are at issue in proximate cause and in the determination of breach. *See generally* P. CANE, ATIYAH'S ACCIDENTS, COMPENSATION AND THE LAW, 60–93 (4th ed. 1987); Leon Green, *The Duty Problem in Negligence Cases,* 28 COLUM. L. REV. 1014 (1928); E. Wayne Thode, *Tort Analysis: Duty-Risk v. Proximate Cause and the Rational Allocation of Functions Between Judge and Jury,* 1977 UTAH L. REV. 1. The carefully chosen words of one court may present a useful starting point:

> [A] court's task in determining "duty" is not to decide whether a particular plaintiff's injury was reasonably foreseeable in light of a particular defendant's conduct, but rather to evaluate more generally whether the category of negligent conduct at issue is sufficiently likely to result in the kind of harm experienced that liability may appropriately be imposed on the negligent party.

> The jury, by contrast, considers "foreseeability" in two more focused, fact-specific settings. First, the jury may consider the likelihood or foreseeability of injury in determining whether, in fact, the particular defendant's conduct was negligent in the first place. Second, foreseeability may be relevant to the jury's determination of whether the defendant's negligence was a proximate or legal cause of the plaintiff's injury.

Ballard v. Uribe, 41 Cal. 3d 564, 573 n.6 (1986).

3. *Generalized "No Duty" Determinations.* The "no-duty" argument may be invoked for a variety of reasons, some of which are internal to the torts system, others of which are not. The most famous example of a systemic concern is the so-called "floodgates" argument, perhaps best expressed in the words of Justice Cardozo that we should be sensitive to exposing defendants to "liability in an indeterminate amount for an indeterminate time to an indeterminate class." *Ultramares Corp. v. Touche, Niven & Co.,* 255 N.Y. 170, 179, (1931). What should be the law and economics perspective on such concerns over indeterminacy?

4. *Perspectives of Judge or Jury. Ballard,* note 2, *supra,* and the *Weirum-Rowland* approach used by Justice Kroninger in *Bigbee* are representative of modern approaches to "duty" determinations. How successfully do the *Weirum-Rowland* factors capture the competing perspectives of modern tort law, particularly corrective justice and law and economics? In *Kentucky Fried Chicken of California, Inc. v. Superior Court*, 14 Cal. 4th 814, 927 P.2d 1260, 59 Cal. Rptr. 2d 756 (1997), Kennard, J., remarked:

> The focus of the duty analysis should not be on the details of a defendant's conduct. The pertinent inquiry is whether a defendant must take steps to avoid causing a given type of harm to the victim. . . . *What* steps a defendant must take to avoid the harm is a question of whether the defendant has met the standard of care by acting reasonably under the circumstances; also, it is a question that arises only after a duty has been found to exist. . . .

> There are at least three good reasons why negligence law has allocated the judgment of the reasonableness of a defendant's conduct to the jury as a matter for case-by-case determination, rather than having courts, under the rubric of "duty," establish as a matter of law fixed and unvarying rules of conduct for various categories of human activity. The first reason arises from the irreducible variety of circumstances which may surround an event that causes harm to someone. Because of this variety, an individualized rather than categorical determination of what constitutes reasonable care to avoid a particular type of harm usually will provide a more precise measure of what conduct is reasonable under the circumstances. . . .

> The greater accuracy that results from determining the propriety of the defendant's conduct by application of the reasonable person standard of care advances the economic function of tort law. The reasonable person standard of negligence liability, by asking whether a reasonable person would have taken additional precautions under the circumstances, examines how the risk of harm from the defendant's activity and the benefits of conducting the activity vary depending upon the precautions taken to avoid the harm. . . . In economic terms, it encourages the optimal level of care on the part of both victims and injurers, optimal being defined as the point at which the cost of any additional precautions will be greater than the benefit of avoiding additional injury. . . . An individualized determination of reasonableness increases efficiency because it allows for the optimal level of care to be determined under the circumstances of each case; it asks not whether in general the cost of additional precautions would be greater than the cost of additional injuries but whether, under the specific

circumstances of the case at hand, additional precautions would have been cost effective. (It asks this question, of course, not formally but intuitively by asking whether a reasonable person would have taken additional precautions to avoid the accident.). . . .

There is a second reason why it is preferable to leave the question of what conduct is required under the circumstances to the jury for an individualized determination, rather than attempting to mandate detailed rules of conduct categorically. Doing so allows successive juries to reassess what precautions are reasonable as social, economic, and technological conditions change over time. . . .

The third reason for allocating the determination of the reasonableness of defendant's care to the jury in a negligence case is that the jury, in addition to providing an individualized judgment of defendant's conduct, also has the potential to bring a wider array of practical experience and knowledge to that task than could a single individual such as a judge. . . .

Id. at 1276-9.

What Perspectives set forth in Chapter 1 are captured in this excerpt? Do you agree with their application?

HILL v. YASKIN
75 N.J. 139 (1977)

CLIFFORD, JUSTICE.

Plaintiff William E. Hill, a Camden police officer, was injured on October 8, 1971, when his police car collided with a vehicle which he was pursuing. The vehicle, owned by defendant Judith A. Yaskin, had been stolen the previous day from a parking lot operated by defendant Camden Parking Services, Inc. (Camden Parking). Suit was commenced against Yaskin and Camden Parking bottomed on the admitted fact that the ignition key had been left in the vehicle while it was parked in the lot. Specifically, the Complaint charged that defendant Yaskin "so negligently and carelessly allowed her motor vehicle to be . . . unattended, so as to allow the unknown driver to take and use the same." As to defendant Camden Parking the charge was that the Yaskin vehicle had been left unattended, with the keys placed in the ignition, on the specific instructions of the lot owner, and that this conduct on the part of Camden Parking constituted negligence.

. . . The trial court granted summary judgment in favor of both defendants and the Appellate Division affirmed. . . .

[Depositions] reveal that on October 7, 1971, defendant Yaskin parked her car in defendant Camden Parking's lot, located in a high crime area, across the street from the building in which she maintained her law office; that although she was a monthly customer, no designated space was reserved for her; and that she was obliged to leave the key in the ignition so the attendant could move it when necessary. We learn further that inasmuch as the lot closed regularly at 5:00 P.M., at which time the attendant departed, any car remaining in the lot at that hour was left with the key under the floor mat or over the visor, with the car doors unlocked. It is to be inferred that this practice was followed on the day in question. When Yaskin went to the lot at about 7:30 or 8:00 P.M., her car was not there and she reported it stolen. The next day plaintiff, while on patrol duty, spotted the car with some youngsters in it. A chase ensued, ending in a collision between the two vehicles.

. . . The depositions also disclose that defendant Yaskin was familiar with the parking routine described above. In addition despite the fact that she had an extra set of keys, she "never thought of" instructing the attendant to lock her vehicle in the event she did not return for it before he departed. The manager of Camden Parking admitted in his deposition that in the past there had been problems with vandalism and theft of cars from this lot. And while Yaskin disputed it, there was testimony indicating that her automobile had previously been stolen from this same lot on at least one prior occasion and perhaps twice before.

. . . While this Court has not yet had occasion to consider the question, there are two decisions of our Appellate Division which are in direct conflict regarding the liability of a person who parks a car on a public street with the key left in the ignition and the car is thereafter stolen and becomes involved in an accident. In *Saracco v. Lyttle,* 11 N.J. Super. 254 (App. Div. 1951), it was held that no jury issue of liability was presented as it was not reasonably to be anticipated that an intermeddler would not only drive the car away but also would later negligently operate it. However, *Zinck v. Whelan,* 120 N.J. Super. 432, 294 A.2d 727 (1972), decided some 21 years later, rejected *Saracco's* rationale and instead held that a jury question of liability was presented where a defendant parked the car overnight, unlocked, with the key left in the ignition and the car was stolen and became involved in an accident.

In the present case, in absolving the car owner of responsibility, the Appellate Division stated that it disagreed with the decision in *Zinck, supra,* and added that it was not convinced that it was fair or just to hold an owner responsible for the consequences of the acts of a car thief. We reverse.

What the issue before us comes down to is whether there was a duty owed to plaintiff by either defendant or both of them. Our approach to this question is taken with an abiding awareness that summary depositions should be upheld only where there exist no issues of material fact, and that all legitimate inferences must be drawn in favor of the party resisting the motion — here, the plaintiff.

In order to ascertain the existence *vel non* of a duty owed by either defendant in the circumstances before us, it is necessary to determine whether or not probable harm to one in the position of this injured plaintiff, a police officer in pursuit of the stolen automobile, should reasonably have been anticipated from defendant's conduct. The issue of foreseeability in this sense must be distinguished from the issue of foreseeability as that concept may be said to relate to the question of whether the specific act or omission of the defendant was such that the ultimate injury to the plaintiff was a reasonably foreseeable result so as to constitute a proximate cause of the injury. Simply put, the distinction is between foreseeability as it affects the duty determination and foreseeability as it is sometimes applied to proximate cause, a critical distinction too often (because too easily) overlooked. Professor Leon Green, in his tidy little Rationale of Proximate Cause (1927), characterizing the failure to make this distinction as "unpardonable" and productive of "interminable confusion," gives us a pointed comment from SALMOND, LAW OF TORTS at 144 (6th ed.): "To treat as a question of remoteness what is really a question as to the existence of negligence or other fault is a fertile source of confusion."

The following from a basic text is as good a statement as any of the concept we seek to emphasize — foreseeability as a "duty" determinant:

> The probability of injury by one to the legally protected interest of another is the basis for the law's creation of a duty to avoid such injury, and foresight of harm lies at the foundation of the duty to use care and therefore of negligence. The broad test of negligence is what a reasonably prudent person would foresee and would do in the light of this foresight under the circumstances. Negligence is clearly relative in reference to the knowledge of the risk of injury to be apprehended. The risk reasonably to be perceived defines the duty to be obeyed; it is the risk reasonably within the range of apprehension, of injury to another person, that is taken into account in determining the existence of the duty to exercise care. In other words, damages for an injury resulting from a negligent act of the defendant may be recovered if a reasonably prudent and careful person should have anticipated, under the same or similar circumstances, that injury to the plaintiff or to those in a like situation would probably result. The most common test of negligence, therefore, is whether the consequences of the alleged wrongful act were reasonably to be foreseen as injurious to others coming within the range of such acts.

> Foresight, not hindsight, is the standard by which one's duty of care is to be judged. The existence of actionable negligence depends, not upon what actually happened, but upon what reasonably might have been expected to happen. Negligence must be determined upon the facts as they appeared at the time, and not by a judgment from actual consequences which were not then to be apprehended by a prudent and competent man. What was reasonably to be foreseen is generally a question for the jury. [57 Am. Jur. 2d *Negligence* § 58 (1970)].

This "duty" aspect of foreseeability was concisely set forth by Judge Conford, in the stolen vehicle context, in *Zinck v. Whelan, supra,* wherein he noted:

> [Basically] the key to duty, negligence and proximate cause in the fact pattern under review is the foreseeability *vel non* to a reasonable man of an unreasonably *enhanced hazard,* when a motor vehicle is left unlocked in a public place with key in the ignition, of both the theft or misappropriation of the vehicle and an ensuing mishandling of it by the taker with death, injury or destruction of property of others lawfully using the highways as the result. If there is such foreseeability, then, on principle, particularly in light of the minimal social utility of the causative conduct of the possessor of the car, a duty arises toward the members of the public using the highways, its breach is

negligence, and the injury is the proximate result of the breach, or so a jury should be permitted to find in the generality of cases.

The *Zinck* court fortified its "enhanced hazard" approach by reference to empirical data indicating the danger involved in leaving ignition keys in unattended vehicles. The continuing validity of such data may be recognized by reference to a recent study conducted by the Law Enforcement Assistance Administration [LEAA]. A report entitled *Preliminary Study of the Effectiveness of Auto Anti-Theft Devices* (Nat'l Inst. of Law Enforcement and Crim. Justice, L.E.A.A., U.S. Dept. of Justice 1975) [hereinafter LEAA Study], indicates that in at least 24% of the cases considered, the means used by a thief to mobilize a stolen car was a key. The study's conclusion on this point was that

> a significant number of the stolen and recovered cars involved keys left in the ignition lock or concealed in the car (under a mat or above the sun visor, for example). It would thus appear that owner/operator action may have directly contributed to a very large proportion of these thefts. [*Id.* at 4.]

This same study further concluded that the accident rate for stolen cars is 47 times greater than the rate for the general public.

With this impressive array of statistical information as a backdrop, we have no hesitancy in concluding that summary judgment should not have been entered in favor of either defendant. As to defendant Camden Parking, while we accept the proposition that a lot operator has the right to fix the hours of business, we cannot lose sight of the fact that this lot was located in a high crime area and had experienced a history of vandalism. Under these special circumstances the unreasonably enhanced hazards attendant upon the defendant lot's method of operation are clear. Camden Parking had a duty, which a jury might determine from all the evidence was breached, to protect users of the highways from the action of a thief who uses the keys left in the vehicle to mobilize it and then to operate it in a negligent fashion, resulting in plaintiff's injuries.

. . . A number of alternative protective measures come to mind . . . some of which are assuredly in effect elsewhere. One not too drastic step would be to require owners to return by five o'clock on pain of being locked out of their cars, thus requiring them to carry the usually available extra set of keys. Another would be to provide for a key drop. Neither of these would appear to require expenditure of inordinate sums of money, certainly not when viewed against the very serious dangers sought to be avoided. . . .

As to defendant Yaskin a similar duty should be borne by her as is cast upon the parking lot. It does not appear — not yet, at least, in the present posture of the record — that the likelihood of theft and the subsequent unhappy occurrence was any the less foreseeable by Yaskin than by her codefendant. While it might be quite a different situation had the theft occurred prior to 5:00 P.M., this defendant knew the lot closed at 5:00 P.M., that her vehicle with the keys in it was unattended thereafter, and for aught we know at this point may have been fully aware of the character of the neighborhood. Once we acknowledge *conceptually* the existence of a duty predicated on foreseeability of an increased hazard of theft and subsequent mishandling of an automobile, it should then become the jury's task to determine whether under the facts of this case that duty was violated by defendant Yaskin and her conduct was a substantial causative factor in the plaintiff's injury.

To be more specific, we would anticipate that at some point in the trial defendant Yaskin would be interrogated about her awareness of the unsavory character of the neighborhood in which she parked her vehicle and about her knowledge of any previous acts of vandalism. (Significantly, for our purposes in reviewing the propriety of summary judgment in her favor, there was not one question put to her on depositions regarding these subjects other than those directed to other incidents of theft of her own vehicle.) The trial judge would, at the appropriate time, instruct the jurors that they should consider whatever information might be elicited in response to such questions, together with all other evidence on the subject, including defendant Yaskin's awareness of and acquiescence in the modus operandi of the lot and her possession of an extra set of keys, in determining whether she should have foreseen that her conduct unreasonably enhanced the hazard of theft of her automobile, thus amounting to a breach of her duty. If so, and if plaintiff's injury proximately resulted therefrom, liability would follow. Mere statement of these propositions demonstrates ample room as well for a defendant's verdict.

Finally, it should be acknowledged that our search here is essentially one for desirable policy. In this area, the issue being whether the plaintiff William Hill's injured interest is one which falls within the protection of the rule he invokes, our function is "altogether an excursion into the domain of policy." Or, as put more succinctly by Chief Justice Weintraub, "[whether] a duty exists is ultimately a question of fairness." *Goldberg v. Housing Auth. of Newark,* 38 N.J. 578, 583, 186 A.2d 291 (1962). As we view the matter, there is nothing unfair in requiring defendants to go to trial on the question of whether they should have foreseen that the leaving of Yaskin's automobile unattended under the circumstances recited above unreasonably increased the hazard of its theft and subsequent mishandling — particularly where that hazard could have so easily been substantially reduced, if not entirely eliminated, by resort to the extra set of keys, a minimal burden at worst.

Judgment reversed. The cause is remanded to the Law Division for trial as to both defendants.

SULLIVAN, J., concurring and dissenting.

I am in full agreement with the part of the majority opinion which holds that summary judgment should not have been granted in favor of Camden Parking. Its method of doing business gave rise to the foreseeable risk that a vehicle left in its custody would be stolen and thereafter become involved in an accident. Therefore it had a duty to take reasonable precautions to guard against this risk. Whether it breached that duty was a jury question.

I part company with the majority when it holds that Judith Yaskin, the owner of the car, had a duty similar to that cast upon the parking lot. Legal responsibility for the consequences of leaving car keys in a vehicle depends on the circumstances.

It is one thing to park a car overnight on a public street with the car doors unlocked and the key left in the ignition, *Zinck v. Whelan,* 120 N.J. Super. 432, 294 A.2d 727 (1972); it is something else to park a car in a garage or parking lot and be required by the attendant to leave the car keys in order to facilitate the shifting of vehicles.

The majority apparently bases its holding on the assumption that the car was stolen from the lot after 5:00 P.M. when the attendant left. It suggests that "it might be quite a different situation had the theft occurred prior to 5:00 P.M." In fact, there is no evidence indicating when the car was taken and, in my opinion, it is equally inferable that the theft took place while the attendant was on duty but was moving cars or his attention was otherwise distracted.

Moreover, since the majority's legal position seems to be that the leaving of the key in the car and the foreseeable consequences therefrom give rise to the duty of care which it would impose on the car owner, the presence or absence of an attendant on the lot would not be controlling and would only make the car owner's conduct less negligent or more negligent.

Many parking lots require that the keys be left with the car in order to facilitate the business of the lot. Absent an extreme situation, not here shown, I would hold that a car owner who parks her car in a parking lot and leaves the key in the ignition at the direction of the attendant is not responsible as a matter of law for the consequences flowing from a theft of the car and its operation by the thief. I would hold that the parking lot requirement was the controlling causal factor.

NOTES

1. Restatement (Second) Torts Section 284 defines negligent misfeasance as "an act which the actor as a reasonable [person] should recognize as involving an unreasonable risk of causing an invasion of an interest of another." This concept of liability attaching to the unreasonable running of a foreseeable risk is central to the law of negligence. In any given case the court (informed by the parties' arguments) may view assessment of foreseeable risk as a matter of duty, legal (proximate) cause, or breach of the standard of care. Does that choice matter?

How did the judges in *Hill* characterize the issue? How can that be determined? By looking to see whether the case is viewed as a matter for the court or the jury? By determining whether the court was making a "categorical" or fact-intensive decision?

2. *A Common Law Rule.* In *McClenahan v. Cooley,* 806 S.W.2d 767 (Tenn. 1991), the court observed:

> The question of a vehicle owner's liability for the consequences of an accident caused by a thief, enabled to misappropriate the vehicle through the presence of a key left in the ignition switch by the owner, is a frequently litigated question upon which there is considerable disagreement among the states. Professor Prosser notes that "[t]he opinions have run the gamut of all possible grounds, ranging from no

duty through no lack of reasonable care to no proximate causation. Actually the problem appears to be a very simple one. Leaving a car [with the key in the ignition] certainly creates a foreseeable likelihood that it will be stolen, which endangers the interests of the owner; but is it so likely that the thief, getting away, will drive negligently, that there is any unreasonable risk of harm to anyone else?" PROSSER AND KEETON, THE LAW OF TORTS, § 44, p. 314 (5th ed. 1984). An accurate summary of the jurisprudence nationwide concerning the topic at hand was recently provided by the Supreme Court of New Mexico:

[A] substantial number of courts have not held owners liable for leaving the keys in their unattended vehicles and for the injuries to third persons as a result of the thefts and subsequent negligent operation of those vehicles. Those courts have concluded either that an owner owes no duty to the general public to guard against the risk of a thief's negligent operation of a vehicle in which the owner left his keys; that the theft and subsequent negligence of the thief could not reasonably be foreseen by the owner as a natural or probable consequence of leaving the keys in the ignition of the car; or have concluded that even if the owner was negligent, his actions were not the proximate cause of the injury because the thief's actions constituted an independent, intervening cause.

An emerging group of jurisdictions, on the other hand, have rejected the contention that an intervening criminal act automatically breaks the chain of causation as a matter of law, concluding instead that a reasonable person could foresee a theft of an automobile left unattended with the keys in the ignition and reasonably could foresee the increased risk to the public should the theft occur. In addition, a few courts, including some of those that earlier denied liability, have indicated a willingness to impose liability upon the owner under special circumstances. Courts looking at special circumstances seek to determine whether an owner's conduct enhanced the probability that his car would be stolen and thus increased the hazard to third persons. Considering special circumstances, then, is just another way of examining the degree of foreseeability of injury and whether the owner is subject to a duty to exercise reasonable care.

This Court is of the opinion that the approach taken by the substantial (and growing) number of jurisdictions representing the minority view is the approach that should be taken in Tennessee, in part because principles of common law negligence long established in this state provide a sufficient analytical framework to dispose of cases with fact patterns similar to the one presented in this appeal . . . Our opinions have recognized that proximate causation is the "ultimate issue" in negligence cases. This is particularly true in cases involving the situation where keys are left in the ignition of an unattended vehicle that is subsequently stolen as a result. . . .

[W]e conclude . . . that leaving a key in the ignition of an unattended automobile in an area where the public has access, be it public or private property, could be found by a reasonable jury to be negligent, whether or not a prohibitory statute is involved. The mere fact that an automobile is parked on private property and no statute is violated should not in all cases dictate a determination of absolute non-liability. The basic issue is foreseeability, both as to proximate causation and superseding intervening cause, and that is a question of fact rather than of law upon which reasonable minds can and do differ, at least where the accident has occurred during the flight of the thief relatively close thereto in time and distance. . . .

Id. at

3. *When Deterrence and Efficient Risk Re-Allocation Combine.* Which of the two defendants in *Hill* had the best opportunity to avoid the accident (or this general type of accident) or provide for the efficient spreading of its costs? Does such an analysis explain the different opinions in the majority opinion and in the dissent?

4. *Foreseeablility Revisited.* In *McClenahan v. Cooley, supra,* the court observed that liability can be imposed on a car owner who leaves the keys in the ignition, "at least where the accident has occurred during the flight of the thief relatively close thereto in time and distance." The chain of proximate cause will be considered broken if the thief negligently injures someone with the stolen car several days after the theft. What if the thief negligently injures someone with the car shortly after the theft, because of the thief's general carelessness, and not as a result of fleeing the scene of the theft?

5. *Perspective?* Ms. Yaskin was a lawyer who "never thought of" asking the lot attendant to lock her car. Did either her gender or profession influence the court?

D. SUPERSEDING OR INTERVENING CAUSES

LODGE v. ARETT SALES CORP.
246 Conn. 563 (1998)

CALIHAN, CHIEF JUSTICE.

The dispositive issue in these appeals is whether the defendants, who negligently caused the transmission of a false fire alarm, are liable to firefighters injured during an accident precipitated by the negligent maintenance and failure of the brakes on the responding fire engine. The plaintiffs are two Waterbury firefighters, the representatives of the estates of two Waterbury firefighters, and three of the firefighters' spouses. They brought this action against three defendants — Baker Protective Services, Inc., Wells Fargo Alarm Services Division (Wells Fargo), Arett Sales Corporation (Arett), and Advanced Automatic Sprinkler Protection Systems, Inc. (Advanced). The plaintiffs alleged that the defendants negligently caused the transmission of a false fire alarm to which the plaintiffs responded. They allege further that, while they were responding to the false alarm, the brakes of their fire engine failed, causing the engine to strike a tree. As a result of the collision, two firefighters died and the surviving plaintiffs suffered serious injuries. The jury returned a verdict against the defendants in favor of the plaintiffs in excess of $4.4 million. The defendants appealed from the judgment of the trial court to the Appellate Court, and we transferred the appeal to this court . . .

The plaintiffs, as employees of the city of Waterbury, were subject to workers' compensation law and received benefits pursuant to the Workers' Compensation Act. . . . Consequently, they have no cause of action against the city for negligence for allowing the brakes to fail. . . . The plaintiffs brought this action against Arett, Advanced and Wells Fargo seeking to hold them liable for the full extent of the plaintiffs' harm owing to the negligent transmission of the false alarm to which the plaintiffs were responding when they were killed or injured.

It cannot be disputed that there was adequate evidence from which the jury could have found that the defendants acted negligently in causing and reporting the false alarm, and the defendants concede that if they owed a duty to the plaintiffs, a breach of that duty could have been found. As a threshold matter, therefore, it is necessary to determine whether, as a matter of law, the defendants owed the plaintiffs a duty of care to protect them from the harm that occurred while they were responding to the false alarm. The defendants argue that they cannot be held to have owed a duty to the plaintiffs because the failure of the engine's brakes, which precipitated the collision, is beyond the scope of the reasonably foreseeable risks created by their negligent conduct. The plaintiffs contend, however, that any collision of a fire engine with any object, for any reason, is a foreseeable risk whenever an engine is responding to an emergency, and, therefore, a duty toward them must be imposed on the defendants. . . .

"Our first step in an analysis of whether a duty exists and the extent of the defendant[s'] duty, therefore, is to determine the foreseeability of the plaintiff[s'] injury. . . ." Both the plaintiffs and the defendants agree that to meet the test of foreseeability, the exact nature of the harm suffered need not have been foreseeable, only the "general nature" of the harm. . . . They diverge, however, with respect to the proper interpretation of the permissible level of generality of the harm. The plaintiffs assert that the general nature of the harm at issue is the possibility of a collision of a fire engine occurring while it is responding to an alarm. They would have us conclude that the brake failure is essentially irrelevant to the determination of foreseeability and should be viewed as no more than one of many possible contributing factors.

The defendants, on the other hand, assert that the general nature of the harm is a collision precipitated by the brake failure of the fire engine owing to negligent maintenance by the city of Waterbury. The defendants argue that by employing a foreseeability test that incorporates such a high level of generality to the harm in this case, the plaintiffs have essentially created a strict liability standard. That is, under the plaintiffs' argument, any accident involving a fire engine responding to a negligently transmitted false alarm would be a basis for imposing liability on the initiator of the alarm, irrespective of the direct cause of the accident. Although the defendants concede that there are certain foreseeable risks of accidents that stem from a fire engine responding to a false alarm, they contend that the failure of the engine's brakes introduced a risk not merely of a different degree, but of a different kind for which they reasonably cannot be held liable. The defendants maintain that the brake failure and the resulting collision were not foreseeable consequences of their negligent conduct.

We agree with the defendants that the analysis of foreseeability logically cannot be extended so far that the term "general harm" incorporates any accident involving a fire engine responding to a false alarm with no consideration given to the direct cause of the accident. It is impractical, if not impossible, to separate the question of duty from an analysis of the cause of the harm when the duty is asserted against one who is not the direct cause of the harm. In defining the limits of duty, we have recognized that "[w]hat is relevant . . . is the . . . attenuation between [the defendant's] conduct, on the one hand, and the consequences to and the identity of the plaintiff, on the other hand". . . . Articulated another way, the attenuation between the plaintiffs' harm and the defendants' conduct is nothing more than a determination of whether the harm was a reasonably foreseeable consequence of the defendants' conduct. It is a well established tenet of our tort jurisprudence that "[d]ue care does not require that one guard against eventualities which at best are too remote to be reasonably foreseeable. *See Palsgraf v. Long Island R. Co.*, 248 N.Y. 339, 345 [1928] . . . [A] defendant [is] not required to take precautions against hazards [that are] too remote to be reasonably foreseeable. Due care is always predicated on the existing circumstances." *Roy v. Friedman Equipment Co.*, 147 Conn. 121, 124 (1960). . . .

Inasmuch as virtually all harms, in hindsight, are "literally 'foreseeable'", *RK Constructors, Inc. v. Fusco Corp.*, 231 Conn. at 386, we might conclude that the engine's brake failure technically was foreseeable. It is for this reason that the law has rejected a literal "foreseeability" test as the fulcrum of duty. . . . "[T]he conclusion that a particular injury to a particular plaintiff or class of plaintiffs possibly is foreseeable does not, in itself, create a duty of care. As we . . . stated in *RK Constructors, Inc. v. Fusco Corp.*, 650 A.2d 153: 'Many harms are quite literally "foreseeable," yet for pragmatic reasons, no recovery is allowed . . . A further inquiry must be made, for we recognize that duty is not sacrosanct in itself, but is only an expression of the sum total of those considerations of policy which lead the law to say that the plaintiff is entitled to protection. . . . While it may seem that there should be a remedy for every wrong, this is an ideal limited perforce by the realities of this world. Every injury has ramifying consequences, like the rippling of the waters, without end. The problem for the law is to limit the legal consequences of wrongs to a controllable degree.'" *Waters v. Autuori*, 676 A.2d 357.

We recognize . . . that the issue of foreseeability cannot be neatly compartmentalized and considered wholly separate from the policy issues that are central to our legal determination of duty . . . We focus our decision, therefore, equally on the policy implications of this case rather than strictly upon the foreseeability of the plaintiffs' harm. For the reasons subsequently discussed, we conclude that the defendants owed no duty to the plaintiffs in these circumstances because: (1) the harm was not reasonably foreseeable; and (2) "the fundamental policy of the law, as to whether the defendant[s'] responsibility should extend to such results", *Jaworski v. Kiernan*, 696 A.2d 332, weighs in favor of concluding that there should be no legal responsibility of the defendants to the plaintiffs under the circumstances.

Notwithstanding the retrospective foreseeability of the possibility of the engine's brake failure, we agree with the defendants that the harm suffered by the plaintiffs qualifies under the category of an unforeseeable consequence. Liability may not be imposed merely because it might have been foreseeable that some accident could have occurred; rather, liability attaches only for reasonably foreseeable consequences. . . . We conclude that the brake failure of a negligently maintained fire engine is beyond the scope of the reasonably foreseeable risks created by the transmission of a false alarm and that legal responsibility for the resulting accident should not extend to these defendants. Negligent transmission of a false alarm, by unnecessarily causing an emergency response, does increase the usual road hazards attendant on the operation of an emergency vehicle on the public roadways. Such increased road hazards might include the danger that the driver of the fire engine or the operators of other vehicles might cause accidents as a result of high rates of speed and congested streets. It might be reasonable in some such circumstances to impose liability on the initiator of the false alarm. It cannot reasonably be said, however, that liability for negligently causing a false alarm should include the risk that the emergency vehicle will be negligently maintained and utilized, causing it to experience brake failure. Imposing liability on these defendants for a harm that they reasonably could not be expected to anticipate and over which they had no control would serve no legitimate objective of the law . . .

In every case in which a defendant's negligent conduct may be remotely related to a plaintiff's harm, the courts must draw a line, beyond which the law will not impose legal liability. Although that line is often amorphous and difficult to discern, we conclude that it has been crossed in this case. The possibility that a city would so negligently maintain its vehicles and that firefighters would operate a fire engine, the mechanical soundness of which was clearly in doubt, is sufficiently remote that a reasonable person should not be expected to anticipate such an event. "To hold otherwise would be to convert the imperfect vision of reasonable foreseeability into the perfect vision of hindsight." *Burns v. Gleason Plant Security, Inc.*, 10 Conn.App. 480, 486 (1987) . . . Consequently, we conclude that the defendants owed the plaintiffs no duty to prevent the harm suffered because that harm was not reasonably foreseeable.

In addition, we are persuaded that liability should not attach because of those policy considerations relating to the underlying purposes of tort recovery. "[T]he fundamental policy purposes of the tort compensation system [are] compensation of innocent parties, shifting the loss to responsible parties or distributing it among appropriate entities, and deterrence of wrongful conduct. . . ." *Mendillo v. Board of Education*, 717 A.2d 1177 (1998). . . . An equally compelling function of the tort system is the "'prophylactic' factor of preventing future harm. . . . The courts are concerned not only with compensation of the victim, but with admonition of the wrongdoer". . . . Under the factual circumstances of this case, we conclude that the benefits to be derived from requiring these defendants to compensate the plaintiffs are outweighed by the costs associated with that compensation.

The potential benefit achieved from the imposition of liability in this case is limited to providing recovery for the plaintiffs from one other than the principal tortfeasor. The plaintiffs have already been compensated for their injuries by the city of Waterbury, as their employer, for injuries sustained in the course of their employment. The fact that the plaintiffs' recovery against the defendants would exceed that which would be available as workers' compensation benefits cannot justify the imposition of liability for an accident that was not a reasonably foreseeable consequence of the defendants' negligent conduct. . . . Because firefighters knowingly engage in a dangerous occupation, we have concluded that they are owed only the limited duty owed to licensees by landowners upon whose property they sustain injury in the course of performing their duty. . . . The policies supporting the application of a narrow scope of duty owed by individual landowners to firefighters counsels us to conclude that it would be inappropriate to establish a broad scope of duty owed by these defendants to guard against unforeseen consequences. It would be irrational to conclude that firefighters are owed a greater duty by individual members of the public while they are en route to the scene of an emergency than when they arrive at the scene. The plaintiffs have been compensated for their risk by society as a whole by way of workers' compensation as well as other statutory benefits provided to injured firefighters. . . . To impose additional liability on the defendants under these circumstances would impose an undue burden on individual members of the public. . . .

The plaintiffs assert that the imposition of liability on the defendants is necessary to achieve a stated purpose of tort law, namely, to encourage alarm companies to use due care in the installation and servicing of their products. We are unpersuaded. The nature of remote monitoring virtually guarantees that some false alarms will occur, regardless of the level of care exercised to avoid such events. Alarm companies already have adequate incentives to avoid negligent conduct that causes false alarms in that they may be held liable for the reasonably foreseeable consequences of their negligent conduct. As noted previously, those consequences may include those accidents that normally and naturally occur as a result of a fire engine's operation under emergency conditions. Consequently, alarm companies already have significant incentives to avoid generating false alarms. Imposing liability for unforeseen consequences would not increase their impetus to act with due care.

Moreover, fire departments regularly receive false alarms, and every emergency response entails a substantial risk that harm may result from the emergency conditions that prevail in answering any alarm. It is an unfortunate aspect of the dangerous nature of a firefighter's duty that he or she is subject to a risk of injury in responding to alarms, whether false or legitimate. The imposition of liability under the circumstances presented here would not appreciably reduce that risk given the absence of a direct causal connection between the negligent conduct of generating a false alarm, and the accident owing to the brake failure of a negligently maintained fire engine. The fact that the alarm was false, in itself, did not contribute to the cause of this accident. Had the alarm been legitimate, the brake failure still would have occurred. No degree of care on the part of the defendants could have prevented the brake failure. Admittedly, but for the alarm, the fire engine probably would not have been on the road at the time of the accident. Although actual causation has always been a prerequisite to liability, it has never been sufficient, in and of itself, to justify the imposition of liability. . . .

Imposing liability on these defendants would have the deleterious effect of exempting the party that is primarily responsible for the plaintiffs' harm from all liability. Pursuant to General Statutes § 31-293(a) . . . the city normally would be entitled to recover the full costs of workers' compensation benefits paid to the plaintiffs from any judgment against these defendants. Such exemption would reward the city for the conduct that directly caused this accident by shifting the entire burden of liability to the shoulders of the defendants for their tangential role in initiating the sequence of events that led to the plaintiffs' injuries. The city is in the best position to ensure the safety of the mechanical equipment used by its firefighters. We decline to interpret the defendants' applicable duty so broadly that the city would be insulated from liability for its failure to do so.

Counterbalancing the limited benefit of providing these plaintiffs with greater compensation than is available through workers' compensation and other statutory disability and survivor benefits are the significant costs that would derive from imposing liability under the facts presented. We frequently have concluded that when the social costs associated with liability are too high to justify its imposition, no duty will be found. . . . If one who initiates a false alarm may be liable for those consequences that are not reasonably foreseeable, but, rather, are significantly attenuated from the original negligent conduct, that liability will impose an unreasonable burden on the public. The costs stemming from this undue burden may include a substantial chilling of the willingness to report an emergency prior to investigating further to determine whether it is legitimate. Such delay may cost precious time, possibly leading to the unnecessary loss of life and property. It also may reduce the willingness of property owners to install alarms for fear of liability. Furthermore, imposing liability for such remote consequences undoubtedly will increase the cost of installing and monitoring alarms. Although those social costs may not be sufficient to prompt us to conclude that public policy dictates that there should be no duty in a case where the harm and the negligence are less attenuated or where the benefits of imposing liability are more substantial, under the circumstances of this case, we find them compelling.

Finally, we note that by concluding that the defendants did not owe a duty of care to these plaintiffs under the factual circumstances presented, we do not create immunity for alarm companies, their clients or subcontractors. Under most circumstances, alarm companies, and their associates, will owe the same duty of care that is expected of any enterprise for those harms that are reasonably foreseeable and within the scope of the risk created by their negligent conduct. We conclude only that, on the facts presented, the defendants cannot be held liable to the plaintiffs for the harm suffered as a result of the brake failure of the city's fire engine simply because the defendants negligently caused the transmission of a false alarm to which the engine was responding. Such unforeseeable consequences are not within the scope of the risk created, and the law cannot countenance the extension of legal responsibility to such an attenuated and unexpected result.

The judgment is reversed and the case is remanded to the trial court with direction to render judgment for the defendants Wells Fargo and Advanced on the plaintiffs' complaints.

NOTES

1. *Jargon and Approach.* Does the court ever use the phrase "superseding cause," a cause that breaks the causal chain and destroys proximate cause? If the decision had been based on the lack of proximate cause because of a superseding cause, what would the superseding cause have been? Is the court's two-pronged approach to duty — foreseeability and policy — appealing? Is a case-specific policy discussion persuasive? Is a court better than a jury at making a case-specific policy analysis?

2. *Intervening Third Parties.* The oft-cited case of *Weirum v. RKO Gen., Inc.,* 15 Cal. 3d 40 (1975), arose out of a promotional campaign by a Los Angeles radio station. As a part of the contest, one of the station's disc jockeys rode in a conspicuous red automobile throughout the Los Angeles metropolitan area. His whereabouts and destination were broadcast and the first person to locate him could win a cash prize. Two teenagers who were unsuccessful in winning at one location followed the disc jockey to his next location, often at high speed. At one point in the "chase," another vehicle was forced off the road, killing an occupant. In a wrongful death action against the radio station, the Supreme Court of California stated:

> . . . It was foreseeable that defendant's youthful listeners, finding the prize had eluded them at one location, would race to arrive first at the next site and in their haste would disregard the demands of highway safety.
>
> It is of no consequence that the harm to decedent was inflicted by third parties acting negligently. Defendant invokes the maxim that an actor is entitled to assume that others will not act negligently. This concept is valid, however, only to the extent the intervening conduct was not to be anticipated. . . . Here, reckless conduct by youthful contestants, stimulated by defendant's broadcast, constituted the hazard to which decedent was exposed. . . .
>
> . . . Defendant is fearful that entrepreneurs will henceforth be burdened with an avalanche of obligations: an athletic department will owe a duty to an ardent sports fan injured while hastening to purchase one of a limited number of tickets; a department store will be liable to injuries incurred in response to a "while-they-last" sale. This argument, however, suffers from a myopic view of the facts presented here. The giveaway contest was no commonplace invitation to an attraction available on a limited basis. It was a competitive scramble in which the thrill of the chase to be the one and only victor was intensified by the live broadcasts which accompanied the pursuit. In the assertedly analogous situations described by defendant, any haste involved in the purchase of the commodity is an incidental and unavoidable result of the scarcity of the commodity itself. In such situations there is no attempt, as here, to generate a competitive pursuit on public streets, accelerated by repeated importuning by radio to be the very first to arrive at a particular destination. Manifestly the "spectacular" bears little resemblance to daily commercial activities.

In *Weirum* (and *Bigbee*, discussed above), does the framing of a broad duty that defendant should be responsible for the actions of a third party essentially preempt any defense argument on intervening cause? At what cost to plaintiff?

E. PREEXISTING CONDITIONS AND OTHER PROBLEMS

Often considered under the rubric of legal or proximate cause is the extent to which the victim's pre-existing condition, or the subsequent conduct of the victim or others, may impact upon the liability of the initial wrongful actor. Some of these issues are considered in the chapter on limited duties that follows. Others are treated in Chapter 12 as an issue of assumption of the risk, contributory negligence or mitigation of damages and, in Chapter 13, as an issue of joint and several liability. The victim's pre-existing condition and the intervening conduct of rescuers are usually discussed in terms of proximate or legal cause.

The law has long recognized that a defendant is liable for those injuries caused by a wrongful act, even though the plaintiff, because of his peculiar or unique condition, suffers injuries greater than a normal person would suffer. This is known as the "thin skull" rule. Often it is restated in the phrase: the defendant takes his plaintiff as he finds him. Of course, the defendant must be negligent; if defendant's conduct does not pose an unreasonable risk of harm, there is no liability. But, once found negligent, the defendant is liable for all plaintiff's injuries.

ANAYA v. SUPERIOR COURT
78 Cal. App. 4th 971 (2000)

. . . Anaya and Vides allege that their 11-year-old daughter, Norma Vides, was with them when their car collided with a Los Angeles City trash truck that was stopped in the number two lane of a road. Injured in the crash, Norma was airlifted by City helicopter; the helicopter crashed and Norma died. Anaya and Vides sued City of Los Angeles and the individual drivers of the trash truck, Ralph Diaz and Gabriel Lara, for, inter alia, wrongful death. They also named Robert Everton, but the complaint does not set forth any facts as to Everton. . . .

Defendants Diaz, Lara, and Everton demurred. Respondent court sustained the demurrer of those defendants on the basis that Norma's death was not foreseeable. . . .

It has long been the rule that a tortfeasor responsible for the original accident is also liable for injuries or death occurring during the course of medical treatment to treat injuries suffered in that accident. In *Ash v. Mortensen* (1944) 24 Cal. 2d 654, 150 P.2d 876, the Supreme Court stated: "It is settled that where one who has suffered personal injuries by reason of the tortious act of another exercises due care in securing the services of a doctor and his injuries are aggravated by the negligence of such doctor, the law regards the act of the original wrongdoer as a proximate cause of the damages flowing from the subsequent negligent medical treatment and holds him liable therefor."

Obviously, if the original tortfeasor is liable for injuries or death suffered during the course of the treatment of injuries suffered in the accident, the original tortfeasor is liable for injuries or death suffered during transportation of the victim to a medical facility for treatment of the injuries resulting from the accident.

In *Pridham v. Cash & Carry Building Center, Inc.* (1976), 116 N.H. 292, Herbert Pridham was injured in an accident that occurred on Cash & Carry's premises and died when the ambulance transporting him to a hospital crashed. The New Hampshire Supreme Court determined that the jury should have been instructed that Cash & Carry was liable for Pridham's death. The New Hampshire Supreme Court explained the principle: "[I]f a tortfeasor's negligence causes harm to another which requires the victim to receive medical, surgical or hospital services and additional bodily harm results from a normal effort of persons rendering such services, whether done in a proper or negligent manner, the original tortfeasor's negligence is a legal cause of the injuries received because of the injured party's involuntary submission to such services. . . ." The allegations that the helicopter malfunctioned and that the manufacturer is strictly liable for the helicopter's malfunction do not establish the manufacturer as a superseding actor. . . .

The demurrer of . . . defendants . . . should have been overruled, because it is foreseeable that, after a traffic collision, the victim's injuries suffered in the collision would require the victim to be transported for medical care to a medical facility (whether by automobile or helicopter). The tortfeasors liable for the original accident that necessitated transportation of the victim of that accident by ambulance are liable in damages for any injuries (or death) suffered by the victim on the way to the hospital. It follows that, on the facts as alleged in the complaint, defendants are liable for Norma's death, which occurred while she was being transported to a medical facility for treatment of injuries suffered in an accident caused by Diaz, Lara, and Everton. Those that built and maintained the helicopter did not become superseding actors. . . .

NOTES

1. *Several Liability.* What would be the result if the applicable jurisdiction did not recognize joint and several liability, and a tortfeasor was only liable for its share of the fault? *See, e.g., Gray v. Ford Motor Co.,* 914 S.W.2d 464 (Tenn. 1996) (initial tortfeasor and subsequent medical tortfeasor are severally liable). How should one allocate fault between the initial tortfeasor and the negligent second injurer?

2. *Unforeseeable Thin Skulls?* By definition, are injuries occurring because of thin skulls or psyches unforeseeable? Did principles of corrective justice call for a special rule to permit recovery for victims in such cases? How would you evaluate the counter argument that those with such conditions have far lower information costs regarding their incidence and severity and, therefore, are in a better position than defendants to insure against their occurrence?

PROBLEMS

6.1

Hotel has a swimming pool open only to guests. State law requires that a lifeguard be on duty at all times when the pool is open for guests. A and B, who are not hotel guests, scale the hotel fence and begin swimming in the pool. A attempts to jump from the diving board, but the board collapses and strikes B, who is rendered unconscious and sinks to the bottom of the pool. There is no lifeguard on duty; the only guest who responds is X, a motel guest who is lounging near the pool, and who jumps in an attempt to save A. However, X cannot swim, and drowns. Is hotel liable to A? To B? To X?

6.2

Attorney is contacted by a family member of X and asked to represent X, who had been arrested but immediately bailed out on a negligent homicide claim arising out of an automobile accident. Unknown to his family, X has a neurosis which places him in great fear of incarceration. At trial of the case, attorney's ineptitude in presenting the defense leads to a guilty verdict. When at the sentencing hearing the judge orders X's incarceration for two years, X immediately sprints out of the courtroom and jumps out of a sixth story courthouse window, falling to his death. Is attorney liable? Would the answer be different if, instead of sprinting out of the courtroom, X, still out on bond after conviction but before beginning the imposed sentence, commits suicide?

6.3

On Superbowl Sunday X is driving on a well-traveled road. His cigarette falls from the ashtray and onto the floor of his vehicle. As he reaches to retrieve it, his car strays into the opposite lane, and as he attempts to overcorrect, his vehicle leaves the road on the right hand side and strikes a utility pole. As a result, fans within a five-mile area of the downed utility pole are unable to view the Superbowl by cable. One of the disgruntled fans attempts to drive to a local bar to watch the game, but is involved in an accident en route. A nearby medical clinic loses power because of the damage to the utility pole and the clinic personnel's prior failure to properly maintain the emergency generator; as a result, patient's condition worsens. What claims should be entertained against X?

6.4

Roder Rentals rented a truck to State Ex, which used the truck to deliver packages to customers. The truck had only one seat, equipped for the driver. The place normally occupied by a front passenger seat was open, allowing the driver to effect deliveries through the open space. The van had exhibited mechanical difficulties (sudden stopping) in the three days before the event in question. State Ex contacted Roder, which told them to return the truck for a replacement at the earliest possible time. The next morning, Sam was instructed to drive the truck to Roder Rentals. As he left State Ex's lot, one of his coworkers, Risky, asked for a ride home (Risky had recently completed an early morning shift). Risky got in the van and stood at the open space. As they proceeded down the interstate, the van suddenly quit and was immediately rear ended by a following motorist. The contact was minimal and Sam was uninjured but Risky, standing in the open space, was propelled out of the vehicle and onto the concrete, where he was struck and killed by another motorist. What claims does Risky's widow have against Roder, State Ex and the following motorist?

Chapter 7

LIMITED DUTIES

A. INTRODUCTION

Preceding chapters have examined the situations in which the law generally deems damage-causing conduct blameworthy — situations in which the actor has intentionally caused injury, or has failed to act as a reasonable person under the circumstances. The law has also imposed a sensible requirement that the damage-causing conduct must be the cause in fact of the injury of which the victim complains. The preceding chapter addressed circumstances when the law, under the rubric of "legal cause" or "proximate cause," some-times does not impose liability upon an actor whose conduct was blameworthy and was the cause in fact of the damage. The limitations upon liability occur because under the circumstances, society may deem it fundamentally unfair to impose liability, or may determine that some other societal policy outweighs the desire to deter certain wrongful conduct or compensate the victims of such conduct. This chapter explores how those policies are applied to limit liability under the concept of "limited duty."

When is a duty owed? Chapter 4 considered the content of the general duty that a person must act as a reasonable person under the circumstances. Chapter 6 offered two very different conceptions of duty in the famous *Palsgraf* case, *supra*, at 302. In his dissent, Justice Andrews articulated a theory that someone owes a duty to the world at large to avoid behavior that could foresee-ably cause injury to anyone. What limits are there on liability for negligence, given Andrews' expansive scope of duty? First, by definition, the defendant must have failed to exercise reasonable care before liability could be imposed. And, second, even if there is a duty owed and a failure to exercise reasonable care, the defendant must have caused the plaintiff's injury — both in-fact and "proximately."

Justice Cardozo's theory of duty is much more limited. He seemed to say (in rather Delphic prose) that a person only owes a duty to behave reasonably towards those persons who are foreseeable victims (foreseeable plaintiffs) of a foreseeable risk of the defendant's act. The differences between the two, as you will recall, are significant, particularly as they affect the role of the judge and jury in deciding a negligence case. But there are also similarities — the under-lying notion for both is that the existence of a duty (whether broadly or nar-rowly) is based upon foreseeability. It is behavior that foreseeably may injure another that gives rise to a duty. As Professor Dobbs has written: "Among strangers . . . the default rule is that everyone owes a duty of reasonable care to others to avoid physical harm." DAN B. DOBBS, THE LAW OF TORTS 578 (2000). The proposed final draft of the REST. 3D TORTS: LIABILITY FOR PHYSICAL HARM § 7(a) provides: "(a) An actor ordinarily has a duty to exercise reasonable care when the actor's conduct creates a risk of physical harm." Arguably that statement eschews foreseeability as a factor in determining duty. *See* W. Jonathan Cardi, *Purging Foreseeability: The New Vision of Duty and Judicial Power in the Proposed Restatement (Third) of Torts*, 58 VAND. L. REV. 739 (2005). That would be a significant change in American tort law.

Are there circumstances where even though harm is foreseeable to the defendant the law does not impose a duty to avoid harm? The answer is yes and those cases are the subject of this Chapter. As the REST. 3D TORTS states in section 7(b): "In exceptional cases, when an articulated countervailing principle or policy warrants denying or limiting liability in a particular class of cases, a court may decide that the defendant has no duty or that the ordinary duty of reasonable care requires modification." REST. 3D TORTS § 7(b). Those cases often involve broad policy decisions applicable not just to the case before the court but also the social impact of such decisionmaking in similar cases.

This chapter considers six such categories of "no duty" or "limited duty" cases: third-party acts such as crimes, the duty to act or lack thereof, negligent infliction of emotional distress, economic loss, prenatal or preconception torts, and owners and occupiers of land. Predictably, a holding that one does not owe a duty to protect against a foreseeable risk of harm may seem unfair or unjust to the injured plaintiff and others. Consequently, courts in these cases have sometimes modified or softened the common law no liability rule. They have sculpted out exceptions, some of which have grown larger with time. Some courts have articulated what they thought were meaningful limits on liability on public policy and fairness grounds while recognizing an obligation to exercise reasonable care in certain cases. Consider whether decisions in these cases reflect value preferences of the presiding and reviewing judges. As you read the cases keep in mind the Perspectives found in Chapter 1, *supra*. Is this an area of tort law that has particular potential to impact on certain women and racial and ethnic minorities? Are juries more or less sensitive to considerations of fairness in this area? Should the jurors' roles be limited here because of the economic or corrective justice impact of decisions related to duty?

B. NO DUTY

Often the issue of whether a duty is owed to the particular person (the *Palsgraf* issue as interpreted by Justice Cardozo) overlaps with broader limited duty issues, such as the duty to act or the interplay of third party criminal acts. The principal case manifests some of that overlap

GIPSON v. KASEY
150 P.3d 228 (Ariz. 2007)

BALES, JUSTICE.

. . . Kasey attended an employee holiday party hosted by the restaurant where he worked. Also present were his co-worker, Nathan Followill, and Followill's girlfriend, Sandy Watters. The restaurant provided beer for the guests. Kasey brought whiskey to the party and he gave shots to others present, including Followill, who was twenty-one years old. Kasey also brought pain pills containing oxycodone, a narcotic drug, which he had been prescribed for back pain. On prior occasions, Kasey had given pain pills to other co-workers for their recreational use.

During the party, Watters asked Kasey for one of his pain pills. Kasey gave Watters eight pills, noting that they were of two different strengths, but not identifying them by name. Although Kasey knew that combining the pills with alcohol or taking more than the prescribed dosage could have dangerous side effects, including death, he did not tell Watters this information.

When Kasey gave the pills to Watters, he knew that she was dating Followill. Kasey also knew that Followill was interested in taking prescription drugs for recreational purposes because Followill had on prior occasions asked Kasey for some of his pills, but Kasey had refused because he thought Followill was "too stupid and immature to take drugs like that."

Shortly after she obtained the pills from Kasey, Watters told Followill she had them, and Followill took the pills from her. As the night progressed, Followill became increasingly intoxicated. Around 1:00 a.m., Watters and Followill left the party. The next morning, Watters awoke to find that Followill had died in his sleep. The cause of death was the combined toxicity of alcohol and oxycodone.

Gipson, Followill's mother, filed a wrongful death action against Kasey. The superior court granted summary judgment for Kasey, finding that he owed Followill no duty of care and that Kasey's conduct had not proximately caused Followill's death because of the intervening acts of Watters and Followill.

The court of appeals reversed, holding that Kasey did owe Followill a duty of care and that disputed facts precluded summary judgment on the issue of proximate cause. . . .

Whether the defendant owes the plaintiff a duty of care is a threshold issue; absent some duty, an action for negligence cannot be maintained. Thus, a conclusion that no duty exists is equivalent to a rule that, for certain categories of cases, defendants may not be held accountable for damages they carelessly cause, no matter how unreasonable their conduct.

In this case, the court of appeals held that Kasey owed Followill a duty of care, based on the totality of the circumstances as reflected in the following factors: (1) the relationship that existed between Kasey and Followill, (2) the foreseeability of harm to a foreseeable victim as a result of Kasey giving eight pills to Watters, and (3) the presence of statutes making it unlawful to furnish one's prescription drugs to another person not covered by the prescription.

Kasey argues that none of these factors support a finding that he owed a duty of care to Followill. Although we disagree with aspects of the analysis of the court of appeals, that court correctly concluded that Kasey owed a duty of care.

Kasey argues that the court of appeals erred by relying on foreseeability of harm because this Court held in *Martinez v. Woodmar IV Condominiums*

Homeowners Ass'n, Inc. that foreseeability should no longer be a factor in determining whether a duty exists. 941 P.2d 218, 223 (Ariz. 1997) Gipson, on the other hand, argues that our prior cases have relied on foreseeability in determining whether a duty is owed. *See, e.g., Donnelly Constr. Co. v. Oberg/ Hunt/Gilleland,* 677 P.2d 1292, 1295 (Ariz. 1984) ("Duty and liability are only imposed where both the plaintiff and the risk are foreseeable to a reasonable person.").

We acknowledge that our case law has created "some confusion and lack of clarity . . . as to what extent, if any, foreseeability issues bear on the initial legal determination of duty." *Riddle v. Ariz. Oncology Servs., Inc.,* 924 P.2d 468, 470 n.3 (App. 1996). To clarify, we now expressly hold that foreseeability is not a factor to be considered by courts when making determinations of duty, and we reject any contrary suggestion in prior opinions.

Whether an injury to a particular plaintiff was foreseeable by a particular defendant necessarily involves an inquiry into the specific facts of an individual case. *See* W. Jonathan Cardi, *Purging Foreseeability: The New Version of Duty and Judicial Power in the Proposed Restatement (Third) of Torts,* 58 VAND. L. REV. 739, 801 (2005). Moreover, foreseeability often determines whether a defendant acted reasonably under the circumstances or proximately caused injury to a particular plaintiff. Such factual inquiries are reserved for the jury. The jury's fact-finding role could be undermined if courts assess foreseeability in determining the existence of duty as a threshold legal issue. *See id.* at 741. Reliance by courts on notions of "foreseeability" also may obscure the factors that actually guide courts in recognizing duties for purposes of negligence liability. *Id.*

Foreseeability, as this Court noted in *Martinez,* is more properly applied to the factual determinations of breach and causation than to the legal determination of duty. 941 P.2d at 223 ("[F]oreseeable danger [does] not dictate the existence of duty but only the nature and extent of the conduct necessary to fulfill the duty."); *cf. Palsgraf v. Long Island R.R.,* 162 N.E. 99, 102 (N.Y. 1928) (Andrews, J., dissenting) (arguing that foreseeability does not determine duty but is a factor in determining proximate cause). We believe that such an approach desirably recognizes the jury's role as factfinder and requires courts to articulate clearly the reasons, other than foreseeability, that might support duty or no-duty determinations. *See* Restatement (Third) of Torts: Liability for Physical Harm § 7 cmt. *j* (Proposed Final Draft No. 1, 2005) ("Third Restatement") (rejecting foreseeability as a factor in determining duty).

Kasey also argues that he did not owe Followill a duty of care because they had no "direct" or "special" relationship. Duties of care may arise from special relationships based on contract, family relations, or conduct undertaken by the defendant. *Stanley v. McCarver,* 92 P.3d 849, 851 (Ariz. 2004). A special or direct relationship, however, is not essential in order for there to be a duty of care.

Under Arizona common law, various categorical relationships can give rise to a duty. These include, but are not limited to, the landowner-invitee relationship, the tavern owner-patron relationship, and those "special relationships" recognized by §315 of the Restatement (Second) of Torts (1965) that create a duty to control the actions of another. None of these relationships existed between Followill and Kasey.

Although a duty of care may result from the nature of the relationship between the parties, we decline to recognize such a duty here based on the particular facts (some of which are disputed) of the relationship between Kasey and Followill. In identifying this relationship as a factor supporting a finding of duty, the court of appeals noted that "[t]hey were co-workers and friends; they had socialized previously; [and] Followill had asked Kasey for pills in the past."

A fact-specific analysis of the relationship between the parties is a problematic basis for determining if a duty of care exists. The issue of duty is not a factual matter; it is a legal matter to be determined *before* the case-specific facts are considered. Accordingly, this Court has cautioned against narrowly defining duties of care in terms of the parties' actions in particular cases. "[A]n attempt to equate the concept of 'duty' with such specific details of conduct is unwise," because a fact-specific discussion of duty conflates the issue with the concepts of breach and causation. *Coburn,* 691 P.2d at 1080; *see also Markowitz,* 706 P.2d at 367 (noting that "the existence of a duty is not to be confused with details of the standard of conduct"). Thus, the court of appeals erred in focusing on the facts of the particular relationship between Kasey and Followill in determining if a duty exists.

A finding of duty, however, does not necessarily depend on a preexisting or direct relationship between the parties. As we explained in *Stanley,* "[t]he requirement of a formalized relationship between the parties has been quietly eroding . . . and, when public policy has supported the existence of a legal obligation, courts have imposed duties for the protection of persons with whom no preexisting 'relationship' existed." 92 P.3d at 851–52 (internal citations omitted).

Having rejected foreseeability as a factor in the duty analysis and declining to recognize a duty based on the particular relationship between the parties, we turn to public policy considerations. Public policy may support the recognition of a duty of care. *See* 92 P.3d at 853 ("We conclude that public policy is better served by imposing a duty in such circumstances to help prevent future harm, even in the absence of a traditional doctor-patient relationship.").

Kasey argues that recognizing a duty here would imply that all people owe a duty of care to all others at all times, a proposition he contends was rejected in *Wertheim v. Pima County,* 122 P.3d 15 (App. 2005) ("We do not understand the law to be that one owes a duty of reasonable care at all times to all people under all circumstances." It is not necessary, however, to frame the issue this broadly to recognize a duty on the part of Kasey. Instead, in this case, Arizona statutes themselves provide a sufficient basis for a duty of care.

It is well settled that "[t]he existence of a statute criminalizing conduct is one aspect of Arizona law supporting the recognition of [a] duty." *Estate of Hernandez v. Ariz. Bd. of Regents,* 866 P.2d 1330, 1339 (Ariz. 1994). Not all criminal statutes, however, create duties in tort. A criminal statute will "establish a tort duty [only] if the statute is 'designed to protect the class of persons, in which the plaintiff is included, against the risk of the type of harm which has in fact occurred as a result of its violation. . . .'" *Id.* (citing W. Page Keeton et al., Prosser and Keeton on the Law of Torts § 36, at 229 n.30).

Several Arizona statutes prohibit the distribution of prescription drugs to persons lacking a valid prescription. As the court of appeals recognized, "[t]hese statutes are designed to avoid injury or death to people who have not been prescribed prescription drugs, who may have no medical need for them and may in fact be endangered by them, and who have not been properly instructed on their usage, potency, and possible dangers." *Gipson,* 129 P.3d at 963. Because Followill is within the class of persons to be protected by the statute and the harm that occurred here is the risk that the statute sought to protect against, these statutes create a tort duty.

Kasey argues that because the legislature did not create a civil duty for a violation of these criminal statutes, a duty does not exist. But this notion was rejected in *Ontiveros:* "[A] duty of care and the attendant standard of conduct may be found in a statute silent on the issue of civil liability." 667 P.2d at 210 (internal citations omitted).

Kasey also contends that because Arizona law does not impose a duty on social hosts who serve alcohol to adults, there should similarly be no duty here. We disagree. Through A.R.S. § 4-301 (2002), the legislature specifically exempted social hosts from liability for harm caused by a consumer of legal drinking age. No similar statute exempts those who improperly give their prescription drugs to others. *Cf. Hernandez,* 866 P.2d at 1338, 1342 (holding that A.R.S. § 4-301 does not preclude recognition of a duty of care to avoid serving alcohol to minors).

Moreover, the reasoning behind the social host no-duty rule does not apply in this context. When a court or legislature adopts a no-duty rule, it generally does so based on concerns that potential liability would chill socially desirable conduct or otherwise have adverse effects. The no-duty rule for social hosts is a prime example. Holding social hosts liable for harm caused by guests to whom they serve alcohol might curb desirable social exchanges. *See, e.g., Keckonen v. Robles,* 705 P.2d 945, 949 (App. 1985) (holding, for policy reasons, that social host owed no duty to person injured by intoxicated guest). In contrast, no recognized social benefit flows from the illegal distribution of prescription drugs. *Cf. Stanley,* 92 P.3d at 853 (observing, in holding that radiologist owed duty of care to examinee despite absence of formal doctor-patient relationship, that there was no apparent public benefit from a no-duty rule).

Kasey additionally argues that because his act of providing pills to Watters was not sufficient by itself to cause harm to Followill, no duty was owed. We reject the suggestion that no duty can exist if the plaintiff's conduct contributed to his injury. *See Hernandez,* 866 P.2d at 1341 ("Nor are considerations of proximate causation a reason to conclude there is no liability as a matter of law in all cases."). Whether the plaintiff's conduct constituted an intervening (or even a superseding) cause of the harm suffered is a question of fact and does not determine whether a duty exists. *See id.; Pratt v. Daly,* 104 P.2d 147 (Ariz. 1940) (finding defendants who provided alcohol to plaintiff's husband, a known alcoholic, liable for loss of consortium to plaintiff).

Alternatively, Kasey argues that this Court should adopt a no-duty rule precluding recovery on the grounds that a person who voluntarily becomes intoxicated and thereby sustains an injury should not be able to recover from the person supplying the intoxicants. We reject this reasoning. Followill's own actions may reduce recovery under comparative fault principles or preclude recovery if deemed a superseding cause of the harm, but those are determinations to be made by the factfinder. For the reasons stated, neither our case law nor considerations of policy justify a blanket no-duty rule that would insulate persons who improperly distribute prescription drugs from tort liability.

We hold that Kasey did owe a duty of care based on Arizona's statutes prohibiting the distribution of prescription drugs to persons not covered by the prescription. Accordingly, we vacate the part of the opinion of the court of appeals that addresses the issue of duty and remand to the superior court for further proceedings consistent with this opinion. [VACATED and REMANDED.]

HURWITZ, JUSTICE, concurring.

The Court correctly applies our precedents in determining that Kasey owed Followill a duty of care. I write briefly to suggest that our analysis of duty might be aided in the future by adopting a different conceptual approach.

The Court's analysis today and in our prior cases largely centers on determining whether we should *impose* a duty on the particular defendant before us. But, as the Court notes, under the common law "every person is under a duty to avoid creating situations which pose an unreasonable risk of harm to others." *Ontiveros v. Borak,* 667 P.2d 200, 209 (Ariz. 1983). Or as the proposed Third Restatement of Torts puts the matter, "[a]n actor ordinarily has a duty to exercise reasonable care when the actor's conduct creates a risk of physical harm." *See* Restatement (Third) of Torts: Liability for Physical Harm § 7(a) (Proposed Final Draft No. 1, 2005) [hereinafter "Third Restatement"].

It thus would seem to make sense for courts to view the duty of reasonable care as the norm, and depart from that norm only in those cases where public policy justifies an exception to the general rule. *See id.* § 7(b) ("In exceptional cases, when . . . policy warrants denying or limiting liability in a particular class of cases, a court may decide that the defendant has no duty or that the ordinary duty of reasonable care requires modification."); 1 DAN B. DOBBS, THE LAW OF TORTS § 227, at 579 (2001) ("[N]o-duty rules should be invoked only when all cases they cover fall substantially within the policy that frees the defendant of liability."); *see also Stagl v. Delta Airlines, Inc.,* 52 F.3d 463, 469 (2d Cir. 1995) (Calabresi, J.) ("[T]he judicial power to modify the general [duty] rule . . . is reserved for very limited situations.") (applying New York law).

A judicial finding that a defendant owes no duty to a plaintiff means that even if the defendant's actions were unreasonable and proximately caused harm to the plaintiff, the plaintiff has no recourse. Such a result should obtain, it seems to me, only when there is a good reason for doing so, and courts finding no duty as a matter of law should be required clearly to identify that reason.

The exemption from liability for social hosts is a good example of a policy-based duty exception. Courts have imposed only limited duties of care upon social hosts serving alcohol because of "staggering" economic and social consequences from adhering to the general rule of reasonable care. *See Keckonen v. Robles,* 705 P.2d 945, 949 (App. 1985).

If the analytic framework suggested by the Third Restatement were applied here, the only issue would be whether there existed a good policy reason to exempt those who distribute prescription drugs to unauthorized users from the general duty of care. As the Court correctly concludes, there is none. Thus, adoption of the Third Restatement approach would not alter the result we reach today.

My tentative sense, however, is that the Third Restatement rubric would simplify our analytical task in future cases and remove some understandable confusion among the bar and lower courts on the duty issue. For example, we have previously stated that the issue of duty depends on "the relationship of the parties." *Markowitz v. Ariz. Parks Bd.,* 706 P.2d 364, 368 (Ariz. 1985). The court of appeals in this case therefore felt constrained to determine whether the relationship between Kasey and Followill, who were co-workers and friends, was sufficient to impose a duty of reasonable care. *Gipson v. Kasey,* 129 P.3d 957, 961 (App. 2006). But, as the Court correctly notes today, a duty of reasonable care is often found even when the parties have no prior relationship at all — in automobile accident cases, for instance.

Under the approach counseled by the Third Restatement, the relationship of the parties is relevant to duty only insofar as it may suggest policy reasons for modifying or eliminating the general duty of reasonable care. Thus, in order to avoid the imposition of excessive costs on possessors of land and to protect property rights, public policy dictates that the landowner's duty to a deliberate trespasser is limited to refraining from willful or wanton injurious conduct. *See, e.g., Barnhizer v. Paradise Valley Unified Sch. Dist. No. 69,* 599 P.2d 209, 210 (Ariz. 1979) (citing Restatement (Second) of Torts § 333 (1965)). And, in some cases in which there is no prior relationship between the parties, public policy may support excusing the defendant from the general duty of reasonable care. *Cf. McCarver,* 92 P.3d at 855 (considering whether imposition of duty on physician to non-patient would "chill" doctors from doing pre-employment examinations).

Despite what appear to me to be the advantages of the Third Restatement approach to duty, the parties in this case have not urged its adoption. We therefore have not had the benefit of argument by counsel or *amici* as to why such an approach would be preferable to our current jurisprudence. Nor has the Third Restatement been finally adopted by the American Law Institute. For those reasons, and because application of the Third Restatement would not in any event change the result today, I leave the issue for another day and concur in the opinion of the Court.

C. LIABILITY FOR THIRD-PARTY ACTS

POSECAI v. WAL-MART STORES, INC.
752 So. 2d 762 (La. 1999)

MARCUS, JUSTICE.

Shirley Posecai brought suit against Sam's Wholesale Club ("Sam's") in Kenner after she was robbed at gunpoint in the store's parking lot. On July 20, 1995, Mrs. Posecai went to Sam's to make an exchange and to do some shopping. She exited the store and returned to her parked car at approximately 7:20 p.m. It was not dark at the time. As Mrs. Posecai was placing her purchases in the trunk, a man who was hiding under her car grabbed her ankle and pointed a gun at her. The unknown assailant instructed her to hand over her jewelry and her wallet. While begging the robber to spare her life, she gave him her purse and all her jewelry. Mrs. Posecai was wearing her most valuable jewelry at the time of the robbery because she had attended a downtown luncheon earlier in the day. She lost a two and a half carat diamond ring given to her by her husband for their twenty-fifth wedding anniversary, a diamond and ruby bracelet and a diamond and gold watch, all valued at close to $19,000.

When the robber released Mrs. Posecai, she ran back to the store for help. The Kenner Police Department was called and two officers came out to investigate the incident. The perpetrator was never apprehended and Mrs. Posecai never recovered her jewelry despite searching several pawn shops.

At the time of this armed robbery, a security guard was stationed inside the store to protect the cash office from 5:00 p.m. until the store closed at 8:00 p.m. He could not see outside and Sam's did not have security guards patrolling the parking lot. At trial, the security guard on duty, Kenner Police Officer Emile Sanchez, testified that he had worked security detail at Sam's since 1986 and was not aware of any similar criminal incidents occurring in Sam's parking lot during the nine years prior to the robbery of Mrs. Posecai. He further testified that he did not consider Sam's parking lot to be a high crime area, but admitted that he had not conducted a study on the issue. The plaintiff presented the testimony of two other Kenner police officers. Officer Russell Moran testified that he had patrolled the area around Sam's from 1993 to 1995. He stated that the subdivision behind Sam's, Lincoln Manor, is generally known as a high crime area, but that the Kenner Police were rarely called out to Sam's. Officer George Ansardi, the investigating officer, similarly testified that Lincoln Manor is a high crime area but explained that Sam's is not considered a high crime location. He further stated that to his knowledge none of the other businesses in the area employed security guards at the time of this robbery.

An expert on crime risk assessment and premises security, David Kent, was qualified and testified on behalf of the plaintiff. It was his opinion that the robbery of Mrs. Posecai could have been prevented by an exterior security presence. He presented crime data from the Kenner Police Department indicating that between 1989 and June of 1995 there were three robberies or "predatory offenses" on Sam's premises, and provided details from the police reports on each of these crimes. The first offense occurred at 12:45 a.m. on March 20, 1989, when a delivery man sleeping in his truck parked in back of the store was robbed. In May of 1992, a person was mugged in the store's parking lot. Finally, on February 7, 1994, an employee of the store was the victim of a purse snatching, but she indicated to the police that the crime was related to a domestic dispute. In order to broaden the geographic scope of his crime data analysis, Mr. Kent looked at the crime statistics at thirteen businesses on the same block as Sam's, all of which were either fast food restaurants, convenience stores or gas stations. He found a total of eighty-three predatory offenses in the six and a half years before Mrs. Posecai was robbed. Mr. Kent concluded that the area around Sam's was "heavily crime impacted," although he did not compare the crime statistics he found around Sam's to any other area in Kenner or the New Orleans metro area.

Mrs. Posecai contends that Sam's was negligent in failing to provide adequate security in the parking lot considering the high level of crime in the surrounding area. Seeking to recover for mental anguish as well as for her property loss, she alleged that after this incident she had trouble sleeping and was afraid to go out by herself at night. After a bench trial, the trial judge held that Sam's owed a duty to provide security in the parking lot because the robbery of the plaintiff was foreseeable and could have been prevented by the use of security. A judgment was rendered in favor of Mrs. Posecai, awarding $18,968 for her lost jewelry and $10,000 in general damages for her mental anguish. . . .

The sole issue presented for our review is whether Sam's owed a duty to protect Mrs. Posecai from the criminal acts of third parties under the facts and circumstances of this case.

This court has adopted a duty-risk analysis to determine whether liability exists under the particular facts presented. Under this analysis the plaintiff must prove that the conduct in question was the cause in fact of the resulting harm, the defendant owed a duty of care to the plaintiff, the requisite duty was breached by the defendant and the risk of harm was within the scope of protection afforded by the duty breached. Under the duty-risk analysis, all four inquiries must be affirmatively answered for plaintiff to recover. . . .

We now join other states in adopting the rule that although business owners are not the insurers of their patrons' safety, they do have a duty to implement reasonable measures to protect their patrons from criminal acts when those acts are foreseeable. We emphasize, however, that there is generally no duty to protect others from the criminal activities of third persons. This duty only arises under limited circumstances, when the criminal act in question was reasonably foreseeable to the owner of the business. Determining when a crime is foreseeable is therefore a critical inquiry.

Other jurisdictions have resolved the foreseeability issue in a variety of ways, but four basic approaches have emerged. The first approach, although somewhat outdated, is known as the specific harm rule. According to this rule, a landowner does not owe a duty to protect patrons from the violent acts of third parties unless he is aware of specific, imminent harm about to befall them. Courts have generally agreed that this rule is too restrictive in limiting the duty of protection that business owners owe their invitees. More recently, some courts have adopted a prior similar incidents test. Under this test, foreseeability is established by evidence of previous crimes on or near the premises. The idea is that a past history of criminal conduct will put the landowner on notice of a future risk. Therefore, courts consider the nature and extent of the previous crimes, as well as their recency, frequency, and similarity to the crime in question. This approach can lead to arbitrary results because it is applied with different standards regarding the number of previous crimes and the degree of similarity required to give rise to a duty. The third and most common approach used in other jurisdictions is known as the totality of the circumstances test. This test takes additional factors into account, such as the nature, condition, and location of the land, as well as any other relevant factual circumstances bearing on foreseeability. As the Indiana Supreme Court explained, "[a] substantial factor in the determination of duty is the number, nature, and location of prior similar incidents, but the lack of prior similar incidents will not preclude a claim where the landowner knew or should have known that the criminal act was foreseeable." *Delta* [*v. Johnson*] *Tau Delta*, 712 N.E.2d at 973. The application of this test often focuses on the level of crime in the surrounding area and courts that apply this test are more willing to see property crimes or minor offenses as precursors to more violent crimes. In general, the totality of the circumstances test tends to place a greater duty on business owners to foresee the risk of criminal attacks on their property and has been criticized "as being too broad a standard, effectively imposing an unqualified duty to protect customers in areas experiencing any significant level of criminal activity." *McClung* [*v. Delta Square Ltd. P'ship*], 937 S.W.2d at 900.

The final standard that has been used to determine foreseeability is a balancing test, an approach which has been adopted in California and Tennessee.... The Tennessee Supreme Court formulated the test as follows: "In determining the duty that exists, the foreseeability of harm and the gravity of harm must be balanced against the commensurate burden imposed on the business to protect against that harm. In cases in which there is a high degree of foreseeability of harm and the probable harm is great, the burden imposed upon defendant may be substantial. Alternatively, in cases in which a lesser degree of foreseeability is present or the potential harm is slight, less onerous burdens may be imposed." *McClung*, 937 S.W.2d at 902. Under this test, the high degree of foreseeability necessary to impose a duty to provide security, will rarely, if ever, be proven in the absence of prior similar incidents of crime on the property.

We agree that a balancing test is the best method for determining when business owners owe a duty to provide security for their patrons. The economic and social impact of requiring businesses to provide security on their premises is an important factor. Security is a significant monetary expense for any business and further increases the cost of doing business in high crime areas that are already economically depressed. Moreover, businesses are generally not responsible for the endemic crime that plagues our communities, a societal problem that even our law enforcement and other government agencies have been unable to solve. At the same time, business owners are in the best position to appreciate the crime risks that are posed on their premises and to take reasonable precautions to counteract those risks.

With the foregoing considerations in mind, we adopt the following balancing test to be used in deciding whether a business owes a duty of care to protect its customers from the criminal acts of third parties. The foreseeability of the crime risk on the defendant's property and the gravity of the risk determine the existence and the extent of the defendant's duty. The greater the foreseeability and gravity of the harm, the greater the duty of care that will be imposed on the business. A very high degree of foreseeability is required to give rise to a duty to post security guards, but a lower degree of foreseeability may support a duty to implement lesser security measures such as using surveillance cameras, installing improved lighting or fencing, or trimming shrubbery. The plaintiff has the burden of establishing the duty the defendant owed under the circumstances.

The foreseeability and gravity of the harm are to be determined by the facts and circumstances of the case. The most important factor to be considered is the existence, frequency and similarity of prior incidents of crime on the premises, but the location, nature and condition of the property should also be taken into account. It is highly unlikely that a crime risk will be sufficiently foreseeable for the imposition of a duty to provide security guards if there have not been previous instances of crime on the business' premises.

In the instant case, there were only three predatory offenses on Sam's premises in the six and a half years prior to the robbery of Mrs. Posecai. The first of these offenses occurred well after store hours, at almost one o'clock in the morning, and involved the robbery of a delivery man who was caught unaware as he slept near Sam's loading dock behind the store. In 1992, a person was mugged while walking through the parking lot. Two years later, an employee of the store was attacked in the parking lot and her purse was taken, apparently by her husband. A careful consideration of the previous incidents of predatory offenses on the property reveals that there was only one other crime in Sam's parking lot, the mugging in 1992, that was perpetrated against a Sam's customer and that bears any similarity to the crime that occurred in this case. Given the large number of customers that used Sam's parking lot, the previous robbery of only one customer in all those years indicates a very low crime risk. It is also relevant that Sam's only operates during daylight hours and must provide an accessible parking lot to the multitude of customers that shop at its store each year. Although the neighborhood bordering Sam's is considered a high crime area by local law enforcement, the foreseeability and gravity of harm in Sam's parking lot remained slight.

We conclude that Sam's did not possess the requisite degree of foreseeability for the imposition of a duty to provide security patrols in its parking lot. Nor was the degree of foreseeability sufficient to support a duty to implement lesser security measures. Accordingly, Sam's owed no duty to protect Mrs. Posecai from the criminal acts of third parties under the facts and circumstances of this case. Having found that no duty was owed, we do not reach the other elements of the duty-risk analysis that must be proven in establishing a negligence claim.

For the reasons assigned, the judgment of the court of appeal is reversed. It is ordered that judgment be rendered in favor of Wal Mart Stores, Inc. d/b/a

Sam's Wholesale Club and against Shirley Posecai, dismissing plaintiff's suit at her cost. [REVERSED.]

NOTES

1. *Bad Stuff Happens.* The rule at common law was that the criminal act of a third person was a superseding cause that relieved the defendant of liability. *See* Chapter 6, *supra*. Of course, if a third-party's criminal act was always a superseding cause, the result was that there was no liability for anyone who might have by her own risky conduct created the opportunity for the criminal act to occur or, put differently, there was no duty to protect against third party criminal acts. Exceptions to the no duty rule arose at common law in cases where the defendant was an innkeeper or common carrier. As seen in the principal case, pressure began to mount on courts to recognize other circumstances in which recognition of a duty might be appropriate. *Posecai* accurately sets forth the main analytical approaches that courts have employed in the business context. The common law rule may still hold firm in other situations. *See, e.g., Dearing v. Baumgardner*, 831 N.E.2d 1187 (Ill. App. 2005) (social host had no duty to protect guest from criminal attack). *Cf. Stuedemann v. Nose*, 713 N.W.2d 79 (Minn. App. 2006) (duty owed by foster home and psychologist but no proximate cause in wrongful death action).

As you have read, the *Posecai* court found that there was no duty under the facts of the case but that there could be a duty owed in a particular case after balancing the relevant factors, including foreseeability. Aren't those factors the court identifies essentially those used in Learned Hand's "negligence" calculus? Aren't they the same factors at stake in *Carroll Towing*? Does that mean that the *Posecai* court has adopted a law and economics approach to duty? Why are these factors relevant to duty?

In concluding that the defendant did not owe a duty to Ms. Posecai, is Justice Marcus adopting Cardozo's approach from *Palsgraf*? Isn't he deciding that, based on the particular facts before the court, the defendant did not owe the plaintiff a duty because the particular risk which arose was not foreseeable? Has the court created a case-by-case exception to the common law no duty rule? That is, has the court merely held that it will decide whether a duty exists to protect against third-party criminal acts on case-by-case basis? Is there something troublesome about that approach to duty? Is it consistent with *Gipson*?

2. *Restating the Common Law.* REST. 3D TORTS § 19 informs us: "The conduct of a defendant can lack reasonable care insofar as it foreseeably combines with or permits the improper conduct of the plaintiff or a third party." Does section 19 turn the common law on its head? Which of the approaches articulated in *Posecai* is adopted by the Third Restatement? Comment *f* to section 19 states, in part:

> The foreseeability of criminal and intentionally harm-causing misconduct invites a more cautious evaluation. The overwhelming majority of persons avoid such conduct almost all the time. Moral codes operate on people in a powerful way; for most people, committing crimes involving personal injury or significant property damage is all but unthinkable.

Moreover, the punishments imposed by the criminal law on people convicted of crime produce a powerful deterrent effect. As a general matter the prospect of criminal conduct is significantly lower than the prospect of negligent conduct. In many situations the possibility of criminal misconduct is so slight that an actor is not negligent for failing to take the possibility into account. . . .

Nevertheless, there is an unfortunate amount of crime in society. Accordingly, in certain situations criminal misconduct is sufficiently foreseeable as to require a full negligence analysis of the actor's conduct. Moreover, the actor may have sufficient knowledge of the immediate circumstances or the general character of the third party to foresee that party's misconduct. For example, if the owner of a gun who leaves it on a table at home knows that a houseguest has a long record of violent crimes, that knowledge supports the claim that owner is negligent in giving the guest access to the gun.

Id. § 19, cmt. *f.*

Does this comment help to answer the question whether the Third Restatement has reversed the common law "no liability" rule?

3. *Does the Same Rule Apply to All?* Should it make a difference that the tortfeasor is a mass murderer? How would you factor that into your analysis? *Lopez v. McDonald's*, 193 Cal. App. 3d 495 (1987), concerned a mass killing at a fast food restaurant. The assailant, armed with a 9 mm. semi-automatic rifle, a semi-automatic 9-mm. pistol and a 12 gauge shotgun, indiscriminately slaughtered 21 patrons and employees before he was killed by a police sharpshooter. He showed no intent to rob the restaurant; as the court put it, "[h]is single apparent purpose was to kill as many people as possible before he himself was slain." 193 Cal. App.3d at 501.

Plaintiffs alleged McDonald's failed to provide adequate safety devices or security personnel to protect customers from dangerous and known risks. The court affirmed the trial court's grant of a defense motion for summary judgment. Are terrorist acts different than other more "mundane" criminal acts? Should airlines, hotels, and communities be obligated to protect against terrorist acts? If your answer to the last question is yes, then based on policy, do you think that obligation or duty should be enforceable in a tort case? If your answer is no to that question, then how is the duty to be enforced?

In the wake of the horrific events of 9/11 Congress passed a statute providing for compensation for victims of the attack. A special master who articulated and applied criteria to determine who was entitled to benefit and the amount of those benefits administered the compensation fund. A discussion of this fund and some of the allocational decisions made by Congress and the special master is contained in Chapter 16, *infra*. While few would argue about the desirability, wisdom, and compassion of this special fund, how about the victims in *Lopez*? Are they less deserving of compensation? What about the victims of Hurricane Katrina? *See, e.g.,* Sherrie Armstrong Tomlinson, Note, *No New Orleanians Left Behind: An Examination of the Disparate Impact of Hurricane Katrina on Minorities,* 38 CONN. L. REV. 1153 (2006).

4. *Nice Folks Can Assume Liability.* Even if there is generally no duty to protect against third party misdeeds, a business owner may assume a duty to exercise reasonable care by hiring security guards. *See, e.g., Harris v. Pizza Hut of Louisiana, Inc.,* 454 So. 2d 1364 (La. 1984). Likewise, perhaps building upon the earlier innkeeper and common carrier cases, a duty to protect against third-party criminal acts may be imposed if there is a special relationship between the victim and the defendant, such as employee/employer. *See, e.g., Lillie v. Thompson,* 332 U.S. 459 (1947). These "special relationship" cases — indeed perhaps this entire section — may be seen as a subset of the affirmative duty to act, discussed below.

5. *Are Blanket Rules Good Policy?* Consider the policy implications of a rule that liability is never imposed for third party criminal acts. What are the implications for a contrary rule, tending to impose liability for such acts on the part of the risk-creator? How do people generally react to the risk of liability? How do businesses react? If for third party criminal acts liability is more likely to be imposed in high crime areas and many high crime areas are also low-income areas, will businesses be reluctant to locate in these high crime/low income areas? If they do locate there, are their prices likely to be higher than they otherwise would be? Is it "fair" for people in high crime/low income areas to pay more for goods and services than people in lower crime/higher income areas? Would that result be consistent with a law and economics approach to negligence? Would a corrective justice approach lead to a different outcome? Is it fair for merchants to pass the cost of guarding against liability for third party criminal acts in high crime areas to patrons in low crime areas? Is this an issue the legislature should step in and regulate or for the courts to "regulate" in the course of deciding cases? If it is a legislative function, how likely is it that the legislature will intervene and how?

How would a critical race theorist analyze a proposed duty to protect against third party misdeeds? Is such a duty racially neutral? Is a feminist perspective particularly relevant to Ms. Posecai's claims? Who was in the best position to prevent valuable jewelry from being stolen, the jewelry wearer or the merchant? What if the question is asked about personal property, rather than "jewelry?" Is B < P x L?

6. *Negligent Entrustment Redux.* If you loan your car to an obviously drunk or incapable individual, should you be liable if the borrower injures a third person while driving your car in an intoxicated state within minutes of borrowing it? One can think of this scenario as a case of negligent entrustment. *See, e.g., Vince v. Wilson,* 561 A.2d 103 (Vt. 1989). In what way is negligent entrustment related to the third party criminal act cases?

There is a recurring, related fact pattern involving an intervening act that has vexed courts and that is discussed in notes dealing with negligence *per se* in Chapter 4, *supra.* Defendant (usually in violation of some statute) leaves his or her keys in the car. A thief steals the car and injures plaintiff while driving the car. Should the defendant car owner be liable? *See Hill v. Yaskin,* 380 A.2d 1107 (N.J. 1977). In *McClenahan v. Cooley,* 806 S.W.2d 767 (Tenn. 1991), the court said that the car owner would be liable where the accident occurred "during the flight of the thief relatively close thereto in time and distance." Both

Hill and *McClenahan* involved the imposition of a common law duty, not negligence *per se.*

6. *Products and Third Party Criminal Acts.* Should the manufacturer or other seller of a product that is dangerous if misused, such as a firearm, be liable if the misuse is arguably foreseeable? The court in *Hamilton v. Beretta U.S.A. Corp.,* 750 N.E.2d 1055 (N.Y. 2001) said no. *See generally* George J. Bentson & Frank J. Vandall, *Legal Control Over The Supply of Handguns: An Analysis of the Issues, With Particular Attention to the Law and Economics of the Hamilton v. Berretta Lawsuit Against Handgun Manufacturers,* 26 PACE L. REV. 305 (2006). Many municipalities have filed suits against firearm manufacturers to recover damages allegedly caused the cities by the misuse of the firearms they had manufactured. *See generally* Thomas C. Galligan, Jr., *Deterrence: The Legitimate Function of the Public Tort,* 58 WASH. & LEE L. REV. 1019 (2001); David Kairys, *Legal Claims of Cities Against the Manufacturers of Handguns,* 71 TEMP. L. REV. 1 (1998).

From an economic perspective, should there be liability in such cases? Should your answer depend on whether the cost of harm caused by the foreseeable criminal acts can reasonably be included in the cost of the product? Or, is it unfair to expect a product's cost to reflect the behavior of wrongdoers? If the cost falls disproportionately on the poor, should a court respond in the context of individual tort cases? Should an appellate court articulate a tort rule to deal with that disproportionate impact? Should there be a different rule for the poor victim as opposed to the rich victim?

How about the liability of the provider of alcohol or other drugs when harm arises?

SCHOOLEY v. PINCH'S DELI MARKET, INC.
951 P.2d 749 (Wa. 1998)

MADSEN, JUSTICE.

On August 25, 1989, Russell Bowser invited five of his friends, all of whom were under 21, over for a party while his parents were out of town. Everyone at the party wanted beer so Bowser, then 19, Lori Schooley, then 18, and the others decided to pool their money and purchase beer. They drove to Pinch's Deli and Bowser and two others entered the store to buy beer. Schooley and the others remained in the car. Bowser purchased four cases of beer. He was not asked to produce identification when purchasing the beer.

After purchasing the beer, Bowser, Schooley, and the others returned to Bowser's house. Schooley drank two or three beers and then consumed an unknown quantity while playing a drinking game with the others. Later, Bowser and one of the other boys carried Schooley to the pool to throw her in. She asked them if she could strip down to her swimsuit, which she had on underneath her clothes, before they threw her in. The boys let her down and she took off her clothes. However, before they could throw her in she dove into the water. The pool was only two feet deep where Schooley dove and consequently she fractured her spinal cord and is now quadriplegic.

Schooley sued Pinch's Deli for damages for negligently selling alcohol to minors. The trial court granted Pinch's motion for summary judgment. . . .

After Congress repealed Prohibition in 1933, the Washington Legislature passed the Washington alcoholic beverage control (WABC) act. In part, this Act prohibits selling alcohol to any minor, or giving or otherwise supplying liquor to any minor. . . .

The issue presented in this case is one of first impression in the State of Washington. To date, we have found that an injured intoxicated minor purchaser and third persons injured by the intoxicated minor purchaser both have a cause of action in negligence against the vendor who sold alcohol to the minor. In this case, however, a somewhat different scenario has occurred; a third person minor who obtained alcohol from a minor purchaser was injured. Thus, the issue here is whether a vendor who sells alcohol to a minor who subsequently furnishes the alcohol to another minor can be held liable for foreseeable alcohol-related injuries arising from the initial sale of alcohol. . . .

We turn first to the contention that Schooley is not within the class of persons protected by the statute. . . .

The WABC Act explicitly prohibits commercial vendors from "selling any intoxicating liquor to any minor." RCW 66.44.320; *see also* RCW 66.44.270(1) ("it is unlawful for any person to sell . . . liquor to any person under the age of twenty-one years . . . ").

Petitioner argues that the statute protects only the immediate minor purchaser, and not other third person minors who may receive the liquor from the minor purchaser. While the legislation focuses primarily on the minor purchaser, the notion that the prohibition against selling liquor to minors imposes a duty toward persons other than the minor purchaser is not a new concept. In *Purchase* [*v. Meyer*, 737 P.2d 661 (Wash. 1997)], we found that third persons injured by a minor purchaser have a cause of action against the liquor vendor stating the vendor's duty extends not only to the minor purchaser but "to members of the general public as well." *Purchase*, [737 P.2d at 666]. To conclude that the commercial vendor's duty extends to third persons whom the minor purchaser injures but not minors with whom the alcohol was shared would be an arbitrary distinction not supported by the recognized purpose of the statute.

We have repeatedly emphasized that "persons under 21 years of age are neither physically nor mentally equipped to handle the consumption of intoxicating liquor." The recognized purpose of legislation prohibiting the sale of alcohol to minors is to protect minors' health and safety interests from their "own inability to drink responsibly" and to protect against the particular hazard of "alcohol in the hands of minors." Because minors who drink commonly do so with other minors, protecting all those injured as a result of the illegal sale of alcohol to minors is the best way to serve the purpose for which the legislation was created, to prevent minors from drinking. Thus, we find that Schooley is part of the protected class.

Petitioner next contends that, although underage, Schooley does not need the protection of the statute. Petitioner cites no authority for this proposition, arguing only that Schooley's history of alcohol consumption supports the conclusion that unlike other minors who are neither physically nor mentally equipped to handle the consumption of alcohol, she had been intoxicated before and was well aware of the effects of alcohol. This argument is without merit. The statute does not provide for such an exception, and, moreover, it is illogical to assume the Legislature would implicitly intend to carve out an exception and allow vendors of alcohol to sell intoxicating liquor to minors who are "experienced" drinkers. Such a conclusion is in direct contradiction to the policy behind the statute that minors as a class are not physically or mentally equipped to handle the consumption of alcohol.

As we found, Schooley is within the protected class and foreseeability serves to define the scope of the duty owed. Where harm to a person protected by a statute is a foreseeable result of the statute's violation, liability may be imposed. Foreseeability is used to limit the scope of the duty owed because actors are responsible only for the foreseeable consequences of their acts. Foreseeability is normally an issue for the trier of fact and will be decided as a matter of law only where reasonable minds cannot differ. Pinch's Deli argues that, as a matter of law, its conduct did not create a foreseeable risk to Schooley because it did not sell alcohol directly to her. We disagree and find that reasonable minds could conclude that a minor purchasing substantial amounts of alcohol would share that alcohol with friends. Thus, it is a question for the jury as to whether under these facts it was foreseeable that the alcohol would be shared with others. Factors that may be considered include, but are not limited to, the amount and character of the beverages purchased, the time of day, the presence of other minors on the premises or in a vehicle, and statements made by the purchaser.

Additionally, the trier of fact must determine whether the harm sustained in this case, diving into the shallow end of a pool, was foreseeable. "[T]he harm sustained must be reasonably perceived as being within the general field of danger covered by the specific duty owed by the defendant." In *Hansen* [*v. Friend*, 824 P.2d 483 (Wash. 1992)], the defendant argued that the duty owed to the plaintiff should be limited only to those minors who drive while intoxicated and not to minors who drown as a result of intoxication. We found that many minors do not drive; thus, it was for the trier of fact to determine whether drowning as result of the intoxication was foreseeable. Likewise, it is for the trier of fact to determine if Schooley's injuries were foreseeable. Thus, we find Schooley is part of the protected class and the jury must determine whether her injuries were a foreseeable result of Pinch's illegal sale of alcohol.

Petitioner argues that even if it owed a legal duty to Schooley, it was not the legal cause of her injuries. Proximate causation is divided into two elements: cause in fact and legal causation. "Cause in fact" refers to the actual, "but for," cause of the injury, i.e., "but for" the defendant's actions the plaintiff would not be injured. Establishing cause in fact involves a determination of what actually occurred and is generally left to the jury. Unlike factual causation, which is based on a physical connection between an act and an injury, legal cause is grounded in policy determinations as to how far the consequences of a defendant's acts should extend. Thus, where the facts are not in dispute, legal causation is for the court to decide as a matter of law.

The focus in the legal causation analysis is whether, as a matter of policy, the connection between the ultimate result and the act of the defendant is too remote or insubstantial to impose liability. . . .

The Court of Appeals indicates the analysis involved in whether a duty is owed to the plaintiff and whether the defendant's actions were the legal cause of the injuries to the plaintiff is identical. The Court of Appeals goes so far in this case as to state that if a duty of care is owed to the plaintiff then legal causation is automatically satisfied. This court has recognized that the issues regarding whether duty and legal causation exist are intertwined. This is so because some of the policy considerations analyzed in answering the question whether a duty is owed to the plaintiff are also analyzed when determining whether the breach of the duty was the legal cause of the injury in question. However, a court should not conclude that the existence of a duty automatically satisfies the requirement of legal causation. This would nullify the legal causation element and along with it decades of tort law. Legal causation is, among other things, a concept that permits a court for sound policy reasons to limit liability where duty and foreseeability concepts alone indicate liability can arise. . . .

Turning to the present case, Washington's policy regarding minors and alcohol is clear. It is illegal to sell minors alcohol and if a vendor breaches this duty it will be responsible for the foreseeable injuries which result. Legislation prohibiting the sale of alcohol to minors was enacted to protect minors' health and safety interests against the effects of alcohol.

Petitioner's main argument as to why it was not the legal cause of Schooley's injuries is that her injuries are too remote and that the legal consequences of the sale of alcohol to the first minor should not extend to minors who share the alcohol with the minor purchaser. The only policy reason given by Petitioner is the fear of unlimited liability, arguing once a vendor has sold the alcohol it has no control over ensuing events.

The alcohol vendor, however, has full control at the point of sale. The duty is not onerous, all the vendor has to do is ask the purchaser for valid identification in order to verify that he or she is of legal age to purchase alcohol. Moreover, the alcohol vendor has within its own control the power to immunize itself from liability for a minor's alcohol-related conduct. If, after a purchaser presents identification, the vendor still has doubts about the purchaser's age the vendor can fill out and have the purchaser sign a certification card complying with RCW 66.20.190. If the vendor completes these simple steps, but, nevertheless, the minor purchases alcohol, the vendor is immune from any criminal or civil liability regarding the sale of alcohol to the minor.

Additionally, even if an alcohol vendor sells alcohol to a minor in violation of the law, other legal concepts exist to prevent Petitioner's fear of unlimited liability. First, foreseeability serves to limit liability by only holding persons liable for the foreseeable consequences of their actions. Thus, an alcohol vendor will be responsible only for the foreseeable consequences of its negligent sale of alcohol.

Second, a minor who purchases, possesses, or consumes alcohol is also in violation of the law and may be found to be contributorily negligent. Moreover, if the minor's intoxication results in that person being more than 50 percent at fault for his or her own injuries then no recovery is allowed.

Finally, the doctrine of superseding cause serves as a significant limitation on a commercial vendor's liability. A defendant's negligence is a proximate cause of the plaintiff's injury only if such negligence, unbroken by any new independent cause, produces the injury complained of. When an independent intervening act of a third person is one which was not reasonably foreseeable then there is a break in the causal connection between the defendant's negligence and the plaintiff's injury. Thus, it is evident that if a commercial vendor negligently sells alcohol the resulting liability will not be endless.

Next . . . Petitioner argues as a matter of policy that Pinch's should not be held liable for Schooley's irresponsible conduct. In *Kelly* [*v. Falin*, 896 P.2d 1245 (Wash. 1995)], we found that RCW 66.44.200, which prohibits selling alcohol to an obviously intoxicated adult, was not intended to shield the drunk driver from responsibility for his or her own actions. Thus, the injured intoxicated adult had no cause of action against the vendor who sold him alcohol. Petitioner in this case argues that, although a minor, she was over the age of 18 and therefore an adult who, like the individual in *Kelly*, should be held responsible for her own actions.

Using this analysis to preclude liability would, however, lead to an illogical and insupportable result whereby alcohol vendors would be absolved of liability when they sell alcohol to persons between the ages of 18 and 21. The Legislature has not created such an exception for those 18 and older. In fact, in *Kelly*, this court emphasized the distinction between minors and adults in the context of commercial vendor liability.

> While commercial vendors have a duty to minors and innocent bystanders, no duty arises when intoxicated adults harm themselves. The distinction between intoxicated adults and intoxicated minors is simple. The Legislature has determined that, unlike adults, "persons under 21 years of age are neither physically nor mentally equipped to handle the consumption of intoxicating liquor. . . .

Petitioner's concern is better addressed as an argument that Schooley was contributorily negligent. As previously noted, the purchase and consumption of alcohol by a person under the age of 21 is illegal and a minor's violation of the statute may be introduced as evidence of that minor's contributory negligence. The issue of contributory negligence is a question for the jury. Finding Petitioner's arguments unpersuasive we conclude that legal cause is satisfied in this case. . . [DECISION OF THE COURT OF APPEALS AFFIRMED.]

NOTES

1. *Statutes and Alcohol. Schooley* reviews the effect of violating a statute in a negligence case and sets forth the relationship between the judicial inquiry of the scope of the harm and legal causation. For present purposes, the case raises issues about the "negligent" provision of alcohol, a person's intervening misconduct (over consumption of the alcohol) and resulting injury. In *Schooley*, the plaintiff is the one who over consumes the alcohol but the plaintiff is not the purchaser of the alcohol. In cases involving the liability of alcohol providers the relationship between the various parties is often critical as is the existence of any relevant legislation. Would the result be different if the minor who purchased the alcohol was the person injured?

Many states have statutes that make it illegal to sell alcohol to any visibly intoxicated person. How is a provider to know if a person is visibly intoxicated? If a provider does violate such a statute should she be liable to someone whom the consumer of the alcohol injures while driving a car under the influence of the provided alcohol? What if the plaintiff is the consumer herself or himself? In *Kelly v. Falin*, 896 P.2d 1245 (Wash. 1995), the court held that a commercial vendor was not liable for serving alcohol to obviously intoxicated adult patrons who later injured themselves as a result of the intoxication. Compare *Jarrett v. Woodward Bros., Inc.*, 751 A.2d 972, 981 (D.C. 2000) (intoxicated underage patron wandered onto a highway and was struck by a car; the court permitted a wrongful death action against the restaurant-bar that served him liquor). If a court was inclined to impose a duty to an alcohol provider, suppose the consumer of the alcohol had been drinking at other establishments before being served by the defendant, how can one be sure that the defendant's provision of alcohol was the cause-in-fact or legal cause of the plaintiff's injury? *See, e.g., Stachniewicz v. Mar-Cam Corp.*, 488 P.2d 436 (Or. 1971) (no cause-in-fact established regarding service to visibly intoxicated person who later injured plaintiff).

A number of other states have enacted statutes for a civil cause of action to someone injured by the intoxicant against someone who served alcohol to a visibly intoxicated person. These statutes are known as Dram Shop Acts. Do such statutes necessarily answer all of the questions asked above? In the absence of a Dram Shop Act, can a court reach the same result under the common law?

2. *Social Hosts.* Should social hosts be treated differently than dram shops (taverns or other establishments serving liquor)? *See Bankston v. Brennan*, 507 So. 2d 1385 (Fla. 1987). What different factors are involved? *Reynolds v. Hicks*, 951 P.2d 761 (Wash. 1998), was a companion case to *Schooley*. There, a minor driver who allegedly became intoxicated at a wedding reception injured the plaintiff. The plaintiff sued the bride and groom. The Washington court held that a social host who furnishes alcohol to a minor does not owe a duty of care to an injured third person. Should the social host be liable if they recklessly serve alcohol to a person? *See Hickingbotham v. Burke*, 662 A.2d 297 (N.H. 1995).

Compare the principal case with *Bell v. Whitten*, 722 So. 2d 1057 (La. App. 1st Cir. 1998) (host minor did not owe duty to deputy sheriff injured by minor to whom host provided alcohol) and *Kapres v. Heller*, 640 A.2d 888 (Pa. 1994) (refusing to hold minor social hosts liable for injuries to another minor resulting from the host's serving alcoholic beverages to the other minor). Louisiana actually has a statute providing that the sale or service of alcohol to a person over 21 is not the proximate cause of any subsequent injury; rather the consumption of the alcohol is the legal cause of any injury. La. R.S. 9:2800.1. Is allocating the risk to the intoxicated driver and *not* the seller or provider the most effective deterrent? Would better deterrence be provided by allocating the risk to *both?* Should the drinker and the server share the responsibility? Is that consistent with a corrective justice approach to torts? Or, would a corrective justice theorist allocate all the fault to the more blameworthy party? How does one define blameworthiness in this context? Is an alcoholic blameworthy?

In *West v. East Tennessee Pioneer Oil Co.*, 172 S.W.2d 545 (Tenn. 2005), the court held that a convenience store owed a duty to another who was injured in an accident with an intoxicated driver where convenience store employees sold gas to a visibly intoxicated driver and helped him pump it.

3. *Broad Rule Versus Tort Liability.* Is the cost of an alcohol related injury one best left to courts in individual cases? Or, is a broader societal response in order? Much progress has been made to make people aware of the risks of drunk driving and over the past fifteen to twenty-five years the police have become much more aggressive in enforcing driving-while-intoxicated laws. Are those broad societal initiatives adequate? Do they speak in favor of or against imposing tort liability? Has raising the legal drinking age to 21 had a beneficial impact? If, yes, then what about increasing the minimum legal drinking age to 30?

D. THE DUTY TO ACT

The common law callously provided that a person owed no duty, in most cases, to take action to aid, help, or rescue another even if injury was foreseeable and the aid could be safely provided. REST. 3D TORTS: LIABILITY FOR PHYSICAL HARM (PROPOSED FINAL DRAFT) § 37 provides in part:

> An actor whose conduct has not created a risk of physical harm to another has no duty of care to the other unless a court determines that one of the affirmative duties provided in § 38-44 is applicable.

Does the rule expressed in the proposed Third Restatement section mean that generally (i.e., unless sections 38-44 apply), one has no duty to help another person? As noted in the proposed draft, that is indeed the traditional rule. Why? Would an economist impose a duty to act if, under the factual circumstances, B was less than P x L? *See Yania v. Bigan*, 155 A.2d 343 (Pa. 1959) (defendant not liable for encouraging another to jump into pit and then refusing help him escape drowning). *See also* Thomas C. Galligan, Jr., *Aiding and Altruism: A Mythopsycholegal Analysis*, 27 U. MICH. J.L. REFORM 439 (1994).

Does the traditional "no duty to act" rule reflect good policy? Does it mean that if I see a baby that I do not know and to whom I am not related lying face down in a puddle on the street that I have no legal duty to stoop down and pick the baby up or at least roll her out of the puddle? Can I just walk by? Why has this so-called freedom not to act been recognized as the general rule of law? Is it to preserve my right as an individual to do as I choose? Is it to limit the power of the state to be able to tell me what I have to do? What about the baby? Have I really caused any injury to the baby if I walk by without stopping to prevent the drowning? But we can say but for my failure to act the baby would not drown when and how it did, can't we? Would a proponent of the law and economics approach to law oppose a limited duty to act? Would a limited duty to act in this factual scenario be consistent with corrective justice? Would it unduly offend my autonomy interest? Would a feminist say that the no duty to act rule is a remnant of an outmoded approach to law? Would a communitarian favor a limited duty to act, eschewing rugged individualism?

Answers to the questions that have been proposed here lead to broader considerations of the duty, no-duty controversy. For example, do I have a duty to help the poor? By making charitable contributions? Would my failure to make a contribution ever be negligence? How would you decide such a question?

The failure to act is sometimes called nonfeasance, in contrast with misfeasance, *i.e.*, the failure to act reasonably in an act already undertaken. Assume I approach an intersection, do not apply my brakes, and collide with a pedestrian, Jane. When Jane sues me for negligence in failing to apply my brakes would you characterize my behavior or lack thereof as misfeasance or nonfeasance? All courts would agree that my failure to apply the brakes was misfeasance in driving, rather than nonfeasance in not braking. Is my failure to act in the baby hypothetical fact-pattern nonfeasance in rescuing or is it misfeasance in walking? Does your answer depend upon how you characterize a citizen's general obligation to the community? As the baby hypothetical suggests, whatever one may conclude about the general no duty to act rule, it is and has been certain that the application of the rule may result in some harsh outcomes and, not surprisingly, the rule is riddled with exceptions.

The next principal case begins consideration of those exceptions but first, consider *Griffith v. Southland Corp.*, 617 A.2d 598 (Md. 1992). An off-duty police officer became the victim of a savage beating while attempting to restore order on the premises of a store owned by the defendant. Defendant's employee was asked to summon aid, refused, and the officer was severely injured. The court stated that the "suggested duty, i.e., to call 911 when there is no imminent risk of danger to the caller, does no violence to the doctrine of *stare decisis*; there is no break from precedent because there is no precedent which permits a bystander to refuse to call 911 when not exposed to imminent danger. Even if there were such an uncivilized and shocking principle, blind allegiance would invite disdain and disrespect for the courts." 617 A2d at 606. *See also Soldano v. O'Daniels*, 141 Cal. App. 3d 443, 190 Cal. Rptr. 310 (1983) (liability imposed on a bar owner who allegedly refused to allow use of his telephone to call police prior to the shooting death of plaintiff's decedent at an eating establishment across the street). Compare *Stangle v. Fireman's Fund Ins. Co.*, 190 Cal. App. 3d 971 (1988) (plaintiff discovered theft of ring immediately after it occurred on defendant's premises and sought to use defendant's telephone to call the police, but defendant's receptionist refused access to her telephone, saying it was "for building use only;" *Soldano* was limited to cases of clear communication of imminent danger of physical harm). Consider whether you can formulate satisfactory guidelines for distinguishing with some consistency appropriate duty and no duty cases.

FARWELL v. KEATON
240 N.W.2d 217 (Mich. 1976)

LEVIN, JUSTICE.

[Wrongful death action brought on behalf of beneficiaries of Farwell estate.] On the evening of August 26, 1966, Siegrist and Farwell drove to a trailer rental lot to return an automobile which Siegrist had borrowed from a friend who worked there. While waiting for the friend to finish work, Siegrist and Farwell consumed some beer. Two girls walked by the entrance to the lot. Siegrist and Farwell attempted to engage them in conversation; they left Farwell's car and followed the girls to a drive-in restaurant down the street.

The girls complained to their friends in the restaurant that they were being followed. Six boys chased Siegrist and Farwell back to the lot. Siegrist escaped unharmed, but Farwell was severely beaten. Siegrist found Farwell underneath his automobile in the lot. Ice was applied to Farwell's head. Siegrist then drove Farwell around for approximately two hours, stopping at a number of drive-in restaurants. Farwell went to sleep in the back seat of his car. Around midnight Siegrist drove the car to the home of Farwell's grandparents, parked it in the driveway, unsuccessfully attempted to rouse Farwell, and left. Farwell's grandparents discovered him in the car the next morning and took him to the hospital. He died three days later of an epidural hematoma.

At trial, plaintiff contended that had Siegrist taken Farwell to the hospital, or had he notified someone of Farwell's condition and whereabouts, Farwell would not have died. A neurosurgeon testified that if a person in Farwell's condition is taken to a doctor before, or within half an hour after, consciousness is lost, there is an 85 to 88 percent chance of survival. Plaintiff testified that Siegrist told him that he knew Farwell was badly injured and that he should have done something.

The jury returned a verdict for plaintiff and awarded $15,000 in damages. The Court of Appeals reversed, finding that Siegrist had not assumed the duty of obtaining aid for Farwell and that he neither knew nor should have known of the need for medical treatment. . . . [We must decide w]hether, on the facts of this case, the trial judge should have ruled, as a matter of law, that Siegrist owed no duty to Farwell? . . . Without regard to whether there is a general duty to aid a person in distress, there is a clearly recognized legal duty of every person to avoid any affirmative acts which may make a situation worse. . . .

Siegrist contends that he is not liable for failure to obtain medical assistance for Farwell because he had no duty to do so.

Courts have been slow to recognize a duty to render aid to a person in peril. Where such a duty has been found, it has been predicated upon the existence of a special relationship between the parties; in such a case, if defendant knew or should have known of the other person's peril, he is required to render reasonable care under all the circumstances.

In *Depue v. Flateu*, 100 Minn. 299, 111 N.W. 1 (1907), the Supreme Court of Minnesota reversed an order of the trial court dismissing the cause of action and said that if the defendants knew their dinner guest was ill, it was for the jury to decide whether they were negligent in refusing his request to spend the night and, propping him on his wagon with the reins thrown over his shoulder, sending him toward home.

The Sixth Circuit Court of Appeals, in *Hutchinson v. Dickie*, 162 F.2d 103, 106 (6th Cir. 1947), said that a host had an affirmative duty to attempt to rescue a guest who had fallen off his yacht. The host controlled the only instrumentality of rescue. The Court declared that to ask of the host anything less than that he attempt to rescue his guest would be "so shocking to humanitarian considerations and the commonly accepted code of social conduct that the courts in similar situations have had no difficulty in pronouncing it to be a legal obligation."

Farwell and Siegrist were companions on a social venture. Implicit in such a common undertaking is the understanding that one will render assistance to the other when he is in peril if he can do so without endangering himself. Siegrist knew or should have known when he left Farwell, who was badly beaten and unconscious, in the back seat of his car that no one would find him before morning. Under these circumstances, to say that Siegrist had no duty to obtain medical assistance or at least to notify someone of Farwell's condition and whereabouts would be "shocking to humanitarian considerations" and fly in the face of "the commonly accepted code of social conduct." . . .

Farwell and Siegrist were companions engaged in a common undertaking; there was a special relationship between the parties. Because Siegrist knew or should have known of the peril Farwell was in and could render assistance without endangering himself he had an affirmative duty to come to Farwell's aid.

The Court of Appeals is REVERSED and the verdict of the jury reinstated.

FITZGERALD, JUSTICE (dissenting).

. . . Plaintiff argues that once having voluntarily undertaken the duty of caring for decedent, defendant could not discontinue such assistance if, in so doing, he left the decedent in a worse position than when such duty was assumed. Defendant's knowledge of the seriousness of decedent's injury and the failure to advise decedent's grandparents, the close personal relationship that existed between defendant and the decedent, and the supposition that the decedent relied upon defendant for assistance leads plaintiff to conclude that defendant did not act "with the reasonable prudence and care of a reasonable man in the same or like circumstances." Defendant's position is that there was no volunteered assumption of duty to care for the safety of the decedent. He argues that the facts within his knowledge on the evening of August 26, 1966, and the evidence introduced at trial failed to establish that defendant should have seen that Richard Farwell had suffered a potentially fatal injury requiring immediate attention.

Defendant did not voluntarily assume the duty of caring for the decedent's safety. Nor did the circumstances which existed on the evening of August 26, 1966, impose such a duty. Testimony revealed that only a qualified physician would have reason to suspect that Farwell had suffered an injury which required immediate medical attention. The decedent never complained of pain and, in fact, had expressed a desire to retaliate against his attackers.

Defendant's inability to arouse the decedent upon arriving at his grandparents' home does not permit us to infer, as does plaintiff, that defendant knew or should have known that the deceased was seriously injured. While it might have been more prudent for the defendant to insure that the decedent was safely in the house prior to leaving, we cannot say that defendant acted unreasonably in permitting Farwell to spend the night asleep in the back seat of his car.

The close relationship between defendant and the decedent is said to establish a legal duty upon defendant to obtain assistance for the decedent. No authority is cited for this proposition other than the public policy observation that the interest of society would be benefited if its members were required to assist one another. This is not the appropriate case to establish a standard of conduct requiring one to legally assume the duty of insuring the safety of another. Recognizing that legal commentaries have expressed moral outrage at those decisions which permit one to refuse aid to another whose life may be in peril, we cannot say that, considering the relationship between these two parties and the existing circumstances, defendant acted in an unreasonable manner. Plaintiff believes that a legal duty to aid others should exist where such assistance greatly benefits society and only a reasonable burden is imposed upon those in a position to help. He contends further that the determination of the existence of a duty must rest with the jury where questions of foreseeability and the relationship of the parties are primary considerations.

It is clear that defendant's nonfeasance, or the "passive inaction or a failure to take steps to protect [the decedent] from harm" is urged as being the proximate cause of Farwell's death. We must reject plaintiff's proposition which elevates a moral obligation to the level of a legal duty, where, as here, the facts within defendant's knowledge in no way indicated that immediate medical attention was necessary and the relationship between the parties imposes no affirmative duty to render assistance. The posture of this case does not permit us to create a legal duty upon one to render assistance to another injured or imperiled party where the initial injury was not caused by the person upon whom the duty is sought to be imposed.

NOTES

1. *Harsh Rules Breed Exceptions: Assumed Duties. Farwell* deals with two potential exceptions to the no duty to act rule. First, even though one may generally have no duty to act to help another person, one may assume a duty. This assumed duty is what we referred to above in note 4, *supra*, following the *Posecai* case when we noted that a merchant might assume a duty to protect against a third party criminal act by hiring security guards. One who assumes a duty to help another must thereafter exercise reasonable care in helping and cannot suspend rescue efforts if to do so would leave the victim worse off or deprive the victim of other available aid.

REST. 3D TORTS § 42 provides:

> An actor who undertakes to render services to another that the actor knows or should know reduces the risk of physical harm to the other

has a duty of reasonable care to the other in conducting the undertaking if:

(a) the failure to exercise such care increases the risk of harm beyond that which existed without the undertaking, or

(b) the person to whom the services are rendered or another relies on the actor's exercising reasonable care in the undertaking.

Id. § 43 provides:

An actor who undertakes to render services to another that the actor knows or should know reduces the risk of physical harm to which a third person is exposed has a duty of reasonable care to the third person in conducting the undertaking if:

(a) the failure to exercise reasonable care increases the risk of harm beyond that which existed without the undertaking;

(b) the actor has undertaken to perform a duty owed by the other to the third person, or

(c) the person to whom the services are rendered, the third party, or another relies on the actor's exercising reasonable care in the undertaking.

And, *id.* § 44 provides:

(a) An actor who, despite no duty to do so, takes charge of another who reasonably appears to be: (1) imperiled and (2) helpless or unable to protect himself or herself has a duty to exercise reasonable care while the other is within the actors' charge.

(b) An actor who discontinues aid or protection is subject to a duty of reasonable care to refrain from putting the other in a worse position than existed before the actor took charge of the other and, if the other reasonably appears to be in imminent peril of serious bodily harm at the time of termination, to exercise reasonable care with regard to the peril before terminating the rescue.

Would a mere promise ever be a sufficient undertaking to impose a duty in tort? *See Thorn v. Deas,* 4 Johns 84 (N.Y. 1809) (joint owner of property who neglected to fulfill promise to obtain insurance for property was not liable to joint owner for loss of property because promise to get insurance was not supported by consideration). Should it? What incentives does an assumed duty rule provide? One generally has no duty to act but if one does act to help, then one assumes a duty to exercise reasonable care.

2. *Special Relationships.* A second potential exception to the no duty to act rule with which *Farwell* also deals is the rule that one has a duty to act if there is a special relationship between the victim and the defendant. *See* REST. 3D TORTS § 40. Some duty-triggering relationships include parent and child; common carrier and passenger; innkeeper and guest; a business owner or other property owner who holds her property open to the public and those legally (and properly) on the property; employer and employee; a school and its students; jailer and prisoner; captain and seaman; and spouse and spouse. *See id.*

§ 40(b). What is the relationship between Siegrist and Farwell? What is the basis of the special relationship — mere friendship? Should friends have a legal duty to help one another? Does your answer turn on whether help or the opportunity to rescue is "easy?" If so, is the no-duty-to-act rule as important as it might at first appear?

3. *Negligent and Innocent Injurers.* Another exception to the no duty to act rule provides that a tortious or innocent injurer has a duty to act to help the person she injured. *See* REST. 3D TORTS § 39.

4. *Statutory Duties.* Some states impose a statutory duty to act to help another. For example, the State of Vermont has enacted a Duty to Aid the Endangered Act, 12 VT. STAT. ANN. § 519. The Act provides in relevant part:

> (a) A person who knows that another is exposed to grave physical harm shall, to the extent that the same can be rendered without danger or peril to himself or without interference with important duties owed to others, give reasonable assistance to the exposed person unless that assistance or care is being provided by others.

> (b) A person who provides reasonable assistance in compliance with subsection (a) of this section shall not be liable in civil damages unless his acts constitute gross negligence or unless he will receive or expects to receive remuneration. Nothing contained in this subsection shall alter existing law with respect to tort liability of a practitioner of the healing arts for acts committed in the ordinary course of his practice.

> (c) A person who willfully violates subsection (a) of this section shall be fined not more than $100.00.

Other states have also enacted statutes imposing limited duties and/or criminalizing the failure to act in certain situations. The Third Restatement is in accord with this position. *See* REST. 3D Torts § 38.

MUNSTERMANN v. ALEGENT HEALTH-IMMANUEL MEDICAL CENTER
716 N.W.2d 73 (Neb. 2006)

GERRARD, JUDGE.

Marty Nuzum murdered his estranged girl friend, Jodi Sue Rowe, on February 12, 2002. The question presented in this appeal is whether Nuzum communicated a serious threat of physical violence against Rowe to the defendants, Nuzum's treating psychiatrist and health care facility, such that the defendants were under a duty to take reasonable precautions to prevent the murder. The jury in this case was unable to reach a verdict, and the district court declared a mistrial. The defendants appeal from the judgment of the district court denying their motion for judgment notwithstanding the verdict. We affirm the district court's denial of the defendants' motion for judgment notwithstanding the verdict, and remand the cause for a new trial . . . . This is an action for wrongful death brought by Carol K. Munstermann, personal representative of Rowe's estate, against Alegent Health-Immanuel Medical

Center (Alegent) and Hudson Hsieh, M.D., Nuzum's treating psychiatrist at Alegent, for their alleged failure to protect or warn Rowe.

The matter went to trial, after which the defendants made a motion for directed verdict, arguing, inter alia, that there was insufficient evidence that Nuzum communicated a serious threat of physical violence against Rowe to the defendants to give rise to a duty to protect or warn Rowe. The motion was denied, and the matter was submitted to the jury, but the jury was unable to reach a verdict. A mistrial was declared, and the defendants moved for a judgment notwithstanding the verdict, which was denied. This appeal followed . . . .

Nuzum was admitted to inpatient care at Alegent on February 4, 2002, when he checked himself in, suffering from depression and suicidal ideations. Nuzum was treated by Hsieh. Nuzum had been treated as an inpatient at Alegent in January 2002, following a suicide attempt. Nuzum had attempted suicide in 1990, 2000, and 2002.

When Nuzum was admitted in January 2002, he was not found to exhibit any homicidal tendencies. Nuzum was examined and observed for homicidal risk factors during his week as an inpatient, and none were found. When Nuzum checked himself back in on February 4, he again denied having homicidal ideations or assaultive behavior. Nuzum was seen by [Dr.] Hsieh on February 5, 2002, with several medical students present, and one of those students, Rebecca Gurney (who is now a medical doctor), transcribed notes for Hsieh. Because those notes are central to the plaintiff's case, they are set forth below in their entirety:

> 2/5/02
>
> M3 transcribing for Dr. Hsieh
>
> Pt was last here ~ 1 mo ago. Pt was to follow up with therapist and take medications. Pt was taking meds. Pt was working, did Ø see therapist. Pt is having problems with girlfriend — she doesn't understand depression. He has been calling into work, doesn't want to get out of bed.
>
> Pt has had suicidal thoughts. He wants to sleep all time, stop thinking.
>
> Thought he would come here before he hurt himself.
>
> Pt was thinking of hurting girlfriend also since she is hurting him. Girlfriend doesn't want to talk about his depression. She won't participate here.
>
> Pt is on Remeron (15 mg) now. Makes him sleep.
>
> Pt doesn't trust himself.
>
> Increase Remeron dose.
>
> [Signed] R. Gurney [M3]

Nuzum was discharged from Alegent on February 7, 2002. His discharge summary indicated that he had recovered from this instance of severe depression and that his suicidal ideations had subsided. Nuzum had been consistently assessed during his stay for homicidal risk factors, and none were present. Nuzum was prescribed medications, instructed on how to follow up with individual psychotherapy, and encouraged to attend community support.

On February 12, 2002, Nuzum murdered Rowe after she came to his apartment to retrieve a set of car keys. Neither Hsieh nor any employee of Alegent acted to warn Rowe or law enforcement that Nuzum might be dangerous.

The primary issue at trial was how to interpret the indication in Gurney's February 5, 2002, notes that Nuzum "was thinking of hurting girlfriend also since she is hurting him." . . .

The threshold inquiry in this appeal is whether the defendants owed the plaintiff a legal duty. This is our first opportunity to address the issues most closely associated with the California Supreme Court's decision in *Tarasoff v. Regents of University of California,* 17 Cal.3d 425, 551 P.2d 334, 131 Cal.Rptr. 14 (1976) (Tarasoff). In *Tarasoff,* the plaintiffs alleged that the defendant therapist had a duty to warn their daughter of the danger posed to her by one of the therapist's patients. The court recognized the general rule that a person owes no duty to control the acts of another. But the court adopted REST. 2D TORTS § 315 at 122 (1965), which provides:

> There is no duty so to control the conduct of a third person as to prevent him from causing physical harm to another unless
>
> (a) a special relation exists between the actor and the third person which imposes a duty upon the actor to control the third person's conduct, or
>
> (b) a special relation exists between the actor and the other which gives to the other a right to protection.

Applying this exception, the *Tarasoff* court held that the relationship between the patient and her therapist was sufficient to support the imposition of an affirmative duty on the defendant for the benefit of third persons. The *Tarasoff* court further held that a therapist's duty to act arises when the therapist determines, or pursuant to the standards of the profession should determine, that the patient presents a serious danger of violence to another.

The vast majority of courts that have considered this issue have accepted the *Tarasoff* analysis. In *Lipari v. Sears, Roebuck & Co.,* 497 F.Supp. 185 (D. Neb. 1980), the U.S. District Court for the District of Nebraska correctly predicted that this court would adopt § 315. . . . Based on that determination, the U.S. District Court concluded that this court would adopt the *Tarasoff* holding as well. In the wake of *Tarasoff,* however, the California Legislature restricted the scope of *Tarasoff* liability. See CAL. CIV. CODE § 43.92 (West Cum. Supp. 2006). Under § 43.92(a), a duty to warn of and protect from a patient's threatened violent behavior arises only "where the patient has communicated to the psychotherapist a serious threat of physical violence against a reasonably identifiable victim or victims." Several states have enacted similar statutes based upon California's example, including Nebraska. . . .

NEB. REV. STAT. § 71-1,336 (Reissue 2003) provides, in relevant part:

(1) There shall be no monetary liability on the part of, and no cause of action shall arise against, any person who is licensed or certified [as a mental health practitioner] for failing to warn of and protect from a patient's threatened violent behavior or failing to predict and warn of and protect from a patient's violent behavior except when the patient has communicated to the mental health practitioner a serious threat of physical violence against himself, herself, or a reasonably identifiable victim or victims.

(2) The duty to warn of or to take reasonable precautions to provide protection from violent behavior shall arise only under the limited circumstances specified in subsection (1) of this section. The duty shall be discharged by the mental health practitioner if reasonable efforts are made to communicate the threat to the victim or victims and to a law enforcement agency.

The parties to this appeal tried this case, and filed their appellate briefs, on the assumption that § 71-1,336 was controlling. That assumption, however, was misplaced. As will be explained in more detail below, the defendant in this case, Hsieh, is a psychiatrist — a physician, licensed pursuant to NEB. REV. STAT. § 71-1,102 to 71-1,107.14 (Reissue 1996 & Cum. Supp. 2000) [and thus 71-1,336 was not controlling in and of itself]. The Nebraska statutes specify the scope of *Tarasoff* liability for psychologists and "mental health practitioners," but do not provide corresponding statutory language for psychiatrists . . .

It is important to note the difference between psychologists and psychiatrists. Psychology is the science dealing with mental processes, both normal and abnormal, and their effects upon behavior. TABER'S CYCLOPEDIC MEDICAL DICTIONARY 1591 (18th ed. 1997). Psychiatry, on the other hand, is the branch of medicine that deals with the diagnosis, treatment, and prevention of mental illness. *Id.* at 1590. In other words, psychiatrists are medical doctors who specialize in mental illness, while psychologists belong to a separate discipline devoted to understanding the human mind and, in clinical psychology, concerned with diagnosing and treating mental disorders. *See id.* at 1591. . . .

In contrast to psychologists and other mental health professionals, psychiatrists, as medical doctors, are licensed pursuant to § 71-1,102 to 71-1,107.14. Those sections contain no equivalent to § 71-1,206.30 or 71-1,336. In short, the duty of psychologists and other mental health professionals to warn and protect third persons is controlled by statute, but a psychiatrist's duty is not addressed by statute, and is still controlled by common law.

After the present appeal was submitted to this court, based upon our consideration of the statutory scheme, we directed the parties to file supplemental briefs addressing whether Hsieh's duty, in his treatment of Nuzum, was controlled by statute. Based upon the reasoning we have set forth above, the parties agree that neither § 71-1,336, nor any other statute, addresses Hsieh's duty in his treatment of Nuzum. The defendants now assert that in the absence of a specifically applicable statute, they owed no duty at all to warn and protect Rowe. The plaintiff insists that in the absence of a statute, the case should have been tried as an ordinary medical malpractice action. We do not accept either of these contentions. . . .

The threshold inquiry in any negligence action, including those involving a duty to warn and protect, is whether the defendant owed the plaintiff a duty. A duty is defined as an obligation, to which the law will give recognition and effect, to conform to a particular standard of conduct toward another. Whether a legal duty exists for actionable negligence is a question of law dependent on the facts in a particular situation. When making that determination a court considers (1) the magnitude of the risk, (2) the relationship of the parties, (3) the nature of the attendant risk, (4) the opportunity and ability to exercise care, (5) the foreseeability of the harm, and (6) the policy interest in the proposed solution.

In this case, we are also mindful of the fact that the determination of a legal duty is fundamentally based in public policy considerations, and it is generally the function of the Legislature to declare what is the law and public policy of this state. Although §71-1,206.30(1) and 71-1,336 "may not be literally applicable, [they are] clearly indicative of legislatively approved public policy." See *Parson v. Chizek*, 272 N.W.2d 48, 51 (Neb. 1978).

Given our prior endorsement of RESTATEMENT (SECOND) OF TORTS §315 (1965), and the clearly articulated public policy expressed in §71-1,206.30(1) and 71-1,336, we conclude that in some circumstances, a special relation may exist between a psychiatrist and patient which imposes a duty upon the psychiatrist to warn or protect a reasonably identifiable victim when a patient has communicated a serious threat of physical violence against that potential victim. However, given the Legislature's decision to limit *Tarasoff* by enacting §71-1,206.30(1) and 71-1,336, we find that the limitations set forth in those sections should also be applied to psychiatrists. The Legislature has made a public policy determination with respect to the *Tarasoff* duty that this court is bound to respect. We see no rational basis for distinguishing the *Tarasoff* duty of psychiatrists from that of psychologists or other mental health practitioners.

Moreover, the analysis of California's identical statutory language, from which the Nebraska statutes were derived, has revealed that the statute is based upon public policy concerns to which our familiar risk-utility test is applicable. The intent of limiting a *Tarasoff* duty to situations in which the patient communicates a serious threat of physical violence was not to overrule *Tarasoff*, but, rather, to preempt an expansive ruling that a therapist can be held liable for the mere failure to predict potential violence by his or her patient. *Ewing v. Goldstein*, 120 Cal. App. 4th 807 (2004). The statutory language represents an effort to strike an appropriate balance between conflicting policy interests. *Id.*

On the one hand, the need to preserve a patient confidence recognizes that effective diagnosis and treatment of a mental illness or an emotional problem is severely undermined when a patient cannot be assured that a statement made in the privacy of his or her therapist's office will not be revealed. *Id.* On the other hand is the recognition that under limited circumstances, preserving a confidence is less important than protecting the safety of someone the patient intends to harm. *Id.* In other words, the statutory language is the result of balancing risk and utility, considering the magnitude of the risk, relationship of the parties, nature of the risk, opportunity and ability to exercise care, foreseeability of the harm, and public policy interest in the proposed solution. Considering our risk-utility test, and the relevant public policy determinations made by the Legislature, we conclude the same duty should be required of psychiatrists as is required of psychologists and other mental health practitioners. We hold, in accord with §71-1,206.30(1) and 71-1,336, that a psychiatrist is liable for failing to warn of and protect from a patient's threatened violent behavior, or failing to predict and warn of and protect from a patient's violent behavior, when the patient has communicated to the psychiatrist a serious threat of physical violence against himself, herself, or a reasonably identifiable victim or victims. The duty to warn of or to take reasonable precautions to provide protection from violent behavior shall arise only under those limited circumstances, and shall be discharged by the psychiatrist if reasonable efforts are made to communicate the threat to the victim or victims and to a law enforcement agency. . . .

With that established, the issue to be confronted in this case is whether Nuzum actually communicated a serious threat of physical violence to the defendants. In that regard, it is important to note that in striking a balance between the protection of third parties and the preservation of medical confidentiality, the statutory language from which our holding is derived is intended to eliminate a therapist's immunity and sanction an invasion into the therapist-patient privilege only in the narrow circumstance in which actual knowledge of potentially grave bodily injury is presented.

The phrase "'serious threat of physical violence'" does not refer to the credibility of a patient's stated intentions, the harm likely to be suffered irrespective of his or her intent, or the gravity of the threatened injury. 15 Cal. Rptr. 3d at 874. The psychiatrist's duty to third parties is not premised on a professional standard of care. Rather, it rests entirely on the fact finder's determination that each factual predicate of the cause of action is satisfied: the existence of a professional relationship, the psychiatrist's actual belief or prediction that the patient poses a serious risk of inflicting grave bodily injury, a reasonably identifiable victim, and the failure to undertake reasonable efforts to warn the victim and a law enforcement agency. *Id.* The question is whether a serious threat of physical violence was actually "communicated" to the psychiatrist. Thus, a duty to warn and protect arises only if the information communicated to the psychiatrist leads the psychiatrist to believe that his or her patient poses a serious risk of grave bodily injury to another.

This does not mean that in an appropriate case, a finder of fact could not conclude that a particular threat of violence was so serious that a defendant could not have believed it to be anything other than credible. Nor does it mean that in some instances, expert testimony might not be helpful to the trier of fact in evaluating a defendant's testimony about whether he or she believed a particular threat of violence to be sincere. It simply means that in determining whether a duty to warn and protect is alleged to have arisen under the holding of this case, the focus should be on whether the patient actually communicated a serious threat of physical violence to his or her psychiatrist. Given that understanding, the evidence in this case is less than clear as to whether Nuzum effectively communicated a serious threat of physical violence. There is little to dispute Hsieh and Gurney's testimony that each understood

Nuzum's statements to indicate that he had, when attempting suicide, been attempting to emotionally hurt Rowe. Wadle [plaintiff's expert] testified that in his opinion, Nuzum was "most likely" referring to physical violence when he made the statement at issue, but Wadle conceded that he had no basis to conclude that the defendants believed Nuzum was making such a threat.

However, the jury instructions given in this case illustrate that the parties and the trial court were working with differing, and mistaken, understandings of what the plaintiff was required to prove. The jury was instructed, without objection, of the exact language of § 71-1,336. But the jury was also instructed, again without objection, that this was "an action based upon a claim of malpractice, sometimes called professional negligence" and that under Nebraska law, the question was whether the defendants had used reasonable care, skill, and knowledge possessed and used under like circumstances by members of the profession engaged in a similar practice in the locality or similar localities. Those instructions were inconsistent with both one another and the duty to warn or protect principles set forth above. Given these instructions, and the evidence supporting liability under one instruction but not the other, it is not surprising that the jury was unable to reach a verdict.

We conclude, given the unsettled state of Nebraska law prior to this opinion, and the uncertainty evident at trial about what standards controlled liability in this case, that it would be inequitable to find that the plaintiff failed, as a matter of law, to meet the burden of proof on liability when the record before us was created without a clear understanding of what, precisely, the plaintiff was required to prove. "There was considerable uncertainty not only as to the existence of a legal duty but also as to the scope of any such duty and the appropriate method of discharging that duty." Thus, the parties were at a considerable disadvantage in marshalling evidence in support of and in defense of the duty to warn or protect claim in the initial trial.

It would be unfair for this court to answer questions of first impression, then retroactively apply those answers without offering the plaintiff an opportunity to meet the bar that has been set. For this reason, we find no merit to the defendants' first assignment of error, arguing that they were entitled to a judgment as a matter of law based upon the lack of a legal duty to warn and protect. For the same reason, however, we conclude that there is merit to the defendants' second assignment of error with respect to the jury instructions. Obviously, on retrial, the jury instructions should reflect the principles of duty explained above. . . .

The defendants also argue that they were entitled to a directed verdict on the issue of causation, contending the evidence was insufficient to support a conclusion that any act or omission of the defendants proximately caused Rowe's murder. The defendants argue Wadle's testimony that the defendants' post discharge provisions for Nuzum were below the standard of care and his opinion that had Rowe "been forewarned of a threat to her by . . . Nuzum, she would have had an opportunity to avoid contact with him and may have lived" are insufficient proof that had the defendants acted to protect or warn Rowe, those efforts would probably have been successful. As a result, the defendants argue that any breach of duty on their part was not the proximate cause of Rowe's death.

However, the same difficulties that make it impossible, on this record, to decide the issue of liability as a matter of law also preclude a finding as a matter of law with respect to proximate cause. An action predicated on a duty to warn and protect is essentially a negligence action. In order to prevail in such an action, a plaintiff must establish the defendant's duty to protect the plaintiff from injury, a failure to discharge that duty, and damages proximately caused by the failure to discharge that duty. In order to prove proximate cause, it is necessary to understand both a defendant's duty, and what the defendant was required to do to discharge that duty — the question is whether the specific act or omission of the defendant was such that the ultimate injury to the plaintiff reasonably flowed from the defendant's alleged breach of duty. The confusion at trial about the defendants' duty, and how that duty was to be discharged, necessarily affected the parties' ability to adduce evidence relevant to proximate cause. Furthermore, the evidence reflects that Rowe was murdered at Nuzum's apartment, where she went to retrieve a set of car keys. When all reasonable inferences are given to the plaintiff, we cannot say, as a matter of law, that reasonable jurors could not conclude that had Rowe been told Nuzum had threatened her, she might not have been in a position where she could be killed. Thus, we find no merit to the defendants' third and final assignment of error. [AFFIRMED.]

NOTES

1. *Special Relationships with Wrongdoers.* With whom did defendant doctors have a special relationship? The victim? The person who caused the harm? REST. 3D TORTS § 41 imposes a duty on certain persons who have a special relationship with a person who poses risks to another. Section 41 (b) identifies the following duty-triggering relationships:

> (1) a parent with dependent children, (2) a custodian with those in its custody, (3) an employer with employees when the employment facilitates the employee's causing harm to third persons, and (4) a mental health professional with patients.

Id. § 41(b).

Consider the ways in which this rule affects the field of psychiatry and those the profession serves.

2. *What's Reasonable?* What if the parents of a dependent child are afraid for their own safety? Would that negate the duty owed by the parents to act for the child's safety or be relevant to the issue of whether there was a breach in their duty of care? *See Cooper v. Meyer*, 365 N.E.2d 201 (Ill. App. 1977). What if an 18 year-old, self-supporting child was still living at home? Would the parents owe a duty to act if they knew the child was dangerous? What evidence indicates dangerousness? In *Eldredge v. Kamp Kachess Youth Serv., Inc.*, 583 P.2d 626 (Wash. 1978), a duty was imposed on the operators of a camp for delinquents when three residents escaped, stole the plaintiff's vehicle and wrecked it.

3. *Did Tarasoff Change Psychiatry?* The genesis of the duty to control patients is *Tarasoff v. Regents of Univ. of Cal.*, 551 P.2d 334, 347 (Cal.1976).

Tarasoff arose out of the events that preceded the killing of Tatiana Tarasoff by Poddar. Plaintiffs alleged that Poddar had confided his intentions to kill Tatiana to a psychologist employed by the defendant university. Although the campus police investigated Poddar, no one warned Tatiana or her parents. Writing for the majority, Justice Tobriner concluded:

> Our current crowded and computerized society compels the interdependence of its members. In this risk-infested society we can hardly tolerate the further exposure to danger that would result from a concealed knowledge of the therapist that his patient was lethal. If the exercise of reasonable care to protect the threatened victim requires the therapist to warn the endangered party or those who can reasonably be expected to notify him, we see no sufficient societal interest that would protect and justify concealment.

In *Schuster v. Altenberg*, 424 N.W.2d 159, 168 (Wis. 1988), the court noted that "the duty which was recognized in *Tarasoff* was not limited to a duty to warn but extended to 'whatever other steps are reasonably necessary under the circumstances.' While the decision is principally noted for its holding, establishing a duty to warn third parties, the duty recognized in *Tarasoff* was significantly broader." Is part of the difficulty in recognizing a duty to act as a consequence of a special relationship to the wrongdoer related to defining what steps a reasonable person would take to control the wrongdoer? As the principal case acknowledges, many states have responded with clarifying legislation. Is this an area better left to the legislature? Why?

4. *Warning!!!* If the information costs imposed on potential victims most concern us, should we require sexual predators, parolees, and others posing risks to post large signs on their homes stating, for example, *DANGEROUS PSYCHOPATH: KEEP YOUR DISTANCE.* Who predicts dangerousness? Would such a condition of probation or parole violate constitutional protection against cruel and unusual punishment, or first amendment guarantees against "forced" speech? The most famous state reaction to such issues is the *New Jersey Registration and Community Notification Law*, N.J.S.A. 2C:7-1 *et seq.* (known as "Megan's Law" in memory of seven-year-old Megan Kanka). Many states have followed New Jersey imposing tough requirements on those who have been adjudicated sexual predators and few if any challenges to these laws raised by the convicted predators have proven successful.

5. *Spreading Disease and Duty.* In *Bradshaw v. Daniel*, 854 S.W.2d 865 (Tenn. 1993), the husband of the plaintiff's deceased was treated for Rocky Mountain spotted fever by defendant doctor. The husband died from the disease, which is caused by tick bites. Although the defendant communicated with the wife during the husband's illness, he never told her of the risk of the disease. Subsequently she contracted and died from the disease, and the plaintiff brought this wrongful death action against the doctor, alleging that the doctor owed the wife a duty to warn of the danger of contracting the disease. Reversing the dismissal of plaintiff's case, the court said the defendant had a legal duty to warn plaintiff's deceased relying, upon *Tarasoff, supra.* In *Rozycki v. Peley*, 489 A.2d 1272 (N.J. Super.1984), the wife of a pedophiliac was held to owe no duty to warn the parents of neighborhood children of her husband's proclivities because she was a layperson, not a medical health professional. *Cf. Pamela L. v. Farmer*, 112 Cal. App. 3d 206 (1980), positing liability on a special relationship created by the wife in inviting minor children into her home knowing her husband was a child molester.

B.N. v. K.K., 538 A.2d 1175 (Md. 1988), arose out of an intimate sexual relationship between a physician and a nurse. The physician had active genital herpes but never disclosed this to the nurse. The nurse contracted the disease. The court concluded, "She was a clearly identified potential victim. . . . As a consequence, Dr. K. had a duty either to refrain from sexual contact with Ms. N. or to warn her of his condition." What is the standard of care in a case such as this? For example, when would a nonphysician be held to have sufficient knowledge of his own status as a carrier? In such a case, would you recommend that defendant argue plaintiff's contributory negligence?

Does the considerable publicity given to AIDS suggest that there is as much a duty to inquire as to the health of a sexual partner as there is to warn? Does a doctor who has tested HIV positive have a duty to warn his patients? If he informs his health care facility, should it revoke or limit his privileges? Recall *Brzoska*, discussed in Chapter 2, *supra*.

6. *Reference Liability?* Plaintiffs' decedent was severely beaten and murdered by a co-worker. His estate sued the co-worker's former employer, alleging that the latter was negligent in failing to give a job reference stating the co-worker's known violent propensities. The defendant said it had not been asked for a reference, but even if it had it would have provided no information other than dates of employment. The defendant had a policy of not providing any further information, apparently out of fear of being sued for defamation. In dismissing the claim, the court held as a matter of law that an employer had no duty to disclose a former employee's "dangerous proclivities to an inquiring prospective employer." *Moore v. St. Joseph Nursing Home, Inc.*, 459 N.W.2d 100 (Mich. 1990). A discussion of the duty to disclose and related employer privilege is included in Chapter14, *infra*.

7. *A Question of Perspective.* Does liability for failure to warn of patient risk over deter doctors? Do the avoidance costs imposed on the psychiatry profession outweigh the dangers averted? What impact does the legal duty to warn have on raising the cost of health care? What is the impact of the imposed duty on allocative efficiency? Can you construct a more efficient rule governing the duty to warn? Should judges or legislatures make the rule?

E.   EMOTIONAL DISTRESS INJURIES

ATLANTIC COAST AIRLINES v. COOK
857 N.E.2d 989 (Ind. 2006)

RUCKER, JUSTICE.

In an action to recover damages for the negligent infliction of emotional distress, Indiana's modified impact rule requires a claimant to demonstrate a direct physical impact resulting from the negligence of another. Where the physical impact is slight, or the evidence of the physical impact is tenuous, we evaluate the alleged emotional distress to determine whether it is not likely speculative, exaggerated, fictitious, or unforeseeable. In this case, we conclude that the emotional distress or mental anguish allegedly suffered by the plaintiffs is speculative, and thus their claim for emotional distress damages must fail.

This case arises from a passenger's behavior onboard an aircraft five months after the September 11th terrorist hijackings of airplanes and less than two months after Richard Reid lit a match onboard a flight from Paris to Miami and attempted to detonate explosives hidden in his shoe. On February 8, 2002 Bryan and Jennifer Cook arrived at the Indianapolis International Airport for a direct flight to New York City. . . . While passengers waited to board, a man later identified as French national Frederic Girard ran toward the gate and abruptly stopped. Mr. Cook observed that the unaccompanied Girard had two tickets in his possession for the flight and that airline security had detained Girard at the boarding gate before allowing him onto the airplane. He further noticed that Girard's face was red and his eyes were bloodshot and glassy.

While boarding the Fairchild Dornier 328, a small airplane with a capacity for thirty-two passengers, Girard ran up the steps and jumped inside. Rather than proceeding to his assigned seat, he attempted to sit in a seat nearest the cockpit but the flight attendant instructed him to sit in the back row. Girard took a seat in the rear of the aircraft but repeatedly pressed the attendant call button and light switch above his head. Prior to take-off, Mr. Cook approached the flight attendant and expressed concern that Girard was a possible security threat. The attendant acknowledged as much and explained that he had directed Girard to sit in the rear of the plane so he could keep an eye on him.

During take-off Girard disregarded instructions to remain seated with his seatbelt fastened. Then during the flight Girard lit a cigarette, disregarding directives from the flight attendant that smoking onboard was prohibited. Despite this admonition Girard was permitted to retain his lighter. Mr. Cook approached three male passengers and asked for their assistance in protecting the flight in the event Girard's behavior grew dangerous. Girard moved about the plane, sat in various empty seats and finally walked up the aisle toward the cockpit. Mr. Cook blocked his path and instructed him to sit. Without any physical contact with Mr. Cook, Girard returned to his seat and lit another cigarette. The flight attendant again told him to extinguish the cigarette, and in response Girard stood and shouted, "Get back! Get back!" At this, Mr. Cook and other passengers approached Girard and ordered him to sit down. Instead Girard stomped his feet and shouted in French. Discernable to the Cooks were the words "World Trade Center," "Americans," and "New York City." Eventually a Delta Airlines employee convinced Girard to sit after speaking to him in French. The employee spent the remainder of the flight sitting across from Girard in the rear of the plane. Ultimately the pilot diverted the flight to Cleveland, Ohio where police placed Girard under arrest. The flight then continued to New York City.

Recalling the events of September 11th, and recalling also a passenger's attempt to detonate a shoe bomb aboard an airplane with the use of a match, the Cooks described their ordeal as one in which they "have never been so scared in their entire lives." Br. of Appellee at 8. The husband and wife filed a complaint in the Perry Township Small Claims Court in Marion County, Indiana. . . . The small claims court entered judgment against the Cooks, and they appealed to the Marion County Superior Court. After both sides conducted discovery, during which the trial court entered an order granting the Cooks' motion to compel discovery of Atlantic Coast's passenger manifest, the defendants filed motions for summary judgment. Atlantic Coast alleged that it was entitled to judgment as a matter of law because . . . the Cooks were not entitled to damages under Indiana's modified impact rule. . . .

After a hearing the trial court . . . determined that . . . the Cooks' claims were not precluded under Indiana's modified impact rule. . . .

. . . Claims for the negligent infliction of mental or emotional distress have long been the subject of scholarly debate. Creating rules, formulating tests, and applying them to address such claims have proven a challenge for most courts. The majority of jurisdictions employ some variation or combination of the following common law limiting tests for evaluating these claims: the "physical injury" rule under which, generally speaking, the plaintiff's emotional distress must be accompanied by a physical injury or symptom; the "zone of danger" rule, under which recovery is limited to those plaintiffs who themselves were not physically injured but were placed in immediate risk of harm by a defendant's negligent conduct which injured another; and the "bystander" test, also sometimes called the "foreseeable bystander" test, which allows recovery to certain plaintiffs that witness the injury or death of a third party (who typically must be a close relative of the bystander) that is caused by the defendant's negligence. The underlying policy reason binding together these judicially created approaches is that absent certain limitations, allowing recovery for mental or emotional distress will open the floodgates to spurious claims.

Before 1991 Indiana followed the rule that damages for mental or emotional distress were recoverable only when accompanied by and resulting from a physical injury. The underlying rationale for this rule was that "absent physical injury, mental anguish is speculative, subject to exaggeration, likely to lead to fictitious claims, and often so unforeseeable that there is no rational basis for awarding damages." *Cullison v. Medley,* 570 N.E.2d 27, 29 (Ind. 1991). But this court modified the rule in *Shuamber v. Henderson.* We held instead:

> When . . . a plaintiff sustains a direct impact by the negligence of another and, by virtue of that direct involvement sustains an emotional trauma which is serious in nature and of a kind and extent normally expected to occur in a reasonable person, . . . such a plaintiff is entitled to maintain an action to recover for that emotional trauma without regard to whether the emotional trauma arises out of or accompanies any physical injury to the plaintiff.

Shuamber v. Henderson, 579 N.E.2d 452, 456 (Ind.1991).

We further expounded upon the contours of what is now commonly referred to as the "modified impact rule" in two cases handed down the same day. In *Conder v. Wood,* 716 N.E.2d 432, 435 (Ind. 1999), we held, "'direct impact' is properly understood as the requisite measure of 'direct involvement' in the incident giving rise to the emotional trauma. Viewed in this context, we find that it matters little how the physical impact occurs, so long as that impact arises from the plaintiff's direct involvement in the tortfeasor's negligent conduct." *Id.* (finding that a pedestrian suffered a direct impact by pounding upon the panels of a truck that was running over her co-worker). In *Ross v. Cheema,* 716 N.E.2d 435, 437 (Ind. 1999), we held, "[i]n causing the requisite physical injuries, the direct impact is properly understood as being 'physical' in nature. Though removing the physical injury element, *Shuamber* in no way altered the 'impact' element of the rule. For purposes of the modified rule, the direct impact sustained by the plaintiff must necessarily be a 'physical' one." *Id.* (rejecting claim that plaintiff sustained the direct physical impact necessary to recover damages for negligent infliction of emotional distress by merely hearing a loud pounding at her door).

As *Shuamber, Conder,* and *Ross* make clear, the modified impact rule maintains the requirement of a direct physical impact. The impact however does not need to cause physical injury to the plaintiff. Additionally the emotional trauma suffered by the plaintiff does not need to result from a physical injury caused by the impact. But how do we assess whether the degree of impact is sufficient to satisfy the requirement of the rule? We have answered this question as follows:

> [W]hen the courts have been satisfied that the facts of a particular case are such that the alleged mental anguish was not likely speculative, exaggerated, fictitious, or unforeseeable, then the claimant has been allowed to proceed with an emotional distress claim for damages even though the physical impact was slight, or the evidence of physical impact seemed to have been rather tenuous.

Bader v. Johnson, 732 N.E.2d 1212, 1221 (Ind. 2000) (finding that mother's continued pregnancy and the physical transformation that her body underwent satisfied the direct impact requirement) (citing *Alexander v. Scheid,* 726 N.E.2d 272, 283–84 (Ind. 2000) (holding that patient suffering from the destruction of healthy lung tissue due to physician's failure to diagnose cancer was sufficient for negligent infliction of emotional distress); *Holloway v. Bob Evans Farms, Inc.,* 695 N.E.2d 991, 996 (Ind. Ct. App. 1998), *trans. not sought* (concluding that restaurant patron's ingestion of a portion of vegetables cooked with a worm was a direct physical impact under the modified impact rule); *Dollar Inn, Inc., v. Slone,* 695 N.E.2d 185, 189 (Ind. Ct. App. 1998), *trans. denied* (finding that hotel guest stabbing herself in the thumb with a hypodermic needle concealed in a roll of toilet paper was sufficient for claim of emotional distress associated with guest's fear of contracting AIDS)).

We acknowledge there have been calls to abandon the impact rule altogether. *See, e.g., Delta Airlines* [*v. Cook,* 821 N.E.2d 400, 401 (Ind. Ct. App. 2005)] (asserting that the reasoning underlying this Court's decision to eliminate the physical injury requirement under the impact rule "also supports eliminating the physical impact requirement under the modified impact rule"); *Ketchmark v. N. Ind. Pub. Serv. Co.,* 818 N.E.2d 522, 526 (Ind. Ct. App. 2004), *trans. not sought* (Crone, J., dissenting) (declaring that, "the time has come to clear the decks of the so-called 'impact rule' and to allow the tort of negligent infliction of emotional distress to stand on its own inherent elements"). Among other things there are concerns that Indiana's impact rule, even as modified, may prohibit some litigants from recovering damages for *bona fide* emotional injury even though there has been no physical impact. These are respectable positions. But this jurisdiction is not alone in grappling with this area of the law for which there is no grand unified theory. We agree with the observations of the California Supreme Court:

> In order to avoid limitless liability out of all proportion to the degree of a defendant's negligence, and against which it is impossible to insure without imposing unacceptable costs on those among whom the risk is spread, the right to recover for negligently caused emotional distress must be limited. . . . [W]e balance the impact of arbitrary lines which deny recovery to some victims whose injury is very real against that of imposing liability out of proportion to culpability for negligent acts. We also weigh in the balance the importance to the administration of justice of clear guidelines under which litigants and trial courts may resolve disputes.

Thing v. La Chusa, 771 P.2d 814, 826–27 (Cal. 1989) (reaffirming California's application of the bystander rule for emotional distress damages). It is our view that the requirements under Indiana's rule are modest and that a less restrictive rule would raise the potential for a flood of trivial suits, pose the possibility of fraudulent claims that are difficult for judges and juries to detect, and result in unlimited and unpredictable liability. We therefore reaffirm that Indiana's impact rule continues to require a plaintiff to demonstrate a direct physical impact resulting from the negligence of another.

This Court has carved out an exception to the physical impact requirement for the negligent infliction of emotional distress. Mindful that the underlying rationale for direct impact is that "it provides clear and unambiguous evidence that the plaintiff was so directly involved in the incident giving rise to the emotional trauma that it is unlikely that the claim is merely spurious," we recognized that there may be circumstances under which a "plaintiff does not sustain a direct impact" but is nonetheless "sufficiently directly involved in the incident giving rise to the emotional trauma that we are able to distinguish legitimate claims from the mere spurious." *Groves v. Taylor,* 729 N.E.2d 569, 572 (Ind. 2000). We thus adopted what is now commonly referred to as the bystander rule. "[W]here the direct impact test is not met, a bystander may nevertheless establish 'direct involvement' by proving that the plaintiff actually witnessed or came on the scene soon after the death or severe injury of a loved one with a relationship to the plaintiff analogous to a spouse, parent, child, grandparent, grandchild, or sibling caused by the defendant's negligent or otherwise tortious conduct." *Id.* at 573. In sum, in order to recover damages for the negligent infliction emotional distress, a plaintiff must satisfy either the modified impact rule or the bystander rule. The elements for each are separate and distinct.

Turning to the case before us, the Cooks do not contend that the bystander rule applies to them. That is, the Cooks do not argue that they witnessed the death or severe injury of a loved one. Rather, their claim rises or falls on whether they suffered a direct physical impact from the alleged negligence of

Atlantic Coast. The Cooks insist they did so and that the physical impact was both actual and constructive. According to the Cooks, breathing the smoke from Girard's lit cigarette and experiencing the vibrations from Girard's stomping feet caused an actual physical impact, and "constructive impact occurred by virtue of the physical effects on the [Cooks'] vital body functions in increased breathing, sweating, pulse, heart rate, adrenaline, and acuteness of the senses." Br. in Opp. to Pet. for Trans. at 4. We first observe that neither this Court nor the Court of Appeals has ever addressed or adopted a theory of "constructive impact" as part of Indiana's impact rule, and we decline to do so today. In any event, citing this Court's opinion in *Alexander,* the Court of Appeals characterized what the Cooks contend amounts to constructive impact as "physical changes" that are "good enough" to satisfy the rule. *Delta Airlines,* 821 N.E.2d at 403.

In *Alexander* the plaintiff sued her physician for failure to diagnose her lung cancer. Among other things she sought damages for emotional distress. Her healthcare providers argued that the plaintiff failed to satisfy the impact rule because the failure to diagnose cancer does not constitute an impact. We disagreed because the impact was not the failure to diagnose: "Rather, allegedly as a result of the defendants' negligence, [the plaintiff] suffered the destruction of healthy lung tissue by a cancerous tumor. . . . This is good enough." *Alexander,* 726 N.E.2d at 284. We decline to equate a physical change resulting from the destruction of healthy lung tissue with what can best be described as the human body's natural responses to fear and anxiety. Indeed, "increased breathing, sweating, pulse, heart rate, adrenaline, and acuteness of the senses" are more descriptive of stress-like symptoms experienced by many passengers during a normal airplane flight that is undergoing turbulence. They simply are not physical changes as anticipated by *Alexander.* Nor are they physical transformations as anticipated by *Bader,* 732 N.E.2d at 1222 (plaintiff's "continued pregnancy and the physical transformation her body underwent as a result, satisfy the direct impact requirement of our modified impact rule").

This leaves for our consideration whether smelling cigarette smoke and feeling floor vibrations satisfy the direct physical impact requirement of the rule. We first observe that at the very least this stretches the outer limits of the impact requirement. Indeed we doubt that most ordinary citizens would think of smelling cigarette smoke and feeling floor vibrations as physical impacts of any kind. But even assuming that in some theoretical sense these experiences may be characterized as physical impact, the impact was certainly very "slight" and "the evidence of physical impact seem[s] to have been rather tenuous." *Bader,* 732 N.E.2d at 1221. We thus explore whether the Cooks' alleged mental anguish is "not likely speculative, exaggerated, fictitious, or unforeseeable." *Id.*

Mr. Cook acknowledges that neither he nor his spouse have sought medical or mental health treatment for their mental or emotional distress. In his deposition . . . Mr. Cook described his emotional state as being "shaken up . . . anxious, just upset" and that he remained so "until [he and his wife] got to New York and got on the ground." App. at 176. Mr. Cook also testified that he was "distraught" and "probably didn't sleep well for at least a week and a half." *Id.*

He further asserted "whenever I get on a flight, I'm concerned that something could happen." *Id.* at 185. According to Mr. Cook, "I will never view things the same as I did before February 8th, '02. I will never view things as — without the concern. I'm not saying it's going to ruin my life, but I will always be — I will always remember it, and I will always — if certain news stories come on, certain things are said, certain situations, when we have terror alerts, and so forth, I will — it will always trigger the memory, and I will always-it will always be in the back of my mind." *Id.*

In her deposition . . . Mrs. Cook, who was seven months pregnant at the time of the incident, reported that after arriving in New York she "was just having lower abdominal pains. Could have been brought on by stress." App. at 227. Further, she reported that she started to feel better, "[o]nce we got home and I got back into my normal routine." *Id.* at 228. Mrs. Cook also testified that she and her husband have traveled by air probably four times since this incident. On those flights Mrs. Cook described her emotional state as "I'm always nervous." *Id.* When asked about the harm she incurred from the flight of February 8, 2002, Mrs. Cook said, "I feared for my life. I thought I was going to die." *Id.* at 230. But she stopped having those fears "[w]hen we landed." *Id.* According to Mrs. Cook, "It bothered me until we landed. It bothered me that it happened. It bothers me every time I get on a plane." *Id.*

Apparently the alleged mental and emotional distress the Cooks experienced manifested itself in fear and anxiety at the time the events were unfolding. But this fear and anxiety were transitory, disappearing once the Cooks completed their flight. Since that time, in their own words, the Cooks have experienced feelings of being "bothered," "concerned," and "nervous." But these feelings about the world around us in general and air travel in particular is the plight of many citizens in this country, living as we do in a post-September 11 environment. As one treatise has explained:

> Complete emotional tranquility is seldom attainable in this world, and some degree of transient and trivial emotional distress is a part of the price of living among people. The law intervenes only where the distress inflicted is so severe that no reasonable [person] could be expected to endure it. The intensity and the duration of the distress are factors to be considered in determining its severity.

REST. 2D TORTS § 46 cmt. j (1965). We do not suggest that the Cooks' fear and anxiety during the flight were trivial. But there was simply nothing before the trial court, and by extension before this Court, suggesting that the Cooks' fear and anxiety were anything other than temporary. And it is pure speculation to assume that the Cooks' later feelings of being bothered, concerned, and nervous are causally related to the events aboard the flight. Because the physical impact in this case was slight to nonexistent, allowing an emotional distress claim to proceed based on the Cooks' lingering mental anguish would essentially abrogate the requirements of Indiana's modified impact rule. In essence we view the alleged mental anguish here as speculative. Accordingly the trial court erred in denying Atlantic Coast's motion for summary judgment on this issue.

We affirm the trial court's denial of Atlantic Coast's motion for summary judgment on the question of federal preemption. We reverse the trial court's grant of summary judgment in favor of Atlantic Coast on the Cooks' breach of contract claim. And we reverse the trial court's denial of Atlantic Coast's motion for summary judgment on the Cooks' claim for emotional distress damages. [REVERSED AND REMANDED.]

NOTES

1. *Analytical Frames for Negligent Infliction Claims.* There are several ways to frame the courts' long-standing antipathy towards emotional distress damages unaccompanied by physical injury. (To some extent, many of the same considerations discussed below can be useful in thinking about recovery for economic losses, discussed in the next section.) The first is to observe an almost inchoate, emotional response to such damages that, perhaps, can be traced to the famous words of Justice Cardozo in *Ultramares Corp. v. Touche*, 174 N.E. 441, 444 (N.Y. 1931). Expressing the danger of expanding the concept of duty to third parties for accountant errors, he recognized in that context, the problem of "liability in an indeterminate amount for an indeterminate time to an indeterminate class." Should such an emotional, intuitive reaction be determinative or must it be critically assessed in light of the micro-economic and social effects of such a no liability rule? Should this long-standing judicial antipathy to recovery for emotional harms now be re-examined given the availability of contemporary psychological and psychiatric knowledge?

A second frame is to see the slowly weakening disapproval of emotional distress recovery as a case study in the evolution of the common law. Here, dissatisfaction with a rule of non-liability engenders a growing number of exceptions (permitting liability) until the exceptional cases outnumber those applying the default rule, prompting a re-examination of that rule. *See generally* EDWARD H. LEVI, AN INTRODUCTION TO LEGAL REASONING (1949). This can also be given a law and economics gloss: Has the default rule ceased to be an efficient one?

A third potential frame is to see emotional distress as a battleground between judges and fact finders. Here, categorical "no-duty" rules are used by judges to keep cases from juries who, in other areas, would be trusted to exercise self-restraint, applying case-by-case limitations based on proximate cause or other considerations.

Finally, attention should be paid to limitations on recovery for emotional distress in the context of tort reform, and particularly damage "caps" on pain and suffering (or noneconomic) injuries. As legislatures impose more stringent caps, frequently not taking into account their disproportionately adverse impact on women and the elderly, so plaintiffs may seek to avoid such strictures by asserting claims as a "bystander" who can make an independent claim for emotional harm. A discussion of some of the tort-reform related considerations concerning recovery for emotional distress can be found in Chapter 16, *infra*.

2. *Physical Injury Rule.* The physical injury or "impact rule" was the first exception to the no recovery rule. The impact rule permits the recovery of emotional injury damages only when the following are present: "(1) a physical impact to the plaintiff; (2) the physical impact causes physical injury to the plaintiff; and (3) the physical injury to the plaintiff causes the plaintiff's mental suffering or emotional distress." *Lee v. State Farm Mut. Ins. Co.,* 272 Ga. 583, 586 (2000). As further noted in *Lee*:

> There are three policy reasons traditionally given for having the impact rule and denying recovery for emotional distress unrelated to physical injuries. First, there is the fear, that absent impact, there will be a flood of litigation of claims for emotional distress. Second, is the concern for fraudulent claims. Third, there is the perception that, absent impact, there would be difficulty in proving the causal connection between the defendant's negligent conduct and claimed damages of emotional distress.

272 Ga. at 587.

3. *"Zone of Danger" Rule.* The "zone of danger" exception applies to an emotionally injured plaintiff who is within the range of physical peril created by the defendant's negligence. Essentially, the "impact" rule is replaced with a "zone of impact" rule. For example, in *Johnson v. District of Columbia,* 728 A.2d 70 (D.C. Cir. 1999), the plaintiff had run hot water in her tub to help alleviate her one-year-old boy's breathing condition. However, her three-year-old daughter entered the bathroom and fell into the tub, sustaining serious burns. The mother, alleging negligence against the apartment complex and the manufacturer of the complex's water heater, claimed for her own emotional distress. The court denied recovery stating:

> Under District of Columbia law, a mother cannot recover for the emotional distress caused by witnessing harm that was negligently inflicted on her child alone. Rather, the District follows the "zone of danger" approach. In order to recover, the plaintiff must show that she was physically endangered by the defendant's negligent activity. The record shows that Johnson failed to present any evidence that she was herself in danger from the hot water. Therefore, this claim could not lie.

Johnson, 728 A.2d at 77.

In *Hansen v. Sea Ray Boats, Inc.,* 830 P.2d 236 (Utah 1992), boat passengers brought suit to recover for negligent infliction of emotional distress as the result of their witnessing other passengers receive electrical shock while in the water. Applying the zone of danger rule, the court said that one of the plaintiffs, who was in the boat, could not recover because she was objectively not within the zone of danger, even though she may have subjectively thought she was. Is this a sensible result or an example of the unfairness wrought by rigid adherence to a "bright line" rule?

4. *"Foreseeable Bystander" Rule.* One of the most widely used exception to the rule of no liability was articulated by the Supreme Court of California in *Dillon v. Legg,* 68 Cal.2d 728 (1968), replacing the "zone of danger" test with one of "reasonable foreseeability" modeled around a "factor analysis":

(1) Whether plaintiff was located near the scene of the accident as contrasted with one who was a distance away from it. (2) Whether the shock resulted from a direct emotional impact upon plaintiff from the sensory and contemporaneous observance of the accident, as contrasted with learning of the accident from others after its occurrence. (3) Whether plaintiff and the victim were closely related, as contrasted with an absence of any relationship or the presence of only a distant relationship.

68 Cal.2d at 740–741.

The liberalized "foreseeable bystander" rule expressed in *Dillon* is not without its problems. For example, most courts applying the bystander rule require that the plaintiff observe the injury to the victim as it happens, not afterwards, in order to recover for negligent infliction of emotional distress. Thus, in *Gendrek v. Poblete*, 654 A.2d 970 (N.J. 1995), parents were not permitted to recover for negligent infliction of emotional distress caused by the alleged malpractice of the defendants in treating their newborn son, since they did not witness the malpractice. Similarly, in *Asaro v. Cardinal Glennon Mem. Hosp.*, 799 S.W.2d 595 (Mo. 1990), a plaintiff mother could not recover for the same reason, where the defendant allegedly committed medical malpractice in the treatment of plaintiff's 5-year-old son. In both cases the plaintiffs witnessed their child's suffering shortly after the alleged malpractice had occurred. Does the present sensory perception requirement effectively rule out recovery for negligent infliction of emotional distress in medical malpractice cases? *See Taylor v. Einstein*, 754 A.2d 650 (Pa. 2000) (mother who was in waiting room of hospital while child underwent surgery in room on the same floor could not recover for emotional distress suffered upon learning of the death of her child and could not recover for intentional infliction of emotional distress from doctor who performed surgery without her permission because she was not present in the room where the surgery took place)

Other cases have struggled with the question how closely the plaintiff (bystander) and direct victim must be related. Almost all courts require a preexisting relationship but not all insist on a "traditional" relationship. For example, *Dunphy v. Gregor*, 642 A.2d 372 (N.J. 1994), concerned Eileen and Michael, an engaged, cohabiting couple (who had a joint checking account and reciprocal life insurance policies). As Michael changed the left rear tire of a friend's car on the shoulder of a highway he was struck by a car driven by the defendant. His body was dragged 240 feet. Eileen had been standing five feet from Michael. After witnessing the accident she cared for and comforted him before he was taken to hospital, where he died. Eileen subsequently underwent psychiatric and psychological treatment for depression and anxiety. The court noted:

> Although novel, applying the standard of an intimate familial relationship to an unmarried cohabitant such as Eileen Dunphy and affording her the protections of bystander liability is hardly unfair. She represents an eminently foreseeable but clearly discrete class of potential plaintiffs. Moreover, the other elements of the bystander cause of action — contemporaneous observation, death or serious injury to the victim, and severe emotional injury to the plaintiff — structure the

kind of "particularized foreseeability" that ensures that the class is winnowed even further and that limitless liability is avoided.

> One can reasonably foresee that people who enjoy an intimate familial relationship with one another will be especially vulnerable to emotional injury resulting from a tragedy befalling one of them. Foreseeability based on that standard . . . preserves the distinction that must be made between ordinary emotional injuries that would be experienced by friends and relatives in general and those 'indelibly stunning' emotional injuries suffered by one whose relationship with the victim 'at the time of the injury, is deep, lasting, and genuinely intimate.

Dunphy, 642 A.2d at 377.

As alluded to in the principal case, *Atlantic Coast Airlines, supra,* the Supreme Court of California has reined in the widely adopted *Dillon* approach. In *Thing v. La Chusa,* 771 P.2d 814 (Cal. 1989), the court rejected the factor analysis, in light of their post-*Dillon* experience with "expansive progression" (*id.* at 821) of liability based on *Dillon*.

> The expectation of the *Dillon* majority that the parameters of the tort would be further defined in future cases has not been fulfilled. Instead, subsequent decisions of the Courts of Appeal and this court, have created more uncertainty. And, just as the "zone of danger" limitation was abandoned in *Dillon* as an arbitrary restriction on recovery, the *Dillon* guidelines have been relaxed on grounds that they, too, created arbitrary limitations on recovery. Little consideration has been given in post-*Dillon* decisions to the importance of avoiding the limitless exposure to liability that the pure foreseeability test of "duty" would create and towards which these decisions have moved.

Id.

As a result of the concerns about limitless recovery expressed by the court, it replaced the factor analysis, that was increasingly operating as a simple foreseeability test, noting:

> We conclude, therefore, that a plaintiff may recover damages for emotional distress caused by observing the negligently inflicted injury of a third person if, but only if, said plaintiff: (1) is closely related to the injury victim; (2) is present at the scene of the injury-producing event at the time it occurs and is then aware that it is causing injury to the victim; and (3) as a result suffers serious emotional distress — a reaction beyond that which would be anticipated in a disinterested witness and which is not an abnormal response to the circumstances.

Thing, 771 P.2d at 829–30.

5. *Direct Victims.* Some courts have dispensed with the limitation on recovery for emotional distress when the defendant owes a duty directly to the plaintiff, essentially holding that such a plaintiff is not a mere "bystander." For example, in *Molien v. Kaiser Found. Hosps.*, 27 Cal. 3d 916 (1980), a patient was mis-diagnosed with syphilis, and advised to tell her husband so that he, too, should be tested. The defendant hospital and doctor were held liable for the husband's distress. *See Roes v. FHP, Inc.*, 985 P.2d 661 (Haw. 1999). The plaintiffs, airline baggage handlers, were exposed to HIV-contaminated blood that leaked from a bag as they were unloading it. Plaintiffs asserted that, at the time of the incident, each of them was suffering from open wounds on their hands. They subsequently tested negative for HIV. They sued FHP, shipper of the blood, for "serious mental distress" which they allegedly suffered between the time of exposure and their discovery that they had not contracted HIV. The court said they could recover without proof of physical injury, as long as their mental distress was of the sort that "a reasonable man, normally constituted, would be unable to cope with." Similarly, in *Williamson v. Waldman*, 696 A.2d 14 (N.J. 1997), where the plaintiff trash collector was stuck by medical needles that had been disposed of negligently, the court said the plaintiff could recover for fear of HIV even though he had not actually been exposed to the virus.

6. *Quantifiable Loss.* Is emotional distress able to be quantified in dollars in the same way that physical harm is? Do people buy insurance against emotional distress? Why not? Do we over deter by holding defendants liable for emotional distress damages? Do we under deter if we don't? How do we decide such questions? Who should decide? How does critical race theory apply in considering whether there ought to be recovery for racial disparities that lead to distress in people of color? Recall the discussion of intentional infliction of emotional distress generated by racially biased conduct in Chapter 2. How do emotional injuries vary by gender? A study of gender in products liability and medical malpractice cases over three decades concluded that women suffered from more reproductive injuries, loss of fertility, and sexual dysfunction than men. *See* THOMAS H. KOENIG & MICHAEL L. RUSTAD, IN DEFENSE OF TORT LAW 117 (2002) (finding that defective products cases redressed chiefly noneconomic injuries to women's reproductive functions). The authors conclude: "Noneconomic damages are the principal source of compensation for reproductive injuries and miscarriages — intangible injuries that cannot be measured in terms of lost wages or imputed earnings." *Id.* at 128. "Non-pecuniary damage awards, for example, compensate the family for the loss of the mother's key role in raising children. Tort reform that limits non-economic damages diminishes the value of women's roles in our society." *Id.* at 126. These issues are given further consideration in Chapter 9, concerning professional liability, and Chapter 10, discussing products liability.

F. ECONOMIC LOSS

AIKENS v. DEBOW
541 S. E.2d 576 (W. Va. 2000)

SCOTT, JUSTICE.

. . . Plaintiff Richard Aikens operates a motel and restaurant known as the Martinsburg Econo-Lodge ("Econo-Lodge"), which is located on Route 901 and can be accessed by exiting from Interstate 81 at the Spring Mills Road exit.

While the Route 901 overpass bridge permits the shortest, most-convenient means of accessing the Econo-Lodge for south-bound travelers traveling on I-81, the establishment can still be accessed through alternate routing. On September 18, 1996, Defendant Robert Debow, a truck driver and employee of Defendant Craig Paving, Inc., was driving a flatbed truck north on I-81 carrying a trackhoe. Because the trackhoe was too high to pass safely under the Route 901 overpass, an accident resulted which caused substantial damage to the bridge. It was closed for nineteen days to make the necessary repairs.

Plaintiff instituted the underlying cause of action on May 28, 1997, seeking recovery for the decreased revenues he experienced due to closure of the Route 901 overpass. Asserting that his reduced revenues were proximately caused by the accident, Plaintiff seeks recovery of $9,000 in lost income.

Arguing that as a matter of law Plaintiff could not recover for his economic losses in the absence of direct bodily injury or property damage, Defendants moved for summary judgment. . . .

Following the circuit court's denial of Defendants' motion for summary judgment, the parties requested and the circuit court agreed to certification. . . .

[That] question, as reformulated, is . . . as follows:

> May a claimant who has sustained purely economic loss as a result of an interruption in commerce caused by negligent injury to the property of a third person recover damages absent either privity of contract or some other special relationship with the alleged tortfeasor?

> We answer this question in the negative. . . .

The resolution of any question of tort liability must be premised upon fundamental concepts of the duty owed by the tortfeasor. . . .

The need to restrict the spatial concept of duty to something less than the limits of logical connection was cogently stated as follows in *In re Exxon Valdez,* No. A89-0095-CV, 1994 WL 182856 (D. Alaska March 23, 1994):

> There is no question but that the Exxon Valdez grounding impacted, in one fashion or another, far more people than will ever recover anything in these proceedings. There is an understandable public perception that if one suffers harm which is perceived to be a result of the conduct of another, the harmed person should be compensated. That perception does not always square up with the institutional guidelines (statutes and case law) under which the court must operate. It is the function of both Congress and the courts (principally the courts of appeal and supreme courts) to determine the extent to which public expectations with respect to financial responsibility are to be realized. Legal liability does not always extend to all of the foreseeable consequences of an accident. In the area of harm to one's body, the reach of what is recoverable is very great. Where one's property is injured, the extent of legal liability is considerable, but not to the same extent as with bodily injury. Where pure economic loss is at issue — not connected with any injury to one's body or property, and especially where that economic

loss occurs in a marine setting — the reach of legal liability is quite limited except as to commercial fishermen.

Were it otherwise, we would have a form of organized anarchy in which no one could count on what rule would apply at any given time or in any given situation.

Id. at 8–9 (emphasis added).

. . . Who draws the line demarcating tort liability? Who, in our society, has the burden of defining the existence and extent of the element of "duty" in tort actions? It necessarily falls to the courts to consider all relevant claims of the competing parties; to determine where and upon whom the burden of carrying the risk of injury will fall; and to draw the line, to declare the existence or absence of "duty," in every case, as a matter of law. The temptation is to accede to the arguments of logical connection in every instance of resulting harm while, in fact, the consequences of pure logic would be socially and economically ruinous.

The sole issue presented for our resolution is whether economic loss from an interruption in commerce in the absence of damage to a plaintiff's person or property is recoverable in a tort action. While this Court has never directly addressed this issue, other jurisdictions, almost without exception, have concluded that economic loss alone will not warrant recovery in the absence of some special relationship between the plaintiff and the tortfeasor. In the seminal decision of *Robins Dry Dock & Repair Co. v. Flint,* 275 U.S. 303 (1927), the United States Supreme Court refused to permit recovery from the dry dock owner when plaintiffs were denied use of a vessel for two weeks because of a third party's act of negligence during the ship's refurbishing. In establishing this long-standing rule of denying recovery in tort for indirect economic injury, Justice Holmes articulated the rationale, based upon English and American precedent, that continues to justify the nonexistence of a legally cognizable or compensable claim for such attenuated injuries even today: "The law does not spread its protection so far." *Id.* at 309. . . .

Where the factual scenario involves a plaintiff's contractual right to use property damaged by a tortfeasor, courts have invoked the RESTATEMENT OF TORTS as a basis for denying causes of action limited to economic damages. In *Philip Morris, Inc. v. Emerson,* 368 S.E.2d 268 (Va. 1988), the plaintiff sought recovery of lost profits to his campground business due to the negligent release of gases from the defendant's property. Citing the well-recognized principle in the RESTATEMENT OF TORTS which recognizes that interference with the ability to contract with third persons is too remote to permit recovery, the court refused to permit recovery of the profits plaintiffs allegedly sustained from his inability to contract with campers for overnight stays. 368 S.E.2d at 282 (citing REST. 2D TORTS § 766 (1979)).

In denying economic damages in the absence of physical impact, courts frequently refer to this element of remoteness between the injury and the act of negligence that is the source of such injury. In *Rickards v. Sun Oil Co.,* 41 A.2d 267 (N.J. Sup. 1945), a case remarkably similar to the one under scrutiny by this Court, plaintiff business owners sought to recover "losses from expectant gains" from a defendant whose barge negligently damaged a drawbridge which served as the only means of access to the island on which plaintiffs' business premises were situated. *Id.* at 268. In granting the defendant's motions to strike the complaints, the court held that "[defendant's] negligent action may be a cause of injury to the plaintiffs, but it is not the natural and proximate effect of such negligence and therefore [is] not actionable." *Id.* . . .

In *General Foods Corp. v. United States,* 448 F. Supp. 111 (D. Md. 1978), the plaintiff manufacturer sought to recover economic damages from the defendant bridge owner for economic damages allegedly arising from the closing of the Penn Central Railroad Bridge over the Chesapeake and Delaware Canal caused by a ship wreck. Citing *Robins Dry Dock* for the proposition that economic losses suffered by the plaintiff in conducting its business, even if proven, are not recoverable damages as a matter of law, the court dismissed plaintiff's complaint, explaining:

> Courts which have addressed this issue have repeatedly expressed concern that a contrary rule would open the door to virtually limitless suits, often of a highly speculative and remote nature. Such suits would expose the negligent defendant to a severe penalty, and would produce serious problems in litigation, particularly in the areas of proof and apportionment of damages.

448 F. Supp. at 113.

In an analogous case, *Nebraska Innkeepers, Inc. v. Pittsburgh-Des Moines Corp.,* 345 N.W.2d 124 (Iowa 1984), the Iowa Supreme Court considered the viability of an action brought by various business owners to recover purely economic losses resulting from the closure of a bridge to repair certain structural defects. Affirming the lower court's grant of summary judgment to defendants, the court recognized, as "uniform[,]" the position of rejecting negligence actions seeking pure economic damages "regardless of how vital to the claimant be the flow of commerce that is interrupted." *Id.* at 126. Critical to the court's ruling was its conclusion that "[e]xceptions to that general rule such as ownership of the bridge, physical injury or direct damages to the claimant's property or person, or a direct contractual relation with the alleged wrongdoer were not factually present here." *Id.*

The recognized necessity of imposing a line of demarcation on actionable theories of recovery serves as another rationale for the denial of purely economic damages. In *Stevenson v. East Ohio Gas. Co.,* 73 N.E.2d 200 (Ohio Ct. App. 1946), the Ohio court held that employees of a neighboring company could not recover lost wages incurred after they were evacuated due to an explosion and fire allegedly caused by the defendant's negligence. The *Stevenson* court reasoned as follows:

> While the reason usually given for the refusal to permit recovery in this class of cases is that the damages are "indirect" or are "too remote" it is our opinion that the principal reason that has motivated the courts in denying recovery in this class of cases is that to permit recovery of damages in such cases would open the door to a mass of litigation which might very well overwhelm the courts so that in the long

run while injustice might result in special cases, the ends of justice are conserved. . . . *Id.* at 203 (emphasis added).

In similar fashion, the Seventh Circuit, in affirming the district court's dismissal of an action seeking economic damages arising from a bridge closing, reasoned that extension of liability in the absence of harm to a plaintiff's person or property would thrust courts into "a field with no sensible or just stopping point." *Leadfree Enterprises, Inc. v. United States Steel Corp.,* 711 F.2d 805, 808 (7th Cir. 1983) (citing *Hass v. Chicago & North Western Ry. Co.,* 179 N.W.2d 885, 888 (Wis. 1970)). The court observed further in *Leadfree Enterprises,* that "in the economic injury case, there is less a fear of fraudulent claims than a sense of wanting to have a sensible stopping point in order to preclude open-ended, crushing liability on a tortfeasor." 711 F.2d at 808; *see also Dundee Cement Co. v. Chemical Labs., Inc.,* 712 F.2d 1166, 1172 (7th Cir. 1983) (discussing policy reasons advocating against permitting third party recovery of economic losses and "conclud[ing] that there is a legitimate fear that a crushing burden of litigation would result from allowing recovery for economic damages like this").

Astutely anticipating the economic chaos that would result from permitting theoretically limitless recovery of economic injury, the court in *Aikens v. Baltimore & Ohio R.R. Co.,* 501 A.2d 277 (Pa. Super Ct 1985), denied recovery for indirect economic losses incurred by employees who lost wages due to the defendant's alleged negligence in causing a train derailment which damaged the plaintiffs' employer's plant. The court affirmed the dismissal of the complaint and opined:

> that allowance of a cause of action for negligent interference with economic advantage would create an undue burden upon industrial freedom of action, and would create a disproportion between the large amount of damages that might be recovered and the extent of the defendant's fault. To allow a cause of action for negligent cause of purely economic loss would be to open the door to every person in the economic chain of the negligent person or business to bring a cause of action. Such an outstanding burden is clearly inappropriate and a danger to our economic system. *Id.* at 279 (citation omitted). . . .

. . . A few jurisdictions have permitted recovery of economic damages without damage to person or property under certain limited circumstances. The New Jersey Supreme Court's approach to this concept is recognized as the leading authority for the minority view and represents a departure from a substantial collection of American and British cases. In *People Express Airlines, Inc. v. Consolidated Rail Corp.,* 495 A.2d 107 (N.J. 1985), the New Jersey court permitted economic recovery where a leak of toxic chemicals from a railway car forced a twelve-hour evacuation of a commercial airline office building adjacent to the site of the leak. *Id.* at 115. The plaintiff sought to recover expenses incurred for flight cancellations, lost bookings and revenue, and certain operating expenses. In permitting the action, the court applied a special foreseeability rule, reasoning that the defendant would be liable only for damages proximately caused and requiring that the defendant must have "knowledge or special reason to know of the consequences of the tortious conduct in terms of the persons likely to be victimized and the nature of the damages likely to be suffered. . . ." *Id.*

Narrowly crafting its decision to apply to a limited and particularized group, the New Jersey court held:

> that a defendant owes a duty of care to take reasonable measures to avoid the risk of causing economic damages, aside from physical injury, to particular plaintiffs or plaintiffs comprising an identifiable class with respect to whom defendant knows or has reason to know are likely to suffer such damages from its conduct. A defendant failing to adhere to this duty of care may be found liable for such economic damages proximately caused by its breach of duty.

Id. at 116. In further explaining its rationale for departure from established doctrine, the New Jersey court noted:

> the close proximity of the North Terminal and People Express Airlines to the Conrail freight yard; the obvious nature of the plaintiff's operations and particular foreseeability of economic losses resulting from an accident and evacuation; the defendants' actual or constructive knowledge of the volatile properties of ethylene oxide; and the existence of an emergency response plan prepared by some of the defendants (alluded to in the course of oral argument), which apparently called for the nearby area to be evacuated to avoid the risk of harm in case of an explosion.

Id. at 118. In fashioning its test, the court in *People Express* determined that liability and foreseeability "stand in direct proportion to one another[:] The more particular is the foreseeability that economic loss will be suffered by the plaintiff as a result of defendant's negligence, the more just is it that liability be imposed and recovery allowed." *Id.* at 116.

An analysis of the facts involved in the *People Express* decision supports the conclusion that the New Jersey court traversed a logical path more closely akin to that navigated in cases involving physical damage to property. Subsequent to the Three Mile Island nuclear incident, plaintiffs similarly asserted claims of temporary loss of use of property and "damage to property" as a result of the intrusion of radioactive materials through the ambient air. In resolving their claims in *Commonwealth of Pennsylvania v. General Public Utilities Corp.,* 710 F.2d 117 (3rd Cir.1983), the United States Court of Appeals for the Third Circuit acknowledged that the complaints did not contain any claim of damages for direct physical damage to any of the plaintiffs' property. *Id.* at 120–21. While the lower court had concluded that the losses claimed were purely economic in nature and unrecoverable, the plaintiffs contended that "increased radioactivity and radioactive materials emitted during the nuclear incident permeated the entire area, and this rendered the public buildings unsafe for a temporary period of time, and constituted a physical intrusion upon the plaintiffs' properties." *Id.* at 122. The plaintiffs maintained that the gaseous intrusion satisfied the requirement of physical harm to justify the recovery of damages in tort. The Third Circuit found that the plaintiffs' contentions were sufficient to defeat a motion for summary judgment, permitting the plaintiffs an opportunity to prove that an invasion by an invisible substance may still constitute a physical damage warranting recovery of economic loss. Similar to the inhabitability problems experienced by the Three Mile Island plaintiffs, the plaintiff's building in *People Express* was rendered uninhabitable by the negligent release of toxic gases. Thus, in *People Express,* the New Jersey court could have reached its decision by reasoning that to render a building uninhabitable by releasing poison gas against it constitutes a direct physical damage to that building.

Analysts of the *People Express* rationale have also criticized the wisdom of that approach by emphasizing that the "Court itself noted the contradictory and inconsistent nature of its reasoning" by acknowledging the inherent limitations to predicating recovery on a principle of particular foreseeability. [*United Textile Workers v.*] *Lear Siegler,* 825 S.W.2d at 86. The *People Express* court stated that "there will arise many similar cases that cannot be resolved by our decision today." 495 A.2d at 117. The court further recognized that:

> some cases will present circumstances that defy the categorization here devised to circumscribe a defendant's orbit of duty, limit otherwise boundless liability and define an identifiable class of plaintiffs that may recover. In these cases, the courts will be required to draw upon notions of fairness, common sense and morality to fix the line limiting liability as a matter of public policy, rather than an uncritical application of the principle of particular foreseeability. *Id.* at 116.

In another case typically referenced as supportive of a minority position on this issue, a California court applied the "special relationship" exception and permitted a restaurant owner to sue for lost profits allegedly caused by a contractor's failure to promptly install and maintain an air conditioner. *J'Aire Corp. v. Gregory,* 598 P.2d 60 (Cal. 1979). The plaintiff introduced evidence that the reliance upon the air conditioning function was repeatedly brought to the defendant's attention. In concluding that such action could be maintained, the court explained that "a contractor owes a duty of care to the tenant of a building undergoing construction work to prosecute that work in a manner which does not cause undue injury to the tenant's business, where such injury is reasonably foreseeable." *Id.* at 66. The court's decision to permit recovery was expressly predicated on the existence of a special relationship: "Where a special relationship exists between the parties, a plaintiff may recover for loss of expected economic advantage through the negligent performance of a contract although the parties were not in contractual privity." *Id.* at 63.

In another case frequently cited as support for the minority position, an employer sought recovery for economic loss sustained as a result of tortious injuries to his employees. *Mattingly v. Sheldon Jackson College,* 743 P.2d 356 (Alaska 1987). Plaintiff's employees were injured when a trench dug by Sheldon Jackson College employees collapsed, which prevented them from cleaning a drainpipe. Plaintiff sought recovery of economic damages as a result of the loss of services of his employees. Pivotal to the Alaska Supreme Court's decision to permit economic recovery in this case was its determination that the plaintiff was a "foreseeable and particularized plaintiff." *Id.* at 361. Although recovery of economic damages was permitted, the court made clear that such recovery is only permitted where it can be established that the defendant owed a duty to "particular plaintiffs or plaintiffs comprising an identifiable class with respect to whom defendant knows or has reason to know are likely to suffer such damages from its conduct." *Id.* at 360 (quoting *People Express,* 495 A.2d at 116).

The special relationship between the plaintiff and the alleged tortfeasor was also emphasized in another case frequently cited for the minority view. In *Hawthorne v. Kober Construction Co.,* 640 P.2d 467 (Mont. 1982), the plaintiff had suffered economic losses due to a delay in the shipment of steel. The court acknowledged that "the action is one for negligence in the performance of a contractual duty." *Id.* at 470. Concluding that such action could be maintained because of the foreseeability of harm, the court relied upon Prosser's textbook reasoning:

> By entering into a contract with A, the defendant may place himself in such a relation toward B that the law will impose upon him an obligation, sounding in tort and not in contract, to act in such a way that B will not be injured. The incidental fact of the existence of the contract with A does not negative the responsibility of the actor when he enters upon a course of affirmative conduct which may be expected to affect the interests of another person. 640 P.2d at 470 (citing PROSSER, LAW OF TORTS, 4th Ed., Section 93.)

After thoroughly considering the intricacies of a potential rule permitting the recovery of economic damages absent physical or personal injury, we conclude that an individual who sustains purely economic loss from an interruption in commerce caused by another's negligence may not recover damages in the absence of physical harm to that individual's person or property, a contractual relationship with the alleged tortfeasor, or some other special relationship between the alleged tortfeasor and the individual who sustains purely economic damages sufficient to compel the conclusion that the tortfeasor had a duty to the particular plaintiff and that the injury complained of was clearly foreseeable to the tortfeasor. The existence of a special relationship will be determined largely by the extent to which the particular plaintiff is affected differently from society in general. It may be evident from the defendant's knowledge or specific reason to know of the potential consequences of the wrongdoing, the persons likely to be injured, and the damages likely to be suffered. Such special relationship may be proven through evidence of foreseeability of the nature of the harm to be suffered by the particular plaintiff or an identifiable class and can arise from contractual privity or other close nexus. . . . Any attempt by this Court to more specifically define the parameters of circumstances which may be held to establish a "special relationship" would create more confusion than clarity.

We base our holding upon our analysis of the complexities of this area of tort law, demonstrated through both historical evolvement and current concerns, and our belief that a hybrid approach must be fabricated to authorize recovery of meritorious claims while simultaneously providing a barrier against limitless liability. The common thread which permeates the analysis of potential economic recovery in the absence of physical harm is the recognition of the underlying concept of duty. Absent some special relationship, the confines of which will differ depending upon the facts of each relationship, there simply is no duty. A thorough examination of the cases comprising what has been referenced as the minority view reveals reasoning similar to ours, which provides the opportunity for recovery only upon a showing of a special relationship between the plaintiff and alleged tortfeasor and narrowly tailors the recovery to conform to the facts of the case under scrutiny.

Our decision under the limited factual scenario presented in this certified question has no impact upon our prior rulings permitting recovery of purely economic damages in negligence actions where a special relationship exists between the plaintiff and the alleged tortfeasor. Our holding in the case sub judice is, in fact, consistent with the rationale underlying such rulings, and we affirm our previous recognition that where a special and narrowly defined relationship can be established between the tortfeasor and a plaintiff who was deprived of an economic benefit, the tortfeasor can be held liable. In cases of that nature, the duty exists because of the special relationship. The special class of plaintiffs involved in those cases were particularly foreseeable to the tortfeasor, and the economic losses were proximately caused by the tortfeasor's negligence.

For example, auditors have been held liable to plaintiffs who bought stock in reliance upon a financial statement negligently prepared for a corporation; surveyors and termite inspectors liable to remote purchasers of property; engineers and architects liable to contractors who relied upon plans negligently prepared for property owners who later hired the contractors; attorneys and notaries public liable to beneficiaries of negligently prepare wills; real estate brokers for failure to disclose defects; and telegraph companies liable to individuals who failed to secure a contract due to the negligent transmission of a message.

We also emphasize that the holding of this case applies strictly to plaintiffs alleging purely economic loss from an interruption in commerce caused by another's negligence. This opinion therefore does not encompass, and has no effect upon, our prior rulings regarding medical monitoring, negligent infliction of emotional distress cases, or nuisance law. . . .

The resolution of this matter of restrictions on tort liability is ultimately a matter of "practical politics." *Palsgraf*, 162 N.E. at 103 (Andrews, J., dissenting). The "law arbitrarily declines to trace a series of events beyond a certain point." *Id.* In other words, it is a question of public policy. The purely economic damages sought by a plaintiff may be indistinguishable in terms of societal entitlement from those damages incurred by the restaurant owner in the next block, the antique dealer in the next town, and all the ripple-effect "losses" experienced by each employer and each resident of every town and village surrounding the location of the initial act of negligence. In crafting a rule to address the issue of economic damages, we have attempted to avoid the expression of a judicial definition of duty which would permit the maintenance of a class action as a result of almost every car wreck and other inconvenience that results to our state's citizenry. . . .

Tort law is essentially a recognition of limitations expressing finite boundaries of recovery. Using the absurdity of these chain-of-reaction but purely logical examples, courts and commentators have expressed disdain for limitless liability and have also cautioned against the potential injustices which might result. This Court's obligation is to draw a line beyond which the law will not extend its protection in tort, and to declare, as a matter of law, that no duty exists beyond that court-created line. It is not a matter of protection of a certain class of defendants; nor is it a matter of championing the causes of a certain class of plaintiffs. It is a question of public policy. Each segment of society will suffer injustice, whether situated as plaintiff or defendant, if there are no finite boundaries to liability and no confines within which the rights of plaintiffs and defendants can be determined. We accept the wise admonition expressed over a century ago, in language both simple and eloquent, proven by the passage of time and the lessons of experience: "There would be no bounds to actions and litigious intricacies, if the ill effects of the negligences of men could be followed down the chain of results to the final effect." *Kahl* [*v. Love,* 37 N.J.L. 5, 8 (N.J. Sup. 1874)]. [CERTIFIED QUESTION ANSWERED.]

NOTES

1. *Limiting Liability.* Clearly there must be some limit to liability for purely economic loss. Ironically, there are many kinds of cases involving recovery of purely economic injuries where courts do not even mention the economic harm rule. For instance consider wrongful death and loss of consortium claims. At least in these cases, someone has suffered a personal injury. But what about attorney or accountant malpractice cases? These are cases where the loss is entirely economic and recovery is routinely allowed with no discussion of the so-called economic loss doctrine. What about misrepresentation cases that do not involve personal injury? Architect malpractice cases in which a contractor or owner seeks to recover increased costs of construction from the architect? Does the opinion in *Aikens* provide a sound basis for making distinctions between plaintiffs who should be able to recover and those who shouldn't? *See generally* Thomas C. Galligan, Jr., *Contortions Along the Boundary Between Contracts and Torts*, 69 TUL. L. REV. 457, 512–20 (1994).

2. *Economic Loss and Law and Economics.* How can a legal system adequately deter conduct if it does not take account of purely economic loss in negligence cases? Negligence holds defendants liable for damages caused by their activities. Does the economic loss rule erode this objective? How does the economic loss rule affect incentives to take care or reduce care? In the *United States v. Carroll Towing Co.* case, discussed in Chapter 4, Judge Hand presented the famous Hand formula in a case involving sinking barges. How would the economic loss doctrine affect the outcome in *Carroll Towing*? How would a pragmatist evaluate the economic loss rule?

G. PRENATAL AND PRECONCEPTION INJURIES

STALLMAN v. YOUNGQUIST
531 N.E.2d 355 (Ill. 1988)

CUNNINGHAM, JUSTICE.

Plaintiff, Lindsay Stallman, brought suit by her father and next friend, Mark Stallman, against defendant Bari Stallman and codefendant Clarence Youngquist (not a party to this appeal) for prenatal injuries allegedly sustained by plaintiff during an automobile collision between Bari Stallman's automobile and the automobile driven by Clarence Youngquist. Defendant Bari Stallman is the mother of plaintiff. Defendant was approximately five months pregnant with plaintiff and was on her way to a restaurant when the collision occurred.

Count II of plaintiff's second amended complaint, the subject matter of this appeal, charged defendant with negligence, the direct and proximate result of which caused the fetus (the unborn plaintiff) to be thrown about in the womb of her mother (defendant) resulting in serious and permanent injury to plaintiff.

The issue whether a cause of action exists by or on behalf of a fetus, subsequently born alive, against its mother for the unintentional infliction of prenatal injuries is an issue of first impression in this court. We begin with a review of the area of tort liability for prenatal negligence as it has developed in regards to third persons. It was not until 1884, in *Dietrich v. Northampton*, 138 Mass. 14 (1884), that such a case came before a court in the United States alleging a cause of action for prenatal injuries. In *Dietrich*, Judge Oliver Wendell Holmes held that the common law did not recognize a cause of action in tort for prenatal injuries to a fetus. Judge Holmes denied that such an action may lie primarily because the fetus "was a part of the mother at the time of the injury, [and] any damage to it which was not too remote to be recovered for at all was recoverable by her." (138 Mass. at 17.) After *Dietrich* and until 1946 [*Bonbrest v. Kotz*, 65 F. Supp. 138 (D.C. 1946)], all courts in the United States which considered the question agreed: no action would lie for injuries sustained by a fetus which became apparent on its birth.

This court was one of the first to consider the question of the liability of third persons for prenatal negligence after the *Dietrich* case. In *Allaire v. St. Luke's Hospital*, 184 Ill. 359 (1900), it was held that no action would lie for injuries to a fetus, only days away from birth, due to the negligence of the defendant hospital where the mother of the plaintiff was a patient awaiting the delivery of the plaintiff. . . .

Allaire is primarily remembered today for the dissent of Mr. Justice Boggs, who asked the question:

Should compensation for his injuries be denied on a mere theory, known to be false, that the injury was not to his [or her] person but to the person of the mother? 184 Ill. at 374 (Boggs, J., dissenting).

The rule recognizing the right to bring an action for injuries inflicted on a fetus by a person not its mother is as pervasive and established now as was the contrary rule before 1946. This court overruled *Allaire* in *Amann v. Faidy*, 415 Ill. 422 (1953), and recognized a cause of action under the wrongful death statute for the death of an infant who, while in a viable condition, sustained a prenatal injury due to the negligence of a third person. Later, in *Rodriquez v. Patti*, 415 Ill. 496 (1953), this court recognized a common law right of action for personal injuries to an infant, a viable fetus, when wrongfully injured due to the negligence of third persons. Much later, in *Chrisafogeorgis v. Brandenberg*, 55 Ill. 2d 368 (1973), this court held that a wrongful death action could be maintained on behalf of a stillborn child who sustained injuries due to the negligence of third persons while a viable fetus.

The early reliance by courts on viability as a point at which with certainty it could be said that the fetus and the woman who is the mother of the fetus are two separate entities proved to be troublesome. Most courts have since abandoned viability as a requirement for a child to bring an action for prenatal injuries inflicted by third persons. . . .

In *Renslow v. Mennonite Hospital*, 67 Ill. 2d 348, (1977), this court rejected viability as a requirement in a cause of action for prenatal injuries suffered by a fetus due to the negligence of third persons. According to the plurality, *Renslow* involved the issue of whether "a child, not conceived at the time negligent acts were committed against its mother, [has] a cause of action against the tortfeasors for its injuries resulting from their conduct." (67 Ill. 2d at 349) The plaintiff in *Renslow* was born jaundiced and suffering from hyperbilirubinemia and required an immediate, complete exchange transfusion of her blood, as well as another such transfusion shortly thereafter. The plaintiff also allegedly suffered permanent damage to various organs, her brain, and her nervous system. This had occurred because eight years before the plaintiff's birth, the defendants (a hospital and a doctor) on two occasions transfused the plaintiff's mother with Rh-positive blood. The plaintiff's mother had Rh-negative blood, which was incompatible with and was therefore sensitized by the Rh-positive blood.

The appellate court, "in a careful and well-reasoned opinion, emphasized that the defendants were a doctor and a hospital, and held that there was no showing 'that the defendants could not reasonably have foreseen that the teenage girl would later marry and bear a child and that the child would be injured as the result of the improper blood transfusion.' (40 Ill. App. 3d 234, 239.)" *Renslow*, 67 Ill. 2d at 350.

The above case law has grown out of circumstances in which the defendant was a third person and not the mother of the plaintiff. Plaintiff in the instant case asserts that she should be able to bring a cause of action for prenatal injuries against her mother just as she would be able to bring a cause of action for prenatal injuries against a third person . . . . In *Grodin* [*v. Grodin*, 301 N.W.2d 869 (Mich. Ct. App. 1980)], a child brought suit against his mother for prenatal negligence. The plaintiff in *Grodin* had developed brown and discolored teeth because the defendant mother had taken tetracycline during the time when she was pregnant with the plaintiff. The suit alleged failure on the part of the mother to request from a doctor a pregnancy test, failure to seek proper prenatal care, and failure to report to a doctor that the mother was taking tetracycline.

The *Grodin* court failed to understand that the question of the application of Michigan's partial abrogation of the parental immunity doctrine was a separate question from that of recognizing a cause of action by a fetus, subsequently born alive, against its mother for the unintentional infliction of prenatal injuries. The *Grodin* court would have the law treat a pregnant woman as a stranger to her developing fetus for purposes of tort liability. The *Grodin* court failed to address any of the profound implications which would result from such a legal fiction and is, for that reason, unpersuasive. . . .

This court has never been asked to decide if, by becoming pregnant, a woman exposes herself to a future lawsuit by or on behalf of the fetus which will become her child. At one time a fetus was seen as only a part of the woman who was the mother of the child. When someone tortiously injured a pregnant woman and her fetus sustained injury as a result, no legal protection would have been extended to the subsequently born child. Today, when the tortious acts of another towards a woman who is or may become pregnant harm a fetus, there is a legally cognizable cause of action for the injury to both the woman and the subsequently born child.

In the path which some courts have taken on the road which has recognized recovery for a child for injuries inflicted on it as a fetus, there has been an articulation of a "legal right to begin life with a sound mind and body". The articulation of this right to recover against third-person tortfeasors has served to emphasize that it is not just the pregnant woman alone who may be harmed by the tortious act of another but also the fetus, whose injuries become apparent at its birth.

It is clear that the recognition of a legal right to begin life with a sound mind and body on the part of a fetus which is assertable after birth against its mother would have serious ramifications for all women and their families, and for the way in which society views women and women's reproductive abilities. The recognition of such a right by a fetus would necessitate the recognition of a legal duty on the part of the woman who is the mother; a legal duty, as opposed to a moral duty, to effectuate the best prenatal environment possible. The recognition of such a legal duty would create a new tort: a cause of action assertable by a fetus, subsequently born alive, against its mother for the unintentional infliction of prenatal injuries.

It is the firmly held belief of some that a woman should subordinate her right to control her life when she decides to become pregnant or does become pregnant: anything which might possibly harm the developing fetus should be prohibited and all things which might positively affect the developing fetus should be mandated under penalty of law, be it criminal or civil. Since anything which a pregnant woman does or does not do may have an impact, either positive or negative, on her developing fetus, any act or omission on her part could render her liable to her subsequently born child. While such a view is consistent with the recognition of a fetus having rights which are superior to those of its mother, such is not and cannot be the law of this State.

A legal right of a fetus to begin life with a sound mind and body assertable against a mother would make a pregnant woman the guarantor of the mind and body of her child at birth. A legal duty to guarantee the mental and physical health of another has never before been recognized in law. Any action which negatively impacted on fetal development would be a breach of the pregnant woman's duty to her developing fetus. Mother and child would be legal adversaries from the moment of conception until birth. The error that a fetus cannot be harmed in a legally cognizable way when the woman who is its mother is injured has been corrected; the law will no longer treat the fetus as only a part of its mother. The law will not now make an error of a different sort, one with enormous implications for all women who have been, are, may be, or might become pregnant: the law will not treat a fetus as an entity which is entirely separate from its mother. . . .

If a legally cognizable duty on the part of mothers were recognized, then a judicially defined standard of conduct would have to be met. It must be asked, By what judicially defined standard would a mother have her every act or omission while pregnant subjected to State scrutiny? By what objective standard could a jury be guided in determining whether a pregnant woman did all that was necessary in order not to breach a legal duty to not interfere with her fetus' separate and independent right to be born whole? In what way would prejudicial and stereotypical beliefs about the reproductive abilities of women be kept from interfering with a jury's determination of whether a particular woman was negligent at any point during her pregnancy?

Holding a third person liable for prenatal injuries furthers the interests of both the mother and the subsequently born child and does not interfere with the defendant's right to control his or her own life. Holding a mother liable for the unintentional infliction of prenatal injuries subjects to State scrutiny all the decisions a woman must make in attempting to carry a pregnancy to term, and infringes on her right to privacy and bodily autonomy . . . . Logic does not demand that a pregnant woman be treated in a court of law as a stranger to her developing fetus.

It would be a legal fiction to treat the fetus as a separate legal person with rights hostile to and assertable against its mother. The relationship between a pregnant woman and her fetus is unlike the relationship between any other plaintiff and defendant. No other plaintiff depends exclusively on any other defendant for everything necessary for life itself. No other defendant must go through biological changes of the most profound type, possibly at the risk of her own life, in order to bring forth an adversary into the world. It is, after all, the whole life of the pregnant woman which impacts on the development of the fetus. As opposed to the third-party defendant, it is the mother's every waking and sleeping moment which, for better or worse, shapes the prenatal environment which forms the world for the developing fetus. That this is so is not a pregnant woman's fault: it is a fact of life. . . .

NOTES

1. *The Duty.* Is the court holding that the mother does not owe a duty to the child or that the mother is immune from suit? Is there a difference in these two conclusions? Is there a practical difference? Is a claim that the pregnant mother was negligently driving different from a claim that she injured the child by taking illegal and dangerous drugs? Wouldn't insurance cover the negligent driving claim? The drug claim may not be covered because it might be an excluded intentional act or tort under the insurance policy. Should that make a difference in the court's ruling? Suppose it was the father who was driving negligently while the pregnant mother was in the car; if the fetus was injured in a resulting collision should the child have a claim against the father? Would the principal case bar this claim? What if the father was a smoker whose smoking while the mother was pregnant allegedly injured the child *in utero*?

2. *An Alternative Conception.* In *Bonte v. Bonte*, 616 A.2d 464 (N.H.1992), the court held:

> Because our cases hold that a child born alive may maintain a cause of action against another for injuries sustained while in utero, and a child may sue his or her mother in tort for the mother's negligence, it follows that a child born alive has a cause of action against his or her mother for the mother's negligence that caused injury to the child when in utero . . .

A dissent countered:

> Such after-the-fact judicial scrutiny of the subtle and complicated factors affecting a woman's pregnancy may make life for women who are pregnant or who are merely contemplating pregnancy intolerable. For these reasons, we are convinced that the best course is to allow the duty of a mother to her fetus to remain a moral obligation which, for the vast majority of women, is already freely recognized and respected without compulsion by law.

Id. at 293.

3. *The Liability of Health Care Providers.* In *Bergstreser v. Mitchell*, 577 F.2d 22 (8th Cir. 1978), the court relied in part upon a prior Missouri case permitting a prenatal cause of action as a predictor of Missouri's approach to preconception injuries. It held that a child stated a cause of action against medical care providers for injuries allegedly sustained as the result of a negligently performed Caesarean section upon the child's mother several years prior to the child's birth. Is it significant that *Bergstreser* was a claim against a health care provider? Should it?

4. *Pre-Conception Fault.* Should it make a difference if the tortiuous act occurred prior to conception? In *Monusko v. Postle*, 175 Mich. App. 269 (1989), a child born with rubella syndrome brought an action against medical care providers who allegedly had failed to test her mother for, or immunize her against, rubella prior to the child's conception. The court held that a duty was owed. What if the parents allege that the child's condition was one that if they had known of it they would have terminated the pregnancy? What if the healthcare provider failed to detect an underlying genetic condition before conception and the parents allege that had known of the underlying genetic condition in the family they never would have gotten pregnant? Consider these issues in light of the next principal case.

5. *Wrongful Death.* The majority of states consider a fetus a person for purposes of their wrongful death statutes. *Compare Aka v. Jefferson Hospital Assn.*, 42 S.W.3d 508 (Ark. 2001) *with Milton v. Cary Med. Center*, 538 A.2d 252 (Me. 1988). In *Light v. Proctor Community Hosp.*, 538 N.E.2d 828 (Ill. 1989), plaintiff brought a wrongful death claim on behalf of her unborn fetus, alleging that defendants were negligent in failing to determine if she was pregnant prior to performing a thyroid scan. Because of the possibility of damage to the fetus by the scanning, plaintiff terminated her pregnancy. The court denied her cause of action because the Illinois wrongful death statute included the following provision: "There shall be no cause of action against a physician or a medical institution for the wrongful death of a fetus caused by an abortion where the abortion was permitted by law and the requisite consent was lawfully given."

BADER v. JOHNSON
732 N.E.2d 1212 (Ind. 2000)

RUCKER, JUSTICE.

[The Johnsons' first child was born with hydrocephalus and severe mental and motor retardation and required extensive medical care until her death at four months of age. When Connie Johnson became pregnant again in 1982, the Johnsons were fearful of bearing another child with congenital defects so they sought consultation with Dr. Bader. Testing showed the pregnancy was normal and the child was born without complication. The Johnsons again sought counseling with Dr. Bader when Ms. Johnson became pregnant again. An amniocentesis performed at 19 1/2 weeks gestation revealed no abnormalities. However, Dr. Bader performed an ultrasound test the same day that revealed a fetus with a larger than expected cavity within the brain and an unusual head shape. Dr. Bader requested her staff to schedule Connie for follow-up testing but due to an office error the testing was not scheduled. The ultrasound report was not forwarded to Mrs. Johnson's treating physician. The child was born with hydrocephalus and other complications and died as a result four months later. The Johnsons alleged negligence in the failure to inform them of the result of the ultrasound test. Defendants moved for summary judgment. The trial court denied the motion. The court began its opinion by refusing to recognize a claim named "wrongful birth" or "wrongful life."]

This jurisdiction has long recognized a physician's duty to disclose to her patient material facts relevant to the patient's decision about treatment. *Boruff v. Jesseph*, 576 N.E.2d 1297, 1299 (Ind. Ct. App. 1991). Although a discussion of this duty has generally arisen in cases involving informed consent and the doctrine of fraudulent concealment, neither of which is alleged here, the underlying premise is still the same. In order for a patient to make an informed decision about her health, she must have the relevant facts at her disposal. If the physician has possession of those facts, then the physician has a duty to disclose them. "This duty arises from the relationship between the doctor and patient, and is imposed as a matter of law as are most legal duties." *Culbertson v. Mernitz*, 602 N.E.2d 98, 101 (Ind. 1992). In this case, the Johnsons allege they consulted Healthcare Providers to obtain information having a direct bearing on Connie's health, namely: a decision to terminate the pregnancy. According to the Johnsons the ultrasound test conducted by Healthcare Providers, revealing pre-natal abnormalities, was precisely the kind of information the couple needed to make an informed decision. For purposes of this summary judgment action we accept the Johnsons' assertions as true. As a matter of law Healthcare Providers owed a duty to the Johnsons to disclose the result of the test. . . . Assuming duty and breach of duty, we next address the third element of a medical malpractice cause of action: compensable injury proximately caused by the breach. According to the Johnsons, as a result of Healthcare Providers' conduct they were not informed of the fetus' condition until it was too late to terminate the pregnancy, resulting in Connie carrying to term and giving birth to a severely deformed child.

An indispensable element of a negligence claim is that the act complained of must be the proximate cause of the plaintiff's injuries. A negligent act is the proximate cause of an injury if the injury is a natural and probable consequence, which in the light of the circumstances, should have been foreseen or anticipated.

On the question of causation, Healthcare Providers make two claims: (1) there is an insufficient nexus between the Johnsons' claimed injury and the alleged act of negligence, and (2) Healthcare Providers did not "cause" the Johnsons' injury. At a minimum, proximate cause requires that the injury would not have occurred but for the defendant's conduct. The "but for" test presupposes that absent the defendant's conduct, a plaintiff would have been spared suffering the claimed injury. The Johnsons' claimed injury is that but for Healthcare Providers' failure to provide them with the result of the ultrasound test, the pregnancy would have been terminated. Whether the Johnsons can carry their burden of proof on this point at trial remains to be seen. However, at this stage of the proceedings the question is whether the Johnsons' carrying to term and giving birth to a severely deformed child can be the natural and probable consequence of Healthcare Providers' breach of duty, which Healthcare Providers should have foreseen or anticipated. This question must be answered affirmatively. Again, for purposes of this summary judgment action only, we accept as true the allegations contained in the Johnsons' complaint and the reasonable inferences to be drawn therefrom. The record shows the Johnsons consulted Healthcare Providers in 1982 when Connie was pregnant with her second child and again in 1991 when she became pregnant with her third child. The consultations were inspired by experiences the Johnsons encountered with their first child who was born with severe defects. The facts most favorable to the Johnsons suggest that Healthcare Providers knew or reasonably should have known that depending on the results of the ultrasound test, the Johnsons would not carry the pregnancy to term. We conclude, therefore that the Johnsons have made a *prima facie* claim of legal causation.

Advancing several public policy arguments, Healthcare Providers contend that even assuming duty, breach, and proximate cause the Johnsons still should not be allowed to pursue their claim. Chief among its arguments is that the court is being called upon "to weigh life (however imperfect) against the non-existence of life as that directly impacts the parents of the child." Brief of Appellant at 20. Characterizing the Johnsons' injury as the birth of a child with congenital defects, Healthcare Providers argue "life, even life with severe defects, cannot be an injury in the legal sense." Brief of Appellant at 24 (quoting *Cowe [v. Forum Group, Inc.]* 575 N.E.2d at 635).

We first observe that the injury claimed in this case is not the child's defects themselves. The Johnsons do not claim that the negligence of Healthcare Providers "caused" their child's defects. Instead, they contend that Healthcare Providers' negligence caused them to lose the ability to terminate the pregnancy and thereby avoid the costs associated with carrying and giving birth to a child with severe defects. In the context of this medical malpractice action, the distinction between causing the Johnsons to forego termination of the troubled pregnancy and causing a defective birth is significant. The former is a matter of causation while the latter goes to the question of damages, which we discuss in more detail in the next section of this opinion. This distinction was amplified in *Cowe* where we were confronted with a claim by a child born to a mentally retarded mother. While in the custody of a nursing home the mother was raped, resulting in the child's birth. The child sued the nursing home contending, among other things, that because of the nursing home's negligence in failing to protect the mother from rape, the child was wrongly born "into a world in which there was no natural parent capable of caring for and supporting him." 575 N.E.2d at 632. We rejected the child's claim on two interrelated grounds: (1) "a general conceptual unwillingness to recognize any cognizable damages for a child born with a genetic impairment as opposed to not being born at all", and (2) "the impossibility of calculating compensatory damages to restore a birth defective child to the position he would have occupied were it not for the defendant's negligence." *Cowe*, 575 N.E.2d at 634. Both interrelated grounds go to the issue of damages. It was in that context we declared "life, even life with severe defects, cannot be an injury in the legal sense." *Cowe*, 575 N.E.2d at 635.

Thus, in *Cowe*, the injury was life itself. And as with numerous other jurisdictions we were unwilling to allow a child plaintiff to proceed with this cause of action, in part because it involved "a calculation of damages dependant upon the relevant benefits of an impaired life as opposed to no life at all . . . a comparison the law is not equipped to make." *Cowe*, 575 N.E.2d at 634. Here, however, the injury is the lost opportunity and ability to terminate the pregnancy. Failure to allow the Johnsons to proceed with their claim would "immunize those in the medical field from liability for their performance in one particular area of medical practice." *Garrison v. Foy*, 486 N.E.2d 5, 8 (Ind. Ct. App. 1985) (recognizing the existence of a cause of action for wrongful pregnancy). We decline to carve out an exception in this case, and see no reason to prohibit the Johnsons from pursuing their claim.

It is a well-established principle that damages are awarded to fairly and adequately compensate an injured party for her loss, and the proper measure of damages must be flexible enough to fit the circumstances. In tort actions generally, all damages directly related to the wrong and arising without an intervening agency are recoverable. In negligence actions specifically, the injured party is entitled to damages proximately caused by the tortfeasor's breach of duty. In order for a negligent act to be a proximate cause of injury, the injury need only be a natural and probable result thereof; and the consequence be one which in light of the circumstances should reasonably have been foreseen or anticipated.

Viewing this case as asserting a tort of "wrongful birth" the trial court determined that the Johnsons could recover the following damages: (1) the extraordinary costs necessary to treat the birth defect, (2) any additional medical or educational costs attributable to the birth defect during the child's minority, (3) medical and hospital expenses incurred as a result of the physician's negligence, (4) the physical pain suffered by the mother, (5) loss of consortium, and (6) the mental and emotional anguish suffered by the parents. The Court of Appeals also viewed this case as one for "wrongful birth." Thus, following the lead from other jurisdictions, with the exception of mental and emotional distress, the Court of Appeals agreed the Johnsons were entitled to recover the foregoing damages. However, we have determined that this case should be treated no differently than any other medical malpractice case. Consequently, we need not evaluate the type of damages that may be allowed in a claimed "wrongful birth" action. Rather, we look at the damages the Johnsons contend they suffered and determine whether, if proven, they be can said to have been proximately caused by Healthcare Providers' breach of duty.

Consolidated and rephrased the Johnsons' complaint essentially sets forth the following damages: (1) hospital and related medical expenses associated with the pregnancy and delivery, (2) costs associated with providing the infant with care and treatment, (3) lost income, (4) emotional distress, and (5) loss of consortium. Indiana subscribes to the general principle of tort law that all damages directly attributable to the wrong done are recoverable. As we have indicated, the Johnsons' claimed injury in this case is the lost opportunity and ability to terminate the pregnancy. In turn, the loss can be measured by the medical and other costs directly attributable to Connie carrying the child to term. In addition to emotional distress damages, which we discuss below, the damages the Johnsons seek are consistent with those naturally flowing from Healthcare Providers' breach of duty. . . .

The underlying rationale for Indiana's traditional impact rule was that "absent physical injury, mental anguish is speculative, subject to exaggeration, likely to lead to fictitious claims, and often so unforeseeable that there is no rational basis for awarding damages." *Cullison v. Medley*, 570 N.E.2d 27, 29 (Ind. 1991). As modified, the rule still requires physical impact as distinguished from physical injury. However, the rationale for requiring some type of physical impact is still the same. Stated somewhat differently, as the United States Supreme Court observed "because the etiology of emotional disturbance is usually not as readily apparent as that of a broken bone following an automobile accident, courts have been concerned . . . that recognition of a cause of action for [emotional] injury when not related to any physical trauma may inundate judicial resources with a flood of relatively trivial claims, many of which may be imagined or falsified, and that liability may be imposed for highly remote consequences of a negligent act." *Consolidated Rail Corporation v. Gottshall*, 512 U.S. 532, 545, (1994).

Indiana's physical impact requirement embraces these concerns. Thus, when the courts have been satisfied that the facts of a particular case are such that the alleged mental anguish was not likely speculative, exaggerated, fictitious, or unforeseeable, then the claimant has been allowed to proceed with an emotional distress claim for damages even though the physical impact was slight, or the evidence of physical impact seemed to have been rather tenuous. . . .

In this case we find that Connie's continued pregnancy and the physical transformation her body underwent as a result, satisfy the direct impact requirement of our modified impact rule. Provided she can prevail on her negligence claim, we see no reason why Connie should not be able to claim damages for emotional distress. By contrast, Ronald did not suffer a direct impact as a result of Healthcare Provider's alleged negligence. We disagree with his argument to the contrary. Rather, at most Ronald is a relative bystander, a classification of potential victims this court has recently adopted in *Groves v. Taylor*, 729 N.E.2d 569, 572–73 (Ind. 2000). Whether Ronald can prevail on his claim for emotional distress damages depends on the evidence adduced at trial. . . .

DICKSON, JUSTICE dissenting:

Actions for "wrongful life" and "wrongful birth" are different from other kinds of negligence actions. . . . The majority opinion, treating the claim as a routine negligence claim, establishes troubling precedent, particularly as to the nature and extent of damages. If such claimants may recover all damages naturally flowing from a medical provider's breach of duty, would this not also include the costs of raising and educating such "unwanted" children? Will the birth of a child with even slight congenital anomalies entitle the parents to claim medical malpractice damages, contending that "if they had only known" their child would have a birth defect, they would have terminated the pregnancy? Will our courts face actions by parents seeking child-rearing costs because the gender of their child was not as expected, when they had sought genetic counseling for the purpose of terminating the pregnancy in the event that the child was of the "wrong" gender? Will defendant health-care providers be entitled to claim a reduction in damages by presenting evidence and arguing that, if the plaintiff-parents had elected to terminate the pregnancy, they would likely have suffered substantial and continuing psychological trauma? Will the process of jury selection (and resulting appeals) become a new battleground for intense disagreements regarding the issue of abortion? These are but a few of the troubling, foreseeable consequences of the majority opinion.

I believe that, because of the resulting complex philosophical, moral, and political implications, this Court should not expand Indiana common law to permit parents to seek damages resulting from the loss of an opportunity to terminate a pregnancy. . . . I therefore dissent and believe that summary judgment should be entered in favor of the defendants.

NOTES

1. *Cause.* Just who caused what injury? In *Wilson v. Kuenzi*, 751 S.W.2d 741, (Mo. 1988), defendant doctor allegedly failed to advise parents in their mid-thirties of the availability of the amniocentesis test for Down's Syndrome. In denying the parents' claim the court said that the doctor had not caused the genetic condition. But the doctor's failure did deprive the plaintiff's of their right to choose to terminate the pregnancy. In that sense did the doctor "cause" the parents to suffer a loss?

2. *What's in a Name?* The court in *Bader* refused to recognize a claim for wrongful birth or wrongful life *per* se and instead chose to treat the parent's claim as a standard tort or malpractice claim without a new label. It always is important to carefully analyze cases and consider exactly who is suing for what. In cases like *Bader*, are the parents the proper plaintiffs? For pregnancy related claims? For medical expenses? For the mother's pain and suffering? Are the parents the proper plaintiffs to recover any damages suffered by the child? Should the parents be able to recover their emotional distress arising from having a child with a "difficult" medical condition? For medical expenses related to the child's medical condition? For the child's enduring life in a compromised state? *See Turpin v. Sortini*, 643 P.2d 954 (Cal. 1982) (genetically harmed child has claim for damages but not for general damages). How do you compare life with some adverse medical condition to no life at all? Should the child be able to recover for being born? Does a child ever have any choice in the matter?

3. *A Child's Claim Against a Parent for Failing to Terminate the Pregnancy.* How should a court respond to an action brought by a child suffering from a hereditary defect against her mother for failing to terminate the pregnancy after being informed of the adverse results of her amniocentesis?

UNIVERSITY OF ARIZONA HEALTH SCIENCES CENTER v. SUPERIOR COURT
667 P.2d 1294 (Ariz. 1983)

FELDMAN, JUSTICE.

. . . The real parties in interest are Patrick Heimann and Jeanne Heimann. . . . The Heimanns claimed that one of the hospital's employees, a doctor, had negligently performed a vasectomy operation upon Patrick Heimann, that as a result Jeanne Heimann became pregnant and on October 4, 1981 gave birth to a baby girl. The Heimanns alleged in the underlying tort action that the vasectomy had been obtained because "already having three children, [they] decided . . . that they desired to have no more children. As a result of this decision they further decided that a vasectomy was the best means of contraception for them." The baby girl is normal and healthy, but the Heimanns argue that they are financially unable to provide for themselves, their other three children and the newest child whose birth was neither planned nor desired. Accordingly, they seek damages from the doctor and his employer. . . .

The first question is whether parents of a child who was neither desired nor planned for but who was, fortunately, normal and healthy, have been damaged at all by the birth of that child. An overview of the authorities indicates rather clearly that the law will recognize at least some types of damage which result from unwanted procreation caused by the negligence of another. The real controversy centers around the nature of the damages which may be recovered. On this issue there are three distinct views.

The first line of authority limits damages by holding that the parents may recover only those damages which occur as the result of pregnancy and birth, and may not recover the cost of rearing the child.

A second view could be characterized as the "full damage" rule and allows the parents to recover all damages and expenses, including the cost of the unsuccessful sterilization procedure, the economic loss from pregnancy, and the economic, physical and emotional cost attendant to birth and rearing the child. These cases appear to be a distinct minority.

A substantial number of cases have adopted a third rule which allows the recovery of all damages which flow from the wrongful act but requires consideration of the offset of benefits. *See* REST. 2D TORTS § 920 (1977). Under this view, the trier of fact is permitted to determine and award all past and future expenses and damages incurred by the parent, including the cost of rearing the child, but is also instructed that it should make a deduction for the benefits that the parents will receive by virtue of having a normal, healthy child. . . .

The hospital claims that the trial court was bound by law to adopt the first view, that the cost of rearing and educating the child are not compensable elements of damage. The Heimanns claim, on the other hand, that the proper rule is the second view, which permits the recovery of all damage and does not permit the jury to consider and offset benefits. We disagree with both positions.

We consider first the strict rule urged by the hospital. Various reasons are given by the courts which adopt the view that damages for rearing and educating the child cannot be recovered. Some cases base their decision on the speculative nature of the necessity to assess "such matters as the emotional effect of a birth on siblings as well as parents, and the emotional as well as pecuniary costs of raising an unplanned and, perhaps, an unwanted child in varying family environments." *Coleman v. Garrison*, 327 A.2d 757, 761 [(Del. Super. Ct. 1974), *aff'd*, 349 A.2d 8 (1975)]. We think, however, that juries in tort cases are often required to assess just such intangible factors, both emotional and pecuniary, and see no reason why a new rule should be adopted for wrongful pregnancy cases. Another reason given for the strict view is the argument that the benefits which the parents will receive from having a normal, healthy child outweigh any loss which the parents might incur in rearing and educating the child. No doubt this is true in many cases, but we think it unrealistic to assume that it is true in all cases. We can envision many situations in which for either financial or emotional reasons, or both, the parents are simply unable to handle another child and where it would be obvious that from either an economic or emotional perspective — or both — substantial damage has occurred.

A third basis for the strict rule is the argument that the "injury is out of proportion to the culpability of the [wrongdoer]; and that the allowance of recovery would place an unreasonable burden upon the [wrongdoer], since it would likely open the way for fraudulent claims. . . ." *Beardsley v. Wierdsma*, 650 P.2d 288, 292 (Wyo. 1982). This, of course, is the hue and cry in many tort cases and in essence is no more than the fear that some cases will be decided badly. Undoubtedly, the system will not decide each case correctly in this field, just as it does not in any field, but here, as in other areas of tort law, we think it better to adopt a rule which will enable courts to strive for justice in all cases rather than to rely upon one which will ensure injustice in many.

The final basis for the strict rule is the one which gives this court greater pause than any of the others. It is well put by the Illinois Supreme Court in *Cockrum v. Baumgartner*, [447 N.E.2d 385, 388–89 (Ill. 1983)]. The court used the following words to justify the denial of recovery of damages for the rearing and educating of the unplanned child:

> . . . [A] parent cannot be said to have been damaged by the birth and rearing of a normal, healthy child . . . [I]t is a matter of universally-shared emotion and sentiment that the intangible but all important, incalculable but invaluable "benefits" of parenthood far outweigh any of the mere monetary burdens involved. Speaking legally, this may be deemed conclusively presumed by the fact that a prospective parent does not abort or subsequently place the "unwanted" child for adoption. On a more practical level, the validity of the principle may be tested simply by asking any parent the purchase price for that particular youngster. Since this is the rule of experience, it should be, and we therefore hold that it is, the appropriate rule of law.

> . . . One can, of course, in mechanical logic reach a different conclusion, but only on the ground that human life and the state of parenthood are compensable losses. In a proper hierarchy of values, the benefit of life should not be outweighed by the expense of supporting it. Respect for life and the rights proceeding from it are the heart of our legal system and, broader still, our civilization.

Id. at 200.

These sentiments evoke a response from this court. In most cases we could join in the "universally shared emotion and sentiment" expressed by the majority of the Illinois court, but we do not believe we hold office to impose our views of morality by deciding cases on the basis of personal emotion and senti- ment, though we realize we cannot and should not escape the effect of human characteristics shared by all mankind. However, we believe our function is to leave the emotion and sentiment to others and attempt to examine the prob- lem with logic and by application of the relevant principles of law. In this case, we believe that the strict rule is based upon an emotional premise and ignores logical considerations. While we recognize that in most cases a family can and will adjust to the birth of the child, even though they had not desired to have it, we must recognize also that there are cases where the birth of an unplanned child can cause serious emotional or economic problems to the parents. We therefore reject the hospital's claim that the cost of rearing and educating the child can never be compensable elements of damage.

We consider next the "full damage" rule urged by the Heimanns. . . . The courts applying this rule have relied on traditional tort principles and determined that the cost of rearing the child is a foreseeable consequence of the physician's negligence and therefore compensable. We agree that these damages are compensable; however, we believe that a rule which does not allow for an offset for the benefits of the parent-child relationship prevents the trier of fact from considering the basic values inherent in the relationship and the dignity and sanctity of human life. We believe that these "sentiments," if they may be called such, are proper considerations for the fact finder in tort cases, whether they be used to mitigate or enhance damages. No doubt ascertaining and assigning a monetary value to such intangibles will be a difficult task, but we do not believe it more difficult than the task of ascertaining the pecuniary and non-pecuniary damages that the parents will experience after the birth of the child. Therefore, we agree with the Illinois Supreme Court that the "full damage" approach is an exercise in mechanical logic and we reject it.

In our view, the preferable rule is that followed by the courts which, although permitting the trier of fact to consider both pecuniary and non-pecuniary elements of damage which pertain to the rearing and education of the child, also require it to consider the question of offsetting the pecuniary and non-pecuniary benefits which the parents will receive from the parental relationship with the child. Some may fear that adoption of such a rule will permit juries to recognize elements of damage which, because of our private philosophy or views of ethics, we, as judges, believe should not be recognized. We feel, however, that the consensus of a cross-section of the community on such important issues is better and more accurately obtained from the verdict of a jury than from the decision of any particular group of that community. A jury verdict based on knowledge of all relevant circumstances is a better reflection of whether real damage exists in each case than can be obtained from use of any abstract, iron-clad rule which some courts would adopt and apply regardless of the circumstances of the particular case.

There may be those who fear that the rule which we adopt will permit the award of damages where no real injury exists. We feel this danger is minimized by giving weight and consideration in each case to the plaintiff's reason for submitting to sterilization procedures. Such evidence is perhaps the most relevant information on the question of whether the subsequent birth of a child actually constitutes damage to the parents. The parents' *preconception* calculation of the reasons for preventing procreation is untainted by bitterness, greed or sense of duty to the child and is perhaps the most telling evidence of whether or to what extent the birth of the child actually injured the parents. For example, where the parent sought sterilization in order to avoid the danger of genetic defect, the jury could easily find that the uneventful birth of a healthy, non-defective child was a blessing rather than a "damage." Such evidence should be admissible, and the rule which we adopt will allow the jury to learn all the factors relevant to the determination of whether there has been any real damage and, if so, how much. We are confident that the inherent good sense of the jury is the best safeguard to "runaway" verdicts and unfounded speculation in the award of damages, provided that the jury is allowed to consider the issues in realistic terms.

It may be argued also that the rule which we adopt will have the unhappy effect of creating situations in which parents will testify to their feeling or opinion that the child is "not worth" the burden of having the rearing. Such testimony could be harmful if or when the child learns of it. "We are not convinced that the effect on the child will be significantly detrimental in every case, or even in most cases; . . . we think the parents, not the courts, are the ones who must weigh the risk. . . ."

We see no reason why ordinary damage rules, applicable to all other tort cases, should not be applicable to this situation. By allowing the jury to consider the future costs, both pecuniary and non-pecuniary, of rearing and educating the child, we permit it to consider all the elements of damage on which the parents may present evidence. By permitting the jury to consider the reason for the procedure and to assess and offset the pecuniary and non-pecuniary benefits which will inure to the parents by reason of their relationship to the child, we allow the jury to discount those damages, thus reducing speculation and permitting the verdict to be based upon the facts as they actually exist in each of the unforeseeable variety of situations which may come before the court. We think this by far the better rule. The blindfold on the figure of justice is a shield from partiality, not from reality.

GORDON, VICE CHIEF JUSTICE (concurring in part and dissenting in part).

. . . The rule of damages established by the majority in this case may indeed be logical and legally scientific. Logic and science may, however, lead to results at variance with public policy. Although I have a very high degree of respect for our country's system of civil justice, and readily admit that our common law concepts of tort liability have caused products manufactured in the United States to be among the safest in the world, I feel that there are some human misfortunes that do not lend themselves to solution by combat in the courtroom. Wrongful pregnancy, in my opinion, is one of those. I believe the rule allowing damages recovery beyond the costs of birth in cases such as these would violate what I consider the public policy of our state in several ways.

As is pointed out in the majority opinion, the prosecution of this type of action requires parents to deny the worth of the child, thus placing the values of the parents over those of the child. Under the "benefits rule," a judgment for the parents is a conclusion by the court that a child is not worth what it takes to raise him or her. This problem has been recognized by several authors who refer to such a child as an "emotional bastard" when attempting to describe the stigma that will attach to the child when he learns the true circumstances of his upbringing. . . .

NOTES

1. *Offset.* How does the jury offset? In *Jones v. Malinowski*, 473 A.2d 429, 436 (Md. 1984), the Court of Appeals of Maryland remarked:

The child rearing costs here in issue are neither too unquantifiable nor too speculative to deny their recovery under settled rules applied by the cases. The computation of such costs requires a routine calculation of reasonably foreseeable expenses that will be incurred by the parents to maintain, support and educate the child to majority age. Such calculations are based on well-recognized economic factors regularly made by actuaries for estate planners and insurance companies; indeed, the expenses associated with raising a child are well appreciated by the average citizen through first hand experience.

See also Zehr v. Haugen, 871 P.2d 1006 (Or. 1994), where the court held plaintiffs could recover the costs of raising a healthy child who was born as a result of a negligent tubal ligation.

2. *The Consequences of Denying Recovery.* Would denying recovery encourage abortion? Does denial of recovery adversely affect the woman's right to decide to have a child? In *Lynch v. Bay Ridge Obstetrical & Gynecological Assocs.* 532 N.E.2d 1239 (N.Y. 1988), the court held that patient stated a claim against her gynecologist, who failed to diagnose her pregnancy and prescribed medication which could cause birth defects, thus forcing the patient to choose between abortion and a potentially defective child. Suppose the victim of a wrongful pregnancy chose abortion over birth; should the defendant be liable for the costs of termination — including the emotional costs?

3. *Adoption Claims.* In *Burr v. Board of County Comm'rs*, 491 N.E.2d 1101 (Oh. 1986), adoptive parents brought an action in fraud against the county adoption division. The 17-month-old boy they adopted had been represented as the son of a young unmarried mother who was leaving the state. In fact, the child's mother was actually a 31-year-old mental patient at the state hospital. The child was born at the institution, and it was presumed that his father also was a mental patient. The child shared many of the same mental impediments as his mother and was diagnosed as suffering from Huntington's Disease, a genetically inherited disease which destroys the central nervous system. The court found that the evidence supported plaintiffs' verdict. *Meracle v. Children's Serv. Soc'y of Wis.*, 437 N.W.2d 532, 537 (Wis. 1989), concerned an action against a private adoption agency which had allegedly told the adoptive parents that although the child's grandmother had died of Huntington's Disease, her father had tested negative, and thus the child was no more at risk than any other child. In fact, there was no reliable test as to inheritance of the disease, and a good chance that the child would inherit it. Five years later the child was diagnosed as suffering from the disease. The court refused the adoptive parents' claim for emotional damages because of an absence of physical manifestation of injury. However, the court permitted the cause of action for extraordinary medical expenses.

H.   OWNERS AND OCCUPIERS OF LAND

This section deals with injuries suffered by those who enter the premises of another when such injuries are related to some condition of the premises. For years, the duty that the occupier of the land owed was based upon the status of the injured person — trespasser, invitee, or licensee. Then the law moved towards a broader reasonable care standard. But old rules die slowly. Moreover, there has been some legislative action in the changing landscape of landowner law, especially in the recreational land area. One may find it hard to contain the boundaries of this section. Welcome, once again, to the uncertain world of the common law and torts in particular.

MALLET v. PICKENS
522 S.E.2d 436 (W. Va. 1999)

McGRAW, JUSTICE.

Appellants Patricia A. Mallett and Ernest R. Mallet appeal a grant of summary judgment entered against them in their tort action, in which they sought damages for an injury Mrs. Mallet sustained when visiting the home of their friends, Selbert Pickens and Anita Pickens. The lower court granted summary judgment on the basis that Mrs. Mallet, as a social guest, was merely a licensee upon the property of the Pickenses, and that the Pickenses had no duty to Mrs. Mallet, save to refrain from willfully or wantonly injuring her. The Mallets appeal, claiming that Mrs. Mallet should be considered an invitee, or, alternatively, that this Court should instead apply a duty of reasonable care upon landowners with respect to all non-trespassing entrants. Because we concur with the Mallets and choose to abolish the common law distinction between licensees and invitees, following the modern trend in the development of premises liability law, we must reverse the decision of the lower court.

On July 23, 1994, the appellants, Patricia and Ernest Mallet, decided to visit their good friends, the Pickens family. Mrs. Pickens had been injured some time before in an auto accident, and the Mallets wanted to wish her well in her recovery. Although the two families often visited one another, the Pickenses did not know that the Mallets were coming to visit that day.

The Pickenses were having work done to their home, so at the time of the visit, the only access to the front door of the house was by way of a set of temporary, wooden stairs, which did not have a railing or banister. Additionally, because of the construction, a masonry block had been left on the ground near the steps. When Mrs. Mallet exited the home after the visit, the stairs shifted under her weight and she fell, striking her head on the block. Mrs. Mallet suffered broken bones in her face that required surgery.

The Mallets' health insurance carrier originally denied Mrs. Mallet's claim, on the basis that a third party (the Pickenses) was at fault, and that the third party should pay the medical bills. The Pickenses submitted their friend's medical bills to their insurance carrier, which denied the claim. The Mallets filed suit, and the lower court granted summary judgment in favor of Mr. and Mrs. Pickens, ruling that Mrs. Mallet was a licensee, and the Pickenses did not breach their duty of care toward Mrs. Mallet, which was merely the duty not to willfully or wantonly injure her . . .

West Virginia common law presently recognizes a difference regarding the duty owed to entrants of land. An entrant of land must fit into the licensee, invitee, or trespasser category and is owed a different duty of care from a landowner, depending upon that status. . . .

From the outset we must bear in mind that the categories of licensee, invitee, and trespasser evolved in a much different time, and in a significantly different legal climate than exists today. Scholars studying the subject regard the English cases of *Parnaby v. Lancaster Canal Co.*, 11 Ad. & E. 223, 113 Eng. Rep. 400 (Ex. 1839), and *Southcote v. Stanley*, 1 H. & N. 247, 156 Eng. Rep. 1195 (Ex. 1856), as the progenitors of the licensee/invitee distinction, soon adopted by jurisdictions in this country . . . .

The ancient precept of "sanctity of property," and the concept of "privity of contract," were the basic principles underpinning the employment of these categories . . . One of the main "benefits," as seen through eyes of the time, of employing the licensee/invitee/trespasser trichotomy was the protection of property owners, who were a privileged minority, from the vagaries of juries, comprised mostly of land entrants and not landowners.

Inherent in such a scheme was the notion that a jury could not be trusted to enter a just verdict; however, we have long ago cast off such suspicion of the jury system:

> Chesterton, the "prince of paradox," framing the experience of two millennia in Tremendous Trifles: The Twelve Men, said:

> "Our civilization has decided, and very justly decided, that determining the guilt or innocence of men [natural or artificial] is a thing too important to be trusted to trained men. It wishes for light upon that awful matter, it asks men who know no more law than I know, but who can feel the things that I felt in the jury box. When it wants a library catalogued, or the solar system discovered, or any trifle of that kind, it uses up its specialists. But when it wishes anything done which is really serious, it collects twelve of the ordinary men standing round. The same thing was done, if I remember right, by the Founder of Christianity." Gilbert K. Chesterton, Tremendous Trifles: The Twelve Men 86–87 (1922).

Delp v. Itmann Coal Co., 342 S. E.2d 219, 223 (W.Va. 1986) (McGraw, J., dissenting). In the case before us, the important matter of liability for Mrs. Mallet's injuries was never presented to the jury; the old scheme served its purpose in limiting juror discretion, effectively eliminating the jury entirely from the consideration of the case. This is the most pernicious side effect of the common law trichotomy, and it is no longer in step with the times.

We must examine the continuing relevance of the common law trichotomy by viewing it in the context of the time in which it was developed. We must not overlook the fact that some of the hoary and "well-established" principles that held sway at the time the common law categories were introduced in the mid-19th Century included, slavery, see *Dred Scott v. Sandford*, 60 U.S. (19 How.) 393, 15 L.Ed. 691 (1856), and a lack of women's suffrage, see *Minor v. Happersett*, 88 U.S. (21 Wall.) 162, 22 L.Ed. 627 (1874) (confining the right of suffrage to males did not deprive women of property without due process of law), both of which, had they not been abandoned, would, to say the least, have had a negative impact on the recent composition of this Court.

Justice Starcher, joined by Justice Workman, recognized in their concurrence in *Self v. Queen* that many "established" rules must give way as society progresses:

> When Justice Oliver Wendell Holmes spoke of "fixed and uniform standards of external conduct" in his 1881 lecture series (now found in THE COMMON LAW (1909)), we must keep in mind that Holmes was writing in a time when the harsh rules of contributory negligence, assumption of the risk, and the fellow-servant doctrine were taking root in the law. These rules, which were once new, shiny principles designed to immunize entrepreneurs and businesses from liability at a time of early industrialization, have since weathered and fallen in the face of time, reason, and a growing intolerance for human suffering that has accompanied the post-industrial era. See *Bradley v. Appalachian Power Co.*, 163 W.Va. 332, 256 S.E.2d 879 (1979) (abolishing contributory negligence rule and adopting modified comparative negligence principles); *King v. Kayak Mfg. Corp.*, 182 W.Va. 276, 387 S.E.2d 511 (1989) (abolishing assumption of risk and adopting comparative assumption of risk); W. VA. CODE, 23-1-1, *et seq.* (abrogating fellow-servant doctrine by providing workers' compensation benefits to workers injured in the course of and as a result of their employment, including injuries by fellow employees).

487 S.E.2d at 299 (Starcher, J., concurring). The outmoded distinction between invitees is just the sort of principle which, though perhaps once an accurate reflection of society's values, no longer comports with our notions of fairness, and for that reason should be abandoned.

Courts, in their efforts to distinguish between licensees and invitees, have felled whole forests and sacrificed them in an often vain attempt to explain the difference. These efforts have resulted in some opinions that strain the credulity of an honest observer. Courts on both sides of the Atlantic have pointed out the confusing complexities encountered when applying the common law classifications:

> A canvasser who comes on your premises without your consent is a trespasser. Once he has your consent, he is a licensee. Not until you do business with him is he an invitee. Even when you have done business with him, it seems rather strange that your duty towards him should be different when he comes up to your door from what it is when he goes away. Does he change his colour in the middle of the conversation? What is the position when you discuss business with him and it comes to nothing? No confident answer can be given to these questions. Such is the morass into which the law has floundered in trying to distinguish between licensees and invitees.

Mariorenzi v. Joseph DiPonte, Inc., 333 A.2d 127, 133 n. 4 (R.I. 1975) (abolishing distinctions between trespasser, licensee, and invitee).

Quite often, the facts of a particular premises liability case will require a departure from Aristotelian logic in its search for common sense realism. The Indiana Court of Appeals demonstrated the mental gymnastics sometimes necessary to hold onto the old distinction in *Markle v. Hacienda Mexican Restaurant*, 570 N.E.2d 969 (Ind. Ct. App. 1991). In *Markle*, the plaintiff decided to eat at a restaurant, but upon driving into the strip mall parking lot where the restaurant was located, stopped when he saw a friend. He got out of his car to transfer an item to the friend's car, and was injured when he stepped into a pothole. Although the court decided that a jury question existed as to the duty the restaurant owed the plaintiff, they found necessary the following exercise in arcane logic:

> We would reach this same result if, for instance, Markle was discussing business with an associate while eating dinner at the restaurant and injured himself in the same parking lot by stepping into the same chuck-hole when going out to his car for some papers to use in the discussion. One could say that Markle stepped out of his role as an invitee — although briefly — by leaving the restaurant to get the papers. However, it is also reasonable that the owners could anticipate patrons would meet to discuss business over dinner. Thus, the question of whether the patron who has left the restaurant to get some papers from his car has stepped out of his role as invitee is one properly left to the trier of fact. Likewise, the question of whether the Shopping Center could have anticipated that Markle — or any other customer — would transact business in the parking lot is one properly left to the trier of fact.

Markle, 570 N.E.2d at 975 n.2. A search of other jurisdictions reveals case after case where a court, bound by the old, common law categories, is forced to ask the wrong question.

The question in instances such as this should not be, "was the plaintiff emblazoned with the magic letters 'L' or 'I' at the moment of injury?," but rather "was the parking lot safe?" Or, alternatively, "did the landowner exercise reasonable care under the circumstances, to ensure that the parking lot was safe for a reasonably foreseeable event, namely, that somebody might walk across it?" Framing the question in this manner is important, because it recognizes that neither landowners nor entrants make decisions with these archaic distinctions in mind. . . .

If we wish for our law to be predictable, and we do, then we have a duty to shape it in such a way that it meshes with the general, reasonable assumptions that people make in their daily lives. Because the common law distinction between invitee and licensee does not meet that standard, it should be discarded.

A growing number of courts have taken Occam's Razor to this problem, in search for a simpler and more predictable rule. Nearly 40 years ago, the Supreme Court of the United States declined to apply the common law categories to admiralty law, and identified the conflict between a feudally-derived liability standard and modern tort theory:

> The distinctions which the common law draws between licensee and invitee were inherited from a culture deeply rooted to the land, a culture which traced many of its standards to a heritage of feudalism. In an effort to do justice in an industrialized urban society, with its complex economic and individual relationships, modern common-law

courts have found it necessary to formulate increasingly subtle verbal refinements, to create subclassifications among traditional common-law categories, and to delineate fine gradations in the standards of care which the landowner owes to each. Yet even within a single jurisdiction, the classifications and subclassifications bred by the common law have produced confusion and conflict. As new distinctions have been spawned, older ones have become obscured. Through this semantic morass the common law has moved, unevenly and with hesitation, towards "imposing on owners and occupiers a single duty of reasonable care in all the circumstances."

Kermarec v. Compagnie Generale Transatlantique, 358 U.S. 625, 630–31 (1959) (footnotes omitted). Clearly the justices underestimated the degree of hesitation, but today we do our part by wading out of the "semantic morass." . . .

Soon after the opinion in *Kermarec*, several states abandoned the old scheme, starting with California in *Rowland v. Christian*, 443 P.2d 561 (Cal. 1968). Over 30 years ago, the California court realized that the old classifications were outmoded:

Complexity can be borne and confusion remedied where the underlying principles governing liability are based upon proper considerations. Whatever may have been the historical justifications for the common law distinctions, it is clear that those distinctions are not justified in the light of our modern society and that the complexity and confusion which [have] arisen is not due to difficulty in applying the original common law rules — they are all to easy to apply in their original formulation — but is due to the attempts to apply just rules in our modern society within the ancient terminology.

Rowland, 443 P.2d at 567. The *Rowland* court could see that application of the old distinction in premises liability cases often yields a result that seems unjust by the standards of today, especially when viewed in light of the general principles of negligence that we employ in other tort cases.

Broad generalizations about the state of premises liability law in other jurisdictions are always subject to caveats and limitations. Several states have special rules for invited social guests; others limit landowner liability via recreational use statutes, or employ a distinction between "active" and "passive" negligence. Having said that, our research reveals that at least 25 jurisdictions have abolished or largely abandoned the licensee/invitee distinction. Among these 25 jurisdictions that have broken with past tradition, at least 17 have eliminated or fundamentally altered the distinction. Another eight of the 25 have eliminated even the trespasser distinction. And, of those retaining the old scheme, judges in at least five of those states have authored vigorous dissents or concurrences arguing for change.

A look at some of these cases provides an example of the logic that persuades us to join the modern trend. In a recent Nebraska case, a father visited his daughter, who worked at a hospital, and injured his back when he slipped on snow-covered stairs as he left the building. The lower court held that, because the father was visiting the daughter, he was a licensee and could not recover in a suit against the hospital. The Supreme Court of Nebraska recognized this absurd result:

> When he was injured, Heins was exiting a county hospital, using the main entrance to the hospital, over the lunch hour. If Heins had been on the hospital premises to visit a patient or purchase a soft drink from a vending machine, he could have been classified as an invitee. . . . However, he came to visit his daughter and was denied recovery as a matter of law.
>
> Thus Heins was denied the possibility of recovering under present law, merely because on this trip to the hospital he happened to be a licensee rather than an invitee. In the instant case, the hospital would undergo no additional burden in exercising reasonable care for a social visitor such as Heins, because it had the duty to exercise reasonable care for its invitees. A patient visitor could have used the same front entrance at which Heins fell and would have been able to maintain a negligence action; however, Heins has been denied the opportunity to recover merely because of his status at the time of the fall.

Heins v. Webster County, 552 N.W. 2d 51, 56 (Neb. 1996). The *Heins* court perceived the obvious question, "did the hospital exercise reasonable care under the circumstances?" The court went on to abolish the common law categories: "We conclude that we should eliminate the distinction between licensees and invitees by requiring a standard of reasonable care for all lawful visitors." *Id*. at 57.

Another recent case in which a court abandoned the old scheme is *Nelson v. Freeland*, 507 S.E.2d 882 (N.C. 1998). In *Nelson*, Mr. Freeland requested that his friend Mr. Nelson pick him up at his home for a business meeting the two were going to attend. In doing so, Mr. Nelson tripped over a stick Mr. Freeland had left lying on his porch. Mr. Freeland won summary judgment, which Mr. Nelson appealed. After a lengthy, exhaustive, and well-written analysis of the history of the common law trichotomy, the North Carolina Supreme Court abandoned the licensee/invitee distinction:

> Given the numerous advantages associated with abolishing the trichotomy, this Court concludes that we should eliminate the distinction between licensees and invitees by requiring a standard of reasonable care toward all lawful visitors. Adoptions of a true negligence standard eliminates the complex, confusing, and unpredictable state of premises-liability law and replaces it with a rule which forces the jury's attention upon the pertinent issue of whether the landowner acted as a reasonable person would under the circumstances.

Nelson, 507 S.E.2d at 892.

Some would argue, and indeed this Court has stated in the past, that the strength of the old system is that it engenders predictability. We are no longer persuaded by this argument. As we noted above, the average person has no idea that such a rule exists. Indeed, in situations such as the case before us, homeowners would probably imagine that if anyone is entitled to protection on their property (and coverage under a homeowners policy), surely their friends and loved ones would qualify. In fact, it is counterintuitive to most lay persons, and many a law student, that those closest to us are not afforded the same protection the law provides to the meter reader or the paper boy. Complicating this confusion among property owners is the fact that an entrant can cascade chameleon-like through the various "colors" of entrant status, from trespasser to licensee to invitee and back, in the course of a single visit.

Today we hold that the common law distinction between licensees and invitees is hereby abolished; landowners or possessors now owe any non-trespassing entrant a duty of reasonable care under the circumstances. We retain our traditional rule with regard to a trespasser, that being that a landowner or possessor need only refrain from willful or wanton injury. Though our decision might seem a radical departure from past cases, in its basic philosophy it is not.

We have held since the 19th Century that: "Negligence is the violation of the duty of taking care under the given circumstances. It is not absolute, but is always relative to some circumstances of time, place, manner, or person." *Dicken v. Liverpool Salt & Coal Co.*, 23 S.E. 2d 582 (W.Va. 1895). Although before today we have allowed the old labels to limit a court's examination of a negligent act, we have recognized that the foreseeability of an injury is dispositive of the duty owed:

> The ultimate test of the existence of a duty to use care is found in the foreseeability that harm may result if it is not exercised. The test is, would the ordinary man in the defendant's position, knowing what he knew or should have known, anticipate that harm of the general nature of that suffered was likely to result?

Sewell v. Gregory, 371 S.E. 2d 82 (W.Va. 1988). In so holding in *Sewell*, we were in accord with Justice Cardozo's celebrated maxim: "The risk reasonably to be perceived defines the duty to be obeyed. . . . " *Palsgraf v. Long Island R. Co.*, 162 N.E. 99, 100 (N.Y. 1928).

We are quick to recognize, however, that foreseeability is not all that the trier of fact must consider when deciding if a given defendant owed a duty to a given plaintiff, even in the absence of the licensee/invitee distinction:

> While the existence of a duty is defined in terms of foreseeability, it also involves policy considerations including "the likelihood of injury, the magnitude of the burden of guarding against it, and the consequences of placing that burden on the defendant."

Harris v. R.A. Martin, Inc., 513 S.E. 2d 170, 174 (W.Va. 1998). Some factors that other jurisdictions have included in the analysis of whether a landowner or occupier has exercised reasonable care under the circumstances include the seriousness of an injury, the time, manner and circumstances under which the injured party entered the premises, and the normal use made of the premises.

We hold that, in determining whether a defendant in a premises liability case met his or her burden of reasonable care under the circumstances to all non-trespassing entrants, the trier of fact must consider (1) the foreseeability that an injury might occur; (2) the severity of injury; (3) the time, manner and circumstances under which the injured party entered the premises; (4) the normal or expected use made of the premises; and (5) the magnitude of the burden placed upon the defendant to guard against injury. . . .

We hold that the invitee/licensee distinction is abandoned. Our cases that rely upon it . . . and their progeny, are overruled to the extent that they rely upon an invitee/licensee distinction. In light of these developments, Mr. and Mrs. Mallet should be afforded another attempt at recovery, and all similar claims, in the future, should be adjudicated under the new standards we have articulated. Accordingly, the lower court's grant of summary judgment is reversed and this case is remanded for proceedings consistent with this opinion. [REVERSED AND REMANDED.]

NOTES

1. *Rowland and Rejection.* In *Rowland v. Christian*, 443 P.2d 561, 567-68 (Cal. 1968), the court stated:

> Although in general there may be a relationship between the remaining factors and the classifications of trespasser, licensee, and invitee, there are many cases in which no such relationship may exist. Thus, although the foreseeability of harm to an invitee would ordinarily seem greater than the foreseeability of harm to a trespasser, in a particular case the opposite may be true. The same may be said of the issue of certainty of injury. The burden to the defendant and consequences to the community of imposing a duty to exercise care with resulting liability for breach may often be greater with respect to trespassers than with respect to invitees, but it by no means follows that this is true in every case. In many situations, the burden will be the same, i.e., the conduct necessary upon the defendant's part to meet the burden of exercising due care as to invitees will also meet his burden with respect to licensees and trespassers. The last of the major factors, the cost of insurance, will, of course, vary depending upon the rules of liability adopted, but there is no persuasive evidence that applying ordinary principles of negligence law to the land occupier's liability will materially reduce the prevalence of insurance due to increased cost or even substantially increase the cost.

Why did the court in *Mallet* preserve the limited duty rule for trespassers? Do you agree with that decision?

2. *Rowland Rejected.* Rowland's rejection of categories has met with rejection in many jurisdictions. *See, e.g., Carter v. Kinney*, 896 S.W.29, 926 (Mo. 1995). In *Adams v. Fred's Dollar Store*, 497 So. 2d 1097, 1102 (Miss. 1986), the court observed: "To adopt such a position now would cause an upheaval of the common law and needlessly inject uncertainty into the realm of commercial and private legal relations. We here reaffirm our intention to follow the common law distinctions."

3. *The Tyranny of Categories.* To what extent should property law classifications be relevant and/or conclusive in defining tort-based liability?

REST. 2D TORTS § 329 states:

> A trespasser is a person who enters or remains upon land in the possession of another without a privilege to do so created by the possessor's consent or otherwise.

Section 330 defines a licensee as "a person who is privileged to enter or remain on land only by virtue of the possessor's consent." REST. 2D TORTS § 330. And, according to REST. 2D TORTS § 332:

> (1) An invitee is either a public invitee or a business visitor.

> (2) A public invitee is a person who is invited to enter or remain on land as a member of the public for a purpose for which the land is held open to the public.

> (3) A business visitor is a person who is invited to enter or remain on land for a purpose directly or indirectly connected with business dealings with the possessor of the land.

In *Coleman v. United Fence Co.*, 668 S.W.2d 536 (Ark. 1984), the plaintiff parked his car on defendant's land without permission. Subsequently, the defendant contracted with a fence company to dig postholes on the defendant's property. The fence company requested that plaintiff remove his car. When plaintiff went to retrieve his car he stepped into a posthole and suffered injuries. The court concluded that plaintiff was a trespasser, on the basis that his failure to remove the car resulted in a continuing trespass. *Stone v. Taffe*, [1974] 3 All E.R. 1016 (C.A.), concerned the aftermath of a private party held in a "pub" by a local lodge of the Royal and Antediluvian Order of Buffaloes. The plaintiff's decedent fell down an unlighted staircase at 1 a.m. The permitted hours for serving alcohol had expired at 10:30 p.m. Both the decedent and the manager of the pub were "Buffs," and members of the lodge met regularly at the pub. The court held that despite the expiration of the lawful time for the serving of alcohol, the decedent had not ceased to be a lawful visitor.

4. *Place of Injury?* Should the extent of a landowner's responsibility depend on whether the plaintiff is or is not on the premises? *See, e.g., Salevan v. Wilmington Park, Inc.*, 72 A.2d 239 (Del. 1950) (pedestrian hit by ball while walking on a street outside baseball park; owner of park was held liable in negligence). In *Mostert v. CBL & Assocs.*, 741 P.2d 1090 (Wyo. 1987), the court deviated from the general rule in concluding that a movie theatre operator had an affirmative duty to advise its patrons of severe weather conditions existing outside of its premises. However, in *Fuhrer v. Gearhart by the Sea, Inc.*, 760 P.2d 874 (Or. 1988), the court affirmed the dismissal of the claim of plaintiff, whose decedent, a hotel guest, drowned while attempting to save some children trapped in an undertow in the adjoining ocean.

5. *Social Guests.* What about a social guest: should he be classified as a licensee or an invitee? In *Younce v. Ferguson*, 724 P.2d 991, 996–97 (Wash. 1986), the plaintiff, who had been a social guest at a "kegger" party for a high school graduation, challenged the trial court's classification of her status as that of a licensee; the court said:

> The explanation usually given by the courts for the classification of social guests as licensees is that there is a common understanding that

the guest is expected to take the premises as the possessor himself uses them, and does not expect and is not entitled to expect that they will be prepared for his reception, or that precautions will be taken for his safety, in any manner in which the possessor does not prepare or take precautions for his own safety, or that of the members of his family. Under the facts of this case, it is hard to imagine how the [defendants] could have prepared or could have been expected to prepare a dairy farm for a kegger party. The trial court correctly identified [plaintiff] as a licensee. She was privileged to enter or remain on the land only by virtue of the owner's consent.

Id. at 996–97.

6. *Open and Obvious.* Sometimes a court will hold that there is no duty (whatever the status) to protect against an open and obvious danger. REST. 2D TORTS § 343A states that a possessor of land is not liable to invitees for a condition on the land "whose danger is known or obvious," unless the possessor should anticipate harm despite such obviousness. In *Harrison v. Taylor*, 768 P.2d 1321 (Idaho 1989), the Supreme Court of Idaho abolished obviousness as a bar to recovery because the bar was inconsistent with the state's comparative negligence rule. *See also Ward v. K Mart Corp.*, 554 N.E.2d 223 (Ill. 1990), where the court held that an occupant's duty of reasonable care encompassed the risk that a customer, while carrying a large bulky item, would walk into the occupant's store. Compare *Eaton v. McLain*, 891 S.W. 2d 587 (Tenn. 1994), where the court held a landowner had no duty to guard against an overnight guest falling down an unlighted basement stairway, when she got up in the dark to go to the bathroom and opened the wrong door. Defendants had no duty to leave a light on in the hall or to lock the basement door. Plaintiff's failure to turn on a light was not reasonably foreseeable, the court said.

7. *Whatever!* Even if a plaintiff is in a jurisdiction where all or some of the categories are still used there may be ameliorative doctrines. One is the doctrine of attractive nuisance under which a landowner may owe a duty to trespassing children under some circumstances. The "attractive nuisance" doctrine arose in American law when the United States Supreme Court allowed recovery to a trespassing child injured while playing on a railroad turntable. *Sioux City & Pacific Railroad Co. v. Stout*, 84 U.S. 657 (1873). It is sometimes known as the "turntable doctrine." The policy which supports the doctrine is that the landowner, rather than the child or the child's parents, is often in the best position to avoid the harm to the child. The rule has been much criticized and generally is limited to artificial conditions on the landowner's premises. Thus in *Hall v. Edlefson*, 498 S.W.2d 514 (Tex. Civ. App. 1973), a Shetland pony from which plaintiff had fallen was held not to be an attractive nuisance as a matter of law. *Hampton v. Hammons*, 743 P.2d 1053, 1061 (Okla. 1987), concerned a five-year-old child who was mauled by his neighbor's pit bull as he was leaving the neighbor's property after rescuing his own puppy which had strayed into the neighbor's yard. The court noted: "The dog . . . was neither [the plaintiff's] reason for crossing the fence nor is a dog an artificial condition. The majority rule is that ordinary domestic creatures cannot constitute attractive nuisances because they are too common to be considered inherently dangerous even to a child."

There is also a so-called "beaten path" exception involving artificial or dangerous conditions and persistent trespassers. In addition to "known" trespassers, the occupier may or should know of habitual trespassing on some limited part of her property; typically this involves the "short cut" or "beaten path" scenario.

8. *Legislative Involvement.* Most states have enacted recreational use statutes immunizing landowners who open their land (oft-times rural land) to (usually uncompensated) uses. Which category of visitor is most affected by the immunity afforded by the typical recreational use statute? What effect does such a statute have in a state that has abrogated the traditional categories? Does it make them applicable again, at least as to certain visitors? In *Jacobsen v. City Of Rathdrum*, 766 P.2d 736 (1988), the court held that one effect of the Idaho recreational use statute was that a recreational user was to be legally treated as a trespasser.

In *Mandel v. United States*, 719 F.2d 963 (8th Cir. 1983), the court dealt with an Arkansas provision excepting from immunity "wilful or malicious failure to guard or warn against a dangerous condition, use, structure, or activity." The court held that the trial judge's grant of summary judgment was erroneous when there was evidence that a warning, which had been recommended by a park ranger, was not posted at the swimming hole, and that park rangers had been aware of the dangers of submerged rocks throughout the river in question.

In an especially harsh decision, the California Supreme Court applied that state's recreational use statute to an eight-year-old plaintiff who accompanied others onto defendant's property and was injured by a dangerous condition of farm equipment on the land. In applying the statute, the court said "whether plaintiff entered the property to play on the equipment, or merely accompanied the other children at play, is immaterial." Nor need the property be "suitable" for recreational purposes in order for the statute to apply. "As the instant case indicates, the concept of 'suitability' is elusive and unpredictable." The court noted, however, that some courts had applied a suitability requirement to exclude "active construction sites" from the coverage of recreational use statutes. *Ornelas v. Randolph*, 847 P. 2d 560 (Cal. 1993). Are recreational use statutes necessary? If their purpose is to encourage land owners to open their land to the public for recreational use or uses, couldn't that policy be a relevant factor in deciding breach? Or is that approach too uncertain?

9. *Professional Rescuers.* Sometimes the person on the defendant's land is a "professional" rescuer such as a police officer, firefighter, or emergency medical technician. In *Flowers v. Rock Creek Terrace Ltd. Pt'ship*, 520 A.2d 361 (Md. 1987), a volunteer fireman fell 12 stories in an apartment building elevator shaft. The defendant building owners, apartment security company and elevator manufacturer argued that they owed no duty of care to a fireman whose injuries arose out of the nature of his occupation. Agreeing with this position, the court examined the theoretical basis for the fireman's rule:

> Many cases emphasize a public policy derived from the unique relationship between firefighters and the public. The courts reason that firemen cannot recover for negligence in starting fires because it is

precisely their duty to take all reasonable measures to protect lives and property from fires.

In addition, some courts have pointed out that firemen receive compensation, such as salary, workers' compensation, and special injury compensation, to fight fires for the public, and that taxpayers should not have to pay such moneys for the firefighting service and then be subject to liability if they call upon the service.

We agree that the fireman's rule is best explained by public policy . . . [I]t is the nature of the firefighting occupation that limits a fireman's ability to recover in tort for work-related injuries. Instead of continuing to use a rationale based on the law of premises liability, we hold that, as a matter of public policy, firemen and police officers generally cannot recover for injuries attributable to the negligence that requires their assistance. This public policy is based on a relationship between firemen and policemen and the public that calls on these safety officers specifically to confront certain hazards on behalf of the public. A fireman or police officer may not recover if injured by the negligently created risk that was the very reason for his presence on the scene in his occupational capacity. Someone who negligently creates the need for a public safety officer will not be liable to a fireman or policeman for injuries caused by this negligence.

We reiterate, however, that firemen and policemen are not barred from recovery for all improper conduct. Negligent acts not protected by the fireman's rule may include failure to warn the firemen of pre-existing hidden dangers where there was knowledge of the danger and an opportunity to warn. They also may include acts which occur subsequent to the safety officer's arrival on the scene and which are outside of his anticipated occupational hazards. [T]he fireman's rule should not apply "when the fireman sustains injuries after the initial period of his anticipated occupational risk, or from perils not reasonably foreseeable as part of that risk." In these situations a fireman or policeman is owed a duty of due care. Moreover, the fireman's rule does not apply to suits against arsonists or those engaging in similar misconduct.

Id. at 368–69.

Thus courts have justified the rule based on premises liability classifications, assumption of the risk, and the fact that professional rescuers receive compensation in the form of worker compensation benefits when injured protecting the public. *See Roberts v. Vaughn*, 587 N.W.2d 249 (Mich. 1998). There, in the course of holding that a volunteer firefighter was not subject to the rule, the court said:

As we have explained, the firefighter's rule is based on considerations of a public policy derived from the unique relationship between professional safety officers and the public. In accordance with that public policy, we concluded that no duty is owed for ordinary negligence because professional safety officers are presumably extensively trained and specially paid to confront dangerous situations in order to protect the public, and that, therefore, these safety officers undertake their profession with the knowledge that their personal safety is at risk. Because of the unique relationship between the public, the safety officer, and those third parties who require the services of the officer, the otherwise applicable duty of care toward the safety officer is replaced by the third party's contribution to tax-supported compensation for those services: when injury occurs, liberal compensation is provided.

Id. at 251.

However, the availability of worker's compensation benefits normally does not bar a worker's tort suit against a non-employer tortfeasor. Why here? Do you suppose that inconsistency is one of the reasons why courts frequently find the professional rescuer rule does not apply?

PROBLEMS

7.1

Local School Board (LSB) has posted numerous signs around the paved playground at Concrete School stating: NO SKATEBOARDING and SKATEBOARDERS WILL BE PROSECUTED. Despite LSB's efforts people continue to skateboard at Concrete School on nights and weekends. After much debate, LSB determined to keep the flood lights on at Concrete School during the night because even though the lights may encourage skateboarding, it is overall safer to have lights on as opposed to having no lights on. Between January 2006 and December 2006, two people were arrested for public intoxication at Concrete School during the evening, one was arrested for possession of marijuana with intent to sell, sixteen were arrested for criminal trespass, and one is arrested for assault. On January 2, 2007, while watching skateboarders, Cindy Mobius is grabbed from behind by two unknown assailants, who stole her purse and her iPod, and then threw her to the ground causing paraplegia. Is LSB liable for Cindy's injuries?

7.2

Cindy's friend, Kelley Fracus, ran away as soon as she saw Cindy thrown down. Had Kelley stayed and called 911, Cindy would have had a 50% less chance of becoming paraplegic. Is Kelley liable for Cindy's injuries? The two assailants turn out to be Jim and Jem Grundy, two violent teens who had been expelled from Concrete School by LSB and ordered to stay away from Concrete School under all circumstances. Is LSB liable to Cindy for not enforcing its ban?

The Grundy boys are 16; their parents know of their violent and dangerous tendencies. Their parents also knew the Grundy boys frequented the Concrete School playground and intended to do so on January 2, 2007. The Grundys testify that they were afraid of their children and could not control them. Are they liable for not calling the police?

7.3

On January 9, 2007, as public outrage grew over the Concrete School attack on Cindy, Holly Truant suffered a disabling injury while skateboarding at Concrete School one hour after school let out. LSB had continued to post signs but took no other action to stop skateboarding at Concrete School. Is LSB liable to Holly?

7.4

Cindy's sister, Emma, was also at Concrete School on the day Cindy was injured. She watched the Grundy's attack her sister and then the Grundys ran at her yelling, swinging their fists, and threatening rape only to turn away when other skateboarders stopped and screamed at them. Now, Emma cannot leave the home, barely eats anything and is on medication to help her sleep. May Emma recover from LSB for her emotional distress?

7.5

Cindy was in love with Xavier Cougar, who was working in the chemistry lab doing advanced research when she was attacked. Xavier loved Cindy as much as she loved him. Indeed they had planned to run off in March, when they both turned 18, get married, and attend Excellent Tech together to study the physics of skateboarding. Xavier was watching out the window when Cindy was injured. Can he recover from LSB for his emotional distress?

7.6

Grainger Plant negligently allowed toxic stuff to escape. 2,000 local residents were exposed to toxic stuff, which is a known carcinogen. All 2,000 filed a class action seeking to recover for their increased risk of developing cancer, medical monitoring costs, and their fear of developing cancer. Can they recover from Grainger?

7.7

During the evacuation, Bjorn Huster, was forced to shut down his music store. The store remained closed for two weeks at exactly the time when the new Mayhem at the Factory album and the new KastAway album were released. Bjorn estimates he lost profits of $150,000 over the two-week closure. Can he recover? Would your answer be different if the toxic stuff physically damaged the CDs in question?

7.8

Remember Cindy? At the time she was assaulted, she was pregnant; Xavier is the baby's father. The baby, Freddy, suffered injuries when Cindy was attacked and was born with adverse medical conditions caused by those prenatal injuries. Can Freddy recover from the Grundys? From LSB? Can Cindy recover? Xavier? Can Cindy and Xavier recover for their emotional distress at "watching" the baby be attacked? For their emotional distress when the child was born?

7.9

Polly Flo was exposed to toxic stuff while she was pregnant. Tests reveal that the toxic stuff caused serious damage to the baby, Dorrin, but Dr. Knownot failed to inform Polly at a time when she could have terminated the pregnancy. Dorrin is born with serious adverse health conditions. Who can recover from Dr. Knownot? Dorrin? Polly? Dorrin's father, Ted? Polly's long-time partner, Mary?

7.10

Are the skateboarders at Concrete School trespassers? What duty of care did LSB owe them? What if Tommy Terrific was injured because of a skateboard-ing accident caused by a hole in negligently maintained concrete? What if the concrete was on a staircase Tommy was trying to surf down?

7.11

Carla Strowth was jogging on a road adjoining a public golf course main-tained by City. Carla was struck in the eye by a golf ball and is now blind in that eye. Carla sued City claiming that the road was too close to the golf course? Is City liable? What questions would you like answers to?

7.12

Carla negligently overdosed on pain killers she was taking after her injury. As she began to lose consciousness, Carla called 911. EMT, Bonnie Breen, was dispatched to Carla's home and began to revive Carla. As Carla came to she was very disoriented and when she saw Bonnie hovering over her, she punched Bonnie in the face, breaking Bonnie's jaw. Is Carla liable to Bonnie?

Chapter 8

LIABILITY WITHOUT FAULT

A. INTRODUCTION

Chapter 4 offered an historical account of the rise of fault liability in the nineteenth century. Vestiges of the earlier "liability without fault" premise also survived. Thus, some jurisdictions imposed liability upon the owner or keeper of an animal for damages caused by the animal, although the owner was neither negligent nor guilty of an intentional tort. Some jurisdictions imposed liability upon an owner of property for damage caused to adjoining landowners by a "non-natural" use of the property.

Courts sometimes applied "fault" principles in such a way as to appear to impose liability *without* fault. For example, a person was guilty of trespass to land if he intended to do the act, which was in fact an entry onto the land of another, although he was reasonable in his belief that he was not trespassing. A conversion could take place, even though the actor believed in good faith that he was not exercising dominion over the property of another. Because a reasonable mistake did not excuse the conduct, the liability was not fault-based. Furthermore, even the embryonic tort of negligence occasionally produced a type of no-fault liability. Thus, a child engaged in an adult activity could be found negligent for failure to conform to the standard of a reasonably prudent adult, although the child lacked the discernment to foresee that the conduct was unreasonably risky. *Res ipsa loquitur* and vicarious liability, including imputed contributory fault, sound in strict liability as well. The modern law of nuisance and environmental liability — the subject of Chapter 11 — is closely related to liability for abnormally dangerous activities.

Modern tort law recognizes yet another form of liability without fault. During the first half of the twentieth century, courts began imposing liability upon non-negligent manufacturers and sellers for damages caused by defective products. The standard for liability did not require a showing of negligence, and differed from the standard for traditional strict liability in that proof of a defective condition or misrepresentation of the product is generally required. See chapter 10, for an exploration of strict liability for defective products.

This chapter examines those forms of strict liability associated with keeping animals and with conducting especially dangerous activities — typically referred to as ultrahazardous or abnormally dangerous activities. Strict liability for abnormally dangerous activities, as it developed from *Rylands v. Fletcher*, [1868] L.R. 3, 19 L.T. 220 (H.L.), is rooted in strict liability for keeping animals, although animals may be no more dangerous than many other instrumentalities. Concepts familiar from fault liability, for example, foreseeability and proximate cause, remain relevant to strict liability, as do policy concerns such as the scope of the duty owed. Thus strict liability does not equate with absolute liability. *Daly v. General Motors Corp.*, 20 Cal.3d 725, 733 (1978) ("From its inception . . . strict liability has never been, and is not now, absolute liability."); *see also* Rest. 3d Torts: Liability for Physical Harm §20 cmt a (Proposed Final Draft No. 1, 2005) ("Strict liability does not signify absolute liability."). This chapter also addresses vicarious liability.

B.   STRICT LIABILITY FOR HARM RELATED TO ANIMALS

The possessor of a wild animal is generally strictly liable for any harm it causes, while the possessor of a domestic animal is liable only if she has reason to know or should know of the animal's dangerous propensities. Section 506 of the Restatement (Second) of Torts defines a domestic animal as one that is "by custom devoted to the service of mankind at the time and in the place in which it is kept." Rest. 2d Torts §506 (2) (1977). The Restatement defines a wild animal as one that is not by custom so devoted. *Id.* §506 (1). *See also* Rest. 3d Torts-PH §22 (P.F.D. No. 1 2005) ("A wild animal is an animal that belongs to a category of animals that have not been generally domesticated and that are likely, unless restrained, to cause personal injury.") Comment *a* to Section 506 states that the term "animal" includes "birds, fish, reptiles and insects." Rest. 2d Torts §506 cmt. *a.* As examples of wild animals, it lists "rattlesnakes, alligators, ostriches or tsetse flies." But "bees are not wild animals," according to comment *b.* Comment *b* also says an elephant in America is a wild animal, "but in Burma it is a domestic animal since elephants are there customarily used as heavy draft animals and for many other common purposes." *Id.*, §506 cmt. *b. See also* REST. 3D TORTS-PH §22 CMT. *b.* (P.F.D. No.1. 2005). The mere fact that a wild animal has been tamed does not change its character, since the owner takes the risk that "at any moment the animal may revert to and exhibit" its dangerous propensities. *Id.*

Are these distinctions between domestic and wild animals satisfactory? Should the distinction be retained in the law?

ISAACS v. POWELL
267 So. 2d 864 (Fla. App. 1972)

McNulty, Judge.

[This case of first impression in Florida poses the question] . . . whether Florida should adopt the general rule that the owner or keeper of a wild animal, in this case a chimpanzee, is liable to one injured by such animal under the strict liability doctrine, i.e., regardless of negligence on his part, or whether his liability should be predicated on his fault or negligence.

Plaintiff-appellant Scott Isaacs was two years and seven months old at the times material herein. His father had taken him to defendants-appellees' monkey farm where, upon purchasing an admission ticket, and as was usual and encouraged by appellees, he also purchased some food to feed the animals. While Scott was feeding a chimpanzee named Valerie she grabbed his arm and inflicted serious injury.

The exact details of how Valerie was able to grab Scott's arm are in dispute. Appellees contend that Scott's father lifted the boy above reasonably sufficient protective barriers to within Valerie's reach, while appellants counter that the barriers and other protective measures were insufficient. But in any case, appellants do not now, nor did they below, rely on any fault of appellees. Rather, they rely solely on the aforesaid generally accepted strict or, as it is sometimes called, absolute liability doctrine under which negligence or fault on the part of the owner or keeper of an animal *ferae naturae* is irrelevant. Appellees, on the other hand, suggest that we should adopt the emerging, though yet minority, view that liability should depend upon negligence, i.e., a breach of the duty of care reasonably called for taking into account the nature and specie of the animal involved. We will consider this aspect of the problem first and will hereinafter discuss the available defenses under the theory we adopt.

The trial judge apparently agreed with the appellees that fault or negligence on the part of the owners of a wild animal must be shown. He charged the jury on causation as follows:

> "The issues for your determination are whether the proximate cause of Scott Isaacs' injuries was the improper protection for paying customers of the defendants in the condition of the cage, and whether the proximate cause was the placing of Scott by his father, Howard Isaacs, within the barrier placed by the defendants for the protection of customers of the defendant."

In other words the trial judge asked the jury to decide whether Scott was injured through the fault of defendants-appellees and/or through the fault of his father. The jury returned a verdict for the defendants; but obviously, it's impossible for us to determine whether, under the foregoing charge, the jury so found because they were unable to find fault on defendants' part, or whether they so found because they believed the cause of Scott's injury to be the fault of the father. If, of course, we adopt the negligence theory of liability there would be no error in submitting both issues to the jury. But we are of the view that the older and general rule of strict liability, which obviates the issue of the owners' negligence, is more suited to the fast growing, populous and activity-oriented society of Florida. Indeed, our society imposes more than enough risks upon its members now, and we are reluctant to encourage the addition of one more particularly when that one more is increasingly contributed to by those who, for profit, would exercise their "right" to harbor wild animals and increase exposure to the dangers thereof by luring advertising. Prosser puts it this way:

> ". . . [Liability] has been thought to rest on the basis of negligence in keeping the animal at all; but this does not coincide with the modern analysis of negligence as conduct which is unreasonable in view of the risk, since it may not be an unreasonable thing to keep a tiger in a zoo. *It is rather an instance of the strict responsibility placed upon those who, even with proper care, expose the community to the risk of a very dangerous thing.* While one or two jurisdictions insist that there is no liability without some negligence in keeping the animal, by far the greater number impose strict liability."(Italics supplied)

Additionally, we observe that Florida has enacted . . . [a statute] relating to dogs, which abrogates the permissive "one bite" rule of the common law. That rule posited that an owner of a dog is liable to one bitten by such dog only if he is chargeable with "scienter," i.e., prior knowledge of the viciousness of the dog. Necessarily, of course, the cause of action therefor was predicated on the negligence of the owner in failing to take proper precautions with knowledge of the dog's vicious propensities. Our statute, however, has in effect imposed strict liability on a dog owner (from which he can absolve himself only by complying with the warning proviso of the statute). It would result in a curious anomaly, then, if we were to adopt the negligence concept as a basis for liability of an owner or keeper of a tiger, while § 767.04, *supra*, imposes potential strict liability upon him if he should trade the tiger for a dog. We are compelled to adopt, therefore, the strict liability rule in these cases.

Concerning, now, available defenses under this rule we share the view, and emphasize, that "strict or absolute liability" does not mean the owner or keeper of a wild animal is an absolute insurer in the sense that he is liable regardless of any fault on the part of the victim. Moreover, we do not think it means he is liable notwithstanding an intervening, efficient independent fault which solely causes the result, as was possibly the case here if fault on the part of Scott's father were the sole efficient cause.

As to the fault of the victim himself, since the owner or keeper of a wild animal is held to a rigorous rule of liability on account of the danger inherent in harboring such animal, it has generally been held that the owner ought not be relieved from such liability by slight negligence or want of ordinary care on the part of the person injured. The latter's acts must be such as would establish that, with knowledge of the danger, he voluntarily brought the calamity upon himself. . .

With regard to an intervening fault bringing about the result we have no hesitancy in expanding the foregoing rule to include as a defense the willful or intentional fault of a third party provided such fault is of itself an efficient cause and is the sole cause. If a jury were to decide in this case, therefore, that the sole efficient cause of Scott's injury was the intentional assumption of the apparent risks on the part of the boy's father and his placing of the boy within reach of the danger, it would be a defense available to appellees. Clearly, though, this defense would be related only to causation and is not dependent upon any theory of imputation of the father's fault to the son, which is now irrelevant in view of the extent of strict liability in these cases and the limited defenses available thereunder.

The judgment is reversed and the cause is remanded for a new trial on the theory of strict liability, and the defenses thereto, as enunciated above.

NOTES

1. *Strict or Absolute?* Why did the Florida court impose strict liability on defendant? Is that liability absolute?

Many courts hold that a municipal zoo is not strictly liable for harm caused by its animals. As the court said in *Denver v. Kennedy*, 476 P.2d 762, 763 (Colo. Ct. App. 1970), strict liability should not apply "where a municipality maintains and operates a zoo for the benefit of the public and in response to the public's obvious desires. In such instance the keeping and displaying of animals which are commonly wild in nature is not an unreasonable or unjustified act." Note that the defendant's "monkey farm" in *Isaacs v. Powell* apparently was not operated by a municipality.

Section 517 of the Restatement (Second) of Torts states that the "rules as to strict liability for dangerous animals do not apply when the possession of the animal is in pursuance of a duty imposed on the possessor as a public officer or employee or as a common carrier." Rest. 2d. Torts §517 (1977). Comment *d* to this section states:

> Even when there is no duty to receive possession of the animal, the possession may be authorized or sanctioned by legislation, under circumstances such as to indicate approval of the activity sufficient to confer immunity from strict liability. Normally this is the case, for example, when under a franchise given to a defendant as a common carrier, it is authorized but not required to accept dangerous animals for transportation. It is likewise usually the case when the legislature grants to a city or other municipal corporation the authority to establish a public zoological garden. On the other hand, it is not every authorization or permission that can be taken to confer immunity, by giving such approval to the activity as to indicate that it is intended that there shall be no strict liability. Thus a permit from a city council to hold a circus will normally not prevent strict liability when one of the lions escapes; nor does the ordinary dog license confer immunity from strict liability for dog bites. The question is one of legislative intention in granting the authorization or sanction in question.
>
> ... [T]he Institute expresses no opinion as to whether the authorization or sanction will relieve the possessor of strict liability.

Id. §517 cmt *d. See also* Rest. 3d Torts-PH §24 cmt *b* (P.F.D. No. 1 2005).

2. *The Domestic Animal with a Vicious Propensity. Isaacs* states that the owner of a domestic animal is liable at common law for injury caused by the animal if she has "prior knowledge" of its viciousness. If such "scienter" exists, then an action can be "predicated on the negligence of the owner in failing to take proper precautions" to prevent such injury.

The case states a minority view in two respects. First, actual knowledge of the animal's viciousness is not required. Section 509 says the owner is liable if she "knows or has *reason to know*" that her domestic animal has "dangerous propensities abnormal to its class" (emphasis added). Rest. 2d Torts §509 (1977). *See also* Rest. 3d Torts-PH §23 (P.F.D. No.1 2005); *Borns ex rel. Gannon v. Voss*, 70 P.3d 262 (Wyo. 2003) (knowledge of dog's dangerous propensity not required in negligence action against owners of dog that bit plaintiff).

Second, once the owner has reason to know or should know of the animal's vicious propensity, the liability for any resulting harm is strict. Rest. 2d Torts § 509 (1977). Liability does not turn on whether the owner "fails to take proper precautions," as *Isaacs* indicates. Section 509 describes such a dangerous domestic animal as one that is abnormally dangerous. *Id.*

3. *The Watchdog.* Section 516 of the Restatement (Second) of Torts states that a person is privileged to use a dog or other animal to protect his property "to the same extent that he is privileged to use a mechanical protective device for those purposes." Rest. 2d Torts § 516 (1977). Comment *b* to this section says that a landowner could "set a ferocious police dog" on a burglar "to terminate a burglarious intrusion." *Id.* § 516 cmt *b*. Does this section correctly restate the spring gun rule? *See Katko v. Briney*, 183 N.W.2d 657 (Iowa 1971) (setting a spring gun is justified only if trespasser was committing a felony of violence or a felony punishable by death or where trespasser was endangering human life by his act).

Comment *a* to section 516 states that the property owner "may be required to post warnings of the presence of a dog on his premises, particularly when the dog is of a character likely to inflict more than trivial harm." *Id.* § 516 cmt *a*. Would a warning be sufficient to protect a landowner from liability for harm caused by a vicious watchdog?

4. *Who is an Animal Possessor?* *Beeler v. Hickman*, 750 P.2d 1282, 1286 (Wash Ct. App. 1988), indicates that a mere possessor, as opposed to an owner, of a vicious dog is not strictly liable for harm caused by the dog. The Second Restatement imposes strict liability for the "possessor" of a wild animal. Rest. 2d Torts § 507 (1977). One who "harbors" a wild or abnormally dangerous domestic animal "is subject to the same liability as if he were in possession of it." *Id.* § 514. Thus the head of a household is liable for harm caused by a household member whom he permits to keep such an animal. However, "a shopkeeper does not harbor dogs that he permits a customer to bring into his shop." *Id.* § 514 cmt *a*. *See also* REST. 3D TORTS-PH § 21 CMT *f* (P.F.D. No.1. 2005).

Possession of land "does not carry with it possession of the indigenous wild animals that are upon it." *Id.* § 508, cmt *a*. Section 508 says a possessor of a wild animal "is not liable for harm done by it after it has gone out of his possession and returned to its natural state as a wild animal indigenous to the locality." *Id.* § 508. But if the animal "is one of a class not indigenous to the locality, its escape does not prevent its possessor from being liable for the harm done by the animal no matter how long after its escape; in this case the risk of liability continues until some third person takes possession of the animal." *Id.* § 507 cmt *d*.

5. *Propensity and Proximate Cause.* Section 507(2) of the Restatement (Second) of Torts states that the possessor of a wild animal is liable only for harm "that results from a dangerous propensity that is characteristic of wild animals of the particular class, or of which the possessor knows or has reason to know." *Id.* § 507(2). Comment *e* states that "if a bear, having escaped, goes to sleep in the highway and is run into by a carefully driven motor car on a dark night, the possessor of the bear is not liable for harm to the motorist in the absence of negligence in its custody." *Id*. §507(2) cmt *e*. Why should "negligence in its custody" change the outcome? *Compare* Rest. 3d Torts-PH §22 cm t*f* (P.F.D. No.1. 2005) ("[I]f the defendant's bear, having escaped, is standing on and blocking a sidewalk when an inattentive child riding a bicycle collides into the bear, the strict-liability rule is not available. . . .In such a case, the defendant is not necessarily free of liability; rather, the defendant's liability is covered by the . . . negligence standard.").

In *Jones v. Utica Mutual Insurance Co.*, 463 So. 2d 1153, 1555 (Fla. 1985), the court interpreted a Florida statute providing: "Owners of dogs shall be liable for any damage done by their dogs to persons." Two young boys tied a small red wagon to Shane, a German shepherd belonging to one of them. Shane chased another dog and the wagon struck the 12-year-old plaintiff as the dog rushed by him. The trial court held that, although the dog exhibited "canine characteristics" when it pursued the other dog, the injury was caused by the attachment of the wagon rather than any such characteristic. *Id*. Reversing, the appellate court commented:

> How is one to determine whether or not an animal's behavior is sufficiently active, or canine, or dispositive of the outcome, so as to render the owner liable for its conduct? When does a dog exercise canine characteristics? There is simply no way to define or administer such a standard and the parties would be at a loss to evaluate when a dog can be found not to have acted like a dog. Is it meaningful to conclude the dog in this case was exhibiting canine characteristics when it chased another dog but acting less like a dog because it was tied to a wagon? We think not. The trial of a suit for damages should never degenerate to a battle of experts giving opinions as to whether a dog exercised canine characteristics or human characteristics.

Id. at 1156.

6. *Negligence Per Se and Strict Liability*. Many jurisdictions have laws prohibiting dog owners from allowing their dogs to be at large except on a leash. The court in *Newport v. Moran*, 721 P.2d 465 (Or. Ct. App. 1985), discussed in Chapter 4, interpreted such a law as not intended to impose negligence *per se* on the owner of a dog at large. According to the court, dog bites and dog-knockdown injuries "were not within the area of risk that the dog-at-large ordinance was designed to avoid." *Id*. at 467. What kind of risks do you suppose the ordinance was designed to avoid? Should a landowner who is injured when he slips and falls on a wet lawn while chasing an unleashed dog from his yard be able to recover from the dog's owner?

7. *Contributory Negligence, Assumption of the Risk, and Strict Liability*. *Isaacs v. Powell* holds that contributory negligence of the plaintiff is no defense, but that assumption of the risk is a bar to plaintiff's recovery. The Second Restatement takes this position both with regard to strict liability for animals and for abnormally dangerous activities. Rest. 2d Torts §515, 523-524 (1977). Should these rules be changed in a jurisdiction that has adopted comparative fault? *See Andrade v. Shiers*, 564 So. 2d 787 (La. Ct. App. 1990) (plaintiff's fault compared to animal owner's strict liability). See chapter 12, *infra*, for a discussion of comparative fault. *See also* Rest. 3d Torts-PH §25 (P.F.D. No.1. 2005).

C. STRICT LIABILITY FOR ABNORMALLY DANGEROUS ACTIVITIES

Rylands v. Fletcher explores theoretical justifications for strict liability doctrine. Compare the reasoning of Justice Blackburn with that of Lord Cairns. Do their opinions ground strict liability on the same logic?

FLETCHER v. RYLANDS [1866]
L.R. 1 Exch. 265 (Ex. Ch.)

Blackburn, J.

[The plaintiff Fletcher leased a coal mine. Partially worked coal seams ran from that parcel under the land of several neighbors. The defendants owned a mill and built a reservoir on leased, neighboring land. The defendants selected competent contractors to construct the reservoir. The defendants were not negligent in failing to discover that old coal workings communicated between the site of the reservoir and the land plaintiff had leased. In December, 1860, a shaft broke open in the reservoir and water flooded the plaintiff's coal mine, which subsequently was abandoned.]

It appears from the statement in the case, that the plaintiff was damaged by his property being flooded by water, which, without any fault on his part, broke out of a reservoir constructed on the defendants' land by the defendants' orders, and maintained by the defendants.

It appears from the statement in the case, that the coal under the defendants' land had, at some remote period, been worked out; but this was unknown at the time when the defendants gave directions to erect the reservoir, and the water in the reservoir would not have escaped from the defendants' land, and no mischief would have been done to the plaintiff, but for this latent defect in the defendants' subsoil. And it further appears, that the defendants selected competent engineers and contractors to make their reservoir, and themselves personally continued in total ignorance of what we have called the latent defect in the subsoil; but that these persons employed by them in the course of the work became aware of the existence of the ancient shafts filled up with soil, though they did not know or suspect that they were shafts communicating with old workings.

It is found that the defendants, personally, were free from all blame, but that in fact proper care and skill was not used by the persons employed by them, to provide for the sufficiency of the reservoir with reference to these shafts. The consequence was, that the reservoir when filled with water burst into the shafts, the water flowed down through them into the old workings, and thence into the plaintiff's mine, and there did the mischief.

The plaintiff, though free from all blame on his part, must bear the loss, unless he can establish that it was the consequence of some default for which the defendants are responsible. The question of law therefore arises, what is the obligation which the law casts on a person who, like the defendants, lawfully brings on his land something which, though harmless whilst it remains there, will naturally do mischief if it escape out of his land. It is agreed on all hands that he must take care to keep in that which he has brought on the land and keeps there, in order that it may not escape and damage his neighbours, but the question arises whether the duty which the law casts upon him, under such circumstances, is an absolute duty to keep it in at his peril, or is . . . merely a duty to take all reasonable and prudent precautions, in order to keep it in, but no more. If the first be the law, the person who has brought on his land and kept there something dangerous, and failed to keep it in, is responsible for all the natural consequences of its escape. If the second be the limit of his duty, he would not be answerable except on proof of negligence, and consequently would not be answerable for escape arising from any latent defect which ordinary prudence and skill could not detect.

Supposing the second to be the correct view of the law, a further question arises subsidiary to the first, viz., whether the defendants are not so far identified with the contractors whom they employed, as to be responsible for the consequences of their want of care and skill in making the reservoir in fact insufficient with reference to the old shafts, of the existence of which they were aware, though they had not ascertained where the shafts went to.

We think that the true rule of law is, that the person who for his own purposes brings on his lands and collects and keeps there anything likely to do mischief if it escapes, must keep it in at his peril, and, if he does not do so, is *prima facie* answerable for all the damage which is the natural consequence of its escape. He can excuse himself by showing that the escape was owing to the plaintiff's default; or perhaps that the escape was the consequence of *vis major*, or the act of God; but as nothing of this sort exists here, it is unnecessary to inquire what excuse would be sufficient. The general rule, as above stated, seems on principle just. The person whose grass or corn is eaten down by the escaping cattle of his neighbour, or whose mine is flooded by the water from his neighbour's reservoir, or whose cellar is invaded by the filth of his neighbour's privy, or whose habitation is made unhealthy by the fumes and noisome vapours of his neighbour's alkali works, is damnified without any fault of his own; and it seems but reasonable and just that the neighbour, who has brought something on his own property which was not naturally there, harmless to others so long as it is confined to his own property, but which he knows to be mischievous if it gets on his neighbour's, should be obliged to make good the damage which ensues if he does not succeed in confining it to his own property. But for his act in bringing it there no mischief could have accrued, and it seems but just that he should at his peril keep it there so that no mischief may accrue, or answer for the natural and anticipated consequences. And upon authority, this we think is established to be the law whether the things so brought be beasts, or water, or filth, or stenches.

The case that has most commonly occurred, and which is most frequently to be found in the books, is as to the obligation of the owner of cattle which he has brought on his land, to prevent their escaping and doing mischief. The law as to them seems to be perfectly settled from early times; the owner must keep them in at his peril, or he will be answerable for the natural consequences of their escape; that is with regard to tame beasts, for the grass they eat and trample upon, though not for any injury to the person of others, for our ancestors have settled that it is not the general nature of horses to kick, or bulls to gore; but if the owner knows that the beast has a vicious propensity to attack man, he will be answerable for that too.

. . . As has been already said, there does not appear to be any difference in principle, between the extent of the duty cast on him who brings cattle on his land to keep them in, and the extent of the duty imposed on him who brings on his land, water, filth, or stenches, or any other thing which will, if it escape, naturally do damage, to prevent their escaping and injuring his neighbour. . . .

. . . But it was further said [in the court below] that when damage is done to personal property, or even to the person, by collision, either upon land or at sea, there must be negligence in the party doing the damage to render him legally responsible; and this is no doubt true, and as was pointed out by [counsel] during his argument before us, this is not confined to cases of collision, for there are many cases in which proof of negligence is essential, as for instance, where an unruly horse gets on the footpath of a public street and kills a passenger; or where a person in a dock is struck by the falling of a bale of cotton which the defendant's servants are lowering, and many other similar cases may be found. But we think these cases distinguishable from the present. Traffic on the highways, whether by land or sea, cannot be conducted without exposing those whose persons or property are near it to some inevitable risk; and that being so, those who go on the highway, or have their property adjacent to it, may well be held to do so subject to their taking upon themselves the risk of injury from that inevitable danger; and persons who by the licence of the owner pass near to warehouses where goods are being raised or lowered, certainly do so subject to the inevitable risk of accident. In neither case, therefore, can they recover without proof of want of care or skill occasioning the accident; and it is believed that all the cases in which inevitable accident has been held an excuse for what *prima facie* was a trespass, can be explained on the same principle, viz., that the circumstances were such as to shew that the plaintiff had taken the risk upon himself. But there is no ground for saying that the plaintiff here took upon himself any risk arising from the uses to which the defendants should choose to apply their land. He neither knew what these might be, nor could he in any way control the defendants, or hinder their building what reservoirs they liked, and storing up in them what water they pleased, so long as the defendants succeeded in preventing the water which they there brought from interfering with the plaintiff's property.

[The defendant mill owner appealed to the House of Lords, which affirmed the judgment of the Exchequer Chamber for the plaintiff. The rationale of the House of Lords, given in the following opinion, differs from that of the Exchequer Chamber. The rationale of the House of Lords is the one widely cited as the basis for this famous opinion.]

RYLANDS v. FLETCHER
[1868] L.R. 3, 19 L.T. 220 (H.L.)

The Lord Chancellor (*Lord Cairns*)

My Lords, the principles on which this case must be determined appear to me to be extremely simple. The Defendants, treating them as the owners or occupiers of the close on which the reservoir was constructed, might lawfully have used that close for any purpose for which it might in the ordinary course of the enjoyment of land be used; and if, in what I may term the natural user of that land, there had been any accumulation of water, either on the surface or underground, and if, by the operation of the laws of nature, that accumulation of water had passed off into the close occupied by the Plaintiff, the Plaintiff could not have complained that that result had taken place. If he had desired to guard himself against it, it would have lain upon him to have done so, by leaving, or by interposing, some barrier between his close and the close of the Defendants in order to have prevented that operation of the laws of nature.

. . . On the other hand if the Defendants, not stopping at the natural use of their close, had desired to use it for any purpose which I may term a non-natural use, for the purpose of introducing into the close that which in its natural condition was not in or upon it, for the purpose of introducing water either above or below ground in quantities and in a manner not the result of any work or operation on or under the land, — and if in consequence of their doing so, or in consequence of any imperfection in the mode of their doing so, the water came to escape and to pass off into the close of the Plaintiff, then it appears to me that if in the course of their doing it, the evil arose to which I have referred, the evil, namely, of the escape of the water and its passing away to the close of the Plaintiff and injuring the Plaintiff, then for the consequence of that, in my opinion, the Defendants would be liable. . . .

My Lords, these simple principles, if they are well founded, as it appears to me they are, really dispose of this case.

The same result is arrived at on the principles referred to by Mr. Justice *Blackburn.* . . . [Lord Cairns quotes the paragraph from Justice Blackburn that begins: "We think that the true rule of law is. . . ." *Fletcher, supra*]

. . . My Lords, in that opinion, I must say I entirely concur. . . .

Lord Cranworth

[I]n considering whether a Defendant is liable to a Plaintiff for damage which the Plaintiff may have sustained, the question in general is not whether the Defendant has acted with due care and caution, but whether his acts have occasioned the damage. And the doctrine is founded on good sense. For when one person, in managing his own affairs, causes, however innocently, damage to another, it is obviously only just that he should be the party to suffer. . . .

NOTES

1. *Escaping Mischief and Non-Natural Use.* Justice Blackburn in the Court of Exchequer said that "the person who for his own purposes brings on his lands and collects and keeps there anything likely to do mischief if it escapes, must keep it in at his peril." Lord Cairns in the House of Lords said that, if a landowner brings onto his land anything which was not on the land in its "natural condition" and the thing escapes from the land causing harm, the landowner will be liable at his "peril" (i.e., strictly liable) for the harm caused by such "non-natural" use of the land. Are Justice Blackburn's and Lord Cairns' formulations of the issue different? Is there a difference between Blackburn's "not-naturally there" and Lord Cairn's "non-natural use"? Notice that both judges agree that escaping cattle and escaping "filth" and "stenches" or "noisome vapors" would result in strict liability and that the escaping waters from defendant's reservoir would also result in strict liability. They both also apparently agree that a natural accumulation of water would *not* result in strict liability, either because the owner did not "bring" the water onto her land or because such an accumulation would not be a "non-natural" use of the land.

In *Read v. J. Lyons & Co.*(1947) A.C. 156 (H.L.), the court held the defendant munitions manufacturer not liable under *Rylands* because the plaintiff, a government inspector, was injured by an explosion on the defendant's premises. *Id.* at 169–170. The explosives therefore did not "escape" from the defendant's land. No such doctrine of escape has been imported into the American law of strict liability for dangerous activities.

2. *Common Usage.* The Restatement of Torts explains how American jurisprudence embraced the strict liability concept of *Rylands v. Fletcher. See* Rest. Torts § 520 (1938); Rest. 2d Torts § 520 (1977). Both of these Restatement sections specify, as a condition for determining strict liability for damages caused by "ultrahazardous" (language used in the first Restatement) or "abnormally dangerous" (language used in the Restatement (Second)) activity, that the activity not be a "matter of common usage." The term "common usage" may be intended to remotely reflect the idea of natural use contained in *Rylands v. Fletcher*, although the Second Restatement probably more nearly reflects this idea in the factor that considers the appropriateness of the activity "to the place where it is carried on." Rest. 2d Torts § 520(e) (1977). Comment *j* makes clear that § 520(e) is intended to reflect the natural-use doctrine of *Rylands*. Rest. 2d Torts § 520(e) cmt. *j* (1977).

Comment *e* of the first Restatement and *i* of the Second Restatement state that an activity is a matter of common usage "if it is customarily carried on by the great mass of mankind or by many people in the community." Rest. Torts § 520 cmt. *e* (1938); Rest. 2d Torts § 520 cmt. *i* (1977). The Restatement gives cars as an example of an activity that has come into such "general use" as to be a common usage. It contrasts blasting and the storage of explosives as not activities of common usage because those activities are carried on by a "comparatively small number of persons." *See also* REST. 3D TORTS-PH § 20 CMT. *j* (P.F.D. No.1. 2005) ("An activity is plainly of common usage if it is carried on by a large fraction of the people in the community.").

Compare these ideas about common usage with the language of Blackburn, J., in *Fletcher v. Rylands*:

> Traffic on the highways, whether by land or sea, cannot be conducted without exposing those whose persons or property are near it to some inevitable risk; and that being so, those who go on the highway, or have their property adjacent to it, may well be held to do so subject to their taking upon themselves the risk of injury from that inevitable danger; and persons who by the licence of the owner pass near to warehouses where goods are being raised or lowered, certainly do so subject to the inevitable risk of accident. In neither case, therefore, can they recover without proof of want of care or skill occasioning the accident; and it is believed that all the cases in which inevitable accident has been held an excuse for what *prima facie* was a trespass, can be explained on the same principle, viz., that the circumstances were such as to shew that the plaintiff had taken the risk upon himself. . . .

Fletcher, L.R. 1 Exch. 265 at 286-287.

3. *Rylands Rejected*. Early American opinions rejected the strict liability of *Rylands v. Fletcher*. *Losee v. Buchanan*, 51 N.Y. 476 (1873), is typical. The *Losee* court said of the *Rylands* decision:

> [It] is in direct conflict with the law as settled in this country. Here, if one builds a dam upon his own premises and thus holds back and accumulates the water for his benefit, or if he brings water upon his premises into a reservoir, in case the dam or the banks of the reservoir give away and the lands of a neighbor are thus flooded, he is not liable for the damage without proof of some fault or negligence on his part.

Losee, 51 N.Y. at 487.

4. *The Renaissance of Rylands v. Fletcher*. According to *Branch v. Western Petr., Inc.,* 657 P.2d 267, 273 (Utah 1982): "Although *Rylands v. Fletcher* was initially rejected by a number of states, its influence has been substantial in the United States. . . . Indeed, the strict liability rule of the first Restatement of Torts was broadened in §519 of the Restatement (Second) of Torts by making it applicable to 'abnormally dangerous activities.'" *SEE* Rest. 2d Torts §519 (1977). *See also* REST. 3D TORTS-PH §20 (P.F.D. No.1. 2005) (RETAINING NOTION THAT ACTIVITY IS NOT ONE OF COMMON USAGE). FURTHERMORE, ACCORDING TO *Peneschi v. National Steel Corp.,* 295 S.E.2d 1 (W. Va. 1982):

> Even jurisdictions that reject *Rylands* by name have accepted and applied it under the cloak of various other theories, with strict liability commonly imposed under the sobriquet of "nuisance." Here too, the relationship of the activity to its surroundings is the controlling factor, so that using explosives in the midst of a city may be an absolute nuisance whereas in a wilderness it is not. . . .

Peneschi, 295 S.E.2d at 5.

State Dep't of Env'l Protection v. Ventron, 468 A.2d 150 (N.J. 1983), concerned the liability of mercury polluters of a state waterway. The New Jersey Supreme Court stated:

We believe it is time to recognize expressly that the law of liability has evolved so that a landowner is strictly liable to others for harm caused by toxic wastes that are stored on his property and flow onto the property of others. Therefore, we . . . adopt the principle of liability originally declared in *Rylands v. Fletcher.* The net result is that those who use, or permit others to use, land for the conduct of abnormally dangerous activities are strictly liable for resultant damages. . . .

Ventron, 468 A.2d at 157.

5. *Blasting and Storage of Explosives.* Even before *Rylands v. Fletcher*, New York applied strict liability for damage done by debris from blasting. *Hay v. Cohoes County*, 2 N.Y. 159 (1849). Why do you suppose there was such a ready acceptance of strict liability in the case of blasting?

In *Booth v. Rome, W. & O.T.R. Co.*, 35 N.E. 592, 596 (N.Y. 1893), the court based blasting liability on a trespass theory, holding that there was no liability for concussion damage from blasting. Finding itself out of line with developing law, New York overruled *Booth* in *Spano v. Perini*, 250 N.E.2d 31 (N.Y. 1969), and imposed strict liability for concussion damage from blasting. "The question . . . was not *whether* it was lawful or proper to engage in blasting but *who* should bear the cost of any resulting damage — the person who engaged in the dangerous activity or the innocent neighbor injured thereby." *Spano*, 250 N.E.2d at 34. In holding that the blaster should be liable, the court appears to be imposing a kind of enterprise liability — that is, a company should bear liability for the damage it causes as a cost of doing business.

The court in *Yukon Equipment, Inc. v. Fireman's Fund Insurance Co.*, 585 P.2d 1206 (Alaska 1978), followed *Exner v. Sherman Power Constr. Co.*, 54 F.2d 510 (2d Cir. 1931), in imposing strict liability for detonation damage resulting from the storage of explosives. "*Exner* has been widely followed," the court said. *Yukon Equipment* quoted the rationale of *Exner* for imposing strict liability:

> The extent to which one man in the lawful conduct of his business is liable for injuries to another involves an adjustment of conflicting interests. . . . When, as here, the defendant, though without fault, has engaged in the perilous activity of storing large quantities of a dangerous explosive for use in his business, we think there is no justification for relieving it of liability, and that the owner of the business, rather than a third party who has no relation to the explosion, other than that of injury, should bear the loss.

Yukon Equip., Inc., 585 P.2d at 1208.

6. *Negligence versus Strict Liability?* Is there a theory under which the *Rylands* defendant should be liable for the negligence of those he employed? See *infra*, for a discussion of vicarious liability. *Bower v. Peate*, [1876] L.R. 1 Q.B.D. 321, 329, held that an employer of an independent contractor could be liable for that actor's negligence.

In the *Clark-Aiken Company v. Cromwell-Wright Company, Inc.*, 323 N.E.2d 876 (Mass. 1975), plaintiff had sued under both negligence and strict liability theories "to recover for damage caused when water allegedly stored behind a dam on the defendant's property was released and flowed onto its property." *Id.* at 877. The court had no problem finding that strict liability and negligence could co-exist as causes of action, stating:

> The fact that a case of strict liability also contains elements of negligence does not preclude the plaintiff from recovering on the basis of strict liability. The distinction is basically one of proof in the particular circumstances. The plaintiff must decide whether it is more economic and feasible to establish negligence under appropriate pleadings, or to prove that the activity in question comes within the parameters of strict liability. The fact that a plaintiff chooses to go forward on one, or possibly both, of these theories does not undercut the existence or vitality of either.

323 N.E. 2d at 883-84.

7. *Enterprise Liability and Corrective Justice.* The next case, *Indiana Harbor Belt Railroad Company v. American Cyanamid Company*, views strict liability as a theory of liability couched in the economic terms of enterprise liability:

> [T]he enterprise should bear the risks of accidents it produces because (1) an enterprise has superior risk-spreading capacity compared to victims who would otherwise bear the costs of accidents [superior risk-spreading ability], and (2) an enterprise is generally better placed to respond to the safety incentives created by liability rules than is the party suffering harm [because of better risk-reducing capacity].

Robert L. Rabin, *Some Thoughts on the Ideology of Enterprise Liability*, 55 Md. L. Rev. 1190, 1190 (1996) (referring to George Priest's writings identifying the theory of enterprise liability). Do the opinions in *Rylands v. Fletcher*, *supra*, premise liability for the escaping water in economic terms? Or, does the perspective of corrective justice and the violation of rights also lend insight to strict liability? See *id.* at 1195-96 (observing that traditional strict liability "is a discourse grounded in ethical norms of interpersonal conduct"). As you read through the strict liability cases, observe the internal tension between superior risk-spreading and better risk-reducing capacity. Will the tortfeasor always be held liable or do fundamental fairness and individual responsibility work to temper tortfeasor liability under strict liability?

INDIANA HARBOR BELT RAILROAD CO. v. AMERICAN CYANAMID CO.
916 F.2d 1174 (7th Cir. 1990)

[The plaintiff railroad yard sued the defendant manufacturer and shipper for the costs of cleaning up a toxic spill. Reversing the district court, the court of appeals, in a decision authored by Judge Posner, held that the defendant was not strictly liable.]

American Cyanamid Company, the defendant in this diversity tort suit governed by Illinois law, is a major manufacturer of chemicals, including acrylonitrile, a chemical used in large quantities in making acrylic fibers, plastics, dyes, pharmaceutical chemicals, and other intermediate and final goods. On

January 2, 1979, at its manufacturing plant in Louisiana, Cyanamid loaded 20,000 gallons of liquid acrylonitrile into a railroad tank car that it had leased from the North American Car Corporation. The next day, a train of the Missouri Pacific Railroad picked up the car at Cyanamid's siding. The car's ultimate destination was a Cyanamid plant in New Jersey served by Conrail rather than by Missouri Pacific. The Missouri Pacific train carried the car north to the Blue Island railroad yard of Indiana Harbor Belt Railroad, the plaintiff in this case, a small switching line that has a contract with Conrail to switch cars from other lines to Conrail, in this case for travel east. The Blue Island yard is in the Village of Riverdale, which is just south of Chicago and part of the Chicago metropolitan area.

The car arrived in the Blue Island yard on the morning of January 9, 1979. Several hours after it arrived, employees of the switching line noticed fluid gushing from the bottom outlet of the car. The lid on the outlet was broken. After two hours, the line's supervisor of equipment was able to stop the leak by closing a shut-off valve controlled from the top of the car. No one was sure at the time just how much of the contents of the car had leaked, but it was feared that all 20,000 gallons had, and since acrylonitrile is flammable at a temperature of 30° Fahrenheit or above, highly toxic, and possibly carcinogenic (*Acrylonitrile*, 9 International Toxicity Update, no. 3, May-June 1989, at 2,4), the local authorities ordered the homes near the yard evacuated. The evacuation lasted only a few hours, until the car was moved to a remote part of the yard and it was discovered that only about a quarter of the acrylonitrile had leaked. Concerned nevertheless that there had been some contamination of soil and water, the Illinois Department of Environmental Protection ordered the switching line to take decontamination measures that cost the line $981,022.75, which it sought to recover by this suit.

One count of the two-count complaint charges Cyanamid with having maintained the leased tank car negligently. The other count asserts that the transportation of acrylonitrile in bulk through the Chicago metropolitan area is an abnormally dangerous activity, for the consequences of which the shipper (Cyanamid) is strictly liable to the switching line, which bore the financial brunt of those consequences because of the decontamination measures that it was forced to take. . . .

. . . The parties agree that the question whether placing acrylonitrile in a rail shipment that will pass through a metropolitan area subjects the shipper to strict liability is, as recommended in Restatement (Second) of Torts § 520, comment *l* (1977), a question of law, so that we owe no particular deference to the conclusion of the district court. They also agree . . . that the Supreme Court of Illinois would treat as authoritative the provisions of the Restatement governing abnormally dangerous activities. The key provision is section 520, which sets forth six factors to be considered in deciding whether an activity is abnormally dangerous and the actor therefore strictly liable.

The roots of section 520 are in nineteenth-century cases. The most famous one is *Rylands v. Fletcher,* 1 Ex. 265, aff'd, L.R. 3 H.L. 300 (1868), but a more illuminating one in the present context is *Guille v. Swan,* 19 Johns. (N.Y.) 381 (1822). A man took off in a hot-air balloon and landed, without intending to, in a vegetable garden in New York City. A crowd that had been anxiously watching his involuntary descent trampled the vegetables in their endeavor to rescue him when he landed. The owner of the garden sued the balloonist for the resulting damage, and won. Yet the balloonist had not been careless. In the then state of ballooning it was impossible to make a pinpoint landing.

Guille is a paradigmatic case for strict liability. (a) The risk (probability) of harm was great, and (b) the harm that would ensue if the risk materialized could be, although luckily was not, great (the balloonist could have crashed into the crowd rather than into the vegetables). The confluence of these two factors established the urgency of seeking to prevent such accidents. (c) Yet such accidents could not be prevented by the exercise of due care; the technology of care in ballooning was insufficiently developed. (d) The activity was not a matter of common usage, so there was no presumption that it was a highly valuable activity despite its unavoidable riskiness. (e) The activity was inappropriate to the place in which it took place — densely populated New York City. The risk of serious harm to others (other than the balloonist himself, that is) could have been reduced by shifting the activity to the sparsely inhabited areas that surrounded the city in those days. (f) Reinforcing (d), the value to the community of the activity of recreational ballooning did not appear to be great enough to offset its unavoidable risks.

These are, of course, the six factors in section 520. They are related to each other in that each is a different facet of a common quest for a proper legal regime to govern accidents that negligence liability cannot adequately control. The interrelations might be more perspicuous if the six factors were reordered. One might for example start with (c), inability to eliminate the risk of accident by the exercise of due care. The baseline common law regime of tort liability is negligence. When it is a workable regime, because the hazards of an activity can be avoided by being careful (which is to say, nonnegligent), there is no need to switch to strict liability. Sometimes, however, a particular type of accident cannot be prevented by taking care but can be avoided, or its consequences minimized, by shifting the activity in which the accident occurs to another locale, where the risk or harm of an accident will be less ((e)), or by reducing the scale of the activity in order to minimize the number of accidents caused by it ((f)). By making the actor strictly liable — by denying him in other words an excuse based on his inability to avoid accidents by being more careful — we give him an incentive, missing in a negligence regime, to experiment with methods of preventing accidents that involve not greater exertions of care, assumed to be futile, but instead relocating, changing, or reducing (perhaps to the vanishing point) the activity giving rise to the accident. The greater the risk of an accident ((a)) and the costs of an accident if one occurs ((b)), the more we want the actor to consider the possibility of making accident-reducing activity changes; the stronger, therefore, is the case for strict liability. Finally, if an activity is extremely common ((d)), like driving an automobile, it is unlikely either that its hazards are perceived as great or that there is no technology of care available to minimize them; so the case for strict liability is weakened.

The largest class of cases in which strict liability has been imposed under the standard codified in the Second Restatement of Torts involves the use of dynamite and other explosives for demolition in residential or urban areas.

Explosives are dangerous even when handled carefully, and we therefore want blasters to choose the location of the activity with care and also to explore the feasibility of using safer substitutes (such as a wrecking ball), as well as to be careful in the blasting itself. Blasting is not a commonplace activity like driving a car, or so superior to substitute methods of demolition that the imposition of liability is unlikely to have any effect except to raise the activity's costs.

Against this background we turn to the particulars of acrylonitrile. Acrylonitrile is one of a large number of chemicals that are hazardous in the sense of being flammable, toxic, or both; acrylonitrile is both, as are many others. A table in the record . . . contains a list of the 125 hazardous materials that are shipped in highest volume on the nation's railroads. Acrylonitrile is the fifty-third most hazardous on the list. . . .

. . . *Siegler v. Kuhlman*, 81 Wash. 2d 448, 502 P.2d 1181 (1972), imposed strict liability on a transporter of hazardous materials, but the circumstances were rather special. A gasoline truck blew up, obliterating the plaintiff's decedent and her car. The court emphasized that the explosion had destroyed the evidence necessary to establish whether the accident had been due to negligence; so, unless liability was strict, there would be no liability — and this as the very consequence of the defendant's hazardous activity . . . .

. . . To begin with, we have been given no reason, whether the reason in *Siegler* or any other, for believing that a negligence regime is not perfectly adequate to remedy and deter, at reasonable cost, the accidental spillage of acrylonitrile from rail cars. Cf. *Bagley v. Controlled Environment Corp.*, 127 N.H. 556, 560, 503 A.2d 823, 826 (1986). Acrylonitrile could explode and destroy evidence, but of course did not here, making imposition of strict liability on the theory of the *Siegler* decision premature. More important, although acrylonitrile is flammable even at relatively low temperatures, and toxic, it is not so corrosive or otherwise destructive that it will eat through or otherwise damage or weaken a tank car's valves although they are maintained with due (which essentially means, with average) care. No one suggests, therefore, that the leak in this case was caused by the *inherent* properties of acrylonitrile. It was caused by carelessness — whether that of the North American Car Corporation in failing to maintain or inspect it, or that of the Missouri Pacific when it had custody of the car, or that of the switching line itself in failing to notice the ruptured lid, or some combination of these possible failures of care. Accidents that are due to a lack of care can be prevented by taking care; and when a lack of care can (unlike *Siegler*) be shown in court, such accidents are adequately deterred by the threat of liability for negligence.

It is true that the district court purported to find as a fact that there is an inevitable risk of derailment or other calamity in transporting "large quantities of anything." 662 F. Supp. at 642. This is not a finding of fact, but a truism: anything can happen. The question is, how likely is this type of accident if the actor uses due care: For all that appears from the record of the case or any other sources of information that we have found, if a tank car is carefully maintained the danger of a spill of acrylonitrile is negligible. If this is right, there is no compelling reason to move to a regime of strict liability, especially one that might embrace all other hazardous materials shipped by rail as well. . . .

NOTES

1. *The Presence of Negligence.* Should the presence of negligence mean that a strict liability claim cannot be brought? One commentator contends that a number of cases support a reading of the Rest. 2d Torts §520 (1977) to mean that the strict liability doctrine for abnormally dangerous activities will not apply if the exercise of reasonable care would prevent the danger. Gerald W. Boston, *Strict Liability for Abnormally Dangerous Activity: The Negligence Barrier*, 36 San Diego L. Rev. 597, 639 (1999). How can one determine if there is an "inability to eliminate the risk" of an abnormally dangerous activity "by the exercise of reasonable care?" Rest. 2d Torts §520(c) (1977). Will expert testimony do the trick? *See* Boston, *supra*, at 636.

2. *The Restatement Position.* Rest. Torts §520 (1938) provides:

An activity is ultrahazardous if it

> (a) necessarily involves a risk of serious harm to the person, land or chattels of others which cannot be eliminated by the exercise of the utmost care, and

> (b) is not a matter of common usage.

Comment *g* to this section states: "In order that an activity may be ultrahazardous it is necessary that it satisfy the conditions stated in both Clauses (a) and (b)." *Id.* §520 cmt *g*.

The Restatement (Second) of Tort's section 520, which replaced that section in the first Restatement, provides:

> In determining whether an activity is abnormally dangerous, the following factors are to be considered:

> (a) existence of a high degree of risk of some harm to the person, land or chattels of others;

> (b) likelihood that the harm that results from it will be great;

> (c) inability to eliminate the risk by the exercise of reasonable care;

> (d) extent to which the activity is not a matter of common usage;

> (e) inappropriateness of the activity to the place where it is carried on; and

> (f) extent to which its value to the community is outweighed by its dangerous attributes.

Comment *f* to this section states:

> In determining whether the danger is abnormal, the factors listed in Clauses (a) to (f) of this Section are all to be considered, and are all of importance. Any one of them is not necessarily sufficient of itself in a particular case, and ordinarily several of them will be required for strict liability. On the other hand, it is not necessary that each of them be present, especially if others weigh heavily. Because of the interplay

of these various factors, it is not possible to reduce abnormally dangerous activities to any definition.

REST. 2D TORTS § 520 CM Tf (1977).

Why do you suppose the second Restatement changed so radically from the position of the first? Is the change in terminology from "ultrahazardous activity" to "abnormally dangerous activity" significant? *See also* Rest. 3d Torts-PH § 20 (P.F.D. No. 1 2005).

3. *Risk-Utility.* Besides emphasizing the likely presence of negligence, the court in *Indiana Harbor Belt Railroad Co. v. American Cyanamid Co.* also stressed risk-utility considerations in determining the inapplicability of strict liability:

> The district judge and plaintiff's lawyer make much of the fact that the spill occurred in a densely inhabited metropolitan area. Only 4,000 gallons spilled; what if all 20,000 had done so? Isn't the risk that this might happen even if everybody were careful sufficient to warrant giving the shipper an incentive to explore alternative routes? Strict liability would supply that incentive. But this argument overlooks the fact that, like other transportation networks, the railroad network is a hub-and-spoke system. And the hubs are in metropolitan areas. Chicago is one of the nation's largest railroad hubs. In 1983, the latest year for which we have figures, Chicago's railroad yards handled the third highest volume of hazardous-material shipments in the nation. East St. Louis, which is also in Illinois, handled the second highest volume. With most hazardous chemicals (by volume of shipments) being at least as hazardous as acryolonitrile, it is unlikely — and certainly not demonstrated by the plaintiff — that they can be rerouted around all the metropolitan areas in the country, except at prohibitive cost. Even if it were feasible to reroute them one would hardly expect shippers, as distinct from carriers, to be the firms best situated to do the rerouting. Granted, the usual view is that common carriers are not subject to strict liability for the carriage of materials that make the transportation of them abnormally dangerous, because a common carrier cannot refuse service to a shipper of a lawful commodity. RESTATEMENT, *supra*, § 521. Two courts, however, have rejected the common carrier exception. *National Steel Service Center, Inc. v. Gibbons*, 319 N.W.2d 269 (Iowa. 1982); *Chavez v. Southern Pacific Transportation Co.*, 413 F. Supp. 1203, 1213–14 (E.D. Cal. 1976). If it were rejected in Illinois, this would weaken still further the case for imposing strict liability on shippers whose goods pass through the densely inhabited portions of the state.

> The difference between shipper and carrier points to a deep flaw in the plaintiff's case. . . . [H]ere it is not the actors — that is, the transporters of acrylonitrile and other chemicals — but the manufacturers, who are sought to be held strictly liable. A shipper can in the bill of lading designate the route of his shipment if he likes, 49 U.S.C. § 11710(a)(1), but is it realistic to suppose that shippers will become students of

railroading in order to lay out the safest route by which to ship their goods? Anyway, rerouting is no panacea. Often it will increase the length of the journey, or compel the use of poorer track, or both. When this happens, the probability of an accident is increased, even if the consequences of an accident if one occurs are reduced; so the expected accident cost, being the product of the probability of an accident and the harm if the accident occurs, may rise. It is easy to see how the accident in this case might have been prevented at reasonable cost by greater care on the part of those who handled the tank car of acryloni-trile. It is difficult to see how it might have been prevented at reason-able cost by a change in the activity of transporting the chemical. This is therefore not an apt case for strict liability.

Indiana Harbor, 916 F.2d at 1180-81.

Why does Judge Posner accept the proposition that strict liability should be available for some activities — those that are "abnormally dangerous" — despite the absence of any negligence on a defendant's part? If negligence is "the baseline common law regime of tort liability," then why should other bases of liability be allowed? If strict liability should sometimes be permitted, is Judge Posner's ruling correct that strict liability does not apply in this case? Do you agree with his reasoning?

4. *Strict Products Liability.* Could the plaintiff have tried the *Indiana Harbor* case on a theory of strict products liability? *See* chapter 10 *infra*. The container of the product, the tank car, was defective. The defendant was only a lessee of the tank car, apparently undertaking by contract to maintain the car. 916 F.2d at 1181. But defendant was the manufacturer and supplier of the acrylonitrile; would the defendant be strictly liable for the container in which it supplied the product? Did the plaintiff suffer physical harm to person or property within the meaning of Rest. 2d Torts § 402A (1965)?

5. *Awareness of Danger Revisited.* In *Perez v. Southern Pacific Transp. Co.*, 883 P.2d 424 (Ariz. Ct. App. 1993), the plaintiff sued for the wrongful death of Anne Perez:

> The undisputed facts are that Anne Perez's death at age 59 in 1991 resulted from mesothelioma, a form of cancer caused by exposure to asbestos. Mesothelioma has a latency period prior to clinically mani-fested symptoms of 25 to 40 years. Perez resided in the family home until her marriage in 1951; the disease was diagnosed in May 1989. Perez's father, Rafael Montenegro, worked for Southern Pacific Railroad in Tucson from 1923 to 1954. From 1931 to 1951, while work-ing as a boilermaker, Montenegro was exposed to asbestos-containing insulation materials used in the repair and maintenance of steam locomotives.
>
> During repair and maintenance, asbestos-containing insulation was removed and reinstalled in the back shop of Southern Pacific's Tucson rail yard. That process created a substantial amount of visible dust in the shop. Montenegro wore his work clothes home and hung them in the family's only bathroom prior to laundering. On occasion, Perez entered Southern Pacific's yard to deliver her father's lunch.

... Southern Pacific contends that liability under this theory is "strict" because it is imposed even when due care has been exercised, but it is not unlimited. We agree.

> The essence of the rule of liability without fault is that if a person in the conduct or maintenance of an enterprise which is lawful and proper in itself deliberately does an act under known conditions and with knowledge that injury will in all probability result to another and injury is sustained by the other as the direct and proximate consequence of the act, the person doing the act and causing the injury is liable in damages even though he acted without negligence. Under the doctrine, liability rests not upon negligence but upon the intentional doing of that which the person knows or should in the exercise of ordinary care know may in the normal course of events reasonably cause loss to another. Liability is automatically imposed upon the tort feasor when damages are sustained by another under such circumstances, even though there was no negligence.

Zampos v. United States Smelting, Refining & Mining Co., 207 F.2d 171, 176 (10th Cir. 1953). In discussing the extent of liability to be imposed under a claim of strict liability for abnormally dangerous activity, W. Page Keeton et al., PROSSER AND KEETON ON THE LAW OF TORTS § 79, at 559 (5th ed. 1984), states:

> It is clear, first of all, that unless a statute requires it, strict liability will never be found unless the defendant is aware of the abnormally dangerous condition or activity, and has voluntarily engaged in or permitted it. Mere negligent failure to discover or prevent it is not enough. . . .

In the present case, the court made extensive findings of fact and law. It imposed strict liability for abnormally dangerous activity, applying the "hindsight" test of *Dart v. Wiebe Manufacturing, Inc.*, 147 Ariz. 242, 709 P.2d 876 (1985). The court's minute entry acknowledged that *Dart* was a products liability case, but applied its "hindsight" test of imputed knowledge for public policy reasons. Although it is attractive to analogize to the risk/benefit factors analysis used in *Dart*, upon which the "hindsight" test is based, we believe it is no more than an attempt to bootstrap that argument onto a totally unrelated legal theory. Without authority to support such an argument, we decline to rule that the "hindsight" test is applicable to a claim for strict liability for abnormally dangerous activity.

In the present case, then, the determination of whether an activity is abnormally dangerous under RESTATEMENT § 520 must be related to the time at which Southern Pacific engaged in the activity being analyzed:

> The liability arises out of the abnormal danger of the activity itself, and the risk that it creates, of harm to those in the vicinity. It is founded upon a policy of law that imposes upon anyone who

for his own purposes creates an abnormal risk of harm to his neighbors, the responsibility of relieving against that harm when it does in fact occur. The defendant's enterprise, in other words, is required to pay its way by compensating for the harm it causes, because of its special, abnormal and dangerous character.

RESTATEMENT (SECOND) OF TORTS § 519 cmt. d.

We believe the court erred as a matter of law in applying the *Dart* hindsight test and therefore reverse and remand. Further proceedings must be based upon the RESTATEMENT test.

Perez, 883 P.2d at 425-27.

Dart v. Wiebe Manufacturing, Inc., 709 P.2d 876 (Ariz. 1985), discussed in *Perez*, was a products liability case alleging strict liability based on the absence of mechanical guards at the nip points of the rollers on a paper shredder and belt conveyor system, used in the recycling of waste paper. In a strict liability case, the court said, "the product is the focus of the inquiry. The quality of the product may be measured not only by the information available to the manufacturer at the time of design, but also by the information available to the trier of fact at the time of trial." *Dart*, 709 P.2d at 881.

6. *Awareness, products, and strict liability.* In commenting on the awareness issue, the court said in the products case of *Brooks v. Beech Aircraft Corp.*, 902 P.2d 54 (N.M. 1995):

In most instances a manufacturer is aware of the risks posed by any given design and of the availability of an alternative design. This case is a perfect example; Dr. Snyder testified that Beech had developed and used a workable shoulder harness prior to the design and manufacture of Mr. Brooks' plane. Thus we disagree with the premise that fairness requires the rejection of strict liability in design cases; when the manufacturer is aware of product risk and alternative designs at the time of supply, it is certainly not unfair to judge the manufacturer's design according to principles of strict liability rather than by conduct at the time of supply.

Further, in those hypothetical instances in which technology known at the time of trial and technology knowable at the time of distribution differ — and outside of academic rationale we find little to suggest the existence in practice of unknowable design considerations — it is more fair that the manufacturers and suppliers who have profited from the sale of the product bear the risk of loss. Given the risk-benefit calculation on which the jury is instructed in New Mexico, and the policy considerations that favor strict products liability, we believe that it is logical and consistent to take the same approach to design defects as to manufacturing flaws. If in some future case we are confronted directly with a proffer of evidence on an advancement or change in the state of the art that was neither known nor knowable at the time the product was supplied, we may at that time reconsider application of a state-of-the-art defense to those real circumstances, properly developed under the proffer with applicable briefs and argument.

Brooks, 902 P.2d at 63.

Why should strict products liability be stricter than strict liability for abnormally dangerous activities?

What sort of awareness is contemplated by *Perez*? The court quotes *Zampos v. United States Smelting, Ref. & Mining Co.*, 206 F.2d 171, 176 (10th Cir. 1953) for the proposition that the defendant must "deliberately" do an act "with knowledge that injury will in all probability result to another." This is recklessness, is it not?

Compare Cambridge Water Co. Ltd. v. Eastern Counties Leather Plc. [1994] 2 A.C. 264 (H.L.) ("foreseeability of the risk" is a prerequisite to recover in strict liability, either in nuisance or under *Rylands v. Fletcher*).

One commentator says:

> The few cases to address the question are in some disagreement, if not disarray, on the question of whether, or to what extent, knowledge of the risks by the defendant is a prerequisite for strict liability for abnormally dangerous activities. One of the premises of strict liability for abnormally dangerous activities seems to be that the defendant deliberately chose to engage in a dangerous activity whose risks were known to the defendant or at least reasonably recognizable by participants in the industry or activity in question.

Joseph H. King, Jr., *Abnormally Dangerous Activities,* 48 Baylor L. Rev. 341, 377 (1996). Are the courts in these cases talking about a form of strict liability that is akin to negligence? Are they measuring the actor's conduct by a risk-utility balancing test? Or will the actor be liable regardless of the risk-utility of the conduct? Of what relevance is the defendant's knowledge in evaluating the basis of liability?

7. *Foreseeability of Intervening Conduct.* In *Yukon Equipment, Inc. v. Fireman's Fund Insurance Co.*, 585 P.2d 1206 (Alaska 1978), the court found the facts as follows:

> A large explosion occurred at 2:47 a.m. on December 7, 1973, in the suburbs north of the City of Anchorage. The explosion originated at a storage magazine for explosives under lease from the federal government to petitioner E.I. du Pont de Nemours and Company, which was operated by petitioner Yukon Equipment, Inc. The storage magazine is located on a 1,870-acre tract of federal land which had been withdrawn by the Department of the Interior for the use of the Alaska Railroad for explosive storage purposes by separate orders in 1950 and 1961. The magazine which exploded was located 3,820 feet from the nearest building not used to store explosives and 4,330 feet from the nearest public highway. At the time of the explosion it contained approximately 80,000 pounds of explosives. The blast damaged dwellings and other buildings within a two-mile radius of the magazine and, in some instances, beyond a two-mile radius. The ground concussion it caused registered 1.8 on the Richter scale at the earthquake observation station in Palmer, some 30 miles away.

> The explosion was caused by thieves. Four young men had driven onto the tract where the magazine was located, broken into the storage magazine, set a prepared charge, and fled. They apparently did so in an effort to conceal the fact that they had stolen explosives from the site a day or two earlier.

Yukon Equipment, Inc., 525 P.2d at 1207.

The suit was brought to recover property damage to nearby property owners caused by the explosion. The trial court granted summary judgment to the plaintiffs on the issue of liability. The state supreme court affirmed on appeal:

> The next question is whether the intentional detonation of the storage magazine was a superseding cause relieving petitioners from liability. . . . The considerations which impel cutting off liability where there is a superseding cause in negligence cases also apply to cases of absolute liability.

> Prior to the explosion in question the petitioners' magazines had been illegally broken into at least six times. Most of these entries involved the theft of explosives. Petitioners had knowledge of all of this.

> . . . The incendiary destruction of premises by thieves to cover evidence of theft is not so uncommon an occurrence that it can be regarded as highly extraordinary. Moreover, the particular kind of result threatened by the defendant's conduct, the storage of explosives, was an explosion at the storage site. Absolute liability is imposed on those who store or use explosives because they have created an unusual risk to others. As between those who have created the risk for the benefit of their own enterprise and those whose only connection with the enterprise is to have suffered damage because of it, the law places the risk of loss on the former. When the risk created causes damage in fact, insistence that the precise details of the intervening cause be foreseeable would subvert the purpose of that rule of law.

Id. at 1211-12.

In *Klein v. Pyrodyne Corp.*, 810 P.2d 917 (Wash. 1991), the court held that Pyrodyne Corp., a pyrotechnic company, could be found strictly liable to spectators for injuries caused by an exploding rocket at a 4th of July fireworks display:

> Pyrodyne argues that even if there is strict liability for fireworks, its liability under the facts of this case is cut off by the manufacturer's negligence, the existence of which we assume for purposes of evaluating the propriety of the trial court's summary judgment. According to Pyrodyne, a rocket detonated without leaving the mortar box because it was negligently manufactured. This detonation, Pyrodyne asserts, was what caused the the misfire of the second rocket, which in turn resulted in the Kleins' injuries. Pyrodyne

reasons that the manufacturer's negligence acted as an intervening or outside force that cuts off Pyrodyne's liability.

In support of its position, Pyrodyne relies upon *Siegler v. Kuhlman*. In *Siegler*, a young woman was killed in an explosion when the car she was driving encountered a pool of thousands of gallons of gasoline spilled from a gasoline truck. This court held that transporting gasoline in great quantities along public highways and streets is an abnormally dangerous activity that calls for the application of strict liability. *Siegler*, 81 Wash. 2d at 459–460. Justice Rosellini concurred, but stated:

> I think the opinion should make clear, however, that the owner of the vehicle will be held strictly liable only for damages caused when the flammable or explosive substance is allowed to escape without the apparent intervention of any outside force beyond the control of the manufacturer, the owner, or the operator of the vehicle hauling it. I do not think the majority means to suggest that if another vehicle, negligently driven, collided with the truck in question, the truck owner would be held liable for the damage.

Siegler, at 460 (Rosellini, J., concurring).

Klein, 810 P.2d at 923-24.

The *Klein* court concluded:

> We hold that intervening acts of third persons serve to relieve the defendant from strict liability for abnormally dangerous activities only if those acts were unforeseeable in relation to the extraordinary risk created by the activity. The rationale for this rule is that it encourages those who conduct abnormally dangerous activities to anticipate and take precautions against the possible negligence of third persons. Where the third person's negligence is beyond the actor's control, this rule, unlike the *Siegler* dicta, nonetheless imposes strict liability if the third person's negligence was reasonably foreseeable. Such a result allocates the economic burden of injuries arising from the foreseeable negligence of third persons to the party best able to plan for it and to bear it — the actor carrying on the abnormally dangerous activity.

Id. at 925.

Should foreseeability of intervening factors be judged by the same standards of awareness of danger discussed in the preceding note?

In *Cadena v. Chicago Fireworks Manufacturing, Co.*, 697 N.E.2d 802 (Ill. App. Ct. 1998), the plaintiff sought damages for injuries suffered at a Fourth of July fireworks display when one of the fireworks misfired and landed in a crowd of spectators, injuring the plaintiffs. The court refused to apply strict liability against the defendants for conducting an abnormally dangerous activity. *Cadena*, 697 N.E.2d at 804-05. It found that "the exercise of reasonable care in displaying fireworks will significantly reduce the risks involved"; that fireworks displays are "a matter of common usage"; that the location of the display (a high school football field) was an appropriate place, in the absence of any allegation to the contrary; and that such displays "are of some social utility to communities." *Id*. at 814.

COPIER BY AND THROUGH LINDSEY v. SMITH & WESSON
138 F.3d 833 (10th Cir. 1998)

The relevant facts of this case are not in dispute. Ms. Copier's ex-husband shot her on March 21, 1991, with a .38 caliber firearm manufactured by defendant-appellee, Smith & Wesson Corp. The shooting, which led to Eldon Copier's conviction for attempted criminal homicide, left Ms. Copier a paraplegic.

Ms. Copier filed her original complaint herein on March 20, 1995 in Utah state court against Smith & Wesson. Her theory of legal liability was based on the tort doctrine of ultrahazardous activity, arguing in particular that since handguns are manufactured to injure or kill people, and since it is a statistical certainty that some handguns are actually used to injure or kill people, the handgun manufacturer should bear strict liability for the resulting damages. She invoked the doctrine of ultrahazardous activity articulated in the Restatement (Second) of Torts § 519 and 520.

Following the filing of her complaint in March 1995 in state court, Ms. Copier died as a result of her injuries on June 24, 1995. Smith & Wesson subsequently removed the case to federal court on August 7, 1995. . . .

On motion of Smith & Wesson, the district court dismissed Ms. Copier's complaint on December 13, 1995, reasoning that its role was to follow, not expand, Utah law, and that Ms. Copier's cause of action was not viable under current Utah law. . . .

. . . Utah law imposes strict liability on one who carries on an abnormally dangerous activity for harm resulting from the activity. *Walker Drug Co., Inc. v. La Sal Oil Co.*, 902 P.2d 1229, 1233 (Utah 1995); Restatement (Second) of Torts § 519 (1976). . . . [The court considers the Restatement factors and concludes "Utah law does not support Ms. Copier's theory of liability of Smith & Wesson."]

. . . None of the above factors is implicated by the *manufacturing* of handguns, as opposed to the use — or rather, the *misuse* — of handguns. For example, in *Walker Drug*, the plaintiffs brought suit because gasoline had leaked from the defendants' gas stations and contaminated the plaintiffs' property. In evaluating the six factors, the Utah Supreme Court considered the danger that would result from the operation of the gas stations — that is, the possibility of leakage of gasoline. It was held that the operation of the gas stations was not an abnormally dangerous activity; they were located in an area of the city where their operation was common, appropriate and of significant value to the community. *Id*. at 1233.

In *Robison v. Robison*, 16 Utah 2d 2, 394 P.2d 876, 877 (1964), the Utah Supreme Court held that the determination of whether the ultrahazardous activity doctrine applied as to injury caused by rock fragments hurled during use by the defendants of dynamite for blasting purposes depended on the circumstances. The court focused on the *use* of dynamite, and not its manufacture. In the instant case, however, Ms. Copier was harmed not by the manufacturing of the Smith & Wesson .38, but by the use of it to shoot her. This distinction is significant, because Ms. Copier's argument essentially collapses all uses of guns into one purpose, which she contends is to injure or kill people. However, Ms. Copier ignores a number of legitimate uses, including self-defense, home protection, and use by law enforcement officers.

We further note that the one case we have found that imposed strict liability upon a handgun manufacturer focused on the unique nature of the firearm in that case, a "Saturday Night Special," which the court characterized as a gun whose 'chief value' . . . is in criminal activity, because of its easy concealability and low price." *See Kelley v. R.G. Industries, Inc.*, 304 Md. 124, 497 A.2d 1143, 1158 (1985). *Kelley* provides little support to Ms. Copier, however, since it actually rejected the application of the ultrahazardous activity doctrine to firearms in general but limited its holding of liability specifically to "Saturday Night Specials."[3] *Id.* at 1147, 1154, 1159. Here, Ms. Copier was shot by a standard .38 caliber pistol and there is no allegation that the gun was easily concealable and designed chiefly for use by criminals.

Ms. Copier relies heavily on several scholarly articles which, she contends, advocate the extension of the ultrahazardous activity doctrine to the manufacturing of firearms. . . . We are not persuaded that the articles support plaintiff-appellant's position that Utah law, or a discernible trend in its decisions, indicate the adoption of her theory.

With respect to the opinion in *In re 101 California Street*, No. 959316 (Cal. Super. 2d Dep't Apr. 10, 1995), which provides the basis for Pearson's article, at least two courts have declined to follow its analysis, noting that while the case may have been correctly decided under its particular facts, it was actually based on a California statute prohibiting the sale, advertising or possession of certain assault weapons, including the specific handgun involved therein. . . .

Ms. Copier's argument, carried to its logical extension, would suggest that the manufacturing of any product that is significantly misused and has great potential for injuring or killing persons should be considered as an ultrahazardous activity. Alcohol production, for example, might be so considered because in any given year, there is a statistical certainty that thousands of people will be killed in alcohol-related accidents. Yet, the Utah Supreme Court has refused to apply strict liability principles to alcohol providers. *See Horton v. Royal Order of the Sun*, 821 P.2d 1167, 1169 (Utah 1991).

In sum, we are convinced that under the state of decisional law in Utah, and of decisions generally, the complaint premised on the ultrahazardous activity doctrine was properly dismissed here. . . .

---

[3] We note, moreover, that the Maryland legislature has since repudiated the liability holding in *Kelley* with respect to "Saturday Night Specials." *See* Md. Ann. Code art. 27 §36-I(h). Additionally, other jurisdictions which have considered the issue have rejected the extension of the ultrahazardous activity doctrine to the manufacturing or sale of firearms. *See, e.g., Hamilton v. Accu-Tek*, 935 F. Supp. 1307, 1324 (E.D.N.Y. 1996) (rejecting the application of the doctrine because it was not an "improper use of land"); *King v. R.G. Industries, Inc.*, 182 Mich. App. 343, 451 N.W.2d 874 (1990) (manufacturer is not liable for criminal misuse of handgun) . . . [the court cites over a dozen cases where the extension of strict liability to the manufacturing and sale of firearms has been rejected].

NOTES

1. *Strict liability for handguns?* Is the court correct in deciding not to apply strict liability for an abnormally dangerous activity to the manufacture of handguns? What about tobacco? How should courts determine if an activity is abnormally dangerous?

2. *Types of Abnormally Dangerous Activities.* Is storage of gasoline in a residential area an abnormally dangerous activity? The courts are divided. *Compare Yommer v. McKenzie,* 257 A.2d 138 (Md. 1969), *with Hudson v. Peavey Oil Co.,* 566 P.2d 175 (Or. 1977). *See Siegler v. Kuhlman,* 502 P.2d 1181 (Wash. 1972) (strict liability for harm caused by the transportation of gasoline on a highway).

A similar division of authority exists as to crop dusting. *Compare Langan v. Valicopters, Inc.,* 567 P.2d 218 (Wash. 1977), *and Gotreaux v. Gary,* 94 So. 2d 293 (La. 1957) *with Lawler v. Skelton,* 130 So. 2d 565 (Miss. 1961).

Strict liability usually is not imposed upon providers of public utility services. *See, e.g., Ferguson v. Northern States Power Co.,* 239 N.W.2d 190 (Minn. 1976) (electrical transmission); *Jennings Buick, Inc. v. Cincinnati,* 384 N.E.2d 303 (Ohio 1978) (water main), and *Mahowald v. Minnesota Gas Co.,* 344 N.W.2d 856 (Minn. 1984) (gas main). *But see Lubin v. Iowa City,* 131 N.W.2d 765 (Iowa 1965) (strict liability for water damage from broken city water main).

The initial rule of strict liability for fires gave way to negligence. The Oregon court has imposed strict liability for "field burning," an activity which is hazardous but which is helpful in clearing land and is essential to the preparation of land for some farming uses. *See Koos v. Roth,* 652 P.2d 1255 (Or. 1982).

The position of Rest. 2d Torts §520A (1977) is that the operator of an aircraft is strictly liability for "physical harm to land or to persons or chattels on the ground" caused by the "ascent, descent or flight of aircraft, or by the dropping or falling of an object from the aircraft." There is no strict liability, however, "to persons themselves participating in aviation, such as the crew or passengers of a falling plane, or the owner of property on it or to persons on another plane which was struck by the defendant's plane." *Id.* §520A cmt *e.* Why? *See also* REST. 3D. TORTS-PH § 20 CM T *k* (P.F.D. No. 1 2005).

The modern trend seems to be away from strict liability for ground damage from falling aircraft, and toward a standard of negligence. *See Crosby v. Cox Aircraft Co.,* 746 P.2d 1198 (Wash. 1987). Apparently this trend is based on the idea that air flight is now a relatively safe means of transportation. Is it? Is the issue of the relative safety of an activity the key for determining whether strict liability should be imposed?

Is strict liability for abnormally dangerous activities a doctrine in search of a unifying principle? Can you provide such a principle? Is there an uneasy tension between the realms of strict tort liability and tort fault liability?

3. *Abnormal Sensitivity.* Section 524A of the Second Restatement states that there is no strict liability for harm caused by an abnormally dangerous activity "if the harm would not have resulted but for the abnormally sensitive character of the plaintiff's activity." Rest. 2d Torts §524A (1977).

In *Foster v. Preston Mill Co.*, 268 P.2d 645 (1954), the court refused to impose strict liability against a blaster whose blasting operations caused plaintiff's frightened mother mink to kill their kittens:

> The relatively moderate vibration and noise which appellant's blasting produced at a distance of two and a quarter miles was no more than a usual incident of the ordinary life of the community. . . .

> It is the exceedingly nervous disposition of mink, rather than the normal risks inherent in blasting operations, which therefore must, as a matter of sound policy, bear the responsibility for the loss here sustained. . . .

Foster, 268 P.2d at 648.

Compare MacGibbon v. Robinson, [1953] 2 D.L.R. 689 (B.C.) (blasting during mink whelping season held unreasonable, where blaster knew of the whelping and the blasting could reasonably have been deferred).

Suppose abnormal heat from defendant's mill damaged a very sensitive type of paper which plaintiff kept for sale on his premises? *See Robinson v. Kilvert*, [1889] L.R. 41 Ch.D. 88 (recovery denied).

Suppose plaintiff establishes an organic gardening farm in an area where her neighbors have grown cotton for generations. As a result of crop dusting of a neighbor's cotton crop, plaintiff's land is damaged so the land can no longer be used to produce organic products. Should the neighbor be held strictly liable? Suppose the damage occurred as a result of negligent dusting?

D. VICARIOUS RESPONSIBILITY FOR THE CONDUCT OF OTHERS

Are there reasons for imposing on someone, who is free from any fault, liability for the tortious conduct of another? Two parties may share a relationship which justifies imposing that liability. This result, often called vicarious liability, imputes the fault or other wrongful conduct of an actor to a party. Vicarious liability attributed to a defendant serves to impose liability; vicarious liability to a plaintiff results in defeating liability or reducing recovery. Perhaps a better term for this blame-shifting would be imputed responsibility.

Although frequently described as a form of strict liability, imputed responsibility or vicarious liability requires that some underlying wrongful conduct exists. Thus, the most nearly accurate term in these situations is imputed fault.

Where the doctrine of strict liability does apply, the non-faulty acts of the agent acting within the scope of her agency can be imputed to her principal as a form of imputed strict liability. Thus, an employer could be liable for damages from blasting caused by the non-faulty acts of its employees acting within the scope of their employment.

1. Imputed Responsibility of the Defendant

What policies might have encouraged courts to impute responsibility for an actor's wrongdoing to a defendant? What limits should be placed on the imputation of responsibility?

LUNDBERG v. STATE
255 N.E.2d 177 (N.Y. 1969)

SCILEPPI, JUDGE.

SANDILANDS WAS EMPLOYED AS A SENIOR ENGINEERING TECHNICIAN BY THE NEW YORK STATE DEPARTMENT OF PUBLIC WORKS. HE WAS PERMANENTLY BASED IN BUFFALO WHERE HE ALSO RESIDED. HOWEVER, SINCE MARCH OF 1965 HE HAD BEEN ASSIGNED TO THE ALLEGHENY RESERVOIR PROJECT NEAR SALAMANCA, ABOUT 80 MILES FROM BUFFALO.

DUE TO THE GREAT DISTANCE BETWEEN THE RESERVOIR AND BUFFALO, SANDILANDS FOUND IT NECESSARY TO STAY AT A HOTEL IN SALAMANCA DURING THE WORK WEEK. GENERALLY, AT THE END OF HIS WORK DAY ON FRIDAY, SANDILANDS WOULD DRIVE HOME TO BUFFALO TO SPEND THE WEEKEND WITH HIS FAMILY, AND ON MONDAY MORNING HE WOULD DRIVE BACK TO THE RESERVOIR IN ORDER TO ARRIVE THERE BEFORE THE START OF HIS WORK DAY. THE STATE REIMBURSED HIM FOR HIS LIVING EXPENSES WHILE HE WAS AWAY FROM HOME AND, IN ADDITION, PAID HIM 9 CENTS A MILE TO COVER THE EXPENSES OF THE TRIP. HE WAS NOT PAID FOR THE TIME HE SPENT TRAVELING TO AND FROM THE SITE, AND IF HE ARRIVED LATE ON MONDAY MORNING, THE TIME HE MISSED WOULD BE DEDUCTED FROM HIS VACATION OR SICK LEAVE.

ON MONDAY, FEBRUARY 14, 1966, AT 7:30 A.M., SANDILANDS WAS DRIVING BACK TO THE RESERVOIR FROM BUFFALO AFTER A HOLIDAY WEEKEND. WHILE ATTEMPTING TO PASS A TRUCK, HIS CAR SKIDDED AND STRUCK THE CAR DRIVEN BY LUNDBERG HEAD ON. LUNDBERG DIED AS A RESULT OF THE INJURIES HE SUSTAINED IN THE ACCIDENT.

SANDILANDS APPLIED FOR AND WAS GRANTED WORKMEN'S COMPENSATION BENEFITS FOR THE INJURIES WHICH HE SUFFERED IN THE ACCIDENT. CLAIMANT, LUNDBERG'S WIDOW, BROUGHT AN ACTION FOR PAIN AND SUFFERING AND WRONGFUL DEATH AGAINST SANDILANDS AND A SIMILAR ACTION AGAINST THE STATE, AS SANDILANDS' EMPLOYER THE ACTION AGAINST SANDILANDS WAS SETTLED FOR $20,000. THE ONE AGAINST THE STATE WENT TO TRIAL AND RESULTED IN A JUDGMENT FOR MORE THAN $73,000. THE APPELLATE DIVISION, FOURTH DEPARTMENT, UNANIMOUSLY AFFIRMED AND THE STATE IS APPEALING.

THE SOLE ISSUE PRESENTED BY THIS APPEAL IS WHETHER THE STATE OF NEW YORK SHOULD BE HELD LIABLE, PURSUANT TO THE DOCTRINE OF *respondeat superior,* for the pain and suffering and wrongful death caused by its employee's negligence. It is our opinion that Sandilands was not acting in the scope of his employment while driving from Buffalo to his work site and that, therefore, the complaint against the defendant State should have been dismissed. Under the doctrine of *respondeat superior,* an employer will be liable for the negligence of an employee committed while the employee is acting in the scope of his employment. An employee acts in the scope of his employment when he is doing something in furtherance of the duties he owes to his employer and where the employer is, or could be, exercising some control, directly or indirectly, over the employee's activities.

As a general rule, an employee driving to and from work is not acting in the scope of his employment. Although such activity is work motivated, the element of control is lacking. An exception to this rule is, that an employee who uses his car in furtherance of his work is acting in the scope of his employment while driving home from his last business appointment, since such a person is working, and is under his employer's control, from the time he leaves the house in the morning until he returns at night. In the instant case, however, the employee was not driving his car in furtherance of his work at the time of the accident. He was engaged in an independent personal activity over which the State had no control. Thus, the general rule applies.

. . . The several cases cited by respondent for the proposition that an employee who is injured while driving to or from a temporary work assignment is entitled to Workmen's Compensation benefits are not applicable to this case. Workmen's Compensation was created to prevent injured workmen from becoming "objects of charity" and to make reasonable compensation for injuries and death caused by job related activities regardless of fault. It is necessary for an employee seeking to obtain compensation benefits to establish only that his injury was caused by an activity related to his job, whereas the doctrine of *respondeat superior* has clearly not received such wide application because of the requirement that the employee be under the control of the employer at the time of the injury.

Accordingly, the order of the Appellate Division should be reversed and the claim against the defendant dismissed.

Burke, Judge, dissenting.

Of particular relevance in this case, as distinguished from the vague and theoretical question of "right to control," is the test for liability posited by former Chief Judge Cardozo: "The test in brief is this: If the work of the employee creates the necessity for travel, he is in the course of his employment, though he is serving at the same time some purpose of his own" (citation omitted). The undisputed facts in the present case clearly indicate that that test has been met. Sandilands' temporary employment at a work site 80 miles from his permanent station and home in Buffalo created the necessity for his travel between Buffalo and the work site. While so traveling, he was clearly acting in furtherance of his employment and this has already been determined by the fact that he has been awarded compensation benefits for the injuries which he received in that same accident. The mere fact that his traveling back and forth was motivated by his desire to see his family occasionally in no way detracts from the fact that the trips would not have been made at all had it not been for his assignment to a distant work site.

In addition, it should be recognized that the fact that the State paid Sandilands' travel expenses for these trips is significant not because it has any relation to some theoretical "right to control" but precisely because it indicates that the State recognized that Sandilands' employment necessitated such travel and acquiesced in his use of his own automobile for that travel. Thus, it is difficult to conclude that it would be somehow "unfair" to impose liability on the State for its employee's negligence when the State itself necessitated the use of the instrumentality through which the death of the claimant's intestate occurred. . . .

NOTES

1. *In the Course of Employment.* Generally an employee is not in the course and scope of his employment while going to and from work. *Robarge v. Bechtel Power Corp.*, 640 P.2d 211 (Ariz. 1982). What if the employer pays the employee's travel expenses to and from work or pays him for the time spent in traveling to and from work? Would this payment indicate that the trip is reasonably in furtherance of the employer's business? *See, e.g., Hinman v. Westinghouse Elec. Co.*, 471 P.2d 988 (Cal. 1970); *Faul v. Jelco*, 595 P.2d 1035 (Ariz. Ct. App. 1979). What if the employee is off duty but "on call?" *See District of Columbia v. Davis*, 386 A.2d 1195 (D.C. Ct. App. 1978).

An employee performing a mission for the employer away from the premises remains in the course and scope of his employment although he makes a trivial departure from his employer's business, such as altering his route for a personal mission. The departure may be so substantial, however, that he is on a "frolic" or "detour" and is no longer within the course and scope of his employment. Under modern business conditions, however, a good many frolics, like the three-martini lunch, may be within the scope of employment.

In *Fruit v. Schreiner*, 502 P.2d 133 (Alaska 1972), Fruit was attending a sales convention of his employer, Equitable Life Assurance Society. *Fruit*, 502 P.2d at 135. He was encouraged by the Society to "socialize" with other life insurance salesmen at the convention in the hope of picking up some useful ideas. *Id.* at 142. At about 11 o'clock one evening he was awakened by friends, who found that he had fully slept off the effect of his lunchtime socializing; shortly thereafter Fruit, using his own car, decided to drive to a bar some miles distant where he thought he would find some out-of-state agents. *Id.* at 136. Finding no colleagues at the bar, he decided to return to the convention center. On the way he skidded across a dividing line and collided with a standing car, crushing the legs of Schreiner, who was standing in front of the car after raising its hood. *Id.* Equitable was held liable to Schreiner. "There was evidence from which the jury could find that he [Fruit] was at least motivated in part by his desire to meet with the out-of-state guests and thus to benefit from their experience so as to improve his abilities as a salesman." *Id.* at 142.

2. *The Role of Alcohol.* When should an employer be liable for intoxicated behavior by an employee?

In *Ira S. Bushey & Sons v. United States*, 398 F.2d 167 (2d Cir. 1968), a drunk crewmember returned to the Coast Guard Ship where he and the rest of the crew were living. *Bushey*, 398 F.2d at 168. At the time, the ship was being overhauled in a floating dry dock. *Id.* The crewman turned several intake valves on the dock, causing the dock to take on a large amount of water. *Id.* As a result, parts of the drydock and ship sank. The drydock owner sued the United States, the employer of the crewman, for damages. The court held the

U.S. could be found responsible for damage caused by the drunk crewman. *Id.* at 171. Although the crewman's actions were not directly motivated by his employment, his intoxication was foreseeable to the employer. The employer should be held to expect risks, to the public also, which arise "out of and in the course of his employment of labor." *Id.* at 172. Thus, it was reasonable to expect that a crewman might be drunk in the workplace, even if his drunkenness was not motivated by work.

Compare *Bell v. Hurstell*, 743 So. 2d 720 (La. Ct. App. 1999). After a meeting with a client at employer's office concluded about 7 p.m., employee went with the client to a lounge and then to a party given by another company with which employer had a business relationship. *Id.* at 721. During that time, employee apparently became intoxicated. At about 11:00 p.m., employee, attempting to drive home, was involved in an accident. The court held that employee was not in the course and scope of her employment at the time of the accident: "an accident, that would not normally be considered as occurring during the course and scope of employment, will not be considered as occurring during the course and scope of employment merely because alcohol, which may have contributed to the accident was consumed (but not required to be consumed as a condition of employment) while the employee-tortfeasor was acting in the course and scope of employment." *Id* at 722.

3. *Failure to Follow Rules.* In *Kuharski v. Somers Motor Lines, Inc.*, 43 A.2d 777 (Conn. 1945), Nihill, a truck driver, stopped at a tavern where he picked up Sophie Kuharski. She went riding with him, and was killed when his truck was involved in an accident. *Id.* Kuharski's estate sued Nihill's employer, which defended on the grounds that Nihill violated company and ICC regulations in allowing Sophie to ride in the truck. *Id.* at 779. In denying this defense, the court said the master is liable for negligent acts of the servant performed in the course of employment, "even though they are not specifically authorized or are at times contrary to instructions." *Id.* In permitting Sophie to board the truck, Nihill was acting outside of his employment, but in then continuing his trip "he was again in the course of it." *Id.*

Do these decisions that find liability seem surprising? What might motivate courts to find defendants responsible for plaintiff's harm in these cases?

4. *Intentional Misconduct.* The plaintiff in *Mary M. v. City of Los Angeles*, 814 P.2d 1341, 1343 (1991), sued the City of Los Angeles on a theory of respondeat superior. While plaintiff was driving home she was stopped by police officer Schroyer. "He was in uniform, wore a badge and a gun, and was driving a marked black-and-white police car. When he detained plaintiff, he sent in a radio message that he was out of his vehicle conducting an investigation." *Id.* at 1342. She performed poorly on the sobriety test, pleaded not to be sent to jail, and Schroyer drove her home. *Id.*

> After entering the house with plaintiff, Sergeant Schroyer told her that he expected "payment" for taking her home instead of to jail. Plaintiff tried to run away, but Schroyer grabbed her hair and threw her on the couch. When plaintiff screamed, Schroyer put his hand over her mouth and threatened to take her to jail. Plaintiff stopped

struggling, and Schroyer raped her. He then left the house. [He was later convicted for rape arising out of this incident.]

Id. at 1342-43.

The court affirmed a jury verdict of $150,000 for the plaintiff against the city, commenting:

> [S]ociety has granted police officers extraordinary power and authority over its citizenry. An officer who detains an individual is acting as the official representative of the state, with all of its coercive power. As visible symbols of that power, an officer is given a distinctively marked car, a uniform, a badge, and a gun. . . . Inherent in this formidable power is the potential for abuse. The cost resulting from misuse of that power should be borne by the community, because of the substantial benefits that the community derives from the lawful exercise of police power.

Id. at 1349. Is this reasoning persuasive or should a line be drawn at imputing responsibility for intentional misconduct?

If the plaintiff in *Mary M.* had sued the city for violation of her civil rights under 42 U.S.C. §1983, she could not have recovered "unless action pursuant to official municipal policy of some nature caused a constitutional tort." *Monell v. Dept. Of Soc. Services*, 436 U.S. 658, 691 (1978). Liability could not be imposed under that section "solely on the basis of the existence of an employer-employee relationship." *Id*. at 692. Why should the federal remedy be more restricted than the state common law remedy?

5. *Intentional and Sexual Misconduct — Title VII and Title IX*. Federal legislation prohibits sex-based discrimination in the workplace (The Equal Employment Act, 42 U.S.C. §2000(e)(1964) — customarily referred to as Title VII) and in federally funded schools (The Education Amendments Act, 20 U.S.C. §1681(A)(1972) — often referred to as Title IX). Sexual harassment rarely will fit within the course and scope of the harassing employee's employment under general principles of vicarious liability. However, the employer may be vicariously liable under these statutes to a victimized employee for an actionable hostile environment created or allowed by a supervisor with immediate or successively higher authority over the employee. *See, e.g., Burlington Industries, Inc. v. Ellerth*, 524 U.S. 742 (1998); *Faragher v. City of Boca Raton*, 524 U.S. 775 (1998). Are these laws examples of vicarious liability, or would they be better described as negligent supervision of the workplace by the employer? For a discussion of the issue, see William R. Corbett, Faragher, Ellerth, *and the Federal Law of Vicarious Liability for Sexual Harassment by Supervisors: Something Lost, Something Gained, and Something to Guard Against*, 7 Wm. & Mary Bill Rts. J. 801 (1999).

SHERARD v. SMITH
778 S.W.2d 546 (Tex. App. 1989)

SEERDEN, JUSTICE.

APPELLANT BROUGHT SUIT FOR WRONGFUL DEATH BASED ON A MOTOR VEHICLE COLLISION WHICH OCCURRED ON JULY 2, 1984. APPELLEE HAD HIRED RENE HINOJOSA TO HAUL GRAIN FROM HIS FARM TO THE ELEVATOR HINOJOSA'S TRUCK WAS LOADED WITH 14 OR 15 TONS OF GRAIN WHEN HE STOPPED IT ON SOUTH PADRE ISLAND DRIVE TO RETRIEVE A SHOVEL THAT HAD FALLEN FROM THE TRUCK. APPELLANT'S SON DROVE HIS VEHICLE INTO THE REAR OF THE TRUCK AND WAS KILLED.

APPELLANT PLEADED THAT APPELLEE WAS NEGLIGENT AND THAT APPELLEE IS VICARIOUSLY LIABLE FOR HINOJOSA'S NEGLIGENCE, ALLEGING THAT HINOJOSA WAS APPELLEE'S AGENT, SERVANT, OR EMPLOYEE. THE TRIAL COURT GRANTED APPELLEE'S MOTION FOR SUMMARY JUDGMENT. WE AFFIRM THE TRIAL COURT'S JUDGMENT.

. . . THE SUMMARY JUDGMENT EVIDENCE SHOWS THAT APPELLEE, CARL SMITH, HAS BEEN A FARMER SINCE 1955. HE RAISES GRAIN IN NUECES COUNTY, TEXAS. SMITH, A RELATIVELY SMALL VOLUME FARMER, CUSTOMARILY HIRES SOMEONE TO HAUL HIS GRAIN FROM THE FARM WHERE IT IS RAISED TO THE GRAIN ELEVATOR WHERE IT IS STORED AND SOLD. APPELLEE HAD USED THE SAME HAULERS FOR A NUMBER OF YEARS, BUT IN 1984, FOR THE FIRST TIME, HE HIRED HINOJOSA TO DO HIS HAULING. PRIOR TO THE WRECK . . . HINOJOSA HAD BEEN HAULING FOR SMITH ABOUT ONE WEEK.

APPELLEE'S MOTION FOR SUMMARY JUDGMENT CONTENDS THAT THE SUMMARY JUDGMENT EVIDENCE ESTABLISHES AS A MATTER OF LAW THAT

1. Hinojosa was an independent contractor and not the agent, servant or employee of appellee. . . .

. . . In light of the authorities cited and the arguments raised by appellee in his first reply point we will only address the matters briefed by appellant. Where there is no dispute as to the controlling facts and only one reasonable conclusion can be inferred, the question of whether one is an "employee" or "independent contractor" is a question of law. To constitute the relationship of employer and employee, the employer must have the right to select, control, and, for misconduct, discharge the employee. An independent contractor is any person who, in the pursuit of an independent business, undertakes to do a specific piece of work for other persons, using his own means and methods, without submitting himself to their control in respect to all details. Recognized tests to determine when one is acting in the capacity of independent contractor are:

1. the independent nature of the business;

2. the obligation to furnish necessary tools, supplies and material to perform the job;

3. the right to control the progress of the work except the final result;

4. the length of time of the employment; and

5. the method of payment — whether by the time or by the job.

It has also been stated that the independent nature of the agreement of employment may be inferred from two circumstances: (1) that the party is engaged in a distinct and generally recognized employment; and (2) that his stipulated remuneration is to be determined by some quantitative standard.

The distinction between an independent contractor and an agent or employee is not always easy to determine, and there is no uniform criterion by which they may be differentiated. Nevertheless, it has often been stated that the test for determining whether a master-servant or independent contractor relationship exists is whether the employer has the "right to control" the details of the work.

. . . Appellee hired Hinojosa to haul his grain from the field to the Corpus Christi Grain Elevator. He agreed to pay him a specific price for each hundred weight of grain hauled. He withheld no monies for any form of taxes nor did he provide any medical or other benefits. He provided no fuel for Hinojosa's truck. The only benefit Hinojosa was to receive for his services was the cash payment based on the amount of grain he delivered to the elevator. While appellee looked at Hinojosa's truck and inquired as to liability insurance coverage at the time of hiring, Hinojosa was responsible for maintenance of the truck and for furnishing any tools or helpers necessary to achieve the task of delivering the grain. The evidence clearly shows that the relationship between appellee and Hinojosa was that of independent contractor-owner rather than employee-employer.

NOTES

1. *Nondelegable Duties.* In *Maloney v. Rath*, 445 P.2d 513 (Cal. 1968), the court found the defendant car owner had a nondelegable duty to maintain her car brakes in proper working condition:

> . . . [W]e have found nondelegable duties in a wide variety of situations and have recognized that the rules set forth in the Restatement of Torts with respect to such duties are generally in accord with California law. Such duties include those imposed by a public authority as a condition of granting a franchise; the duty of a condemning agent to protect a severed parcel from damage; the duty of a general contractor to construct a building safely; the duty to exercise due care when an ". . . independent contractor is employed to do work which the employer should recognize as necessarily creating a condition involving an unreasonable risk of bodily harm to others unless special precautions are taken." *Courtell v. McEachan*, 51 Cal. 2d 448, 457, 334 P.2d 870, 874 (1951); the duty of landowners to maintain their property in a reasonably safe condition and to comply with applicable safety ordinances and the duty of employers and suppliers to comply with the safety provisions of the Labor Code.

> Section 423 of the Restatement (Second) of Torts provides that "One who carries on an activity which threatens a grave risk of serious bodily harm or death unless the instrumentalities used are carefully . . . maintained, and who employs an independent contractor to . . .

maintain such instrumentalities, is subject to the same liability for physical harm caused by the negligence of the contractor in . . . maintaining such instrumentalities as though the employer had himself done the work of . . . maintenance." Section 424 provides that: "One who by statute or by administrative regulation is under a duty to provide specified safeguards or precautions for the safety of others is subject to liability to the others for whose protection the duty is imposed for harm caused by the failure of a contractor employed by him to provide such safeguards or precautions." Both of these sections point to a nondelegable duty in this case. The statutory provisions regulating the maintenance and equipment of automobiles constitute express legislative recognition of the fact that improperly maintained motor vehicles threaten "a grave risk of serious bodily harm or death." The responsibility for minimizing that risk or compensating for the failure to do so properly rests with the person who owns and operates the vehicle. He is the party primarily to be benefited by its use; he selects the contractor and is free to insist upon one who is financially responsible and to demand indemnity from him; the cost of his liability insurance that distributes the risk is properly attributable to his activities; and the discharge of the duty to exercise reasonable care in the maintenance of his vehicle is of the utmost importance to the public.

In the present case it is undisputed that the accident was caused by a failure of defendant's brakes that resulted from her independent contractor's negligence in overhauling or in thereafter inspecting the brakes. Since her duty to maintain her brakes in compliance with the provisions of the Vehicle Code is nondelegable, the fact that the brake failure was the result of her independent contractor's negligence is no defense.

Maloney, 445 P.2d at 516-17.

The *Maloney* result was rejected in *Hackett v. Perron,* 402 A.2d 193 (N.H. 1979). However, courts have found a variety of non-delegable duties, including construction or repair of a building, Rest. 2d Torts § 422 (1965); *Misiulis v. Milbrand Main. Corp.,* 218 N.W.2d 68 (Mich. Ct. App. 1974); failing to clear a roadway, *Westby v. Itasca County,* 290 N.W.2d 437 (Minn. 1980); work imposed by a public authority as a condition of granting a franchise, *E.R. Harding Co. v. Paducah S. Ry.,* 271 S.W. 1046 (Ky. 1925); the duty of a landowner to maintain his property in a reasonably safe condition, *Snyder v. Southern California Edison,* 285 P.2d 912 (Cal. 1955); the duty to comply with applicable safety ordinances, Rest. 2d Torts, § 424 (1965); property owner statutory duty to provide safe scaffolding for independent contractors and workers, *Gordon v. Eastern Ry. Supply, Inc.,* 626 N.E.2d 912 (N.Y. 1993); city ordinance duty of landlord to install fire detector, *Shump v. First Cont.-Robinwood Assoc.,* 644 N.E.2d 291 (Ohio 1994).

2. *Collateral Negligence.* In *Otero v. Jordon Restaurant Enterprises,* 895 P.2d 243, 244 (N.M. 1995), a patron sued the owner of a restaurant for injuries sustained when metal bleachers, constructed by an independent contractor to allow viewing of a large television screen, collapsed. The court discussed the collateral negligence doctrine:

> [A]n exception to an exception. That is, the general rule is that an employer is not liable for the negligence of an independent contractor. . . . [However,] an owner of property is liable for the negligence of an independent contractor in building or making repairs to structures on that property, once the owner resumes possession. In turn, those exceptions are also subject to an exception — that the owner is not liable for collateral negligence of the contractor or the contractor's employees. . . .

> . . . [Collateral negligence] is limited to negligence that produces a temporarily unsafe condition while the work is in progress. . . .

> . . . Here, Defendant had a nondelegable duty to exercise reasonable care that the bleachers were in a safe condition. The contractor's negligent assembly, therefore, made the complete structure unsafe and affected the result that the owner was under a duty to attain — a result of reasonably safe premises. This was not a situation involving an unsafe condition created only while the work was ongoing. We conclude, as a matter of law, that the negligence of the independent contractor was not collateral negligence, and therefore Defendant is liable for that negligence.

Otero, 895 P.2d at 246-47.

3. *Highly Dangerous Activities.* The Restatement contains several apparently overlapping exceptions to the "independent contractor" rule. One is work which creates a peculiar risk of physical harm to others unless special precautions are taken. Rest. 2d Torts § 416 (1965). Another is § 423, which imposes liability upon the principal for "an activity which threatens a grave risk of serious bodily harm or death unless the instrumentalities used are carefully constructed and maintained. . . ." *Id.* § 423. A third is § 427, work "involving a special danger to others which the employer knows or has reason to know to be inherent in or normal to the work. . . ." *Id.*, § 427. Finally, § 427A makes the principal liable if he employs a contractor to engage in an "abnormally dangerous" activity. *Id.* § 427A.

Should the principal be liable to the employees of a contractor whom he engages to perform an "inherently dangerous" activity? The cases are divided. *King v. Shelby Rural Elec. Coop.,* 502 S.W.2d 659 (Ky. 1973) (yes); *New Mexico Elec. Serv. Co. v. Montanez,* 551 P.2d 634 (N.M. 1976) (no). *See* Francis M. Dougherty, *Liability of an Employer with regards to Inherently Dangerous Work for Injuries to Employees of Independent Contractor,* 34 A.L.R.4th 914 (1984). An owner is likely to contract with another to perform an "inherently dangerous" activity because the owner lacks knowledge of how the activity can be done safely. In such a situation, can the imposition of liability upon the owner foster deterrence? Might the cost of the activity be spread to the enterprise through the contract price? Would it make more sense to impose liability upon the owner only if the contractor's actions which expose the contractor's employees to risks are "obviously improvident" and the principal becomes aware of them? *See, e.g., Scindia Steam Nav. Co. v. De Los Santos,* 451 U.S. 156 (1981).

A principal remains liable for the torts of an independent contractor whom he employs to engage in an "illegal activity." *See King v. Loessin,* 572 S.W.2d 87 (Tex. App. 1978).

In *Falls v. Scott,* 815 P.2d 1104, 1110 (Kan. 1991), the court said defendant landowner could be liable to the plaintiff for damages caused by a "bush hog" mowing machine operated by an independent contractor. The machine threw a piece of wire that struck plaintiff, an adjoining landowner, in the eye. The court cited Rest. 2d Torts § 427 as the basis for liability:

> One who employs an independent contractor to do work involving a special danger to others which the employer knows or has reason to know to be inherent in or normal to the work, or which he contemplates or has reason to contemplate when making the contract, is subject to liability for physical harm caused to such others by the contractor's failure to take reasonable precautions against such danger.

Falls, 572 S.W.2d at 1109.

It also cited § 519-520 as an apparently additional basis of liability. Recall § 519 and 520 of the Second Restatement, *supra,* set out the test for determining whether an activity is abnormally dangerous. Are the bases of liability under § 427 and 519-520 the same?

4. *Imputed Responsibility to Hospitals.* If a health care provider — such as a nurse — is an employee of a doctor or of a hospital, then the doctor or hospital will be vicariously liable for the torts of its employee committed within the scope of employment.

Frequently, however, health care providers are independent contractors, and in that situation there is a tendency to impose vicarious liability based variously on theories of ostensible or apparent agency, estoppel, and nondelegable duty.

The doctrine of ostensible agency or apparent authority is widely applied to hospital emergency room services that are provided by independent contractors. *See, e.g., Paintsville Hosp. Co. v. Rose,* 683 S.W.2d 255 (Ky. 1985).

In a non-emergency situation, the issue of reliance by the patient under an apparent-agent theory can become complicated. In *Sztore v. Northwest Hosp.,* 496 N.E.2d 1200, 1200 (Ill. App. Ct. 1986), the plaintiff underwent a radical mastectomy at defendant hospital in 1975, and subsequently "received radiation therapy during approximately 31 daily sessions at the x-ray department located in defendant hospital." In 1981 she learned "that her right brachial plexus had been permanently damaged as a result to overexposure to radiation in 1975." *Id.* at 1201.

She sued the hospital, which claimed that "the staff of the hospital's x-ray department were neither its actual nor its apparent agents." *Id.* The appellate court reversed a summary judgment for the defendant, holding "that when a person goes to a full service hospital for care and treatment, he or she does so in reliance on the reputation of the institution and the skill and expertise of its personnel." *Id.* at 1202. Patients are "generally unaware of the independent status of the treating physicians," and should not be bound by "secret limitations" contained in a contract between the hospital and physician. *Id.*

Should a hospital, or a doctor, ever tell a patient that the doctor or other medical personnel are independent contractors? If they did, would the patient understand what she was being told? The application of doctrine such as nondelegable duty and ostensible or apparent agency to hospitals for the torts of independent contractor health providers is discussed further in Chapter 9, *infra*.

5. *Imputed Responsibility to Doctors.* A patient in *Long v. Hacker*, 520 N.W.2d 195, 198 (Neb. 1994), brought a medical malpractice action against surgeon Hacker for operating on the wrong vertebra in patient's spine. Dr. Hacker contended that the operation decision was based on an x-ray furnished by a radiologist. The trial court erroneously instructed the jury on "efficient intervening cause," the appellate court said:

> The instruction on efficient intervening cause is improper because Hacker, as head surgeon, was ultimately responsible for any negligent acts or omissions on behalf of himself or the operating team. Hacker might have been negligent in his acts or omissions. The radiologist might have been negligent in his acts or omissions. It is irrelevant in what sequence these negligent acts or omissions might have occurred, because Hacker is ultimately liable for the negligence. Hacker may not escape liability by presenting the negligence of another as an efficient intervening cause.

Long, 520 N.W.2d at 201.

Could this case also have been tried on ostensible or apparent agency?

6. *Partnership.* Generally, one partner is liable for the tortious acts of another partner committed within the scope of the partnership business. *Client's Security Fund v. Grandeau*, 526 N.E.2d 270 (N.Y. 1988). In *Thompson v. Gilmore*, 888 S.W.2d 715, 716-717 (Mo. Ct. App. 1994), the court said a partner could be liable for the tortious act of another partner (negligently allowing the statute of limitations to run on a claim) that occurred after the partnership was dissolved, where the attorney-client relationship of the plaintiff with the partnership was entered into prior to the dissolution. The law "applicable today in Missouri and elsewhere," the court said, is that "dissolution does not relieve the partners for performance of contracts theretofore made." *Id.* at 716.

7. *Car Owner Liability.* A number of jurisdictions impose vicarious liability on the "head of a household" who maintains a car for family use under the "family purpose doctrine." *See, e.g., Camper v. Minor*, 915 S.W.2d 437, 447 (Tenn. 1996) (holding that "the head of a household who maintains a motor vehicle for the general use and convenience of the family is liable for the negligence of any member of the family driving the vehicle, provided the driver received express or implied consent").

Yet another means of imposing vicarious liability is by statutes mandating the use of "omnibus" clauses in automobile liability insurance policies. These clauses "typically extend the definition of the term 'insured' to include 'the named insured and any resident of the household' and 'any other person using such automobile . . . with the permission of the named insured.'" Fowler V. Harper et al., The Law of Torts §8.13 & n.34, at 598 (2d ed. 1986).

8. *Common Carrier Liability.* In *Gilstrap v. Amtrak*, 998 F.2d 559 (8th Cir. 1993), an employee on defendant's train sexually assaulted plaintiff passenger. Finding the defendant vicariously liable under Washington law, the court said a common carrier is "liable for tortious acts committed by its employee against a passenger" even if the employee is acting "outside the scope of his or her employment." *Gilstrap*, 998 F.2d at 561. In support of this proposition, the court cited the Restatement (Second) of Agency which provides:

> [A] master or other principal may be in such relation to another that he has a duty to protect such other from harm although not caused by an enterprise which has been initiated by the master of by things owned or possessed by him. This duty may be created by contract, as where one agrees to protect another, or may be imposed by law as incident to a relation voluntarily entered into, *as the relation of carrier and passenger,* or by statute. . . . [T]he fact that the one to whom the performance of the duty is delegated acts for his own purposes and with no intent to benefit the principal or master is irrelevant.

REST. 2D AGENCY §214 CMT *e* (1958) (emphasis added). The American Law Institute provided the following illustration: "P, a railroad, employs A, a qualified conductor, to take charge of a train. A assaults T, a passenger. P is subject to liability to T." *Id.* §214 cmt e, Illus. 3. Does this imputed responsibility differ from a common carrier's duty under negligence to protect passengers from assaults by employees?

9. *Imputed Responsibility to Franchisors.* In *O'Banner v. McDonald's Corp.*, 653 N.E.2d 1267 (Ill. App. Ct. 1995), a customer injured in a bathroom slip-and-fall incident brought a personal injury action against the franchisor. Holding that the trial judge improperly granted summary judgment for the franchisor, the state court of appeals observed that:

> We see no reason to limit the apparent agency theory of vicarious liability to a hospital setting. Just as patients naturally depend upon their chosen hospital to supervise and take responsibility for the conduct of those who work within the facility, it is logical to conclude that many members of the public have come to believe that franchisors such as McDonald's Corporation are ultimately responsible not only for the quality of the food, but also for the condition of the premises in which it is served. McDonald's Corporation's extensive and visible reach into every aspect of its franchisee's businesses makes such a belief natural. The license agreement included in the record illustrates this fact. Under its terms McDonald's Corporation has undertaken a substantial effort to assure that it alone controls how the public perceives its franchised restaurants.

McDonald's Corporation's "system" is described in its license agreements as being "comprehensive" in scope and offering the public a "uniform" atmosphere. Only designated food and beverages may be served at franchised restaurants. Franchisees are required to use prescribed equipment, building layouts and designs. McDonald's Corporation dictates the level of quality, service and cleanliness throughout the system. All restaurant employees are required to wear uniforms designated by McDonald's Corporation. McDonald's Corporation also dictates management, advertising and personnel policies and additionally runs "Hamburger University," a training facility where its franchisees are required to train their managers. Presumably the employees responsible for maintaining the bathroom facilities where plaintiff was injured wore "McDonald's uniforms" and were required to follow McDonald's prescribed standards of "quality, service and cleanliness."

We find the degree of control exercised by the McDonald's Corporation over its franchisee, including the control exercised over the way in which the franchisee's business is promoted and advertised, to create the potential for members of the public to be misled as to the entity responsible for maintaining the restaurant facilities. The record indicates that McDonald's Corporation is the entity responsible for the relentless stream of commercials which permeate the media, promoting McDonald's restaurants as providing a safe, clean and wholesome atmosphere. It is a question of fact as to whether this type conduct could lead a person such as the plaintiff to enter the premises in reliance upon McDonald's reputation for quality and upon a belief that he was, in fact, dealing with an agent of the McDonald's Corporation.

O'Banner, 653 N.E.2d at 1271.

The state supreme court affirmed summary judgment for the defendant in *O'Banner*, because the plaintiff gave "no indication as to why he went to the restaurant in the first place." *O'Banner v. McDonald's Corp.*, 670 N.E.2d 632, 635 (Ill. 1996). Does this omission in the record reflect a failure by counsel?

2. Imputed Responsibility of the Plaintiff

Imputing responsibility to a defendant expands potential theories of liability and fosters recovery by an injured plaintiff. Does the doctrine of imputed responsibility make sense when it is applied to the injured plaintiff?

LaBIER v. PELLETIER
665 A.2d 1013 (Me. 1995)

Roberts, Justice.

. . . [Monique Pelletier injured Joseph LaBier (age four years and eight months) when her car hit the bicycle he was riding. Joseph's mother Nyla talked with a neighbor as she watched her son ride up and down the neighbor's steeply sloping driveway. On one of his trips down the driveway, Joseph's feet slipped off the pedals of his bike and he lost control, veering into the street. Pelletier estimated her speed at 20 to 25 m.p.h., within the legal limit for that residential neighborhood. She evidently accelerated as she approached the home where Joseph had been playing and her view was unobstructed.]

LaBier's father sued Pelletier on behalf of Joseph, claiming that her negligence caused Joseph's injuries. Pelletier alleged the comparative negligence of Joseph and Nyla as an affirmative defense, and brought a counterclaim against Nyla for contribution, alleging that Nyla's failure to properly supervise Joseph caused the accident. At trial, the court instructed the jury, over LaBier's objection, to consider both Nyla's negligence and Joseph's negligence, and to return a verdict in favor of Joseph only if it found that the combined causative negligence of Joseph and Nyla was less than the causative negligence of Pelletier. The jury found that Joseph was not negligent; that both Nyla and Pelletier were negligent; and that Nyla's negligence was greater than Pelletier's. It therefore awarded no damages to Joseph. The court entered a judgment on the verdict and dismissed Pelletier's counterclaim against Nyla as moot. LaBier's appeal followed.

Although we have stated that the negligence of a parent may be imputed to a child, the parties cite no case, and we find none, in which we have relied exclusively on the doctrine of imputed parental negligence to bar recovery for a child. The instant case squarely presents for the first time the question whether the doctrine of imputed parental negligence is or ought to be the law of Maine.

As the facts of this case demonstrate, the doctrine of imputed parental negligence may deprive an innocent child of a remedy for his injuries. Modern authorities recognize that it is fundamentally unfair to deprive an injured child of a remedy because of actions by the parent that the child is unable to control. As the Supreme Court of Montana recognized over eighty years ago:

> [T]he negligence of the parent, guardian, or custodian is not imputable to the child, because it is in no way responsible for the danger, had no volition in establishing the relation of privity with the person whose negligence it is sought to impute to it, and should not be charged with the fault of such person in allowing it to be exposed to danger which it had not the capacity either to know or to avoid.

Flaherty v. Butte Elec. R.R., 40 Mont. 454, 107 P. 416, 418 (1910). The unfairness of imputed parental negligence is amplified by the fact that in cases like this one the doctrine enables an admittedly blameworthy party to escape liability. Because the policies that support the doctrine, even if valid, fail to justify the unfair result that the doctrine produces, we reject the doctrine of imputed parental negligence. Instead, we adopt the approach of the Restatement, which provides that "[a] child who suffers physical harm is not barred from recovery by the negligence of his parent, either in the parent's custody of the child or otherwise." Restatement (Second) of Torts § 488 (1965).

Pelletier argues that the doctrine of imputed parental negligence grows from the theory of unity between parent and child, similar to the common law fiction of legal unity between husband and wife. Pelletier maintains that the parent is therefore the agent of the child. She relies on *Merchant v. Mansir*, 572 A.2d 493 (Me. 1990), which adopts Restatement (Second) of Torts § 316 (1965), to support her argument that "the parent is the child, and the child the parent in terms of facing both liability and harm vis-à-vis the outside world."

We disagree. In *Black v. Solmitz*, 409 A.2d 634, 635 (Me. 1979), we held for the first time that children may sue their parents. In so doing, we put to rest any possibility that parent and child might be one legal entity. We realized that the common law recognized "no conception of any unity of parent and minor child comparable to the conception of unity of husband and wife." *Id.* at 637. Contrary to Pelletier's contention, "the common law . . . never has made the parent vicariously liable as such for the conduct of the child." W. Page Keeton et al., Prosser and Keeton on the Law of Torts § 123, at 913 (5th ed. 1984) (hereinafter Prosser). Indeed, Prosser refers to the supposed agency of the parent to look after the child as "the sheerest nonsense." *Id.* § 74, at 532.

Pelletier's reliance on *Merchant* and Restatement (Second) of Torts § 316 is misplaced. In *Merchant*, we did not hold that parents are liable for the torts of their children, as Pelletier suggests. We stated that parents may be liable in limited circumstances to third persons who are injured as a result of a breach of a duty of supervision, *citing* Restatement (Second) of Torts § 316. *Merchant*, 572 A.2d at 494. Moreover, the Restatement specifically rejects Pelletier's contention that the parent and child are a single entity for comparative negligence purposes, noting that "[t]he family relation between the parent and child does not so identify the two as to make the parent's negligence a bar to the child's recovery or child's negligence a bar to the parent's recovery." Restatement (Second) of Torts § 488, comment *a* (1965).

Pelletier also argues that imputed parental negligence is necessary to prevent parents from reaping a windfall from their own negligence. Although Pelletier's windfall argument may once have had some validity, modern legal developments have rendered it anachronistic. Historically, the nonparental defendant was unable to seek contribution from a joint tortfeasor who was the plaintiff's parent because a defendant could seek contribution only from a party against whom the plaintiff had a cause of action. Because parents were immune from suit by their children in many jurisdictions, that rule effectively prevented nonparental negligent parties from seeking contribution.

That historical justification for the doctrine of imputed parental negligence has been absent in Maine at least since *Bedell v. Reagan*, 159 Me. 292, 192 A.2d 24 (1963). In that case, we held that the existence of interspousal immunity would not prevent a third-party claim for contribution against a negligent spouse although that spouse was then immune from suit by the injured spouse. Presumably the same analysis was applicable to a third-party claim against a negligent parent who was then immune from suit by a child. The abrogation of parental immunity in *Black*, however, combined with modern third-party practice eliminated any potential unfairness to the nonparental defendant. Accordingly, Pelletier's counterclaim for contribution must be reinstated, and in that context the comparison of the negligence of Pelletier to that of Nyla properly placed before the jury.

Moreover, Pelletier's argument that any tort recovery by a minor child will relieve the parent's obligation to provide for the child is inaccurate. The common law imposes a duty on parents to support their children. The existence of the child's own income or property does not relieve the parent of that duty. In an appropriate case the court may restrict the application of the proceeds of suit for the protection of a minor plaintiff.

Even if the parent might realize some incidental benefit from the child's recovery, it is unfair to remedy that problem by shifting the windfall to the nonparental tortfeasor, thereby stripping the innocent child of any recovery against a negligent nonparental defendant.

Finally, Pelletier contends that a change in a long-standing principle of tort law must be left to the Legislature. "It is fundamental that the rules of common law which are court-made rules can be changed by the court when it becomes convinced that the policies upon which they are based have lost their validity or were mistakenly conceived." *Pendexter*, 363 A.2d at 749. "When principles fail to produce just results, [we have] found a departure from precedent necessary to fulfill [our] role of reasoned decision making." *Adams v. Buffalo Forge Co.*, 443 A.2d 932, 935 (Me. 1982). Assuming that the doctrine of imputing a parent's negligence to the child has been a long-standing principle of Maine tort law, it has outlived whatever limited usefulness it might once have had.

Our decision today adopts the modern view that unanimously rejects the doctrine of imputed parental negligence as "not only unsound, but absurd and inhuman." *Denver City Tramway v. Brown*, 57 Colo. 484, 143 P. 364, 368 (1914). According to Prosser:

> [T]his barbarous rule, which denied to the innocent victim of the negligence of two parties any recovery against either, and visited the sins of the fathers upon the children, was accepted in several American States until it was at one time very nearly the prevailing rule; but it now is abrogated, by statute or by decision everywhere except in Maine, where it should be hoped that it will not long survive.

PROSSER § 74, AT 531-32.

BECAUSE THE TRIAL COURT IN THIS CASE INSTRUCTED THE JURY TO IMPUTE THE NEGLIGENCE OF NYLA TO JOSEPH IN DETERMINING WHETHER JOSEPH WAS ENTITLED TO RECOVERY AGAINST PELLETIER, WE MUST VACATE THE JUDGMENT IN FAVOR OF PELLETIER.

NOTES

1. *Imputation of Child's Fault to the Parent.* Recognizing a division of authority, the court in *Handeland v. Brown*, 216 N.W.2d 574, 579 (Iowa 1974), refused to impute a child's negligence to the father, in an action by the father for medical expenses, loss of services, companionship and society against a tortfeasor who injured the child. The court noted but rejected Rest. 2d Torts §494 (1965):

> The plaintiff is barred from recovery for an invasion of his legally protected interest in the health or life of a third person which results from the harm or death of such third person, if the negligence of such third person would have barred his own recovery.

Handeland, 216 N.W.2d at 575. The Restatement contemplates a situation where contributory negligence is a complete bar. Would the same result be reached in a jurisdiction applying comparative fault?

2. *Loss of Consortium.* In *Tuggle v. Allright Parking Sys., Inc.,* 922 S.W.2d 105 (Tenn. 1996), the court, in reducing a spouse's claim for loss of consortium by the comparative fault of the other spouse, observed that:

> [A] small number of jurisdictions view a claim for loss of consortium as an essentially different and independent cause of action from the physically injured spouse. Based on that premise, those jurisdictions apply the rule that the recovery awarded the spouse claiming loss of consortium is not affected by the fault of the physically injured spouse.
>
> The clear majority of jurisdictions, however, hold that a loss of consortium award must be reduced, and may be barred, by the comparative fault of the physically injured spouse.

Tuggle, 922 S.W.2d at 108-109.

The court gave as the rationale for the majority rule:

> [T]here must be a tort which gives rise to a cause of action that must be maintained by the [physically] injured spouse in order for the non-injured spouse to claim a loss of consortium. In other words, the loss of consortium claim is dependent upon the negligent injury of the other spouse who has the primary tort cause of action.

Id.

The court added that the imputed-fault approach also fostered family harmony:

> If a claim for loss of consortium were viewed as totally independent of the other spouse's personal injury claim, there would be no reason to preclude one spouse from suing another for loss of consortium or to prohibit the primary tortfeasor sued in a consortium claim from impleading the spouse who suffered the personal injuries.

Id.

Compare *Massengale v. Pitts,* 737 A.2d 1029 (D.C. 1999) (contributory negligence of spouse does not affect other spouse's consortium claim).

3. *Impact of Comparative Fault and Joint and Several Liability.* The problems of imputed contributory negligence may disappear when a jurisdiction adopts pure comparative fault and abolishes joint and several liability among joint tortfeasors. In such a case, the fault of each person will be quantified, and the victim can recover from the nonparental or nonemployer tortfeasor only for the percentage of fault chargeable to that tortfeasor. But some courts will not allocate fault to a party against whom the plaintiff has no legal claim, *e.g.,* because of immunity. *See Ridings v. Ralph M. Parsons Co.,* 914 S.W. 2d 79 (Tenn. 1996) (employer workers' compensation immunity).

PROBLEMS

8.1

Orialle took her dog, suspected of having contracted the rabies virus, to a veterinary clinic for quarantine and observation. The dog escaped from the clinic. A week after its escape, the dog bit Viola on a public highway. After being bitten, Viola ran from the dog and while running was stung to death by Ballimore's bees. Discuss the possible liability of the clinic, Orialle, and Ballimore to Viola's estate.

8.2

The Restatement (Second) of Torts, discussing strict liability for "abnormally dangerous activity," prescribes the weighing of several factors to determine whether an activity is abnormally dangerous. Several of these factors resemble the elements of Judge Learned Hand's *Carroll Towing Company* formula for measuring whether conduct is negligent (Chapter 4, *supra*). Which Restatement factor or factors is/are different from the elements of negligence?

8.3

Quick Pizza, Inc. grants franchises for the operation of "Pizza Quick" restaurants. In exchange for the franchise fee, the franchisee receives the benefit of national and cooperative local advertising (Quick Pizza, Inc. subsidizes the local franchisee's advertising in an amount up to 10% of the gross advertising, or $5,000, whichever is greater). Quick Pizza, Inc. also provides training of the franchisee and its employees for the initial startup of the franchise restaurant, and makes semiannual inspections. The franchise agreement gives Quick Pizza, Inc., the right to cancel the franchise if the restaurant is not operated within the general minimum standards adopted by Quick Pizza, Inc. Quick Pizza, Inc. also sells restaurant supplies to the franchisee; however, the franchisee is only obligated to purchase $10,000 per year in supplies, and may obtain other supplies elsewhere.

The national advertising, and the franchisor's policy, provide that a pizza will be delivered to a customer's home or place of business within 20 minutes after the order is placed; if it is not, the customer receives the pizza without charge. The local franchisee in the present case, Mr. Jones, employs college students and other young people to deliver his pizzas. The delivery person must furnish her own vehicle and pay all of her expenses. She is provided with a portable "Pizza Quick" sign which she is required to display atop her vehicle while delivering pizzas. Jones pays the delivery person a fee of 25% of the cost of the pizza for each order delivered; however, if the order is not delivered within the 20-minute period, the delivery person receives no fee. Jones provides delivery persons with a map showing the shortest routes to areas from which orders frequently are placed, but he does not require that any particular route be taken. A delivery person is not required to work a given schedule, but must be available three evenings a week to retain her position. Jones also requires that each delivery person have a valid driver's license and maintain the minimum compulsory insurance required by law ($10,000 each person, $20,000 each accident).

On the day in question, Simoni, a college graduate student, is delivering a pizza for Jones. However, he notices that he has left his driver's license at his home. Because the delivery is a "gimme," *i.e.,* one in which delivery can easily be made in 5 to 10 minutes, and is in the neighborhood where he lives, Simoni decides to drop by his home and pick up his license en route to the customer's residence. He turns off the most direct route from the pizza restaurant to the customer, and begins the three-block detour to his house. In the second block, he fails to observe a stop sign, enters the intersection, and strikes a vehicle driven by Kildare. Kildare, a young physician, is rendered a quadriplegic in the accident.

Discuss Kildare's claims against Quick Pizza, Inc. (the franchisor) and Jones (the franchisee).

8.4

Wife, husband and child were involved in an automobile collision with defendant, another automobile driver. Wife was driving the family car, and husband and child were passengers in the car, at the time of the collision. Wife was 20% at fault, and defendant 80% at fault. Husband and child were injured in the collision.

Child sues wife (his mother) and the other driver for damages resulting from his personal injuries. Husband sues his wife and the other driver for his personal injuries, the child's medical expenses and loss of the child's services and companionship, loss of the wife's consortium, and damage to the family car. Should the wife's fault be imputed to the husband's or the child's claims? If so, which claims?

Chapter 9

PROFESSIONAL LIABILITY

A. INTRODUCTION

The most common types of tort claims for negligent provision of services are those brought against professionals, and generally are called malpractice claims. Professional malpractice claims apply negligence and occasionally intentional tort principles to typically complex factual situations in cases that frequently turn on expert testimony.

Of the malpractice or professional liability claims, the more frequent and most controversial is medical malpractice. According to the Institute of Medicine between 48,000 and 98,000 Americans die in hospitals every year because of preventable medical errors. One million more are injured.[1] In other areas of tort law, such as products liability (discussed in Chapter 10, *infra*), the courts have developed rules that shift most of the risks associated with an activity (such as using products) away from plaintiffs (consumers) to defendants (product sellers). In contrast, the somewhat conservative law of professional liability shifts relatively few risks away from patients to healthcare providers. This observation seems to run counter to our familiarity with widely reported malpractice "crises" of the 1970s, 1980s, and late 1990s and frequent legislative reforms apparently premised on a belief that the malpractice system is shifting *too many* risks to doctors, hospitals, and managed care organizations. These legislative retrenchments are discussed in Chapter 16.

B. THE PROFESSIONAL RELATIONSHIP

IRVIN v. SMITH
272 Kan. 112 (2001)

ABBOTT, JUSTICE.

. . . Irvin was born 6 weeks premature with hydrocephalus, a condition which required the surgical placement of a ventriculoperitoneal or "VP" shunt. The shunt is a pump with a tube. The tube extends from the brain to the abdomen. The purpose of the shunt is to drain excess cerebrospinal fluid from the skull. Once the fluid is drained from the brain, it is reabsorbed into the body through the abdomen. Without the shunt, Irvin would die. With a properly operating shunt, however, a hydrocephalic can live a normal life. The shunt was placed in Irvin at 2 days of age by her neurosurgeon, Dr. Edwin MacGee.

---

[1] Institute of Medicine, Committee on Quality of Health Care in America, To Err Is Human: Building a Safer Health System (Linda Kohn et al., eds. 1999).

On October 15, 1995, 12-year-old Irvin began experiencing flu-like symptoms and seizures. She also complained of neck and back pain. On October 18, Irvin was transported by life flight from Bob Wilson Memorial Hospital in Ulysses, Kansas, to St. Luke's Hospital in Kansas City, Missouri. At St. Luke's, Irvin was examined by MacGee to determine whether the shunt was working properly. During the 12 years the shunt had been in place, MacGee had performed two other surgeries on the shunt.

On October 19, MacGee determined there was no shunt malfunction. MacGee recalled speaking to an unidentified radiologist about the shunt. . . . On October 21, Irvin was discharged and went home. The x-rays taken at St. Luke's, however, revealed at trial that the distal end of the shunt tubing had pulled up into the abdomen wall due to Irvin's growth, intermittently blocking the flow of cranial fluid into the abdominal cavity.

On October 23, 1995, MacGee wrote Dr. Michael Shull, Irvin's pediatrician in Garden City, Kansas, and told him that the "shunt appeared to be working well."

Irvin's seizures, nausea, vomiting, and neck and back pain soon returned. On November 12, Irvin was admitted to St. Catherine's Hospital in Garden City, Kansas. At St. Catherine's Hospital, Irvin was examined by Shull. Shull worried that the shunt had malfunctioned. X-rays were taken of Irvin's chest and abdomen. The radiologist concluded that no abnormalities were present and reported nothing wrong with the shunt tubing . . .

Irvin continued to experience nausea, vomiting, neck pain, and seizures on November 13 and 14. On November 14, Shull ordered Irvin to be transported by life-flight from St. Catherine's Hospital to Wesley Medical Center (Wesley) in Wichita, Kansas. Prior to her transfer, Shull spoke with Smith, a pediatric intensivist, at Wesley. Shull and Smith discussed Irvin's condition, history, symptoms, Shull's concern about her seizures, and the possibility of a shunt malfunction . . .

Smith admitted Irvin at Wesley with x-ray films which showed the outlet or "tip" of her shunt embedded in the muscle of her abdominal wall in a position requiring that it be repaired. Smith testified that he could not remember whether he looked at the x-ray films, however. He admitted that had he looked at the films he would have seen that the shunt needed to be repaired. Smith explained that he could not remember looking at the x-ray films because he was led to believe that a radiologist in Garden City had already read the x-rays and had concluded that they were "negative." No doctor in Garden City ever looked at Irvin's x-ray films.

On November 14, Smith made a telephone call to obtain a "neurological consult" from Gilmartin, a child neurologist, because Smith thought that Gilmartin was "the best consultant to use to help evaluate Ashley." Gilmartin and Smith discussed performing a shuntogram. A shuntogram is a procedure which involves injection of a radioactive isotope into the shunt to check for shunt blockage. After the consultation, a shuntogram and EEG were ordered for the following morning to be performed by Gilmartin and Smith. Gilmartin and Smith planned to do the shuntogram the next morning because Irvin appeared stable, alert, and conscious between seizures. Neither Smith nor

Gilmartin believed that her symptoms indicated an impending shunt malfunction.

The next morning, November 15, Irvin was alert, awake, and verbal. At approximately 8:45 a.m., however, prior to any tests being performed to determine the status of the shunt, Irvin's condition deteriorated, became critical, and required that she be resuscitated and intubated.

At approximately 11:30 a.m., Irvin's condition became worse as her pupils dilated and became unresponsive to light. The shuntogram was finally performed, and it was determined that the shunt was obstructed. Surgery was performed to correct the shunt malfunction.

Prior to undergoing the shuntogram procedure, Irvin suffered permanent and severe brain damage . . . Since her discharge, Irvin has received continuous care, treatment, and rehabilitation. Irvin's condition requires that she be fed through a gastrostomy tube. Irvin is unable to walk or speak, is incontinent, and requires full-time care.

[Plaintiffs field suit against multiple health care providers, including Dr. Gilmartin] Gilmartin moved for summary judgment, arguing that he owed no duty to Irvin as there was no physician-patient relationship. The district court agreed and granted summary judgment in favor of Gilmartin . . .

The plaintiff in a medical malpractice case bears the burden of proof in establishing the elements of the negligence claim. The existence of the duty of care is dependent on the existence of a physician-patient relationship . . .

Courts have concluded, as has this court, that whether a physician-patient relationship exists is generally a question of fact for the jury . . .

A physician-patient relationship may be found and summary judgment may be considered, however, "where the facts are shown by such clear, palpable, and undisputed evidence that the jury could reasonably draw but one conclusion." *Walker v. Jack Eckerd Corp.*, 209 Ga. App. 517, 524 (1993).

Generally, a physician-patient relationship is created only where the physician personally examines the patient. *Millard v. Corrado*, 14 S.W.3d 42, 49 (Mo. App. 1999). A physician's indirect contact with a patient, however, does not preclude the finding of a physician-patient relationship. *Adams v. Via Christi Regional Med. Center*, 270 Kan. 824, 835, 19 P.3d 132 (2001) . . . A physician-patient relationship may be found where a physician is contacted by someone on behalf of the patient. *Reynolds*, 277 Ill. App. 3d 80, 85 (1996). Indeed, an implied physician-patient relationship may be found where the physician gives advice to a patient by communicating the advice through another health care professional. *Campbell v. Haber*, 274 A.D.2d 946, 946-47, 710 N.Y.S.2d 495 (2000).

A physician who gives an "informal opinion," however, at the request of a treating physician, does not owe a duty to the patient because no physician-patient relationship is created. *See Oliver v. Brock*, 342 So.2d 1, 4 (Ala. 1976) (no physician-patient relationship found where physician never met with patient, did not even know the patient's name, and merely conversed with treating physician on "gratuitous" basis); *Hill v. Kokosky*, 186 Mich. App. 300,

304, 463 N.W.2d 265 (1990) (opinion directed at treating physician to do with "as he saw fit" does not create physician-patient relationship); *Reynolds,* 277 Ill. App. 3d at 85 (informal opinion from consulting physician at request of treating physician does not create physician-patient relationship); *Lopez v. Aziz*, 852 S.W.2d 303, 306 (Tex. Civ. App. 1993) (physician cannot be liable where he or she merely consulted with treating physician and nothing more). A physician who assumes the role of treating the patient, however, can be liable for medical malpractice. *Tumblin [v. Ball-Incon Glass Packing Corp.* 324 S.C. 359, 365 (Ct. App. 1996)], 324 S.C. 359, at 365 (1996) . . .

In the present case, Irvin argues that the undisputed facts show that there was a physician-patient relationship between Gilmartin and Irvin and that the district court erred in granting summary judgment in favor of Gilmartin. The facts, Irvin argues, show that Gilmartin received a lengthy telephone call from Smith during which they engaged in a detailed conversation about the condition, care, and treatment of Irvin. Gilmartin was called because of his experience and expertise as a pediatric neurologist. Gilmartin was not an employee of the hospital and was not "on call" the night he received the phone call from Smith. As a result of the conversation, Gilmartin testified he had a "complete picture of Ashley Irvin's presentation" and that he had surmised that Irvin's condition was "stable." Gilmartin further testified that he and Smith "jointly developed a plan for the evaluation of Ashley Irvin" and that he assumed primary responsibility for performing the shuntogram tests the next day.

Before receiving a call from Smith on November 14, 1995, Gilmartin had never had contact with Irvin or her family and had no involvement of any kind in her medical care. Clearly up to that point, there was no physician-patient relationship. Gilmartin was not "on call" on November 14, 1995, and was subject to no contractual obligation which would require him to attend any patients at Wesley.

During the evening of November 14, 1995, Smith called Gilmartin and asked him to perform a consultation on Irvin. The working diagnosis at the time was new onset seizure disorder, with concern over possible shunt malfunction. The two doctors discussed the case and it was agreed that Gilmartin would see the patient the next morning, carry out a formal consultation, and assist in conducting the diagnostic test known as a shuntogram. Gilmartin's position is that he had no duty as a physician until he assumed a physician-patient relationship with Irvin on the morning of November 15, 1995. Without a legal duty, there can be no compensable negligence.

Whether a physician owes a legal duty to a patient under a particular circumstance is a question of law. It is not a question of fact or of negligence. Absent the existence of a physician-patient relationship, there can be no liability for medical malpractice . . .

Here, the sole involvement of Gilmartin was as a private practitioner who had been asked to carry out a consultation the following day. The formal consultation refers to a full bedside review of the case which includes a physical examination of the patient. At the time Gilmartin spoke with Smith, Gilmartin had not examined Irvin, had not reviewed her hospital chart, and had never spoken with either her or her parents. The only information he had was what he had been told by Smith. There is no claim that Gilmartin entered any orders in the case or took any other action other than discussing the case in general terms with Smith and agreeing to consult the next day. This, by itself, does not create a physician-patient relationship.

This case, to a large extent, boils down to public policy concerns. The type of telephone conversation that took place here takes place on a frequent basis in the medical profession and is vital to the treatment of patients. For the courts to discourage such conversations is not to the patients' or the public's best interests.

Courts have used great caution when responding to requests that they recognize legal duties within this medically important but legally ambiguous world of the curbside consultation. Indeed, the published decisions are unanimous in agreeing that extension of the physician-patient relationship to include this type of informal consultation would be contrary to public policy. "Imposition of liability under these circumstances would not be prophylactic but instead counter-productive by stifling efforts at improving medical knowledge. *Rainer v. Grossman,* 31 Cal. App. 3d 539, 544 (1973). A good expression of these public policy concerns appears in *Reynolds v. Decatur Memorial Hosp.,* 277 Ill. App. 3d 80, 86 (1996), as follows:

> Plaintiffs suggest that what needs to be done is to find a physician-patient relationship to result from every such conversation. The consequence of such a role would be significant. It would have a chilling effect upon practice of medicine. It would stifle communication, education and professional association, all to the detriment of the patient. The likely effect in adopting plaintiffs' argument also would be that such informal conferences would no longer occur.

Courts have taken these public policy concerns to heart and have routinely refused to extend liability for medical malpractice to doctors who have acted solely in the role of an informal or curbside consultant. This has been true even when the doctors' involvement in giving advice to the attending physician has been very extensive. In *NBD Bank v. Barry*, 223 Mich. App. 370 (1997), for example, the patient's attending physician, Dr. Miller, contacted the defendant, Dr. Barry, "on multiple occasions" asking his opinion of the patient's case. Not only did Barry discuss the case and make recommendations to Miller, he apparently even reviewed the chart once with Miller. However, Barry did not formally consult on the case and never contacted or examined the patient. In upholding summary judgment for Barry, the court concluded that contacts with Miller fell into the context of an informal consultation which did not create a physician-patient relationship with the patient. Absent such a relationship, Barry owed no duty of care to the patient. While he had offered opinions to Miller, these "were simply recommendations that Miller was free to accept or reject." 223 Mich. App. at 373.

The same result was reached in *Reynolds*, 277 Ill. App. 3d 80, a case with facts strikingly similar to the present case. There, a young boy who came to the emergency room had a history of falling at home. A pediatrician, Dr. Bonds, was called to the emergency room and assessed the child. The child had a fever of 102 degrees. At this point, Bonds called a colleague, Dr. Fulbright, and gave him a run down on the child's condition. Fulbright asked if the child had a stiff neck; Bonds checked and reported that he did. At the conclusion of the conversation, Fulbright recommended that a spinal tap be performed to rule out meningitis or a similar infectious process; this was done by Bonds. Unfortunately, the child was ultimately found to have had a spinal cord injury as opposed to an infectious process. His injuries left him permanently quadriplegic. The plaintiffs' expert witnesses in the case alleged that Fulbright had been negligent in making recommendations without first examining the patient. In rejecting this claim, the trial court granted summary judgment to Fulbright. On appeal, the court upheld the summary judgment concluding that there was no evidence that Fulbright had ever developed a physician-patient relationship with the patient. Of particular importance to this case, the court concluded that the law does not "require a physician to enter into a physician-patient relationship with every person treated in the hospital whose treating physician might make an informal inquiry about that case." 277 Ill. App. 3d at 86.

We conclude that Gilmartin was under no legal duty to go to the hospital on November 14, 1995; thus, his failure to do so cannot constitute a breach of duty to support a claim of negligence . . . [AFFIRMED].

LOCKETT, J., dissenting.

. . . The majority asserts that the sole involvement of Gilmartin was as a private practitioner who had been asked to carry out a formal consultation the following day. The majority states that a formal consultation requires (1) a full bedside review of the case and (2) a physical examination of the patient. The majority notes that at the time Gilmartin spoke with Smith, Gilmartin had not examined Irvin, had not reviewed her hospital chart, and had never spoken with her or her parents. The only information he had was what Smith had told him. The majority observes that there is no claim that Gilmartin entered any orders in the case or took any other action other than discussing the case in general terms with Smith and agreeing to "formally" consult the next day.

After disregarding facts favorable to the plaintiff and our prior law that the creation of the physician-patient relationship is a question of fact, the majority reveals its intent to create public policy . . .

Citing *Millard v. Corrado*, 14 S.W.3d 42, 49 (Mo. App. 1999), the majority asserts that generally, a physician-patient relationship is created only where the physician personally examines the patient. The majority then acknowledges our contrary statement in *Adams v. Via Christi Regional Medical Center*, 270 Kan. 824, 835 (2001), that a physician's indirect contact with a patient does not preclude the finding of a physician-patient relationship. The majority acknowledges that a physician-patient relationship does not require a formal contract and may be implied by the circumstances. It notes that a physician-patient relationship may be found where a physician is contacted by someone on behalf of the patient. The majority states that an implied physician-patient relationship may be found where the physician gives advice to a patient by communicating the advice through another health care professional.

Ignoring the law it has just acknowledged, the majority asserts that a physician who gives an informal opinion at the request of a treating physician does not owe a duty to the patient because no physician-patient relationship is created. It points out that a physician cannot be liable where he or she merely consults with a treating physician and nothing more.

. . . The record on appeal shows that Gilmartin was called by Irvin's treating physician, Smith because of Gilmartin's experience and expertise as a pediatric neurologist. Gilmartin was not an employee of the hospital and was not "on call" the night he received the phone call from Smith. Gilmartin and Smith had a detailed conversation about the condition, care, and treatment of Irvin. The majority fails to take into account Gilmartin's testimony that during the telephone conversation Gilmartin and Smith "jointly developed a plan for the evaluation of Ashley Irvin," and Gilmartin agreed to assume primary responsibility for performing the shuntogram tests the next day . . .

Most confusing is the majority's broad statement that a physician who gives an "informal opinion" at the request of a treating physician does not owe a duty to the patient because no physician-patient relationship is created. The majority fails to note the difference between an "informal opinion" and a "formal opinion." It also fails to recognize that there are consulting physicians whose role in a patient's case is limited to offering an opinion or suggestion to the treating physician and there are consulting physicians who advise treating physicians by aiding them in formulating a treatment plan for the patient . . .

I find the reasoning in *Diggs v. Arizona Cardiologists, Ltd.*, 198 Ariz. 198 (Ariz. App. 2000), to be persuasive. After an emergency room physician consulted with the cardiologist, he released the patient who died of a heart attack 3 hours later. The *Diggs* court found that the cardiologist who informally consulted with the emergency room physician owed a duty of care to the patient brought to the hospital with severe chest pain. It noted that the lack of an express contractual physician-patient relationship between the cardiologist and the patient was not dispositive. It then observed that only the cardiologist had the expertise to interpret the echocardiogram to rule out myocardial infarction on the basis of the electrocardiogram and determine further treatment.

The *Diggs* court reasoned that the cardiologist was in a unique position to prevent further harm to the patient. The cardiologist, with his superior knowledge and experience, was in the best position to correct any error in the emergency room doctor's diagnosis . . .

The *Diggs* court, taking the undisputed facts and all inferences therefrom in a light most favorable to Diggs, found that the consulting doctor undertook to provide his expertise to the treating physician, knowing that it was necessary for the protection of Diggs and that the treating physician would rely on it. The treating physician needed the specialized knowledge of the expert. The record indicated that the treating physician did not exercise independent judgment as to Diggs' diagnosis; rather, he subordinated his professional judgment to that of the specialist. The court concluded that the specialist effectively became a provider of medical treatment to Diggs and that relationship gave rise to a duty of reasonable care . . .

To reach its conclusion, the majority characterized Gilmartin's involvement as an informal consultant and cites the public policy of encouraging physicians to converse with other physicians regarding patient care. To reach its goal, the majority ignores the fact that Gilmartin's involvement was more than informal. It was Gilmartin's assessment and recommendations for care that directly influenced the course of Irvin's treatment. Gilmartin, in consultation with Smith, determined that a shuntogram was necessary and agreed to perform the shuntogram the next day. These facts indicate a physician-patient relationship. During the telephone conversation, it was Gilmartin and Smith's decision to wait until the next day to perform the shuntogram on Irvin. The decision to delay medical treatment caused Irvin's injuries. Under our present law, Gilmartin should not be relieved of his physician-patient relationship merely because he had not yet met Irvin. The decision that delayed the care and treatment of Irvin until the next morning was based on Gilmartin's experience and expertise.

The district court's grant of summary judgment to Gilmartin should be reversed. Gilmartin's actions on the night of November 14 and his agreement to perform the shuntogram on Irvin the next day are sufficient facts to submit to the jury the question of whether Gilmartin had a physician-patient relationship with Irvin.

NOTES

1. *Fact or Law?* Did the majority opinion in *Irvin* consider the question of whether a physician-patient relationship existed to be one of fact or law? What about the dissenter? If the majority favored a bright line rule for consultations, what are the operational criteria?

2. *Third Parties' Physicians.* Frequently, patients interact with physicians acting on behalf of third parties, such as a life insurer or an employer. In such case what relationship and duties are created? In *Webb v. T.D.*, 951 P.2d 1008 (Mont. 1997), the plaintiff who suffered a work-related back injury, was referred to an orthopedic surgeon by the workers' compensation insurance carrier of the employer. The surgeon examined her and reviewed a CAT scan he had ordered. He then contacted her by letter ("I have reviewed the CAT scan, and it looks excellent. There is no evidence of a ruptured disc") and cleared her return to work. Subsequently, she suffered an additional back injury and brought an action against the surgeon for negligent diagnosis. The surgeon argued the absence of a physician-patient relationship. Reversing the defendant's summary judgment the court noted:

> We do not, by this opinion, conclude that physicians retained by third parties who perform independent medical examinations have the same duty of care that a physician has to his or her own patient. The scope of the duty attendant to an independent medical examination must necessarily be developed on a case-by-case basis . . .

> What we do hold, in this case, is that a health care provider . . . who is retained by a third party to do an independent medical examination has the following duties:

> 1. To exercise ordinary care to discover those conditions which pose an imminent danger to the examinee's physical or mental well-being and

take reasonable steps to communicate to the examinee the presence of any such condition; and

2. To exercise ordinary care to assure that when he or she advises an examinee about her condition following an independent examination, the advice comports with the standard of care for that health care provider's profession.

Is this a matter of duty or of standard of care? Can the third party's physician avoid the duty by eschewing direct communications with the patient?

3. *Doctors Refusing to Treat.* AMA, PRINCIPLES OF MEDICAL ETHICS (2001) VI provides:

A physician shall, in the provision of appropriate patient care, except in emergencies, be free to choose whom to serve, with whom to associate, and the environment in which to provide medical care.

At common law a general rule that healthcare providers do not owe a positive duty to treat has long been applied in favor of physicians. For example, in *Childs v. Weis,* 440 S.W.2d 104 (Tex. Civ. App. 1969), a pregnant woman went to an emergency room complaining of bleeding and contractions. The nurse on duty telephoned the non-employee emergency room doctor who was on call and told him of the symptoms. The doctor told the nurse to tell the woman to contact her own doctor and to get his advice. The woman left the hospital, and an hour later gave birth in her car to a child who died within a few hours. The court held that no evidence had been presented which would support a finding of the creation of a physician-patient relationship. However, in essentially similar cases, hospital records or other evidence tending to indicate some direct contact between the physician and patient have been held to preclude summary judgment on the issue of whether a relationship had been established. *See Easter v. Lexington Mem. Hosp.,* 303 N.C. 303 (1981); *Willoughby v. Wilkins,* 65 N.C. App. 626 (1983).

4. *Abandonment.* Decoding whether there is a physician-patient relationship has importance beyond cases turning on when or if a relationship *commenced.* Physicians who fail to treat patients whom they have not terminated may be liable for the tort of abandonment. In *Marshall v. Klebanov*, 188 N.J. 23 (2006), the patient was being treated for depression by the defendant psychiatrist. She went to the doctor's office for a scheduled appointment but left before being seen by the doctor, allegedly because she did not have money to pay for the visit and the office did not accept credit cards. Two days later she committed suicide. The defendant argued that a state statute that limited mental health practitioners' *Tarasoff* liability (see the discussion in Chapter 7) afforded him immunity. The court held that the statute did not apply "if the practitioner abandons a seriously depressed patient and fails to treat the patient in accordance with accepted standards of care in the field."

5. *Hospitals Refusing Patients.* The position at common law was stated in *Birmingham Baptist Hosp. v. Crews,* 229 Ala. 398, 157 So. 224, 225 (1934), a case dealing with a highly contagious patient who was stabilized, but then told to leave the hospital. The court held that a private hospital "owes the public no duty to accept any patient not desired by it . . . [and it need not] assign any reason for its refusal to accept a patient for hospital service." Some courts have suggested a broader rule of liability applies to hospitals that have emergency rooms by analogy to REST. 2D TORTS § 323 because a refusal to treat "might well result in worsening the condition of the injured person, because of the time lost in a useless attempt to obtain medical aid." *Wilmington General Hospital v. Manlove*, 174 A.2d 135 (Del. 1961). Other courts have relied on broader public policy grounds evidenced by state regulation of hospitals. See *Guerrero v. Copper Queen Hosp.*, 537 P.2d 1329 (Ariz. 1975).

The modern position is informed by the *Emergency Medical Treatment and Active Labor Act* (EMTALA), 42 U.S.C. § 1395, which requires Medicare-participating hospitals that offer emergency services to, "provide for an appropriate medical screening examination within the capability of the hospital's emergency department." If the hospital "determines that the individual has an emergency medical condition or is in active labor" it must "stabilize the medical condition" or "provide for treatment of the labor." Any subsequent transfer of the patient requires the consent of the receiving facility. EMTALA is enforced through civil penalties and suspension or termination of the hospital's Medicare provider agreement. In addition, an individual patient who is harmed by breach of these provisions has a private right of action against the hospital. As interpreted by the federal courts, however, EMTALA generally protects against discriminatory treatment of uninsured or impecunious patients rather than imposing any broader negligence-based duty of care. See the summary of recent case law in *Morgan v. N. Miss. Med. Ctr., Inc.*, 458 F. Supp. 2d 1341 (S.D. Ala. 2006):

> [T]he law is clear that EMTALA does not establish a federal medical malpractice cause of action. See *Harry v. Marchant*, 291 F.3d 767, 770 (11th Cir. 2002)(EMTALA "was not intended to be a federal malpractice statute"); *Hoffman v. Tonnemacher*, 425 F. Supp. 2d 1120, 1130 (E.D. Cal. 2006)("EMTALA does not establish a federal malpractice cause of action nor does it establish a national standard of care). Claims that a physician or other health care provider failed properly to detect or discern the existence or severity of an emergency medical condition are not generally redressable under EMTALA, but are instead relegated to the state-law province of medical malpractice law. *See, e.g., Marshall v. East Carroll Parish Hosp. Service Dist.*, 134 F.3d 319, 323 (5th Cir. 1998) ("a treating physician's failure to appreciate the extent of the patient's injury or illness, as well as a subsequent failure to order an additional diagnostic procedure, may constitute negligence or malpractice, but cannot support an EMTALA claim").

Id. at 1352.

6. *Racial, Ethnic, and Class Disparities.* To what extent has the general common law rule requiring a consensual relationship between physician (or healthcare institution) and patient caused or exacerbated the disparities in healthcare access and quality that affect large numbers of the poor and those in minority groups? Rather than merely deterring "patient dumping," has EMTALA had the unintended result of providing an emergency room-based "safety net" for those without health insurance?

C. STANDARDS AND EVIDENCE

From the first reported malpractice cases, it has been clear that the pre-dominant standard is "custom," which must be established through expert testimony. *Slater v. Baker & Stapleton,* 2 Wils. K.B. 359, 95 Eng. Rep. 860, 863 (1767); *Cross v. Guthery,* 2 Root 90, 91 (Conn. 1794). If a medical defendant's conduct complies with the relevant customary medical standards, then she cannot be found liable merely because an expert medical witness testifies that "he personally" would have pursued a different course. *Boyce v. Brown,* 77 P.2d 455 (Ariz. 1938).

There has long been a debate whether this customary standard is "local" or "national" and, therefore, whether the testifying experts should be drawn from a local or national pool. The famous case of *Small v. Howard,* 128 Mass. 131 (1880), involved a plaintiff who had suffered a severe glass wound to his wrist, severing both arteries and tendons. The defendant was a physician and sur-geon in a country town of some 2500 inhabitants. An eminent surgeon resided within four miles. Defendant treated plaintiff for ten days but did not refer him to any other surgeon. Over the plaintiff's objection, the jury was instructed that the defendant, "undertaking to practice as a physician and surgeon in a town of comparatively small population, was bound to possess that skill only which physicians and surgeons of ordinary ability and skill, practicing in similar localities, with opportunities for no larger experience, ordinarily pos-sess." The jury found for the defendant and the Massachusetts Supreme Court affirmed, stating:

> It is a matter of common knowledge that a physician in a small coun-try village does not usually make a specialty of surgery, and, however well informed he may be in the theory of all parts of his profession, he would, generally speaking, be but seldom called upon as a surgeon to perform difficult operations. He would have but few opportunities of observation and practice in that line such as public hospitals or large cities would afford.

Most courts now apply a national standard of care. For example, in *Hall v. Hilbun,* 466 So. 2d 856, 870 (Miss. 1985) (given in Chapter 4), the court stated:

> We would have to put our heads in the sand to ignore the "nationaliza-tion" of medical education and training. Medical school admission standards are similar across the country. Curricula are substantially the same. Internship and residency programs for those entering medi-cal specialties have substantially common components. Nationally uniform standards are enforced in the case of certification of special-ists. Differences and changes in these areas occur temporally, not geo-graphically.

Id. at 870.

Hall adopted the following statement of the standard of care:

> The duty of care, as it thus emerges from considerations of reason and fairness, when applied to the facts of the world of medical science and

practice, takes two forms: (a) a duty to render a quality of care consonant with the level of medical and practical knowledge the physician
may reasonably be expected to possess and the medical judgment he
may be expected to exercise, and (b) a duty based upon the adept use
of such medical facilities, services, equipment and options as are reasonably available.

Id. at 872.

As to the first duty the court saw no reason to place any geographic limitations on the expert who could testify or the substance of that testimony. As to
the second duty the court noted:

> Before the witness may go further, he must be familiarized with the
> facilities, resources, services and options available. This may be done
> in any number of ways. The witness may prior to trial have visited the
> facilities, etc. He may have sat in the courtroom and listened as other
> witnesses described the facilities. He may have known and over the
> years interacted with physicians in the area. There are no doubt many
> other ways in which this could be done, but, significantly, we should
> allow the witness to be made familiar with the facilities (and customs)
> of the medical community in question via a properly predicated and
> phrased hypothetical question.

> Once he has become informed of the facilities, etc. available to the
> defendant physician, the qualified medical expert witness may express
> an opinion what the care duty of the defendant physician was and
> whether the acts or omissions of the defendant physician were in com-
> pliance with, or fell substantially short of compliance with, that duty.

Id. at 875.

A few jurisdictions (some because of legislative mandate) continue to
instruct on a locality standard. For example, in *Estate of Hagedorn v. Peterson*,
690 N.W.2d 84 (Iowa 2004), the court gave the following instruction, "A physician must use the degree of skill, care, and learning ordinarily possessed and
exercised by other physicians in similar circumstances. The locality of practice
in question is one circumstance to take into consideration but is not an absolute limit upon the skill required." Affirming a defense verdict the court noted,
"the facilities, personnel, services, and equipment reasonably available to a
physician continue to be circumstances relevant to the appropriateness of the
care rendered by the physician to the patient." Does not *Hall v. Hilbun* adequately incorporate this into a national standard? Wherein lies the practical
distinction?

The obvious effect of a national standard of care is to provide the litigants
with the widest possible pool of experts. Does it favor expert-shopping plaintiffs over defendants? Does this therefore translate into a greater redistribution of medical care injuries? Are there any other justifications for a national
standard of care? Consider the purposes and goals of both alternatives.

NOWATSKE v. OSTERLOH
198 Wis. 2d 419 (1996)

ABRAHAMSON, JUDGE.

. . . One morning the plaintiff noticed an area of blurred vision in his right eye. He was referred to the defendant, a retina specialist in Oshkosh, who diagnosed him as having a retinal detachment . . .

The defendant elected to conduct a relatively common procedure, known as scleral buckling, in an effort to reattach the retina. Buckling procedures may raise the intraocular pressure (IOP) in the eye, resulting in blindness.

Prior to placement of the buckle with permanent sutures, the defendant checked the IOP in the plaintiff's eye with his finger and then proceeded to attach the buckle. Subsequently, he again checked the IOP with his finger and concluded that it was within an acceptable range. The parties dispute whether the defendant should have used a tonometer rather than his finger to check the plaintiff's IOP.

On the morning following surgery, the defendant conducted a post-operative visit to assess the success of his surgery. The parties dispute whether the defendant measured the IOP. The defendant tested the plaintiff's vision with an ophthalmoscope, shining a light into the eye to check its response. Noting a normal "back-off" response to the light, he concluded that the surgery had been successful. The parties dispute whether the defendant should have also asked the plaintiff directly whether he could see out of his right eye . . .

By the next morning, the swelling around the plaintiff's eye had subsided. Because the defendant had not indicated when the plaintiff's vision would return, the plaintiff remained unconcerned about his continuing inability to see out of his right eye. At the plaintiff's scheduled follow-up appointment, however, the defendant informed the plaintiff that he would be permanently blind in the right eye . . .

During a five-day jury trial in January 1993, the plaintiff introduced expert testimony suggesting that if the defendant had utilized reasonable care, the plaintiff would not have lost his eyesight. The defendant, in turn, introduced expert testimony suggesting that the defendant had exercised ordinary care and that a high IOP was not the cause of the plaintiff's blindness.

At the defendant's request and over the plaintiff's objection, the circuit court used various paragraphs from the standard jury instruction pertaining to medical malpractice, Wis JI-Civil 1023, to instruct the jury. In response to the verdict question asking whether the defendant was negligent, the jury answered "no," thus returning a verdict in his favor. The circuit court entered a judgment dismissing the complaint. [Plaintiff argues that the malpractice instruction was erroneous and prejudicial] . . .

[T]he first paragraph of the circuit court's medical malpractice instruction to the jury in this case reads as follows:

> In treating Kim Nowatske, Dr. Osterloh was required to use the degree of care, skill, and judgment which is usually exercised in the same or similar circumstances by the average specialist who practices the

specialty which Dr. Osterloh practices, having due regard for the state of medical science at the time Kim Nowatske was treated. The burden in this case is on the plaintiffs to prove that Dr. Osterloh failed to conform to this standard.

The plaintiff's principal objection to this paragraph is that it defines the standard of care as that care usually exercised by the average physician practicing within the same specialty. According to the plaintiff the instruction thus equates the reasonable care required by law with customary medical care as defined by the medical profession, regardless of whether what is customary in the profession reflects what is reasonable in the wake of current medical science.

Because the medical profession is allowed to set its own definition of reasonable behavior in accordance with the customs of the profession, argues the plaintiff, what counts as an exercise of due care is established as a matter of law by doctors rather than as an issue to be resolved by the jury. Under Wis JI-Civil 1023, the plaintiff continues, all a defendant doctor need do is demonstrate that the methods used in treating the patient were customary in the medical profession. Even if the challenged custom is unreasonable and outdated, claims the plaintiff, the fact that it is "usually exercised in the same or similar circumstances by the average physician" is sufficient to shield clearly negligent conduct and negligent practitioners from liability.

The plaintiff is correct in suggesting that physicians, like all others in this state, are bound by a duty to exercise due care. Every person in Wisconsin must conform to the standard of a reasonable person under like circumstances; so too, then, "the duty of a physician or surgeon is to exercise ordinary care." *Scaria v. St. Paul Fire & Marine Ins. Co.*, 68 Wis. 2d 1, 11 (1975). As the amicus brief of the State Medical Society of Wisconsin correctly states, "the basic standard — ordinary care — does not change when the defendant is a physician. The only thing that changes is the makeup of the group to which the defendant's conduct is compared." Brief for the State Medical Society of Wisconsin as Amicus Curiae at 2 . . .

Thus physicians are required to exercise ordinary care, a standard to which they have been held since early Wisconsin case law. In *Reynolds v. Graves*, 3 Wis. 371, 375-76 (1854), a physician's duty of care was alternately expressed as the obligation "to use reasonable professional skill and attention" and "to use due and reasonable skill and diligence" in an effort to cure the patient . . .

[E]arly cases demonstrate that the standard of ordinary care applicable to all people in this state applies to physicians in this state as well. Subsequent case law has confirmed and amplified what these early cases announced.

The cases also demonstrate, as the plaintiff urges, that should customary medical practice fail to keep pace with developments and advances in medical science, adherence to custom might constitute a failure to exercise ordinary care. The court explained its aversion to equating custom with reasonable care in abolishing the locality rule. The locality rule, observed the court, allowed a small group, through its "laxness or carelessness," to "establish a local standard of care that was below that which the law requires." *Shier v. Freedman*, 58 Wis. 2d 269, 280 (1973). But "negligence," the court continued, "cannot be excused on the ground that others in the same locality practice the same kind of negligence. No degree of antiquity can give sanction to usage bad in itself." *Id.* Since technological changes insured that there was no longer any "lack of opportunity for a physician or surgeon to keep abreast of the advances made in his profession and to be familiar with the latest methods and practices adopted," *id.*, the court concluded that the reasons prompting the abolition of the locality rule elsewhere applied "with equal logic and persuasion in Wisconsin." *Shier*, 58 Wis. 2d at 283.

Wis JI-Civil 1023 incorporates the reasoning of *Shier*, not only by defining reasonable care as that "which is usually exercised in the same or similar circumstances by the average physician" but also by requiring that this definition of care itself be shaped by a "due regard for the state of medical science at the time plaintiff was treated." If what passes for customary or usual care lags behind developments in medical science, such care might be negligent, despite its customary nature . . .

The defendant interprets the same jury instruction language as applying "a dynamic standard" to professionals because the standard "changes as the state of knowledge of the profession changes." Brief for Defendant at 17. "Absent a dynamic standard," the defendant continues, "the law could not adjust to changes and improvement in medical science." *Id.* at 18. At oral argument before this court, counsel for the defendant stated that if a particular custom in the medical profession failed to keep pace with what developments in medical science had rendered reasonable, the plaintiff could introduce evidence demonstrating that the custom in question constituted negligent conduct.

We agree with the parties and the Medical Society that while evidence of the usual and customary conduct of others under similar circumstances is ordinarily relevant and admissible as an indication of what is reasonably prudent, customary conduct is not dispositive and cannot overcome the requirement that physicians exercise ordinary care.

The standard of care applicable to physicians in this state can not be conclusively established either by a reflection of what the majority of practitioners do or by a sum of the customs which those practitioners follow. It must instead be established by a determination of what it is reasonable to expect of a professional given the state of medical knowledge at the time of the treatment in issue.

We recognize that in most situations there will be no significant difference between customary and reasonable practices. In most situations physicians, like other professionals, will revise their customary practices so that the care they offer reflects a due regard for advances in the profession. An emphasis on reasonable rather than customary practices, however, insures that custom will not shelter physicians who fail to adopt advances in their respective fields and who consequently fail to conform to the standard of care which both the profession and its patients have a right to expect.

The issue then is whether the first paragraph of the instruction conveys the correct legal message that the defendant is held to a standard of reasonable care, skill and judgment and that reasonable care, skill and judgment are not necessarily embodied by the customary practice of the profession but rather represent the practice of physicians who keep abreast of advances in medical knowledge.

We conclude that the first paragraph of Wis JI-Civil 1023, read in conjunction with the remainder of the instructions given, conveys this message. The first paragraph speaks of the degree of care, skill, and judgment usually exercised in the same or similar circumstances by the average specialist. The second paragraph expressly states that a physician must use reasonable care. The third paragraph cautions that even a physician who has chosen a recognized method of treatment can nevertheless be found negligent for failing to exercise "the required care, skill, and judgment in administering the method" chosen. And much like the first paragraph of the plaintiff's proposed instruction, the first paragraph of the instruction given requires that in determining the degree of care, skill and judgment required of a physician, "due regard" should be given to "the state of medical science." The phrase "due regard for the state of medical science" tells the jury that a reasonably competent practitioner is one who keeps up with advances in medical knowledge . . .

The word "average" is problematic, as we explain more fully below. Viewed as a whole, however, the instruction given does not imply that the degree of care, skill and judgment expected of a doctor is set by the customs of the profession. Consequently, we disagree with the plaintiff's claim that the first paragraph of Wis JI-Civil 1023 allows medical custom to be dispositive regarding what constitutes reasonable medical care.

Nevertheless, the plaintiff's arguments demonstrate that this pattern jury instruction could be improved, and we conclude that the instruction should be revised . . .

The instruction's failure to define negligence is exacerbated by its use of the word "average" to denote the subset of physicians with whom an alleged tortfeasor is to be compared. The fallacy in the "average" formulation is that it bears no intrinsic relation to what is reasonable. As the American Law Institute stated in its commentary to § 299A REST. 2D TORTS (1965), "those who have less than . . . average skill may still be competent and qualified. Half of the physicians of America do not automatically become negligent in practicing medicine . . . merely because their skill is less than the professional average." . . .

On reflection, we too have reservations about the reference to "average" in Wis JI-Civil 1023 and conclude that this word should be eliminated. Loaded as it is with mathematical connotations, the word could distract a jury from its true purpose in a medical malpractice case: an investigation of whether the alleged tortfeasor exercised reasonable care. Reasonable care cannot be established by determining whether a physician provided care above or below the mean of the medical profession, but rather must be determined by assessing whether a patient received the standard of care he or she might reasonably expect from that practitioner, with due regard for the state of medical science at the time of treatment.

The second paragraph of the circuit court's medical malpractice instruction to the jury in this case reads as follows:

A physician does not guarantee the results of his care and treatment. A physician must use reasonable care and is not liable for failing to use the highest degree of care, skill, and judgment. Dr. Osterloh cannot be found negligent simply because there was a bad result. Medicine is not an exact science. Therefore, the issue you must decide in determining whether Dr. Osterloh was negligent is not whether there was a bad result but whether he failed to use the degree of care, skill, and judgment which is exercised by the average physician practicing the sub-specialty of retinal surgery.

. . . The plaintiff characterizes the paragraph as argumentative, however, because it allegedly accords undue emphasis to the defendant's case by repeatedly telling the jury what is not negligent without ever explaining what negligence is. . . .

Compounding the second paragraph's allegedly disproportionate emphasis on behavior which is not negligent, argues the plaintiff, the facts in this case did not merit giving the first sentence of that paragraph. Although the first sentence simply states that a doctor does not guarantee a favorable result, the plaintiff never claimed that the defendant was guaranteeing results . . .

Finally the plaintiff contends that by repeatedly emphasizing forms of behavior which are not negligent, Wis JI-Civil 1023 ignores this court's admonition that an instruction "should not give undue prominence to the contention of one party without giving equal prominence to the contention of the other party." *Kuklinski v. Dibelius*, 267 Wis. 378, 381 (1954).

We agree with the plaintiff that the circuit court need not have given the instruction's "no guarantee" language and we acknowledge that the second paragraph of Wis JI-Civil 1023 largely defines negligence through what is not negligent. Nevertheless, we conclude that the instruction is not erroneous . . .

When read in the context of both the remaining portions of Wis JI-Civil 1023 and the instructions as a whole, any alleged bias in the second paragraph of this instruction is readily dissipated. As the defendant points out in his brief to this court, the fifth paragraph of Wis JI-Civil 1023, which addresses the relation between negligence and cause and which was also given at trial, could be perceived as demonstrating a bias in favor of the plaintiff. Similarly, as the defendant suggested in oral argument before this court, one could conclude that the damages instructions given to the jury at trial were erroneous because of their focus on the plaintiff's suffering.

We would reject such arguments, as we reject the one made here by the plaintiff. While jury instructions can appear to be biased or argumentative when read in isolation, the litmus test applied by this court when reviewing such instructions is whether that bias persists when the instructions are read together. Read together with the remaining instructions given by the circuit court, the second paragraph of Wis JI-Civil 1023 passes that test. We therefore conclude that the second paragraph of Wis JI-Civil 1023 as given in this case was not erroneous . . .

To sum up, we conclude that these . . . paragraphs of Wis JI-Civil 1023, read as a whole and in conjunction with the other instructions given in this case, were not erroneous. At the same time, however, we recognize that the plaintiff has pointed to a number of ways in which the first three paragraphs of Wis JI-Civil 1023 might be clarified and thereby improved. Hence even though we hold that the pattern jury instruction was not erroneous in this case, we also conclude that it should be revised. [REMANDED.]

NOTES

1. *Customary Care.* In *The T.J. Hooper,* 60 F.2d 737 (2d Cir. 1932) (evidence of custom is admissible but not dispositive), explored in Chapter 4, the court refused to allow an industry to set its own standards. How would you justify a different rule for the learned professions? Is *Nowatske* successful in closing the gap between how professionals and industry are treated?

2. *From Custom to Reasonable Care.* How should the court react if there is evidence that the entire medical profession and, therefore, the customary practice has fallen behind? The well-known case of *Helling v. Carey,* 519 P.2d 981 (Wash. 1974), is one of the few to address the issue. There the defendant ophthalmologist failed to give a routine pressure test for glaucoma to the 32-year-old plaintiff. Expert testimony established that it was the universal custom not to give the test to patients under the age of 40. The court stated:

> Under the facts of this case, reasonable prudence required the timely giving of the pressure test to this plaintiff. The precaution of giving this test to detect the incidence of glaucoma to patients under 40 years of age is so imperative that irrespective of its disregard by the standards of the ophthalmology profession, it is the duty of the courts to say what is required to protect patients under 40 from the damaging results of glaucoma.

Id. at 519.

Does the *Helling* approach do away with the need for expert testimony, or does it merely change the weight of the testimony offered?

3. *Instructing on "Errors of Judgment".* In *Rogers v. Meridian Park Hosp.,* 307 Or. 612, (1989), the Supreme Court of Oregon reviewed an "error of judgment" instruction which had preceded a defense verdict, observing:

> ... If the term "judgment" refers to choices between acceptable courses of treatment, then the term "error in judgment" is a contradiction in itself. Use of any acceptable alternative would not be an "error." Witnesses may continue to use terms such as "exercise of judgment." But the court should not instruct the jury in such terms; such instructions not only confuse, but they are also incorrect because they suggest that substandard conduct is permissible if it is garbed as an "exercise of judgment."

Id. at 620.

4. *Schools of Thought.* Frequently, malpractice defendants rely on the fact that medical science often recognizes more than one approach or technique, recognized by the so-called "schools of thought" jury instruction. How many physicians, and of what prominence, does it take to make a "school of thought"?

Is the test quantitative (a "considerable number" of physicians) or qualitative (a "considerable number" of "reputable and respected" physicians)? In *Jones v. Chidester*, 610 A.2d 964 (Pa. 1992), the court concluded:

> Where competent medical authority is divided, a physician will not be held responsible if in the exercise of his judgment he followed a course of treatment advocated by a considerable number of recognized and respected professionals in his given area of expertise.

> In recognizing this doctrine, we do not attempt to place a numerical certainty on what constitutes a "considerable number." The burden of proving that there are two schools of thought falls to the defendant. The burden, however, should not prove burdensome. The proper use of expert witnesses should supply the answers. Once the expert states the factual reasons to support his claim that there is a considerable number of professionals who agree with the treatment employed by the defendant, there is sufficient evidence to warrant an instruction to the jury on the two "schools of thought." It then becomes a question for the jury to determine whether they believe that there are two legitimate schools of thought such that the defendant should be insulated from liability.

5. *External Indicia of Reasonable Care.* Parties to malpractice litigation increasingly seek to bolster or substitute expert testimony on the standard of care with external "standards. They may be found in medical journals, treatises, or Clinical Practice Guidelines (including "best practices" such as decision "trees" for diagnosis or treatment, based on best available scientific evidence). Two issues in their use arise: first, whether the materials constitute inadmissible hearsay evidence and, second, whether such data can substitute for expert testimony. Representative is *Morlino v. Medical Ctr.*, 152 N.J. 563 (1998), where the issue was whether the pharmaceutical package inserts found in the Physicians Desk Reference (PDR) were admissible as evidence of a physician's standard of care. The court stated:

> [D]rug manufacturers do not design package inserts and PDR entries to establish a standard of medical care. Manufacturers write drug package inserts and PDR warnings for many reasons including compliance with FDA requirements, advertisement, the provision of useful information to physicians, and an attempt to limit the manufacturer's liability. After a drug has been on the market for a sufficient period of time, moreover, physicians may rely more on their own experience and the professional publications of others than on a drug manufacturer's advertisements, inserts, or PDR entries.

> Those considerations highlight the reasons expert testimony must accompany the introduction of PDR warnings to establish the applicable standard of care in prescribing a drug. Additionally, expert testimony often is needed to explain the information contained in package inserts or the PDR. Drug manufacturers write explanations and warnings for doctors, not the general public. Comprehension of the terms and their significance may depend on medical expertise.

Accordingly, we hold that package inserts and PDR references alone do not establish the standard of care. It follows that a physician's failure to adhere to PDR warnings does not by itself constitute negligence. Reliance on the PDR alone to establish negligence would both obviate expert testimony on an issue where it is needed and could mislead the jury about the appropriate standard of care.

Similarly, a party may not generally introduce a treatise into evidence as a substitute for expert testimony. As we recently stated when considering the admissibility of learned treatises under [exceptions to the state's hearsay rules] a learned treatise's use as "substantive evidence is limited to situations in which an expert is on the stand and available to explain and assist in the application of the treatise if desired." *Jacober v. St. Peter's Medical Ctr.*, 128 N.J. 475, 491 (1992) (citing *Fed. R. Evid.* 803(18) advisory committee's note).

In *Hinlicky v. Dreyfuss*, 6 N.Y.3d 636 (2006), the patient died of a heart attack following an operation to remove plaque buildup in her carotid artery. The defendant anesthesiologist testified that he had decided not to send her for a preoperative cardiac evaluation based on the risk "score" he had given her when applying clinical guidelines published by American Heart Association (AHA) and the American College of Cardiology (ACC), and an accompanying flow chart or algorithm. Over hearsay objection the trial judge allowed the doctor to testify as to the nature and use of the guidelines and admitted them as evidence. The court affirmed the defense verdict, noting that the trial judge had properly admitted the guidelines as demonstrative evidence going to the witness's own conduct. However, the court rejected the invitation to determine whether guidelines would be admissible "under the professional reliability exception to the hearsay rule, which enables an expert witness to provide opinion evidence based on otherwise inadmissible hearsay . . ."

6. *Beyond Reasonable Care — Strict Liability*. In *Helling v. Carey*, discussed above, the majority opinion applied a reasonable rather than customary care standard. Concurring in the result Judge Utter noted:

> [W]e as judges, by using a negligence analysis, seem to be imposing a stigma of moral blame upon the doctors who, in this case, used all the precautions commonly prescribed by their profession in diagnosis and treatment. Lacking their training in this highly sophisticated profession, it seems illogical for this court to say they failed to exercise a reasonable standard of care. It seems to me we are, in reality, imposing liability, because, in choosing between an innocent plaintiff and a doctor, who acted reasonably according to his specialty but who could have prevented the full effects of this disease by administering a simple, harmless test and treatment, the plaintiff should not have to bear the risk of loss. As such, imposition of liability approaches that of strict liability.

Strict liability is routinely applied in other fact-patterns where parties are in informational asymmetry regarding risks or have similar risk-shifting mechanisms available such as insurance. See Chapter 8 (Strict Liability for Ultrahazardous Activities) and Chapter 10 (Products Liability). The courts, however, have generally been reluctant to move towards strict liability for professionals. Why is this so? In contrast, there has been some limited experimentation with alternate liability models through legislation. For example, *The Virginia Birth-Related Neurological Injury Compensation Act*, VA. CODE § 38.2-5000 (Supp. 1989), introduced a no-fault compensation scheme in the case of a "birth-related neurological injury." Such an injury is defined as:

> [i]njury to the brain or spinal cord of an infant caused by the deprivation of oxygen or mechanical injury occurring in the course of labor, delivery or resuscitation in the immediate post-delivery period in a hospital which renders the infant permanently nonambulatory, aphasic, incontinent, and in need of assistance in all phases of daily living (§ 38.2-5001).

Claims are heard by the state's "Industrial Commission" (§ 38.2-5003) and the claimant benefits from:

> A rebuttable presumption . . . that the injury alleged is a birth-related neurological injury where it has been demonstrated, to the satisfaction of the Industrial Commission, that the infant has sustained a brain or spinal cord injury caused by oxygen deprivation or mechanical injury, and that the infant was thereby rendered permanently nonambulatory, aphasic and incontinent (§ 38.2-5008.A.1).

What questions are raised by Virginia's scheme? Does it primarily benefit patients, physicians or malpractice insurers?

At a time when there is considerable concern about the level of medical error, how should the courts reformulate the medical standard of care to increase healthcare quality and safety? Is any major change to "ordinary care" or in the direction of strict liability impossible, given the politics of the malpractice crises? Some of these issues (including Virginia's statutory alternative) are more fully explored in Chapter 16.

LOCKE v. PACHTMAN
446 Mich. 216 (1994)

MALLETT, JUDGE.

. . . On August 5, 1981, plaintiff Shirley Locke underwent a vaginal hysterectomy with entocele and rectocele repair at the University of Michigan Hospital.[2] The procedure was performed by defendant, Dr. Judith Pachtman, then a fourth-year resident in gynecology. Codefendant, Dr. James Roberts, was the attending physician and was present for most of the surgery.

Dr. Pachtman testified that she performed the first two procedures, the hysterectomy and entocele repair, without complication, although the entocele repair took longer than expected. Following the entocele repair, Dr. Roberts left the room to attend another operation that had been previously scheduled.

---

[2] As explained at trial, an entocele is an out-pouching or hernia of the peritoneal cavity where the bowel protrudes into the area between the vagina and the rectum. A rectocele is a hernial protrusion of the rectum through the posterior vaginal wall.

Dr. Pachtman then began the rectocele repair. Upon Dr. Pachtman's initial insertion into the levator ani muscle, the needle she was using broke. One-half to two-thirds of the needle, a length of about 1.5 cm, broke off and lodged somewhere within that muscle. Dr. Pachtman searched unsuccessfully for the broken portion of the needle for fifteen to twenty minutes. At that time, Dr. Roberts returned and joined Dr. Pachtman in searching for the needle fragment.

Drs. Pachtman and Roberts utilized a silver probe to x-ray the affected area, in an attempt to locate the broken portion of the needle. After ascertaining the approximate location of the fragment, they decided to close the old incision and to continue their search through a new incision. After unsuccessfully searching for the needle for another forty-five minutes to one hour, they abandoned the search and closed the second incision. Both doctors indicated that they felt it was in the plaintiff's best interest to terminate the surgery at that point, even though they had failed to locate the needle fragment.

Plaintiff testified that after the surgery Dr. Pachtman informed her of the needle breakage and stated that the needle was entrenched in the muscle and therefore could remain there without causing her any problems. However, after experiencing considerable pain and discomfort, plaintiff consulted with another physician, Dr. Frances Couch. Dr. Couch advised removing the needle fragment, and, subsequently, she performed the surgical procedure, successfully locating and removing the broken portion of the needle.

Plaintiff filed suit against Drs. Pachtman and Roberts, alleging negligence on various grounds, including the use of a needle that they knew or should have known was too small and failing to locate and remove the needle fragment . . .

In testimony presented at trial, plaintiff's expert witness, Dr. Couch, was unable to identify any negligent conduct on the part of either Dr. Pachtman or Dr. Roberts. Dr. Couch also stated that she could not give an opinion regarding the adequacy of the needle size, because she had never viewed the needle intact. She explained that she could not identify the size of the needle without viewing the needle in its entirety.

When questioned generally regarding the cause of needle breakage and its relation to the standard of care, Dr. Couch made two separate statements. At one point Dr. Couch stated that the standard of care did not relate to needle breakage at all, but rather to how one dealt with it, suggesting that needle breakage was simply one of the risks of surgery. Later, without relating this point to a standard of care, she noted that a surgeon's "incorrect technique" often causes a needle to break. When asked to describe what she meant by incorrect technique, Dr. Couch described instances in which a surgeon fails to manipulate the needle correctly, such as by inserting it at the wrong angle or applying too much force. Dr. Couch also testified that she had previously had a needle break while performing surgery.

In addition to Dr. Couch's expert testimony, plaintiff introduced evidence regarding a number of statements allegedly made by Dr. Pachtman following the surgery.

Plaintiff's brother, Reverend Gary Heniser, testified that, while he was at the hospital visiting his sister, Dr. Pachtman told him, "'I knew the needle was too small when I used it.'"

Coplaintiff Danny Locke testified that Dr. Pachtman had also spoken to him about the surgery: "[S]he told me that it was her fault, that she used the wrong needle, and she was sorry."

Finally, Shirley Locke testified that Dr. Pachtman had told her:

"I knew that needle was too small when the new scrub nurse handed it to me. It wasn't her fault because she was new, but I chose to use it anyway and it's my fault and I am really sorry. . . ."

. . . At the close of plaintiff's proofs, the trial court granted defendants' motion for directed verdict on the ground that plaintiff had failed to make a *prima facie* showing regarding the standard of care. Plaintiff's motion for a new trial was denied . . .

Plaintiff argues that the lower courts erred in finding that she had failed to demonstrate the standard of care applicable to defendants' conduct. Plaintiff contends that expert testimony was sufficient to establish this point, and, further, that the standard of care and breach of that standard were inferable under the doctrine of res ipsa loquitur and because the alleged negligence was within the common understanding of the jury.

We agree with the lower courts' determination that no *prima facie* showing was made, and therefore we affirm the directed verdict entered for the defendants. . . .

Plaintiff argues first that the standard of care attributable to Dr. Pachtman was established by way of expert testimony. This Court has long recognized the importance of expert testimony in establishing a medical malpractice claim, and the need to educate the jury and the court regarding matters not within their common purview. As we have previously explained:

In a case involving professional service the ordinary layman is not equipped by common knowledge and experience to judge of the skill and competence of that service and determine whether it squares with the standard of such professional practice in the community. For that, the aid of expert testimony from those learned in the profession involved is required. [*Lince v. Monson,* 363 Mich. 135, 140 (1961).]

While we have recognized exceptions to this requirement, the benefit of expert testimony, particularly in demonstrating the applicable standard of care, cannot be overstated.

In this case, plaintiff contends that the standard of care applicable to Dr. Pachtman was established by Dr. Couch's expert testimony. For this point, plaintiff relies on Dr. Couch's statement that needle breakage often occurs because of the surgeon's "incorrect technique." Plaintiff asserts that this testimony, coupled with Dr. Pachtman's admissions regarding use of a needle she knew to be too small, were sufficient to establish the standard of care and breach of that standard.

Dr. Couch's testimony with regard to the standard of care associated with needle breakage was rather confused. At one point she suggested that needle breakage was merely one of the risks of surgery, and that needle breakage did not ordinarily signal a violation of the standard of care . . .

Dr. Couch later testified that needle breakage may be attributable to a surgeon's "incorrect technique" . . .

[I]t is . . . questionable whether Dr. Couch's latter testimony on this point was sufficient to establish a standard of care with regard to "incorrect technique." Dr. Couch, while presenting one way in which needles break, never went so far as to relate that discussion to a standard of care. In effect, she never explained what a reasonably prudent surgeon would do, in keeping with the standards of professional practice that might not have been done by Dr. Pachtman. Accordingly, the jury would have had no standard against which to measure Dr. Pachtman's conduct. This factor, coupled with the conflicting nature of Dr. Couch's testimony, leads us to believe that the standard of care was not sufficiently established.

We further note that Dr. Couch's explanation of how and why needles break, even had it established a standard of care, provides little support for the specific theory of negligence advanced by plaintiff in her complaint and at trial. While plaintiff argued that the needle broke in this case because it was of an inadequate size for the area to be sutured, Dr. Couch's description of "incorrect technique" leading to needle breakage related to the way the chosen needle is positioned and manipulated, regardless of its size. Dr. Couch did acknowledge at one point that there is such a thing as using a needle that is too small or too weak for a particular task. However, she never related this to her theory of "incorrect technique," nor did she indicate that the needle utilized by defendants was of an inappropriate size. We find her statement, either standing alone or in conjunction with her testimony regarding incorrect technique, to be insufficient to establish a standard of care. Therefore, no *prima facie* showing was made.

Plaintiff next argues that the statements allegedly made by Dr. Pachtman were themselves sufficient to establish the standard of care and breach of that standard. Plaintiff contends that her case is governed by this Court's decision in *Orozco v. Henry Ford Hosp.*, 408 Mich. 248 (1980), and that, under the reasoning presented in *Orozco*, the lower courts erred in finding that defendant's admissions alone were insufficient to establish the standard of care.

Plaintiff's reliance upon *Orozco* is misplaced. In *Orozco*, the plaintiff testified that during his hernial surgery he heard one of the surgeons say, "Oops, I cut in the wrong place." *Id.* at 254. Following the surgery, one of his testicles atrophied. At trial, an expert witness testified that this injury was likely due to an impairment of the blood supply to the testicles during the surgery.

At the close of Orozco's proofs, the trial court granted the defendants' motion for a directed verdict, and the Court of Appeals affirmed, finding that the plaintiff had failed to make a *prima facie* showing of the applicable standard of care. This Court reversed the Court of Appeals by per curiam opinion. The Court found that expert testimony was not necessary because jury members would be able to determine, from their own common knowledge, whether the defendants' actions violated the applicable standard of care. As the Court explained:

> Here Orozco offered the fact of the injury, a medical explanation of how that injury likely occurred, and an admission by the surgeon that he cut in the wrong place.
>
> Paraphrasing Lince, "[t]he question is whether the action of defendants conformed to standards of good practice in the community. Common knowledge and the experience of ordinary laymen do . . . equip them to give the answer in a case such as this" when an expert testifies that the likely cause of injury was an impairment of the blood supply to the testicles in the course of the operation and the plaintiff testifies that the surgeon said, "Oops, I cut in the wrong place." [408 Mich. at 253-254. (Emphasis in original.)]

As is indicated above, the Court in *Orozco* did not rely exclusively upon the defendant's *admission* to find that a *prima facie* showing had been made. Rather, the Court found that on the basis of that admission and corroborating expert testimony the jury could determine *from their own common knowledge* whether the defendants' actions conformed to standards of professional practice . . .

Turning to the present case, we hold that the lower courts correctly concluded that Dr. Pachtman's statements were insufficient to make a *prima facie* showing. While the statements may have indicated Dr. Pachtman's belief that she made a mistake or acted in error, a jury could not reasonably infer from those statements alone that Dr. Pachtman's actions did not conform to the standard of professional practice for the community as a whole.

Unlike the situation presented in *Orozco,* the standard of care associated with needle choice and needle breakage is not accessible to the jury absent expert guidance. Plaintiff has provided no guidance with regard to what options were available to Dr. Pachtman and which of them she should have chosen. In short, there was no testimony regarding what a reasonably prudent surgeon would have done in Dr. Pachtman's situation. We agree with the Court of Appeals determination that the jury should not be left to speculate in this regard. It is precisely to avoid such speculation that expert testimony is ordinarily required.

Accordingly, without diminishing the holding in *Orozco,* we decline to extend it to the present case, in which the standard of care associated with the alleged negligence is not within the common knowledge of the jury, it cannot be reasonably inferred from the admissions alone, and where no further evidence was presented linking Dr. Pachtman's admissions to the standard of care. While it is conceivable that in some circumstances a doctor defendant's extrajudicial admissions could present *prima facie* evidence of breach of the standard of care, that is not the case here.

Plaintiff next argues that even if expert testimony was insufficient, her case against Dr. Pachtman should have proceeded to the jury on the theory of res ipsa loquitur. Specifically, plaintiff contends, under this doctrine, a *prima facie* case was made, with regard to both the needle breakage and the fact that defendant terminated the surgery without having recovered the needle. The lower courts rejected these arguments, as do we.

As previously noted, while expert testimony is the traditional and the preferred method of proving medical malpractice, exceptions to the need for expert testimony have been recognized. One such exception involves the doctrine of res ipsa loquitur. If a plaintiff's case satisfies the dictates of this doctrine, then the case may proceed to the jury without expert testimony.

This Court's decision in *Jones v. Porretta,* 428 Mich. 132 (1987), marked the Court's first explicit adoption and application of res ipsa loquitur in the medical malpractice context. In *Jones,* the Court cited the following four factors as necessary to a res ipsa loquitur claim:

> (1) the event must be of a kind which ordinarily does not occur in the absence of someone's negligence;
>
> (2) it must be caused by an agency or instrumentality within the exclusive control of the defendant;
>
> (3) it must not have been due to any voluntary action or contribution on the part of the plaintiff. . . .
>
> (4) [e]vidence of the true explanation of the event must be more readily accessible to the defendant than to the plaintiff. [*Id.* at 150-151.]

In the medical malpractice context, the crucial element, and that most difficult to establish, will often be the first factor, i.e., that the event is of a kind that does not ordinarily occur in the absence of negligence. A bad result will not *itself* be sufficient to satisfy that condition. As the Court explained:

> This does not mean that a bad result cannot be presented by plaintiffs as part of their evidence of negligence, but, rather, that, standing alone, it is not adequate to create an issue for the jury. *Something more is required, be it the common knowledge that the injury does not ordinarily occur without negligence or expert testimony to that effect.* [*Id.* at 154. (Emphasis added.)]

Therefore, the fact that the injury complained of does not ordinarily occur in the absence of negligence must either be supported by expert testimony or must be within the common understanding of the jury. Neither standard was met here.

Plaintiff first argues that expert testimony was sufficient for the jury to find that needle breakage does not ordinarily occur without negligence. We disagree. Even plaintiff's own expert acknowledged at one point that needle breakage is one of the risks of surgery, suggesting that faulty equipment might be a cause of breakage. Therefore no *prima facie* showing was made.

In the alternative, plaintiff contends that no expert testimony is required because it is within the common understanding of the jury that needles do not ordinarily break absent negligence. For this theory, plaintiff relies on this Court's holding in *LeFaive v. Asselin,* 262 Mich. 443 (1933). In *LeFaive,* the Court held that a jury could determine, without the aid of expert testimony, that the defendant's action in inadvertently leaving a needle within the plaintiff's incision violated the applicable standard of care.

Plaintiff's analogy to *LeFaive* is inapposite. In *LeFaive,* the act of leaving the needle within the incision was one of carelessness, from which negligence may easily be discerned. However, a far different situation is presented where a needle breaks off, and the surgeon, despite attempts to locate the fragment is *unable* to. One could not reasonably conclude, on the basis of common knowledge, that such an event does not ordinarily occur in the absence of negligence. Where negligence is not inferable through common knowledge, and where no expert testimony was presented to the effect that the event complained of would not ordinarily occur without negligence, plaintiff's res ipsa loquitur claim must fail.

Lastly, plaintiff contends that a *prima facie* case was made against Dr. Pachtman because the negligence alleged was so gross as to be within the common understanding of the jury.

This Court has previously held that expert testimony may not be required when

> [T]he lack of professional care is so manifest that it would be within the common knowledge and experience of the ordinary layman that the conduct was careless and not conformable to the standards of professional practice and care employed in the community. [*Sullivan v. Russell,* 417 Mich. 398, 407 (1983), quoting *Lince,* 363 Mich. at 141.]

However, . . . we do not find the standard of care with relation to Dr. Pachtman's allegedly negligent use of an inadequately sized needle to be within the common understanding of the jury. Nor do we find the standard of care applicable to defendants' decision to terminate the surgery, without having recovered the needle, to be ascertainable by the jury without the aid of expert testimony. [AFFIRMED]

LEVIN, JUSTICE (dissenting).

I agree with the majority that expert medical testimony concerning the standard of care and a breach was required. I also agree that the plaintiff did not establish a jury submissible question of fact on the basis of res ipsa loquitur or on the basis that the evidence of negligence was within the common understanding of the jury.

I would hold, however, that Dr. Judith A. Pachtman's statements to the effect that she knew the needle that broke during surgery was too small when it was handed to her, and when she used it, were *prima facie* evidence of the standard of care and breach.

The question presented is whether Pachtman's statements — in effect admitting error but not in lawyer jargon such as "standard medical practice in this community" — are *prima facie* evidence of the standard of care and breach.

Plaintiff, Shirley Locke testified that Pachtman said that she knew the needle was too small when the new scrub nurse handed it to her, and Danny Locke testified that Pachtman said that she knew the needle was too small when she used it. Drawing all reasonable inferences in favor of Shirley Locke, a jury could reasonably conclude that Pachtman's statements conveyed her expert medical view that it was not sound medical practice in her community to use the particular needle she used in the surgery she was performing . . .

Cases from other jurisdictions indicate that statements like Pachtman's — that confess error with reasonable specificity — are *prima facie* evidence of the standard of care and breach.

In *Greenwood v. Harris,* 362 P.2d 85, 87–88 (Okla., 1961), the plaintiff alleged that the physician erroneously diagnosed her pregnancy as a tumor, and then performed unnecessary surgery that left the plaintiff with an unsightly and painful scar. The plaintiff's only evidence concerning the standard of care was the physician's statements to the plaintiff and her husband that he "should have made more tests," and that he "wasn't satisfied with the lab report [and] *should have had the tests run again,* . . . should have made some other tests." (Emphasis added.) The Oklahoma Supreme Court held that those statements alone were *prima facie* evidence of the standard of care and breach . . .

In *Woronka v. Sewall,* 320 Mass. 362, 364 (1946), the plaintiff claimed that her physician negligently exposed the skin on her buttocks to irritating chemicals during the delivery of a child. The plaintiff's only evidence of the standard of care and breach was the physician's statements to the plaintiff and her husband that the plaintiff's burns resulted from "negligence when they [the plaintiff and the physician] were upstairs [in the delivery room]," and that the plaintiff's injury apparently occurred when a chemical solution was allowed to stay in contact with her skin for "too long a period." The physician argued that the word "negligence" did not supply the essential elements justifying a finding of liability . . .

In *Greenwood* and *Woronka,* the physicians' statements indicated with relative precision how they had erred. In *Greenwood,* the physician, in effect, confessed error in failing to administer certain tests for a second time in the face of inconclusive results, and, in *Woronka,* the physician stated that he improperly permitted the plaintiff's buttocks to stay in contact with a chemical irritant.

Other state supreme courts have found that the standard of care was not established by statements that fail to explain with relative precision what the physician should have done . . .

I conclude, consistent with precedent from other jurisdictions, that Pachtman's statement satisfied Locke's burden of presenting *prima facie* evidence of the standard of care and breach . . .

NOTES

1. *Exclusive Control.* In *Kambat v. St. Francis Hospital,* 89 N.Y.2d 489 (1997), a laparotomy pad measuring 18-by-18 inches was removed from the plaintiff several months after an abdominal hysterectomy. The defendants argued that they had followed standard procedures and counted the lap pads as they were removed, and argued that plaintiff must have swallowed the pad in question. The trial court refused to give a *res ipsa* instruction. The court reversed a defense verdict stating:

[P]laintiffs' evidence that similar pads were used during decedent's surgery, that decedent was unconscious throughout the operation, that laparotomy pads are not accessible to patients and that it would be anatomically impossible to swallow such pads sufficed to allow the jury to conclude that defendants had exclusive control of the laparotomy pad. . . .

Plaintiffs were not obligated to eliminate every alternative explanation for the event. Defendants' evidence that they used due care and expert testimony supporting their competing theory that decedent might have had access to laparotomy pads and inflicted the injury upon herself by swallowing the pad merely raised alternative inferences to be evaluated by the jury in determining. The undisputed fact remained in evidence that a laparotomy pad measuring 18 inches square was discovered in decedent's abdomen [from which an inference of negligence could reasonably have been drawn]

2. *Patent Error.* There are some circumstances in which expert testimony is not essential to the plaintiff's recovery. For example, in *Hammer v. Rosen,* 7 N.Y.2d 376 (1960), there was evidence that a psychiatrist who had treated a schizophrenic for some seven years had beaten her on several occasions. In answer to the defendant's objection that plaintiff had supplied no expert testimony that this constituted malpractice, the court stated that, "the very nature of the acts complained of bespeaks improper treatment and malpractice."

Wilson v. Martin Mem. Hosp., 232 N.C. 362 (1950), arose out of a botched childbirth. The court observed that "[w]hen the evidence of lack of ordinary care is patent and such as to be within the comprehension of laymen, requiring only common knowledge and experience to understand and judge it, expert testimony is not required." Consider also *Ohligschlager v. Proctor Community Hosp.,* 55 Ill. 2d 411 (1973), holding that expert testimony was not necessary when a doctor deviated from a manufacturer's recommendation as to the concentration in which a drug should be administered. While the patient may not require expert testimony to create a *prima facie* case of negligence in patent error cases, does it follow that the defendant cannot use such testimony to rebut the allegation? In *Houserman v. Garrett*, 902 So. 2d 670 (Ala. 2004), a gauze pad had been placed under the patient's uterus during surgery but not removed, causing damage and necessitating additional surgery. Testimony at trial established that the defendant surgeon had used a three-part check before closing the site: a visual inspection, a manual inspection (by feel), and a numerical count conducted by a nurse. The surgeon objected to jury instructions that contained the phrases, "the physician who conducted the surgery bears the responsibility for removing all foreign objects from the patient's body" and "[t]he fact that . . . physicians . . . routinely delegate the task of accounting for foreign objects and relying on counts given to them . . . does not relieve the physician of the liability for such foreign objects left inside the patient's body." Reversing, the court stated, "[P]roof of a retained object creates a *prima facie* case of negligence, the burden then shifts to the defendant physician, who, upon presenting substantial evidence of the applicable standard of care and his or her compliance with it, may be found by the jury not to have been negligent." Is that an efficient method of dealing with foreign object or other patent error cases?

3. *Expert Testimony Foundation for a Res Ipsa Loquitur Instruction.* In *Mireles v. Broderick,* 117 N.M. 445 (1994), the plaintiff sued her anesthesiologist when she suffered numbness in her right arm (ulnar neuropathy) after undergoing a bilateral mastectomy. Her expert testified that her injury "in all probability, occurred while she was under anesthesia for [the] surgery." He testified further that an anesthesiologist should properly position and cushion the arm to avoid compression and should monitor the arm during surgery to be sure that proper positioning and cushioning are maintained while the patient is unconscious, and that such an injury was totally preventable by proper care. The trial judge refused a res ipsa instruction and the jury found for the defendant. Reversing and remanding, the court stated:

> Dr. Broderick argues that, because of the rule that negligence of medical providers generally must be proved by expert testimony, *res ipsa loquitur* is limited in malpractice cases to the common-knowledge exception . . . He argues that only when the inference of negligence is within the common reservoir of knowledge of the jurors may the jury be charged on the *res ipsa loquitur* doctrine. . . .

> Dr. Broderick's argument loses sight of the dispositive principle at issue in the application of *res ipsa loquitur*. *Res ipsa loquitur* describes a set of conditions to be met before an inference of negligence may be drawn. As such, the central issue is not whether common knowledge alone is sufficient to establish an inference of negligence. Rather, the issue is whether there is a factual predicate sufficient to support an inference that the injury was caused by the failure of the party in control to exercise due care. The requisite probability of negligence may exist independently of the common knowledge of the jurors. The common-knowledge exception to the expert testimony rule may inform but does not delimit the application of *res ipsa loquitur*.

> We join the growing consensus of courts from other jurisdictions and adopt scholarly commentary to hold that the foundation for an inference of negligence may be formed by expert testimony that a certain occurrence indicates the probability of negligence. . . .

4. *Multiple Defendants and a Possible Conspiracy of Silence. Ybarra v. Spangard,* 25 Cal. 2d 486 (1944), concerned a patient who awoke from an appendectomy experiencing pain around the neck and shoulders. Plaintiff brought suit against several hospital employees and members of the operating team. Defendants resisted the application of *res ipsa loquitur* on the basis that there were *several* defendants and *multiple* instrumentalities. Intimating that to give force to such objections would make *res ipsa* of doubtful utility in the modern medical context, the court concluded:

> [W]here a plaintiff receives unusual injuries while unconscious and in the course of medical treatment, all those defendants who had any control over his body or the instrumentalities which might have caused the injuries may properly be called upon to meet the inference of negligence by giving an explanation of their conduct.

5. *Admissions and Apologies.* As follows from *Locke v. Pachtman* only in the rare case will the doctor's statement satisfy the *prima facie* requirements for negligence. However, even if insufficient, standing alone, to establish the *prima facie* case, such statements are generally admissible. This is problematic as health quality reformers and organizations such as Joint Commission on Accreditation of Healthcare Organizations (JCAHO) favor admissions and even apology. As a result, many states have passed so-called "Apology Statutes." For example, the Illinois statute, 735 ILCS 5/8-1901(b), provides:

> Any expression of grief, apology, or explanation provided by a health care provider, including, but not limited to, a statement that the health care provider is "sorry" for the outcome to a patient, the patient's family, or the patient's legal representative about an inadequate or unanticipated treatment or care outcome that is provided within 72 hours of when the provider knew or should have known of the potential cause of such outcome shall not be admissible as evidence in any action of any kind in any court or before any tribunal, board, agency, or person. The disclosure of any such information, whether proper, or improper, shall not waive or have any effect upon its confidentiality or inadmissibility. . . .

Is an apology always an admission? Would the Illinois statute bar an admission? Why favor apologies? *See generally* Jennifer K. Robbennolt, *What We Know and Don't Know About the Role of Apologies in Resolving Health Care Disputes*, 21 Ga. St. U.L. Rev. 1009 (2005)(discussing critical empirical evidence comparing apology to acceptance of responsibility).

6. *Costly Litigation.* Should there be a streamlined compensation scheme for "foreign object," patent error, or common experience cases?

D. CONSENT AND RISK DISCLOSURE

PERNA v. PIROZZI
92 N.J. 446 (1983)

Pollock, Judge.

. . . On the advice of his family physician, Thomas Perna entered St. Joseph's Hospital on May 8, 1977 for tests and a urological consultation. Mr. Perna consulted Dr. Pirozzi, a specialist in urology, who examined Mr. Perna and recommended that he undergo surgery for the removal of kidney stones.

Dr. Pirozzi was associated with a medical group that also included Drs. Del Gaizo and Ciccone. The doctors testified at trial that their medical group customarily shared patients; no doctor had individual patients, and each doctor was familiar with all cases under care of the group. Further, it was not the practice of the group to inform patients which member would operate; the physicians operated as a "team," and their regular practice was to decide just prior to the operation who was to operate. If, however, a patient requested a specific member of the group as his surgeon, that surgeon would perform the operation. Nothing indicated that Mr. Perna was aware of the group's custom of sharing patients or of their methods for assigning surgical duties.

Although Mr. Perna had never consulted with Dr. Del Gaizo or Dr. Ciccone, he had been treated by Dr. Pirozzi previously in conjunction with a bladder infection. According to Mr. Perna, he specifically requested Dr. Pirozzi to perform the operation. None of the defendants directly contradicted Mr. Perna's testimony. However, Dr. Ciccone testified that he met with Mr. Perna on May 16 and, without discussing who would operate, explained that two members of the medical group would be present during the operation. The following day, in the presence of a urological resident, Mr. Perna executed a consent form that named Dr. Pirozzi as the operating surgeon and authorized him, with the aid of unnamed "assistants," to perform the surgery. In this context, the term "assistants" refers to medical personnel, not necessarily doctors, who aid the operating surgeon. The operation was performed on May 18 by Dr. Del Gaizo, assisted by Dr. Ciccone. Dr. Pirozzi was not present during the operation; in fact, he was not on duty that day. At the time of surgery, Dr. Del Gaizo and Dr. Ciccone were unaware that only Dr. Pirozzi's name appeared on the consent form.

Mr. Perna first learned of the identities of the operating surgeons when he was readmitted to the hospital on June 11 because of post-surgical complications. Subsequently, Mr. and Mrs. Perna filed suit for malpractice against all three doctors, alleging four deviations from standard medical procedure concerning the diagnosis, treatment and surgery performed by the defendants. They further alleged that there was a failure to obtain Mr. Perna's informed consent to the operation performed by Dr. Del Gaizo. That is, plaintiffs claimed that Mr. Perna's consent to the operation was conditioned upon his belief that Dr. Pirozzi would be the surgeon . . .

We now address the nature of the claim resulting from the performance of the operation by a physician other than the one named in the consent form, so called "ghost surgery." If the claim is characterized as a failure to obtain informed consent, the operation may constitute an act of medical malpractice; if, however, it is viewed as a failure to obtain any consent, it is better classified as a battery.

Informed consent is a negligence concept predicated on the duty of a physician to disclose to a patient information that will enable him to "evaluate knowledgeably the options available and the risks attendant upon each" before subjecting that patient to a course of treatment. *Canterbury v. Spence,* 464 F.2d 772, 780 (D.C. Cir.), *cert. den.,* 409 U.S. 1064 (1972) . . . Under the doctrine, the patient who consents to an operation is given the opportunity to show that the surgeon withheld information concerning "the inherent and potential hazards of the proposed treatment, the alternatives to that treatment, if any, and the results likely if the patient remains untreated." *Canterbury v. Spence, supra,* 464 F.2d at 787–88. If the patient succeeds in proving that the surgeon did not comply with the applicable standard for disclosure, the consent is vitiated.

In an action predicated upon a battery, a patient need not prove initially that the physician has deviated from a professional standard of care. Under a battery theory, proof of an unauthorized invasion of the plaintiff's person, even if harmless, entitles him to nominal damages. The plaintiff may further recover for all injuries proximately caused by the mere performance of the operation, whether the result of negligence or not. If an operation is properly performed, albeit by a surgeon operating without the consent of the patient, and the patient suffers no injuries except those which foreseeably follow from the operation, then a jury could find that the substitution of surgeons did not cause any compensable injury. Even there, however, a jury could award damages for mental anguish resulting from the belated knowledge that the operation was performed by a doctor to whom the patient had not given consent. Furthermore, because battery connotes an intentional invasion of another's rights, punitive damages may be assessed in an appropriate case.

The plaintiffs here do not challenge the adequacy of the disclosure of information relating to risks inherent in the operation performed. Nor do they contend that Mr. Perna would have decided not to undergo the operation if additional facts had been provided to him. In short, they concede Perna consented to an operation by Dr. Pirozzi. However, plaintiffs contend that two other surgeons operated on him without his consent. If that contention is correct, the operating surgeons violated the patient's right to control his own body.

Any non-consensual touching is a battery. Even more private than the decision who may touch one's body is the decision who may cut it open and invade it with hands and instruments. Absent an emergency, patients have the right to determine not only whether surgery is to be performed on them, but who shall perform it. A surgeon who operates without the patient's consent engages in the unauthorized touching of another and, thus, commits a battery. A non-consensual operation remains a battery even if performed skillfully and to the benefit of the patient. The medical profession itself recognizes that it is unethical to mislead a patient as to the identity of the doctor who performs the operation. *American College of Surgeons, Statements on Principles*, § I.A. (June 1981). Participation in such a deception is a recognized cause for discipline by the medical profession. By statute, the State Board of Medical Examiners is empowered to prevent the professional certification or future professional practice of a person who "[h]as engaged in the use or employment of dishonesty, fraud, deception, misrepresentation, false promise or false pretense. . . ." N.J.S.A. 45:1-21. Consequently, a statutory, as well as a moral, imperative compels doctors to be honest with their patients.

A different theory applies to the claim against Dr. Pirozzi. As to him, the action follows from the alleged breach of his agreement to operate and the fiduciary duty he owed his patient. With respect to that allegation, the Judicial Council of the American Medical Association has decried the substitution of one surgeon for another without the consent of the patient, describing that practice as a "deceit."[3] A patient has the right to choose the surgeon who will operate on him and to refuse to accept a substitute. Correlative to that right is the duty of the doctor to provide his or her personal services in accordance with the agreement with the patient. *Judicial Council of the American Medical Ass'n*, Op. 8.12 (1982).

Few decisions bespeak greater trust and confidence than the decision of a patient to proceed with surgery. Implicit in that decision is a willingness of the patient to put his or her life in the hands of a known and trusted medical doctor. Sometimes circumstances will arise in which, because of an emergency, the limited capacity of the patient, or some other valid reason, the doctor cannot obtain the express consent of the patient to a surrogate surgeon. Other times, doctors who practice in a medical group may explain to a patient that any one of them may perform a medical procedure. In that situation, the patient may accept any or all the members of the group as his surgeon. In still other instances, the patient may consent to an operation performed by a resident under the supervision of the attending physician. The point is that a patient has the right to know who will operate and the consent form should reflect the patient's decision. Where a competent patient consents to surgery by a specific surgeon of his choice, the patient has every right to expect that surgeon, not another, to operate.

The failure of a surgeon to perform a medical procedure after soliciting a patient's consent, like the failure to operate on the appropriate part of a patient's body, is a deviation from standard medical care. It is malpractice whether the right surgeon operates on the wrong part or the wrong surgeon operates on the right part of the patient. In each instance, the surgeon has breached his duty to care for the patient. Where damages are the proximate result of a deviation from standard medical care, a patient has a cause of action for malpractice. Although an alternative cause of action could be framed as a breach of the contract between the surgeon and the patient, generally the more appropriate characterization of the cause will be for breach of the duty of care owed by the doctor to the patient. The absence of damages may render

---

[3] The Judicial Council of the American Medical Association has declared:

> To have another physician operate on one's patient without the patient's knowledge and consent is a deceit. The patient is entitled to choose his own physician and he should be permitted to acquiesce in or refuse to accept the substitution . . . It should be noted that it is the operating surgeon to whom the patient grants consent to perform the operation. The patient is entitled to the services of the particular surgeon with whom he or she contracts. The surgeon, in accepting the patient is obligated to utilize his personal talents in the performance of the operation to the extent required by the agreement creating the physician-patient relationship. He cannot properly delegate to another the duties which he is required to perform personally.

> Under the normal and customary arrangement with private patients, and with reference to the usual form of consent to operation, the surgeon is obligated to perform the operation, and may use the services of assisting residents or other assisting surgeons to the extent that the operation reasonably requires the employment of such assistance. If a resident or other physician is to perform the operation under the guidance of the surgeon, it is necessary to make a full disclosure of this fact to the patient, and this should be evidenced by an appropriate statement contained in the consent.

> If the surgeon employed merely assists the resident or other physician in performing the operation, it is the resident or other physician who becomes the operating surgeon. If the patient is not informed as to the identity of the operating surgeon, the situation is "ghost surgery."

Judicial Council of the American Medical Ass'n, Op. 8.12 (1982).

any action deficient, but the doctor who, without the consent of the patient, permits another surgeon to operate violates not only a fundamental tenet of the medical profession, but also a legal obligation.

The judgment below is reversed and the matter remanded for trial consistent with our opinion. On remand, the court shall conduct a new pretrial conference at which all parties should have the opportunity to amend their pleadings to conform to this opinion. [REVERSED AND REMANDED]

NOTES

1. *Battery or Negligence?* In *Mink v. University of Chicago,* 460 F. Supp. 713, 717 (N.D. Ill. 1978), women were given DES during their prenatal care by the defendant as part of a study to determine the value of the drug as a miscarriage preventative. The women were not told that they were part of an experiment or the identity of the drug. Defendants argued that plaintiffs' allegations suggested negligence-based informed consent. The court concluded:

> The plaintiffs did not consent to DES treatment; they were not even aware that the drug was being administered to them. They were the subjects of an experiment whereby non-emergency treatment was performed upon them without their consent or knowledge.

> ... The plaintiffs in this action are in a different position from patients who at least knew they were being given some form of drug. The latter must rely on a negligence action based on the physician's failure to disclose inherent risks; the former may bring a battery action grounded on the total lack of consent to DES drug treatment.

Id. at 717.

Do you agree? Wasn't there consent to the ingestion of *some* drug?

2. *Effect of Consent Forms.* IOWA CODE § 147.137 provides:

A consent in writing to any medical or surgical procedure or course of procedures in patient care which meets the requirements of this section shall create a presumption that informed consent was given. A consent in writing meets the requirements of this section if it:

> 1. Sets forth in general terms the nature and purpose of the procedure or procedures, together with the known risks, if any, of death, brain damage, quadriplegia, paraplegia, the loss or loss of function of any organ or limb, or disfiguring scars associated with such procedure or procedures, with the probability of each such risk if reasonably determinable.

> 2. Acknowledges that the disclosure of that information has been made and that all questions asked about the procedure or procedures have been answered in a satisfactory manner ...

Do you interpret this statute as going to the issues of battery, informed consent, or both? Assume that a surgery patient signed a consent form such as one contemplated by this statute; would that, without more, dispose of both questions of "consent" (to the "technical" battery of the surgery) and "adequate disclosure" (for the purposes of determining informed consent)? Would your answer differ dependent on whether you were considering a "professional standard" rather than "patient expectations" jurisdiction?

3. *Dignitary Loss or Un-provable Error?* Why do plaintiffs complain about essentially interpersonal lapses (e.g., lack of consent or failure to advise of risks) in cases where there has been an adverse result?

LARGEY v. ROTHMAN
540 A.2d 504 (N.J. 1988)

PER CURIAM.

In [the] course of a routine physical examination plaintiff's gynecologist, Dr. Glassman, detected a "vague mass" in her right breast. The doctor arranged for mammograms to be taken. The radiologist reported two anomalies to the doctor: an "ill-defined density" in the subareolar region and an enlarged lymph node or nodes, measuring four-by-two centimeters, in the right axilla (armpit). The doctor referred plaintiff to defendant, a surgeon. Defendant expressed concern that the anomalies on the mammograms might be cancer and recommended a biopsy. There was a sharp dispute at trial over whether he stated that the biopsy would include the lymph nodes as well as the breast tissue. Plaintiff claims that defendant never mentioned the nodes.

Plaintiff submitted to the biopsy procedure after receiving a confirmatory second opinion from a Dr. Slattery. During the procedure defendant removed a piece of the suspect mass from plaintiff's breast and excised the nodes. The biopsies showed that both specimens were benign. About six weeks after the operation, plaintiff developed a right arm and hand lymphedema, a swelling caused by inadequate drainage in the lymphatic system. The condition resulted from the excision of the lymph nodes. Defendant did not advise plaintiff of this risk. Plaintiff's experts testified that defendant should have informed plaintiff that lymphedema was a risk of the operation. Defendant's experts testified that it was too rare to be discussed with a patient.

Plaintiff and her husband . . . advanced two theories of liability . . . They claimed that they were never told that the operation would include removal of the nodes and therefore that procedure constituted an unauthorized battery. Alternatively, they claimed that even if they had authorized the node excision, defendant was negligent in failing to warn them of the risk of lymphedema, and therefore their consent was uninformed. The jury specifically rejected both claims.

. . . *In Schloendorff v. The Soc'y of the N.Y. Hosp.,* 211 N.Y. 125 (1914), Justice Cardozo announced a patient's right to be free of uninvited, unknown surgery, which constitutes a trespass on the patient: "Every human being of adult years and sound mind has a right to determine what shall be done with his own body; and a surgeon who performs an operation without his patient's consent commits an assault, for which he is liable in damages." 211 N.Y. at 129–130. Earlier case law recognized that theories of fraud and misrepresentation would sustain a patient's action in battery for an unauthorized intervention . . . Although that cause of action continues to be recognized in New

Jersey, . . . there is no "battery" claim implicated in the appeal because the jury determined as a matter of fact that plaintiff had given consent to the node excision performed by Dr. Rothman.

Although the requirement that a patient give consent before the physician can operate is of long standing, the doctrine of *informed* consent is one of relatively recent development in our jurisprudence. It is essentially a negligence concept, predicated on the duty of a physician to disclose to a patient such information as will enable the patient to make an evaluation of the nature of the treatment and of any attendant substantial risks, as well as of available options in the form of alternative therapies . . .

Anglo-American law starts with the premise of thorough self-determination. It follows that each man is considered to be master of his own body, and he may, if he be of sound mind, expressly prohibit the performance of life-saving surgery, or other medical treatment. A doctor might well believe that an operation or form of treatment is desirable or necessary but the law does not permit him to substitute his own judgment for that of the patient by any form of artifice or deception.

. . . [T]he doctrine of informed consent came to be adopted and developed in other jurisdictions, which, until 1972, followed the "traditional" or "professional" standard formulation of the rule. Under that standard, as applied by the majority of the jurisdictions that adopted it, a physician is required to make such disclosure as comports with the prevailing medical standard in the community — that is, the disclosure of those risks that a reasonable physician in the community, of like training, would customarily make in similar circumstances. A minority of the jurisdictions that adhere to the "professional" standard do not relate the test to any kind of community standard but require only such disclosures as would be made by a reasonable medical practitioner under similar circumstances. In order to prevail in a case applying the "traditional" or "professional" standard a plaintiff would have to present expert testimony of the community's medical standard for disclosure in respect of the procedure in question and of the defendant physician's failure to have met that standard.

In both the majority and minority formulations the "professional" standard rests on the belief that a physician, and *only* a physician, can effectively estimate both the psychological and physical consequences that a risk inherent in a medical procedure might produce in a patient . . .

It was the "professional" standard that this Court accepted when, twenty years ago, it made the doctrine of informed consent a component part of our medical malpractice jurisprudence. *See Kaplan v. Haines,* 51 N.J. 404, *aff'g* 96 N.J. Super, 242 (1968). In falling into step with those other jurisdictions that by then had adopted informed consent, the Court approved the following from the Appellate Division's opinion in *Kaplan*:

> The authorities . . . are in general agreement that the nature and extent of the disclosure, essential to an informed consent, depends upon the medical problem as well as the patient. Plaintiff has the burden to prove what a reasonable medical practitioner of the same school and same or similar circumstances, would have disclosed to his patient and the issue is one for the jury where, as in the case *sub judice,* a fact

issue is raised upon conflicting testimony as to whether the physician made an adequate disclosure. [96 N.J. Super., at 257.]

In 1972 a new standard of disclosure for "informed consent" was established in *Canterbury v. Spence,* 464 F.2d 772 (D.C. Cir. 1972). The case raised a question of the defendant physician's duty to warn the patient beforehand of the risk involved in a laminectomy, a surgical procedure the purpose of which was to relieve pain in plaintiff's lower back, and particularly the risk attendant on a myelogram, the diagnostic procedure preceding the surgery. After several surgical interventions and hospitalizations, plaintiff was still, at the time of trial, using crutches to walk, suffering from urinary incontinence and paralysis of the bowels, and wearing a penile clamp.

The *Canterbury* court announced a duty on the part of a physician to "warn of the dangers lurking in the proposed treatment" and to "impart information [that] the patient has every right to expect," as well as a duty of "reasonable disclosure of the choices with respect to proposed therapy and the dangers inherently and potentially involved." *Id.* at 782. The court held that the scope of the duty to disclose

> must be measured by the patient's need, and that need is the information material to the decision. Thus the test for determining whether a particular peril must be divulged is its materiality to the patient's decision: all risks potentially affecting the decision must be unmasked. And to safeguard the patient's interest in achieving his own determination on treatment, the law must itself set the standard for adequate disclosure. [*Id.* at 786–787]

The breadth of the disclosure of the risks legally to be required is measured, under *Canterbury,* by a standard whose scope is "not subjective as to either the physician or the patient," *id.* at 787; rather, "it remains *objective* with due regard for the patient's informational needs and with suitable leeway for the physician's situation." *Ibid.* (emphasis added). A risk would be deemed "material" when a reasonable patient, in what the physician knows or should know to be the patient's position, would be "likely to attach significance to the risk or cluster of risks" in deciding whether to forego the proposed therapy or to submit to it. *Ibid* . . .

Taken together, the reasons supporting adoption of the "prudent patient" standard persuade us that the time has come for us to abandon so much of the decision by which this Court embraced the doctrine of informed consent as accepts the "professional" standard. To that extent *Kaplan v. Haines,* 51 N.J. 404, *aff'g* 96 N.J. Super. 242, is overruled.

. . . At the outset we are entirely unimpressed with the argument, made by those favoring the "professional" standard . . . that the "prudent patient" rule would compel disclosure of *every* risk (not just *material* risks) to *any* patient (rather than the *reasonable* patient). As *Canterbury* makes clear,

> [t]he topics importantly demanding a communication of information are the inherent and potential hazards of the proposed treatment, the alternatives to that treatment, if any, and the results likely if the patient remains untreated. The factors contributing significance to the

dangerousness of a medical technique are, of course, the incidence of injury and the degree of harm threatened. [464 F.2d at 787–788.]

The court in *Canterbury* did not presume to draw a "bright line separating the significant [risks] from the insignificant"; rather, it resorted to a "rule of reason," *id.* at 788, concluding that "[w]henever nondisclosure of particular risk information is open to debate by reasonable minded men, the issue is one for the finder of facts." The point assumes significance in this case because defendant argues that the risk of lymphedema from an axillary node biopsy is remote, not material. Plaintiff's experts disagree, contending that she should have been informed of that risk. Thus there will be presented on the retrial a factual issue for the jury's resolution: would the risk of lymphedema influence a prudent patient in reaching a decision on whether to submit to the surgery?

Perhaps the strongest consideration that influences our decision in favor of the "prudent patient" standard lies in the notion that the physician's duty of disclosure "arises from phenomena apart from medical custom and practice": the patient's right of self-determination. *Canterbury, supra,* 464 F.2d at 786-787. The foundation for the physician's duty to disclose in the first place is found in the idea that "it is the prerogative of the patient, not the physician, to determine for himself the direction in which his interests seem to lie." *Id.* at 781. In contrast the arguments for the "professional" standard smack of an anachronistic paternalism that is at odds with any strong conception of a patient's right of self-determination. *Id.* at 781, 784, 789.

. . . We therefore align ourselves with those jurisdictions that have adopted *Canterbury's* "prudent patient" standard. [REVERSED AND REMANDED.]

NOTES

1. *Professional or Patient Standard?* A slight majority of jurisdictions utilizes the professional or customary standard for informed consent cases. What are the arguments given in *Largey* in support of the "prudent patient" standard? What arguments can be made in favor of the professional standard?

2. *The Persistent Role of Expert Testimony.* In *Winkjer v. Herr*, 277 N.W.2d 579 (N.D. 1979), plaintiff unsuccessfully appealed from an adverse summary judgment in an informed consent case. Irrespective of whether a custom or patient expectations standard applied the court noted:

> Under either an objective or subjective duty of disclosure, expert medical testimony is generally necessary to identify the risks of treatment, their gravity, likelihood of occurrence, and reasonable alternatives. The necessity for expert testimony is particularly so when such information is outside the common knowledge of laymen.
>
> A duty to disclose can arise only if the physician knew or should have known of the risks to be disclosed. Also, a physician is not required to disclose all possible risks and dangers of the proposed procedure but only those that are significant in terms of their seriousness and likelihood of occurrence. There is no need to disclose risks of little consequence, those

that are extremely remote, or those that are common knowledge as inherent in the treatment. If a risk was not known to exist, clearly a physician cannot be held liable for failure to inform his patient.

The plaintiff did not offer expert testimony to refute the showing of the defendant that there was no genuine issue of fact as to a known risk to be disclosed . . . There can be no liability for a physician to disclose a risk that was unknown in the manner in which a particular drug or treatment was prescribed.

In *Winkjer* and other cases that use the patient standard, expert evidence of what reasonable physicians consider adequate disclosure is admissible, but not dispositive. *See, e.g.*, *Martin v. Richards*, 192 Wis.2d 156, 174 (1995).

3. *The Limits of Informed Consent.* In *Morgan v. MacPhail*, 550 Pa. 202 (1997), the court held that the doctrine of informed consent applies only to invasive (e.g., surgical) procedures on the basis that "the performance of a surgical procedure upon a patient without his consent constitutes a technical assault or a battery because the patient is typically unconscious and unable to object. . . . The patient, appellants urge, has the right to make an informed choice as to electing to undergo a medical procedure after having been presented with the alternatives and the risks attendant to each alternative. This argument, however, flies in the face of the traditional battery theory. It is the invasive nature of the surgical or operative procedure involving a surgical cut and the use of surgical instruments that gives rise to the need to inform the patient of risks prior to surgery."

Contrast *Truman v. Thomas*, 27 Cal. 3d 285 (1980), which concerned a patient who died of cervical cancer. The action was brought against her family physician for failing to inform the decedent of the risks associated with failing to undergo a diagnostic test (a pap smear). The defendant argued that the risk disclosure duty only applies when a patient consents to a procedure. The court replied, "The duty to disclose was imposed . . . so that patients might meaningfully exercise their right to make decisions about their own bodies. The importance of this right should not be diminished by the manner in which it is exercised. Further, the need for disclosure is not lessened because patients reject a recommended procedure."

In *Johnson v. Kokemoor*, 199 Wis.2d 615 (1996), the question presented was whether the trial court had erred by admitting evidence that the defendant, prior to receiving the patient's consent to clip an aneurysm, failed to divulge the extent of his experience in performing this type of operation; did not compare the morbidity and mortality rates for this type of surgery among experienced surgeons and inexperienced surgeons; and failed to refer the plaintiff to a tertiary care center staffed by physicians more experienced in performing the same surgery. The Supreme Court of Wisconsin held that the evidence was properly admitted. The court stated: "The prudent patient standard . . . is incompatible with such a bright line rule" and that "what a physician must disclose is contingent upon what, under the circumstances of a given case, a reasonable person in the patient's position would need to know in order to make an intelligent and informed decision. The question of whether certain information is material to a patient's decision and therefore requires disclosure is "rooted in the facts and circumstances of the particular case in which it arises." 199 Wis.2d at 639.

4. *Informed Causation.* In an informed consent case the plaintiff is arguing that the physician negligently failed to adequately disclose the risk of a procedure and the risk occurred. Plaintiff must also prove that the alleged negligence was causally related to his consent to the procedure. Consider the advantages and disadvantages of objective and subjective standards for considering whether the consent was informed. In *Cheung v. Cunningham,* 214 N.J. Super. 649 (1987), the majority opinion stated: "The fault of the objective standard is that plaintiff must for all practical purposes prove that *any* reasonable person placed in the same position would necessarily withhold consent even though plaintiff may have withheld consent and thereby have avoided injury" and described the result as "the antithesis of the doctrine of informed consent which is intended to protect the individual patient's right to decline treatment . . . " The concurrence countered: "adoption of the subjective test in the present context would have the potential of converting each patient into a litigant and would promote a doctor-adversarial relationship as opposed to a doctor-patient status, thereby increasing malpractice litigation and escalating medical costs." Which view is more persuasive?

5. *Escalating Liability.* The informed consent doctrine is one of the few major *doctrinal* developments in the last half-century of malpractice law. *Largey* quotes Justice Cardozo's well-known statement that "[e]very human being of adult years and sound mind has a right to determine what shall be done with his own body." Do some or all of the perspectives — Corrective Justice, Critical Race Theory, Critical Feminism — explain how that aspiration translated into the modern law of Informed Consent? In contrast, do the perspectives of Law and Economics or Pragmatism explain why a slight majority of jurisdictions use a *physician* standard to determine this *patient* interest in autonomy?

E. ADDITIONAL LIABILITY THEORIES

ROSENBLIT v. ZIMMERMAN
166 N.J. 391 (2001)

Long, Judge.

. . . Plaintiff Erin Rosenblit, a registered nurse, sought treatment from defendant, Dr. John F. Zimmerman, Jr., a chiropractor, for midback pain early in 1992. In January and February of 1992, and again in May and June of 1992, Dr. Zimmerman treated Rosenblit with chiropractic manipulation. In manipulation, Zimmerman placed one hand under Rosenblit's chin, the other hand on the back of her skull, and moved her backward by pulling up on her chin. After her third or fourth visit, Rosenblit developed new symptoms, including neck pain, headaches, nausea, and ringing in her ears. Rosenblit testified that even after bringing those complaints to Dr. Zimmerman's attention, he attempted the same type of neck manipulation during a subsequent visit.

Rosenblit went to other doctors in an attempt to determine what was wrong with her. Dr. Jerome Cottler, who saw Rosenblit in October 1994, found C1-C2 instability in her neck on the basis of X rays of plaintiff's neck that revealed a space between the C1 and C2 vertebrae greater than two millimeters. She underwent orthopaedic surgery in January 1995 to fuse two cervical vertebrae in her spine. Rosenblit testified that the symptoms that brought her to seek treatment from defendant in the first place were not relieved until after the fusion surgery.

In 1995, Rosenblit sued Dr. Zimmerman, and Health First Chiropractic Clinic in which Dr. Zimmerman was a partner, alleging malpractice. She obtained a copy of her medical chart from Dr. Zimmerman's office prior to commencing the malpractice lawsuit. During discovery, Rosenblit received another copy of her chart from Dr. Zimmerman and realized that it was different from the one she already had in her possession. The altered chart made it appear that she was improving with the treatment administered by the doctor; that her complaints about neck pain after the treatment were really complaints about mid-back pain; and that she was satisfied with the treatment when she left his care. The original unaltered chart, however, revealed that Rosenblit was not gradually improving and that she was dissatisfied with her condition when she last visited Dr. Zimmerman. When Dr. Zimmerman was confronted with that discrepancy at his deposition, he explained that when he was served with the summons and complaint, almost two years after treating Rosenblit, he decided to recopy the chart to make it more legible. After he recopied the chart, he destroyed the originals. A comparison of the two charts, however, shows alterations that are plainly not the result of recopying. With respect to those alterations, Dr. Zimmerman testified at his deposition that he wanted to make the records more complete, and that he remembered details that he had never recorded earlier.

After discovering that a second set of altered medical records existed, Rosenblit amended her complaint to include counts for spoliation and fraudulent concealment of evidence based upon Dr. Zimmerman's conduct. The trial court bifurcated the malpractice counts from the spoliation and fraudulent concealment counts. All claims, however, were tried before the same jury, with the malpractice case proceeding first.

Before the malpractice portion of the trial began, the trial court barred evidence of Dr. Zimmerman's alteration of the medical chart, except if used to impeach his credibility as a witness. Predictably, defense counsel did not call Dr. Zimmerman to the stand, and Rosenblit therefore was barred from referring to the altered records, or to Zimmerman's deposition acknowledging and attempting to explain the alterations.

The malpractice trial proceeded with Rosenblit's original chart being placed in evidence, and Dr. Zimmerman stipulating that Rosenblit's version of the chiropractic treatment that he provided was true. Both parties presented expert witnesses about whether or not Dr. Zimmerman's treatment of Rosenblit was within the accepted standard of care.

That testimony need not be recounted here except to observe that it constituted the proverbial battle of the experts. The jury returned a verdict in favor of Dr. Zimmerman on the issue of negligence, never reaching the proximate cause question.

Over defense counsel's objections, the spoliation and fraudulent concealment trial proceeded before the same jury. During that trial, Rosenblit presented the altered records, and Dr. Zimmerman's deposition testimony explaining why he altered and then destroyed her records . . .

The jury returned a verdict in favor of Rosenblit, and awarded her $421.75 in compensatory damages, and $500,000 in punitive damages . . .

Thereafter, Rosenblit appealed from the judgment in the malpractice action on the ground that the jury should have been permitted to consider Dr. Zimmerman's alteration of her medical records, regardless of his decision not to take the stand. Dr. Zimmerman cross-appealed from the fraudulent concealment verdict, maintaining that Rosenblit could not sustain that cause of action because she had the accurate records in her possession and thus the alteration and destruction of the medical records did not impair her ability to file or prove her malpractice case . . .

Spoliation, as its name implies, is an act that spoils, impairs or taints the value or usefulness of a thing. *BLACK'S LAW DICTIONARY* 1409 (7th ed.1999) . . .

When spoliation occurs, the law has developed a number of civil remedies, the purpose of which is to make whole, as nearly as possible, the litigant whose cause of action has been impaired by the absence of crucial evidence; to punish the wrongdoer; and to deter others from such conduct.

The best known civil remedy that has been developed is the so-called spoliation inference that comes into play where a litigant is made aware of the destruction or concealment of evidence during the underlying litigation. Since the seventeenth century, courts have followed the rule "omnia praesumuntur contra spoliatorem," which means "all things are presumed against the destroyer." *Hirsch v. General Motors Corp.*, 266 N.J. Super. 222, 258 (Law Div. 1993).

Courts use the spoliation inference during the underlying litigation as a method of evening the playing field where evidence has been hidden or destroyed. It essentially allows a jury in the underlying case to presume that the evidence the spoliator destroyed or otherwise concealed would have been unfavorable to him or her. Commentators have characterized the spoliation inference as a powerful tool.

A second and more traditional remedy generally available against a party who destroys evidence is the discovery sanction. For instance, where a party fails to comply with a discovery demand or request, [our rules provide] that the court may order that designated facts be taken as established, refuse to permit the disobedient party to support or oppose designated claims or defenses, prohibit the introduction of designated matters into evidence, dismiss an action, or enter judgment by default. That rule further provides that the court may order the delinquent party to pay reasonable expenses resulting from his or her conduct, including attorney's fees.

Another remedy for the destruction of litigation evidence is a separate tort action against the spoliator. Two distinct types of conduct have been identified in other jurisdictions as potentially subjecting a miscreant to a tort remedy: intentional spoliation and negligent spoliation. Because the conduct of Dr. Zimmerman in this case was entirely purposeful, we confine our discussion to the tort remedy for intentional spoliation.

Several jurisdictions have recognized a new tort of intentional spoliation of evidence. . . .

Some courts have refused to recognize any tort action to remedy spoliation, holding instead that the evidentiary rules, along with adverse inferences will suffice. That, of course, is true only if the spoliation is discovered in time for the underlying litigation, or so soon afterward that the litigant has an opportunity under the rules to seek relief from judgment and retry his or her case.

Other courts have refused to recognize a new tort because they conceive of spoliation as remediable under existing tort principles. New Jersey falls into that category . . .

Viviano v. CBS, Inc., 251 N.J. Super. 113 (App. Div. 1991), *certif. denied,* 127 N.J. 565 (1992) properly denominated the conduct of destruction of litigation evidence as spoliation and, in so doing, cited cases and commentaries that recognized an independent tort remedy for that conduct . . . *Viviano* did not recognize a novel cause of action for spoliation, but identified a pre-existing tort remedy for that conduct: fraudulent concealment . . .

We fully approve of that approach . . . The elements that must be established by a plaintiff in such a fraudulent concealment action are:

> (1) That defendant in the fraudulent concealment action had a legal obligation to disclose evidence in connection with an existing or pending litigation;

> (2) That the evidence was material to the litigation;

> (3) That plaintiff could not reasonably have obtained access to the evidence from another source;

> (4) That defendant intentionally withheld, altered or destroyed the evidence with purpose to disrupt the litigation;

> (5) That plaintiff was damaged in the underlying action by having to rely on an evidential record that did not contain the evidence defendant concealed.

. . . A party's access to the remedies we have catalogued will depend upon the point in the litigation process that the concealment or destruction is uncovered. If it is revealed in time for the underlying litigation, the spoliation inference may be invoked. In addition, the injured party may amend his or her complaint to add a count for fraudulent concealment. As the trial court realized here, those counts will require bifurcation because the fraudulent concealment remedy depends on the jury's assessment of the underlying cause of action. In that instance, after the jury has returned a verdict in the bifurcated underlying action, it will be required to determine whether the elements of the tort of fraudulent concealment have been established, and, if so, whether damages are warranted. Further, the plaintiff may be awarded discovery sanctions if the court determines that they are justified in light of the outcome in the fraudulent concealment trial.

If, however, the spoliation is not discovered until after the underlying action has been lost or otherwise seriously inhibited, the plaintiff may file a separate tort action. In such an action, plaintiff will be required to establish the elements of the tort of fraudulent concealment. To do so, the fundamentals of the underlying litigation will also require exposition. Unless such an action is allowed, a belatedly discovered spoliation claim would be without a meaningful remedy. Obviously the plaintiff in such an action also could recover discovery sanctions if the court determines that they are warranted in light of the jury verdict.

Neither the spoliation inference nor a separate tort action was appropriate in this case because Rosenblit not only uncovered the concealment prior to the malpractice trial, but was fortunate enough to have obtained copies of the original records. Thus the evidence was not absent when it was required and there was no need to presume what the original record entailed. Nor was there a basis for a separate tort action for losses sustained as a result of missing evidence . . . [S]uch an action cannot be maintained when the evidence the spoliator sought to hide or destroy has come to light in time for the underlying litigation.

Because the records Dr. Zimmerman altered were fully aired during the malpractice litigation, its outcome could not have been affected by the attempted spoliation. Thus, there was no basis for a fraudulent concealment action against him. Accordingly, we reverse the judgment entered upon that jury verdict.

That conclusion does not end the matter however, because an error took place during the malpractice action that requires a retrial. That error was the trial court's circumscription of Rosenblit's right to apprise the jury of Dr. Zimmerman's alteration of her medical records . . .

Dr. Zimmerman was not just a witness. He was a party to the action, and subject to [our rule] that provides that a statement made by a party opponent may be offered against him or her in evidence. The alteration of Rosenblit's medical records constituted a verbal act by Dr. Zimmerman tantamount to a statement that was evidential against him under the rule . . .

[T]he alteration evidence would have had a substantial impact on Dr. Zimmerman's case. But that is what happens when there is powerful and persuasive evidence. That does not mean, as Dr. Zimmerman has argued, that it should be excluded . . . Absent extraordinary circumstances, evidence of intentional alteration or destruction of medical records by a physician accused of malpractice should not be excluded under *N.J.R.E.* 403 . . .

In short, Rosenblit did not receive a fair trial in the underlying malpractice action. Indeed, the importance of the alteration evidence to the jury was underscored by its large award of punitive damages to Rosenblit in the later, albeit improper, spoliation case. By that verdict, the jury effectively signaled that it would have ruled differently in the malpractice case had it been aware of Dr. Zimmerman's efforts to cover up his actions. Thus, exclusion of that evidence in the malpractice trial clearly had the potential to affect the outcome unjustly.

. . . [E]vidence of the alteration to show constant improvement by Rosenblit was also relevant to whether Zimmerman breached the appropriate standard of care by continuing manipulations on her after she brought her claims of neck pain, nausea and ear-ringing to his attention. Malpractice could arise not only in the method of manipulation performed by Dr. Zimmerman, but also in his continued use of that method on Rosenblit after the injury about which she complained. Consequently, the error was not harmless. We thus reverse the judgment in the malpractice action and remand that case for a new trial consonant with the evidentiary principles to which we have adverted . . .

The judgment entered on the jury verdict for spoliation is reversed. The judgment in the malpractice action is reversed and that matter is remanded for trial. [REVERSED AND REMANDED.]

NOTES

1. *Spoiling for a Fight.* Why would a court approve of this additional tort cause of action when there are already procedural remedies available to the litigant? In *Rosenblit* the court setout five elements for the spoliation tort — on which did the plaintiff's case fail?

2. *Contracting for Specific Medical Results.* In the leading case of *Sullivan v. O'Connor,* 296 N.E.2d 183, 186 (Mass. 1973), the plaintiff recovered on an express warranty theory after alleging that the defendant plastic surgeon had promised to enhance her beauty and improve her appearance. Nevertheless, the court cautioned:

> It is not hard to see why the courts should be unenthusiastic or skeptical about the contract theory. Considering the uncertainties of medical science and the variations in the physical and psychological conditions of individual patients, doctors can seldom in good faith promise specific results. Therefore it is unlikely that physicians of even average integrity will in fact make such promises. Statements of opinion by the physician with some optimistic coloring are a different thing, and may indeed have therapeutic value. But patients may transform such statements into firm promises in their own minds, especially when they have been disappointed in the event. . . .

3. *Outrage.* In his classic book, EXPLORATIONS IN QUALITY ASSESSMENT AND MONITORING, Vol. 1, *The Definition of Quality and Approaches to Its Assessment* (1980), Avedis Donabedian identified the quality management of patient care as having both "technical" and "interpersonal" aspects. This chapter primarily concentrates on the "technical" aspects — diagnosis, treatment, surgery, etc. However, the causes of action considered in this section (and, to an extent, in the section dealing with Consent) deal with more "interpersonal" issues.

Occasionally the relationship between a physician and a patient will become severely strained, as in "abandonment" scenarios.

In some cases the dysfunction will be expressed legally by an action for "outrage" or intentional infliction of emotional distress in accordance with REST. 2D TORTS § 46(2), discussed in Chapter 2. Is the use of this tort satisfactory for addressing breakdowns in the doctor/patient relationship? Consider *Lucchesi v. Stimmell*, 149 Ariz. 76 (1986), where a doctor specializing in high risk pregnancies failed to attend his patient's labor notwithstanding his alleged promise to be present. The patient's baby was stillborn and its head had been severed during the delivery. The parent plaintiffs also alleged that subsequent to the birth the doctor had failed to inform them of the full details surrounding their child's birth. The court held the trial court had erred in granting the defendant's motion for summary judgment and that there was "a factual issue so that a jury should have had an opportunity to decide whether defendant's conduct was outrageous and whether plaintiff suffered severe emotional distress."

Compare *Taylor v. Albert Einstein Med. Ctr.*, 562 Pa. 176 (2000), where a 16-year-old died during an invasive diagnostic procedure. The patient's mother alleged that she had only consented to a specific cardiologist performing the procedure, not the less experienced doctor who actually performed it. The mother was in a hospital waiting room during the procedure but she could hear the defibrillator alarm sound when her daughter's heart stopped. The court held that the mother's action for outrage based on the alleged representation by the cardiologist that his colleague would perform the procedure failed because "[p]resence is a crucial element of the tort because an individual who witnesses outrageous or shocking conduct directed at a third-party has no time in which to prepare himself/herself for the immediate emotional impact of such conduct . . . By way of comparison, the emotional effects are generally lessened where the individual learns of the outrageous conduct long after its occurrence and by means other than through his or her own personal observations."

4. *Privacy and Confidentiality.* Of increasing importance in modern healthcare litigation are allegations of invasions of privacy and breach of confidence. In the former, the patient is claiming that the healthcare provider improperly *collected* information. In the latter, the complaint goes to the *dissemination* of the data.

In *Doe v. Roe,* 400 N.Y.S.2d 668, 676-677 (Sup. Ct. 1977), a former patient of a psychiatrist alleged that a book subsequently published by the psychiatrist contained verbatim her most personal disclosures. The court stated, "Every patient, and particularly every patient undergoing psychoanalysis, has a right of privacy . . . Despite the fact that in no New York case has such a right been remedied due, most likely, to the fact that so few physicians violate this fundamental obligation, it is time that the obligation not only be recognized but that the right of redress be recognized as well." The court continued: "What label we affix to this wrong is unimportant . . . What is important is that there must be the infliction of intentional harm, resulting in damage without legal excuse or justification."

In *Humphers v. First Interstate Bank,* 298 Or. 706 (1985), a patient consented to the adoption of her daughter at birth. Twenty-one years later, the daughter, wishing to contact her natural mother, discovered the identity of the delivering physician. Agreeing to help her, the physician gave her a letter which stated, untruthfully, that he had treated her mother with the drug diethylstilbestrol (DES) and thus, daughter and mother needed to be put in contact with each other. Armed with this letter, the daughter was able to breach the confidentiality of her birth and adoption records and contact her natural mother. The court held that the emotionally distressed mother stated a cause of action for breach of confidence.

Today, considerable attention focuses on the so-called HIPAA privacy regulations (*Privacy of Individually Identifiable Health Information,* 45 CFR 164.500 *et seq.*). However, these regulations apply only to the dissemination of patient data (and are thus mislabeled as "privacy" regulations), contain many exceptions, and do not permit a private right of action. *See generally* Nicolas P. Terry & Leslie P. Francis, *Ensuring The Privacy and Confidentiality of Electronic Health Records,* 2007 U. ILL. L. REV. 681.

5. *Proliferation of Causes of Action.* With judicial expansion of claims to address informed consent, spoliation, breach of confidence, etc., are the courts soberly exploring the reach of malpractice liability or endorsing patient frustration with core, negligence-based malpractice doctrine? Do these novel or alternative theories of liability constitute a backlash against prevalent tort reform that has made the core malpractice case ever more difficult to win? Is this a modern battle ground between, for example, Law and Economics and Corrective Justice perspectives on the role of Tort law?

F. LIABILITY OF HEALTHCARE INSTITUTIONS

BURLESS v. WEST VIRGINIA UNIVERSITY HOSPITALS, INC.
215 W.Va. 765 (2004)

DAVIS, JUSTICE.

. . . Each of the two cases consolidated for purposes of this opinion involve a woman who gave birth to her child at West Virginia University Hospitals (WVUH) under circumstances that she alleges resulted in severe birth defects to her child . . . [In each case the plaintiff had received allegedly negligent care from physicians employed by the West Virginia University Board of Trustees ("the BOT"). Both (Ms. Burless and Ms. Pritt) had signed WVUH consent forms that stated: "I understand that the faculty physicians and resident physicians who provide treatment in the hospital are not employees of the hospital." Plaintiffs claimed that WVUH was vicariously liable for the BOT physicians and in both cases the trial courts granted summary judgment to WVUH.] . . .

There are four general factors which bear upon whether a master-servant relationship exists for purposes of the doctrine of *respondeat superior:* (1) Selection and engagement of the servant; (2) Payment of compensation; (3) Power of dismissal; and (4) Power of control. The first three factors are not essential to the existence of the relationship; the fourth, the power of control, is determinative. *Paxton v. Crabtree,* 184 W.Va. 237 (1990) . . .

[The plaintiffs] and WVUH have directed us to numerous portions of the voluminous record in this case in support of their contrasting contentions on this issue. We have thoroughly considered each of the *Paxton* factors in light of the particular facts of this case and the evidence in the record to which we were directed. We conclude that the considerable evidence contained in the record admits of only one reasonable conclusion, the BOT resident physicians who treat patients at WVUH are not agents or employees of WVUH . . .

Accordingly, we find no error in the circuit courts decisions to grant summary judgment to WVUH on the issue of actual agency.

[The plaintiffs] next assert that the circuit courts erred in finding no apparent agency[4] relationship between the doctors who treated them and WVUH. Because we have explained in the previous section that we find no *actual* agency relationship in these cases, we have concluded that the doctors were, in fact, independent contractors. Our cases have recognized that, as a general rule, "[i]f [a physician] is found to be an independent contractor, then the hospital is not liable for his [or her] negligence."

. . . As with most general rules, there are exceptions to the independent contractor rule . . .

In the hospital/physician context, this Court has heretofore established that even where a physician charged with negligence is an independent contractor, the hospital may nevertheless be found vicariously liable where the complained of treatment was provided in an emergency room. *See* Syl. pt. 1, *Torrence v. Kusminsky,* 185 W.Va. 734, 408 S.E.2d 684 (1991) ("Where a hospital makes emergency room treatment available to serve the public as an integral part of its facilities, the hospital is estopped to deny that the physicians and other medical personnel on duty providing treatment are its agents. Regardless of any contractual arrangements with so-called independent contractors, the hospital is liable to the injured patient for acts of malpractice committed *in its emergency room,* so long as the requisite proximate cause and damages are present.") (emphasis added). Although we have addressed using a theory of apparent agency to overcome the physician/independent contractor rule in the context of emergency room treatment, we have never expressly defined such a rule for use outside of the emergency room setting. We do so now.

---

[4] [The plaintiffs] refer to this element of their claim as "ostensible agency" instead of "apparent agency." The two terms are commonly used interchangeably. *See Baptist Mem'l Hosp. Syst. v. Sampson,* 969 S.W.2d 945, 947 n. 2 (Tex.1998) (collecting cases) (commenting that "[m]any courts use the terms ostensible agency, apparent agency, apparent authority, and agency by estoppel interchangeably. As a practical matter, there is no distinction among them."). *See generally Blacks Law Dictionary* 62 (7th ed. 1999) (noting in definition of "agency by estoppel" that it is "[a]lso termed *apparent agency; ostensible agency, agency by operation of law.*"). For ease of reference, we will refer to the doctrine as "apparent agency," unless quoting an authority using an alternate term.

1. Hospital/Physician Apparent Agency Outside the Emergency Room Setting. The public's confidence in the modern hospital's portrayal of itself as a full service provider of health care appears to be at the foundation of the national trend toward adopting a rule of apparent agency to find hospitals liable, under the appropriate circumstances, for the negligence of physicians providing services within its walls . . .

In order to set out a specific test for finding liability based upon apparent agency in a hospital/physician context, we consider the tests that have been adopted in other jurisdictions. The California appellate court in *Mejia v. Community Hosp. of San Bernardino*, 99 Cal. App. 4th 1448, 1453 (2002), summarized the tests that are used as follows:

> Although the cases discussing ostensible agency use various linguistic formulation to describe the elements of the doctrine, in essence, they require the same two elements: (1) conduct by the hospital that would cause a reasonable person to believe that the physician was an agent of the hospital, and (2) reliance on that apparent agency relationship by the plaintiff.

99 Cal. App. 4th at 1453. Looking at some of the specific tests that have been adopted, we note that the Appellate Court of Illinois has said

> [f]or a hospital to be held liable under an apparent agency theory, a plaintiff must establish that: "'(1) the hospital, or its agent, acted in a manner that would lead a reasonable person to conclude that the individual who was alleged to be negligent was an employee or agent of the hospital; (2) where the acts of the agent create the appearance of authority, the plaintiff must also prove that the hospital had knowledge of and acquiesced in them; and (3) the plaintiff acted in reliance upon the conduct of the hospital or its agent, consistent with ordinary care and prudence.'" [*Scardina v. Alexian Brothers Med. Ctr.*, 308 Ill. App. 3d 359, 363–64 (1999)] . . .

. . . [W]e now hold that for a hospital to be held liable for a physician's negligence under an apparent agency theory, a plaintiff must establish that: (1) the hospital either committed an act that would cause a reasonable person to believe that the physician in question was an agent of the hospital, or, by failing to take an action, created a circumstance that would allow a reasonable person to hold such a belief, and (2) the plaintiff relied on the apparent agency relationship.

2. Hospital's Actions or Inactions. The first element of our test requires evidence that the hospital either committed an act that would cause a reasonable person to believe that the physician in question was an agent of the hospital, or, by failing to take an action, created a circumstance that would allow a reasonable person to hold such a belief. This portion of the test focuses on the acts of the hospital and is generally satisfied when "the hospital 'holds itself out' to the public as a provider of care." *Mejia v. Community Hosp. of San Bernardino*, 99 Cal. App. 4th 1448, 1453 (2002). *See also Collins v. Gettysburg Hosp.*, 55 Pa. D.&C. 4th 174,184 (2001) (explaining that whether a hospital "holds out" a physician as its employee typically refers to a hospital acting or omitting to act "in some way which leads the patient to a reasonable belief he is being treated by the hospital or one of its employees."). However, "the hospital need not make express representations to the patient that the treating physician is an employee of the hospital; rather a representation also may be general and implied." *Sword v. NKC Hosps. Inc.,* 714 N.E.2d 142, 151 (Ind. 1999). *See also Kashishian v. Al-Bitar,* 194 Wis.2d 722, 728 (1995) ("There . . . need not be an 'express representation' that the person alleged to be negligent is an employee for the doctrine of apparent authority to apply."). One court has explained that "[i]n order to prove this element, it is not necessary to show an express representation by the hospital. . . . Instead, a hospital is generally deemed to have held itself out as the provider of care, unless it gave the patient contrary notice." *Mejia,* 99 Cal. App. 4th at 1454. The "contrary notice" referred to by the *Mejia* court generally manifests itself in the form of a disclaimer. As one court has acknowledged, "[a] hospital generally will be able to avoid liability by providing *meaningful written notice* to the patient, acknowledged at the time of admission." *Sword v. NKC Hosps., Inc.,* 714 N.E.2d 142, 152. It has been said that "[l]iability under apparent agency. . . will not attach against a hospital where the patient knows, or reasonably should have known, that the treating physician was an independent contractor." *Scardina,* 308 Ill. App.3d at 364. Thus, a hospital's failure to provide a meaningful written notice may constitute "failing to take an action" and thereby allowing a reasonable person to believe that a particular doctor is an agent of the hospital. Conversely, absent other overt acts by the hospital indicating an employer/employee relationship, an unambiguous disclaimer by a hospital explaining the independent contractor status of physicians will generally suffice to immunize the hospital from being vicariously liable for physician conduct.

Turning to the cases before us, the circuit courts in both cases relied on the disclaimers signed by [the plaintiffs] in granting summary judgment in favor of WVUH. In addition, the circuit court considering Ms. Pritt's case summarily concluded that WVUH had not "held the physicians out to be its employees." We disagree with these conclusions.

The disclaimer that WVUH required both [the plaintiffs] to sign stated: "I understand that the faculty physicians and resident physicians who provide treatment in the hospital are not employees of the hospital." WVUH contends that this "disclaimer" was sufficient to unequivocally inform [the plaintiffs] that the physicians treating them were not employees of the hospital. We disagree.

We do not find the disclaimer language used by WVUH, which indicated that "faculty physicians and resident physicians who provide treatment in the hospital" are independent contractors, was sufficient to support a grant of summary judgment in their favor. The WVUH disclaimer provision presupposes that all patients can distinguish between "faculty physicians," "resident physicians" and any other type of physician having privileges at the hospital. In other words, for this disclaimer to be meaningful, a patient would literally have to inquire into the employment status of everyone treating him or her . . .

Consequently, it was improper for the circuit court to grant summary judgment in favor of WVUH. [The plaintiffs] have established a genuine question of material fact as to whether WVUH has either committed an act that would cause a reasonable person to believe that the physician in question was an agent of the hospital, or, by failing to take an action, created a circumstance that would allow a reasonable person to hold such a belief.

3. Reliance. The reliance prong of the apparent agency test is a subjective molehill. "Reliance . . . is established when the plaintiff 'looks to' the hospital for services, rather than to an individual physician." *Mejia,* 99 Cal.App.4th at 1453. It is "sometimes characterized as an inquiry as to whether 'the plaintiff acted in reliance upon the conduct of the hospital or its agent, consistent with ordinary care and prudence.'" *Sword,* 714 N.E.2d at 151. This factor "simply focuses on the 'patient's belief that the hospital or its employees were rendering health care.'" *Jennison v. Providence St. Vincent Med. Ctr.,* 174 Or.App. 219, 230 (2001). However, this portion of the test also requires consideration of the "reasonableness of the patient's [subjective] belief that the hospital or its employees were rendering health care." *Sword v. NKC Hosps. Inc.,* 714 N.E.2d at 152. "This . . . determination is made by considering the totality of the circumstances, including . . . any special knowledge the patient[/plaintiff] may have about the hospital's arrangements with its physicians." *Id.*

[The plaintiffs] provided evidence indicating that they believed that the physicians treating them were employees of WVUH.

In the deposition testimony of Ms. Burless she stated her belief that the people treating her at the hospital were employees, as follows: "Q. Did anyone do anything to make you believe that they were employees of WVU Hospital? A. They were all wearing their coats and name tags and in the building, so, you know, you know they're — they work there, they're employees." In the affidavit submitted by Ms. Pritt in opposition to WVUH's motion for summary judgment, the following was stated:

> 2. At the West Virginia University Hospitals, I was assigned doctors who treated me and consulted me through my prenatal care, surgery and delivery of my son Adam.

> 3. Throughout all of my treatment and consultations, I believed that the doctors and nurses who treated me and spoke to me were employees of the West Virginia University Hospitals.

[The plaintiffs] have also established a genuine question of material fact on the issue of their reliance on the apparent agency relationship between WVUH and their treating physicians. Consequently, on the issue of apparent agency, it is clear that summary judgment should not have been granted in favor of WVUH.

For the reasons explained above, we find that the circuit courts correctly granted summary judgment on this issue of actual agency, however they erred in granting summary judgment to WVUH on the issue of apparent agency. Accordingly, the orders of the circuit courts are affirmed in part, reversed in part, and this case is remanded for further proceedings consistent with this opinion. [AFFIRMED IN PART, REVERSED IN PART AND REMANDED.]

MAYNARD, CHIEF JUSTICE, concurring, in part, and dissenting, in part:

. . . I believe the record clearly shows that there was no apparent agency. First, [the plaintiffs] signed an unambiguous disclaimer that stated: "I understand that the faculty physicians and resident physicians who provide treatment in the hospital are not employees of the hospital." The majority opinion, in discounting this disclaimer, reasons that "[t]he WVUH disclaimer provision presupposes that all patients can distinguish between 'faculty physicians,' 'resident physicians' and any other type of physician having privileges at the hospital." This reasoning baffles me. If *both* faculty physicians *and* resident physicians are non-employees, why is it necessary to distinguish between them? Second, the evidence demonstrates that neither [plaintiff] relied on any representation by the hospital that their physicians' status was that of agent. Finally, the evidence shows that Ms. Burless chose her own physician, and Ms. Pritt could have rejected the hospital's choice and chosen another physician. For these reasons, I would have affirmed the circuit court's grant of summary judgment on behalf of the hospital on the issue of apparent agency.

NOTES

1. *Liability for Independent Physicians.* Large numbers of physicians who work in hospitals (or for other healthcare institutions such as HMOs) are independent contractors who have been granted "staff privileges" to treat patients within the institution.

Courts have used an array of legal doctrines to create exceptions to the general rule that healthcare institutions are not vicariously liable for such independent contractors. These doctrines include apparent or ostensible agency (*see, e.g., Jackson v. Power*, 743 P.2d 1376 (Alaska 1987); *Sheldon v. Damle*, 2004 R.I. Super. LEXIS 160 (2004)); liberally interpreting the "control" exercised by a hospital over a physician (*see, e.g., Berel v. HCA Health Servs.*, 881 S.W.2d 21 (Tex. Ct. App. 1994)); and non-delegable duty (*see, e.g., Simmons v. Tuomey Reg'l Med. Ctr.*, 341 S.C. 32 (2000)).

However, a minority of jurisdictions does not recognize some or all of these theories. For example, in *Sanchez v. Medicorp Health System*, 270 Va. 299, 307-08 (2005), an emergency room case, the court stated: "[W]e have not previously imposed vicarious liability on an employer for the negligence of an independent contractor on the basis of apparent or ostensible agency, or agency by estoppel. We find no reason to do so in the specific context presented in this case." What are the reasons that lead a court to embrace the minority and majority positions?

2. *Apparent Reliance.* Once a court recognizes the apparent agency doctrine as applicable to hospitals or other healthcare institutions the cases turn on: (1) whether the hospital has committed an act that would cause a reasonable person to believe that the physician in question was its employee or agent: and (2) whether the patient relied on the hospital's conduct.

As in *Burless*, an express representation is not always required; rather, the first element may be satisfied if the hospital generally holds itself out as a provider of care but does not inform the patient that independent contractors actually offer the care. What is the content of the second consideration — reliance? In *York v. Rush-Presbyterian-St. Luke's Medical Center*, 222 Ill.2d 147, 202, 204–05 (Ill. 2006), the court upheld the plaintiffs' verdict even though the patient was himself a retired orthopedic surgeon and his son was an anesthesiology resident at the defendant hospital. The court ruled that a finding of reliance is proper unless "a patient knows, or should have known, that the allegedly negligent physician is an independent contractor." Dissenting, Justice Garman remarked: "The majority . . . dilutes the "reliance" element of apparent authority claims against hospitals. Under the position adopted by the majority, the fact a plaintiff sought care from a specific physician is now virtually inconsequential in determining whether a hospital is vicariously liable for the negligence of an independent contractor physician. In effect, as long as the plaintiff can satisfy the "holding out" element of his apparent authority claim, he may recover from the hospital. This approach . . . promises to significantly expand the scope of apparent authority liability."

3. *Fun with Disclaimers.* The court in *Pamperin v. Trinity Memorial Hospital*, 423 N.W.2d 848, 849-50 (Wis. 1988), observed:

> When a hospital does not inform incoming patients which, if any, care or service is provided by independent contractors, and not by employees or agents, a patient should be able to look to the hospital for the negligence of the physician retained by the hospital to provide medical care. Moreover, because complete medical care consists of both direct care and support services, liability should attach regardless of whether the physician who is negligent is treating the patient directly or assisting in treating the patient by providing support services invisible to the patient. . . .

As courts have become more aggressive with their application of the apparent agency doctrine, hospitals have included language in their admissions or general consent forms purporting to inform patients which, if any, care or service is provided by independent contractors rather than by hospital employees. Why was the language in *Burless* ineffective?

Even if such language is sufficient to counter a tort claim, it may not be as effective in contract law. In *Pope v. Winter Park Healthcare Group, Ltd.*, 939 So. 2d 185, 190 (Fla. App. 5th Dist. 2006), the plaintiffs brought an action against a hospital for the alleged negligence of an "on-call" neonatologist. The consent form signed by the plaintiffs included the following:

> I recognize that the physicians who practices [sic] at WPMH are not employees or agents of the hospital but are independent physicians; the hospital may delegate to these independent physicians those services physicians normally provide; and any questions relating to care my physician has given or ordered should be directed to him/her.

Holding that there was an express contract between the plaintiffs and the hospital the court stated:

> Under the law of tort, the hiring of an independent contractor, unless done negligently, precludes liability because the hiring party has no duty to an injured third party to procure non-negligent performance of the independent contractor. However, delegation of a *contractual* duty

to an independent contractor does not eliminate the duty. Section 318 of the REST. 2D CONTRACTS sets forth the controlling principle of law:

> . . . (3) Unless the obligee agrees otherwise, neither delegation of performance nor a contract to assume the duty made with the obligor by the person delegated discharges any duty or liability of the delegating obligor. (emphasis added.)
>
> There is no language in this contract between Winter Park Hospital and the Popes of any assent by Mrs. Pope that the delegation of Winter Park Hospital's duty to provide the necessary medical treatment to independent contractor physicians will discharge the hospital from its contractual obligations. Acknowledgement on the part of Mrs. Pope that the duty to provide "medical or surgical treatments" can be delegated to an independent physician does not constitute an agreement on the part of Mrs. Pope to discharge Winter Park Hospital from any contractual duty it assumed. Delegation and discharge are two different things entirely, performed by different contracting parties. Contractual language of discharge should be clear, yet the only language in the form that may even obliquely refer to discharge is the final sentence, which provides that "questions" relating to the physician's care should be directed to the physician.

Pope, 939 So.2d at 191.

In general, how should courts respond to disclaimers and other documents that patients are given to sign? It is well established that outright disclaimers of liability are against public policy. *See, e.g., Tunkl v. Regents of University of Cal.*, 60 Cal.2d 92 (1963) (court held invalid a release of liability that plaintiff signed as a "Condition of Admission.") How should the courts react to forms that, for example, tell the patient that a planned surgery was "not a generally accepted procedure."

4. *Is This Any Way to Run a Liability System?* Some judges have displayed understandable frustration at the current state of the law. For example, concurring in *Roessler v. Novak*, 858 So.2d 1158, 1163-65 (Fla. App. 2nd Dist. 2003), Chief Judge Altenbernd stated:

> [O]ur twenty-year experiment with the use of apparent agency as a doctrine to determine a hospital's vicarious liability for the acts of various independent contractors has been a failure. Patients, hospitals, doctors, nurses, other licensed professionals, risk managers for governmental agencies, and insurance companies all need to have predictable general rules establishing the parameters of vicarious liability in this situation. Utilizing case-specific decisions by individually selected juries to determine whether a hospital is or is not vicariously liable for the mistakes of a radiology department, an emergency room, or some other corporate entity that has been created as an independent contractor to provide necessary services within the hospital is inefficient, unpredictable and, perhaps most important, a source of avoidable litigation. Our society can undoubtedly function well and provide insurance coverage to protect the risks of malpractice if there

is either broad liability upon the hospital for these services as nondelegable duties or if liability is restricted to the independent contractor. The uncertainty of the current system, however, does not work. The supreme court or the legislature needs to simplify the rules of liability in this area . . .

[H]ospitals should be vicariously liable as a general rule for activities within the hospital where the patient cannot and does not realistically have the ability to shop on the open market for another provider. Given modern marketing approaches in which hospitals aggressively advertise the quality and safety of the services provided within their hospitals, it is quite arguable that hospitals should have a nondelegable duty to provide adequate radiology departments, pathology laboratories, emergency rooms, and other professional services necessary to the ordinary and usual functioning of the hospital. The patient does not usually have the option to pick among several independent contractors at the hospital and has little ability to negotiate and bargain in this market to select a preferred radiology department. The hospital, on the other hand, has great ability to assure that competent radiologists work within an independent radiology department and to bargain with those radiologists to provide adequate malpractice protections for their mutual customers. I suspect that medical economics would work better if the general rule placed general vicarious liability upon the hospital for these activities. Thus, I would consider adopting a theory of nondelegable duty. . . .

The Supreme Court of Alaska took a similar approach in *Jackson v. Power,* 743 P.2d 1376, 1385 (Alaska 1987), holding that a hospital which had a duty to provide emergency care pursuant to Joint Committee on the Accreditation of Hospitals accreditation standards and its own internal regulations could not avoid vicarious liability by delegating that duty to an independent contractor. The court stated:

Not only is this rule consonant with the public perception of the hospital as a multifaceted health care facility responsible for the quality of medical care and treatment rendered, it also treats tort liability in the medical arena in a manner that is consistent with the commercialization of American medicine.

GAFNER v. DOWN E. COMMUNITY HOSP.
735 A.2d 969 (Me. 1999)

SAUFLEY, JUDGE.

. . . On May 27, 1990, Janet Gafner gave birth to her second child, Shannon, at Down East Community Hospital. William Gafner is Janet's husband and Shannon's father. Cynthia Sammis, M.D., was Janet's physician during Shannon's birth. During the delivery, Shannon's shoulders became lodged behind her mother's pubic bone. The Gafners allege that Shannon suffered a brachial plexus injury resulting from Dr. Sammis's negligence in responding to the medical emergency. They filed a notice of claim . . . alleging that Shannon's injury was caused by the professional negligence of Sammis and the Hospital . . .

We turn then to the final issue in this matter [the appeal from the summary judgment entered by the Superior Court in favor of Down East Community Hospital on the Gafners' claims against the Hospital for professional negligence], whether we should adopt into the common law of the State of Maine a cause of action against hospitals and other medical facilities referred to as "corporate liability."

. . . For purposes of this analysis, we accept the Gafners' factual assertion that the Hospital "failed to have in place at the time of Shannon Gafner's birth a written policy *requiring mandatory consultation*" with a specialist in high risk births. *See Thompson v. Nason Hosp.,* 527 Pa. 330, 591 A.2d 703, 707 (Pa. 1991). No duty to promulgate such policies existed at common law, nor has the Legislature placed such a duty on the Hospital. Nonetheless, the Gafners ask us to recognize a duty on the part of a hospital to adopt rules and policies controlling the actions of independent physicians practicing within its walls.

. . . [The] Gafners rely heavily on the analysis of the Pennsylvania Supreme Court in *Thompson.* There, the court adopted a theory of corporate liability, allowing a hospital to be held liable if it "failed to monitor and review medical services provided within its facilities." *Id.* at 708. The court suggested that a hospital's duties could be separated into four general areas:

> (1) a duty to use reasonable care in the maintenance of safe and adequate facilities and equipment; (2) a duty to select and retain only competent physicians; (3) a duty to oversee all persons who practice medicine within its walls as to patient care; and (4) a duty to formulate, adopt and enforce adequate rules and policies to ensure quality care for the patients. *Id.* at 707.

Some form of this cause of action has been adopted in many other states, and is largely recognized as stemming from the decision of the Illinois Supreme Court in *Darling v. Charleston Community Memorial Hospital,* 33 Ill. 2d 326 (1965). Proponents of the theory present a number of justifications in its support. Most prominent is the concept that hospitals are no longer viewed as the mere physical facilities in which doctors do their work, but are rather viewed as comprehensive healthcare centers that "provide and monitor all aspects of health care." *See* David H. Rutchik, Note, The *Emerging Trend of Corporate Liability: Courts' Uneven Treatment of Hospital Standards Leaves Hospitals Uncertain and Exposed,* 47 VAND. L. REV. 535, 538 (1994). Thus,

> because hospitals offer comprehensive medical services within a corporate structure, courts have found that the public reasonably may rely on the hospital itself as a health-care provider. The public expects to be treated and cured by the hospital rather than by particular nurses or other employees who provide patient care, Accordingly, patients often believe that the various health-care practitioners within the hospital render care collectively on the hospital's behalf. . . . The increased public reliance on sophisticated, profit-generating hospitals [is] a major reason for imposing corporate liability.

Id. at 539. Other rationales offered in justification for the doctrine of corpo-rate liability include the belief that "a hospital is in the best position to moni-tor and control its staff physicians." *See* Rutchik, 47 VAND. L. REV. at 549.

Notably, the theory is also understood to have been generated by the "judi-cial desire to place liability on the party most able to pay." *See* Gregory T. Perkes, Casenote, *Medical Malpractice — Ostensible Agency and Corporate Negligence,* 17 ST. MARY'S L.J. 551, 573 (1986).

This evolving theory of liability, however, has not been universally embraced. At least one critic has decried the result as misguided economic policy making on the part of the courts. *See, e.g., Thompson.* 591 A.2d at 709 (Flaherty, J., dis-senting). Declaring the cause of action to represent a "deep pocket" approach, Justice Flaherty offered the following observations:

> In adopting this new theory of liability, the majority is making a
> monumental and ill-advised change in the law of this Commonwealth.
> The change reflects a deep pocket theory of liability, placing financial
> burdens upon hospitals for the actions of persons who are not even
> their own employees. At a time when hospital costs are spiraling
> upwards to a staggering degree, this will serve only to boost the health
> care costs that already too heavily burden the public. Traditional theo-
> ries of liability, such as respondeat superior, have long proven to be
> perfectly adequate for establishing corporate responsibility for torts.
> [591 A.2d at 709 (Flaherty, J., dissenting)].

The balancing of interests implicated by the changing nature of hospitals has been undertaken in some depth by the Legislature. Consistent with the growing recognition of an independent duty on the part of hospitals to assure the credentials of physicians practicing with their facilities, the Legislature has considered the relationship between hospitals and physicians and has placed very specific duties upon hospitals. Among those duties is the obligation to assure that "provider privileges extended or subsequently renewed to any physician are in accordance with those recommended by the medical staff as being consistent with that physician's training, experience and professional competence." 24 M.R.S.A. § 2503(2) (1990). To date, however, the Legislature has not chosen to place upon hospitals a specific duty to regulate the medical decisions of the physicians practicing within the facility.

Nonetheless, the Gafners would have us incorporate into Maine law a theory of corporate liability for failure to have explicit policies in place controlling the actions of independent physicians. This formulation of the theory of liability has only been recognized by a few jurisdictions. Instead, most courts that have recognized the cause of action referred to as corporate liability have grounded the claim upon the responsibility of the facility to assure that physicians prac-ticing in the facility are properly credentialed and licensed. For example, in *Pedroza v. Bryant,* 677 P.2d 166, 168-69 (Wash. 1984), the Washington Supreme Court gave the following description of its theory of corporate liability:

> The doctrine of corporate negligence has . . . been utilized by courts to
> require hospitals to exercise reasonable care to insure that the physi-
> cians selected as members of hospital medical staffs are competent.

[Those courts] have also held that hospitals have a continuing duty to review and delineate staff privileges so that incompetent staff physicians are not retained . . .

In contrast, the Gafners' proposed theory of "corporate liability" has not yet gained significant acceptance in other jurisdictions and has not been addressed by our own Legislature. Moreover, no study of the effects of such a change in the law has been undertaken. Creating a duty that would place external controls upon the medical judgments and actions of physicians should not be undertaken without a thorough and thoughtful analysis.

We decline to create such a duty from whole cloth and therefore decline to recognize the cause of action suggested by the Gafners. There are a number of reasons for our refusal to accept the Gafners' theory of liability against the Hospital. Private hospitals in Maine are extensively regulated. The Legislature has created duties and guidelines for the actions of those hospitals in a number of areas. Before the expansion of tort liability into an area that has been significantly controlled by the Legislature, we should allow the Legislature to address the policy considerations and determine whether imposing such a duty constitutes wise public policy.

Moreover, creating a duty on the part of hospitals to control the actions of those physicians who have traditionally been considered independent contractors may shift the nature of the medical care provided by those physicians. In an area as replete with the possibility of unexpected or unintended consequences as this, we should exercise restraint in the use of our authority to create new causes of action . . .

In sum, there exist serious and unanswered public policy questions regarding the wisdom of requiring hospitals to control the medical judgments and actions of independent physicians practicing within their facilities. Those questions implicate both quality of care and economic considerations. We will not lightly adopt a new theory of liability in an area of such significant concern for the public health. We decline to do so here. [AFFIRMED]

NOTES

1. *Specifics of Corporate Hospital Liability.* In *Thompson v. Nason Hospital*, 591 A.2d 703, 707-08 (Pa. 1991), the court went beyond the "four general areas" cited in *Gafner*, stating:

Today, we take a step beyond the hospital's duty of care delineated in [earlier case law] in full recognition of the corporate hospital's role in the total health care of its patients. In so doing, we adopt as a theory of hospital liability the doctrine of corporate negligence or corporate liability under which the hospital is liable if it fails to uphold the proper standard of care owed its patient. In addition, we fully embrace the aforementioned four categories of the hospital's duties. It is important to note that for a hospital to be charged with negligence, it is necessary to show that the hospital had actual or constructive knowledge of the defect or procedures which created the harm . . .

2. *The Limits of Corporate Liability.* Some jurisdictions deny a cause of action for corporate or institutional liability on technical grounds. For example, in *Daly v. Aspen Center for Women's Health, Inc.*, 134 P.3d 450 (Colo. App. 2005), the court refused to allow the action as it was inconsistent with state law prohibiting corporations from practicing medicine; this is the so-called "corporate practice" doctrine. Some courts, while generally recognizing corporate liability, limit its operation. In *Pedroza v. Bryant,* 101 Wash. 2d 226 (1984), the court declined to extend corporate negligence principles to the treatment of patients by hospital staff members in the staff members' private offices off the hospital premises. What arguments in favor of extending staff liability could be made on this issue? What if the hospital had actual notice of previous malpractice committed outside the hospital premises? Most courts that have considered the issue have refused to extent the corporate negligence doctrine to the provision of informed consent. With what justification?

3. *What's the Point?* Does refusing to recognize full corporate liability merely perpetuate the *respondeat superior* battles seen in *Burless* and similar cases? If the hospital or HMO is to be generally liable for patient care does it make any sense to continue to allow suit against individual physicians? Consider how these choices affect publicly supported institutions or poor patients.

G. DUTIES, CAUSATION, AND DAMAGES

Many of the issues that arise in professional liability cases are similar to those raised in "general" negligence cases. As a result courts have been called on to determine questions about the extent of the "duties" owed by healthcare providers. Although it might once have been true that the existence of a physician-patient relationship was a *sine qua non* to a medical malpractice action, most people today would expect to encompass actions by third parties within that general rubric. For example, in *Freese v. Lemmon,* 210 N.W.2d 576 (Iowa 1973), a pedestrian struck by a motorist who was in the midst of a seizure brought an action against the motorist's physician for alleged failure to diagnose the cause of the motorist's previous seizure and to warn him not to drive. The court held that the allegations constituted a cause of action against the physician.

The duty inquiry, discussed in Chapter 7, also reaches the question of cognizable damages. Thus, in *Bader v. Johnson*, 732 N.E.2d 1212 (Ind. 2000), plaintiffs sued healthcare professionals for negligent failure to disclose ultrasound results showing abnormalities in their unborn child. The child died several months after birth due to congenital birth defects. They alleged that the wife would have terminated the pregnancy had they known the test results. Defendants argued that Indiana did not recognize the tort of "wrongful birth." The court replied that nothing analytical was gained by using the "wrongful birth" label and that the issue was whether the plaintiffs' emotional distress injuries were cognizable. Relying on Indiana's modified "impact rule" the court ruled that the mother's "continued pregnancy and the physical transformation her body underwent as a result, satisfy the direct impact requirement of our modified impact rule." In contrast, the court suggested that the father was likely a "bystander."

Complex causal issues are central to most professional liability cases and frequently center on expert testimony. Some helpful guidance as to the major causal issues that may arise is provided in *Joshi v. Providence Health Sys. of Oregon Corp.*, 2006 Ore. LEXIS 1344 (2006). There the court provided an overview of causal tools, noting that "The 'but-for' test for causation, in which a plaintiff must demonstrate that the defendant's negligence more likely than not caused the plaintiff's harm, applies to the majority of cases," that the standard for cause in fact was "reasonable probability," and that "[a]ny showing of causation less than a reasonable probability would be merely a possibility and, therefore, insufficient . . . " The "substantial factor" test, the court concluded, had not supplanted "but-for," but applies in cases where the plaintiff is alleging concurrent causes (arising, for example, where multiple healthcare defendants are involved or in an automobile accident followed by allegedly negligent emergency room care). Finally, the court noted the "lost chance of survival theory" may apply in negligent diagnosis cases. In such cases a "substantial factor" test applies and the plaintiff must demonstrate that the defendant's negligence caused (by reasonable probability) the diminution of the plaintiff's chance of survival.

The quantum of recovery has been extensively modified by malpractice "crisis" legislation (discussed in Chapter 16). For example, California has a "hard cap" of $250,000 for "noneconomic losses" (mostly considered as plaintiff's pain and suffering), see Cal. Civ. Code § 3333.2.

Questions related to the type of damages that plaintiff may recover still emerge, as reflected in *Bader, supra,* (emotional damages). In *Dillon v. Evanston Hospital*, 199 Ill. 2d 483 (2002), the defendant failed to completely remove a catheter used in chemotherapy. The catheter fragment migrated to the plaintiff's heart and the risks of removing it were higher than its present risk to the patient. Defendant complained of the court's instruction that the jury could award plaintiff damages for "the increased risk of future injuries." Noting the common law's historic antipathy to "future injuries" the court reversed the jury verdict because of improper jury instructions. However, using an analogy to loss of chance cases," it suggested that such damages might be available, saying "a plaintiff must be permitted to recover for *all* demonstrated injuries. The burden is on the plaintiff to prove that the defendant's negligence increased the plaintiff's risk of future injuries. A plaintiff can obtain compensation for a future injury that is not reasonably certain to occur, but the compensation would reflect the low probability of occurrence."

H.   LIABILITY OF OTHER PROFESSIONALS

DONAHUE v. SHUGHART, THOMSON & KILROY, P.C.
900 S.W.2d 624 (Mo. 1995)

HOLSTEIN, JUDGE.

Mary Donahue and Sundy McClung appeal a dismissal of their legal malpractice claim. In their petition they assert that because of the defendant attorneys' malpractice, an attempted testamentary transfer failed. Among other grounds for relief, they claim to have standing to bring this action even though they were not the clients of the attorneys involved . . . The order of dismissal is affirmed in part, reversed in part and the cause remanded . . .

Defendant J. Harlan Stamper is an attorney and shareholder of the defendant law firm Shughart, Thomson & Kilroy, P.C. (law firm). Gerald E. Stockton died in November 1988. For many years prior to his death, Mr. Stamper had been an attorney to Mr. Stockton. In 1979, Mr. Stockton established a living trust naming himself as trustee. The beneficiaries of the trust included persons other than Mary Donahue and Sundy McClung.

In May 1988, Stockton explained to Stamper that he was entering the hospital for surgery. He sent Stamper $150,000.00 in checks on the trust account made payable to Mary Donahue and Sundy McClung. Stamper was directed to see to it that Donahue and McClung received the proceeds of the checks on the trust account when Stockton died. Stockton also directed Stamper to prepare a deed to his home transferring a fifty percent interest in the home to Donahue, effective on Stockton's death. Donahue and McClung were the sole intended beneficiaries of these transfers.

In September 1988, Stockton gave Stamper another check drawn on the trust in the amount of $100,000.00 payable to "Mary Donahue, G. E. Stockton, J,T,W,R,O,S, [sic] J. Harlan Stamper, Trustee." Mr. Stamper understood that Stockton wanted Mary Donahue to receive the proceeds of this check upon his death. On October 26, 1988, Stamper was informed that Stockton's death was imminent. Stamper then sought advice from others in his law firm on how to make the checks and deed effective. He and other law firm attorneys attempted to take action to effectuate Stockton's wishes, including the recording of the deed. Stockton died November 5, 1988. The steps taken to effectuate the transfers were brought into question by declaratory judgment action, which resulted in an opinion by the Missouri court of appeals holding the transfers were invalid.

The plaintiffs filed an amended petition asserting two theories of legal malpractice . . . The first legal malpractice theory is that Stamper and the law firm were acting as attorneys for Donahue and McClung and acted negligently in that representation. The second legal malpractice theory alleges that Stamper and the law firm violated their professional duties to Stockton and the trust. All counts of the amended petition were dismissed.

The four elements of a legal malpractice action are: "(1) that an attorney-client relationship existed; (2) that defendant acted negligently or in breach of contract; (3) that such acts were the proximate cause of the plaintiffs' damages; (4) that but for defendant's conduct the plaintiffs would have been successful in prosecution of their [underlying] claim." *Boatright v. Shaw*, 804 S.W.2d 795, 796 (Mo. App. 1990). In count I of their amended petition, plaintiffs allege that in late September or early October 1988, Donahue, on behalf of herself and McClung, then a minor, met with Stamper to seek legal advice regarding negotiation of the checks and recording of the deed. They further allege that while acting as their attorney, Stamper incorrectly advised them that there was no need to negotiate the checks at that time. The plaintiffs allege that at a subsequent meeting on October 27, 1988, Stamper and other attorneys with the law firm incorrectly advised them that if plaintiffs followed their instructions, the negotiation of the May checks, the second Donahue check, and the transfer of fifty percent interest in Stockton's home would all be effective and binding. It is further alleged that because Stamper and others with the law firm failed to perform any research between the meeting in late September 1988 and October 26, 1988, the transfers were ineffective . . .

The more complicated question is whether the intended beneficiaries, in this case, Donahue and McClung, have standing to bring a legal malpractice action against Stamper and the law firm because the lawyers failed to effectuate a transfer in accordance with the wishes of their client, Stockton . . . As previously noted, one required element of a legal malpractice action is that an attorney-client relationship existed between the plaintiff and defendant. *Rose v. Summers, Compton, Wells & Hamburg*, 887 S.W.2d 683, 686 (Mo. App. 1994). Plaintiffs contend that, although they are not clients of defendants, they have met such requirement by pleading that they were the intended beneficiaries of the client's action and that such fact, accompanied by other recognized elements of a legal malpractice claim, suffice to establish the element of attorney-client relationship.

There are cases in Missouri indicating that circumstances may exist where an attorney will be held liable to third parties for the attorney's unprofessional conduct. For example, there are exceptional cases involving fraud, collusion, or malicious or tortious acts by the attorney that might justify liability to third parties. But to date, no Missouri case has held that intended beneficiaries of a will have a cause of action against the attorney when the intended beneficiary is damaged as a result of attorney negligence.

In comparable circumstances, this Court held that an indemnitor of a surety could sustain, in the absence of privity of contract, an action against an architect-defendant who allegedly failed to exercise ordinary care in certifying the amount of material furnished and labor performed. *Westerhold v. Carroll*, 419 S.W.2d 73, 76 (Mo. 1967). The appellants here argue that the *Westerhold* reasoning should apply to legal malpractice actions.

In *Westerhold*, the Court applied a case-by-case balancing of factors test established by *Biakanja v. Irving*, 320 P.2d 16, 19 (Cal. 1958), to determine whether as a matter of policy a defendant would be held liable to a third person not in privity under a surety contract. *Westerhold*, 419 S.W.2d at 81. Those factors are:

> The extent to which the transaction was intended to affect the plaintiff, the foreseeability of harm to [the plaintiff], the degree of certainty that the plaintiff suffered injury, the closeness of the connection between the defendant's conduct and the injury suffered, the moral blame attached to the defendant's conduct, and the policy of preventing future harm.

Id. This Court concluded that all the factors were satisfied except the one involving "moral blame" and allowed the plaintiff to maintain the action.

Courts of other states have considered whether an attorney can be held liable for negligence to a person other than the client. Generally, the analysis begins with the historical rule requiring privity of contract to maintain an action for professional negligence. Ronald E. Mallen and Jeffrey M. Smith, *Legal Malpractice* § 7.4, at 364 (3d ed. 1993). However, "the vast majority of modern decisions have favored expanding privity beyond the confines of the attorney-client relationship where the plaintiff was intended to be *the* beneficiary of the lawyer's retention." *Id.*, § 7.10, at 379.

The balancing test cited in *Westerhold* was used by the California Supreme Court to determine whether non-client beneficiaries of a will could maintain a legal malpractice action. *Lucas v. Hamm*, 56 Cal. 2d 583 (Cal. 1961). There the court reiterated the *Biakanja* factors but eliminated, without explanation, the factor concerning "moral blame." Perhaps the rationale for excluding moral blame is that such factor is subsumed by the concept that a duty is owed from one whose conduct is culpable to one who is innocent but injured by such culpability. The *Lucas* court also added the factor of whether the expansion of liability would impose an undue burden on the legal profession. 364 P.2d at 688. That balancing test has been cited with approval by most jurisdictions which have considered the issue. Mallen and Smith, *supra*, § 7.11, at 383.

The second theory commonly used to establish liability to those not in strict privity with the defendant-attorney is based on the concept of a third party beneficiary contract. *See* Mallen and Smith, *supra*, § 7.11, at 382, and *Flaherty v. Weinberg*, 492 A.2d 618, 621 (Md. 1985). Under that approach, the inquiry is whether the intent of the client to benefit the non-client was the direct purpose of the attorney-client transaction or relationship. The third party beneficiary approach focuses the existence of a duty entirely on whether the plaintiff was the person intended to be benefited by the legal services and does not extend to those incidentally deriving an indirect benefit. Neither does it extend to those in an adversarial relationship with the client. Under this theory, it is difficult to conceive of a situation where the lawyer will be held liable for a failed gift or testamentary transfer while the client is still living and competent. Commentators have suggested that even in those jurisdictions which have followed the balancing approach of *Lucas*, the predominant inquiry has generally involved the criterion of whether the principal purpose of the attorney's retention to provide legal services was for the specific benefit of the plaintiff.

The two most common approaches do not appear to be irreconcilable. The first factor of the balancing test addresses the extent to which the transaction was intended to benefit the plaintiff and bears a remarkable resemblance to the third party beneficiary theory. The question of whether the client had a specific intent to benefit the plaintiff plays an important role in determining if a legal duty exists under the balancing of factors test. The first factor identified in *Westerhold* and *Lucas* should be modified to reflect that the factor weighs in favor of a legal duty by an attorney where the client *specifically intended* to benefit the plaintiffs. With that modification, that approach is an appropriate method for determining an attorney's duty to non-clients. The weighing of factors allows consideration of relevant policy concerns and is consistent with prior case law, as expressed in *Westerhold*. Concurrently, the ultimate factual issue that must be pleaded and proved is that an attorney-client relationship existed in which the client specifically intended to benefit the plaintiff.

The primary arguments against allowing a non-client to bring a legal malpractice action are the possibility that liability will extend to an unlimited class of individuals and will interfere with the attorney-client relationship. These concerns are addressed by proper application of the modified balancing of factors approach. If the transaction was specifically intended to benefit the plaintiff, liability is not extended to an unlimited class and it does not interfere with the attorney-client relationship, particularly where the client is deceased or incompetent. A benefit that is merely incidental or indirect will not satisfy this factor. Neither will a benefit to one in an adversarial relationship to the client be sufficient to satisfy the factor. Within the bounds of the law, the attorney's duty is solely to advance the client's interest. Further, recognizing liability to an intended beneficiary of a testamentary transfer does not unduly burden the legal profession when liability is limited to those the client intended but is no longer able to benefit and where no other remedy exists to prevent harm to the beneficiaries. Additionally, extending liability under such circumstances is necessary to prevent future harm because no individual is likely to bring the action if the intended beneficiaries are not allowed to do so. The testator's estate will have little incentive to challenge the action and, therefore, the potential for liability to intended beneficiaries is likely to encourage attorneys to exercise care in drafting and executing testamentary instruments.

To summarize, the Court concludes that the first element of a legal malpractice action may be satisfied by establishing as a matter of fact either that an attorney-client relationship exists between the plaintiff and defendant or an attorney-client relationship existed in which the attorney-defendant performed services specifically intended by the client to benefit plaintiffs. As a separate matter, the question of legal duty of attorneys to non-clients will be determined by weighing the factors in the modified balancing test. The factors are:

(1) the existence of a specific intent by the client that the purpose of the attorney's services were to benefit the plaintiffs.

(2) the foreseeability of the harm to the plaintiffs as a result of the attorney's negligence.

(3) the degree of certainty that the plaintiffs will suffer injury from attorney misconduct.

(4) the closeness of the connection between the attorney's conduct and the injury.

(5) the policy of preventing future harm.

(6) the burden on the profession of recognizing liability under the circumstances.

Applying these six factors here, the pleadings state that Stockton's primary purpose in writing the checks and preparing and signing the deed was to benefit the plaintiffs and, aside from Stockton's desire that his property be distributed according to his directions after his death, no benefit to him is apparent. It is clear that plaintiffs cannot be characterized as incidental or indirect beneficiaries. Negligent advice or preparation of testamentary documents was almost certain to cause plaintiffs injury. The conduct of Stamper and the law firm was directly connected to the injury. Future harm may only be prevented by allowing intended beneficiaries of failed testamentary transfers some avenue of recovery in malpractice claims, particularly where the estate has interests inconsistent with those of the intended beneficiaries. The legal profession will not be unduly burdened by being required to act competently toward identifiable persons that a client specifically intends to benefit when such persons have no other viable remedy and where such persons are not in an adversarial relationship to the client. The Court concludes that the facts as pleaded here are sufficient to assert a breach of a legal duty and to state a cause of action in a lawyer malpractice action . . . [Affirmed in Part, Reversed in Part and Cause Remanded.]

NOTES

1. *Third Party "Clients."* After *Donahue*, which do you believe to be the more efficient approach: a balancing test or a bright-line rule? What concerns are raised by each of these choices?

2. *Common Knowledge.* As in medical malpractice cases, almost all legal malpractice cases will require expert testimony on the standard of care. In *Bowman v. Doherty*, 235 Kan. 870 (1984), the plaintiff was arrested for writing a worthless check. At his initial appearance the judge advised him of his rights to an attorney and continued the case. Knowing he was to be out of town on a skiing trip, plaintiff telephoned defendant attorney who had represented him on prior matters. The attorney said he would take care of the matter but allegedly failed to arrange a continuance with the court. As a result, the plaintiff was arrested and imprisoned for aggravated failure to appear. In the ensuing legal malpractice case the defendant argued that trial court erred in denying his motion for directed verdict because the plaintiff failed to present expert testimony that the attorney had deviated from the professional standard of care. Although a retrial was ordered on other grounds the court addressed the expert evidence issue as follows:

> There is a common knowledge exception to the rule requiring expert testimony in malpractice cases. Expert testimony is not necessary where the breach of duty on the part of the attorney, or his failure to use due care, is so clear or obvious that the trier of fact may find a deviation from the appropriate standard of the legal profession from its common knowledge . . . .

> Doherty was hired to represent Bowman in an alleged criminal check case . . . Bowman's loss of freedom, for failure to appear before the court when required, was due to Doherty's deviation from the appropriate standard for an attorney [and] fell within the common knowledge exception to the rule requiring expert legal testimony.

3. *Standard of Care for Lawyers.* The locality rule has been described as "peculiar" to medical malpractice doctrine. *Morrison v. MacNamara,* 407 A.2d

555 (D.C. 1979). Tennessee, which uses a statutorily mandated locality rule for medical malpractice, has confronted the question in legal malpractice cases. In *Chapman v. Bearfield*, 2006 Tenn. LEXIS 990 (2006), the court disposed of the issue as follows:

> This Court allows an attorney with a Tennessee law license to practice anywhere in the state. An attorney practicing in Tennessee, then, must exercise the ordinary care, skill, and diligence commonly possessed and practiced by attorneys *throughout the state*. Indeed, while there may be local *rules of practice* within the various judicial districts of our State, there are no local *standards of care*. There is only one standard of care for attorneys practicing in Tennessee: a statewide standard. By extension, an expert who opines in a legal malpractice case about an attorney's adherence to our professional standard of care must be familiar with the statewide professional standard of care.
>
> Defendant argues that the medical malpractice locality rule should be extended to legal malpractice actions. However, the locality rule for medical malpractice is a creature of statute. *See* TENN. CODE ANN. § 29-26-115(a)(1) (Supp. 2005) (standard of care relates to "the community in which the defendant practices or in a similar community"). Neither this Court nor the legislature has created a similar standard for the legal profession, and we decline to create one here.
>
> We also believe the adoption of a statewide professional standard of care for attorneys who practice law in Tennessee is good policy. Three concerns motivate our conclusion. First, if a local professional standard of care prevailed, plaintiffs might have difficulty proving their legal malpractice cases because local attorneys might not be willing to speak against their colleagues. Second, local variations in the standard of care could create an inefficient and inequitable morass of professional standards of care, reducing the likelihood that some attorneys would face malpractice claims while increasing the likelihood for others. Finally, the emergence of the Internet as a primary tool for legal research undercuts historical transportation and communications arguments favoring local variations in the standard of care. We join those states which have accepted these and other rationales for maintaining a statewide standard of professional care for their attorneys.

Lazy Seven Coal Mines v. Stone & Hinds, 813 S.W.2d 400 (Tenn. 1991), noted that jurisdictions were in agreement that the Code of Professional Responsibility does not give rise to a private cause of action for damages. The court quoted with approval the following reasons for that rule given in *Bob Godfrey Pontiac, Inc. v. Roloff*, 630 P.2d 840 (Ore. 1981):

> (a) The statute or Code of Professional Responsibility was not intended to create a private cause of action. On the contrary, the sole intended remedy for a violation of such a statute or code is the imposition of discipline by disbarment, suspension or reprimand of the offending attorney.
>
> (b) Other remedies, such as malicious prosecution, adequately protect the public from harassment or abuse by unprofessional lawyers.

(c) To expose attorneys to actions for damages for breach of ethical duties imposed by such statutes and codes would be contrary to the "obvious public interest" in affording every citizen "the utmost freedom of access to the courts."

630 P.2d at 848.

However, the *Lazy Seven Coal Mines* court also noted:

> Even though, as set forth above, the Code does not define standards for civil liability, the standards stated in the Code are not irrelevant in determining the standard of care in certain actions for malpractice. The Code may provide guidance in ascertaining lawyers' obligations to their clients under various circumstances, and conduct which violates the Code may also constitute a breach of the standard of care due a client. However, in a civil action charging malpractice, the standard of care is the particular duty owed the client under the circumstances of the representation, which may or may not be the standard contemplated by the Code.

813 S.W.2d at 405.

Should the standard of care expected of an attorney reflect the various strategies that could be used in a trial? According to *Smith v. Lewis,* 530 P.2d 589, 595 (Cal. 1975):

> [A]n attorney engaging in litigation may have occasion to choose among various alternative strategies available to his client, one of which may be to refrain from pressing a debatable point because potential benefit may not equal detriment in terms of expenditure of time or resources or because of calculated tactics to the advantage of his client. But, as the Ninth Circuit put it somewhat brutally in *Pineda v. Craven,* 424 F.2d 369, 372 (9th Cir. 1970): "There is nothing strategic or tactical about ignorance. . . ."

Id. at

As in the case of physicians, extreme professional misconduct by lawyers is policed by REST. 2D TORTS § 46. For example, in *Singleton v. Foreman*, 435 F.2d 962, 971 (5th Cir. 1970), the court held that plaintiff stated a cause of action for intentional infliction of emotional distress based on allegations that the defendant divorce attorney had forced her into an oppressive contingent fee agreement at a time when she was already distraught, demanded her jewelry and coat as security for his retainer, was abusive and oppressive when she attempted to discuss the settlement of her divorce, and threatened her with ruin if she attempted to change lawyers.

For another situation in which medical and legal malpractice draw together, consider *Cohen v. Lipsig,* 459 N.Y.S.2d 98 (1983), in which it was held that there was a triable issue of fact as to whether plaintiff had given informed consent to his attorney's choice of outside trial counsel.

4. *Accountants' Duties to Non-Clients.* As in legal malpractice cases such as *Donahue,* the question arises as to what "duty" limitations apply in malpractice cases against accountants. The accountancy cases are to an extent still ruled from the grave by Justice Cardozo's opinion in *Ultramares Corp. v. Touche, Niven & Co.*, 255 N.Y. 170 (1931), disallowing a negligence action against an accounting firm brought by a plaintiff who had neither contractual privity nor a relationship "so close as to approach that of privity." *Id.* at xxx. Famously, Cardozo stated: "If liability for negligence exists, a thoughtless slip or blunder, the failure to detect a theft or forgery beneath the cover of deceptive entries, may expose accountants to a liability in an indeterminate amount for an indeterminate time to an indeterminate class." *Id.* at 179. This "actual foresight" rule was adopted by REST. 2D TORTS § 552.

In *Thayer v. Hicks*, 243 Mont. 138 (1990), the defendant accountant rendered a "clean" opinion on a company's balance sheet following an audit that was relied upon by the company's purchaser. As the court noted:

> The question most courts grapple with today is not whether an accountant owes a duty of care to third parties but, rather, just how far the duty extends. In dealing with this issue, courts have employed three different approaches. The first approach limits the duty of care to those third parties who are actually known to the accountant, the second limits the duty to those who are actually foreseen and the third expands the duty to all those who are reasonably foreseeable . . .

Id. at 144-46.

> At least four jurisdictions have expanded an accountant's duty to third parties beyond the "actually foreseen" class of the Restatement. These jurisdictions apply ordinary negligence rules when dealing with the question of the scope of liability, holding that an accountant owes a duty to all who might reasonably and foreseeably obtain and rely upon the accountant's work product.

> Because the facts of the present case meet the strictest of the three formulations of an account-ant's duty of care to non-clients, we see no need to adopt a more liberal standard at this time.

Id. at

Given evidence that the accountant may have failed to comply with generally accepted auditing standards or generally accepted accounting principles, the *Thayer* court noted:

> Accountants and auditors have a duty to exercise the same degree of care, skill and competence as that exercised by other reasonably competent members of the profession in the same or similar circumstances . . . Evidence of national rules and codes followed by members of the profession may aid the jury in determining whether the proper degree of care was exercised, however, any deviation from the national guidelines, no matter how slight, does not automatically constitute negligence.

Id. 150-51.

In the wake of the Enron Corp., WorldCom Inc., and other scandals Congress passed the *Sarbanes-Oxley Act of 2002* (Pub. L. No. 107-204, 116 Stat. 745), providing an array of new or modified accounting, audit, and disclosure rules and additional civil and criminal penalties for transgressors. Should the common law respond by increasing its scope of duty and standard of care rules?

5. *Clergy and Church Negligence. Roman Catholic Diocese v. Morrison*, 905 So. 2d 1213, 1237, 1248 (Miss. 2005), involved parents' action against a church administration for alleged sexual molestation of children by the defendant's priest. Allegedly, after the parents learned of allegations of molestation and confronted church officials, the priest was allowed to remain in the parish and continued to abuse children. The church argued, *inter alia*, that the First Amendment's Free Exercise Clause deprived civil courts of jurisdiction over plaintiffs' complaint. The court responded:

> We are satisfied that the cloak of religion, which does not shield religious institutions from civil responsibility for fraud or breach of contract, surely cannot serve to shield such institutions from civil responsibility for more abhorrent conduct such as sexual molestation of a child. Nor should it shield those who fail in their duty to protect children from it . . .

> Neither the Doctrine of Church Autonomy nor jurisdictional arguments shall serve to prevent the [plaintiffs] from pursuing their causes of action in our civil courts. The civil and criminal laws which protect children from abuse and allow those who are abused to be compensated for the damage they suffer, are neutral, generally applicable laws. They have, at best, a *de minimis* effect on any religious organization's internal, ecclesiastical matters. We find no credibility in the argument that immunity from liability for damages caused by pedophiles should be grounded in religious faith, doctrine, practice or belief, regardless of any theory under which that argument is advanced.

Id. at

Courts have been more reluctant to recognize an action for "clergy malpractice," that is a tort claim arising out of advising or counseling. An exception is *Destefano v. Grabrian*, 763 P.2d 275 (Colo. 1988), where a priest who was providing marriage-counseling services to a couple developed an intimate relationship with the wife. Consider what claims are able to be asserted against the Diocese and the priest who engages in a sexual liaison with his counseling subject. In *Grabarian* the court reversed and remanded for a determination of whether the priest's conduct was outrageous and whether the diocese had negligently failed to supervise the priest.

6. *Good Luck on the Bar Exam!* The overwhelming majority of courts that have considered a cause of action for educational malpractice have rejected it. *See Finstad v. Washburn University of Topeka*, 845 P.2d 685 (Kan. 1993). The seminal case is *Ross v. Creighton University*, 740 F. Supp. 1319 (N.D. Ill. 1990), where the court wrote:

> Admittedly, the term "educational malpractice" has a seductive ring to it; after all, if doctors, lawyers, accountants and other professionals can be held liable for failing to exercise due care, why can't teachers? The answer is that the nature of education radically differs from

other professions. Education is an intensely collaborative process, requiring the interaction of student with teacher. A good student can learn from a poor teacher; a poor student can close his mind to a good teacher. Without effort by a student, he cannot be educated. Good teaching method may vary with the needs of the individual student. In other professions, by contrast, client cooperation is far less important; given a modicum of cooperation, a competent professional in other fields can control the results obtained. But in education, the ultimate responsibility for success remains always with the student. Both the process and the result are subjective, and proof or disproof extremely difficult . . .

It also must be remembered that education is a service rendered on an immensely greater scale than other professional services. If every failed student could seek tort damages against any teacher, administrator and school he feels may have shortchanged him at some point in his education, the courts could be deluged and schools shut down . . . This is not to say that the mere worry that litigation will increase justifies a court's refusal to remedy a wrong; it is to say that the real danger of an unrestrained multiplication of lawsuits shows the disutility of the proposed remedy. If poor education (or student laziness) is to be corrected, a common law action for negligence is not a practical means of going about it.

Is this reasoning persuasive? Are there opportunities for reconsidering these arguments in light of class, race, or gender-based perspectives?

PROBLEMS

9.1

Two male infants, "Baby Jones" and "Baby Smith," were born within minutes of each other at City Hospital. Incorrectly marked identification bracelets were placed on each child, and the nursing staff gave "Baby Jones" to Ms. Smith and "Baby Smith" to Ms. Jones for feeding and family photographs. The hospital discovered the mistake when the infants were five days old. Both infants are in perfect health. The extremely distraught Jones and Smith families have contacted their attorneys. You are the general counsel for City Hospital. What is the Hospital's exposure, and on what theories of liability? Would you recommend that your client litigate these claims?

9.2

Attorney Bright interviewed Victim, a prospective client who wanted to sue her former lawyer, Superficial, for legal malpractice. Bright's interview with Victim and her follow-up investigation revealed that Superficial represented Victim in a dental malpractice suit against Dentist. After Dentist removed a wisdom tooth, Victim was left without feeling in portions of her lower jaw.

Victim claimed that the loss of feeling was caused when Dentist negligently damaged a nerve during oral surgery. Although Dentist denied negligence, she did admit that the loss of feeling in Victim's jaw was a result of the surgery. Dentist contended, however, that the loss of feeling was a risk inherent in the surgery, that she had fully advised Victim of this risk prior to the surgery, and that Victim had consented to the surgery with full knowledge of the risk. Victim claimed Dentist never advised her of such a risk. The case went to trial before Judge Callous, who entered a judgment for Dentist.

Bright believes that Superficial made three critical errors in representing Victim in her dental malpractice case. First, he did not demand a jury trial. Second, he retained an expert witness who was on the faculty of a prestigious, out-of-town dental school and who had outstanding academic credentials, but who had never been in private practice. Third, Superficial never discussed with Victim the decision to forego a jury trial and retain an academic expert witness who had never been in private practice. Bright is confident that she can get an attorney from the local community to testify that in a dental malpractice case such as this one, it is customary in the local community for a plaintiff's attorney to request a jury trial and to retain an expert witness with private practice experience. Bright doubts that she can get anyone to testify as to a custom to discuss these tactical decisions with the client, although Bright feels strongly that such a discussion is mandated by ethical and legal considerations.

You are a new associate employed by Bright. Identify the legal and factual issues that will be presented by a legal malpractice case against Superficial, and, in light of your critical assessment of the law and the facts, advise Bright of the chance of getting the case to the jury.

9.3

Patient, 18-year-old, was admitted to the hospital for a Caesarian-section delivery of her third child. In the course of several prior discussions with her obstetrician-gynecologist (Ob-Gyn), Patient learned that she and her husband had incompatible blood types, a condition which posed an escalating threat to each successive child she conceived. As a result Patient initiated discussions with Ob-Gyn about various contraceptive techniques. Ob-Gyn suggested that Patient undergo a hysterectomy, but Patient rejected that option as too final. During the successful delivery of the third child, Ob-Gyn asked Patient's husband whether he should perform a bilateral tubal ligation on Patient. The husband said that he and his wife had discussed that procedure and that the doctor should perform the procedure. When Patient discovers what happened, she brings a battery action against Ob-Gyn. What arguments should Ob-Gyn make? How successful will they be?

9.4

Patient consulted defendant urologist Dr. Harry for treatment of his kidney stones. Dr. Harry advised surgery. Patient requested that Dr. Harry perform the operation, and executed a consent form listing Dr. Harry as operating surgeon. Dr. Harry explained the risk of complications to Patient before

Patient signed the consent form. Although Dr. Harry had treated him previously, Patient was unaware that Dr. Harry was in a "group" practice and "shared" patients with his partner, Dr. Charles. Plaintiff underwent the surgery; however, he suffered severe post-operative complications. Upon readmission to the hospital for further treatment of these complications, Patient learned that *Dr. Charles had performed his operation* and that on the day of the operation, Dr. Harry was in West Germany taking delivery of his new sports car.

You are Patient's attorney. Your client is not only suffering from post-operative complications but is extremely angry! Your preliminary investigations suggest that there is a high statistical correlation between the complications suffered by Patient and the type of operation performed. You realize that this is the first case in your jurisdiction involving what is known as "ghost surgery," where one doctor performs an operation for another without the patient's consent. You know that your state's Supreme Court has consistently held that actions brought by patients complaining about the conduct of their physicians sound *only in tort* and not in contract, misrepresentation, fraud or deceit.

What doctrinal approaches will you take in your suit against Dr. Harry and Dr. Charles? What case law will you draw on by way of analogy? What are your strongest *nondoctrinal* arguments?

9.5

In April 2004, Greg House, a 64-year-old violinist with a history of lower back pain consulted with Dr. Cuddy, a member of an independent surgical group. After performing several diagnostic tests, Dr. Cuddy recommended that Mr. House undergo a laminectomy and a partial discectomy. The surgery was intended to excise the posterior arch of the vertebrae, known as the lamina, and an intervertebral disc in order to relieve compression of the nerves of the spine.

On June 8, 2004, Dr. Cuddy met with Dr. Chase, a general surgeon at Grace Memorial Hospital. Dr. Cuddy showed House's chart to Dr. Chase and asked him whether he foresaw any particular problems with the upcoming back surgery. Dr. Chase said: "No, it should be routine," a remark that Dr. Cuddy noted in House's chart.

The surgery took place on June 9, 2004, at Princeton-Plainsboro Teaching Hospital, Anystate, where Dr. Cuddy had surgical privileges. His resident, Dr. Cameron, assisted him. While working to remove the lamina from the lower portion of one of the lumbar vertebrae, known as L5, using manual bone-cutting instruments called rongeurs, Dr. Cuddy inadvertently nicked the dura, the tough fibrous membrane covering the spinal cord; and created a one millimeter tear in it, a relatively common complication of such surgery. Through the hole in the dura Dr. Cuddy could see the arachnoid, a thin, delicate, cobweb-like membrane that lies beneath the dura and encloses the spinal cord; however, no cerebrospinal fluid was leaking out and no nerves had been damaged.

Dr. Cuddy then moved to the upper portion of L5 and attempted to continue using the rongeurs. However, the fact that Mr. House's dura was thinner than normal and very nearly stuck to the underside of the lamina made it difficult to separate the dura adequately from the bone. Although used by a relatively small number of innovative surgeons, Dr. Cuddy determined that a high-speed, turbine, hand-operated drill would be the most effective way of thinning the lamina to a thickness that would allow him to pick away the remaining bone with special instruments, and intended to use a small piece of cotton, known as a cottonoid, to protect the already exposed dura. His surgical nurse, Nurse Wilson, an employee of Princeton-Plainsboro Hospital, was unable to place the cottonoid between the dura and the bone due to the inadequate spatial conditions. Instead she laid the cottonoid on the exposed dura next to the bone while Dr. Cuddy drilled and Dr. Cameron operated the suction instrument. Either because of the placement of the cottonoid or the angle of the suction device, the drill encountered a piece of bone of uneven consistency, which caused the drill to jump and land in the dural sac between the bone and the cottonoid near the area that had already been torn. The drill severed several of Mr. House's nerves, specifically those responsible for bowel and bladder control. The collision between drill and bone caused a piece of bone to break off and migrate from the specific location of the surgery; although he searched for the fragment Dr. Cuddy was unable to recover it. Dr. Cuddy removed the nerves from the drill, put them back in the dural sac, sutured it closed, placed fibrin glue over it, and continued on with the operation, the remainder of which was successful. Immediately following the surgery Dr. Cuddy met with Mrs. House family and said he was "very sorry that something had gone so wrong with the surgery." However, in his post-surgical notes Dr. Cuddy made no mention of the missing bone fragment.

Subsequently Dr. Foreman, a Princeton-Plainsboro urologist, treated Mr. House. Dr. Foreman confirmed that Mr. House has lost bladder and bowel function and some sexual function with no hope of regaining them. Dr. Foreman also performed a scan that discovered the bone chip that had migrated from the L5 immediate area and was now lodged near the nerves where they exited the spinal cord. According to Dr. Foreman any further surgery to remove the chip is contraindicated. Mr. House's injuries have caused him to suffer chronic pain and episodes of depression. He was forced to retire from his position with the Anystate Symphony Orchestra.

Mr. House has filed suit against Princeton-Plainsboro Hospital, Cuddy's surgical group, Nurse Wilson, Dr. Cameron, and Dr. Chase, alleging lack of informed consent and clinical negligence. What specific allegations will plaintiff likely argue? What issues likely will arise? Discuss how a court would resolve the claims and issues you identify.

9.6

Freda and Doris were involved in an intersectional collision in Anytown. Neither was insured. Doris filed a negligence action against Freda. Freda saw a TV commercial that advertised the services of Grabbit, a personal injury lawyer. Impressed, she employed Grabbit to handle her defense. Grabbit personally investigated the circumstances surrounding the accident. His first inclination was to use a comparative negligence defense. However, on reflection he decided on an "all or nothing" approach. He omitted the comparative negligence defense and elected to fight Doris' claim on the basis of factual causation. The jury returned a verdict of $200,000 against Freda, forcing her into both bankruptcy and a mental hospital. Grabbit did not lodge an appeal within the period permitted under Anystate rules. When he decided against using the comparative negligence approach, Grabbit destroyed all records of his investigation of the accident. After the jury verdict, Grabbit refused to return Freda's telephone calls.

Freda wants to bring an action against Grabbit. What approaches would you recommend? What legal issues would arise? How should they be resolved?

Chapter 10

PRODUCTS LIABILITY

A. INTRODUCTION

Products liability concerns the legal liability of manufacturers and other sellers for injuries caused by defective products. Manufacturers, distributors, retailers, and others in the distribution chain are potentially liable if they market products posing unreasonable danger to users or consumers.

Products liability evolved as a legal hybrid on the borderline between contract and tort (sometimes identified as "contort"). In a modern products liability lawsuit, the plaintiff typically will plead a number of alternative theories. Thus, a "products liability action" may be:

> any action against a manufacturer or seller for recovery of damages arising out of personal injury, death, or property damage allegedly caused by a defective product whether the action is based in strict tort liability, strict products liability, negligence, misrepresentation, breach of express or implied warranty, or any other theory or combination of theories. TEX. CIV. PRAC. & REM. CODE §82.001(2).

Products liability is an example of a field where there is considerable crossover between contract and torts. Indeed, Prosser dubbed warranty law as "a freak hybrid born of the illicit intercourse of tort and contract." William L. Prosser, *The Assault on the Citadel (Strict Liability to the Consumer)*, 69 YALE L.J. 1099, 1126 (1960). Products liability is not a unitary theory like medical malpractice. In the typical products liability case, plaintiff will assert causes of action in contracts (express warranties, implied warranty of merchantability, fitness for a particular purpose) as well as torts (negligence, strict liability, misrepresentation). A plaintiff injured by a defective stepladder, for example, may file a complaint charging the defendant manufacturer with negligent design, misrepresentation, breach of warranty (express and implied warranty of merchantability), and strict products liability.

In order to understand the heterogeneity of products liability law, it is necessary to examine its history. Products liability was slow to develop because of the barrier of privity — the requirement that a buyer have a direct contractual relationship with the seller or be barred from recovery in either warranty or negligence. During the first decades of the twentieth century American consumers purchased goods from national manufacturers and the privity doctrine insulated manufacturers from most claims.

Products liability was jump-started by *MacPherson v. Buick Motor Co.*, 111 N.E. 1050, 1053 (1916), which overturned the privity doctrine established in *Winterbottom v. Wright,* 152 Eng. Rep. 402 (1842), in negligence cases. Prior to *MacPherson*, even though privity had barred most claims, a few courts had created exceptions for products imminently or inherently dangerous, such as fire arms or poisons. Justice Cardozo creatively used these exceptions to craft a broader liability rule, reasoning:

> If the nature of a thing is such that it is reasonably certain to place life and limb in peril when negligently made, it is then a thing of danger. Its nature gives warning of the consequences to be expected. If to the element of danger there is added knowledge that the thing will be used by persons other than the purchaser, and used without new tests, then, irrespective of contract, the manufacturer of this thing of danger is under a duty to make it carefully.

Modern products liability reached its nadir in the mid 1960s with the development of strict products liability. The doctrine of *res ipsa loquitur* had already found robust application in cases concerning defective products cases (*see, e.g., Escola v. Coca Cola Bottling Co. of Fresno*, 150 P.2d 436 (Cal. 1944)), but the most influential doctrine had been contractual. Implied warranties, such as the requirement of "merchantable quality" (now set forth in Art. § 2-314 of the Uniform Commercial Code) placed an obligation on sellers to sell only goods of "merchantable quality" or goods that meet the ordinary consumer's expectations and are fit for their ordinary purpose.

This chapter starts with the early efforts of the court and the drafters of the Restatement (Second) Torts to build products liability doctrine around a *product*-centric (rather than *conduct*-centric) approach.

Thereafter, the story of products liability involves two interwoven plots. One of the themes involves the struggle of courts and commentators to clarify how strict liability should be fashioned appropriately to reach cases involving products that are injurious without making the seller absolutely liable for product-related harm. The focus of that struggle has been on defining defect. A product may be dangerously defective due to (1) *a manufacturing defect*; (2) *a design defect* or; (3) *a failure of a manufacturer to warn of a danger or instruct on the proper use of the product.*

A second theme has played out in the case law, state legislatures and law reviews, as well as in the more recent Third Restatement about whether products liability is a true strict liability tort or retains considerable amounts of the fault-based doctrine of negligence. The usage of language like foreseeability, feasibility and reasonableness intimates a fault basis that belies a strict liability basis.

As you read these materials also note: (1) the doctrinal differences that have evolved in jurisdictions over how to determine if a product is "defective" (e.g., "consumer expectations" vs. "risk-utility") and how, even in the same jurisdiction, that approach may vary depending on the type of defect (manufacture, design, or warning) being discussed; (2) the extent to which limitations on recovery have been imposed through rules such as the "obvious risk" doctrine or because of the peculiarities of a particular distribution chain (e.g., one involving a government contractor or a health professional), and (3) How discrete rules have evolved to deal with specific types of products or accidents (e.g., food, prescription drugs, and automobiles).

B. THE DEVELOPMENT OF MODERN PRODUCTS LIABILITY

GREENMAN v. YUBA POWER PRODUCTS, INC.
377 P.2d 897 (Cal. 1963)

TRAYNOR, JUDGE.

Plaintiff brought this action for damages against the retailer and the manufacturer of a Shopsmith, a combination power tool that could be used as a saw, drill, and wood lathe. He saw a Shopsmith demonstrated by the retailer and studied a brochure prepared by the manufacturer. He decided he wanted a Shopsmith for his home workshop, and his wife bought and gave him one for Christmas in 1955. In 1957 he bought the necessary attachments to use the Shopsmith as a lathe for turning a large piece of wood he wished to make into a chalice. After he had worked on the piece of wood several times without difficulty, it suddenly flew out of the machine and struck him on the forehead, inflicting serious injuries . . .

After a trial before a jury, the court ruled that there was no evidence that the retailer was negligent or had breached any express warranty and that the manufacturer was not liable for the breach of any implied warranty. Accordingly, it submitted to the jury only the cause of action alleging breach of implied warranties against the retailer and the causes of action alleging negligence and breach of express warranties against the manufacturer. The jury returned a verdict for the retailer against plaintiff and for plaintiff against the manufacturer in the amount of $65,000. The trial court denied the manufacturer's motion for a new trial and entered judgment on the verdict. [On appeal the manufacturer argued that a technical provision of the warranty code barred plaintiff's action] . . .

[T]o impose strict liability on the manufacturer under the circumstances of this case, it was not necessary for plaintiff to establish an express warranty as defined in [the warranty code] A manufacturer is strictly liable in tort when an article he places on the market, knowing that it is to be used without inspection for defects, proves to have a defect that causes injury to a human being. Recognized first in the case of unwholesome food products, such liability has now been extended to a variety of other products that create as great or greater hazards if defective.

Although in these cases strict liability has usually been based on the theory of an express or implied warranty running from the manufacturer to the plaintiff, the abandonment of the requirement of a contract between them, the recognition that the liability is not assumed by agreement but imposed by law, and the refusal to permit the manufacturer to define the scope of its own responsibility for defective products make clear that the liability is not one governed by the law of contract warranties but by the law of strict liability in tort. Accordingly, rules defining and governing warranties that were developed to meet the needs of commercial transactions cannot properly be invoked to govern the manufacturer's liability to those injured by its defective products unless those rules also serve the purposes for which such liability is imposed.

We need not recanvass the reasons for imposing strict liability on the manufacturer . . . The purpose of such liability is to insure that the costs of injuries resulting from defective products are borne by the manufacturers that put such products on the market rather than by the injured persons who are powerless to protect themselves. Sales warranties serve this purpose fitfully at best. In the present case, for example, plaintiff was able to plead and prove an express warranty only because he read and relied on the representations of the Shopsmith's ruggedness contained in the manufacturer's brochure. Implicit in the machine's presence on the market, however, was a representation that it would safely do the jobs for which it was built. Under these circumstances, it should not be controlling whether plaintiff selected the machine because of the statements in the brochure, or because of the machine's own appearance of excellence that belied the defect lurking beneath the surface, or because he merely assumed that it would safely do the jobs it was built to do. It should not be controlling whether the details of the sales from manufacturer to retailer and from retailer to plaintiff's wife were such that one or more of the implied warranties of the sales act arose. To establish the manufacturer's liability it was sufficient that plaintiff proved that he was injured while using the Shopsmith in a way it was intended to be used as a result of a defect in design and manufacture of which plaintiff was not aware that made the Shopsmith unsafe for its intended use . . . [AFFIRMED.]

NOTES

1. *Strict Liability Restated*. Two years after *Greenman*, the American Law Institute followed suit and adopted strict liability. State after state adopted The Second Restatement's section 402A, either by statute or through judicial decision-making. According to section 402A:

> (1) One who sells any product in a defective condition unreasonably dangerous to the user or consumer or to his property is subject to liability for physical harm thereby caused to the ultimate user or consumer, or to his property, if

> (a) the seller is engaged in the business of selling such a product, and

> (b) it is expected to and does reach the user or consumer without substantial change in the condition in which it is sold.

> (2) The rule stated in Subsection (1) applies although

> (a) the seller has exercised all possible care in the preparation and sale of his product, and

> (b) the user or consumer has not bought the product from or entered into any contractual relation with the seller.

REST. 2D TORTS § 402A (1965).

2. *Plaintiff's Prima Facie Case*. What are the elements of the § 402A action that plaintiff must address?

Section 402A imposes liability only for those defective products that are "unreasonably dangerous" to "the ordinary consumer who purchases it, with the ordinary knowledge common to the community as to its characteristics." REST. 2D TORTS § 402A, comment *i*. Design defects cases are the most challenging for the plaintiff to prove. Section 402A requires a plaintiff to prove that a product was defectively designed because it failed to perform in accordance with the consumer's or user's reasonable expectations. Under this "consumer expectation" test, the plaintiff must prove that the product did not safely perform the job or function for which it was made, contrary to the consumer's or user's reasonable expectations. For example, an automobile would be defective if it were designed so that its brakes did not hold in situations where a driver would reasonably expect the brakes to hold. The consumer expectations test has generally been in retreat and replaced by risk/utility. *See, e.g., Prentis v. Yale Mfg.*, 365 N.W.2d 176, 184 (Mich. 1984).

Today, most courts expect the plaintiff to prove defective design through a risk/utility test in which the plaintiff bears the burden of proving that the product's risks outweigh its utility in light of various factors. *See, e.g., Azzarello v. Black Bros. Co.*, 391 A.2d 1020 (Pa. 1978); *Turner v. General Motors Corp.*, 584 S.W.2d 844, 847 (Tex. 1979). Some states give the plaintiff the option to prove design defect through two alternative tests for determining design defect liability: (1) the consumer expectation analysis; and (2) a balancing test that inquires whether a product's risks outweigh its benefits. *See, e.g., Lamkin v. Towner,* 138 Ill.2d 510, 528 (1990). *See also Barker v. Lull Engineering Co.,* 20 Cal.3d 413, 427-28 (1978) (reversing burden of proof in favor of plaintiff on risk-utility option).

3. *Product-Centricity*. Some courts have refused to attach an "unreasonably dangerous" definition of defect, drawing upon the language in Section 402A, because they think that it unduly injects negligence concepts (as do terms like foreseeability and unreasonableness) into the strict tort liability inquiry. Section 402A(2)(a) itself says that the seller's reasonable care is *not* dispositive of a products liability action. Note the words of the Supreme Court of Oregon in the leading case of *Phillips v. Kimwood Mach. Co.*, 525 P.2d 1033, 1036-39 (Or. 1974):

> The problem with strict liability of products has been one of limitation. No one wants absolute liability where all the article has to do is to cause injury. To impose liability there has to be something about the article which makes it dangerously defective without regard to whether the manufacturer was or was not at fault for such condition. A test for unreasonable danger is therefore vital. A dangerously defective article would be one which a reasonable person would not put into the stream of commerce if he had knowledge of its harmful character. The test, therefore, is whether the seller would be negligent if he sold the article knowing of the risk involved. Strict liability imposes what amounts to constructive knowledge of the condition of the product.

> . . . To some it may seem that absolute liability has been imposed upon the manufacturer since it might be argued that no manufacturer could reasonably put into the stream of commerce an article which he realized might result in injury to a user. This is not the case, however. The

manner of injury may be so fortuitous and the chances of injury occurring so remote that it is reasonable to sell the product despite the danger. In design cases the utility of the article may be so great, and the change of design necessary to alleviate the danger in question may so impair such utility, that it is reasonable to market the product as it is, even though the possibility of injury exists and was realized at the time of the sale. Again, the cost of the change necessary to alleviate the danger in design may be so great that the article would be priced out of the market and no one would buy it even though it was of high utility. Such an article is not dangerously defective despite its having inflicted injury.

. . . It is apparent that the language being used in the discussion of the above problems is largely that which is also used in negligence cases, i.e., "unreasonably dangerous," "have reasonably anticipated," "reasonably prudent manufacturer," etc. It is necessary to remember that whether the doctrine of negligence, ultrahazardousness, or strict liability is being used to impose liability, the same process is going on in each instance, i.e., weighing the utility of the article against the risk of its use. Therefore, the same language and concepts of reasonableness are used by courts for the determination of unreasonable danger in products liability cases.

The *Phillips* court raises two concepts familiar in discussing the law of negligence; the requirement that the defendant has foreseen the risk (foreseeability) and the reasonableness of the defendant's conduct (standard of care). How does the court describe the approach to these concepts for products liability cases so as to create a strict liability rather than negligence-based tort?

4. *Multiple Restatements?* Published two years after *Greenman*, REST. 2D TORTS §402A provided little more than a doctrinal skeleton that the courts have fleshed out over four decades. The Third Restatement is a far more substantial creature. For the most part the new Restatement effectively synthesizes the doctrinal complexity and sophistication that resulted from the four decades of judicial attention to products liability law. However, the Third Restatement's standard for judging defectiveness (particularly design defectiveness) is highly controversial. For a classic critique see Jerry J. Phillips, *Symposium on Generic Products Liability: The Unreasonably Unsafe Product and Strict Liability*, 72 CHI.-KENT L. REV. 129 (1996).

REST. 3D TORTS §2 states that a product

contains a design defect when the foreseeable risks of harm posed by the product could have been reduced or avoided by the adoption of a reasonable alternative design by the seller or other distributor, or a predecessor in the commercial chain of distribution, and the omission of the reasonable alternative design renders the product not reasonably safe.

This new test for design defect replaces the consumer expectation test with a risk utility test. Moreover, §2 makes proof of *reasonable* alternative design an absolute requirement for liability for all design defect cases. Without such proof, there is no liability. The Reporters to the Third Restatement stated that "very substantial authority supports the proposition that [the] plaintiff must establish a reasonable alternative design in order for a product to be adjudged defective in design." *Id.* § 2, Reporters' Note to cmt. *c*. However, another survey of state law concluded that the requirement to prove an alternative design was a minority position with only Alabama and Maine clearly adopting an absolute requirement of alternative design evidence. *See* John F. Vargo, *The Emperor's New Clothes: The American Law Institute Adorns A "Newcloth" For Section 402a Products Liability Design Defects — A Survey of the States Reveals a Different Weave*, 26 U. MEM. L. REV. 493 (1996).

Section 402A of the Restatement (Second) of Torts swept the country whereas few states have adopted the Third Restatement's "reasonable alternative design" requirement. Most design defect cases will go to the jury when the plaintiff introduces cogent evidence of a *feasible* alternative design (a strict liability concept) *See General Motors Corp. v. Edwards*, 482 So. 2d 1176, 1191 (Ala. 1985) ("plaintiff must prove that a safer, practical, alternative design was available to the manufacturer"). Few jurisdictions, however, require evidence of *reasonable* alternative design (a negligence concept). Further, most jurisdictions hold that a feasible alternative design is merely one of several factors that the jury may consider in determining whether a product design is defective. *See e.g., Banks v. ICI Americas, Inc.*, 450 S.E.2d 671, 674 (Ga. 1994), Should a manufacturer be liable for marketing a product with a defective design notwithstanding the fact that there are no safer alternative designs in existence? Can a product be marketed with a defective design even though no feasible alternative design is available? *See Phipps v. General Motors Corp.*, 363 A.2d 955 (Md. 1976) (holding that liability can still attach).

For some, the new Restatement is no more than a tardy recognition that products liability was merely a "tweaked" child of negligence. For others, it is an attempt to lead the courts away from the strict liability system that had been developed, and returning to negligence. So far, most courts have rejected the new Restatement's approach to defectiveness, which is why this chapter continues to rely on § 402A.

5. *Who Should Bear The Risk?* As with other torts actions the core question in products liability cases concerns the level of risk that defendants (here sellers, including manufacturers) should bear compared to plaintiffs (here consumers). What factors or criteria can we use to answer that question? Why should a product manufacturer bear a greater share of risks vis-à-vis a consumer than, say a doctor bears regarding a patient, or an automobile driver owes a pedestrian? Why have legislatures intervened in this area, "interfering" with the common law development of products liability in response to calls for tort "reform"?

CATERPILLAR TRACTOR CO. v. BECK
593 P.2d 871 (Alaska 1979)

CONNOR. JUDGE.

On June 24, 1973, Derald Allen Beck was killed when the Caterpillar 944 front-end loader which he was operating rolled over an embankment. Decedent's widow, Paula Beck, brought this action against Caterpillar Tractor

Company (hereinafter Caterpillar) for the wrongful death of her husband. Beck contended that Caterpillar's failure to equip the 944 loader with a roll-over protective shield (hereinafter ROPS) constituted a design defect in the loader, and because of that defect, Derald Beck suffered fatal injuries. Following a jury verdict in favor of Beck, judgment was entered against Caterpillar in the amount of $408,594.50. Caterpillar appeals from this judgment, specifying several errors by the trial court . . .

Although there were no witnesses to the accident, an investigating state trooper testified that Derald Beck was apparently "roading" the loader in reverse, with the bucket in a raised position. The road was dirt and gravel with soft shoulders and wound around the side of a hill. On one side of the road there was an embankment of approximately seven feet. The trooper estimated that Beck was traveling at approximately 10 to 15 miles per hour as he proceeded up the road, but the loader then sank into the road shoulder and came almost to a complete stop. The loader apparently rolled over on its side and then flipped over 180 degrees and fell down the embankment. Beck was crushed beneath the loader, pinned between the steering wheel and part of the seat. The fiberglass canopy was flattened out and parts of it were broken off . . .

A ROPS is an overhead protective canopy which is constructed to withstand a roll-over and, thus, protect the operator from being crushed. In addition, a ROPS can decrease the risk of a roll-over. There was no dispute at trial that a ROPS, as developed at the time of the accident, would have saved Derald Beck's life. Beck would not have been crushed and a ROPS may have even prevented the loader from overturning. There was also no dispute that it is best from a cost and technological standpoint to have a ROPS installed by the loader manufacturer at the time of initial production. However, there was con- siderable dispute about the availability of a ROPS at the time Caterpillar produced this loader in 1964.

Various types of protective canopies were used in the heavy equipment industry for many years prior to the development of a ROPS, particularly in the logging industry. These canopies provided protection primarily from inclement weather and falling objects. Such devices were known in the indus- try by the name FOPS, falling object protective shield or structure. These shields were manufactured by several auxiliary equipment manufacturers at the time the 944 loader was produced. A FOPS did not have the capability to withstand a roll-over.

A consulting safety engineer, Ovid Holmes, appearing as an expert for Beck, testified that the heavy equipment industry began testing ROPS devices as early as 1961. Holmes had not heard of a FOPS, but testified that he believed that some of the canopies developed in the 1950's did have roll-over protection capability. Although other front-end loader manufacturers did not supply a ROPS as part of the standard equipment at that time, several auxiliary equip- ment manufacturers did offer them . . .

Caterpillar, at the time of design and production of the 944 loader, made a "deliberate decision" not to install any kind of protective canopy whatsoever on the 944 as part of its basic design. It did begin testing the ROPS concept in 1966. By that time, several auxiliary equipment manufacturers were regularly producing ROPS. In response to various state and federal regulations promulgated shortly thereafter, Caterpillar, in 1969, began installing ROPS as part of the basic vehicle model. No ROPS was ever made part of the 944 model manufactured by Caterpillar and the 944 loader went out of production in 1968 before Caterpillar began adding ROPS to its loaders . . .

Appellant Caterpillar contends in this appeal that the trial court erred by . . . improperly instructing the jury on the law of strict liability for alleged design defects and refusing to define "defect" for the jury . . .

Caterpillar contends that the trial court erred in instructing the jury that "[a] design defect is one in which the product, however perfectly manufactured, incorporates or fails to incorporate a design feature with the result that injury is proximately caused thereby." Caterpillar argues that the instruction misconstrues the law of strict liability in that it essentially instructs the jury on absolute liability: it does not instruct the jury that they must first find a defect in the product nor does it give the jury guidance in determining whether a defect exists. In addition, Caterpillar urges that we define the term "defective" for cases involving design defect, preferably by use of a standard which balances the risk presented by the product in light of the product's utility. Beck, in response, argues that the jury was properly instructed on the necessity of finding a defect before it could fix liability and that the term "defect" need not be defined beyond its inherent meaning . . .

Although courts and commentators have struggled with diverse approaches to strict products liability, most authorities appear to agree that manufacturers are not absolute insurers of their products. Strict liability will not impose legal responsibility simply because a product causes harm. A product must be defective as marketed if liability is to attach, and "defective" must mean something more than a condition causing physical injury.

The instruction at issue stated that plaintiff Beck alleged that a design defect caused the death of Derald Beck and then proceeded to state that a product is defectively designed when an injury results from a design feature (or the lack of a design feature). Essentially, the jury was instructed that there must be proof of a defect in the product's design in order for liability to attach, and that proof of an injury could suffice to prove a defect. If such defect proximately caused the injury, strict liability is imposed. This is a tautology and tantamount to an instruction of absolute liability.

Beck argues that the instruction was proper because it "simply advises the jury that a design defect is a defect resulting from a design feature." However, it is not just any design feature yielding an injury which will result in the imposition of legal responsibility for the incidents of such injury. A product is not necessarily defective merely because an injury occurred . . .

Caterpillar also contends that the jury was inadequately instructed on the meaning of design defect. Since a manufacturer's strict liability depends upon the meaning of defective, Caterpillar urges us to develop particular standards for assessing a product's defectiveness.

Design defects present the most perplexing problems in the field of strict products liability because there is no readily ascertainable external measure of defectiveness. While manufacturing flaws can be evaluated against the intended design of the product, no such objective standard exists in the design defect context. Beck argues that, despite the lack of an external standard in design defect cases, the word "defect" has an inherent meaning; *i.e.,* a flaw or incompleteness. Therefore, when jurors are instructed that they must find a defect to impose liability, they realize that the product must be faulty. However, we believe that the dictionary meaning of the word "defect" is insufficient to fully explain to the jury when a manufacturer should incur legal responsibility for his product's design . . .

In the strict liability context, the term "defect" is "neither self-defining nor susceptible to a single definition applicable in all contexts." *Barker v. Lull Engineering Co., Inc.,* 573 P.2d 443, 453 (Cal. 1978). The varied purposes and the theoretical underpinnings of implied warranty and strict liability in tort have generated five main tests for product defectiveness: (1) the "deviation from the norm" test; (2) the "reasonable fitness for intended purpose" test; (3) the Restatement test; (4) the "risk/utility analysis" test; and (5) the recent test proposed by the California Supreme Court in *Barker v. Lull Engineering Co., Inc., supra* . . .

Under the "deviation from the norm" test, the product is classified as defective because it does not match the quality of most similar products. While this test may be reliable in a case involving a manufacturing defect, it is inadequate for those cases where the plaintiff contends that an entire product line is defectively designed. Comparison with similar products manufactured by others, while helpful, would be improper if used as the definitive test for ascertaining a defect. The test may also be overinclusive in some fact settings; *e.g.,* where "unavoidably unsafe products" are involved. In addition, the burden of proving the deviation would fall on the plaintiff. Since one of the major goals of strict products liability is to relieve the plaintiff of the burdensome evidentiary requirements of the negligence cause of action, this test would unduly burden the plaintiff.

The "unfitness for intended purpose" test of defectiveness originated "as a basis for deciding when purchasers could recover from sellers for intangible financial and commercial losses" resulting from frustration of the purchaser's expectations as to what the product would do. It was intended as a test to determine when a manufacturer would be liable for injuries caused by its products; but the adaptation of the test from commercial expectations suggests that the only basis for liability is consumer expectations. Accordingly, plaintiffs are more likely to recover when the danger is hidden than when it is patent. This is unacceptable because we have already determined that any distinction between patent and latent defects is unnecessarily restrictive to plaintiffs. Also, this test operates to shield a defendant from liability as long as the product does not fall below the ordinary customer's expectations as to the product's safety. Consumer expectations are a factor to be considered in determining defectiveness, but the public policy supporting strict liability would be poorly served if consumer expectations were the sole boundary of liability.

The REST. 2D §402A, provides a two-prong test for the seller's liability. Defectiveness is established if the product leaves the seller's hands in an "unreasonably dangerous" condition and such condition is not contemplated by the ultimate consumer. Thus, recovery would not be allowed for obvious or generally known dangers. Although the Restatement test improves upon the deficiencies of the above tests, we adhere to our previously expressed view that the "unreasonably dangerous" terminology of the Restatement unnecessarily limits the scope of liability and unduly increases the plaintiff's burden of proof . . .

The focus of strict products liability is on the condition of the product, not on the manufacturing and marketing decision of the defendant. Therefore, indiscriminate use of reasonableness language will confuse the strict liability standard by introducing inessential attention to the conduct of the defendant, even if actual knowledge of the harmful condition is presumed rather than proven. Nor do we think it necessary to have a two-tier system where the trial judge, before giving the case to the jury, must first find that it would be reasonable for the jury to find for the plaintiff. Given proper instructions, we believe a jury can determine from the evidence whether a defect exists or not.

The California Supreme Court held in *Barker v. Lull Engineering Co., Inc., supra*, that:

> [A] trial judge may properly instruct the jury that a product is defective in design (1) if the plaintiff demonstrates that the product failed to perform as safely as an ordinary consumer would expect when used in an intended or reasonably foreseeable manner, or (2) if the plaintiff proves that the product's design proximately caused his injury and the defendant fails to prove . . . that on balance the benefits of the challenged design outweighed the risk of danger inherent in such design.

573 P.2d at 457-58. This dual approach was conceived in recognition of the multiplicity of "injury-producing deficiencies" encompassed within the word "defect" . . .

The *Barker* test represents a composite of the most workable features of each of the other tests. The first prong of the *Barker* test — that a product is defectively designed if it fails "to perform as safely as an ordinary consumer would expect when used in an intended or reasonably foreseeable manner" — incorporates notions of the implied warranty of fitness for reasonable use, a primary concept in the evolution of strict products liability, but eases the burden of proof on the plaintiff. In a cause of action based upon a warranty of fitness and merchantability, the plaintiff would have to prove the breach by pinpointing the actual defect. Under the *Barker* test, the plaintiff need only show, for strict liability to apply, that he used the product in an intended or reasonably foreseeable fashion and the product failed to perform in that capacity as safely as expected. Thus, this test, while giving content to the meaning of "defect," preserves the policies we expressed in *Clary*.

The second prong of the Barker definition encompasses those situations, such as the lack of a safety device which is presented here, where the product satisfies ordinary consumer expectations as to its general use but is still "defective" in that its design exposes the user or bystander to "excessive preventable danger." What is excessive preventable danger must turn on the facts of each case. With the focus off the ordinary consumer's expectations, the trier of fact balances the risk and the social utility of the product. This requires a weighing of various factors. Therefore, where necessary, the trial court may instruct the jury that if "on balance, the benefits of the challenged design outweigh the risk of danger inherent in such design," no liability will attach.

Although we believe that a balancing process is inevitable in certain design defect cases, we in no way intend to diminish our adherence to the goals of strict products liability. Therefore, we also agree with the position taken by *Barker* regarding the allocation of the burden of proof:

> Inasmuch as . . . a manufacturer who seeks to escape liability for an injury proximately caused by the product's design on a risk-benefit theory should bear the burden of persuading the trier of fact that its product should not be judged defective, the defendant's burden is one affecting the burden of proof, rather than simply the burden of producing evidence. (citations omitted)

573 P.2d at 455. We hold that the plaintiff need only show that he was injured and that the injury was proximately caused by the product's design. The defendant may then avoid liability for a defectively designed product by proving by a preponderance of the evidence that, "on balance, the benefits of the challenged design outweigh the risk of danger inherent in such design." *Barker, supra* at 458. This will require the fact-finder to consider and compare a number of competing factors, including but not limited to,

> the gravity of the danger posed by the challenged design, the likelihood that such danger would occur, the mechanical feasibility of a safer alternative design, the financial cost of an improved design, and the adverse consequences to the product and to the consumer that would result from an alternative design.

573 P.2d at 455. Besides lessening the burdens of the plaintiff's *prima facie* case, this allocation puts the burden of producing the relevant complex and technical evidence on the party who has the most access to and is the most familiar with such evidence.

Beck protests that adding further content to the meaning of product defectiveness will be a retreat to negligence concepts, will increase the plaintiff's burden of proof, and will create a distinction between manufacturing and design defects . . . Negligence concepts will not dilute the plaintiff's case because the trier of fact will concentrate on the nature of the product in determining defectiveness rather than upon the conduct of the defendant.

> Thus, the fact that the manufacturer took reasonable precautions in an attempt to design a safe product or otherwise acted as a reasonably prudent manufacturer would have under the circumstances, while perhaps absolving the manufacturer of liability under a negligence theory, will not preclude the imposition of liability under strict liability principles if, upon hindsight, the trier of fact concludes that the product's design is unsafe to consumers, users, or bystanders. (citation omitted)

Barker, supra, 573 P.2d at 457. The plaintiff's *prima facie* case in strict liability will not be made more onerous. The plaintiff's *prima facie* case essentially remains the same whether the defect is one in manufacturing or in design. Our holding merely reflects that the concept of defectiveness covers a diversity of product characteristics and, because we are not willing to affix liability solely on the basis of an injury-producing product, we will allow the trial courts to formulate instructions which elucidate the concept of "defect" in the particular circumstances presented.

In summary then, we hold that the instruction approved in *Clary* will in many cases suffice. However, in those cases where the meaning of "defect" will be unduly vague, particularly in design defect cases, the trial court may formulate instructions which define the legal concept of "defect" for the jury. Following the guidelines set by the *Barker* court, we hold that the trial court may instruct the jury that a product is defectively designed if:

> (1) the plaintiff proves that the product failed to perform as safely as an ordinary consumer would expect when used in an intended or reasonably foreseeable manner, or (2) the plaintiff proves that the product's design proximately caused injury and the defendant fails to prove, in light of the relevant factors, that on balance the benefits of the challenged design outweigh the risk of danger inherent in such design.

573 P.2d at 452. Because the jury here was erroneously instructed on causation as the primary definition of defect, the judgment entered against appellant Caterpillar must be reversed . . . [REVERSED].

NOTES

1. *Risk-Utility.* Under *Greenman* and the REST. 2D TORTS § 402A approach, liability does not turn on the manufacturer's lack of reasonable care. Under pure strict liability theory, the product is on trial, not the knowledge or conduct of the manufacturer. In searching for an appropriate product-centric test (determining when a product is "defective") the courts have struggled with defining the liability standard that requires a lesser showing of fault than negligence, but does not impose "absolute" liability on the manufacturer or other seller. As *Caterpillar* and *Barker* illustrate, a significant part of this debate has revolved around whether "defective" or "unreasonably dangerous" should be based upon the consumer expectation test, a risk-utility test, or some combination of the two. Why has the construction of a test posed such difficulty?

2. *A Combination Approach.* The *Barker-Caterpillar* solution of combining the two tests as options has been rarely adopted. However, the risk-utility test, standing on its own and with the burden on plaintiff, has been adopted in a large number of jurisdictions, particularly in design defect cases. Does the use of such a balancing test suggest that there is little or no distinction between negligence and strict products liability theories, at least as courts have defined strict products liability? Does the test necessarily lead to a different result if, for example, the court excludes evidence of manufacturer conduct and focuses on whether a safer product could have been designed?

3. *Consumer Expectations.* The Restatement (Second) test for defectiveness is whether the product was more dangerous than which an ordinary consumer would expect. The test has been criticized for both asking too much and too little of a manufacturer. For instance, if a consumer expected a product that was not very safe a consumer expectation test might result in no liability even though the manufacturer could easily and cheaply have made the product safer. Alternatively, if a consumer expected a product to be extraordinarily safe, she might expect a perfect product even though it was technologically or economically impossible or impractical for the manufacturer to make such a safe product.

How does one establish consumer expectations? By lay testimony? By expert testimony? If by expert testimony, what would be the basis for the expert's opinion? An opinion poll of consumers? The expert's view of what consumers *should* expect?

The Restatement (Third) displaces the consumer expectation test with the risk utility test. In section 2, consumer expectation is just one factor to be considered when weighing and balancing the magnitude and probability of the foreseeable risks of harm, along with factors such as production costs, its effect on product longevity, maintenance, repair, and aesthetics; and the range of consumer choice among products. *See* REST. 3D TORTS § 2, cmts *b* & *g*.

4. *Re-Restated.* The Restatement (Third) of Torts essentially abandons the consumer expectation test in design and warning cases as the substantive basis for liability. But the comments provide, in relevant part: "although consumer expectations do not constitute an independent standard for judging the defectiveness of product designs, they may substantially influence or even be determinative on risk-utility balancing in judging whether the omission of the proposed alternative design renders the product not reasonably safe." *Id.*, § 2, cmt. *g*. Additionally, the consumer expectation test remains viable in cases involving food. *See* REST. 3D TORTS § 7.

5. *Tort or Warranty?* The "strict" or product-centric nature of warranty law may have pushed tort law towards strict liability for defective products in the sixties, but in the decades that followed the drafting of the Restatement (Second), claims for breach of warranty (while frequently appearing as additional counts in products cases) have taken a backseat to tort law, viewed by courts as secondary or even duplicative of principal claims. However, in *Denny v. Ford Motor Co.*, 662 N.E.2d 730 (N.Y. 1995), the New York Court of Appeals rejected the defendant's argument that the warranty claim had been subsumed in the tort strict product liability claim. The court said, in part: "The continued vitality of the warranty approach is evidenced by its retention and expansion in New York's version of the Uniform Commercial Code. . . . The existence of this statutory authority belies any argument that the breach of implied warranty remedy is a dead letter. . . ." *Denny*, 662 N.E. 2d at 734.

UCC Art 2-314 provides: "Merchantability means that the goods shall be reasonably suited for the ordinary purpose for which goods of that description are sold." The consequence of the court recognizing the warranty-based approach was its recognition of a consumer expectations approach based on the language in UCC 2-314. Was the *Denny* court seeking to insulate future strict products liability from erosion to negligence by providing a warranty-based strict liability remedy alternative in the event that the Third

Restatement's adoption of a negligence-like doctrine created a less favorable environment for consumers? *See e.g., Castro v. QVC Network, Inc.* 139 F.3d 114 (2d Cir. 1998) (opinion of Calabresi, J., in which the consumer expectation test is used to provide the basis for liability under the warranty claim).

6. *Horses for Courses.* Do these competing tests for measuring "defectiveness" in strict products liability make more sense when framed by discrete allegations of defective manufacture, design or warning? That is, does a consumer expectations test make more sense as a standard for defective manufacture, while risk-utility is more appropriate for design defect cases? If so, which test should be used for failure to warn cases? Is it better to view consumer expectations as appropriate for simple products (or simple defects) while risk-utility is more valuable in dealing with more complex cases? Why? Is it because jurors may not be capable of understanding the complexities of some products?

7. *Of Contort and Misrepresentation.* A number of jurisdictions have adopted REST. 2D TORTS § 402B, which states that a seller is liable for making a misrepresentation of material fact concerning the character or quality of the product. Section 402B is a powerful products liability theory because it, too, is based upon strict liability. If a seller makes a safety misrepresentation (even innocently or non-negligently) and the consumer justifiably relies upon the misrepresentation and suffers personal injury, liability attaches. *See generally* Jerry J. Phillips, *Symposium on Generic Products Liability: the Unreasonably Unsafe Product and Strict Liability*, 72 CHI.-KENT. L. REV. 129 (1996) (discussing the "fourth" products liability theory of misrepresentation and explaining its relationship with "warnings" cases).

The classic § 402B case is *Hauter v. Zogarts*, 14 Cal. 3d 104 (1975), in which the plaintiff was hit on the head by golf ball while using a golf training device called the "Golfing Gizmo." Plaintiff recovered not by showing a defect in the product, but under § 402B, on the basis that the packaging contained the legend "COMPLETELY SAFE BALL WILL NOT HIT PLAYER."

8. *Law or Economics?* Clearly, the risk-utility test balances interests in a manner that is reminiscent of the Learned Hand test for negligence (discussed in Chapter 4). That test has been fundamental in shaping our conception of an economic analysis of tort law. Does the use of an explicit risk-utility jury instruction by courts formally validate that economic analysis? More importantly, does the burden-shifting employed in some jurisdictions suggest a judicial recognition of the informational asymmetry between consumers and manufacturers?

C. DEFECTIVENESS

WILLIAMS v. SMART CHEVROLET CO.
730 S.W.2d 479 (Ark. 1987)

HOLT, CHIEF JUSTICE.

[Appeal from grant of defendants' motions for directed verdict.] . . . Looking at the evidence in the light most favorable to Williams, there was testimony by Williams that she purchased her new Chevrolet Camaro Z-28 from Smart [her Chevrolet dealer] on September 12, 1984, and noticed after a few days that the driver's side door was difficult to close and would work loose after being shut and locked. She returned the car to Smart for repairs and told them about the problem with the door. Smart returned the car to her and, according to Williams, told her the car was fixed. The door continued to work loose. On October 4, 1984, Williams was driving about 10 miles per hour down a straight, level, gravel road when her door, which she testified she specifically remembered shutting and locking with the power locks, suddenly came open. Williams said she fell out of the car, injuring herself. The car went into a ditch but was not damaged. Immediately after the accident, Williams noticed that the driver's door latch mechanism had one of the three securing screws hanging partially out. She returned the car to Smart to be fixed. The door, however, continued to work loose, but it never came open again. She sold the car some fourteen months later.

Williams also offered the testimony of her mother, her sister, and a friend that they rode in the car before and after the accident and noticed that the door would work loose.

Mike Keller, assistant technical director of American Interplex Corp., was Williams' expert witness. He testified that he worked on the car for two or three days in July, 1985, and test drove it on all types of roads and was never able to get the door to come all the way open, including when he tried to force it open. He testified he found no defective parts which would cause the door to fail and come open. He explained that the word "defective" excludes parts which had been abraded or otherwise damaged by external factors. Keller stated that the driver's side striker bolt, as compared to the striker bolt on the passenger door, had one or two additional shims and had two separate wear patterns, as opposed to one on the passenger side. Keller said this indicated to him that the latch mechanism had engaged at different places on the striker bolt. In addition, the driver's side door latch was abraded and the jaws of the rotor were flared wider, which he believed was caused by uneven contact of the striker bolt with the rotor jaws. Keller testified that this all resulted in an alignment problem with the door. He explained, however, that his examination of the vehicle did not indicate anything that would have allowed the door to come open and he could not document that it had ever previously been in a condition that would cause that to occur.

. . . The doctrine of strict liability does not change the burden of proof as to the existence of a flaw or defect in a product, but it does do away with the necessity of proving negligence in order to recover for injuries resulting from a defective product. The plaintiff still has the burden of proving that a particular defendant has sold a product which he should not have sold and that it caused his injury. We further explained in *Southern Co. v. Graham*, 271 Ark. 232 (1980), *quoting* PROSSER, TORTS, § 102, p. 672 (4th Ed. 1971):

> The difficult problems are those of proof by circumstantial evidence. Strictly speaking, since proof of negligence is not in issue, res ipsa loquitur has no application to strict liability; but the inferences which are the core of the doctrine remain, and are not less applicable. The plaintiff is not required to eliminate all other possibilities, and so prove his case beyond a reasonable doubt . . . [I]t is enough that he makes out a preponderance of probability. . . .

> [I]n the absence of direct proof of a specific defect, it is sufficient if a plaintiff negates other possible causes of failure of the product, not attributable to the defendant, and thus raises a reasonable inference that the defendant, as argued here, is responsible for the defect.

The plaintiff is not required to prove a specific defect when common experience tells us that the accident would not have occurred in the absence of a defect. The mere fact of an accident, standing alone, does not make out a case that the product was defective, nor does the fact that it was found in a defective condition after the event. But the addition of other facts tending to show that the defect existed before the accident may make out a sufficient case . . .

Here . . . we cannot say that when a car door suddenly flies open while the car is traveling on a gravel road at 10 miles per hour common experience tells us that it could not have happened absent a defect. Therefore, we examine the evidence to see to what extent Williams negated other causes of the accident. Williams stated that she is positive she shut and locked the door and that she was driving slowly and the road was straight. She testified she was not wearing her seat belt and that, when she saw the door open, she turned to her left and hit the brakes and her left hand came off of the steering wheel. She then fell to the ground, landing on her left hip and the left side of her face. The foregoing does not adequately negate any cause of the accident due to driver error or control. Furthermore, she had an expert examine the car, but he could not say that any of the problems he found were defects or that they would cause the door to come open. The expert's testimony was inconclusive as to the existence of any defect and tended to support the theory that the accident was due to driver error.

. . . [A]ppellant's proof does not go beyond suspicion or conjecture nor raise a reasonable inference that the defect was the cause of the accident. We . . . affirm the trial court's action in granting the motions for directed verdict. [AFFIRMED.]

NOTES

1. *Circumstantial Evidence of Defect.* As noted in *Williams*, plaintiff may establish the existence of a defect (defect-in-fact) with direct or circumstantial evidence. This is confirmed in REST. 3D TORTS § 3, that provides:

> It may be inferred that the harm sustained by the plaintiff was caused by a product defect existing at the time of sale or distribution, without proof of a specific defect, when the incident that harmed the plaintiff:
>
> (a) was of a kind that ordinarily occurs as a result of product defect; and
>
> (b) was not, in the particular case, solely the result of causes other than product defect existing at the time of sale or distribution.

2. *The Nature of the Manufacturing Claim.* REST. 3D TORTS § 2(a) states that a product is defective if it "contains a manufacturing defect when the product departs from its intended design even though all possible care was exercised in the preparation and marketing of the product." Note how the plaintiff's claim in *Williams* is not that the entire product line was defective but only that there was a problem with her particular automobile. She is claiming there was something about this car that was different and more dangerous than it was intended to be. In manufacturing defect cases there is symmetry between the manufacturer's intentions and the consumer's expectations as to the product. Is that why most manufacturing defect cases turn on proof of factual issues, such as: What was the defect? When did the defect exist? Was the manufacturer responsible for the defect? Did the defect cause the accident?

3. *Date of Defect.* The general rule is that the defendant supplier is not subject to products liability unless the product is defective when it leaves his control. *Consider Mickle v. Blackmon,* 252 S.C. 202 (1969), *later app.*, 255 S.C. 136 (1970), where the defendant car manufacturer was held liable for injuries resulting when, just months after the car was sold, the protective knob on the stick gearshift of the car deteriorated from exposure to sun rays. The plaintiff was impaled on the lever when she was thrown against it in an accident, causing the knob to shatter. Did the defect "exist" when it left the control of the manufacturer?

4. *Manufacturing Versus Design Defect.* One court has described the manufacturing-design defect distinction as follows:

> A defect in manufacture is, of course, quite different from a defect in design. The latter focuses upon whether the product was designed to perform as safely as an ordinary consumer would expect or whether the risk of danger inherent in the design outweighed the benefits of the design. The former focuses on whether the particular product involved in the accident was manufactured in conformity with the manufacturer's design.

Dierks v. Mitsubishi Motors Corp., 208 Cal. App. 3d 352 (1989). But what if many products in the product line somehow deviated from their intended design? In *American Tobacco Co. v. Grinnell*, 951 S.W.2d 420 (Tex. 1997), plaintiffs filed a mismanufacture claim against a tobacco company. Apparently, all the cigarettes manufactured by defendant contained allegedly harmful chemical residues from the tobacco curing process. The defendant argued that since all of its cigarettes contained the chemical residues the claim was really a design claim. The Texas Supreme Court rejected that argument, noting that the chemical residues were not specified in the design specifications for the cigarettes.

5. *The Hot Coffee Debate.* One of the most famous products liability cases (and one of the few to affect popular culture in a significant way.) is *Liebeck v. McDonald's Restaurants, P.T.S., Inc.* (N.M. Dist. Ct. Aug. 18, 1994),[1] discussed in Chapter 1. A 79-year-old female car passenger ordered coffee from a McDonalds drive-through in Albuquerque. With the car stationary she pulled on the lid to add creamer, but spilled the entire cup on her lap and suffered third degree burns. After a seven-day trial the jury awarded her $2.9 million, including $2.7 million in punitive damages (probably representing 2 days of the defendant's coffee revenues). The trial judge reduced the punitive award to $480,000 (three times the compensatory award) and reportedly the parties eventually settled the case for less than $600,000. The case (particularly the original damage award) was widely reported and remains the subject of considerable debate. Several positions can be taken on the case: (1) It is an outlier (or false positive), possibly explained by the severity of the plaintiff's injuries, the fact that it was a negligence case (based on evidence that the defendant knew of similar accidents), or the consequence of defendant's aggressive trial tactics following an intransigent decision not to settle the case. (2) It is proof of a torts system that is out of control, compensating for one-in-a-million chance accidents arising from obvious risks, with excessive damage awards that defeats society's expectation of personal responsibility for accidents. (3) It is a correctly decided case because the coffee was (allegedly) hotter than the industry standard and the warning on the cup was too small to convey this danger to consumers, including 700 others who sustained injuries before this case.

Other courts have been less than sympathetic to plaintiffs in such suits. *McMahon v. Bunn-O-Matic Corp.*, 150 F.3d 651 (7th Cir. 1998), was a case with similar facts, but brought against the manufacturer of the coffee maker. Judge Easterbrook noted:

> It is easy to sympathize with [plaintiff], severely injured by a common household beverage — and, for all we can see, without fault on her part. Using the legal system to shift the costs of this injury to someone else may be attractive to the [plaintiffs], but it would have bad consequences for coffee fanciers who like their beverage hot. First party health and accident insurance deals with injuries of the kind [plaintiff] suffered without the high costs of adjudication, and without potential side effects such as lukewarm coffee. We do not know whether the [plaintiffs] carried such insurance . . . but we are confident that Indiana law does not make [defendant] and similar firms insurers through the tort system of the harms, even grievous ones, that are common to the human existence.

---

[1] For some of the debating points see http://en.wikipedia.org/wiki/McDonald's_coffee_case#_note-0; Andrea Gerlin, *A Matter of Degree: How a Jury Decided That a Coffee Spill Is Worth $2.9 Million*, WALL ST. J., September 1, 1994 at A1; *Urban legends and Stella Liebeck and the McDonald's coffee case*, http://www.overlawyered.com/2005/10/urban_legends_and_stella_liebe. html.

As you consider the design and warning cases that follow reconsider how *you* would decide a "hot coffee" case.

POTTER v. CHICAGO PNEUMATIC TOOL CO.
694 A.2d 1319 (Conn. 1997)

KATZ, ASSOCIATE JUSTICE.

. . . The plaintiffs claim that they were injured in the course of their employment as shipyard workers at the General Dynamics Corporation Electric Boat facility . . . as a result of using pneumatic hand tools manufactured by the defendants. Specifically, the plaintiffs allege that the tools were defectively designed because they exposed the plaintiffs to excessive vibration. . . .

The defendants appeal from the judgment rendered on jury verdicts in favor of the plaintiffs . . .

The plaintiffs were employed at Electric Boat as "grinders," positions which required use of pneumatic hand tools to smooth welds and metal surfaces. In the course of their employment, the plaintiffs used various pneumatic hand tools, including chipping and grinding tools, which were manufactured and sold by the defendants. The plaintiffs' use of the defendants' tools at Electric Boat spanned approximately twenty-five years, from the mid-1960s until 1987. The plaintiffs suffer from permanent vascular and neurological impairment of their hands, which has caused blanching of their fingers, pain, numbness, tingling, reduction of grip strength, intolerance of cold and clumsiness from restricted blood flow. As a result, the plaintiffs have been unable to continue their employment as grinders and their performance of other activities has been restricted. The plaintiffs' symptoms are consistent with a diagnosis of hand arm vibration syndrome. Expert testimony confirmed that exposure to vibration is a significant contributing factor to the development of hand arm vibration syndrome, and that a clear relationship exists between the level of vibration exposure and the risk of developing the syndrome . . .

Ronald Guarneri, an industrial hygienist at Electric Boat, testified that he had conducted extensive testing of tools used at the shipyard in order to identify occupational hazards. This testing revealed that a large number of the defendants' tools violated the limits for vibration exposure established by the American National Standards Institute (institute), and exceeded the threshold limit promulgated by the American Conference of Governmental and Industrial Hygienists (conference).

Richard Alexander, a mechanical engineering professor at Texas A & M University, testified that because machinery vibration has harmful effects on machines and on people, engineers routinely research ways to reduce or to eliminate the amount of vibration that a machine produces when operated. Alexander discussed various methods available to control vibration, including isolation (the use of springs or mass to isolate vibration), dampening (adding weights to dampen vibrational effects), and balancing (adding weights to counterbalance machine imbalances that cause vibration). Alexander testified that each of these methods has been available to manufacturers for at least thirty-five years.

Alexander also stated that, in 1983, he had been engaged by another pneumatic tool manufacturer to perform testing of methods by which to reduce the level of vibration in its three horsepower vertical grinder. The vertical grinder had a live handle, which contained hardware for the air power, and a dead handle, which vibrated significantly more than the live handle because it weighed less. Alexander modified the design by inserting rubber isolation mounts between the handles and the housing, and by adding an aluminum rod to the dead handle to match the weight of the two handles. As a result of these modifications, which were published in 1987, Alexander achieved a threefold reduction in vibration levels.

The plaintiffs also presented the testimony of Charles Suggs, a research engineer at North Carolina State University, who has been investigating machinery vibration reduction since the 1960s. In 1968, Suggs published the first of several papers in which he discussed his success in reducing vibration hazards in chain saws by inserting rubber mounts between the handle and chain saw body. In the 1970s, he also published a series of articles reporting how he had reduced vibration by 70 percent in tools without handles by wrapping the tools with a resilient foam rubber material and a metal sleeve. Additionally, in 1988, Suggs tested the defendants' die grinders and, by applying the same technique, reduced the levels of vibration by between 35 and 60 percent. Additional facts will be presented as warranted.

After a six-week trial, the trial court rendered judgment on jury verdicts in favor of the plaintiffs. . . . This appeal and cross appeal followed. . . .

We first address the defendants' argument that the trial court improperly failed to render judgment for the defendants notwithstanding the verdicts because there was insufficient evidence for the jury to have found that the tools had been defectively designed. Specifically, the defendants claim that, in order to establish a *prima facie* design defect case, the plaintiffs were required to prove that there was a feasible alternative design available at the time that the defendants put their tools into the stream of commerce. We disagree . . .

Products liability law has . . . evolved to hold manufacturers strictly liable for unreasonably dangerous products that cause injury to ultimate users. Nevertheless, strict tort liability does not transform manufacturers into insurers, nor does it impose absolute liability. . . . As the Wisconsin Supreme Court has pointed out, "[f]rom the plaintiff's point of view the most beneficial aspect of the rule is that it relieves him of proving specific acts of negligence and protects him from the defenses of notice of breach, disclaimer, and lack of privity in the implied warranty concepts of sales and contracts." *Dippel v. Sciano*, 37 Wis.2d 443, 460 (1967). Strict tort liability merely relieves the plaintiff from proving that the manufacturer was negligent and allows the plaintiff to establish instead the defective condition of the product as the principal basis of liability. . . .

Although courts have widely accepted the concept of strict tort liability, some of the specifics of strict tort liability remain in question. In particular, courts have sharply disagreed over the appropriate definition of defectiveness in design cases. As the Alaska Supreme Court has stated: "Design defects present the most perplexing problems in the field of strict products liability because there is no readily ascertainable external measure of defectiveness. While manufacturing flaws can be evaluated against the intended design of the product, no such objective standard exists in the design defect context." *Caterpillar Tractor Co. v. Beck*, 593 P.2d 871, 880 (Alaska 1979).

Section 402A imposes liability only for those defective products that are "unreasonably dangerous" to "the ordinary consumer who purchases it, with the ordinary knowledge common to the community as to its characteristics." 2 Restatement (Second) § 402A, comment (i). Under this formulation, known as the "consumer expectation" test, a manufacturer is strictly liable for any condition not contemplated by the ultimate consumer that will be unreasonably dangerous to the consumer . . .

In *Barker v. Lull Engineering Co.*, 20 Cal.3d 413, 435 (1978), the California Supreme Court established two alternative tests for determining design defect liability: (1) the consumer expectation analysis; and (2) a balancing test that inquires whether a product's risks outweigh its benefits. Under the latter, otherwise known as the "risk-utility," test, the manufacturer bears the burden of proving that the product's utility is not outweighed by its risks in light of various factors. Three other jurisdictions have subsequently adopted California's two-pronged test, including the burden-shifting risk-utility inquiry.

Other jurisdictions apply only a risk-utility test in determining whether a manufacturer is liable for a design defect. . . .

This court has long held that in order to prevail in a design defect claim, "[t]he plaintiff must prove that the product is unreasonably dangerous." *Giglio v. Connecticut Light & Power Co.*, 180 Conn. 230, 234 (1980). We have derived our definition of "unreasonably dangerous" from comment (i) to § 402A, which provides that "the article sold must be dangerous to an extent beyond that which would be contemplated by the ordinary consumer who purchases it, with the ordinary knowledge common to the community as to its characteristics." This "consumer expectation" standard is now well established in Connecticut strict products liability decisions.

The defendants propose that it is time for this court to abandon the consumer expectation standard and adopt the requirement that the plaintiff must prove the existence of a reasonable alternative design in order to prevail on a design defect claim. We decline to accept the defendants' invitation.

In support of their position, the defendants point to the . . . Rest. 3d Torts, which provides that, as part of a plaintiff's *prima facie* case, the plaintiff must establish the availability of a reasonable alternative design. Specifically, § 2(b) of the Restatement (Third) provides: "[A] product is defective in design when the foreseeable risks of harm posed by the product could have been reduced or avoided by the adoption of a reasonable alternative design by the seller or other distributor, or a predecessor in the commercial chain of distribution, and the omission of the alternative design renders the product not reasonably safe." The reporters to the Restatement (Third) state that "[v]ery substantial authority supports the proposition that [the] plaintiff must establish a reasonable alternative design in order for a product to be adjudged defective in design." § 2, reporters' note to comment (c).

We point out that this provision of the Draft Restatement (Third) has been a source of substantial controversy among commentators. . . . Contrary to the rule promulgated in the Draft Restatement (Third), our independent review of the prevailing common law reveals that the majority of jurisdictions *do not* impose upon plaintiffs an absolute requirement to prove a feasible alternative design.

In our view, the feasible alternative design requirement imposes an undue burden on plaintiffs that might preclude otherwise valid claims from jury consideration. Such a rule would require plaintiffs to retain an expert witness even in cases in which lay jurors can infer a design defect from circumstantial evidence. Connecticut courts, however, have consistently stated that a jury may, under appropriate circumstances, infer a defect from the evidence without the necessity of expert testimony. . . .

Moreover, in some instances, a product may be in a defective condition unreasonably dangerous to the user even though no feasible alternative design is available. In such instances, the manufacturer may be strictly liable for a design defect notwithstanding the fact that there are no safer alternative designs in existence. . . . Accordingly, we decline to adopt the requirement that a plaintiff must prove a feasible alternative design as a sine qua non to establishing a *prima facie* case of design defect.

Although today we continue to adhere to our long-standing rule that a product's defectiveness is to be determined by the expectations of an ordinary consumer, we nevertheless recognize that there may be instances involving complex product designs in which an ordinary consumer may not be able to form expectations of safety. . . . In such cases, a consumer's expectations may be viewed in light of various factors that balance the utility of the product's design with the magnitude of its risks. We find persuasive the reasoning of those jurisdictions that have modified their formulation of the consumer expectation test by incorporating risk-utility factors into the ordinary consumer expectation analysis. . . . Thus, the modified consumer expectation test provides the jury with the product's risks and utility and then inquires whether a reasonable consumer would consider the product unreasonably dangerous. As the Supreme Court of Washington stated in *Seattle-First National Bank v. Tabert*, 86 Wash. 2d 145, 154 (1975), "[i]n determining the reasonable expectations of the ordinary consumer, a number of factors must be considered. The relative cost of the product, the gravity of the potential harm from the claimed defect and the cost and feasibility of eliminating or minimizing the risk may be relevant in a particular case. In other instances the nature of the product or the nature of the claimed defect may make other factors relevant to the issue." Accordingly, under this modified formulation, the consumer expectation test would establish the product's risks and utility, and the inquiry would then be whether a reasonable consumer would consider the product design unreasonably dangerous.

In our view, the relevant factors that a jury *may* consider include, but are not limited to, the usefulness of the product, the likelihood and severity of the danger posed by the design, the feasibility of an alternative design, the financial cost of an improved design, the ability to reduce the product's danger without impairing its usefulness or making it too expensive, and the feasibility of spreading the loss by increasing the product's price . . .

Although today we adopt a modified formulation of the consumer expectation test, we emphasize that we do not require a plaintiff to present evidence relating to the product's risks and utility in every case. . . . Accordingly, the ordinary consumer expectation test is appropriate when the everyday experience of the particular product's users permits the inference that the product did not meet minimum safety expectations.

Conversely, the jury should engage in the risk-utility balancing required by our modified consumer expectation test when the particular facts do not reasonably permit the inference that the product did not meet the safety expectations of the ordinary consumer. . . . Furthermore, instructions based on the ordinary consumer expectation test would not be appropriate when, as a matter of law, there is insufficient evidence to support a jury verdict under that test. In such circumstances, the jury should be instructed solely on the modified consumer expectation test we have articulated today.

In this respect, it is the function of the trial court to determine whether an instruction based on the ordinary consumer expectation test or the modified consumer expectation test, or both, is appropriate in light of the evidence presented. In making this determination, the trial court must ascertain whether, under each test, there is sufficient evidence as a matter of law to warrant the respective instruction.

With these principles in mind, we now consider whether, in the present case, the trial court properly instructed the jury with respect to the definition of design defect for the purposes of strict tort liability. The trial court instructed the jury that a manufacturer may be strictly liable if the plaintiffs prove, among other elements, that the product in question was in a defective condition, unreasonably dangerous to the ultimate user. The court further instructed the jury that, in determining whether the tools were unreasonably dangerous, it may draw its conclusions based on the reasonable expectations of an ordinary user of the defendants' tools. Because there was sufficient evidence as a matter of law to support the determination that the tools were unreasonably dangerous based on the ordinary consumer expectation test, we conclude that this instruction was appropriately given to the jury. . . .

The jury heard testimony that Guarneri, Electric Boat's industrial hygienist, had performed extensive testing of tools used at the shipyard, which tests revealed that a large number of the defendants' tools violated the institute's limits for vibration exposure and exceeded the conference's threshold limit. The jury also heard substantial testimony with respect to various methods, including isolation, dampening and balancing, available to reduce the deleterious effects of vibration caused by the defendants' tools. Moreover, there was expert testimony that exposure to vibration is a significant contributing factor to the development of hand arm vibration syndrome and that a clear relationship exists between the level of vibration exposure and the risk of developing the syndrome. Viewing the evidence in a light favorable to supporting the jury's verdicts, as we must, we conclude that the jury properly determined that the defendants' tools had been defectively designed. . . .

Although we have concluded [on other grounds] that a new trial is necessary, we address the defendants' final claim because it is likely to arise on retrial. The defendants argue that the trial court improperly instructed the jury that the "state-of-the-art defense" was restricted to the plaintiffs' failure to warn claim. Specifically, the defendants assert that the trial court improperly prevented the jury from considering the state-of-the-art defense in the context of the plaintiffs' claim of defective design. In response, the plaintiffs argue that the state-of-the-art defense has no place in a strict products liability action because it improperly diverts the jury's attention from the product's condition to the manufacturer's conduct. The plaintiffs further assert that even if the trial court improperly declined to provide the instruction with respect to the design defect claim, the defendants have failed to prove that it constituted harmful error. Although we agree with the defendants that state-of-the-art evidence applies to design defect claims as well as to failure to warn claims, we disagree that such evidence constitutes an affirmative defense to the plaintiffs' design defect claims.

The following additional facts are relevant to this issue. The defendants presented testimony that they produced the safest and highest quality tools that they were able to design. Robert Marelli, superintendent of tools and equipment at Electric Boat, testified that the defendants' tools were the best for Electric Boat's purposes and that Electric Boat would be in a "tough situation" if faced with the prospect of having to replace them.

Conversely, the plaintiffs presented evidence that a chipping hammer manufactured by Atlas Copco, which had a reduced vibration design, was available in 1976. A Chicago Pneumatic interoffice memorandum dated October, 1974, provided that, "[u]nless we at least keep pace with the technological developments of major competitors like Atlas Copco, we certainly face a prospect of loss of market share." The plaintiffs also presented another Chicago Pneumatic interoffice memorandum dated May, 1974, which outlined various devices designed to isolate vibration developed by Chicago Pneumatic in conjunction with Caterpillar Tractor Company.

The trial court instructed the jury that "state of the art is defined as the level of scientific and technological knowledge existing at the time the product in question was designed for manufacture." The court also instructed the jury that a manufacturer cannot be held to standards that exceed the limit of scientific advances and technology existing at the time of manufacture and, therefore, the defendants could not be found liable if they had proven compliance with the state of the art. The trial court, however, limited the applicability of the state-of-the-art defense solely to the plaintiffs' failure to warn claims. The defendants took timely exception to the court's limitation of the state-of-the-art defense to only the failure to warn claims.

In *Tomer v. American Home Products Corp.*, 170 Conn. 681, 687 (1976), this court recognized the applicability of state-of-the-art evidence to failure to warn claims, stating that "[s]ince the defendants could not be held to standards which exceeded the limits of scientific advances existing at the time of their allegedly tortious conduct, expert testimony tending to show the scope of duties owed could have been properly limited to scientific knowledge existing at that time." The question of whether state-of-the-art evidence similarly applies to design defect claims, however, is a matter of first impression for this court.

We begin our analysis of this issue by recognizing that the term "state of the art" has been the source of substantial confusion. . . .

The majority of courts, however, have defined state-of-the-art evidence as the level of relevant scientific, technological and safety knowledge existing and reasonably feasible at the time of design. . . .

We also recognize that courts are divided on the issue of whether state-of-the-art evidence is admissible in design defect claims. Several courts have concluded that such evidence is inadmissible in design defect claims because it improperly focuses on the reasonableness of the manufacturer's conduct, which is irrelevant in a strict products liability action. . . . Conversely, other courts, in construing relevant state tort reform statutes, have stated that a manufacturer's proof of state-of-the-art evidence constitutes a complete defense to a design defect claim.

Nevertheless, the overwhelming majority of courts have held that, in design defect cases, state-of-the-art evidence is relevant to determining the adequacy of the product's design.

The plaintiffs assert that state-of-the-art evidence has no place in a strict products liability action because it improperly focuses the jury's attention on the manufacturer's conduct. We disagree. We adopt the majority view and hold that such evidence is relevant and assists the jury in determining whether a product is defective and unreasonably dangerous. . . . [W]e conclude that state of the art is a relevant factor in considering the adequacy of the design of a product and whether it is in a defective condition unreasonably dangerous to the ordinary consumer. In defining the term state of the art, we adhere to our precedent in *Tomer* and to the majority view, which characterize state of the art as the level of relevant scientific, technological and safety knowledge existing and reasonably feasible at the time of design.

Furthermore, we point out that state of the art refers to what is technologically feasible, rather than merely industry custom. . . . Accordingly, "[a] manufacturer may have a duty to make products pursuant to a safer design even if the custom of the industry is not to use that alternative." *O'Brien v. Muskin Corp.*, 94 N.J. 169, 182-83 (1983).

We now apply these principles to the standards for determining design defectiveness that we have addressed in part I of this opinion. Under the ordinary consumer expectation standard, state-of-the-art evidence "helps to determine the expectation of the ordinary consumer." *Bruce v. Martin-Marietta Corp.*, 544 F.2d 442, 447 (10th Cir. 1976). For example, in approving the trial court's admission of state-of-the-art evidence, the court in *Bruce* stated: "A consumer would not expect a Model T to have the safety features which are incorporated in automobiles made today. The same expectation applies to airplanes. [The p]laintiffs have not shown that the ordinary consumer would expect a plane made in 1952 to have the safety features of one made in 1970." *Id.* at 447. In other words, state-of-the-art evidence supplies the jury with a relevant basis on which to determine what the ordinary consumer would expect with respect to safety features available at the time of manufacture.

Furthermore, under the modified consumer expectations standard we have set forth today, such evidence would be admissible as a factor properly to be considered as part of the risk-utility calculus. . . . [S]uch evidence is a relevant factor on both sides of the risk-utility equation: the risks that the product presents to consumers in light of the availability of other safety measures, and the utility of the product in comparison to feasible design alternatives. Accordingly, state-of-the-art evidence constitutes one of several relevant factors to assist the jury in determining whether a reasonable consumer would consider the product design unreasonably dangerous.

In summary, we agree with the defendants insofar as they argue that the trial court improperly limited the applicability of state-of-the-art evidence to the plaintiffs' failure to warn claims. In our view, state-of-the-art evidence is relevant to the determination of whether a particular product design is unreasonably dangerous. We disagree with the defendants' contention, however, that proof of compliance with the state of the art constitutes an affirmative defense to a design defect claim.

We emphasize that although state-of-the-art evidence may be dispositive on the facts of a particular case, such evidence does not constitute an affirmative defense that, if proven, would absolve the defendant from liability. . . . In other words, compliance with state of the art would not, as a matter of law, warrant a judgment for a defendant. . . . For this reason, we believe that state-of-the-art evidence is "better characterized as rebuttal evidence than as a defense." *Owens-Corning Fiberglas Corp. v. Caldwell*, 818 S.W.2d 749, 752 (Tex. 1991).

We therefore conclude that state-of-the-art evidence is merely one factor for the jury to consider under either the ordinary or modified consumer expectation test. Accordingly, if on remand the trial court concludes that sufficient evidence has been produced to warrant an instruction, the jury may properly consider the state of the art in determining whether the defendants' tools were defectively designed and unreasonably dangerous. . . . [REVERSED AND REMANDED.]

NOTES

1. *"Defectiveness" Tests Revisited.* Consider, once again, the tests for determining whether a product is defective in light of *Potter*. There is the consumer expectation test (whether treated as a standard under a warranty or tort claim); there is the risk-utility test (the substantive implications of which depend upon the relevance and effect of how the jurisdiction treats the admissibility of so-called "state-of-the-art" evidence). And some jurisdictions provide that a plaintiff can establish defect under either the consumer expectation test or the risk-utility test (some requiring the defendant to prove no liability under the risk utility test, others requiring the plaintiff to prove risk outweighs utility). Taking a somewhat different path, *Potter* adopts a modified consumer expectation test. Under *Potter*, the consumer expectation test sets the standard but risk and utility are relevant to a determination of whether the product is more dangerous than a reasonable consumer would expect.

2. *The Core of the Design Claim — The Feasible Alternative Design. Potter* rejects a blanket rule requiring that the plaintiff must establish a feasible alternative design for the product in question. In practice, however, most plaintiffs in most design defect cases *will* introduce expert testimony directed at establishing that very issue. Indeed, a careful plaintiff's lawyer would always want to have expert testimony on alternative designs, if such testimony existed. *Potter* took issue with a blanket rule that would *require* every plaintiff to establish a feasible alternative design. Why? What are the exceptional cases where a court would want the question of design defectiveness to go to the jury even without evidence of feasible alternative design? Cases involving simple/obvious defects? Simple products which are understandable to lay persons? Products which are so dangerous that they should not be placed into distribution at all, notwithstanding the absence of a substitute product or design, because they expose unacceptable risks that cannot be avoided by a safer product (so-called product line defects)?

3. *Retrenchment — The Reasonable Alternative Design.* Section 2(b) of the Third Restatement provides that a product "is defective in design when the foreseeable risks of harm posed by the product could have been reduced or avoided by the adoption of a reasonable alternative design by the seller or other distributor, or a predecessor in the commercial chain of distribution, and the omission of the alternative design renders the product not reasonably safe . . . " REST. 3D TORTS § 2(b). Note that this goes further than requiring a feasible alternative design (rejected in *Potter*) and requires that the alternative design is "reasonable" and would have reduced or avoided the "foreseeable risks of harm." Section 2(b) therefore clearly injects negligence concepts — both a conduct-centric consideration (was the alternate design "reasonable"?) and a requirement that the risk was or reasonably foreseeable (actual or constructive foresight, rather than the imputed foresight recognized in cases such as *Phillips v. Kimwood Mach. Co.*, discussed *supra*).

4. *Unreasonably Dangerous Products.* How should a court approach a dangerous product that cannot be made safer or for which there may be no safe substitute? For example, cases involving asbestos, cigarettes, handguns, tequila, some prescription drugs, or even very fast cars. The REST. 2D TORTS § 402A, cmt. *i* recognizes that many products cannot be made safely but are not unreasonably dangerous. It continues:

> Good whiskey is not unreasonably dangerous merely because it will make some people drunk, and is especially dangerous to alcoholics; but bad whiskey, containing a dangerous amount of fusel oil, is unreasonably dangerous. Good tobacco is not unreasonably dangerous merely because the effects of smoking may be harmful, but tobacco containing something like marijuana may be unreasonably dangerous. Good butter is not unreasonably dangerous merely, because if such be the case, it deposits cholesterol in the arteries and leads to heart attacks; but bad butter, contaminated with poisonous fish oil, is unreasonably dangerous.

In contrast, REST. 3D torts § 2, cmt. *d*, provides:

> The requirement in Subsection (b) that plaintiff show a reasonable
> alternative design applies in most instances even though the plaintiff
> alleges that the category of product sold by the defendant is so danger-
> ous that it should not have been marketed at all . . . Common and
> widely distributed products such as alcoholic beverages, firearms, and
> above-ground swimming pools may be found to be defective only upon
> proof of the requisite conditions in Subsection (a), (b), or (c).

Are there other theories available to attack an entire product line other than
the products liability design claim? In addition to warning and design claims,
plaintiffs are increasingly attacking the way in which products are marketed
under misrepresentation or non-disclosure theories or under general negligence theories. What about the claim that manufacturing and selling a particular product is an ultrahazardous or abnormally dangerous activity that
ought to expose the producer or seller to strict or absolute liability? *See, e.g.,*
Kelley v. R.G. Indus., 304 Md. 124 (1985) (Selling "Saturday Night Special"
handgun not an unreasonably dangerous activity, but possibly subject to strict
products liability); *City of Phila. v. Beretta U.S.A. Corp.,* 277 F.3d 415 (3d Cir.
Pa. 2002) (public nuisance theory inapplicable to the lawful distribution of
handguns). *Cf. City of Gary v. Smith & Wesson,* 801 N.E.2d 1222 (Ind. 2003)
(public nuisance claim against handgun manufacturers, distributors, and dealers in which city alleged dealers engaged in illegal sales about which distributors and manufacturers were aware of but failed to curtail). Further exploration
of this controversy can be found in Chapter 8 *supra.*

5. *State of the Art.* A product is not defective or non-defective in the abstract;
rather, defect is defined by the context of use. The question of defectiveness
may be contextualized by the obviousness of the risk it poses or whether the
use to which the plaintiff put it was foreseeable. One of the most contentious
issues in products cases is the state of the technology or "art" when the product
was put into the chain of distribution. In most design defect cases this issue is
framed as one of admissible evidence. When a manufacturer argues "state of
the art" he may be seeking to introduce evidence (1) of scientific unknowability
of the risks posed by the product, (2) that other manufacturers used similar
designs, or (3) that there was no available technology to make the product
safer. How should the court in a design case deal with objections to such
evidence?

HOOD v. RYOBI AMERICA CORP.
181 F.3d 608 (4th Cir. 1999)

WILKINSON, CHIEF JUDGE.

Wilson M. Hood lost part of his thumb and lacerated his leg when he
removed the blade guards from his new Ryobi miter saw and then used the
unguarded saw for home carpentry. Hood sued Ryobi, alleging that the company failed adequately to warn of the saw's dangers and that the saw was
defective. Applying Maryland products liability law, the district court granted
summary judgment to Ryobi on all claims.

The saw and owner's manual bore at least seven clear, simple warnings not to operate the tool with the blade guards removed. The warnings were not required to spell out all the consequences of improper use. Nor was the saw defective — Hood altered and used the tool in violation of Ryobi's clear warnings. Thus we affirm the judgment.

Hood purchased a Ryobi TS-254 miter saw in Westminster, Maryland on February 25, 1995, for the purpose of performing home repairs. The saw was fully assembled at the time of purchase. It had a ten-inch diameter blade mounted on a rotating spindle controlled by a finger trigger on a handle near the top of the blade. To operate the saw, the consumer would use that handle to lower the blade through the material being cut.

Two blade guards shielded nearly the entire saw blade. A large metal guard, fixed to the frame of the saw, surrounded the upper half of the blade. A transparent plastic lower guard covered the rest of the blade and retracted into the upper guard as the saw came into contact with the work piece.

A number of warnings in the operator's manual and affixed to the saw itself stated that the user should operate the saw only with the blade guards in place. For example, the owner's manual declared that the user should "KEEP GUARDS IN PLACE" and warned: "ALWAYS USE THE SAW BLADE GUARD. Never operate the machine with the guard removed"; "NEVER operate this saw without all guards in place and in good operating condition"; and "WARNING: TO PREVENT POSSIBLE SERIOUS PERSONAL INJURY, NEVER PERFORM ANY CUTTING OPERATION WITH THE UPPER OR LOWER BLADE GUARD REMOVED." The saw itself carried several decals stating "DANGER: DO NOT REMOVE ANY GUARD. USE OF SAW WITHOUT THIS GUARD WILL RESULT IN SERIOUS INJURY"; "OPERATE ONLY WITH GUARDS IN PLACE"; and "WARNING . . . DO NOT operate saw without the upper and lower guards in place."

The day after his purchase, Hood began working with the saw in his driveway. While attempting to cut a piece of wood approximately four inches in height Hood found that the blade guards prevented the saw blade from passing completely through the piece. Disregarding the manufacturer's warnings, Hood decided to remove the blade guards from the saw. Hood first detached the saw blade from its spindle. He then unscrewed the four screws that held the blade guard assembly to the frame of the saw. Finally, he replaced the blade onto the bare spindle and completed his cut.

Rather than replacing the blade guards, Hood continued to work with the saw blade exposed. He worked in this fashion for about twenty minutes longer when, in the middle of another cut, the spinning saw blade flew off the saw and back toward Hood. The blade partially amputated his left thumb and lacerated his right leg.

Hood admits that he read the owner's manual and most of the warning labels on the saw before he began his work. He claims, however, that he believed the blade guards were intended solely to prevent a user's clothing or fingers from coming into contact with the saw blade. He contends that he was unaware that removing the blade guards would permit the spinning blade to detach from the saw. But Ryobi, he claims, was aware of that possibility. In fact, another customer had sued Ryobi after suffering a similar accident in the mid-1980s.

On December 5, 1997, Hood sued several divisions of Ryobi in the United States District Court for the District of Maryland. Hood raised claims of failure to warn and defective design under several theories of liability. On cross-motions for summary judgment the district court entered judgment for the defendants on all claims, finding that in the face of adequate warnings Hood had altered the saw and caused his own injury. *Hood v. Ryobi N. Am., Inc.*, 17 F. Supp. 2d 448 (D.Md. 1998). Hood appeals.

A manufacturer may be liable for placing a product on the market that bears inadequate instructions and warnings or that is defective in design . . . Hood asserts that Ryobi failed adequately to warn of the dangers of using the saw without the blade guards in place. Hood also contends that the design of the saw was defective. We disagree on both counts.

Hood first complains that the warnings he received were insufficiently specific. Hood admits that Ryobi provided several clear and conspicuous warnings not to operate the saw without the blade guards. He contends, however, that the warnings affixed to the product and displayed in the operator's manual were inadequate to alert him to the dangers of doing so. In addition to Ryobi's directive "never" to operate a guardless saw, Hood would require the company to inform of the actual consequences of such conduct. Specifically, Hood contends that an adequate warning would have explained that removing the guards would lead to blade detachment.

We disagree. Maryland does not require an encyclopedic warning. Instead, "a warning need only be one that is reasonable under the circumstances." *Levin v. Walter Kidde & Co.*, 248 A.2d 151, 153 (1968). A clear and specific warning will normally be sufficient — "the manufacturer need not warn of every mishap or source of injury that the mind can imagine flowing from the product." *Liesener v. Weslo, Inc.*, 775 F. Supp. 857, 861 (D.Md. 1991); *see Levin*, 248 A.2d at 154 (declining to require warning of the danger that a cracked syphon bottle might explode and holding "never use cracked bottle" to be adequate as a matter of law). In deciding whether a warning is adequate, Maryland law asks whether the benefits of a more detailed warning outweigh the costs of requiring the change.

Hood assumes that the cost of a more detailed warning label is minimal in this case, and he claims that such a warning would have prevented his injury. But the price of more detailed warnings is greater than their additional printing fees alone. Some commentators have observed that the proliferation of label detail threatens to undermine the effectiveness of warnings altogether. *See* James A. Henderson, Jr. & Aaron D. Twerski, *Doctrinal Collapse in Products Liability: The Empty Shell of Failure to Warn*, 65 N.Y.U. L. REV. 265, 296–97 (1990). As manufacturers append line after line onto product labels in the quest for the best possible warning, it is easy to lose sight of the label's communicative value as a whole. Well-meaning attempts to warn of every possible accident lead over time to voluminous yet impenetrable labels — too prolix to read and too technical to understand.

By contrast, Ryobi's warnings are clear and unequivocal. Three labels on the saw itself and at least four warnings in the owner's manual direct the user not to operate the saw with the blade guards removed. Two declare that "serious injury" could result from doing so. This is not a case where the manufacturer has failed to include any warnings at all with its product. Ryobi provided warnings sufficient to apprise the ordinary consumer that it is unsafe to operate a guardless saw — warnings which, if followed, would have prevented the injury in this case.

It is apparent, moreover, that the vast majority of consumers do not detach this critical safety feature before using this type of saw. Indeed, although Ryobi claims to have sold thousands of these saws, Hood has identified only one fifteen-year-old incident similar to his. Hood has thus not shown that these clear, unmistakable, and prominent warnings are insufficient to accomplish their purpose. Nor can he prove that increased label clutter would bring any net societal benefit. We hold that the warnings Ryobi provided are adequate as a matter of law.

Hood's defective design claim is likewise unpersuasive. Hood's injuries were the direct result of the alterations he made to the saw — alterations that directly contravened clear, unambiguous warnings. And such alterations defeat a claim of design defect.

This rule has been expressed alternatively as one of duty and one of causation. First, a manufacturer is only required to design a product that is safe for its reasonably foreseeable uses. If that duty is met, the product is simply not defective. Second, if a consumer alters a product in a way that creates a defect, the consumer's conduct rather than the manufacturer's is the proximate cause of any ensuing accident. Under either rationale, a post-sale product alteration will defeat a design defect claim if that alteration leads directly to the plaintiff's injury.

Hood admits that he altered the table saw by removing the blade guards from the unit's frame, and he acknowledges that the alteration led directly to his injuries. Hood asserts, however, that Ryobi should have foreseen that consumers might operate its saws with the guards removed. Hood notes that the operation of equipment without safety guards is a frequently cited OSHA violation. And, as noted, Ryobi itself has faced litigation on one other occasion for the same type of accident that befell Hood. In short, Hood contends that Ryobi should have designed its saw to operate equally well with the guards in place or removed.

We disagree. Maryland imposes no duty to predict that a consumer will violate clear, easily understandable safety warnings such as those Ryobi included with this product. For example, a manufacturer need not foresee that a consumer might store a gasoline can in his basement in contravention of clear warning labels. *Simpson v. Standard Container Co.*, 527 A.2d 1337, 1341 (Md. App. 1987) ("'Where warning is given, the seller may reasonably assume that it will be read and heeded; and a product bearing such a warning, which is safe for use if it is followed, is not in defective condition, nor is it unreasonably dangerous'" (quoting REST. 2D TORTS § 402A cmt. j)). Nor must a manufacturer foresee that a worker will shove his arm into a conveyor machine to repair it without first shutting the machine down, again in violation of "explicit written warnings." . . . When a consumer injures himself by using a product — or, as in this case, by altering it — in violation of clear, unmistakable, and easy-to-follow warnings, it is the consumer's own conduct that causes the injury . . . The manufacturer is not liable under a design defect theory

We recognize that the American Law Institute has recently underscored the concern that comment j of the Second Restatement, read literally, would permit a manufacturer of a dangerously defective product to immunize itself from liability merely by slapping warning labels on that product. See REST. 3D TORTS § 2 cmt. l & Reporter's Note. We are all afflicted with lapses of attention; warnings aimed simply at avoiding consumer carelessness should not absolve a manufacturer of the duty to design reasonable safeguards for its products. *See Id.* cmt. l, illus. 14 (when warning could not eliminate the possibility of accidental contact with a dangerous shear point, decal declaring "keep hands and feet away" does not bar a design defect claim).

The Maryland courts have already made clear, however, that warnings will not inevitably defeat liability for a product's defective design. *See Klein v. Sears, Roebuck & Co.*, 608 A.2d 1276, 1282–83 (Ct. Spec. App. 1992) (such warnings as "never leave tool running unattended" and "do not place fingers or hands in the path of the saw blade" are too vague to defeat manufacturer's liability for failing to include blade guards on its saws). Maryland has thus sought to encourage manufacturers to rid their products of traps for the unwary, while declining to hold them responsible for affirmative consumer misuse.

This case involves much more than a consumer's inevitable inattention. Rather, Hood took affirmative steps to remove the safety guards from his saw and — in contravention of warnings which were "clear, direct, simple, unequivocal, unmistakable, definite, and easy to understand and obey" — then used the saw to cut several pieces of wood. Hood's own conduct thus caused his injury and defeats any claim that the saw is defective in design.

Warned never to operate his miter saw without the blade guards in place, Hood nonetheless chose to detach those guards and run the saw in a disassembled condition. We hold that Ryobi is not liable for Hood's resulting injuries under any of the theories of recovery raised here. [AFFIRMED.]

NOTES

1. *Foreseeable Use.* It is a fundamental principle of products liability law that the defectiveness of a product must be determined in the context of the product's foreseeable use. It is plaintiff's burden to establish that his use of the product was objectively foreseeable. Even if the plaintiff's use is within the ambit of objective foreseeability his *particular* use or other conduct associated with the accident could break the chain of causation or give rise to an affirmative defense available to defendant seller, based on his comparative fault.

2. *Warnings and Design.* The conventional wisdom is that a manufacturer may be liable for failure to warn of a defect in his product, although the product is not "defective" in manufacture or design. *See Teagle v. Fischer & Porter Co.*, 570 P.2d 438, 442 (Wash. 1977) ("A product may be faultlessly manufactured and designed, yet still not be reasonably safe when placed in the hands of the ultimate user without first giving an adequate warning concerning the manner in which to safely use the product.")

What is the purpose of a warning in such a case? Is it to make a dangerous (though not necessarily defective) product, such as power tool, safe or safer for use? Is it to put a plaintiff on notice that she is about to use an irremediably dangerous product, such as a prescription drug, thus informing his choice as to whether to use the product at all? Are both of these informational objectives relevant, depending on the product?

3. *Adequacy of Warning.* In manufacturing defect cases liability turns on the manufacturer's expectations. In design defect cases the question of defectiveness usually is addressed by reference to consumer expectations or risk-utility. But, how should courts determine whether a product is defective for failure to warn? Two types of cases present — those where there is no warning and those where plaintiff alleges that the warning provided is inadequate. How can a plaintiff establish that a warning is inadequate? Must the plaintiff suggest an alternative, "adequate" warning? What criteria apply? What evidence should be adduced? When is the question of adequacy for the court? For the jury?

4. *Strict Liability or Negligence?* Concerns over the adequacy of a standard plus doubts about whether there can be imputed foresight have stoked a long debate over whether the failure to warn claim is one of negligence or strict liability. A pure negligence system would require actual or constructive knowledge of the risk by the manufacturer and judge the warning by reference to the manufacturer's conduct. A pure strict liability approach would impute to the manufacturer the foresight of harm (as in design cases) and determine adequacy by reference to the safety of the product (rather than the conduct of the manufacturer). REST. 3D TORTS § 2(c) provides that a product has a warning defect:

> [w]hen the foreseeable risks of harm posed by the product could have been reduced or avoided by the provision of reasonable instructions or warnings by the seller or other distributor, or a predecessor in the commercial chain of distribution, and the omission of the instructions or warnings renders the product not reasonably safe.

Does that language sound like negligence or strict liability?

5. *Constructive or Imputed Foresight?* Most courts have not imputed foresight in warning cases. *See, e.g., Olson v. Prosoco, Inc.*, 522 N.W.2d 284, 289 (Iowa 1994). *Cf. Phillips v. Kimwood Mach. Co.*, 525 P.2d 1033, 1037-38 (Or. 1974) (imputed foresight in design defect cases). Is that because it is illogical to require a manufacturer to warn against an unknowable or undiscoverable risk?

Yet, not all courts concede a purely negligence approach to the issue, instead holding manufacturers to the standard of an expert (*see, e.g., Carlin v. Superior Court*, 13 Cal. 4th 1104, 1112-13 (1996) ("a manufacturer could not escape liability under strict liability principles merely because its failure to warn of a known or reasonably scientifically knowable risk conformed to an industry-wide practice of failing to provide warnings that constituted the standard of reasonable care.") or switching the burden of persuasion on the issue of "unknowability" to the manufacturer (*see, e.g., Shanks v. Upjohn Co.*, 835 P.2d 1189, 1200 (Alaska 1992) ("the manufacturer is strictly liable unless the defendant manufacturer can prove that the risk was scientifically unknowable at the time the product was distributed to the plaintiff"). A small number even impose imputed foresight. *See, e.g., Ayers v. Johnson & Johnson Baby Prods. Co.*, 818 P.2d 1337, 1346 (Wash. 1991).

6. *Safety of the Product or Conduct of the Manufacturer?* According to *Anderson v. Owens-Corning Fiberglas Corp.*, 53 Cal. 3d 987, 1002–1003 (1991), quoted in the next principal case, "failure to warn in strict liability differs markedly from failure to warn in the negligence context." Does the explanation given there provide a sound or, at least, workable distinction?

D. PARTICULAR PRODUCTS OR SELLERS

CARLIN v. SUPERIOR COURT
13 Cal. 4th 1104 (1996)

MOSK, ACTING CIRCUIT JUDGE.

. . . In our recent decision in *Anderson v. Owens-Corning Fiberglas Corp.* (1993) 53 Cal. 3d 987, we held generally that manufacturers are strictly liable for injuries caused by their failure to give warning of dangers that were known to the scientific community at the time they manufactured and distributed the product: "Whatever may be reasonable from the point of view of the manufacturer, the user of the product must be given the option either to refrain from using the product at all or to use it in such a way as to minimize the degree of danger." (*Id.* at p. 1003.) In so doing, we expressly applied to manufacturers of *all* products the same rule of strict liability for failure to warn of known or reasonably scientifically knowable risks that we previously applied specifically to manufacturers of prescription drugs. (*Id.* at p. 1000; *see Brown v. Superior Court* (1988) 44 Cal. 3d 1049 (hereafter *Brown.*) The Upjohn Company (hereafter Upjohn), a manufacturer of prescription drugs, urges us to now reject the strict liability standard under *Anderson* for cases involving failure to warn of known or reasonably scientifically knowable risks from prescription drugs, and adopt a new standard of simple negligence for that industry only. We discern no sound basis for doing so. Accordingly, we affirm the judgment of the Court of Appeal.

Plaintiff Wilma Peggy Carlin (hereafter Carlin) brought an action for damages against Upjohn for injuries she assertedly sustained from ingesting the drug Halcion, which was prescribed for her by a physician between 1987 and 1992. She claimed, as relevant here, that Upjohn was strictly liable for failing "properly to prepare and/or warn of the dangerous propensities of Halcion." She specifically alleged that Upjohn "knew that the drug Halcion was defective . . . [,] that those who were prescribed Halcion and took the same would experience, and did experience, severe physical, mental, and emotional damages/injuries and yet, notwithstanding this knowledge, [it] despicably, and in willful and conscious disregard of the safety of those who were prescribed Halcion and of the plaintiff herein, without giving any notice of the defect to the purchasers of Halcion, placed and persisted in placing Halcion into the stream of commerce. . . .

Upjohn demurred, alleging, inter alia, that Carlin failed to state facts sufficient to constitute a cause of action for strict liability . . .

In *Anderson*, we summarized prior case law and outlined the general principles of strict liability as they have been applied by California courts for over three decades. As we explained therein, under our doctrine of strict liability, first announced in *Greenman v. Yuba Power Products, Inc.* (1963) 59 Cal. 2d 57, a manufacturer "'is strictly liable in tort when an article he places on the market, knowing that it is to be used without inspection for defects, proves to have a defect that causes injury to a human being.' . . . 'The purpose of such liability is to insure that the costs of injuries resulting from defective products are borne by the manufacturers that put such products on the market rather than by the injured persons who are powerless to protect themselves.' . . . Strict liability, however, was never intended to make the manufacturer or distributor of a product its insurer. 'From its inception, . . . strict liability has never been, and is not now, *absolute* liability. . . .'" (*Anderson, supra*, 53 Cal. 3d at pp. 994-995)

We specifically addressed the issue "whether knowledge, actual or constructive, is a component of strict liability on the failure-to-warn theory." (*Anderson, supra*, 53 Cal. 3d at p. 990.) We concluded that it is. "The California courts, either expressly or by implication, have to date required knowledge, actual or constructive, of potential risk or danger before imposing strict liability for a failure to warn." (*Id.* at p. 991.) We affirmed that "California is well settled into the majority view that . . . knowledge or knowability is a component of strict liability for failure to warn." (*Id.* at p. 1000.)

Although *Anderson* involved an action against a manufacturer of asbestos, we relied extensively on cases involving a variety of products, including prescription drugs. In particular, we were guided by our prior decision in *Brown* in which we refused to extend strict liability to the failure to warn of risks that were unknown or *unknowable* at the time of distribution. "As we stated [in *Brown*], if a manufacturer could not count on limiting its liability to risks that were known or knowable at the time of manufacture or distribution, it would be discouraged from developing new and improved products for fear that later significant advances in scientific knowledge would increase its liability. . . . [A] manufacturer is not strictly liable for injuries caused by a prescription drug so long as it was properly prepared and accompanied by warnings of its dangerous propensities that were either known or scientifically knowable at the time of distribution." (*Anderson, supra*, 53 Cal. 3d at p. 999.) . . .

We recognized that the knowledge or knowability requirement for failure to warn infuses some negligence concepts into strict liability cases. Indeed, in the failure-to-warn context, strict liability is to some extent a hybrid of traditional strict liability and negligence doctrine. As we explained, however, "the claim that a particular component 'rings of' or 'sounds in' negligence has not precluded its acceptance in the context of strict liability." (*Ibid*.) Indeed, "the strict liability doctrine has incorporated some well-settled rules from the law of negligence and has survived judicial challenges asserting that such incorporation violates the fundamental principles of the doctrine." (*Id*. at p. 1002.) Thus, although *Anderson*, following *Brown*, incorporated certain negligence concepts into the standard of strict liability for failure to warn, it did not thereby adopt a simple negligence test.

"[F]ailure to warn in strict liability differs markedly from failure to warn in the negligence context. Negligence law in a failure-to-warn case requires a plaintiff to prove that a manufacturer or distributor did not warn of a particular risk for reasons which fell below the acceptable standard of care, i.e., what a reasonably prudent manufacturer would have known and warned about. Strict liability is not concerned with the standard of due care or the reasonableness of a manufacturer's conduct. The rules of strict liability require a plaintiff to prove only that the defendant did not adequately warn of a particular risk that was known or knowable in light of the generally recognized and prevailing best scientific and medical knowledge available at the time of manufacture and distribution. Thus, in strict liability, as opposed to negligence, the reasonableness of the defendant's failure to warn is immaterial. Stated another way, a reasonably prudent manufacturer might reasonably decide that the risk of harm was such as not to require a warning as, for example, if the manufacturer's own testing showed a result contrary to that of others in the scientific community. Such a manufacturer might escape liability under negligence principles. In contrast, under strict liability principles the manufacturer has no such leeway; the manufacturer is liable if it failed to give warning of dangers that were known to the scientific community at the time it manufactured or distributed the product." (*Anderson, supra*, 53 Cal. 3d at pp. 1002-1003, fn. omitted.) Similarly, a manufacturer could not escape liability under strict liability principles merely because its failure to warn of a known or reasonably scientifically knowable risk conformed to an industry-wide practice of failing to provide warnings that constituted the standard of reasonable care.

We explained the policy behind our strict liability standard for failure to warn as follows: "'When, in a particular case, the risk qualitatively (e.g., of death or major disability) as well as quantitatively, on balance with the end sought to be achieved, is such as to call for a true choice judgment, *medical or personal*, the warning must be given . . . ' Thus, the fact that a manufacturer acted as a reasonably prudent manufacturer in deciding not to warn, while perhaps absolving the manufacturer of liability under the negligence theory, will not preclude liability under strict liability principles if the trier of fact concludes that, based on the information scientifically available to the manufacturer, the manufacturer's failure to warn rendered the product unsafe to its users." (*Anderson, supra*, 53 Cal. 3d at p. 1003, italics added, quoting *Davis v. Wyeth Laboratories, Inc.* (9th Cir. 1968) 399 F.2d 121, 129-130 [applying strict liability to a manufacturer of prescription drugs].) . . .

We are unpersuaded by Upjohn's argument that a strict liability standard for failure to warn about known or reasonably scientifically knowable risks from prescription drugs is inconsistent with federal regulatory policy. Upjohn concedes that FDA regulations do not expressly preempt common law tort remedies for failure to warn or occupy the entire field of regulation. As numerous courts have concluded, Congress evinced no intention of preempting state tort liability for injuries from prescription drugs. . . .

We disagree with Carlin's argument, however, that FDA regulations are essentially irrelevant in a common law action for failure to warn. We reiterate that strict liability for failure to warn *is not absolute liability*. Under *Anderson*, drug manufacturers are not strictly liable for a risk that was not known or reasonably scientifically knowable. In this context, it is significant that the FDA *precludes* drug manufacturers from warning about every conceivable adverse reaction; they may warn only if there exists significant medical evidence of a possible health hazard. They are also specifically precluded from warning of adverse reactions when differences of opinion exist within the medical community with regard to potential adverse reactions. (*See* 21 C.F.R. § 201.57(d) & (e) (1996) [requiring that warnings shall only be of known hazards, not theoretical hazards]; *id.*, § 1.21(c)(1) [prohibiting the inclusion of differing opinions regarding contraindications, precautions, adverse reactions, and other product hazards on drug warning labels].) At the same time, however, they are required to "describe serious adverse reactions and potential safety hazards, limitations in use imposed by them, and steps that should be taken if they occur. The labeling shall be revised to include a warning as soon as there is reasonable evidence of an association of a serious hazard with a drug; a causal relationship need not have been proved." (*Id.*, § 201.57(e).)

In appropriate cases, FDA action or inaction, though not dispositive, may be admissible under *Anderson* to show whether a risk was known or reasonably scientifically knowable. Similarly, a drug manufacturer could present evidence to show that there was no "reasonably scientifically knowable risk" because, at the time of distribution, the cause of the alleged adverse effect was too speculative to have been reasonably attributable to the drug by a scientist conducting state-of-the-art research. Thus, when a plaintiff's claim is based on an allegation that a particular risk was "reasonably scientifically knowable," an inquiry may arise as to what a reasonable scientist operating in good faith should have known under the circumstances of the evidence. As we emphasized in *Anderson*, we do not altogether reject strict liability in the failure-to-warn context — for drugs or any other products — simply because some considerations of reasonableness sounding in negligence may be required. (*Anderson, supra*, 53 Cal. 3d at pp. 1001-1002.)

Moreover, in the case of an alleged "known" risk, if state-of-the-art scientific data concerning the alleged risk was fully disclosed to the FDA and it determined, after review, that the pharmaceutical manufacturer was *not permitted to warn* — e.g., because the data was inconclusive or the risk was too speculative to justify a warning — the manufacturer could present such evidence to show that strict liability cannot apply; the FDA's conclusion that there was, in effect, no "known risk" is controlling. (See *Feldman v. Lederle Laboratories* (1991) 125 N.J. 117, 132 ["conflict preemption" occurs when compliance with both federal and state requirements is impossible].)

We are also unpersuaded by Upjohn's assertion that applying strict liability to claims of injury for failure to warn will inevitably result in manufacturers inundating consumers with warnings of even speculative risks from prescription drugs. In *Finn v. G. D. Searle & Co.* (1984) 35 Cal. 3d 691, 701 [200 Cal. Rptr. 870, 677 P.2d 1147], we addressed the potential problems of overlabeling: "[E]xperience suggest[s] that if every report of a possible risk, no matter how speculative, conjectural, or tentative, imposed an affirmative duty to give some warning, a manufacturer would be required to inundate physicians indiscriminately with notice of any and every hint of danger, thereby inevitably diluting the force of any specific warning given." (See *Anderson, supra,* 53 Cal. 3d at p. 1002, citing *Finn.*) The application of the failure-to-warn theory to pharmaceuticals requires determinations whether available evidence established a causal link between an alleged side effect and a prescription drug, whether any warning should have been given, and, if so, whether the warning was adequate. These are issues of fact involving, inter alia, questions concerning the state of the art, i.e., what was known or reasonably knowable by the application of scientific and medical knowledge available at the time of manufacture and distribution of the prescription drug. They also necessarily involve questions concerning whether the risk, in light of accepted scientific norms, was more than merely speculative or conjectural, or so remote and insignificant as to be negligible. . . .

Nor does Upjohn offer any sound public policy rationale for departing from *Anderson* concerning the liability of manufacturers of prescription drugs for failure to warn of known or reasonably scientifically knowable risks. Thus, we are unpersuaded by the argument, purportedly derived from our reasoning in *Brown*, that manufacturers of prescription drugs should be exempt from the strict liability duty to warn because they might otherwise refrain from developing and marketing drugs, including "cutting-edge vaccines to combat human immunodeficiency virus (HIV)" and other diseases. Our rationale in *Brown*, which involved strict liability for *design defects*, is inapplicable: unlike strict liability for design defects, strict liability for failure to warn does not potentially subject drug manufacturers to liability for flaws in their products that they have not, and could not have, discovered. Drug manufacturers need only warn of risks that are *actually known or reasonably scientifically knowable.*

Upjohn offers no clear or sufficient basis for concluding that research and development will inevitably decrease as a result of imposing strict liability for failure to warn of *known or reasonably scientifically knowable* risks; indeed, requiring manufacturers to internalize the costs of failing to determine such risks may instead *increase* the level of research into safe and effective drugs. In any event, we see no reason to depart from our conclusion in *Anderson* that the manufacturer should bear the costs, in terms of preventable injury or death, of its own failure to provide adequate warnings of known or reasonably scientifically knowable risks. As we observed: "Whatever may be reasonable from the point of view of the manufacturer, the user of the product must be given the option either to refrain from using the product at all or to use it in such a way as to minimize the degree of danger." (*Anderson, supra,* 53 Cal. 3d at p. 1003.) Although *Anderson* itself involved a nondrug, asbestos, our conclusion therein applies with equal force to prescription drugs. [AFFIRMED.]

KENNARD, JUDGE, Concurring and Dissenting.

... The majority holds that a prescription drug manufacturer is liable in tort for all drug-related injuries about which it did not warn, provided only that the risk of injury was either actually known or in some manner scientifically ascertainable by the manufacturer when it distributed the drug. In his dissent, by contrast, Justice Baxter proposes that a prescription drug manufacturer be held liable for failure to warn of possible drug-related injuries only if the person injured by the drug succeeds in proving that the manufacturer's decision not to warn was unreasonable.

I find neither approach entirely satisfactory. Combining what I view as the best features of both, I would hold that initially, to establish a *prima facie* case, a person seeking damages for drug-related injures on a failure-to-warn theory need prove only that at the time of distribution the manufacturer either knew or should have learned, through the application of commonly accepted scientific methods and reasonably available technologies, of the particular risk of harm; but I would hold also that after the party seeking recovery makes this showing, the manufacturer may defend on the basis that it acted reasonably, in light of all relevant considerations, in not warning of the particular risk. . . .

I would require the plaintiff in a prescription drug case to show that at the time of the manufacturer's distribution of the drug evidence of a risk of harm from the drug was considered credible in the relevant scientific community or that a reasonable scientist would have investigated the possibility of a risk and the investigation would have resulted in scientifically credible evidence of the risk's existence. Evidence of a risk would be scientifically credible if the data upon which it is based, the methodology employed, and its conclusions identifying the existence of a risk comply with generally accepted scientific methodology and analysis. Scientific evidence that postulates the possibility of a risk or that is otherwise speculative or conjectural would be inadequate. Also, the relevant inquiry relates to the credibility of the scientific evidence in light of accepted scientific norms, not to the personal professional beliefs or preferences of an otherwise qualified expert . . .

To satisfy its burden, the manufacturer would have to show that its failure to warn was reasonable in relation to the identified risk. The manufacturer, for instance, could introduce evidence that the risk did not pose a serious threat to health, that it was remote, that the number or relative severity of other risks justified a failure to warn, or that the scientific association between the drug and the risk was weak. The manufacturer's compliance with product safety statutes or regulations such as those of the FDA would also be relevant, but not necessarily controlling. The same is true of industry standards and practices to the extent they relate to the reasonableness of the manufacturer's decision not to warn.

In my view, this allocation of the burden of proof is appropriate given the manufacturer's superior access to and capability of evaluating the relevant scientific information; it also furthers a goal of products liability law of relieving injured consumers from evidentiary burdens that may be too onerous.

Is this solution perfect? Perhaps not. But it does attempt to strike a fair balance between two distinct public interests: compensating consumers injured by defective products, and encouraging the development of prescription drugs, many of which are life sustaining and lifesaving.

BAXTER, JUDGE, dissenting.

. . . I conclude that the same important public policy considerations relating to the development, marketing, and availability of prescription drugs that led this court in *Brown* to conclude that principles of strict liability (and breach of warranty liability) generally applicable to "design defects" should not be extended to manufacturers of prescription drugs, should apply as well to fail-ure-to-warn defects. I would therefore hold in this case that it is solely under negligence principles that a prescription drug manufacturer may be held liable for failure to warn . . .

I note that related provisions in the American Law Institute's tentative draft of the Restatement Third of Torts pertaining to products liability buttress my conclusion that the drafters of the Restatement have long viewed, and continue to view, failure-to-warn liability in prescription drug cases as requiring applica-tion of a *negligence* standard of liability. . . . Clearly, by incorporating concepts of "reasonableness" and "foreseeability" into the new standard, the drafters of the new Restatement intend to impose a standard of care *sounding in negligence* in failure-to-warn actions involving prescription drugs. . . .

[I]n the warning context, as in the design-defect context, the existence and role of the federal Food and Drug Administration (FDA) provides a justifica-tion for distinguishing prescription drugs from other products, because one of the FDA's primary functions is to evaluate the necessity and adequacy of warnings provided by prescription drug manufacturers . . . In the prescription drug industry, however, a manufacturer is not left to its own resources to decide whether the risk of harm is such as to require a warning. Rather, the FDA plays a significant role in determining whether a warning must be pro-vided, and, if so, the specific content of the warning.

It seems clear that the FDA regulations applicable to prescription drugs and their accompanying warnings, and various factors such as the presence or absence of a prior FDA approval requirement, whether FDA approval has been obtained for a particular warning, or whether authorization has been obtained to forego the furnishing of a warning altogether — are all highly relevant in determining liability in actions for failure to warn brought against prescrip-tion drug manufacturers under state tort laws, and of necessity will require inquiry into the *reasonableness* of the manufacturer's individualized conduct in its efforts to comply with the FDA warning requirements, and the *foresee-ability* of the need for such warnings in the first instance. Concepts such as "reasonableness" and "foreseeability" are fundamentally rooted in negligence doctrine. To fail to apply them, and instead hold prescription drug manufactur-ers *strictly liable* for failing to warn of the risks of harm associated with their products, would effectively preclude consideration of evidence highly relevant to the question of fault in the failure-to-warn context . . .

[S]ubjecting prescription drug manufacturers to a strict liability standard for failure to warn would create a risk of inhibiting or delaying the develop-ment and marketing of new drugs that is comparable to the risk that the court in *Brown* determined was contrary to the public interest . . .

Admittedly, under a negligence standard, some consumers of prescription drugs may be denied compensation for injuries resulting from the absence of warnings of risks of harm that were scientifically knowable but reasonably not known by the manufacturer at the time a prescription drug was sold. Nevertheless, I conclude, as did this court in *Brown*, that on balance the public is better served by increasing the likely availability of affordable, highly beneficial prescription drugs than by extending a strict liability cause of action for monetary compensation to those persons who are injured despite the reasonable actions of prescription drug manufacturers.

NOTES

1. *Unavoidably Dangerous Products.* REST. 2D TORTS § 402A, cmt. *k*, provides:

> There are some products which, in the present state of human knowledge, are quite incapable of being made safe for their intended and ordinary use. These are especially common in the field of drugs . . . Such a product, properly prepared, and accompanied by proper directions and warning, is not defective, nor is it unreasonably dangerous. The same is true of many other drugs, vaccines, and the like, many of which for this very reason cannot legally be sold except to physicians, or under the prescription of a physician . . . The seller of such products, again with the qualification that they are properly prepared and marketed, and proper warning is given, where the situation calls for it, is not to be held to strict liability for unfortunate consequences attending their use, merely because he has undertaken to supply the public with an apparently useful and desirable product, attended with a known but apparently reasonable risk.

REST. 2D TORTS § 402A, cmt. *k*.

Does comment k apply to all strict products liability claims or does it suggest different treatment for design rather than manufacturing defect or failure to warn cases?

2. *Unavoidable Dangerousness Applied.* Most courts have applied comment k to prescription drugs and medical devices and held that a seller is not be liable for unknown risks its product posed or for failing to warn of those risks. *See, e.g., Terhune v. A. H. Robins Co.*, 90 Wash. 2d 9 (1978). However, in *Hill v. Searle Labs., Div. of Searle Pharmaceuticals, Inc.*, 884 F.2d 1064 (8th Cir. 1989), the court, reversing summary judgment for the defendant, held that comment K did not apply to the intrauterine device CU-7. The comment should apply, said the court, only in those circumstances "when it is shown that the product is incapable of being made safe given the present state of human knowledge but possesses such a high degree of social need so that its use is warranted, provided warnings are adequate." *Id.* at 1068. The example of the Pasteur treatment for rabies, given in the comment, "suggests that only special products, those with exceptional social need, fall within the gamut of comment *k*." *Id.*

3. *Restated and Expanded.* REST. 3D TORTS § 6 is devoted entirely to prescription drugs and medical devices. Section 6 provides in part:

(a) A manufacturer of a prescription drug or medical device who sells or otherwise distributes a defective drug or medical device is subject to liability for harm to persons caused by the defect. A prescription drug or medical device is one that may be legally sold or otherwise distributed only pursuant to a health-care provider's prescription.

(b) For purposes of liability under Subsection (a), a prescription drug or medical device is defective if at the time of sale or other distribution the drug or medical device:

(1) contains a manufacturing defect as defined in § 2(a); or

(2) is not reasonably safe due to defective design as defined in Subsection (c); or

(3) is not reasonably safe due to inadequate instructions or warnings as defined in Subsection (d).

(c) A prescription drug or medical device is not reasonably safe due to defective design if the foreseeable risks of harm posed by the drug or medical device are sufficiently great in relation to its foreseeable therapeutic benefits that reasonable health-care providers, knowing of such foreseeable risks and therapeutic benefits, would not prescribe the drug or medical device for any class of patients.

4. *Preemption or Presumption.* In most cases manufacturer compliance (or for that matter non-compliance) with a state or federal regulation as to, say, the provision of warnings will be admissible but not conclusive. Compare a Michigan statute that provides (subject to some limited exceptions):

In a product liability action against a manufacturer or seller, a product that is a drug is not defective or unreasonably dangerous, and the manufacturer or seller is not liable, if the drug was approved for safety and efficacy by the United States food and drug administration, and the drug and its labeling were in compliance with the United States food and drug administration's approval at the time the drug left the control of the manufacturer or seller.

MCL § 600.2946(5). *See Taylor v. Smithkline Beecham Corp.*, 658 N.W.2d 127 (Mich. 2003) (upholding constitutionality of statute). While Michigan so far is alone in taking this position, the FDA itself has asserted the position that its labeling requirements have a pre-emptive effect, stating: "FDA approval of labeling under the act . . . preempts conflicting or contrary State law." Requirements on Content and Format of Labeling for Human Prescription Drug and Biological Products, 21 C.F.R. 201, 314, 601 (effective June 30, 2006). This was held insufficient to preempt a state warning action in *McNellis v. Pfizer, Inc.*, 2006 U.S. Dist. LEXIS 70844 (D.N.J. Sept. 29, 2006) but another court has agreed with the FDA. *Compare Colacicio v. Apotex*, Inc. 432 F. Supp. 2d 514 (E.D. Pa. 2006). For an exploration of the FDA's position and the changing judicial interpretation of preemption in the light of pressures for tort reform, see Chapter 16.

REST. 3D TORTS §4 details the general, non-drug/device rule in design and warning cases that "(a) a product's noncompliance with an applicable product safety statute or administrative regulation renders the product defective with respect to the risks sought to be reduced by the statute or regulation" whereas "(b) a product's compliance with an applicable product safety statute or administrative regulation is properly considered in determining whether the product is defective with respect to the risks sought to be reduced by the statute or regulation, but such compliance does not preclude as a matter of law a finding of product defect." *Compare* TENN. CODE ANN. §29-28-104:

> Compliance by a manufacturer or seller with any federal or state statute or administrative regulation existing at the time a product was manufactured and prescribing standards for design, inspection, testing, manufacture, labeling, warning or instructions for use of a product, shall raise a rebuttable presumption that the product is not in an unreasonably dangerous condition in regard to matters covered by these standards.

5. *Learned Medical Intermediaries.* Products law has long endorsed the fiction that the consumer of a prescription drug or medical device is the physician not the patient. In failure to warn cases this led to the "learned intermediary" doctrine. In the words of one court:

> In cases involving complex products, such as those in which pharmaceutical companies are selling prescription drugs, the learned intermediary doctrine applies. Under the learned intermediary doctrine, a manufacturer's duty to warn is limited to an obligation to advise the prescribing physician of any potential dangers that may result from the use of its product. This standard is 'an understandable exception to the Restatement's general rule that one who markets goods must warn foreseeable ultimate users of dangers inherent in his products.' As such, we rely on the expertise of the physician intermediary to bridge the gap in special cases where the product and related warning are sufficiently complex so as not to be fully appreciated by the consumer. . . . 'Under the "learned intermediary doctrine" the adequacy of [the defendant's] warning is measured by its effect on the physician, . . . to whom it owed a duty to warn, and not by its effect on [the consumer].'

Toole v. Baxter Healthcare Corp., 235 F.3d 1307, 1313-14 (11th Cir. 2000). In such cases the manufacturer will be insulated from liability and any patient redress will be limited to a negligence action (for negligent prescribing or failure to disclose the risks associated with the drug) against the prescribing physician.

REST. 3D TORTS §6(d)(2) recognizes that there will be exceptional cases requiring warnings to the patient "when the manufacturer knows or has reason to know that health-care providers will not be in a position to reduce the risks of harm in accordance with the instructions or warnings." As a result courts frequently have required warnings to be provided in cases involving mass immunizations or where the warnings are explicitly directed at patients. The most controversial emerging area for potential manufacturer liability is direct-to-consumer marketing of drugs by pharmaceutical manufacturers. In *Perez v. Wyeth Laboratories, Inc.*, 734 A.2d 1245, 1246-47 (N.J. 1999), the New Jersey Supreme Court observed:

> Our medical-legal jurisprudence is based on images of health care that no longer exist. At an earlier time, medical advice was received in the doctor's office from a physician who most likely made house calls if needed. The patient usually paid a small sum of money to the doctor. Neighborhood pharmacists compounded prescribed medicines. Without being pejorative, it is safe to say that the prevailing attitude of law and medicine was that the "doctor knows best." *Logan v. Greenwich Hosp. Ass'n*, 191 Conn. 282, 465 A.2d 294, 299 (1983).
>
> Pharmaceutical manufacturers never advertised their products to patients, but rather directed all sales efforts at physicians. In this comforting setting, the law created an exception to the traditional duty of manufacturers to warn consumers directly of risks associated with the product as long as they warned health-care providers of those risks.
>
> For good or ill, that has all changed. Medical services are in large measure provided by managed care organizations. Medicines are purchased in the pharmacy department of supermarkets and often paid for by third-party providers. Drug manufacturers now directly advertise products to consumers on the radio, television, the Internet, billboards on public transportation, and in magazines . . .
>
> The question in this case, broadly stated, is whether our law should follow these changes in the marketplace or reflect the images of the past. We believe that when mass marketing of prescription drugs seeks to influence a patient's choice of a drug, a pharmaceutical manufacturer that makes direct claims to consumers for the efficacy of its product should not be unqualifiedly relieved of a duty to provide proper warnings of the dangers or side effects of the product.

6. *Product Equality.* Do all types of products or product users receive equal treatment from the torts system? For example, does liability attach more regularly to products (e.g., power tools, heavy equipment) that primarily injure men, while courts have been slower to break down barriers to liability for contraceptive drugs and devices? Recall the discussion of *Perez* in Chapter 1.

ROYER v. CATHOLIC MEDICAL CENTER
741 A.2d 74 (N.H. 1999)

BROCK, CIRCUIT JUDGE.

. . . The plaintiffs have pleaded the following facts. In September 1991, Ira Royer underwent total knee replacement surgery at CMC. As part of the procedure, a prosthetic knee, provided by CMC, was surgically implanted. In April

1993, Royer complained to his doctor that the pain in his knee was worse than it had been before the surgery. His doctors determined that the prosthesis was defective, and in June 1993 Royer underwent a second operation in which the prosthesis was removed, and a second prosthesis inserted.

Ira Royer initially brought suit against Dow Corning Corp., Dow Corning Wright, Inc., and Wright Medical Technologies, Inc., the companies that had allegedly designed and manufactured the defective prosthesis. Subsequently, Dow Corning commenced federal bankruptcy proceedings, and the plaintiffs filed a second writ against CMC, alleging that CMC was strictly liable to Ira because it had sold a prosthesis with a design defect that was in an unreasonably dangerous condition, and liable to Rachel who suffered a loss of consortium.

The defendant moved to dismiss, arguing, inter alia, that it was not a "seller of goods" for purposes of strict products liability, and that absent the strict liability claim, Ira's claim and the loss of consortium claim could not stand. The trial court granted the motion, finding that CMC was not, as a matter of law, engaged in the business of selling prosthetic devices. On appeal, the plaintiffs contend that this finding was error . . .

Although we have adopted a cause of action for strict products liability, we have recognized limits to the doctrine . . . In *Bruzga v. PMR Architects*, 141 N.H. 756, 761-63 (1997), we rejected an argument that strict liability should extend to architects and building contractors who allegedly designed and "manufactured" a defective building. After determining that the reasons supporting strict liability did not apply to architects and contractors, we concluded that architects and contractors provide a professional service. Although we acknowledged that a building contractor "supplies" a structure to the purchaser, we declined to extend strict products liability to contractors because they are "engaged primarily in the rendition of a service."

A majority of the jurisdictions that have addressed whether a health care provider who supplies a defective prosthesis is subject to strict liability have declined to extend strict liability, similarly reasoning that the health care provider primarily renders a service, and that the provision of a prosthetic device is merely incidental to that service. *See, e.g., Cafazzo v. Cent. Medical Health Services*, 668 A.2d 521, 524-25 (1995); . . . The defendant urges us to adopt this rationale.

The plaintiffs argue, however, that the distinction between selling products and providing services is a legal fiction. The defendant, according to the plaintiffs, acted both as a seller of the prosthetic knee and as a provider of professional services in the transaction. Because the defendant charged separately for the prosthesis and earned a profit on the "sale," the plaintiffs argue that the defendant should be treated no differently than any other distributor of a defective product. The defendant, according to the plaintiffs, primarily supplied a prosthesis, while the surgeon provided the professional "services."

Although a defendant may both provide a service and sell a product within the same transaction for purposes of strict liability, see REST. 2D TORTS § 402A, comment *f* at 350, the dispositive issue in this case is not whether the defendant "sold" or transferred a prosthetic knee, but whether the defendant was an entity "engaged in the business of selling" prosthetic knees so as to warrant the imposition of liability without proof of legal fault . . . We find the reasoning of both *Bruzga* and the majority of courts that have declined to extend strict liability to health care providers who supply defective prostheses to be persuasive.

"The essence of the relationship between hospital and patient is the provision of professional medical services necessary to effectuate the implantation of the [prosthesis] . . . " *Hector v. Cedars-Sinai Medical Center*, 225 Cal.Rptr. 595, 599 (1986). "[T]he patient bargains for, and the hospital agrees to make available, the human skill and physical material of medical science to the end that the patient's health be restored." *Perlmutter v. Beth David Hospital*, 123 N.E.2d 792, 794 (1954). That the hospital charges a fee for the prosthesis and transfers possession does not transform the character of the hospital-patient relationship. "The thrust of the inquiry is thus not on whether a separate consideration is charged for the physical material used in the exercise of medical skill, but what service is performed to restore or maintain the patient's health." *Cafazzo*, 668 A.2d at 524.

We cannot agree that this distinction is merely a legal fiction. "[T]he essence of the transaction between the retail seller and the consumer relates to the article sold. The seller is in the business of supplying the product to the consumer. It is that, and that alone, for which he is paid." *Hoff v. Zimmer, Inc.*, 746 F. Supp. 872, 875 (W.D.Wis.1990). A patient, by contrast, does not enter a hospital to "purchase" a prosthesis, "but to obtain a course of treatment in the hope of being cured of what ails him." *Perlmutter*, 123 N.E.2d at 796. Indeed, "to ignore the ancillary nature of the association of product with activity is to posit surgery, or . . . any medical service requiring the use of a physical object, as a marketing device for the incorporated object." *Cafazzo*, 668 A.2d at 524.

We decline to ignore the reality of the relationship between Ira Royer and CMC, and to treat any services provided by CMC as ancillary to a primary purpose of selling a prosthetic knee. Rather, the record indicates that in addition to the prosthesis, Royer was billed for a hospital room, operating room services, physical therapy, a recovery room, pathology laboratory work, an EKG or ECG, X rays, and anesthesia. Thus, it is evident that Ira Royer entered CMC not to purchase a prosthesis, but to obtain health care services that included the implantation of the knee, with the overall objective of restoring his health. *See St. Mary Medical Center, Inc. v. Casko*, 639 N.E.2d 312, 315 (Ind. Ct. App. 1994). Necessary to the restoration of his health, in the judgment of his physicians, was the implantation of the prosthesis. We do not find this scenario, as the plaintiffs urge, analogous to one in which a plaintiff purchases a defective tire from a retail tire distributor and has the distributor install the tire. *Cf. Perlmutter*, 123 N.E.2d at 795-96.

Moreover, the policy rationale underlying strict liability, as in *Bruzga*, does not support extension of the doctrine under the facts of this case. With respect to the inherent difficulty of proving negligence in many products liability cases, this rationale fails in the context of non-manufacturer cases alleging a design defect. Because "ordinarily there is no possibility that a distributor other than the manufacturer created a design defect[,] . . . strict liability would impose liability when there is no possibility of negligence." *Parker v.*

St. Vincent Hosp., 919 P.2d 1104, 1108-09 (N.M. App. 1996). The plaintiffs do not allege in this case that the defendant altered the prosthesis in any way. Further, holding health care providers strictly liable for defects in prosthetic devices necessary to the provision of health care would likely result in higher health care costs borne ultimately by all patients and "place an unrealistic burden on the physicians and hospitals of this state to test or guarantee the tens of thousands of products used in hospitals by doctors," *Ayyash v. Henry Ford Health Systems*, 533 N.W.2d 353, 356 (1995). Additionally, "research and innovation in medical equipment and treatment would be inhibited." *Cafazzo*, 668 A.2d at 527. We find that the "peculiar characteristics of medical services[,] . . . [which] include the tendency to be experimental, . . . a dependence on factors beyond the control of the professional[,] and a lack of certainty or assurance of the desired result," *Cafazzo*, 668 A.2d at 527, outweigh any reasons that might support the imposition of strict liability in this context.

"In short, medical services are distinguished by factors which make them significantly different in kind from the retail marketing enterprise at which 402A is directed." *Id.* We conclude that where, as here, a health care provider in the course of rendering health care services supplies a prosthetic device to be implanted into a patient, the health care provider is not "engaged in the business of selling" prostheses for purposes of strict products liability. Accordingly, the trial court did not err in granting the defendant's motion to dismiss. [AFFIRMED].

NOTES

1. *Sales of Products or Goods versus Provision of Services.* It is hornbook law that there is a distinction between sales of products or goods and provision of services. The provider of services is only liable if he or she is actually negligent. Consistent with these general rules, section 19 of the Third Restatement applies to products — that is, tangible personal property. REST. 3D TORTS § 19(a). Services are not products. *Id.* § 19(b). What was the rule argued for by the plaintiff in *Royer*?

2. *Statutory Characterizations.* Many states have blood shield statutes often dating from the early days of strict liability and legislative concern over hepatitis litigation. In *Samson v. Carolina-Georgia Blood Center,* 297 S.C. 409 (1989), a case brought by a woman alleging that she had contracted the human immunodeficiency virus from a blood transfusion, the South Carolina Supreme Court held that the state blood shield statute prevented blood from being treated as a product for the purpose of strict products liability law. REST. 3D TORTS § 19(c), states that human blood and human tissue are not subject to the rules of the Restatement.

3. *Sellers or Manufacturers?* At common law and under § 402A, strict products liability applied to "One who sells any product . . . if . . . the seller is engaged in the business of selling such a product." REST. 3D TORTS § 20 states:

(a) One sells a product when, in a commercial context, one transfers ownership thereto either for use or consumption or for resale leading to ultimate use or consumption. Commercial product sellers include, but are not limited to, manufacturers, wholesalers, and retailers.

(b) One otherwise distributes a product when, in a commercial transaction other than a sale, one provides the product to another either for use or consumption or as a preliminary step leading to ultimate use or consumption. Commercial nonsale product distributors include, but are not limited to, lessors, bailors, and those who provide products to others as a means of promoting either the use or consumption of such products or some other commercial activity.

(c) One also sells or otherwise distributes a product when, in a commercial transaction, one provides a combination of products and services and either the transaction taken as a whole, or the product component thereof, satisfies the criteria in Subsection (a) or (b).

4. *A Prescribed Exception.* Note, however, that § 6(e) exempts retail pharmacists unless "at the time of sale or other distribution the drug or medical device [the drug or device] contains a manufacturing defect" or "at or before the time of sale or other distribution of the drug or medical device the retail seller or other distributor fails to exercise reasonable care and such failure causes harm to persons." Several courts have viewed the pharmacist's relative immunity as a corollary of the learned intermediary rule. *See, e.g., McKee v. American Home Prods. Corp.*, 782 P.2d 1045, 1055-56 (Wash. 1989): "The pharmacist still has a duty to accurately *fill* a prescription and to be alert for clear errors or mistakes in the prescription. The pharmacist does not, however, have a duty to question a judgment made by the physician as to the propriety of a prescription or to warn customers of the hazardous side effects associated with a drug, either orally or by way of the manufacturer's package insert."

5. *State Statutes.* Some states have moved away from the common law rule imposing liability on "innocent" non-manufacturer sellers in the chain of distribution. For example the Missouri statute provides that "[a] defendant whose liability is based solely on his status as a seller in the stream of commerce may be dismissed from a products liability claim" so long as the defendant shows that "another defendant, including the manufacturer, is properly before the court," and that "total recovery may be had for plaintiff's claim" from the other defendants. § 537.762 R.S.Mo. How does the state statute considered in the principal case set forth below differ?

6. *Articulated Justice?* What is the appropriate application of principles of corrective justice to drugs and devices provided by healthcare providers? How would you justify the sale-service distinction to an injured patient?

KOLARIK v. CORY INT'L CORP.
721 N.W.2d 159 (Iowa 2006)

CARTER, JUSTICE.

... Plaintiff has alleged that he opened a jar of pimento-stuffed, green olives, which had been imported and sold at wholesale by defendants. He alleges that he used several of these olives, which bore the label Italica Spanish Olives, in the preparation of a salad and, when eating the salad, bit down on an olive pit or pit fragment and fractured a tooth.

The motion papers reveal that defendants are importers and wholesalers of Spanish olives grown by various Spanish companies. They obtain bulk shipments of pimento-stuffed, green olives shipped in 150-kilogram drums to their plant in Norfolk, Virginia. There, the drums are emptied and the olives are washed and placed in a brine solution in glass jars suitable for retail sale under various names including Italica Spanish Olives. When defendants receive the olives, they are inspected for general appearance, pH, and acid level. Defendants rely on their Spanish suppliers for quality control of the pitting and stuffing process ...

In sustaining defendants' motion for summary judgment, the district court concluded that defendants were immune from plaintiff's strict liability claim and implied-warranty-of-merchantability claim by reason of IOWA CODE section 613.18(1)(a) (2001). That statute provides:

> 1. A person who is not the assembler, designer, or manufacturer, and who wholesales, retails, distributes, or otherwise sells a product is:
>
> > a. Immune from any suit based upon strict liability in tort or breach of implied warranty of merchantability which arises solely from an alleged defect in the original design or manufacture of the product.

IOWA CODE § 613.18(1)(a).

Plaintiff urges that section 613.18(1)(a) does not apply to his strict liability and breach-of-implied-warranty-of-merchantability claim. He contends that defendants were assemblers of the olives at issue here, thus removing them from the immunity provisions of the statute. The assembling occurs, he asserts, when defendants remove bulk olives from drums and repackage them in jars. We disagree that this repackaging process excludes defendants from the immunity granted by the statute.

We are convinced that the assemblers exclusion contained in section 613.18(1)(a) is aimed at those situations in which an assembling process has some causal connection to a dangerous condition in the product that gives rise to a strict-liability claim or a product condition that constitutes a breach of an implied warranty of merchantability. Because the repackaging of the olives by defendants did not contribute to the condition that underlies plaintiff's product-liability claim, defendants are afforded the immunity granted by the statute.

In the alternative, plaintiff argues that section 613.18(1)(a) does not apply because olives are not a "product" as that term is used in that statute. This argument is premised on his assertion that a product is something that has been produced by human action. He contends that no human action has produced the olives that defendants import and sell. In his written argument, plaintiff states this point as follows:

> No producer can mix ingredients or connect component pieces in order to create an olive. The creation of an olive is a phenomenon of nature over which no human can exercise control or influence. Thus, olives are neither assembled, designed, nor manufactured.

To the contrary, we are reasonably certain that human effort does play a role in the growing and commercial distribution of olives. A standard legal dictionary defines "product" as follows:

> Something that is distributed commercially for use or consumption and that is usually (1) tangible personal property (2) the result of fabrication or processing, and (3) an item that has passed through a chain of commercial distribution before ultimate use or consumption.

BLACK'S LAW DICTIONARY 1225 (7th ed. 1999). We are satisfied that agricultural commodities may be products as that term is used in section 613.18(1)(a). That statute is aimed at situations giving rise to product liability actions and food products may produce such claims. *See* REST. 3D TORTS § 7 (1998) (one engaged in the business of selling or distributing food products is subject to liability for harm to persons caused by defective product). Consequently, the district court did not err in applying that statute to bar plaintiff's strict-liability and breach-of-implied-warranty-of-merchantability claims . . .

Much of the argument of both parties with regard to plaintiff's negligence claim turns on the decision in *Brown v. Nebiker*, 229 Iowa 1223 (1941). In that case, the plaintiff's decedent, a restaurant patron, swallowed a bone while eating a pork chop. The bone lodged in his esophagus and complications from the surgical removal that followed led to the patron's death. The patron's personal representative sued the restaurant owner on theories of implied warranty and negligence. At the trial, several witnesses testified that they had ordered pork chops at the same restaurant on the same evening and that the pork chops were served with the bone left intact.

The district court directed a verdict for the defendant on both the warranty and negligence claims. On appeal this court held that the common-law warranty that flows to patrons of a restaurant protected them against food that was unfit for human consumption and against having foreign objects in the food. The court held that pork chops served with the bones in were not unfit for human consumption and that, because bones are naturally contained in pork, they do not constitute a foreign object. On the negligence claim, we indicated that a restaurant owes no duty to its patrons to serve meat that is entirely free of bones that are natural to the product.

In seeking to overturn the district court's grant of summary judgment on his negligence claim, plaintiff urges that, irrespective of its natural components, a food product may be marketed in a manner in which the consumer's reasonable expectations will be that certain natural components of the product have been removed. He asserts that this is the case with respect to the pimento-stuffed olives at issue in the present case.

Defendants seek to uphold the district court's summary judgment by espousing the virtues of *Brown v. Nebiker*'s pronouncements concerning consumer expectations as to the natural components of food products. They argue in their brief, "[s]urely there is no one who does not recognize, if he thinks at all, that natural products may well be present, such as bones in fish and meat and pits in olives and seeds in oranges."

We are unable to attribute any more to the *Brown v. Nebiker* decision than a recognition that, when pork chops are served in their natural state with the bone left in the meat, the presence of bone fragments must be anticipated. The opinion sheds little light on the requirements placed on a seller of food products in various stages of preparation or processing. We share the views expressed by the Wisconsin Supreme Court with regard to this matter:

> The "foreign-natural" test . . . does not recommend itself to us as being logical or desirable. It is true one can expect a T-bone in T-bone steak, chicken bones in roast chicken, pork bone in a pork chop, pork bone in spare ribs, a rib bone in short ribs of beef, and fish bones in a whole baked or fried fish, but the expectation is based not on the naturalness of the particular bone to the meat, fowl, or fish, but on the type of dish served containing the meat, fowl, or fish. There is a distinction between what a consumer expects to find in a fish stick and in a baked or fried fish, or in a chicken sandwich made from sliced white meat and in roast chicken. The test should be what is reasonably expected by the consumer in the food as served, not what might be natural to the ingredients of that food prior to preparation.

Betehia v. Cape Cod Corp., 103 N.W.2d 64, 68-69 (Wis. 1960) . . .

We find the principle applied by the Wisconsin court in *Betehia* with respect to restaurant food to be equally applicable to situations involving processed foods contained in cans or jars. In *Bryer v. Rath Packing Co.*, 156 A.2d 442 (Md. Ct. App. 1959), a child's throat was injured by a chicken bone while she was eating chow mein in a school cafeteria, which had purchased the chow mein in sealed cans from the defendant food processor. The trial court directed a verdict in favor of the defendant. In reversing that judgment, the Maryland Court of Appeals stated:

> The obligation of the packer of food to the ultimate consumer is to exercise such care in its preparation that the product will not cause injury to the consumer, and the amount of care that is required is commensurate with the danger to the life or health of the consumer that may foreseeably result from such lack of care. In the instant case the packer of the chicken set its own standard of care and increased the necessary amount of care by expressly representing on the cans sold that the product was ready to serve and boned. By its advertising it was saying to the ultimate consumer that this was chicken from which the bones had been removed, and this assurance which it must have foreseen would be relied on (as indeed it was in the case before us, as the cafeteria manager explicitly testified), required it to exercise as much care as would enable users to rely with reasonable safety on the assurance. This is not to say that the packer was an insurer, for it is

clear, and agreed, that in the form of action brought it is not. The question is whether due care was exercised under the circumstances.

Bryer, 156 A.2d at 446. Similar reasoning was applied in *Wood v. Waldorf System, Inc.*, 83 A.2d 90, 93 (R.I. 1951), a case involving a chicken bone in a can of chicken soup.

We are satisfied that, in the case of processed foods, consumers may develop reasonable expectations that certain components of food products in their natural state that serve to impede human consumption will be removed. Specifically, we believe that the purchaser of pimento-stuffed olives may reasonably anticipate that the olive pits have been removed. We need not decide whether this expectation would create an implied warranty of merchantability because such a claim is precluded by statute in the present case. We are convinced, however, that a seller of stuffed olives must be cognizant that consumers will assume that the olives will be free from pits and act on that assumption in consuming the product. Consistent with that expectation, a seller must exercise reasonable care to assure that this expectation is realized. The district court erred in rejecting plaintiff's negligence claim by reliance on the natural component principle that was applied in *Brown v. Nebiker*.

In reviewing the motion papers to ascertain whether issues of material fact otherwise remain concerning plaintiff's negligence claim, we are satisfied that it does not appear that defendants were in any manner negligent in the processing of the olives that contained the pit that caused harm to the plaintiff. We conclude, however, that a genuine issue of material fact does exist with respect to plaintiff's claim that defendants were negligent in not warning against the possible presence of pits or pit fragments in the jar of olives.

Defendants' quality control officer testified in his deposition that the pitting process is not one hundred percent effective. He indicated that the presence of an occasional pit or pit fragment in the stuffed olives is inevitable because the machine that does the pitting will fail to remove a pit if the olive has an abnormal shape. Given this circumstance, we conclude that a trier of fact might find that reasonable care by a wholesale seller of stuffed olives would include providing a warning on the label that pits or pit fragments might be encountered. A claim based on that theory should have survived summary judgment. [AFFIRMED IN PART, REVERSED IN PART, AND REMANDED.]

NOTES

1. *Food*. REST. 3D TORTS § 7 provides that "a harm-causing ingredient of the food product constitutes a defect if a reasonable consumer would not expect the food product to contain that ingredient." Most jurisdictions now use this "reasonable consumer expectations test," with the foreign-natural rule now in retreat in even its traditional strongholds. (*See Porteous v. St. Ann's Cafe & Deli*, 713 So. 2d 454 (La. 1998) (foreign-natural distinction rejected in case where plaintiff damaged a tooth as a result of biting onto a pearl contained in an oyster sandwich, but court found for restaurant on basis of its compliance with reasonable care).

As a practical matter, what defects in foods would attract liability under a reasonable expectations test but not the foreign-natural rule?

2. *A Less Tasty Variant.* In *Mexicali Rose v. Superior Court*, 822 P.2d 1292, 1303 (Ca. 1992), the plaintiff brought strict liability and negligence actions against a restaurant after he sustained throat injuries when he swallowed a one-inch chicken bone contained in an enchilada. The court adopted the following rules:

> If the injury-producing substance is natural to the preparation of the food served, it can be said that it was reasonably expected by its very nature and the food cannot be determined unfit or defective. A plaintiff in such a case has no cause of action in strict liability or implied warranty. If, however, the presence of the natural substance is due to a restaurateur's failure to exercise due care in food preparation, the injured patron may sue under a negligence theory.

> If the injury-causing substance is foreign to the food served, then the injured patron may also state a cause of action in implied warranty and strict liability, and the trier of fact will determine whether the substance (i) could be reasonably expected by the average consumer and (ii) rendered the food unfit or defective.

3. *Component Parts.* Where a product is defective the manufacturer should be liable, but what about the manufacturers of component parts that were incorporated into the injury-causing product? REST. 3D TORTS § 5 states:

> One engaged in the business of selling or otherwise distributing product components who sells or distributes a component is subject to liability for harm to persons or property caused by a product into which the component is integrated if:

> (a) the component is defective in itself, as defined in this Chapter, and the defect causes the harm; or

> (b)(1) the seller or distributor of the component substantially participates in the integration of the component into the design of the product; and

> (2) the integration of the component causes the product to be defective, as defined in this Chapter; and

> (3) the defect in the product causes the harm.

4. *Predecessors and Successors.* According to REST. 3D TORTS § 12:

> A successor corporation or other business entity that acquires assets of a predecessor corporation or other business entity is subject to liability for harm to persons or property caused by a defective product sold or otherwise distributed commercially by the predecessor if the acquisition:

> (a) is accompanied by an agreement for the successor to assume such liability; or

> (b) results from a fraudulent conveyance to escape liability for the debts or liabilities of the predecessor; or

(c) constitutes a consolidation or merger with the predecessor; or

(d) results in the successor becoming a continuation of the predecessor.

In contrast, a few jurisdictions impose more extensive liability on successor corporations under the so-called "product line" theory. The justification for this approach was explained in *Ray v. Alad Corp.*, 560 P.2d 3, 9 (Cal. 1977), as resting on:

(1) the virtual destruction of the plaintiff's remedies against the original manufacturer caused by the successor's acquisition of the business, (2) the successor's ability to assume the original manufacturer's risk-spreading role, and (3) the fairness of requiring the successor to assume a responsibility for defective products that was a burden necessarily attached to the original manufacturer's good will being enjoyed by the successor in the continued operation of the business.

In *Lefever v. K.P. Hovnanian Enters.*, 734 A.2d 290 (NJ 1999), the New Jersey Supreme Court applied the product line theory in a case where the assets had been purchased in a sale pursuant to federal bankruptcy law but where the bankruptcy court had not specifically addressed the question of future products liability claims.

Notwithstanding the majority rule set forth in § 12, REST. 3D TORTS § 13 contemplates possible liability on the successor for *negligent* failure to warn about defects in the predecessors' products. In what circumstances should such liability be imposed?

5. *Automobile Accidents.* Some specific types of products raise discrete issues for the courts not because (as is the case with prescription drugs and devices) they raise distinct policy issues or employ unique distribution models, but rather because recurring fact patterns consistently raise discrete, practical difficulties. For example, it has been argued that automobiles are complex products and so particularly unsuitable for application of the consumer expectations test for defectiveness. Thus, in *Soule v. GMC*, 882 P.2d 298, 310 (Cal. 1994), the Supreme Court of California, that typically allows for a dual instruction on consumer expectations or risk-benefit under *Barker v. Lull Engineering Co., Inc.*, 573 P.2d 443 (Cal. 1978), said that such an instruction should not be given in a complex design case because:

An ordinary consumer of automobiles cannot reasonably expect that a car's frame, suspension, or interior will be designed to remain intact in any and all accidents. Nor would ordinary experience and understanding inform such a consumer how safely an automobile's design should perform under the esoteric circumstances of the collision at issue here. Indeed, both parties assumed that quite complicated design considerations were at issue, and that expert testimony was necessary to illuminate these matters. Therefore, injection of ordinary consumer expectations into the design defect equation was improper.

Cf. GMC v. Farnsworth, 965 P.2d 1209 (Alaska 1998) (consumer expectations test appropriate in case dealing with allegation of defective seat belt system that permitted "submarining" of occupant during collision.).

Many automobile accident cases also involve difficult issues of concurrent causation where the argument is made that the design of the vehicle (for example, inadequate safety restraints or crash protection) is only one cause; the other is the negligent driving of another motorist or the plaintiff himself. In these cases the result turns on whether the plaintiff or the manufacturer has the burden of persuasion on the role of the vehicle defect in causing the "enhanced" injuries (i.e., those injuries that would have been avoided if the vehicle had, for example, non-defective crash protection). The majority approach, adopted by REST. 3D TORTS § 16 cmt. *d*, was approved in *Farnsworth,* where the court noted:

> Although both [approaches] are logically defensible, we find the majority rule more compelling for policy reasons. We agree with [plaintiff] that it should be the proven wrongdoer who must bear the burden of limiting its liability; it would be unfair to require a plaintiff who has already proved that a defect was a substantial factor in causing his or her injuries to try another case based upon what might have happened absent the defect.

965 P.2d at 1220.

E. LIMITS ON LIABILITY

CALLES v. SCRIPTO-TOKAI CORP.
864 N.E.2d 249 (Ill. 2007)

BURKE, JUSTICE.

. . . On March 31, 1998, plaintiff Susan Calles resided with her four daughters, Amanda, age 11, Victoria, age 5, and Jenna and Jillian, age 3. At some point that night, Calles left her home with Victoria to get videos for Amanda. When she left, the twins were in bed and Amanda was watching television. Calles returned to find fire trucks and emergency vehicles around her home. It was subsequently determined by a fire investigator, Robert Finn, that Jenna had started a fire using an Aim N Flame utility lighter Calles had purchased approximately one week earlier. The Aim N Flame was ignited by pulling a trigger after an "ON/OFF" switch was slid to the "on" position. As a result of the fire, Jillian suffered smoke inhalation. She was hospitalized and died on April 21.

Calles, individually and as administrator of Jillian's estate, filed suit in the circuit court of Cook County against Tokai, designer and manufacturer of the Aim N Flame, and Scripto-Tokai, distributor (collectively Scripto), alleging that the Aim N Flame was defectively designed and unreasonably dangerous because it did not contain a child-resistant safety device. According to the complaint, a safety device was available, inexpensive, and would have reduced the risk that children could ignite the lighter. Calles' claims sounded in strict liability, negligence, and breach of the implied warranties of merchantability and fitness for a particular purpose . . .

In support of its motion for summary judgment, Scripto offered the deposition testimony of Calles and Robert Finn, the fire inspector. In her deposition, Calles admitted she was aware of the risks and dangers presented by lighters in the hands of children, and, for this reason, she stored the Aim N Flames on the top shelf of her kitchen cabinet. Calles further admitted that the Aim N Flame operated as intended and expected.

In opposition to Scripto's motion for summary judgment, Calles offered affidavits from several experts including John Geremia, a chemical and mechanical engineer; Tarald Kvlseth, a mechanical and industrial engineer; William Kitzes, a board-certified product safety manager; Richard Dahlquist, an electrical engineer; and Carol Pollack-Nelson, an engineering psychologist. All of these experts opined that the Aim N Flame was defective and unreasonably dangerous because it lacked a child-resistant design. They also opined that a technologically and economically feasible alternative design, which included a child-resistant safety device, existed at the time the Aim N Flame was manufactured. Several of the experts averred that Scripto was aware of the desirability of a child-safety device because it knew children could operate the Aim N Flame. Further, according to these experts, Scripto owned the technology to make the Aim N Flame child resistant in 1994 and 1995.

With respect to the cost of an alternative design, Kvlseth noted that the Consumer Product Safety Commission, the regulatory body for lighters, in a proposed rule dated September 30, 1998, estimated the increased cost of adding a safety device to the lighter would be $0.40 per unit. However, it was Kvlseth's opinion that, had the feature been incorporated into the original design, the cost would have been negligible.

Calles also offered evidence of the dangerousness of lighters in the hands of children and Scripto's awareness of such dangers. She introduced into evidence statistics showing the number of previous fires started by children with lighters (both utility and cigarette), the number of deaths and injuries that had occurred each year as a result of fires started by children, and the reduction in cost to society that would be derived from the addition of child-resistant safety devices on the lighters. Calles further pointed to Scripto's answers to interrogatories, in which Scripto admitted they had been named as defendants in 25 lawsuits filed between 1996 and 2000 for injuries that occurred between 1992 and 1999 under circumstances similar to this case.

The trial court granted summary judgment in favor of Scripto . . .

On appeal, the appellate court affirmed in part and reversed in part. With respect to strict liability, the appellate court held that the Aim N Flame "does not qualify as the kind of especially simple device for which the result of the risk-utility balancing is too obvious for trial." Accordingly, the appellate court reversed the trial court's grant of summary judgment in favor of Scripto . . .

In *Suvada v. White Motor Co.,* 32 Ill.2d 612, 622-23, 210 N.E.2d 182 (1965), this court adopted the strict liability doctrine set forth in section 402A of the Second Restatement of Torts . . . The test outlined in section 402A for determining whether a product is "unreasonably dangerous" is known as the consumer-expectation or consumer-contemplation test. This test provides that a product is "unreasonably dangerous" when it is "dangerous to an extent beyond that which would be contemplated by the ordinary consumer who purchases it, with the ordinary knowledge common to the community as to its characteristics." RESTATEMENT (SECOND) OF TORTS § 402A, Comment *i,* at 352 (1965).

Under the consumer-expectation test, a plaintiff must establish what an ordinary consumer purchasing the product would expect about the product and its safety. This is an objective standard based on the average, normal, or ordinary expectations of the reasonable person; it is not dependent upon the subjective expectation of a particular consumer or user.

The consumer-expectation test was originally applied to manufacturing defects, but soon came to be applied to design-defect issues as well. Over time, the applicability of the consumer-expectation test to design-defect cases was questioned, primarily because it became apparent that consumers might not be aware of what to expect regarding the safety of certain products. *See Barker v. Lull Engineering Co.,* 20 Cal. 3d 413, 427-28 (1978). Accordingly, this court in *Lamkin v. Towner,* 138 Ill. 2d 510, 528 (1990), adopted a second, alternative test for design defect cases known as the risk-utility, or risk-benefit, test. *See Blue v. Environmental Engineering, Inc.,* 215 Ill.2d 78, 91 (2005) (noting this court "understood the problem[s associated with application of the consumer-expectation test to design-defect cases] and recognized a second, alternative test").

In *Lamkin,* this court held that a plaintiff may demonstrate a product has been defectively designed "in one of two ways." One way a plaintiff may demonstrate a design defect is to present evidence that the product fails to satisfy the consumer-expectation test. Alternatively, a plaintiff may demonstrate a design defect by presenting evidence that the risk of danger inherent in the challenged design outweighs the benefits of such design. *Lamkin,* 138 Ill. 2d at 529.

The rationale for employing two tests was explained in *Barker.* There, the court noted that "at a minimum a product must meet ordinary consumer expectations as to safety to avoid being found defective." (Emphases omitted.) *Barker,* 20 Cal. 3d at 426 n. 7. However, "the expectations of the ordinary consumer cannot be viewed as the exclusive yardstick for evaluating design defectiveness because '[i]n many situations . . . the consumer would not know what to expect, because he would have no idea how safe the product could be made.' [Citation.]" *Barker,* 20 Cal.3d at 430. Thus, even if a product satisfies ordinary consumer expectations, "if through hindsight the jury determines that the product's design embodies 'excessive preventable danger,' or, in other words, if the jury finds that the risk of danger inherent in the challenged design outweighs the benefits of such design," a product may be found defective in design. *Barker,* 20 Cal. 3d at 430. *See also Soule v. General Motors Corp.,* 8 Cal. 4th 548, 567, 882 P.2d 298, 308, 34 Cal. Rptr. 2d 607, 617 (1994) (refining *Barker* test and holding that the "consumer expectations test is reserved for cases in which the everyday experience of the product's users permits a conclusion that the product's design violated minimum safety assumptions," (emphases omitted) but that "the risks and benefits of a challenged design must be carefully balanced whenever the issue of design defect goes beyond the common experience of the product's users").

Since *Lamkin,* this court has continued to employ these two tests when determining whether a product is unreasonably dangerous. We now turn to them . . .

As noted above, under the consumer-expectation test, a plaintiff may prevail if he or she demonstrates that the product failed to perform as an ordinary consumer would expect when used in an intended or reasonably foreseeable manner. In the case at bar, there is a threshold question. Whose expectations control, *i.e.,* the adult purchaser or the child user? Calles argues we must apply the consumer-expectation test from the point of view of a child. We disagree.

For purposes of the consumer-expectation test, "ordinary" modifies consumer. Ordinary means "[r]egular; usual; normal; common." BLACK'S LAW DICTIONARY 989 (5th ed.1979). See also 1 MADDEN & OWEN ON PRODUCTS LIABILITY §8:3, at 71 (Supp.2006) (ordinary consumer "applies to the customary or usual consumer of the product"). Several courts in other jurisdictions have held that the "ordinary consumer" of a lighter is an adult, not a child. In light of these cases, we hold that the ordinary consumer of a lighter, such as the Aim N Flame here, is an adult-the typical user and purchaser. Therefore, the expectations regarding the Aim N Flame's use and safety must be viewed from the point of view of the adult consumer.

We now consider whether the Aim N Flame meets the consumer-expectation test. The purpose of a lighter, such as the Aim N Flame, is to produce a flame. Clearly then, the ordinary consumer would expect that, when the trigger is pulled, a flame would be produced. Here, the Aim N Flame was not used in its intended manner, *i.e.,* by an adult. Thus, the question is whether it was used in a reasonably foreseeable manner. We find that it was.

An ordinary consumer would expect that a child could obtain possession of the Aim N Flame and attempt to use it. Thus, a child is a reasonably foreseeable user. Likewise, an ordinary consumer would appreciate the consequences that would naturally flow when a child obtains possession of a lighter. Specifically, an ordinary consumer would expect that the Aim N Flame, in the hands of a child, could cause the result that occurred here-the starting of a fire that led to injury to a child.

Under the facts of this case, the Aim N Flame performed as an ordinary consumer would expect-it produced a flame when used in a reasonably foreseeable manner, *i.e.,* by a child. This leads to the inescapable conclusion that the ordinary consumer's expectations were fulfilled. In other words, the Aim N Flame did not fail to perform as an ordinary consumer would expect when used in a reasonably foreseeable manner. Thus, as a matter of law, no fact finder could conclude that the Aim N Flame was unreasonably dangerous under the consumer-expectation test. Therefore, Calles cannot prevail under this theory.

This does not end our analysis however. Though the Aim N Flame satisfies the consumer-expectation test, it may, nonetheless, be deemed unreasonably dangerous under the risk-utility test.

Under the risk-utility test, a plaintiff may prevail in a strict liability design-defect case if he or she demonstrates that the magnitude of the danger outweighs the utility of the product, as designed. *Lamkin,* 138 Ill.2d at 529. Stated differently, "[t]he utility of the design must therefore be weighed against the risk of harm created" and "[i]f the likelihood and gravity of the harm outweigh the benefits and utilities of the product, the product is unreasonably dangerous." 63A Am.Jur.2d *Products Liability* § 978, at 146-47 (1997).

Relying on *Scoby v. Vulcan-Hart Corp.,* 211 Ill.App.3d 106 (1991), Scripto argues there is a "simple product" exception to the application of the risk-utility test. In other words, Scripto contends that, when a product is deemed "simple," the risk-utility test need not be employed. We disagree.

In *Scoby,* an individual was injured while working in a restaurant kitchen when he slipped and fell and his arm became submerged in hot oil contained in an open deep-fat fryer. The plaintiff sued the fryer manufacturer, alleging a design defect, and argued for liability under the risk-utility test. Relying on *Lamkin,* the manufacturer argued that, because the danger at issue was not "excessive," the risk-utility test should not be utilized.

The *Scoby* court agreed with the defendant. Noting that hot oil in a fryer was an open and obvious danger and that, for efficient kitchen operation, it was often necessary to keep a lid off the fryer, the *Scoby* court concluded:

> "We do not deem that *Lamkin* or other cases applying aspects of the danger-utility test intend that all manufacturers . . . should be subject to liability depending upon a trier of fact's balancing under that test . . . Somewhere, a line must be drawn beyond which the danger-utility test cannot be applied. Considering not only the obvious nature of any danger here but, also, the simple nature of the mechanism involved, we conclude the circuit court properly applied only the consumer-user contemplation test." *Scoby,* 211 Ill.App.3d at 112.

In support of their position that summary judgment was properly granted in their favor, Scripto also cites to *Todd v. Societe Bic, S.A.,* 21 F.3d 1402 (7th Cir. 1994), wherein the court applied the *Scoby* exception to facts very similar to those in the case at bar. In *Todd,* a two-year-old child died when a four-year-old child used a Bic lighter to start a fire in the two-year-old's bedroom. The plaintiff filed a strict liability design-defect claim against the manufacturer, alleging the lighter was unreasonably dangerous because it did not contain a child-resistant safety device. The district court granted summary judgment in favor of the manufacturer and the plaintiff appealed. The Seventh Circuit Court of Appeals affirmed, concluding that the lighter was not unreasonably dangerous under the consumer-expectation test because it performed exactly as a consumer would expect-it produced a flame when activated.

The *Todd* court then observed that this court had adopted a second test in strict liability design-defect cases, the risk-utility test. The court also observed, however, that in *Scoby,* a simple-product exception to application of this test had been adopted. Noting that this court had not yet addressed the *Scoby* exception, the *Todd* court opined that this court "would not apply the risk-utility test to simple but obviously dangerous products." *Todd,* 21 F.3d at 1412. The *Todd* court then concluded the lighter was a simple product and, for that reason, the risk-utility test was not applicable . . .

Upon close examination of *Scoby,* we find that it uses "simple" and "open and obvious" as separate components. However, in our view, the dangers associated with a product that is deemed "simple" are, by their very nature, open and obvious. We conclude, then, that *Scoby's* adoption of a "simple product" exception is nothing more than the adoption of a general rule that a manufacturer will not be liable for open and obvious dangers.

A majority of courts have rejected the notion that the open and obvious danger of a product is an absolute defense to a defective-design claim in strict liability. We, too, recognized this principle in *Blue,* when this court stated:

> "In strict products liability cases, the open and obvious nature of the risk is just one factor to be considered in the range of considerations required by the risk-utility test, and it will only serve to bar the liability of the manufacturer where it outweighs all other factors to be considered in weighing the inherent design risks against the utility of the product as manufactured." *Blue,* 215 Ill. 2d at 103.

. . . As one case has held, the obviousness of a risk inherent in a product, *simple or nonsimple,* does not by itself obviate a manufacturer's liability. *Cacevic v. Simplimatic Engineering Co.*, 241 Mich. App. 717, 725 (2000).

Policy reasons also support rejection of a *per se* rule excepting simple products with open and obvious dangers from analysis under the risk-utility test. Adoption of such a rule would essentially absolve manufacturers from liability in certain situations even though there may be a reasonable and feasible alternative design available that would make a product safer, but which the manufacturer declines to incorporate because it knows it will not be held liable. This would discourage product improvements that could easily and cost-effectively alleviate the dangers of a product. A *per se* rule would also frustrate the policy of preventing future harm which is at the heart of strict liability law. See 1 MADDEN & OWENS ON PRODUCT LIABILITY § 8:3, at 447 (noting that the consumer-expectation test limited by the open and obvious doctrine "perniciously rewards manufacturers for failing to adopt cost-effective measures to remedy obviously unnecessary dangers to human life and limb").

Accordingly, we hold that the open and obvious danger of a product does not create a *per se* bar to a manufacturer's liability, nor does it preclude application of the risk-utility test. Rather, the open and obvious nature of a danger is one factor that may be weighed in the risk-utility test. We reject *Scoby's* adoption of a *per se* rule excepting simple products with open and obvious dangers from analysis under the risk-utility test. Accordingly, we reject Scripto's assertion that only the consumer-expectation test applies here. We now consider whether Calles presented sufficient evidence under the risk-utility test to withstand summary judgment.

Under the risk-utility test, a court may take into consideration numerous factors. In past decisions, this court has held that a plaintiff may prove a design defect by presenting evidence of "the availability and feasability of alternate designs at the time of its manufacture, or that the design used did not conform with the design standards of the industry, design guidelines provided by an authoritative voluntary association, or design criteria set by legislation or governmental regulation." *Anderson v. Hyster Co.*, 74 Ill.2d 364, 368 (1979). . .

John W. Wade, dean and professor of law, emeritus, Vanderbilt University School of Law, has also identified several factors relevant when engaging in risk-utility analysis. These factors include:

"(1) The usefulness and desirability of the product-its utility to the user and to the public as a whole.

(2) The safety aspects of the product-the likelihood that it will cause injury, and the probable seriousness of the injury.

(3) The availability of a substitute product which would meet the same need and not be as unsafe.

(4) The manufacturer's ability to eliminate the unsafe character of the product without impairing its usefulness or making it too expensive to maintain its utility.

(5) The user's ability to avoid danger by the exercise of care in the use of the product.

(6) The user's anticipated awareness of the dangers inherent in the product and their availability, because of general public knowledge of the obvious condition of the product, or of the existence of suitable warnings or instructions.

(7) The feasibility, on the part of the manufacturer, of spreading the loss by setting the price of the product or carrying liability insurance."

J. Wade, *On The Nature of Strict Tort Liability for Products,* 44 MISS. L.J. 825, 837-38 (1973).

Wade's factors have been adopted and relied upon by numerous jurisdictions, including our own appellate court.

Lastly, we find that when assessing the utility of a product, the following factors may also be relevant: "(1) the appearance and aesthetic attractiveness of the product; (2) its utility for multiple uses; (3) the convenience and extent of its use, especially in light of the period of time it could be used without harm resulting from the product; and (4) the collateral safety of a feature other than the one that harmed the plaintiff." AMERICAN LAW OF PRODUCTS LIABILITY 3D § 28:19, at 28-30 through 28-31 (1997).

Although we have listed a number of factors which courts may consider when assessing risk-utility, we do not mean to imply that the list is exclusive. The factors cited merely illustrate those that may assist a court and jury in evaluating whether a design is unreasonably dangerous. A plaintiff need not present proof on each of the factors. In the first instance, the court must balance factors it finds relevant to determine if the case is a proper one to submit to the jury. Once this threshold determination has been met, it is up to the fact finder to determine the importance of any particular factor, and its "relevance, and the relevance of other factors, will vary from case to case." *See* RESTATEMENT (THIRD) OF TORTS: PRODUCTS LIABILITY §2, Comment *f*, at 23 (1998). We now apply those factors identified above to the evidence presented in the case at bar.

After reviewing the evidence presented, we find the only factor which favors Calles and a finding of unreasonably dangerous is the second Wade factor-safety aspects. Calles presented specific and detailed evidence as to the likelihood of injury and the seriousness of injury from lighters which do not have child-safety devices.

Factors which would favor *Scripto* and a finding that the product is not unreasonably dangerous are the first and sixth Wade factors-the utility of the Aim N Flame and the user's awareness of the dangers. As to the utility of the Aim N Flame, it is both useful and desirable to society as a whole-it serves as an inexpensive alternative source of fire. Moreover, compared to other sources of fire, such as matches, it is more convenient and longer lasting since it is a multiuse product. The lighter may also be safer since it will extinguish if dropped on the floor while lit, unlike a match. With respect to the user's awareness of the dangers, there is no question, based on Calles' deposition testimony, that it was obvious to her that the lighter could come into the hands of a child and the dangers and risks that situation would pose.

In connection with the remaining relevant factors, we find that these neither weigh for nor against a finding of unreasonably dangerous. Calles claims that a substitute product was available, but the only evidence she relies upon is the fact Bic introduced a child-resistant utility lighter in March 1998, the very same month of the incident here. This is insufficient to demonstrate that a substitute product was available at the time of the manufacture of the Aim N Flame.

Calles offered expert affidavits regarding the availability and feasibility of an alternative design, including product impairment and cost factors, along with industry standards. Each expert opined, in a conclusory fashion, that a feasible alternative design existed. Kvlseth identified three alternative designs.

Scripto argues that, although Kvlseth set forth these alternative designs, he failed to give a basis for his feasability determination, nor did he show that these alternative designs met regulatory standards. In this regard, Scripto notes that the Consumer Product Safety Commission (CPSC), the regulatory body for these products, required safety devices on cigarette lighters beginning in 1994, but exempted utility lighters. It was not until 1999 that CPSC required safety devices on utility lighters. CPSC exempted utility lighters because it was concerned about "flashbacks" (the build up of gas and resultant sudden flash when a lighter was not ignited properly). Specifically, CPSC feared that if a child-resistant device on a utility lighter needed to be reset between attempts, this could cause a delay in ignition, resulting in the increased risk of flashback. Scripto maintains that this concern shows that some of the child-resistant options proffered by Kvlseth in his affidavit were not, in fact, feasible. Scripto also disputes Calles' claim that there would be no impairment to the Aim N Flame from modification with a child-resistant safety device since she cites no evidence in support of her argument.

With respect to the cost feasability, Calles offered evidence through Kvlseth's affidavit. According to Kvlseth,

> "the CPSC [Consumer Product Safety Commission] in the Proposed Rule dated September 20, 1998, has estimated that the rule will likely increase the cost of manufacturing utility lighters by about $0.40 per unit. The defendants have indicated that such a cost increase would only be a few cents per lighter. However, had a utility lighter . . . been originally designed to be effectively child resistant, . . . then the incremental cost due to an effective child-resistancy feature would have been negligible."

. . . Lastly, with respect to the user's ability to avoid the danger, Calles testified she put the Aim N Flames on the top shelf of her kitchen cabinet. However, she also acknowledged she could have left them on the counter. As Scripto maintains, the appellate court embraced the former testimony, despite contradictory evidence. This is a factual determination we cannot make.

Based on a review of the foregoing factors, reasonable persons could differ on the weight to be given the relevant factors, particularly where additional proofs are necessary, and thus could differ on whether the risks of the Aim N Flame outweigh its utility. Therefore, reasonable persons could differ as to whether the Aim N Flame is unreasonably dangerous, and we cannot say that Scripto was entitled to judgment as a matter of law . . .

We find there is no *per se* rule excepting application of the risk-utility test where a product is deemed simple and its dangers are open and obvious. We also find that there are material questions of law and fact that preclude us from finding, as a matter of law, that the Aim N Flame was not unreasonably dangerous under the risk-utility test . . . [APPELLATE COURT JUDGMENT AFFIRMED.]

JUSTICE KARMEIER, specially concurring:

. . . I disagree with the reasoning behind the majority's rejection of the simple-product exception. I would hold that whatever its merits, the exception has no application in this case because the Aim N Flame lighter is not a simple product. Consequently, the majority properly evaluates the plaintiff's claim under the risk-utility test . . .

The majority concludes that while *Scoby* used "simple" and "open and obvious" as separate components, the dangers associated with a "simple" product are, by their very nature, open and obvious. Consequently, the majority concludes that the simple-product exception set forth in *Scoby* is nothing more than the adoption of a general rule that a manufacturer will not be liable for open and obvious dangers, a position this court rejected in *Blue v. Environmental Engineering*, 215 Ill. 2d 78, 103 (2005).

I am not persuaded by the majority's reasoning. As the majority acknowledges, the *Scoby* court treated simplicity of the product and the openness and obviousness of the danger as separate elements. As envisioned by *Scoby,* the simple-product exception applies only when the product is simple *and* the dangers are open and obvious. In other words, under the simple-product exception, the openness and obviousness of a product's dangers will not *per se* preclude liability *unless the product is also a simple one.* The majority's view that the simple-product exception is nothing more than a general rule that a manufacturer will not be liable for open and obvious dangers essentially reads the "simple" component out of the simple-product exception. Consequently, the majority rejects the simple-product exception without ever addressing its merits.

Although I disagree with the majority's rejection of the simple-product exception, I would hold that it does not preclude application of the risk-utility test in this case because the Aim N Flame is not a simple product. Applying that test, I agree with the majority that there was sufficient evidence to raise a genuine material issue of fact with respect to the question of whether a feasible alternative design was available. Consequently, summary judgment on the strict liability count was improper . . .

NOTES

1. *Simple vs. Complex Products and Consumer Expectations.* Recall that in *Soule v. General Motors Corp.*, 882 P.2d 298, 310 (Cal. 1994), discussed above, the court held that a "consumer expectations" instruction should not be given in a complex design case, noting that:

> An ordinary consumer of automobiles cannot reasonably expect that a car's frame, suspension, or interior will be designed to remain intact in any and all accidents. Nor would ordinary experience and understanding inform such a consumer how safely an automobile's design should perform under the esoteric circumstances of the collision at issue here. Indeed, both parties assumed that quite complicated design considerations were at issue, and that expert testimony was necessary to illuminate these matters.

Is the simple-complex product dichotomy raised in *Calles* of the same type? Does it go to the same issue?

2. *Obviousness and Risk-Utility.* In *Sperry-New Holland, a Div. of Sperry Corp. v. Prestage*, 617 So. 2d 248 (Miss. 1993), an agricultural worker was pulled into the discharge auger of a combine harvester when his un-tucked jersey became entangled on a bolt as he was climbing over the back of the combine trying to unclog a tank. The jury decided in his favor after the judge had instructed on risk-utility. The defendant appealed arguing that a consumer expectations instruction should have been given, but the court affirmed. The case is noteworthy because, typically, defendants will prefer a risk-utility instruction compared to consumer expectations. The likely explanation is that the defendant considered that the consumer expectations test would be more "friendly" to their argument that the plaintiff had encountered and open and obvious risk. *Calles* appears to confirm that reading. Once risk-utility is instructed upon, defendant's obvious risk argument becomes less compelling because, as recognized in both *Sperry-New Holland* and *Calles*, that characteristic of the product is simply one factor to consider in applying the risk-utility test.

3. *Design and Warning Contrasted.* In the design context, it is widely held that an obvious danger does not make a product reasonably safe. Obviousness is "only a factor to be considered" on the issues of defective design and "whether plaintiff used that degree of reasonable care required by the circumstances." *Auburn Machine Works v. Jones*, 366 So. 2d 1167, 1169 (Fla. 1979). However, in warning cases most courts state that there is no duty to warn of an obvious risk within the common knowledge of the user. As you read the following case consider what rationale exists for this distinction.

KLEN v. ASAHI POOL, INC.
643 N.E.2d 1360 (Ill. App. 1994)

GORDON, JUSTICE.

Plaintiff's products liability action was brought against the Defendants as sellers and manufacturers of a swimming pool (Asahi), a swimming pool liner (Doughboy), and a trampoline (Andy's Sales). The Plaintiff was injured when he dove from the trampoline into an above-ground swimming pool and was rendered a quadriplegic. The Plaintiff alleged that the Defendants were liable to him for their failure to warn of the risk of permanent neurological injury presented by their products' intended and foreseeable uses and that the lack of warnings was the proximate cause of his injury.

The facts derived from the pleadings, affidavits and depositions of the parties are not in dispute. At the time of Plaintiff's injury, the trampoline had been placed adjacent to the swimming pool by the owners of the pool and trampoline, the Monroes, who were the Plaintiff's neighbors. The Plaintiff was 14 years old, although he was to turn fifteen in three days. The Plaintiff arrived at the Monroe's house accompanied by several teenage friends. He swam in the pool for approximately 15 to 30 minutes. He stood in and walked around the perimeter of the pool and knew the water was chest deep. He knew that the sides of the pool were approximately four feet high.

At some point, the individuals at the Monroe's house began using the trampoline as a springboard for diving into the pool. John Monroe bounced on the trampoline and did a somersault dive from the trampoline into the pool. Some of the Plaintiff's friends dove head first from the trampoline into the pool and instructed the Plaintiff as to how to do the same. After watching John Monroe and his friends bounce on the trampoline and dive into the pool, Plaintiff got on the trampoline and began bouncing. As he had been instructed by the others to do, he bounced three times on the trampoline and propelled himself head first into the pool. Plaintiff hit the bottom of the pool and suffered permanent neurological injury. There is no dispute that the Plaintiff was attempting a "shallow" or surface dive not a vertical dive.

Plaintiff had taken swimming and diving lessons with the Lockport Park District for seven years, beginning in second grade. He had learned to swim and dive into both deep and shallow water. He learned the difference between deep and shallow dives and learned that certain dives would be appropriate in deep water but not shallow water. Plaintiff had experience in swimming in other above-ground pools that were approximately the same size, shape and depth as the Monroes' pool; and he had experience in using a small exercise trampoline.

Plaintiff stated that he understood that it was possible to dive into shallow water without injury by executing a flat, racing type dive that others had performed safely on the night he was injured. He believed the dive he was attempting was safe.

Upon the foregoing facts, the Defendants moved for summary judgment. The trial court granted summary judgment to Doughboy, the pool liner manufacturer, and to Andy's Sales, the trampoline manufacturer, holding that those products were "conditions" and not "causes" of Plaintiff's injuries. The court denied summary judgment to Asahi, the pool manufacturer, holding that whether the risk of quadriplegia is open and obvious to a 14 year old is a question of fact to be resolved by the jury . . .

A duty to warn of an unreasonably dangerous condition extends to the use of the product by an ordinary person with the ordinary knowledge common to the community regarding the characteristics of the product. The duty to warn is determined using an objective standard, i.e., the awareness of an ordinary person, and is normally a question of law, although when the record is in dispute, it becomes a question of fact.

The duty to warn analysis, which is an objective one, should focus on the typical user's perception and knowledge. The plaintiff's subjective knowledge is immaterial to the antecedent determination of an open and obvious danger. The plaintiff's knowledge is relevant to the issue of proximate cause; that is, whether the defendant's failure to warn was the legal or proximate cause of the plaintiff's injury; and to the issue of assumption of risk.

Several Illinois cases have decided the duty to warn issue with reference to the plaintiffs' subjective knowledge finding no duty to warn where the reason for warning, which is to apprise a party of a danger of which he has no knowledge, is lacking. To the extent that there is a reliance on the plaintiff's knowledge for purposes of determining a duty to warn, we would disagree with these cases since the plaintiff's personal awareness of the risk is irrelevant to the determination of whether a danger is open and obvious as a matter of common knowledge and perception . . .

Applying the ordinary person standard, courts have held that there was no duty to warn of the open and obvious risk of installing a metal tower and antenna in close proximity to electrical wires; slipping on wet flooring while wearing shoes; slipping on ice buildup inside a refrigeration truck; riding a motorcycle; tripping over a vacuum cleaner cord; and not being able to see behind an opaque ventilation curtain. Since the risk of injury was open and obvious as a matter of common knowledge and perception, the products in these cases could not be deemed unreasonably dangerous or defective so as to establish a duty to warn or resultant breach of that duty. *See Smith v. American Motors Sales, Corp.* (1991), 215 Ill.App.3d 951.

A question of fact was found to exist as to the obviousness of the danger of consuming cleaning fluid in *Jonescue v. Jewel Home Shopping Service* (1973), 16 Ill. App. 3d 339. In *Jonescue*, the plaintiff sought recovery under theories of strict liability and negligence based on the manufacturer's failure to warn against ingestment of the cleaning product. The court found that the manufacturer could be liable for an unintended but reasonably foreseen use of the product where there was no adequate warning given as to its dangerous propensities. The court stated:

> "When a danger is fully obvious and generally appreciated, nothing of value is added by a warning. Thus, there is no duty to warn against patent dangers . . .

> On the other hand, there is some evidence from which a jury could infer that users of the Jetco cleaner might not recognize illness or injury to the extent of that suffered by [the plaintiff] as an obvious consequence of ingesting the cleaner. . . .

> The more serious the consequences resulting from the foreseeable but unintended use of a product such as the Jetco cleaner involved here, the less expected and hence the less obvious those consequences would appear to the user." 16 Ill. App. 3d at 345-47.

See also Fuller v. Fend-All Co. (1979), 70 Ill. App. 3d 634 (obviousness of dangers associated with safety glasses without side shields was disputable such that defendant's duty to warn could not be decided as a matter of law).

In the instant case, the trial court denied summary judgment to Asahi, the manufacturer of the pool, holding that a question of fact existed as to whether the risk of quadriplegia was open and obvious to a 14 year old and "whether or not a 14 year old is chargeable with knowledge of circumstances that people who are adults who have experience would be chargeable." Asahi argues that the trial court erred in applying a subjective standard to the duty to warn. Defendant Asahi and one of the amicus briefs filed in the instant appeal argue that the issue of whether an open and obvious danger exists should be decided using an adult standard of reasonableness. They argue that, although distinctions have been made in the context of premises liability cases with respect to whether a danger is open and obvious to children, those cases are irrelevant to products liability cases. Asahi further argues that the trial court erred in suggesting that a subjective standard, based upon the plaintiff's own knowledge, be applied to determine whether the risk was open and obvious to him.

We do not agree with Asahi's contention that the trial court in the instant case applied a subjective standard, based on the plaintiff's knowledge, to the question of whether the danger of diving into an above-ground pool was open and obvious. While, it does appear that the trial court distinguished the obviousness of the danger to an adult from the obviousness of the same danger to a fourteen-year-old, this distinction did not change the standard from an objective one to a subjective one. Rather, the standard remained an objective one, but the reasonable person standard was that of a reasonable child of fourteen years of age rather than a reasonable adult . . .

Having determined that an objective fourteen-year-old standard of reason-ableness should be applied to the instant case, the question now becomes whether, in accordance with that standard, the risk of paraplegia from per-forming shallow dives, also known as flat or surface dives, into an above-ground pool, having a depth of about four feet, was open and obvious as a matter of law. If it was, defendant Asahi would have been entitled to summary judgment . . .

The plaintiff in the instant case argues that the pleadings, affidavits, and depositions submitted establish a question of fact as to the whether the risk of injury when performing "shallow" dives, that is, flat or surface dives, into an above-ground swimming pool is obvious to the reasonable fourteen-year-old. Moreover, the Plaintiff contends that there is a general belief that dives into shallow water are appropriate and safe. The plaintiff cites to a survey pur-ported to have been done by a defense expert, which indicates that nearly half of those surveyed were unaware of the possibility of permanent neurological injury from diving and to evidence from Plaintiff's expert that hundreds of thousands of Americans dive into shallow water while not appreciating the extreme danger and believing that such dives are safe and appropriate. The Plaintiff argues that the deposition testimony from several occurrence wit-nesses, which included other children and the adult hosts and adult guests, shows that the risk of permanent neurological injury from diving into an above-ground pool was not open and obvious to them. Finally, the plaintiff cites to his own lack of knowledge regarding the risk of permanent neurological injury; however, as stated above, the duty to warn is determined objectively with reference to the ordinary person's common knowledge.

No Illinois products liability case has held that the danger of executing a shallow dive into a shallow pool is open and obvious as a matter of law. A conclusion against a finding of obvious danger was impliedly reached in *Erickson v. Muskin Corp.* (1989), 180 Ill. App. 3d 117, when the manufacturer of the pool was held liable for a failure to warn of the dangers of diving into it. In Erickson, the jury was asked to answer a special interrogatory and, using an objective, reasonable person standard, found that the above-ground swim-ming pool in that case was unreasonably dangerous because it lacked a warn-ing regarding the dangers of diving into it. The issue on appeal in *Erickson* was whether the defendant swimming pool manufacturer could raise the adult plaintiff's assumption of risk as an affirmative defense, and the court held that it could . . .

In a negligent failure to warn case decided by another jurisdiction, the dan-ger of serious spinal cord injury from executing a flat dive into the shallow water of an above-ground pool was held not to be open and obvious to a reason-able adult as a matter of law. In *Corbin v. Coleco Industries, Inc.* (7th Cir. 1984), 748 F.2d 411, a case which involved a 27-year-old adult and which was decided under Indiana law, the court stated:

> The crucial point made in this testimony is that even though people are generally aware of the danger of diving into shallow water, they believe that there is a safe way to do it, namely, by executing a flat, shallow dive. If people do in fact generally hold such a belief, then it cannot be said, as a matter of law, that the risk of spinal injury from

diving into shallow water is open and obvious. Whether a danger is open and obvious depends not just on what people can see with their eyes but also on what they know and believe about what they see. In particular, if people generally believe that there is a danger associated with the use of a product, but that there is a safe way to use it, any danger there may be in using the product in the way generally believed to be safe is not open and obvious."

748 F.2d at 417-18.

To the extent *Corbin* finds that the danger of executing a flat or "shallow" dive by an adult is not open and obvious, we do not reach that conclusion here nor do we necessarily agree that it would not be open and obvious to an adult. (*See Dowen v. Hall* (1989), 191 Ill. App. 3d 903.) We do believe, however, that the reasoning in *Corbin* does have application with respect to minors and is in accord with our court's treatment of minors in *Schellenberg* and *Leonard*.

For similar reasons we distinguish *Glittenberg v. Doughboy Recreational Industries* (1992), 441 Mich. 379, a case relied upon by Defendant Asahi and in one of the amicus briefs. *Glittenberg* also dealt with adult plaintiffs, and the four-justice majority in that case held as a matter of law that there was no duty upon the manufacturer to warn of the dangers of diving into shallow swimming pools since the danger of injury was "readily apparent or easily discoverable upon casual inspection by the average user of ordinary intelligence." (441 Mich. at 395.) Moreover, we note that there is a strong dissent in that case which states:

> A reasonable person, viewing the plaintiffs' evidence as a whole, could conclude that a significant number of catastrophic injuries occur, that the swimming pool industry has been aware of the potential for such injuries for a number of years and in many instances provided warnings with the product, and that the likely consuming public does not appreciate either the general risk of diving in shallow water in an above-ground swimming pool or the specific risk of quadriplegic injury occurring during a shallow dive assumed by the uninformed diver to be safe . . .

> Performance of a shallow dive, while it is evidence that the diver recognizes a need to modify his actions in response to a perceived danger, is also evidence that divers incorrectly perceive that execution of a shallow dive is sufficient protection from the danger presented by diving in a shallow above-ground swimming pool.

Glittenberg, 441 Mich. at 415-16 (Levin, J. dissenting).

Based upon the pleadings, affidavits, and evidence submitted by the parties in the case at bar, and based upon the cases they have cited to support their respective positions, it is by no means evident that, as a matter of law, the dangers of "shallow" or surface diving into a shallow pool are open and obvious to minors . . .

It would further seem that, having made the determination that the risk of executing "shallow" or surface dives is not open and obvious to minors as a matter of law, the jury could then be asked to redetermine this question as an issue of fact. In addition, the defense is not precluded from raising the subjective awareness of the plaintiff as a question of fact with respect to assumption of risk (*Erickson v. Muskin Corp*. (1989), 180 Ill. App. 3d 117 (jury applied subjective standard, what the plaintiff actually knew, to issue of assumption of risk)) and proximate cause.

For the foregoing reasons, the denial of summary judgment to Defendant Asahi is affirmed; the grant of summary judgment to Defendant Doughboy is reversed; the grant of summary judgment to Andy's Sales is affirmed and the cause is remanded for further proceedings.

NOTES

1. *Judge or Jury?* According to REST. 3D TORTS § 2 cmt. *j*:

> In general, a product seller is not subject to liability for failing to warn or instruct regarding risks and risk-avoidance measures that should be obvious to, or generally known by, foreseeable product users. When a risk is obvious or generally known, the prospective addressee of a warning will or should already know of its existence. Warning of an obvious or generally known risk in most instances will not provide an effective additional measure of safety. Furthermore, warnings that deal with obvious or generally known risks may be ignored by users and consumers and may diminish the significance of warnings about non-obvious, not-generally-known risks. Thus, requiring warnings of obvious or generally known risks could reduce the efficacy of warnings generally. When reasonable minds may differ as to whether the risk was obvious or generally known, the issue is to be decided by the trier of fact.

Cf. Glittenberg v. Doughboy Recreational Industries, 491 N.W.2d 208, 217 (Mich. 1992), where the court observed:

> [W]hen a defendant claims that it owes no duty to warn because of the obvious nature of a danger, a court is required, as a threshold matter, to decide that issue. The court must determine whether reasonable minds could differ with respect to whether the danger is open and obvious. If reasonable minds cannot differ on the 'obvious' character of the product-connected danger, the court determines the question as a matter of law. If, on the other hand, the court determines that reasonable minds could differ, the obviousness of risk must be determined by the jury. (note and citation omitted)

2. *Sophisticated Users*. Related to the issue of obvious risk and the "learned intermediary" rule in prescription drug cases is the so-called "sophisticated intermediary" defense. Here, a manufacturer supplies a product to an intermediary complete with warnings. The intermediary passes on the product but without warnings. According to *Natural Gas Odorizing v. Downs*, 685 N.E.2d 155, 163-64 (Ind. Ct. App. 1997) (citations omitted):

> The duty to warn stems from the view that a product manufacturer should have superior knowledge of its product. However, under the "sophisticated user" exception, there is no duty to warn when the dangers posed by the product are already known to the user. That

exception has been extended to limit the duty to warn the ultimate user when the product is sold to a "knowledgeable" or "sophisticated intermediary."

To determine whether a manufacturer has satisfied its duty to warn by relying upon a sophisticated intermediary, courts should consider the following factors:

> The likelihood or unlikelihood that harm will occur if the [intermediary] does not pass on the warning to the ultimate user, the trivial nature of the probable harm, the probability or improbability that the particular [intermediary] will not pass on the warning and the ease or burden of the giving of the warning by the manufacturer to the ultimate user.

Further, for the exception to apply, the intermediary must have knowledge or sophistication equal to that of the manufacturer or supplier, and the manufacturer must be able to rely reasonably on the intermediary to warn the ultimate consumer. Reliance is only reasonable if the intermediary knows or should know of the product's dangers. Actual or constructive knowledge may arise where either the supplier has provided an adequate explicit warning of such dangers or information of the product's dangers is available in the public domain. . . .

Whether a manufacturer has discharged its duty under the sophisticated intermediary doctrine is almost always a question for the trier of fact. The manufacturer's reliance on the intermediary's alleged sophistication may be more or less reasonable given the product's nature, complexity and associated dangers, the likelihood that the intermediary will communicate warnings to the ultimate consumer, the dangers posed to the ultimate consumer by an inadequate or nonexistent warning, and the feasibility of requiring the manufacturer to directly warn the product's ultimate consumers.

3. *Government Contractors.* Suppose the federal government specifies the design of a product for military or other government purposes and someone is injured as a result of that design and sues the manufacturer which complied with the government specifications. Can a state hold the manufacturer liable? The Supreme Court considered this issue in *Boyle v. United Technologies Corp.*, 487 U.S. 500 (1988). There, a Marine helicopter pilot was killed in a crash. His father sued the helicopter manufacturer that claimed it had complied with the government's specifications. In upholding the government contractor defense in a 5-4 decision, Justice Scalia stated:

> Liability for design defects in military equipment cannot be imposed, pursuant to state law, when (1) the United States approved reasonably precise specifications; (2) the equipment conformed to those specifications; and (3) the supplier warned the United States about the dangers in the use of the equipment that were known to the supplier but not to the United States. The first two of these conditions assure that the suit is within the area where the policy of the "discretionary function" would be frustrated, *i.e.,* they assure that the design feature in question was considered by a Government officer, and not merely by

the contractor itself. The third condition is necessary because, in its absence, the displacement of state tort law would create some incentive for the manufacturer to withhold knowledge of risks, since conveying that knowledge might disrupt the contract but withholding it would produce no liability. We adopt this provision lest our effort to protect discretionary functions perversely impede them by cutting off information highly relevant to the discretionary decision.

487 U.S. at 512-13.

4. *Reading and Heeding.* Restatement (Second) of Torts §402A comment j noted: "Where warning is given, the seller may reasonably assume that it will be read and heeded ... " In some jurisdictions this has given rise to two rules, one for cases in which plaintiff is alleging an absence of warning and one for cases in which plaintiff argues that a warning is inadequate. REST. 2D TORTS §402A, cmt *j*. As summarized by one court:

> [A] majority of jurisdictions recognize a rebuttable presumption that if a product comes with a warning, the user will read and heed the warning. When applied, the presumption operates to the benefit of the manufacturer where adequate warnings are provided because the manufacturer receives the benefit of the doubt that the warning provided is effective in alerting the user of the product's potential danger. Where no warning is given, the presumption operates in favor of the user by presuming the user would have read, understood, and heeded the warning. The practical effect of the presumption is to relieve a plaintiff of the burden of proving proximate cause.

Tuttle v. Lorillard Tobacco Co., 377 F.3d 917, 925 n.5 (8th Cir. 2004).

5. *Cause in Fact.* Several courts have puzzled over the appropriate response to cases in which plaintiff has been injured by a generic product manufactured (often several decades before) by many defendants. The issue has arisen in asbestos cases (*see, e.g., Black v. Abex Corp.*, 603 N.W.2d 182 (N.D. 1999)), but most controversially in cases involving the drug diethylstilbestrol (DES), a synthetic hormone prescribed as a miscarriage preventative in the 1950s and allegedly responsible for ovarian cancer in the daughters of the patients who were prescribed the drug. Almost 200 companies manufactured the drug, but by the time suits were brought by the "DES daughters" in the 1970s most of these companies had ceased to exist or had been absorbed into other entities. Faced with the apparent impossibility of a plaintiff daughter meeting her causation burden by identifying her mother's drug manufacturer, several jurisdictions endorsed novel approaches (*see, e.g., Collins v. Eli Lilly Co.*, 116 Wis. 2d 166 (1984); *Hymowitz v. Eli Lilly & Co.* 73 N.Y.2d 487 (1989)). The most famous was the so-called market-share liability introduced by the Supreme Court of California in *Sindell v. Abbott Laboratories*, 26 Cal. 3d 588 (1980). Loosely based on the alternative liability doctrine introduced in *Summers v. Tice*, 33 Cal. 2d 80 (1948), the market share approach requires plaintiff to join enough manufacturers to constitute a "substantial share" of the DES market. Thereafter the burden shifts to the defendants to prove that they were not the manufacturer. A manufacturer who fails that burden would be severally liable on the basis of its market share. However, most courts have rejected such novel theories and insisted that plaintiff bear the burden of identifying the supplier of the product alleged to have caused her injury. *See, e.g., Smith v. Eli Lilly & Co.,* 560 N.E.2d 324, 344-45 (Ill. 1990). The court stated:

> [T]he majority of plausible defendants have not been or cannot be brought before the court. Those who are present have the difficult burden of establishing their share of a market. The companies which cannot prove their share will be made to pay the unattributed portion of the damages, thus paying the damages which rightfully belong to companies which are insolvent, not amenable to suit in the jurisdiction or for some other reason are not before the court. *Sindell* justified its ruling in part on the belief that over the run of the cases a company's liability would approximate the harm it caused. However, this is a purely illusory assumption. . . .
>
> We have not in the past been hesitant to develop new tort concepts; however, in this instance we decline to do so because of the infirmities in the proposed theory. Furthermore, this is too great a deviation from a tort principle which we have found to serve a vital function in the law, causation in fact, especially when market share liability is a flawed concept and its application will likely be only to a narrow class of defendants.

Market share liability is discussed more generally in Chapter 6.

6. *Economic Loss.* According to REST. 3D TORTS § 21(a): "harm to persons or property includes economic loss if caused by harm to . . . the plaintiff's person." What would such a loss be? Consequential damages, such as loss of wages? Business losses?

What, however, if the loss is the cost of the product itself when it is destroyed or damaged in an accident (e.g., a vehicle's defective braking system causes accident that injures driver)? Or suppose the *only* loss is the product itself when a design defect leads to its failure (e.g., a defective braking system renders the vehicle un-drivable).

Section 21(c) includes in the definition of recoverable economic loss "the plaintiff's property other than the defective product itself." REST. 3D TORTS § 21 (c). The Third Restatement drafters explain the distinction on the basis that "[w]hen a product defect results in harm to the product itself, the law governing commercial transactions sets forth a comprehensive scheme governing the rights of the buyer and seller . . . " regarding repair or replacement costs and any consequential losses. *Id.* cmt. *d*. However, as the drafters note:

> A somewhat more difficult question is presented when the defect in the product renders it unreasonably dangerous, but the product does not cause harm to persons or property. In these situations the danger either (1) never eventuates in harm because the product defect is discovered before it causes harm, or (2) eventuates in harm to the product itself but not in harm to persons or other property. A plausible argument can be made that products that are dangerous, rather than merely ineffectual, should be governed by the rules governing products liability law. However, a majority of courts have concluded that the

remedies provided under the Uniform Commercial Code — repair and replacement costs and, in appropriate circumstances, consequential economic loss — are sufficient . . .

Id.

Applying this approach in *Clarys v. Ford Motor Co.*, 592 N.W.2d 573 (N.D. 1999), the Supreme Court of North Dakota denied products liability recovery when a van manufactured by the defendant ignited and burned in a parking lot. Why is it that courts allow both tort and breach of contract remedies (e.g., breach of the implied warranty of merchantability under UCC §2-314) in personal injury cases, yet deny torts claims for damage to the product?

PROBLEMS

10.1

An 11-year-old boy purchased a slingshot, manufactured by defendant and sold at retail for $1. The slingshot was packaged so as to appeal to children. The boy shot a pebble from the slingshot at a tree, and the pebble ricocheted, hitting plaintiff, a 12-year-old neighbor, in the eye and blinding that eye.

You have been appointed as counsel for the manufacturer of the slingshot. Can plaintiff recover from the manufacturer in products liability? What would be the likely causes of action? What argument could you make to defend against a claim that the slingshot was defectively designed? What would the plaintiff's burden be under the Restatement (Third) Torts? Assume further that the manufacturer's advertising stated that the slingshot was safe for children of all ages. What defenses would you use to counter the plaintiff's claims?

10.2

In *Denny v. Ford Motor Co.*, the court stated: "[I]t is apparent that the causes of action for strict products liability and breach [of] . . . warranty . . . are not identical . . . and that the latter is not necessarily subsumed by the former . . . "

UCC Article 2 recognizes three distinct types of warranties which have to do with the performance of the goods: (1) §2-313, Express Statements made by sellers that go to the "basis of the bargain;" (2) §2-314, The Implied Warranty of Merchantability that goods are fit for their ordinary purpose and are at least fair, average and have other reasonable performance standards; and (3) §2-315, The Implied Warranty of Fitness for a Particular Purpose that goods conform to the promise made by a seller that they will fulfill a particular purpose made known to the seller.

What would a plaintiff need to prove using UCC, §2-314? If the seller knows or has reason to know of a particular purpose, UCC, §2-315's fitness warranty applies. Why would a plaintiff choose to bring an action in warranty rather than tort, or vice versa? Is the implied warranty claim closer to strict liability or negligence?

10.3

Buyer purchased a small dog, together with a collar and leash, from Pet Shop. A week later, Buyer was walking the dog in the park when the dog saw Plaintiff some 50 feet away and lunged at her, breaking the dog collar. The dog, freed from the collar, ran to the plaintiff and bit her on her leg. Plaintiff contracted rabies as a result of the dog bite. Does the injured woman have a valid products liability claim against Pet Shop? Against the collar and leash manufacturer? How would the claim differ if brought under a consumer expectation test, risk-utility, or the Restatement (Third). What defenses would likely be raised to this products liability case?

10.4

Buzz Beater is a star baseball player at State University. Buzz wants to become a pro baseball player. Consequently, unlike his teammates, he does not use aluminum bats, which are legal in amateur baseball. He uses wooden bats, like the pros use. One day in batting practice, Buzz's bat, made by Wooden Bat Co. (WBC), shatters and a splinter blinds him in one eye. Analyze Buzz's design claims against WBC.

10.5

Imogene entered a restaurant and ordered a martini. After she had drunk the martini down in a couple of gulps, she upended the glass and bit down lustily on the olive that had been in the martini, and broke her dental bridge on a pit in the olive. The olive used in the martini had been purchased by restaurant from Olivia Co. in a jar labeled "pitted olives."

Discuss Imogene's potential products liability claims against restaurant and Olivia for dental damage.

10.6

Shelly and Peggy attend a minor league hockey game. During the second period a hungry Shelly purchases an order of nachos from an aisle vendor. The vendor asks Shelly whether he wants "hot cheese sauce." Peggy replies, "Yes, as spicy as possible." Shelly passes the nachos to Peggy but she fails to get good purchase on the plate, which falls into her lap where the cheese sauce burns her legs. Peggy brings a products liability claim against the stadium. What issues arise?

10.7

A miscreant injected a lethal chemical into the bottle of a pharmaceutical product that once had been sold as a prescription drug but was, at the time of this tampering, sold over the counter. The miscreant surreptitiously opened the bottle of the product on a shelf of X pharmacy, injected the chemical, and then reclosed the bottle. The product was manufactured by Y company.

Plaintiff's deceased bought the bottled product after it had been tampered with, and died from ingesting the product.

Can plaintiff recover against either X or Y for the death of her deceased?

10.8

Brake Co. manufactured brakes to be installed in Small Truck Co.'s D 1000 truck. Pierre purchased a D 1000 for use in his pizza business, Pierre's Pizza's. The pizza business is Pierre's sole means of support and it is a sole proprietorship, i.e. it is not a partnership, corporation, or limited liability company. While delivering pizzas one night, the brakes in the D 1000 mysteriously failed and the truck crashed. The truck was totaled in the crash and Pierre suffered grievous personal injuries which prevent him from working. Also destroyed in the crash were an in-dash CD player that the dealer had installed in the truck when Pierre purchased it and a rare Salvador Dali painting Pierre kept stored behind the driver's seat; the painting is worth $2,000,000. Pierre estimates he has lost $20,000 in pizza sales because of his injury and the loss of the truck. What claims for what injuries does Pierre have against Brake Co. and Small Truck Co.?

10.9

Bill is driving home from a bar late at night. He pulls over to obey flashing red and blue "police lights" on a following vehicle. In fact, the occupants of the "police car" are carjackers. They assault Bill and steal his car. Bill brings suit against Impressions, Inc., the manufacturers of the "police lights" alleging design defect and arguing that the benefits of the light as designed were outweighed by its inherent risks. What argument(s) should Impressions, Inc., make?

10.10

Billy Bob purchased two "laptop" computers from the online store of their manufacturer, Tex Computing, Inc. He put one in his second floor home study and used the other in his office and when traveling. Two months ago Billy Bob received a letter from Tex notifying him that the batteries (that were manufactured by a third-party, Soko, Inc.) in a small number of laptops exhibited symptoms of overheating and offering to replace his batteries free of charge. The next week, and before he was able to exchange his batteries, Billy Bob had an important sales presentation to give out of town. Just prior to boarding his outbound flight airline representatives announced that Tex laptops were not permitted on the airplane because of safety concerns. Billy Bob had to leave his laptop in an airport locker. Without his computer his sales presentation did not go so well, and he lost the contract he was bidding on. On his return he retrieved his laptop and drove home, to discover that what remained of his smoldering house was surrounded by emergency vehicles that had been called to deal with a serious fire that, according to a later investigation by the fire department, had started on the second floor. His home office was completely destroyed and neither fire department nor insurance investigators have been able to identify the specific cause of the fire, although they considered the source to be "electrical." Billy Bob is considering a products liability claim against Tex. What issues arise?

Chapter 11

NUISANCE AND ENVIRONMENTAL TORTS

A. INTRODUCTION

Nuisance has been available as the basis of a cause of action for a very long time. It is usually associated with the invasion of one's interest in land. An important distinction between trespass and nuisance is that a trespass requires an invasion of land whereas a nuisance does not. To oversimplify, an action for trespass to land protects exclusive possession of the land and an action for private nuisance protects use and enjoyment of the land. A nuisance may involve annoyances, such as sounds or smells that harm or offend a person or her sensitivities. The pivotal consideration of a nuisance claim is whether the conduct of the defendant results in an unreasonable interference with the plaintiff's use and enjoyment of the land. A nuisance may be either private or public. A nuisance is considered public if it interferes with the right of a person to use property as a member of the public as distinguished from the private use of property, although there is sometimes an overlapping or blurring of a public and private nuisance. Just as with products liability, a nuisance action can be based on negligence, intentional misconduct, or strict liability. Where strict liability is involved, the nuisance action parallels liability for abnormally dangerous conduct as described in Section 520 of the Second Restatement. REST. 2D TORTS § 520. Thus, a case such as *Rylands v. Fletcher*, [1868] L.R. 3, 19 L.T. 220 (H.L.), can be viewed as a nuisance action.

The Torts student may well wonder what purpose a nuisance action serves that is not already provided for by existing law. Where there is no abnormally dangerous activity or negligence, a nuisance claim may fill a hiatus not covered by an action in trespass. The injunctive remedy is used in nuisance probably more than in any other tort action. The law of nuisance highlights risk-utility analysis in a way not always present in tort law generally. Moreover, resolution of a nuisance claim requires a court or jury to decide whose value preferences will prevail when incompatible claims are made for the use of land or public space. A homeless person sleeping in a soiled and smelly blanket in a public library to escape freezing weather may disturb other users of the library by his appearance and smell, but is he making an unreasonable use of public space? In some circumstances statutes or regulations mandate or guide the determination of nuisance, but often the conflict over the use of land must be resolved by a judge or jury based on an assessment of community values.

Environmental torts are of more recent origin than nuisance. The term environmental tort is used loosely to cover a congeries of ideas including land, water and air pollution and damage, toxic and radioactive injury, and the like. Such claims often involve the tort of nuisance, but they are more expansive and pervasive. They frequently involve mass torts, and implicate the class action remedy. A CIVIL ACTION (1995), the best selling book by Jonathan Haar (later made into a movie), offers an illuminating and heart wrenching portrayal of the impact that toxic injuries have on individuals, families and communities. Woburn, a small community in Massachusetts, experienced an unexpectedly high number of leukemia cases and other injuries, primarily in children. A number of families who have children suffering from leukemia set out to prove that their injuries were caused by a toxic substance that made its way into water wells, after being surreptitiously and illegally dumped in a neighborhood site. The problems confronted by the families and their zealous lawyer highlight the challenges that toxic tort cases present to the legal system. Discovery in toxic tort cases often reveals that there are an indeterminate number of potential plaintiffs who may have been hurt, multiple potential defendants who may have contributed to the contamination of the environment, and even though there is strong scientific evidence that links the suspected toxin to a disease or illness, there may be scant scientific evidence to prove that it caused an injury to any particular plaintiff. Moreover, the passage of time from the alleged wrongful conduct and the manifestation of injuries make proof of causation even more difficult, and compel reconsideration as to whether the established statute of limitations for bringing tort claims works fairly when applied to toxic tort action. In addition, the nature of global business operations and the transport of toxic substances augurs for an increasing number of toxic tort claims with international implications. Environmental claims are a hallmark of tort litigation in the second half of the twentieth century, and may well come to dominate tort litigation in the twenty-first century. Nuisance and toxic tort litigation raise issues relevant to law and economics, corrective justice, social justice, critical theory, feminism, and more.

This chapter begins with the core questions flowing from competing claims for incompatible uses of land and then delves into the procedural, substantive, and jurisprudential issues that arise out of more complex nuisance and toxic tort litigation.

B. NUISANCE: ASSESSING REASONABLENESS OF LAND USE

LANGAN v. BELLINGER
611 N.Y.S.2d 59 (N.Y. App. D.v. 1994)

WEISS, JUSTICE.

Appeal from an order of the Supreme Court (Hughes, J.), entered May 21, 1993 in Schoharie County, which, *inter alia*, granted defendant's cross motion for summary judgment dismissing the complaint.

This lawsuit demonstrates that what may be music to the ears of some can, in certain circumstances, be a nuisance to the ears of others. Plaintiffs, who reside in the Village of Schoharie, Schoharie County, have commenced this action against their neighbor, the Presbyterian Church of the Town of Schoharie, seeking injunctive relief "from playing hourly chimes on a daily basis beginning at 8:00 o'clock in the forenoon and ending at 8:00 o'clock in the afternoon and from playing carillon music on a daily basis at 12:00 o'clock in the afternoon and at 6:00 o'clock in the afternoon," which plaintiff Julie Langan[4] avers "is a complete disruption of [her] family life, prevents a child from sleeping, and invades the privacy of [her] residence and creates unnecessary stress." The complaint characterizes the foregoing to be both a private nuisance and a violation of an ordinance of the Village of Schoharie. Plaintiffs moved by order to show cause for a preliminary injunction, in response to which defendant cross-moved for summary judgment dismissing the complaint. Supreme Court denied plaintiffs' motion, granted defendant's cross motion and dismissed the complaint. We affirm.

One may be liable for a private nuisance where the wrongful invasion of the use of another's land is intentional and unreasonable. The elements of such a private nuisance are "(1) an interference substantial in nature, (2) intentional in origin, (3) unreasonable in character, (4) with a person's property right to use and enjoy land, (5) caused by another's conduct in acting or failing to act" (*Copart Indus. v. Consolidated Edison Co. of N.Y.*, 41 N.Y.2d 564, 570, 394 N.Y.S.2d 169, 362 N.E.2d 968; *see*, Restatement (Second) of Torts, § 822). We note that the complaint appears to be defective in that it fails to allege two of the basic elements of private nuisance, i.e., that the interference is substantial in nature or that it is unreasonable in character. For this reason alone, dismissal of the complaint would be appropriate.

Nonetheless, we similarly find dismissal on the ground found by Supreme Court to be proper. Defendant's moving papers included the sworn affidavit of and report by Wayne Sikora, an expert in noise management, which showed that the sound levels emanating from the bells and chimes were no greater than the sound from a passing automobile, of which some 6500 passed plaintiffs' properties each day. This document, together with affidavits from the pastor of the church, defense counsel and affidavits from 15 other Village residents who found the bells and chimes to be pleasant, as well as an affidavit from the Village Mayor and Village Attorney showing there was no violation of an ordinance, constituted a prima facie showing of entitlement to summary judgment.

In opposition, plaintiffs offered only their own affidavits and that of their attorney, all of which were lacking in objective evidence to either rebut the opinion of defendant's expert or demonstrate that the music and chimes constituted a nuisance. Because plaintiffs failed to meet their burden of coming forward with proof in evidentiary form to demonstrate the existence of factual issues requiring a trial, summary judgment dismissing the complaint was entirely appropriate. We further note that opposition which rests only on discrepancies between opposing papers and relates solely to matters of credibility of conflicting opinions of experts will not suffice.

Finally, we find that Supreme Court correctly denied plaintiffs' applications for preliminary injunctive relief in the absence of any demonstration of the probability of success in the lawsuit.

---

[4] Langan and the other plaintiff, Ernest Eggers, both reside approximately 250 feet from the church.

NOTES

1. Significant harm to neighbors may change the result in a finding that an activity constitutes a nuisance. In *Harford Penn-Cann Service, Inc. v. Zymblosky*, 549 A.2d 208 (Pa. 1988) a business created such a vast amount of dust that the neighbors experienced health problems and lost business. The court found a nuisance and issued an injunction.

2. The character of the neighborhood often proves to be the most influential finding in a nuisance case. *Anderson v. Guerrein Skyway Amusement Co.*, 29 A.2d 682 (Pa. 1943) involved fifty-four plaintiffs who succeeded in having a drive-in theater's operation declared a nuisance on the ground that it operated with bright lights and loud noise inconsistent with the residential character of the neighborhood and prevented plaintiffs from sleeping. In contrast, the plaintiffs in *Karpiak v. Russo*, 676 A.2d 270 (Pa. Super. 1996), sued defendants for dust and noise created by defendants' landscaping business. The court denied plaintiffs' claims, declaring "this noise *is not out of character with the area* since appellants admitted that Saltsburg Road is traveled heavily with trucks, buses, and cars, which make the same noises as the [complaining neighbor's] machinery which consists of backhoes, loaders, and trucks." *Id.* at 274.

HENDRICKS v. STALNAKER
380 S.E.2d 198 (W. Va. 1989)

NEELY, JUSTICE.

Walter S. Stalnaker, defendant below, appeals from a decision by the Circuit Court of Lewis County declaring a water well drilled on his property to be a private nuisance to Harry L. Hendricks and Mary Hendricks, plaintiffs below. The Hendrickses, owners of the property adjacent to that of Mr. Stalnaker, were refused a Health Department permit for a septic system located within 100 feet of Mr. Stalnaker's water well. The Circuit Court of Lewis County, based on a jury verdict, found the water well to be a private nuisance and ordered its abatement. On appeal, Mr. Stalnaker argues that because his water well was not an unreasonable use of his land, he is not liable for the effects on the Hendrickses' property. We agree and, therefore, reverse the decision of the circuit court.

Mr. Stalnaker owns approximately 10 acres of land situated on Glady Fork Road, Lewis County. In 1985, Mr. Stalnaker constructed his home on a 2.493 acre portion of the tract, and had two water wells dowsed. One well was located behind his house and the other, near the Hendrickses' property. The rear well was near land disturbed by a former strip mine and, therefore, the well produced poor quality water. Except for a small section of land near the Hendrickses' property — the location of the second "dowsed" well — most of Mr. Stalnaker's home tract had been disturbed by a strip mine. In August 1985, Mr. Stalnaker spent approximately $3,000 in an unsuccessful attempt to treat the water from the rear well.

In 1984, the Hendrickses purchased approximately 2.95 acres adjacent to Mr. Stalnaker's property for a home site or a trailer development. On

31 December 1985, Mr. Hendricks met with the Lewis County sanitarian to determine locations for a water well and a septic system. The Health Department requires a distance of 100 feet between water wells and septic systems before it will issue permits. Because the Hendrickses' land was too hilly or had been disturbed in order to build a pond, the only location for a septic system on the tract was near Mr. Stalnaker's property. On 13 January 1986, the Hendrickses contacted the county sanitarian to visit their property to complete the septic system permit application. The county sanitarian said because of snowy weather he would come out later in the week.

On 13 January 1986, Mr. Stalnaker called the sanitarian and was told about the Hendrickses' proposed septic system. Mr. Stalnaker was also told that the county sanitarian would be unavailable on 14 January 1986 but could meet with him on 15 January 1986. On 14 January 1986, Mr. Stalnaker contacted a well driller, who applied for and received a well drilling permit for the second well from the assistant sanitarian. The well was completed on 25 January 1986 but was not connected to Mr. Stalnaker's home until January 1987.

On 15 January 1986, the county sanitarian informed Mr. Hendricks that no permit for his proposed septic system could be issued because the absorption field for his septic system was within one hundred feet of Mr. Stalnaker's water well. Mr. Hendricks did install a septic system without a permit in January 1987; however, the system was left inoperative pending the outcome of this suit.

The Hendrickses filed suit in the Circuit Court of Lewis County on 29 January 1987 requesting (1) the water well be declared a private nuisance, (2) the nuisance be abated, and (3) damages. In a bifurcated trial, the jury found that the water well was a private nuisance and the trial judge ordered it to be abated. On the issue of damages the jury found for the defendant and awarded no damages.

In the past we have broadly described what constitutes a nuisance:

A nuisance is anything which annoys or disturbs the free use of one's property, or which renders its ordinary use or physical occupation uncomfortable. . . . A nuisance is anything which interferes with the rights of a citizen, either in person, property, the enjoyment of his property, or his comfort. . . . A condition is a nuisance when it clearly appears that enjoyment of property is materially lessened, and physical comfort of persons in their homes is materially interfered with thereby.

Martin v. Williams, 141 W. Va. 595, 610-611, 93 S.E.2d 835, 844 (1956). Also cited in *Mahoney v. Walter*, 157 W. Va. 882, 205 S.E.2d 692 (1974) (automobile salvage yard); *Sharon Steel Corp. v. City of Fairmont*, 175 W. Va. 479, 334 S.E.2d 616 (1985) (regulation of hazardous waste); *Sticklen v. Kittle*, 168 W. Va. 147, 287 S.E.2d 148 (1981) (construction of a high school near an airport). This definition of nuisance includes acts or conditions that affect either the general public or a limited number of persons. In *Hark v. Mountain Fork Lumber Co.*, 127 W. Va. 586, 595-96, 34 S.E.2d 348, 354 (1945), we defined a public nuisance as that which "affects the general public as public, and [a private nuisance as that which] injures one person or a limited number of persons only."

In order clearly to delineate between a public nuisance and a private nuisance, we define a private nuisance as a substantial and unreasonable interference with the private use and enjoyment of another's land. The definition of private nuisance includes conduct that is intentional and unreasonable, negligent or reckless, or that results in [sic] an abnormally dangerous conditions or activities in an inappropriate place. Recovery for a private nuisance is limited to plaintiffs who have suffered a significant harm to their property rights or privileges caused by the interference.

Early West Virginia cases indicate that the existence of a private nuisance was determined primarily by the harm caused. *Medford v. Levy*, 31 W. Va. 649, 8 S.E. 302 (1888) (cooking odors); *Flanagan v. Gregory and Poole, Inc.*, 136 W. Va. 554, 67 S.E.2d 865 (1951) (inadequate culvert). Gradually the focus included an examination of the reasonableness of the property's use. *See McGregor v. Camden*, 47 W. Va. 193, 34 S.E. 936 (1899) (required an examination of the location, capacity and management of oil and gas well); *Pope v. Edward M. Rude Carrier Corp.*, 138 W. Va. 218, 75 S.E.2d 584 (1953) (transportation of explosives); *Martin, supra* (used automobile lot); *State ex rel. Ammerman v. City of Philippi*, 136 W. Va. 120, 65 S.E.2d 713 (1951) (tire recapping business); *Ritz v. Woman's Club of Charleston*, 114 W. Va. 675, 173 S.E. 564 (1934) (noise); *Harless v. Workman*, 145 W. Va. 266, 114 S.E.2d 548 (1960) (coal dust).

In the area of public nuisance, we have made explicit that an examination of the "reasonableness or unreasonableness of the use of property in relation to the particular locality" is a fair test to determine the existence of a public nuisance. Similarly, any determination of liability for a private nuisance must include an examination of the private use and enjoyment of the land seeking protection and the nature of the interference.

Because the present case concerns conduct that is not a negligent, reckless, or abnormally dangerous activity, our discussion of private nuisance is limited to conduct that is intentional and unreasonable. An interference is intentional when the actor knows or should know that the conduct is causing a substantial and unreasonable interference. Restatement (Second) of Torts § 825 (1979). The unreasonableness of an intentional interference must be determined by a balancing of the landowners' interests. An interference is unreasonable when the gravity of the harm outweighs the social value of the activity alleged to cause the harm. Restatement (Second) of Torts §§ 827 and 828 (1979) list some of the factors to be considered in determining the gravity of the harm and the social value of the activity alleged to cause the harm.[1] However, this balancing

---

[1] The Restatement (Second) of Torts § 827 (1979) lists the following "gravity of harm" factors: (a) The extent of the harm involved; (b) the character of the harm involved; (c) the social value that the law attaches to the type of use or enjoyment invaded; (d) the suitability of the particular use or enjoyment invaded to the character of the locality; and (e) the burden on the person harmed of avoiding the harm. The Restatement (Second) of Torts § 828 lists the following "utility of conduct" factors: (a) the social value that the law attaches to the primary purpose of the conduct; (b) the suitability of the conduct to the character of the locality; and; (c) the impracticability of preventing or avoiding the invasion.

["An intentional invasion of another's interest in the use and enjoyment of land is unreasonable if the harm resulting from the invasion is severe and greater than the other should be required to bear without compensation." Restatement (Second) of Torts § 829.]

to determine unreasonableness is not absolute. Additional consideration might include the malicious or indecent conduct of the actor. Restatement (Second) of Torts § 829. . . .

In the case before us, the Hendrickses' inability to operate a septic system on their property is clearly a substantial interference with the use and enjoyment of their land. The record indicates that the installation of the water well was intentional, but there was no evidence that the installation was done so as maliciously to deprive the Hendrickses of a septic system. Mr. Stalnaker wanted to insure himself of an adequate water supply and found no alternative to the well he dug.

The critical question is whether the interference, the installation of a water well, was unreasonable. Unreasonableness is determined by balancing the competing landholders' interests. We note that either use, well or septic system, burdens the adjacent property. Under Health Department regulations, a water well merely requires non-interference within 100 feet of its location. In the case of a septic system, however, the 100 foot safety zone, extending from the edge of the absorption field, may intrude on adjacent property. Thus, the septic system, with its potential for drainage, places a more invasive burden on adjacent property. Clearly both uses present similar considerations of gravity of harm and social value of the activity alleged to cause the harm. Both a water well and a septic system are necessary to use this land for housing; together they constitute the in and out of many water systems. Neither party has an inexpensive and practical alternative. The site of the water well means quality water for Mr. Stalnaker and the Hendrickses have only one location available for their septic system.

In the case before us, we are asked to determine if the water well is a private nuisance. But if the septic system were operational, the same question could be asked about the septic system. Because of the similar competing interests, the balancing of these landowners' interests is at least equal or, perhaps, slightly in favor of the water well. Thus, the Hendrickses have not shown that the balancing of interests favors their septic system. We find that the evidence presented clearly does not demonstrate that the water well is an unreasonable use of land and, therefore, does not constitute a private nuisance.

Although questions of fact are normally for the jury, when the material facts are not disputed and only one inference may be drawn from them by reasonable minds, the factual questions at issue become questions of law for the court.

We find that because the evidence is not disputed and only one interference is reasonable, the trial court should have held as a matter of law that the water well was not a private nuisance.

Accordingly, for the reasons stated above, the judgment of the Circuit Court of Lewis County is reversed and the case is remanded for entry of an order consistent with this opinion.

NOTES

1. *Perspectives on a Nuisance.* In footnote 2 of the principal case the court observed: "In a factually similar case, the Supreme Court of Oklahoma held that a sewage lagoon created within 100 feet of a neighbor's water well was a 'willful' injury to the adjacent property and awarded attorneys' fees. The court reasoned that under an Oklahoma statute the sewage lagoon actively burdened adjacent property whereas the water well was a non-invasive burden. *Schaeffer v. Schaeffer*, 743 P.2d 1038 (Okla. 1987). In the absence of a statute, what result is justified in *Hendricks* using an economic efficiency analysis? Does a corrective justice or social justice analysis lead you to the same result?

2. *First in Time User.* What weight should the court give to the fact that a land user was first in time in the way in which she used her property? In *Spur Indus., Inc. v. Del E. Webb Dev. Co.*, 494 P.2d 700 (Ariz. 1972), plaintiff Webb's residential housing development grew until it came within smelling distance of defendant Spur's previously rural cattle feedlot, which thus became a nuisance to the residential area. Defendant was required to relocate or shut down. However, "[h]aving brought people to the nuisance to the foreseeable detriment of Spur, Webb must indemnify Spur for a reasonable amount of the cost of moving or shutting down." How should the conflict be resolved in a situation similar to *Spur Industries*, but lacking a solvent developer or other financially responsible person toward whom the court could shift the costs of relocation?

3. *Nuisance and Governmental Takings.* If a state or the federal government takes private property, it is required, under the Fifth and Fourteenth Amendments of the federal Constitution as well as under state constitutions, to provide just compensation for the taking. *See Jackson v. Metrop. Knoxville Airport Authority*, 922 S.W.2d 860 (Tenn. 1996) (claim of noise, vibration, and pollution from nearby airport flights Constituted *prima facie* cause of action for inverse condemnation). But the government may take a property interest without compensation if the interest constitutes a nuisance. *Erb v. Maryland Dep't of the Environment*, 676 A.2d 1017 (Md. App. 1996).

SPRING-GAR COMMUNITY CIVIC ASSOCIATION, INC. v. HOMES FOR THE HOMELESS, INC.,
135 Misc. 2d 689; 516 N.Y.S.2d 399 (1987 N.Y. Misc.)

ZELMAN, JUSTICE.

The present case involves the difficult question of housing for the homeless, and one community's partial opposition thereto.

. . .

Springfield Gardens is a fine residential community composed basically of one-family homes. Into this community, a nonprofit corporation, Homes for the Homeless, Inc., wants to thrust approximately 715 homeless people.

Springfield Gardens, a community of approximately 3,000 people, is represented in this action by Spring-Gar Community Civic Association, Inc., an association formed in 1968, and by J. Clifford Gadsden, individually and as chairman of the Spring-Gar Community Civic Association. It has approximately 500 members who are homeowners in the Springfield Gardens community, a community bounded by South Conduit Avenue on the north, Rockaway Boulevard on the southwest, and Springfield Boulevard on the southeast. One of the stated purposes of the association is "to protect and promote the best interests of the residents of the area." It is for this purpose that the association and its chairman, J. Clifford Gadsden, both as Chairman and individually as a homeowner in the Springfield Gardens area, bring suit to permanently enjoin Homes for the Homeless from depositing what has to be considered a very substantial number of homeless people into this area. The community believes that the large number of homeless people will seriously and adversely affect the existing patterns of population growth, distribution and concentration, and the character of the community and the neighborhood. Accordingly, they fear the value of their homes will be reduced.

The Springfield Gardens community at the present time does not have an overabundance of hospital facilities, educational facilities, or police protection. The sudden addition of a substantial number of people, be they homeless or otherwise, would seem to pose a potential for strain on a multitude of services in the community, including those already mentioned. It is for these reasons, among others, that the plaintiffs oppose the sudden dumping of 715 people into the community.

The object of the community's opposition in this action is defendant Homes for the Homeless, a nonprofit corporation, which corporation is an interfaith project of the Cathedral of St. John the Divine in New York City. Recognizing that there is a problem in New York City when it comes to providing shelter for the homeless, Homes for the Homeless' stated purpose is to help fill a need for more private sector involvement in the problems of the homeless. Their program is designed to provide temporary housing for homeless families, together with counseling, job training, and other social services programs, and to assist such families in obtaining permanent housing. The stated objective of this homeless project is to make homeless families as independent as possible and to reestablish them in the community through assistance in locating permanent residencies and jobs.

Homes for the Homeless has leased a building in Springfield Gardens and has named the property the Saratoga Inter-Faith Inn. The property, formerly known as the Holiday Inn, is located on Rockaway Boulevard, Queens County. It is bounded on three sides by commercial buildings, and on the fourth, across Rockaway Boulevard, by Kennedy Airport. The closest homeowners in Springfield Gardens are approximately two blocks away. Mr. Gadsen's home is approximately one-half mile away. The Saratoga has 259 residential units.

Homes for the Homeless plans on using the facility to provide housing solely for family units, approximately 200 such units, one family to a room. Families of two, three, or four will occupy one room for that family. It is anticipated that there will be no more than 450 children, of which approximately 200 will be teen-agers. Under its operational plan, there will be a comprehensive range of programs and social services. Such programs include child care assistance, job training, family counseling, and help in locating housing. As now planned, there is to be a staff of 141, including internal security. The facility is considered by the Human Resources Administration of the City of New York as a Tier II facility, with communal dining areas and sanitary facilities.

Homes for the Homeless has never operated a facility of this magnitude. In fact, they have only operated one other facility in The Bronx, which facility is limited to 70 families.

Under recent court decisions, the City of New York is obligated to provide housing for the homeless. To meet this need the Human Resources Administration of the city itself operates some emergency housing, but the majority of the apparently 4,700 families per night it aids are placed in privately run facilities, like the Saratoga. Funding is provided by the Human Resources Administration to the Saratoga for its housing of homeless facilities with aid to dependent children funds. These funds represent 50% from the Federal Government, 25% from the State, and 25% from city funds. In addition, the Human Resources Administration, in part, supervises the operation of the Saratoga. Accordingly, the City of New York and various officers of city agencies are named as defendants.

The people of Springfield Gardens do not oppose homeless people. The people of Springfield Gardens do not even oppose having homeless people being introduced into their community, a community that already has accepted other types of smaller shelters. What the people of Springfield Gardens do oppose is the sudden introduction of very large numbers of people, viz., approximately 715, into this community of approximately 3,000. This court can understand and definitely sympathizes with the people of Springfield Gardens.

THE LAW

The plaintiffs' complaint sets forth three causes of action. Count I alleges a public and private nuisance. Count II claims environmental violations under the SEQRA and CEQA laws. Count III states that the local community was not notified as required by the Social Services Law.

Though sympathizing with the plaintiffs, this court finds itself constrained to follow the law, and, accordingly, the plaintiffs' complaint for a permanent injunction must be dismissed.

COUNT I — THE NUISANCE CLAIMS

Plaintiffs, in their complaint, alleged that the use of the Saratoga Inn by defendant Homes for the Homeless as a residence for very large numbers of homeless individuals will constitute a menace to the public health, safety, moral and general welfare and well-being of the residents of Springfield Gardens and to the homeless people who would reside at this facility, thereby creating a public and private nuisance. Plaintiffs further allege that they will sustain irreparable damages in that the operation and maintenance of a residential shelter for the homeless will greatly inconvenience and restrict plaintiffs' use and enjoyment of their property and that the value of their property will depreciate. These allegations do not support a cause of action for either a public or private nuisance.

The maintenance and operation of a residential facility for homeless families is not a nuisance *per se*. Rather, facilities such as the Saratoga Inn have become public necessities, which are lawful in character and in the public interest. (*See*, Social Services Law §41; 18 NYCRR part 900; *see also, Matter of Tafnet Realty Corp. v. City of New York*, 118 Misc. 2d 498.) Homeless families with children are entitled to emergency shelter on both constitutional and statutory grounds, and the courts lack the power to condition or limit the number of homeless persons a facility can accommodate. (*See, McCain v. Koch*, 117 AD2d 198, *mot to vacate stay denied as unnecessary* 68 NY2d 713; *cf., Matter of Lamboy v. Gross*, 129 Misc 2d 564, *affd* 126 AD2d 265 [1st Dept 1987].) The court, therefore, may not enjoin the maintenance and operation of the Saratoga Inn based upon plaintiffs' uncertain apprehensions, conjectural injuries, and mere speculation that a facility of this kind will be maintained in such a manner as to constitute a nuisance. (*See*, 42 NY Jur, Nuisance, §54.)

A public nuisance "is an offense against the State and is subject to abatement or prosecution on application of the proper governmental agency. It consists of conduct or omissions which offend, interfere with or cause damage to the public in the exercise of rights common to all in a manner such as to offend public morals, interfere with use by the public of a public place or endanger or injure the property, health, safety or comfort of a considerable number of persons" (*Copart Indus. v. Consolidated Edison Co.*, 41 NY2d 564, 568 [1977]).

Thus, such nuisance would exist if there is a substantial interference with the common rights of the public at large. Such activity would violate a public law or rule and for this reason would be considered to be a public nuisance. The plaintiffs have been unable to offer evidence that shows that the Saratoga Inn creates a public nuisance. The reason for that is probably because the Saratoga Inn has not opened its doors for a substantial period of time so that we can evaluate its impact on the community. One major argument advanced by the plaintiffs was that the value of the property in the community will decrease. An expert testified that in his opinion, because of the oversaturation of people in the area, there could be a possible increase in crime and this would cause the value of real estate to fall.

When a public nuisance is found, such invasion of public rights is to be left to be remedied by public officials. (*Burns Jackson Miller Summit & Spitzer v. Lindner*, 59 NY2d 314 [1983].) However, unfortunately for a private party to sue for a public nuisance, the private party must show that that party has suffered some "special damage" from the alleged public nuisance, separate and apart from any injury suffered by the public generally. Otherwise, the party does not have standing to sue. (*Burns Jackson Miller Summit & Spitzer v. Lindner, supra; Wakeman v. Wilbur*, 147 NY 657 [1895]; *Queens County Business Alliance v. New York Racing Assn.*, 98 AD2d 743 [1983]; *Copart Indus. v. Consolidated Edison Co., supra.*)

Assuming, arguendo, that plaintiffs have established a public nuisance claim, which they have not, the next question to consider is whether they have standing to bring this cause of action, i.e., whether they have suffered special damages. The leading case in this area is *Burns Jackson (supra)*. In *Burns Jackson*, two New York law firms brought suit on behalf of all professional and business entities in New York City against the Transport Workers Union and union officials as a result of their illegal transit strike in 1980. The action sought loss of business profits for these businesses that rely upon public transportation serving the city and have been damaged. Their claim was predicated, among other claims, on a private cause of action for a public nuisance, the transit strike. The Court of Appeals denied their claim, stating the following (at 334-335): "When the injury claimed to be peculiar is of the same kind suffered by all who are affected, when it 'is common to the entire community' (*Francis v. Schoellkopf*, 53 NY 152, 154), or, as Prosser put it (52 Va L Rev, p 1015), 'it becomes so general and widespread as to affect a whole community,' the injury is not peculiar and the action cannot be maintained. . . . The economic loss which results from a transit strike is not recoverable in a private action for public nuisance because the class includes all members of the public who are affected by the strike."

In the case at bar, the plaintiffs have not shown how they would be damaged in a way that is different from the rest of the community. Therefore, the same result reached in *Burns Jackson (supra)* must be reached here.

A private nuisance is one that substantially threatens an interference with the use or enjoyment of land. This interference may be as a result of an intentional act, a negligent act, or as a result of an act based on absolute liability. Such nuisance is one that threatens one person or relatively few persons. Once this invasion or interference occurs, the private nuisance gives rise to a course of action against the person or persons whose action or lack of action causes the invasion or interference. (*See, Copart Indus. v. Consolidated Edison Co., supra.*)

In the case at bar, the plaintiffs have not established during the trial of this action that the land possessed by any individual, or few individuals, in the community was harmed by the establishment or operation of the Saratoga. . . .

COUNT II — THE ENVIRONMENTAL CLAIMS

Plaintiffs, in their second cause of action, base their request for injunctive relief upon the assertion that defendants' policy and decisions to use the Saratoga Inn as a facility for a large number of homeless families, and to provide funding to this facility are actions which may have a significant affect on the environment, so that under the provisions of SEQRA, and the regulations promulgated thereunder (6 NYCRR part 617) and City Environmental Quality Review (CEQR), the actions should have been preceded by an environmental impact statement. (*See*, ECL 8-0105, 8-0109.) The city defendants assert that SEQRA and CEQR are inapplicable as there has been no governmental action in connection with the establishment and operation of the Saratoga Inn, as defined by ECL 8-0105 (4) (i), (ii) and 6 NYCRR 617.2 (b). The city claims that the Human Resource's Administration's referral of homeless families to the Saratoga Inn, and the use of Aid to Dependent Children shelter funds to reimburse the Saratoga Inn for a family's stay do not constitute "planning activity" or "funding" under the environmental statutes and regulations. It is further asserted that even if the referral of homeless families to a particular private shelter were deemed a "policy" and therefore an "action" under SEQRA, defendants would not be required to fill [sic] an environmental impact statement, as such an action constitutes "Type II" activity, under 6 NYCRR 617.13, and therefore has no significant effect on the environment. Finally, it is asserted that even if an "action" exists which is not exempt under Type II actions, injunctive relief pending SEQRA review should not be granted, under the emergency exemptions of CEQR 4 (h) and 6 NYCRR 617.2 (o) (6), although there has been no actual declaration of an emergency by the city agencies.

It is undisputed that SEQRA and CEQR applies only to government actions and decision-making and that purely private activity is not subject to environmental review. (*See*, ECL 8-0105.) Plaintiffs therefore cannot seek injunctive relief against Homes for The Homeless, a private corporation on the basis of alleged SEQRA and CEQR violations.

The initial determination to be made under SEQRA and CEQR is whether an environmental impact statement is required, which in turn depends on whether an action may or will have a significant effect on the environment. (ECL 8-0109 [2]; CEQR 7 [a].) It is clear from the express terms of the statutes and regulations that the term environment is broadly defined and includes "existing patterns of population concentration, distribution, or growth, and existing community or neighborhood character." (ECL 8-0105 [6]; CEQR 1 [f]; 6 NYCRR 617.2 [k]; *see, Chinese Staff & Workers Assn. v. City of New York*, 68 NY2d 359; *Matter of Jackson v. New York State Urban Dev. Corp.*, 67 NY2d 400.)

Turning now to the city defendants, the court finds unpersuasive their assertion that their activities in connection with the operation and use of the Saratoga Inn as a facility for homeless families does not constitute an "action." It is clear that the Human Resources Administration and the Department of Social Services, in providing assistance to needy families, actively houses homeless families in the Saratoga Inn and other facilities and are not mere referral agencies. Rather, it is the policy of the city to house homeless families in facilities such as the Saratoga Inn, and therefore this policy constitutes an action within the meaning of SEQRA (ECL 8-0105 [4]; *see, Midtown S. Preservation v. City of New York*, NYLJ, Jan. 5, 1987, at 6, col 5; *see also, McCain v. Koch*, 117 AD2d 198, *supra; Slade v. Koch*, 135 Misc 2d 283). The court further finds that the change in the use of Saratoga Inn from a transient hotel (the former Holiday Inn) to a facility for homeless families may have a check on the existing population patterns and neighborhood patterns, so as to require the city at the very least to make a threshold determination as to the environmental impact of its actions under SEQRA and CEQR. (*Cf., Chinese Staff & Workers Assn. v. City of New York, supra; Matter of Jackson v. New York Urban Dev. Corp., supra; Midtown S. Preservation v. City of New York, supra.*) The city defendants are therefore required to follow the environmental review procedures mandated by SEQRA and CEQR.

In view of the fact that the city has yet to make such a threshold determination, the court makes no determination as to whether the city's actions fall within Type II actions, and therefore are exempt. . . . Furthermore, as no environmental procedures have been undertaken it is premature for the court, at this time, to consider whether the social and economic impact factors have been properly identified, assessed and applied.

Plaintiffs' request for an injunction until such time as defendants have conducted a complete review of the environmental impact of its actions however is denied. Defendants assert that even if they are required to follow the SEQRA and CEQR procedures an emergency exists with respect to the use of the Saratoga Inn because the protection and preservation of the life and health of homeless families and children require immediate action which cannot await the usual procedures set forth in CEQR (6 NYCRR part 617). Although there has been no declaration of emergency as regards the use of the Saratoga Inn, it is beyond dispute that the plight of the homeless in New York City is so life threatening and of such proportions as to come within the meaning of the applicable emergency provisions of CEQR 4 (h) and 6 NYCRR 617.2 (o) (6), so as to provide some dispensation from the requirements generally governing environmental standards. (*Matter of Gerges v. Koch*, 62 NY2d 84; *Matter of Board of Visitors — Marcy Psychiatric Center v. Coughlin*, 60 NY2d 14; *Vann v. Koch*, NYLJ, Feb. 20, 1987, at 16, col 4; *Greenpoint Renaissance Enter. Corp. v. City of New York*, Sup Ct, Kings County, Feb. 24, 1987, Hutcherson, J.)

The court recognizes the valid concerns and fears of the community that the establishment of this facility may bring serious ecological, sociological and economic problems affecting the quality of life for the residents of Springfield Gardens. However, on a motion for injunctive relief the court is required to consider and balance the equities of the parties and where, as here, to deny access to homeless families to the Saratoga Inn would present a far more serious harm than that which could result to the community, a balancing of the equities favors the homeless. . . .

COUNT III — THE NOTICE CLAIM

Plaintiffs' third cause of action, which alleges that the defendants failed to provide plaintiffs with ample notice and information as to the projection of the Saratoga Inn, as a facility for homeless families, pursuant to section 43 (11) of the Social Services Law and 18 NYCRR 800.4 has merit. The testimony was that Sister Joan Kirby and Emmanuel Stern were listed as speakers at a meeting of Community Board No. 13 on June 23, 1986. The testimony of the chairwoman was that their appearance was listed as an item and that neither speaker could answer amply questions that were put to them. There is no question in the court's mind that there should have been more involvement with the community. It was up to the parties to hold community-wide public hearings instead of "dumping" such a large project on the community. It is up to the legislative and executive branches of the government to present to the community all the information they can before going ahead and disregarding their needs.

Though this court is constrained to decide the case as it did, the court does so with a heavy heart. The court does not believe that overburdening a community, as will be done here, is just. Accordingly, it asks the Legislature to address the issue. At the very least, the Legislature should promulgate laws that will provide the community with the right to a hearing on any proposed homeless shelter, rather than mere notice of intent to act, when such action is planned. The Legislature should also establish laws that would prevent large numbers of homeless from being placed into any one particular area. In fact, a City Council Committee, the Select Committee on the Homeless, has recommended to the Mayor of the City of New York that no shelter should contain more than 100 families. Such recommendation should be enacted into law. It is for the Legislature, not for the courts, to so act.

Lastly, this court is concerned not only about the people of Springfield Gardens, but also the homeless as well. This court is not unmindful that the housing being provided to the homeless at the Saratoga, though far from the least desirable, is also far from ideal. It is concerned that families are being placed into a room for the homeless which is immediately surrounded on three sides by commercial and industrial plants including freight forwarders and cargo terminals, with trucks going in, out, and around, all the time. On the fourth side lies Rockaway Boulevard, a major roadway that is now considered part of the Nassau-Queens Expressway. This court views this location as being highly dangerous for its residents who desire to leave the premises by foot. Further, the fact that families must share one room, including children sleeping with their parents, and children of the opposite sex sleeping together, is certainly not healthy, and cries out for relief. Moreover, the fact that the housing is merely transitory does not insure continuity and stability in the education of children.

The Comptroller of the City of New York, the Honorable Harrison J. Goldin, in a report dated April 23, 1987 entitled, Room to Spare But Nowhere to Go, set forth a better solution of this problem wherein he stated: "The City owns approximately 3700 occupied buildings which it seized for nonpayment of taxes; they contain about 4000 vacant apartments. We inspected 445 of these apartments in 85 different occupied rem buildings; it would cost under 9 million dollars to rehabilitate them all." This would give permanent housing to the homeless, it would stop shunting families and children from one inhumane shelter to another. These people by temporary housing are denied stable environments. Temporary housing fragments social and educational needs. The city needs an intensive city-wide rehabilitation program to meet the problem on a permanent basis. In the long run, this would save more money by addressing the problem head on.

Accordingly, plaintiffs' request for a permanent injunction is denied without prejudice to renewing its application should there come a time when special damages can be proven, and defendants' cross motion to dismiss the complaint is granted.

The city is directed to initiate an environmental proceeding under SEQRA and CEQA consistent with this decision.

NOTES

1. *Class Issues.* Professor Jane Baron has thrown light on the competing property use claims in the context of homelessness by challenging policy makers to envision living in the world without property. *See* Jane Baron, *Property* *and No Property*, 42 HOUS. L. REV. 1425 (2006). For example, without a living space identified as yours, where would you leave your clothes, go to the bathroom, cook your meals, etc? Professor Baron argues persuasively that people with no property face a legal regime that tells them what they cannot do but gives almost no protection or rights to do something. In the context of nuisance law, the claim of a homeless person to use public space in a particular way may adduce different answers to the issue of reasonable use, depending on one's perspective having some property, however limited, vs. having no property. A social justice evaluation of reasonableness of the use of land requires looking at the competing claims from multiple perspectives. Which tort theory best illuminates the issues that the court in the principal case had to resolve?

2. *Race Issues.* Race issues further complicate the public policy issues raised by nuisance and toxic tort claims. Evidence continues to emerge that communities comprised of a majority of poor people, working-class people, or people of color endure a disproportionate exposure to toxins in the environment. Consequently, class and race issues lurk in the background of many toxic tort cases. *See* Rachel Godsil, *Viewing the Cathedral from Behind the Color Line: Property Rules, Liability Rules and Environmental Racism*, 53 EMORY LAW J. 1807 (2004) (examining nuisance theory in light of microeconomic theory and recounting the role of government in promoting racially segregated community and withholding equal environmental protection from communities of color). If the operators of the homeless shelter or the neighborhood opponents of the shelter offered evidence of the racial composition of the residents of the shelter, would it be relevant to any legal issues that the court must resolve in deciding the nuisance claim?

3. *Gender Issues.* In some cases, the activity is alleged to be a nuisance or constitute a toxic tort because it exposes women to an increased risk of injury. *See, e.g., Ruff v. Ensign-Bickford Indus.*, 168 F. Supp. 2d 1271 (D.Utah 2001); *German v. Federal Home Loan Mortg. Corp.*, 885 F. Supp. 537 (S.D.N.Y 1995). Should the court take into account the disproportionate impact of an activity on women? See Chapter 1, *supra*.

4. *Cultural Perspectives.* In a review of the book A CIVIL ACTION, one commentator observed: "A Civil Action is a window on an emerging cultural obsession with the American tort system. At the close of the twentieth century more and more American tort cases are mass torts and, with increasing frequency pit class action plaintiffs against Fortune 500 corporations and large government bureaucracies." Robert Blomquist, *Bottomless Pit: Toxic Trials, The American Legal Profession and Popular Perceptions of the Law*, 81 CORNELL L. REV. 953, 985 (1996). Should the tort system take into account differentials in power and wealth of the litigants? If so, what remedies should be adopted in cases of vast disparities in power or wealth?

## C.	NUISANCE AND RELATED ENVIRONMENTAL TORTS: IDENTIFYING COGNIZABLE HARM

GOLEN v. THE UNION CORP.
718 A.2d 298 (Pa. Super. 1998)

OLSZEWSKI, JUDGE.

This appeal presents the question of whether private nuisance provides a remedy for a landowner who cannot sell his or her property because of neighboring environmental contamination, when the contamination does not otherwise affect the landowner's use of the property. The trial court granted appellees' motion for summary judgment, finding that private nuisance does not provide a remedy. We affirm.

Both appellants' and appellees' property are located in an industrial section of Philadelphia. During the 1970's, appellees' property was used for recycling electrical transformers, which contaminated the property with polychlorinated biphenyls (PCBs). As a result of this contamination, the property was listed on the National Priorities List (NPL) of the Comprehensive Environmental Response, Compensation and Liability Act[1] ("CERCLA" or "Superfund"). Although the contamination leaked into the Delaware River, there is no evidence that it migrated to appellants' property.

Appellants' property was used as a waste transfer station including the treatment of some hazardous waste. Appellants learned of appellees' property NPL status in 1983. Appellants attempted to sell their property in 1991, but claim they were unable to find a buyer because of appellees' NPL listing. Appellants concede that their ability to use the property has not otherwise changed.

Appellants filed a private nuisance suit, based upon the inability to sell the property. In response, appellees filed a motion for summary judgment, which the trial court granted. This appeal followed.

When considering an order for summary judgment, our standard of review is well settled. We must view the record in the light most favorable to the non-moving party, and all doubts as to the existence of a genuine issue of material fact must be resolved against the moving party. Summary judgment will be granted only in those cases which are free and clear from doubt. Our scope of review is plenary.

Appellants admit that their land is not contaminated and that aside from alienability, their use of the property remains unaffected. Nevertheless, appellants argue that they are entitled to relief under a theory of private nuisance. In tort, one may be damaged but not suffer a legal injury. Although appellants have clearly alleged damages, we must decide whether they were a result of a compensable injury. We conclude that they are not.

---

[1] 42 U.S.C.S §§ 9601-9675.

This Commonwealth follows the Restatement (Second) of Torts' formulation of private nuisance. The Restatement defines a private nuisance as "a nontrespassory invasion of another's interest in the private use and enjoyment of land." 4 Restatement Torts, 2d, § 821D, p. 100. Appellants claim that the interest invaded was their ability to sell their property. We find, however, that this is not the type of injury contemplated by the Restatement.

Admittedly, a broad reading of the Restatement definition could include appellants' claim. It has been noted that the concept of nuisance is broad enough to encompass virtually all harms. Thus, courts must determine sensible limits to liability under this potentially sweeping concept. After careful consideration, we conclude that private nuisance only recognizes injuries that require physical presence on the property in order to be perceived.

We recognize that alienability and diminution of property value are relevant means to calculate damages in a nuisance suit. These concepts are not, however, cognizable injuries of themselves.

The physical presence requirement is supported in the text of the Restatement:

b. *Interest in use and enjoyment of land* . . . The phrase "interest in the use and enjoyment of land" is used in this Restatement in a broad sense. It comprehends not only the interests that a person may have in the actual present use of land for residential, agricultural, commercial, industrial and other purposes, but also his interests in having the present use value of the land unimpaired by changes in its physical condition. . . . "Interest in use and enjoyment" also comprehends the pleasure, comfort and enjoyment that a person normally derives from the occupancy of land. Freedom from discomfort and annoyance while using land is often as important to a person as freedom from physical interruption with his use or freedom from detrimental change in the physical condition of the land itself. This interest in freedom from annoyance and discomfort in the use of land is to be distinguished from the interest in freedom from emotional distress. . . . The latter is purely an interest of personality and receives limited legal protection, whereas the former is essentially an interest in the usability of land and, although it involves an element of personal tastes and sensibilities, it receives much greater legal protection. Restatement Torts, 2d, § 821D comment b., p. 101.

Although the comment requires "interest in use and enjoyment of land" to be read broadly, this broad reading is entirely within the confines of uses of land that arise while occupying property. It defines the interest in terms of occupancy, physical interruption, and physical condition. These terms denote land uses that are enjoyed while a person is actually present on the property. Nowhere in the comment is there the merest allusion to abstract property rights such as ability to sell. This ability can be enjoyed regardless of one's occupancy of the land as land sales may occur without the parties ever entering the property. We find the ability to sell more like an injury against personality, which the Restatement specifically rejects. Both are types of harm that, though connected with the property in some way, manifest independent of presence on the property.

Pennsylvania caselaw involving private nuisance is consistent with this view. All of the cases relate to an interference of the enjoyment of the property while on the premises. *See, e.g., Harford Penn-Cann Service, Inc. v. Zymblosky*, 378 Pa. Super. 578, 549 A.2d 208 (Pa. Super. 1988) (dust from truck stop sufficient to constitute nuisance where health problems to employees resulted); *Karpiak v. Russo*, 450 Pa. Super. 471, 676 A.2d 270 (Pa. Super. 1996) (dust from a business not a nuisance where no health problems or effect on daily activities resulted); *Township of Bedminster v. Vargo Dragway, Inc.*, 434 Pa. 100, 253 A.2d 659 (Pa. 1969) (excessive noise from a racetrack in a residential area found to be a nuisance in fact). No case allows for as expansive a protection as appellants advocate.

Finally, accepting appellants' theory of private nuisance would constitute poor policy. If we were to allow recovery in this case, we would open the proverbial floodgates. Anytime a property owner engaged in an activity that ostensibly reduced surrounding property values, liability would attach. Hence, a property owner opening an unpopular public housing project or an AIDS clinic would be strictly liable for a decline in surrounding property values. Such a rule would allow unfounded prejudices to dictate property use, which is clearly unacceptable. Although hazardous waste contamination is undeniably pernicious, when such contamination only affects a property owner's ability to sell his or her property, a nuisance action does not exist.

Moreover, the rule proposed by appellants would impose almost limitless liability on a property owner for an undesirable use. Instantly, if appellants recover so can every other neighbor who claims difficulty selling his or her property, regardless of proximity to appellees. This Court has condemned this type of unlimited liability.

In conclusion, we find that appellants' claim of inability to sell property is, by itself, insufficient to establish a private nuisance. This claim amounts to damage without legal injury, or *damnum absque injuria*, and is therefore merit less.

NOTES

1. *Significant Harm.* Rest. 2d Torts § 821F provides:

> There is liability for a nuisance only to those to whom it causes significant harm, of a kind that would be suffered by a normal person in the community or by property in normal condition and used for a normal purpose.

2. *Property That Can't be Sold.* Is an interference with the ability to sell the property a significant harm? It is clearly a harm to one's economic interest. But is there a way in which it should be viewed as a significant harm to the present use and enjoyment of the property? Can you think of a persuasive argument from an economic efficiency perspective?

3. *Perspectives.* The court in *Golen* expresses concerns that a limit must be drawn on nuisance claims and that recognizing a diminution in land value loss — absent an interference with present use — would open a Pandora's box, adversely impacting land uses such as "an unpopular public housing project or an AIDS clinic." Critically assess this argument from perspectives of economic efficiency, corrective justice, and social justice.

D. ASSESSING PROOF AND FASHIONING REMEDIES

BOOMER, v. ATLANTIC CEMENT COMPANY, INC.,
257 N.E.2d 870 (N.Y. 1970)

BERGAN, JUSTICE.

Defendant operates a large cement plant near Albany. These are actions for injunction and damages by neighboring land owners alleging injury to property from dirt, smoke and vibration emanating from the plant. A nuisance has been found after trial, temporary damages have been allowed; but an injunction has been denied.

The public concern with air pollution arising from many sources in industry and in transportation is currently accorded ever wider recognition accompanied by a growing sense of responsibility in State and Federal Governments to control it. Cement plants are obvious sources of air pollution in the neighborhoods where they operate.

But there is now before the court private litigation in which individual property owners have sought specific relief from a single plant operation. The threshold question raised by the division of view on this appeal is whether the court should resolve the litigation between the parties now before it as equitably as seems possible; or whether, seeking promotion of the general public welfare, it should channel private litigation into broad public objectives.

A court performs its essential function when it decides the rights of parties before it. Its decision of private controversies may sometimes greatly affect public issues. Large questions of law are often resolved by the manner in which private litigation is decided. But this is normally an incident to the court's main function to settle controversy. It is a rare exercise of judicial power to use a decision in private litigation as a purposeful mechanism to achieve direct public objectives greatly beyond the rights and interests before the court.

Effective control of air pollution is a problem presently far from solution even with the full public and financial powers of government. In large measure adequate technical procedures are yet to be developed and some that appear possible may be economically impracticable.

It seems apparent that the amelioration of air pollution will depend on technical research in great depth; on a carefully balanced consideration of the economic impact of close regulation; and of the actual effect on public health. It is likely to require massive public expenditure and to demand more than any local community can accomplish and to depend on regional and interstate controls.

A court should not try to do this on its own as a by-product of private litigation and it seems manifest that the judicial establishment is neither equipped in the limited nature of any judgment it can pronounce nor prepared to lay down and implement an effective policy for the elimination of air pollution. This is an area beyond the circumference of one private lawsuit. It is a direct responsibility for government and should not thus be undertaken as an incident to solving a dispute between property owners and a single cement plant — one of many — in the Hudson River valley.

The cement making operations of defendant have been found by the court at Special Term to have damaged the nearby properties of plaintiffs in these two actions. That court, as it has been noted, accordingly found defendant maintained a nuisance and this has been affirmed at the Appellate Division. The total damage to plaintiffs' properties is, however, relatively small in comparison with the value of defendant's operation and with the consequences of the injunction which plaintiffs seek.

The ground for the denial of injunction, notwithstanding the finding both that there is a nuisance and that plaintiffs have been damaged substantially, is the large disparity in economic consequences of the nuisance and of the injunction. This theory cannot, however, be sustained without overruling a doctrine which has been consistently reaffirmed in several leading cases in this court and which has never been disavowed here, namely that where a nuisance has been found and where there has been any substantial damage shown by the party complaining an injunction will be granted.

The rule in New York has been that such a nuisance will be enjoined although marked disparity be shown in economic consequence between the effect of the injunction and the effect of the nuisance.

The problem of disparity in economic consequence was sharply in focus in *Whalen v. Union Bag & Paper Co.* (208 N.Y. 1). A pulp mill entailing an investment of more than a million dollars polluted a stream in which plaintiff, who owned a farm, was "a lower riparian owner." The economic loss to plaintiff from this pollution was small. This court, reversing the Appellate Division, reinstated the injunction granted by the Special Term against the argument of the mill owner that in view of "the slight advantage to plaintiff and the great loss that will be inflicted on defendant" an injunction should not be granted (p. 2). "Such a balancing of injuries cannot be justified by the circumstances of this case," Judge Werner noted (p. 4). He continued: "Although the damage to the plaintiff may be slight as compared with the defendant's expense of abating the condition, that is not a good reason for refusing an injunction" (p. 5).

Thus the unconditional injunction granted at Special Term was reinstated. The rule laid down in that case, then, is that whenever the damage resulting from a nuisance is found not "unsubstantial," viz., $100 a year, injunction would follow. This states a rule that had been followed in this court with marked consistency (*McCarty v. Natural Carbonic Gas Co.*, 189 N.Y. 40; *Strobel v. Kerr Salt Co.*, 164 N.Y. 303; *Campbell v. Seaman*, 63 N.Y. 568).

There are cases where injunction has been denied. *McCann v. Chasm Power Co.* (211 N.Y. 301) is one of them. There, however, the damage shown by plaintiffs was not only unsubstantial, it was non-existent. Plaintiffs owned a rocky bank of the stream in which defendant had raised the level of the water. This had no economic or other adverse consequence to plaintiffs, and thus injunctive relief was denied. Similar is the basis for denial of injunction in *Forstmann* v. *Joray Holding Co.* (244 N.Y. 22) where no benefit to plaintiffs could be seen from the injunction sought (p. 32). Thus if, within *Whalen* v. *Union Bag & Paper Co.* (*supra*) which authoritatively states the rule in New York, the damage to plaintiffs in these present cases from defendant's cement plant is "not unsubstantial", an injunction should follow.

Although the court at Special Term and the Appellate Division held that injunction should be denied, it was found that plaintiffs had been damaged in various specific amounts up to the time of the trial and damages to the respective plaintiffs were awarded for those amounts. The effect of this was, injunction having been denied, plaintiffs could maintain successive actions at law for damages thereafter as further damage was incurred.

The court at Special Term also found the amount of permanent damage attributable to each plaintiff, for the guidance of the parties in the event both sides stipulated to the payment and acceptance of such permanent damage as a settlement of all the controversies among the parties. The total of permanent damages to all plaintiffs thus found was $185,000. This basis of adjustment has not resulted in any stipulation by the parties.

This result at Special Term and at the Appellate Division is a departure from a rule that has become settled; but to follow the rule literally in these cases would be to close down the plant at once. This court is fully agreed to avoid that immediately drastic remedy; the difference in view is how best to avoid it. . . .

One alternative is to grant the injunction but postpone its effect to a specified future date to give opportunity for technical advances to permit defendant to eliminate the nuisance; another is to grant the injunction conditioned on the payment of permanent damages to plaintiffs which would compensate them for the total economic loss to their property present and future caused by defendant's operations. For reasons which will be developed the court chooses the latter alternative.

If the injunction were to be granted unless within a short period — e.g., 18 months — the nuisance be abated by improved methods, there would be no assurance that any significant technical improvement would occur.

The parties could settle this private litigation at any time if defendant paid enough money and the imminent threat of closing the plant would build up the pressure on defendant. If there were no improved techniques found, there would inevitably be applications to the court at Special Term for extensions of time to perform on showing of good faith efforts to find such techniques.

Moreover, techniques to eliminate dust and other annoying by-products of cement making are unlikely to be developed by any research the defendant can undertake within any short period, but will depend on the total resources of the cement industry Nationwide and throughout the world. The problem is universal wherever cement is made.

For obvious reasons the rate of the research is beyond control of defendant. If at the end of 18 months the whole industry has not found a technical solution a court would be hard put to close down this one cement plant if due regard be given to equitable principles.

On the other hand, to grant the injunction unless defendant pays plaintiffs such permanent damages as may be fixed by the court seems to do justice between the contending parties. All of the attributions of economic loss to the properties on which plaintiffs' complaints are based will have been redressed.

The nuisance complained of by these plaintiffs may have other public or private consequences, but these particular parties are the only ones who have sought remedies and the judgment proposed will fully redress them. The limitation of relief granted is a limitation only within the four corners of these actions and does not foreclose public health or other public agencies from seeking proper relief in a proper court.

It seems reasonable to think that the risk of being required to pay permanent damages to injured property owners by cement plant owners would itself be a reasonable effective spur to research for improved techniques to minimize nuisance.

The power of the court to condition on equitable grounds the continuance of an injunction on the payment of permanent damages seems undoubted. (See, e.g., the alternatives considered in *McCarty* v. *Natural Carbonic Gas Co., supra*, as well as *Strobel* v. *Kerr Salt Co., supra*.)

The damage base here suggested is consistent with the general rule in those nuisance cases where damages are allowed. "Where a nuisance is of such a permanent and unabatable character that a single recovery can be had, including the whole damage past and future resulting therefrom, there can be but one recovery" (66 C. J. S., Nuisances, § 140, p. 947). It has been said that permanent damages are allowed where the loss recoverable would obviously be small as compared with the cost of removal of the nuisance (*Kentucky-Ohio Gas Co.* v. *Bowling*, 264 Ky. 470, 477).

The present cases and the remedy here proposed are in a number of other respects rather similar to *Northern Indiana Public Serv. Co.* v. *Vesey* (210 Ind. 338) decided by the Supreme Court of Indiana. The gases, odors, ammonia and smoke from the Northern Indiana company's gas plant damaged the nearby Vesey greenhouse operation. An injunction and damages were sought, but an injunction was denied and the relief granted was limited to permanent damages "present, past, and future" (p. 371).

Denial of injunction was grounded on a public interest in the operation of the gas plant and on the court's conclusion "that less injury would be occasioned by requiring the appellant [Public Service] to pay the appellee [Vesey] all damages suffered by it than by enjoining the operation of the gas plant; and that the maintenance and operation of the gas plant should not be enjoined" (p. 349).

The Indiana Supreme Court opinion continued: "When the trial court refused injunctive relief to the appellee upon the ground of public interest in the continuance of the gas plant, it properly retained jurisdiction of the case and awarded full compensation to the appellee. This is upon the general equitable principle that equity will give full relief in one action and prevent a multiplicity of suits" (pp. 353-354).

It was held that in this type of continuing and recurrent nuisance permanent damages were appropriate. See, also, *City of Amarillo* v. *Ware* (120 Tex. 456) where recurring overflows from a system of storm sewers were treated as the kind of nuisance for which permanent depreciation of value of affected property would be recoverable.

There is some parallel to the conditioning of an injunction on the payment of permanent damages in the noted "elevated railway cases" (*Pappenheim* v. *Metropolitan El. Ry. Co.*, 128 N. Y. 436, and others which followed). Decisions in these cases were based on the finding that the railways created a nuisance as to adjacent property owners, but in lieu of enjoining their operation, the court allowed permanent damages.

Judge Finch, reviewing these cases in *Ferguson* v. *Village of Hamburg* (272 N. Y. 234, 239-240), said: "The courts decided that the plaintiffs had a valuable right which was being impaired, but did not grant an absolute injunction or require the railway companies to resort to separate condemnation proceedings. Instead they held that a court of equity could ascertain the damages and grant an injunction which was not to be effective unless the defendant failed to pay the amount fixed as damages for the past and permanent injury inflicted." (*See also*, *Lynch* v. *Metropolitan El. Ry. Co.*, 129 N.Y. 274; *Van Allen* v. *New York El. R. R. Co.*, 144 N. Y. 174; *Cox* v. *City of New York*, 265 N.Y. 411, and similarly, *Westphal* v. *City of New York*, 177 N.Y. 140.)

Thus it seems fair to both sides to grant permanent damages to plaintiffs which will terminate this private litigation. The theory of damage is the "servitude on land" of plaintiffs imposed by defendant's nuisance. (See *United States* v. *Causby*, 328 U.S. 256, 261, 262, 267, where the term "servitude" addressed to the land was used by Justice Douglas relating to the effect of airplane noise on property near an airport.)

The judgment, by allowance of permanent damages imposing a servitude on land, which is the basis of the actions, would preclude future recovery by plaintiffs or their grantees (*see Northern Indiana Public Serv. Co.* v. *Vesey, supra*, p. 351).

This should be placed beyond debate by a provision of the judgment that the payment by defendant and the acceptance by plaintiffs of permanent damages found by the court shall be in compensation for a servitude on the land.

Although the Trial Term has found permanent damages as a possible basis of settlement of the litigation, on remission the court should be entirely free to re-examine this subject. It may again find the permanent damage already found; or make new findings.

The orders should be reversed, without costs, and the cases remitted to Supreme Court, Albany County to grant an injunction which shall be vacated upon payment by defendant of such amounts of permanent damage to the respective plaintiffs as shall for this purpose be determined by the court.

DISSENT:

JASEN, J. (dissenting). I agree with the majority that a reversal is required here, but I do not subscribe to the newly enunciated doctrine of assessment of permanent damages, in lieu of an injunction, where substantial property rights have been impaired by the creation of a nuisance.

It has long been the rule in this State, as the majority acknowledges, that a nuisance which results in substantial continuing damage to neighbors must be enjoined. (*Whalen* v. *Union Bag & Paper Co.*, 208 N.Y. 1; *Campbell* v. *Seaman*, 63 N.Y. 568; see, also, *Kennedy* v. *Moog Servocontrols*, 21 NY 2d 966.) To now change the rule to permit the cement company to continue polluting the air indefinitely upon the payment of permanent damages is, in my opinion, compounding the magnitude of a very serious problem in our State and Nation today.

In recognition of this problem, the Legislature of this State has enacted the Air Pollution Control Act (Public Health Law, §§ 1264-1299-m) declaring that it is the State policy to require the use of all available and reasonable methods to prevent and control air pollution (Public Health Law, § 1265). . . .

The harmful nature and widespread occurrence of air pollution have been extensively documented. Congressional hearings have revealed that air pollution causes substantial property damage, as well as being a contributing factor to a rising incidence of lung cancer, emphysema, bronchitis and asthma.

The specific problem faced here is known as particulate contamination because of the fine dust particles emanating from defendant's cement plant. The particular type of nuisance is not new, having appeared in many cases for at least the past 60 years. (See *Hulbert* v. *California Portland Cement Co.*, 161 Cal. 239 [1911].) It is interesting to note that cement production has recently been identified as a significant source of particulate contamination in the Hudson Valley. This type of pollution, wherein very small particles escape and stay in the atmosphere, has been denominated as the type of air pollution which produces the greatest hazard to human health. We have thus a nuisance which not only is damaging to the plaintiffs but also is decidedly harmful to the general public.

I see grave dangers in overruling our long-established rule of granting an injunction where a nuisance results in substantial continuing damage. In permitting the injunction to become inoperative upon the payment of permanent damages, the majority is, in effect, licensing a continuing wrong. It is the same as saying to the cement company, you may continue to do harm to your neighbors so long as you pay a fee for it. Furthermore, once such permanent damages are assessed and paid, the incentive to alleviate the wrong would be eliminated, thereby continuing air pollution of an area without abatement.

It is true that some courts have sanctioned the remedy here proposed by the majority in a number of cases, but none of the authorities relied upon by the majority are analogous to the situation before us. In those cases, the courts, in denying an injunction and awarding money damages, grounded their decision on a showing that the use to which the property was intended to be put was primarily for the public benefit. Here, on the other hand, it is clearly established that the cement company is creating a continuing air pollution nuisance primarily for its own private interest with no public benefit.

This kind of inverse condemnation (*Ferguson* v. *Village of Hamburg*, 272 N.Y. 234, may not be invoked by a private person or corporation for private gain or advantage. Inverse condemnation should only be permitted when the public is primarily served in the taking or impairment of property. (*Matter of New York City Housing Auth.* v. *Muller*, 270 N.Y. 333, 343; *Pocantico Water Works Co.* v. *Bird*, 130 N. Y. 249, 258.) The promotion of the interests of the polluting cement company has, in my opinion, no public use or benefit.

Nor is it constitutionally permissible to impose servitude on land, without consent of the owner, by payment of permanent damages where the continuing impairment of the land is for a private use. (See *Fifth Ave. Coach Lines* v. *City of New York*, 11 N Y 2d 342, 347; *Walker* v. *City of Hutchinson*, 352 U.S. 112.) This is made clear by the State Constitution (art. I, § 7, subd. [a]) which provides that "[private] property shall not be taken for *public use* without just compensation" (emphasis added). It is, of course, significant that the section makes no mention of taking for a *private* use.

In sum, then, by constitutional mandate as well as by judicial pronouncement, the permanent impairment of private property for private purposes is not authorized in the absence of clearly demonstrated public benefit and use.

I would enjoin the defendant cement company from continuing the discharge of dust particles upon its neighbors' properties unless, within 18 months, the cement company abated this nuisance.

It is not my intention to cause the removal of the cement plant from the Albany area, but to recognize the urgency of the problem stemming from this stationary source of air pollution, and to allow the company a specified period of time to develop a means to alleviate this nuisance.

I am aware that the trial court found that the most modern dust control devices available have been installed in defendant's plant, but, I submit, this does not mean that *better* and more effective dust control devices could not be developed within the time allowed to abate the pollution.

Moreover, I believe it is incumbent upon the defendant to develop such devices, since the cement company, at the time the plant commenced production (1962) was well aware of the plaintiffs' presence in the area, as well as the probable consequences of its contemplated operation. Yet, it still chose to build and operate the plant at this site.

In a day when there is a growing concern for clean air, highly developed industry should not expect acquiescence by the courts, but should, instead, plan its operations to eliminate contamination of our air and damage to its neighbors.

Accordingly, the orders of the Appellate Division, insofar as they denied the injunction, should be reversed, and the actions remitted to Supreme Court, Albany County to grant an injunction to take effect 18 months hence, unless the nuisance is abated by improved techniques prior to said date.

NOTES

1. *Permanent Pollution?* The court in *Boomer* concluded: "Thus it seems fair to both sides to grant permanent damages to plaintiffs which will terminate this private litigation. The theory of damage is the 'servitude on land' of plaintiffs imposed by defendant's nuisance. The judgment, by allowance of permanent damages imposing a servitude on land, which is the basis of the actions, would preclude future recovery by plaintiffs or their grantees. This should be placed beyond debate by a provision of the judgment that the payment by defendant and the acceptance by plaintiffs of permanent damages found by the court shall be in compensation for a servitude on the land." *Boomer*, 257 N.E.2d at 875. Should a court use its power to authorize permanent pollution?

2. *Balancing the Equities.* The *Boomer* court offered the following advice to the trial court: "Although the Trial Term has found permanent damages as a possible basis of settlement of the litigation, on remission the court should be entirely free to re-examine this subject. It may again find the permanent damage already found; or make new findings." Boomer, 257 N.E. 2d at 875. What new findings should the court consider making?

3. *Electromagnetic Field (EMF) Litigation.* Numerous claims have been made regarding alleged EMF injuries:

According to a July 1992 article in *Science* magazine, as many as 20 million people presently may be exposed to higher than normal levels of EMF just from the 642,000 circuit miles of high-voltage transmission lines in the United States alone. (Normal levels are said to range from 5 mg to 1.5 mg.) An additional 12,600 circuit miles of such transmission lines were scheduled for construction by the year 2000.

Added to the number of people exposed to EMF from household or workplace electrical wiring, appliances, and other sources, the scope is immense. (An electric razor, for example, can generate a magnetic field of as much as 200 mg at five inches.)

Concern about EMF health effects go back at least three decades. The first studies, conducted in the Soviet Union 30 years ago, suggested a link between exposure to electric fields and certain chronic afflictions such as headaches, fatigue and nausea. Research in the West proceeded throughout the 1970s without replicating the Soviet results and gaining little attention.

Then, in 1979 the results of a major epidemiological study on EMF conducted in the Denver area were published. They seemed to show an association between exposure to EMF from powerlines and increased incidence of childhood cancer, though serious questions have since arisen about the methodology used.

Over 35 major studies conducted since then in this country and abroad have produced results best characterized as inconclusive and sometimes conflicting. A 1990 analysis by the Environmental Protection Agency of previous studies on EMF exposure and the incidence of cancer concluded only that an increasing amount of data show "a consistent pattern of response which suggests, but does not prove, a causal link."

Meanwhile, a report released by the White House Office of Science and Technology Policy claimed that "there is no convincing evidence in the published literature to support the contention that exposures to . . . EMF generated by sources such as household appliances, video display terminals and local powerlines are demonstrable health risks." Still, the studies have succeeded in arousing public concern.

An understanding of the obstacles confronting EMF research begins with the nature of ailments attributed to EMF exposure. Those most often cited are various forms of cancer, particularly childhood leukemia. A myriad of other disorders, including birth defects, miscarriages, and neurological dysfunctions also are alleged to result from exposure to EMF.

But the pathology of these afflictions is poorly understood. Causes are obscure and may be rooted in multiple environmental as well as hereditary factors.

Roy W. Krieger, *On the Line*, A.B.A. J. 42 (Jan. 1994).

4. *Repetitive Stress Injury*. A major breakthrough in repetitive stress injury litigation was reported in the American Bar Journal:

> Three plaintiffs were a charm for a Brooklyn jury in a lawsuit against Digital Equipment Corp. Their $5.9 million award is the first jury verdict against a keyboard manufacturer for repetitive stress injuries suffered by office workers.
>
> The jury found in December that the defendant failed to warn the three plaintiffs about the dangers of using the Digital LK201 keyboard. The injured women had experienced wrist and spinal ailments after using the product. *Madden v. Digital Equipment Corp.*, No. 94-CV1427 (E.D.N.Y.)(1997). U.S. District Judge Jack Weinstein had denied a defense motion to sever the three cases, making the defense job triply difficult. Digital alleged one plaintiff's injuries were caused by existing medical conditions and another by hobbies. In the third case, it claimed there were no injuries.
>
> The company, headquartered in Maynard, Mass., plans to move to set aside the verdict and to appeal if the motion is denied. "One verdict is not a trend, by any definition," says Digital's lead lawyer, Kenneth J. King of Beatie, King & Abate in New York City.
>
> But the lead attorney for the plaintiffs says the award should not be portrayed as an aberration because several hundred keyboard cases brought by his firm have resulted in settlements. "It's a bigger picture than [the manufacturers] are letting on," says Steven J. Phillips of Levy Phillips & Konigsberg in New York City.
>
> The firm has about 900 pending repetitive stress injury cases, the majority of which are against keyboard manufacturers. Symptoms of

RSI range from numbness and tingling sensations to severe pain; the malady currently consumes about one-third of all workers compensation dollars. Many RSI sufferers have carpal tunnel syndrome, which causes pain in the hand, wrist and lower arm.

Eric Milstone, *Keyed Up, Repetitive Stressed Out*, A.B.A. J. 22 (Feb. 1997).

E.   THE STATUTE OF LIMITATIONS

JACK CLINE v. ASHLAND, INC., ET AL.
2007 Ala. LEXIS 5 (Ala. 2007)

SEE, JUSTICE.

[The majority of the Court affirmed the grant of summary judgment dismissing the plaintiff's claim, without an opinion.]

Jack Cline appeals from the summary judgment entered by the Jefferson Circuit Court, which held that Cline's claims are barred by the statute of limitations. On October 14, 2005, this Court affirmed the summary judgment without an opinion. Cline applied for a rehearing. We granted his application and heard oral argument. This Court today affirms the summary judgment on rehearing, without an opinion, and I write specially to explain why I concur in its decision to do so. Cline alleges that from 1968 to 1987, while he was working for Griffin Wheel Company of Bessemer, he was exposed to the chemical benzene. He retired from Griffin Wheel in 1995, and he was diagnosed with acute myelogenous leukemia ("AML") on October 7, 1999. On April 6, 2001, Cline sued Ashland, Inc.; Chevron Phillips Chemical L.P., the successor in interest to Chevron Chemical Company, LLC; and ExxonMobil Corporation, alleging that the defendants manufactured and/or supplied the benzene to which he was exposed during the course of his employment at Griffin Wheel. He alleges that the defendants are responsible for his developing AML and are liable under the Alabama Extended Manufacturer's Liability Doctrine ("the AEMLD"). The defendants moved for a summary judgment, arguing that Cline's claims are barred by the applicable statute of limitations. Cline argued that the statute of limitations did not begin to run until he was diagnosed with AML. The trial court entered a summary judgment in favor of the defendants, holding that the applicable statute of limitations began to run in 1987, when Cline was last exposed to the benzene. Cline appealed the trial court's summary judgment as to his AEMLD claim, and this Court affirmed the summary judgment, without an opinion. Cline applied for a rehearing, which this Court granted.

In 1979, in *Garrett v. Raytheon Co.*, 368 So. 2d 516 (Ala. 1979), this Court considered the case in which Jerry Garrett sued several companies, claiming that he had unknowingly been exposed to massive amounts of radiation from 1955 to 1957 because, he argued, the companies had negligently designed certain radar systems where he worked. He did not experience any health problems as a result of the radiation exposure until March 1975, when his hair suddenly turned white and then fell out. He consulted several doctors but it was not until March 1977 that a radiologist told him that his earlier radiation exposure had caused his health problems. Although Garrett brought his action within 1 year of the radiologist's diagnosis, he did so more than a year after the first manifestation of his health problems and more than 20 years after his last exposure to the radiation. At the time this Court decided *Garrett*, the applicable statute of limitations required that "[a]ctions for any injury to the person or rights of another not arising from contract and not specifically enumerated in this section" be commenced within one year from accrual. § 6-2-39(a)(5), Ala. Code 1975. In *Garrett*, this Court held that "the statute of limitations of one year began to run when [the] plaintiff was last exposed to radiation and the plaintiff's ignorance of the tort or injury, there being no fraudulent concealment, does not postpone the running of the statute until the tort or injury is discovered." 368 So. 2d at 521.

The *Garrett* court invited the legislature to respond. The legislature responded by enacting Act No. 79-468, Ala. Acts 1979. Act No. 79-468 provided a discovery rule for cases in which a person has been injured by a toxic substance over a period of time. § 6-5-502, Ala. Code 1975. Under the discovery rule, the statute of limitations did not begin to run until the date the plaintiff discovered, or should have discovered, the injury. § 6-5-502, Ala. Code 1975. The legislature, however, provided in Act No. 79-468 that if any part of the Act was declared unconstitutional, then the entire Act would become inoperative. § 6-5-504, Ala. Code 1975. In accordance with this limitation, this Court invalidated the entire Act when it held that a particular section of Act No. 79-468 concerning a rule of repose was unconstitutional. With Act No. 79-468 no longer in effect, the law reverted to the "last exposure" rule declared in *Garrett*. Since then, the legislature has acted in the toxic-tort area, but has limited the scope of the subsequent act to injuries resulting from exposure to asbestos. § 6-2-30(b), Ala. Code 1975. The Alabama Legislature also has considered, and thus far chosen not to adopt, proposals that would provide a discovery rule in cases of the nature of this one.

This Court also has consistently chosen to continue to follow *Garrett*'s "last exposure" rule. See, e.g., *Moore v. Glover*, 501 So. 2d 1187, 1190 (Ala. 1986) ("[T]his Court's opinion in *Garrett v. Raytheon Co.*, 368 So. 2d 516 (Ala. 1979), settled the question of the 'accrual' of a plaintiff's claim in a radiation exposure case for purposes of determining when the applicable statute of limitations begins to run. . . ."); *Hubbard v. Liberty Mut. Ins. Co.*, 599 So. 2d 20, 21 n.2 (Ala. 1982) ("[I]t seems to be settled in Alabama that the 'date of injury,' which starts the running of the statutory period of limitations in a continuous exposure case, occurs when the plaintiff was last exposed to the chemical or condition causing his injuries.").

The legislature has acted in this area both by enacting legislation and by considering, and thus far not adopting, proposed legislation. See §§ 6-5-500 through -504, Ala. Code 1975. . . . The power "to declare what the law shall be" is a legislative power, and this Court will not revisit an area of the law in which the legislature has already acted. *City of Daphne v. City of Spanish Fort*, 853 So. 2d 933, 942 (Ala. 2003).

The determination of when the statute of limitations ought to begin to run in toxic-substance-exposure cases depends on a weighing of competing public policies. We seek in Alabama to compensate those who have been injured. Ala. Const. 1901, Art. I, § 13 ("[T]hat every person, for any injury done him . . . shall have a remedy by due process of law; and right and justice shall be administered without sale, denial, or delay."). On the other hand, we also seek to avoid stale claims and the injustice such claims can engender. *Travis v. Ziter*, 681 So. 2d 1348, 1355 (Ala. 1996) ("At its core, the statute of limitations advances the truth-seeking function of our justice system, promotes efficiency by giving plaintiffs an incentive to timely pursue claims, and promotes stability by protecting defendants from stale claims."). The proper balance between these competing public policies requires a weighing, and "[i]t is well established that '"[t]he Legislature is endowed with the exclusive domain to formulate public policy in Alabama. . . ."'" *Leonard v. Terminix Int'l Co.*, 854 So. 2d 529, 534 (Ala. 2002) (citations omitted). . . .

HARWOOD, JUSTICE (dissenting).

In their special concurrences to this Court's decision to affirm the trial court's summary judgment in this appeal without an opinion, Justice See and Justice Smith emphasize that it is the role of the legislature, not this Court, to declare public policy. I quite agree. Indeed, the legislature has already acted and declared the public policy applicable to this case, by means of the interaction of two provisions of the Code of Alabama. Section 6-2-30(a), Ala. Code 1975, provides, in pertinent part, that "[a]ll civil actions must be commenced after the cause of action has accrued within the period prescribed . . . and not afterwards. . . ." Section 6-2-38(l), Ala. Code 1975, provides that an action of the type Jack Cline has filed "must be brought within two years." Therefore, the legislatively declared public policy is that an action such as Cline's can be filed (within the two-year limitations period) only after the cause of action has accrued. By this dissent, I do not presume to advocate a contrary public policy; I simply attempt to honor the public policy the legislature has declared, by correctly construing the statutory language "cause of action has accrued" in § 6-2-30(a) in accord with traditional principles of tort law.

Neither special concurrence takes the position that the construction given that language in *Garrett v. Raytheon Co.*, 368 So. 2d 516 (Ala. 1979), was in accord with those principles and true to the legislature's intent. They simply take the position, in support of which they offer reasoned argument, that any change from the rule set out in *Garrett* must, at this late date, be left exclusively to the legislature. For the reasons I set forth hereinafter, I respectfully disagree.

First, however, these three miscellaneous points: Although Justice See fairly states the basic facts underlying Cline's tort claim, it is appropriate to note that it is undisputed that acute myelogenous leukemia can be caused by exposure to benzene, which this Court described in *Shell v. Union Oil Co.*, 489 So. 2d 569, 570 (Ala. 1986), as "a carcinogen known to cause leukemia." Also,

Cline made the alternative argument before the trial court and on original submission on this appeal that his "last exposure" in 1999 to benzene contained in the product of an alleged "joint tortfeasor" of the present appellees should serve to delay the running of the statute of limitations as to them as well. Because this contention was not revisited in Cline's brief in support of his application for rehearing, it was thereby waived and will not now be considered. *Birmingham News Co. v. Horn*, 901 So. 2d 27, 77 (Ala. 2004). Last, the defendants have not attempted to argue that the natural history of acute myelogenous leukemia is such that Cline must have been suffering from it, i.e., that he must have actually experienced a manifest, present injury in connection with it, before his October 7, 1999, diagnosis. Accordingly, Cline's action filed on April 6, 2001, was timely under the two-year statute of limitations, if the commencement of the running of that statute is measured from October 7, 1999, or any other time within two years before April 6, 2001.

Relevant Caselaw and Legislation.

In *Garrett, supra,* Jerry Kenneth Garrett filed an action in 1978 against seven companies he alleged had designed, manufactured, or serviced certain radar systems with which he had had contact from 1955 to 1957; he asserted that because of the defective condition of those systems, he unknowingly had been exposed to massive dosages of dangerous radiation. He had experienced no symptoms or health problems until March 1975. He then consulted numerous doctors, but the nature of his problems was not diagnosed until March 1977 when a radiologist advised him that his problems were the result of his earlier radiation exposure. Garrett's action was filed within one year of that diagnosis, but more than one year after the first manifestation of his health problems and more than two decades after his last exposure to the radiation. Then, as now, § 6-2-30, Ala. Code 1975, required that all civil actions must be commenced within the statutorily prescribed limitations period "after the cause of action has accrued" (emphasis supplied). The then applicable statute of limitations, former § 6-2-39(a)(5), required "[a]ctions for any injury to the person or rights of another not arising from contract and not specifically enumerated in this section" to be commenced within one year from accrual. (That provision was recodified as § 6-2-38(l) when the limitations period was increased to two years in 1985.)

The opinion of the five-member *Garrett* majority (four Justices dissented) commenced: "When does the statute of limitations begin to run for injuries suffered as a result of radiation exposure? We conclude that it begins to run when the plaintiff is exposed to radiation and an injury occurs." 368 So. 2d at 517–18 (emphasis supplied). However, the majority then collapsed injury into exposure, holding that "the statute of limitations of one year began to run when plaintiff was last exposed to radiation and plaintiff's ignorance of the tort or injury, there being no fraudulent concealment, does not postpone the running of the statute until the tort or injury is discovered." The Court justified this conclusion by stating, "[i]f plaintiff was *not injured* in 1955–1957 then defendant committed *no negligent act* at that time which *resulted in injury* and defendant would not be liable. If plaintiff did become injured or damaged at that time, then the statute of limitations has run." 368 So. 2d at 521. The Court similarly reasoned, "*[d]amage* must have occurred at the time of exposure else defendant would not be liable. It is simply that all the progressive nature of the injury has not made itself manifest at the time of the last exposure." 368 So. 2d at 520. As Justice Shores observed in her dissent, "[t]he majority opinion assumes that the injury occurred simultaneously with the plaintiff's exposure to the radiation." 368 So. 2d at 526. She disagreed, stating that "[t]he defendant's exposure of the plaintiff to radiation would not create a cause of action in the plaintiff until injury resulted from that exposure." 368 So. 2d at 526. Justice Jones in his dissenting opinion on application for rehearing likewise explained that the holding of the majority "reduces date of injury (and thus accrual of the cause of action) to a legal conclusion without regard to when the injury in fact occurs." 368 So. 2d at 528.

Leading up to its conclusion that "[t]he injury in this case occurred on the date or dates of exposure," 368 So. 2d at 520, the majority acknowledged that

> there are cases where the act complained of does not itself constitute a legal injury at the time, but plaintiff's injury only comes as a result of, and in furtherance and subsequent development of, the act defendant has done. In such cases, the cause of action accrues, and the statute of limitation begins to run, 'when, and only when, the damages are sustained.'

368 So. 2d at 519. The countervailing rule was explained by the Court as follows:

> If the act of which the injury is the natural sequence is of itself a legal injury to plaintiff, a completed wrong, the cause of action accrues and the statute begins to run from the time the act is committed, be the actual damage (then apparent) however slight, and the statute will operate to bar a recovery not only for the present damages but for damages developing subsequently and not actionable at the time of the wrong done; for in such a case the subsequent increase in the damages resulting gives no new cause of action.

368 So. 2d at 519 (quoting *Home Ins. Co. v. Stuart-McCorkle*, 291 Ala. 601, 608, 285 So. 2d 468, 473 (1973), quoting in turn *Kelley v. Shropshire*, 199 Ala. 602, 604-05, 75 So. 291, 292 (1917)).

The majority's explanation that Garrett's radiation exposure fell within the second class of cases because the "defendant committed no negligent act at that time which resulted in injury and defendant would not be liable," 368 So. 2d at 521, and "[d]amage must have occurred at the time of exposure else defendant would not be liable," 368 So. 2d at 520, seems to me to be no more than circular reasoning that ignores the first class of cases. Indeed, to my best attempt to follow the reasoning of the *Garrett* majority, it represents judicial public policy-making of the type the majority in this case now rightfully decries.

*   *   *

Garrett's last-exposure rule is purely a "court made" rule, because § 6-2-30 then provided, and § 6-2-30(a) now provides, only that civil actions must be commenced within the applicable limitations period "after the cause of action has accrued." The *Garrett* Court simply declared, as a matter of policy rather than scientific fact, that a toxic-exposure cause of action accrues contemporaneously with the last exposure to the toxic substance, it being judicially deemed that an injury has occurred at that time as a matter of law.

Neither *Garrett* nor any of its progeny articulate any scientific basis for that conclusion, and certainly the defendants in the present case do not argue that benzene exposure, even up through a last exposure, is known to cause concurrently some actual damage at the cellular level or otherwise to inflict an objectively ascertainable bodily injury.

Although it is undisputed that "the Legislature has the inherent power to enact a statute of limitations establishing the period within which a claim must be brought," *Baugher v. Beaver Constr. Co.*, 791 So. 2d 932, 934 n.1 (Ala. 2000), the question presented by this appeal is whether this Court should reexamine its construction in *Garrett* of the operative phrase in § 6-2-30, "after the cause of action has accrued" and interpret it differently than it did in *Garrett* for toxic-substance-exposure cases.

The Doctrine of Stare Decisis, and When Change in the Law is the Role of the Judiciary

* * *

Given the legislative history recited earlier, particularly the legislature's prompt response to this Court's decision in *Garrett* by enacting Act No. 79-468 (Ala. Code 1975, §§ 6-5-500 through -504) so as to register its disagreement with the holding in Garrett, I do not view the legislature's failure to act further than it has done in this area to constitute its approval of the construction this Court has placed on the statutory term "accrued" in toxic-exposure cases. Since *Garrett*, this Court has again and again reaffirmed the proposition acknowledged but ignored in *Garrett* — that there are cases where the defendant's act does not cause a contemporaneous injury to the plaintiff, but an injury later manifests as a result of, and in furtherance and subsequent development of, the defendant's act. See, e.g., *Ex parte Stonebrook Dev., LLC*, 854 So. 2d 584 (Ala. 2003); *Hinton ex rel. Hinton v. Monsanto*, 813 So. 2d 827 (Ala. 2001); *Payton v. Monsanto*, 801 So. 2d 829 (Ala. 2001); *Ex parte Floyd*, 796 So. 2d 303 (Ala. 2001); System *Dynamics Int'l, Inc. v. Boykin*, 683 So. 2d 419 (Ala. 1996); *Smith v. Medtronic, Inc.*, 607 So. 2d 156 (Ala. 1992); and *Payne v. Alabama Cemetery Ass'n, Inc.*, 413 So. 2d 1067 (Ala. 1982). In *Hinton*, the Court was asked in a certified question from a federal district court whether Alabama law recognized a cause of action for medical monitoring following hazardous-substance exposure when the plaintiffs were not claiming any present injury or illness. Based on that precise set of facts, the Court concluded that Alabama law "provides no redress for a plaintiff who has no present injury or illness" because, as the plurality opinion explained, "Alabama law has long required a manifest, present injury before a plaintiff may recover in tort." 813 So. 2d at 831-32, 829.

* * *

7 "It is a basic principle of tort law that in negligence cases, the plaintiff must suffer actual injury; the threat of future harm, not yet real-

ized, is not enough. W. PAGE KEETON ET AL., THE LAW OF TORTS § 30 at 165 (5th ed. 1984). . . ."

As things now stand, and as left in placed by the majority in this case, the law in this State would seem to be this: A person exposed to a toxic substance having the potential to cause disease on a delayed basis, but who has suffered no manifest, present injury within two years thereafter, may not file an action within that two-year period. *Hinton, supra*; *Southern Bakeries, supra*. If, after two years, that same person in fact suffers an injury from the exposure and files an action, the action will be dismissed on the basis that it should have been filed earlier. Thus, no matter when the person attempts to file the action, it is either too soon or too late. This is a classic Catch-22,[6] and one that would seem to violate Art. 1, § 13, Ala. Const. 1901, which provides, in pertinent part, "that every person for any injury done him . . . shall have a remedy by due process of law."

Perhaps, however, I am mistaken in understanding that the interaction of the rule in *Garrett* and our more recent caselaw serves to disallow the maintenance of a personal-injury tort claim after exposure to a toxic substance but in advance of a manifest, present injury. After all, as noted earlier, Justice Jones forecast in his dissent in *Garrett* that "one so exposed can bring his action within the year [now two years] of last exposure without medical proof of . . . damage — injury being presumed as a matter of law." 368 So. 2d at 528. In fact, the defendants embraced this view of the Garrett rule when they asserted in their initial brief to this Court that Cline "was entitled to sue these defendants for his exposure to benzene at Griffin Wheel from the first day he was exposed to benzene there to any time up to and including the day two years after he was last exposed there to benzene supplied by the defendants. . . ." (Appellee's brief, p. 43.) If this then is the correct state of the law, why could not the plaintiff in such a situation, after asserting a "*Garrett* injury," claim as additional damage mental anguish stemming from his or her fear of subsequently developing disease? And why could not the plaintiff in such a case, if asserting claims of fraudulent suppression, misrepresentation, and/or wantonness (as in *Southern Bakeries, supra*), additionally maintain a demand for punitive damages? All without any proof of any manifest, present injury.

The number of persons eligible to file an action if all that is required is some period of exposure to a toxic substance is potentially huge. *See Ex parte BASF Corp.*, [Ms. 1051060, Oct. 27, 2006] So. 2d, 2006 Ala. LEXIS 306 (Ala. 2006) (1600 plaintiffs); *Ex parte Flexible Prods.* Co., 915 So. 2d 34 (Ala. 2005) (1675 plaintiffs); and *Ex parte Monsanto Co.*, 862 So. 2d 595 (Ala. 2003) (3500 plaintiffs).

I submit that under either view of the implications of the *Garrett* rule, the law is confounded; thus, a continued blind obedience to that rule, simply in deference to stare decisis, does not serve the law, but rather greatly disserves it. As the Court explained in *Ex parte First Alabama Bank*, 883 So. 2d 1236, 1245 (Ala. 2003):

---

[6] "Catch-22: a frustrating situation in which one is trapped by contradictory regulations or conditions." *Random House Webster's Unabridged Dictionary* (2d ed. 2001).

"Justice Houston, writing specially in *Southern States Ford, Inc. v. Proctor*, 541 So. 2d 1081 (Ala. 1989), embraced a useful standard for weighing the need for change against the advantages of settled principles of law under the doctrine of stare decisis. He posed the question as follows: whether the ratio decidendi of earlier precedent would '"hypothetically be consented to today by the conscience and the feeling of justice of the majority of all those whose obedience is required by [that] rule of law?"' *Southern States Ford, Inc.*, 541 So. 2d at 1093 (quoting Laun, *Stare Decisis*, 25 Va. L.Rev. 12, 22 (1938))."

Surely the conscience and feeling of justice of the majority of those whose obedience would be required to a rule that says an action filed by a victim of delayed-onset injury from toxic-substance exposure will always be disallowed as either premature or too mature would be shocked. On the other hand, similar shock would surely be the reaction of the majority of those required to accept a rule that would permit anyone and everyone exposed to a toxic substance to maintain a tort action even though that person had not yet suffered, and statistically would probably never suffer, any health problem as a result of that exposure.

Based on the foregoing analyses, I conclude that the *Garrett* construction of the § 6-2-30(a) phrase "after the cause of action has accrued" in toxic-substance-exposure situations should be corrected, that it should be corrected now, and that this Court should undertake the correction rather than abdicating that responsibility to the legislature.

Construction of "Accrued"

The proper construction of the term "accrued" in § 6-2-30(a) in the context of toxic-substance-exposure cases should honor the rule that a cause of action accrues only when there has occurred a manifest, present injury. I understand "manifest" in this context to mean an injury manifested by observable signs or symptoms or the existence of which is medically identifiable. "Manifest" in this sense does not mean that the injured person must be personally aware of the injury or must know its cause or origin. All that is required is that there be in fact a physical injury manifested, even if the injured person is ignorant of it for some period after its development. . . .

The defendants argue that apart from the statute-of-limitations issue there were failure-of-proof bases on which the trial court should have entered a summary judgment in their favor, and this Court could rely on those bases to affirm that judgment. They acknowledge that the trial court did not reach those issues, but they invoke the principle of appellate procedure that this Court may affirm the judgment of a trial court on any valid ground presented by the record, regardless of whether the ground was considered, or even if it was rejected, by the trial court. See *Unum Life Ins. Co. of America v. Wright*, 897 So. 2d 1059, 1082 (Ala. 2004). Because I would not affirm the summary judgment here based on a statute-of-limitations ground, it behooves me to explain why I do not explore the option of affirming that judgment based on other grounds.

This Court unhesitatingly resorts to the device of affirming a trial court's judgment on an alternative basis if to do otherwise would have us apply an incorrect rule of law to the parties' circumstances. See *Blue Cross & Blue Shield of Alabama v. Hodurski*, 899 So. 2d 949, 960 (Ala. 2004). Nonetheless, the decision to affirm a trial court's ruling on an alternative basis is discretionary with the appellate court. *E.g., Tualatin Valley Builders Supply, Inc. v. TMT Homes of Oregon, Inc.*, 179 Or. App. 575, 41 P.3d 1006 (2002); *Frady v. Morrow*, 169 Or. App. 250, 255-56, 9 P.3d 141, 144 (2000); and *Busch v. Graphic Color Corp.*, 169 Ill. 2d 325, 662 N.E.2d 397, 214 Ill. Dec. 831 (1996). I would decline to exercise our discretion to invoke that principle under the circumstances presented by this case. It was necessarily clear to the trial court, obliged as it was to apply the last-exposure rule of *Garrett*, that the case had to be dismissed because the statute of limitations had expired. Thus, it was not just that the trial court failed to consider other possible bases for entering a summary judgment, it was effectively precluded from doing so.

The defendants principally argue that Cline's evidence failed sufficiently to establish the element of causation required under the Alabama Extended Manufacturer's Liability Doctrine, but the trial court's reliance on the *Garrett* rule effectively eliminated causation as an issue. That is to say, if a last exposure effects a legally cognizable injury as a matter of law, then one need not prove actual causation. Additionally, Cline's counsel asserts, and submits arguably supportive materials, that he forwent fully developing certain evidentiary aspects once it became evident that the trial judge was going to dispose of the case on the basis of the statute of limitations, and Cline's counsel came to understand that counsel for the defendants was in agreement that the planned appeal would focus solely on that issue.

Presumably because of its determination early on that *Garrett* clearly would require a dismissal of the claims against the defendants, the trial court did not address certain challenges they made to the admissibility and adequacy of some of Cline's evidentiary submissions. Because the construction of "accrued" in §6-2-30(a) that I advocate as the proper one would so alter the analytical approach the trial court would have taken had it had the benefit of that rule, I would deem it appropriate to afford the trial court the opportunity to address on the merits the defendants' evidentiary-challenge arguments.

Retroactive Versus Prospective Application of the New Standard Proposed by this Dissent

[The Justice sets forth his reasons for a new accrual rule for toxic-substance-exposure cases is in order.]

. . . .

My view of the proper construction to be accorded the term "accrued" in §6-2-30(a) in the context of toxic-substance-exposure cases would establish a new principle of law by overruling clear past precedent on which litigants may have relied. This consideration weighs in favor of a prospective application of the principle, as does the purpose of time limitations for filing actions. On the other hand, Cline, as the prevailing party in bringing about a change in the law should be rewarded for his efforts and to deny him the benefit of the new rule would have a chilling effect on litigants who desire to challenge existing rules of law that are in need of reform. Weighing the merits and demerits of the possible options for effectuating the new rule, I would recommend that it be accorded a completely prospective operation, save only for its application in Cline's case, where it would apply retroactively. Therefore, except for Cline, only those persons whose last exposure to a toxic substance, and first manifest injury resulting from that exposure, occurred within two years of the opinion adopting the new rule would be entitled to have the accrual of their cause of action determined according to the new rule.

By this approach, there would be no "flood gates of litigation" opened, and only if the legislature chose to refrain from any action for many years would there eventually develop the potential for a significant lag time between last exposure and manifest, present injury. Likewise, this approach would answer the concerns of the specially concurring Justices about the presentation of "stale" claims. Claims could become stale, in the sense of there being a significant temporal separation between cause and effect, only if the legislature is satisfied with the new rule and forgoes for a decade or more any legislative adjustment. (It bears noting, moreover, that under the *Garrett* rule, a claim is "fresh" only at a time when it is not actionable, and when it finally becomes actionable, upon the occurrence of a manifest, present injury, it is necessarily impermissibly "stale" under the statute of limitations.)

I do not seek to preempt the legislature by having this Court correct the erroneous *Garrett* rule. I simply take the position that the Court, having created the rule, should assume the responsibility for overruling it and replacing it with a rule that conforms to established principles for determining when a tort cause of action accrues. Thereafter, the Court having corrected its own mistake, I would welcome further legislative action aimed at providing any different rules for accrual, including those incorporating a "discovery" feature, that the legislature might determine to be in order. I therefore would reverse the trial court's judgment and remand this case to the trial court so that it might gauge the accrual of Cline's Alabama Extended Manufacturer's Liability Doctrine cause of action under the new rule, as well as consider the other grounds the defendants asserted in support of their motion for a summary judgment.

LYONS, WOODALL, and PARKER, JJ., concur.

NOTES

1. *Starting the Statute to Run.* As the principal case reveals, courts split on the proper rule to apply to determine when a statute of limitations begins to run in a toxic tort case. The majority of states have adopted a discovery rule to ease the harsh effects of a strict application of the statute of limitations However, there is significant variation as to what events will commence the running of the statute of limitations: some hold that the statute begins to run when the plaintiff discovers or reasonably should have discovered the injury. *See, e.g., Wells v. Radiator Specialty Co.*, 413 F. Supp. 2d 778 (S.D. Miss. 2006); some, like New York, provide that the statute of limitations for a toxic tort plaintiff begins to run when the plaintiff discovers the physical condition for which she is seeking damages, *not* when the plaintiff discovers the link between the toxic substance and her condition. *See, e.g., Matter of New York*

County DES Litigation, 678 N.E.2d 474 (N.Y. 1997); *Styles v. Goord*, 367 F. Supp. 2d 473, 475 (W.D.N.Y. 2005); N.Y.C.P.L.R. §214-c(2); other states follow a "two-step" trigger version of the discovery rule, holding that the statute of limitations begins to run only when the plaintiff knows of both the nature of her injury and its cause. *See, e.g., In re Latex Gloves Prods. Liab. Litig.*, 134 F. Supp. 2d 425 (E.D. Pa. 2001); *Goodwin v. Bayer Corp.*, 624 S.E.2d 562 (W.Va. 2005).Other states apply a third variation of the discovery rule, under which the statute of limitations begins to run at the point when a plaintiff should have discovered "(1) their injury; (2) its cause; and (3) the existence of a cause of action." *Soutiere v. Betzdearborn, Inc.* 189 F. Supp. 2d 183, 190 (D. Vt. 2002); *see also James v. Montoya*, 963 P.2d 993 (Wyo. 1998). Adopting a variation on the third approach, Alaska declared that the statute of limitations does not begin to run until the plaintiff "discovers, or reasonably should discover, all of the elements of his cause of action," which in toxic tort cases is usually not until "the plaintiff's disease manifests itself in an illness." *Sopko v. Dowell Schlumberger, Inc.*, 21 P.3d 1265, 1271 (Alaska 2001).

2. *Last Exposure Rule.* A distinct minority of states continues to follow the last-exposure rule adopted by the Alabama court in *Cline, supra.* As noted in *Cline, supra*, a statutorily — created discovery rule does exist for victims of asbestos exposure. Ala. Code. 1975 §6-2-30. The Alabama legislature also enacted legislation providing a discovery rule for persons injured by toxic substances over time, but Alabama's Supreme Court found the act containing the discovery rule unconstitutional, affirming that Alabama follows the last-exposure rule in *Garrett* (discussed in *Cline, supra*).

3. *Perspectives.* Tied into the question of fairness of the running of the statue is the question when a person can be reasonably expected to know he has suffered an injury caused by a toxic substance. Consider the plaintiffs in A CIVIL ACTION, *supra*, who in some cases had no idea they had been exposed to toxic substances until several years after the fact. What tort theory justifies requiring someone to pinpoint the exact date of their last exposure to a toxic substance? Do you agree with the majority of states that have adopted a discovery rule for these kinds of cases?

4. *Public Policies.* In his concurring opinion in *Cline, supra*, Justice See identifies competing public policies that should be weighed in determining when the statute of limitations ought to run. These include compensating victims on the one hand and avoiding stale claims and "the injustice such claims can engender" on the other. 2007 Ala. LEXIS at 7. Are there any other public policies that should be considered in determining when the statute of limitations begins to run in toxic tort actions? How should a court determine what constitutes a "stale claim?" Consider the fact that certain diseases, such as one form of lung cancer caused by inhaling asbestos dust, may take up to *forty years* to incubate. *See Hamilton v. Asbestos Corp.*, 998 P.2d 403, 407 (Cal. 2000).

5. *Race and Class Issues.* As noted in the beginning of this chapter, people of color, working-class people, and low-income families suffer disproportionate exposure to environmental toxins. One study found, for example, that three out of every five African Americans and Lationas/os were living in communities with uncontrolled toxic waste sites. Tseming Yang, *Environmental*

Regulation, Tort Law and Environmental Justice: What Could Have Been, 41 WASHBURN L.J. 607, 609 (2002). Poor communities are prime targets for siting of hazardous waste sites. *Id.* at 611. A Government Accounting Office study found that in eight Southeastern states, a significant portion of the population surrounding the hazardous sites studied were living in poverty and that African Americans comprised 90% of this population. General Accounting Office, Rep. No. RCED-83-1968, Siting of Hazardous Waste Landfills and Their Correlation With Racial and Economic Status of Surrounding Communities (1983), available at http://archive.gao.gov/d48t13/121648.pdf.

6. *Additional Reading.* For more on toxic torts generally, see Anthony Z. Roisman et al., *Preserving Justice: Defending Toxic Tort Litigation*, 51 FORDHAM ENV'L. LAW. J. 191 (2004); David G. Owen, *Special Defenses in Modern Products Liability Law*, 70 MO. L. REV. 1 (2005). For more about the public policies behind statutes of limitations see Suzette M. Malveaux, *Statutes of Limitations: A Policy Analysis in the Context of Reparations Litigation*, 74 GEO. WASH. L. REV. 68 (2005); Tyler T. Ochoa & Andrew J. Wistrich, *The Puzzling Purposes of Statutes of Limitation*, 23 PAC. L.J. 453 (1997). Regarding the application of the discovery rule to loss of consortium claims, see Paul Davis Fancher, Note, *To Have and Not Hold: Applying the Discovery Rule to Loss of Consortium Claims Stemming from Premarital, Latent Injuries*, 53 VAND. L. REV. 685 (2000). For additional reading on environmental justice, see Alex Geisinger, *Rethinking Environmental Justice Regulation: A Modest Proposal for Penalty Return*, 55 SYRACUSE L. REV. 33 (2004).

PROBLEMS

11.1

Plaintiffs who resided in homes a few blocks away from a mine reuse dump suffered physical symptoms of headaches, nausea, and dizziness from defendant's release of noxious, poisonous, and foul-smelling gases emanating from the dump. Do the neighbors have a valid claim for a private or public nuisance? What additional information, if any, would you need to answer the question? *Cf. Evans v. Moffat*, 192 Pa. Super. 204, 160 A.2d 465 (1960).

11.2

Defendant operates a race track where noise from drag cars is heard three miles away in a residential faming community. People who lived one mile away could not hear themselves talk and had their windows rattle from noise. Is the defendant liable to any of the residents based on the law of torts governing nuisance claims? *Cf. Bedminster Township v. Vargo Dragway, Inc.*, 434 Pa. 100, 253 A. 2d 659 (1969).

11.3

A family of 8, after being evicted during the winter, and unable to find a shelter in which they felt safe, began seeking refuge from the cold in various places within the community of Goodhope, a suburban town with a population of about 10,000. At various times during a three week period they snuck into the garage of a private home, the garage of a shopping mall, a public library, and the town courthouse. The city attorney is considering seeking an injunction based on allegations of a continuing trespass, private nuisance, and public nuisance. You are employed by the Legal Services for the Poor, a non profit organization and you have been asked to defend the homeless family. What arguments will you make? Assess the likelihood of mounting a successful legal defense to the nuisance claims.

11.4

Weschester Associates owns a six-story apartment building immediately adjacent to electric power lines operated by Boston Edison Company. Magnetic fields generated by Edison's power lines have caused distorted images and disruption on the computer monitor screens of tenants who lease space in the building. Boston has a legal right to generate electricity in the power lines. It has not been able to find a way to deliver service to its customers without disrupting the computers. Does Westchester have a valid claim of nuisance? Does it turn on which company was carrying on its business first? If the court finds a nuisance, should it grant an injunction? Award damages? Both or neither? What rights, if any, do the tenants have and against whom? *Compare Westchester Associates, Inc. v. Boston Edison Company*, 712 N.E.2d 1145 (Mass. 1999)

11.5

Plaintiffs worked as employees in a nuclear power plant licensed to operate under federal law. The plant was in violation of its license because it had failed to report "an unplanned release of quantities of fission products in excess of allowable limits," in violation of 42 U.S.C. §2133(f). The release occurred from cigarette smoking damage caused by one of the employees, a cigarette smoker. Prior to the release, it was not scientifically knowable that such damage could be caused by smoking.

About half of the employees smoked while at work. All the employees suffered injury from the workplace smoking. They were also all injured by the unplanned release of fission products.

Please discuss the claims the employees may have against the nuclear plant, and against the manufacturers of the cigarettes smoked by the employees.

Chapter 12

AFFIRMATIVE DEFENSES TO NEGLIGENCE

A. INTRODUCTION

The same policies which lead courts to impose liability upon a defendant whose unreasonable and risky conduct damages the plaintiff lead them to look at the reasonableness of the plaintiff's conduct that contributed to the injury. In order to deter accidents, tort law encourages potential accident victims to take reasonable care for their own protection. It is arguably inefficient to compensate a victim for damages caused in part by her own conduct falling below the standard of conduct. In addition, the community's sense of justice or fairness may be offended by a rule that imposes all of the loss on one of two people whose unreasonably risky conduct coalesces to cause damage to one of them. Plaintiff misconduct might take one of several forms. The plaintiff (1) may have failed to act as a reasonable person for her own safety, and her substandard conduct was a cause in fact of her injuries, or (2) may have knowingly and voluntarily assumed the risk that defendant would not act reasonably toward her, or (3) may have failed to act as a reasonable person for her own safety, and her failure did not contribute to the occurrence of the accident, but enhanced her damages. The material in this chapter examines how the law treats negligence of a plaintiff who contributes to an accident or injury.

The legal solution to this problem has been made difficult by the prevalent idea, until modern times, that the law could not quantify unreasonably risky conduct. If the unreasonably risky conduct of two persons combined to cause an indivisible injury, the burden of the loss could be placed upon only one of them. The common law approach was to place all of the burden on one of the parties, instead of dividing responsibility as is done under the modern law of comparative fault. Alternatively, the law could divide the loss between them on a per capita basis. Maritime law in collision cases adopted this solution; thus, when two vessels collided and both were at fault, the damages were divided equally between the vessel owners. *The Schooner Catherine v. Dickinson*, 511 U.S. (17 How.) 170 (U.S. 1854). Now comparative fault has spread to both land and water.

The law encourages litigation near in time to the relevant injury so that memories are fresh, fact-finding is potentially more accurate and defendants can get on with their lives. These policies are behind the universal rule that a plaintiff must file her claim within the applicable statute of limitations. In the last forty years or so statute of limitations issues have gotten more complex because, increasingly, some injuries — such as latent diseases or medical conditions — do not reveal themselves for many years. Most tort statutes of limitation range between one and three years. Courts and legislatures have adopted "a discovery rule" in many latent disease cases, for example, where the latent illness does not manifest itself for many decades. A statute of limitations permits the defendant to rationally determine their potential liabilities. In that sense it may encourage efficient planning but it may allow a person to escape liability for injuries they caused another.

Thirdly, this chapter deals with another type of defense normally based upon the defendant's status — immunity. Some actors are immune from tort liability, either generally, or to certain victims. A few jurisdictions hold that one spouse cannot sue the other for most torts though the clear trend has been to abolish spousal immunity. Some jurisdictions have partially abolished immunity and permitted lawsuits where the husband and wife are separated or divorced. The purpose of spousal immunity has been the preservation of domestic peace and tranquility. Nevertheless, how much spousal immunity can there be when an abusive husband batters his wife? Similarly, the trend is for children to be able to sue their parents in tort.

A state may be immune from any tort suit by its citizens or noncitizens just as a spouse may be shielded from a tort suit by his or her spouse. Immunity has the same effect as an affirmative defense, such as consent, privilege, or contributory negligence. The major distinction is that an affirmative defense bars recovery because the actor's conduct, under the circumstances, was not tortious, while immunity bars recovery solely because of the status of the actor or his relationship to the victim. Tort immunities once flourished; however, the trend since World War II has been to abolish or severely limit them. Today charitable immunity is on the decline. The public policy purpose of charitable immunities was to preserve charitable resources. Some jurisdictions have enacted tort reforms making charities fully liable for their torts, but place caps on the amount of liability. The *Federal Tort Claims Act*, 28 U.S.C. § 1346(b), enacted in 1946, permits suits against the United States for any "negligent or wrongful act or omission of any employee of the Government while acting within the scope of his office or employment, under circumstances where the United States, if a private person, would be liable to the claimant . . .".

This trend towards abolishing or limiting immunities has been fueled partly by the availability of liability insurance by which the defendant can reduce the impact of tort liability. Another important factor in the general demise of the immunity concept has been the realization that the justifications for immunity do not now (if they ever did) outweigh its societal costs, such as the loss of deterrence of risky conduct and the unfair imposition of losses upon innocent victims. The erosion of immunity may have abated more recently in the age of tort reform.

B. PLAINTIFF'S FAULT

1. Contributory Negligence

BUTTERFIELD v. FORRESTER
11 East 60, 103 Eng. Rep. 926 (K.B. 1809)

This was an action on the case for obstructing a highway, by means of which obstruction the plaintiff, who was riding along the road, was thrown down with his horse, and injured, etc. At the trial before Bayley J. at Derby, it appeared that the defendant, for the purpose of making some repairs to his house, which was close by the road side at one end of the town, had put up a pole across this part of the road, a free passage being let by another branch of street in the same direction. That the plaintiff left a public house not far distant from the place in question at 11 o'clock in the evening in August, when they were just beginning to light candles, but while there was light enough left to discern the obstruction at 100 yards distance: and the witness, who proved this, said that if the plaintiff had not been riding very hard he might have observed and avoided it: the plaintiff however, who was riding violently, did not observe it, but rode against it, and fell with his horse and was much hurt in consequence of the accident; and there was no evidence of his being intoxicated at the time. On this evidence Bayley J. directed the jury, that if a person riding with reasonable and ordinary care could have seen and avoided the obstruction; and if they were satisfied that the plaintiff was riding along the street extremely hard, and without ordinary care, they should find a verdict for the defendant: which they accordingly did.

Vaughan Serjt. now objected to this direction, on moving for a new trial and referred to Buller's Ni. Pri. 26(a), where the rule is laid down, that "if a man lay logs of wood across a highway; though a person may with care ride safely by, yet if by means thereof my horse stumble and fling me, I may bring an action."

Bayley, Justice.

The plaintiff was proved to be riding as fast as his horse could go, and this was through the streets of Derby. If he had used ordinary care he must have seen the obstruction; so that the accident appeared to happen entirely from his own fault.

Lord Ellenborough, Chief Justice.

A party is not to cast himself upon an obstruction which has been made by the fault of another, and avail himself of it, if he do not himself use common and ordinary caution to be in the right. In cases of persons riding upon what is considered to be the wrong side of the road, that would not authorise another purposely to ride up against them. One person being in fault will not dispense with another's using ordinary care for himself. Two things must concur to support this action, an obstruction in the road by fault of the defendant, and no want of ordinary care to avoid it on the part of the plaintiff.

[Per Curiam. Rule refused.]

NOTES

1. *The Meaning of Butterfield. Butterfield* led to the common law rule that plaintiff's unreasonably risky conduct barred his recovery. Why was recovery barred?

(a) Because defendant did not owe a duty to a plaintiff who acted unreasonably for his own safety? But can the unreasonableness of the foreseeable risk which defendant creates be based on the conduct of the person who ultimately encountered the risk? And if so, then plaintiff fault is not a defense but a failure of duty.

(b) Defendant's conduct was not unreasonable, in the light of plaintiff's action? But doesn't that mean that the plaintiff has not proved breach? And, if so, once again plaintiff fault is not an affirmative defense but a failure of the plaintiff's *prima facie* case.

(c) Plaintiff's conduct, and not defendant's, was the legal or proximate cause of plaintiff's injury? Does that mean the plaintiff has not proven proximate or legal cause, again a failure of the *prima facie* case rather than an affirmative defense? But what if the conduct of plaintiff and defendant also caused injury to a third person? Could the third person recover from the plaintiff but not from the defendant?

(d) Plaintiff's unreasonable conduct is an affirmative defense?

2. *Under Deterrence of Defendants.* The rule that the plaintiff's contributory negligence barred recovery was a harsh one. A plaintiff even slightly at fault recovered nothing. The rule did provide a deterrent to plaintiffs, but what about defendants? What impact did the rule have on deterrence of the negligent defendant? Does the "all or nothing" rule of contributory negligence or some form of comparative negligence lead to optimal deterrence?

3. *Ameliorative Doctrines.* Predictably, the common law developed various ameliorative devices to allow negligent plaintiffs to recover. For instance, many of the "rules" you considered in Chapter 4, dealing with the standard of care, had their origin in contributory negligence cases. These included: momentary forgetfulness or sudden emergency, the standard of care for those with physical differences, and the children's standard of care. Should these standards of care rules still apply in a jurisdiction that has adopted comparative fault?

Other cases held that even though the plaintiff may have breached the appropriate standard of care, the plaintiff's negligence was not a cause-in-fact or legal cause of the plaintiff's injuries. Thus, the risk that plaintiff would fall between a truck and a wall did not encompass a risk of being injured by a metal hook protruding from the side of the truck. *See Furukawa v. Ogawa*, 236 F.2d 272 (9th Cir. 1956). Theoretically, the defendant must still prove that the plaintiff was negligent and that proof would require that the defendant establish all the elements of negligence.

Other courts held that even though a plaintiff might have been negligent, the defendant's duty included the risk of the plaintiff's negligence. Or put differently, the defendant had a duty to protect the plaintiff from its own negligence. For example in *Boyer v. Johnson*, 360 So. 2d 1164 (La. 1978), the court held that a person who hired a child to work in a dangerous setting in violation of the child labor laws owed a duty to protect the child from the child's own negligence. Thus the parents of a deceased child who was killed while driving a truck containing fireworks could recover even though the child may have negligently driven the truck. Should decisions like these survive the adoption of comparative fault?

Another device used to avoid the harsh rule of the contributory negligence bar was to let the jury decide the issue. Perhaps a jury which knew that contributory negligence barred recovery, was unlikely to find the plaintiff contributorily negligent except in those cases in which his conduct was particularly egregious; or, if the plaintiff's conduct was unreasonably risky and contributed to his injury, a jury could attempt to achieve rough justice by finding that the plaintiff was not contributorily negligent but reduce the award of damages to account for the plaintiff's misconduct. This second approach was *de facto* comparative negligence; it was well recognized by attorneys and by judges, who often conveniently refused an *additur* sought by plaintiff or a *remittitur* sought by defendant. But what about a jury that was not aware of the underlying contributory negligence rule or the jury that took the judge's instructions seriously. Could any system that relied upon the jury's covert knowledge or that winked at its disregard for the technicalities of the law ever be fair, transparent, and consistent?

If defendant's conduct was more reprehensible than negligence, contributory negligence ordinarily was not a defense. Thus a determination that the defendant was guilty of "recklessness" or "willful and wanton" conduct would permit an escape from the contributory negligence bar. Courts also generally held that contributory negligence was not a defense to an intentional tort. *See, e.g., Graves v. Graves*, 531 So. 2d 817 (Miss. 1988).

4. *Last Clear Chance.* Additionally, if both plaintiff and defendant engaged in unreasonably risky conduct, but defendant's conduct continued after plaintiff was no longer able to avoid the accident, courts allowed the plaintiff to escape the contributory negligence bar by finding that the defendant had the "last clear chance" to avoid the accident. The doctrine had its genesis in the "groans, ineffably and mournfully sad, of Davies' dying donkey." *Fuller v. Illinois C.R.R.*, 100 Miss. 705, 717, 56 So. 783 (1911). The Davies referred to was the plaintiff in *Davies v. Mann*, 10 M. & W. 547, 152 Eng. Rep. 588 (Exch. 1842). In that case, the plaintiff recovered on these facts:

> Plaintiff, having fettered the fore feet of an ass belonging to him, turned it into a public highway, and at the time in question the ass was grazing on the off side of a road about eight yards wide, when the defendant's wagon, with a team of three horses, coming down a slight descent, at what the witness termed a smartish pace, ran against the ass, knocked it down, and the wheels passing over it, it died soon after. . . . [The trial judge instructed the jury] that though the act of the plaintiff, in leaving the donkey on the highway so fettered as to prevent his getting out of the way of carriages traveling along it, might be illegal, still, if the proximate cause of the injury was attributable to the want of proper conduct on the part of the driver of the wagon, the action was maintainable against the defendant; and [the trial judge] directed them, if they thought that the accident might have been avoided by the exercise of ordinary care on the part of the driver, to find for the plaintiff.

These jury instructions were held to be proper. The doctrine of "last clear chance" was adopted in some form in nearly every state. There were four situations: (1) the plaintiff is helpless, and the defendant discovers the plaintiff's peril, but unreasonably fails to avoid the injury, *see* REST. 2D TORTS §479; (2) the plaintiff is inattentive and the defendant discovers the plaintiff's peril, but unreasonably fails to avoid the injury, *id.* §480; (3) the plaintiff is helpless and the defendant unreasonably fails to discover plaintiff's peril, *id.* §479; and (4) the plaintiff is inattentive and the defendant unreasonably fails to discover plaintiff's peril. *See Meyers v. Louisiana*, 637 S.W.2d 219 (Mo. App. 1982). Most states applied the last clear chance doctrine to situations (1) through (3), but very few applied it to (4). Why do you suppose the doctrine was seldom applied to (4)? Does the rule make for trouble or is it based on good sense?

2. Comparative Fault

LI v. YELLOW CAB CO.
532 P.2d 1226 (Cal. 1975)

SULLIVAN, JUSTICE.

In this case we address the grave and recurrent question of whether we should judicially declare no longer applicable in California courts the doctrine of contributory negligence, which bars all recovery when the plaintiff's negligent conduct has contributed as a legal cause in any degree to the harm suffered by him, and hold that it must give way to a system of comparative negligence, which assesses liability in direct proportion to fault. As we explain in detail *infra*, we conclude that we should. In the course of reaching our ultimate decision we conclude that: (1) the doctrine of comparative negligence is preferable to the "all-or-nothing" doctrine of contributory negligence from the point of view of logic, practical experience, and fundamental justice; (2) judicial action in this area is not precluded by the presence of section 1714 of the CIVIL CODE, which has been said to "codify" the "all-or-nothing" rule and to render it immune from attack in the courts except on constitutional grounds; (3) given the possibility of judicial action, certain practical difficulties attendant upon the adoption of comparative negligence should not dissuade us from charting a new course — leaving the resolution of some of these problems to future judicial or legislative action; (4) the doctrine of comparative negligence should be applied in this state in its so-called "pure" form under which the assessment of liability in proportion to fault proceeds in spite of the fact that the plaintiff is equally at fault as or more at fault than the defendant; and finally, (5) this new rule should be given a limited retrospective application. [The court briefly recited the facts involving a two-car collision.] . . .

"Contributory negligence is conduct on the part of the plaintiff which falls below the standard to which he should conform for his own protection, and which is a legally contributing cause cooperating with the negligence of the defendant in bringing about the plaintiff's harm." REST. 2D TORTS, §463. Thus the American Law Institute, in its second restatement of the law, describes the kind of conduct on the part of one seeking recovery for damage caused by negligence which renders him subject to the doctrine of contributory negligence. What the effect of such conduct will be is left to a further section, which states the doctrine in its clearest essence: "Except where the defendant has the last clear chance, the plaintiff's contributory negligence *bars recovery* against a defendant whose negligent conduct would otherwise make him liable to the plaintiff for the harm sustained by him." REST. 2D TORTS, § 467. (Italics added.)

This rule, rooted in the long-standing principle that one should not recover from another for damages brought upon oneself, has been the law of this state from its beginning. . . .

It is unnecessary for us to catalogue the enormous amount of critical comment that has been directed over the years against the "all-or-nothing" approach of the doctrine of contributory negligence. The essence of that criticism has been constant and clear: the doctrine is inequitable in its operation because it fails to distribute responsibility in proportion to fault. Against this have been raised several arguments in justification, but none have proved even remotely adequate to the task. The basic objection to the doctrine — grounded in the primal concept that in a system in which liability is based on fault, the extent of fault should govern the extent of liability — remains irresistible to reason and all intelligent notions of fairness.

Furthermore, practical experience with the application by juries of the doctrine of contributory negligence has added its weight to analyses of its inherent shortcomings: "Every trial lawyer is well aware that juries often do in fact allow recovery in cases of contributory negligence, and that the compromise in the jury room does result in some diminution of the damages because of the plaintiff's fault. But the process is at best a haphazard and most unsatisfactory one." Prosser, *Comparative Negligence*, 41 CAL. L. REV. 1, 4 (1953).

It is in view of these theoretical and practical considerations that to this date 25 states have abrogated the "all-or-nothing" rule of contributory negligence and have enacted in its place general apportionment *statutes* calculated in one manner or another to assess liability in proportion to fault. In 1973 these states were joined by Florida, which effected the same result by *judicial* decision. We are likewise persuaded that logic, practical experience, and fundamental justice counsel against the retention of the doctrine rendering contributory negligence a complete bar to recovery — and that it should be replaced in this state by a system under which liability for damage will be borne by those whose negligence caused it, in direct proportion to their respective fault.

The foregoing conclusion, however, clearly takes us only part of the way. It is strenuously and ably urged by defendants and two of the amici curiae that whatever our views on the relative merits of contributory and comparative negligence, we are precluded from making those views the law of the state by judicial decision. Moreover, it is contended, even if we are not so precluded, there exist considerations of a practical nature which should dissuade us from embarking upon the course which we have indicated. We proceed to take up these two objections in order. . . .

[The court concluded that § 1714 of the CIVIL CODE, which provided that every person is responsible for his own negligence except where a person by the want of ordinary care has "brought the injury upon himself," merely announced "existing common law principles . . . with a distinct view toward continuing judicial evolution."]

We are thus brought to the second group of arguments which have been advanced by defendants and the amici curiae supporting their position. Generally speaking, such arguments expose considerations of a practical nature which, it is urged, counsel against the adoption of a rule of comparative negligence in this state even if such adoption is possible by judicial means.

The most serious of these considerations are those attendant upon the administration of a rule of comparative negligence in cases involving multiple parties. One such problem may arise when all responsible parties are not brought before the court: it may be difficult for the jury to evaluate relative negligence in such circumstances, and to compound this difficulty such an evaluation would not be res judicata in a subsequent suit against the absent wrongdoer. Problems of contribution and indemnity among joint tortfeasors lurk in the background.

A second and related major area of concern involves the administration of the actual process of fact-finding in a comparative negligence system. The assigning of a specific percentage factor to the amount of negligence attributable to a particular party, while in theory a matter of little difficulty, can become a matter of perplexity in the face of hard facts. The temptation for the jury to resort to a quotient verdict in such circumstances can be great. These inherent difficulties are not, however, insurmountable. Guidelines might be provided the jury which will assist it in keeping focused upon the true inquiry, and the utilization of special verdicts or jury interrogatories can be of invaluable assistance in assuring that the jury has approached its sensitive and often complex task with proper standards and appropriate reverence.

The third area of concern, the status of the doctrines of last clear chance and assumption of risk, involves less the practical problems of administering a particular form of comparative negligence than it does a definition of the theoretical outline of the specific form to be adopted. Although several states which apply comparative negligence concepts retain the last clear chance doctrine, the better reasoned position seems to be that when true comparative negligence is adopted, the need for last clear chance as a palliative of the hardships of the "all-or-nothing" rule disappears and its retention results only in a windfall to the plaintiff in direct contravention of the principle of liability in proportion to fault.

As for assumption of risk, we have recognized in this state that this defense overlaps that of contributory negligence to some extent and in fact is made up of at least two distinct defenses. "To simplify greatly, it has been observed . . . that in one kind of situation, to wit, where a plaintiff *unreasonably* undertakes to encounter a specific known risk imposed by a defendant's negligence, plaintiff's conduct, although he may encounter that risk in a prudent manner, is in reality a form of contributory negligence. . . . Other kinds of situations within the doctrine of assumption of risk are those, for example, where plaintiff is held to agree to relieve defendant of an obligation of reasonable conduct toward him. Such a situation would not involve contributory negligence, but rather a reduction of defendant's duty of care." *Grey v. Fibreboard Paper Prod. Co.*, 418 P.2d 153, 156 (Cal. 1966). We think it clear that the adoption of a system of comparative negligence should entail the merger of the defense of assumption of risk into the general scheme of assessment of liability in proportion to fault in those particular cases in which the form of assumption of risk involved is no more than a variant of contributory negligence.

Finally there is the problem of the treatment of willful misconduct under a system of comparative negligence. In jurisdictions following the "all-or-nothing" rule, contributory negligence is no defense to an action based upon a claim of willful misconduct, and this is the present rule in California. . . . The thought is that the difference between willful and wanton misconduct and ordinary negligence is one of kind rather than degree in that the former involves conduct of an entirely different order, and under this conception it might well be urged that comparative negligence concepts should have no application when one of the parties has been guilty of willful and wanton misconduct. It has been persuasively argued, however, that the loss of deterrent effect that would occur upon application of comparative fault concepts to willful and wanton misconduct as well as ordinary negligence would be slight, and that a comprehensive system of comparative negligence should allow for the apportionment of damages in all cases involving misconduct which falls short of being intentional. The law of punitive damages remains a separate consideration.

The existence of the foregoing areas of difficulty and uncertainty (as well as others which we have not here mentioned) has not diminished our conviction that the time for a revision of the means for dealing with contributory fault in this state is long past due and that it lies within the province of this court to initiate the needed change by our decision in this case. Two of the indicated areas (i.e., multiple parties and willful misconduct) are not involved in the case before us, and we consider it neither necessary nor wise to address ourselves to specific problems of this nature which might be expected to arise. As the Florida court stated with respect to the same subject, "it is not the proper function of this Court to decide unripe issues, without the benefit of adequate briefing, not involving an actual controversy, and unrelated to a specific factual situation." *Hoffman v. Jones*, 280 So. 2d 431, 439 (Fla. 1973).

Our previous comments relating to the remaining two areas of concern (i.e., the status of the doctrines of last clear chance and assumption of risk, and the matter of judicial supervision of the finder of fact) have provided sufficient guidance to enable the trial courts of this state to meet and resolve particular problems in this area as they arise. As we have indicated, last clear chance and assumption of risk (insofar as the latter doctrine is but a variant of contributory negligence) are to be subsumed under the general process of assessing liability in proportion to fault, and the matter of jury supervision we leave for the moment within the broad discretion of the trial courts.

Our decision in this case is to be viewed as a first step in what we deem to be a proper and just direction, not as a compendium containing the answers to all questions that may be expected to arise. Pending future judicial or legislative developments, we are content for the present to assume the position taken by the Florida court in this matter: "We feel the trial judges of this State are capable of applying [a] comparative negligence rule without our setting guidelines in anticipation of expected problems. The problems are more appropriately resolved at the trial level in a practical manner instead of a theoretical solution at the appellate level. The trial judges are granted broad discretion in adopting such procedures as may accomplish the objectives and purposes expressed in this opinion." 280 So. 2d at 439–440.

It remains to identify the precise form of comparative negligence which we now adopt for application in this state. Although there are many variants, only the two basic forms need be considered here. The first of these, the so-called "pure" form of comparative negligence, apportions liability in direct proportion to fault in all cases. This was the form adopted by the Supreme Court of Florida in *Hoffman v. Jones*, and it applies by statute in Mississippi, Rhode Island, and Washington. Moreover it is the form favored by most scholars and commentators. The second basic form of comparative negligence, of which there are several variants, applies apportionment based on fault *up to the point* at which the plaintiff's negligence is equal to or greater than that of the defendant — when that point is reached, plaintiff is barred from recovery. Nineteen states have adopted this form or one of its variants by statute. The principal argument advanced in its favor is moral in nature: that it is not morally right to permit one more at fault in an accident to recover from one less at fault. Other arguments assert the probability of increased insurance, administrative, and judicial costs if a "pure" rather than a "50 percent" system is adopted, but this has been seriously questioned.

We have concluded that the "pure" form of comparative negligence is that which should be adopted in this state. In our view the "50 percent" system simply shifts the lottery aspect of the contributory negligence rule to a different ground. As Dean Prosser has noted, under such a system "[it] is obvious that a slight difference in the proportionate fault may permit a recovery; and there has been much justified criticism of a rule under which a plaintiff who is charged with 49 percent of the total negligence recovers 51 percent of his damages, while one who is charged with 50 percent recovers nothing at all." Prosser, *Comparative Negligence, supra*, 41 CAL. L. REV. 1, 25. In effect "such a rule distorts the very principle it recognizes, i.e., that persons are responsible for their acts to the extent their fault contributes to an injurious result. The partial rule simply lowers, but does not eliminate, the bar of contributory negligence." Juenger, *Brief for Negligence Law Section of the State Bar of Michigan in Support of Comparative Negligence as Amicus Curiae, Parsonson v. Constr. Equip. Co.*, 18 WAYNE L. REV. 3, 50. . . .

For all of the foregoing reasons we conclude that the "all-or-nothing" rule of contributory negligence as it presently exists in this state should be and is herewith superseded by a system of "pure" comparative negligence, the fundamental purpose of which shall be to assign responsibility and liability for damage in direct proportion to the amount of negligence of each of the parties. Therefore, in all actions for negligence resulting in injury to person or property, the contributory negligence of the person injured in person or property shall not bar recovery, but the damages awarded shall be diminished in proportion to the amount of negligence attributable to the person recovering.

The doctrine of last clear chance is abolished, and the defense of assumption of risk is also abolished to the extent that it is merely a variant of the former doctrine of contributory negligence; both of these are to be subsumed under the general process of assessing liability in proportion to negligence. Pending future judicial or legislative developments, the trial courts of this state are to use broad discretion in seeking to assure that the principle stated is applied in the interest of justice and in furtherance of the purposes and objectives set forth in this opinion. . . .

CLARK, JUSTICE (dissenting).

. . . I dispute the need for judicial — instead of legislative — action in this area. The majority is clearly correct in its observation that our society has changed significantly during the 103-year existence of section 1714. But this social change has been neither recent nor traumatic, and the criticisms leveled by the majority at the present operation of contributory negligence are not new. I cannot conclude our society's evolution has now rendered the normal legislative process inadequate.

Further, the Legislature is the branch best able to effect transition from contributory to comparative or some other doctrine of negligence. Numerous and differing negligence systems have been urged over the years, yet there remains widespread disagreement among both the commentators and the states as to which one is best. This court is not an investigatory body, and we lack the means of fairly appraising the merits of these competing systems. Constrained by settled rules of judicial review, we must consider only matters within the record or susceptible to judicial notice. That this court is inadequate to the task of carefully selecting the best replacement system is reflected in the majority's summary manner of eliminating from consideration *all but two* of the many competing proposals — including models adopted by some of our sister states. . . .

NOTES

1. *The Rise of Comparative Fault.* The concept of comparing the fault of the parties and dividing the otherwise indivisible loss on the basis of such a comparison developed slowly. Georgia adopted a form of comparative fault in the nineteenth century. The Mississippi legislature adopted comparative fault in 1910. In the *Federal Employer's Liability Act* in 1908, Congress provided that in an action by an employee against a railroad employer, "the fact that the employee may have been guilty of contributory negligence shall not bar a recovery, but the damages shall be diminished by the jury in proportion to the amount of negligence attributable to such employee." In 1920, Congress extended comparative negligence to actions by seamen against their employers in *The Jones Act*.

Acceptance of the concept that the finder of fact can quantify fault tolled the death knell for the contributory negligence bar in most states. By the mid-1960s the issue was no longer whether comparative negligence would supersede the contributory negligence bar, but whether the change would come from the legislatures or from the courts, and what type of comparative negligence would be adopted. Today, all but a handful of states have some from of comparative fault.

2. *Types of Comparative Fault.* As the *Li* case indicates, there are two major kinds of comparative negligence: "pure," in which plaintiff may recover as little as 1% of his damages, *see, e.g., Sutton v. Piasecki Trucking, Inc.,* 451 N.E.2d 481 (N.Y. 1983) (plaintiff allocated 99% of the fault was entitled to recover 1% of his damages), and "modified," in which plaintiff may not recover if his percentage of fault equals or exceeds that of the defendant. The "modified" plan is the most popular. Twenty plus states have adopted one kind of "modified" plan — sometimes called the New Hampshire or the "50-50" plan: plaintiff may recover the amount of his damages multiplied by the defendant's percentage of fault, if the plaintiff's negligence does not exceed that of the defendant. If it does, plaintiff is barred from recovery. This Minnesota statute represents the "50-50" plan:

> Contributory fault does not bar recovery in an action by any person or the person's legal representative to recover damages for fault resulting in death, in injury to person or property, or in economic loss, if the contributory fault was not greater than the fault of the person against whom recovery is sought, but any damages allowed must be diminished in proportion to the amount of fault attributable to the person recovering. The court may, and when requested by any party shall, direct the jury to find separate special verdicts determining the amount of damages and the percentage of fault attributable to each party and the court shall then reduce the amount of damages in proportion to the amount of fault attributable to the person recovering.

MINN. STAT. ANN. § 604.01(1).

Other states follow the Georgia or "49-51" plan: plaintiff may recover the amount of his damages, multiplied by the defendant's percentage of fault, only if the plaintiff's negligence is less than that of defendant. For example, Arkansas law provides:

> (b)(1) If the fault chargeable to a party claiming damages is of a lesser degree than the fault chargeable to the party or parties from whom the claiming party seeks to recover damages, then the claiming party is entitled to recover the amount of his or her damages after they have been diminished in proportion to the degree of his or her own fault.

> (2) If the fault chargeable to a party claiming damages is equal to or greater in degree than any fault chargeable to the party or parties from whom the claiming party seeks to recover damages, then the claiming party is not entitled to recover such damages.

ARK. STAT. ANN. § 16-64-122(b).

Other states and federal maritime law use the "pure" comparative negligence approach. Some jurisdictions have changed from one plan to another.

What might motivate a legislature to switch from "pure" comparative negligence to a modified plan? From a "49-51" plan to a "50-50" plan?

What is the underlying basis of the modified plans? Once the plaintiff's fault reaches a certain level, the defendant did not cause the plaintiff's injuries? If the defendant is 51% at fault he caused the plaintiff's injuries but if he is 51% at fault he did not cause its injuries? No cause in fact? Or no legal cause? Or perhaps once the plaintiff's fault reaches the prohibited level, the defendant owes no duty? Or do the rules just reflect unrefined policy choices?

Of course the defendant must still prove that the plaintiff was at fault. *See* REST. 3D TORTS: APPORTIONMENT OF LIABILITY § 5.

3. *Comparing Fault.* What if the plaintiff's conduct is reckless, willful or wanton, and the defendant is merely negligent? *See, e.g., Barker v. Kallash*, 468 N.E.2d 39 (N.Y.1984) (15-year-old, injured when pipe bomb he was making exploded in his hands, could not recover against 9-year-old who sold gun powder used in bomb); *Symone T. v. Lieber*, 613 N.Y.S.2d 404 (N.Y. App. 1994) (12-year-old victim could not recover against health care provider because she criminally sought abortion during 25th week of pregnancy). What if both plaintiff and defendant are reckless or willful or wanton? Once again it would seem that the Restatement (Third) would apportion. *See id.*, cmt. *c.*

4. *Punitive Damages and Comparative Fault.* Can plaintiff's negligence be used to reduce exemplary or punitive damages? The majority rule is that it may not. Why is that so?

5. *The Mechanics of Comparing Fault.* The REST. 3D TORTS: APPORTIONMENT OF LIABILITY § 8 provides:

> Factors for assigning percentages of responsibility to each person whose legal responsibility has been established include:
>
> (a) the nature of the person's risk-creating conduct, including any awareness or indifference with respect to the risks created by the conduct and any intent with respect to the harm created by the conduct; and
>
> (b) the strength of the causal connection between the person's risk-creating conduct and the harm.

How does one determine the strength of the causal connection? How should fault be allocated in "second accident" cases, where one defendant's fault caused the accident but another defendant's fault increased the damages therefrom? *See Campbell v. Louisiana Department of Transportation & Development*, 648 So. 2d 898 (La. 1995) ("In apportioning fault the trier of fact shall consider both the nature of the conduct of each party . . . and the extent of the causal relation between the conduct and the damages claimed.").

6. *The Impact of Comparative Fault on Res Ipsa.* When plaintiff's contributory negligence barred plaintiff's recovery, the general rule used to be that *res ipsa* did not apply if the plaintiff's conduct contributed to his own injury. Should *res ipsa* apply if the plaintiff is partly at fault in a comparative fault jurisdiction? *See Giles v. City of New Haven*, 619 A.2d 476 (Ct. 1993) (with the adoption of comparative negligence, a plaintiff can be a negligent participant in the events leading up to the injuries suffered without depriving plaintiff of the use of the doctrine of *res ipsa*, as long as plaintiff was not the sole cause of the injuries).

7. *Comparative Fault and Set-Offs.* If two parties are injured in an accident and each is entitled to recover from the other for example under principles of pure comparative fault, should the court make separate awards to each, or should it set off the lesser award against the greater one and render only one judgment for the difference in favor of the party with the greater award? Assume: the first party suffers $10,000 damages and is guilty of 40% of the fault; the second party suffers $5,000 damages and is guilty of the remaining 60%. Should there be two awards, one to the first party in the amount of $6,000, and one to the second party in the amount of $2,000? Or should there be only one award to the first for $4,000? Suppose one of the parties files for bankruptcy? Suppose only one of the parties has liability insurance? Suppose both have liability insurance? REST. 3D § 9 provides:

> If two parties are liable to each other in the same suit, each party is entitled to a setoff of any recovery owed by the other party, except that, in cases in which one or both of the parties has liability insurance, setoff does not reduce the payment of a liability insurer unless an applicable rule of law or statute so provides.

8. *Instructing the Jury.* With a general verdict, the jury reports whether it finds for the plaintiff or the defendant, and if it finds for the plaintiff, the jury also reports the total amount of damages it has awarded. Such a verdict will reflect (although it will not reveal) the jury's determination as to comparative fault, and the result is similar to pre-comparative days when juries often were allowed to make *ad hoc* comparisons of fault. Many jurisdictions permit or require a special verdict, in which the jury answers specific questions, and the judge determines the appropriate judgment in light of the jury's answers. Such a verdict might ask these questions:

Was the defendant negligent?

If so, was the plaintiff negligent?

If you find both parties negligent, state in percentages (totaling 100%) the causal negligence of each party?

Plaintiff _____

Defendant _____

State the total amount of damages sustained by plaintiff. $ _____

A jury presented with a special verdict but untutored in the effect of its responses may provide answers which will produce a result different from that which they intended. In a pure comparative negligence state, the jury may not know that the judge will further reduce the amount of damages by the percentage of fault that the jury assigned to the plaintiff. In a state using a modified plan, the jury may not know that the victim will be uncompensated if it assesses 50% or more of the fault to him. Should the jury be told the effect of its answers to special interrogatories? What philosophy might be reflected by an affirmative answer to that question? By a negative one? The cases divide on this issue. *Compare Schabe v. Hampton Bays Union Free Sch. Dist.*, 103 A.D.2d 418 (N.Y. App. Div. 1984), *with Smith v. Gizzi*, 564 P.2d 1009 (Okla. 1977).

3. Assumption of the Risk

SCHUTKOWSKI v. CAREY
725 P.2d 1057 (Wyo. 1986)

BROWN, JUSTICE.

Appellant Barbara Schutkowski, a skydiving student injured during her first jump, filed a negligence complaint against appellees Dwain Carey and Robert Rodekohr, her skydiving instructors. The district court, in a summary judgment for appellees, found that a "Release and Indemnity Agreement" signed by appellant excused the instructors from all liability for injury, including consequences arising from negligence. On appeal Ms. Schutkowski raises the following issues:

"1. Did the trial court err in determining that the contracting parties intended for the release to excuse appellees from liability caused by their negligence?

"2. Did error occur in failing to strictly construe the release as merely excusing liability for injuries that ordinarily and inevitably occur without fault?

"3. Did the trial court err in following the rationale of a minority view?"

We will affirm.

The basic facts are undisputed. Appellant employed appellees to teach her to sky dive. Before her first jump, she signed an agreement releasing appellees from all claims for personal injury resulting from parachuting and related activities. On July 1, 1979, appellant made her first parachute jump, flying with instructor Carey and pilot Rodekohr. During a difficult landing some distance from the target Ms. Schutkowski suffered back, arm and leg injuries. She filed an action charging that Carey and Rodekohr were negligent in failing to warn her of the risks of parachuting, and failing to adequately instruct and direct her during skydiving procedures.

In their answers to the complaint and subsequent motions for summary judgment, appellees contended that appellant's claims were barred by the liability release agreement. In this document Ms. Schutkowski acknowledged that for consideration and permission to participate in the course,

> . . . I, Barbara Schutkowski of Cheyenne, Wy for myself, my heirs . . . do hereby *fully and forever release* and discharge the said Cheyenne Parachute Club and Bob Rodekohr, Cheyenne, Wy, and their divisions, and their employees . . . and *all persons whomsoever directly or indirectly liable, from any and all other claims and demands*, actions, and

causes of action, damages, costs, loss of services, expenses, and any and all other claims of damages whatsoever both in law and in equity, on account of, or *in any way resulting from, personal injuries*, conscious suffering, death, or property damages sustained by me, arising out of aircraft flights, parachute jumps, or any other means of lift, ascent, or descent from an aircraft . . . on the ground or in flight, and meaning and intending to include herein all such personal injuries, conscious suffering, death or property damage resulting from or in any way connected with or arising out of instructions, training, and ground or air operations incidental thereto, and in consideration of the foregoing premises I . . . hereby expressly stipulate, covenant and agree to indemnify and hold forever harmless the said Cheyenne Parachute Club . . . from any and all actions . . . and any and all other claims for damages whatsoever which may hereafter arise . . . from my negligent, willful or wanton, or intentional act or actions.

The terms of this release and indemnification agreement are contractual and not a mere recital and contain the entire agreement between the parties hereto. (Emphasis added.)

The district court found that the agreement released appellees from liability for negligence. An order granting summary judgment for defendants was entered from which Ms. Schutkowski appeals. . . .

Wyoming courts enforce exculpatory clauses releasing parties from liability for injury or damages resulting from negligence if the clause is not contrary to public policy. Generally, specific agreements absolving participants and proprietors from negligence liability during hazardous recreational activities are enforceable, subject to willful misconduct limitations. *Cain v. Cleveland Parachute Training Center*, 457 N.E.2d 1185 (Ohio 1983). The Ohio court observed in *Cain*:

A participant in recreational activity is free to contract with the proprietor of such activity so as to relieve the proprietor of responsibility for damages or injuries to the participant caused by the negligence of the proprietor, except when caused by willful or wanton misconduct. *Id.* at 1187.

In *Jones v. Dressel*, [623 P.2d 370 (Colo. 1981)], the Colorado Supreme Court developed a four-part test to determine whether a negligence exculpatory clause is valid. Pennsylvania courts have also adopted standards which closely parallel those in the Colorado case. *Liability Assur. Corporation v. Greenville Business Men's Assoc.*, 224 A.2d 620 (Pa. 1966). In reaching its determination a court considers (1) whether a duty to the public exists; (2) the nature of the service performed; (3) whether the contract was fairly entered into; and (4) whether the intention of the parties is expressed in clear and unambiguous language. Only exculpatory agreements meeting these requirements are enforceable.

Private recreational businesses generally do not qualify as services demanding a special duty to the public, nor are their services of a special, highly necessary nature. The California Supreme Court, in *Tunkl v. Regents of University of Cal.*, 60 Cal. 2d 92, 32 Cal. Rptr. 33, 36, 383 P.2d 441, 445–446 (1963), described the elements of an agreement affecting the public interest:

> [The agreement] concerns a business of a type generally thought suitable for public regulation. The party seeking exculpation is engaged in performing a service of great importance to the public, which is often a matter of practical necessity for some members of the public. The party holds himself out as willing to perform this service for any member of the public who seeks it . . . As a result of the essential nature of the service, in the economic setting of the transaction the party invoking exculpation possesses a decisive advantage of bargaining strength against any member of the public who seeks his services . . . .

The service provided by appellees was not a matter of practical necessity for any member of the public. It was not an essential service, so no decisive bargaining advantage existed. Further, no evidence suggests that appellant was unfairly pressured into signing the agreement or that she was deprived of an opportunity to understand its implications. The agreement meets the first three criteria for determining if the exculpatory clause is valid.

Finally, we must determine if the release clearly shows the intent to eliminate appellee's liability for negligent acts. Public policy disfavors clauses exculpating liability for negligence, and a court must closely scrutinize such clauses. The exculpatory clause must clearly and unequivocally demonstrate the parties' intent to eliminate liability for negligence. The question here is whether "negligence" or other specific words are required to clearly show intent.

Courts disagree on the specific language needed to show such intent. In some jurisdictions the word "negligence" or equally precise language is required in order to bar liability for negligent acts. While these jurisdictions may reluctantly accept contracts absolving parties from liability for negligence, they insist on exacting, "unequivocal" language.

Conversely, the absence of the word "negligence" is not fatal to an exculpatory clause in many courts if the terms of the contract clearly show intent to extinguish liability. The facts in *Cain v. Cleveland Parachute Training Center*, *supra*, were very similar to the case before us. A sky diving student signed a liability release stating:

> . . . I covenant for myself, my estate, executor, heirs, and assigns not to file suit or initiate any claim procedure in respect to any personal injuries, property damages, or losses I may experience or sustain arising directly or indirectly out of my activities hereunder.

Id. at 1186. The Ohio court, while narrowly construing the language of the exculpatory clause, found that it expressed an intent to limit liability for negligence even though the words used did not include "negligence."

Jurisdictions which interpret exculpatory language based on the clear intent of the parties rather than specific "negligence" terminology better characterize Wyoming law. . . .

Considering all of the language of the agreement in context, it is clear that the parties' intent was to release appellees from liability for negligence. The contract wording focuses particular attention on the unconditional nature of the exculpatory agreement. It specifically and repeatedly exempts appellants from any responsibility for potential consequences. By signing the release, Barbara Schutkowski voluntarily waived her potential claims against

> all persons whomsoever directly or indirectly liable, from *any and all* . . . claims and demands, actions and causes of action . . . and *any and all other claims* of damages *whatsoever both in law and in equity*, and *in any way* resulting from, personal injuries. . . .

Common sense is one of the leading characteristics of contract interpretation and construction. In construing this contract the nature of the service and the purpose of the release must be considered. In *Gross v. Sweet*, [400 N.E.2d 306, 313 (N.Y. 1979)], a parachuting case similar to this one, the well-reasoned dissent contends:

> The activity on which plaintiff was about to embark under the tutelage of defendants was a hazardous one at best, but virtually the only claims that he might have had against them [the defendants] should he sustain personal injuries or property damage would be claims resulting from fault or negligence of defendants. The majority reads the agreement 'merely as driving home the fact that the defendant was not to bear any responsibility for injuries that ordinarily and inevitably would occur, without any fault of the defendant, to those who participate in such a physically demanding sport.' But of what significance or practical effect is such a release? It is difficult to conceive of any claim other than one predicated on negligence; personal injuries or property damage occasioned without negligence by one or both of the defendants would give rise to no cause of action at all. The release then, if construed as not including claims predicated on negligence, releases nothing and is meaningless and a nullity . . . [A] requirement that there be included the word "negligence" or a description of the specific acts of misconduct pleaded in the complaint (as plaintiff would contend for) would be a reversion to the semantic stereotypes, which we have now abjured. . . .

In this case it is difficult to envision any claim other than one based on negligence that appellant might have had against appellees. If it was not the intent of the parties to release appellees from liability for negligent acts, we see little purpose in the Release and Indemnity Agreement.

Adult private parties should not enter into a contract for hazardous recreational services lightly. The agreement language is unambiguous; it clearly shows that appellant intended to relinquish all liability claims she might have against appellees. We will enforce the exculpatory clause. [AFFIRMED.]

THOMAS, CHIEF JUSTICE (dissenting).

. . . I would opt for the line of authority which requires that the word "negligence" be included in an exculpatory agreement such as this. This requirement is most likely to alert the other party to the extent of the release which he is granting in the contract, which usually is prepared in advance. In many respects this simply would seem to be fair. . . .

[T]he result may well be deemed appropriate with respect to parachuting activities. I wonder how comfortable this court and others will feel with such a rule when it is invoked in favor of day care centers; youth activity organizations; health clubs; public or private schools; landlords; or any of a myriad of activities to which this concept logically can be extended. Because of my concern with the public policy implications of this holding by the court, which I submit may be rather far-reaching, I would vote to reverse the disposition by the trial court and require that if one is to be released from the consequences of his own negligence the release must say exactly that and use the word negligence specifically.

NOTES

1. *Express Assumption of the Risk.* Assumption of the risk encompasses two concepts: express and implied assumption of the risk. One, express assumption of the risk, is contractual: as the parties enter into a relationship, the tort victim, by express agreement, relieves the defendant of any duty to protect the victim against specified risks. The other is a tort concept: a person who knowingly and voluntarily assumes the risk of harm from another's conduct may not recover the damages he sustains from such conduct.

Contractual assumption of the risk contemplates an agreement between the parties. The agreement is usually in writing and prepared in advance by a party seeking relief from tort liability in exchange for providing goods or services to the other. The principal considerations in contract law are: (1) Did the parties agree? (2) What did they agree to? (3) Were they free to agree to that, or does the law make such an agreement invalid? The latter two considerations, reflected in the *Schutkowski* opinion, dominate judicial treatment of contractual assumption of the risk. There must be a "meeting of the minds," *i.e.*, the parties must be aware that they are entering into a contract affecting their rights. Thus, where a patron is presented with a ticket which contains an exculpatory clause, the courts will not find express contractual assumption of the risk unless the patron knew of the nature of the agreement contained in the ticket. *See, e.g., Kermarec v. Compagnie Generale Transatlantique,* 358 U.S. 625 (1959).

Often the issue concerns the scope of the plaintiff's consent. *See Turnbough v. Ladner,* 754 So. 2d 467 (Miss. 2000) (release stating: "I understand that diving with compressed air involves inherent risks [including] decompression sickness," did not demonstrate that plaintiff accepted exposure to injury caused by instructor's negligence in failing to follow basic safety guidelines).

Generally, the REST. 3D TORTS: APPORTIONMENT OF LIABILITY § 2 recognizes a contractual limitation of liability. It provides:

> When permitted by contract law, substantive law governing the claim, and applicable rules of construction, a contract between the plaintiff and another person absolving the person from liability for future harm

bars the plaintiff's recovery from that person for the harm, unlike a plaintiff's negligence, a valid contractual limitation on liability does not provide an occasion for the factfinder to assign a percentage of responsibility to any party or other person.

The common law has established varying guidelines for determining if an agreement is against public policy. Does the Restatement (Third) preclude consideration of such guidelines and public policy? The court in *Hawkins v. Peart*, 37 P.2d 1062 (Utah 2001), held a parent lacked the authority to release the defendant horse riding business from liability for negligent injury of the parent's child. The parent's indemnity provision, agreeing to hold the defendant harmless, was unenforceable as against public policy. Should disclaimers of liability for intentional or wilful misconduct be void as against public policy?

LA. CIV. CODE ART. 2004 takes a different approach. It provides: "Any clause is null that, in advance, excludes or limits the liability of one party for causing physical injury to another party."

2. *Attorney Limitation of Liability.* ABA Model Rule 1.8(h) states that a lawyer shall not limit her malpractice liability by agreement, "unless permitted by law and the client is independently represented in making the agreement."

HOWELL v. CLYDE
620 A.2d 1107 (Pa. 1993)

FLAHERTY, JUSTICE.

Daniel Howell was attending a party at his neighbors' house and was injured when a fireworks cannon owned by the host-neighbors exploded. Howell then sued the neighbors, Theodore and Pamela Clyde, for damages associated with his injuries. The Court of Common Pleas of Clearfield County entered an involuntary nonsuit at the close of plaintiff's evidence, holding that Howell had assumed the risk of injury and was, therefore, barred from recovery. On appeal, Superior Court reversed and remanded for a new trial, . . . holding that the trial court could have granted the nonsuit only if Howell's evidence failed to demonstrate that the Clydes breached a duty which they owed to Howell. Further, Superior Court stated that a nonsuit could not be granted on the basis of assumption of risk because the evidence did not show that Howell knew of the existence of the specific risk he was alleged to have taken.

The evidence established that there was conversation at the party concerning a fireworks cannon fabricated by Clyde's grandfather. The guests, including Howell, visually inspected the cannon and expressed an interest in firing it. Howell went to his residence next door to retrieve black powder for use in the cannon, and upon returning with two cans of black powder, Howell held a flashlight while Clyde filled the bore of the cannon half full of black powder. Howell stood back approximately 40 feet while Clyde ignited the cannon, which exploded, injuring Howell. . . .

Ten years ago in *Rutter v. Northeastern Beaver County School District*, 437 A.2d 1198 (Pa. 1981), a plurality of this court sought to abolish the doctrine of assumption of risk, except where expressly preserved by statute, or in cases of express assumption of risk, or cases brought under 402A (strict liability). A major concern was that the complexity of analysis in assumption of risk cases makes it extremely difficult to instruct juries, who must decide not only questions related to negligence, but also whether the affirmative defense of assumption of risk operates to bar recovery altogether. Additionally, the plurality stated:

> [T]he difficulties of using the term "assumption of risk" outweigh the benefits. The issues should be limited to negligence and contributory negligence. Those are the problems in the case at bar and in all cases brought on a negligence theory. There is no need to introduce further complications. The policy reasons which once existed to preserve the doctrine because of its use in the master-servant cases no longer exist. Furthermore, as is indicated in the *Pennsylvania Suggested Standard Jury Instructions*, "cases which have evoked the doctrine to deny plaintiff's recovery would have produced the same result either by (1) the court's determination that, as a matter of law, defendant owed plaintiff no duty, or, by (2) the jury's determination that plaintiff's own negligent conduct was a substantial factor in bringing about the harm he suffered."

496 Pa. at 613, 437 A.2d 1198.[2] Additionally, the plurality in *Rutter* stated:

> As is indicated in § 496C, comment g [of the RESTATEMENT SECOND OF TORTS], the implicit decision to assume the risk can be either reasonable

---

[2] As described in the Restatement Second of Torts, § 496A, the four types of assumption of risk are as follows: 1. In its simplest form, assumption of risk means that the plaintiff has given his express consent to relieve the defendant of an obligation to exercise care for his protection, and agrees to take his chances as to injury from a known or possible risk. The result is that the defendant, who would otherwise be under a duty to exercise such care, is relieved of that responsibility, and is no longer under any duty to protect the plaintiff. As to such express assumption of risk, see § 496B. 2. A second, and closely related, meaning is that the plaintiff has entered voluntarily into some relation with the defendant which he knows to involve the risk, and so is regarded as tacitly or impliedly agreeing to relieve the defendant of responsibility, and to take his own chances. Thus a spectator entering a baseball park may be regarded as consenting that the players may proceed with the game without taking precautions to protect him from being hit by the ball. Again the legal result is that the defendant is relieved of his duty to the plaintiff. As to such implied assumption of risk, see § 496C. 3. In a third type of situation the plaintiff, aware of a risk created by the negligence of the defendant, proceeds or continues voluntarily to encounter it. For example, an independent contractor who finds that he has been furnished by his employer with a machine which is in dangerous condition, and that the employer, after notice, has failed to repair it or to substitute another, may continue to work with the machine. He may not be negligent in doing so, since his decision may be an entirely reasonable one, because the risk is relatively slight in comparison with the utility of his own conduct; and he may even act with unusual caution because he is aware of the danger. The same policy of the common law which denies recovery to one who expressly consents to accept a risk will, however, prevent his recovery is such a case. As to such implied assumption of risk, see § 496C. As to the necessity that the plaintiff's conduct be voluntary, see § 496E. 4. To be distinguished from these three situations is the fourth, in which the plaintiff's conduct in voluntarily encountering a known risk is itself unreasonable, and amounts to contributory negligence. There is thus negligence on the part of both plaintiff and defendant; and the plaintiff is barred from recovery, not only by his implied consent to accept the risk, but also by the policy of the law which refuses to allow him to impose upon the defendant a loss for which his own negligence was in part responsible. (See § 467.)

or unreasonable. Since the Pennsylvania comparative negligence statute is designed to apportion liability on the basis of fault, not to bar
plaintiff's recovery if it can be shown that he had any degree of fault
at all, the absolute bar to plaintiff's recovery effected by the application of types 2 and 3 [of assumption of risk], without regard to the
reasonableness of plaintiff's action, tends to frustrate the purpose of
the comparative negligence statute.

496 Pa. at 616, n. 6, 437 A.2d at 1210, n. 6. Finally, type 4 of assumption of the
risk, where both plaintiff and defendant are negligent to some degree, also
frustrates the policies behind our comparative negligence statute, where plaintiff is not barred from recovery unless his own negligence is greater than 50%.

Two years after *Rutter* this court again had occasion to address the assumption of risk problem in *Carrender v. Fitterer*, 469 A.2d 120 (Pa. 1983). In that
case, a plaintiff visiting a medical clinic in order to receive treatment for a
back ailment parked in the clinic lot next to a sheet of ice. When she returned
to her car, she slipped on the ice and was injured. The evidence disclosed that
there were areas in the lot which were not ice-covered and that plaintiff saw
the ice next to her car and appreciated the danger that she might fall. Mr.
Chief Justice Roberts, writing for a unanimous court, held that where plaintiff's uncontradicted evidence was that the danger posed by the ice was both
obvious and known, the defendant reasonably expected that the danger would
be avoided. Plaintiff, therefore, failed to establish a duty essential to a prima
facie case of negligence and the defendant clinic was entitled to a judgment
notwithstanding the verdict as a matter of law.

In explaining the relationship between assumption of risk and the duty
owed an invitee by a possessor of land, Mr. Justice Roberts wrote:

When an invitee enters business premises, discovers dangerous conditions which are both obvious and avoidable, and nevertheless proceeds
voluntarily to encounter them, the doctrine of assumption of risk operates merely as a counterpart to the possessor's lack of duty to protect
the invitee from those risks. . . . By voluntarily proceeding to encounter
a known or obvious danger, the invitee is deemed to have agreed to
accept the risk and to undertake to look out for himself. . . . It is precisely because the invitee assumes the risk of injury from obvious and
avoidable dangers that the possessor owes the invitee no duty to take
measures to alleviate those dangers. Thus, to say that the invitee
assumed the risk of injury from a known and avoidable danger is simply another way of expressing the lack of any duty on the part of the
possessor to protect the invitee against such dangers. *See Jones v.
Three Rivers Management Corp.*, 394 A.2d 546 (Pa. 1978) (operator of
baseball park owes no duty to guard against common, frequent, and
expected risks of baseball; duty extends only to foreseeable risks not
inherent in baseball activity). 469 A.2d at 125.

It should be noted that in *Carrender* there was no question as to whether the injured party knew of the risk. This is significant because one of the problems in an assumption of risk analysis is determining what the plaintiff knew and whether the plaintiff's course of action was voluntarily and deliberately taken. Because there was no question in *Carrender* as to whether the risk was intelligently and voluntarily taken, the court was able to decide that there was no duty as a matter of law.

As Mr. Justice Roberts pointed out in *Carrender*, an assumption of risk analysis may, in an appropriate case, be "merely a counterpart" to a duty analysis. . . . In other words, cases like *Carrender* may be analyzed from the point of view of duty, or assumption of risk, or ordinary negligence law, each of which overlaps with the others (i.e., a duty analysis may entail a consideration of assumption of risk and ordinary negligence principles).

The present case may also be analyzed from different perspectives. . . .

If the case is viewed from the perspective of a duty analysis, the evidence presented at trial establishes that Howell voluntarily encountered a known risk, thereby obviating any duty which might otherwise have been owed him by Clyde. Under this analysis, the case is controlled by the assumption of risk principle that one who voluntarily undertakes a known risk thereby releases the defendant from any duty of care.

A second analysis is that Howell was negligent in participating in the cannon episode and that his negligence must be compared with Clyde's. 42 Pa.C.S. § 7102 provides:

(a) General rule. —

In all actions brought to recover damages for negligence resulting in death or injury to person or property, the fact that the plaintiff may have been guilty of contributory negligence shall not bar a recovery by the plaintiff or his legal representative where such negligence was not greater than the causal negligence of the defendant or defendants against whom recovery is sought, but any damages sustained by the plaintiff shall be diminished in proportion to the amount of negligence attributed to the plaintiff.

Such a comparison is for the jury, and if Clyde is found to be negligent, Howell will recover at least some proportion of his damages so long as his negligence does not exceed Clyde's.

A third analysis is that this is a type 4 assumption of risk case. Type 4 assumption of risk, as defined by the Restatement, is that in which:

the plaintiff's conduct in voluntarily encountering a known risk is itself unreasonable, and amounts to contributory negligence. There is thus negligence on the part of both plaintiff and defendant; and the plaintiff is barred from recovery, not only by his implied consent to accept the risk, but also by the policy of the law which refuses to allow him to impose upon the defendant a loss for which his own negligence was in part responsible.

Thus, under a type 4 analysis, a plaintiff who negligently assumes a risk is barred from recovery because he was, in part, at fault.

Fourth, the case may be analyzed as a type 2 or 3 assumption of risk case. . . .

In type 2, Howell may be said to have voluntarily entered into "some relation" with Clyde which he knows to involve risk (i.e., the joint enterprise of firing the cannon); and in type 3, Howell may be said to have voluntarily proceeded to encounter a risk created by Clyde's cannon, seeing the risk of injury as slight, and proceeding cautiously, nonetheless, because of the risk.

Which of these analyses should prevail? It is, perhaps, easiest to determine which should not. Assumption of risk type 4 should no longer be a part of the law of Pennsylvania since it plainly conflicts with the legislative policy underlying the comparative negligence act. One's recovery, under the comparative negligence act, is to be reduced by the amount of his own negligence so long as it does not exceed that of the defendant; it is not to be barred, as in assumption of risk type 4, by the mere existence of any amount of negligence. Assumption of risk type 4, therefore, should be abolished.

A more complex question is whether assumption of risk types 2 and 3 can co-exist with comparative negligence. Arguably, they cannot. Again, the policy underlying a comparative process is inimical to the policy underlying the complete bar of assumption of risk. I believe, however, that a better approach is to recognize the social utility of assumption of risk and continue its viability, albeit in a modified form.

In assumption of risk types 2 and 3 a plaintiff has voluntarily and intelligently undertaken an activity which he knows to be hazardous in ways which subsequently cause him injury. His choice to undertake this activity may or may not be regarded as negligent. His negligence or lack of negligence, however, is not the operative fact; rather, the operative fact is his voluntary choice to encounter the risk. The theoretical underpinning of these types of assumption of risk is that as a matter of public policy one who chooses to take risks will not then be heard later to complain that he was injured by the risks he chose to take and will not be permitted to seek money damages from those who might otherwise have been liable. This policy is distinct from the public policy underlying negligence recovery, which is, in essence, that recovery should be permitted on the basis of fault. Fault has no relevance in assumption of risk types 2 and 3.

Assumption of risk types 2 and 3, then, deal with situations not treated by comparative negligence. In comparative negligence, each of the parties must have been negligent: there must be negligence on both sides to compare. In assumption of risk types 2 and 3, the plaintiff may or may not have been negligent in encountering the risk. He is barred from recovery not because of his negligence, but because of the policy that a person may not recover for injuries which he himself has chosen to risk.

If types 2 and 3 assumption of risk were to be abolished, this idea would be lost. But the policy against recovery for "self-inflicted" injuries remains as viable today as it ever was. Because it is desirable to preserve the public policy behind assumption of risk types 2 and 3, but to the extent possible, remove the difficulties of application of the doctrine and the conflicts which exist with our comparative negligence statute, to the extent that an assumption of risk analysis is appropriate in any given case, it shall be applied by the court as a part of the duty analysis, and not as part of the case to be determined by the jury.[10] This approach preserves the public policy behind the doctrine while at the same time alleviating the difficulty of instructing a jury on voluntariness, knowledge, and scope of the risk.

Under this approach the court may determine that no duty exists only if reasonable minds could not disagree that the plaintiff deliberately and with the awareness of specific risks inherent in the activity nonetheless engaged in the activity that produced his injury. Under those facts, the court would determine that the defendant, as a matter of law, owed plaintiff no duty of care.

If, on the other hand, the court is not able to make this determination and a nonsuit is denied, then the case would proceed and would be submitted to the jury on a comparative negligence theory. Under this approach, subject to the exceptions set out in footnote 10, assumption of the risk would no longer be part of the jury's deliberations or instructions.

In the case at bar, the Court of Common Pleas was not in error in concluding, as a matter of law, that Howell had assumed the risk of injury. Howell voluntarily participated in a dangerous activity, knowing that the ignition of gunpowder is inherently dangerous and might cause injury to himself or others. Although the court granted the nonsuit on the basis of an assumed risk rather than because of an absence of duty, the analysis, nonetheless, is substantially the same. Since Howell voluntarily assumed the risk of injury, Clyde owed him no duty. It was error, therefore, for Superior Court to remand the case for a new trial. . . .

Nix, Chief Justice, (dissenting).

Today the majority decides to preserve assumption of the risk as an affirmative defense in negligence cases despite the fact that, for the purposes of this case, the doctrine lost its viability when the General Assembly passed the Comparative Negligence Act. Therefore, I dissent. . . .

. . . Assumption of the risk is not expressly mentioned as being affected [by Pennsylvania's Comparative Negligence Act]. Indeed, nowhere does the Act make such an express statement. Nevertheless, it is clear that the General Assembly contemplated that assumption of the risk would be modified by the Act. This is readily apparent from the subsection addressing the sport of downhill skiing. The relevant portion of that provision states that "[t]he doctrine of

---

[10]An exception to this holding which, in essence, abolishes assumption of risk as affirmative defense, is that in cases involving express assumption of risk, or cases brought pursuant to 402A (strict liability theory), or cases in which assumption of risk is specifically preserved by statute, assumption of risk remains a viable affirmative defense.

voluntary assumption of the risk as it applies to downhill skiing injuries and damages is not modified by subsection (a). . . ." 42 PA.C.S.A. § 7102 (c)(2). The very existence of this provision and the unique way in which it is written indicate that the General Assembly recognized that Subsection 7102(a) would have an effect on the assumption of the risk doctrine, at least when the defense is raised in connection with the plaintiff's voluntary conduct. Otherwise, there would be no need to enact Subsection 7102(c).

This Court is obligated to give effect to all the provisions of a statute, 1 PA. C.S.A. § 1921(a), and the only way to give effect to Subsection (c)(2) of the Comparative Negligence Act is to conclude that Subsection 7102(a) modifies the assumption of the risk defense in some way. The nature of the modification can be determined by analyzing the overall purpose that the Comparative Negligence Act seeks to achieve. In broad terms, the Act expresses three legislative judgments. First, it rejects the idea that a plaintiff who may be partially responsible for his injuries should be precluded from recovery notwithstanding the conduct of others whose negligence contributed to the event. Second, it embraces the idea that any recovery should be reduced in proportion to the plaintiff's share of responsibility for his injuries. Third, it denies recovery only when the plaintiff is more responsible than the defendant(s) for his injuries.

These three legislative judgments are frustrated by the doctrine of assumption of the risk. Assumption of the risk erects a threshold bar to recovery, regardless of how insignificant a role the plaintiff's conduct may have played in producing his injuries. Given the fundamental incompatibility between the Comparative Negligence Act and the doctrine of assumption of risk, there would be no way to achieve what the General Assembly sought to accomplish by passing the Comparative Negligence Act unless this Court concludes that, except in downhill skiing cases, assumption of the risk as an affirmative defense is no longer viable in this Commonwealth. . . .

In order to achieve its policy objectives, the majority declares that the pivotal consideration is to be whether the plaintiff's decision to encounter a known risk is voluntary. However, when the General Assembly passed the Comparative Negligence Act, it embraced negligence, not voluntariness, as the touchstone of analysis. As the Act's very name implies, courts and juries are statutorily required to evaluate the plaintiff's conduct in terms of negligence and to compare it with that of the defendant(s).[2] This is an entirely legitimate policy judgment, and this Court is obligated to effectuate that decision. . . .The majority's arrogant refusal to do so constitutes a blatant attempt to usurp a legislative power. . . .

---

[2] Of course the plaintiff's voluntariness may be weighed in considering his negligence. However, in that situation, voluntariness is one of several factors, while the majority treats it as the dispositive consideration.

NOTES

1. *Implied Assumption of the Risk,* If one is aware that another will not protect her from a risk created by the other's conduct, but one nevertheless voluntarily encounters that risk, it may be implied that the person encountering the risk has (albeit tacitly) agreed to assume the risk of injury from that conduct. At common law, implied assumption of the risk was a defense that barred all recovery. The defendant was required to plead and prove assumption of the risk as an affirmative defense. This involves a twofold burden. First, the plaintiff must have known and appreciated the specific risk created by defendant's conduct. The test was subjective: plaintiff's knowledge and appreciation, and not that of a reasonable person, was the test. *See, e.g., Desai v. Silver Dollar City, Inc.*, 493 S.E.2d 540 (Ga. App. 1997) (amusement park patron, injured when she stepped from a raft and was struck by an oncoming raft, knew and appreciated the risk).

Second, the plaintiff must have voluntarily encountered the risk. *See, e.g., Marshall v. Ranne*, 511 S.W.2d 255 (Tex. 1974) (plaintiff going from his home to his car did not assume the risk of being bitten by defendant's animal). *Cf. Muldovan v. McEachern*, 523 S.E.2d 566 (Ga. 1999) (decedent, while intoxicated and knowing handgun was loaded, took part in game of Russian Roulette and was killed by a co-player; held, voluntary assumption of the risk).

Implied "assumption of the risk," in the broadest sense, encompasses several concepts. Some are the now familiar concepts of duty and breach. Every person assumes the risk that he will be injured by conduct of another which will not be faulty, either because the defendant acted reasonably, or because the injury was not within the scope of the risks which the law protects from faulty conduct. This concept — assumption of the risk of injury by conduct for which the law does not hold the actor liable — often is called "primary assumption of the risk." *See* Fleming James, *Assumption of the Risk*, 61 YALE L. J. 141 (1952).

Often, primary assumption of the risk is applied to the inherent risks of recreational activities and the contemplated risks of sports experienced by the participants and spectators. What is the rationale for concluding that the defendant owes no legal duty other than for reckless or intentional conduct in organized sports and recreational activities? Is it knowledge of the risks by the plaintiff or simply that the activity is inherently dangerous? *See, e.g., Goodlett v. Kalishek*, 223 F.3d 32 (2d Cir. 2000) (air racing accident; "knowledge plays a role but inherence is the sine qua non"). In light of the recklessness standard that many courts apply, can it be said that the safety objective in sports and recreational activity is undervalued? Being hit by a foul ball?

2. *Effect of Comparative Negligence.* A person who voluntarily encounters a known risk usually is not acting as a reasonable person for his own safety, and is contributorily negligent. When contributory negligence barred all recovery, it was not necessary to distinguish it from assumption of the risk; in either event, the plaintiff took nothing. The adoption of comparative negligence in nearly all of the states has prompted a careful analysis of the various forms of "assumption of the risk" developed at common law. In some jurisdictions, comparative negligence was adopted by judicial fiat and sometimes did not address assumption of risk. In other jurisdictions, the legislation adopting comparative negligence was silent on the future of the doctrine of assumption of the risk. In jurisdictions where comparative negligence has been adopted by the court or where the state legislation (or court) adopting comparative negligence is silent on the future of the doctrine of assumption of the risk, courts have attempted to resolve how best to effectuate comparative negligence principles while preserving the common law effect of the somewhat competing and overlapping tort goals and values expressed in the doctrine of assumption of risk. *See, e.g., Davenport v. Cotton Hope Plantation Horizontal Prop.*, 333 S.C. 71, 508 S.E. 2d 565 (1998) (condo unit owner fell on steps unlit because of broken flood lights; assumption of risk as "absolute defense" seen as inconsistent with comparative negligence); *Churchill v. Pearl River Basin Development*, 757 So. 2d 940 (Miss. 1999) (15-year-old diver struck head on river bottom, breaking neck; assumption of risk subsumed in comparative negligence).

4. *The Penalties of Doctrinal Simplification.* Louisiana adopted pure comparative negligence and subsequently abolished assumption of the risk as a defense. *Murray v. Ramada Inns, Inc.*, 521 So. 2d 1123 (La. 1988).

5. *Statutory Insulation From Comparative Treatment.* Some states (like Pennsylvania, as mentioned in *Howell)* have comparative negligence statutes that explicitly retain the absolute bar to recovery in assumption of risk cases dealing with certain recreational activities. What purpose is served by these insulating statutes? *See Madison v. Wyoming River Trips, Inc.*, 31 F. Supp.2d 1321 (Wyo. 1997) (defendant company not liable for river rafting risk of jostling).

6. *The Passing of Assumption of Risk.* With the wholesale adoption of comparative negligence, assumption of the risk is fading from the American legal scene. It was never a popular defense. Some states even abolished it before comparative negligence came into favor. *See, e.g., McGrath v. American Cyanamid Co.*, 196 A.2d 238 (N.J. 1963). Whether the plaintiff's fault is called negligence or (implied) assumption of the risk, might there still be instances in comparative fault jurisdictions in which the plaintiff's fault is so outrageous that there should be no recovery even from a defendant who has failed to exercise reasonable care? The United States Supreme Court has said yes. *Exxon Co. v. Sofec, Inc.* , 517 U.S. 830 (1996). *See also* FRANK L. MARAIST & THOMAS C. GALLIGAN, JR., ADMIRALTY IN NUTSHELL (5th ed. 2005). In such a case could the court say that the defendant had no duty to protect the plaintiff from the risk which arose? Or that the defendant was not negligent vis-à-vis the plaintiff's conduct? Or that the defendant was not the legal cause of the plaintiff's injuries? Would refusing recovery be consistent with a jurisdiction's adoption of comparative fault? Would it matter if the comparative fault scheme were modified comparative fault? How and why? *See generally* Joseph H. King, Jr., *Outlaws and Outlier Doctrines: The Serious Misconduct Bar in Tort Law*, 43 WILLIAM AND MARY L. REV. 1011 (2002).

4. Avoidable Consequences

TANBERG v. ACKERMAN INVESTMENT CO.
473 N.W.2d 193 (Iowa 1991)

McGIVERIN, CHIEF JUSTICE.

This case presents the issue of whether a plaintiff's failure to follow medical advice to reasonably attempt to lose weight to decrease back pain, thereby mitigating his damages, can be considered fault under Iowa's comparative fault statute. The court of appeals thought plaintiff's failure to lose weight was not such fault. We disagree and, therefore, vacate the decision of the court of appeals and affirm the district court judgment.

Plaintiff Bruce A. Tanberg was a guest at the Best Western Starlite Village motel, located in Ames, on August 7, 1987. On that date, while attempting to exit the whirlpool bathtub located in the bathroom of his motel room to turn off the whirlpool jets, plaintiff fell and injured his back.

Plaintiff sued defendant Ackerman Investment Co., d/b/a Best Western Starlight Village (Best Western), owner and operator of the motel, for injuries he allegedly sustained as a result of his fall. He asserted that defendant had been negligent in several respects. Plaintiff claimed injury to his back and continual pain resulting from the fall. Best Western answered plaintiff's petition by denying that it had been negligent and asserting several affirmative defenses, including that plaintiff was at fault in causing the accident and by failing to mitigate his damages by losing weight after the fall. . . .

At trial, the following evidence was presented in support of defendant's theory that plaintiff failed to mitigate his damages by losing weight after the accident. Plaintiff was five feet eleven inches tall and weighed 309 pounds at the time of the accident; testimony of Dr. Terman, plaintiff's treating physician, that he thought plaintiff's main problem was his obesity and recommended that he lose weight and referred plaintiff to a dietitian for a special diet; testimony of Dr. Noran, plaintiff's treating neurologist, that he thought losing weight could theoretically decrease the pain plaintiff was experiencing in his back because weight loss should reduce some of the load on the spine and in the long run decrease plaintiff's risk of developing more serious problems with his back; testimony of Dr. Dry, plaintiff's initial treating physician, that he did not disagree with Dr. Noran's testimony and, while he could not say that losing weight would probably decrease plaintiff's back pain, he thought carrying around excess weight might strain a person's back; and, plaintiff's testimony that Dr. Pratt advised him to lose thirty to forty pounds after the accident, that all his doctors advised him to lose weight to relieve his back pain and that he had not been as faithful in following his diets as he should have been.

The court, over plaintiff's objection, detailed plaintiff's duty to exercise ordinary care in following reasonable medical advice in instruction 19, which stated:

> Defendant claims plaintiff was at fault by failing to exercise ordinary care
> to follow reasonable medical treatment. Evidence has been introduced

that damages could have been reduced to some extent if Mr. Tanberg followed his doctor's advice and lost weight. An injured person has no duty to undergo serious or speculative medical treatment, but, if by slight expense and by slight inconvenience, a person exercising ordinary care could have reduced the damages, he has a duty to do so.

Plaintiff's objection to instruction 19 as relevant was as follows . . .

This is violative of the law in Iowa, where you take the plaintiff as they find them, the eggshell plaintiff rule. They took this man in his overweight condition, and he should not be penalized with any percentage of fault because of his overweight condition. Had there been a suggestion of an operation that would make him feel better, that instruction may be applicable, but it is not applicable in this case.

The jury found plaintiff 70% at fault for his damages and defendant 30% at fault for plaintiff's damages. Based on the jury's assessment that the plaintiff was liable for a greater percentage of the fault than defendant, the court entered judgment for defendant. See IOWA CODE § 668.3(1). . . .

IOWA CODE section 668.1(1) provides:

1. As used in this chapter, "fault" means one or more acts or omissions that are in any measure negligent or reckless toward the person or property of the actor or others, or that subject a person to strict tort liability. The term also includes breach of warranty, unreasonable assumption of risk not constituting an enforceable express consent, misuse of a product for which the defendant otherwise would be liable, and unreasonable failure to avoid an injury or to mitigate damages. . . .

We, therefore, hold that unreasonable failure to attempt to lose weight pursuant to medical advice can be assessed as fault if weight loss will mitigate damages. We do not hold that a plaintiff must actually lose weight in order to mitigate damages; there must, however, be a reasonable attempt to do so. Since Tanberg was not "as faithful in following his diets as he should have been," a jury could find he did not reasonably mitigate damages. Compare *Fuches v. S.E.S. Co.*, 459 N.W.2d 642, 643–644 (Iowa App. 1990) (failure to undergo an operation that would mitigate damages may be assessed as fault); *Miller* [*v. Eichhorn*], 426 N.W.2d at 643 (failure to undergo additional chiropractic treatment may be assessed as fault). We do, however, note that before the mitigation instruction is given, defendant has the burden of showing substantial evidence that plaintiff's weight loss would have mitigated his damages and that requiring plaintiff to lose weight was reasonable under the circumstances.

Our decision is in accord with other jurisdictions that have considered a plaintiff's failure to lose weight as a mitigating factor when weight loss will lessen damages.

These jurisdictions review each case to determine if failure to lose weight should be treated as a mitigating factor. *See, e.g., Kratzer* [*v. Capital Marine Supply, Inc.,*] 645 F.2d at 483–484 (trial court properly did not consider the defendant's argument that the plaintiff failed to mitigate his damages by losing weight where the plaintiff was not placed on any doctor-administered weight reduction program and, although doctor told the plaintiff to lose weight, the benefits of weight loss were uncertain); *Muller* [*v. Lykes Bros. S.S. Co.,*] 337 F. Supp. at 706–707 (by failing to follow the competent medical advice of his doctors, the plaintiff has neglected his duty to minimize damages); *Anglin* [*v. Grisamore*], 386 S.E.2d at 53 (not error to instruct that plaintiff could be assessed fault for failure to lose weight when no dispute existed that the surgery was unsuccessful due to plaintiff's inability or unwillingness to restrict her diet in accordance with instructions given to her); *Butler v. Anderson*, 295 S.E.2d 216, 217 (1982) (mitigation instruction regarding the plaintiff's failure to lose weight was not error where medical evidence was introduced establishing that the plaintiff's back and leg pain was caused by her obesity); *Close* [*v. State*], 90 A.D.2d at 599–600, 456 N.Y.S.2d at 439 (failure to lose weight was improperly treated as a mitigating factor where the claimant made a good faith effort to lose weight); *Armellini* [*v. Ansley,*] 605 S.W.2d at 309 (trial court did not err in refusing to instruct on mitigation of damages for failure to lose weight where there was no evidence of plaintiff's failure to follow a diet and exercise routine nor of the results the doctors expected if the plaintiff followed the prescribed routine).

Under the present record we find no error in the trial court giving instruction 19 to the jury. . . . [JUDGMENT OF TRIAL COURT AFFIRMED.]

NOTES

1. *Mitigation or Comparative Fault.* The *Tanberg* court treated plaintiff's failure to mitigate as comparative fault. The Iowa statute required this result. Thus, plaintiff was denied all recovery under Iowa's modified comparative fault statute since his fault exceeded that of the defendant. The REST. 3D § 3, cmt. *b* also would treat avoidable consequences as an apportionment issue. Contrariwise, the court in *Ostrowski v. Azzara*, 545 A.2d 148 (N.J. 1988), said failure to mitigate should not be treated as contributory negligence for comparative fault purposes. Under that state's modified comparative fault rule, with its fifty percent qualifier for recovery, the plaintiff could be barred entirely. The court said that the doctrine of avoidable consequences, or failure to mitigate damages, should not be given that barring effect. Contributory negligence arises when the plaintiff is negligent "before the defendant's wrongdoing has been completed." *Id.* at 152. The doctrine of avoidable consequences comes into play where "the defendant's wrong has been committed. Which makes more sense, the Iowa approach? The Restatement (Third) approach or the New Jersey rule? Does a jury assess failure to mitigate in terms of fault, or cause? Why does it matter?

The plaintiff in, *Bokte v. Mine Safety Appliance Corp.*, 611 A.2d 1174 (Pa. 1992), suffered post-traumatic stress disorder as a result of defendant's negligence. The testimony provided that his emotional distress could have been substantially reduced had he sought "counseling and drug therapy for anxiety," as he was advised by his doctor to do. He did not, however, seek such treatment. The fact that he "was resistant to treatment does not disqualify him from receiving compensation," the court said. "It is clear that where a claimant's rejection of treatment is part of his emotional injuries, he may recover damages in spite of the failure to receive treatment." *Id.* at 167, n.2.

2. *Religious Reservations.* The plaintiff's deceased wife, a Jehovah's Witness, received severe injuries in an automobile accident. *Munn v. Algee*, 924 F.2d 568 (5th Cir. 1991). She refused blood transfusions on religious grounds, and died approximately eight hours after the accident. There was testimony that she would have survived if she had received the transfusions. The jury returned no damages for wrongful death. In upholding this verdict, the court said a "strong case can be made" *id.* at 575, that allowing the jury to assess the reasonableness of a religious belief — as was apparently done here — violates the first amendment freedom of religion. However, no error occurred, the court said, because the deceased's husband interjected religion into the case, seeking to explain his wife's conduct." Whose religious interests were at stake, those of the deceased wife or those of her husband as beneficiary of her estate? If he had not been a Jehovah's Witness, could the religious rights of a deceased person be violated?

3. *Duty to Seek Other Employment.* What if the injury prevents the plaintiff from pursuing his pre-accident employment but he can be retrained to perform other employment, and refuses to do so? *See, e.g., McGinley v. United States*, 329 F. Supp. 62 (E.D. Pa. 1971) (45-year-old plaintiff, suffering back injury precluding future employment as stevedore, had no duty to obtain employment as waterfront checker when it would take a long time to complete necessary schooling). Would your answer be different if plaintiff was required to undergo an operation that would cause significant pain? Would the likelihood of success have any bearing on your decision? What policy factors are involved in this assessment?

4. *Immediate Replacement of Property Damage.* The doctrine of "avoidable consequences" or the "duty to mitigate damages" applies to property damage and personal injuries. The doctrine may be the genesis of the rule that if the property is destroyed, the owner may not recover for loss of use because he can immediately replace it. Is this rule realistic? If your car was totally destroyed in an accident, are you in a position to purchase a replacement on the same day? Within a week?

5. *The Seat Belt Defense.* If a victim fails to act reasonably before an accident, and his risky conduct contributes to the happening of the accident, he is contributorily negligent, and his recovery is barred or reduced under principles of comparative or contributory negligence. What if the plaintiff's unreasonably risky pre-accident conduct does not contribute to the accident, but increases his harm from the accident? The most common situation is the failure to use a seat belt. Before the era of quantification of fault, courts were reluctant to bar recovery for failure to use seat belts. Because seat belts were not standard equipment in all vehicles, some worried about the "invidious discrimination" of such a defense. The main reason for the judicial reluctance probably was the difficult issue of cause in fact which would arise: can the judicial process properly allocate the damages caused by the accident and the damages caused by the failure to use the seat belt? Some state legislatures have addressed the matter. LA. REV. STAT. 32:295.1 (E) provides:

> E. In any action to recover damages arising out of the ownership, common maintenance, or operation of a motor vehicle, failure to wear a safety belt in violation of this Section shall not be considered evidence of comparative negligence. Failure to wear a safety belt in violation of this Section shall not be admitted to mitigate damages.

C. STATUTES OF LIMITATIONS AND REPOSE

APGAR v. LEDERLE LABORATORIES
588 A.2d 380 (N.J. 1991)

PER CURIAM.

[Kelly Ann Apgar was born on August 19, 1961. She sued defendants] alleging that between January 1963 and April 1964 she ingested certain tetracycline-based antibiotic drugs manufactured and distributed by defendants; that those drugs were defective as not being reasonably safe for their intended use by pediatric consumers, particularly in their "known potential for tooth discoloration consequent to infant ingestion," and that defendants are liable [for Apgar's tooth discoloration caused by the defendants' products. Ms. Apgar's complaint was grounded on] theories of strict products liability, failure to warn; negligent failure to warn; breach of warranty; misbranding, deceptive packaging and false labeling, all in violation of state statutory standards, federal regulations, and Food and Drug Administration requirements; and unconscionable commercial practice, fraud, and misrepresentation, all in contravention of the New Jersey Consumer Fraud Act. [In their answers to Ms. Apgar's complaint, the defendants raise the statute-of-limitations defense. While still in grammar school, Apgar noticed that her permanent teeth were discolored.] In junior high school, she learned from her dentist that medicine she had taken as an infant had caused the discoloration. [She visited the Johnson & Johnson Dental Clinic for an evaluation and learned that the tooth discoloration had been caused by medication and that the damage was permanent. Ms. Apgar's mother informed her that she had taken Mysteclin.

By the time that Ms. Apgar had graduated from high school in 1979, she thought that medication she had ingested had caused the tooth discoloration. After graduating from college, Ms. Apgar read an article in the November 7, 1985 edition of *The Star-Ledger*, about a successful litigant in a tooth-discoloration case. In November or December 1985 she consulted the attorney for that litigant about bringing an action against the defendants. That was about three years prior to the filing of her complaint.]

In April 1986, plaintiff obtained her treatment records from Dr. Coggleshall, which indicated that in 1961 she had been prescribed Declomycin, a tetracycline antibiotic manufactured by Lederle Laboratories. On November 14, 1986, Dr. Minier informed Ms. Apgar's attorney that, according to his records, in 1963 and 1964 he had prescribed three types of tetracycline antibiotics for

Kelly: Panalba, manufactured by Upjohn; Achromycin V, manufactured by Lederle; and Signemycin, manufactured by Pfizer, Inc.

On March 22, 1988, Kelly Ann Apgar sued Lederle. On October 25, 1988 she amended the complaint to join Upjohn and Pfizer as defendants. The trial court denied the defendants' motions for summary judgment based on the statute of limitations. The Appellate Division denied defendants' motion for leave to appeal. The Supreme Court granted leave to appeal.

Held: Kelly Ann Apgar's cause of action accrued well in advance of the two years prior to the time she filed her complaint; hence, her claim is time-barred.]

The statute of limitations for personal-injury actions is two years. . . . If the injured plaintiff is under the age of twenty-one years when the cause of action accrues, [she has two years from the date of her twenty-first birthday to file her cause of action.] . . . To avoid the "harsh result that otherwise would flow from a mechanical application of the statute of limitations," *Visgisiano v. Ashland Chem. Co.*, 107 N.J. 416, 426 . . . the "discovery rule" was developed. [That rule] delays "the accrual of the cause of action until the plaintiff learns or reasonably should learn, the existence of the state of facts which may equate in law with a cause of action." *Ibid* . . .

In this case, Ms. Apgar knew by the time she reached her twenty-first birthday that her teeth had been discolored and, based on information from several dentists, that medication she had taken as a child had produced the staining. . . . [Therefore,] the statute of limitations expired on August 19, 1984, two years after plaintiff's twenty-first birthday. Inasmuch as she did not begin suit until March 22, 1988, her claim is time-barred. . . .

Even if the plaintiff is given the benefit of the date on which she read the *Star-Ledger* article and consulted her attorney around November or December 1985, she still does not come within the time limitations period.

[The specific identity of a potential defendant is not a requirement for commencing a cause of action. Ms. Apgar can file a complaint naming "John Doe" defendants if the actual identity of the wrongdoer is unknown. Here, the identities of defendants were readily ascertainable from Ms. Apgar's physicians' records.] . . .

Judgment of the Appellate Division is reversed and the matter is remanded to the Law Division for entry of judgment in favor of defendants. [Reversed and Remanded]

NOTES

1. *Statute of Limitations vs. Statutes of Repose.* A statute of limitations bars claims after they have arisen Recently in *Grisham v. Phillip Morris, U.S.A., Inc.,* 151 P.3d 1151 (Ca. 2007), the court answered a certified question from the Ninth Circuit Court of Appeals and held that personal injury claims arising from smoking accrued when the plaintiff discovered her illness and not earlier when she suffered economic injury. The court also said that by 1988 people were presumed to know that smoking caused addiction and disease but that the presumption was rebuttable. Florida has a "delayed discovery" doctrine which generally provides that the statute of limitations does not begin to run until the victim either knows or reasonably should know of the wrongful act giving rise to the cause of action. *See Herndon v. Graham*, 767 So.2d 1179 (Fla. 2000).

2. *The John Doe Defendant.* The *Apgar* court said lack of knowledge of the defendant's identity does not stop the statute of limitations from running, since the plaintiff "can file a complaint naming 'John Doe' defendants if the actual identity of the wrongdoer is unknown." Not all states permit the filing of a John Doe complaint. If they do not, then would reasonable discovery of the defendant also be part of the discovery rule?

Suppose the plaintiff sues the wrong defendant? Under the federal rules, the correct defendant must be sued within the statutory period, unless state law allows a more liberal period or unless the correct defendant is sued typically within 120 days after the statute has run and the correct defendant knows of the suit, should know the wrong person has been sued, and has not been prejudiced by the delay. FED. R. EVID. 4(m), 15(c)(3). Why should a plaintiff be permitted to keep refiling if she is unable to obtain service of process, Rule 4(m), but not if she sues the wrong defendant? If the defendant intentionally conceals his identity, then the running of the statute of limitations may be tolled (or stopped) on grounds of equity. *See, e.g., Martinelli v. Bridgeport Roman Catholic Diocesan Corp.*, 196 F.3d 409 (2d Cir. 1999).

The *Apgar* court said that case did not present "the kind of difficulties the 'discovery rule' may have caused the Court in other contexts," citing *Graves v. Church & Dwight Co.*, 115 N.J. 256 (1989). In a 4-3 decision the *Graves* majority said the plaintiff did not discover that defendant's bicarbonate of soda was the tortious cause of his stomach rupture until much later after the rupture occurred. While he associated the rupture with the taking of the soda, he had no reason to know that his injury was attributable to the "fault of another" (i.e., the soda manufacturer). Only later did medical research establish the causal link.

The *Graves* court said the plaintiff's case was not like that of *Burd v. N.J. Tel. Co.*, 76 N.J. 284 (1978). The court in a 4-3 decision held in *Burd* that the facts supported a finding that the plaintiff should have known defendant's glue caused his heart attack, and that he failed to sue thereafter within the statutory period.

3. *Splitting Claims.* In *Potts v. Celotex Corp.*, 796 S.W.2d 678 (Tenn. 1990), the plaintiff developed asbestosis from exposure to defendant's product, and later developed mesothelioma. Recognizing a division of authority, the court said plaintiff's discovery of his asbestosis did not start the statute running on his mesothelioma claim, even though both diseases were caused by exposure to asbestos. *See also Sopha v. Owens-Corning Fiberglas Corp.*, 601 N. W. 2d 627 (Wis. 1999) (diagnosis of a non-malignant asbestos-related injury did not trigger statue of limitations with respect to another asbestos-related injury). An even more dramatic illustration of the principle of the *Potts* case is found in *Seale v. Gowans*, 923 P.2d 1361 (Utah 1996). There the defendant doctor negligently failed to diagnose plaintiff's breast cancer in 1987. In 1988 plaintiff discovered this negligence and underwent a radical mastectomy. Pathological studies of the removed area showed that the malignancy had spread to eight of her twenty lymph nodes. She then underwent radiation and hormone therapy to increase the likelihood of complete recovery. All subsequent tests remained negative until the summer of 1991, when it was discovered that the cancer had spread to her left hip. The court said that the statute of limitations began to run for the hip cancer in 1991, not in 1988 when she discovered this misdiagnosis and the metastasis of the cancer to her lymph nodes. While the cancer in the lymph nodes "increased the risk that the cancer would recur," defendant failed to produce any evidence that plaintiff suffered any "actual present damages" to her hip in 1988. Although "the cancer's spread resulted in a dramatic decrease in Ms. Seale's chance of survival," there was no cause of action for the hip cancer until she discovered she had suffered actual injury to the hip.

4. *Legal Malpractice and the Running of the Statute of Limitations.* The cases divide on when an injury occurs for purposes of legal malpractice, in the context of prosecution or defense of a lawsuit. Does it occur when the alleged negligent act is committed, or not until exhaustion of appeals of the underlying suit?

5. *Other Claims.* A medical malpractice statute of limitations may be tolled by continued treatment of the plaintiff by the defendant doctor. Dan B. Dobbs, The Law of Torts, § 220 (2000). Continuous wrongs may delay the tolling of the statute of limitations in sexual harassment suits involving ongoing misconduct. *Cusseaux v. Pickett*, 652 A.2d 789 (N.J. 1994) (in a spousal abuse claim, the court said the statute of limitations could be tolled by the ongoing nature of the tort).

DUNLEA v. DAPPEN
924 P.2d 196 (Haw. 1996)

Moon, Chief Justice

Dunlea, who was born in 1947, alleges that she was the victim of incestuous rape at the hands of her natural father, Dappen. She has direct and detailed memory of sexual assaults that occurred between 1961 and 1964, when she was between the ages of fourteen and seventeen years old, while living with her father in Ventura, California. She also alleges memories, beginning at age five, of heinous assaults by a faceless attacker whom she now realizes was Dappen.

In 1964, Dunlea reported the incestuous rape to a California Highway Patrolman. After an investigation, she was removed from Dappen's custody and placed in a foster home. Dappen, apparently, was never prosecuted.

In 1991, Dappen told Dunlea's sister that he was still angry with Dunlea and would never forgive her for what happened in 1964. When the statement was repeated to Dunlea, it triggered a severe emotional reaction because Dunlea had interpreted her father's statement as blaming her for falsely accusing him if incest. One week later, she called Dappen at his Maui residence to confront him about the statement. Dappen was "very angry" and repeated to Dunlea that he would never forgive her for what she did to him. The conversation with Dappen prompted Dunlea to begin therapy. Although Dunlea "has been haunted by depression, thoughts of suicide, shame, disgust, and denial," which have "greatly damaged every facet of [her] life," it was only through therapy that she allegedly discovered that these feelings were symptomatic of a psychological illness caused by her father's incestuous rape.

[In 1992, Dunlea filed a suit against her father seeking, among other things, to recover damages for childhood sexual abuse (CSA). The applicable Hawaii statute of limitations provided that actions for injury to persons or property must be instituted "within two years after the cause of action accrued", except that if a person is under 18 years of age when the action accrues she can bring suit at any time within two years after reaching majority.]

In this case, Dunlea alleged that it was only after she sought psychological counseling that she became aware that Dappen's acts caused her psychological injury and illness. On appeal, Dappen asserts, in his answering brief, that, because Dunlea does not contend that she repressed all memory of the abuse and her complaint makes clear that she was aware of the wrongful nature of Dappen's acts, the circuit court correctly determined that the statute of limitations began to run when Dunlea reached the age of majority and that any action commenced after 1972 was barred . . .

We are persuaded by the reasoning of those courts that, having considered the application of either statutory or judicially created discovery rules to claims of CSA, have determined that the issue of when a plaintiff discovered, or reasonably should have discovered, that she or he was psychologically injured and that the injury was caused by CSA is a question of fact for the jury.

For example, in *Hammer v. Hammer*, 142 Wis. 2d 257, 418 N.W.2d 23 (Wis. Ct. App. 1987), the plaintiff did not deny that she had always had conscious recollection of sexual abuse by her father, or that she had reported the abuse to her mother when she was fifteen years old. She alleged, however, that,

> because of the psychological distress caused by the abuse and the coping mechanisms which resulted, she was unable to perceive or know the existence or nature of her psychological and emotional injuries. These manifestations continued to operate on her long after the incidents of sexual molestation had ended, preventing her from perceiving her psychological and emotional injuries and their connection to her father's earlier acts, and causing her to resist and reject any suggestions that she obtain psychological counseling or legal advice.

Id., 418 N.W.2d at 25. The Wisconsin Court of Appeals reversed the trial court's order granting the defendant's motion to dismiss on statute of limitations grounds. The court, after reviewing the psychological effects of incestuous abuse and previous applications of the judicially adopted discovery rule, held, "as a matter of law, that a cause of action for incestuous abuse will not accrue until the victim discovers, or in the exercise of reasonable diligence should have discovered, the fact and cause of the injury." *Id.*, 418 N.W.2d at 26. The court went on to state:

> In concluding that the discovery rule is applicable, however, we do not decide the factual question of when [plaintiff] discovered or should have discovered her injuries and their cause. Since the trial court rejected the applicability of the discovery rule, this question was not answered. Thus, because genuine issues of material fact remain open, including when [plaintiff's] cause of action accrued, we reverse and remand this matter for trial.

Id. at 27 (footnote omitted). The Supreme Court of North Dakota reached a similar result in *Osland v. Osland*, 442 N.W.2d 907 (N.D. 1989) . . .

Other jurisdictions have reached the same results when interpreting statutory provisions codifying the discovery rule for CSA claims. In *Sellery*, 55 Cal. Rptr. 2d 706, the California Court of Appeals held that, under CAL. C.C.P. § 340.1, a plaintiff need not allege repression of memory to delay the accrual of her or his cause of action. The trial court had granted defendants' motion for summary judgment based on its finding that the plaintiff's "claims were time barred 'by reason of her admitted conscious memory of torts committed as to her during her minority.'" *Id.*, 55 Cal. Rptr. 2d at 709. The court of appeals reversed, stating:

> Nothing in section 340.1 requires that memories of abuse be repressed as a prerequisite to a delayed discovery claim. To the contrary, to satisfy delayed discovery plaintiff need only allege the onset of psychological injury or illness after the age of majority and that he commenced his action within three years of the time he discovered or reasonably should have discovered such psychological injury or illness was caused by the childhood sexual abuse.

Id., 55 Cal Rptr. 2d at 711–12 . . .

Because we agree that the issue of when Dunlea discovered, or should have discovered, that her alleged injuries were caused by Dappen's alleged actions is a question of fact for the jury, we cannot hold as a matter of law that Dunlea ascertained her alleged injuries and their causal link to Dappen's alleged actions more than two years before she asserted her claim, or that her failure to recognize her alleged injuries and the cause of those injuries sooner was unreasonable. Certainly, a reasonable jury could find that Dunlea filed suit within two years of discovering her allege injuries and the cause of those injuries, given their nature and circumstances. We therefore hold that the motion to dismiss was wrongly granted. Accordingly, we vacate the circuit court's dismissal of count III and remand this case for trial on Dunlea's CSA claim. . . .

NOTES

1. *Repressed Memory.* Noting the division of authority as to when the statute of limitations begins to run on claims involving alleged repressed memory of childhood sexual abuse, the court in *Fager v. Hundt*, 610 N.E.2d 246 (Ind.

1993), applied the doctrine of fraudulent concealment to stop the defendant from asserting a statute of limitations defense. The doctrine applies, the court said, when the defendant has deceived the plaintiff or concealed material facts preventing discovery of the cause of action. ELIZABETH LOFTUS & KATHERINE KETCHUM, THE MYTH OF REPRESSED MEMORY (1995), questions the reliability of repressed-memory testimony. Are the problems here any greater than in other areas of memory recall? *See also* Robert Timothy Reagan, *Scientific Consensus on Memory Repressions and Recovery,* 51 RUT. L. REV. 275 (1999) (admissibility of recovered repressed memory testimony).

2. *Statutes of Repose.* States have enacted statutes of repose for medical malpractice, building construction, products liability and warranty claims. The periods generally expire after a fixed date, typically 4–12 years after the date of treatment, building completion, or product sale, and the like. Statutes of repose may expire before the plaintiff has reason to know she has been injured or even before she has been injured. Repose statutes variously provide for: (1) an absolute bar to all claims; (2) a presumption of no negligence, rebuttable by a preponderance of the evidence or by clear and convincing evidence; (3) a bar to strict liability actions (in products cases); (4) a limitation of liability to the product's "useful life"; or (5) both a useful life provision and some form of repose provision. Some states adopted "useful life" statutes to address the problem of "open-ended liability for aging products." See, e.g., *Hodder v. Goodyear Tire & Rubber Co.*, 426 N.W. 2d 826 (Minn. 1988). The *Hodder* court reviewed MINN. STAT. § 604.03, subd. 1 (1986), which provides: "it is a defense to a claim against a designer, manufacturer, distributor or seller of the product or a part thereof, that the injury was sustained following the expiration of the ordinary useful life of the product". It found the statute's useful life concept "ambiguous." Florida enacted a statute of repose requiring claimants alleging abuse or incest to commence actions either 7 years after the state of majority or within 4 years after the plaintiff left the dependency of the abuser. *See* FLA. STAT. ANN. § 95.11(7) (2007).

There is a division of authority as to the constitutionality of statutes of repose. *See Lee v. Gaufin*, 867 P.2d 572 (Utah 1993) (medical malpractice); *Hazine v. Montgomery Elevator Co.*, 861 P.2d 625 (Ariz. 1993) (products liability). Courts striking down such statutes do so because of the harshness of cutting off a claim before the plaintiff could ever bring a suit. *See generally* McGovern, *The Variety, Policy and Constitutionality of Products Liability Statutes of Repose*, 30 AM. U. L. REV. 579 (1981). Another controversy related to statutes of repose concerns the post-sale duty to warn about defects in products. *See* chapter 10, *supra*. How would a corrective justice scholar respond to the imposition of a statute of repose for product-related claims? What response would be taken by a law and economics proponent? Are there race or gender considerations raised by the decision to enact a general statute of repose?

D. IMMUNITIES

1. Sovereign Immunity

The *Federal Tort Claims Act*, passed in 1946, provides for suit against the United States:

§ 1346. United States as defendant

(b)(1) [The United States district courts] shall have exclusive jurisdiction of civil actions on claims against the United States, for money damages, accruing on and after January 1, 1945, for injury or loss of property, or personal injury or death caused by the negligent or wrongful act or omission of any employee of the Government while acting within the scope of his office or employment, under circumstances where the United States, if a private person, would be liable to the claimant in accordance with the law of the place where the act or omission occurred. . . .

§ 2674. Liability of United States

The United States shall be liable, respecting the provisions of this title relating to tort claims, in the same manner and to the same extent as a private individual under like circumstances, but shall not be liable for interest prior to judgment or for punitive damages. . . .

With respect to any claim under this chapter, the United States shall be entitled to assert any defense upon judicial or legislative immunity which otherwise would have been available to the employee of the United States whose act or omission gave rise to the claim, as well as any other defenses to which the United States is entitled. . . .

§ 2675. Disposition by federal agency as prerequisite; evidence

(a) An action shall not be instituted upon a claim against the United States for money damages for injury or loss of property or personal injury or death caused by the negligent or wrongful act or omission of any employee of the Government while acting within the scope of his office or employment, unless the claimant shall have first presented the claim to the appropriate Federal agency and his claim shall have been finally denied by the agency. . . . The failure of an agency to make final disposition of a claim within six months after it is filed shall, at the option of the claimant any time thereafter, be deemed a final denial of the claim for purposes of this section. . . .

(b) Action under this section shall not be instituted for any sum in excess of the amount of the claim presented to the federal agency, except where the increased amount is based upon newly discovered evidence not reasonably discoverable at the time of presenting the claim to the federal agency, or upon allegation and proof of intervening facts, relating to the amount of the claim.

(c) Disposition of any claim by the Attorney General or other head of a federal agency shall not be competent evidence of liability or amount of damages.

. . .

§ 2679. Exclusiveness of remedy

(b)(1) The remedy against the United States provided [herein] for injury or loss of property, or personal injury or death arising or resulting from the negligent or wrongful act or omission of any employee of the Government while acting within the scope of his office or employment is exclusive of any other civil action or proceeding for money damages by reason of the same subject matter against the employee whose act or omission gave rise to the claim or against the estate of such employee. Any other civil action or proceeding for money damages arising out of or relating to the same subject matter against the employee or the employee's estate is precluded without regard to when the action or omission occurred.

(2) Paragraph (1) does not extend or apply to a civil action against an employee of the Government —

(A) which is brought for violation of the Constitution of the United States. . . .

§ 2680. Exceptions

The provisions of this chapter and section 1346(b) of this title shall not apply to —

(a) Any claim based upon an act or omission of an employee of the Government, exercising due care, in the execution of a statute or regulation, whether or not such statute or regulation be valid, or based upon the exercise or performance or the failure to exercise or perform a discretionary function or duty on the part of a federal agency or an employee of the Government, whether or not the discretion involved be abused. . . .

(h) Any claim arising out of assault, battery, false imprisonment, false arrest, malicious prosecution, abuse of process, libel, slander, misrepresentation, deceit, or interference with contract rights: Provided, That, with regard to acts or omissions of investigative or law enforcement officers of the United States Government, the provisions of this chapter and section 1346(b) of this title shall apply to any claim arising, on or after the date of the enactment of this proviso, out of assault, battery, false imprisonment, false arrest, abuse of process, or malicious prosecution. For the purpose of this subsection, "investigative or law enforcement officer" means any officer of the United States who is empowered by law to execute searches, to seize evidence, or to make arrests for violations of Federal law. . . .

(j) Any claim arising out of the combatant activities of the military or naval forces, or the Coast guard, during time of war.

NOTES

1. *Federal Sovereign Immunity.* The federal sovereign enjoyed immunity from the early days of the Republic. *See Osborn v. President, Dirs. & Co. of Bank*, 22 U.S. (9 Wheat.) 738 (1824). General waiver of that immunity took a long time to develop. In 1887, the *Tucker Act* permitted suit in federal court and assessment of liability against the federal sovereign on contract claims. Congress sometimes enacted legislation permitting a particular plaintiff to sue. In 1920, Congress waived sovereign immunity for torts committed by merchant vessels owned by or operated for the *United States in The Suits in Admiralty Act*. 46 U.S.C.A. § 30901 et seq.. However, there was no comprehensive waiver of sovereign immunity from tort claims until after World War II, when Congress adopted the *Federal Tort Claims Act* (FTCA).

2. *Administrative Relief.* Under the FTCA the plaintiff must first present his claim to the appropriate federal agency, and cannot bring a suit until the claim is denied. 28 U.S.C. § 2675. However, the claim is treated as denied if the agency takes no action within six months. There is a two-year statute of limitations on claims under the FTCA. 28 U.S.C. § 2401(b). Is this a reasonable time limit?

3. *Exclusive Jurisdiction.* Federal courts have exclusive subject matter jurisdiction over a tort claim against the federal government. § 1346(b)(1). Except for constitutional and other expressly authorized tort claims, the exclusive remedy under the FTCA is against the federal government, and not against the government employee. 28 U.S.C. § 2679(b).

4. *Strict Liability and Intentional Torts.* The FTCA waives immunity as to a "negligent or wrongful act or omission." 28 U.S.C. § 1346(b)(1); it does not waive the sovereign's immunity from strict liability. *Laird v. Nelms*, 406 U.S. 797 reh. denied, 409 U.S. 902 (1972). Note, also, that the act does not waive immunity to certain intentional torts, § 2680(h). Consider these provisions in light of the Perspectives discussed in Chapter 1.

STENCEL AERO ENGINEERING CORP. v. UNITED STATES
431 U.S. 666 (1977)

CHIEF JUSTICE BURGER delivered the opinion of the Court.

We granted certiorari in this case to decide whether the United States is liable under the *Federal Tort Claims Act*, 28 U.S.C. § 2674, to indemnify a third party for damages paid by it to a member of the Armed Forces injured in the course of military service.

On June 9, 1973, Captain John Donham was permanently injured when the egress life-support system of his F-100 fighter aircraft malfunctioned during a mid-air emergency. Petitioner, Stencel Aero Engineering Corp., manufactured the ejection system pursuant to the specifications of, and by use of certain components provided by, the United States. Pursuant to the *Veterans' Benefits Act*, 38 U.S.C. § 321 *et seq.*, made applicable to National Guardsmen by 32 U.S.C. § 318, Captain Donham was awarded a lifetime pension of approximately $1,500 per month. He nonetheless brought suit for the injury in the Eastern District of Missouri claiming damages of $2,500,000. Named as defendants, inter alia, were the United States and Stencel. Donham alleged that the emergency eject system malfunctioned as a result of the "negligence and carelessness of the defendants individually and jointly."

Stencel then cross-claimed against the United States for indemnity, charging that any malfunction in the egress life-support system used by Donham was due to faulty specifications, requirements, and components provided by the United States or other persons under contract with the United States. The cross-claim further charged that the malfunctioning system had been in the exclusive custody and control of the United States since the time of its manufacture. Stencel therefore claimed that, insofar as it was negligent at all, its negligence was passive, while the negligence of the United States was active.

Accordingly it prayed for indemnity as to any sums it would be required to pay to Captain Donham.

The United States moved for summary judgment against Donham, contending that he could not recover under the Tort Claims Act against the Government for injuries sustained incident to military service. *Feres v. United States*, 340 U.S. 135, 95 L. Ed. 152, 71 S. Ct. 153 (1950). The United States further moved for dismissal of Stencel's cross-claim, asserting that *Feres* also bars an indemnity action by third party for monies paid to military personnel who could not recover directly from the United States.

The District Court granted the Government's motions, holding that *Feres* protected the United States both from the claim of the serviceman and that of the third party. Both claims were therefore dismissed for lack of subject-matter jurisdiction. Stencel appealed this ruling to the Court of Appeals for the Eighth Circuit and that court affirmed. We granted certiorari.

In *Feres v. United States*, *supra*, the Court held that an on-duty serviceman who is injured due to the negligence of Government officials may not recover against the United States under the Federal Tort Claims Act. During the same Term, in a case involving injuries to private parties, the Court also held that the Act permits impleading the Government as a third-party defendant, under a theory of indemnity or contribution, if the original defendant claims that the United States was wholly or partially responsible for the plaintiff's injury. *United States v. Yellow Cab Co.*, 340 U.S. 543, 95 L. Ed. 523, 71 S. Ct. 399 (1951). In this case we must resolve the tension between *Feres* and *Yellow Cab* when a member of the Armed Services brings a tort action against a private defendant and the latter seeks indemnity from the United States under the Tort Claims Act, claiming that Government officials were primarily responsible for the injuries.

Petitioner argues that "[the] Federal Tort Claims Act waives the Government's immunity from suit in sweeping language." *United States v. Yellow Cab Co.*, *supra*, at 547. Petitioner therefore contends that, unless its claim falls within one of the express exceptions to the Act, the Court should give effect to the congressional policy underlying the Act, which is to hold the United States liable under state-law principles to the same extent as a similarly situated private individual. However, the principles of *Yellow Cab* here come into conflict with the equally well-established doctrine of *Feres v. United States*. It is necessary, therefore, to examine the rationale of *Feres* to determine to what extent, if any, allowance of petitioner's claim would circumvent the purposes of the Act as there construed by the Court.

Feres was an action by the executrix of a serviceman who had been killed when the barracks in which he was sleeping caught fire. The plaintiff claimed that the United States had been negligent in quartering the decedent in barracks it knew to be unsafe due to a defective heating plant. While recognizing the broad congressional purpose in passing the Act, the Court noted that the relationship between a sovereign and the members of its Armed Forces is unlike any relationship between private individuals. 340 U.S. at 141–142. There is thus at least a surface anomaly in applying the mandate of the Act that "[the] United States shall be liable . . . in the same manner and to the same extent as a private individual under like circumstances. . . ." 28 U.S.C. § 2674. Noting that the effect of the Act was "to waive immunity from recognized causes of action and . . . not to visit the Government with novel and unprecedented liabilities," 340 U.S. at 142, the Court concluded:

> [T]he Government is not liable under the Federal Tort Claims Act for injuries to servicemen where the injuries arise out of or are in the course of activity incident to service. Without exception, the relationship of military personnel to the Government has been governed exclusively by federal law. We do not think that congress, in drafting this Act, created a new cause of action dependent on local law for service-connected injuries or death due to negligence. We cannot impute to Congress such a radical departure from established law in the absence of express congressional command. *Id.* at 146.

In reaching this conclusion, the Court considered two factors: First, the relationship between the Government and members of its Armed Forces is "'distinctively federal in character,'" *id.*, at 143, citing *United States v. Standard Oil Co.*, 332 U.S. 301, 91 L. Ed. 2067, 67 S. Ct. 1604 (1947); it would make little sense to have the Government's liability to members of the Armed Services dependent on the fortuity of where the soldier happened to be stationed at the time of the injury. Second, the Veterans' Benefits Act establishes, as a substitute for tort liability, a statutory "no fault" compensation scheme which provides generous pensions to injured servicemen, without regard to any negligence attributable to the Government. A third factor was explicated in *United States v. Brown*, 348 U.S. 110, 112 (1954), namely, "[t]he peculiar and special relationship of the soldier to his superiors, the effects of the maintenance of such suits on discipline, and the extreme results that might obtain if suits under the Tort Claims Act were allowed for negligent orders given or negligent acts committed in the course of military duty. . . ." We must therefore consider the impact of these factors where, as here, the suit against the Government is not brought by the serviceman himself, but by a third party seeking indemnity for any damages it may be required to pay the serviceman.

Clearly, the first factor considered in *Feres* operates with equal force in this case. The relationship between the Government and its suppliers of ordnance is certainly no less "distinctively federal in character" than the relationship between the Government and its soldiers. The Armed Services perform a unique, nationwide function in protecting the security of the United States. To that end military authorities frequently move large numbers of men, and large quantities of equipment, from one end of the continent to the other, and beyond. Significant risk of accidents and injuries attend such a vast undertaking. If, as the Court held in *Feres*, it makes no sense to permit the fortuity of the *situs* of the alleged negligence to affect the liability of he Government to a serviceman who sustains service-connected injuries, it makes equally little sense to permit that *situs* to affect the Government's liability to a Government contractor for the identical injury.

The second factor considered by *Feres* is somewhat more difficult to apply. Petitioner argues that the existence of a generous military compensation scheme is of little comfort to it. It is contended that, although it may be fair to prohibit direct recovery by servicemen under the Act, since they are assured of compensation regardless of fault under the Veterans' Benefits Act, petitioner as a third-party claimant should not be barred from indemnity for damages which it may be required to pay to the serviceman, and as to which it has no alternative federal remedy.

A compensation scheme such as the Veterans' Benefits Act serves a dual purpose: it not only provides a swift, efficient remedy for the injured serviceman, but it also clothes the Government in the "protective mantle of the Act's limitation-of-liability provisions." See *Cooper Stevedoring Co. v. Fritz Kopke, Inc.*, 417 U.S. 106, 115, 40 L. Ed. 2d 694, 94 S. Ct. 2174 (1974). Given the broad exposure of the Government, and the great variability in the potentially applicable tort law, the military compensation scheme provides an upper limit of liability for the Government as to service-connected injuries. To permit petitioner's claim would circumvent this limitation, thereby frustrating one of the essential features of the Veterans' Benefits Act. As we stated in a somewhat different context concerning the Tort Claims Act: "To permit [petitioner] to proceed . . . here would be to judicially admit at the back door that which has been legislatively turned away at the front door. We do not believe that the [Federal Tort Claims] Act permits such a result." *Laird v. Nelms*, 406 U.S. 797, 802 (1972).

Turning to the third factor, it seems quite clear that where the case concerns an injury sustained by a soldier while on duty, the effect of the action upon military discipline is identical whether the suit is brought by the soldier directly or by a third party. The litigation would take virtually the identical form in either case, and at issue would be the degree of fault, if any, on the part of the Government's agents and the effect upon the serviceman's safety. The trial would, in either case, involve second-guessing military orders, and would often required members of the Armed Services to testify in court as to each other's decisions and actions. This factor, too, weighs against permitting any recovery by petitioner against the United States.

We conclude, therefore, that the third-party indemnity action in this case is unavailable for essentially the same reasons that the direct action by Donham is barred by *Feres*. The factors considered by the *Feres* court are largely applicable in this type of case as well; hence, the right of the third party to recover in an indemnity action against the United States recognized in *Yellow Cab*, must be held limited by the rationale of *Feres* where the injured party is a serviceman. Since the relationship between the United States and petitioner is based on a commercial contract, there is no basis for a claim of unfairness in this result.

NOTES

1. *The Feres Doctrine.* The *Feres* doctrine bars "indirect" claims, such as loss of consortium and wrongful death, by a soldier's beneficiaries. It also bars the claims of family members for mental anguish caused by the injury to a soldier's relative. *De Font v. United States*, 453 F.2d 1239 (1st Cir.), *cert. denied*, 407 U.S.

910 (1972). Consider these statutory limitations from the social justice, corrective justice and law and economics perspectives discussed in Chapter 1.

LINDGREN v. UNITED STATES
665 F.2d 978 (9th Cir. 1982)

MUECKE, DISTRICT JUDGE

On September 28, 1974, plaintiff Eric A. Lindgren was water skiing on a section of the Colorado River, south of Parker Dam. While making a run, plaintiff's ski struck the river bottom, throwing plaintiff forward and causing him serious physical injury.

Plaintiffs filed their First Amended Complaint on February 26, 1979. The complaint named the United States as defendant and sought damages pursuant to the *Federal Tort Claims Act* (FTCA), 28 U.S.C. §§ 1346(b) and 2671 *et seq.*, for personal injury, negligent infliction of emotional distress and loss of consortium. Plaintiffs' complaint alleged that the U.S. Bureau of Reclamation, the agency in control at Parker Dam, had artificially altered the flow, the water level and the riverbed configuration of the Colorado River, and had thereby created a dangerous condition for users of the river. Plaintiffs further alleged that the Bureau had knowledge of the recreational use of the river and of the hazards posed to such users by the Bureau's alteration; it was alleged that despite this knowledge, the Bureau had failed to post any warnings as to the dangerous condition of the river.

On May 25, 1979, the United States moved for summary judgment. The Government's motion was based, in part, on the discretionary function exemption to the FTCA, 28 U.S.C. § 2680(a), which provides in pertinent part:

> The provisions of this Chapter and Section 1346(b) of this title shall not apply to — (a) Any claim . . . based upon the exercise or performance or the failure to exercise or perform a discretionary function or duty on the part of a federal agency or an employee of the Government, whether or not the discretion involved be abused.

On August 9, 1979, the trial court entered summary judgment in the Government's favor. In so doing, the Court held that the operation of Parker Dam constituted a discretionary activity within the meaning of the above statute and cited *Spillway Marina, Inc. v. United States*, 445 F.2d 876 (10th Cir. 1971).

Plaintiffs do not contest the trial court's conclusion as to the discretionary character of dam operations. Their sole contention is that the Government's failure to warn was not such an activity, and therefore that the trial court erred in entering summary judgment in the Government's favor.

It may well be that the trial court's ultimate conclusion as to the discretionary character of the Government's failure to warn was correct. It may also be that even if the Government's failure is found nondiscretionary, the trial court will conclude that under the present circumstances the Government was under no duty to warn. The problem with the Court's ruling was its assumption that simply because the hazard which allegedly caused plaintiff's injury was created through the exercise of a discretionary function, the Government's failure to warn of the hazard was also discretionary. The trial court's *per se* approach to the issue was in error.

The leading decision interpreting the discretionary function exemption is *Dalehite v. United States*, 346 U.S. 15, 73 S. Ct. 956, 97 L. Ed. 1427 (1953). In that case, the Court established that the purpose of the exemption was to permit the Government to make planning-level decisions without fear of suit . . .

Although the *Dalehite* Court declined to define the outer limits of "discretion," it did go so far as to hold that discretion

> includes more than the initiation of programs and activities. It also includes determinations made by executives or administrators in establishing plans, specifications or schedules of operations. Where there is room for policy judgment and decision, there is discretion. It necessarily follows that acts of subordinates carrying out the operations of government in accordance with official directions cannot be actionable. If it were not so, the protection of § 2680(a) would fail at the time it would be needed, that is, when a subordinate performs or fails to perform a causal step, each action or nonaction being directed by the superior exercising, perhaps abusing, discretion.

Id. at 35–36, 73 S. Ct. 968. (Footnote omitted.)

Although *Dalehite* remains an important statement of the policy behind the discretionary function exemption, subsequent decisions by the Supreme Court and various circuit courts have operated to narrow *Dalehite's* definition of the term "discretion."

The prevailing test in the Ninth Circuit asks whether the act or omission occurred on the "planning level" of governmental activity or on the "operational level":

> Not every discretionary act is exempt. Obviously, attending to many day-to-day details of management involves decisions and thus some element of discretion. The exercise of this kind of discretion does not fall within the discretionary function exemption. The distinction generally made in the application of the discretionary function exemption is between those decisions which are made on a policy or planning level, as opposed to those made on an operational level.

Thompson v. United States, 592 F.2d 1104, 1111 (9th Cir. 1979). . . .

NOTES

1. *Drawing Elusive Lines.* There may be no more elusive concept in American law than the "discretionary function" exception to the waiver of sovereign immunity. The purpose of the exception is to avoid infringement upon the power and operations of the executive. If the decision is clearly one of policy, such as whether to engage in a certain activity, the matter will be "discretionary," and the immunity will apply. As *Lindgren* illustrates, the government may be liable for negligent failure to warn that it has exercised a discretionary function which will expose others to an unreasonable risk of harm. *Martin v.*

United States, 546 F.2d 1355 (9th Cir. 1976), *cert. den.*, 432 U.S. 906, (1977), or in failing to gather the data necessary for an intelligent exercise of the discretionary function. *Payton v. United States*, 679 F.2d 475 (5th Cir. 1982). The Coast Guard may not be liable for failing to erect or operate a lighthouse, but it may be liable for letting the light go out or in failing to warn that the lighthouse is not operating. *See, e.g., Indian Towing Co. v. United States*, 350 U.S. 61 (1955).

HACKING v. TOWN OF BELMONT
736 A.2d 1229 (N.H. 1999)

BROCK, C.J.

This is an interlocutory appeal by the defendants, the Town of Belmont and the Shaker Regional School District, from a ruling of the Superior Court denying their motion to dismiss. The plaintiffs, Nancy and Charles Hacking, Jr., have asserted several theories of negligence against the defendants for injuries that their daughter, Chelsea Hacking, sustained in a basketball game. We affirm in part, reverse in part, and remand.

The plaintiffs have alleged the following facts. On or about January 27, 1995, when she was a sixth grade student at the Canterbury Elementary School, Chelsea participated in a girls basketball game against a team from the Belmont Elementary School. During that game, which was organized by the defendants and/or the Town of Canterbury, the referees, coaches, instructors, and employees of the defendants permitted the game to escalate out of control. Belmont players twice knocked Chelsea down and stepped on her leg. As a result, she suffered permanent injury to her left leg, underwent surgery and other medical treatment, and will require future medical care.

[The plaintiffs sued alleging several grounds of negligence. Defendants moved to dismiss on the grounds that they were immune under the discretionary function doctrine, and the trial court denied the motion to dismiss.]

The defendants' first allegation of error requires us to review once again the doctrine of discretionary function immunity. In *Merrill v. Manchester*, 114 N.H. 722, 729, 332 A.2d 378, 383 (1974), we abrogated the doctrine of municipal immunity. In so doing, we established that as a general rule, municipalities are "subject to the same rules as private corporations if a duty has been violated and a tort committed." *Id.* at 730, 332 A.2d at 383.

As an exception to the general rule, however, we held that municipalities are immune from liability for acts and omissions that constitute "the exercise of an executive or planning function involving the making of a basic policy decision which is characterized by the exercise of a high degree of official judgment or discretion." *Id.* at 729, 332 A.2d at 383. We have recognized that "[c]ertain essential, fundamental activities of government must remain immune from tort liability so that our government can govern." *Mahan v. N.H. Dep't of Admin. Services*, 141 N.H. 747, 750, 693 A.2d 79, 82 (1997) (decided under the discretionary function exception to the State's waiver of sovereign immunity). Accordingly, in evaluating whether the trial court erred, we must "distinguish between planning or discretionary functions and functions that are purely ministerial." *Bergeron v. City of Manchester*, 140 N.H. 417, 421, 666 A.2d 982, 984 (1995).

We have refused to adopt a bright line rule to determine whether conduct constitutes discretionary planning or merely the ministerial implementation of a plan. See *id.* at 421, 666 A.2d at 985; *Gardner v. City of Concord*, 137 N.H. 253, 258, 624 A.2d 1337, 1340 (1993). We have, however, adopted the following test:

> When the particular conduct which caused the injury is one character-
> ized by the high degree of discretion and judgment involved in weigh-
> ing alternatives and making choices with respect to public policy and
> planning, governmental entities should remain immune from liability.

Bergeron, 140 N.H. at 421, 666 A.2d at 984. In applying this test, "[w]e dis-
tinguish policy decisions involving the consideration of competing economic, social, and political factors from operational or ministerial decisions required to implement the policy decisions." *Mahan*, 141 N.H. at 750, 693 A.2d at 82.

To the extent that the plaintiffs challenge the defendants' decisions regard-
ing the training and supervision of the coaches and referees, the defendants are immune from liability. There is no question that the decision whether or not to have a fifth and sixth grade girls basketball program is characterized by a high degree of discretion in making public policy and planning choices. Likewise, the decisions regarding what training and supervision to provide those whom the defendants chose to run the program are planning decisions requiring a high degree of discretion. Cf. *Bergeron*, 140 N.H. at 425, 666 A.2d at 987 (because ultimate decision regarding traffic controls at intersection was discretionary, intermediate decision regarding whether to have staff keep track of accidents at intersection also discretionary). These decisions necessarily involved the most prudent allocation of municipal resources, and thus the weighing of "competing, economic, social, and political factors." *Mahan*, 141 N.H. at 750, 693 A.2d at 82; cf. *Phillips v. Thomas*, 555 So. 2d 81, 85 (Ala. 1989) (defendant entitled to discretionary function immunity for negligent training and supervision claim); *Brooks v. Logan*, 127 Idaho 484, 903 P.2d 73, 77 (1995) (school district entitled to discretionary function immunity for failure to train staff to prevent student suicide); *Erskine v. Commissioner of Corrections*, 682 A.2d 681, 686 (Me. 1996) (defendants' actions in training and supervising personnel protected by discretionary immunity); *Miller v. Szelenyi*, 546 A.2d 1013, 1021 (Me. 1988) (proper supervision and control of employees required exer-
cise of discretion). Accordingly, the trial court should have dismissed Count III, and we reverse its decision with respect to that count . . . .

The defendants assert that they are entitled to immunity for their decisions regarding not only the training and supervision of the coaches and referees, but also the selection of the coaches and referees. In arguing that the trial court erred on this issue, the defendants state that the plaintiffs' claim for negligent training and supervision should have been dismissed in part because the decision to rely on parent volunteers as referees and coaches was discretionary. Count III, however, alleges only that the defendants "failed to properly train and supervise" the referees and coaches. Moreover, plaintiffs' counsel conceded at oral argument that they had not alleged negligent selection of

referees and coaches. Accordingly, we find it unnecessary to address whether the selection of the referees or coaches was entitled to immunity.

The defendants next argue that the decisions made by the referees and coaches in the course of the game were entitled to discretionary function immunity. Decisions such as whether to call a foul, whether to replace one player with another, or whether a team has scored, according to the defendants, are inherently discretionary and require the weighing of alternatives. The defendants contend that discretionary function immunity should extend not only to "high-level" decisions, but to decisions made at any level when those decisions "involve the weighing of alternatives regarding the implementation or allocation of municipal resources." Accordingly, the defendants argue that the decisions of the referees and coaches are precisely the sort of decision that ought to be afforded immunity. The only conduct that should be considered ministerial, according to the defendants, is conduct that involves the mere execution of a set task, requiring no independent judgment.

Although the level of government at which a decision is made is not dispositive of whether the municipality is entitled to immunity, ministerial conduct is not limited to conduct requiring no judgment whatsoever. Indeed, "it would be difficult to conceive of any official act, no matter how directly ministerial, that did not admit of some discretion in the manner of its performance, even if it involved only the driving of a nail." 18 E. MCQUILLIN, MUNICIPAL CORPORATIONS §53.04.10, at 157 (3d ed. rev. 1993) (quotation and brackets omitted); see also *Whitney v. City of Worcester*, 373 Mass. 208, 366 N.E. 2d 1210, 1217 (1977) (distinction is not merely between discretionary and non-discretionary functions as all functions involve some degree of judgment). While "[n]ot all governmental decisions involving an element of discretion fall within the discretionary function exception," the exception does apply "when a decision entails governmental planning or policy formulation, involving the evaluation of economic, social, and political considerations." *Mahan*, 141 N.H. at 751, 693 A.2d at 83.

Assuming the truth of the plaintiffs' allegations, we conclude that the decisions of the referees and coaches, while perhaps involving some discretion and judgment, were not decisions that concerned municipal planning and public policy. These decisions did not involve the weighing of competing social, economic, or political factors. Rather, the plaintiffs have alleged negligence on the part of the referees and coaches in the implementation of the school basketball program.

The discretionary function exception "was not designed to cloak the ancient doctrine of [municipal] immunity in modern garb." *Adriance*, 687 A.2d at 241. Elevating the decisions of referees and coaches in the course of an elementary school basketball game to the level of governmental planning or policy formulation would indeed undermine the rule of *Merrill* establishing immunity as the exception. Accordingly, we hold that the trial court did not err in denying the motion to dismiss on the grounds that the decisions of the referees and coaches were not entitled to discretionary function immunity . . .

NOTES

1. *Public Duty.* The public duty doctrine (a duty owed to all is a duty owed to none) has been used as a doctrine parallel to that of discretionary immunity. In *Riss v. City of New York*, 240 N.E. 2d 860 (N.Y. App. 1968), the court held the city of New York had no duty to provide police protection to a woman who had been repeatedly threatened by a would-be suitor. But compare *DeLong v. Erie County*, 455 N.Y. S.2d 887 (App. Dir. 1982), and *Beal for Martinez v. City of Seattle*, 954 P.2d 237 (Wash. 1998), where the defendant governmental entities could be found liable for the negligent performance of their special duties assumed by the adoption of an emergency 911 call system. Often the "public duty" doctrine is an issue in cases involving the government's duty to act. In *Osborn v. Mason County*, 134 P.2d 197, 202 (Wa. 2006) the Washington Supreme Court said:

> Because a public entity is liable in tort "to the same extent as if it were a private person or corporation," . . . the public duty doctrine does not — cannot — provide immunity from liability. Rather it is a "focusing tool" we use to determine whether a public entity owed a duty to be a "nebulous public" or a particular individual. The public duty doctrine simply reminds us that a public entity — like any other defendant — is liable in negligence only if it has a statutory or common law duty of care. And its "exceptions" indicate when a statutory or common law duty exists. "The question whether an exception to the public duty doctrine applies is thus another way of asking whether the State has a duty to the plaintiff." In other words, the public duty doctrine helps us distinguish proper legal duties from mere hortatory "duties."

Is the court saying that the public duty doctrine adds nothing? Do you agree? Does the public duty doctrine tend to operate in a manner that affects disproportionately certain kinds of claims? Is it likely to affect identifiable groups like women, minorities, or the poor more than others? Consider this doctrine from the standpoint of the Perspectives included in Chapter 1.

2. *The Eleventh Amendment.* The eleventh amendment to the United States Constitution provides in effect that no state can be sued for damages in a federal court. The U.S. Supreme Court has extended that immunity to suits against states in state courts for violation of federal law. The United States Supreme Court, in a series of 5-4 decisions, *Alden v. Maine*, 527 U.S. 706 (1999); *College Sav. Bank v. Florida Prepaid Postsecondary Educ. Expense Bd.*, 527 U.S. 666 (1999); *Kimel v. Florida Board of Regents,* 120 S. Ct. 631 (2000); and *Board of Trustees v. Garrett*, 121 S. Ct. 955 (2001) has dramatically restricted the power of individuals to seek money damages against states for injuries resulting form violation of federal law. In *Alden* the Court held that Congress lacked power under Article I of the U.S. Constitution to authorize suits against the states without the states' consent. Here the Court denied a claim by state probation officers against the State of Maine for violation of the overtime provisions of the Fair Labor Standards Act. The eleventh amendment, said the Court, is "convenient shorthand" for state sovereign immunity that "neither derives from nor is limited by the terms of the Eleventh Amendment."

In *Florida Prepaid*, the Court said neither the patent clause (Art. I, §8, cl. 8) nor the fourteenth amendment of the United States Constitution authorized Congress to abrogate state sovereign immunity in suits for state infringement of the federal patent law. The Court held in *Kimel* that Congress lacked the power under the fourteenth amendment to authorize suits against a state for violation of the Age Discrimination in Employment Act. *Garrett* held a state could not be sued for violation of the Americans with Disabilities Act.

2. Individual Immunities

LLMD OF MICHIGAN, INC. v. JACKSON-CROSS CO.
740 A.2d 186 (Pa. 1999)

ZAPPALA, JUSTICE.

This is an appeal by LLMD of Michigan, Inc., a general partner trading as Wintoll Associates Limited Partnership (Wintoll), from the Superior Court's order affirming the order of the Philadelphia County Common Pleas Court, which granted summary judgment in favor of Jackson-Cross Company (Appellee) in an action for professional malpractice. For the following reasons, we reverse.

In 1989, Wintoll commenced an action in the United States District Court for the Eastern District of Pennsylvania against Marine Midland Realty Credit Corporation and USLife Life Insurance Company, alleging breach of contract arising out of the defendants' failure to provide financing for the purchase and rehabilitation of an industrial facility in Springfield, Michigan. After the lawsuit was filed, Robert Swift, Esquire, Wintoll's attorney, contacted Charles Seymour, chairman of Jackson-Cross, to engage Seymour's services as Wintoll's expert on the issue of the lost profits suffered as a result of the defendants' breach of their financing commitment for the industrial rehabilitation project. On December 28, 1990, Seymour responded with a proposal outlining the scope of services that he would perform for Wintoll and the fees that would be charged for those services. The proposal contemplated that Seymour would quantify the damages sustained because of the lenders' failure to close under the mortgage commitments; prepare a signed report outlining what was done, stating the conclusions and supporting them; and participate in pre- trial conferences, depositions and trial. By letter dated January 4, 1991, Wintoll's attorney accepted Seymour's proposal.

Wintoll was subsequently provided with a calculation of the lost profits, which Jackson-Cross estimated to be $6 million. The calculation was prepared by David Anderson, an employee of Jackson-Cross, using a computerized accounting spreadsheet program. The federal trial began on November 24, 1992. Seymour was called by Wintoll to testify as an expert witness on the lost profits calculation on December 7, 1992 and provided his opinion as to the damages sustained by Wintoll.

On cross-examination, defense counsel established that Anderson's lost profits calculation contained a mathematical error that completely undermined the basis for the Jackson-Cross calculation of Wintoll's damages. Seymour conceded that the calculation was wrong because of the error that had been made. Because Seymour had not performed the calculations himself, he was unable to explain the mathematical error in the calculations or to recalculate the lost profits by correcting the error while on the stand. Defense counsel requested that Seymour's opinion be stricken from the record because it was based on inaccurate numbers and on erroneous mathematical calculations. The trial judge granted the motion to strike Seymour's testimony and instructed the jury to completely disregard the testimony during its deliberations.

Without Seymour's testimony, Wintoll's evidence relating to lost profits consisted of the testimony of Leon Winitsky and Michael Winitsky, principals of Wintoll, and a calculation by Wintoll of its estimated profits. The day after Seymour's testimony was stricken, Wintoll accepted a settlement offer from the federal defendants for approximately $750,000. Jackson-Cross subsequently provided Wintoll with a corrected computation of estimated lost profits, which indicated such damages amounted to $2.7 million.

On January 14, 1993, Wintoll filed a civil action in the Philadelphia County Common Pleas Court against Jackson-Cross, asserting causes of action for breach of contract and professional malpractice. Wintoll asserted that Jackson-Cross had breached its agreement to furnish expert services in connection with the federal lawsuit by failing to deliver an accurate or workmanlike lost profits computation, and had failed to exercise the degree of care and skill ordinarily exercised by experts in the field of real estate counseling and computation of lost profits in real estate transactions. Wintoll alleged that it would have received a judgment for lost profits in an amount in excess of $2.7 million plus interest but for the conduct of Jackson-Cross. Wintoll sought damages for the estimated lost profits and reimbursement of the fees paid to Jackson-Cross for its services.

Jackson-Cross filed preliminary objections in the nature of a demurrer to the complaint, which were overruled. In its answer and new matter, Jackson-Cross asserted, inter alia, that Wintoll's causes of action were barred by the doctrine of witness immunity. The immunity issue was then raised by Jackson-Cross in a motion for judgment on the pleadings. The motion was denied. Jackson-Cross renewed the issue in a motion for summary judgment, which was also denied. On June 7, 1996, an order was entered by the common pleas court denying reconsideration of the summary judgment motion.

On July 1, 1996, Jackson-Cross filed a second motion for summary judgment. Jackson-Cross asserted that (1) Wintoll's claim was non-justiciable because the federal action had been settled prior to a jury verdict; (2) Wintoll's settlement of the federal action severed the causal link between the striking of Seymour's testimony and the alleged damages; (3) the pro tanto release given by Wintoll to the additional defendant applied to Jackson-Cross as an agent; and (4) Wintoll had failed to state a claim for breach of contract. The second summary judgment motion was granted by order dated July 10, 1996. Judgment was entered in favor of Jackson-Cross and the case was dismissed.

On appeal, the Superior Court affirmed the order granting summary judgment on different grounds. The Superior Court concluded that the doctrine of witness immunity barred Wintoll's action against Jackson-Cross. We granted Wintoll's petition for allowance of appeal to address the issue of whether the doctrine of witness immunity extends to bar professional malpractice actions against professionals hired to perform services related to litigation.

Wintoll challenges the ruling of the Superior Court, asserting that the witness immunity doctrine should not be extended so as to bar professional malpractice actions against an expert retained by a party to litigation. Wintoll contends that privately retained and compensated experts should not be immunized from their own negligence, and that the policy concerns underlying the witness immunity doctrine are not advanced by extending immunity under such circumstances. Jackson-Cross asserts that the Superior Court's decision should be affirmed because it is based upon sound public policy.

In *Binder v. Triangle Publications, Inc.*, 442 Pa. 319, 275 A.2d 53 (Pa. 1971), we recognized, in the context of a defamation action, that participants in judicial proceedings have an absolute privilege for communications related to the proceedings.

> [S]tatements by a party, a witness, counsel, or a judge cannot be the basis of a defamation action whether they occur in the pleadings or in open court. The reasons for the absolute privilege are well recognized. A judge must be free to administer the law without fear of consequences. This independence would be impaired were he to be in daily apprehension of defamation suits. The privilege is also extended to parties to afford freedom of access to the courts, to witnesses to encourage their complete and unintimidated testimony in court, and to counsel to enable him to best represent his client's interests. Likewise, the privilege exists because the courts have other internal sanctions against defamatory statements, such a perjury or contempt proceedings.

See also *Post v. Mendel*, 510 Pa. 213, 507 A.2d 351, 354 (Pa. 1986) ("The origin of the rule was the great mischief that would result if witnesses in courts of justice were not at liberty to speak freely, subject only to the animadversion of the court. . . . The rule is inflexible that no action will lie for words spoken or written in the course of giving evidence.")

The United States Supreme Court addressed the policy concerns underlying the witness immunity doctrine in the oft-cited decision of *Briscoe v. LaHue*, 460 U.S. 325 (1983):

> The immunity of parties and witnesses from subsequent damages liability for their testimony in judicial proceedings was well established in English common law. Some American decisions required a showing that the witness' allegedly defamatory statements were relevant to the judicial proceeding, but once this threshold showing had been made, the witness had an absolute privilege. The plaintiff could not recover even if the witness knew the statements were false and made them with malice.

In the words of one 19th-century court, in damages suits against witnesses, "the claims of the individual must yield to the dictates of public policy, which requires that the paths which lead to the ascertainment of truth should be left as free and unobstructed as possible." A witness' apprehension of subsequent damages liability might induce two forms of self-censorship. First, witnesses might be reluctant to come forward to testify. And once a witness is on the stand, his testimony might be distorted by the fear of subsequent liability. Even within the constraints of the witness' oath there may be various ways to give an account or to state an opinion. These alternatives may be more or less detailed and may differ in emphasis and certainty. A witness who knows that he might be forced to defend a subsequent lawsuit, and perhaps to pay damages, might be inclined to shade his testimony in favor of the potential plaintiff, to magnify uncertainties, and thus to deprive the finder of fact of candid, objective, and undistorted evidence. But the truthfinding process is better served if the witness' testimony is submitted to "the crucible of the judicial process so that the fact-finder may consider it, after cross-examination, together with the other evidence in the case to determine where the truth lies."

The witness immunity doctrine has been applied by the Superior Court in actions other than for defamation when the court has determined that the extension of immunity is in furtherance of the policy underlying the doctrine. See *Clodgo v. Bowman*, 411 Pa. Super. 267, 601 A.2d 342, 345 (Pa. Super. 1992), appeal granted, 532 Pa. 640, 614 A.2d 1138 (Pa. 1992), appeal dismissed as having been improvidently granted, 533 Pa. 352, 625 A.2d 612 (Pa. 1993), ("The form of the cause of action is not relevant to application of the privilege. Regardless of the tort contained in the complaint, if the communication was made in connection with a judicial proceeding and was material and relevant to it, the privilege applies.") *Moses v. McWilliams*, 379 Pa. Super. 150, 549 A.2d 950, 957 (Pa. Super. 1988) ("While it is true that immunity from civil liability in judicial proceedings has been applied most frequently in defamation actions, many courts, including those in Pennsylvania, have extended the immunity from civil liability to other alleged torts when they occur in connection with judicial proceedings.")

In this case, the Superior Court stated that it was required to analyze and decide the case in light of its decision in *Panitz v. Behrend*, 429 Pa. Super. 273, 632 A.2d 562 (Pa. Super. 1993), allocatur denied, 539 Pa. 694, 653 A.2d 1232 (Pa. 1994). *Panitz* involved a medical doctor who was retained by a law firm to provide services as an expert witness in a lawsuit by plaintiffs who alleged that they had suffered from formaldehyde in building materials. The law firm anticipated that the expert would be cross-examined about the lack of formaldehyde sensitization in cigarette smokers who regularly were exposed to much greater concentrations of formaldehyde than were the plaintiffs. Prior to trial, the expert provided the law firm with deposition transcripts from an unrelated case in which the expert had testified about the lack of sensitization in smokers.

At trial, the expert proffered her opinion that the plaintiffs' injuries had been caused by formaldehyde present in building materials. The expert conceded on cross-examination, however, that she could not explain the apparent inconsistency about the lack of sensitization in cigarette smokers. After trial, the expert indicated that she had realized before her testimony that her prior analysis of the lack of sensitization in cigarette smokers was inaccurate.

When a defense verdict was returned, the law firm refused to pay the expert for her services. The expert then brought an action to recover her fees. The law firm filed a counterclaim seeking damages resulting from the defense verdict, alleging negligence and misrepresentation regarding the expert's trial testimony. Preliminary objections to the counterclaim were sustained and the counterclaim was dismissed.

The Superior Court affirmed the order dismissing the counterclaim, finding that the expert was immune from liability for the testimony which she gave. The court found that the policy of encouraging witnesses to give frank and truthful testimony would be advanced by application of the witness immunity doctrine. The court reasoned that the primary purpose of expert testimony was to assist the factfinder in understanding complicated matters, rather than to assist one party in winning a case. "Having testified truthfully in the judicial process, a witness should not thereafter be subjected to civil liability for the testimony which he or she has given." 632 A.2d at 563. The Superior Court concluded that liability could not be imposed upon an expert who is persuaded on cross-examination by conflicting evidence that some or all of the expert's opinion testimony was inaccurate.

In this case, the Superior Court determined that *Panitz* was dispositive and concluded that the witness immunity doctrine bars Wintoll's professional negligence action against Jackson-Cross. We find *Panitz* to be distinguishable, however. In *Panitz*, the expert witness offered her opinion as to the cause of the plaintiffs' formaldehyde sensitization but testified during cross-examination that she could not explain the lack of such sensitization in cigarette smokers. The theories that the expert witness had previously articulated to explain the inconsistency had been discounted by the expert prior to trial. While the expert's testimony on cross-examination may have defeated the expectation of plaintiffs' counsel that she would be able to account for the inconsistency, the expert offered her opinion based upon her knowledge of formaldehyde sensitization.

It is imperative that an expert witness not be subjected to litigation because the party who retained the expert is dissatisfied with the substance of the opinion rendered by the expert. An expert witness must be able to articulate the basis for his or her opinion without fear that a verdict unfavorable to the client will result in litigation, even where the party who has retained the expert contends that the expert's opinion was not fully explained prior to trial. Application of the witness immunity doctrine in *Panitz* was consistent, therefore, with the two-fold policy of the doctrine: to ensure that the path to the truth is left as free and unobstructed as possible and to protect the judicial process.

We are unpersuaded, however, that those policy concerns are furthered by extending the witness immunity doctrine to professional negligence actions which are brought against an expert witness when the allegations of negligence are not premised on the substance of the expert's opinion. We perceive a significant difference between *Panitz* and Wintoll's claim in this case that Jackson-Cross had been negligent in performing the mathematical calculations required to determine lost profits. The goal of ensuring that the path to truth is unobstructed and the judicial process is protected, by fostering an atmosphere where the expert witness will be forthright and candid in stating his or her opinion, is not advanced by immunizing an expert witness from his or her negligence in formulating that opinion. The judicial process will be enhanced only by requiring that an expert witness render services to the degree of care, skill and proficiency commonly exercised by the ordinarily skillful, careful and prudent members of their profession.

Therefore, we find that the witness immunity doctrine does not bar Wintoll's professional malpractice action against Jackson-Cross. We caution, however, that our holding that the witness immunity doctrine does not preclude claims against an expert witness for professional malpractice has limited application. An expert witness may not be held liable merely because his or her opinion is challenged by another expert or authoritative source. In those circumstances, the judicial process is enhanced by the presentation of different views. Differences of opinion will not suffice to establish liability of an expert witness for professional negligence.

Accordingly, we reverse the order of the Superior Court and remand for disposition of the remaining issues. [REVERSED AND REMANDED.]

CAPPY, JUSTICE, dissenting.

The majority premises its opinion largely on its conclusion that the situation presented in the matter *sub judice* is distinguishable from that with which the Superior Court was faced in *Panitz v. Behrend*, 429 Pa. Super. 273, 632 A.2d 562 (Pa. Super. Ct. 1993). The majority categorizes the suit filed against the expert witness in *Panitz* as one which attacked the "substance" of the expert's opinion; in contrast, the majority asserts that the suit in the matter presently before the court is premised on the allegation that the expert was "negligen[t] in formulating [his] opinion." The majority finds this distinction to be crucial. It concludes that while a suit may not be filed on the basis that the "substance" of an expert witness' testimony was unacceptable, an expert witness may be sued on the basis that the expert was negligent in formulating the opinion tendered at trial. In my opinion, the majority's attempts to distinguish *Panitz* ring hollow. Furthermore, I believe that the distinction formulated by the majority is an unworkable and radical departure from our accepted law regarding witness immunity. I therefore am compelled to dissent.

In the underlying lawsuit in *Panitz*, the expert witness, Elaine Panitz ("Panitz"), tendered her medical opinion on direct examination in favor of the plaintiffs; this was in accord with her pre-trial communications with the Behrend firm which represented the plaintiffs in the underlying lawsuit. On cross-examination, however, Panitz conceded that her opinion was inconsistent with the available scientific data. After trial, Panitz admitted that she had realized prior to trial that her pro-plaintiffs medical opinion was inaccurate; yet Panitz had failed to inform the Behrend firm that she had changed her opinion.

Contrary to the majority's characterization of *Panitz*, I believe that the lawsuit filed against Panitz was premised on the allegation that she had been negligent in formulating her opinion, and was not an attack on the substance of the opinion she offered on cross-examination. In fact, there is a lengthy discussion in the Superior Court opinion concerning the contention by the Behrend firm in its suit against Panitz that "it was not the in-court testimony that caused the loss but the pre-trial representations about what the in-court testimony would be." *Panitz*, 632 A.2d at 565. Clearly, the Behrend firm sued Panitz premised upon Panitz's negligent failure to inform them that she had changed her opinion prior to trial; I see nothing in *Panitz* which would indicate that the Behrend firm sued Panitz on the basis that they somehow disagreed with the substance of her opinion.

Furthermore, I find that the test proposed by the majority is simply unworkable. In my opinion, there is no bright line between what constitutes an attack on the "substance" of an expert's opinion and what constitutes a challenge premised on the expert's negligence in formulating that opinion. I believe that there is a great gray area which lies between these two points, and distinguishing between them will be quite difficult. This difficulty has, in my opinion, been amply illustrated by the varying analyses of *Panitz* offered by the majority and by this author in the matter *sub judice*. I fear that by establishing this unworkable distinction, we will be sowing confusion in the lower courts and the practicing bar.

Rather than adopting such a test, I would continue to adhere to our established rule that there is no civil liability for statements made by witnesses in a legal proceeding. This straightforward rule advances the laudable and long-recognized policy goal of "encourag[ing] [the witness'] complete and unintimidated testimony in court. . . ." *Binder v. Triangle Publications, Inc.*, 442 Pa. 319, 275 A.2d 53, 56 (Pa. 1971). Furthermore, I agree with the position as ably stated by the Superior Court in *Panitz* that there "is no reason for refusing to apply the privilege to friendly experts hired by a party." *Panitz*, 632 A.2d at 565. "To allow a party to litigation to contract with an expert witness and thereby obligate the witness to testify only in a manner favorable to the party, on threat of civil liability, would be contrary to public policy." *Id.* at 565–66.

For the foregoing reasons, I respectfully dissent.

NOTES

1. *Absolute and Conditional Immunities.* It is generally held that legislators are absolutely immune from liability for tortious acts committed within the scope of their jurisdiction. *Sanchez v. Coxon*, 854 P.2d 126 (Ariz. 1993). Absolute tort immunity is also widely extended to judicial officers acting within the scope of their jurisdiction. *See Stump v. Sparkman*, 435 U.S. 349 (1978); *cf. Zarcone v. Perry*, 572 F.2d 52 (2d Cir. 1978). The exact scope of this immunity is not always clear. *See Wagshal v. Foster*, 28 F.3d 1249 (D.C. Cir. 1994), applying "absolute quasi-judicial immunity . . . to mediators and case evaluators in the Superior Court's [alternative dispute resolution] process." Absolute immunity has been extended to prosecuting attorneys, *Knapper v. Connick*, 681 So. 2d 944 (La. 1996), and to public defenders. *Dziubak v. Mott*, 503 N.W. 2d 771

(Minn. 1993). Courts widely hold that court witnesses are absolutely immune from civil liability for their testimony. *Panitz v. Behrend*, 632 A.2d 562 (Pa. Super. 1993).

The President of the United States is absolutely immune from liability for torts committed while acting as president. *Nixon v. Fitzgerald*, 457 U.S. 731 (1981) (5-4 decision). See *Clinton v. Jones*, 520 U.S. 681 (1997), holding that the president can be sued while in the presidential office for torts allegedly committed prior to taking such office. Executive officers, however, do not enjoy absolute immunity. Federal officials "performing discretionary functions generally are shielded from liability for civil damages insofar as their conduct does not violate clearly established statutory or constitutional rights of which a reasonable person would have known." *Harlow v. Fitzgerald*, 457 U.S. 800, 818 (1982). A state executive officer is entitled to qualified immunity "dependent upon the scope of discretion and responsibilities of the office and all the circumstances as they reasonably appeared at the time of the action on which liability is sought to be based." *Scheuer v. Rhodes*, 416 U.S. 232 (1974). Why have the courts accorded to different state actors different kinds of immunities and privileges?

2. *The Return of Individual Immunity.* There are many state statutes protecting non profit organizations and volunteers. For example, TENN. CODE ANN. §§ 48-58-601(c) provides, in part:

> (c) All directors, trustees or members of the governing bodies of nonprofit cooperatives, corporations, clubs, associations and organizations described in subsection (d), whether compensated or not, shall be immune from suit arising from the conduct of the affairs of such cooperatives, corporations, clubs, associations or organizations. Such immunity from suit shall be removed when such conduct amounts to willful, wanton or gross negligence.

Congress enacted the *Volunteer Protection Act of 1997*, 42 U.S.C. 14501. Unless the Act is expressly rejected by a state, the Act immunizes volunteers to nonprofit organizations or to governmental entities from negligence. A volunteer is defined in the Act, 42 U.S.C. § 14805(6), as an individual who performs services for a nonprofit organization or a governmental entity without compensation "other than reasonable reimbursement or allowance for expenses actually incurred," and without receiving "any other thing of value in lieu of compensation, in excess of $500 per year, and such term includes a volunteer serving as a director, officer, trustee, or direct service volunteer."

Are such protective statutes necessary? Consider their value from social justice and corrective justice perspectives.

3.   Charitable Immunity

In the mid-nineteenth century, American courts established the doctrine that a charity was immune from tort liability. The doctrine was based upon the English decision in *Feoffees of Heriot's Hosp. v. Ross*, 13 C & F 507, 8 Eng. Rep. 1508 (1846), which was repudiated in its own jurisdiction within a generation. *See Mersey Docks Trustees v. Gibbs*, 11 H.L. Cas. 686, 11 Eng. Rep.

1500 (1866); PROSSER & KEETON ON TORTS § 132 (5th ed. 1984). However, the doctrine persisted in America. One major justification probably was the fear that use of donated funds to pay tort judgments would greatly reduce charitable giving. Another justification was the perceived ingratitude of the charity patient who "bit the hand that fed him" by seeking tort damages. The argument also was offered that because a charity was performing a governmental function, it was entitled to the same immunity as the government enjoys from tort liability. By the twentieth century, however, conditions affecting the charitable immunity had changed greatly. When the doctrine arose, charitable hospitals were a major source of health care, open to all patients and funded primarily by donations. By the twentieth century, the state had become a major health care provider, and charitable donations were motivated as much by tax considerations as by any other reason. The ascendancy of the idea that fair spreading of the risks of negligent conduct is an important societal policy, and the ready availability of liability insurance, helped seal the fate of charitable immunity.

A substantial majority of jurisdictions have abolished charitable immunity. *Abernathy v. Sisters of St. Mary's*, 446 S.W.2d 599 (Mo. 1969). Other jurisdictions have limited the immunity to suits by beneficiaries of the charity. *See, e.g.,* N.J. STAT. ANN. §§ 2A:53A-7 and 53A-8 (West). Are the nonprofit and volunteer protection statutes discussed above a partial revival of something like sovereign immunity? What are the implications of these developments from a law and economics perspective

4. Family Immunities

CATES v. CATES
156 Ill. 2d 76 (1993)

FREEMAN, JUSTICE

On June 9, 1985, Heather Cates, aged 4 years, was a passenger in an automobile driven by her father, Timothy Cates. At the time, Cates was transporting his girlfriend, her minor son and Heather to his home for the evening. As Cates' auto approached an intersection of two State highways, it collided with an automobile driven by Phillip Darwin. Heather was seriously injured as a result of the accident. At the time of the incident, Cates was exercising his visitation privileges as a noncustodial parent.

Heather, as plaintiff, by her mother and next friend, Nancy Cates Schmittling, filed a negligence action in the circuit court of St. Clair County against Phillip Darwin's estate and Keeley and Sons, Inc., a construction company engaged in repairing the highway area around the collision site at the time of the accident. Heather subsequently amended her complaint, naming [her father] as an additional defendant and alleging that [her mother] had assigned to [her the mother's rights] against [her father] for medical expenses and other costs expended in Heather's behalf. State Farm Mutual Automobile Insurance Company, [the mother's] insurer, intervened as a subrogor against all defendants to recover uninsured motorist's benefits paid to [the mother] under her policy.

[Defendant] Cates filed a motion for summary judgment, alleging that the parent-child immunity doctrine precluded Heather's negligence action as well as the subrogation action. The trial court granted Cates' motion for summary judgment with respect to both actions, stating that "[i]t is difficult to determine that the purpose of the parental immunity doctrine would be served by applying it to the facts of this case," but that it was obliged to follow precedent. . . .

The court of appeals abolished parental immunity "in case of automobile negligence." The appellate court misperceived the effect of several of our pronouncements. We do not, however, reverse its decision. We must yet consider whether the parent-child tort immunity doctrine bars plaintiff's automobile negligence action.

Defendant argues that the parent-child tort immunity doctrine is long-standing in Illinois and recognized as applying in negligence cases by all appellate court districts. . . . Defendant argues that: (1) preservation of the parent-child relationship is recognized in Illinois as a worthy public policy goal; (2) the immunity's purpose is to protect parent and child from an opportunity to engage in fraud and collusion; (3) the elimination of the immunity will threaten parents' authority to discipline and control their children; (4) abrogation of the immunity would allow courts to second-guess the exercise of parental discretion in day-to-day family matters; (5) the doctrine as it stands applies to custodial and noncustodial parents; and (6) the immunity should be applied irrespective of the existence of liability insurance.

Plaintiff responds that the originally recognized policy bases for the immunity, the preservation of family harmony and prevention of collusion and fraud, do not sufficiently justify its application in automobile negligence cases. Plaintiff contends that an automobile negligence action brought by a very young child against her father does not disrupt family harmony where divorce has already occurred. Plaintiff further contends that it is the injury itself, and not the subsequent legal action to remedy those damages, which disrupts family harmony. Moreover, according to plaintiff, any possibility of collusion and fraud in such cases is easily overcome by resort to discovery, cross-examination, review of evidence and a heightened degree of skepticism. Plaintiff also argues that in this case fraud and collusion are virtually impossible because the extent of Heather's injuries are independently ascertainable. . . .

The parent-child tort immunity doctrine was unknown at English common law and arose in American case law as the result of three decisions, often termed "the great trilogy" (*Hewlett*, 68 Miss. 703, 9 So. 885 (married, minor child barred from suing mother for malicious imprisonment in insane asylum); *McKelvey v. McKelvey*, 111 Tenn. 388, 77 S.W. 664 (1903) (minor child barred from suing parent for cruel and inhumane punishment); *Roller v. Roller*, 37 Wash. 242, 79 P. 788 (1905) (minor child barred from suing father for rape)). These cases articulated several public policies to justify the immunity: preservation of family harmony, preservation of parental authority to control children by way of analogy to spousal immunity, and the avoidance of a depletion of family assets to the detriment of the injured child's siblings (commonly referred to as the "family exchequer" rationale), *Dunlap v. Dunlap* (1930), 150 A. 905, 909, 84 N.H. 352, 361. Because most of the justifications for the immunity concerned the relationship of a parent to a minor child under his custody and control and for whose support he was responsible, the immunity did not generally apply to an adult child or emancipated minor children. RESTATEMENT (SECOND) OF TORTS § 895G, Comment d, at 428 (1979).

Despite the development of the immunity against parent-child tort litigation, both English and American common law has always allowed contract and property actions between parent and child. . . . Other nineteenth century authority indicates that prior to the immunity, children were allowed to sue their parents for both negligent and intentional torts. . . .

A sizeable number of jurisdictions (approximately 25) have fully abrogated the doctrine and applied a standard limiting parent-child liability by relying on either *Goller v. White* (1963), 20 Wis. 2d 402, 122 N.W.2d 193 (*Goller* standard), or *Gibson v. Gibson*, 3 Cal. 3d 914, 92 Cal. Rptr. 288, 479 P.2d 648 (1971) (reasonable parent standard). . . .

Under the *Goller* standard, a child may sue his parent for negligent conduct except where the conduct involves "an exercise of parental authority [or] an exercise of ordinary parental discretion with respect to the provision of food, clothing, housing, medical and dental services, and other care." *Goller*, 20 Wis. 2d at 413, 122 N.W.2d at 198. The first limitation embraces the area of parental discipline; and the second has been interpreted as concerning only the performance of legal duties and not moral duties, such as a duty to supervise. *Thoreson v. Milwaukee & Suburban Transport Co.*, 56 Wis. 2d 231, 246–47, 201 N.W.2d 745, 753 (1973). Arguably, under the *Goller* standard, a child could not sue his parent for a failure to maintain the family residence in some manner (for instance, a failure to secure carpeting).

In California, courts apply a reasonable parent standard to test the viability of all negligence actions between parent and child. *Gibson*, 3 Cal. 3d at 922, 479 P.2d at 653, 92 Cal. Rptr. at 293 ("what would an ordinarily reasonable and prudent parent have done in similar circumstances?"). And in New York, a child may sue his parent for negligent conduct except that a parent's failure to supervise the child is not recognized as an actionable tort; there exists no legal duty on the part of parents to supervise their children. *Holodook*, 36 N.Y.2d at 50–51, 324 N.E.2d at 346, 364 N.Y.S.2d at 871. . . .

In contrast, Illinois stands in that group of jurisdictions, a minority, which have partially abrogated the doctrine by carving out exceptions to it. The approach taken by Illinois and this group of jurisdictions, however, is considered problematic, as the law which develops is often inconsistent and arbitrary. . . .

Illinois courts have relied consistently on three major public policy considerations for the parent-child tort immunity doctrine: (1) the preservation of family harmony, (2) the discouragement of fraud and collusion, and (3) the preservation of parental authority and discipline. . . . Illinois courts have more consistently espoused the preservation of family harmony rationale. . . .

Yet, Illinois courts have narrowed the doctrine, by creating exceptions to it, where the doctrine's public purposes do not appear to be served. This court "modif[ied]" the immunity doctrine by recognizing an exception in an automobile accident case where willful and wanton misconduct was alleged. . . . *Nudd*, 7 Ill. 2d at 619, 131 N.E.2d 525. . . .

Illinois courts . . . have carved out additional exceptions to the immunity in the area of negligence. An exception to the immunity rule is now recognized where a child sues a deceased parent. *Johnson v. Myers*, 2 Ill. App. 3d 844, 277 N.E.2d 773 (1972) (when the family relationship is dissolved by death, the policy basis for the immunity doctrine ceases to exist as well); but see *Marsh v. McNeill*, 136 Ill. App. 3d 616, 622, 91 Ill. Dec. 249, 483 N.E.2d 595 (1985) (parent-child tort immunity barred wrongful death action by representative of deceased parents' estates against living daughter tortfeasor). Another exception allows children to sue grandparents. *Gulledge v. Gulledge*, 51 Ill. App. 3d 972, 10 Ill. Dec. 42, 367 N.E.2d 429 (1977) (rationale behind immunity loses persuasive force when family relations more distant than parent-child are involved). . . .

Illinois courts also reject application of the parent-child tort immunity doctrine as a bar to third-party contribution actions against allegedly negligent parents. . . .

Another exception allows a parent-child negligence action where the alleged duty is owed to the general public. See *Cummings v. Jackson*, 57 Ill. App. 3d 68, 14 Ill. Dec. 848, 372 N.E.2d 1127 (1978) (breach of duty owed to general public is not as disruptive of family unity as breach of duty owed to family members). This exception is in keeping with . . . the view that the immunity is insupportable as applied to conduct outside the parent-child relationship. It also suggests the confinement of the immunity to actions based on conduct constituting a breach of parental or family duties. . . .

. . . A public policy based on the principle of preserving family harmony necessarily argues against every kind of intrafamily litigation. The allowance of a variety of intrafamily negligence actions by exception reveals that the family harmony rationale, an apparently absolute principle, is in fact balanced against other considerations or is not, as a practical matter, a viable consideration. . . . In truth, the traditional policy of family harmony is no longer viable. . . . The focus has shifted to a concern with preventing litigation concerning conduct intimately associated with the parent-child relationship. The exceptions consistently demonstrate that where the family relationship is dissolved or where that relationship has ceased to exist with respect to conduct giving rise to the injury, the immunity will not be applied. This is so because the immunity exists only to further the parent-child relationship, and where that relationship is not impacted, the policies supporting the doctrine lose their persuasive strength . . . The exceptions themselves thereby tend to highlight the arbitrariness of the traditional underlying public policies.

Both the traditional family harmony and collusion rationales are accordingly diminished. If negligence actions between parent and child are maintainable where the alleged duty is owed to the general public or where the conduct is beyond the parental relationship, these policies offer little support . . .

The notion that parent-child tort immunity promotes family harmony in the area of negligence, the justification most relied on, has now been largely discounted. Without exception, legal scholars recognize that, more often than not, it is the injury if anything which disrupts the family. (See 17 LOY. U. CHI. L. J. at 307; Rooney & Rooney, *Parental Tort Immunity: Spare the Liability, Spoil the Parent*, 25 NEW ENG. L. REV. 1161, 1165 (1991). Providing a child an avenue to obtain redress of those injuries does not work against family harmony. Even in the small percentage of cases where a parent or child has no liability insurance and injuries are serious, or in the case where an older child would perhaps bring an action to challenge the parent's authority, the suit cannot preserve harmony which, apparently, does not exist; the law does not have that capacity. . . .

The impact of liability insurance on the traditional rationales for the immunity cannot be ignored. It is now generally recognized that the existence of liability insurance eliminates the actual adversity of parent and child in negligence actions. . . . Where liability insurance is present, the parent and child are only nominally adverse; the "real" defendant is the insurer. Further, negligence actions between parent and child are rarely brought, except in cases where insurance is present. This is not to say that liability should be allowed simply because liability insurance exists. We agree with defendant in that respect. Liability should be allowed where the reasons for its preclusion do not exist for whatever reason. The fact that liability insurance significantly undercuts a traditional basis for the rule is a reality, however, which must be considered by courts. . . .

The widespread existence of insurance and the resulting diminished adversity of parties impacts on the traditional policies against collusion and fraud. Defendant argues that the parent-child relationship is threatened by presenting it with an opportunity to collude and defraud. Numerous authorities have pointed out that even in cases where collusion and fraud may exist, our adversarial legal system, through its skilled attorneys, discovery, examinations and evidentiary reviews, is adequately equipped to deal with such problems and does so daily in other intrafamily litigations and areas of law. We believe this to be generally true. The stronger argument against this rationale is that it forms an insufficient basis to deny redress to a whole class of litigants. . . . A rule which seeks to incidentally attack fraud by withholding legal protection for all claimants, regardless of the justice of their claims, "employs a medieval technique which, however satisfying it may be to defendants, is scarcely in keeping with the acknowledged function of a modern legal system." Leflar & Sanders, *Mental Suffering and its Consequence — Arkansas Law*, 7 U. ARK. L. SCH. BULL. 43, 60 (1939).

The fact that our legislature has abolished the husband-wife tort immunity doctrine also demonstrates a reluctance to adhere to both the traditionally espoused bases for intrafamily immunities. . . . [Although] the two doctrines are fundamentally different, spousal immunity being based on the legal unity of husband and wife, each doctrine has been typically supported by the same public policies. . . .

Defendant argues that abolishing the immunity doctrine will allow divorced parents to utilize parent-child negligence litigation as a battlefield for their continuing animosities and to promote disharmony between a noncustodial parent and the child. This argument lacks merit. Divorced parents have not taken such advantage of negligence actions which are allowed based on the recognized exceptions to the immunity rule. Nor do divorced parents appear to have taken advantage of the absence of the immunity rule in third-party contribution situations.

Recognizing that a child's injury is more likely the cause of any family disharmony as opposed to the institution of a suit, defendant also argues that any suit thus serves to exasperate that existing disharmony and should therefore be disallowed. We disagree. If the injury has disharmonized the family, an action can potentially relieve it. Further, this argument harkens back to the original fiction that regardless of the apparent family disharmony, a suit makes things worse rather than better. . . .

. . . We are convinced that the immunity doctrine is supported today by other public policy concerns. Courts should not be involved in deciding matters between parent and child which concern decisions which those persons are uniquely equipped to make because of that relationship; to allow otherwise would unnecessarily and obtrusively inject courts into family matters which they are ill-equipped to decide. Such matters, by definition, involve parental discretion in discipline, supervision and care. We are also convinced that those underlying policies ought to determine the scope of the immunity. . . .

We believe the . . . appropriate inquiry . . . would not concern whether "family purposes" were furthered by a parent's conduct, but whether the alleged conduct concerns parental discretion in discipline, supervision and care of the child. . . . The immunity should afford protection to conduct inherent to the parent-child relationship; such conduct constitutes an exercise of parental authority and supervision over the child or an exercise of discretion in the provision of care to the child. These limited areas of conduct require the skills, knowledge, intuition, affection, wisdom, faith, humor, perspective, background, experience, and culture which only a parent and his or her child can bring to the situation; our legal system is ill-equipped to decide the reasonableness of such matters.

The standard we have thus developed focuses primarily on conduct inherent to the parent-child relationship, which conduct we describe by approximating the *Goller* standard without its enumerated duties. Such a standard is consistent with other jurisdictions which have abrogated the immunity in order to achieve greater clarity in the area of parent-child negligence. The standard we have created is not, however, as extreme because we do not fully abrogate the immunity, but rely on an exception. Our standard also allows a broader area of negligent conduct to remain immunized. Thus, under our standard, parental discretion in the provision of care includes maintenance of the family home, medical treatment, and supervision of the child. A child may attempt to sue a parent alleging that the child fell on a wet, freshly mopped floor in the home, but the immunity would bar such an action because the parent was exercising his discretion in providing and maintaining housing for the child.

We note as well that parents in Illinois must conform their treatment of their children within certain socially acceptable limits or face criminal and civil actions by the State. Such actions are instituted regardless of the fact that parental authority is thereby circumscribed. Further, there is no immunity as applied to the area of intentional torts. . . . There yet exists limits to parental authority beyond those recognized here.

In this case, we are asked to consider whether the immunity doctrine bars plaintiff's action which alleged the negligent operation of an automobile by a parent. Applying the standard we have created, we conclude that the negligent operation of an automobile is not conduct inherent in the parent-child relationship; such conduct does not represent a parent's decision-making in disciplining, supervising or caring for his child. . . . The duty which Cates owed in operating his vehicle on State highways was owed to the general public and not to Heather as his child. The negligent operation of a vehicle even when exercising visitation privileges does not constitute conduct inherent to the parent-child relationship. The parent-child tort immunity doctrine cannot be applied to bar a negligence action alleging such conduct.

We disagree with defendant's argument that eliminating the immunity in automobile negligence cases will threaten parental authority to discipline children or inject courts into matters concerning the exercise of parental discretion. A child's action against her father for the negligent operation of an automobile does not usurp the father's authority to discipline her. Neither does such action allow a court to second-guess the father's exercise of discretion in day-to-day matters which bear on the parent-child relationship. . . .

In sum, the parent-child tort immunity doctrine developed in an era which was vastly different from the present; our society has changed in myriad and countless ways. The parent-child relationship has been both beneficially and detrimentally affected by these changes. We seek in this instance to uphold and preserve that which forms an integral component of that relationship, parental authority and discretion. Yet, we must also consider the very real needs to our children in today's world. In this regard, we are mindful that the parent-child tort immunity doctrine was created by the courts and it is especially for them to interpret and modify the doctrine to correspond with prevailing public policy and social needs. . . . [AFFIRMED].

NOTES

1. *Old Fashioned.* The most effective argument in favor of parental immunity may be its antiquity. More than half of the states have abrogated the parental immunity from the children's claims. Some abrogations have been partial: there is no immunity from intentional torts, *Federhoff v. Federhoff*, 473 S.W.2d 978 (Tex. 1971), or from "willful, wanton or reckless conduct," *Attwood v. Estate of Attwood*, 633 S.W.2d 366 (Ark. 1982), or from gross negligence, *Rodebaugh v. Grand Trunk W.R.R.*, 145 N.W.2d 401 (Mich. App.1966); no immunity after death of parent or child, *MFA Mut. Ins. Co. v. Howard Const. Co.*, 608 S.W.2d 535 (Mo. App. 1980), or the emancipation of the child, *Carriceto v. Carriceto*, 384 S.W.2d 85 (Ky. 1964); no immunity in action for wrongful death of other parent, *Harlan Nat'l Bank v. Gross*, 346 S.W.2d 482 (Ky. 1961); no immunity to persons *in loco parentis*, such as a stepparent,

Gillett v. Gillett, 335 P.2d 736 (Cal. 1959); no immunity to a divorced parent who does not have custody of the child, *Fugate v. Fugate*, 582 S.W.2d 663 (Mo. 1979), or to a deceased parent, *Davis v. Smith*, 126 F. Supp. 497 (E.D. Pa. 1954); no immunity in automobile cases, *Nocktonick v. Nocktonick*, 611 P.2d 135 (Kan. 1980); *Jilani v. Jilani*, 767 S.W.2d 671 (Tex. 1988), particularly if the parent is driving while intoxicated, *Winn v. Gilroy*, 681 P.2d 776 (Or. 1984); no immunity to the extent the parent is protected by liability insurance, *Williams v. Williams*, 369 A.2d 669 (Del. 1976); *Ard v. Ard*, 414 So. 2d 1066 (Fla. 1982).

A number of states, as in the principal case, abolish parental immunity except in the case of the exercise of parental authority, supervision, or care and custody. *Broadwell v. Holmes*, 871 S.W.2d 471 (Tenn. 1994). Others abolish the immunity entirely. *See Broadbent v. Broadbent*, 907 P.2d 43 (Ariz. 1995). Louisiana preserves parental immunity but the child may sue the parent the child reaches the age of majority and a guardian can bring suit on the child's behalf against a parent's insurance provider.

While a child may not have an action against her parent for negligent supervision, see *Holodook v. Spencer*, 324 N.E.2d 338 (N.Y. 1974). A third-party sued by the child may have a claim for contribution against the parent for negligent supervision of the child. *See Nolechek v. Gesuale*, 385 N.E.2d 1268 (N.Y. 1978). Not all courts would allow such a third party claim.

2. *Parent Versus Child.* Are the same considerations present in determining whether a child can sue a parent, as in determining whether a parent can sue a child? The Restatement (Second) would draw no distinction, except for the caveat that the repudiation of the immunity "does not establish liability for an act or omission that, because of the parent-child relationship, is otherwise privileged or is not tortious." REST. 2D TORTS § 895G.

3. *Sibling Immunity.* RESTATEMENT 2D § 895H states: "Brothers and sisters or other kin are not immune from tort liability to one another by reason of that relationship." Why should the sibling or other kin relationship be treated differently from the parent-child relationship?

4. *Interspousal Immunity.* The doctrine of interspousal immunity has been totally abrogated in more than half the states. *See, e.g., Heino v. Harper*, 759 P.2d 53 (Ore. 1988); *Davis v. Davis*, 657 S.W.2d 753 (Tenn. 1983). However, it has been reaffirmed in some states. *See Raisen v. Raisen*, 379 So. 2d 352 (Fla. 1979); *Price v. Price*, 732 S.W.316 (Tex. 1987). Some jurisdictions have only partially abrogated the immunity, for example, permitting suit if the tortfeasor-spouse's conduct is intentional or outrageous, *Lusby v. Lusby*, 390 A.2d 77 (Md. 1978), or in motor vehicle accident cases. *Surratt v. Thompson*, 183 S.E.2d 200 (Va. 1971); *Digby v. Digby*, 388 A.2d 1 (R.I. 1978).

Where there is no interspousal immunity, what should be the result if the wife brings an action against her husband for damages she sustains because he provides unwholesome food at the family dinner table? Negligently invests the family savings? Can we draw a meaningful distinction between negligent spouse-injuring activities "within the family circle" and "in the outside world?" Is it likely that interspousal immunity disproportionately affects claims likely to be asserted by women?

What if the tort occurs before, but the claim is brought against the spouse after the marriage? What if the tort occurs during the marriage, but the marriage subsequently is dissolved by death? By divorce? If a spouse is immune from tort liability to the other spouse, then theoretically the tort does not arise, and the subsequent dissolution of the marriage cannot revive it. However, if the immunity does not prevent the tort from arising, but merely bars enforcement during the marriage, then the victim spouse arguably may maintain the action after the dissolution of the marriage.

In most states the victim may not bring a direct action against the tortfeasor's liability insurer, but first must obtain judgment against the tortfeasor. If the insured tortfeasor is immune, then the victim is unable to obtain the judgment that triggers the insurer's liability. If there is no immunity, there is a danger of collusion between the spouses to obtain recovery from the insurer. About one fifth of the states permit a direct action by the tort victim against the insurer. If the interspousal immunity prevents the tort from arising, then the victim should not be able to recover against the insurer. However, if the immunity only bars suit, can the spouse-victim recover from the liability insurer in a direct action? *See, e.g., Soirez v. Great American Ins. Co.*, 168 So. 2d 418 (La. App. 1964), permitting suit against the liability insurer. A court which permits a direct action against the liability insurer of an immune spouse may describe the immunity as "personal" between the spouses. Is this a reason, or a conclusory statement?

Some liability policies exclude coverage for suits between spouses. Is such an exclusion against a state's public policy? *See, e.g., American Family Mut. v. Ward,* 789 S.W.2d 791 (Mo. 1990) (explicit provision of an automobile liability policy excluding coverage for injuries to a person related to the operator of the vehicle does not violate public policy). *See also Bishop v. Allstate*, 623 S.W.2d 865 (Ky. 1981); *Allstate v. Farmers Mut.*, 444 N.W.2d 676 (Neb. 1989).

5. Employer Immunity

Perhaps the most significant practical immunity of all is the employer's immunity from negligence actions by employees injured in the course and scope of their employment. The immunity arises out of worker's compensation statutes which grant the worker injured in the course and scope of employment a right to recover no-fault worker's compensation benefits from the employer. The employer's immunity was the trade-off for the benefits. The benefits normally entail 2/3 of lost wages for the period of disability or a defined period, medical benefits, and perhaps some set amount for permanent partial disability, such as the loss of a finger.

Not all employers are covered and significant issues may arise in either a worker's compensation case or a tort case involving whether the worker was in the course and scope of employment, The immunity does not apply to a non-employer third party tortfeasor. And, if the employee recovers in tort from a third party tortfeasor, the employer may recover any workers compensation benefits paid and may receive a credit against future workers' compensation liability. Courses in employment law further explore this important immunity and its practical and theoretical ramifications.

PROBLEMS

12.1

Emma, 13, was riding her bicycle on the wrong side of the street when she was hit by Foster, who was driving his car. Foster was not paying attention because he was adjusting his satellite radio. If Foster had been paying attention, he would not have hit Emma. May Emma recover from Foster? Was Emma at fault? May Emma recover if she was 1% at fault? 25% at fault? 49% at fault? 50% at fault? 51% at fault? 99% at fault? Assume that Emma is in a pure contributory negligence jurisdiction? Would your answer change if Emma was in a 50-50 jurisdiction?

12.2

As Rhoda Rush approached the access road to the expressway, her regular route to work, she noticed her gas gauge registered empty. Since she was late for work, she decided to take the risk that she could make the three-mile drive without running out of gas. After driving two miles on the expressway, her engine stopped running because the vehicle was out of gas. Unfortunately, Rhoda's vehicle was in the passing lane at the time, and the traffic on her right precluded her from steering onto the shoulder of the highway. She activated her hazard lights and steered the car to a halt in the passing lane. The car immediately following Rhoda swerved into the other lane to avoid an accident.

Rhoda sat in her car for a minute as the traffic sped by, awaiting a break in the traffic that would permit her to exit the car. Before she could do so, another car driven by Paula Pushy struck the rear of Rhoda's car, totally destroying it and seriously injuring Rhoda. Paula told investigating officers she was attempting to pass a trailer truck and had just turned into the passing lane when she sighted Rhoda's car 20 feet in front of the truck. However, there was evidence that Paula was driving 65 mph when she pulled into the passing lane. The speed limit was 55 mph on the expressway.

Should Rhoda recover from Paula all of her damages, part of her damages, or none of her damages? What answer would be mandated by the cases set forth in this chapter? What approach do you consider the best, and why?

12.3

Oscar Owner left his convertible, with the key in the ignition, in the parking lot of a liquor store. Immediately thereafter, Tillie Teenager, a 14-year-old with a long history of car thefts, walked by, saw the convertible, jumped in it and drove away. Within a few blocks, Tillie sped around a sharp curve, lost control of the car and crashed into a car driven by Ann Taylor. Ann could have avoided the accident by taking evasive action, but she panicked when she saw Tillie heading toward her. A state statute provides:

> Any driver who, in a public place, leaves his automobile unattended with the key in the ignition shall be guilty of a misdemeanor and, upon conviction, shall be fined not less than $10 nor more than $100.

Discuss the rights and liabilities of the parties: (a) in a pure comparative negligence jurisdiction; (b) in a modified comparative negligence jurisdiction. Which scheme is preferable? Why?

12.4

Lonnie is 17 but looks older. Lonnie went bungie jumping at Gord's Gorge and signed a release form which Gord provided. The release provided that the undersigned (Lonnie) understood the risks inherent in bungie jumping and absolved Gord from responsibility for any injuries which occurred in the course of the activity. Lonnie suffered a back injury in the course of his jumping. May he sue Gord or does the release resolve the issue? What if Lonnie proves that Gord was somehow negligent in the way he hooked up the ropes — does the release bar Lonnie's claim?

12.5

Before entering a race, runner signs a form which provides that "as a consideration for permission to compete in the race, runner waives all claims she has or may have against race sponsor for damages sustained as a result of her participation in the race." While running the prescribed route along a wooded area, runner is abducted and raped by an intruder; reasonable care by race sponsor may have prevented the rape. Does the release bar recovery against race sponsor? Suppose, instead, runner's child, viewing the race, is injured by the negligence of the race sponsor. Does the release bar the runner's claim for loss of consortium with, or mental anguish over the injury to, her child?

12.6

Cynthia went to a minor league baseball game and was injured when she was hit by a foul ball. What facts would you want to know in analyzing Cynthia's claim?

12.7

Dorian was exposed to ABC asbestos while working in a shipyard during the 1940s. He developed asbestosis in 1997 and sued ABC for asbestos injuries and fear of developing cancer. In November 2007, Dorian developed mesothelioma, a cancer caused by exposure to asbestos. Dorian filed suit against ABC for the cancer in January 2006. Is Dorian's claim timely?

12.8

Jones was injured when Smith lost control of the car that Smith was driving and in which Jones was a passenger. At the time of the accident Smith was driving 50 mph in a 35 mph zone. Jones was aware that Smith was speeding but said nothing. What issues? What result?

Would your response be different if Jones were Smith's wife? If Jones and Smith were co-workers and Jones were Smith's supervisor?

Assume Smith was intoxicated and Jones was aware of the intoxication; nevertheless, he continued to ride with Smith, and was injured in an accident caused by Smith's intoxication. What issues? What result?

12.9

Horace was a mentally disturbed young man who told his father that he was going to burn down a house in their town. When the father asked which house, Horace said he did not know or care which house but he was going to do it. Horace's father called the police and told them what Horace said. The police came by, asked Horace a few questions and left. That night Horace burned down the Langley home. The Langleys sued the police department. Liability?

12.10

Adam was teaching his 16-year-old son, Seth, to drive. Seth got nervous, lost control of the car, and had a head on wreck with Castle. Castle sued Seth and Adam. Adam sued Seth. Seth sued Adam. What causes of action? What defenses?

12.11

A city police officer killed a teenager by shooting him in the back as the teenager was attempting to escape from the scene of a robbery. What facts would you need to know to determine if the teenager's survivors or estate would have a valid tort action for the shooting against the police officer, the city, or the police officer's spouse?

Claims for contribution normally do not exist if the tortfeasors are severally, rather than jointly, liable. Each such tortfeasor is liable only for his portion of the damages.

Punitive damages normally are imposed severally, rather than jointly, so that no contribution or indemnity for such damages is permitted. Indeed, an intentional tortfeasor may not be able to recover either contribution or indemnity, even for compensatory damages, from another joint tortfeasor, apparently on the ground that an intentional wrongdoer should not as a matter of policy be able to invoke the equitable remedy of contribution or indemnity.

As discussed below, and more fully in Chapter 16 on Tort Reform, the common law approach of holding a concurrent tortfeasor responsible for the entire harm has evoked vigorous debate and disagreement among legislators, courts and commentators, focusing on social justice. The common law rule rested on the value judgment that the plaintiff should collect all of her damages from tortfeasors and any risk that one of the tortfeasors cannot pay his fair share of the judgment should be borne by the wrongdoers. The contrasting view that has gained an increasing number of supporters over the past decade is that it is unfair to make a joint tortfeasor pay more than a fair proportionate share of damages that were caused by concurring tortfeasors. This rationale has been supported by the widespread adoption of comparative fault; the reasoning is that if a tortfeasor is not liable for the plaintiff's fault, why should she be liable for another tortfeasor's fault? The rationale has been applied, however, even where the plaintiff is free of fault. The result of the clash over social justice in tort cases involving multiple tortfeasors has produced a variety of approaches among the states. The Restatement (Third) of Torts § 17 (2000) highlights the conflict and takes no position on the issue. Comment c to § 17 states:

> . . . there is currently no majority rule on this question, although joint and several liability has been substantially modified in most jurisdictions both as a result of the adoption of comparative fault and tort reform during the 1980s and 1990s. Nevertheless, five different versions of joint and several, several, and combinations of the two are presented in the five separate and independent Tracks that follow this section.

REST. 3D TORTS § 17, cmt. c.

The tracks described by the Restatement are:

- Track A, a pure joint and several liability;

- Track B, a pure several-liability approach;

- Track C, which begins with joint and several liability but applies comparative negligence to take into account the plaintiff's responsibility; then reallocates the share of an insolvent tortfeasor to the parties in proportion to their comparative responsibility;

- Track D, which imposes joint and several liability on all parties whose responsibility exceeds a specified threshold; and

- Track E, which uses the type of harm suffered by the plaintiff to make the joint and several liability determination — e.g., hold parties jointly and severally liable for economic losses, but only severally liable for non-economic losses.

In light of the myriad of approaches the practicing lawyer may face less of a challenge than law students, professors, and legislators because the practicing lawyer may sometimes be satisfied with knowing which approach her jurisdiction follows. However, a student of the law (and the skillful practitioner) who seeks to understand the reasons for the rules and to assess whether the rules promote good public policy faces a daunting task to make sense of this controversial area of tort law. Moreover, the lawyer who focuses on the approach of a particular jurisdiction will inevitably encounter problems when his client travels to another state or is involved in an accident with a person from another state. Conflicts of laws principles may compel an understanding of whether state laws differ and why in order to assess the rights and liabilities of the parties.

In reviewing the cases and problems in this chapter, attempt to answer the following questions and articulate the policy justifications for your answers. First, should the traditional common law rule that imposes joint and several liability on concurrent tortfeasors be retained? If the traditional rule is changed, should it be abolished in totality or partially? If retained partially, in what circumstances should one tortfeasor be responsible for paying the entire damages? Should a settlement with one concurrent tortfeasor reduce the plaintiff's right to recover all or part of the damage claim against other concurrent tortfeasors? Should the existence of the settlement be excluded from evidence presented to a jury against another tortfeasor in all circumstances? Should a concurrent tortfeasor always have the right to recover from other tortfeasors payments made to the plaintiff that exceed the settling tortfeasor's fair share? How should fair share be determined? If the settling defendant enters into an agreement (commonly referred to as a "Mary Carter Agreement") requiring him to cooperate with the plaintiff in some manner in the subsequent litigation against other joint tortfeasors, should that agreement be declared void as against public policy? If the cooperation agreement is allowed in the jurisdiction should the joint tortfeasors, the court, and/or the jury be informed of the terms of the settlement agreement? Will different perspectives on tort law — e.g., law and economics, corrective justice, or social justice prompt courts and scholars to endorse different approaches to allocating the risk of non-collection in joint tortfeasor cases?

We begin our study of these important questions with a review of the meaning of joint and several liability and the effect of applying that classification to independent actors.

B. JOINT AND SEVERAL LIABILITY

GLOMB v. GLOMB
530 A.2d 1362 (Pa. Super. Ct. 1987)

MONTEMURO, JUDGE.

Appellants John and Marie Glomb challenge the denial of their post-trial motions. A jury found that the Glombs had negligently hired and retained appellee Sherry Ginosky to care for the Glombs' one-year-old daughter, appellee Tia Marie Glomb. Tia Marie, through her guardian ad litem, instituted this action against her parents, who in turn joined Ms. Ginosky as an additional defendant. We address two issues on appeal: (1) whether the trial court properly refused to allow the jury to apportion liability between the Glombs and Ms. Ginosky; and (2) whether the $1.5 million jury verdict in favor of Tia Marie was excessive. None of the Glombs' arguments on these issues convince us that we should disturb the judgment of the Beaver County Court of Common Pleas. We therefore affirm.

The evidence at trial established the following facts. Tia Marie is the only child of John and Marie Glomb. At the time of Tia Marie's birth, both John and Marie worked full-time. John's employment required him to travel away from home up to six days a week. Marie worked Monday through Friday from 7:00 in the morning until 5:30 or 6:00 in the evening. The Glombs therefore employed baby-sitters to provide in-home care for Tia Marie during the work week. Sometime during the summer of 1982, Tia Marie's second baby-sitter quit on short notice because of ill health. In need of an immediate replacement, the Glombs hurriedly hired Sherry Ginosky at the beginning of August, 1982. Within two or three weeks, the Glombs began to notice problems. Small bruise marks appeared on Tia Marie's face and body. When asked about the marks, Ms. Ginosky would offer explanations that John Glomb found implausible. On one occasion, John observed that his daughter seemed afraid of Ms. Ginosky. After the Glombs discovered a large, hand-shaped bruise on Tia Marie's leg in late October of 1982, John threatened to discharge Ms. Ginosky if any more bruises appeared. Two days after this warning, however, Tia Marie suffered grave injuries to her face and head while in the care of Ms. Ginosky. The paramedics whom Ms. Ginosky summoned to the Glomb residence on the morning of November 3, 1982 found the child unconscious. Ms. Ginosky explained that Tia Marie had tripped over a toy and struck her head on a child's rocking chair. While unconscious, Tia Marie experienced periodic seizures during which she stopped breathing. Her face and head were severely bruised, and she remained in the hospital for nearly two weeks. Since her discharge from the hospital, Tia Marie has required extensive physical rehabilitation to remedy the effects of the brain damage she suffered. The parties agree that Sherry Ginosky intentionally inflicted these injuries upon her charge.

As a result of the November 3, 1982 incident, the court appointed a guardian ad litem for Tia Marie. The guardian filed a complaint on Tia Marie's behalf against John and Marie Glomb. The Glombs immediately joined Ms. Ginosky as a third party defendant. Following a trial at which Ms. Ginosky was neither present nor represented by counsel, the trial court directed the jury to find that Ms. Ginosky had "intentionally injured" Tia Marie and that the Glombs therefore "are entitled to indemnification" from Ms. Ginosky. The court refused, however, to instruct the jury on apportionment of liability between Ms. Ginosky and the Glombs. At sidebar, the court informed counsel that the Glombs could seek "indemnification" from Ms. Ginosky in a separate proceeding if the Glombs ultimately bore the burden of satisfying a judgment.

The jury returned with a $1.5 million verdict against both the Glombs and Ms. Ginosky, jointly and severally. The trial court denied the Glombs' motions for post-trial relief, and this timely appeal followed the entry of judgment. Although a three-judge panel of this court decided to affirm the judgment, we granted the Glombs' petition for reargument before the court en banc. . . .

As this case clearly illustrates, a decision to impose "joint and several" liability upon multiple tort-feasors, rather than to "apportion" liability between them, can alter significantly the risks of tort litigation. Imposition of joint and several liability enables the injured party to satisfy an entire judgment against any one tort-feasor, even if the wrongdoing of that tort-feasor contributed only a small part to the harm inflicted. Apportionment of liability, on the other hand, limits the liability of each tort-feasor to that portion of the harm which he or she caused. Thus, if the court imposes joint and several liability, and if only one of the joint tort-feasors is financially responsible, the injured party can attempt to recover the full measure of damages against that single source. The financially responsible tort-feasor who satisfies more than his or her equitable share of the joint liability then bears the risk of recovering the excess from his or her less responsible fellow tort-feasors. If, however, the court decided to apportion liability, the *injured party* bears the risk that the financial irresponsibility of one tort-feasor will defeat a complete recovery. By asserting that the court should apportion liability, the Glombs seek to avoid the risk that Ms. Ginosky, their fellow tort-feasor, will lack the resources to satisfy her share of the $1.5 million verdict.

A court can direct the apportionment of liability among distinct causes only when the injured party suffers distinct harms or when the court is able to identify "a reasonable basis for determining the contribution of each cause to a single harm." Restatement (Second) of Torts § 433A(1) (1965). In the present case, the parties agree that Tia Marie has suffered a single harm. The availability of apportionment therefore hinges upon whether the party who seeks it can demonstrate some logical, reasonable or practical basis for assigning discrete portions of the over-all liability to discrete causes. Determining whether a "logical, reasonable or practical" basis for apportionment exists necessarily requires the court to consider the unique circumstances of each case. Although most single personal injuries defy objective apportionment, *see Capone v. Donovan,* 332 Pa. Super. 185, 480 A.2d 1249, 1251 (1984), we should not allow one party to bear an entire liability if the particular facts of the case will support a reasonable alternative. On the other hand, we cannot allow an arbitrary apportionment merely to avoid imposition of entire liability. A court should not limit the innocent plaintiff's ability to recover the full measure of damages unless the court has some reasonable basis for doing so. *See* Restatement (Second) of Torts § 433A comments h and i. . . .

The negligence of the Glombs worked in tandem with the deliberate misconduct of Ms. Ginosky to cause a single harm to Tia Marie. Although the Glombs did not act in concert with Ms. Ginosky, they acted concurrently with her. Their ongoing neglect of Tia Marie's welfare facilitated the ultimate infliction of the actionable harm. This case therefore differs from such cases in which one party adds to or aggravates an injury already caused by another party. Had the Glombs heeded the signs of danger, they could have averted the harm altogether. Moreover, had Ms. Ginosky not acted upon the opportunity that the Glombs created, the Glombs' breach of duty would have constituted *injuria absque damno,* a mere legal wrong without loss or damage. The drafters of the Restatement (Second) of Torts recognized that a court cannot direct apportionment between a party whose misconduct facilitates the infliction of a harm and a party who actually inflicts that harm:

One defendant may create a situation upon which the other may act later to cause the harm. One may leave combustible material, and the other set it afire; one may leave a hole in the street, and the other drive into it. Whether there is liability in such a case may depend upon the effect of the intervening agency as a superseding cause . . . *but if the defendant is liable at all, he is liable for the entire indivisible harm which he has caused.*

Restatement (Second) of Torts § 433A comment i (emphasis added). The facilitative negligence of the Glombs in the present case is akin to the facilitative negligence of the party who leaves combustible material for another to ignite.

In *Wade v. S. J. Groves & Sons Co.,* 283 Pa. Super. 464, 424 A.2d 902 (1981), we refused to apportion damages under circumstances analogous to those in the present case. The defendant landowners in *Wade* had permitted the co-defendant contractor to use their property as a landfill. During heavy rainfall, waste from the landfill washed onto the plaintiff's adjoining property. We reversed the trial court's decision to apportion ten percent of the resulting liability to the landowners and ninety percent to the contractor. We observed that the landowners "did not cause ten percent or any other reasonably identifiable percentage of the dirt or fill to be deposited on the [plaintiff's] land" and that the court therefore lacked a reasonable basis for the apportionment. . . .

NOTES

1. *Concurrent Tortfeasors.* The *Glomb* case represents the typical situation for imposition of joint liability, i.e., where the tortious conduct of two or more tortfeasors concurs to produce what is essentially an indivisible injury. Tort "reformers" have most notably sought to do away with joint liability in this situation. For a discussion of reform efforts to change joint and several liability, see chapter 16, *infra,* at 1024.

2. *Concert of Activity.* Where two or more persons consciously act together to commit a tort, the common law has classically applied joint liability to the actors. *See, e.g., Bierczynsky v. Rogers*, 239 A.2d 218 (Del. Super. 1968) (automobile race). This is so even though the resulting damages are practically divisible. A Latin maxim is used to describe such joint action: *qui facit per alium facit per se* (he who acts through another acts himself). REST. 2D TORTS § 876 (1979) provides that a person is liable for the tortious acts of another if he:

> (a) does a tortious act in concert with the other or pursuant to a common design with him, or

> (b) knows that the other's conduct constitutes a breach of duty and gives substantial assistance or encouragement to the other so to conduct himself, or

> (c) gives substantial assistance to the other in accomplishing a tortious result and his own conduct, separately considered, constitutes a breach of duty to the third person.

Should the tort reformers attempt to abolish joint liability in the case of concerted activity? Why has this not been the central focus of tort reformers?

3. *Vicarious Liability.* Reconsider the concept of vicarious liability. This is also a classic situation for imposing joint liability upon the servant who is actually at fault, and upon the master who is vicariously liable for the servant's fault. REST. 2D AGENCY §§ 234-245. The principle is most commonly applied to impose liability upon a corporation for the tortious acts of its employees acting within the scope of their employment. The principle also would impose liability upon a principal for the negligence of an independent contractor performing a nondelegable duty. REST. 2D TORTS §§ 416-429; REST. 3D TORTS § 23. Should this be a subject for tort reform?

4. *Successive Tortfeasors.* Ordinarily, successive tortfeasors cause separate harms and the law treats their acts as separate torts. Often, however, the otherwise unrelated conduct of the successive tortfeasors impacts upon the same victim at different times but causes or enhances the same harm. In such a case, the first tortfeasor may be liable for all of the damages if the second tortfeasor's conduct was within the scope of the risks of the first tortfeasor's conduct. The classic example is when a health care provider negligently treats a victim's tort injury. There, courts generally hold the original tortfeasor for the increased injury. *See, e.g., Doyle v. Piccadilly Cafeterias*, 576 So. 2d 1143 (La. App. 1991). But what if successive conduct, not within the scope of the risks of either tortfeasor's conduct, produces an indivisible harm? Courts sometimes "divide" the indivisible harm. *See, e.g., Hess v. Sports Publishing Co.*, 520 So. 2d 472 (La. App. 1988) (trial court properly allowed jury to apportion damages suffered by plaintiff in two different automobile accidents that happened one month apart from each other).

5. *Where Grounds of Liability Differ.* The Glombs in *Glomb v. Glomb* were guilty of negligence, while the babysitter was guilty of an intentional tort. The Glombs argued they should not be held jointly liable with the babysitter because the grounds of liability differed. The court rejected this argument, relying on *Svetz for Svetz v. Land Tool Co.*, 513 A.2d 403 (Pa. Super. 1986). There, after plaintiff's deceased was killed in a motorcycle accident, plaintiff sued the manufacturer of the helmet that the deceased was wearing, alleging that the manufacturer was strictly liable for selling a defective helmet which was allegedly a substantial cause of the deceased's death. The court held it was proper to join in the suit as joint tortfeasors the tavern keeper who allegedly negligently served the deceased alcoholic beverages before the accident, and another motorcyclist who was racing with the decedent at the time of the accident.

McINTYRE v. BALENTINE
833 S.W.2d 52 (Tenn. 1992)

DROWOTA, JUSTICE.

In this personal injury action, we granted Plaintiff's application for permission to appeal in order to decide whether to adopt a system of comparative fault. . . . We now replace the common law defense of contributory negligence with a system of comparative fault. . . .

In the early morning darkness of November 2, 1986, Plaintiff Harry Douglas McIntyre and Defendant Clifford Balentine were involved in a motor vehicle accident resulting in severe injuries to Plaintiff. The accident occurred in the vicinity of Smith's Truck Stop in Savannah, Tennessee. As Defendant Balentine was traveling south on Highway 69, Plaintiff entered the highway (also traveling south) from the truck stop parking lot. Shortly after Plaintiff entered the highway, his pickup truck was struck by Defendant's Peterbilt tractor. At trial, the parties disputed the exact chronology of events immediately preceding the accident.

Both men had consumed alcohol the evening of the accident. After the accident, Plaintiff's blood alcohol level was measured at .17 percent by weight. Testimony suggested that Defendant was traveling in excess of the posted speed limit.

Plaintiff brought a negligence action against Defendant Balentine. Defendant answered that Plaintiff was contributorily negligent, in part due to operating his vehicle while intoxicated. After trial, the jury returned a verdict stating: "We, the jury, find the plaintiff and the defendant equally at fault in this accident; therefore, we rule in favor of the defendant." . . .

[T]oday's holding renders the doctrine of joint and several liability obsolete. Our adoption of comparative fault is due largely to considerations of fairness: the contributory negligence doctrine unjustly allowed the entire loss to be borne by a negligent plaintiff, notwithstanding that the plaintiff's fault was minor in comparison to defendant's. Having thus adopted a rule more closely linking liability and fault, it would be inconsistent to simultaneously retain a rule, joint and several liability, which may fortuitously impose a degree of liability that is out of all proportion to fault.

Further, because a particular defendant will henceforth be liable only for the percentage of a plaintiff's damages occasioned by that defendant's negligence, situations where a defendant has paid more than his "share" of a judgment will no longer arise, and therefore the Uniform Contribution Among

Tort-feasors Act, T.C.A. §§ 29-11-101 to 106 (1980), will no longer determine the apportionment of liability between codefendants. . . .

Fairness and efficiency require that defendants called upon to answer allegations in negligence be permitted to allege, as an affirmative defense, that a nonparty caused or contributed to the injury or damage for which recovery is sought. In cases where such a defense is raised, the trial court shall instruct the jury to assign this nonparty the percentage of the total negligence for which he is responsible. However, in order for a plaintiff to recover a judgment against such additional person, the plaintiff must have made a timely amendment to his complaint and caused process to be served on such additional person. Thereafter, the additional party will be required to answer the amended complaint. The procedures shall be in accordance with the Tennessee Rules of Civil Procedure. . . .

NOTES

1. *Retrenchment by the* McIntyre *Court.* In three decisions issued on the same date, the Tennessee Supreme Court substantially retrenched the several liability holding of *McIntyre.* In *Camper v. Minor*, 915 S.W.2d 437 (Tenn. 1996), the court held that the owner of a car was vicariously liable under the automobile family purpose doctrine for the tort of the car's user. In *Owens v. Truckstops of America, Inc.*, 915 S.W.2d 420 (Tenn. 1996), the court held that joint and several liability applied to all strictly liable product suppliers in the chain of distribution. In *Ridings v. Ralph M. Parsons Co.*, 914 S.W.2d 79 (Tenn. 1996), the court held that a tortfeasor was not entitled to allocate fault to an immune party (in this case, plaintiff's employer). Later, in *Brown v. Wal-Mart*, 12 S.W.3d 785 (Tenn. 2000), the court said fault could not be allocated to an unidentifiable tortfeasor. In *Turner v. Jordan*, 957 S.W.2d 815 (Tenn. 1997), the court refused to apportion fault to a foreseeable intentional tortfeasor. But, reversing this trend, the court held fault could be allocated to an immune state-employee tortfeasor, *Carroll v. Whitney*, 29 S.W.3d 14 (Tenn. 2000), and to a tortfeasor against whom a statute of repose had run, *Dotson v. Blake*, 29 S.W. 3d 26 (Tenn. 2000). Similarly, the court in *Johnson v. Settle*, 2001 Tenn. App. LEXIS 412, held that the concept of intervening cause survived the holding in *McIntyre* and consequently a defendant is not liable if he only furnishes the condition by which the injury is made possible and the accident is produced by the intervention of a distinct and unrelated cause of the injury.

2. *Joint and Several Versus Several Liability.* The advent of comparative negligence has prompted a change in joint liability for joint tortfeasors, particularly related to concurrent joint tortfeasors. As noted in the introduction to this Chapter, the states are scattered all over the board on approaches to joint and several liability. For an effort to identify the approach taken by the various states see the Reporters' Note to Sec. 17 of the Restatement (Third) of Torts, designating which states probably fall into the 5 tracks that the Reporters use to try to categorize the disparate approaches.

3. *The Case for Retaining Joint Liability After the Adoption of Comparative Fault.* In *Coney v. J.L.G. Indus.*, 454 N.E.2d 197 (Ill. 1983), the court gave these reasons for retaining joint liability after the adoption of comparative fault:

(1) The feasibility of apportioning fault on a comparative basis does not render an indivisible injury "divisible" for purposes of the joint and several liability rule. A concurrent tortfeasor is liable for the whole of an indivisible injury when his negligence is a proximate cause of that damage. In many instances, the negligence of a concurrent tortfeasor may be sufficient by itself to cause the entire loss. The mere fact that it may be possible to assign some percentage figure to the relative culpability of one negligent defendant as compared to another does not in any way suggest that each defendant's negligence is not a proximate cause of the entire indivisible injury.

(2) In those instances where the plaintiff is not guilty of negligence, he would be forced to bear a portion of the loss should one of the tortfeasors prove financially unable to satisfy his share of the damages.

(3) Even in cases where a plaintiff is partially at fault, his culpability is not equivalent to that of a defendant. The plaintiff's negligence relates only to a lack of due care for his own safety while the defendant's negligence relates to a lack of due care for the safety of others; the latter is tortious, but the former is not.

(4) Elimination of joint and several liability would work a serious and unwarranted deleterious effect on the ability of an injured plaintiff to obtain adequate compensation for his injuries.

4. *Insolvent or Immune Tortfeasors.* Where, as is often the case, there is comparative contribution on the basis of percentages of fault, and all of the tortfeasors are known and solvent, the abolition of joint liability makes no difference; each tortfeasor will end up paying only his or her share. But what if one or more of the joint tortfeasors is insolvent, or a "phantom," or immune from suit by the plaintiff and, as in many workplace accidents, also immune from contribution claims. What if plaintiff's claim against one of the tortfeasors is barred by the statute of limitations? Upon whom should the risk of such missing or immune tortfeasors fall? Under full joint and several liability, all of the risk is borne by the solvent, known tortfeasors; under total abolition of joint and several, all of the risk is borne by the plaintiff. Is this a fair result? What if the plaintiff is free from fault? Not free from fault? Guilty of fault greater than that of the known, solvent tortfeasor? Do the reasons given by the Illinois court in note 3, *supra*, adequately treat the "fairness" issue from both sides? *See, e.g., Bartlett v. New Mexico Welding Supply, Inc.*, 646 P.2d 579 (1982 N.M.), where the court observed that several liability is based on "the concept on which pure comparative negligence is based — that fairness is achieved by basing liability on a person's fault." The court pointed out that causation, as well as fault, could be apportioned. "If the jury can do one, it can do the other." The court concluded that as between one plaintiff and one defendant, the plaintiff should bear the risk of the defendant's insolvency; "on what basis does the risk shift if there are two defendants, and one is insolvent?" The court saw no reason why joint and several liability should be "retained in our pure comparative negligence system on the basis that a plaintiff must be favored."

Where there is joint liability or limited joint liability, a crucial issue may be whether the fault of a non-party (an immune or "phantom" tortfeasor, or one who has settled with the plaintiff) should be quantified. It makes a difference, because the failure to allocate such fault will result in some of the burden falling upon the party tortfeasor. In *Gauthier v. O'Brien*, 618 So. 2d 825 (La. 1993), the court held the immune employer's fault should not be quantified, and, if quantified, should be reallocated among all other blameworthy parties proportionately. This view reflects the position of Uniform Comparative Fault Act (1977) § 2(d). After the *Gauthier* decision the legislature stepped in and declared that the fault of all parties, including the immune employer, should be quantified. *See* LA. CIV. CODE ANN. art. 2323 (1996), discussed in Frank L. Maraist and Thomas C. Galligan, Jr. *Burying Caesar: Civil Justice Reform and the Changing Face of Louisiana Tort Law*, 71 TUL. L. REV. 339 (1996).

The court in *Newville v. Montana Dep't of Pub. Serv.*, 883 P.2d 793 (Mont. 1994), held that allocation of fault to a nonparty violated substantive due process. A statute permitted juries to consider the negligence of settling parties, persons immune from suit, and anyone else who may have been at fault. The court said the statute unfairly allowed a defendant to blame nonparties late in the trial, thus forcing the plaintiff to develop a last-minute defense:

> [T]here is no reasonable basis for requiring plaintiffs to examine jury instructions, marshal evidence, make objections, argue the case, and examine witnesses from the standpoint of unrepresented parties, particularly when they do not know until the latter part of the trial that defendants will seek to place blame on unrepresented persons.

5. *Several Liability and "Second Accident" Successive Tortfeasors.* In *Whitehead v. Toyota Motor Corp.*, 897 S.W.2d 684 (Tenn. 1995), the plaintiff was injured by his own negligence in a car accident, and his injuries allegedly were increased because of a defective seat belt in the vehicle he was driving. The court said the damages should be divided between the negligent cause of the accident and the "enhanced injury" caused by the defective seat belt. Would such a division be made regardless of who or what caused the initial injury, or whether the initial cause was attributable to a person acting without fault?

The court gave the hypothetical example of a negligent person suffering $100,000 damages in an accident, $50,000 of which were allegedly caused by a defective seat belt. The manufacturer of the seatbelt "could not be liable for the first $50,000 in damages, which would have been incurred even if the seat belt had been properly manufactured and installed."

But would the manufacturer be liable for the entire second $50,000, or only that portion thereof attributable to its own fault? Surely the second $50,000 was caused by the joint fault of the manufacturer and of the person or entity that caused the accident.

Whenever there are multiple concurrent tortfeasors in a several-liability jurisdiction, should the division of liability be made first on the basis of cause, then on the basis of fault? Fault and cause are not the same, are they? Can one really compare causation without also comparing fault, especially when one also hears the evidence of fault? *See, e.g., Howard v. Allstate Ins. Co.*, 520 So. 2d 715 (La. 1988).

6. *Several Liability Where Grounds of Liability Differ.* In the *Whitehead* case, note 5, *supra,* liability was apportioned between a negligent plaintiff and a strictly liable defendant. May liability be apportioned between a negligent and an intentional tortfeasor? *See Reichert v. Alter*, 875 P.2d 379 (N.M. 1994).

C. CONTRIBUTION AND INDEMNITY

A tortfeasor by contract may be entitled to recover from a third person all of the sums he has paid to the tort victim. This is contractual indemnity, and is governed generally by the rules of contract law. A tortfeasor also may be entitled to tort-based indemnity, particularly where the basis of his liability differs in kind or in great degree from that of other tortfeasor. In addition, a joint tortfeasor who pays more than his proportionate share of the victim's damages is entitled to recover the excess through a tort form of subrogation usually called contribution. Of course, where joint liability is abolished, no tortfeasor will pay more than his share, and the contribution remedy does not apply. This section explores tort indemnity and contribution.

Section 886B(2) of the Second Restatement states that indemnity (full recovery) is proper when:

(a) The indemnitee was liable only vicariously for the conduct of the indemnitor;

(b) The indemnitee acted pursuant to directions of the indemnitor and reasonably believed the directions to be lawful;

(c) The indemnitee was induced to act by a misrepresentation on the part of the indemnitor, upon which he justifiably relied;

(d) The indemnitor supplied a defective chattel or performed defective work upon land or buildings as a result of which both were liable to the third person, and the indemnitee innocently or negligently failed to discover the defect;

(e) The indemnitor created a dangerous condition of land or chattels as a result of which both were liable to the third person, and the indemnitee innocently or negligently failed to discover the defect;

(f) The indemnitor was under a duty to the indemnitee to protect him against the liability to the third person.

The history of contribution is reviewed in AMERICAN LAW OF PRODUCT LIABILITY §§ 52.14, 52.21, 52.22 (3d ed. 1987):

At common law, contribution among joint tortfeasors did not exist. This general rule . . . prohibits one of several joint tortfeasors from enforcing contribution from the others who participated in the wrong. This position is based on the maxim that one cannot make one's own misconduct the ground for an action in one's own favor. . . .

Several jurisdictions, adopting the position of the [1995] Uniform Contribution Among Tortfeasors Act, provide by statute that a tortfeasor's liability for contribution arising from products liability litigation is to be based upon pro rata shares determined without regard to the relative degrees of fault of the tortfeasors. Some statutes stipulate that the shares shall be equal shares, while another formulation refers to the tortfeasors as being equally bound to bear the common burden. . . .

[T]he system of pro rata allocation as the basis for contribution, being simpler and easier to administer, may be more likely to lead the parties themselves to reach a settlement on their own. It is, however, somewhat arbitrary on occasion and generally less fair than apportionment based on comparative percentages of fault. . . .

The 1939 version of the Uniform Contribution Among Tortfeasors Act includes an optional provision that relative degrees of fault of the joint tortfeasors are to be considered in determining pro rata shares when equal distribution among them of the common liability would be inequitable because of disproportionate degrees of fault. This provision . . . is in effect in four states, and several others have adopted similar formulations calling for consideration of relative fault in determining pro rata shares. In some jurisdictions, the requirement is that contribution be based on proportional shares, with consideration of relative degrees of fault, or on the negligence or relative fault of the persons against whom recovery is allowed. The Uniform Comparative Fault Act, which has been adopted in Iowa and Washington, declares that the basis for contribution is each person's equitable share of the obligation. Legislation in New Mexico now defines a pro rata share by reference to the ratio between the tortfeasor's percentage of fault and the total percentage of fault attributable to all tortfeasors. Other formulations, apparently to the same effect, include references to comparative fault, comparative negligence, equitable or proportionate shares, or a combination of these. The statutory formula for calculating the right to contribution according to relative degrees of fault has been described by the courts as comparative contribution or comparative causation.

The Restatement (Third) of Torts, Apportionment of Liability, § 23 would resolve the issue of contribution in this manner:

(a) When two or more persons are or may be liable for the same harm and one of them discharges the liability of another by settlement or discharge of judgment, the person discharging the liability is entitled to recover contribution from the other, unless the other previously had a valid settlement and release from the plaintiff.

(b) A person entitled to recover contribution may recover no more than the amount paid to the plaintiff in excess of the person's comparative share of responsibility.

(c) A person who has a right of indemnity against another person under §22 does not have a right of contribution against that person and is not subject to liability for contribution to that person.

REST 3D TORTS, APPORTIONMENT OF LIABILITY, § 23 (2000).

PROMAULAYKO v. JOHNS MANVILLE SALES CORP.
562 A.2d 202 (N.J. 1989)

POLLOCK, JUSTICE.

The sole issue on this appeal is whether an intermediate distributor in a chain of distribution should indemnify the ultimate distributor when both are strictly liable in tort to the injured plaintiff. The Law Division granted indemnification to the ultimate distributor, but the Appellate Division reversed. We granted certification, and now reverse the judgment of the Appellate Division.

The underlying facts are that the decedent, John Promaulayko (Promaulayko), contracted asbestosis while working for Ruberoid Corporation from 1934 to 1978 at its South Bound Brook plant. During that period, Ruberoid purchased asbestos from Leonard J. Buck, Inc. (Buck), Asbestos Corporation Limited (Asbestos), and various other suppliers. Included in the asbestos sold by Buck to Ruberoid's South Bound Brook plant was 96.5 tons of Soviet asbestos, which Buck purchased from Amtorg Trading Corporation (Amtorg). The asbestos was packaged in 100-pound bags that did not warn of the dangers of asbestosis.

Apparently neither Amtorg nor Buck ever took possession of the bags, which were shipped from the Soviet Union to the United States where Ruberoid took possession of them. The jury determined in answer to a special interrogatory that Amtorg had supplied all of the Soviet asbestos that caused Promaulayko's injuries. After Promaulayko's death, his wife, plaintiff, Marie Promaulayko, instituted wrongful death, N.J.S.A. 2A:31-1 to -6, and survivor's, N.J.S.A. 2A:15-3, actions, naming as defendants, among others, Amtorg, Buck, and Asbestos. Only Buck and Amtorg are involved in the present appeal.

Buck, a corporation of the State of Delaware, is a broker of mineral products, whose brokerage of asbestos at the time of its sales to Ruberoid accounted for less than one percent of its business. Amtorg is a New York corporation founded in 1924 to promote trade between the United States and the Soviet Union. Its employees are Soviet citizens, the majority of whom remain in the United States for three or four years before returning to jobs in the Soviet Ministry of Foreign Trade. By 1930, Amtorg served as broker for eighty-six percent of the Soviet products entering the United States. At present, Amtorg serves as a direct agent for Soviet business interests and channels the majority of Soviet trade to the United States.

At the conclusion of the trial, the jury dismissed plaintiff's wrongful-death claim, apparently because Promaulayko died from a heart attack unrelated to his asbestosis. The jury awarded $60,000 to Promaulayko's estate on the survivor's action, and $40,000 to plaintiff on her *per quod* claim. In reaching that result, the jury provided the following answers to special interrogatories:

6. Considering that all of the fault that proximately contributed to John Promaulayko's asbestosis is 100%, what percentage of that total fault is attributable to:

(a) Leonard J. Buck, Inc. 25%

(b) Amtorg Trading Corp. 10%

(c) Asbestos Corp. Ltd. (also known as Johnson's Company Ltd.) 65%

TOTAL 100%

7a. Was all (100%) of the asbestos fiber sold by Leonard J. Buck, Inc., which proximately contributed to John Promaulayko's asbestosis sold to Buck by Amtorg Trading Corp.?

Yes X No. _____   _____

Based on the jury's answer that Amtorg had supplied Buck with all of the asbestos that had caused Promaulayko's asbestosis, the trial court granted Buck indemnification from Amtorg. The court rejected Amtorg's argument that Buck was not entitled to indemnification because the jury's answer to interrogatory 6 indicated that Buck was more at fault than Amtorg. Although the court acknowledged the inconsistencies in the answers to interrogatories 6 and 7a, it concluded that if the jury made a mistake, it was in answer to interrogatory 6, which dealt with the difficult issue of the allocation of fault. By contrast, the answer to the simple factual issue posed by interrogatory 7a established that Amtorg had supplied all the Soviet asbestos that Buck sold to Ruberoid's South Bound Brook plant.

The Appellate Division reversed, ruling that one in the position of a retailer, such as Buck, could obtain indemnification only from the manufacturer who produced the defective product and not from an intermediate distributor such as Amtorg. Underlying that determination was the court's conclusion that indemnity is based on the difference between the primary liability of the manufacturer and the secondary liability of distributors lower in the chain of distribution. The court reasoned that the

> trial court's order requiring Amtorg to indemnify Buck is not based on any primary fault of Amtorg. Instead, it is based on Amtorg's proximity to the manufacturer. The jury's finding that Amtorg sold to Buck all of the asbestos fiber Buck sold Ruberoid placed Amtorg closer to the manufacturer in the chain of distribution than was Buck. Both Amtorg and Buck, however, were blameless in terms of conduct that created the defect in the product. The fact that Amtorg supplied Buck with all of the asbestos Buck distributed to Ruberoid does not change the kind or character of Amtorg's liability from secondary to primary. Here, it is clear that the manufacturer, a Russian Company, created the defect by not placing a warning on the product. Common law indemnification is based on equitable principles designed to further the ends of justice by allowing a party whose liability is merely constructive, technical, imputed or vicarious to be indemnified by the party who caused the defect. A retailer or distributor is permitted to be indemnified by the manufacturer because the manufacturer created the defect and the distributor or retailer is generally blameless.

The purpose of indemnification is restitution to prevent an active wrongdoer from being unjustly enriched by having another party discharge the obligation of the active wrongdoer. . . . Where, as here, the distributors' liability is based upon a common failure to detect the defect in the product and this failure merely continued the defect created by the manufacturer, we perceive of no valid reason to shift the liability of one distributor to another distributor through common law indemnification. Because Buck and Amtorg were both without personal fault, indemnification would create, rather than prevent, unjust enrichment.

The court concluded that the proper method ameliorating its otherwise "harsh" result was to modify the award based on the Comparative Negligence Act, N.J.S.A. 2A:15-5.1 to 5.3. Consequently, it molded the verdict in accordance with the jury's answer to interrogatory 6, the result of which is that Asbestos would pay sixty-five percent; Buck, twenty-five percent; and Amtorg, ten percent of the total $100,000 award.

Two basic principles underlie the development of strict liability in tort. The first principle is the allocation of the risk of loss to the party best able to control it. The second is the allocation of the risk to the party best able to distribute it. We have expressly applied those general principles to asbestosis cases. Accordingly, the essence of a *prima facie* case of liability is proof that defendant placed a defective product in the stream of commerce. As a matter of law, the seller is presumed to know of the defect, so the injured party need not prove that the manufacturer was negligent or knew of the defect. Even in a failure-to-warn case, the cause is essentially one in strict liability into which negligence creeps to the limited extent of analyzing the reasonableness of the defendant's conduct on the assumption that it knew of the defect. Although the focus remains on the product, the defendant satisfies its obligation by proving that it "acted in a reasonably prudent manner in marketing the product or in providing the warnings given." *Feldman v. Lederle Laboratories,* 97 N.J. 429, 451, 479 A.2d 374 (1984).

In a strict-liability action, liability extends beyond the manufacturer to all entities in the chain of distribution. Although a distributor and a retailer may be innocent conduits in the sale of the defective product, they remain liable to the injured party. The net result is that the absence of the original manufacturer or producer need not deprive the injured party of a cause of action.

In the absence of an express agreement between them, allocation of the risk of loss between the parties in the chain of distribution is achieved through common-law indemnity, an equitable doctrine that allows a court to shift the cost from one tortfeasor to another. The right to common-law indemnity arises "without agreement, and by operation of law to prevent a result which is regarded as unjust or unsatisfactory." W. Keeton, D. Dobbs, R. Keeton, & D. Owen, Prosser & Keeton on the Law of Torts §51 at 341 (5th ed. 1984) (Prosser & Keeton). One branch of common-law indemnity shifts the cost of liability from one who is constructively or vicariously liable to the tortfeasor who is primarily liable. A corollary to this principle is that one who is primarily at fault may not obtain indemnity from another tortfeasor. Consistent with this principle, actions by retailers against manufacturers have been recognized in this State for twenty years.

In the present case, we consider the application of the principles underlying strict liability in tort to a claim for common-law indemnification by one distributor against a distributor higher in the chain. Here, the claim is not between two parties, one of which is primarily liable and the other liable only secondarily or vicariously. Both Amtorg and Buck are liable to plaintiff because of their relationship to the product as it proceeded down the chain of distribution. We have not previously considered the issue, and it has received scant attention from commentators and other courts.

The Mississippi Supreme Court, however, has indicated that one distributor may recover from another distributor closer to the source of distribution. In the Mississippi case, the nephew of a soft-drink purchaser recovered from a distributor for personal injuries caused by a bottle that broke when it fell from a defective carton. In affirming the judgment, the court noted that "[m]ore generally, in the strict liability era, each party from the retail seller on up the chain has a potential right of indemnity (assuming of course that all of the elements of the claim for indemnity are met) against the person or firm who sold the product to him as well as against all others on up the chain to the designer or manufacturer of the product or the component part found unreasonably dangerously defective." [*Coca Cola Bottling Co. v. Reeves,* 486 So. 2d 374, 379 n.4 (Miss. 1986).]

Similarly, in a Missouri case where a consumer recovered against a retailer for injuries caused by the collapse of a defective crutch, the retailer was awarded indemnification from the manufacturer. *Welkener v. Kirkwood Drug Store Co.,* 734 S.W.2d 233 (1987). In approving indemnification against the manufacturer, the Missouri Court of Appeals stated that it "agree[d] with the authorities which hold that a seller lower in the chain of distribution who sells a product without actual or constructive knowledge of a defect and who has no duty to inspect is entitled to indemnity against one higher in the chain, such as the manufacturer." *Id.* at 242; *see K-Mart Corp. v. Chairs, Inc.,* 506 So. 2d 7 (Fla. Dist. Ct. App.), *rev. denied,* 513 So. 2d 1060 (1987) (allowing common law indemnification against distributor and manufacturer of a defective swing set); *cf.* Restatement of the Law of Restitution § 98(b), comment (1936) (as between two innocent parties, one without fault is entitled to indemnification from another who is primarily responsible for injuries caused by the condition of chattels).

In allowing claims for common law indemnification by one party in the chain of distribution against a party higher up the chain, these courts have proceeded in a manner consistent with the principle of allocating the risk of loss to the party better able to control the risk and to distribute its costs. The approach is consistent also with the principle of focusing on the defective product as it proceeds down the chain of distribution. In general, the effect of requiring the party closest to the original producer to indemnify parties farther down the chain is to shift the risk of loss to the most efficient accident avoider. Passing the cost of the risk up the distributive chain also fulfills, as a general rule, the goal of distributing the risk to the party best able to bear it. The manufacturer to whom the cost is shifted can distribute that cost among all purchasers of its product. Similarly, a wholesale distributor can generally pass the risk among a greater number of potential users than a distributor farther down the chain. When viewed in terms of these economic consequences, the principle of unjust enrichment, on which the Appellate Division relied, similarly supports the allocation of the risk to the distributor closest to the manufacturer.

Although our analysis has proceeded along the lines of strict liability in tort, our reasoning is consistent with the principles underlying commercial law. Nothing in the Uniform Commercial Code precludes one party in a distributive chain from seeking indemnification from a party higher up the chain for breach of implied warranties of merchantability, N.J.S.A. 12A:2-314, or of fitness for a particular purpose, N.J.S.A. 12A:2-315. Permitting indemnification from the next party in the distributive chain also is consistent with the former Sales Act, N.J.S.A. 46:30-21, which was in effect at the time of the sale from Amtorg to Buck in 1947. *See Griffin v. James Butler Grocery Co.,* 108 N.J.L. 92, 97, [156 A. 636] (N.J. Sup. Ct. 1931) (retailer held liable under implied warranty created in section 15 of Sale of Goods Act had action against manufacturer who sold it adulterated peaches); *General Home Improvement Co. v. American Ladder Co., Inc.,* 26 N.J. Misc. 24, [56 A.2d 116 (1947)] (purchaser of a ladder could recover from seller and manufacturer on express and implied warranties when purchaser had to pay workmen's compensation claim to employee who fell when ladder broke), *overruled on other grounds, Henningsen,* 32 N.J. at 416 (1947). Other jurisdictions have also allowed recovery on implied warranties that extend from one party to another down the chain of distribution. *See Klein v. Asgrow Seed Co.,* 246 Cal. App. 2d 87, 54 Cal. Rptr. 609 (1966) (tomato grower recovered judgment for breach of warranty against seed grower; indemnification allowed by each party in the chain of distribution against party higher in the chain); *McSpedon v. Kunz,* 271 N.Y. 131, 2 N.E.2d 513 (1936) (customer developed trichinosis after eating pork chops and recovered judgment against butcher for breach of implied warranty; indemnification allowed for butcher against supplier, and for supplier against packer); *Aldridge Motors Inc. v. Alexander,* 217 N.C. 750, 9 S.E.2d 469 (1940) (retail car dealer successfully sued wholesale car dealer based on implied warranty when consumer obtained damages from retailer); *Hellenbrand v. Bowar,* 16 Wis. 2d 264, 114 N.W.2d 418 (1962) (buyer of feed for lactating sows brought action under express and implied warranty against seller, seller brought implied warranty against his supplier, supplier brought warranty cross claim against distributor, the manufacturer not involved in action; all judgments against party higher in distributive chain affirmed); *see also* N.J.S.A. 12A:2-607(5)(a) (permits buyer to vouch in its seller when third party brings suit against buyer based on the product).

In the present case, Amtorg was closer than Buck to the producer of the asbestos in the Soviet Union. As between the two of them, Amtorg is better positioned "to put pressure on" the producer to make the product safe. Here, the defect was the absence of a warning of the dangers of asbestosis when the bags were placed in the stream of commerce. Because of Amtorg's relationship to Soviet commerce in general and to the producer in particular, it is more likely that it, rather than Buck, will be able to persuade the producer to provide an adequate warning. Further, Amtorg is better able to shift the cost of the loss to the asbestos producer and to require that producer to reflect the cost of injury in the price of its product.

Conceivably, a set of facts might arise in which the party at the end of the distributive chain will be a better risk-bearer than a party higher in the chain. As a general rule, however, we expect indemnification to follow the chain of distribution. Finally, we recognize that parties in a distributive chain may contract for a different allocation of the risk of loss. For example, one distributor may expressly agree to disclaim or waive any right of indemnification against a distributor farther up the chain. In the present case, the parties did not make any such agreement, and we are satisfied that Buck is entitled to indemnification from Amtorg, the distributor that was interposed between Buck and the producer of the product.

Amtorg contends that it should not be obliged to indemnify Buck because of the answer to special interrogatory 6, in which the jury found Buck twenty-five per cent at fault and Amtorg only ten per cent at fault for Promaulayko's injuries. The trial court apparently submitted this interrogatory because of the cross claims for contribution. According to the trial court, the jury's determination did not represent a finding of fault in the negligence sense. Instead, it was a finding of "sterile fault" assigned in a strict-liability case to intermediate parties in a distributive chain. This finding led the trial court to conclude that the jury's allocation of fault was probably based on the fact that Buck was closer in the chain to Ruberoid. As previously indicated, however, the liability of Buck and Amtorg to plaintiff stems from their relative roles as conduits for the distribution of the defective product. In answer to interrogatory 7, the jury found that Amtorg had supplied to Buck 100% of that product. As between Buck and Amtorg, then, Amtorg should accept the responsibility for Buck's liability to plaintiff. Thus, the jury's finding of fault with respect to a possible claim for contribution does not change Buck's right to indemnification from Amtorg. Nothing in the Joint Tortfeasors Contribution Act, N.J.S.A. 2A:53A-1 to-5, or the Comparative Negligence Act, N.J.S.A. 2A:15-5.1 to-5.3, would alter that result.

Here, the injured party sued two distributors, neither of which altered or even possessed the product as it proceeded from the producer to the ultimate purchaser. In this context, the appropriate vehicle for allocating responsibility between the distributors is indemnification, not contribution. It follows that the trial court should not have asked the jury to determine the various percentages of fault attributable to Buck and Amtorg. The right of the downstream distributor to indemnification from the upstream distributor existed as a matter of law. Consequently, the court should have determined that right following the entry of the jury verdict against defendants.

The judgment of the Appellate Division is reversed, and the matter is remanded to the Law Division for the entry of judgment permitting indemnification by Buck against Amtorg.

NOTES

1. *Contribution and Willful Misconduct.* Section 1(c) of the UCTA (1955) states: "(c) There is no right of contribution in favor of any tortfeasor who has intentionally [willfully or wantonly] caused or contributed to the injury or wrongful death." This provision has been adopted in a number of states.

Should a negligent or strictly liable defendant be permitted to recover contribution from an intentional co-tortfeasor? Or could such a defendant obtain indemnity (full recovery)? Some jurisdictions recognize a right of indemnity by a "passively" negligent tortfeasor against an "actively" negligent tortfeasor. *See Vertecs Corp. v. Reichhold Chem. Co.*, 661 P.2d 619 (Alaska 1983) (abolishing the active-passive doctrine because it had proven elusive and difficult to apply).

2. *No Contribution Against One Who is Not a Co-Tortfeasor.* In *General Motors Corp. v. Doupnik,* 1 F.3d 862 (9th Cir. 1993) plaintiff sued General Motors (GM) for injuries resulting from the defective design of an automobile. He was awarded $6,668,212, reduced to $1,333,642 because he was found to be 80% at fault and the defendant was only 20% at fault. The evidence indicated that Doupnik had been drinking prior to the accident. He lost control of the car while driving. Defective welds in a pillar post of the car caused the body of the car to collapse on the driver's side, rendering Doupnik a quadriplegic. Doupnik's wife sued GM for loss of consortium, and recovered $1 million. The court refused to impute the husband's negligence to the wife, so as to reduce her recovery by 80%.

Thereafter, GM brought an action against the husband to recover 80% of the $1 million paid to the wife. The court denied the claim for "equitable indemnity," saying that there can be no such indemnity unless both the prospective indemnitor (husband) and indemnitee (GM) are jointly and severally liable to the plaintiff. Since the husband did not owe a duty of care to his wife to avoid depriving her of his loss of consortium, the husband was not liable to GM for equitable indemnity.

Some courts have held that a tortfeasor who is immune from tort liability to the plaintiff is not liable for contribution to a co-tortfeasor. Other courts permit such contribution, reasoning that the immunity does not prevent the tort from arising, but merely bars suit between the parties to the immunity. *See* Prosser and Wade On Torts § 50, p. 339 n. 32 (5th ed. 1984). Would the latter rule permit recovery by GM against husband Doupnik?

Recall the "successive" tortfeasors discussed *supra.* Should one be entitled to contribution from the other? *See* the discussion in *District of Columbia v. Washington Hospital Center*, 722 A.2d 332 (D.C. App. 1998).

3. *Contribution Between Tortfeasor and Contract Breacher.* In products liability it is not uncommon for parties held liable in tort and breach of warranty to obtain contribution between themselves. *See, e.g., Wolfe v. Ford Motor Co.,* 434 N.E.2d 1008 (Mass. 1982). Since warranty and strict tort liability are closely allied, *see Kennedy v. The City of Sawyer, Kan.*, 618 P.2d 788 (Kan. 1980), warranty-negligence contribution may be viewed as liability between two types of tortfeasors.

4. *Indemnity Up the Chain of Product Distribution. Promaulayko* upheld the widely recognized view that a business product supplier, held liable for the distribution of a defective product, generally is entitled to indemnity, or full recovery over, against the business supplier who supplied it the defective product. *See also Kelly v. Hanscom Bros., Inc.*, 331 A.2d 737 (Pa. Super. Ct. 1974) (indemnity of strictly liable retailer against wholesaler for breach of implied warranty). Presumably, however, if both parties were negligent, contribution would be appropriate.

In *Casey v. Westinghouse Elevator Co.*, 651 F. Supp. 258 (S.D. Ill. 1986), the underlying complaint concerned a child whose hand was caught in an escalator manufactured by Westinghouse and installed in a May Centers, Inc. shopping mall. May cross-claimed against Westinghouse, seeking "upstream" implied indemnity. The court held that:

> [T]he passage of [Illinois'] Contribution Act eliminates the need for "upstream" implied indemnity. This Court finds that the Contribution Act achieves fair and equitable results in the apportionment of fault without imposing the artificial requirements, and total shifting of responsibility, of implied indemnity. To permit the remedies of implied indemnity to coexist with those of contribution would be in contravention of the express purposes, and not in keeping with the legislative history, of the Contribution Act, namely to encourage settlements and apportion fault.

5. *Respondeat Superior Indemnity.* In *American Nat'l Bank v. Columbus Cuner-Cabrini Med. Center*, 609 N.E.2d 285 (Ill. 1995), the court held that a principal, found vicariously liable for the tort of its agent, was entitled to indemnity from the agent. Is there any principal-agent situation where contribution would be the appropriate remedy of the principal against the agent? What about the employment relationship: should the vicariously liable employer be entitled to indemnification from the employee whose fault triggered the vicarious liability?

6. *Partial Indemnity.* In *In re Consolidated Vista Hills Retaining Wall Litig. (Amrep Southwest, Inc., Defendant-Third Party-Plaintiff v. Shollenbarger Wood Treating, Inc., Third-Party-Defendant)*, 893 P.2d 438 (N.M. 1995), the defendant construction firm, Amrep, was held liable to homeowners for using improperly treated construction materials in their homes, and the firm filed a third-party claim against the materials supplier, Shollenbarger. The trial court held Amrep was not entitled to traditional indemnification of full recovery over, since it was partially at fault. On appeal, the court said there was a factual issue as to whether Amrep was only passively at fault, and Shollenberger actively at fault. If such a passive-active situation existed, Amrep would be entitled to traditional indemnification:

> Under traditional indemnification an indemnitee is entitled to be made whole by a third party such as the primary wrongdoer. Traditional indemnification differs from contribution in that contribution requires each joint tortfeasor to share a common liability. Further, contribution was not recognized at common law. In essence, traditional indemnification is a judicially created common-law right that grants to one who is held liable an all-or-nothing right of recovery from a third party; contribution is a statutorily created right that allows proportional distribution of liability as between the parties at fault.

Traditional indemnification would appear to apply only when there is some independent, preexisting legal relationship between the indemnitee and indemnitor. The right to indemnification may be established through an express or implied contract, or "may . . . arise without agreement, and by operation of law to prevent a result which is regarded as unjust or unsatisfactory." W. Page Keeton et al., *Prosser and Keeton on the Law of Torts* 51, at 341 (5th ed. 1984).

The right to indemnification may arise through vicarious or derivative liability, as when an employer must pay for the negligent conduct of its employee under the doctrine of respondeat superior or when a person is directed by another to do something that appears innocent but is in fact wrongful. Further, traditional indemnification principles apply in both negligence and strict liability cases involving persons in the chain of supply of a product, and in breach of warranty cases, *Schneider Nat'l, Inc. v. Holland Hitch Co.*, 843 P.2d 561, 587 (Wyo. 1992). *See generally* Restatement (Second) of Torts §886B (1977) (listing situations in which parties may be entitled to indemnification). In this case an independent, preexisting legal relationship between Amrep and Shollenbarger is established by their respective positions in the chain of distribution of a product. Thus, provided it could prove all of the requisite elements, Amrep would be entitled to seek indemnification.

The purpose of traditional indemnification is to allow a party who has been held liable without active fault to seek recovery from one who was actively at fault. Thus the right to indemnification involves whether the conduct of the party seeking indemnification was passive and not active or in pari delicto with the indemnitor. . . .

If Amrep were at fault, the court said, then it might be entitled to partial, or proportional, indemnification from Shollenbarger:

A growing number of courts are applying comparative fault principles to indemnification claims and replacing the all-or-nothing rule of traditional indemnification with a system of apportioning damages according to relative fault. *See, e.g., Allison v. Shell Oil Co.*, 495 N.E.2d 496, 500–01 (Ill. 1986) (declaring that active/passive doctrine is replaced by system applying comparative-fault principles); *Schneider Nat'l, Inc. v. Holland Hitch Co.*, 843 P.2d 561, 576–77 (Wyo. 1992) (recognizing Wyoming's acceptance of relative-fault doctrine over the "all-or-nothing rule"). Amrep refers to the application of comparative fault to indemnification claims as "comparative indemnification;" Shollenbarger entitles it "equitable implied comparative indemnity;" we shall refer to the doctrine as "proportional indemnification."

Proportional indemnification has its genesis in jurisdictions that did not adopt a system of contribution among tortfeasors. *See Schneider Nat'l, Inc.*, 843 P.2d at 573. Other state courts adopted proportional indemnification because they were frustrated with inadequate contribution statutes. Restatement (Second) of Torts §886B cmt. m (1977). In most cases, the adoption of proportional indemnification has followed a state's legislative or judicial rejection of contributory negligence and adoption of comparative fault. *See, e.g., American Motorcycle Ass'n v. Superior Court*, 578 P.2d 899, 918 (Cal. 1978) (en banc); *Allison*, 495 N.E.2d at 501 ("Active-passive indemnity, like contributory negligence, perpetuates inequality by its inability to apportion loss and its refusal to grant any relief whatsoever to a party whose conduct is considered 'active' regardless of how much or little other tortfeasors are at fault."); *cf. Herndon*, 716 F.2d at 1332 (stating that when "states have adopted the comparative negligence approach, the indemnity principles in those states have changed from the traditional all or nothing approach [to] damages measured by the degree of comparative fault of all the parties").

D. SETTLEMENTS

A settlement is a contract by which parties resolve a dispute either before or after the commencement of litigation over the dispute. For a number of reasons, the law generally encourages settlements. One, of course, is the usual subsequent reduction of animosity between the parties involved and their families. The most important is judicial efficiency and the resulting proper allocation of resources. The generally accepted estimate is that about 95% of all suits filed are settled before trial; without such a result, the judicial system would require a vast expansion and the delay between the filing of suit and trial would become intolerable.

Essentially, a settlement is a contract between the parties, and is governed by the appropriate contract law. Some types of settlement agreements may violate public policy because they have a negative impact upon the judicial system or produce unfairness to others. This result usually occurs in cases involving partial settlement by one of the multiple parties involved in the litigation; the most important issue which arises is the impact which the settlement will have upon the non-settling parties, both at trial and in any subsequent judgment. Recall that the common law rule provided that a settlement and release of one joint tortfeasor had the legal effect of releasing all of them. The modern rule codified in a statute in most states seeks to encourage settlements by providing that a release of one tortfeasor effectuates a release of others only to the extent provided in the settlement agreement and release. REST. 3D TORTS § 40.

The most common type of a release provides that the settling tortfeasor is released to the extent of his pro rata or proportionate share. Under the UCTA, a pro rata release protects the settling defendant from claims for contribution by other joint tortfeasors. At the same time the non-settling tortfeasors are able to reduce their potential liability by the proportionate share of the settling defendant. The plaintiff takes a risk that she received adequate payment for the proportionate share of the party she released. If it turns out based on a later determination by the jury or the court that the tortfeasor who settled was responsible for a higher proportion of the damages than she paid, the plaintiff is out of luck.

An alternative type of release, pro tanto, provides that the settling defendant is released to the extent of the amount of money she paid for the release. This leaves the settling defendant potentially liable to contribution claims of other joint tortfeasors if it turns out the amount the released defendant paid did not satisfy her proportionate share.

BECKER v. CROUNSE CORP.
822 F. Supp. 386 (W.D. Ky. 1993)

HEYBURN, DISTRICT JUDGE.

The parties dispute this Court's jurisdiction and propose differing sources of applicable law in this admiralty case arising from a boating accident on the Ohio River. The motions submitted for decision require this Court to determine whether it possesses subject matter jurisdiction; whether it must apply federal or state law; and whether Defendants may pursue a cross-claim demanding contribution from a party who has settled his liability to Plaintiffs.

Plaintiff Virgil Becker was a passenger in a fishing boat sailing on the Ohio River between Kentucky and Illinois, near Smithland Pool, on June 25, 1989. Plaintiff's son, Third-Party Defendant Randall Becker, piloted the vessel that day. A large wave allegedly struck the boat and capsized it, injuring Plaintiff and destroying the vessel. Plaintiffs allege that the negligent operation of three nearby commercial barges combined to create the damaging surge of water. Plaintiff and his wife, Plaintiff Ruby Joleen Becker, who alleges loss of consortium resulting from the accident, settled their claims against Randall Becker for $45,000.00 in March, 1990. Plaintiffs, who are Illinois residents, filed suit in the courts of Kentucky on June 22, 1992. They named as Defendants the owners of the three barges: Crounse Corporation, a Kentucky enterprise, operator of the vessel *Zelda Humphrey*; M/G Transport Services, an Ohio corporation, operator of the *Michael Conaton*; and Midsouth Towing, a Florida concern, operator of the *Anne B*. Defendants removed the litigation to this Court soon thereafter. They also asserted cross-claims against Randall Becker, demanding contribution from him in the event Defendants are held liable for the injuries sustained by Plaintiffs. . . .

The final issue which the Court must consider is whether Defendants may pursue their claims against a settling third-party defendant. Regardless of the answer, the Court must fashion a fair process for apportioning fault and damages in this case.

Plaintiffs settled their claims against Randall Becker for $45,000.00 in March, 1990 and released him from any further liability for their injuries. (Answer of Randall Becker, Ex.A.) Randall Becker now offers this settlement as grounds for judgment on the pleadings against Defendants' Third Party Complaint, which seeks contribution from Becker to defray any damages they may be required to pay Plaintiffs. Randall Becker contends that admiralty law discharges a settling joint tortfeasor from liability for contribution to other wrongdoers, and that Defendants cannot collect reimbursement from him under any circumstances.

Prevailing admiralty law offers no uniform doctrine which disposes of the controversy presented here. The Supreme Court has not yet addressed the liability of settling tortfeasors for contribution to their non-settling cohorts; the Sixth Circuit has taken no clear stance in the area; and the other Circuits are divided. One court which surveyed the conflicting pronouncements in this field was moved to "sympathize with the district court's difficulties in finding guidance from controlling authority on the settlement bar issue. There is none." *Miller v. Christopher*, 887 F.2d 902, 903 (9th Cir. 1989). There are, nevertheless, certain long-established admiralty principles which provide direction in evaluating the options available, and there is no lack of advice from the Circuit Courts regarding possible solutions to the issue at hand.

Maritime tort law seeks first to assure full compensation to victims for their injuries. That policy dictates the general imposition of joint and several liability upon multiple wrongdoers whose negligence precipitates an accident. As the Supreme Court has commented, this maritime doctrine "is in accord with the common law, which allows an injured party to sue a tortfeasor for the full amount of damages for an indivisible injury that the tortfeasor's negligence was a substantial factor in causing, even if the concurrent negligence of others contributed to the incident." *Edmonds v. Compagnie Generale Transatlantique*, 443 U.S. 256, 260, 99 S. Ct. 2753, 2756, 61 L. Ed. 2d 521 (1979). The Court acknowledged the possible inequity threatened by a doctrine which allows a plaintiff to demand that a less-culpable wrongdoer bear a disproportionate share of the plaintiff's damages. Nevertheless, the Court insisted that such consequences would "not justify allocating more of the loss to the innocent [victim]" by limiting that victim's recovery to an amount based on the individual wrongdoer's relative share of fault. There can be little doubt that, as between the plaintiff and several wrongdoers, the plaintiff should be able to insist upon a full recovery from any tortfeasor, regardless of that tortfeasor's comparative liability.

The harsh consequences of a joint and several liability system are tempered, though, by the centuries-old admiralty principles of comparative liability and contribution. Maritime law rejected long ago the common law rules against contribution, and adopted instead a "doctrine of ancient lineage providing that . . . mutual wrongdoers shall share equally the damages sustained by each. . . ." *Cooper Stevedoring Co. v. Fritz Kopke, Inc.*, 417 U.S. 106, 110, 94 S. Ct. 2174, 2176, 40 L. Ed. 2d 694 (1974). The admiralty courts recognized that "a 'more equal distribution of justice' can best be achieved by ameliorating the common-law rule against contribution which permits a plaintiff to force one of two wrongdoers to bear the entire loss, though the other may have been equally or more to blame." *Cooper* at 111 [94 S. Ct. at 2177]. In recent years the Supreme Court further refined these rules by declaring that the liability of joint tortfeasors for maritime injury "is to be allocated among the parties proportionately to the comparative degree of their fault. . . ." *United States v. Reliable Transfer*, 421 U.S. 397, 411, 44 L. Ed. 2d 251, 95 S. Ct. 1708, 1715 (1975). In this manner, "contribution remedies the unjust enrichment of the concurrent tortfeasor" who temporarily escapes responsibility for damages under the joint and several liability system. Though the plaintiff may choose to collect damages from a single wrongdoer, it is clear that joint wrongdoers may assure a more equitable division of liability among themselves by allocating their comparative fault and pursuing contribution remedies.

When applied in a litigation context, the doctrines of joint and several liability and comparative contribution ably serve the admiralty policies of protection for victims and fairness between defendants. All the defendants are present to dispute their liability under such circumstances, and all are prepared to bear the consequences of an adverse verdict. Each defendant is fully conscious of the possibility that he or she may be held to pay the full amount of the plaintiff's damages, and presumably has chosen this exposure based upon the defendant's anticipation of a favorable verdict. But these doctrines of joint and several liability and contribution may yield uncertain results when one joint tortfeasor chooses to settle with the plaintiff before litigation, leaving the other wrongdoer to proceed to trial alone.

Courts have struggled with the problems created by these twin principles of admiralty recovery. Admiralty's comparative contribution principle leaves the settling defendant exposed to additional liability even after settlement, since that defendant may be required to share the damages paid by the non-settling joint tortfeasor after the latter's unsuccessful trial. Such continued exposure undermines one of the principal benefits sought through settlement. Contribution liability also permits the plaintiff effectively to collect, by a circuitous route, more money from the settling defendant than the plaintiff had agreed to take originally. Contribution from settling defendants would therefore seem to contradict "the interest the courts have in encouraging settlements" in admiralty cases. *Tankrederiet Gefion v. Hyman-Michaels Co.*, 406 F.2d 1039, 1043 (6th Cir. 1969). These considerations moved the Eighth Circuit to adopt a "proportional fault" system which excuses the settling defendant from contribution liability and holds the non-settling defendant liable only for damages representing that defendant's comparative share of fault. *Associated Elec. Coop. v. Mid-America Transp. Co.*, 931 F.2d 1266, 1271 (8th Cir. 1990). The Eighth Circuit's approach retains admiralty law's comparative liability principle, but allocates the defendants' shares of fault at the trial stage rather than during the traditional post-trial contribution action. Advancing the allocation procedure allows the court to calculate the defendants' liability to the plaintiff in the form of a percentage share of the plaintiff's total damages. Since the non-settling defendant will pay no more than his or her individual portion of the plaintiff's recovery, that defendant will have no need to demand additional funds from the settling defendant through the comparative contribution process. Adoption of proportional liability as between the defendants and the plaintiff necessarily prevents the application of joint and several liability, since that doctrine presupposes the right of a plaintiff to demand damages from one wrongdoer in excess of that wrongdoer's relative fault. The Eighth Circuit proposed its reform in the belief that its new system would "not discourage defendants from settling by subjecting them to the risk of contribution suits from non-settling defendants," and would deter "collusive settlements by limiting the plaintiff's recovery against non-settling defendants to a sum accurately reflecting such defendants' negligence." *Assoc'd Elec.* at 1271.[1]

The Eighth Circuit's proportional fault system is notable for its adaptation of admiralty's policy of assuring fairness between defendants to the somewhat novel context of settling and non-settling joint tortfeasors. A non-settling defendant may be ordered to pay no more than its comparative share of the plaintiff's damages — which, indeed, is the maximum any defendant should pay after the combined application of joint and several liability and comparative contribution. A plaintiff "loses" only if the plaintiff accepts from the settling defendant an amount which is less than that defendant's actual share of the plaintiff's damages. Yet even this result need not inevitably be considered "unfair": the plaintiff accepted a fixed sum in exchange for foregoing the chance of a more favorable outcome at trial, and the balancing of risks undertaken by the plaintiff likely produced an equitable settlement, if not an actuarially precise result. And it seems likely that the risk of improvident settlements will be balanced, over time, by the occasional receipt of an overly-generous settlement in which the settling defendant pays more than would have been ordered at trial.

Despite the merits of the Eighth Circuit's approach, the recent trend among those Circuit Courts which have addressed the issue has been to reject the proportional fault system. *See, e.g., In re Amoco Cadiz*, 954 F.2d 1279 (7th Cir. 1992), *and Great Lakes Dredge & Dock v. Miller*, 957 F.2d 1575 (11th Cir. 1992). The Seventh Circuit contended that the proportional fault approach "in particular is no panacea," since the necessity of determining each wrongdoer's precise share of liability "creates a substantial possibility of extended collateral litigation." *Amoco Cadiz*, 954 F.2d at 1318. This additional litigation is complicated by the absence of the settling defendant who, under the proportional fault system, cannot be held liable for contribution and therefore has no incentive to participate in the trial. Plaintiffs additionally may decide to settle for a particular amount, not because that amount accurately reflects the settling defendant's share of fault, but because that amount represents the maximum which a near-insolvent opponent can afford to pay. The elimination of joint and several liability under such circumstances, as required by the proportional fault system, would prevent the plaintiff from recovering an amount sufficient to make the plaintiff whole. "Why should the judicial system invest so heavily in adjusting accounts among wrongdoers?" asked the *Amoco* court: "Neither justification for the tort system — compensation of victims and the creation of incentives to take care — would be served" by the proportional fault approach. *Id.*

---

[1] The Eighth Circuit rejected a modified approach, which it called a "contribution bar" system. That approach would require the non-settling defendant to pay the plaintiff's full damages, less a *pro tanto* credit for any amount paid by the settling defendant. The non-settling defendant, however, could have no contribution from the settling defendant to align the amounts paid with the defendants' comparative fault. This Court agrees with the Eighth Circuit's reasoning. A "contribution bar" approach would amplify the harshest aspect of joint and several liability (solitary responsibility for the plaintiff's damages, regardless of comparative fault) while eliminating admiralty law's ameliorative doctrine of comparative contribution.

The proportional fault system's abolition of joint and several liability may constitute its most significant flaw. The Supreme Court in *Edmonds* pointedly rejected the application of proportional fault and reaffirmed admiralty law's long standing commitment to the joint and several liability principle. *Edmonds*, 443 U.S. at 268–69 [99 S. Ct. at 2760–61]. The Court in *Edmonds* examined the plight of a longshoreman injured by the concurrent negligence of his employer and a shipowner. *Edmonds*, 443 U.S. at 258, 99 S. Ct. at 2755. The plaintiff collected workers compensation benefits from his employer, the payment of which excused the employer from any further liability. The longshoreman ultimately collected 90% of his total damages from the shipowner, even though that defendant accounted for only 20% of the negligence resulting in the plaintiff's injury. The shipowner urged the Court to prevent the imposition of this unfair burden by adopting a proportional fault system.

The Court acknowledged "the sound arguments supporting division of damages between parties before the court on the basis of their comparative fault." *Id*. at 271 [99 S. Ct. at 2762]. But the Court concluded that the elimination of joint and several liability could create its own inequities by reducing a plaintiff's total recovery and thereby shifting the burden of loss to the victim. The Supreme Court's ringing endorsement of the application of joint and several liability cannot easily be brushed aside; indeed, several courts have declared themselves unable to rebut the reasoning employed in the *Edmonds* case.

The courts readily acknowledge, though, that *Edmonds* does not preclude the adoption of a proportionate fault system in a context not involving the application of workers compensation. The Eighth Circuit insisted that the *Edmonds* rule should not govern litigation in which one party has avoided liability by settlement rather than by the payment of statutorily required benefits. *Associated Elec.*, 931 F.2d at 1270–71. The Supreme Court itself suggested a single distinction between a plaintiff who has settled and a plaintiff who has received workers compensation when the Court acknowledged that "[g]enerally, workers' compensation benefits are not intended to compensate for an employee's entire losses." *Edmonds*, 443 U.S. at 261 [99 S. Ct. at 2756] (fn. 9). Under ordinary circumstances, a settlement payment clearly *is* intended to compensate the plaintiff for all losses attributable to the settling party's negligence. The need for joint and several liability, with its attendant possibility of a disproportionate recovery, seems less urgent when a plaintiff has already received a payment calculated to reimburse an appropriate share of the plaintiff's total losses.

Consequently, this Court is confronted with much advice and little guidance on the matter at issue in this case. The traditions and teachings of admiralty law seek to promote the following interests in order of preference:

(1) Full recovery by Plaintiffs;

(2) Fairness among Defendants of varying culpability; and

(3) Settlement of cases.

The Court believes that a "hybrid" approach which draws upon the best elements of traditional admiralty doctrines and the evolving standards of comparative negligence best crafts an equitable remedy for all concerned. The principles of this "hybrid" approach are as follows:

(1) The Court would apply the principle of joint and several liability in all cases in which no defendant settled.

(2) Fault would be apportioned among the defendants to achieve fairness among the defendants. The plaintiff would continue to be entitled to collect judgment *in toto* from any defendant which is adjudged at fault. The paying defendant could then exercise its right of proportionate contribution.

(3) If a plaintiff chooses to settle with one or more defendants, that plaintiff does so with the knowledge that the settling defendants' proportionate share of the award, as determined by the jury, will be excluded from the judgment.

(4) However, even in the case where a plaintiff has settled with one or more defendants, the plaintiff would still obtain a joint and several judgment against any and all remaining defendants for that amount which remains after the settling defendants' share of the award is excluded. The non-settling defendants retain their right of proportionate contribution, which they may exercise only against other non-settling defendants.

By this "hybrid" method, the interests of all important parties are protected and promoted. Plaintiff may preserve joint and several liability against all Defendants by simply not settling. And, if a partial settlement is advantageous, even that settlement does not extinguish Plaintiff's joint and several rights against the remaining Defendants. At the same time, Defendants would have some incentive to settle, because by settlement they may gain complete peace and protection against continued litigation with co-defendants.

Certainly, a plaintiff could be harmed by a wrong judgment about settlement. But that is always possible. However, the "hybrid method" assures that plaintiff will not be hurt by an unfair operation of law, but only by bad judgment in settling. Finally, the "hybrid method" is consistent with the traditional mandates and preferences of admiralty law as set forth in *Edmonds* and *Cooper* and the method recognizes the best and most tested principles of comparative negligence which have evolved in recent years.

For the reasons stated above, the Court is entering an Order herewith sustaining the Third-Party Defendant's Motion to Dismiss.

NOTES

1. *Settler Immunity?* Many, perhaps most, courts recognize that a settlement by a tortfeasor, if fair, insulates a jointly liable settler from any claim for contribution by a joint tortfeasor. *See Rufolo v. Midwest Marine Contr., Inc.*, 6 F.3d 448 (7th Cir. 1993); *Cook v. Stansell*, 411 S.E.2d 844 (W. Va. 1991). Not all do, however. In *Boca Grande Club v. Polackwich*, 990 F.2d 606 (11th Cir. 1993), the court said that under maritime law, "a tortfeasor is not precluded from seeking contribution from a joint tortfeasor who has settled."

In *Hager v. Marshall*, 505 S.E.2d 640 (W. Va. 1998), the court discussed "good faith" settlements in this manner:

> Settlements are presumptively made in good faith. A defendant seeking to establish that a settlement made by a plaintiff and a joint tortfeasor lacks good faith has the burden of doing so by clear and convincing evidence. Because the primary consideration is whether the settlement arrangement substantially impairs the ability of remaining defendants to receive a fair trial, a settlement lacks good faith only upon a showing of corrupt intent by the setting plaintiff and joint tortfeasor, in that the settlement involved collusion, dishonesty, fraud or other tortious conduct.
>
> Some factors that may be relevant to determining whether a settlement lacks good faith are: (1) the amount of the settlement in comparison to the potential liability of the settling tortfeasor at the time of settlement, in view of such considerations as (a) a recognition that a tortfeasor should pay less in settlement than after an unfavorable trial verdict, (b) the expense of litigation, (c) the probability that the plaintiff would win at trial, and (d) the insurance limits and solvency of all joint tortfeasors; (2) whether the settlement is supported by consideration; (3) whether the motivation of the settling plaintiff and settling tortfeasor was to single out a non-settling defendant or defendants for wrongful tactical gain; and (4) whether there exists a relationship, such as family ties or an employer-employee relationship, naturally conducive to collusion.

13-14

Where the non-settling tortfeasor otherwise would have been entitled to contribution from the settling tortfeasor, courts usually compensate by granting the non-settling tortfeasor a credit against the judgment ultimately rendered against him. There are three principal ways to calculate the amount of the credit: (1) the dollar amount paid in settlement; (2) a percentage of the total compensatory damages equal to the percentage of fault attributable to the settler, or (3) a pro capita reduction equal to the number of tortfeasors (*e.g.*, if there are three defendants and one settles, the total liability per capita is reduced by one-third, regardless of the amount paid or the percentage of fault of the settler).

Id. at

Which method is fairest? To whom?

2. *Settlement and Assignment of Rights of Contribution.* Normally a full settlement of the claimant's damages by a tortfeasor extinguishes any further claims of the claimant against a joint tortfeasor, although the settler will have a claim for contribution against the joint tortfeasor. However, if the settler settles only his own liability, he has no claim for contribution but the claimant retains a claim against the co-tortfeasor — reduced by the amount of credit attributable to the settlement.

In *Robarts v. Diaco*, 581 So. 2d 911 (Fla. App. 1991), a doctor, sued for malpractice, settled the claim against himself and also settled the plaintiff's negligence claim against the treating hospital. As part of the settlement agreement, the doctor assigned to the plaintiff any claim for contribution it might have against the hospital. The applicable contribution statute provided in part:

> A tortfeasor who enters into a settlement with a claimant is not entitled to recover contribution from another tortfeasor whose liability for the injury or wrongful death is not extinguished by the settlement or in respect to any amount paid in a settlement which is in excess of what was reasonable.

The court concluded that

> the assignment of the doctors' rights of contribution in this case is not invalid merely because it was assigned to the original plaintiff in the tort action who may or may not have received full compensation for the injuries sustained by reason of the tort. If the assigning tortfeasor should choose to bestow a "windfall" upon the plaintiff by reason of such an assignment, that is a matter of contract between those parties.

Id. at 9-10.

How could the doctor have anything to assign unless he extinguished the liability of the hospital to the plaintiff? If the doctor did extinguish the hospital's liability to the plaintiff, then what claim does the plaintiff have against the hospital by way of assignment? What if the joint tortfeasor settles with the plaintiff and takes an assignment of the plaintiff's rights against the other joint tortfeasor? May the settling tortfeasor recover more than the amount he paid to settle? For an exploration of the possibilities associated with settlement, see *Woodfield v. Bowman*, 193 F.3d 354 (5th Cir. 1999).

3. *Overpayment.* The United States Supreme Court has held that a settlement deduction based on the percentage of fault of the settler, rather than the amount paid in settlement, by another should be made, even though this might result in the plaintiff recovering more than his total damages. *McDermott, Inc. v. AmClyde*, 511 U.S. 202 (1994). *Accord, Charles v. Giant Eagle Mkts.*, 522 A.2d 1 (Pa. 1987). *Compare Snowden v. D.C. Transit Sys.*, 454 F.2d 1047 (D.C. Cir. 1971), where a non-settling tortfeasor received a credit for the amount paid in settlement by one who was ultimately exonerated from liability.

Where joint liability has been abolished, a non-settling tortfeasor is not entitled to a credit for any settlement made; the non-settler's liability is limited to its degree of fault. In such a context, the court in *Roland v. Bernstein*, 828 P.2d 1237 (Ariz. App. 1991), observed that if the plaintiff had "made a disadvantageous settlement, she would have borne that consequence." Conversely, "it would be anomalous to give the benefit of an advantageous settlement, not to the plaintiff who negotiated it, but to the non-settling tortfeasor. . . . Those considerations have led most courts considering this question to apply the rule we are adopting."

4. *The Workers' Compensation Problem.* Where a worker injured in the course of employment receives workers' compensation benefits and then brings a third-party action for the same injury, should the third party be given a credit for the compensation payments, or a right of contribution against the employer whose fault contributed to the worker's injury? Bear in mind in this context that the employer normally has a right of subrogation against the third party to recover any workers' compensation benefits paid.

The courts take three approaches to this issue: (1) there is no credit given, and the employer retains its right of subrogation. *Hudson v. Union Carbide Corp.*, 620 F. Supp. 563 (N.D. Ga. 1985); (2) the third-party receives a credit, and the employer's subrogation lien is reduced, by the percentage of the employer's fault, with the maximum credit being the amount of benefits paid. *Kotecki v. Cyclops Welding Corp.*, 585 N.E.2d 1023 (Ill. 1991); *Lambertson v. Cincinnati Corp.*, 257 N.W.2d 679 (Minn. 1977); (3) the third-party has a right of contribution against the employer equal to the percentage of the employer's fault, which may eliminate the subrogation lien and extend beyond that amount, depending upon the percentage of employer fault. *Dole v. Dow Chem. Co.*, 282 N.E.2d 288 (N.Y. App. 1972), codified in N.Y. Gen'l Oblig. Law § 15-108 (1989).

Which approach is fairest? To whom?

What result in a several liability context (i.e., where joint liability has been abolished)? The court in *Ridings v. Ralph M. Parsons Co.*, 914 S.W.2d 79 (Tenn. 1996), held that the third party is not entitled to a reduction of its liability based on any percentage of fault attributable to the employer. The rationale for several liability is that fault may be attributable only to those persons against whom the plaintiff has tort claim. In the court's view, fault cannot be attributable to the employer because the employee has no cause of action against the employer under the express provisions of the workers' compensation statute.

5. *Settlement in the Indemnity Context.* The courts are divided over whether a plaintiff's settlement with an indemnitor extinguishes the indemnitee's claim for indemnity against the indemnitor. *Compare Dunn v. Kanawha County Bd. of Educ.*, 459 S.E.2d 151 (W. Va. 1995), *with Anne Arundel Med. Center v. Condon*, 649 A.2d 1189 (Md. 1994), holding that the release of the indemnitor releases the indemnitee as a matter of law. The *Anne Arundel* court points out that termination "of the claims against the agent extinguishes the derivative claim against the principal."

Insurance liability is a form of indemnity; should the plaintiff's release of the insured bar further recovery from the insurer? Would it make any difference if the plaintiff could maintain a direct action against the insurer? What public policy is promoted by the rule that a release of the indemnitor results in a release of the indminitee?

HESS v. ST. FRANCIS REGIONAL MEDICAL CENTER
869 P.2d 598 (Kan 1994)

LOCKETT, JUSTICE.

Plaintiff Ralph Hess appeals the jury's finding for the defendant, St. Francis Regional Medical Center (St. Francis), in a negligence action, claiming the trial court erred in: (1) allowing into evidence his pretrial settlement with other defendants. . . .

Hess, an employee of Vulcan Materials (Vulcan), was injured on the job. After Hess settled his workers compensation claim, Vulcan terminated Hess' employment. Hess sued Vulcan, his former employer, for retaliatory discharge and for negligently failing to properly notify medical personnel of the caustic nature of the liquid that caused his burns. He also sued Chris Cookson, the plant nurse for Vulcan, and St. Francis for failing to act on the information from his employer that he had been burned by a caustic liquid. Without admitting liability for its conduct or action, Vulcan paid Hess $15,000 and waived its right to subrogate medical expenses and other workers compensation benefits previously paid to Hess. After the settlement, all the defendants except St. Francis were dismissed as parties to the action. However, at trial, the jury could still assess the fault of the defendants that had been dismissed. . . .

The jury found Vulcan 100% at fault. The trial court entered judgment in favor of St. Francis. Hess appealed to the Court of Appeals. This court, on its own motion, transferred the case to its docket. . . .

Prior to trial, Hess settled with Vulcan and its employees. He dismissed his claims against them. Hess proceeded to trial against the remaining defendant, St. Francis. The jury was to compare the fault of the defendants who had been dismissed from the action.

Over Hess' objection, during cross-examination of Eric Phillips, Phillips informed the jury that Vulcan had been sued and had settled with Hess prior to trial. During cross-examination of Hess, the matter of settlement was also raised. St. Francis' attorney asked Hess if he had sued and settled with his employer. Hess admitted that he had sued and settled with his employer. St. Francis' attorney then asked if Hess had received $231,819.85 in workers compensation benefits from his employer. Hess stated he had received workers compensation but did not know the total amount. The attorney then asked Hess if he was seeking to recover expenses from St. Francis that had already been paid by Vulcan in the settlement. (It is not clear if Hess answered that question.) Finally, in the cross-examination of Dr. Jost, the doctor acknowledged that Vulcan had been sued by Hess.

It has been consistently held that offers of settlement and evidence of pretrial settlements with other parties to the action are generally inadmissible. There are two statutes which specifically concern the admissibility of evidence concerning settlement negotiations and settlements. K.S.A. 60-452 provides in part that evidence a person has, in compromise, furnished money or any other thing to another who claims to have sustained loss or damage is inadmissible to prove his or her liability for the loss or damage or any part of it. K.S.A. 60-453 states that evidence a person has accepted or offered or promised to accept a sum of money or any other thing in satisfaction of a claim is inadmissible to prove the invalidity of the claim or any part of it. K.S.A. 60-452 is concerned with possible prejudice to a party on the issue of liability. K.S.A. 60-453 is concerned with protecting the plaintiff's claim. The public policy behind these statutes is to promote settlement. *Ettus v. Orkin Exterminating Co.*, 233 Kan. 555, 567, 665 P.2d 730 (1983).

In *Lytle v. Stearns*, 250 Kan. 783, 830 P.2d 1197 (1992), this court discussed: (1) the disclosure of settlement agreements to the jury; (2) the admissibility of evidence regarding a settlement; (3) that the statements and defenses set out in the pleadings are not admissible as admissions; and (4) the cross-examination of a lay party witness regarding theories asserted against a party no longer in the lawsuit.

Lytle involved a survival and wrongful death action filed by the estate of the deceased against multiple defendants. Deborah K. Lytle was a passenger in a car involved in a head-on automobile collision. Deborah was transferred from the accident scene to a hospital by ambulance. At the hospital, Deborah went into cardiac and respiratory arrest and died. Deborah's estate brought an action against the driver of the car she had been riding in, the hospital, and the ambulance driver. Other parties were impled into the lawsuit by the ambulance driver for comparative negligence purposes. Prior to trial, the estate settled with all defendants except the ambulance driver. Each of the settling defendants denied liability and stated that the payment of the specified amount to the plaintiff should not be construed as an admission of liability. The release and settlement agreements each contained a confidentiality provision.

Prior to trial, the plaintiff filed a motion *in limine* to prohibit the remaining defendant from referring directly or indirectly to any dismissal of parties who had previously been named as defendants. The defendant opposed the motion, claiming that *Ratterree v. Bartlett*, 238 Kan. 11, 707 P.2d 1063 (1985), allowed the fact of settlement to be admitted into evidence. The *Ratterree* court had held that where any defendant has entered into a confidential settlement and the settling defendant is a witness at the trial of the remaining defendants or remains a party, the trial court shall disclose to the jury the existence and content of the settlement unless the court finds the disclosure will create substantial danger of undue prejudice, of confusing of the issues, or of otherwise misleading the jury. The trial court in *Lytle* denied the motion but precluded the defendant from mentioning the settlements. Later in the trial, the court informed the jury of the settlement.

On appeal, the plaintiff argued (1) that *Ratterree* applies only to sliding-scale agreements where the settling defendant retains an interest in the judgment and (2) that K.S.A. 60-452 and K.S.A. 60-453 prohibit evidence of compromise, settlement, or invalidity of a claim. The *Lytle* court noted the rule stated in *Ratterree* is broad enough to include any confidential settlement in any tort action involving multiple defendants when the settling defendant is a witness and either remains a party to the action or retains some financial interest in the litigation. 250 Kan. at 791 [830 P.2d 1197]. The *Lytle* court pointed out that *Ratterree* involved a sliding-scale settlement, also known as a *Mary Carter* agreement, which most courts insist be disclosed due to the possibility of prejudice or collusion because the settling defendant's liability is decreased depending on the outcome of the trial. The *Lytle* court noted that the statutory purpose of K.S.A. 60-452 and K.S.A. 60-453 is to promote settlements. The *Lytle* court observed that none of the settling defendants in that case were still parties to the litigation, nor did they have a financial stake in the outcome or a claim against the remaining defendant and they had always denied that they were negligent. The court held under the facts it was error to admit the evidence of the settlements. As in *Lytle*, the settlement between Hess and Vulcan was not a *Mary Carter* agreement and should not have been disclosed to the jury. . . .

St. Francis also maintains that evidence of the settlement was relevant to show the bias of the witness Phillips, and that Hess' theory of his injury changed after the settlement. St. Francis asserts that the probative value of the fact of settlement outweighed its prejudicial value and that the admissibility of this evidence was within the discretion of the court.

We disagree. Although an employee of Vulcan was a witness, Vulcan was not a party to the action, having been dismissed. Vulcan had paid an agreed amount and waived its subrogation rights to any damages recovered by Hess from St. Francis. Vulcan had no financial interest in the litigation by virtue of its waiver of subrogation rights. Because Vulcan waived subrogation, its monetary liability was fixed; therefore, evidence of the settlement was not relevant to show bias.

In addition, Hess' theory of his injury did not change. His petition alleged liability under five separate causes of action involving Vulcan, its employees, and St. Francis. The claims were that Vulcan and its employees either intentionally or negligently failed to inform the hospital's medical personnel caustic was involved or, in the alternative, that St. Francis negligently treated Hess if the hospital staff had been informed caustic was involved. The pretrial order noted Hess had settled his claims with all defendants except St. Francis. Hess' only remaining claim was the fourth cause of action pled in his petition.

The admission of the evidence of settlement was not within the discretion permitted a trial court, and it should not have been admitted. . . .

NOTES

1. *Evidence of Settlement.* The courts divide on the admissibility of evidence of settlement with a joint tortfeasor. *Compare Tritsch v. Boston Edison Co.*, 293 N.E.2d 264 (Mass. 1973) (admissible) *with DeLude v. Rimek*, 115 N.E.2d 561 (Ill. App. 1953) (inadmissible). The Federal Rules of Evidence, adopted by many states, provide:

> Evidence of (1) furnishing or offering or promising to furnish, or (2) accepting or offering or promising to accept, a valuable consideration in compromising or attempting to compromise a claim which was disputed as to either validity or amount, is not admissible to prove liability for or invalidity of the claim or its amount. Evidence of conduct or statements made in compromise negotiations is likewise not admissible. This rule does not require the exclusion of any evidence otherwise discoverable merely because it is presented in the course of compromise negotiations. This rule also does not require exclusion when the evidence is offered for another purpose, such as proving bias or prejudice of a witness, negativing a contention of undue delay, or proving

an effort to obstruct a criminal investigation or prosecution. Fed. R. Evid. 408.

The Advisory Committee's Note to this Rule states:

> As a matter of general agreement, evidence of an offer to compromise a claim is not receivable in evidence as an admission of, as the case may be, the validity or invalidity of the claim. As with evidence of subsequent remedial measures, dealt with in Rule 407, exclusion may be based on two grounds. (1) The evidence is irrelevant, since the offer may be motivated by a desire for peace rather than from any concession of weakness of position. The validity of this position will vary as the amount of the offer varies in relation to the size of the claim and may also be influenced by other circumstances. (2) A more consistently impressive ground is promotion of the public policy favoring the compromise and settlement of disputes. While the rule is ordinarily phrased in terms of offers of compromise, it is apparent that a similar attitude must be taken with respect to completed compromises when offered against a party thereto. This latter situation will not, of course, ordinarily occur except when a party to the present litigation has compromised with a third person.

2. *"Mary Carter" Agreements.* A "Mary Carter" agreement, named after *Booth v. Mary Carter Paint C.,* 202 So. 2d 8 (Fla. Dist. Ct. App. 196) a case that upheld this type of settlement arrangement, is a settlement by one of two or more defendants in which the settlement is conditioned on the outcome against the other defendants. It is controversial because the settling defendant has the potential of benefiting financially if the plaintiff prevails against the non-settling defendant. For example, the conditional settler might agree to pay $50,000 unless the other defendant or defendants are found liable for $50,000 or more, in which event the conditional settler would be released from liability. Or the settler might agree to pay $50,000, with her liability reduced dollar for dollar for every dollar over $50,000 which the plaintiff recovers from the nonsettling defendant (e.g., if the co-defendant is found liable for $75,000, the settler would only be liable for $25,000). The possible "Mary Carter" arrangements are myriad. The essence of the agreement is that the settler defendant's liability is dependent upon the outcome of the subsequent trial against the non-settler defendant, thus pitting the settler against the non-settler. The settler may remain a defendant in the case, a situation which is especially insidious if the jury does not know of the settler's interest in the outcome.

In *Reager v. Anderson,* 371 S.E.2d 619, 629 (W. Va. 1988), the court summarized the four essential features of a Mary Carter agreement:

> (1) The agreeing defendant(s) must remain in the action in the posture of defendant(s); (2) The agreement must be kept secret; (3) The agreeing defendant(s) guarantee to the plaintiff a certain monetary recovery regardless of the outcome of the action; and (4) The agreeing defendant(s)' liability is decreased in direct proportion to the increase in the non-agreeing defendant(s)' liability.

Some courts have held that a "Mary Carter" agreement is void as against public policy. *See, e.g., Elbaor v. Smith,* 845 S.W.2d 240 (Tex. 1992). Other courts hold that the jury should be informed of the existence of a "Mary Carter" agreement. *See, e.g., Hatfield v. Continental Imports, Inc.,* 610 A.2d 446 (Pa. 1992). Should the jury be informed of the terms of the agreement? *See, e.g., Thibodeaux v. Ferrell Gas Inc.,* 717 So. 2d 668 (La. App. 1998).

3. *Financial Interest in Outcome.* Note that the court in *Hess* said that evidence of plaintiff's settlement with his employer was not admissible because the employer did not retain a financial interest in the plaintiff's claim against the hospital. The employer had waived its workers' compensation subrogation lien. If such lien had not been waived, presumably evidence of the employer settlement would be admissible, at least if a representative of the employer testified in the case. Would the plaintiff be such a representative for this purpose?

4. *A High-Low Agreement.* A "high-low" agreement is one in which the plaintiff agrees to accept a maximum amount if the jury awards that amount or more against the defendant, and the defendant agrees to pay a minimum amount if the jury awards that amount or less. The parties agree to accept a jury award between the minimum and maximum amounts. In *Beng v. Pirez,* 636 A.2d 101 (N.J. Super 1994), a defendant agreed to pay the plaintiff a minimum of $45,000, and a maximum of $62,500 if the jury awarded that much or more against the defendant. In upholding this agreement, the court said:

"No assertion is made that the parties' agreement is a "Mary Carter" agreement, a settlement device which has been restricted or even invalidated in many jurisdictions because it secretly and unfairly allies one defendant with plaintiff to the prejudice of the other defendant." In this case, the outcome of the high-low agreement was independent of the outcome against the co-defendant.

PROBLEMS

13.1

Fred Flash left the keys in the ignition of his new red sports car for a minute while he entered the office of a self-service gas station to pay for a gasoline purchase. Bob Bold, 17 years of age, happened by and could not resist taking a "joy ride" in Fred's car. Accompanied by his 10-year-old brother, Tim, Bob drove at speeds ranging as high as 70 mph on city streets until he crashed into another automobile driven by Martha Madd, seriously injuring her and totally destroying her automobile. Tim also suffered serious physical injuries. This was the fourth time Bob had stolen a car and had been involved in an accident while driving it. Each time his parents had paid for the damages quickly in an effort to avoid the matter being reported to their insurance company or to the police.

Martha and Tim want to collect the entire amount of their damages from Fred Flash because they consider him the most culpable for leaving his keys in the car. Will they be permitted to do so?

13.2

A municipal bus crossed the center line of the highway and hit a car head-on, killing the driver of the car. Evidence showed that the bus driver was intoxicated at the time of the accident. Should the municipality be held jointly and severly liable to the deceased's estate for compensatory and punitive damages?

13.3

John and Jim, while racing their cars down a city street, forced the plaintiff's car off the road, damaging plaintiff's car. When plaintiff got out of his car to inspect the damages, he stepped on a live fallen electrical wire and was electrocuted. The wire had been negligently installed too close to another electrical wire by Electric Co., some 10 years earlier. The two wires had rubbed against each other over the years because of their being blown together by the wind, until eventually the insulation was worn from the wires and one of them ultimately broke as a result of the wear. The City had agreed with Electric Co. periodically to inspect and maintain the line installed by Electric Co., but the City had never done so.

Discuss the possible tort claims of plaintiff's estate against John, Jim, Electric Co., and City in a jurisdiction with joint and several liability, and in a jurisdiction with several liability.

13.4

On the day before jury selection in a product liability and negligence case, two of three defendants offered to settle P's personal injury action for $1 million, with defendant A paying $100,000 (her maximum liability insurance coverage) and B paying $900,000. The relevant facts of the underlying case are that P suffered serious bodily injury in an automobile accident that occurred after A, while driving her automobile, suffered a heart attack and lost consciousness. A's automobile crossed the median of the highway and collided with an automobile driven by P, knocking P's automobile into a truck owned by B that had been parked on the shoulder of the highway in violation of state and local laws. P suffered paralysis from the waist down as a result of the accident. C, the non-settling defendant, is a Drug Manufacturer who sold a pain treatment drug that A had been taking for 3 months prior to the accident. P alleges that the drug was sold with inadequate warnings as to the risk of causing heart attacks and the inadequate warning was a proximate cause of the accident. C has vowed to never settle this claim. The parties agree that P who was 60 years old at the time of the accident has suffered an income loss (past and future) of approximately $500,000.00, his medical expenses (past and future) will exceed $1 million and P has experienced and will continue to experience substantial pain and suffering for the remainder of his life. P is inclined to accept the $1 million. Negotiate the non-monetary terms of the settlement, including the following points:

What type of Release should the parties agree to: Pro tanto or pro rata?

In addition to the payment of money the parties may want to include other material provisions in their settlement agreement such as confidentiality of the settlement or an obligation of cooperation of the released party at the trial against the other joint tortfeasors. If a confidentiality clause is included in the agreement should disclosure to non-settling defendant, court, and/or public be required? Permissible?

What obligations should the Released Defendants have to participate in the trial if the other tortfeasors do not settle?

What other important terms should be covered in the settlement agreement and the release?

13.5

Plaintiff sued employee for employee's tortious acts. He also sued employee's employer for vicarious liability for the employee's acts, and for negligence in hiring and supervising the employee.

Employer subsequently entered into an agreement with plaintiff providing that employer would pay plaintiff $10,000.00 for her separate tort claim against employer, provided however, that employer would be released from plaintiff's vicarious liability claim if employee were found liable. The agreement provided that plaintiff would look solely and exclusively to employee's assets and insurance to collect any judgment rendered against an employee.

How should the court handle this agreement? If the employee is found liable, may she receive contribution from her employer?

Chapter 14

BUSINESS AND COMMUNICATIVE TORTS

A. INTRODUCTION

This chapter examines both business and communicative torts. Business or economic torts concern misrepresentation, appropriation of name or likeness and trade secrets, and interference with contract or business. Communicative torts include defamation and invasion of privacy. These claims may overlap, and they pertain to areas covered in other chapters of the book such as professional liability, products liability, and damages. *See* chapters 9, 10, 11, and 15. Typically the damages highlighted in this chapter are economic, psychic, and dignitary and do not involve physical injury. However, such damages are by no means unique to the torts considered here. Statutes regulate some of the claims addressed in this chapter although the primary focus will be common-law tort remedies. Notably, the claims also intersect with contractual remedies, raising fundamental issues about the relationship of contract and tort.

The business and other economic claims involved in this chapter raise basic questions about the advantages and limitations of competition and a free market economy. Questions of equity and fairness, as well as efficiency and autonomy, also underlie the subject matter, thus bringing into focus some of the foundational aspects of the law of torts. The communicative torts, which include defamation, an area in which the United States Supreme Court has frequently intervened and recognized constitutional restrictions based on First Amendment speech considerations, also reflect value choices. In defamation the Court has utilized the fault requirement as a way of protecting speech and has all but rejected strict liability. It is unclear whether such requirements apply to other communicative torts. Disputes arising in the context of using the Internet have begun to shape the discussion in both business and communicative torts, adding complexities to the subject matter. New business ventures and relationships continue to challenge courts and legislatures to resolve the tensions among competing values like speech, autonomy, privacy, and "justice, equity and fair dealing." W. Page Keeton, *Fraud — Concealment and Non-Disclosure*, 15 TEX. L. REV. 1, 31 (1936), discussed on p. 794, *infra*.

The chapter begins with the business and economic disputes and then focuses on the communicative-based claims.

PART 1 — BUSINESS AND ECONOMIC TORTS

B. INTENTIONAL MISREPRESENTATION/DECEIT

ALEXANDER v. MEDUNA
47 P. 3d 206 (Wyo. 2002)

KITE, JUSTICE.

James and Rita Alexander (the sellers) sold their home of many years to Donald and Linda Meduna and Meduna Red Angus Ranch Trust (the buyers). Before contracting, the buyers viewed the property and were advised by the sellers there was no groundwater seepage or structural defects. The basement flooded shortly after the buyers took possession. At the bench trial, an engineer testified he discovered evidence of long-term structural damage under paneling and carpet and in crawl spaces. The trial court found the sellers' fraudulent representations induced the buyers to contract and awarded punitive damages. We affirm in part, reverse in part, and remand for correction of the compensatory damages associated with the Northwest Rural Water District hookup.

In February 1996, the sellers listed their home of over twenty years, including approximately forty acres of land, a residence, and a mobile home office, for sale through Alexander Realty with Mrs. Alexander as the listing broker. The buyers and their real estate agent first viewed the property on or about December 9, 1996.

The real estate agent prepared a purchase offer for the buyers within approximately one day of the first property showing. A copy of a property condition statement completed by Mrs. Alexander was delivered to the buyers before they made their first offer and was attached to all offers that went back and forth between the parties.

The buyers did not have professional inspections performed. The property closing occurred on or about April 11, 1997, and the buyers did not take physical possession until approximately June 10, 1997. . . .

In the latter part of June 1997, the buyers experienced a number of problems including flooding in the residence basement, roof disrepair, and leakage in the mobile home office; the inability to grow any produce in the garden; and the discovery the Northwest Rural Water District hookup costs would be in excess of $8,000. They filed a lawsuit against the sellers seeking recovery on two causes of action: (1) fraud and deceit and (2) infliction of severe emotional distress. After a lengthy bench trial, the trial court found the buyers had proved the sellers' multiple, intentional fraudulent misrepresentations by clear and convincing evidence but had not established intentional infliction of emotional distress by a preponderance of the evidence. Subsequent to a punitive damages hearing, the trial court awarded the buyers judgment and damages of $100,840.94, attorney fees of $38,045, costs of $9,228.42, and punitive damages of $25,000. The sellers appealed. . . .

At trial, the buyers' expert witness, a registered professional engineer, testified regarding his July 1997 inspection of the property, his written report based on that inspection, and what, in his opinion, caused the structural damages and defects. The gist of his testimony was that the problems had existed for a long period of time. He noted evidence of water damage in the basement including heavy salt deposits and peeling paint on the basement walls, extensively rusted and corroded heat registers, spalling of the masonry and significant alkali deposits in the west crawl space, and bulging of the east and west walls. The engineer opined that excessive migrating groundwater and inadequate subsurface drainage away from the residence existing for not less than three to five years caused water to permeate the inadequately damp proofed foundation walls, swelling the soil and causing the east and west walls to buckle inward. He also concluded the damage was not caused by excessive lawn watering. He testified the foundation walls would have to be exposed, sandblasted, and damp proofed to prevent complete failure. This would require emptying the basement; removing the electrical wiring, plumbing, and carpeting; and excavating the soil from the foundation perimeter. Cracks and heaves in the basement floor would likewise need repair. He noted the excavation would disrupt the existing landscaping which would require repair after the foundation was secured. . . .

An experienced building contractor testified he saw bulging of the east basement wall which was causing the center wall support to move and the center-bearing wall to wrinkle at the basement ceiling. He also observed cracks and heaves in the floor, metal heat registers severely rotted from water and salts coming through the walls, and heavy salt deposits on the walls where the buyers had removed the paneling just after they moved into the house.

Mr. Meduna and his real estate agent testified that the sellers knew the buyers needed to generate supplemental income from the property by using the mobile home office as a business and selling produce and crops from the garden and other acreage. Before entering into the contract, the sellers showed them around the property including the residence, a separate workshop, the mobile home office, the garden, the irrigated acreage, and a pig barn. The sellers each made representations regarding the property condition and suitability for the buyers' stated needs. Neither Mr. Meduna nor his agent saw visible evidence of water damage. They were not shown the crawl spaces, and the walls of two bedroom closets could not be seen because they were covered over by boxes and other items. During the showing, as witnessed by the real estate agent, the sellers represented to the buyers that: (1) the basement had water leakage due to a water softener defect and a downspout malfunction, both of which had been repaired; (2) the garden had been fertilized and was sufficiently productive to permit Mrs. Alexander to can produce; and (3) Northwest Rural Water District water could be accessed at the property line by the road for approximately a $2,000 tap fee and a $1,500 trench cost. The buyers received the property condition statement listing only the two repaired leakage incidents prior to making their initial offer. That statement also provided:

> The undersigned Seller . . . completes and executes this Addendum to such listing contract in order to comply with Seller's obligation to reasonably discover and fully disclose to all parties any and all informa-

tion regarding the condition of such property, does hereby make the following statement and representation concerning the present description and condition of subject property.

The buyers relied heavily on the sellers' oral and written representations of the property condition in making an offer to purchase and believed the disclosures were honest and complete.

. . . The sellers' former housekeeper testified that, approximately six years prior to the house sale, she periodically cleaned salt residue off the basement carpet. The former owner of the home testified that, during the time he lived in the home, he installed paneling in only one basement bedroom and did no other paneling or painting; the groundwater level was significantly below the foundation level; and there were no irrigation lines in place.

Mrs. Alexander initially testified she was unaware of any excessive water issues in her former home. However, she later admitted the sellers recarpeted the basement many times during their twenty-year residency but denied that the frequent replacement was due to excessive groundwater leakage. She acknowledged as a realtor she was aware that sellers are required to fully disclose any known property defects on the property condition statement. She also eventually acknowledged she was aware of the salt buildup on the basement walls and this was a defect she had failed to disclose. Mrs. Alexander initially testified the sellers did not panel or paint the basement prior to offering the property for sale but then equivocated stating she was not sure whether they had made the improvements. She testified the water leakage could have come from over watering the lawn or wet weather and she had advised the buyers not to water the lawn area for more than fifteen minutes at a time. She acknowledged she told the buyers she had grown and canned produce from the garden and still had canned goods in the basement. However, she admitted this was over ten years ago and did not specifically recall whether she had advised the buyers of this fact.

Mr. Alexander similarly denied knowledge of the water leakage issue or efforts on his part to conceal the water damage through cosmetic repairs of the walls and floors. His testimony regarding paneling and painting was equivocal as well. In due course, he conceded he was aware of the salt deposits and did not advise the buyers of this orally or on the property condition statement.

. . . The trial court found the buyers' expert witness was qualified to present technical evidence regarding the condition of the property, causation of structural damages, and defects. This testimony was deemed credible and unrefuted. Conversely, the trial court found Mr. Alexander testified in a conflicting manner regarding certain matters and rejected portions of his testimony. Further, certain aspects of the sellers' testimony, by which they endeavored to exonerate their misrepresentations and failure to disclose, were found not to be credible.

The trial court determined: (1) The sellers were, or reasonably should have been, aware of, and failed to disclose, defects and damage to the basement foundation, walls, floor, and heat registers; (2) the sellers bolstered the buyers' trust in their representations through statements during the initial showing that two excessive water incidents had been corrected and by pointing out an indention of the living room floor; (3) undisclosed leaks and buckling in the mobile home office would require extensive repairs; (4) the sellers were aware of the buyers' interest in water from Northwest Rural Water District and represented the fees would be $3,500, though the actual expense was in excess of $8,000; (5) the sellers failed to disclose the garden had not grown crops in ten years and soil sterilizing weed killer had been applied; (6) the buyers relied on the property condition statement representation that the identified problems had been fully repaired and there were no other defects whatsoever; and (7) neither the preprinted contract nor the standard inspection clause language was negotiated. The trial court found the clear and convincing evidence demonstrated the sellers made material misrepresentations regarding structural defects, both verbally and through the property condition statement, and breached their duty to disclose all defects which, if known, would have caused the buyers not to rely upon the property condition statement and, to their detriment, subsequently purchase the property.

In contrast, the trial court determined the buyers (A) acted in good faith and reasonably relied on the sellers' representations in purchasing the property; (B) were attentive at the initial showing; and (C) believed, as did their real estate agent, that the information disclosed in the property condition statement was candid and accurate. Despite reasonable efforts to mitigate the damages, the buyers sustained special and specific damages for repair and restoration in the total amount of $100,840.94, attorney fees, and costs. The trial court further found the sellers' conduct was willful, wanton, and in reckless disregard of the buyers' rights which entitled the buyers to a hearing on punitive damages.

The sellers contend the trial court's finding of clear and convincing evidence of fraud was erroneous due to its reliance on an unqualified expert, the failure to disclose does not constitute fraudulent misrepresentation, the duty to disclose was delegated to the buyers by contract, and fraud was not established by the evidence. . . .

The sellers contend failure to disclose a fact does not constitute fraud. However, they ignore the reality that they acknowledged making a number of false statements. It is in light of these false statements that the nondisclosures became part and parcel of the fraudulent acts:

> Conduct or words which tend to produce an erroneous impression may satisfy the plaintiff's burden. *In addition, even if someone is not under a duty to speak, if he does speak, he is under a duty to speak truthfully and to make a full and fair disclosure.* Reliance is reasonable when false representations have occurred prior to the execution of the contract which is sought to be avoided or for which damages are sought to be recovered.

. . . By way of example, Mrs. Alexander acknowledged the sellers' duty to complete the property condition statement honestly and fully. Both sellers acknowledged they knew of the salt deposits, and yet they failed to disclose this information on the property condition statement, thereby making an affirmative false statement. Likewise, they admitted they advised the buyers of two specific excess water incidents but failed to advise them of any other defects. They also acknowledged saying the garden was in good condition but not advising the buyers the soil had been sterilized and nothing had been grown in over ten years. The trial court determined the sellers' disclosures, both verbally at the initial showing of the property and in the written property condition statement, reinforced the buyers' confidence the property was in good condition as the sellers reported.

The foregoing list of the sellers' misleading statements and actions is . . . illustrative of the definitive point that, regardless of whether there was a duty, once the sellers started making disclosures, they had a duty to do so completely and truthfully.

. . . [T]he overarching issue [is] whether the evidence relied upon by the trial court reaches the level of clear and convincing evidence of fraud. Clear and convincing evidence is the "kind of proof which would persuade a trier of fact that the truth of the contention is highly probable." *MacGuire v. Harriscope Broadcasting Co.,* 612 P.2d 830, 839 (Wy. 1980). . . . This definition, although broad and subjective in nature, in most circumstances provides sufficient guidance to the finder of fact. . . .

The buyers' trial evidence had sufficient character and integrity to meet the objective "clear and convincing" evidence standard described in *Weigand* [*v. Union National Bank of Witchita,* 610 P.2d 572 (Kan. 1980)] The buyers' witnesses testified very specifically and precisely. None of their witnesses, except Mr. Meduna and perhaps his real estate agent, had any personal interest or apparent bias. Their testimony was internally consistent and corroborated other testimony and evidence received.

On the other hand, the sellers' testimony was fraught with internal inconsistencies, and even acknowledgement of some degree of misrepresentation and failure to disclose. . . .

Further, the sellers provided no evidence or expert witness to challenge the qualifications or expertise of the buyers' expert, the integrity of his inspection method, or his observations and conclusions. The trial court accurately found this evidence was unrefuted. . . .

The evidence the trial court relied upon constituted clear and convincing evidence that (1) both sellers made false representations intended to induce the buyers to offer to purchase the property and enter into a contract to purchase, (2) the buyers reasonably believed the sellers' representations as to the property condition were true, and (3) the buyers relied on the false representations and suffered damages.

Before leaving this issue, we briefly address the wording of the trial court's findings that the sellers "were aware or reasonably should have been aware" of the defects and damage to the west wall and heat registers, the serious east wall bulge, and the basement floor. At first glance, the language appears to apply an incorrect standard as the sellers had to have intended to defraud the buyers; therefore, they had to know of the defects they failed to disclose or misrepresented. In light of the record as a whole, we believe the language "were aware or reasonably should have been aware" was responsive to the sellers' implausible explanations. We conclude the trial court was endeavoring in a diplomatic manner to address the untruthful nature of the sellers' testimony. The trial court unquestionably determined there was clear and convincing evidence of fraud because the sellers knew of the defects and purposely made misrepresentations regarding the property condition to induce the buyers, to their significant detriment, to make a purchase offer and enter into a purchase contract. These findings are supported by clear and convincing evidence and are sufficient.

. . . Affirmed in part, reversed in part, and remanded for correction of the judgment consistent with this opinion.

NOTES

1. *The Restatement Position on Deceit.* REST. 2D TORTS §525 states:

> One who fraudulently makes a misrepresentation of fact, opinion, intention or law for the purpose of inducing another to act or to refrain from action in reliance upon it, is subject to liability to the other in deceit for pecuniary loss caused to him by his justifiable reliance upon the misrepresentation.

The Restatement provides that a misrepresentation is "fraudulent" if the maker of the statement:

> (a) knows or believes that the matter is not as he represents it to be,
>
> (b) does not have the confidence in the accuracy of his representation that he states or implies, or
>
> (c) knows that he does not have the basis for his representation that he states or implies.

REST. 2D TORTS §526.

As the principal case reflects, plaintiff bears the burden of persuasion by clear and convincing evidence that misrepresentation has occurred. Plaintiff must prove the defendant's misrepresentation was made with knowledge of its falsity or that it was made in reckless disregard of its accuracy. Note that the Restatement here uses "purpose" rather than "intent." Compare REST. 2D §531, which uses intent when it emphasizes that there must be an expectation of influencing conduct:

> One who makes a fraudulent misrepresentation is subject to liability to the persons or classes of persons whom he intends or has reason to expect to act or to refrain from action in reliance upon the misrepresentation, for pecuniary loss suffered by them through their justifiable reliance in the type of transaction in which he *intends* or has reason to expect their conduct to be influenced. (Emphasis added.)

2. *Damages for Intentional Misrepresentation.* Note that Section 525 of the Restatement states that the maker of the misrepresentation will be liable for pecuniary loss cause by justifiable reliance. REST. 2D TORTS §525. Does this explain why the trial court in *Meduna* rejected damages for emotional distress? Could damages for misrepresentation and for the intentional infliction of emotional distress overlap, permitting recovery for both pecuniary and non-economic damages?

Should punitive damages be available in such a case? Might punitive damages and compensatory damages overlap? *See State Farm Mutual Automobile Insurance Co. v. Campbell*, 538 U.S. 408, 426 (2003) (noting compensatory damages may contain a "punitive element").

3. *Materiality. Reed v. King*, 145 Cal. App. 3d 261 (1983) raised the issue whether in the sale of a house, the seller must disclose it was the site of a multiple murder. In *Reed,* neither King nor his real estate agents (the other named defendants) told the purchaser that a woman and her four children had been murdered there ten years earlier. Reed learned of the gruesome story from a neighbor after the sale and sued seeking rescission and damages. The appellate court reversed the trial court's ruling on defendants' demurrer for failure to state a cause of action. The court found:

> King and his real estate agent knew the event materially affected the market value of the house when they listed it for sale. They represented to Reed the premises were in good condition and fit for an "elderly lady" living alone. They did not disclose the fact of the murders. At some point King asked a neighbor not to inform Reed of that event. . . . Reed paid $76,000, but the house is only worth $65,000 because of its past.

Id. at 264. The court observed that generally a seller of real property has a duty to disclose to the buyer "facts materially affecting the value or desirability of the property which are known or accessible only to him" if he knows such facts "are not known to, or within the reach of the diligent attention and observation of the buyer." . . . *Id.* at 265. *See* REST. 2D TORTS §538. The matter is material if:

> (a) a reasonable man [or woman] would attach importance to its existence or nonexistence in determining his [or her] choice of action in the transaction in question; or

> (b) the maker of the representation knows or has reason to know that its recipient regards or is likely to regard the matter as important. . . ."

4. *Actionable Misrepresentation — The Tort Distinguished from Conduct.* In an effort to clarify the settings where courts would recognize the tort of misrepresentation, one court observed:

> The tort of fraudulent misrepresentation is often surrounded by unnecessary confusion, because misrepresentations themselves often play large roles in a variety of other torts. . . . A misrepresentation is the essence of torts such as defamation, interference with contractual relations, and malicious prosecution. A malicious, outrageous lie may even give rise to a cause of action for intentional infliction of emotional distress. . . . However, not every misrepresentation gives rise to a cause of action for fraudulent misrepresentation. The origin of fraudulent misrepresentation lies in the common law action of deceit [which prior to the eighteenth century] was not available unless the misrepresentation was part of some contractual dealing between parties. [Although today deceit can] be independent of any contractual relationship . . . the torts of deceit and fraudulent misrepresentation have been limited

to cases involving business or financial transactions between parties. . . . *See* W. PROSSER, TORTS § 105 (4th ed. 1971). . . .

Neurosurgery and Spine Surgery, S.C. v. Goldman, 790 N.E.2d 925 (Ill. App. Ct. 2003) (rejecting claim for misrepresentation when the parties had no financial or business connection). As the court noted, the tort applies to interference with financial or commercial interests where a party suffers a pecuniary loss. *See also* D. Dobbs § 9.2(4), at 559-60 (2d ed. 1993)(noting that there may be emotional distress associated with the invasion of an economic interest but the usual rule is that plaintiff must show pecuniary loss and the damages are limited to such pecuniary loss with no recovery for emotional distress). Why is there such a limitation today? Consider your answer in light of responses that might be offered by law and economics and feminist commentators.

C.   NONDISCLOSURE OR CONCEALMENT

OBDE v. SCHLEMEYER
353 P.2d 672 (Wash. 1960)

FINLEY, JUDGE

Plaintiffs, Mr. and Mrs. Fred Obde, brought this action to recover damages for the alleged fraudulent concealment of termite infestation in an apartment house purchased by them from the defendants, Mr. and Mrs. Robert Schlemeyer. Plaintiffs assert that the building was infested at the time of the purchase; that defendants were well apprised of the termite condition, but fraudulently concealed it from the plaintiffs.

After a trial on the merits, the trial court entered findings of fact and conclusions of law sustaining the plaintiffs' claim, and awarded them a judgment for damages in the amount of $3,950. The defendants appealed.

. . . The Schlemeyers concede that, shortly after they purchased the property from a Mr. Ayars on an installment contract in April 1954, they discovered substantial termite infestation in the premises. The Schlemeyers contend, however, that they immediately took steps to eradicate the termites, and that, at the time of the sale to the Obdes in November 1954, they had no reason to believe that these steps had not completely remedied the situation. We are not convinced of the merit of this contention.

The record reveals that when the Schlemeyers discovered the termite condition they engaged the services of a Mr. Senske, a specialist in pest control. He effected some measures to eradicate the termites, and made some repairs in the apartment house. Thereafter, there was no easily apparent or surface evidence of termite damage. However [the trial court's findings are considered as established fact as follows]:

> Senske had advised Schlemeyer that in order to obtain a complete job it would be necessary to drill the holes and pump the fluid into all parts of the basement floors as well as the basement walls. Part of the basement was used as a basement apartment. Senske informed

Schlemeyer that the floors should be taken up in the apartment and the cement flooring under the wood floors should be treated in the same manner as the remainder of the basement. Schlemeyer did not care to go to the expense of tearing up the floors to do this and therefore this portion of the basement was not treated.

Senske also told Schlemeyer even though the job [was] done completely, including treating the portion of the basement which was occupied by the apartment, to be sure of success, it would be necessary to make inspections regularly for a period of a year. Until these inspections were made for this period of time the success of the process could not be determined. Considering the job was not completed as mentioned, Senske would give Schlemeyer no assurance of success and advised him that he would make no guarantee under the circumstances.

. . . The pattern thus established is hardly compatible with the Schlemeyers' claim that they had no reason to believe that their efforts to remedy the termite condition were not completely successful.

The Schlemeyers urge that, in any event, as sellers, they had no duty to inform the Obdes of the termite condition. They emphasize that it is undisputed that the purchasers asked no questions respecting the possibility of termites. They rely on a Massachusetts case involving a substantially similar factual situation, *Swinton v. Whitinsville Sav. Bank*, 42 N.E.2d 808 (Mass. 1942). Applying the traditional doctrine of *caveat emptor* — namely, that, as between parties dealing at arms length (as vendor and purchaser), there is no duty to speak, in the absence of a request for information — the Massachusetts court held that a vendor of real property has no duty to disclose to a prospective purchaser the fact of a latent termite condition in the premises.

Without doubt, the parties in the instant case were dealing at arms length. Nevertheless, and notwithstanding the reasoning of the Massachusetts court above noted, we are convinced that the defendants had a duty to inform the plaintiffs of the termite condition. In *Perkins v. Marsh,* 37 P.2d 689 (Wash.1934), a case involving parties dealing at arms length as landlord and tenant, we held[:]

> Where there are concealed defects in demised premises, dangerous to the property, health or life of the tenant, which defects are known to the landlord when the lease is made, but unknown to the tenant, and which a careful examination on his part would not disclose, it is the landlord's duty to disclose them to the tenant before leasing, and his failure to do so amounts to a fraud.

We deem this rule to be equally applicable to the vendor purchaser relationship. *See* [W. Page Keeton, Fraud — Concealment and Non-Disclosure,] 15 Tex. Law Review (December 1936) 1, 14–16. . . . In this article Professor Keeton also aptly summarized the modern judicial trend away from a strict application of *caveat emptor* by saying:

> It is of course apparent that the content of the maxim "caveat emptor," used in its broader meaning of imposing risks on both parties to a transaction, has been greatly limited since its origin. When Lord Cairns stated in *Peek v. Gurney* that there was no duty to disclose

facts, however censurable their non-disclosure may be, he was stating the law as shaped by an individualistic philosophy based upon freedom of contract. It was not concerned with morals. In the present stage of the law, the decisions show a drawing away from this idea, and there can be seen an attempt by many courts to reach a just result in so far as possible, but yet maintaining the degree of certainty which the law must have. The statement may often be found that if either party to a contract of sale conceals or suppresses a material fact which he is in good faith bound to disclose then his silence is fraudulent.

The attitude of the courts toward non-disclosure is undergoing a change and contrary to Lord Cairns' famous remark it would seem that the object of the law in these cases should be to impose on parties to the transaction a duty to speak whenever justice, equity, and fair dealing demand it. . . .

A termite infestation of a frame building, such as that involved in the instant case, is manifestly a serious and dangerous condition. One of the Schlemeyers' own witnesses, Mr. Hoefer, who at the time was a building inspector for the city of Spokane, testified that " . . . if termites are not checked in their damage, they can cause a complete collapse of a building, . . . they would simply eat up the wood." Further, at the time of the sale of the premises, the condition was clearly latent — not readily observable upon reasonable inspection. . . . Under the circumstances, we are satisfied that "justice, equity, and fair dealing," to use Professor Keeton's language, demanded that the Schlemeyers . . . inform prospective purchasers, such as the Obdes, of the condition, regardless of the latter's failure to ask any questions relative to the possibility of termites. . . .

NOTES

1. *The Restatement Approach to Nondisclosure.* The traditional rule is that one is under no duty to disclose facts. *See* DAN B. DOBBS, DOBBS ON TORTS § 481 (2000). The Restatement (Second) of Torts § 551 states:

(1) One who fails to disclose to another a fact that he knows may justifiably induce the other to act or refrain from acting in a business transaction is subject to the same liability to the other as though he had represented the nonexistence of the matter that he has failed to disclose, if, but only if, he is under a duty to the other to exercise reasonable care to disclose the matter in question.

(2) One party to a business transaction is under a duty to exercise reasonable care to disclose to the other before the transaction is consummated,

(a) matters known to him that the other is entitled to know because of a fiduciary or other similar relation of trust and confidence between them; and

(b) matters known to him that he knows to be necessary to prevent his partial or ambiguous statement of the facts from being misleading; and

(c) subsequently acquired information that he knows will make untrue or misleading a previous representation that when made was true or believed to be so; and

(d) the falsity of a representation not made with the expectation that it would be acted upon, if he subsequently learns that the other is about to act in reliance upon it in a transaction with him; and

(e) facts basic to the transaction, if he knows that the other is about to enter into it under a mistake as to them, and that the other, because of the relationship between them, the customs of the trade or other objective circumstances, would reasonably expect a disclosure of those facts.

REST. 2D TORTS § 551.

Which of these provisions applies to the misconduct alleged in *Obde*? Why does the court refer us to Keeton's language on "justice equity and fair dealing"? Do those words lead us with sufficient certainty to an understanding when a duty to disclose arises? Should the duty be limited to those who are in a fiduciary relationship? *See also* Michelle Oberman, *Sex, Lies, and the Duty to Disclose*, 47 ARIZ. L. REV. 871 (2005).

2. *The Boundary Between Intentional and Negligent Misrepresentation.* Note that the nondisclosure section of the Restatement set forth extends liability for nondisclosure to one who is "under a duty to the other to exercise reasonable care to disclose" certain information. REST. 2D TORTS § 551. Is nondisclosure a tort governed by negligence? REST. 2D TORTS § 552 cmt. *a* indicates that liability for negligent misrepresentation is narrower than that for intentional misrepresentation. "When there is no intent to deceive but only good faith coupled with negligence, the fault of the maker of the misrepresentation is sufficiently less to justify a narrower responsibility for its consequences." *Id.*

Must there be an "intent to deceive"? Is there a difference between having an intent to deceive and deceit? *See Nielson v. Adams*, 388 N.W.2d 840 (Neb. 1986) (defendant cannot avoid liability by arguing no intent to deceive on any relevant point). For a general discussion of negligent misrepresentation, see DAN B. DOBBS, DOBBS ON TORTS § 472 (2002). *See also* Jean Braucher, *Deception, Economic Loss and Mass Market Customers: Consumer Protection Statutes as Persuasive Authority in the Common Law of Fraud*, 48 ARIZ. L. REV. 829 (2006) (noting "fuzzy line" between intentional and negligent misrepresentation).

D. LIABILITY TO THIRD PARTIES FOR MISREPRESENTATION

IDAHO BANK & TRUST CO. v. FIRST BANCORP OF IDAHO
772 P.2d 720 (Idaho 1989)

SHEPARD, CHIEF JUSTICE.

This case presents the question of the liability of a certified public accounting firm to a person not a party to the auditing contract. Main Hurdman contracted with First Bank & Trust to examine and give an opinion on the financial statements of First Bank & Trust. That audit was completed and an opinion provided to First Bank & Trust. At a later time, as a result of a buyout, Bancorp gained control over First Bank & Trust. In connection with that transaction, Bancorp obtained a loan from Idaho Bank & Trust. In connection with that loan, Bancorp provided Idaho Bank & Trust with the aforesaid audit report prepared by Main Hurdman.

Thereafter, First Bank & Trust was placed in receivership, and Bancorp defaulted upon its loan payments to Idaho Bank & Trust. The present action was brought by Idaho Bank & Trust against Bancorp and Main Hurdman. Upon motion, Main Hurdman was dismissed as a party, that order of dismissal was certified for appeal, and the only matter before this Court is the liability, if any, of Main Hurdman to Idaho Bank & Trust [for negligence].

. . . [T]he issue here is stated by the appellant as "[s]hould an independent accountant, who certifies an audit of an entity, be liable to those who detrimentally rely upon the audit?" Thus, we are presented with a question which falls within a classic pattern, and presents the question originally treated in *Ultramares Corp. v. Touche*, 255 N.Y. 170, 174 N.E. 441 (1931). In *Ultramares* a certified public accountant examined and audited the financial statements of a customer, and failed to discover that an account receivable exhibited on those statements was nonexistent. The certified statements indicated the customer's net worth of over one million dollars, when in fact the customer was insolvent. The plaintiff, relying on that statement, loaned money to the firm. The firm later filed for bankruptcy. The New York court refused to hold the auditor liable to all persons who foreseeably would rely on the negligently audited financial statements, reasoning:

> If liability for negligence exists, a thoughtless slip or blunder, the failure to detect a theft or forgery beneath the cover of deceptive entries, may expose accountants to a liability in an indeterminate amount for an indeterminate time to an indeterminate class. The hazards of the business conducted on these terms are so extreme as to enkindle doubt whether a flaw may not exist in the implication of a duty that exposes to these consequences.

The rule as stated in *Ultramares* has been applied by other courts.

Other jurisdictions have departed from the doctrine of *Ultramares*, holding that public accountants may be liable to third parties, not always precisely identifiable, but who belong to a limited class of persons whose reliance on the accountant's representations is specially foreseen.

More recently the New York court, in *Credit Alliance Corp. v. Arthur Andersen & Co.*, 483 N.E.2d 110, 493 N.Y.S.2d 435 (1985), has reaffirmed the basic principles articulated in *Ultramares*, but has interpreted the *Ultramares* doctrine to include noncontractual parties when certain other prerequisites are satisfied, *i.e.*,

> 1. the accountants must have been aware that the financial reports were to be used for a particular purpose or purposes;
>
> 2. in the furtherance of which a known party or parties was intended to rely; and
>
> 3. there must have been some conduct on the part of the accountants linking them to that party or parties, which evinces the accountants' understanding of that party or parties' reliance.

Hence, the New York court has expanded its traditional rule set forth in *Ultramares*. We agree and adopt the extension of the traditional rule as expounded in *Credit Alliance*.

Plaintiff urges this Court to adopt the imposition of liability in accordance with the *Restatement* and *Restatement (Second) of Torts*. Section 552[2] of the *Restatement (Second) of Torts* limits the liability of a professional who has made a negligent misrepresentation for loss suffered:

> a. by the person or one of a limited group of persons for whose benefit and guidance he intends to supply the information or knows that the recipient intends to supply it; and
>
> b. through reliance upon it in a transaction that he intends the information to influence or knows that the recipient so intends or in a substantially similar transaction.

When applied to an audit, the *Restatement* thus limits the person or persons to whom the auditor owes a duty to intended identifiable beneficiaries and to any unidentified member of the intended class of beneficiaries. We decline to adopt the *Restatement* standard. . . .

NOTES

1. *Foreseeability and Intent in Defining the Boundaries of Liability.* How does the rule in *Idaho Bank & Trust* differ from that found in the Restatement (Second) of Torts? The reasoning of *Idaho Bank & Trust* was essentially followed in *Bily v. Arthur Young and Co.*, 834 P.2d 745 (Cal. 1992), despite a vigorous dissent. The majority said an auditor should be liable to third parties (i.e., those who are not clients) for negligent representation only when the statement is made with intent to induce reliance by the plaintiff, or by a particular class of persons to whom plaintiff belongs, in a specific transaction or type of transaction that the auditor intended to influence. Intent includes situations where the "defendant knows with substantial certainty that plaintiff, or the particular class of persons to which plaintiff belongs, will rely on the representation in the course of the transaction." *Id.* at 773.

But liability for fraudulent misrepresentation, the court said, extends to any reasonably foreseeable plaintiff. The concern about potential "unlimited liability for mere errors or oversights and the uncertain connection between investment and credit losses and the auditor's report pale as policy factors when intentional misconduct is in issue." *Id.* Is the court in *Bily* suggesting that causation requirements should be relaxed whenever any intentional tort is involved or is it just talking about misrepresentation? In either case, how much relaxation should there be? Is the court suggesting that the potential plaintiffs are more likely to be considered "foreseeable" if the person making the misrepresentation is acting with the purpose or intent to deceive?

The plaintiff attorney in *Stewart v. Jackson & Nash*, 976 F.2d 86 (2d Cir. 1992), stated a claim against her employer law firm for fraudulently inducing her to accept employment with the defendant by promising an opportunity to practice environmental law, an avenue which did not exist or materialize. The fraud, which occurred prior to her termination, was not barred by the at-will employee rule, because the fraud caused the plaintiff to leave a good practice and to spend two years where she was unable to work in her specialty. The court ruled that the statute of frauds did not bar the claim, because fraudulent misrepresentation and the employment contract "are distinct and separable." *Id.* at 88. But the plaintiff failed to state a claim for negligent misrepresentation because under New York law a plaintiff can recover for negligent misrepresentation "only where the defendant owes her a fiduciary duty" and because the complaint asserted "no facts which would establish such a fiduciary duty." *Id.* at 90. Why do you think the court sought to limit liability to fiduciary relationships? Why should such a duty be required for purposes of bringing a claim for negligent misrepresentation?

2. *Liability to Third Parties under* Ultramares. In *Ultramares*, discussed in *Idaho Bank & Trust*, the court observed that when the conduct constitutes fraud or deceit, liability to foreseeable plaintiffs for economic loss has long been recognized. Why shouldn't professionals like auditors (or lawyers) be subject to liability for economic loss to particularly foreseeable plaintiffs for negligent misrepresentations? In *H. Rosenblum, Inc. v. Adler*, 461 A.2d 138 (N.J. 1983), the court reached this result, in part by recognizing that accounting firms "are presently liable to purchasers of securities in public offerings when they have misstated a material fact in the financial statements." *Id.* at 151. The court also noted that "auditors have apparently been able to obtain liability insurance covering these risks or otherwise to satisfy their financial obligations." *Id.* Moreover, it reasoned: "The imposition of a duty to foreseeable users may cause accounting firms to engage in more thorough reviews. This duty might entail setting up stricter standards and applying closer supervision, which should tend to reduce the number of instances in which liability would ensue." *Id.* at 152.

Notably, the New Jersey legislature intervened, responding to *Rosenblum*. *See, e.g.,* N.J.S.A. 2A:53A-25(b)(2)(a) (2007). Under subsection (b)(2)(a) of the statute, the accountant must know when engaged, or must thereafter agree with the client that his work will be made available to a "specifically identified" claimant "in connection with a specified transaction made by the claimant." And under subsection (b)(2)(b), the accountant must have known that the claimant "intended to rely" on his services "in connection with that specified transaction." Moreover, there can be no liability unless the accountant used words or conduct "directly expressed to the claimant" that establishes for the accountant an understanding of the claimant's intended reliance on his work. *See* N.J.S.A 2A:53A-25(b)(2)(c), discussed in *E. Dickerson & Son, Inc. v. Ernst & Young, LLP*, 361 N.J. Super. 362 (App. Div. 2003) (reviewing the effects of the legislation).

3. *The Impact of Enron.* In considering whether and how to circumscribe the liability of auditors — or other professionals — should we consider the Enron debacle and the failure of auditors to uncover the sham corporate schemes that caused employees and investors millions of dollars in losses? The Enron case is reported at *Newby v. Enron Corp.* (*In re Enron Corp. Securities, Derivative, and ERISA Litigation*), 2005 U.S. Dist. LEXIS 4494 (S.D. Tex. 2005).

Following the wake of Enron, Congress enacted legislation redefining corporate directors' responsibilities to avoid the oversight lapses that had led to massive corporate abuses. P.L. 107-204, 116 Stat. 745 (July 30, 2002), Sarbanes-Oxley Act. For more on Sarbanes-Oxley, *see* Larry Cata Backer, *In the Wake of Corporate Reform: One Year in the Life of Sarbanes-Oxley — A Critical Review Symposium Issue: Surveillance and Control: Privatizing and Nationalizing Corporate Monitoring After Sarbanes-Oxley,* 2004 MICH. ST. L. REV. 327. *See generally* William S. Lerach, *Plundering America: How American Investors Got Taken for Trillions by Corporate Insiders — The Rise of the New Corporate Kleptocracy,* 8 STAN. J. L. BUS. & FIN. 69 (2002); David Leonhardt, *The Nation: Winners, Losers and Liars: The Long Boom's Ugly Side,* N.Y. TIMES, May 12, 2002, at A1; Kurt Eichenwald, *A Higher Standard for Corporate Advice,* N.Y. TIMES, Dec. 23, 2002, at A1. *See also* Charlie Cray & Lee Drutman, *Linking Corporate Law with Progressive Social Movements: Corporations and the Public Purpose: Restoring the Balance,* 4 SEATTLE J. SOC. JUST. 305 (2005); Jacqueline Lang Weaver, *Can Energy Markets be Trusted? The Effects of the Rise and Fall of Enron on Energy Markets,* 4 HOUS. BUS. & TAX. L.J. 1, 145-149 (2004).

For further reading on third party liability for accountants, see Nanneska N. Hazel, *Depending Upon the Care of Strangers: Professionals' Duty to Third Parties for Negligent Misrepresentations,* 33 TEX. TECH. L. REV. 1073 (2002); Jay M. Feinman, *Liability of Accountants for Negligent Auditing: Doctrine, Policy, and Ideology,* 31 FLA. ST. U. L. REV. 17 (2003); Ken Brown & Ianthe Jeanne Dugan, *Sad Account: Andersen's Fall from Grace is a Tale of Greed and Miscues — Pushed to Boost Revenue, Auditors Acted as Sellers, Warred with Consultants — 'Three Pebbles and a Boulder,'* WALL ST. J., June 7, 2002, at A1.

4. *Strict Liability for Parties in Privity.* In contrast with the rule in *Idaho Bank & Trust* regarding misrepresentations affecting third parties, parties in privity of contract may be subject to strict liability solely for economic loss. *Richard v. A. Waldman & Sons,* 232 A.2d 307 (Conn. 1967). Restatement §552C provides for strict liability, limited to out-of-pocket damages, for pecuniary loss resulting from a material misrepresentation made by one and relied on by another "in a sale, rental or exchange transaction."

See also REST 2D TORTS § 402B (strict liability for false representations of product attributes); *Crocker v. Winthrop Labs.*, 514 S.W.2d 429 (Tex. 1974) (drug company liable when addiction-prone patient became dependent on drug it represented as safe as aspirin and patient consequently died); *Kirby v. B.I. Inc.*, No. 4:98-CV-1136-Y, 2003 U.S. Dist. LEXIS 16964, 2003 WL 227694 (N.D. Tex. 2003) (ankle monitor manufacturer liable for misrepresenting that any tampering with monitor would be detected and failing to communicate that if ankle unit was removed outside the detection range no one would be alerted, which resulted in monitor wearer murdering decedent).

5. *The Intersection of Misrepresentation and Contract.* The court in *Stamp v. Honest Abe Log Homes, Inc.*, 804 S.W.2d 455 (Tenn. App. 1990), said the parol evidence rule does not apply to negligent misrepresentation, as opposed to breach of contract. The misrepresentation in this case occurred during the negotiation of the sale of a log home, and concerned the competence of a recommended contractor. Where does contract end and tort begin? *See* Robert Prentice, *Contract-Based Defenses in Securities Fraud Litigation: A Behavioral Analysis*, 2003 U. ILL. L. REV. 337 (2003). *Cf. Wallis v. Smith*, 22 P.3d 682 (N.M. Ct. App. 2001) (sexual partner of child's mother brought misrepresentation claim against mother for falsely stating she was practicing birth control at the time she became pregnant; court dismissed claim in light of (1) public policy of child support; (2) its view that father's attempt to apply "traditional" contract and tort principles to this context was unconvincing).

DAVIS v. BOARD OF COUNTY COMM'RS
987 P.2d 1172 (N.M. Ct. App. 1999)

BOSSON, JUDGE.

As a matter of first impression under New Mexico common law, we decide whether an employer owes prospective employers and foreseeable third persons a duty of reasonable care not to misrepresent material facts in the course of making an employment recommendation about a present or former employee, when a substantial risk of physical harm to third persons by the employee is foreseeable. . . .

Mesilla Valley Hospital (MVH), a psychiatric hospital in Dona Ana County, employs mental health technicians for a variety of patient-care functions, such as restraining patients, taking patients on walks, and providing staff coverage at night. MVH hired Joseph "Tinie" Herrera (Herrera) as a mental health technician on January 20, 1995. Plaintiff, a young woman undergoing psychiatric therapy, was admitted to MVH as a patient on February 26 of that same year, and Herrera was assigned to work with her. Plaintiff asserts that Herrera initially managed to ingratiate himself into her confidence, and then, over a period of about two weeks, Herrera subjected Plaintiff to escalating incidents of sexual harassment, sexual assault, and other physical abuse committed under the guise of psychiatric therapy. . . .

Prior to working at MVH, Herrera was employed for some time as a detention sergeant and classification officer at the Dona Ana County Detention Center (Detention Center). According to Plaintiff, MVH's decision to hire Herrera was based in part on unqualified, favorable recommendations from Herrera's supervisors at the Detention Center, Frank Steele and Al Mochen. Steele was the director and Mochen was the captain and assistant director of the Detention Center, both of whom had supervisory authority over Herrera. The accuracy of these favorable recommendations goes to the heart of Plaintiff's suit against the County.

Of particular importance to the accuracy of the recommendations is a report authored by Steele after Herrera was investigated for allegedly sexually harassing female inmates under his authority at the Detention Center. The Detention Center first became aware of sexual complaints against Herrera in 1993, when a female inmate alleged that Herrera had sexually harassed her. Steele gave Herrera a written reprimand based on the 1993 allegation which also indicated that an additional complaint of this nature could result in Herrera's termination. Thereafter, on February 4, 1994, another female inmate filed a sexual harassment grievance against Herrera for incidents that had occurred between 1990 and 1992. She alleged that Herrera had helped her in exchange for demanding and receiving sexual favors. Although Herrera denied the allegations, he was placed on administrative leave on February 8, 1994. Steele then had the County Sheriff's Department conduct an investigation of Herrera, and on April 5, 1994, Steele authored a report of the results of that investigation.

According to Steele's report, Herrera was accused of inappropriate sexual behavior with female inmates that took various forms. The accusations included making statements with sexual overtones, and stating his desire for sex. Reportedly, Herrera received sexual favors from inmates in return for helping them. On more than one occasion, he was observed taking female inmates to his office and closing the door, allegedly for the purpose of conducting interviews. Steele's report also made specific reference to a pornographic video and condoms which were found in Herrera's desk, and he was observed with underwear belonging to a juvenile.

While not all the allegations against Herrera could be confirmed, the report concluded that Herrera's conduct and performance of duty had been "questionable" and "suspect." Accordingly, Steele recommended disciplinary action against Herrera seeking to have him suspended without pay as well as demoted and reassigned. On April 5, 1994, Steele informed Herrera that he intended to seek disciplinary action at a hearing scheduled for April 12, 1994.

On April 8, 1994, Herrera resigned rather than proceed with the scheduled hearing. Upon his resignation, Herrera asked Steele for a letter of recommendation for prospective employment. On April 11, 1994, only six days after recommending discipline, Steele wrote a positive endorsement of Herrera that omitted any reference to either the reprimand, the subsequent allegations of sexual harassment, the results of the investigation, or the recommended discipline. The letter was written on county letterhead, which Steele signed as the Detention Center administrator, and stated:

To Whom It May Concern:

This letter will introduce to you, Joseph V. Herrera. I have had the distinct pleasure of working with Tinie Herrera for the past two years. In my opinion he is an excellent employee and supervisor for the . . . Center. In developing social programs for the inmate population, he displayed considerable initiative and imagination. Tinie was instrumental in the Department's maintenance program and was involved in remodeling projects. I know that this Department will suffer for his leaving. Employees of his caliber are difficult to find. I am confident that you would find Tinie to be an excellent employee. Should you need verbal confirmation of his ability, I would deem it a pleasure to respond to any inquiries that you may have.

Sincerely,

[Signed]

. . .

On December 5, 1994, Herrera applied for employment with MVH and included Steele's letter of recommendation. According to Plaintiff, MVH called the Detention Center seeking further information about Herrera, and Mochen told MVH that Herrera was a good person and a hard worker whom he would definitely rehire. Mochen was aware of Herrera's past when he allegedly gave this verbal recommendation. Mochen denied talking to MVH. According to Plaintiff, MVH's decision to hire Herrera was based in part on these unqualified, favorable recommendations from Steele and Mochen, an allegation which, as yet, remains unproven, and as with other causation issues, remains part of Plaintiff's burden to prove at trial. . . .

The County argues that the law does not require employers to divulge their reasons for an employee's termination or resignation and that it would be against public policy to impose such a duty, especially in favor of an unknown third party outside the line of communication with a prospective employer. Plaintiff agrees that employers may remain silent if they wish. . . . However, once employers elect to give references and offer recommendations, then, according to Plaintiff, employers have a common-law duty to exercise reasonable care so as not to misrepresent an employee's record when, to do so, would create a foreseeable risk of physical injury to third parties.

Thus, two initial questions are before this Court. First, we must consider whether employers who do not remain silent, those electing to recommend employees, owe any such duty of reasonable care in regard to what they say and how they say it. If so, then we must decide whether such employers owe a duty of care to third parties as well as the prospective employer to whom the recommendation is given. We limit our discussion to the present circumstances involving a substantial, foreseeable risk of physical harm to third parties by the employee if reasonable care is not exercised about what is said when an employer elects to make an unqualified recommendation, and we decide that employers do owe such a duty to third parties.

We begin with general principles. As our Supreme Court has succinctly stated, "Policy determines duty." *Torres v. State*, 894 P.2d 386, 389 (N. Mex.

1995). Based on considerations of policy, the court determines whether a defendant owes a duty of care to a class of persons with respect to a particular type of risk of harm. . . .

As an accepted legal proposition, there is generally no affirmative duty to prevent criminal acts by a third party in the absence of some special relationship or statutory duty. However, it is also a general proposition that "'every person has a duty to exercise ordinary care for the safety of others[,]'" when that person does choose to act. *Lerma ex rel. Lerma v. State Highway Dep't*, 117 N.M. 782, 784, 877 P.2d 1085, 1087 (1994). . . .

Few jurisdictions have directly addressed duty in the context of misleading employer references. Of those few, several have concluded that, although employers generally may not have an affirmative duty to disclose negative information about employees, employers may be held liable for negligent misrepresentations, or misleading half-truths, about those employees who present a foreseeable risk of physical harm to others, and the duty of care extends to third parties foreseeably at risk.

The recent California Supreme Court opinion in *Randi W.*, 929 P.2d 582 (Cal. 1997), is closely analogous and provides persuasive guidance for our case. In *Randi W.*, various officials at different school districts gave gratuitous recommendations "containing unreserved and unconditional praise" of a former employee, despite their knowledge of complaints involving sexual misconduct at his prior employment. The employee was subsequently hired as a vice-principal where he was accused of sexually assaulting a thirteen-year-old student. A unanimous court adopted Sections 310 and 311 of the Restatement, holding that the recommending school officials owed a duty of care to third-party students "not to misrepresent the facts in describing the qualifications and character of a former employee, if making these misrepresentations would present a substantial, foreseeable risk of physical injury to the third persons." *Randi W.*, 60 Cal. Rptr. 2d 263, 929 P.2d at 591. "Having volunteered this information, defendants were obliged to complete the picture by disclosing material facts regarding charges and complaints of [the teacher]'s sexual improprieties." *Id.*

. . . Comments c and d of Section 310 of the Restatement involving liability to third persons are incorporated into Section 311. *See* § 311 cmt. f. Section 311 states:

Negligent Misrepresentation Involving Risk of Physical Harm

(1) One who negligently gives false information to another is subject to liability for physical harm caused by action taken by the other in reasonable reliance upon such information, where such harm results

  (a) to the other, or

  (b) to such third persons as the actor should expect to be put in peril by the action taken.

(2) Such negligence may consist of failure to exercise reasonable care

  (a) in ascertaining the accuracy of the information, or

  (b) in the manner in which it is communicated.

The rule of Section 311 extends to anyone undertaking to give information to a person who "knows or should realize that the safety of the person of [sic] others may depend upon the accuracy of the information." *Id.* § 311 cmt. b; *see also id.* § 310. . . . A misrepresentation under Section 311 may breach a duty of care owed not only to the person to whom it is addressed, and whose conduct it is intended to influence, but also a duty of care owed to third parties whom the speaker should recognize as likely to be imperiled by action taken in reliance upon the misrepresentation. *See id.* § 310 cmt. c.

In the context of this case, we accept the principles set forth in Section 311, as they apply to an employer's duty of care in making employment references and the circumstances under which that duty extends to foreseeable third parties. We find those principles harmonious with the general propositions of New Mexico law that govern duty of care and duty to third parties. Cases cited by the County for a narrower rule are easily distinguished or unpersuasive. . . .

Applying the foregoing principles to the case before us, we see nothing in the facts as alleged that would make the assault and battery suffered by Plaintiff either too remote as a matter of policy or unforeseeable as a matter of law. The County's agents could have remained silent in response to requests for information about Herrera. Instead, they elected to recommend him in a manner distorted by misrepresentations and half-truths. The employment recommendations of Steele and Mochen provided unqualified praise of Herrera as an excellent employee of a caliber that is "difficult to find," and yet they omitted disciplinary action both taken and recommended by these same officers against Herrera. The disciplinary action came as a result of allegations, a subsequent investigation, and a resulting report in which Steele was directly involved, which constitutes far more than mere gossip or innuendo. The information in the report concerned abuse of power and sexual abuse of women who were directly under Herrera's control at the Detention Center which bears a direct correlation to the potential risks female patients would incur if they were placed under Herrera's control at MVH. The parallels are compelling. We are not persuaded that reasonable people, who had the information possessed by Steele and Mochen, could not have foreseen potential victims like Plaintiff, and could not have foreseen how the omission of objective information, like Steele's report and the disciplinary actions taken, would not pose a threat of physical harm to persons like plaintiff. We emphasize that ultimately the question of foreseeability will be for the jury to decide. We only decline to say categorically that such injuries to people like Plaintiff are unforeseeable as a matter of law. . . .

Thus, in applying the principles set forth in Section 311 of the Restatement, we determine that Steele and Mochen did owe a duty of care, once they elected to make employment recommendations for Herrera, in regard to what they said and what they omitted from their references. We also conclude that such a duty was owed to plaintiff as a third-party victim, under the circumstances of this case. We intend our holding to be narrow. We decline to speculate on how different facts and circumstances, such as the lapse of time between the referral and the assault, might affect this duty, and where "social policy" might compel us "to draw the line against otherwise unlimited liability." *Solon*, 829 P.2d at 648, 652. Plaintiff has a claim pursuant to that duty unless the County can persuade us by additional arguments that the duty of care should not apply in this case. . . .

The County argues that plaintiff's claim is not actionable because of plaintiff's lack of reliance. It is true, of course, that Steele and Mochen never represented any information about Herrera directly to Plaintiff and, of course, plaintiff could not have relied on the statements made to MVH, that Herrera was an "excellent employee," of which she was not aware. However, plaintiff's lack of reliance is immaterial.

A victim of physical violence need not rely on the negligent misrepresentation, or even be a party to it, as long as the injury is a result of the recipient's reliance on the employer's misrepresentation. *See* Restatement, *supra* §§ 310 cmt. c, 311 cmt. d, illus 8 & 324A. . . . Plaintiff has presented evidence to support the allegation, if found credible by a jury, that her injury resulted from MVH's reliance on the misleading employee reference from the County's supervisory employees, and this is sufficient to present an actionable claim under these circumstances. . . .

The County further argues that, taken literally, Steele and Mochen did not misrepresent anything to MVH, because MVH never specifically asked for the reasons for Herrera's resignation. However, "if the [employer] does speak, he must disclose enough to prevent his words from being misleading." We are not persuaded by the County's position on this point. "In other words, half of the truth may obviously amount to a lie, if it is understood to be the whole." [Prosser and Keeton on the law of Torts §106, at 738.]

Finally, the County argues that public policy should dissuade us from imposing such a duty on employers. According to the County, a duty of accurate representation will become an invitation to litigate. In our view, however, we have sufficiently restricted the duty so as not to encourage extensive litigation. We do, however, find intriguing another of the County's policy arguments that any expansion of a tort duty will have a chilling effect on employer willingness to give references, whether good or bad, and society's interest in reliable information will suffer.

We agree with the County that public policy supports full and accurate disclosure of non-confidential information by employers. . . . Full and accurate disclosure regarding employees with violent and dangerous propensities promotes a safe work environment, and a productive workforce benefits both employees and employers. The past several years have seen considerable academic commentary embracing this same policy of encouraging full and accurate disclosure by employers. One incentive suggested to encourage employer disclosure is legislation to shield employers from employee defamation lawsuits when making a good-faith effort to produce accurate information about their former employees.

New Mexico's common law reflects just such a policy of encouraging employer disclosure by recognizing a "qualified or conditional privilege [against a defamation claim] to make statements about its employee or former employee if for a proper purpose and to one having a legitimate interest in the statements." *Baker v. Bhajan*, 117 N.M. 278, 282, 871 P.2d 374, 378 (1994). . . .

We acknowledge that, at the margins, the common-law duty we recognize in this opinion may discourage some employment referrals. But that impact should be minimal. The duty not to misrepresent applies only in cases of foreseeable physical harm. The vast majority of cases will involve pejorative information in the hands of an employer that does not create a risk of foreseeable physical harm and accordingly does not implicate this duty to disclose. When physical harm by the employee is foreseeable, the employer who discloses will be protected against defamation by the qualified privilege. However, even if some overly cautious employers are deterred unnecessarily from volunteering helpful information and elect to remain silent, we determine that silence may be preferable under these circumstances to what [occurred] in this case. In the face of silence from a former employer, the prospective employer can still conduct its own investigation; silence renders the employer no worse off. In contrast, the prospective employer who is misled may relax its own guard; it may not investigate as thoroughly, and may end up worse off than if it had received no information at all. On balance, therefore, the policy gains of imposing a duty not to misrepresent under these limited circumstances outweigh the potential consequences of inhibiting employer disclosure. . . .

NOTES

1. *Employers' Duty to Disclose and the Restatement (Second) of Torts §311.* In *Richland School District v. Mabton School District*, 45 P.3d 580 (Wash. Ct. App. 2002), the Washington court of appeals did not adopt REST. 2D TORTS § 311 as a basis for negligent misrepresentation. Mabton School District wrote a letter of recommendation for one of its former janitors, failing to mention his history of reprimands or criminal charges for child molestation. Richland School District hired the janitor, but later fired him for making false statements on his employment application. Richland then sued Mabton for damages due to Mabton's negligent misrepresentation. Specifically, Richland claimed that Mabton owed them a duty to make accurate recommendations for its former employee, especially when those recommendations were for potential employment around children. In affirming the trial court's grant of summary judgment for the defendant school district Mabton, the court of appeals stated that, unlike the plaintiffs in *Davis, supra*, and *Randi W.* (cited in *Davis*), "Richland cannot show that Mabton's alleged misrepresentations presented a substantial, foreseeable risk of physical injury or that any person suffered physical harm." 45 P.3d at 587.

2. *Tension of Limited Duty/Defamation (Shades of* Tarasoff*).* Cases involving duties to third parties often arise in the education context. Recently, in *Fishpaw v. Francisco*, No. 05AP-861, 2006 Ohio App. LEXIS 3402, 2006 Ohio 3450 (Ohio App. 2006), the plaintiff parents brought suit against a day care provider and a day care provider referral service after the parents' infant was abused by the day care provider. The court rejected the parents' claim for negligent misrepresentation against the day care referral service, holding that it owed no cognizable legal duty to the parents.

3. *More on Duty/Defamation.* For more on the complex relationship between an employer's duty of accurate representation, employer willingness to write recommendations, and employers' fear of defamation suits, see Connie Swemba, *"To Tell the Truth, the Whole Truth, and Nothing But the Truth":* *Employment References and Tort Liability*, 33 U. Tol. L. Rev. 847 (2002). How can this tension be resolved? Consider your answer from law and economics and social justice perspectives.

E.   APPROPRIATION OF INTANGIBLE PROPERTY IN GENERAL

MIDLER v. FORD MOTOR CO.
849 F.2d 460 (9th Cir. 1988)

Noonan, Circuit Judge.

This case centers on the protectibility of the voice of a celebrated chanteuse from commercial exploitation without her consent. Ford Motor Company and its advertising agency, Young & Rubicam, Inc., in 1985 advertised the Ford Lincoln Mercury with a series of nineteen 30 or 60 second television commercials in what the agency called "The Yuppie Campaign." The aim was to make an emotional connection with Yuppies, bringing back memories of when they were in college. Different popular songs of the seventies were sung on each commercial. The agency tried to get "the original people," that is, the singers who had popularized the songs, to sing them. Failing in that endeavor in ten cases the agency had the songs sung by "sound alikes." Bette Midler, the plaintiff and appellant here, was done by a sound alike.

Midler is a nationally known actress and singer. She won a Grammy as early as 1973 as the Best New Artist of that year. Records made by her since then have gone Platinum and Gold. She was nominated in 1979 for an Academy award for Best Female Actress in *The Rose*, in which she portrayed a pop singer. *Newsweek*, in its June 30, 1986 issue described her as an "outrageously original singer/comedian." *Time* hailed her in its March 2, 1987 issue as "a legend" and "the most dynamic and poignant singer-actress of her time."

When Young & Rubicam was preparing the Yuppie Campaign it presented the commercial to its client by playing an edited version of Midler singing "Do You Want To Dance," taken from the 1973 Midler album, "The Divine Miss M." After the client accepted the idea and form of the commercial, the agency contacted Midler's manager, Jerry Edelstein. The conversation went as follows: "Hello, I am Craig Hazen from Young and Rubicam. I am calling you to find out if Bette Midler would be interested in doing . . . ?" Edelstein: "Is it a commercial?" "Yes." "We are not interested."

Undeterred, Young & Rubicam sought out Ula Hedwig whom it knew to have been as one of "the Harlettes," a backup singer for Midler for ten years. Hedwig was told by Young & Rubicam that "they wanted someone who could sound like Bette Midler's recording of [Do You Want To Dance]." She was asked to make a "demo" tape of the song if she was interested. She made an a cappella demo and got the job.

At the direction of Young & Rubicam, Hedwig then made a record for the commercial. The Midler record of "Do You Want To Dance" was first played to her. She was told to "sound as much as possible like the Bette Midler record," leaving out only a few "aahs" unsuitable for the commercial. Hedwig imitated Midler to the best of her ability.

After the commercial was aired Midler was told by "a number of people" that it "sounded exactly" like her record of "Do You Want To Dance." Hedwig was told by "many personal friends" that they thought it was Midler singing the commercial. . . .

Neither the name nor the picture of Midler was used in the commercial; Young & Rubicam had a license from the copyright holder to use the song. At issue in this case is only the protection of Midler's voice. The district court described the defendants' conduct as that "of the average thief." They decided, "If we can't buy it, we'll take it." The court nonetheless believed there was no legal principle preventing imitation of Midler's voice and so gave summary judgment for the defendants. Midler appeals.

The First Amendment protects much of what the media do in the reproduction of likenesses or sounds. A primary value is freedom of speech and press. The purpose of the media's use of a person's identity is central. If the purpose is "informative or cultural" the use is immune; "if it serves no such function but merely exploits the individual portrayed, immunity will not be granted." Felcher and Rubin, "Privacy, Publicity and the Portrayal of Real People by the Media," 88 Yale L.J. 1577 1596 (1979). Moreover, federal copyright law preempts much of the area. "Mere imitation of a recorded performance would not constitute a copyright infringement even where one performer deliberately sets out to simulate another's performance as exactly as possible." Notes of Committee on the Judiciary, 17 U.S.C.A. § 114(b). It is in the context of these First Amendment and federal copyright distinctions that we address the present appeal.

Nancy Sinatra once sued Goodyear Tire and Rubber Company on the basis of an advertising campaign by Young & Rubicam featuring "These Boots Are Made For Walkin'," a song closely identified with her; the female singers of the commercial were alleged to have imitated her voice and style and to have dressed and looked like her. The basis of Nancy Sinatra's complaint was unfair competition; she claimed that the song and the arrangement had acquired "a secondary meaning" which, under California law, was protectable. This court noted that the defendants "had paid a very substantial sum to the copyright proprietor to obtain the license for the use of the song and all of its arrangements." To give Sinatra damages for their use of the song would clash with federal copyright law. Summary judgment for the defendants was affirmed. *Sinatra v. Goodyear Tire & Rubber Co.*, 435 F.2d 711, 717–718 (9th Cir. 1970). If Midler were claiming a secondary meaning to "Do You Want To Dance" or seeking to prevent the defendants from using that song, she would fail like Sinatra. But that is not this case. Midler does not seek damages for Ford's use of "Do You Want To Dance," and thus her claim is not preempted by federal copyright law. Copyright protects "original works of authorship fixed in any tangible medium of expression." 17 U.S.C. § 102(a). A voice is not copyrightable.

The sounds are not "fixed." What is put forward as protectable here is more personal than any work of authorship.

Bert Lahr once sued Adell Chemical Co. for selling Lestoil by means of a commercial in which an imitation of Lahr's voice accompanied a cartoon of a duck. Lahr alleged that his style of vocal delivery was distinctive in pitch, accent, inflection, and sounds. The First Circuit held that Lahr had stated a cause of action for unfair competition, that it could be found "that defendant's conduct saturated plaintiff's audience, curtailing his market." *Lahr v. Adell Chemical Co.*, 300 F.2d 256, 259 (1st Cir. 1962). That case is more like this one. But we do not find unfair competition here. One-minute commercials of the sort the defendants put on would not have saturated Midler's audience and curtailed her market. Midler did not do television commercials. The defendants were not in competition with her.

California Civil Code section 3344 is also of no aid to Midler. The statute affords damages to a person injured by another who uses the person's "name, voice, signature, photograph or likeness, in any manner." The defendants did not use Midler's name or anything else whose use is prohibited by the statute. The voice they used was Hedwig's, not hers. The term "likeness" refers to a visual image not a vocal imitation. The statute, however, does not preclude Midler from pursuing any cause of action she may have at common law; the statute itself implies that such common law causes of action do exist because it says its remedies are merely "cumulative."

The companion statute protecting the use of a deceased person's name, voice, signature, photograph or likeness states that the rights it recognizes are "property rights." *Id.* § 990(b). By analogy the common law rights are also property rights. Appropriation of such common law rights is a tort in California. *Motschenbacher v. R.J. Reynolds Tobacco Co.*, 498 F.2d 821 (9th Cir. 1974). In that case what the defendants used in their television commercial for Winston cigarettes was a photograph of a famous professional racing driver's racing car. The number of the car was changed and a wing-like device known as a "spoiler" was attached to the car; the car's features of white pinpointing, an oval medallion, and solid red coloring were retained. The driver, Lothar Motschenbacher, was in the car but his features were not visible. Some persons, viewing the commercial, correctly inferred that the car was his and that he was in the car and was therefore endorsing the product. The defendants were held to have invaded a "proprietary interest" of Motschenbacher in his own identity.

Midler's case is different from Motschenbacher's. He and his car were physically used by the tobacco company's ad; he made part of his living out of giving commercial endorsements. But, as Judge Koelsch expressed it in *Motschenbacher*, California will recognize an injury from "an appropriation of the attributes of one's identity." It was irrelevant that Motschenbacher could not be identified in the ad. The ad suggested that it was he. The ad did so by emphasizing signs or symbols associated with him. In the same way the defendants here used an imitation to convey the impression that Midler was singing for them.

Why did the defendants ask Midler to sing if her voice was not of value to them? Why did they studiously acquire the services of a sound-alike and instruct her to imitate Midler if Midler's voice was not of value to them? What they sought was an attribute of Midler's identity. Its value was what the market would have paid for Midler to have sung the commercial in person.

. . . A voice is as distinctive and personal as a face. The human voice is one of the most palpable ways identity is manifested. We are all aware that a friend is at once known by a few words on the phone. At a philosophical level it has been observed that with the sound of a voice, "the other stands before me." D. Ihde, *Listening and Voice* 77 (1976). A fortiori, these observations hold true of singing, especially singing by a singer of renown. The singer manifests herself in the song. To impersonate her voice is to pirate her identity.

We need not and do not go so far as to hold that every imitation of a voice to advertise merchandise is actionable. We hold only that when a distinctive voice of a professional singer is widely known and is deliberately imitated in order to sell a product, the sellers have appropriated what is not theirs and have committed a tort in California. Midler has made a showing, sufficient to defeat summary judgment, that the defendants here for their own profit in selling their product did appropriate part of her identity.

NOTES

1. *Evaluating Damages for Appropriation.* On remand, a jury awarded Bette Midler $400,000. Note, 37 WAYNE L. REV. 1683, 1686 (1991). The verdict was affirmed on appeal, 944 F.2d 909 (9th Cir. 1991), *cert. denied, Young & Rubican, Inc. v. Midler,* 503 U.S. 951 (1992). How do you think the damages were proven? Why would a celebrity see the suit as worth the inevitable costs of litigating? Another voice appropriations case arose in *Waits v. Frito-Lay, Inc.,* 978 F.2d 1093 (9th Cir. 1992), *cert. denied, Frito Lay, Inc. v. Waits,* 506 U.S. 1080 (1993). This suit involved Tom Waits, also a popular singer with a distinctive gravely voice and singing style, who was vociferous about his unwillingness to participate in product commercials. Applying *Midler,* the court upheld a jury verdict for $2.5 million, consisting of $100,000 for the fair market value of plaintiff's services, $200,000 for "injury to his peace, happiness and feelings," $75,000 for injury to "goodwill, professional standing and future publicity value," $2 million in punitive damages, and attorneys' fees.

2. *Secondary Meaning vs. Right of Publicity.* In *Carson v. Here's Johnny Portable Toilets, Inc.,* 698 F.2d 831 (6th Cir. 1983), Johnny Carson, the television entertainer whose introduction on his show each weeknight for nearly twenty years had been "Here's Johnny," sued the defendant portable toilet company alleging unfair competition under §43(a) of the Lanham Act, 15 U.S.C. §1125(a), and invasion of privacy and publicity rights. The appellate court agreed with the trial court's determination that Carson had failed to satisfy the "likelihood of confusion test" under the Lanham Act. Citing *Frisch's Restaurants, Inc. v. Elby's Big Boy, Inc.,* 670 F.2d 642 (6th Cir. 1982), the court recognized eight factors to be balanced in determining whether a likelihood of confusion exists among consumers of goods involved in a §43(a) action: (1) strength of the plaintiff's mark; (2) relatedness of the goods; (3) similarity of the marks; (4) evidence of actual confusion; (5) marketing channels used;

(6) likely degree of purchaser care; (7) defendant's intent in selecting the mark; and (8) likelihood of expansion of the product lines.

The district court had noted that "Here's Johnny" was not such a strong mark that its use for other goods should be entirely foreclosed. Moreover, although the defendant had intended to capitalize on the phrase popularized by Carson, it had not intended to deceive the public into believing Carson was connected with the product. In addition, the court found little evidence of actual confusion and no evidence that defendant's use of the phrase had damaged plaintiff. Having rejected the Lanham Act claim, the court also concluded that the facts did not amount to an invasion of any of the interests protected by the right of privacy. However, the court reversed the district court's rejection of the right of publicity allegation, stating "a celebrity has a protected pecuniary interest in the commercial exploitation of his identity. If the celebrity's identity is commercially exploited, there has been an invasion of his right whether or not his "name or likeness" is used. Carson's identity may be exploited even if his name, John W. Carson, or his picture is not used." *Id.* at 835.

What is the relationship between the interest being protected under the right of privacy in *Carson* and the "secondary meaning" doctrine which in *Midler* was held to conflict with federal copyright law? Carson had never registered "Here's Johnny" as a trademark.

3. *Common Law Copyright.* In *Desny v. Wilder*, 299 P.2d 257 (Cal. 1956), plaintiff sought compensation from Billy Wilder, mogul movie producer and director, contending that a story plot based in part on an actual event which plaintiff had researched, constructed, and tried to pitch to Wilder through Wilder's secretary became the basis of a film. The court found the claim cognizable, noting:

> An idea is usually not regarded as property, because all sentient beings may conceive and evolve ideas throughout the gamut of their powers of cerebration and because our concept of property implies something which may be owned and possessed to the exclusion of all other persons . . . The principles above stated do not, however, lead to the conclusion that ideas cannot be a subject of contract. . . . Obviously the defendants here used someone's script in preparing and producing their photoplay. That script must have had value to them [and] it closely resembles plaintiff's synopsis. Ergo, plaintiff's synopsis appears to be a valuable literary composition. Defendants had an unassailable right to have their own employe[e]s conduct the research . . . and prepare a story based on those facts and to translate it into a script for the play. But equally unassailable . . . is plaintiff's position that defendants had no right — except by purchase on the terms he offered — to acquire and use the synopsis prepared by him.

Id. at 265-72.

See also Levin v. Gap, Inc., 1998 U.S. Dist. LEXIS 20378 (S.D.N.Y. Dec. 30, 1998) (plaintiff's property rights were not violated after he submitted an idea for a Gap Kids clothing line for Barbie dolls which Gap rejected, but began manufacturing a Gap Barbie doll three years later); *Metro-Goldwyn Mayer Studios Inc. v. Grokster*, 545 U.S. 913 (2005) (free software distributors liable for third-party infringement).

4. *The First-Sale Doctrine.* In *Allison v. Vintage Sports Plaques*, 136 F.3d 1443 (11th Cir. 1998), well known sports persons, Hershiser and Allison, were unsuccessful in seeking damages from Vintage Sports for appropriation of their names and likenesses. Defendant purchased trading cards from licensed card manufacturers and distributors and, without altering the cards in any way, framed them, labeling each plaque with an identification plate bearing the name of the player or team represented. In addition to the mounted trading card, some of the plaques featured a clock with a sports motif. Vintage marketed each plaque as a "Limited Edition" and an "Authentic Collectible." Vintage had no licensing agreement that granted the right to use the appellants' names or likenesses for commercial purposes and never paid a royalty or commission, though presumably the plaintiffs had licensing agreements, royalties from the card manufacturers and distributors for the initial sale of the cards to Vintage.

The court concluded that the first-sale doctrine protected defendant's use of these playing cards. The first-sale doctrine provides that once the holder of an intellectual property right consents to the sale of copies of his work, he may not thereafter exercise the distribution right with respect to such copies. This doctrine applies to copyright, patent, and trademark law, as well as to the rights of publicity, and would apply in this case since the court concluded that Vintage's plaques are merely the cards themselves repackaged, rather than products separate and distinct from the trading cards they incorporate. It believed it to be "unlikely that anyone would purchase one of Vintage's plaques for any reason other than to obtain a display of the mounted cards themselves." *Id.* at 1451. What about the cards with the clocks? Suppose the pictures were given to Vintage Sports, or Vintage Sports found them. Would the first-sale doctrine still apply? *See Almeida v. Amazon.com, Inc.*, 456 F.3d 1316 (11th Cir. 2006) (the court rejected plaintiff's contention that permission to use her photograph did not extend to its use on defendant's website in furtherance of its book sales of a second edition; defendant functioned as an Internet equivalent to traditional bookstore and did not use plaintiff's image for commercial purpose of "directly promoting a product or service" in violation of Florida's statutory provisions relating to misappropriation with felonious intent).

5. *The Right of Publicity and Parody.* Because of popular interest in professional sports, sports figures are attractive subjects for enterprising commercial ventures and parodies. Should their highly visible profiles and newsworthiness leave them without recourse if they prefer to define how they are depicted? We will discuss speech-related considerations for public figures more generally in a later part of this chapter. As for a right of publicity, compare *Montana v. San Jose Mercury News, Inc.*, 40 Cal. Rptr. 2d 639 (Cal. App. 1995) (posters drawn from news accounts of football player Montana's feats in Super Bowl XXIII and XXIV were constitutionally protected speech, precluding claim of appropriation of name and likeness) with e.g., *Abdul-Jabbar v. GMC*, 85 F.3d 407 (9th Cir. 1996) (basketball star sued alleging his likeness was improperly used in defendant's ad without his consent, in violation of common-law right of publicity). In the *Abdul-Jabbar* case, the defendant had used Abdul-Jabbar's formerly used name in a television advertisement aired during a nationally televised basketball tournament. The court concluded that a person's interest in a former name continues and its use requires consent. Abdul-

Jabbar's basketball record at the time he used the other name was not so newsworthy as to be automatically privileged.

F. APPROPRIATION OF TRADE SECRETS

BRIEFING.COM v. JONES
126 P.3d 928 (Wyo. 2006)

VOIGT, JUSTICE.

Plaintiff, Briefing.com, is a California corporation that provides analysis of stock and fixed income markets for use by professional and individual investors. Plaintiff, Richard Green, is the President of Briefing.com and is a member of Briefing.com's board of directors. The Briefing.com website was started in 1995. Mr. Green owns approximately 51 percent of Briefing.com's outstanding shares and is Briefing.com's majority shareholder.

StreetAccount LLC is a Wyoming limited liability company whose members include defendants Gregory Jones and Cynthia Dietzmann. Plaintiffs allege that Defendant StreetAccount LLC is [a] direct competitor of Briefing.com in the internet-based market analysis industry. Defendants Jones and Dietzmann are citizens of the State of Wyoming. Mr. Jones and Ms. Dietzmann currently own approximately 10 percent and 1.1 percent, respectively, of the outstanding shares of Briefing.com.

Mr. Jones and Ms. Dietzmann are former employees of Briefing.com. While employed with Briefing.com, they worked in the company's Jackson, Wyoming office. Ms. Dietzmann was employed by Briefing.com for approximately seven years as a market analyst until her resignation in or about late February or early March 2003. Mr. Jones was employed by Briefing.com from approximately November 1996 through late February or early March 2003. Plaintiffs allege that in addition to being an employee of Briefing.com, Mr. Jones was also a member of Briefing.com's board of directors for approximately six years until his resignation from that position in April 2003.

Plaintiffs allege that, based on their former positions with Briefing.com, Defendants . . . knew of Briefing.com's work and proprietary studies in developing Briefing.com's themes and designs. More specifically, Plaintiffs allege that, as employees . . . Jones and Dietzmann had inside access to certain of the company's confidential information and data regarding the internet-based market analysis trade.

Plaintiffs allege that while working for Briefing.com, Ms. Dietzmann developed a list of market contacts that Briefing.com used to obtain market information that could be displayed on its website [and] that such market contact information [was] developed by Ms. Dietzmann . . . pursuant to her employment with Briefing.com, and is therefore the sole property of Briefing.com [which] Plaintiffs allege . . . Ms. Dietzmann did not return . . . to the company, either before or after her resignation. As a result, Plaintiffs allege that Defendants misappropriated certain of Briefing.com's trade secrets and/or confidential information in order to form and operate a competing business.

... Plaintiffs asserted a common-law cause of action against Defendants for misappropriation of trade secrets and/or confidential information. . . . Defendants moved to dismiss Count V of the SAC on the grounds that Wyoming law does not recognize a cause of action for misappropriation of trade secrets. Alternatively, Defendants requested that the issue be certified to the Wyoming Supreme Court for a determination as to whether such a cause of actions [sic] exists under Wyoming law. . . .

. . . A cause of action for misuse of trade secrets was first recognized by Roman law, and was well known to the common law. Trade secret laws have their genesis in society's need to encourage innovation and to foster standards of trust in the marketplace:

> The basis of the law as to trade secrets, apart from breach of contract, is the abuse of confidence or an impropriety in the means of procurement of information. Trade secrets are protected to encourage the development of new inventions, processes, and business techniques, to protect against breaches of faith and the use of improper methods to obtain information, and to maintain standards of loyalty and trust in the business community. An employee owes a duty of fidelity to an employer while the worker is employed by that employer, even where the employment is at will and even though the worker has not signed an agreement not to use trade secrets acquired by the employee; therefore, an employee will be restrained from using the employer's trade secrets learned during employment. Moreover, one who knowingly and for his or her own interests helps employees to violate their duty of fidelity and trust to their employer with respect to trade secrets is also liable to the employer, and will be restrained from use of the confidential information.

54A Am.Jur.2d *Monopolies, Restraints of Trade, and Unfair Trade Practices* § 1114 (1996 and Supp. 2005). At the same time, however, trade secret law has recognized a counterbalancing need for free competition:

> It has been said that the law of trade secrets is the result of balancing two conflicting elements essential to society. On the one hand, there is a strong policy favoring free competition, thus entitling an employee to use the skill and knowledge of his trade or profession which he has learned in the course of his employment, for the benefit of himself and the public, if he does not violate a contractual or fiduciary obligation in doing so. On the other hand, in order to promote the progress of science and the useful arts, the law provides certain protections to an originator, one of these being the law protecting trade secrets.

P. Guthrie, Annotation, Employee's Duty, in Absence of Express Contract, Not to Disclose or Use in New Employment Special Skills or Techniques Acquired in Earlier Employment, 30 A.L.R.3d 631, § 2 at 636 (1970 and Supp. 2005). . . .

Today, there are three primary manifestations of trade secret law. The first is the formulation of the common law tort set forth in [RESTAT. TORTS, § 757 at 1–2 (1939)]:

§ 757. Liability for Disclosure or Use of Another's Trade Secret-General Principle.

One who discloses or uses another's trade secret, without a privilege to do so, is liable to the other if

(a) he discovered the secret by improper means, or

(b) his disclosure or use constitutes a breach of confidence reposed in him by the other in disclosing the secret to him, or

(c) he learned the secret from a third person with notice of the facts that it was a secret and that the third person discovered it by improper means or that the third person's disclosure of it was otherwise a breach of his duty to the other, or

(d) he learned the secret with notice of the facts that it was a secret and that its disclosure was made to him by mistake.

This version of the common law tort has been supplanted by sections now found in the Restatement (Third) of Unfair Competition (1995). The authors of the Restatement explain that change as follows:

> Part 1 of the Division covered Interference by Trade Practices and included Chapters 34 (The Privilege to Engage in Business), 35 (Confusion of Source) and 36 (Miscellaneous Trade Practices). The rules relating to liability for harm caused by unfair trade practices developed doctrinally from established principles in the law of Torts, and for this reason the decision was made that it was appropriate to include these legal areas in the Restatement of Torts, despite the fact that the fields of Unfair Competition and Trade Regulation were rapidly developing into independent bodies of law with diminishing reliance upon the traditional principles of Tort law. In the more than 40 years since that decision was initially made, the influence of Tort law has continued to decrease, so that it is now largely of historical interest and the law of Unfair Competition and Trade Regulation is no more dependent upon Tort law than it is on many other general fields of the law and upon broad statutory developments, particularly at the federal level. The Council formally reached the decision that these chapters no longer belong in the Restatement of Torts, and they are omitted from this Second Restatement. . . .

4 Restatement (Second) of Torts, Division Nine, Introductory Note at 1–2 (1979).

The commentary accompanying the trade secret provisions now found in the Restatement (Third) of Unfair Competition make it clear that development of these provisions was not meant to be a "sea change" in the law, but was meant to accommodate the law to developments in the commercial world, especially those wrought by the increased mobility of employees during the industrial revolution. *See* Restatement (Third) of Unfair Competition, *supra,* at 425–426. The prohibition against misuse of trade secrets remains a common law cause of action, formulated through case decision, just as before. These new sections provide as follows:

§ 39. Definition of Trade Secret

A trade secret is any information that can be used in the operation of a business or other enterprise and that is sufficiently valuable and secret to afford an actual or potential economic advantage over others.

§ 40. Appropriation of Trade Secrets

One is subject to liability for the appropriation of another's trade secret if:

(a) the actor acquires by means that are improper under the rule stated in § 43 information that the actor knows or has reason to know is the other's trade secret; or

(b) the actor uses or discloses the other's trade secret without the other's consent and, at the time of the use or disclosure,

(1) the actor knows or has reason to know that the information is a trade secret that the actor acquired under circumstances creating a duty of confidence owed by the actor to the other under the rule stated in § 41; or

(2) the actor knows or has reason to know that the information is a trade secret that the actor acquired by means that are improper under the rule stated in § 43; or

(3) the actor knows or has reason to know that the information is a trade secret that the actor acquired from or through a person who acquired it by means that are improper under the rule stated in § 43 or whose disclosure of the trade secret constituted a breach of a duty of confidence owed to the other under the rule stated in § 41; or

(4) the actor knows or has reason to know that the information is a trade secret that the actor acquired through an accident or mistake, unless the acquisition was the result of the other's failure to take reasonable precautions to maintain the secrecy of the information.

§ 41. Duty of Confidence

A person to whom a trade secret has been disclosed owes a duty of confidence to the owner of the trade secret for purposes of the rule stated in § 40 if:

(a) the person made an express promise of confidentiality prior to the disclosure of the trade secret; or

(b) the trade secret was disclosed to the person under circumstances in which the relationship between the parties to the disclosure or the other facts surrounding the disclosure justify the conclusions that, at the time of the disclosure,

(1) the person knew or had reason to know that the disclosure was intended to be in confidence, and

(2) the other party to the disclosure was reasonable in inferring that the person consented to an obligation of confidentiality.

§42. Breach of Confidence by Employees

An employee or former employee who uses or discloses a trade secret owned by the employer or former employer in breach of a duty of confidence is subject to liability for appropriation of the trade secret under the rule stated in §40.

§43. Improper Acquisition of Trade Secrets

"Improper" means of acquiring another's trade secret under the rule stated in §40 include theft, fraud, unauthorized interception of communications, inducement of or knowing participation in a breach of confidence, and other means either wrongful in themselves or wrongful under the circumstances of the case. Independent discovery and analysis of publicly available products or information are not improper means of acquisition.

§44. Injunctions: Appropriation of Trade Secrets

(1) If appropriate under the rule stated in Subsection (2), injunctive relief may be awarded to prevent a continuing or threatened appropriation of another's trade secret by one who is subject to liability under the rule stated in §40.

(2) The appropriateness and scope of injunctive relief depend upon a comparative appraisal of all the factors of the case, including the following primary factors:

(a) the nature of the interest to be protected;

(b) the nature and extent of the appropriation;

(c) the relative adequacy to the plaintiff of an injunction and of other remedies;

(d) the relative harm likely to result to the legitimate interests of the defendant if an injunction is granted and to the legitimate interests of the plaintiff if an injunction is denied;

(e) the interests of third persons and of the public;

(f) any unreasonable delay by the plaintiff in bringing suit or otherwise asserting its rights;

(g) any related misconduct on the part of the plaintiff; and

(h) the practicality of framing and enforcing the injunction.

(3) The duration of injunctive relief in trade secret actions should be limited to the time necessary to protect the plaintiff from any harm attributable to the appropriation and to deprive the defendant of any economic advantage attributable to the appropriation.

§45. Monetary Relief: Appropriation of Trade Secrets

(1) One who is liable to another for an appropriation of the other's trade secret under the rule stated in §40 is liable for the pecuniary loss to the other caused by the appropriation or for the actor's own pecuniary gain resulting from the appropriation, whichever is greater, unless such relief is inappropriate under the rule stated in Subsection (2).

(2) Whether an award of monetary relief is appropriate and the appropriate method of measuring such relief depend upon a comparative appraisal of all the factors of the case, including the following primary factors:

(a) the degree of certainty with which the plaintiff has established the fact and extent of the pecuniary loss or the actor's pecuniary gain resulting from the appropriation;

(b) the nature and extent of the appropriation;

(c) the relative adequacy to the plaintiff of other remedies;

(d) the intent and knowledge of the actor and the nature and extent of any good faith reliance by the actor;

(e) any unreasonable delay by the plaintiff in bringing suit or otherwise asserting its rights; and

(f) any related misconduct on the part of the plaintiff.

Restatement (Third) of Unfair Competition, *supra*, at 425-527.

. . . [The court also noted that the National Conference of Commissioners on Uniform State Laws had produced a Uniform Trade Secrets Act, intended to be legislatively adopted. *See Uniform Trade Secrets Act with 1985 Amendments* § 1, 14 U.L.A., 537 (2005). Some version of the UTSA has been adopted by forty-four states and the District of Columbia. The states not listed in 14 Uniform Laws Annotated, *supra*, at 529-30 as having adopted the UTSA are Massachusetts, New Jersey, New York, North Carolina, Texas, and Wyoming. All of these states but Wyoming, however, provide in some manner for a cause of action for misuse of trade secrets.]

Wyoming is the only jurisdiction in the United States that has not given specific legislative or judicial recognition to a tort cause of action for misuse of trade secrets. This Court has discussed the related issue of covenants not to compete or to use employers' trade secrets, but we have not directly addressed the Restatement of Torts § 757, or either of the more modern formulations of trade secret law. *See Hopper v. All Pet Animal Clinic, Inc.*, 861 P.2d 531, 539 (Wyo. 1993) and *Ridley v. Krout*, 63 Wyo. 252, 180 P.2d 124, 127 (1947). Nevertheless, trade secret protection is a well-established principle in this state. For instance, W.R.C.P. 26(c)(1)(G) protects trade secrets during the pre-trial discovery process in civil cases. And the legislature has recognized the sanctity of trade secrets in numerous statutes. . . . Clearly, the concept of trade secret protection is firmly embedded in the existing law of Wyoming.

Perhaps this entire discussion should have been shortened to the dual observation that (1) misuse of trade secrets is a recognized common law cause of action; and (2) the Wyoming legislature adopted the common law over 100 years ago. Wyo. Stat. Ann. § 8-1-101 (LexisNexis 2005). . . .

The question is not so much whether this Court should "adopt" a cause of action for misuse of trade secrets. Rather, the question is whether this Court should declare that such a cause of action exists in the common law that has been statutorily adopted in this State. . . .

[T]his Court has repeatedly recognized the dynamic nature of the common law:

That court best serves the law which recognizes that the rules of law which grew up in a remote generation may in the fullness of experience be found to serve another generation badly, and which discards the old rule when it finds that another rule of law represents what should be according to the established and settled judgment of society, and no considerable property rights have become vested in reliance upon the old rule. It is thus great writers upon the common law have discovered the source and method of its growth, and in its growth found its health and life. It is not and it should not be stationary. Change of this character should not be left to the Legislature.

. . . Misuse or misappropriation of a trade secret as a tort was part of the common law adopted by the Wyoming legislature as the "rule of decision" for this State. The numerous statutes listed above recognizing the confidentiality of trade secrets in particular contexts reveal the legislature's commitment to trade secret protection, yet they do not constitute such a "covering of the whole field" as to evidence legislative intent to abrogate the common law rule. . . . Furthermore, as Wyoming has advanced into the modern commercial world along with the rest of the United States, its people have the same need for trade secret protection as do the rest of the people of the country. Consequently, we have no hesitation in declaring that the tort of misuse or misappropriation of trade secrets is part of the law of this jurisdiction. Furthermore, because it represents the common law cause of action in its modern and most appropriate version, we adopt the cause of action as it appears in Restatement (Third) of Unfair Competition, *supra*, §§ 39 through 45.

[The majority concluded that (1) The common law cause of action for misappropriation of trade secrets and/or confidential information when former employees of a company are alleged to have misappropriated their former employer's trade secrets and/or confidential information to start a competing business is part of the common law in the State of Wyoming; and (2) The elements of the cause of action are those contained in Restatement (Third) of Unfair Competition, *supra*, §§ 39 through 45.]

HILL, CHIEF JUSTICE, dissenting, in which GOLDEN, JUSTICE, joins.

I respectfully dissent because I perceive that the protection of trade secrets and other confidential economic information developed by employers has become an increasingly complex issue that is fraught with technicalities and permeated with vital public policy issues. I would have answered the certified questions in the negative and referred the responsibility for answering those questions to the legislature. Wyo. Const. art. 2, § 1 provides: "The powers of the government of this state are divided into three distinct departments: The legislative, executive and judicial, and no person or collection of persons charged with the exercise of powers properly belonging to one of these departments shall exercise any powers properly belonging to either of the others, except as in this constitution expressly directed or permitted."

The majority expressly recognizes the complexities of the issues at hand, that the Restatement of Torts § 757 has been deprived of the essence of its vitality, and that this Court does not have authority to adopt the Uniform Trade Secrets Act (UTSA). The vast majority of jurisdictions now use UTSA, or other legislative enactments, to govern this area of law. Prior to this litigation, Wyoming was alone in not having given recognition to a civil remedy to protect trade secrets. Wyoming will now be alone in adopting the Restatement (Third) of Unfair Competition as the vehicle for filling in this gap. It is my conviction that the Restatement (Third) of Unfair Competition so closely resembles a system of statutes, akin to UTSA, that the adoption of it as the governing law in Wyoming is a usurpation of the Legislature's authority and responsibility.

NOTES

1. *The Contours of Secrecy.* Comment *f* to Restatement (Third) of Unfair Competition, section 39 (1995) gives some sense of the conceptualization of trade secrets, beginning with the self-evident statement: "To qualify as a trade secret, the information must be secret" though acknowledging that "secrecy . . . need not be absolute." The Restatement further provides:

> The rule stated in this Section requires only secrecy sufficient to confer an actual or potential economic advantage on one who possesses the information. Thus, the requirement of secrecy is satisfied if it would be difficult or costly for others who could exploit the information to acquire it without resort to the wrongful conduct proscribed under §40. Novelty in the patent law sense is not required. Although trade secret cases sometimes announce a "novelty" requirement, the requirement is synonymous with the concepts of secrecy and value as described in this Section and the correlative exclusion of self-evident variants of the known art.

> Information known by persons in addition to the trade secret owner can retain its status as a trade secret if it remains secret from others to whom it has potential economic value. Independent discovery by another who maintains the secrecy of the information, for example, will not preclude relief against an appropriation by a third person. Similarly, confidential disclosures to employees, licensees, or others will not destroy the information's status as a trade secret. Even limited non-confidential disclosure will not necessarily terminate protection if the recipients of the disclosure maintain the secrecy of the information.

> Information that is generally known or readily ascertainable through proper means (*see* §43) by others to whom it has potential economic value is not protectable as a trade secret. . . . [I]nformation readily ascertainable from an examination of a product on public sale or display is not a trade secret. . . . [I]t is the secrecy of the claimed trade secret as a whole that is determinative. The fact that some or all of the components of the trade secret are well-known does not preclude protection for a secret combination, compilation, or integration of the individual elements.

> The theoretical ability of others to ascertain the information through proper means does not necessarily preclude protection as a trade

secret. Trade secret protection remains available unless the information is readily ascertainable by such means.

Circumstantial evidence is admissible to establish that information is not readily ascertainable through proper means and hence is eligible for protection as a trade secret. Precautions taken by the claimant to preserve the secrecy of the information . . . , the willingness of licensees to pay for disclosure of the secret, unsuccessful attempts by the defendant or others to duplicate the information by proper means, and resort by a defendant to improper means of acquisition are all probative of the relative accessibility of the information. When a defendant has engaged in egregious misconduct in order to acquire the information, the inference that the information is sufficiently inaccessible to qualify for protection as a trade secret is particularly strong. . . .

REST. 3D UNFAIR COMP. at § 39 (1995).

2. *The Relation of Trade Secrets to Patent and Copyright Law.* Federal patent law does not preempt state trade secret law. *Kewanee Oil Co. v. Bicron Corp.*, 416 U. S. 470 (1974). The requirement of secrecy, the Court said, makes it unlikely that the policy of inducing public disclosure in exchange for patent protection will be undermined. But if the information is in the public domain or is readily ascertainable from public sources, patent law preempts any state law that substantially interferes with the use of such information. *Bonito Boats, Inc. v. Thunder Craft Boats, Inc.*, 489 U.S. 141 (1989).

3. *Injunctive Relief.* The court in *PepsiCo, Inc. v. Redmond*, 54 F.3d 1262 (7th Cir. 1995), upheld the trial court's issuance of an injunction against disclosure of trade secrets by Redmond, a former managerial employee of PepsiCo. The fierce beverage-industry competition between Quaker, producer of the sports drink, "Gatorade," and PepsiCo, which produced a competitor drink, "All Sport," formed the backdrop of this dispute. Defendant Redmond worked for PepsiCo in its Pepsi-Cola North America division ("PCNA") from 1984 to 1994 and was a General Manager of a lucrative business unit covering all of California at the time he was courted by Quaker.

Redmond's relatively high-level position at PCNA gave him access to inside information and trade secrets and, like other PepsiCo management employees, he had signed a confidentiality agreement with PepsiCo, stating that he would not disclose at any time, to anyone other than officers or employees of PepsiCo, nor make use of, confidential information relating to the business and obtained while in PepsiCo's employ. Redmond was courted by another former PepsiCo employee to become Vice President–On Premise Sales for Gatorade. Redmond did not then accept the offer but continued to negotiate for more money and kept his dealings with Quaker secret from most of his colleagues at PCNA until after he accepted the position of Vice President-Field Operations for Gatorade. When Redmond finally informed his employer, PepsiCo sued, seeking a temporary restraining order to enjoin Redmond from assuming his duties at Quaker and to prevent him from disclosing trade secrets or confidential information to his new employer.

At the preliminary injunction hearing PepsiCo offered evidence of a number of trade secrets and confidential information it desired protected and to which

Redmond was privy. The evidence included its annual Strategic Plan concerning competition and financial goals and business strategies; its Annual Operating Plan outlining growth expectations and proposed initiatives, and pricing information; and "attack plans" for specific markets. PepsiCo also offered evidence of PCNA trade secrets regarding innovations in its selling and delivery systems.

The court found that the issuance of an injunction was justified in part because employment of Redmond by Quaker would probably cause him to breach his confidentiality agreement with PepsiCo. Lack of a time limitation did not invalidate the confidentiality agreement. *Id.* at 1272 n.10.

Though "PepsiCo has not brought a traditional trade secret case, in which a former employee has knowledge of a special manufacturing process or customer list and can give a competitor an unfair advantage by transferring the technology or customers to that competitor," the court found an injunction justified because "Redmond cannot help but rely on PCNA trade secrets as he helps plot Gatorade and Snapple's new course, and . . . these secrets will enable Quaker to achieve a substantial advantage by knowing exactly how PCNA will price, distribute, and market its sports drinks and new age drinks and being able to respond strategically." *Id.* at 1270. Although this type of trade secret problem may arise less often, it nevertheless falls within the realm of trade secret protection under the present circumstances.

For these reasons the court affirmed "the district court's order enjoining Redmond from assuming his responsibilities at Quaker through May 1995, and preventing him forever from disclosing PCNA trade secrets and confidential information." *Id.* at 1272. Why wasn't the defendant forever enjoined from working for Quaker? Conversely, why wasn't the injunction against disclosure sufficient without the need for the temporary injunction against employment?

4. *Publication of Trade Secrets.* In *Rockwell Graphic Systems, Inc. v. DEV. Industries*, 925 F.2d 174 (7th Cir. 1991), the plaintiff, a manufacturer of printing presses and parts, sued its competitor and the competitor's president, a former employee of the plaintiff, for misappropriation of trade secrets. The plaintiff had made certain piece — part drawings available to other manufacturers, but it claimed that in doing so these drawings maintained their status as trade secrets. The Seventh Circuit agreed, touching off more than ten years of multi-million dollar litigation. *See Goss Graphics Systems v. DEV Industries, Inc.*, 267 F.3d 624 (7th Cir. 2001).

BENDINGER v. MARSHALLTOWN TROWEL CO.
994 S.W.2d 468 (Ark. 1999)

GLAZE, JUSTICE.

This case involves an action alleging a violation of the Arkansas Trade Secrets Act, Ark. Code Ann. §§ 4-75-601 *et seq.* (Repl. 1996), and, alternatively, a violation of a covenant not to compete. . . . The chancellor enforced the restrictive covenant, thereby prohibiting Bendinger from working for Marshalltown's competitor, Kraft Tool Company, for two years. Nonetheless, the chancellor refused to permanently enjoin Bendinger under the Act from employment with Kraft or any other competitor. Both parties appealed the chancellor's order. . . .

Marshalltown [engages in] the production and sale of trowels and related merchandise. Bendinger is an industrial engineer who was hired to work for Marshalltown beginning July 15, 1970, when he graduated from college in Iowa. When he began his employment, no written employment document was executed, but on March 22, 1978, at Marshalltown's request, he signed the following agreement:

> Without [Marshalltown's] prior written consent, [Bendinger] shall not use or disclose at any time, either during or subsequent to his employment hereunder, any secret or confidential information, whether patentable or not, which is disclosed or known to [Bendinger], as a consequence of his said employment except as may be required in the performance of [Bendinger's] duties to [Marshalltown].

> [Bendinger], shall not, for a period of two years following the termination of [his] employment with [Marshalltown], directly or indirectly render service to a business competitor of [Marshalltown].

. . . Marshalltown expanded its business facilities and opened a new plant in Fayetteville whose construction Bendinger was transferred to oversee. . . .

In 1993, Marshalltown advised Bendinger by memoranda that he was being replaced as factory manager and being demoted to the position of facilities manager. His demotion was purportedly due to his lack of motivation and imagination, as well as his inability to deal effectively with those employees he supervised. . . . Displeased with Marshalltown's actions, Bendinger . . . responded to a blind newspaper advertisement in the *Northwest Arkansas Times* . . . , placed by Kraft Tool Company of Kansas, [seeking] an individual highly qualified in the manufacturing of hand tools.

Bendinger told Kraft of his restrictive employment agreement with Marshalltown, and eventually notified Marshalltown of his job search efforts. Marshalltown reacted by refusing to release Bendinger from his employment agreement. . . . On April 17, 1997, Bendinger . . . resigned from Marshalltown, and the following day, he entered into an oral employment agreement with Kraft to serve as its plant manager. Upon taking the job with Kraft, both Bendinger and Kraft sued for declaratory judgment . . . and asked the Kansas court to declare Bendinger's restrictive-covenant agreement void.

In response, Marshalltown filed suit against Bendinger and Kraft in the Washington County Chancery Court, seeking enforcement of the parties' two-year restrictive covenant, and also alleging that Bendinger's misappropriation of Marshalltown's trade secrets should be held a violation of the Arkansas Trade Secrets Act. . . . Marshalltown obtained an ex parte temporary restraining order (TRO) enjoining Bendinger from working at Kraft. . . . After the hearing, the chancellor set aside the TRO and allowed Bendinger to work for Kraft, but imposed a protective order on the parties to secure Marshalltown's proprietary information.

... [T]he chancellor issued his decree, denying Marshalltown's request for a permanent injunction under the Trade Secrets Act because the proof was insufficient to show that either Bendinger or Kraft misappropriated Marshalltown's trade secrets. Nonetheless, the chancellor found Marshalltown's and Bendinger's restrictive covenant enforceable, and directed that Bendinger could not work for Kraft or any other competitor for a period of two years, commencing from the date of the chancellor's decree.

... Bendinger submits that it was error to uphold the [restrictive covenant], as the chancellor found no proof of either actual or threatened misappropriation of Marshalltown's trade secrets by either Bendinger or Kraft [and insists] that Arkansas courts have never upheld a covenant not to compete where the employee has not engaged in some act to harm his former employer or where the new employer has not already benefitted (sic) from an unfair competitive advantage. . . . Alternatively, Bendinger argues that the contract is not enforceable since it failed to contain a reasonable geographic limitation.

Noncompetition clauses in employment contracts have been the source of litigation for over 500 years. Under early English common law, courts were hostile to employee covenants not to compete and regarded them as contrary to public policy. For at least 250 years, the most cited case on common-law restraints of trade has been *Mitchel v. Reynolds*, 1 P. Wms. 181, 24 Eng. Rep. 347 (Q.B. 1711), which sought a unifying principle to guide judicial decisions in all subsequent cases involving enforcement of a covenant not to compete. *Id*. In that case, Lord Maclesfield noted that there was a presumption that all restraints of trade are invalid, but nonetheless held that the presumption could be overcome . . . by a showing of reasonableness. . . . Arkansas has followed the trend in this area by requiring a party challenging the validity of a covenant to show that it is unreasonable and contrary to public policy. Without statutory authorization, or some dominant policy justification, a contract in restraint of trade is unreasonable if it is based on a promise to refrain from competition that is not ancillary to a contract of employment or to a contract for the transfer of goodwill or other property. However, the law will not protect parties against ordinary competition. This court has recognized that covenants not to compete in *employment* contracts are subject to stricter scrutiny than those connected with a *sale of a business*. We review cases involving covenants not to compete on a case-by-case basis. Furthermore, the court reviews chancery cases *de novo* and does not reverse a finding of fact by the chancery court unless it is clearly erroneous. . . .

We hold that the failure of the covenant to contain a geographic restriction in this case renders it overbroad. In its brief, Marshalltown contends that the failure to supply a geographic restriction was reasonable since Marshalltown competes with Kraft on a nationwide basis and because Marshalltown has established an international market. . . . [W]here a company is actually engaged in nation-wide activities, nation-wide protection would appear to be reasonable and proper. *See, e.g., Harwell Enterprises, Inc. v. Heim*, 173 S.W.2d 316 (N.C. 1970). Accord *Sigma Chemical Company v. Harris*, 794 F.2d 371 (8th Cir. 1986) (enforcing restrictive covenant lacking a geographical limitation based on Missouri law which permits enforcement where the breach occurs within an area in which the restriction would be clearly reasonable, even though the terms of the agreement impose a larger and unreasonable restraint). . . .

During oral argument, Marshalltown clarified its position and explained its restrictive covenant banned Bendinger from working for any company it considered a "competitor." Marshalltown defines "competitor" as "any company in the trowel industry that is in competition with Marshalltown for sales in the United States, regardless of where that company is located." [Although] Marshalltown suggests that the use of the word "competitor" in its agreement with Bendinger supplies a sufficient geographic restriction . . . that term as Marshalltown wishes to define it is not contained in the covenant, and we are unable to rewrite the restrictive covenant to supply it. The court has held that the contract must be valid as written, and the court will not apportion or enforce a contract to the extent that it might be considered reasonable. . . . In this case, there is no . . . inherent limitation in Bendinger's employment agreement with Marshalltown, and we do not agree that the term "competitor," by itself, provides a reasonable restriction. . . . Bendinger is precluded from *any* work within the trowel industry under Marshalltown's definition of "competitor." Accordingly, we believe that the chancellor clearly erred in finding that the failure of the parties' restrictive covenant to contain a geographic limitation was reasonable. Therefore, we reverse the chancellor's order because the employment agreement is overbroad. . . .

The chancellor below found Marshalltown possessed . . . trade secrets. Despite the existence of the trade secrets, the chancellor expressly determined that there was no proof that either Bendinger or Kraft would misappropriate the confidential information. Marshalltown submits that Bendinger's employment with Kraft will result in the inevitable disclosure of such information. Marshalltown points out that a number of courts have found that where an employee's knowledge and skills are inextricably tied up with his employer's trade secrets and the subsequent employment poses a substantial risk that the first employer's trade secrets will be used, such inevitable disclosure will justify an injunction against the competitive employment. . . .

Recently, this court adopted the inevitable-disclosure rule in *Cardinal Freight Carriers v. J.B. Hunt Transportation Services*, 336 Ark. 143, 152, 987 S.W.2d 642, 646. In that case, we recognized that a number of federal cases dealing with trade secrets have held that a plaintiff may prove a claim of trade-secrets misappropriation by demonstrating that a defendant's new employment will inevitably lead him to rely on the plaintiff's trade secrets. Because we have adopted the inevitable-disclosure rule, the only question to resolve is whether Bendinger's employment with Kraft will result in a situation where Bendinger will inevitably rely on Marshalltown's trade secrets. After considering the evidence and testimony before the chancellor, we cannot hold he was clearly erroneous in finding that there is no evidence of any actual, threatened, or inevitable misappropriation. . . .

. . . Bendinger's answers to certain interrogatories showed how Bendinger could not avoid incorporating his special knowledge of Marshalltown's sale information and manufacturing processes into his work with Kraft. In other words, . . . Bendinger would be constantly using the knowledge and experience gained at Marshalltown as a reference for his work with Kraft. Other witnesses, including some employees of Kraft, testified that Bendinger chairs daily morning and afternoon production meetings during which employees discuss engineering matters relating to product quality, equipment problems, and changes in manufacturing processes. During these daily meetings, Marshalltown insists Bendinger will be exposed to issues relating to his engineering background and will inevitably result in Bendinger divulging Marshalltown's trade secrets to Kraft.

On the other hand, Bendinger testified that he had only a general working knowledge of Marshalltown's machines and processes, and that he did not have in his possession any of the company's machine designs or blueprints. Bendinger candidly requested "guidance" from the chancellor as to what was Marshalltown's proprietary information so that he could avoid violating the parties' employment agreement. Bendinger also offered testimony that Kraft circulated a memo pertaining to Bendinger's employment detailing his personal situation and instructed employees that Bendinger was not to be consulted in relation to his prior employment with Marshalltown. In the end, the chancellor found Bendinger's testimony believable, specifically stating in his decree that Bendinger appeared to be an "honest, honorable person who respects Marshalltown's rights to protect its trade secrets." The chancellor also determined that Bendinger had some knowledge of Marshalltown's trade secrets, but that knowledge was "minimal at best," and that Bendinger lacked access to Marshalltown's customer and vendor lists, its blueprints, machine and product drawings, secret formula, or any other written information or material. In the chancellor's judgment, Bendinger's vast *general* knowledge of the trowel industry, as opposed to his engineering expertise, was of far greater value to Kraft than any knowledge of the four trade secrets he purportedly had.

. . . Given the fact that we review a chancellor's findings according to the clearly erroneous standard, we cannot say that the chancellor in this case erred in determining that there was no proof of actual, threatened, or inevitable misappropriation. The . . . mere fact a person assumes a similar position at a competitor does not, without more, make it inevitable that he will use or disclose trade secrets. While Bendinger has assumed a position with a competitor of Marshalltown's, that position is managerial in nature and does not require him to use his engineering expertise. So, Bendinger has not even assumed a *similar position* which would render the disclosure of Marshalltown's trade secrets inevitable. We also note, as did the Seventh Circuit Court of Appeals in *AMP, Inc.* [*v. Heishhacker,* 823 F.2d 1199, 1202 (7th Cir. 1987)], that the right of an individual to follow and pursue the particular occupation for which he is best trained is a most fundamental right. Our society is extremely mobile and our free economy is based upon competition; one who has worked in a particular field cannot be compelled to erase from his mind all of the *general* skills, knowledge and expertise acquired through his experience. Restraints cannot be lightly placed upon an employee's right to compete in the area of his greatest worth. Because Bendinger is only using his *general* knowledge gained through his education and his twenty-seven years of experience in the trowel industry, he poses no threat to Marshalltown's trade secrets. For these reasons, we affirm the chancellor's refusal to issue Marshalltown an injunction permanently enjoining Bendinger from working for Kraft or any other competitor. . . .

NOTES

1. *What's in a Name?* The defendant hair stylists in *Renee Beauty Salons, Inc. v. Blose-Venable*, 652 A.2d 1345 (Pa. Super. 1995), left plaintiff's hair-styling concern and set up a competing business. Defendants then solicited customers they had serviced while working for the plaintiff. The court said there was no trade secret violation:

> [T]he business of hair styling, like most service industries, requires the compilation of customer information. Many stylists maintain records of customers' names, telephone numbers, hair styling preferences and the like. So, too, in this case, Renee utilized a client record card, which bore at the bottom the notation that the "card and its information is [sic] the sole property of Renee Beauty Salons, Inc. It is forbidden for any employee or third party to misuse or steal salon information." Eventually, Renee's card system was replaced by a computer system which stored the data on a computer disk. There was no evidence presented, and defendants denied, that defendants had removed the disk to obtain customer information, or had used the computer to print customer lists. Instead, defendants testified that through repeatedly servicing the same customers, as well as through personal contacts with the clients, who in many cases were friends and relatives of defendants, they had memorized the names of the customers. Each stylist, then, when they left Renee for Apropos, compiled from memory a list of their customers, i.e., their friends and relatives, which was then used by the former employees to solicit business for their new venture, Apropos. To consider this information, easily obtainable through any number of sources, the "sole property of Renee Beauty Salons, Inc." is to stretch the trade secret doctrine to the point of unrecognizability.

Id. at 1349.

In *Gary Van Zeeland Talent v. Sandas*, 267 N.W.2d 242 (Wis. 1978), the defendant Sandas worked for the plaintiff talent agency, Gary Van Zeeland, which booked musical groups in nightclubs and other entertainment places. Defendant left plaintiff intending to start a competing agency, and he took with him a list of names of Van Zeeland's customers, but he did not take their addresses or any booking information. The court said there was no appropriation of trade secrets:

> Van Zeeland acknowledged that it would be relatively simple to prepare a customer list — the names of the clubs — in comparison to the more difficult task of matching appropriate talent with those clubs. There is no assertion that any list which matched bands with customers was taken. Van Zeeland admitted that a list of customers without detailed information about club preferences would be relatively useless.

Id. at 245.

In *Ed Nowogroski Insurance, Inc. v. Rucker*, 971 P.2d 936 (Wash. 1999), the issue was whether a former employee could be found liable for appropriation of customer names by memorizing the names rather than taking a customer list from a former employer. The court recognized a division of authority on the issue of whether there could be appropriation by memorization. It held that under the Uniform Trade Secrets Act, it made no difference whether the information was documentary or memorized. A trade secret, said the court, is:

> a compilation of information that derives independent economic value from not being generally known or readily ascertainable to others and subject to reasonable efforts to maintain secrecy. . . . If an employee was privy to a secret formula of a manufacturing company, which was valuable and kept secret, it should not cease to be a trade secret if an employee committed it to memory.

Id. at 947-48.

2. *Confidential and Proprietary Business Information.* The plaintiff Warner-Lambert Co. stated a cause of action for misappropriation of business information against defendant Execuquest Corp. in *Warner-Lambert Co. v. Execuquest Corp.*, 691 N.E.2d 545 (Mass. 1998). Defendant provided executive employee search services. Over several days, Execuquest agents made numerous telephone calls to various Warner-Lambert offices throughout the United States. The Execuquest agents misrepresented themselves by using various aliases and titles, including misrepresenting themselves as employees in Warner-Lambert's corporate headquarters. The Execuquest callers requested information from the various Warner-Lambert offices, including names, addresses, telephone numbers, and positions of managerial employees and of minority and female sales representatives. Warner-Lambert employees disclosed some of this information to the callers. This ruse is known as "pretexting."

3. *Employment Agreements.* In *Bendinger*, the restrictive covenant was unenforceable because it contained no geographic restriction. Recall the conclusion of the court in *PepsiCo v. Redmond*, given above, that the confidentiality agreement there involved was not void for lack of durational or geographical limitations. But in *Gary Van Zeeland Talent*, also discussed above, the court said an employment agreement prohibiting disclosure of the agency's customer list, without limitation in time or place, was an "unreasonable restraint of trade." Do the different results in *PepsiCo Gary* and *Van Zeeland Talent* turn on the fact that *Pepsico* involved valid trade secrets while *Gary Van Zeeland Talent* did not? What explains the difference in treatment of employment restrictions in *Bendinger* and *PepsiCo*? Did the court in *Bendinger* seem overprotective of Bendinger's autonomy interests in a "mobile and free economy," when it concluded he posed no threat to Marshalltown's trade secrets?

See also Vaske v. DuCharme, McMillen & Assoc., 757 F. Supp. 1158 (D. Colo. 1990) (no cause of action for wrongful discharge where employment was terminated because of employee's refusal to sign a non-competition agreement).

4. *Trade Secret Commentary.* For a thoughtful discussion of trade secrets and democratic development, including the implications of thinking reflected in the Restatement (Third) of Unfair Competition (1995), see David S. Levine, *Secrecy and Unaccountability: Trade Secrets in our Public Infrastructure*, 59 FLA. L. REV. 135 (2007).

G. WRONGFUL INTERFERENCE WITH CONTRACT OR BUSINESS RELATIONS

FRED SIEGEL CO., L.P.A. v. ARTER & HADDEN
707 N.E.2d 853 (Ohio 1999)

MOYER, CHIEF JUSTICE.

The determinative issues in this case are (1) whether it was error for the trial court to grant summary judgment in favor of Karen Bauernschmidt and Arter & Hadden as to Siegel's claim of tortious interference with contract, and (2) whether it was error for the trial court to grant summary judgment in favor of Karen Bauernschmidt and Arter & Hadden as to Siegel's claim of misappropriation of trade secrets. [The court of appeals reversed the trial court.]

Tortious interference with contract. We reaffirm the elements of the tort of tortious interference with contract as enumerated in paragraph two of the syllabus of *Kenty v. Transamerica Premium Ins. Co.*, 650 N.E.2d 863 (Ohio 1995). They are (1) the existence of a contract, (2) the wrongdoer's knowledge of the contract, (3) the wrongdoer's intentional procurement of the contract's breach, (4) the lack of justification, and (5) resulting damages.

In *Kenty* we quoted with approval [REST. 2D TORTS], § 766, which provides: "One who intentionally and *improperly* interferes with the performance of a contract (except a contract to marry) between another and a third person by inducing or otherwise causing the third person not to perform the contract, is subject to liability to the other for the pecuniary loss resulting to the other from the failure of the third person to perform the contract." (Emphasis added.) *Kenty*, 650 N.E.2d at 866. Only improper interference with a contract is actionable, as reflected in the fourth element of the tort. . . . Thus, even if an actor's interference with another's contract causes damages to be suffered, that interference does not constitute a tort if the interference is justified. "The issue in each case is whether the interference is improper or not under the circumstances; whether, upon a consideration of the relative significance of the factors involved, the conduct should be permitted without liability, despite its effect of harm to another." [REST. 2D TORTS § 767, cmt. *b*.] We today reaffirm *Kenty* and hold that establishment of the fourth element of the tort of tortious interference with contract, lack of justification, requires proof that the defendant's interference with another's contract was improper.

Bauernschmidt and Arter & Hadden contend that the record creates no genuine issue of material fact, and that they are entitled to summary judgment in that they were justified in contacting clients of Fred Siegel and soliciting them to change legal representation. They cite several Disciplinary Rules contained in the Code of Professional Responsibility and argue that their actions fall within those rules. They further assert that they are entitled to summary judgment because a client has a legal right to terminate an existing attorney-client relationship, with or without cause, and to hire a new attorney. *Reid, Johnson, Downes, Andrachik & Webster v. Lansberry*, 629 N.E.2d 431 (Ohio 1994). . . .

Appellants argue that DR 2-102(A)(2) authorizes a lawyer to distribute professional announcement cards stating "new or changed associations or addresses, change of firm name, or similar matters pertaining to the professional offices of a lawyer or law firm." However, in this case, appellant Bauernschmidt exceeded the authorization of DR 2-102. In her letters to Siegel clients she not only provided information as to her change of law firms, but also expressed a willingness to continue providing legal services at the new firm ("I would like for us to continue our professional relationship. When you need assistance or have questions, please contact me."). She thereby solicited Siegel clients to change legal representation.

We note that American Bar Association Model Rule of Professional Conduct 7.3(c) implies that an attorney may solicit professional employment by making a direct written communication to persons with whom the lawyer has a "family or prior professional relationship," without labeling it "Advertising Material." However, the corresponding Ohio rule, DR 2-101(F)(2)(e), provides that where written direct mail solicitations are made to persons who may be in need of specific legal services, the mailing must include the recital "ADVERTISEMENT ONLY," of specified size and color, both in the text and on the envelope. No exception from this requirement is expressly included in DR 2-101 for communications to family and past clients. However, the Board of Commissioners on Grievances and Discipline in Opinion No. 98-5 (Apr. 3, 1998) expressed the view that a departing attorney may notify clients of his or her departure from a law firm, identify his or her new location of practice, and indicate a willingness to provide services at the new location without violating ethical standards.

Appellants further argue that Bauernschmidt not only was permitted but had an ethical duty to inform clients with whom she had worked of her departure from Siegel. They cite DR 2-110(A)(2), which imposes a duty upon an attorney who intends to "withdraw from employment" to first "take[ ] reasonable steps to avoid foreseeable prejudice to the rights of his client, including giving due notice to his client, allowing time for employment of other counsel, delivering to the client all papers and property to which the client is entitled, and complying with applicable laws and rules." However, we do not accept appellants' contention that this rule is applicable to the case at bar.

Bauernschmidt herself acknowledged that the parties for whom she worked while an associate at the Siegel firm were not "her" clients but were clients of Fred Siegel Co., L.P.A. Although her work as an employee of that firm resulted in the establishment of an attorney-client relationship with Siegel clients, Bauernschmidt had never entered into a contractual agreement with those clients under which she personally was obligated to provide legal services. DR 2-110 is designed to avoid the danger of a client being left unrepresented upon an attorney's withdrawal. These dangers were not generated when Bauernschmidt left the Siegel firm. Because Bauernschmidt was never employed by Siegel clients, she did not withdraw from employment by them, and DR 2-110 is simply not applicable.

Moreover, the fact that a client has a right to discharge his or her attorney, pursuant to *Reid, Johnson*, does not, of itself, provide a competing attorney with justification for encouraging the client to exercise that right, and thus does not necessarily preclude a finding that a tortious interference with contract has occurred.

. . . In any event, we reject the suggestion that the propriety of an attorney's conduct for purposes of a tortious interference analysis should be determined solely by application of the Disciplinary Rules. The purpose of disciplinary actions is to protect the public interest and to ensure that members of the bar are competent to practice a profession imbued with the public trust. These interests are different from the purposes underlying tort law, which provides a means of redress to individuals for damages suffered as a result of tortious conduct. Accordingly, violation of the Disciplinary Rules does not, in itself, create a private cause of action. . . .

. . . Moreover, the power to determine violations of the Disciplinary Rules is reserved to this court. Were we to hold that a lawyer's compliance with the Code of Professional Responsibility is an absolute defense to a claim of tortious interference with contract, we would effectively be delegating our authority to determine violations of the Disciplinary Rules to the trial courts. Rather, consistent with our adoption in *Kenty* of Restatement Section 766, which sets forth the elements of tortious interference with contract, the propriety of the appellants' conduct in contacting Siegel's clients and suggesting that they follow Bauernschmidt to Arter & Hadden should be determined by applying relevant legal tests [and we] therefore adopt Section 767 of the Restatement, which provides guidelines to be followed in determining whether an actor's interference with another's contract is improper. Accordingly, . . . consideration should be given to the following factors: (a) the nature of the actor's conduct, (b) the actor's motive, (c) the interests of the other with which the actor's conduct interferes, (d) the interests sought to be advanced by the actor, (e) the social interests in protecting the freedom of action of the actor and the contractual interests of the other, (f) the proximity or remoteness of the actor's conduct to the interference, and (g) the relations between the parties.

Within this framework the standards defined in the Disciplinary Rules, which govern the conduct of all attorneys, are relevant in determining the propriety of an attorney's conduct in a tortious interference claim pursuant to the Restatement. See Comment *c* to Section 767, at 32 ("Violation of recognized ethical codes for a particular area of business activity or of established customs or practices regarding disapproved actions or methods may also be significant in evaluating the nature of the actor's conduct as a factor in determining whether his interference with plaintiff's contractual relations was improper or not.").

The standards of the Disciplinary Rules are relevant to, but not determinative of, the propriety of an attorney's conduct for purposes of a tortious interference with contract claim. Similarly relevant are the interests of clients in being fully apprised of information relevant to their decisionmaking in choosing legal representation and appellants' interests in engaging in constitutionally protected free speech.

Moreover, Section 768 of the Restatement provides that fair competition may constitute a proper ground, or justification, for an interference with an existing contract that is terminable at will. Thus, where an existing contract is terminable at will, and where all the elements of Section 768 of the Restatement are met, a competitor may take action to attract business, even if that action results in an interference with another's existing contract. Where a defendant in an action for tortious interference with contract establishes that his or her conduct falls within Section 768, the factfinder need not balance the factors set forth in Section 767. See Section 767, Comment *a*, at 27 ("The specific applications in [Section 768] supplant the generalization expressed in [Section 767].")

We today adopt Section 768 of the Restatement and accordingly hold that establishment of the privilege of fair competition, as set forth in Section 768 of the Restatement, will defeat a claim of tortious interference with contract where the contract is terminable at will.

. . . Pursuant to Section 768, competition is proper if (a) the relation between the actor (here Bauernschmidt and Arter & Hadden) and his or her competitor (here Siegel) concerns a matter involved in the competition between the actor and the other, and (b) the actor does not employ wrongful means, and (c) his action does not create or continue an unlawful restraint of trade, and (d) his purpose is at least in part to advance his interest in competing with the other. Thus, appellants would be entitled to summary judgment pursuant to Section 768 only if the record establishes that each of those elements was met.

We do not find the existence of any genuine issue of fact in this case as to the establishment of elements (a), (c), and (d) as outlined above. We find, however, that the record before us reflects unresolved issues of fact as to whether Bauernschmidt and Arter & Hadden employed wrongful means in competing with Siegel. The evidence is ambiguous as to whether Bauernschmidt and Arter & Hadden used information acquired through improper means in their competitive efforts, *e.g.*, information protected as trade secrets, or information as to Siegel's fee arrangements with clients that may have been wrongfully disclosed. Further proceedings are required to determine whether appellants employed wrongful means within the contemplation of Restatement Section 768 in competing against Siegel. . . .

The question whether a particular knowledge or process is a trade secret is, however, a question of fact to be determined by the trier of fact upon the greater weight of the evidence. *Valco Cincinnati, Inc. v. N & D Machining Serv., Inc.*, 492 N.E.2d 814, at 819 (Ohio 1986).

[The court reviews state law and concludes that], listings of names, addresses, or telephone numbers that have not been published or disseminated, or otherwise become a matter of general public knowledge, constitute trade secrets if the owner of the list has taken reasonable precautions to protect the secrecy of the listing to prevent it from being made available to persons other than those selected by the owner to have access to it in furtherance of the owner's purposes.

Siegel claims that Bauernschmidt and Arter & Hadden tortiously misappropriated the information contained in Siegel's client list and used it for their own economic gain. We find that genuine issues of material fact exist precluding entry of summary judgment in appellants' favor on this claim. The record demonstrates that the Siegel client list was maintained on a computer that was protected by a password. Hard copies of the list were stored within office filing cabinets, which were sometimes locked. Fred Siegel testified during deposition that he "probably" had told employees that the client list information was confidential and not to be removed from the office.

These facts raise a genuine issue of material fact as to whether Siegel took reasonable actions to ensure that only authorized persons had access to his client list for authorized uses. . . . In this case, a question of fact exists as to whether the appellants, in effect, "independently invented" their own list of property owners, resulting in a list similar to the Siegel list, or whether they simply used Siegel's computer-generated client list.

Where information is alleged to be a trade secret, a factfinder may consider, e.g., the amount of effort or money expended in obtaining and developing the information, as well as the amount of time and expense it would take for others to acquire and duplicate the information. The Siegel client list was sixty-three pages in length and included the names of property owners, contact persons, addresses, and telephone numbers of hundreds of clients. The extensive accumulation of property owner names, contacts, addresses, and phone numbers contained in the Siegel client list may well be shown at trial to represent the investment of Siegel time and effort over a long period.

The purpose of Ohio's trade secret law is to maintain commercial ethics, encourage invention, and protect an employer's investments and proprietary information. That purpose would be frustrated were we to except from trade secret status any knowledge or process based simply on the fact that the information at issue was capable of being independently replicated. . . .

COOK, JUSTICE, dissenting.

I believe that the trial court correctly granted summary judgment in favor of Bauernschmidt in this case. . . . First, Siegel clients with whom Bauernschmidt worked were not just Siegel's clients, but also Bauernschmidt's clients. Second, the information developed by Siegel as a "client list" may be protectable as a trade secret, but the identities of Bauernschmidt's clients cannot be trade secrets. Third, Bauernschmidt was therefore entitled, upon leaving Siegel, to contact those clients with whom she had worked while with the Siegel firm. Fourth, use of the "client list" by Bauernschmidt for purposes of preparing a mailing to the clients with whom she worked while with the Siegel firm would not amount to misappropriation of the trade secret properties of the Siegel client list. . . .

NOTES

1. *Interference with One's Own Contractual Relation?* Do you agree with the dissenting judge that the "client list" which was developed for the purposes of preparing a mailing to clients with whom Bauernschmidt worked would not amount to trade secret property of the Siegel firm? Does it appear that attorneys and law firms are treated differently by courts than other professionals in this area?

It is hornbook law that the tort of wrongful interference does not apply to one interfering with one's own contractual or business relationship. Alex B. Long, *Tortious Interference*, 84 MINN. L. REV. 863, 885 (2000). In *Trimble v. City and County of Denver*, 697 P.2d 716 (Colo. 1985), the court said an employer was a third person, with respect to one employee's interference with another employee's contractual relationship with their common employer.

2. *Rejection of the Tort of Interference.* Should courts continue to recognize the tort of intentional interference with existing or prospective business? Doesn't it hamper free competition? *See Trau-Med of Am., Inc. v. Allstate Ins. Co.*, 71 S.W.3d 691 (Tenn. 2002) (adopting the tort of interference).

3. *Interference with an Existing Contract and Interference with Prospective Economic Advantage.* One may *not* intentionally interfere with an existing contract solely for the purposes of competition. *Lumley v. Gye*, 2 El. & Bl. 216, 118 Eng. Rep. 749 (Q. B. 1853). One *may* interfere with existing contracts for valid policy reasons, however. For example, in *Brimelow v. Casson*, [1924] 1 Ch. 302, the court upheld the right of the defendant labor organizers to induce theater owners to breach their performance contracts with the plaintiff show producer, to force the producer to pay better wages to his chorus dancers.

In *Macklin v. Robert Logan Assocs.*, 639 A.2d 112 (Md. 1994), the defendant was held not guilty of wrongful interference by inducing, (for competitive reasons) a lessor to terminate the lease on 90 days notice. Defendant was liable, however, for wrongfully appropriating plaintiff's trade name when it took over plaintiff's business in the leasehold.

The court recognized the distinction between interference with contract and interference with prospective economic advantage:

> When the existing contract is not terminable at will, inducing its breach, even for competitive purposes, is itself improper and, consequently, not "just cause" for damaging another in his or her business. . . . The situation is entirely different when the existing contract is one terminable at will or at the option of the party importuned. Where the contract is one terminable at will by the party who refuses to continue performance, there is a broader right to interfere. . . .

Id. at 120. The court further explained:

> Where the decision whether to terminate or continue a contract with the plaintiff rests solely in the discretion of the third party, it is not improper or wrongful conduct for one in competition with the plaintiff to provide that third party with a reason for exercising his or her discretion. See *Mac Enters., Inc. v. Del E. Webb Dev. Co.*, 645 P.2d 1245, 1250 (Ariz. Ct. App. 1982) (no tortious interference where landlord had right to cancel its lease with tenant). No matter with what motive or intention a defendant may have acted, it cannot be said in that situation that he or she acted improperly or wrongfully so long as he or she was legitimately competing for the subject of the contract.

Id.

4. *Trade Secrets Commentary.* For more on trade secrets generally, see, for example, Michael Risch, *Why Do We Have Trade Secrets?*, 11 MARQ. INTELL. PROP. L. REV. 1 (2007); Robert G. Bone, *A New Look at Trade Secret Law: Doctrine in Search of Justification*, 86 CAL. L. REV. 241 (1998); *see also* Donald P. Harris, *Sexual Harassment: Limiting the Affirmative Defense in the Digital Workplace*, 39 U. MICH J.L. REFORM 73 (2005) (discussing the types of technology that companies use to guard against misappropriation of trade secrets). For more on wrongful interference with business relations, see, e.g., Orrin K. Ames III, *Tortious Interference with Business Relationships: The Changing Contours of this Commercial Tort*, 35 CUMB. L. REV. 317 (2004); T. Leigh Anenson, *Creating Conflicts of Interest: Litigation as Interference with the Attorney-Client Relationship*, 43 AM. BUS. L.J. 173 (2006).

Business and communicative torts are significantly affected by new technology, particularly the Internet. The notes and principal cases in this chapter show that new technology, particularly the Internet, significantly affect business and communicative torts, including what constitutes a representation, or a communication, and what is a secret. Technological innovations have also shaped intellectual property conceptions. Are traditional torts equipped to handle these new developments? *See, e.g.,* Michael L. Rustad & Thomas H. Koenig, *The Tort of Negligent Enablement of Cybercrime*, 20 BERKELEY TECH. L. J. 1553 (2005) (proposing new tort of negligent enablement which will hold software vendors accountable for defending products and services that pave the way for third-party criminals who exploit known vulnerabilities).

PART 2 — COMMUNICATIVE TORTS

H. DEFAMATION

The common law affords protection against written and spoken defamatory communications that adversely affect reputation. Can you imagine a context in which it is defamatory to call someone Black or Latino? White? Female? Male? Gay? Straight? What values does law support in finding reputational harm in these settings?

The Restatement (Second) of Torts § 558 (1977) articulates the *prima facie* elements of defamation as:

(a) a false and defamatory statement concerning another;

(b) an unprivileged publication to a third party;

(c) fault amounting at least to negligence on the part of the publisher; and

(d) either actionability of the statement irrespective of special harm or the existence of special harm caused by publication.

The U.S. Supreme Court transformed the law of defamation by its holding in *New York Times Co. v. Sullivan*, 376 U.S. 254 (1964), *infra*. The Court ruled that defamation law implicates the freedom of speech protected under the First Amendment. The changes arose in cases involving media-based communications about public officials and public figures. Now *Sullivan's* reach extends further, addressing communications which are the subject of public concern, privileges, and the kinds of damages that are recoverable. In other areas the impact is less certain. It is unclear, for example, the extent to which the Court's constitutional rulings affect the actions of private individuals. Nor is it settled how constitutional concerns will impact on other communicative torts. The Supreme Court's rulings in this area of tort law impact state courts and legislatures since many First Amendment speech protections apply to the states through the Fourteenth Amendment.

A consequence of *Sullivan* and its progeny is a wide diversity of approaches to defamation and other communicative torts in areas that lie at the margins of the Supreme Court rulings. For example, states have taken widely varying positions on whether strict liability can govern private communications about private persons. The diversity of views reflects the controversy about the proper balance between speech and reputational protection, among other interests. In a Special Note at the beginning of the chapters on defamation, the Reporters of the Restatement (Second) of Torts recognize the transformative nature of *Sullivan*, as well as *Gertz v. Robert Welch, Inc.*, 418 U.S. 323 (1974), and the likely risk that, in this evolving area, a provision of the Restatement might become outdated or questionable. *See* Reporter's Notes on Scope of Division 5 (1977).

After examining some of the traditional understandings of what is actionable under the law of libel and slander, this chapter considers the *Sullivan* case and explores some of the principal ways that case and its progeny have affected the law of defamation. It then looks at other communicative torts, especially privacy-related torts. Notably, technology and the advent of the Internet as a principal mode of communication promise to dramatically affect the law in this area.

1. The Prima Facie Case

The Vermont court's treatment of defamation in *Lent v. Huntoon*, below, presents a view of common-law defamation claims.

LENT v. HUNTOON
470 A.2d 1162 (Vt. 1983)

UNDERWOOD, JUSTICE.

Defendants appeal from a verdict and judgment [based on a jury finding them] liable for defamation and award[ing] plaintiff a total of $40,000 in compensatory and punitive damages. We affirm the judgment.

. . . Plaintiff worked for Huntoon Business Machines, Inc. (Huntoon Corporation) from 1964 until his employment was terminated in 1977 — a period of thirteen years. During that time he worked his way up to the position of service manager. At the time he was hired, in 1964, the plaintiff informed defendant H. J. Huntoon (Huntoon) that he was on probation for a criminal conviction and that he had once been confined to the base for a period of time for a minor offense during his service in the Air Force. Defendants hired plaintiff with full knowledge of these events.

In the early part of 1977, plaintiff informed Huntoon that he would be leaving his job at Huntoon Corporation as he was moving to Florida. . . . He offered to stay on long enough to train his successor. Shortly thereafter, and without any prior notice, Huntoon told plaintiff that he was discharged.

Plaintiff was unable to sell his house and so decided to remain in Rutland. In August of 1977, he started his own business equipment sales and service business, Lent Business Machines. Early in March of 1978, plaintiff was awarded a cash register sales and service franchise formerly held by the Huntoon Corporation. Thus, plaintiff and Huntoon Corporation became direct competitors. About this same time, plaintiff became aware that defendants sent a letter to the cash register franchise customers who were formerly serviced by Huntoon Corporation and for whose business both the plaintiff and defendants were then vying. The letter, which indicated that plaintiff had been discharged for "sound business reasons," formed the basis of plaintiff's libel count. Plaintiff asserted that the letter, taken in its totality, was defamatory since it implied that he was fired because of some dishonesty or incompetence. There was evidence that the letter caused plaintiff to become estranged from some of his customers, to suffer physical and emotional malaise, and to neglect his business to the point where it nearly collapsed.

About this time, plaintiff became aware of numerous verbal statements made about him by Huntoon to customers sought after by both plaintiff and defendants. Testimony revealed that these statements asserted that plaintiff had a criminal "record a mile long," had stolen merchandise from the defendants, had stolen money from the cash register of Huntoon Corporation, was an incompetent serviceman, and was generally untrustworthy. Testimony indicated that most of these statements were made by Huntoon in competitive business situations. Plaintiff asked Huntoon to stop making the statements, apparently to no avail, as there was further testimony that some of the statements were made even after plaintiff's lawsuit was initiated. Some testimony indicated that the defendants were fully satisfied with plaintiff's work prior to termination and had never complained about any thefts by plaintiff prior to his leaving Huntoon Corporation. Defendants also knew he intended to leave his job voluntarily and was not fired. . . .

Defamation is comprised of the complementary torts of libel and slander. Although these torts evolved from different antecedents, both were eventually cognizable in the King's courts in England prior to reception of the common law in Vermont. Because of the permanence of the written word, libel was considered the more serious tort, with slander, or the spoken word, considered the less serious. The distinction between written and spoken defamation has resulted in a host of special rules with corresponding special legal terminology. Herein lies much of the confusion which abounds even today.

Libel is generally considered "actionable *per se*"; that is, the plaintiff need not allege or prove that he or she suffered any "special damages" as a direct or proximate result of the libel. Special damages, in short, are presumed. Special damages have a unique connotation in the law of defamation. Special damages are those of a pecuniary nature, and historically they have included loss of customers or business, loss of contracts, or loss of employment. In addition,

> modern decisions have shown some tendency to liberalize the old rule, and to find pecuniary loss when the plaintiff has been deprived of benefit which has a more or less indirect financial value to him. Thus the loss of the society, companionship and association of friends may be sufficient when . . . [they] can be found to have a money value.

REST. 2D TORTS § 575 comment b, at 198 (1977).

Slander, on the other hand, is generally not actionable *per se*; that is, special damages are not presumed and must be alleged and proven. Several kinds of slander, however, were identified at English common law as more serious than others and these were held to be actionable *per se*. Spoken defamation involving (1) imputation of a crime, (2) statements injurious to one's trade, business or occupation, or (3) charges of having a loathsome disease were deemed slander *per se* and were actionable without proof of special damages. The decisions of our Court are in accord with this common law exception. Most American jurisdictions added . . . a fourth exception: charging a woman to be unchaste. Thus "actionable *per se*" simply means special damages need not be proved in libel actions or in those slander actions which fall into one of the exceptions categorized as slander *per se*.

The general elements of a private action for defamation (libel and/or slander) are: (1) a false and defamatory statement concerning another; (2) some negligence, or greater fault, in publishing the statement; (3) publication to at least one third person; (4) lack of privilege in the publication; (5) special damages, unless actionable *per se*; and (6) some actual harm so as to warrant compensatory damages.

For reasons probably lost in history, a special rule of procedure developed for the trial of a defamation action. Once the plaintiff's evidence was in, the court had to determine whether the written or spoken words were defamatory as a matter of law. If the court was in doubt because the connotation of the written or spoken words was ambiguous, then the court had to submit the question to the jury to decide. In libel actions, when the court determined that the written words were libelous as a matter of law, the term "libel *per se*" was used. This unfortunate terminology when used in conjunction with such terms as "slander *per se*" and "actionable *per se*" has greatly confused courts and counsel. "Libel *per se*" simply means defamatory as a matter of law. Since all libel is actionable *per se*, it makes no difference whether the court rules that the written words are defamatory as a matter of law, or that the written words are ambiguous and the jury determines that there is defamation; in each instance special damages need not be proven.

A further complication in the semantics of defamation law arose when the courts embarked upon the "spurious" concept of a "libel per quod." This rule only served to compound an already confusing area of the law of torts. Being written, libel is generally evaluated by examining the four corners of the writing itself. A letter or newspaper article can be introduced at trial and its defamatory nature determined by judge or jury as appropriate. Some writings, however, are seemingly innocent in and of themselves, and resort must be had to extrinsic evidence to determine if they have defamatory qualities. If the writing together with the extrinsic evidence constitutes defamation, such a writing is referred to as "libel per quod" in several American jurisdictions. These jurisdictions require that special damages be proven for libel per quod, unless the libel falls into one of the exceptions we previously mentioned as constituting slander *per se*. Thus, under this rule, the simple fact that extrinsic evidence must be used to prove the defamatory nature of a libel prevents it from being "actionable *per se*" and special damages must be proven.

A scholarly debate concerning libel per quod took place before the [Second Restatement] was published. Thereafter, section 569 of the Restatement reflects the simpler rule and rejects any notion of libel per quod.

Vermont's reported decisions do not recognize libel per quod, and we adhere to the wisdom of that course today. We hold that libel, whether defamatory on the face of the writing alone or with the aid of extrinsic evidence, is actionable *per se*. Our previous use of the term libel *per se* in no way, directly or inferentially, encompasses the rule of libel per quod. In the appropriate circumstances we recognize that libel *per se* may be found either solely from the writing or from the writing together with extrinsic evidence. Similarly the question of whether an ambiguous writing is defamatory or not is a jury question under either set of circumstances.

Given the great confusion in this area, we urge the future use of the term "libel as a matter of law" in situations where "libel *per se*" has been used in the past. "Libel as a matter of law" and where appropriate "slander as a matter of law" accurately identify the issue as one of law for the preliminary determination of the trial court.

In the case before us the pleadings include one count sounding in libel and one count sounding in slander. Two defenses to these allegations of defamation are raised: truth and privilege. Truth, of course, defeats the action and is a complete defense to defamation. The privilege raised here is a conditional privilege which may be overcome by a showing of malice. The defendants allege a privilege to protect their legitimate business interests. This privilege is recognized in [REST. 2D TORTS], *supra*, §595 comment d, and we hold it to be applicable in Vermont. The burden of proving the privilege is on the defendants. A showing of malice, however, may defeat the conditional privilege, Prosser, Handbook of the Law of Torts, at 794, but in such instance the plaintiff must show malice by clear and convincing proof. In this sense malice may be either actual or implied. The court will infer malice upon a showing that the defendant knew the statement was false or acted with reckless disregard of its truth. Actual malice includes spiteful or wanton conduct.

This case also raises the issue of general and punitive damages in defamation. At the outset, we must observe that even though libel and some forms of slander are actionable *per se* and special damages need not be proven, a plaintiff can no longer recover general damages without a showing of some harm. In *Gertz v. Robert Welch, Inc.*, [418 U.S. 323 (1974), *later app.,* 680 F.2d 527 (7th Cir. 1982) *cert. denied* 459 U.S. 1226 (1983)], the United States Supreme Court noted that state remedies for defamation must be restricted "to compensation for *actual injury*." 418 U.S. at 349 (emphasis added). This, of course, applies to general or compensatory damages that "include impairment of reputation and standing in the community, personal humiliation, and mental anguish and suffering." . . . We are persuaded and now hold that liability for defamation must logically be based on some showing of harm to the plaintiff. Thus, Vermont will require defamation plaintiffs to demonstrate some "actual harm" as a prerequisite to recovering general damages. . . . In summary, defamation that is actionable *per se* will require some showing of actual harm, but not of special damages before recovery of general, or compensatory, damages. This sound rule is reflected in the [REST. 2D TORTS] § 621. Finally, this case raises the question of punitive damages. Once general (compensatory) damages are established, punitive damages may be awarded on a showing of actual malice, but actual malice may not be considered to enhance compensatory damages. . . . Malice supporting punitive damages may be shown by proving that the defendant repeated the defamatory statement, especially when the repetition occurred after commencement of the lawsuit.

Once malice sufficient to entitle plaintiff to punitive damages has been shown, the plaintiff may present evidence of defendant's financial condition: "Where exemplary damages are awardable . . . the defendant's pecuniary ability may be considered in order to determine what would be a just punishment for him." *Kidder v. Bacon*, 74 Vt. 263, 274, 52 A. 322, 324 (1902).

[Turning to the bases of appeal, the court found the trial court committed no error in denying defendant's motions for j.n.o.v., for a new trial, and for remittitur.]

NOTES

1. *Special Damage.* Suppose that plaintiff becomes ill as a result of the defamation and is hospitalized and incurs substantial medical expenses. Are there grounds for special damage?

2. *Malice.* The *Huntoon* court does not fully and accurately address the requirements for proof of malice where the First Amendment is implicated. For further discussion of malice, see *New York Times Co. v. Sullivan*, 376 U.S. 254 (1964); *Gertz v. Robert Welch, Inc.,* 418 U.S. 323 (1974); *Dun & Bradstreet v. Greenmoss Builders*, 472 U.S. 749 (1985), *infra*.

3. *Slander Per Se.* The *Huntoon* court lists four types of slander that were considered actionable *per se* at common law, that is, actionable without proof of special damages. Are these meaningful categories today, distinguishing settings in which reputational harm should be presumed? In *Ward v. Zelikovsky*, 623 A.2d 285 (N.J. Super. 1993), the court held that accusing someone of "hating Jews" was as much an "assault upon reputation" as one of the four common-law types of slander *per se*, and was therefore actionable without proof of special damages. It characterized the common-law categories as "arbitrary and archaic," and the result of "historical accident." The court adopted a new standard: whether the spoken words were "so injurious that the court will presume, without further proof, that plaintiff's reputation has been thereby impaired." However, a year later the New Jersey Supreme Court reversed, holding that it will "not expand the four slander *per se* categories and that defendant's 'anti-Semitic' statement does not come within any of the four traditional categories of slander *per se.*" *Ward v. Zelikovsky*, 643 A.2d 972, 986 (N.J. 1994). The court further stated: "the trend should be toward elimination not expansion of the *per se* categories." *Id.* at 984. Which approach do you think is better? *See also Wilson v. Harvey*, 842 N.E.2d 83 (Ohio Ct. App. 2005). The victim of a college prank filed an action against defendant students for using computer-generated fliers depicting plaintiff as a homosexual and giving his name, phone number and e-mail address. The court concluded that the evidence did not support a cause of action since it is not libel *per se* to be called gay because being gay is neither a crime nor a disease, and being considered gay did not injure the plaintiff in his trade or occupation. With no special damages, the victim of such a prank was not able to maintain an action for libel per quod. Does the superior court's standard offered in *Ward, supra,* satisfy constitution-related concerns that require some showing of harm? *See* Dean R. Knight, *"I'm Not Gay — Not That There's Anything Wrong with That!"* 37 VICTORIA WELL. L. REV. 249 (2006).

4. *Reputational Harm?* The REST. 2D TORTS § 559 (1977) defines a communication as defamatory "if it tends so to harm the reputation of another as to lower him in the estimation of the community or deter third persons from associating or dealing with him." In *Lenz Hardware, Inc. v. Wilson*, 729 N.E.2d 338 (N.Y. 2000), the defendant was a member of a limited liability company that operated St. Johnsville Hardware, a store competing locally with Lenz Hardware, a store owned by plaintiff. Defendant placed an advertisement in the local shopper newspaper which in large print compared St. Johnsville prices with those of plaintiff's store and invited customers to "Compare & Save." In considerably smaller print, it listed both stores' prices for a number of household items and then stated:

> "No Coupon Necessary at St. Johnsville Hardware. We have friendly, fast service. We Speak English, Plumbing, Farming and Dabble in Pig Latin."

Lenz Hardware brought a defamation action, asserting that the phrase, "We Speak English," falsely implied that Lenz Hardware's vice-president, an American citizen of Korean origin, was not conversant in English. The court held the lower court's dismissal of the complaint was proper. "Giving the phrase a natural reading in the context presented," the court found the ad not "reasonably susceptible of a defamatory connotation." *Id.* at 339. *See also Smith v. Sch. Dist. of Philadelphia*, 112 F. Supp. 2d 417 (E.D. Pa. 2000) (calling person "racist and anti-semitic" though unflattering is "non-fact based rhetoric").

The plaintiff in *Golub v. Enquirer/Star Group, Inc.*, 681 N.E.2d 1282 (N.Y. 1997), contended that the defendant defamed plaintiff's decedent, a public relations consultant, by stating in an article that the decedent had cancer. In dismissing the claim, the court said: "the statement did not impugn, or even relate to, any particular talent or ability needed to perform in decedent's profession as a publicist." *Id.* at 1283. Nor did the statement impute a loathsome disease, since cancer "is neither contagious nor attributed in any way to socially repugnant conduct." . . . *Id.*

Courts have held that the defamatory nature of the communication should be assessed in the context of the whole statement. *See, e.g., Knievel v. ESPN,*

393 F.3d 1068 (9th Cir. 2005). The court held that a photograph of Evel Knievel bearing the caption: "Evel Knievel proves that you're never too old to be a pimp" that was published on ESPN's "extreme sports" website was not defamatory since the website, when viewed as a whole, did not impute that Knievel was actually soliciting prostitution.

5. *Publication.* Publication is a term of art in defamation law, referring to any form of communication of the defamatory statement to a third party. Thus publication may be spoken or written. Courts have rejected the notion of compelled self-publication. *Sullivan v. Baptist Mem. Hosp.*, 995 S.W.2d 569 (Tenn. 1999). A former hospital employee claimed that in seeking new employment she was compelled to disclose the allegedly erroneous and defamatory reasons for her termination. The court said it sided with the majority of states addressing the issue which do not recognize self-publication as constituting publication for defamation purposes, "even when the publication is compelled in the employment setting." *Id.* at 573. The court noted that the rule would conflict with Tennessee's employment-at-will doctrine. Under that doctrine, an employer has no duty to investigate before terminating an employee, and can terminate "at any time for good cause, bad cause, or no cause." *Id.* at 574.

The court also observed that recognition of such a self-publication rule "would chill communications in the work place" and "negatively affect grievance procedures intended to benefit the discharged employee." *Id.* at 573. The only way an employer could avoid potential litigation would be to say nothing to the employee or to third persons about the reasons for termination. For a discussion of the problems employers face if they do not remain silent but do not divulge information about an employee's past, see *Davis v. Board of County Comm'rs*, 987 P.2d 1172 (N.M. Ct. App. 1999), discussed *supra,* at p. 801.

An employer who does divulge information about conduct which poses a risk of harm in future employment is privileged to make the disclosure. The *Baptist Memorial Hospital* court argued that permitting recovery under a self-publication rule would also conflict with TENN. CODE ANNOT. §50-1-105, which provides that an employer can be liable only for knowing or reckless falsity in communicating "upon request by a prospective employer or a current or former employee . . . information about a current or former employee's job performance." Compliance with this statute raises a presumption of good faith, and mere negligence is not enough to rebut the presumption in favor of the employer's good faith. In contrast, defamation may be proven by establishing that a party published a false and defaming statement with reckless disregard for the truth *or* with negligence in failing to ascertain the truth. *Cweklinsky v. Mobil Chem. Co.*, 837 A.2d 759 (Conn. 2004) is in accord with the approach of the Tennessee courts. In *Cweklinsky* the court found that public policy considerations, including concern about the chilling effect on communication in the workplace, outweighed the employee's equity and fairness concerns. *See* also Connie Swenba, *"To Tell the Truth, the Whole Truth and Nothing but the Truth": Employment References and Tort Liability*, 33 U. TOL. L. REV. 847 (2002) (discussing intersection of defamation and employer's duty to disclose).

6. *Inadvertent Publication.* If the defendant knows that another person is in the habit of opening plaintiff's mail, and sends plaintiff a libelous letter that is opened and read by that other person, as the court in *Roberts v. English Mfg. Co.*, 155 Ala. 414, 46 So. 752 (1908) held, that letter can be a publication. However, in *McNichol v. Grandy*, [1931] 1 D.L.R. 225, 230, the Canadian supreme court concluded there was no actionable publication of a defendant's defamation of the plaintiff if the defamatory statement is made to the plaintiff herself and is "accidentally" overheard by a third person, provided the defendant did not intend, or have "reason to know or to suspect that any other person was within hearing." Do the holdings in *Roberts* and *McNichol* square with more recently recognized constitutional protections considered below?

2. Constitutional Dimensions of Defamation

NEW YORK TIMES CO. v. SULLIVAN
376 U.S. 254 (1964)

MR. JUSTICE BRENNAN delivered the opinion of the Court.

[Respondent L. B. Sullivan was a public official, criticized for his official conduct. He served as one of three elected Commissioners of the City of Montgomery, Alabama. This position supervised the police. Petitioners were "Negroes and Alabama clergymen" and the New York Times Company, publisher of the New York Times, a daily newspaper.

Respondent alleged he had been libeled by statements in a full-page advertisement carried in the New York Times on March 29, 1960. Entitled "Heed Their Rising Voices," the ad solicited support for non-violent protests during the civil rights movement.

The Court presented the following facts:]

Of the 10 paragraphs of text in the advertisement, the third and a portion of the sixth were the basis of respondent's claim of libel. They read as follows:

Third paragraph:

"In Montgomery, Alabama, after students sang 'My Country, 'Tis of Thee' on the State Capitol steps, their leaders were expelled from school, and truckloads of police armed with shotguns and tear-gas ringed the Alabama State College Campus. When the entire student body protested to state authorities by refusing to re-register, their dining hall was padlocked in an attempt to starve them into submission."

Sixth paragraph:

"Again and again the Southern violators have answered Dr. King's peaceful protests with intimidation and violence. They have bombed his home almost killing his wife and child. They have assaulted his person. They have arrested him seven times — for 'speeding,' 'loitering' and similar 'offenses.' And now they have charged him with 'perjury' — a *felony* under which they could imprison him for *ten years*. . . .*"

Although neither of these statements mentions respondent by name, he contended that the word "police" in the third paragraph referred to him as the Montgomery Commissioner who supervised the Police Department, so that he was being accused of "ringing" the campus with police. He further claimed that the paragraph would be read as imputing to the police, and hence to him, the padlocking of the dining hall in order to starve the students into submission. As to the sixth paragraph, he contended that since arrests are ordinarily made by the police, the statement "They have arrested [Dr. King] seven times" would be read as referring to him; he further contended that the "They" who did the arresting would be equated with the "They" who committed the other described acts and with the "Southern violators." Thus, he argued, the paragraph would be read as accusing the Montgomery police, and hence him, of answering Dr. King's protests with "intimidation and violence," bombing his home, assaulting his person, and charging him with perjury. Respondent and six other Montgomery residents testified that they read some or all of the statements as referring to him in his capacity as Commissioner.

It is uncontroverted that some of the statements contained in the two paragraphs were not accurate descriptions of events which occurred in Montgomery. Although Negro students staged a demonstration on the State Capitol steps, they sang the National Anthem and not "My Country,' 'Tis of Thee." Although nine students were expelled by the State Board of Education, this was not for leading the demonstration at the Capitol, but for demanding service at a lunch counter in the Montgomery County Courthouse on another day. Not the entire student body, but most of it, had protested the expulsion, not by refusing to register, but by boycotting classes on a single day; virtually all the students did register for the ensuing semester. The campus dining hall was not padlocked on any occasion, and the only students who may have been barred from eating there were the few who had neither signed a preregistration application nor requested temporary meal tickets. Although the police were deployed near the campus in large numbers on three occasions, they did not at any time "ring" the campus, and they were not called to the campus in connection with the demonstration on the State Capitol steps, as the third paragraph implied. Dr. King had not been arrested seven times, but only four; and although he claimed to have been assaulted some years earlier in connection with his arrest for loitering outside a courtroom, one of the officers who made the arrest denied that there was such an assault.

On the premise that the charges in the sixth paragraph could be read as referring to him, respondent was allowed to prove that he had not participated in the events described. Although Dr. King's home had in fact been bombed twice when his wife and child were there, both of these occasions antedated respondent's tenure as Commissioner, and the police were not only not implicated in the bombings, but had made every effort to apprehend those who were. Three of Dr. King's four arrests took place before respondent became Commissioner. Although Dr. King had in fact been indicted (he was subsequently acquitted) on two counts of perjury, each of which carried a possible five-year sentence, respondent had nothing to do with procuring the indictment.

Respondent made no effort to prove he had suffered pecuniary loss as a result of the advertisement.... [No one] at the Times made an effort to confirm the accuracy of the [advertisement], either by checking it against recent Times news stories relating to some of the described events or by any other means. ...

The trial judge submitted the case to the jury under instructions that the statements in the [advertisement] were "libelous *per se*" and were not privileged, so that petitioners might be held liable if the jury found that they had published the advertisement and that the statements were made "of and concerning" respondent. The jury was instructed that, because the statements were libelous *per se*, "the law ... implies legal injury from the bare fact of publication itself," "falsity and malice are presumed," "general damages need not be alleged or proved but are presumed," and "punitive damages may be awarded by the jury even though the amount of actual damages is neither found nor shown." An award of punitive damages — as distinguished from "general" damages, which are compensatory in nature — apparently requires proof of actual malice under Alabama law, and the judge charged that "mere negligence or carelessness is not evidence of actual malice or malice in fact, and does not justify an award of exemplary or punitive damages." He refused to charge, however, that the jury must be "convinced" of malice, in the sense of "actual intent" to harm or "gross negligence and recklessness," to make such an award, and he also refused to require that a verdict for respondent differentiate between compensatory and punitive damages. The judge rejected petitioners' contention that his rulings abridged the freedoms of speech and of the press that are guaranteed by the First and Fourteenth Amendments. [A jury ... awarded him damages of $500,000, the full amount claimed, against all the petitioners, and the Supreme Court of Alabama affirmed.]

... We reverse the judgment. We hold that the rule of law applied by the Alabama courts is constitutionally deficient for failure to provide the safeguards for freedom of speech and of the press that are required by the First and Fourteenth Amendments in a libel action brought by a public official against critics of his official conduct. We further hold that under the proper safeguards the evidence presented in this case is constitutionally insufficient to support the judgment for respondent. ...

Respondent relies heavily, as did the Alabama courts, on statements of this Court to the effect that the Constitution does not protect libelous publications. Those statements do not foreclose our inquiry here. None of the cases sustained the use of libel laws to impose sanctions upon expression critical of the official conduct of public officials. ... In *Beauharnais v. Illinois*, 343 U.S. 250, [96 L. Ed. 919, 72 S. Ct. 725 (1952)] the Court sustained an Illinois criminal libel statute as applied to a publication held to be both defamatory of a racial group and "liable to cause violence and disorder." But the Court was careful to note that it "retains and exercises authority to nullify action which encroaches on freedom of utterance under the guise of punishing libel"; for "public men, are, as it were, public property," and "discussion cannot be denied and the right, as well as the duty, of criticism must not be stifled." ...

The general proposition that freedom of expression upon public questions is secured by the First Amendment has long been settled by our decisions. ...

Mr. Justice Brandeis, in his concurring opinion in *Whitney v. California,* 274 U.S. 357, 375-376, (1927) gave the principle its classic formulation:

> Those who won our independence believed . . . that public discussion is a political duty; and that this should be a fundamental principle of the American government. . . . Believing in the power of reason as applied through public discussion, they eschewed silence coerced by law — the argument of force in its worst form. Recognizing the occasional tyrannies of governing majorities, they amended the Constitution so that free speech and assembly should be guaranteed.

Thus we consider this case against the background of a profound national commitment to the principle that debate on public issues should be uninhibited, robust, and wide-open, and that it may well include vehement, caustic, and sometimes unpleasantly sharp attacks on government and public officials. The present advertisement, as an expression of grievance and protest on one of the major public issues of our time, would seem clearly to qualify for the constitutional protection. The question is whether it forfeits that protection by the falsity of some of its factual statements and by its alleged defamation of respondent. . . .

The constitutional protection does not turn upon "the truth, popularity, or social utility of the ideas and beliefs which are offered." *N.A.A.C.P. v. Button,* 371 U.S. 415 [(1963)]. As Madison said, "Some degree of abuse is inseparable from the proper use of every thing; and in no instance is this more true than in that of the press." 4 Elliot's Debates on the Federal Constitution (1876), p. 571. In *Cantwell v. Connecticut,* 310 U.S. 296 [(1940)], the Court declared:

> In the realm of religious faith, and in that of political belief, sharp differences arise. In both fields the tenets of one man may seem the rankest error to his neighbor. To persuade others to his own point of view, the pleader, as we know, at times, resorts to exaggeration, to vilification of men who have been, or are, prominent in church or state, and even to false statement. But the people of this nation have ordained in the light of history, that, in spite of the probability of excesses and abuses, these liberties are, in the long view, essential to enlightened opinion and right conduct on the part of the citizens of a democracy.

That erroneous statement is inevitable in free debate, and that it must be protected if the freedoms of expression are to have the "breathing space" that they "need . . . to survive," *N.A.A.C.P. v. Button,* 371 U.S. at 433, was also recognized by the Court of Appeals for the District of Columbia Circuit in *Sweeney v. Patterson,* 128 F.2d 457, 458 (D.C. Cir. 1942), *cert. denied,* 317 U.S. 678. Judge Edgerton spoke for a unanimous court which affirmed the dismissal of a Congressman's libel suit based upon a newspaper article charging him with anti-Semitism in opposing a judicial appointment. He said:

> Cases which impose liability for erroneous reports of the political conduct of officials reflect the obsolete doctrine that the governed must not criticize their governors. . . . The interest of the public here outweighs the interest of appellant or any other individual. The protection of the public requires not merely discussion, but information. Political conduct and

views which some respectable people approve, and others condemn, are constantly imputed to Congressmen. Errors of fact, particularly in regard to a man's mental states and processes, are inevitable. . . . Whatever is added to the field of libel is taken from the field of free debate.

Injury to official reputation affords no more warrant for repressing speech that would otherwise be free than does factual error. Where judicial officers are involved, this Court has held that concern for the dignity and reputation of the courts does not justify the punishment as criminal contempt of criticism of the judge or his decision. This is true even though the utterance contains "half-truths" and "misinformation." *Pennekamp v. Florida,* 328 U.S. 331, 342, 343, n. 5, 345 [(1946)]. Such repression can be justified, if at all, only by a clear and present danger of the obstruction of justice. . . . If judges are to be treated as "men of fortitude, able to thrive in a hardy climate," *Craig v. Harney,* 331 U.S. 367, 376 (1947), surely the same must be true of other government officials, such as elected city commissioners. Criticism of their official conduct does not lose its constitutional protection merely because it is effective criticism and hence diminishes their official reputations.

If neither factual error nor defamatory content suffices to remove the constitutional shield from criticism of official conduct, the combination of the two elements is no less inadequate. This is the lesson to be drawn from the great controversy over the Sedition Act of 1798, 1 Stat. 596, which first crystallized a national awareness of the central meaning of the First Amendment. . . . That statute made it a crime, punishable by a $5,000 fine and five years in prison, "if any person shall write, print, utter or publish . . . any false, scandalous and malicious writing or writings against the government of the United States, or either house of the Congress . . . , or the President . . . , with intent to defame . . . or to bring them, or either of them, into contempt or disrepute; or to excite against them, or either or any of them, the hatred of the good people of the United States." The Act allowed the defendant the defense of truth, and provided that the jury were to be judges both of the law and the facts. Despite these qualifications, the Act was vigorously condemned as unconstitutional in an attack joined in by Jefferson and Madison. In the famous Virginia Resolutions of 1798, the General Assembly of Virginia resolved that it

> doth particularly protest against the palpable and alarming infractions of the Constitution, in the two late cases of the 'Alien and Sedition Acts,' passed at the last session of Congress. . . . [The Sedition Act] exercises . . . a power not delegated by the Constitution, but, on the contrary, expressly and positively forbidden by one of the amendments thereto — a power which, more than any other, ought to produce universal alarm, because it is levelled against the right of freely examining public characters and measures, and of free communication among the people thereon, which has ever been justly deemed the only effectual guardian of every other right.

4 Elliot's Debates, *supra,* pp. 553-554. . . .

There is no force in respondent's argument that the constitutional limitations implicit in the history of the Sedition Act apply only to Congress and not to the States. It is true that the First Amendment was originally addressed only to action by the Federal Government, and that Jefferson, for one, while denying the power of Congress "to control the freedom of the press," recognized such a power in the States. See the 1804 Letter to Abigail Adams quoted in *Dennis v. United States,* 341 U.S. 494, 522, n. 4 [(1951)] (concurring opinion). But this distinction was eliminated with the adoption of the Fourteenth Amendment and the application to the States of the First Amendment's restrictions.

What a State may not constitutionally bring about by means of a criminal statute is likewise beyond the reach of its civil law of libel. The fear of damage awards under a rule such as that invoked by the Alabama courts here may be markedly more inhibiting than the fear of prosecution under a criminal statute. Alabama, for example, has a criminal libel law which subjects to prosecution "any person who speaks, writes, or prints of and concerning another any accusation falsely and maliciously importing the commission by such person of a felony, or any other indictable offense involving moral turpitude," and which allows as punishment upon conviction a fine not exceeding $500 and a prison sentence of six months. Alabama Code, Tit. 14, §350. Presumably a person charged with violation of this statute enjoys ordinary criminal-law safeguards such as the requirements of an indictment and of proof beyond a reasonable doubt. These safeguards are not available to the defendant in a civil action. The judgment awarded in this case — without the need for any proof of actual pecuniary loss — was one thousand times greater than the maximum fine provided by the Alabama criminal statute, and one hundred times greater than that provided by the Sedition Act. And since there is no double-jeopardy limitation applicable to civil lawsuits, this is not the only judgment that may be awarded against petitioners for the same publication. Whether or not a newspaper can survive a succession of such judgments, the pall of fear and timidity imposed upon those who would give voice to public criticism is an atmosphere in which the First Amendment freedoms cannot survive. . . .

The state rule of law is not saved by its allowance of the defense of truth. . . .

A rule compelling the critic of official conduct to guarantee the truth of all his factual assertions — and to do so on pain of libel judgments virtually unlimited in amount — leads to a comparable "self-censorship." Allowance of the defense of truth, with the burden of proving it on the defendant, does not mean that only false speech will be deterred. Even courts accepting this defense as an adequate safeguard have recognized the difficulties of adducing legal proofs that the alleged libel was true in all its factual particulars. . . . Under such a rule, would-be critics of official conduct may be deterred from voicing their criticism, even though it is believed to be true and even though it is in fact true, because of doubt whether it can be proved in court or fear of the expense of having to do so. They tend to make only statements which "steer far wider of the unlawful zone." *Speiser v. Randall,* 357 U.S. [513, 526 (1958)]. The rule thus dampens the vigor and limits the variety of public debate. It is inconsistent with the First and Fourteenth Amendments.

The constitutional guarantees require, we think, a federal rule that prohibits a public official from recovering damages for a defamatory falsehood relating to his official conduct unless he proves that the statement was made with "actual malice" — that is, with knowledge that it was false or with reckless disregard of whether it was false or not. . . .

We hold today that the Constitution delimits a State's power to award damages for libel in actions brought by public officials against critics of their official conduct. Since this is such an action, the rule requiring proof of actual malice is applicable. While Alabama law apparently requires proof of actual malice for an award of punitive damages, where general damages are concerned malice is "presumed." Such a presumption is inconsistent with the federal rule. . . . Since the trial judge did not instruct the jury to differentiate between general and punitive damages, it may be that the verdict was wholly an award of one or the other. But it is impossible to know, in view of the general verdict returned. Because of this uncertainty, the judgment must be reversed and the case remanded.

. . . [W]e consider that the proof presented to show actual malice lacks the convincing clarity which the constitutional standard demands, and hence that it would not constitutionally sustain the judgment for respondent under the proper rule of law. The case of the individual petitioners requires little discussion. Even assuming that they could constitutionally be found to have authorized the use of their names on the advertisement, there was no evidence whatever that they were aware of any erroneous statements or were in any way reckless in that regard. The judgment against them is thus without constitutional support.

As to the Times, we similarly conclude that the facts do not support a finding of actual malice. The statement by the Times' Secretary that, apart from the padlocking allegation, he thought the advertisement was "substantially correct," affords no constitutional warrant for the Alabama Supreme Court's conclusion that it was a "cavalier ignoring of the falsity of the advertisement [from which] the jury could not have but been impressed with the bad faith of The Times, and its maliciousness inferable therefrom." The statement does not indicate malice at the time of the publication; even if the advertisement was not "substantially correct" — although respondent's own proofs tend to show that it was — that opinion was at least a reasonable one, and there was no evidence to impeach the witness' good faith in holding it. The Times' failure to retract upon respondent's demand, although it later retracted upon the demand of Governor Patterson, is likewise not adequate evidence of malice for constitutional purposes. Whether or not a failure to retract may ever constitute such evidence, there are two reasons why it does not here. *First,* the letter written by the Times reflected a reasonable doubt on its part as to whether the advertisement could reasonably be taken to refer to respondent at all. *Second,* it was not a final refusal, since it asked for an explanation on this point — a request that respondent chose to ignore. Nor does the retraction upon the demand of the Governor supply the necessary proof. . . .

Finally, there is evidence that the Times published the advertisement without checking its accuracy against the news stories in the Times' own files. The mere presence of the stories in the files does not, of course, establish that the Times "knew" the advertisement was false, since the state of mind required for actual malice would have to be brought home to the persons in the Times' organization having responsibility for the publication of the advertisement. With respect to the failure of those persons to make the check, the record shows that they relied upon their knowledge of the good reputation of many of those whose names were listed as sponsors of the advertisement, and upon the letter from A. Philip Randolph, known to them as a responsible individual, certifying that the use of the names was authorized. There was testimony that the persons handling the advertisement saw nothing in it that would render it unacceptable under the Times' policy of rejecting advertisements containing "attacks of a personal character"; their failure to reject it on this ground was not unreasonable. We think the evidence against the Times supports at most a finding of negligence in failing to discover the misstatements, and is constitutionally insufficient to show the recklessness that is required for a finding of actual malice. . . .

We also think the evidence was constitutionally defective in another respect: it was incapable of supporting the jury's finding that the allegedly libelous statements were made "of and concerning" respondent. . . .

. . . [T]he Supreme Court of Alabama . . . in holding that the trial court "did not err in overruling the demurrer [of the Times] in the aspect that the libelous matter was not of and concerning the [plaintiff,]" based its ruling on the proposition that:

> We think it common knowledge that the average person knows that municipal agents, such as police and firemen, and others, are under the control and direction of the city governing body, and more particularly under the direction and control of a single commissioner. In measuring the performance or deficiencies of such groups, praise or criticism is usually attached to the official in complete control of the body.

This proposition has disquieting implications for criticism of governmental conduct. . . . The present proposition would sidestep this obstacle by transmuting criticism of government, however impersonal it may seem on its face, into personal criticism, and hence potential libel, of the officials of whom the government is composed. . . . Raising as it does the possibility that a good-faith critic of government will be penalized for his criticism, the proposition relied on by the Alabama courts strikes at the very center of the constitutionally protected area of free expression. We hold that such a proposition may not constitutionally be utilized to establish that an otherwise impersonal attack on governmental operations was a libel of an official responsible for those operations. Since it was relied on exclusively here, and there was no other evidence to connect the statements with respondent, the evidence was constitutionally insufficient to support a finding that the statements referred to respondent.

The judgment of the Supreme Court of Alabama is reversed and the case is remanded to that court for further proceedings not inconsistent with this opinion.

NOTES

1. *The Public Person and Constitutional or "Actual" Malice. New York Times Co. v. Sullivan* required a public official to prove constitutional or "actual" malice. The Court applied this rule to defamation plaintiffs who are public figures in *Curtis Publishing Co. v. Butts,* 388 U.S. 130 (1967). In *Garrison v. Louisiana,* 379 U.S. 64 (1964), the Court said that proof of constitutional malice requires a showing that a false publication was made with a "high degree of awareness of . . . probable falsity." As examples of such awareness, the Court in *St. Amant v. Thompson,* 390 U.S. 727 (1968), stated:

> The defendant in a defamation action brought by a public official cannot, however, automatically insure a favorable verdict by testifying that he published with a belief that the statements were true. The finder of fact must determine whether the publication was indeed made in good faith. Professions of good faith will be unlikely to prove persuasive, for example, where a story is fabricated by the defendant, is the product of his imagination, or is based wholly on an unverified anonymous telephone call. Nor will they be likely to prevail when the publisher's allegations are so inherently improbable that only a reckless man would have put them in circulation. Likewise, recklessness may be found where there are obvious reasons to doubt the veracity of the informant or the accuracy of his reports.

Id. at 732.

In *Rosenblatt v. Baer,* 383 U.S. 75 (1966), the Court required proof of "actual" malice because the manager of a public ski resort was a public official. "Where a position in government has such apparent importance that the public has an independent interest in the qualifications and performance of the person who holds it, beyond the general public interest in the qualifications and performance of all government employees," the person is a public official. How far down the public employment line do these cases extend speech protections? Would a public elementary school teacher be included? Would the school secretary or a maintenance worker employed by city hall?

In *Posadas v. City of Reno*, 851 P.2d 438 (Nev. 1993), the defendant issued an allegedly false press release stating that the plaintiff police officer had lied under oath. The court indicated that *New York Times* "actual malice" can be established in part by showing "ill will" on the part of the defendant toward the plaintiff. How much proof of actual knowledge or reckless disregard of falsity must be presented before proof of ill will can tip the balance? *See Freedom Newspapers v. Cantu*, 168 S.W.3d 847 (Tex. 2005). In *Cantu* former sheriff sued the newspaper and two former employees alleging that two articles about a candidate debate in which plaintiff had participated were defamatory. The sheriff had distinguished himself as being bilingual and bicultural; the newspaper's headline read "no Anglo can be sheriff" and this quote and a similar comment in the article were attributed to the sheriff. After the sheriff objected to the word "Anglo," the paper printed a second article. The court concluded that a reasonable reader would have understood that the part of the statement printed without quotations and the other with quotations would indicate paraphrasing or interpretation of the sheriff's remarks. Therefore proof that he did not make the exact remarks attributed to him, standing alone, was not evidence of actual malice.

In *Harte-Hanks Communication, Inc. v. Connaughton,* 491 U.S. 657 (1989), the Court concluded that the jury had properly found by clear and convincing evidence that the defendant acted with constitutional malice in printing the false and defamatory article. The plaintiff, an unsuccessful candidate for the office of municipal judge, sued defendant for printing a story before the election stating in effect that plaintiff had bribed a witness to testify that the incumbent's director of court services had repeatedly accepted bribes in return for judicial favors. The story was based on a newspaper interview with the witness' sister, who said she was present at the plaintiff's meeting with the witness. Although the defendant interviewed the plaintiff before printing the story, it made no attempt to talk to the witness. The Court ruled in plaintiff's favor after an exhaustive de novo review of the facts. *See Hearst Corp v. Skeen*, 159 S.W.3d 633 (Tex. 2005) (publication under deadline pressure is not enough to show actual malice in an article about a public figure).

2. *Defamation of a Large Group.* In *Neiman-Marcus v. Lait,* 13 F.R.D 311 (D.C.N.Y. 1952), the court held that a group of 382 saleswomen, who had been defamed as a group, was so large that no individual saleswoman could bring an action. One commentator would permit each member of a group of not more than twenty-five persons to assert a defamation claim against a speaker if the speaker insinuated individual blameworthiness of the group members and if the statement were untrue as to the claimant and as to most members of the group. Joseph H. King, Jr., *Reference to the Plaintiff Requirement in Defamatory Statements Directed at Groups*, 35 WAKE FOREST L. REV. 343 (2000).

3. *Belief in the Falsity of a Defamatory Statement.* The *Sullivan* Court said that the evidence did not indicate that any of the witnesses believed the alleged charges against Commissioner Sullivan in the New York Times' article. Would this be an independent basis for finding an absence of libel?

4. *Vicarious Liability.* The *Sullivan* Court refused to impute to the New York Times advertising department the knowledge of its filing department about prior stories in the newspaper that would have indicated the falsity of some of the statements in the *Sullivan* case. Would application of the doctrine of corporate vicarious liability have required such an imputation? Why would the Court refuse to take such a position?

5. Not surprisingly the *Sullivan* case continues to spawn a great deal of commentary. *See, e.g.,* David A. Anderson, *Rethinking Defamation*, 48 ARIZ. L. REV. 1047 (2006); R. Kenton Bird, *The Ad That Changed Libel Law: Judicial Realism and Social Activism in* New York Times v. Sullivan, 9 COMM. L. & POL'Y 489 (2004); Kristian D. Whitten, *The Economics of Actual Malice: A Proposal for Legislative Change to the Rule of* New York Times v. Sullivan, 32 CUMB. L. REV. 519 (2001); David A. Anderson, *Is Libel Law Worth Reforming?*, 140 U. PA. L. REV. 487 (1991); Anthony Lewis, New York Times v. Sullivan *Reconsidered: Time to Return to "The Central Meaning of the First Amendment,"* 83 COLUM. L. REV. 603 (1983).

GERTZ v. ROBERT WELCH, INC.
418 U.S. 323 (1974)

MR. JUSTICE POWELL delivered the opinion of the Court.

. . . In 1968 a Chicago policeman named Nuccio shot and killed a youth named Nelson. The state authorities prosecuted Nuccio for the homicide and ultimately obtained a conviction for murder in the second degree. The Nelson family retained petitioner Elmer Gertz, a reputable attorney, to represent them in civil litigation against Nuccio.

Respondent publishes American Opinion, a monthly outlet for the views of the John Birch Society. Early in the 1960's the magazine began to warn of a nationwide conspiracy to discredit local law enforcement agencies and create in their stead a national police force capable of supporting a Communist dictatorship. As part of the continuing effort to alert the public to this assumed danger, the managing editor of American Opinion commissioned an article on the murder trial of Officer Nuccio [by] a regular contributor to the magazine. In March 1969 respondent published the resulting article under the title "FRAME-UP: Richard Nuccio And The War On Police." The article purports to demonstrate that the testimony against Nuccio at his criminal trial was false and that his prosecution was part of the Communist campaign against the police.

In his capacity as counsel for the Nelson family in the civil litigation, petitioner attended the coroner's inquest into the boy's death and initiated actions for damages, but he neither discussed Officer Nuccio with the press nor played any part in the criminal proceeding. Notwithstanding petitioner's remote connection with the prosecution of Nuccio, respondent's magazine portrayed him as an architect of the "frame-up." According to the article, the police file on petitioner took "a big, Irish cop to lift." The article stated that petitioner had been an official of the "Marxist League for Industrial Democracy, originally known as the Intercollegiate Socialist Society, which has advocated the violent seizure of our government." It labeled Gertz a "Leninist" and a "Communist-fronter." It also stated that Gertz had been an officer of the National Lawyers Guild, described as a Communist organization that "probably did more than any other outfit to plan the Communist attack on the Chicago police during the 1968 Democratic Convention."

These statements contained serious inaccuracies. The implication that petitioner had a criminal record was false. Petitioner had been a member and officer of the National Lawyers Guild some 15 years earlier, but there was no evidence that he or that organization had taken any part in planning the 1968 demonstrations in Chicago. There was also no basis for the charge that petitioner was a "Leninist" or a "Communist-fronter." And he had never been a member of the "Marxist League for Industrial Democracy" or the "Intercollegiate Socialist Society."

The managing editor of American Opinion made no effort to verify or substantiate the charges against petitioner. Instead, he appended an editorial introduction stating that the author had "conducted extensive research into the Richard Nuccio Case." And he included in the article a photograph of petitioner and wrote the caption that appeared under it: "Elmer Gertz of Red

Guild harasses Nuccio." Respondent placed the issue of American Opinion containing the article on sale at newsstands throughout the country and distributed reprints of the article on the streets of Chicago.

Petitioner filed a diversity action for libel in the United States District Court for the Northern District of Illinois. He claimed that the falsehoods published by respondent injured his reputation as a lawyer and a citizen. . . . [R]espondent filed a pretrial motion for summary judgment, claiming . . . petitioner was a public official or a public figure and that the article concerned an issue of public interest and concern. For these reasons, respondent argued, it was entitled to invoke the privilege enunciated in *New York Times Co. v. Sullivan,* 376 U.S. 254 (1964). Under this rule respondent would escape liability unless petitioner could prove publication of defamatory falsehood "with 'actual malice' — that is, with knowledge that it was false or with reckless disregard of whether it was false or not." Respondent claimed that petitioner could not make such a showing and submitted a supporting affidavit by the magazine's managing editor. The editor denied any knowledge of the falsity of the statements concerning petitioner and stated that he had relied on the author's reputation and on his prior experience with the accuracy and authenticity of the author's contributions to American Opinion. . . .

Following [a $50,000] jury verdict . . . the District Court concluded that the *New York Times* standard should govern this case even though petitioner was not a public official or public figure. It accepted respondent's contention that that privilege protected discussion of any public issue without regard to the status of a person defamed therein. Accordingly, the court entered judgment for respondent notwithstanding the jury's verdict. . . .

Petitioner appealed to contest the applicability of the *New York Times* standard to this case. Although the Court of Appeals for the Seventh Circuit doubted the correctness of the District Court's determination that petitioner was not a public figure, it did not overturn that finding. It agreed with the District Court that respondent could assert the constitutional privilege because the article concerned a matter of public interest, citing this Court's intervening decision in *Rosenbloom v. Metromedia, Inc.,* [403 U.S. 29 (1971)]. The Court of Appeals read *Rosenbloom* to require application of the *New York Times* standard to any publication or broadcast about an issue of significant public interest, without regard to the position, fame, or anonymity of the person defamed, and it concluded that respondent's statements concerned such an issue. After reviewing the record, the Court of Appeals endorsed the District Court's conclusion that petitioner had failed to show by clear and convincing evidence that respondent had acted with "actual malice" as defined by *New York Times.* There was no evidence that the managing editor of American Opinion knew of the falsity of the accusations made in the article. In fact, he knew nothing about petitioner except what he learned from the article. The court correctly noted that mere proof of failure to investigate, without more, cannot establish reckless disregard for the truth. Rather, the publisher must act with a "'high degree of awareness of . . . probable falsity.'" *St. Amant v. Thompson,* 390 U.S. 727, 731 (1968). . . . The evidence in this case did not reveal that respondent had cause for such an awareness. The Court of Appeals therefore affirmed. For the reasons stated below, we reverse. . . .

We begin with the common ground. Under the First Amendment there is no such thing as a false idea. However pernicious an opinion may seem, we depend for its correction not on the conscience of judges and juries but on the competition of other ideas.[7]

But there is no constitutional value in false statements of fact. Neither the intentional lie nor the careless error materially advances society's interest in "uninhibited, robust, and wide-open" debate on public issues. They belong to that category of utterances which "are no essential part of any exposition of ideas, and are of such slight social value as a step to truth that any benefit that may be derived from them is clearly outweighed by the social interest in order and morality." . . .

The need to avoid self-censorship by the news media is, however, not the only societal value at issue. . . .

The legitimate state interest underlying the law of libel is the compensation of individuals for the harm inflicted on them by defamatory falsehood. We would not lightly require the State to abandon this purpose, for as Mr. Justice Stewart has reminded us, the individual's right to the protection of his own good name "reflects no more than our basic concept of the essential dignity and worth of every human being — a concept at the root of any decent system of ordered liberty. The protection of private personality, like the protection of life itself, is left primarily to the individual States under the Ninth and Tenth Amendments. But this does not mean that the right is entitled to any less recognition by this Court as a basic of our constitutional system." *Rosenblatt v. Baer,* 383 U.S. 75, 92 (1966) (concurring opinion). . . .

The *New York Times* standard defines the level of constitutional protection appropriate to the context of defamation of a public person. Those who, by reason of the notoriety of their achievements or the vigor and success with which they seek the public's attention, are properly classed as public figures and those who hold governmental office may recover for injury to reputation only on clear and convincing proof that the defamatory falsehood was made with knowledge of its falsity or with reckless disregard for the truth. This standard administers an extremely powerful antidote to the inducement to media self-censorship of the common-law rule of strict liability for libel and slander. And it exacts a correspondingly high price from the victims of defamatory falsehood. Plainly many deserving plaintiffs, including some intentionally subjected to injury, will be unable to surmount the barrier of the *New York Times* test. Despite this substantial abridgment of the state law right to compensation for wrongful hurt to one's reputation, the Court has concluded that the protection of the *New York Times* privilege should be available to publishers and broadcasters of defamatory falsehood concerning public officials and public figures. We think that these decisions are correct, but we do not find their holdings justified solely by reference to the interest of the press and broadcast media in immunity from liability. Rather, we believe that the *New*

---

[7] As Thomas Jefferson made the point in his first Inaugural Address: "If there be any among us who would wish to dissolve this Union or change its republican form, let them stand undisturbed as monuments of the safety with which error of opinion may be tolerated where reason is left free to combat it."

York Times rule states an accommodation between this concern and the limited state interest present in the context of libel actions brought by public persons. For the reasons stated below, we conclude that the state interest in compensating injury to the reputation of private individuals requires that a different rule should obtain with respect to them.

Theoretically, of course, the balance between the needs of the press and the individual's claim to compensation for wrongful injury might be struck on a case-by-case basis. . . . But this approach would lead to unpredictable results and uncertain expectations, and it could render our duty to supervise the lower courts unmanageable. Because an *ad hoc* resolution of the competing interests at stake in each particular case is not feasible, we must lay down broad rules of general application. Such rules necessarily treat alike various cases involving differences as well as similarities. . . .

With that caveat we have no difficulty in distinguishing among defamation plaintiffs. The first remedy of any victim of defamation is self-help — using available opportunities to contradict the lie or correct the error and thereby to minimize its adverse impact on reputation. Public officials and public figures usually enjoy significantly greater access to the channels of effective communication and hence have a more realistic opportunity to counteract false statements than private individuals normally enjoy. Private individuals are therefore more vulnerable to injury, and the state interest in protecting them is correspondingly greater.

More important than the likelihood that private individuals will lack effective opportunities for rebuttal, there is a compelling normative consideration underlying the distinction between public and private defamation plaintiffs. An individual who decides to seek governmental office must accept certain necessary consequences of that involvement in public affairs. He runs the risk of closer public scrutiny than might otherwise be the case. And society's interest in the officers of government is not strictly limited to the formal discharge of official duties. As the Court pointed out in *Garrison v. Louisiana,* 379 U.S. [64, 77 (1964)], the public's interest extends to "anything which might touch on an official's fitness for office. . . . Few personal attributes are more germane to fitness for office than dishonesty, malfeasance, or improper motivation, even though these characteristics may also affect the official's private character."

Those classed as public figures stand in a similar position. Hypothetically, it may be possible for someone to become a public figure through no purposeful action of his own, but the instances of truly involuntary public figures must be exceedingly rare. For the most part those who attain this status have assumed roles of special prominence in the affairs of society. Some occupy positions of such persuasive power and influence that they are deemed public figures for all purposes. More commonly, those classed as public figures have thrust themselves to the forefront of particular public controversies. . . . In either event, they invite attention and comment.

Even if the foregoing generalities do not obtain in every instance, the communications media are entitled to act on the assumption that public officials and public figures have voluntarily exposed themselves to increased risk of injury from defamatory falsehood concerning them. No such assumption is justified with respect to a private individual. He has not accepted public office or assumed an "influential role in ordering society." *Curtis Pub. Co. v. Butts,* 388 U.S. [130 (1967)] (Warren, C.J., concurring in result). He has relinquished no part of his interest in the protection of his own good name, and consequently he has a more compelling call on the courts for redress of injury inflicted by defamatory falsehood. Thus, private individuals are not only more vulnerable to injury than public officials and public figures; they are also more deserving of recovery.

For these reasons we conclude that the States should retain substantial latitude in their efforts to enforce a legal remedy for defamatory falsehood injurious to the reputation of a private individual. The extension of the *New York Times* test proposed by the *Rosenbloom* plurality would abridge this legitimate state interest to a degree that we find unacceptable. And it would occasion the additional difficulty of forcing state and federal judges to decide on an *ad hoc* basis which publications address issues of "general or public interest" and which do not — to determine, in the words of Mr. Justice Marshall, "what information is relevant to self-government." We doubt the wisdom of committing this task to the conscience of judges. Nor does the Constitution require us to draw so thin a line between the drastic alternatives of the *New York Times* privilege and the common law of strict liability for defamatory error. The "public or general interest" test for determining the applicability of the *New York Times* standard to private defamation actions inadequately serves both of the competing values at stake. On the one hand, a private individual whose reputation is injured by defamatory falsehood that does concern an issue of public or general interest has no recourse unless he can meet the rigorous requirements of *New York Times.* This is true despite the factors that distinguish the state interest in compensating private individuals from the analogous interest involved in the context of public persons. On the other hand, a publisher or broadcaster of a defamatory error which a court deems unrelated to an issue of public or general interest may be held liable in damages even if it took every reasonable precaution to ensure the accuracy of its assertions. And liability may far exceed compensation for any actual injury to the plaintiff, for the jury may be permitted to presume damages without proof of loss and even to award punitive damages.

We hold that, so long as they do not impose liability without fault, the States may define for themselves the appropriate standard of liability for a publisher or broadcaster of defamatory falsehood injurious to a private individual. This approach provides a more equitable boundary between the competing concerns involved here. It recognizes the strength of the legitimate state interest in compensating private individuals for wrongful injury to reputation, yet shields the press and broadcast media from the rigors of strict liability for defamation. At least this conclusion obtains where, as here, the substance of the defamatory statement "makes substantial danger to reputation apparent." This phrase places in perspective the conclusion we announce today. Our inquiry would involve considerations somewhat different from those discussed above if a State purported to condition civil liability on a factual misstatement whose content did not warn a reasonably prudent editor or broadcaster of its defamatory potential. . . . Such a case is not now before us, and we intimate no view as to its proper resolution.

Our accommodation of the competing values at stake in defamation suits by private individuals allows the States to impose liability on the publisher or broadcaster of defamatory falsehood on a less demanding showing than that required by *New York Times*. This conclusion is not based on a belief that the considerations which prompted the adoption of the *New York Times* privilege for defamation of public officials and its extension to public figures are wholly inapplicable to the context of private individuals. Rather, we endorse this approach in recognition of the strong and legitimate state interest in compensating private individuals for injury to reputation. But this countervailing state interest extends no further than compensation for actual injury. For the reasons stated below, we hold that the States may not permit recovery of presumed or punitive damages, at least when liability is not based on a showing of knowledge of falsity or reckless disregard for the truth.

The common law of defamation is an oddity of tort law, for it allows recovery of purportedly compensatory damages without evidence of actual loss. Under the traditional rules pertaining to actions for libel, the existence of injury is presumed from the fact of publication. Juries may award substantial sums as compensation for supposed damage to reputation without any proof that such harm actually occurred. The largely uncontrolled discretion of juries to award damages where there is no loss unnecessarily compounds the potential of any system of liability for defamatory falsehood to inhibit the vigorous exercise of First Amendment freedoms. Additionally, the doctrine of presumed damages invites juries to punish unpopular opinion rather than to compensate individuals for injury sustained by the publication of a false fact. . . . [T]he States have no substantial interest in securing for plaintiffs such as this petitioner gratuitous awards of money damages far in excess of any actual injury. . . .

[W]e are attempting to reconcile state law with a competing interest grounded in the constitutional command of the First Amendment. It is therefore appropriate to require that state remedies for defamatory falsehood reach no farther than is necessary to protect the legitimate interest involved. It is necessary to restrict defamation plaintiffs who do not prove knowledge of falsity or reckless disregard for the truth to compensation for actual injury. We need not define "actual injury," as trial courts have wide experience in framing appropriate jury instructions in tort actions. Suffice it to say that actual injury is not limited to out-of-pocket loss. Indeed, the more customary types of actual harm inflicted by defamatory falsehood include impairment of reputation and standing in the community, personal humiliation, and mental anguish and suffering. Of course, juries must be limited by appropriate instructions, and all awards must be supported by competent evidence concerning the injury, although there need be no evidence which assigns an actual dollar value to the injury.

We also find no justification for allowing awards of punitive damages against publishers and broadcasters held liable under state-defined standards of liability for defamation. In most jurisdictions jury discretion over the amounts awarded is limited only by the gentle rule that they not be excessive. . . . Like the doctrine of presumed damages, jury discretion to award punitive damages unnecessarily exacerbates the danger of media self-censorship, but, unlike the former rule, punitive damages are wholly irrelevant to the state interest that justifies a negligence standard for private defamation actions. They are not compensation for injury. Instead, they are private fines levied by civil juries to punish reprehensible conduct and to deter its future occurrence. In short, the private defamation plaintiff who establishes liability under a less demanding standard than that stated by *New York Times* may recover only such damages as are sufficient to compensate him for actual injury.

Notwithstanding our refusal to extend the *New York Times* privilege to defamation of private individuals, respondent contends that we should affirm the judgment below on the ground that petitioner is either a public official or a public figure. There is little basis for the former assertion. Several years prior to the present incident, petitioner had served briefly on housing committees appointed by the mayor of Chicago, but at the time of publication he had never held any remunerative governmental position. Respondent admits this but argues that petitioner's appearance at the coroner's inquest rendered him a "de facto public official." Our cases recognize no such concept. Respondent's suggestion would sweep all lawyers under the *New York Times* rule as officers of the court and distort the plain meaning of the "public official" category beyond all recognition. We decline to follow it.

Respondent's characterization of petitioner as a public figure raises a different question. That designation may rest on either of two alternative bases. In some instances an individual may achieve such pervasive fame or notoriety that he becomes a public figure for all purposes and in all contexts. More commonly, an individual voluntarily injects himself or is drawn into a particular public controversy and thereby becomes a public figure for a limited range of issues. In either case such persons assume special prominence in the resolution of public questions.

Petitioner has long been active in community and professional affairs. He has served as an officer of local civic groups and of various professional organizations, and he has published several books and articles on legal subjects. Although petitioner was consequently well known in some circles, he had achieved no general fame or notoriety in the community. None of the prospective jurors called at the trial had ever heard of petitioner prior to this litigation, and respondent offered no proof that this response was atypical of the local population. We would not lightly assume that a citizen's participation in community and professional affairs rendered him a public figure for all purposes. Absent clear evidence of general fame or notoriety in the community, and pervasive involvement in the affairs of society, an individual should not be deemed a public personality for all aspects of his life. It is preferable to reduce the public-figure question to a more meaningful context by looking to the nature and extent of an individual's participation in the particular controversy giving rise to the defamation.

In this context it is plain that petitioner was not a public figure . . . and his participation related solely to his representation of a private client. He took no part in the criminal prosecution of Officer Nuccio. Moreover, he never discussed either the criminal or civil litigation with the press and was never quoted as having done so. He plainly did not thrust himself into the vortex of this public issue, nor did he engage the public's attention in an attempt to influence its outcome. We are persuaded that the trial court did not err in refusing to characterize petitioner as a public figure for the purpose of this litigation.

We therefore conclude that the *New York Times* standard is inapplicable to this case and that the trial court erred in entering judgment for respondent. Because the jury was allowed to impose liability without fault and was permitted to presume damages without proof of injury, a new trial is necessary. We reverse and remand for further proceedings in accord with this opinion.

[BLACKMUN, J., who joined in the plurality opinion in *Rosenbloom,* nevertheless concurred in the opinion here as follows.]

Although the Court's opinion in the present case departs from the rationale of the *Rosenbloom* plurality, in that the Court now conditions a libel action by a private person upon a showing of negligence, as contrasted with a showing of willful or reckless disregard, I am willing to join, and so join, the Court's opinion and its judgment for two reasons:

1. By removing the specters of presumed and punitive damages in the absence of *New York Times* malice, the Court eliminates significant and powerful motives for self-censorship that otherwise are present in the traditional libel action. By so doing, the Court leaves what should prove to be sufficient and adequate breathing space for a vigorous press. What the Court has done, I believe, will have little, if any, practical effect on the functioning of responsible journalism.

2. The Court was sadly fractionated in *Rosenbloom.* A result of that kind inevitably leads to uncertainty. I feel that it is of profound importance for the Court to come to rest in the defamation area and to have a clearly defined majority position. . . . If my vote were not needed to create a majority, I would adhere to my prior view. A definitive ruling, however, is paramount. . . .

NOTES

1. *Actual Injury Versus Special Damage.* The *Gertz* Court said the private plaintiff, who seeks recovery on the basis of a showing of fault that is less than that of constitutional or "actual malice," must prove "actual injury." That injury is not the same as that of "special damage," which is typically required for recovery in slander *per quod.* "Actual injury" under *Gertz* can be shown by proving mental anguish and suffering, which alone is insufficient to establish "special damage."

2. *Vicarious Liability Revisited.* The author of the American Opinion article about Mr. Gertz likely wrote with constitutional malice (knowing falsity, or reckless disregard of the truth). Why was that malice not imputed to the defendant publisher?

3. *Public Official and Public Figure Compared.* In *Jenoff v. Hearst Corp.,* 644 F.2d 1004 (4th Cir. 1981), the defendant newspaper allegedly libeled plaintiff Jenoff, an informant for the Baltimore Police Department, by writing that he had broken into the office of a criminal defense attorney and that the statements of certain key witnesses had disappeared from the office at that time.

Affirming a judgment for the plaintiff, the court found he was neither a public official nor a public figure. One need not hold a "formal public position" in order to be a public official, the court said. *Id.* at 1006. One may participate in some governmental enterprise to such an extent as to require that he be classified as a public official. *Id.* But as an informant for the police department, Jenoff played such a "minor role" in a "government enterprise" as to "preclude the public official characterization." *Id.* Nor was Jenoff a voluntary public figure since he enjoyed no special access to the media, other than that which may have been created by the defamatory publications. He assumed no prominence in any public controversy, except as a result of the charges leveled against him. *Id.* at 1007. The court observed that it is established that "those charged with defamation cannot, by their own conduct, create their own defense by making the claimant a public figure." *Id.* (citing *Hutchinson v. Proxmire,* 443 U.S. 111, 135 (1979)). The court concluded that if Jenoff was considered to be a public figure in this context, then "all informants, by virtue of that status, become public figures." *Id.* The use of such "subject-matter classifications" to define the contours of constitutionally protected defamation has been authoritatively rejected. *See Hutchinson v. Proxmire,* 443 U.S. 111, 135 (1979); *Time, Inc. v. Firestone,* 424 U.S. 448 (1976). The court further noted that Jenoff never sought to influence the resolution of any public issue. Would this be determinative of his status or merely a factor in defining a public figure? *See Wolston v. Reader's Digest Ass'n,* 443 U.S. 157, 169 (1979) (Blackmun, J., concurring) ("The Court seems to hold . . . that a person becomes a limited-issue public figure only if he literally or figuratively 'mounts a rostrum' to advocate a particular view").

4. *Burden of Proof.* In a 5-4 decision, the United States Supreme Court in *Philadelphia Newspapers, Inc. v. Hepps,* 475 U.S. 767 (1986), held that the private plaintiff in a defamation suit involving a matter of public concern has the burden of proving falsity of the defamation. The burden lies with the public plaintiff in a matter of public concern, said the Court, to show falsity by "clear and convincing evidence." The Court left open the question of whether the rule of the case applied to nonmedia defendants. The dissent thought it sufficient if the plaintiff showed fault on the part of the defendant. It simply did not "understand, however, why a character assassin should be given an absolute license to defame by means of statements that can neither be verified nor disproved." *Id.* at 785.

3. Private Parties and Matters

DUN & BRADSTREET, INC. v. GREENMOSS BUILDERS, INC.
472 U.S. 749 (1985)

JUSTICE POWELL announced the judgment of the Court and delivered an opinion, in which JUSTICE REHNQUIST and JUSTICE O'CONNOR joined.

In *Gertz v. Robert Welch, Inc.,* 418 U.S. 323 . . . (1974), we held that the First Amendment restricted the damages that a private individual could obtain from a publisher for libel that involved a matter of public concern. More specifically, we held that in these circumstances the First Amendment prohibited awards of presumed and punitive damages for false and defamatory statements unless the plaintiff shows "actual malice," that is, knowledge of falsity or reckless disregard for the truth. The question presented in this case is whether this rule of *Gertz* applies when the false and defamatory statements do not involve matters of public concern.

Petitioner Dun & Bradstreet, a credit reporting agency, provides subscribers with financial and related information about businesses. All the information is confidential; under the terms of the subscription agreement the subscribers may not reveal it to anyone else. On July 26, 1976, petitioner sent a report to five subscribers indicating that respondent, a construction contractor, had filed a voluntary petition for bankruptcy. This report was false and grossly misrepresented respondent's assets and liabilities. That same day, while discussing the possibility of future financing with its bank, respondent's president was told that the bank had received the defamatory report. He immediately called petitioner's regional office, explained the error, and asked for a correction. In addition, he requested the names of the firms that had received the false report in order to assure them that the company was solvent. Petitioner promised to look into the matter but refused to divulge the names of those who had received the report.

After determining that its report was indeed false, petitioner issued a corrective notice on or about August 3, 1976, to the five subscribers who had received the initial report. The notice stated that one of respondent's former employees, not respondent itself, had filed for bankruptcy and that respondent "continued in business as usual." Respondent told petitioner that it was dissatisfied with the notice, and it again asked for a list of subscribers who had seen the initial report. Again petitioner refused to divulge their names.

Respondent then brought this defamation action in Vermont state court. It alleged that the false report had injured its reputation and sought both compensatory and punitive damages. The trial established that the error in petitioner's report had been caused when one of its employees, a 17-year-old high school student paid to review Vermont bankruptcy pleadings, had inadvertently attributed to respondent a bankruptcy petition filed by one of respondent's former employees. Although petitioner's representative testified that it was routine practice to check the accuracy of such reports with the businesses themselves, it did not try to verify the information about respondent before reporting it.

After trial, the jury returned a verdict in favor of respondent and awarded $50,000 in compensatory or presumed damages and $300,000 in punitive damages. . . .

[The trial court granted a new trial, but the state supreme court reversed and reinstated the jury verdict, holding that *Gertz* did not apply to a nonmedia defendant.]

As an initial matter, respondent contends that we need not determine whether *Gertz* applies in this case because the instructions, taken as a whole, required the jury to find "actual malice" before awarding presumed or punitive damages. The trial court instructed the jury that because the report was libelous *per se*, respondent was not required "to prove actual damages . . . since damage and loss [are] conclusively presumed." It also instructed the jury that it could award punitive damages only if it found "actual malice." Its only other relevant instruction was that liability could not be established unless respondent showed "malice or lack of good faith on the part of the Defendant." Respondent contends that these references to "malice," "lack of good faith," and "actual malice" required the jury to find knowledge of falsity or reckless disregard for the truth — the "actual malice" of *New York Times, Co. v. Sullivan*, 376 U.S. 254 (1964) — before it awarded presumed or punitive damages.

We reject this claim because the trial court failed to define any of these terms adequately. It did not, for example, provide the jury with any definition of the term "actual malice." In fact, the only relevant term it defined was simple "malice."[3] And its definitions of this term included not only the *New York Times* formulation but also other concepts such as "bad faith" and "reckless disregard of the [statement's] possible consequences." The instructions thus permitted the jury to award presumed and punitive damages on a lesser showing than "actual malice." Consequently, the trial court's conclusion that the instructions did not satisfy *Gertz* was correct, and the Vermont Supreme Court's determination that *Gertz* was inapplicable was necessary to its decision that the trial court erred in granting the motion for a new trial. We therefore must consider whether *Gertz* applies to the case before us.

In *New York Times Co. v. Sullivan, supra*, the Court for the first time held that the First Amendment limits the reach of state defamation laws. That case concerned a public official's recovery of damages for the publication of an advertisement criticizing police conduct in a civil rights demonstration. As the Court noted, the advertisement concerned "one of the major public issues of our time." *Id.*, at 271. Noting that "freedom of expression *upon public questions* is secured by the First Amendment," *id.*, at 269 (emphasis added), and that "debate *on public issues* should be uninhibited, robust, and wide-open," *id.*, at 270 (emphasis added), the Court held that a public official cannot recover damages for defamatory falsehood unless he proves that the false statement was made with "'actual malice' — that is, with knowledge that it was false or with reckless disregard of whether it was false or not," *id.*, at 280. In later cases, all involving public issues, the Court extended this same constitutional protection to libels of public figures, *e.g.*, *Curtis Publishing Co. v. Butts*, 388 U.S. 130 (1967), and in one case suggested in a plurality opinion that this constitutional rule should extend to libels of any individual so long as the defamatory statements involved a "matter of public or general interest," *Rosenbloom v. Metromedia, Inc.*, 403 U.S. 29, 44 (1971) (opinion of BRENNAN, J.).

---

[3] The full instruction on malice reads as follows:

"If you find that the Defendant acted in a bad faith towards the Plaintiff in publishing the Erroneous Report, *or* that Defendant intended to injure the Plaintiff in it business, *or* that it acted in a willful, wanton or reckless disregard of the rights and interests of the Plaintiff, the Defendant has acted maliciously and the privilege is destroyed. *Further*, if the Report was made with reckless disregard of the possible consequences, *or* if it was made with the knowledge that it was false *or* with the reckless disregard of its truth or falsity, it was made with malice."

In *Gertz v. Robert Welch, Inc.*, 418 U.S. 323 (1974), we held that the protections of *New York Times* did not extend as far as *Rosenbloom* suggested. In *Gertz*, we held that the fact that expression concerned a public issue did not by itself entitle the libel defendant to the constitutional protections of *New York Times*. These protections, we found, were not "justified solely by reference to the interest of the press and broadcast media in immunity from liability." 418 U.S., at 343. Rather, they represented "an accommodation between [First Amendment] [concerns] and the limited state interest present in the context of libel actions brought by public persons." In libel actions brought by private persons we found the competing interests different. Largely because private persons have not voluntarily exposed themselves to increased risk of injury from defamatory statements and because they generally lack effective opportunities for rebutting such statements, we found that the State possessed a "strong and legitimate . . . interest in compensating private individuals for injury to reputation." *Id.*, at 348–349. Balancing this stronger state interest against the same First Amendment interest at stake in *New York Times*, we held that a State could not allow recovery of presumed and punitive damages absent a showing of "actual malice." Nothing in our opinion, however, indicated that this same balance would be struck regardless of the type of speech involved.[4]

We have never considered whether the *Gertz* balance obtains when the defamatory statements involve no issue of public concern. To make this determination, we must employ the approach approved in *Gertz* and balance the State's interest in compensating private individuals for injury to their reputation against the First Amendment interest in protecting this type of expression. This state interest is identical to the one weighed in *Gertz*. There we found that it was "strong and legitimate." 418 U.S., at 348. . . .

The First Amendment interest, on the other hand, is less important than the one weighed in *Gertz*. . . . [S]peech on matters of purely private concern is of less First Amendment concern. As a number of state courts, including the court below, have recognized, the role of the Constitution in regulating state libel law is far more limited when the concerns that activated *New York Times* and *Gertz* are absent.[5] In such a case,

---

[4] The dissent states that "[a]t several points the Court in *Gertz* makes perfectly clear [that] the restrictions of presumed and punitive damages were to apply in all cases." Given the context of *Gertz* however, the Court could have made "perfectly clear" only that these restrictions applied in cases involving *public speech*. In fact, the dissent itself concedes that "*Gertz* . . . focused largely on defining the circumstances under which protection of the central First Amendment value of robust debate of *public issues* should mandate plaintiffs to show actual malice to obtain a judgment and actual damages. . . ."

The dissent also incorrectly states that *Gertz* "specifically held, 'both' that the award of presumed and punitive damages on less than a showing of actual malice is not a narrowly tailored means to achieve the legitimate state purpose of protecting the reputation of private persons . . . ," and that "unrestrained presumed and punitive damages were 'unnecessarily' broad . . . in relation to the legitimate state interests." Although the Court made both statements, it did so only within the context of public speech. Neither statement controls here. What was "not . . . narrowly tailored" or was "'unnecessarily' broad" with respect to public speech is not necessarily so with respect to the speech now at issue. Properly understood, *Gertz* is consistent with the result we reach today.

[5] As one commentator has remarked with respect to "the case of a commercial supplier of credit information that defames a person applying for credit" — the case before us today — "If the first

"[t]here is no threat to the free and robust debate of public issues; there is no potential interference with a meaningful dialogue of ideas concerning self-government; and there is no threat of liability causing a reaction to self-censorship by the press. The facts of the present case are wholly without the First Amendment concerns with which the Supreme Court of the United States has been struggling." *Harley-Davidson Motorsports, Inc., v. Markley*, 568 P.2d 1359, 1363 (Or. 1977). . . .

The only remaining issue is whether petitioner's credit report involved a matter of public concern. In a related context, we have held that "[w]hether . . . speech addresses a matter of public concern must be determined by [the expression's] content, form, and context . . . as revealed by the whole record." *Connick v. Myers*, [461 U.S.], at 147–148. These factors indicate that petitioner's credit report concerns no public issue. It was speech solely in the individual interest of the speaker and its specific business audience. This particular interest warrants no special protection when — as in this case — the speech is wholly false and clearly damaging to the victim's business reputation. Moreover, since the credit report was made available to only five subscribers, who, under the terms of the subscription agreement, could not disseminate it further, it cannot be said that the report involves any "strong interest in the free flow of commercial information." There is simply no credible argument that this type of credit reporting requires special protection to ensure that "debate on public issues [will] be uninhibited, robust, and wide-open." *New York Times Co. v. Sullivan*, 376 U.S., at 270.

In addition, the speech here, like advertising, is hardy and unlikely to be deterred by incidental state regulation. It is solely motivated by the desire for profit, which, we have noted, is a force less likely to be deterred than others. Arguably, the reporting here was also more objectively verifiable than speech deserving of greater protection. In any case, the market provides a powerful incentive to a credit reporting agency to be accurate, since false credit reporting is of no use to creditors. Thus, any incremental "chilling" effect of libel suits would be of decreased significance.

We conclude that permitting recovery of presumed and punitive damages in defamation cases absent a showing of "actual malice" does not violate the First Amendment when the defamatory statements do not involve matters of public concern. Accordingly, we affirm the judgment of the Vermont Supreme Court.

[BURGER, C.J., AND WHITE, J., concurred in the judgment. They believed *Gertz* should be overruled. They did not think the Constitution should be applied where the "ordinary private citizen" was the plaintiff. They agreed that the holding in *Gertz* should be limited to those situations in which the defamation dealt with a matter of public importance.]

[JUSTICES BRENNAN, MARSHALL, BLACKMUN, and STEVENS dissented, asserting that the case was controlled by *Gertz*.]

---

amendment requirements outlined in *Gertz* apply, there is something clearly wrong with the first amendment or with *Gertz*." Shiffrin, The First Amendment and Economic Regulation: Away From a General Theory of the First Amendment, 78 Nw. U. L. Rev. 1212, 1268 (1983).

NOTES

1. *The Scope of* Dun & Bradstreet. When the matter is not one of public concern, can the court impose strict liability? *Compare Snead v. Redland Aggregates*, 998 F.2d 1325, 1334 (5th Cir. 1993) (court left to states to determine the standard of fault to apply in private figure cases where subject matter is of private concern), *with Levinsky's Inc. v. Wal-Mart Stores, Inc.,* 127 F.3d 122 (1st Cir. 1997) (unclear whether First Amendment prohibits a state from imposing strict liability in defamtion cases brought by private plaintiffs concerning statements implicating private concerns). Can the state place the burden of proof on whomever it chooses? Remove the defense of truth? Make "pure opinion" actionable as defamation? In the absence of a matter of public concern, what speech-related interests might lead courts to preclude the state from acting in any of these settings? *See* Tom Bennigson, *Nike Revisited: Can Commercial Corporations Engage in Non-Commercial Speech?*, 39 CONN. L. REV. 379 (2006); Steven G. Gieseler, *Information Cascades and Mass Media Law*, 3 FIRST AMEND. L. REV. 301 (2005).

The Fair Credit Reporting Act, 15 U.S.C § 1681, requires that a credit agency disclose on request to any reported consumer debtor the names of any recipients of the credit report. This act does not apply, however, to reports in connection with the issuance of commercial credit. 4 BUS. TORTS § 33.08[1], at 33–52 (J. Zamore, ed. 1989). Why do you suppose the defendant in *Dunn & Bradstreet* was unwilling to furnish the plaintiff with the names of the persons who received the credit report?

In a footnote in *Dun & Bradstreet, supra*, the Court noted that, according to the Fifth Circuit, most states provide a qualified privilege against libel suits for commercial and credit reporting agencies; however, in those states that do not do so, there is a thriving credit reporting business and commercial transactions are not inhibited. *See Hood v. Dun & Bradstreet, Inc.* 486 F.2d 25, 32 n.18 (1973), *cert. denied*, 415 U.S. 985 (1974) (comparing empirical study of commercial transactions in Boise, Idaho, where there is no privilege, and Spokane, Washington, where there is one).

In *Johnson v. Johnson*, 654 A.2d 1212 (R.I. 1995), plaintiff brought a slander action against her former husband for calling her a "whore" in a public place. Though the trial court found the statement "essentially truthful," it was made with "spite or ill will." Such a finding was sufficient to support a compensatory award of $5,000, but the punitive award of $20,000 was struck because the statement was made "under enormous provocation" and therefore the award did not meet "the rigorous standard which we set for punitive damages." The *Johnson* court recognized that in *Garrison v. Louisiana*, 379 U.S. 64 (1964), the U.S. Supreme Court "held that the *New York Times* rule absolutely prohibits punishment of truthful criticism of public officials," even if the statements are made with "hatred, ill will or enmity or a wanton desire to injure." But here, the court said, "we are not dealing with public officials, public figures, or even matters of public concern." Citing *Dun & Bradstreet*, the court said that damages may be awarded in accordance with state law where "the defamatory statements made by defendant were not matters of public concern." 654 A.2d at 1216.

2. *Single and Multiple Publications.* REST. 2d TORTS (1977) §577A states:

(1) Except as stated in Subsections (2) and (3), each of several communications to a third person by the same defamer is a separate publication.

(2) A single communication heard at the same time by two or more third persons is a single publication.

(3) Any one edition of a book or newspaper, or any one radio or television broadcast, exhibition of a motion picture or similar aggregate communication is a single publication.

(4) As to any single publication,

(a) only one action for damages can be maintained;

(b) all damages suffered in all jurisdictions can be recovered in the one action; and

(c) a judgment for or against the plaintiff upon the merits of any action for damages bars any other action for damages between the same parties in all jurisdictions.

The comments to this section state that if defendant makes the same defamatory statement about plaintiff on three separate occasions, once to one person and twice to another person, plaintiff has three causes of action. But if defendant makes the statement to an audience of a thousand persons, plaintiff has only one cause of action. *Id.* §577A, cmts. *a* & *b*.

Note that one edition of a book or newspaper constitutes a single publication, even though hundreds of different people may read the publication at different times. But the repetition of a radio or TV broadcast, and each showing of a movie, constitute separate publications. *Id.* §577A, cmt. *d*.

The advent of the Internet has made this area of defamation even more complicated. *See, e.g.,* 47 U.S.C. §230 of the 1996 Communications Decency Act, interpreted in *Barrett v. Rosenthal,* 146 P.3d 510 (Cal. 2006). The provision protects private blocking and screening of offensive material, and includes protection for users who did not generate content and for Internet Service Providers (ISPs) from civil suits for the defamatory effects that Internet communications may have. In *Barrett,* the California supreme court held that an Internet user who is not a provider is immune from prosecution for republication of defamatory content on the Internet, in part because imposing liability would "chill online speech." *Id.* at 525. *See also Churchill v. State,* 876 A.2d 311 (N.J. Super. Ct. App. Div. 2005) (single publication rule for mass-published information, relevant to material published on the Internet for statute of limitations purposes). *See generally* Anthony Michael Ciolli, *Defamatory Internet Speech: A Defense of the Status Quo,* 24 QUINNIPIAC L. REV. 1 (2006).

3. *The Actual Malice Requirement and the Private Plaintiff.* In *Turf Lawnmower Repair, Inc. v. Bergen Record Corp.,* 655 A.2d 417, 423-24 (N.J. 1995), the New Jersey court noted that "forty-two jurisdictions in the United States hold that negligence is the standard for private plaintiffs to recover against a media defendant even when the subject matter is of public concern." States are free to impose a higher (more protective) standard, however, and

Colorado, Indiana, New Jersey, and Kansas use the actual malice standard in such cases.

The court in *Turf* decided to change its rule for private plaintiffs. The "negligence standard is the most appropriate standard with regard to businesses involved with an everyday product or service." *Id.* at 435. But the actual malice standard would be used with regard to plaintiff businesses "whose practices allegedly constitute consumer fraud, impinge on the health and safety of New Jersey's citizenry, or comprise activity within a highly regulated industry." *Id.*

4. Fact vs. Opinion

LUND v. CHICAGO AND NORTHWESTERN TRANSPORTATION COMPANY
467 N.W.2d 366 (Minn. App. 1991)

MULALLY, JUDGE.

Richard Lund sued his employer for defamation and infliction of emotional distress. Concluding that the allegedly defamatory statements were constitutionally protected expressions of opinion and that Lund had not established the elements for a claim of emotional distress, the trial court entered summary judgment in favor of the employer. Lund appeals. We affirm.

On August 29, 1988, various employees of the Chicago and Northwestern Transportation Company (C&NW) participated in a "brainstorming session" to discuss general problems and concerns. Such meetings were commonly held and were part of the company's effort to promote open communication. Richard Lund, an employee of C&NW and the plaintiff in this action, was not present at the meeting.

A C&NW manager, Ray Peterson, compiled his notes of the meeting into a typed, four-page memorandum. Most of the 85, numbered entries concerned employees' complaints with management's practices and responses to problems. However, line 66 of the memorandum read as follows:

FAVORITISM, DICK LUND, SICK, MOVE-UPS, BROWN NOSE,
SHIT HEADS

The memorandum was posted on the company bulletin board, and additional copies were sent to other company offices. Upon Lund's request, C&NW removed the memorandum. Although unauthorized, copies of the memorandum were reposted, apparently by Lund's coworkers. The company removed those copies as well.

After the initial posting, employees verbally harassed Lund. There were also two instances when some unidentified person placed a foreign substance (analyzed as a pepper derivative) in Lund's coffee. Lund claims to have experienced various emotional and physical problems arising from these incidents. His absences, which Lund contends were due to sickness, almost doubled in 1989 over 1988 or 1987.

Lund sued C&NW, claiming defamation and infliction of emotional distress. On C&NW's motion for summary judgment, the trial court concluded that the challenged portion of the memorandum was protected either under the first amendment, as opinion, or by a qualified privilege. Concluding also that the facts did not support Lund's claims for emotional distress, the court granted C&NW's motion. Lund appeals, arguing that the memorandum is not entitled to constitutional protection and that material issues of fact preclude summary judgment. . . .

To be defamatory, a statement must be communicated to someone other than the plaintiff, must be false, and must tend to harm the plaintiff's reputation in the community. Since the United States Supreme Court decided *Gertz v. Robert Welch, Inc.*, 418 U.S. 323 (1974), numerous courts, including the Minnesota Supreme Court, have held that expressions of opinion, even if defamatory, are constitutionally protected. *See Janklow v. Newsweek, Inc.*, 788 F.2d 1300, 1302 (8th Cir.), *cert. denied*, 479 U.S. 883 (1986). The federal circuit courts developed a four-factor test to distinguish opinion from fact, which considered 1) the statement's precision and specificity; 2) the statement's verifiability; 3) the social and literary context in which the statement was made; and 4) the statement's public context. *See Janklow*, 788 F.2d at 1302–03.

In *Milkovich v. Lorain Journal Co.*, 497 U.S. 1 (1990), the Supreme Court recently reviewed the issue of opinion protection. The Court rejected the lower courts' "artificial dichotomy between 'opinion' and fact," holding that not all statements of opinion are constitutionally protected. Recognizing that expressions of opinion may imply assertions of objective facts, the Court concluded that only opinions relating to matters of public concern that are incapable of being proven true or false, and statements that cannot reasonably be interpreted as stating actual facts, are constitutionally protected.

In *Hunt v. University of Minnesota*, 465 N.W.2d 88 (Minn. App. 1991), this court construed *Milkovich* as narrowing, but not abolishing, the constitutional protection for opinions. The *Hunt* court also emphasized that cases applying the federal courts' four-factor test, although not binding after *Milkovich*, are still helpful for determining when a statement implies actual facts that can be proven false.

The opinion-fact determination is a question of law. Applying the four-factor test of *Janklow*, the trial court determined that the words contained in line 66 were clearly statements of opinion.

We agree. In *Lee v. Metropolitan Airport Comm'n*, 428 N.W.2d 815 (Minn. App. 1988), coworkers had referred to the plaintiff as a "fluffy," a "bitch," and flirtatious. This court held that such comments regarding Lee's social life and personal characteristics were, as a matter of law, too imprecise in nature to be actionable defamatory statements.

Whether office gossip or railroad shop vernacular, like the statements in *Lee*, the terms in line 66 lack precision and specificity. Furthermore, in the context of the setting in which they were spoken, this lack of precision and specificity blunts any connotation of conduct sufficiently reprehensible to constitute defamation, whether measured by constitutional or common law standards. As the trial court recognized, two of the terms, "move-ups" and "shit heads," are plural and do not necessarily apply to Lund exclusively. Moreover, the underlying facts to be inferred from these terms are unclear. Although uncomplimentary, "shit heads" does not suggest verifiably false facts about Lund.

The terms "favoritism" and "brown nose" require a similar conclusion. They are not themselves factual assertions, and it is unclear what, if any, underlying facts they imply. Even if the terms are viewed as hybrid statements of opinion and fact, we conclude that the ambiguous implications of the words prevent them from being proven true or false. We hold that the statements were constitutionally protected expressions of opinion and, therefore, not actionable. . . . [In an accompanying footnote the court noted that a "state's substantial interest in providing remedies for defamation *per se* can outweigh the admittedly less weighty, constitutional concerns in a 'private' case," but in statements such as the employee grievances at issue here which "are clearly opinions, the state's interest fades and the first amendment predominates."]

C&NW also claims that the statements in the memorandum are conditionally privileged. Because we decide that C&NW's statements are constitutionally protected, we need not address whether they are also entitled to a qualified privilege.

[The court also concluded that Lund could not recover for intentional or negligent infliction of emotional distress because the statements did not "reach the requisite level of severity. Line 66, although vulgar, is not especially shocking or egregious."]

CRIPPEN, JUDGE (dissenting).

Opinions, the trial court concluded, are "absolutely protected" under the first amendment and are not actionable. We ought not sustain this mistaken statement.

The United States Supreme Court never has held that purely private communications — those involving private plaintiffs and private issues — are subject to the same constitutional protections as communications involving public claimants or public issues. To the contrary, its decisions extending first amendment law to defamation cases consistently have been in the context of public comments or public parties. Moreover, since 1985 the Court has affirmatively indicated that in the absence of such a public context, a defamation action is not constitutionally significant, but rather is governed by state common law.

In *Dun & Bradstreet, Inc. v. Greenmoss Builders*, 472 U.S. 749 (1985), a plurality of the Court stated that speech on purely private matters is of less first amendment concern, and therefore, the state's interest in protecting individual reputations is not necessarily overcome by constitutional considerations. Whether speech addresses a matter of public concern is to be determined by the content, form and context of the expression as revealed by the whole record. In *Dun & Bradstreet*, a confidential credit report sent to only five subscribers was held to be purely private speech.

The Court clarified the *Dun & Bradstreet* plurality opinion a year later in *Philadelphia Newspapers, Inc. v. Hepps*, 475 U.S. 767 (1986). One can discern, the Court observed, two forces that may "reshape the common-law landscape to conform to the First Amendment."

The first is whether the plaintiff is a public official or figure, or is instead a private figure. The second is whether the speech at issue is of public concern . . . When the speech is of exclusively private concern and the plaintiff is a private figure, as in *Dun & Bradstreet*, the constitutional requirements do not necessarily force any change in at least some of the features of the common-law landscape. *Id.* at 775.

The internal business communication at issue in this appeal is of purely private concern. The plaintiff is a private figure. Thus, we should determine the dispute according to state common law principles rather than constitutional law. . . .

Generally, the common law considers actionable many statements of opinion. . . .

The First Restatement lists three categories in a section entitled "types of defamatory communication": (1) statements of fact; (2) expressions of opinion upon known or assumed facts; and (3) expressions of opinion upon undisclosed facts. Restatement of Torts §§ 565-567. Thus, under the First Restatement:

> A defamatory communication may be made by derogatory adjectives or epithets as well as by statements of fact. Thus, it is defamatory to add to an accurate statement of another's innocent conduct, an adjective or epithet which characterizes it as reprehensible.

Id. § 566, comment a.

Defamation may consist of "words which, while couched in the form of epithets or adjectives, carry an implied accusation that the other has been guilty of some specific type of reprehensible conduct." *Id.* § 567, comment a. In addition, common law defamation can occur when one utters what the First Restatement labels "harsh judgments on undisclosed facts." *Id.* § 567, comment b. Such statements "leave it open to doubt as to whether they are intended to imply conduct, the direct accusation of which would be defamatory, or whether they are intended to express a harsh judgment on conduct, the direct accusation of which would not necessarily be defamatory." *Id.* For all these statements of opinion, including "harsh judgments," the Restatement requires the defendant to prove that the "harsh judgment" is either true or privileged as fair comment under section 606.[18] *Id.; see id.* § 606.

---

[18] The Restatement suggests that calling another a hypocrite, without stating any conduct on which one bases this opinion, would be actionable unless privileged as fair comment. Restatement of Torts § 567, comment b (illustration). Thus, common law support is even lacking for the "rhetorical hyperbole" doctrine, outlined by the Court in *Milkovich v. Lorain Journal Co.*, 497 U.S. 1, 110 S.Ct. 2695, 111 L.Ed.2d 1 (1990). In cases appropriately governed by constitutional law principles, the Supreme Court has found statements not actionable in defamation if in categories of "rhetorical hyperbole" or "imaginative expression," statements that cannot reasonably be

It is the First Restatement, not the Second, which offers primary guidance in deciding this case. . . . Applying common law principles just outlined, the "opinion" at issue here is actionable. The epithets published by respondent characterize appellant's conduct as reprehensible, and as an employment problem requiring correction. Moreover, the labels imply that appellant has sought and obtained favors inappropriately, so much so in fact to make him an obnoxious employee. These statements place upon respondent the burden to prove truth or privilege. . . .

NOTES

1. *Actionable Opinion.* In *Milkovich v. Lorain Journal Co.*, 497 U.S. 1 (1990), a local newspaper accused the plaintiff, a high school wrestling coach, of lying at a judicial hearing held to determine whether the coach's team should be disqualified from the state competition on the grounds that the coach had incited a brawl at a match with a rival team. The Court said the accusation was capable of being proved true or false and therefore was actionable. A dissent argued that the article was protected speech because it was filled with cautionary language, and it was evident that the author "had no unstated reasons for concluding that Milkovich perjured himself. Furthermore, the tone and format of the piece notify readers to expect speculation and personal judgment." *Id.* at 32.

2. *Nonactionable Opinion.* In *Vail v. The Plain Dealer Publishing Co.*, 649 N.E.2d 182 (Ohio 1995), a columnist for the defendant newspaper wrote an article attacking plaintiff, a candidate for the Ohio Senate. The article appeared in the "Commentary" section of the newspaper, and described defendant as a "gay-basher," "neo-numbskull," "bigot," and a hate monger who engaged in a "homosexual diatribe" and fostered "homophobia." The court said these statements were constitutionally protected speech: "Based upon the totality of the circumstances, we are convinced that the ordinary reader would accept this column as opinion and not as fact."

In *Avins v. White*, 627 F.2d 637 (3d Cir. 1980), the Delaware Law School dean sued the ABA accreditation team in defamation for its description of the law school: "The most important deficiency is an intangible one; there is an academic ennui that pervades the institution. The intellectual spark is missing in the faculty and the students." The court held this was nonactionable opinion. Opinion aside, how could this statement be construed to be "of and concerning" the dean? Reconsider *New York Times, Inc., v. Sullivan, supra.* Rejecting the claim, the *Avins* court said the statements "more closely approximate a critic's review of an institution rather than a particular individual." *Id.* at 643.

---

interpreted as stating actual facts about a person. *Id.* at 17, 110 S.Ct. at 2704–06; *see National Ass'n of Letter Carriers v. Austin*, 418 U.S. 264, 284–86, (1974) (use of the word "traitor" in literary definition of a union "scab" not basis for defamation action because used as mere rhetorical hyperbole, in loose figurative sense as imaginative expression); *Greenbelt Cooperative Publishing Ass'n v. Bresler*, 398 U.S. 6, 13-14, (use of the word "blackmail" to describe a negotiating position not basis for defamation action because used as rhetorical hyperbole and a "vigorous epithet").

3. *Book Reviews and Other Literata.* The author of a book brought an action for libel against a newspaper publisher in *Moldea v. New York Times Company,* 22 F.3d 310 (1994). The action was based on a book review of plaintiff's book INTERFERENCE. The reviewer said: "But there is too much sloppy journalism to trust the bulk of this book's 512 pages — including its whopping 64 pages of footnotes."

The reviewer gave examples of what he considered sloppy journalism in the book. The court found the review nonactionable, taking into account "the fact that the challenged statements appeared in the context of a book review, and were solely evaluations of a literary work."

In *Mashburn v. Collin,* 355 So. 2d 879 (La. 1977), the court held a newspaper columnist's opinion regarding the food at plaintiff's restaurant was privileged. The columnist described the food as: "T'ain't Creole, t'ain't Cajun, t'ain't French, t'ain't country American, t'ain't good." *Id.*

4. *Libel-Proof Plaintiffs?* The plaintiff, Dr. Jack Kevorkian, sued the defendants, American Medical Association and others, alleging they had defamed him by calling him a killer and a criminal in connection with his assisted suicide activities. Reversing the trial court, the court of appeals found the statements were opinion. It also found plaintiff was libel-proof, since "his reputation in the community, if not the nation, is such that the effect of more people calling him either a murderer or a saint is de minimis." *Kevorkian v. AMA,* 602 N.W.2d 233 (Mich. 1999). The trial court rendered its opinion on May 21, 1997, and the appellate court rendered its opinion on August 6, 1999. Before the appellate decision was rendered, on March 26, 1999, Dr. Kevorkian was convicted of second degree murder in connection with the assisted suicides. What effect, if any, should this conviction have had on the case?

Is the line between actionable and nonactionable drawn with clarity in these cases?

Consider whether inconsistency in courts' treatment of statements as opinions or facts might adversely affect individuals seeking protection based on their status or group-based identity such as race or class. Return to the perspectives offered in Chapter 1, *supra,* to support your thinking.

5. *Interrelationship of Privacy, Libel, and Intentional Infliction of Emotional Distress.* How are privacy, libel, and intentional infliction of emotional distress claims interrelated? In *Hustler Magazine v. Falwell,* 485 U.S. 46 (1988), Jerry Falwell, a nationally, known minister who was active as a commentator on politics and public affairs, sued Hustler Magazine on all three theories. A jury awarded damages based on intentional infliction of emotional distress. The U.S. Supreme Court reversed the jury award, noting: "[T]his claim cannot, consistently with the First Amendment, form a basis for the award of damages when the conduct in question is the publication of a caricature such as the ad parody involved here." *Id.* at 57. An action for intentional infliction of emotional distress could not be upheld when the underlying publication would not support an action for defamation.

In *Esposito-Hilder v. SFX Broadcasting, Inc.* 236 A.D.2d 186 (N.Y. App. Div. 1997), the court considered whether "conduct which is not actionable as defamation, by reason of being an expression of opinion, [could] nonetheless be the subject of an action for intentional infliction of emotional distress?" The court concluded that "where (a) the aggrieved party is a private individual rather than a public figure, (b) the conduct in question involved no matter of public interest or concern, and (c) the status of the parties as business competitors is relevant to an evaluation of defendants' conduct insofar as an intent to injure is concerned" the aggrieved party could bring a claim for intentional infliction of emotional distress. *Id*. at 187.

The case arose out of a disc jockey routine called the "Ugliest Bride" contest in which the disc jockey ordinarily made derogatory comments about the brides in the newspapers and invited the same commentary from the audience. According to plaintiff, defendants deviated from their ordinary routine on the day her photograph was in the newspaper by disclosing her full name and place and position of employment, as well as the identity of, and her relations with, her superiors. She heard this broadcast as did her supervisors and colleagues, and claimed that as a result of its outrageously offensive content, she experienced extreme emotional distress exacerbated by its occurrence at the time because she was a newlywed.

Defendants contended that the claim was actually one for defamation which would fail as constitutionally protected speech. The court characterized the expression as "pure, subjective opinion," acknowledging that it is well-settled law that "expressions of an opinion 'false or not, libelous or not, are constitutionally protected and may not be the subject of private damage actions.'" *Id*. at 189 (court's citations omitted). However, though intentional infliction of emotional distress has "received very little judicial solicitude" the claims have often failed because the alleged conduct was not sufficiently outrageous. *Id*. "[W]e conclude that under the unique factual circumstances herein presented, the [trial court] properly denied defendants' motion, and we affirm." *Id*.

The court noted that in *Howell v. New York Post Co.*, 612 N.E.2d 699 (1993), the New York court considered the "relationship between the potentially overlapping nature of intentional infliction of emotional distress and invasion of the right to privacy," and observed that the tort of emotional distress "is as limitless as the human capacity for cruelty. The price for this flexibility in redressing utterly reprehensible behavior, however, is a tort that, by its terms, may overlap other areas of the law, with potential liability for conduct that is otherwise lawful." *Howell*, 612 N.E.2d at 702. The New York Appellate Division attached significance to several determinative factors in this case. "First, plaintiff is a private individual and not a 'public figure.' Second, the nature of the communications made by defendants involved a matter of virtually no 'public interest'; there is an inference that defendants' conduct represented a deliberate intent to inflict injury upon plaintiff based upon the claimed unprecedented expansion of its standard 'routine' of the 'Ugliest Bride' contest to include particulars concerning plaintiff's name, employer, supervisors and the like, and the fact that the parties are business competitors in the radio broadcast industry." *Esposito-Hilder*, 236 A.D. at 190. In this case, "[i]n the quest for the proper accommodation between the right of redress for infliction of injury and the freedoms of speech and expression protected by the 1st Amendment, we have determined that the State's relatively strong interest in compensating individuals for harm outweighs the relatively weak 1st Amendment protection to be accorded defendants." *Id.* It noted that among the forms of communication, broadcasting enjoys the "most limited 1st Amendment protection." *Id.* (citing *FCC v. Pacifica Foundation*, 438 U.S. 726, 727 (1978)).

In *Esposito-Hilder*, the court observed that defendants sought to avoid liability by characterizing their conduct as protected comedic expression, adding:

> we note that comedic expression does not receive absolute 1st Amendment protection. Instead, it can be actionable where 'humor is used in an attempt to disguise an attempt to injure' (*Frank v. National Broadcasting Co.*, 119 A.D.2d 252, 261–262). The allegations of the amended complaint allege an intent to injure, which satisfies the limited inquiry before us.

Id. at 191. The Appellate Division noted finally that its decision "does no more than permit plaintiff's lawsuit to proceed. Whether and to what extent the allegations of her complaint ultimately satisfy the stringent requirements for the tort will be determined upon further proceedings." *Id.*

5. Privilege

ARNEJA v. GILDAR
541 A.2d 621 (D.C. 1988)

GALLAGHER, SENIOR JUDGE.

[Both appellant and appellee are attorneys. They were representing opposing parties in a landlord-tenant dispute involving the interpretation of the small landlord exemption of the Rental Housing Act of 1980. On behalf of the tenants, appellant filed a petition with the District of Columbia Rental Accommodations Office challenging an exemption from rent control granted to the landlord's property.]

The alleged slanderous statements were uttered while both parties and their clients were present in a hearing room at the Rental Accommodations Office, awaiting the imminent arrival of the hearing examiner to adjudicate the dispute.

Before the hearing examiner arrived, appellee concededly made the following unsolicited remarks to appellant:

> You're unnecessarily pursuing this case. You don't understand the law. Where did you go to law school; you should go back to law school before you practice law. You don't understand. You better learn your English, go to elementary school.

Appellant asserts that these statements were *ad hominem* attacks on his ethnicity and educational background, which were said with malice to impugn his professional capacity as a lawyer. . . . [The appellant was born in India and earned several degrees there but his formal legal training was in English and he has spoken English since he was a child]. Appellant claims that, as a result, he suffered pecuniary losses as well as humiliation and embarrassment before his clients. Appellee, on the other hand, asserted that his statements were intended to lead to a settlement of the dispute, *viz.*, to induce appellant to cease the litigation by highlighting his supposed incredulous position.

After a hearing on appellee's motion for summary judgment, the trial court found the alleged defamatory statements to be sufficiently related to the underlying dispute — the interpretation of a statute — to fall within the protective scope of the absolute privilege, which affords attorneys absolute immunity from liability for statements made in the course of a judicial proceeding. The trial judge found "a very strong connection between the words alleged to have been said by [appellee] and the procedure that was involved in this landlord and tenant case." He further opined that "the English language is an issue" in disputes involving opposing interpretations of a statute. In addition, the trial judge considered that the physical location and temporal proximity of the parties — sitting in a hearing room awaiting the imminent arrival of the examiner — justified concluding the statements were made preliminary to a judicial proceeding. . . .

In this jurisdiction, an attorney "is protected by an absolute privilege to publish false and defamatory matter of another" during the course of or preliminary to a judicial proceeding, provided the statements bear some relation to the proceeding. *Mohler v. Houston,* 356 A.2d 646, 647 (D.C. 1976) (per curiam); *see* Restatement (Second) of Torts § 586 (1977).[24] The privilege affords an attorney absolute immunity from actions in defamation for communications related to judicial proceedings. The determination of whether a communication is privileged is a question of law for the court. For the absolute immunity of the privilege to apply, two requirements must be satisfied: (1) the statement must have been made in the course of or preliminary to a judicial proceeding; and (2) the statement must be related in some way to the underlying proceeding.

The scope of the absolute privilege has been extended to encompass quasi-judicial proceedings conducted by administrative agencies. The shield of absolute immunity extends to adversarial proceedings conducted before administrative agencies "because it enables participants to state and support their positions without instilling a fear of retaliation, i.e., an action for damages." *Sturdivant* [*v. Seaboard Service System, Ltd.,* 459 A.2d 1058, 1060 (D.C. 1983).] We therefore conclude that the proceeding conducted before the Rental Accommodations Office constituted a proceeding within the gambit of the judicial privilege.

A more difficult question is whether the defamatory statements occurred "preliminary to" that administrative proceeding. According to the American Law Institute, "communications preliminary to a proposed judicial proceeding" includes [sic] "conferences and other communications preliminary to the proceeding." Restatement (Second) of Torts § 586 & comment a (1977). Given

---

[24] The Restatement provides:

   An attorney at law is absolutely privileged to publish defamatory matter concerning another in communications preliminary to a proposed judicial proceeding, or in the institution of, or during the course and as part of, a judicial proceeding in which he participates as counsel, if it has some relation to the proceeding. Restatement (Second) of Torts § 586 (1977).

that the parties were involved in litigation, present in a hearing room, and awaiting commencement of the proceeding to adjudicate their dispute, we believe the trial court did not err in concluding the statements were made preliminary to a judicial proceeding.[25]

The issues of fact disputed by appellant, *viz.*, that (1) no settlement discussions transpired in the hearing room, and (2) the remarks were ethnic slurs, are not controlling in determining whether, as a matter of law, appellee is entitled to the immunity of absolute privilege. Furthermore, the motive of appellee in uttering these remarks is irrelevant under the doctrine of absolute privilege.[26]

Although we must recognize the absolute privilege in this instance, we naturally do not wish to be understood as condoning remarks such as those concededly (for purposes of the motion) made by appellee. Attorneys do not possess a license to defame their adversaries in the course of a judicial proceeding. The immunity of the absolute privilege supports the public policy of allowing counsel to zealously represent a client's interests without fear of reprisal through defamation actions.[27] A separate public policy concern, however, is the integrity and civility of legal proceedings, especially as perceived by the public. A potential alternative mechanism available to deal with outrageous conduct by an attorney in lieu of an action for damages in slander may be the policing function of the Bar Disciplinary Committee.

Affirmed.

PRYOR, CHIEF JUDGE, dissenting.

. . . Recognizing, as does the majority, that it is difficult to draw a boundary for this absolute privilege, I am unable to distinguish this case from a similar scenario which occurs in the hallway or just outside of the courthouse. . . . I think in this case, in particular, it is a question of fact whether there was a

---

[25] The parties' physical presence in the hearing room substantially affects our analysis of the issue. If these same remarks were uttered outside the courtroom, a different question might be presented on the issue of absolute privilege, depending upon the particular circumstances. *See, e.g., Petrus v. Smith*, 91 A.D.2d 1190, 459 N.Y.S.2d 173 (1983) (absolute privilege may not extend to statements made outside the courthouse); *Sussman v. Damian*, 355 So. 2d 809 (Fla. Dist. Ct. App. 1977) (statements made on elevator held not absolutely privileged).

[26] Malice or improper motive is a relevant consideration, under some circumstances reserved for a jury, when addressing the applicability of the qualified privilege, as distinguished from the absolute privilege involved here.

[27] The necessity of the absolute privilege to protect comments related to judicial and administrative proceedings does not mean that attorneys disposed toward dispensing verbal abuse during proceedings may do so with impunity. It goes without saying that courts and agencies should insist upon decent conduct by attorneys appearing before them, as a matter of civility and courtroom decorum. The various regulatory bodies, whether they be judicial commissions or an arm of the Bar, would reasonably be expected to understand and support any sensible exercise of discipline by the presiding judge or hearing officer pertaining to such conduct. Trial judges, after all, are not mere spectators in the courtroom. Quite naturally, they have the duty to preside over an orderly courtroom and move cases along. While ours is an adversary system, this too has its limitations. The two factors, the adversary system and the search for justice in a civil way, are quite capable of being balanced.

conference or even a discussion between the lawyers or whether this was a circumstance where one attorney was simply unilaterally abusing the other. . . .

I would remand for resolution of the factual question which I have noted.

NOTES

1. *Other Judicial Immunities.* A judicial officer enjoys a similar absolute privilege. See REST. 2d TORTS §585. So do witnesses. *Id.* §588.

Court reporters, however, are not entitled to an absolute judicial immunity. In *Antoine v. Byers & Anderson*, 508 U.S. 429 (1993), the Court said a court reporter could be held liable for damages in negligently failing to provide a complete transcript of public proceedings, resulting in a delay of appellate review for over four years.

2. *Executive and Legislative Immunity.* Executive officials may enjoy complete common-law immunity from liability for statements and actions closely related to the performance of their official duties. *Mosley v. Observer Pub. Co.*, 619 A.2d 343 (Pa. Super. 1993). They may not have such an immunity, however, from liability for the commission of constitutional torts. *Williams v. Brooks*, 945 F.2d 1322 (5th Cir. 1991).

The court in *Williams*, on the other hand, said that federal legislators have an immunity only as broad as the Speech or Debate Clause of the United States Constitution. U.S. CONST. art. I, sec. 6[1]. The clause did not protect a television interview by the defendant Congressman.

3. *The Privilege to Repeat Privileged Statements.* The court in *Rosenberg v. Helinski*, 616 A.2d 866 (Md. 1992), held that a psychologist, whose expert in-court testimony in a child custody matter supporting the mother's accusation that the father had sexually abused the child, was privileged to repeat the substance of this testimony to journalists waiting for him outside the courtroom. Similarly, in *Doe v. Kohn Nast & Graf*, 866 F. Supp. 190 (E.D. Pa. 1994), where the plaintiff filed suit alleging he had been wrongfully fired, the defendant was privileged to report to the press what its answer to the suit would be.

Rosenberg and *Kohn Nast* are in sharp contrast with *Bochetto v. Gibson*, 860 A.2d 67 (Pa. 2004). In *Bochetto*, a nonprofit group sued its former law firm for malpractice and faxed a copy of the initial complaint to a freelance journalist who wrote about legal issues. When the journalist published the complaint, the law firm sued for defamation and libel, claiming that many of the allegations of the complaint were false. The court held that the defamation defendants could be liable because the act of faxing a copy of the complaint to the media was neither made in the normal course of judicial proceedings nor pertinent to resolving an issue of those proceedings. While the court recognized the ruling could make it more difficult for journalists to obtain information about trials, the court ruled that "the privilege is not meant to promote the airing of pleadings to the media. Rather, the privilege is only meant to promote the airing of issues and facts during judicial proceedings." *Id.* at 73.

In *Rothman v. Jackson*, 49 Cal. App. 4th 1134 (Cal. App. 1996), music star Michael Jackson called a press conference at which he accused an attorney, who was suing him on behalf of a minor, of committing defamation and extortion after an unknown person leaked sensational material related to the case to the press. The attorney in turn sued Jackson for libel and defamation, but the trial court granted a demurrer, holding that Jackson's statements were privileged because they related to ongoing litigation. The appellate court reversed. The court reasoned that in order to be privileged, out-of-court statements that are designed to achieve the object of litigation not only must replicate the subject matter of in-court statements, but must actually have some functional purpose toward achieving litigational goals. Jackson's belief that the claims were baseless, coupled with his desire for public vindication, did not make his statements privileged merely because this paralleled his goals in the litigation.

What about the situation in which the repeater is not the same person as the original, privileged speaker? The Court in *Doe v. McMillan*, 412 U.S. 306 (1973), held that the Speech or Debate Clause privilege did not extend to printers who, acting at the order of a congressional committee, prepared for publication a committee report that allegedly invaded the privacy of some of those named in the report.

Notably, if a defamation is foreseeably repeated, the defamer is liable for the repetition. REST. 2D TORTS § 576 (1977).

4. *Neutral Reportage.* The issue in *Bartnicki v. Vopper*, 532 U.S. 514 (2001), was whether, under state and federal wiretap statutes, the defendant radio station and an individual could be held civilly liable for receiving and disclosing the contents of plaintiffs' cellular phone conversation on a matter of public concern that defendants knew or had reason to know had been illegally intercepted and recorded by an unknown person or persons. Defendants did not encourage or participate in the recording. The Court held defendants could not be found liable; to do so would violate their First Amendment rights. The majority believed that enforcement of 18 U.S.C. § 2511(1)(c), which prohibits such disclosure, would not appreciably reduce illegal wiretaps, and that the plaintiffs' interest in privacy was outweighed by the public or general interest in the matter disclosed (views on a controversial labor dispute).

Two concurring justices thought the "narrow" holding was justified regarding a matter of "unusual public concern" involving plaintiffs who were "limited public figures." *Id.* at 535-36. Three dissenters thought the majority, in order to protect an "amorphous concept" of "public concern," rode roughshod over legislative findings, that the statutes deterred "clandestine invasions of privacy," and that an important right of privacy was at stake. *Id.* at 553.

5. *Conditional Privileges.* There are many common-law conditional privileges that protect the speaker unless the privilege is abused. An abuse occurs when the speaker is guilty of common-law malice. States define common-law malice in a variety of ways and the state conceptions do not always have the same meaning as actual or constitutional malice as those terms are used in *New York Times* and *Gertz*.

For example, in *Staples v. Bangor Hydro-Electric. Co.*, 629 A.2d 601 (Me. 1993), the court held that an intra-company defamation is a publication that is entitled to a qualified privilege. The privilege is not available to a defendant who makes a statement with knowledge, or reckless disregard, of falsity, or with a "high degree of awareness of probable falsity or serious doubt as to the truth of the statement." Nor does the privilege apply if the defendant "acted out of ill will" toward the plaintiff. In contrast, in *Bickford v. Tektronix, Inc.*, 842 P.2d 432 (Or. 1992), the court said an intra-company defamation was a privileged publication, but that the "privilege may be abused if the speaker does not believe that the statement is true or lacks reasonable grounds to believe that it is true."

Why do some state or public actors but not others have the benefit of a qualified or conditional privilege while others (like judges) enjoy absolute privilege? Are immunities and conditional privileges correlated with power or status-related considerations that are mostly remnants of old common-law customs or are there other meaningful considerations behind the immunities? For a more in-depth discussion of immunities, see Chapter 12, *supra*.

In *Miller v. Servicemaster by Rees*, 851 P.2d 143 (Ariz. Ct. App. 1992), the court held that the plaintiff employee was privileged to report what she perceived to be sexual harassment. A privilege exists if there is "an obligation to speak." The privilege is abused if the defendant made the statement "knowing it was false or with reckless disregard of its truth," or if the plaintiff can show "excessive publication" by the defendant. *Id.* at 145. Excessive publication typically refers to statements not reasonably necessary to assert the privilege.

It is widely held that a person is privileged to report a suspected crime to the police. *See Williams v. Bell Tel. Labs Inc.*, 623 A.2d 234 (N.J. 1993). Again, the privilege can be lost if common-law malice is found.

I. INVASION OF PRIVACY

PETA v. BOBBY BEROSINI, LTD.
895 P.2d 1269 (Nev. 1995)

SPRINGER, JUSTICE.

In this litigation respondent Berosini claims that two animal rights organizations, People for the Ethical Treatment of Animals (PETA) and Performing Animal Welfare Society (PAWS), and three individuals defamed him and invaded his privacy. Judgment was entered by the trial court on jury verdicts on the libel and invasion of privacy claims in the aggregate amount of $4.2 million. This appeal followed. We conclude that the evidence was insufficient to support the jury's verdict and, accordingly, reverse the judgment. . . .

[Defendants secretively videotaped plaintiff Berosini "preparing" his orangutans backstage for public performance. This preparation consisted of grabbing, slapping, punching, and shaking the animals, and hitting them with a black rod approximately a foot in length. Plaintiff did not deny this treatment, but stated that it was necessary to calm the animals down and get them ready for their public performance. No one was present at these "preparatory" sessions except the plaintiff and his assistants. The defendants later had the video shown on local TV in an attempt to combat what they considered to be cruelty to animals.]

Berosini claims that one of the Stardust dancers, Ottavio Gesmundo, has intruded upon his "seclusion" backstage, before his act commenced. We support the need for vigilance in preventing unwanted intrusions upon our privacy and the need to protect ourselves against the Orwellian nightmare that our "every movement [be] scrutinized." The question now to be examined is whether Gesmundo's inquiring video camera gives cause for concern over privacy and gives rise to a tort action against Gesmundo for invasion of Berosini's privacy.

Although the problems which the tort of intrusion seeks to remedy are well-recognized, the tort of intrusion has only recently gained the attention of this court. . . .

The Restatement, [2d of Torts § 652B], upon which this court has previously relied for guidance in this area, formulates the tort of intrusion in terms of a physical invasion upon the "solitude or seclusion" of another, the rationale being that one should be protected against intrusion by others into one's private "space" or private affairs. To Prosser, these torts were personal injury actions, and he saw as examples of tortious activity the meddling conduct of eavesdroppers, the unpermitted opening of others' mail, and the making of illegal searches and seizures. Simply put, the intrusion tort gives redress for interference with one's "right to be left alone."

To recover for the tort of intrusion, a plaintiff must prove the following elements: 1) an intentional intrusion (physical or otherwise); 2) on the solitude or seclusion of another; 3) that would be highly offensive to a reasonable person.

In order to have an interest in seclusion or solitude which the law will protect, a plaintiff must show that he or she had an actual expectation of seclusion or solitude and that that expectation was objectively reasonable. Thus, not every expectation of privacy and seclusion is protected by the law. "The extent to which seclusion can be protected is severely limited by the protection that must often be accorded to the freedom of action and expression of those who threaten that seclusion of others." 2 Fowler V. Harper, et al., *The Law of Torts*, § 9.6, at 636 (2d ed. 1986). For example, it is no invasion of privacy to photograph a person in a public place; or for the police, acting within their powers, to photograph and fingerprint a suspect. Bearing this in mind, let us examine Berosini's claimed "right to be left alone" in this case and, particularly, the nature of Berosini's claim to seclusion backstage at the Stardust Hotel.

Berosini's "Invasion of Privacy" claim in his Second Claim for Relief contains no factual averments and . . . [t]he only factual allegations that appear to have any relation to the intrusion tort are found in paragraph 12 . . . , a paragraph that . . . reads as follows:

12. Defendant GESMUNDO unlawfully trespassed onto the Stardust Hotel with a video camera in July, 1989. Video cameras and other recording equipment are strictly prohibited at the Stardust Hotel. Defendant GESMUNDO unlawfully filmed Plaintiff BEROSINI disciplining the orangutans without the Plaintiff's knowledge or consent and just after Defendant GESMUNDO and others agitated the orangutans.

The focus, then, of Berosini's intrusion upon seclusion claim is Gesmundo's having "trespassed onto the Stardust Hotel with a video camera" and having "unlawfully filmed Plaintiff Berosini disciplining the orangutans without the Plaintiff's knowledge or consent." It is of no relevance to the intrusion tort that Gesmundo trespassed onto the Stardust Hotel, and it is of no moment that Gesmundo might have "unlawfully" filmed Berosini, unless at the same time he was violating a justifiable expectation of privacy on Berosini's part. The issue, then, is whether, when Gesmundo filmed Berosini "disciplining the orangutans without the Plaintiff's knowledge or consent," Gesmundo was intruding on "the solitude or seclusion" of Berosini.

The primary thrust of Berosini's expectation of privacy backstage at the Stardust was that he be left alone with his animals and trainers for a period of time immediately before going on stage. Berosini testified that "as part of his engagement with the Stardust," he demanded that "the animals be left alone prior to going on stage." Throughout his testimony, over and over again, he stresses his need to be alone with his animals before going on stage. Berosini's counsel asked him what his "purpose" was in requiring that he be "secured from the other cast members and people before [he] went on stage." Berosini's answer to this question was: "I have to have the attention . . . I have to know how they think. I cannot have them drift away with their mind. . . ."; and, further, "it is very important that before the show I have the orangutans' attention and I can see what they think before I take him [sic] on stage. . . ." Significantly, Berosini testified that his "concern for *privacy* was *based upon the animals*" and that his "main concern is that [he] have no problems going on stage and off stage," that is to say that no one interfere with his animals in any way immediately before going on stage. (emphasis added) . . . He never expressed any concern about backstage personnel merely seeing him or hearing him during these necessary final preparations before going on stage; his only expressed concern was about possible interference with his pre-act training procedures and the danger that such interference might create with respect to his control over the animals. Persons who were backstage at the Stardust could hear what was going on when "Berosini [was] disciplining his animals," and, without interfering with Berosini's activities, could, if they wanted to, get a glimpse of what Berosini was doing with his animals as he was going on stage.

What is perhaps most important in defining the breadth of Berosini's expectation of privacy is that in his own mind there was nothing wrong or untoward in the manner in which he disciplined the animals, as portrayed on the videotape, and he expressed no concern about merely being seen or heard carrying out these disciplinary practices. To Berosini all of his disciplinary activities were completely "justified." He had nothing to hide — nothing to be private about. Except to avoid possible distraction of the animals, he had no reason to exclude others from observing or listening to his activities with the animals.

Berosini testified that he was not "ashamed of the way that [he] controlled [his] animals"; and he testified that he "would have done the same thing if people were standing there because if anybody would have been standing there, it was visible. It was correct. It was proper. It was necessary."

As his testimony indicates, Berosini's "concern for privacy was based upon the animals," and not upon any desire for sight/sound secrecy or privacy or seclusion as such; and he "would have done the same thing if people were standing there." The supposed intruder, Gesmundo, was in a real sense just "standing there." By observing Berosini through the eye of his video camera, he was merely doing what other backstage personnel were also permissibly doing. The camera did not interfere in any way with Berosini's pre-act animal discipline or his claimed interest in being "secured from the other cast members and people before [he] went on stage." Having testified that he would have done the same thing if people were standing there, he can hardly complain about a camera "standing there."

If Berosini's expectation was, as he says it is, freedom from distracting intrusion and interference with his animals and his pre-act disciplinary procedures, then Gesmundo's video "filming" did not invade the scope of this expectation. Gesmundo did not intrude upon Berosini's expected seclusion. . . . For this reason the tort of intrusion cannot be maintained in this case.

On the question of whether Gesmundo's camera was highly offensive to a reasonable person, we first note that this is a question of first impression in this state. As might be expected, "the question of what kinds of conduct will be regarded as a 'highly offensive' intrusion is largely a matter of social conventions and expectations." J. Thomas McCarthy, *The Rights of Publicity and Privacy*, §5.10(A)(2) (1993). For example, while questions about one's sexual activities would be highly offensive when asked by an employer, they might not be offensive when asked by one's closest friend. . . . "While what is 'highly offensive to a reasonable person' suggests a standard upon which a jury would properly be instructed, there is a preliminary determination of 'offensiveness' which must be made by the court in discerning the existence of a cause of action for intrusion." *Miller v. National Broadcasting Co.*, 187 Cal. App. 3d 1463, 232 Cal. Rptr. 668, 678 (1986). . . . A court considering whether a particular action is "highly offensive" should consider the following factors: "the degree of intrusion, the context, conduct and circumstances surrounding the intrusion as well as the intruder's motives and objectives, the setting into which he intrudes, and the expectations of those whose privacy is invaded." [*Id.*] at 679.

Three of these factors are of particular significance here and, we conclude, militate strongly against Berosini's claim that Gesmundo's conduct was highly offensive to a reasonable person. These factors are: the degree of the alleged intrusion, the context in which the actions occurred, and the motive of the supposed intruder. First, we note the nonintrusive nature of the taping process in the instant case. Berosini was concerned with anyone or anything interfering with his animals prior to performance. The camera caused no such interference. Neither Berosini nor his animals were aware of the camera's presence. If Gesmundo had surprised Berosini and his animals with a film crew and had caused a great commotion, we might view this factor differently. On the contrary, it appears from these facts that any colorable privacy claims arose not from the actual presence of the video camera but from the subsequent use to which the video tape was put.

Secondly, as has been discussed fully above, the context in which this allegedly tortious conduct occurred was hardly a model of what we think of as "privacy." We must remember that the videotaping did not take place in a private bedroom . . . or in a hospital room . . . or in a restroom . . . , or in a young ladies' dressing room . . . , or in any other place traditionally associated with a legitimate expectation of privacy. Rather, Gesmundo filmed activities taking place backstage at the Stardust Hotel, an area where Gesmundo had every right to be, and the filming was of a subject that could be seen and heard by any number of persons. This was not, after all, Berosini's dressing room; it was a holding area for his orangutans.

Finally, with regard to Gesmundo's motives, we note that Gesmundo's purpose was not to eavesdrop or to invade into a realm that Berosini claimed for personal seclusion. Gesmundo was merely memorializing on tape what he and others could readily perceive. Unlike the typical intrusion claim, Gesmundo was not trying to pry, he was not trying to uncover the covered-up. Although Berosini envisioned Gesmundo to be engaged in a conspiracy with others (as put in the Answering Brief) "to put an end to the use of animals in entertainment," . . . the conspiracy charges in Berosini's complaint were dismissed. Furthermore, even if Gesmundo was conspiring to put an end to the use of animals in entertainment, this is not the kind of motive that would be considered highly offensive to a reasonable person. Many courts, and Professor Prosser, have found the inquiry into motive or purpose to be dispositive of this particular element of the tort. *See Prosser and Keeton on Torts* § 117 at 856 (W. Page Keeton, ed., 5th ed. 1984). . . .

While we could reverse Berosini's intrusion upon seclusion judgment solely on the absence of any intrusion upon his actual privacy expectation, we go on to conclude that even if Berosini had expected complete seclusion from prying eyes and ears, Gesmundo's camera was not "highly offensive to a reasonable person" because of the nonintrusive nature of the taping process, the context in which the taping took place, and Gesmundo's well-intentioned (and in the eyes of some, at least, laudable) motive. If Berosini suffered as a result of the videotaping, it was not because of any tortious intrusion, it was because of subsequent events that, if remediable, relate to other kinds of tort actions than the intrusion upon seclusion tort.

[The court also found that there was no defamation, and that plaintiffs did not tortiously appropriate defendant's name or identity for commercial purposes.] [This case was overruled in part by *City of Las Vegas Downtown Redevelopment Authority v. Hecht*, 940 P.2d 134 (Nev. 1997) (regarding a question of judicial disqualification)].

NOTES

1. *Trespass or Privacy?* Recall the treatment of trespass to realty in Chapter 2. How is this privacy tort different from trespass?

REST. 2D TORTS § 652B provides:

> One who intentionally intrudes, physically or otherwise, upon the solitude or seclusion of another or his private affairs or concerns, is subject to liability to the other for invasion of his privacy, if the intrusion would be highly offensive to a reasonable person.

Two ABC television reporters used false resumes to get jobs at Food Lion Supermarkets, where they videotaped without plaintiff's knowledge or permission unwholesome food handling practices. *Food Lion, Inc. v. Capital Cities/ABC, Inc.*, 194 F.3d 505 (4th Cir. 1999). Some of the video footage was later used by ABC in a Prime Time Live broadcast that was sharply critical of Food Lion. Food Lion sued ABC and collected nominal damages for breach of their duty of loyalty and trespass committed by the ABC reporters. The truth of the broadcast was never in issue. The court refused, however, on First Amendment free speech grounds, to uphold a substantial verdict for publication damages allegedly resulting from the broadcast. With regard to the publication damages, allegedly consisting of harm to plaintiff's business, the court held that *Hustler Magazine v. Falwell*, 485 U.S. 46 (1988) barred the claim. 194 F.3d at 522. *Hustler Magazine*, the court said, required a public figure plaintiff to prove "actual" malice under the defamation standard of *New York Times v. Sullivan*, 376 U.S. 254 (1964), in order to recover publication damages, a standard Food Lion was not prepared to meet. 194 F.3d at 523.

2. *The Manner of Intrusion.* The circumstances determine whether there has been a tortious intrusion into seclusion. There may be such an intrusion by secretly recording and photographing conversations with a person in his home, *Dietemann v. Time, Inc.*, 449 F.2d 245 (9th Cir. 1971), or by secretly videotaping conversations of an employee at work, *Sanders v. ABC*, 978 P.2d 67 (Cal. 1999). But there was no actionable intrusion into seclusion where an insurance investigator trespassed onto private club property and photographed the plaintiffs — one of whom was a plaintiff in a personal injury lawsuit. The plaintiffs were on or near a yacht in a public waterway and in open view to the public. *Furman v. Sheppard*, 744 A.2d 583, 586-87 (Md. Ct. Spec. App. 2000).

A television cameraman's presence at and filming of events at an accident scene was not an actionable invasion of privacy, the court held, in *Shulman v. Group W Productions, Inc.*, 955 P.2d 469 (Cal. 1998). But the cameraman's recording and filming of events in the rescue helicopter may have been an invasion of privacy, since a patient's conversation with a healthcare provider in the course of treatment, including emergency treatment, carries a traditional and legally well-established expectation of privacy. *Id.* at 492. Should motive matter, as was suggested in *Berosini, supra*?

3. *Other Intrusions.* The court in *Veeder v. Kennedy*, 589 N.W.2d 610 (S.D. 1999), described the tort of alienation of affections for marital intrusion as an offshoot of the common-law tort for depriving a master of his quasi-proprietary interest in his servant. However, in this suit by the husband against his wife's lover and employer, the court found sufficient evidence existed so that "reasonable minds could differ" as to whether the alleged conduct met the elements of the alienation of affections tort. The court concluded that the trial court had not erred in denying a motion for directed verdict favoring the defendants. *Id.* at 617. Although 34 states, including the District of Columbia, had statutorily abolished the tort, only five states had done so judicially and the court refused to join those state courts rejecting the claim. In states like South Dakota that do continue to recognize the tort, the elements of alienation of affections are: (1) wrongful conduct of the defendant; (2) loss of affection or consortium; and (3) a causal connection between such conduct and loss. *Id.* at 615. *See Pickering v. Pickering*, 434 N.W.2d 758, 762-63 (S.D. 1989) (citing *Pankratz v. Miller*, 401 N.W.2d 543, 546 (S.D. 1987);and *Hunt v. Hunt*, 309 N.W.2d 818, 820 (S.D. 1981)).

In *O'Neil v. Schuckardt*, 733 P.2d 693 (Idaho 1986), plaintiff O'Neil as well as his five children recovered against the Fatima Crusade, a fundamentalist sect of the Catholic Church, and individual leaders of the Crusade, for invasion of marital privacy. Plaintiff alleged that defendants maliciously caused his wife to divorce him because he was not a member of the Crusade. O'Neil could not recover for alienation of affections, however, because the court determined that the tort was outmoded and against public policy. *Id.* at 698. Therefore the court affirmed the ruling of the trial court, and abolished the cause of action in Idaho.

How does alienation of affections differ from invasion of privacy in the context of this lawsuit? The *O'Neil* court said an invasion of privacy occurs when one "intentionally intrudes, physically or otherwise, upon the solitude or seclusion of another or his private concerns or affairs." *Id.* Was there such an intrusion there?

The court in the principal case said that the challenged conduct did not intrude into Berosini's privacy because in his mind "there was nothing wrong or untoward" with the way in which he dealt with his animals, and because others witnessed his dealings with the animals. If this rationale were applied to the *O'Neil* claim, would it result in a denial of recovery? Does *O'Neil* concern a privacy interest, or some other sort of interest?

4. *Invasion of Privacy and the Hospital-Patient Relationship.* In *Biddle v. Warren General Hospital*, 715 N.E. 2d 518 (Ohio 1999), the court held that a hospital and its attorneys could be held liable, the hospital for breach of the duty of patient confidentiality and the attorneys for inducing such breach. By agreement between the hospital and its attorneys, the hospital furnished the attorneys medical information regarding patients who had not paid their medical bills, so the attorneys could determine if the patients might be eligible for SSI (Supplementary Security Income) benefits that could be used toward payment of the patients' medical bills. If the attorneys determined the patients were eligibile, they would contact the patients in an attempt to file for recovery of the benefits. The hospital paid the attorneys a contingent fee on any benefits recovered by the hospital.

Patients filed class action claims for breach of patient confidentiality and the court said these were cognizable claims. The patients had not given their consent for release of the information to the attorneys who were representing the hospital.

5. *Random Publication as Privacy Invasion. Roshto v. Hebert*, 439 So. 2d 428 (La. 1983) involved the publication of an article as a "Page from Our Past," a feature of the newspaper that unwittingly brought to light plaintiff's criminal conviction twenty-five years previously for which he had been pardoned. Noting similarities and differences between this case and *Cox Broadcasting Corp. v. Cohn*, 420 U.S. 469 (1975) (no recovery for television report of a rape victim despite state's statute making it unlawful to publish a rape victim's name), the court concluded that in this case the publication of factual information, though disruptive to plaintiff, was not intentionally injurious or abusive; more than insensitivity or carelessness is required for recovery of damages "when the publication is truthful, accurate and non-malicious." *Roshto, supra*, 439 So. 2d at 432.

RASMUSSEN v. SOUTH FLORIDA BLOOD SERVICE, INC.
500 So. 2d 533 (Fla. 1987)

BARKETT, JUSTICE.

. . . On May 24, 1982, petitioner, Donald Rasmussen, was sitting on a park bench when he was struck by an automobile. He sued the driver and alleged owner of the automobile for personal injuries he sustained in the accident. While hospitalized as a result of his injuries, Rasmussen received fifty-one units of blood via transfusion. In July of 1983, he was diagnosed as having "Acquired Immune Deficiency Syndrome" (AIDS) and died of that disease one year later. In an attempt to prove that the source of this AIDS was the necessary medical treatment he received because of injuries sustained in the accident, Rasmussen served respondent, South Florida Blood Service (Blood Service), with a subpoena duces tecum requesting "any and all records, documents and other material indicating the names and addresses of the [51] blood donors." (South Florida Blood Service is not a party to the underlying personal injury litigation, and there has been no allegation of negligence on the part of the Blood Service).

The Blood Service moved the trial court to either quash the subpoena or issue a protective order barring disclosure. That court denied the motion and ordered the Blood Service to disclose the subpoenaed information. On certiorari review, the Third District Court of Appeal, applying the balancing test that courts have traditionally performed under the Florida discovery rules, concluded that the requested material should not be discovered. Although we agree with respondent's contention that Rasmussen's blood donors' rights of privacy are protected by state and federal constitutions, we need not engage in the stricter scrutiny mandated by constitutional analysis. We find that the interests involved here are adequately protected under our discovery rules and approve the decision of the district court. This opinion in no way changes or dilutes the compelling state interest standard appropriate to a review of state action that infringes privacy rights under article I, section 23 of the Florida Constitution as established in *Winfield v. Division of Pari-Mutuel Wagering, Dep't. of Business Regulation*, 477 So.2d 544, 547 (Fla. 1985).

The potential for invasion of privacy is inherent in the litigation process. Under the Florida discovery rules, any nonprivileged matter that is relevant to the subject matter of the action is discoverable. Fla. R. Civ. P. 1.280(b)(1). The discovery rules also confer broad discretion on the trial court to limit or prohibit discovery in order to "protect a party or person from annoyance, embarrassment, oppression, or undue burden or expense." Fla. R. Civ. P. 1.280(c). Under this authority, a court may act to protect the privacy of the affected person.

In deciding whether a protective order is appropriate in a particular case, the court must balance the competing interests that would be served by granting discovery or by denying it. Thus, the discovery rules provide a framework for judicial analysis of challenges to discovery on the basis that the discovery will result in undue invasion of privacy. This framework allows for broad discovery in order to advance the state's important interest in the fair and efficient resolution of disputes while at the same time providing protective measures to minimize the impact of discovery on competing privacy interests. . . .

The Supreme Court first recognized a right of privacy based on the United States Constitution in *Griswold v. Connecticut,* 381 U.S. 479 (1965). This right of privacy has been described as "the most comprehensive of rights and the right most valued by civilized man." *Stanley v. Georgia,* 394 U.S. 557, 564 (1969) (citing *Olmstead v. United States,* 277 U.S. 438, 478 (1928) (Brandeis, J., dissenting)). In recent cases, the Court has discussed the privacy right as one of those fundamental rights that are "'implicit in the concept of ordered liberty' such that 'neither liberty nor justice would exist if [they] were sacrificed.'" *Bowers v. Hardwick,* 478 U.S. 186 (1986) [other citations omitted]. . . . *See Roe v. Wade,* 410 U.S. 113, 147 (1973). In *Whalen v. Roe,* 429 U.S. 589, 599-600 (1977), the Supreme Court specifically recognized that the right to privacy encompasses at least two different kinds of interests, "the individual interest in avoiding disclosure of personal matters, and . . . the interest in independence in making certain kinds of important decisions." In *Nixon v. Administrator of General Services,* 433 U.S. 425, 457-458 (1977), the Supreme Court reaffirmed the confidentiality strand of privacy. Lower federal courts have recognized that the essential core of this zone of privacy is the right "to prevent disclosure of . . . identity in a damaging context." *E.g., Lora v. Board of Education,* 74 F.R.D. 565, 580 (1977). These cases clearly establish that the federal right to privacy extends protection in some circumstances against disclosure of personal matters.

Moreover, in Florida, a citizen's right to privacy is independently protected by our state constitution. In 1980, the voters of Florida amended our state constitution to include an express right of privacy. Art. V, §23, Fla. Const.[38] In approving the amendment, Florida became the fourth state to adopt a strong, freestanding right of privacy as a separate section of its state constitution, thus providing an explicit textual foundation for those privacy interests

---

[38] Article I, section 23, Florida Constitution, provides:

   Right of Privacy. — Every natural person has the right to be let alone and free from governmental intrusion into his private life except as otherwise provided herein. This section shall not be construed to limit the public's right of access to public records and meetings as provided by law.

inherent in the concept of liberty which may not otherwise be protected by specific constitutional provisions.

Although the general concept of privacy encompasses an enormously broad and diverse field of personal action and belief, there can be no doubt that the Florida amendment was intended to protect the right to determine whether or not sensitive information about oneself will be disclosed to others. The proceedings of the Constitution Revision Commission reveal that the right to informational privacy was a major concern of the amendment's drafters. At the opening session of Florida's 1977-78 Constitution Revision Commission, then Chief Justice Ben F. Overton remarked:

> Who, ten years ago, really understood that *personal* and financial *data* on a substantial part of our population could be collected by government or business and held for easy distribution by computer operated information systems? There is a public concern about how personal information concerning an individual citizen is used, whether it be collected by government or by business. The subject of individual privacy and privacy law is in a developing stage . . . It is a new problem that should probably be addressed. (Emphasis added.)

Address by Chief Justice Ben F. Overton to the Constitution Revision Commission (July 6, 1977). Thus, a principal aim of the constitutional provision is to afford individuals some protection against the increasing collection, retention, and use of information relating to all facets of an individual's life.

It is now known that AIDS is a major health problem with calamitous potential. At present, there is no known cure and the mortality rate is high. As noted by the court below, medical researchers have identified a number of groups which have a high incidence of the disease and are labeled "high risk" groups. Seventy-two percent of all AIDS victims are homosexual or bisexual males with multiple sex partners and seventeen percent are intravenous drug users. Other high risk groups are hemophiliacs (1 percent), heterosexual partners of AIDS victims (1 percent), and blood transfusion recipients (1 percent).

As the district court recognized, petitioner needs more than just the names and addresses of the donors. His interest is in establishing that one or more of the donors has AIDS or is in a high risk group. Petitioner argues that his inquiry may never go beyond comparing the donors' names against a list of known AIDS victims, or against other public records (e.g., conviction records in order to determine whether any of the donors is a known drug user). He contends that because a limited inquiry *may* reveal the information he seeks, with no invasion of privacy, the donors' privacy rights are not yet at issue. We find this argument disingenuous. As we have already noted, the discovery rules allow a trial judge upon good cause shown to set conditions under which discovery will be given. Some method could be formulated to verify the Blood Service's report that none of the donors is a known AIDS victim while preserving the confidentiality of the donors' identities. However, the subpoena in question gives petitioner access to the names and addresses of the blood donors with no restrictions on their use. There is nothing to prohibit petitioner from conducting an investigation without the knowledge of the persons in question. We cannot ignore, therefore, the consequences of disclosure to nonparties, including the possibility that a donor's co-workers, friends, employers, and others may be queried as to the donor's sexual preferences, drug use, or general life-style.

The threat posed by the disclosure of the donors' identities goes far beyond the immediate discomfort occasioned by third party probing into sensitive areas of the donors' lives. Disclosure of donor identities in any context involving AIDS could be extremely disruptive and even devastating to the individual donor. If the requested information is released, and petitioner queries the donor's friends and fellow employees, it will be functionally impossible to prevent occasional references to AIDS. . . . We wish to emphasize that although the importance of protecting the privacy of donor information does not depend on the special stigma associated with AIDS, public response to the disease does make this a more critical matter. By the very nature of this case, disclosure of donor identities is "disclosure in a damaging context." *See Lora,* 74 F.R.D. at 580. We conclude, therefore, that the disclosure sought here implicates constitutionally protected privacy interests.

Our analysis of the interests to be served by denying discovery does not end with the effects of disclosure on the private lives of the fifty-one donors implicated in this case. Society has a vital interest in maintaining a strong volunteer blood supply, a task that has become more difficult with the emergence of AIDS. The donor population has been reduced by the necessary exclusion of potential blood donors through AIDS screening and testing procedures, as well as by the unnecessary reduction in the donor population as a result of the widespread fear that donation itself can transmit the disease. In light of this, it is clearly "in the public interest to discourage any serious disincentive to volunteer blood donation." *Rasmussen,* 467 So. 2d at 804. Because there is little doubt that the prospect of inquiry into one's private life and potential association with AIDS will deter blood donation, we conclude that society's interest in a strong and healthy blood supply will be furthered by the denial of discovery in this case. In balancing the competing interests involved, we do not ignore Rasmussen's interest in obtaining the requested information in order to prove aggregation of his injuries and obtain full recovery. We recognize that petitioner's interest parallels the state's interest in ensuring full compensation for victims of negligence. However, we find that the discovery order requested here would do little to advance that interest. The probative value of the discovery sought by Rasmussen is dubious at best. The potential of significant harm to most, if not all, of the fifty-one unsuspecting donors in permitting such a fishing expedition is great and far outweighs the plaintiff's need under these circumstances.

NOTES

1. *Problems of Proof.* Was it possible for the court to construct an appropriate discovery remedy in this case?

2. *Videotapes.* Congress in 1988 passed the Videotape Privacy Act, 18 U.S.C. § 2710. If a videotape service provider releases without authorization, warrant, demand, or court order "personally identifiable information concerning any consumer of such provider," the provider can be liable to "any person aggrieved" by such a release, for actual damages, punitive damages, attorneys' fees, and such other "equitable relief as the court determines to be appropriate." The provider must destroy such information "as soon as practicable, but no later than one year from the date the information is no longer necessary for the purposes for which it was collected."

3. *What is Newsworthy?* In *McNutt v. New Mexico State Tribune Co.*, 538 P.2d 804 (N.M. Ct. App. 1975), *cert. denied*, 540 P.2d 248 (N.M. 1975), plaintiff law-enforcement officers were engaged in a gun battle, at a place called Black Mesa, with two individuals who were attempting to steal dynamite from a highway construction site. Both individuals, later determined to be members of a group called the Black Berets, were killed in the gun battle. The *Tribune* carried an article covering the events at Black Mesa which gave the names and home addresses of the plaintiff officers. Prior to publishing the article, the city editor of the newspaper called several of the officers, including plaintiffs McNutt and Urioste, seeking information for the piece. The officers told him that they had been instructed not to discuss the matter, and they referred him to their superiors. The editor replied that he was going to print their names and addresses because they would not cooperate in giving the details he sought. Despite the officers' protestations for their families' sake, the editor published the information and several of the officers and family members received anonymous phone calls threatening violence.

Plaintiffs alleged that the publication of their names and addresses was done maliciously, and they sought punitive as well as actual damages. The court held the claims were not available since the publication was privileged because of newsworthiness. It drew upon *Jenkins v. Dell Publishing Co.*, 251 F.2d 447 (3d Cir. 1958), agreeing with its observation that:

> [i]n the verbal and graphic publication of news, it is clear that information and entertainment are not mutually exclusive categories. A large part of the matter which appears in newspapers and news magazines today is not published or read for the value or importance of the information it conveys. Some readers are attracted by shocking news. Others are titillated by sex in the news. Still others are entertained by news which has an incongruous or ironic aspect. Much news is in various ways amusing and for that reason of special interest to many people. Few newspapers or news magazines would long survive if they did not publish a substantial amount of news on the basis of entertainment value of one kind or another. This may be a disturbing commentary upon our civilization, but it is nonetheless a realistic picture of society of which courts in shaping new juristic concepts must take into account. In brief, once the character of an item as news is established, it is neither feasible nor desirable for a court to make a distinction between news for information and news for entertainment in determining the extent to which publication is privileged.

538 P.2d at 809. The court added that "reports of current criminal activities are the legitimate province of a free press." *Id.*, quoting *Briscoe v. Reader's Digest Assoc.*, 483 P.2d 34 (1971). The *McNutt* court rejected the plaintiffs'

assertion that publication of their addresses was not newsworthy or necessary to the report, stating:

> If an individual participates in a newsworthy event, proper identification of that individual is an essential part of the story. It is the usual practice in newspaper accounts to identify persons by giving their names and addresses so as to avoid confusion because many individuals have identical names.

McNutt, supra, 538 P.2d at 809. The court found it immaterial whether the editor "harbored ill will toward the plaintiff officers," concluding that such a harboring does not constitute *New York Times* "actual malice." *Id.* at 810.

In contrast, in *Diaz v. Oakland Tribune, Inc.,* 139 Cal. App. 3d 118 (Cal. 1983), the court permitted an action for invasion of privacy by a transsexual whose gender corrective surgery was exposed. Diaz had kept the surgery secret from all but her immediate family and closest friends. By all outward appearances Diaz looked like a woman and was accepted by the public as a woman. According to her therapist, her physical and psychological identities were in harmony as a result of the surgery. She changed her name to Toni Ann Diaz. While enrolled in one of the colleges of the Peralta Community College District, plaintiff was elected student body president. Near the middle of her term as student body president, Diaz became embroiled in a controversy in which she charged the college administrators with misuse of student funds. An issue of the *Tribune* quoted Diaz's charge that her signature had improperly been "rubber stamped" on checks drawn from the associated students' account. *Id.* at 124. Subsequently, an article in the *Alameda Times-Star*, a daily newspaper, mentioned Diaz in connection with the charge of misuse of student body funds and the reporter added:

> More Education Stuff: The students at the College of Alameda will be surprised to learn that their student body president, Toni Diaz, is no lady, but is in fact a man whose real name is Antonio. . . . Now I realize, that in these times, such a matter is no big deal, but I suspect his female classmates in P.E. 97 may wish to make other showering arrangements.

Id. The court found that plaintiff's sex change was not a matter of public record. The evidence revealed that Diaz took affirmative steps to conceal this fact by changing her driver's license, social security number, and high school records, and by lawfully changing her name. The court found the information about sexual identity was a private matter and, though it recognized the defense of newsworthiness, the court found the defense inapplicable where the publicity is so offensive as to constitute a "morbid and sensational prying into private lives for its own sake." *Id.* at 126. Whether a publication is or is not newsworthy depends upon contemporary community mores and standards of decency. This is largely a question of fact, which a jury is uniquely well-suited to decide. Defendants had also argued that, as the first female student body president of the College, Diaz was a public figure, and the fact of her sexual identity was a newsworthy item as a matter of law. The court responded:

the extent to which Diaz voluntarily acceded to a position of public notoriety and the degree to which she opened her private life are questions of fact. As student body president, Diaz was a public figure for some purposes. However . . . we cannot state that the fact of her gender was newsworthy *per se*.

Contrary to defendants' claim, we find little if any connection between the information disclosed and Diaz's fitness for office. . . . Nor does the fact that she was the first woman student body president, in itself, warrant that her entire private life be open to public inspection. The public arena entered by Diaz is concededly small. Public figures more celebrated than she are entitled to keep some information of their domestic activities and sexual relations private. . . . The tenor of the article was by no means an attempt to enlighten the public on a contemporary issue. . . .

Id. at 134–35. Are the *McNutt* and *Diaz* courts' views on the balance between privacy and newsworthiness reconcilable? *See also Zacchini v. Scripps-Howard Broadcasting Co.*, 433 U.S. 562 (1977). In a 5-4 decision, the Supreme Court held the Constitution did not prevent an action by the petitioner against the respondent television station for filming his fifteen-second "human cannonball" act without permission while petitioner performed at the Geauga County Fair, and then broadcasting the performance on the evening news program. The Court reasoned that the broadcast of a film of petitioner's entire act pose a substantial threat to the economic value of that performance. On remand, the Ohio Supreme Court held that Zacchini stated a cause of action for commercial appropriation of the right of publicity. 376 N.E.2d 582 (1978).

3. *Survival of the Claim.* The cases vary widely on whether the right of publicity survives one's death and is inheritable. Some cases hold there is no right of survival, others find the existence of the right depends on whether the deceased commercially exploited her name or likeness during her lifetime, and still others conclude that there is an unqualified right of survival. *See* discussion in *Martin Luther King, Jr. Center for Social Change v. American Heritage Products,* 694 F.2d 674 (11th Cir. 1983).

In *Lugosi v. Universal Pictures*, 603 P.2d 425 (Cal. 1979), the heirs of the deceased movie actor Bela Lugosi sought damages for and an injunction against the use of Lugosi's Count Dracula character. The court denied the claim, stating that the right of privacy is "protectable during one's lifetime but it does not survive the death of Lugosi." *Id.* at 428. Subsequently, California passed the Astaire Celebrity Image Protection Act, codified at Cal. Civ. Code §3344.1 (2007), granting heirs the right to sue for protection of the "name, voice, photograph, or likeness" of a deceased person for 70 years after the person's death.

4. *The Celebrity and the Unknown Person.* The privacy tort here being considered — more aptly described as the right of publicity — actually is a business tort, and is treated in detail on in the Business and Economics Torts section of this chapter.

Private individuals, as well as celebrities, have a right to protect their names and likeness. In *Staruski v. Continental Telephone Co.*, 581 A.2d 266 (Vt. 1990), a sales and service representative sued her employer for featuring her in a newspaper advertisement without her consent. It contained a photograph of the plaintiff smiling broadly and saying, "Hi, I'm Cindy Staruski," with text that describes her job and says it has been "exciting and reassuring to know that Continental continues to expand its equipment and services to meet its obligation to serve you." The jury awarded plaintiff $1,000 in compensatory and $3,500 in punitive damages. Reversing the trial court's JNOV, the supreme court said recovery does not turn on the fame of the person whose identity has been appropriated. *Id.* at 269.

In *Tellado v. Time-Life Books*, 643 F. Supp. 904, 909 (D.N.J. 1986), the court held that a publisher may be liable for misappropriation of likeness for using a photograph of the plaintiff, without his permission, in promotional material for a series of books on the Vietnam War. The photograph showed the plaintiff as an anguished soldier in Vietnam, but neither his name nor his face was well known to the public. The REST. 2D TORTS § 652C recognizes recovery for persons who are not famous.

What damages are recoverable if the person is not famous? In *Faber v. Condecor, Inc.*, 477 A.2d 1289 (N.J. Super. Ct. App. Div. 1984), a family and a photographer brought suit after the defendant corporation appropriated a photograph of the family without the family's consent. The court noted that even if the injury suffered is mental distress alone, the plaintiff is entitled to recover damages based on a tortious invasion of privacy.

DIAMOND SHAMROCK REFINING AND MARKETING CO. v. MENDEZ
844 S.W.2d 198 (Tex. 1992)

PHILLIPS, CHIEF JUSTICE.

In this action, an employee claims that his employer committed the torts of "false light" invasion of privacy and intentional infliction of emotional distress by circulating information about his termination among his fellow employees. The trial court rendered judgment on a jury verdict for the plaintiff on both theories. The court of appeals held that no evidence supported the jury's verdict as to intentional infliction of emotional distress, but it affirmed the judgment of the trial court under the false light theory. We reverse the judgment of the court of appeals and remand for a new trial on Mendez's false light theory.

Roque Mendez was a chief operator at the Diamond Shamrock oil refinery in Three Rivers, Texas. . . . Mendez was ordered by his supervisor to clean up debris that had been left in his work area, including loose nails discarded by carpenters. He became angry at being assigned the clean-up task, which he perceived to be outside the scope of his ordinary duties. While he was cleaning, Mendez threw some of the nails, the value of which was less than five dollars, into a box and put the box into his lunch bag. He then placed the bag on a shelf while he finished cleaning. When he was finished he went to the clock house, which was on company property, placed the bag on a table, clocked out, and left the refinery.

After Mendez departed, a security officer found his lunch bag and noticed that it contained the nails. The security staff reported the finding to Wayne Billings, Human Resource and Administrative Manager, and John Hoffman, Plant Manager. Billings telephoned Mendez and asked him to return to the refinery. Confronted by Billings and Hoffman, Mendez identified the bag as his own. When asked to explain, Mendez described how he had become angered by his supervisor's order and rudeness and how he simply threw the nails into the box and threw the box into the bag. Hoffman then told Mendez that the bag contained company property and that it appeared that Mendez was stealing. When Hoffman asked whether Mendez agreed, Mendez replied, "I guess so." Hoffman then terminated Mendez and left the room. Left alone with Mendez, Billings asked why Mendez had not simply asked for a "gate pass" to take the nails off the premises. Mendez replied, "I don't know, Wayne. I guess I messed up."

Word of Mendez's termination spread quickly in Three Rivers. Many people with whom Mendez spoke during the next few weeks, including potential employers, knew that he had been terminated for stealing. As a result, he claims to have suffered significant financial and emotional setbacks.

Mendez filed suit against Diamond Shamrock on September 1, 1987, nearly two years after his termination. In his original petition, he alleged defamation, breach of contract, bad faith and unfair dealing, and violation of certain constitutional rights. Later, he added claims for malicious and wrongful termination, intentional or reckless infliction of emotional distress, negligence, and invasion of privacy comprising the embarrassing disclosure of personal facts and placing the plaintiff in a false light in the public eye. Mendez did not pursue his defamation claim, presumably because he did not bring it within the applicable one-year limitations period. The trial court submitted questions to the jury on only two theories of liability: intentional infliction of emotional distress and false light invasion of privacy. With respect to false light, the court submitted the following question to the jury:

> Did the Defendant, Diamond Shamrock, by and through its employees, invade the privacy of the Plaintiff, Roque Mendez? You are instructed that the Defendant may invade the privacy of the Plaintiff if it publicized matters which placed him in a false light before the public that would be highly offensive to a reasonable person. . . .

The jury found for Mendez on both the false light and intentional infliction of emotional distress counts, awarding him $460,000 in damages: $260,000 for past and future lost wages, $100,000 for mental anguish, and $100,000 for loss of reputation. The trial court rendered judgment on the jury verdict.

On appeal to the court of appeals, Diamond Shamrock argued that the trial court erred by failing to include the element of actual malice in its instruction to the jury on false light invasion of privacy. The court of appeals affirmed the judgment, holding that negligence, rather than actual malice, should be the standard in false light suits by private individuals. Further, Diamond Shamrock could not complain of the absence of a negligence instruction, since it had not requested one. Although the court also held that there was no evidence that Diamond Shamrock intentionally inflicted emotional distress on Mendez, it affirmed the judgment of the trial court because it rested on alternate grounds.

This court has never expressly held that a tort for false light invasion of privacy exists in Texas, although we have recognized that it is one of the four usual categories of private actions for invasion of privacy. Although amicus curiae urge us to reject the false light tort, we do not reach this issue, as it has not been adequately presented by the parties. Even assuming the availability of this cause of action, however, Mendez would not be entitled to recover on the record before us, as he did not submit all the essential elements of the false light tort.

The Restatement (Second) of Torts §652E defines the false light tort to include an actual malice requirement as follows:

One who gives publicity to a matter concerning another that places the other before the public in a false light is subject to liability to the other for invasion of his privacy if

(a) the false light in which the other was placed would be highly offensive to a reasonable person, and

(b) the actor had knowledge of or acted in reckless disregard as to the falsity of the publicized matter and the false light in which the other would be placed.

[T]he Texas courts of appeals that have recognized this tort have applied the actual malice standard, as have most courts in other jurisdictions. . . . *But see Jones v. Palmer Communications, Inc.*, 440 N.W.2d 884, 898 (Iowa 1989), *Crump v. Beckley Newspapers, Inc.*, 320 S.E.2d 70, 90 (W. Va. 1984), adopting a negligence standard. Thus, if the tort of false light invasion of privacy exists in Texas, it requires a showing of actual malice as an element of recovery. Because the trial court's instruction omitted an element of Mendez's cause of action, Diamond Shamrock properly preserved error by objecting. Since Mendez failed to establish an essential element of the false light cause of action under the Restatement and the preponderance of case law, the court of appeals' judgment in favor of Mendez on this claim must be reversed.

Because of the conflict between jurisdictions regarding the proper standard of conduct, and because this Court has not yet either recognized or disapproved the tort, we remand this cause of action for a new trial in the interest of justice, giving Mendez an opportunity to prove actual malice and Diamond Shamrock an opportunity to object to the theory of recovery in its entirety. . . .

The court of appeals reversed the trial court's judgment that Diamond Shamrock intentionally inflicted emotional distress on Mendez, finding no evidence of such an infliction. By cross-point, Mendez urges us to reverse this holding.

The Restatement (Second) of Torts § 46 (1965) defines the tort of intentional infliction of emotional distress as follows:

> One who by extreme and outrageous conduct intentionally or reck-lessly causes severe emotional distress to another is subject to liability for such emotional distress . . .

We have never recognized this tort, but a number of Texas courts of appeals have done so, . . . as have courts in many other jurisdictions. We need not decide in this case whether the tort exists in Texas, because Mendez failed to offer more than a scintilla of evidence of an essential element of the tort as it has been recognized in lower courts of this state and in courts of other jurisdictions, the presence of outrageous conduct.

Mendez argues that Diamond Shamrock's tortious conduct occurred not by terminating him, but by falsely depicting him in the community as a thief. Even if Mendez's charges are taken as true, however, this conduct is not sufficiently outrageous to raise a fact issue. Restatement [(scecond) of Torts] § 46, comment d, describes conduct reaching the level of "outrageousness" necessary for liability for intentional infliction of emotional distress in these terms:

> Liability has been found only where the conduct has been so outrageous in character, and so extreme in degree, as to go beyond all possible bounds of decency, and to be regarded as atrocious, and utterly intolerable in a civilized community.

There is no evidence that Diamond Shamrock's conduct met this standard. We need not condone or agree with Diamond Shamrock's actions to conclude that, as a matter of law, they fall short of being "beyond all possible bounds of decency," "atrocious," and "utterly intolerable in a civilized community." While there may obviously be instances where a termination is accompanied by behavior of this sort, there would be little left of the employment-at-will doctrine if an employer's public statement of the reason for termination was, so long as the employee disputed that reason, in and of itself some evidence that a tort of intentional infliction of emotional distress had been committed. The court of appeals did not err in denying Mendez recovery on this ground.

For the foregoing reasons, we affirm the judgment of the court of appeals against Mendez on the ground of intentional infliction of emotional distress. We reverse the judgment of the court of appeals in favor of Mendez on the ground of false light, and remand that claim to the trial court for a new trial.

GONZALEZ, JUSTICE, concurring and dissenting.

. . . The false light action, as it has been defined by the Restatement, permits recovery for injuries caused by publicity that unreasonably places the plaintiff in a false light before the public. Restatement (Second) of Torts § 652A (1977). Although not explicitly required by the Restatement definition, most jurisdictions, including the lower Texas courts that have recognized the action, require that a statement be false if it is to be cognizable under the false light doctrine. The falsity requirement is sensible, considering that the "revelation of private facts" invasion of privacy tort purports to grant relief for the disclosure of true statements that adversely affect the subject. *But see* Thomas I. Emerson, *The Right of Privacy and Freedom of the Press*, 14 HARV. C.R.-C.L. REV. 329, 345 (1979) (the truth or falsity of statements giving rise to liability for false light should not matter; rather, false light cases should be treated the same as embarrassing disclosure cases).

If we were to recognize a false light tort in Texas, it would largely duplicate several existing causes of action, particularly defamation. . . .

[L]ike false light, defamatory statements must be false in order to be actionable.

Furthermore, the elements of damages that have been recognized in false light actions are similar to those awarded for defamation. The principal element of actual damages for false light claims is typically mental anguish . . . but physical illness and harm to the plaintiff's commercial interests have also been recognized. These are essentially the types of damages sought in defamation actions. Thus many, if not all, of the injuries redressed by the false light tort are also redressed by defamation. *See Kapellas v. Kofman*, 459 P.2d 912, 921 n.16 (1969) ("since the complaint contains a specific cause of action for libel, the privacy count, if intended [as a false light count] is superfluous and should be dismissed.").

The false light tort also overlaps with some of the other, better recognized, privacy torts. *See, e.g.*, Harry Kalven, Jr., *Privacy in Tort Law — Were Warren and Brandeis Wrong?*, 31 LAW & CONTEMP. PROBS. 326, 332 (1966) (noting the potential overlap of false light and appropriation); *Lerman v. Flynt Distributing Co.*, 745 F.2d 123, 135 (2d Cir. 1984) ("while not specifically alleged in her complaint, [plaintiff's right to publicity] action presents a classic false light claim"). Finally, as we observed in *Billings v. Atkinson*, 489 S.W.2d 858, 860 (Tex. 1973), "some of the right of privacy interests have been afforded protection under such traditional theories as libel and slander, wrongful search and seizure, eavesdropping and wiretapping, and other similar invasions into the private business and personal affairs of an individual."

A few commentators have attempted to delineate the theoretical differences between false light invasion of privacy and other torts, particularly defamation. As one notes:

> In defamation cases the interest sought to be protected is the objective one of reputation, either economic, political, or personal, in the outside world. In privacy cases the interest affected is the subjective one of injury to the inner person . . . in defamation cases, where the issue is truth or falsity, the marketplace of ideas furnishes a forum in which the battle can be fought. In privacy cases, resort to the marketplace simply accentuates the injury.

Thomas I. Emerson, *The Right of Privacy and Freedom of the Press*, 14 HARV. C.R.-C.L. L. REV. 329, 333 (1979). . . . But a number of other scholars have argued that false light and defamation are nearly identical or even indistinguishable. *See, e.g.*, BRUCE W. SANFORD, *supra*, § 11.4.1 at 567 (2d ed. 1991) ("Legally, placing someone in a false light amounts to little more than defamation"); ROBERT D. SACK, LIBEL, SLANDER, AND RELATED PROBLEMS 394 (1980) (where the circumstances would support an action for "false light" invasion of privacy, plaintiffs may often successfully use libel or slander in addition or instead); John W. Wade, *Defamation and the Right of Privacy*, 15 VAND. L. REV. 1093, 1121 (1962) ("the great majority of defamation actions can now be brought for invasion of privacy . . . the action for invasion of privacy may come to supplant the action for defamation"); William L. Prosser, *Privacy*, 48 CAL. L. REV. 383, 400 (1960) ("there has been a good deal of overlapping of defamation in the false light cases, and apparently either action, or both, will very often lie").

In practice, the theoretical distinctions between false light and defamation have proven largely illusory. Of the six false light cases considered by Texas courts of appeals, all were brought, or could have been brought, under another legal theory. . . .

. . . In essence, Mendez asks this Court to afford him relief under a false light theory simply because he was prevented by limitations from prevailing on a defamation theory. In response, we should adopt this reasoning of the North Carolina Supreme Court . . . :

> The recognition of claims for relief for false light invasions of privacy would reduce judicial efficiency by requiring our courts to consider two claims for the same relief which, if not identical, would not differ significantly.

Renwick v. News & Observer Publishing Co., 312 S.E.2d 405, 413, *cert. denied*, 469 U.S. 858 (1984). . . .

As discussed above, the false light tort bears remarkable similarities to defamation. However, the torts are not wholly identical for two reasons: (1) defamation actions are subject to a number of procedural requirements to which invasion of privacy actions are not subject, and (2) certain publications not actionable under a defamation theory might be actionable under false light. Far from persuading me that these distinctions justify a separate tort, I believe they demonstrate that adopting a false light tort in this state would unacceptably derogate constitutional free speech rights under both the Texas and the United States Constitution. [The dissenter next outlines the procedural and substantive hurdles of proving a defamation case in Texas]. *See also* RESTATEMENT (SECOND) OF TORTS § 652E, comment e (1977) (listing other possible limitations on the defamation action, including bond posting requirements and proof of special damages). . . .

Every defamation action that the law permits necessarily inhibits free speech. As the Supreme Court stated with respect to political speech in *New York Times v. Sullivan*, 376 U.S. 254, 272 (1964), "[w]hatever is added to the field of libel is taken from the field of free debate." While less compelling, these same considerations are also at play in private, non-political expression. Thus, the defamation action has been narrowly tailored to limit free speech as little as possible.

Courts in many jurisdictions have preserved their protection of speech by holding false light actions to the same strictures as defamation actions. As the Restatement (Second) of Torts § 652E, comment e, reasons:

when the false publicity is also defamatory . . . it is arguable that limitations of long standing that have been found desirable for the action for defamation should not be successfully evaded by a proceeding upon a different theory of later origin, in the development of which the attention of the courts has not been directed to the limitations.

Several courts have followed this reasoning, particularly regarding the applicable limitations period. Permitting plaintiffs to bring actions for false light without the limits established for defamation actions may inhibit free speech beyond the permissible range.

. . . On balance, the marginal benefit to be achieved by permitting recovery against non-defamatory speech not addressed by any existing tort would be outweighed by the probable chilling effect on speech and, in some cases, on freedom of the press, that would result from recognition of the false light tort.

For the reasons expressed in this opinion, we should reverse and render this cause and expressly decline to recognize the tort of false light.

NOTES

1. *Negligent Infliction of Emotional Distress?* In *Hustler Magazine, Inc. v. Falwell*, 485 U.S. 46 (1988), the Court said that an action for intentional infliction of emotional distress would not lie where defendant's parody was nondefamatory. But in *Diamond Shamrock, supra*, the court held that an action for false light might be available although a claim for intentional infliction of emotional distress would not. Could the plaintiff have recovered for negligent infliction of emotional distress?

2. *Possible Constitutional Limitations.* In *Time, Inc. v. Hill*, 385 U.S. 374 (1967), the U.S. Supreme Court held that "actual" (constitutional) malice must be proved in order to recover for false light invasion of privacy. Subsequently, in *Gertz, supra*, the Court held that only negligent misstatement need be shown for defamation in the case of a nonpublic plaintiff, at least where the substance of the defamatory statement "makes substantial danger to reputation apparent." *Dun & Bradstreet, supra*, however, suggests that First Amendment strictures may not apply if the defamatory matter is not one of public concern. Where does all of this leave false light invasion of privacy?

3. *Restricting the Reach of False Light?* A statute in California requires that plaintiff prove special damages in the case of defamatory language that is not libelous on its face. The court in *Fellows v. National Enquirer, Inc.*, 721 P.2d 97, 107-08 (Cal. 1986), said the statute also applied to false light invasion of privacy, since the statute "manifests a legislative determination that liability imposed for a publication which affords no warning of its defamatory nature, and has not caused actual pecuniary injury, would place too great a burden on the editorial process and would hamper the free dissemination of the news." Many states provide that in an action for defamation the plaintiff can only recover special damages, unless he first asks the defendant for a retraction which the defendant refuses to make. *See Freedom Newspapers, Inc. v. The*

Superior Court, 842 P.2d 138 (Cal. 1992). Would the same rule apply to false light invasion of privacy?

4. *The Nonlibelous "False Light" Invasion of Privacy.* One can make a false statement about someone where the statement is unwelcome although nondefamatory. Thus in *Time, Inc. v. Hill*, and in *Cantrell v. Forest City Publishing Co.*, discussed in *Mendez*, *supra*, the false light statements implied that the plaintiffs were heroes. *See Mitchell v. Globe Int'l Publ'g Co.*, 817 F. Supp. 72 (W.D. Ark. 1993), *appeal dismissed*, 14 F.3d 607 (8th Cir. 1993), *cert. denied*, 510 U.S. 931 (1993). A photograph of the plaintiff, a 96-year old woman, was used to illustrate a story in a tabloid newspaper about "Paper Gal, Audrey Wiles" who became pregnant at age 101 by one of her customers, a reclusive millionaire she met on her paper route. In fact, the plaintiff made her living running a newspaper stand and delivering newspapers in a small town in Arkansas. Plaintiff was awarded $650,000 in compensatory and $850,000 in punitive damages against the defendant newspaper for false light invasion of privacy and intentional infliction of emotional distress but the compensatory award was reduced to $150,000, and the judgment affirmed for $1 million. Is it likely anyone who knew Mrs. Mitchell believed the story about her in the tabloid, and thought less well of her? What damages did she suffer?

PROBLEMS

14.1

Wife brought suit against her husband for damages resulting from contracting herpes from him as a result of sexual intercourse between them before their marriage. Her future husband knew he had relations with another woman who had the disease but said nothing to his future wife and did not see a doctor to confirm one way or another. Can Wife recover?

14.2

Buyer (B) proposes to purchase Greenacre from Seller (S), a young woman. S knows there has been discussion for years about the possibility of condemning the property to make way for a new road. S also knows that the area is cavernous, and that Greenacre had once been used to perform illegal abortions and the fetuses were disposed of on the premises. S tells B none of these facts prior to purchase of the property.

During the course of negotiations S and B become engaged and they marry. After the marriage and purchase of Greenacre, B discovers the foregoing facts about Greenacre and also discovers that S has a history of insanity in her family. B becomes distraught over these discoveries. The abortion clinic background of Greenacre disturbs him because of his religious beliefs, and because it affects the salability of the property to persons of the same religious faith as B (which is the dominant faith in that area). A few months after B makes the discoveries, the state institutes eminent domain proceedings against Greenacre to obtain the property. Thereafter S gives birth to a mentally unstable child, conceived before B learned of S's family history of insanity.

Assuming no tort immunity, discuss B's possible tort claims against S.

14.3

Patient was hospitalized for lung cancer, and a successful operation was performed to remove the cancerous growth. Prior to the operation, Patient was given a CAT scan to determine whether the cancer had metastasized to her brain. The results revealed no cancer. Doctor, who performed the scan, submitted a bill of $129 to Medicare as his charges for performing the scan. In the "Diagnosis" box of the Medicare reimbursement form, Doctor wrote "brain tumor." He did this, instead of writing "rule out brain tumor," because on several previous occasions a "rule out" diagnosis had resulted in the form being returned unpaid.

Medicare paid a portion of the bill, and a statement for the balance was sent to Patient's private, secondary insurance company for payment. The company paid the balance, and as a routine matter sent a copy of the statement and certificate of payment to Patient's home. The certificate indicated that the payment had been made for a CAT scan resulting in the diagnosis of a brain tumor. Patient's Husband received the letter containing the certificate from the insurance company, opened and read it, and laid it on the dining room table. Later, Patient read the certificate. Erroneously believing that brain tumor was invariably fatal, Patient became deeply depressed and took her own life.

Discuss a possible wrongful death claim by Patient's estate and a claim by Husband against Doctor.

14.4

Robby agreed to secretly videotape his friend Barry having sexual relations with assorted women, on the assurance of Barry's attorney, Omer, that it was legal to do so. Eventually the women found out about the videotaping, and some of them sued Robby for invasion of privacy and outrageous conduct. Robby settled these claims, and then brought this suit against Omer, alleging negligent misrepresentation in representing that the videotaping was legal. In his deposition Robby states that he did the videotaping for Barry as "a really good friend," received no payment for the work, and that he did not do the work out of "a desire to protect a financial interest he had with Barry." Does Robby have a viable claim for negligent misrepresentation? *See* Rest. 2d Torts §552.

14.5

Having delivered a healthy child, Plaintiff seeks recovery against defendant for pain and suffering, loss of income, and emotional distress resulting from defendant's misrepresentation to her that he was "single," and "incapable of impregnating her" because he had "undergone a vasectomy." Plaintiff alleges that in reliance upon these representations, which were false, she engaged in a "personal relationship" with defendant, became pregnant as a result, and gave birth to a normal, healthy child. Who should prevail and why?

14.6

Defendant makes a car capable of traveling at speeds of 150 mph. The highest lawful speed in the United States is 80 mph. Defendant advertises the car as "the fastest thing on wheels," and sponsors television commercials showing the car involved in extraordinary feats of speed and maneuverability. The advertisement says "This is the car of REAL MEN."

Joe Public bought one of these cars. While driving it at a speed well in excess of 100 mph, and while under the influence of alcohol, Public lost control of the car and hit and killed plaintiff's deceased who was standing in a yard near the road where Public was driving.

Discuss the possible liability of the defendant car manufacturer to the estate of plaintiff's deceased for wrongful death.

14.7

Entertainer made a cassette in which he imitated the voice of the President of the United States. The imitation was nearly perfect. In the cassette, he lampooned the President, capitalizing on all his snafus and gaffes. Entertainer made substantial profits in the sale of this cassette. Entertainer also sold a wristwatch which he had designed, with the hands of the watch consisting of a cartoon likeness of the President's body and face. He derived substantial profits from the sale of this watch.

The Stetson hat is a famous brand of Western-style hat. John Stetson, who is unrelated to the Stetson hat manufacturer, decides to manufacture his own hats, which he sold at his outlet store under the advertising name of "John Stetson Hats." Mr. Stetson also opened a motel next to his hat store called "The Worst Western Motel." There is a national motel chain called "Best Western Motels."

Does the President have a tort action against Entertainer?

Does either the original Stetson or Best Western have a tort action against John Stetson?

14.8

One night, over a few beers, Chris Marlow told his neighbor, Bill Shakespeare, about a plot he had in mind for a new play called "Hamlet." Chris got the basic idea for the play from Hollingshed's history book, but he had embroidered it by adding a subplot involving Hamlet's girlfriend Ophelia and her father Polonius. Chris told Bill that he decided to portray Hamlet as "not all there, you know, sort of half-baked." He intended to imply an incestuous attraction of Hamlet for his mother as a motive for Hamlet's strong dislike for his stepfather, Claudius. Chris also planned a play-within-a-play scene in which

Claudius' guilt for the death of Hamlet's father would be strongly suggested by Claudius' reaction to the scene. The play was to begin with the appearance to Hamlet of the ghost of Hamlet's father, who would tell Hamlet that Claudius had poisoned him. Hamlet was to be killed in the end by a poisoned rapier in a sword fight with Ophelia's brother, Laertes.

When Chris sobered up some months later, he realized that his neighbor Bill had written and produced a highly successful play called "Hamlet" which incorporated all the ideas Chris had previously related to Bill — plus many fine speeches ("To be or not to be," and the like) which were original with Bill.

Has Chris a valid claim against Bill for wrongful appropriation of property?

14.9

Michele, a paralegal, worked for Smokem Tobacco Co., a cigarette manufacturer. In her capacity as a paralegal, she had access to Company documents indicating that Smokem's research had established twenty years before her employment that tobacco was carcinogenic and addictive, and that Smokem had consciously controlled nicotine levels in its cigarettes to make them addictive. Smokem considered these documents to be trade secrets. It publicly denied that cigarettes were either carcinogenic or addictive. When she began working for Smokem, Michele had signed an agreement not to reveal any trade secrets that she might learn about at Smokem. She knew that Smokem considered these documents to be trade secrets.

Smokem notified Michele that her termination was a consequence of her "violent public anti-smoking stance." She had written and spoken against the cigarette industry, describing it as "corrupt" and "evil" and "a No.1 health hazard."

Before her termination, Michele had secretly made copies of the above documents. After her termination, she sold copies of these documents to plaintiffs' attorneys who were able to use them with devastating effect in cigarette-smoking tort litigation against Smokem.

Does Smokem have a valid claim against Michele for wrongful appropriation of trade secrets? Does Michele have a valid claim against Smokem for wrongful discharge?

14.10

Defendant company employed a woman who was extraordinarily productive and efficient. Her performance evaluations consistently substantially outstripped those of everyone else in the company. The president of the company terminated the woman's employment. When she asked the reason for her termination, the president said in the presence of other employees: "You show up the rest of us and make us all look bad. Moreover, you are married and have children, and I believe you are a terrible wife and mother because u spend too much time at work with men and a woman's place is in the home." Does the woman have a valid claim for defamation?

14.11

Defendant trained a chimpanzee to follow plaintiff about and make obscene gestures. Is this libel or slander?

Finally, defendant hired an airplane pilot to sky-write obscene remarks in the air about the plaintiff. Libel or slander?

14.12

In connection with their divorce proceeding, wife charged the husband-plaintiff, a prominent psychologist, with sexually molesting their daughter. After the court dismissed this charge, the husband-plaintiff later appeared on a TV talk show and discussed his divorce case. During the course of the discussion, the wife-defendant stood up in the audience and stated to plaintiff: "You are lying. You raped your child and you know you did." Plaintiff suffered great emotional distress as a result of the statement.

Discuss plaintiff's possible defamation claim against the wife-defendant.

14.13

Patron says to Librarian: "You have a book on your shelf that libels me" (naming the book), "and if you don't remove it right away, I'll sue you for libel."

If the librarian does not remove the book, can the librarian and the library be found liable for republication?

14.14

Suppose Commissioner Sullivan had been explicitly named as the one responsible for the libelous matters alleged in the newspaper article. If the Times refused to print a retraction after being notified of the alleged libel by Commissioner Sullivan, would it be guilty of republication?

14.15

Leading Law Firm called up Distinguished Professor to seek his opinion about a job applicant to the Firm, Molly Student. Molly was first in her class, and editor-in-chief of the law review. Professor said, "I can't put my finger on it; but after years of experience in this business, my visceral reaction is that she will not make a good lawyer."

On the basis of this negative recommendation by Professor, for whom the Firm had the highest regard, Firm did not make Molly a job offer.

Can Molly recover in defamation against Professor?

14.16

A cellular telephone conversation of plaintiffs, two identifiable local teachers' union representatives, was covertly taped by an unknown person. In that conversation, union contract negotiations with the school district were discussed. One of the plaintiffs said that if the school district did not "move" for a 3% wage increase, "we're gonna have to go to their homes . . . to blow off their front porches, we'll have to do some work on some of those guys."

The tape of the conversation was anonymously turned over to the defendant radio station and its reporter, who published the tape on the radio news-public affairs talk show. Plaintiffs sued defendants for damages resulting from defendants' violation of federal and state wiretap statutes. The statutes made it a crime, and provided a civil cause of action, inter alia, for anyone to "use or disclose intercepted communications and who had reason to know that the information was received through an illegal interception." The United States intervened in the case and argued that the federal statute had the twofold purpose of "denying the wrongdoer the fruits of his labor" and "eliminating the demand for those fruits by third parties."

The court said the First Amendment protected the defendants from liability, where the record was "devoid of any allegation that the defendants encouraged or participated in the interception in a way that would justify characterizing them as 'wrongdoers'. . . . The public interest and newsworthiness of the conversation broadcast and disclosed by the defendants are patent." A dissent faulted the defendants for broadcasting the conversation without making any effort to ensure its authenticity, authorization, or prior press release.

See Bartnicki v. Vopper, 200 F.3d 109 (3d Cir. 1999), *aff'd*, 532 U.S. 514 (2001).

14.17

A candidate for the U.S. Presidency learns that her opponent's wife had a lesbian affair while in elementary school. The candidate also learns that her opponent once said in privacy to his closest friend that he "doubted the existence of a Supreme Being," although the opponent attends church regularly and faithfully adheres to a strong moral code. The candidate publicizes these items of information about her opponent during the election campaign. The candidate wins the election.

Does the opponent have a cause of action against the winner for invasion of privacy? How would the opponent prove his case, and what would be the measure of damages? Does the opponent's wife have such an action?

Chapter 15

TORT REMEDIES

A. INTRODUCTION

> "Tort law divorced from damages is like Hamlet without
> the Prince of Denmark."
>
> — Thomas F. Lambert Jr.

In the vast majority of tort cases, the ultimate goal of the plaintiff is an award of money damages. Exceptions most often involve lawsuits asserting nuisance, trespass, a toxic tort, and commercial business cases where the plaintiff often seeks an injunction. Traditionally, tort damages are divided into nominal, compensatory, and punitive damages. Nominal damages represent a symbolic remedy awarded in intentional torts cases where the plaintiff is unable to prove actual loss or injury. Nominal damages affirm the merit of the plaintiff's intentional tort claim, but leave her with empty pockets. In negligence and strict liability actions plaintiff is required to prove actual damages as an essential part of her claim. As you know, the *prima facie* case for negligence is: duty, breach, causation, and damages. Similarly, in a strict products liability case, the plaintiff must prove that a product is defective and causally connected to the plaintiff's personal injury or property damage. Tort damages serve four purposes:

(1) to compensate, for harms;

(2) to determine rights;

(3) to punish wrongdoers and deter wrongful conduct; and

(4) to vindicate parties and deter retaliation or violent and unlawful self-help.

REST. 2d TORTS § 901.

When a plaintiff seeks an award of money damages the ability of the legal system to promote justice turns not only on who wins the case but also on the size of the award if the plaintiff prevails. If the case involves a claim limited to property damages, the size of the award rarely induces a public debate. In contrast, if the claim involves a personal injury, an award of a substantial sum of money often evokes media coverage and widespread public debate as to whether justice has been served and whether the tort system is malfunctioning. The reason for the different responses to awards in personal injury cases and property damage cases is simple: There is a market for the replacement of property and the market provides a reference for evaluating whether the award makes sense. From a remedial and corrective justice perspective, the goal of tort law is to place the plaintiff back in the position he was in before being victimized by tortious conduct. A money award that allows the repair or replacement of property rests on objective evidence that everyone can assess. The specific elements for which a plaintiff seeks damage in a personal injury case include losses for items such as emotional distress, physical pain and suffering, loss of ability to enjoy life and disfigurement — elements that are not susceptible to measurement in the market.

Moreover, even when a market exists for elements of damages such as medical expenses and lost wages, great uncertainties arise as to how to measure the losses. This is because the common law requires a lump sum award, taking into account, once and for all, past, present, and future losses. Experts often disagree as to what would have happened in the plaintiff's future if she had not been seriously injured or killed. It is thus not surprising that a multi-million dollar award for a brain-damaged baby evokes intense debate as to its legal justification, reflecting the perspectives and value preferences of the observers.

In torts such as assault, false imprisonment, and defamation, juries may award nonpecuniary damages compensating *dignitary loss*. In a tortious wrongful discharge case, for example, the plaintiff may be compensated for the stigma and self-doubt arising from the loss of a job. *See, e.g., Dotson v. United States*, 87 F.3d 682, 689 (5th Cir. 1996) (stress stigma and self doubt resulting from discriminatory firing are traditional harms associated with personal injury and are excludable for purposes of income taxation). "The value that is placed upon the dignitary loss is a question for the jury, subject, of course, to review by the courts." *Herrera v. Valentine*, 653 F.2d 1220 (8th Cir. 1981). "Compensatory damages for the injury to dignity which follows from an intentional blow, or even from a slander, must not be confused with, or regarded as, punitive damages." *Hernandez v. Lattimore*, 454 F. Supp. 763, 767 (S.D.N.Y. 1978). Punitive damages are awarded as societal damages in addition to "dignitary loss already provided as part of compensatory damages." *Id.* In dignitary torts such as the invasion of privacy, defamation, or civil rights torts, nominal damages is in effect, a "public declaration that the plaintiff is right and improperly treated." REST. 2D TORTS § 901, Illus. c.

The indeterminate nature of dignitary, noneconomic damages and punitive damages has served as fertile ground for debates among jurors, judges, law professors, economists, and legislators as to whether the measurement of personal injury awards makes sense in light of the established tort goals of deterrence, corrective justice, and social justice and makes sense from an economics perspective. Some argue that the system encourages accident victims to sue in the hope of finding a sympathetic jury that will award a "pot of gold." Others argue that empirical evidence has identified under compensation as the real problem; the torts system compensating only a very small percentage of accident victims injured by tortfeasors. Plaintiffs are not entitled to the recovery of attorneys fees under the American system of civil justice and therefore the structure of the system encourages pursuing suits that are significant enough to generate damages for the plaintiff and payment for the attorney's work. *See* Dan B. Dobbs, LAW OF REMEDIES § 3.10 (2d ed. 1993). *See* REST. 2D TORTS § 914, cmt *a*.

This chapter presents cases, materials, and notes that prompt the student to begin a critical assessment of the competing claims and arguments about the proper goals and functions of a compensatory or punitive damage award. In addition to posing questions from the perspectives of law and economics and corrective justice, this chapter examines the role of race, gender, ethnicity, or national origin in tort damages. Finally, practical considerations concerning the role of insurance and attorneys' fees are highlighted as critical and complementary aspects of a torts compensation system.

B. COMPENSATION FOR MONETARY LOSSES: SPECIAL DAMAGES

Compensatory damages are subdivided into economic losses such as lost earning capacity — categorized as special damages — and noneconomic damages, often referred to as pain and suffering damages — categorized as general damages. This section describes the law governing special damages, including calculation alternatives. The next section will address general damages.

REST. 2D TORTS § 906 provides: "Compensatory damages that will not be awarded without proof of pecuniary loss include compensation for (a) harm to property, (b) harm to earning capacity, and (c) the creation of liabilities." Economic damages compensate the plaintiff for injuries to his person or property and may include medical bills, past and future earnings, and other direct economic expenses. Lost past or future income, lost earning capacity, business economic losses, and diminished value of property are common categories of economic loss.

Special damages typically encompass measurable economic losses that are direct, reasonable, and expectable items of loss from an injury. In all personal injury actions where future damages are awarded, the court adjusts the award to reflect the present value of the sum. If the jury decides to award damages, they must determine what amount of money will fairly compensate the plaintiff. For each item of loss, the jury must determine the nature, extent, and duration of the injury. Tort damages may be broadly divided into easily computed *special damages* such as the cost of hospital care, rehabilitation, supplies, ambulance services, or medical devices used in treatment. Special damages for burial and funeral expenses are an important component of tort recovery in nursing home neglect cases where the plaintiff is rarely alive at the time a case is tried. In a medical liability case where the plaintiff suffers hemiplegia or partial paralysis, special damages may include the cost of 24-hour care and residential placement in a nursing home. *See generally* FRANK M. MCCLELLAN, MEDICAL MALPRACTICE: LAW, TACTICS, AND ETHICS 101–35 (1994).

Past medical expenses are recoverable as part of the special damages award. The plaintiff may receive the reasonable expense of necessary medical care from the time of the accident to the trial. Medical care may include nursing care, drugs, x-rays, medical devices and the like. Past medical expenses are relatively easy to compute, at least when compared to future medical expenses. Future medical expenses are an item of economic loss but inflation and present value must be taken into account. In order to award future medical expenses, a jury must find the expense is reasonably necessary and reasonably certain to occur. In that process of determination the plaintiff's current life expectancy must be taken into account as well as the probability that the medical expenses will continue into the future. Compensatory awards for future losses will frequently involve difficult conceptual problems fixing the loss period, reducing the award to present value, and adjusting for inflation. DAN B. DOBBS, THE LAW OF TORTS 1056 (2000). However, "[o]nce the appropriate interest rate and the time of the future losses are determined, the reduction is simply mathematical." *Id.* at 1057. An infant suffering severe brain damage, will for example, require the cost of 24-hour care for decades. Live-in attendant care alone can cost millions of dollars projected over seven decades or more as life expectancy increases.

As you read the principal case, consider what methodology should be used in determining damage awards. How should the annual inflation rate be taken into account? Which items of damages are classifiable as special damages? Should damage awards for consortium also be adjusted for present value? How can juries determine future expenses by a "reasonable certainty?" What methodology should be used in determining future compensatory damages? Should expert testimony be required?

GLEASON v. KUEKER
641 N.W.2d 553 (Iowa App. 2001)

VAITHESWARAN JUSTICE.

A jury awarded Mary Gleason and her husband damages in their personal injury action against Gary Kueker. The damages included an award for future medical expenses. Kueker contends the jury did not reduce this award to present value. We disagree and affirm.

Kueker rear-ended Gleason's car at a stoplight. Gleason sued for injuries sustained in the accident and her husband David sued for loss of consortium. Dr. Jennifer Rasmussen, a chiropractor who treated Mary Gleason for neck, shoulder, and back pain testified at trial. She opined that the accident resulted in a thirty-two percent whole body impairment rating. She also opined Gleason's condition would worsen and she would eventually need surgery. Dr. Rasmussen stated she released Gleason from her care after fourteen visits because she was unable to do anything for her. Gleason also called Michael Kaus, a physical therapist who treated her. He opined Gleason needed ongoing physical therapy.

The plaintiffs did not call an economic expert to testify about damages. Instead, Gleason herself estimated the damages she believed she had sustained. She testified her post-accident medical expenses totaled $17,607.59. Based on this figure, and a life expectancy of thirty years, she approximated her future health costs at $130,000. Gleason stated she arrived at this approximation as follows: "Past health care costs divided by four years times 30 years equals $132,00.57 or last month health costs times 12 times 30 years and that comes to $131,400." [The Gleasons introduced standardized mortality tables reflecting a life expectancy for Mary of 30.3 years].

The jury returned a verdict of $299,324.84 for Mary Gleason, $126,400 of which was allocated to future medical expenses. Kueker moved for a new trial and remittitur. The district court denied both motions. This appeal followed. On appeal, Kueker challenges only the future medical expenses award.

[The jury specified the following damages]:

Past Medical Expenses $17,607.59

Future Medical Expenses $126,400.00

Loss of time (earnings) $3,604.25

Loss of future earning capacity $11,713.00

Past loss of full body $10,000.00

Future loss of full body $100,000.00

Past pain and suffering $5,000.00

Future pain and suffering $25,000.00.

David Gleason received $1000 for past loss of consortium and $4000 for future loss of consortium. Kueker challenges the district court's denial of his motion for new trial as it relates to the jury's award of future medical expenses. Our scope of review on this issue is for abuse of discretion . . . A denial of remittitur is generally also reviewed for abuse of discretion . . . However, where the question is whether the jury followed the law, we believe our review is on error.

Iowa law requires an award for future damages in a personal injury action to be reduced to present value. . . . The key question is whether the jury followed the instruction. Kueker contends it did not. He points out that the jury's award of $126,400 for future medical expenses is roughly equal to Gleason's past yearly medical expenses multiplied by her life expectancy, less the costs of the chiropractic care that was no longer needed. The Gleasons respond that Kueker's attempt to parse the future medical expense award amounts to speculation. Both parties raise cogent arguments. To resolve their competing claims, we find it necessary to examine the theory and practice behind present value reductions of future damage awards.

Present value analysis is the method used to determine the value today of future losses or expenses . . . It accounts for the reality that "money has the power to earn money." JACOB A. STEIN, 2 STEIN ON PERSONAL INJURY DAMAGES § 6:16 (3d ed.1997). Plaintiffs can realize earnings through the investment of an advance lump sum award, which effectively over-compensates them for their injuries if the award is not discounted. *See Beaulieu v. Elliott*, 434 P.2d 665, 671 (Alaska 1967). A countervailing consideration, however, is inflation, which devalues future damage awards. *Id.* at 671. The United States Supreme Court has recognized that "ours is not an inflation-free economy" and "anticipated price inflation . . . certainly affects market rates of return." *See Jones & Laughlin Steel Corp. v. Pfeifer*, 462 U.S. 523 (1983). Therefore, the modern consensus is that present value reductions should take into account future inflationary pressures. In other words, the rate by which an award is discounted should be offset by an anticipated inflation rate. 22 Am.Jur.2d

Damages § 144 (1988). Iowa recognizes this economic reality. *Schnebly,* 217 N.W.2d at 728; *see also Schmitt v. Jenkins Truck Lines, Inc.,* 170 N.W.2d 632, 658 (Iowa 1969) (upholding expert testimony on present value reduction which took into account both inflation and increased productivity of economy).

Although there is a growing consensus that anticipated inflation should be considered in a present value analysis, there is little agreement on the preferred methodology . . . Courts generally have adopted one of three approaches: (1) the current dollar earnings and current interest rate or "inflate-discount" method; (2) the real earnings and real interest rate or "real interest rate" method; and (3) the "total offset" method. *See* Curran, 72 CONNECTICUT B.J. at 377; Michael I. Krauss and Robert A. Levy, *Calculating Tort Damages for Lost Future Earnings,* 31 GONZAGA L. REV. 325, 341 (1996). The first approach projects future damages with inflation built in. The second approach projects damages without inflation and discounts those damages at an interest rate that does not have inflation built in (real interest rate). *Id.* The third approach assumes that the discount rate is completely neutralized or offset by the inflation rate.

. . . Our legislature has not mandated a particular approach to discount future awards to present value, nor has it prescribed a discount rate to be applied by the fact-finder. . . . Although our highest court has not explicitly mandated a particular methodology, it has affirmed the use of the total offset approach where there is evidence from which to conclude that the discount and inflation rates are the same. . . . Additionally, the court has rejected use of the legal rate of interest to reduce future damages to their present value, adopting instead the rate "found by the jury from the evidence to be fairly expected from reasonably safe investments which a person of ordinary prudence, but without particular financial experience or skill, could make in the locality." 99 N.W.2d 287, 291 (Iowa 1959).

Finally, the court has reaffirmed its faith in the jury to make the present value reduction based on all the relevant facts and circumstances shown by the evidence. . . . While certain courts have questioned the wisdom of relegating such a complex economic calculation to a jury, others have noted that the use of economics in a litigation setting is in any event less than exact and the determination should be left to the sound discretion of the jury. . . . Iowa appears to have endorsed the "sound discretion" approach. Turning now to the facts of this case, it becomes evident that we must adopt the Gleasons' position. Although Kueker compellingly argues that the numbers reflect no present value reduction, to adopt his position would require us to speculate as to the jury's calculations. We decline to do so.

We must assume that the jury acted in accordance with its instruction and made a determination of present value. . . . The jury very well could have determined from Mary Gleason's medical billing records that the cost of medical care was rising at a higher rate than the prevailing interest rate, justifying a complete offset of the two and adoption of the approximate figure offered by Gleason. *See Burgess v. Mid-Florida Service,* 609 So. 2d 637, 638 (Fl. Ct.App.1992) (noting jury's failure to arrive at present value calculation smaller than future damages award did not necessarily prove failure to follow instructions but may have been "consistent with an intentional determination that the present value is equal to future damages by application of a 'total offset' calculation.") In the alternative, the jury could have reduced Mary Gleason's $130,000 figure to $126,400 not because it was taking into account the assumptions suggested by Kueker, but because it believed inflation would not offset the discount rate. Because there was some evidence from which the jury could have made this present value determination, we conclude the future medical expense award should be affirmed. The district court did not abuse its discretion in denying Kueker's motion for new trial and did not err in rejecting his request for remittitur. [AFFIRMED].

NOTES

1. *Methods for Discounting Future Earnings.* Damages for future loss of earnings are reduced to present value because, at time of trial, the plaintiff is awarded a lump sum representing the earnings he would have received later. Present value is determined by calculating how much money the plaintiff would need presently in order to enable her to invest at interest so as to recover her full value of expectable damages when they occur at a later date. The interest-rate discount is usually reduced to take account of expected inflation. *See Jones & Laughlin Steel Corp. v. Pfeifer*, 462 U.S. 523 (1983). Courts are not in agreement about what methodology should be used for determining the discount rate for future wages or medical costs:

> 1. Calculate the lost income stream by excluding the effects of inflation and the real interest rate by fixing the difference between the market rate of interest and the anticipated rate of inflation; 2. Calculate the size of the lost income stream by including the effects of inflation and discounting by the market interest rate; [or] 3. Calculate the value of pecuniary damages by employing a zero discount rate (the total offset approach).

Scott v. United States, 884 F.2d 1280, 1285 (9th Cir. 1989) (discussing alternative methods used to compute future wages and medical services under the Federal Torts Claim Act). An expert economist may, for example, testify as to the market rate of interest for treasury bonds and the inflation for that same period in calibrating future wages or medical costs. Some courts find it improper to use historical increases in wages as the yardstick for determining inflation when determining the discount rate. *Id*. at 1287. Another approach is to treat the interest rate as offset by inflation, so that no reduction to present value need be made. *See Kaczkowski v. Bolubasz*, 421 A.2d 1027 (Pa. 1980) (adopting the total offset method rather than discounting future damages awards to present value based on rationale that interest earned on invested money will be offset by inflation).

The common law rule is that the plaintiff may not recover for prejudgment interest. DAN B. DOBBS, THE LAW OF TORTS 1062 (2000). Some states now permit prejudgment interests in tort actions. "Some are narrower and cover only wrongful death actions or claims involving fraud, malice or oppression." *Id*.

Experts may also testify to lost earning capacity. Because this award is for loss of earning capacity, the victim need not be employed at the time of the accident. Thus, a child victim may be entitled to recover loss of earning capacity on the basis of the minimum wage. Greater recovery may be too speculative, although the court may give the jury wide discretion.

2. *Commodifying Special Damages:* Special damages are "objectively verifiable monetary losses including medical expenses, loss of earnings, burial costs, loss of use of property, costs of repair or replacement, costs of obtaining substitute domestic services, loss of employment and loss of business or employment opportunities." *Scalice v. Performance Cleaning Sys.,* 57 Cal. Rptr. 2d 711, 716 (Cal. Ct. App. 1996) (quoting California's workers' compensation statute). The monetization of future damages is less straightforward. The discounting for future damages requires the finder of fact to determine the appropriate term for the future loss along with the interest rate that should be used for making the present value determination. Experts reduce damages to future worth to determine future damages and thus "[t]he jury should determine from the evidence what interest could be fairly expected from safe investments which a person of ordinary prudence, but without particular financial experience or skill, could make in that locality." Daniel F. Sullivan, *Discount Rate for Future Damages,* 8 AM JUR. PROOF OF FACTS 2D 1 (2006). This rule has been explicitly adopted in some jurisdictions and others have adopted substantially similar language." *Id.* The standard methodology determines the discount rate "measured by the highest net rate of interest that the testimony shows can be had on money safely invested." *Id.* Alaska, however, reflects a minority rule in measuring future damages; "the discount rate is measured by the rate of interest that could be 'fairly expected' from safe investments." *Id.*

Discounting to present value is a very rough-and-ready method of calculating damages. Obviously, the accuracy of this calculation would depend on the type of present worth in dollars of these future damages. Juries are instructed that they must reduce any award for future awards for the amount of the expenses that the plaintiff would have incurred in making those earnings. If there is a future loss of earnings, for example, the jury is instructed to reduce the award to present value by considering the interest that the plaintiff could earn on the amount of the award because the plaintiff can earn interest.

3. *A Statistical Approach to Lost Earning Capacity.* Future wages present the same problem of methodology. Wages, like future medical expenses, must be proven to a "reasonable certainty." A statute may prescribe the use of certain work life or life expectancy tables. Courts usually take judicial notice of mortality tables in general use in the insurance industry. *See* Annot., 50 A.L.R.2d 419 (1986). The parties may introduce evidence as to normal work life or life expectancy of the particular plaintiff in the particular industry, and may rebut with evidence that the plaintiff had a different life expectancy. *See, e.g., Christiansen v. Hollings,* 112 P.2d 723 (Cal. Ct. App. 1941).

4. *Expert Testimony on Future Damages.* Courts give plaintiffs' counsel considerable discretion in methods related to testimony about future earnings or medical costs. In *Reager v. Anderson,* 371 S.E.2d 619 (W. Va. 1988), a 13-year-old boy suffered leg and head injuries from a fall from a cliff. The physician who examined him did not detect signs of impeded circulation and his failure to diagnose resulted in the boy suffering an amputation of his leg. In the subsequent medical malpractice action, the court determined that an economist's expert testimony specifying five alternative scenarios was properly admitted evidence:

> With respect to loss of future earnings, the undisputed testimony of the plaintiffs'/appellees' economic expert and vocational rehabilitation expert indicates that the loss of future earnings would range from $192,236.00 to $1,154,942.00; within that range are figures of $301,043.00, $502,547.00 and $918,426.00, depending upon the vocational scenario . . . the jury believed, would best apply to the patient. The five vocational scenarios given to the jury, one of which must apply, were: (1) The patient chooses not to attend college but can hold a job; or . . . (2) The patient chooses to attend college, graduates and can hold a job; or (3) The patient begins college, cannot finish due to medical reasons but can hold a nonskilled job; or (4) The patient attends college and graduates but cannot hold a job thereafter due to medical problems; or (5) The patient chooses not to attend college and for medical reasons cannot hold a job. For each scenario, jobs were listed for a person with both legs and without one leg, and an average income was computed each way. The differences between average annual income with both legs and average annual income without one leg were multiplied by the expected number of work-force years and were reduced to present value.

Id. at 626.

The court found that these scenarios were admissible evidence and the weight to be given to this evidence was for the jury to decide. *Id.* at 626 (stating that even if these special damages were not considered, the case supported a jury verdict of $1,500,000).

5. *Future Medical Expenses.* Courts permit plaintiffs to calculate future medical expenses based upon the history of medical expenses that have accrued as of the time of the trial. Weber v. Trinidad, 2007 WL 663707 (Conn. Super. Ct., Feb. 14, 2007). The defendant in *Marchetti v. Ramirez*, 673 A.2d 567 (Conn. Ct. App. 1996), objected to submission of the issue of plaintiff's future medical expenses to the jury, in the absence of evidence that it was "reasonably probable" that such expenses would be incurred. In overruling the objection, the court said:

> It is not speculation or conjecture to calculate future medical expenses based upon the history of medical expenses that have accrued as of the trial date; particularly when there is also a degree of medical certainty that future medical expenses will be necessary. . . .

> Where the doctor testifies that the injured party *might* need future treatment and the injured party testifies he still suffers pain, that testimony is sufficient for consideration of the element of future medical expense. Here, there was testimony that the plaintiff might incur future medical expenses, and the plaintiff testified that he still suffers pain. Therefore, the jury could properly award future medical damages.

Id. at 571.

C. COMPENSATION FOR NON-PECUNIARY LOSSES: GENERAL DAMAGES

As mentioned earlier, compensatory damages encompass both noneconomic and economic damages. The previous section focused on economic damages, using the "special damages" terminology often used by courts. This section will focus on "general damages," which are also called noneconomic damages. REST. 2D TORTS § 905 states "Compensatory damages that may be awarded without proof of pecuniary loss include compensation (a) for bodily harm, and (b) for emotional distress."

In *Gleason* the jury awarded the plaintiff past and future pain and suffering as well as consortium damages. All of these items are classified as general damages sometimes referred to as "pain and suffering" "noneconomic," or "non-pecuniary" damages. Recall the case of *Palsgraf v. Long Island R. Co.*, 162 N.E. 99 (N.Y. 1928). Helen Palsgraf's injuries were predominately noneconomic damages. She "stammered quite a good deal. . . . had insomnia, depression of spirits and crying spells." WILLIAM H. MANZ, THE PALSGRAF CASE: COURTS, LAW, AND SOCIETY IN 1920S NEW YORK 48 (2005). The "traumatic hysteria" might today be diagnosed as a "post-traumatic stress disorder." *Id.* Mrs. Palsgraf's traumatic hysteria injury would be classified as general damages.

Professor Ellen Pryor notes that courts use many different terms when referring to general damages:

> Tort law has many terms for suffering, including general damages, noneconomic damages, pain and suffering, mental anguish, impair-ment, loss of the enjoyment of life, and loss of companionship and society. All these terms signify forms of human suffering: from pain; from injury and shock; from loss of ability, mobility, or livelihood; from the loss of a loved one; from the recognition that life will never be the same. Each year the vast tort engine processes tens of thousands of claims for suffering. The players in the tort system — the plaintiff's lawyer, the defense lawyer, and the insurance company and its adjust-ers — articulate, investigate, measure, probe, argue, gather evidence, strategize, monetize, and bargain over these claims for suffering.

Ellen Pryor, *The Challenge of Noneconomic Damages in Civil Litigation: Noneconomic Damages, Suffering, and the Role of the Plaintiff's Lawyer*, 55 DEPAUL L. REV. 563, 563 (2006).

Plaintiffs frequently use experts to give the jury a basis for determining the plaintiff's diminished enjoyment of life, impairment of faculties, or pain and suffering. However, it is difficult to determine the monetary value for a violin-ist who lost her arm in a mass transit accident. What amount will compensate a young child whose face was flesh-fused by a dangerously defective drain cleaner? How should a jury determine the mental pain of losing a limb or other disfigurement? A tort victim who loses a limb suffers past, present, and future physical and mental pain and suffering as well as lost self-esteem.

Pain and suffering awards may include compensation for disfigurement, infertility, or reproductive injuries. The loss of consortium or sexual intimacy is a another type of noneconomic damage for which the plaintiff may collect monetary compensation. To prevail on a claim of loss of *consortium*, a plaintiff must show, among other things, that one spouse suffered an injury that deprived the other spouse of some benefit that formerly existed in the marriage.

A tort plaintiff may receive compensation for the aggravation of a preexisting ailment or condition. The reasonable value of a plaintiff's loss of services, society, companionship, and conjugal relationship is also recoverable if causally connected to the defendant's tortious conduct. A jury must monetize the loss of these intangible relationships as they may accrue in the future. In the loss of a child, a jury may compensate the plaintiff for what a minor child might have contributed. The reasonable value of present, past, and future suffering as a result of the injury are recoverable. Professor Neil Vidmar and his colleagues found a correlation between noneconomic damages and severity of injury in an empirical study of medical malpractice awards in New York, Florida and California:

> [T]he general damages portion of awards was positively related to severity of plaintiff injury. That is, the more serious the injury the higher the mean and median levels of general damages. The exception to this trend was that in cases involving death the mean and median awards tended to be substantially lower than in cases of very serious permanent disabilities. That finding is consistent with [other empirical research]. While these verdict statistics provide no information on the actual basis of the jury's decisions, there is no evidence that these decisions result from caprice or unwarranted sympathy.

Neil Vidmar, *Medical Malpractice Lawsuits: An Essay On Patient Interests, The Contingency Fee System, Juries, And Social Policy*, 38 LOY. LA. L. REV. 1217, 1242 (2005).

General damages are difficult to measure, but most courts take the view that full compensation demands recovery for emotional distress. When emotional distress accompanies physical injury, it is part of the recovery for personal injury. Special problems arise, however, when the predominant or sole basis for recovery is for emotional distress.

WRY v. DIAL
503 P.2d 979 (Ariz. Ct. App. 1972)

[Plaintiff was rescued from a fire in an automobile in the aftermath of an automobile accident negligently caused by the defendant]. Unanimous verdicts were rendered by the jury in favor of the appellees Joe H. Dial and Arrah L. Dial in the sum of $3,500,000 and in favor of the appellees David L. Hudnall and Patricia B. Hudnall in the sum of $401,750.

Appellants Wry filed a motion for new trial or for remittitur, both of which were denied by the trial judge. The appeal from the judgment and from the trial court's denial of their motions. . . . Because of the questions involved, we deem it necessary to set forth the facts at length considered in the light most favorable to upholding the verdict of the jury. They are as follows: On August 6,

1971, Joe Dial and Arrah Dial, husband and wife, were 32 and 29 years of age respectively. They had lived in Tucson for five years and had a one-year-old daughter. Arrah Dial was a graduate of the University of Redlands and had a master's degree in education from the University of Arizona. Joe Dial was a graduate of the University of Redlands and had a master's degree in electrical engineering. All Joe Dial needed for his Ph.D. degree was the completion of his dissertation, which he was in the process of writing. While working at this, he was employed part-time as a researcher for Dr. Paul Johnson at the University of Arizona. Dr. Johnson's particular field was physiology. Because of Joe Dial's expertise in the field of electrical engineering, he was working with Dr. Johnson to develop special instrumentation in the field of microcirculation.

Dr. Johnson testified that he was delighted with Joe Dial because he had a good capability for designing instruments, seeing improvements that were needed and how this should be accomplished. Dial was instrumental in developing two separate instruments which the laboratory is now using. . . . Although Dr. Johnson had worked for the past ten years with several engineers, he felt that Joe Dial was exceptional in that he was able to communicate with him across the barrier of engineering to biology and medicine. . . . He was very easy to talk to and seemed quite stable. He had no major problems and seemed to relate to people easily. It was easy to talk to Joe. He understood and was able to concentrate very well on subjects that were being discussed.

Because of Dial's growing interest in the relationship between engineering and medicine, it was arranged for him to enter the physiology department after he received his Ph.D. degree in electrical engineering to spend at least two years working in the research laboratory with Dr. Stewart, a professor of physiology specializing in neurophysiology. His salary at that time would have been approximately $9000 with some fringe benefits. . . . Joe Dial was very active athletically. He and his wife both played tennis about three times a week. He played basketball, baseball and belonged to a volleyball group which met on Thursday evenings. He rode his bicycle to and from work every day, and had a morning physical fitness program. He and his wife did a lot of hiking, backpacking and camping . . .

Joe Dial was extremely intelligent, creative, and took great pride in his creativity. He was also a very calm person with a lot of self-assurance. . . . On August 6, 1971, Joe Dial was brought to the emergency room of St. Mary's Hospital as a result of the automobile collision which caused his automobile to catch fire. He was first seen by Dr. Morton Aronoff, a specialist in plastic and reconstructive surgery. At that time Dial was severely burned, primarily around his face, neck, shoulders and back. He was admitted immediately to the hospital's Burn Unit. Dr. Charles Elkins was immediately called to see him in regard to possible brain injury because of his comatose condition. Dr. Elkins thought he was suffering from severe concussion and examined him for an intracranial injury or blood clot formation.

An electroencephalogram was performed and was somewhat abnormal. Dr. Elkins was of the opinion that Dial was suffering from a concussion and not a neurological problem. After Dr. Aronoff satisfied himself that the head injury need not be attended to immediately by a neurosurgeon, he concerned himself with the burns. His diagnosis was that Joe Dial had first, second and third degree burns of his face, neck, mouth, arms, back and legs, and had a cerebral concussion.

His initial examination revealed that Dial had severe burns over his entire face, neck and ears. The inside of his mouth, his tongue and his tonsils were also burned and Dial developed signs of respiratory obstruction. The inside of his throat, the inside of his mouth and his entire face began to swell. Because of the swelling he was taken to surgery on August 7. Prior to the operation a general anesthesia was not given because Dial was irrational, comatose, and every so often made wild gestures his arms and legs. A few intravenous drugs were given to obtain a local the doctor performed a tracheotomy to relieve the doctor performed a tracheotomy to relive Dial's breathing. The tracheotomy consisted of making a cut in the base of Dial's neck and putting a tube into his air passage.

Prior to the tracheotomy Dial had to be treated for shock. This involving putting a catheter in his bladder to monitor his urinary output. A catheter also had to be inserted into one of his veins to give him fluid in the form of electro-lytes and cholines to prevent shock and to maintain him. For the first two or three days of hospitalization Joe Dial was in a state of coma and did not respond, even to painful stimulation.

During that time he was receiving moderate sedation because of his head injury. On the third, fourth and fifth days he went into a state of stupor. He was irrational to a great degree, his movements were uncoordinated, and he thrashed around. On the fifth post-operative day the tracheotomy tube was removed. The swelling inside Dial's mouth and neck subsided and he was able to breathe on his own. At that point he was able to talk and respond rationally to questions. Approximately six or seven days following the injury Dr. Aronoff commenced his routine burn treatment. This involved taking Dial twice daily on a cart to a tank of water solution and putting him in the tank. The burnt skin was then washed and 'debrided.' The debriding was done by nurses and consisted of pulling off the dead portions of skin with forceps. Many times this would require sedation by morphine prior to going into the tank because of the pain occasioned in the debriding operation. The debriding is necessary to pre-vent infection. Following the debriding his burns were covered with a sulfamy-lon cream. This cream contains acid and burns a great deal. Dial was not able to tolerate the side effect of burning, and after a while Dr. Aronoff had to change to a terramycin cream. The debriding procedure is so extremely painful that patients undergoing the treatment begin to hate their nurses and doctors. . . . . Dial then developed a full thickness or third degree loss of the skin on his forehead, lost the outer two-thirds of his left eyebrow completely, and lost the skin of his left upper eyelid. The skin over the nose and especially the left half of the nose was deeply burned. A great portion of his upper lip was deeply burned as was his chin.

On September 3, 1971, almost a month after the accident, Joe Dial was taken to surgery under general anesthesia and an intermediate skin graft was made. An intermediate thickness skin graft is an area of skin which is 15/1000 of an inch thick. It was taken from the patient and applied to the burned raw areas of his left upper and lower eyelids, his left cheek, his forehead and his nose. . . . .

Dial felt as if he were in a jail and that the nurses who took him to the tank twice a day were torturing him. Because of this emotional deterioration, Dr. Aronoff felt that it would be better if Dial had some raw ungrafted areas on his body to be treated in his office rather than in a hospital.

After he was discharged from the hospital Joe Dial commenced office visits to Dr. Aronoff. Dr. Aronoff observed large red healed areas on Dial's back and neck and found that they bothered him a great deal because they were tender, painful and itched a great deal. Drugs are sometimes used to sedate the patient, but it is usually impossible to control the itching. He further noticed that Joe Dial was developing an ectopia of the left lower eyelid, which is a drawing down of the eyelid. The result of this ectopia was an exposure of the eyeball. Subsequently, this happened to the upper eyelid exposing the upper eyeball. Shortly thereafter the doctor discovered that Dial was a 'keloid scar former.' This meant that the scars grew beyond their original confines. They became raised up above the level of the skin and invaded normal skin. The scars appeared bright red and when touched turned white from the acute inflammatory response. The scars began to tighten up into a tight band and drew his normal tissues out of configuration. Dial also developed a severe contracture of the upper lip due to his keloidal scar tendency causing it to be drawn up and everted so that it was turned inside out. This interfered with his saliva control and eating.

On September 27, 1971, Dr. Aronoff noted that Joe Dial was very upset emotionally and psychologically. He further noted that Dial's whole life appeared to have been shattered by the accident. Dial's condition seemed to suddenly dawn upon him, and he had a very severe emotional breakdown, especially when told by Dr. Aronoff that he would have to go back into the hospital for more grafting of his eyelids and lip. Dial was readmitted to the hospital on October 5, 1971, for a skin graft and to release the contractures of his upper lip and eyelid. This was done under local anesthesia. A full thickness graft was taken from the left postauricular area, which is the area behind the left ear, and this was applied to the defect of his left upper eyelid and to the defect created on the lip. He was kept in the hospital until October 12, 1971. When the sutures were removed from his graft it appeared that the doctor's purpose had been accomplished and the patient was able to close his eye and mouth. As the skin grafting continued, however, further difficulty was encountered. Because of Dial's keloidal scar tendencies the donor sites also developed keloidal scars.

On October 24th, Dial was admitted to the hospital for a four-day stay. At that time the doctor was concerned with the left lower eyelid and again noted that it was beginning to contract quite severely. The doctor stated that because of the keloidal scar tendency he could not nonchalantly decide to do a split thickness graft on any given area to correct the problem, since he would be creating another problem at the donor site. He therefore had to consider that in order to cure one problem he was creating another and taking a like risk. A graft was performed on Dial's upper left eyelid. On November 15, 1971, Dr. Aronoff noted that the grafts were doing well but that the contracture around the mouth and the scars were getting worse. The lower lip was being drawn down and the inner corner of the left eye was beginning to contract.

Dial also developed an abscess in the upper lip where the doctor had placed a graft, and this had to be drained. Dial was again admitted to the hospital on December 1, 1971, and surgery was performed under local anesthesia. The scar contracture around the corner of his mouth and upper lip was cut out completely, allowing his mouth to return to a normal configuration.

In January of 1972, Dial developed a severe contracture of the nose and corners of his left eye. He was admitted once again to the hospital for the purpose of grafting. Two-thirds of the skin of his nose, the corner of his eye, and the adjacent cheek on the left side were excised completely and a split-thickness graft was taken from the inside of his right arm. No attempt was made to correct the distortion of the nose at that time. The graft took well and the corners of his eyes improved considerably compared to their former condition. The donor site of the inside right upper arm became red, raw, tender and raised above the level of the surrounding skin and became quite a problem. An attempt was made to treat the keloidal scars by injections of cortisone and steroids. On two occasions his neck scars were injected because they were beginning to contract quite severely. At this point Joe Dial had grafts all over the left side of his face and was going to need, in the words of Dr. Aronoff, '. . . an awful lot of treatment further.' The doctor had a neck splint fashioned for Dial to keep his neck straight up in order to avoid a contracture of the skin of the left side of his neck which would have contracted down and become deformed if the splint were not worn.

Since the scars on Dial's nose and the corners of his eyes still presented a problem, Dr. Aronoff made a model of Dial's face, a moulage. From this moulage the doctor fashioned a mask made of orthoplast, a malleable material. This mask was worn to keep pressure on the scars, with experience showing that such pressure on keloidal scar tissue does tend to have some beneficial effect. The mask looks like a white Halloween mask with eyes cut out. Pressure was also applied on Dial's arms in the form of Ace bandages. The bandages were wrapped around his arms continuously, with intermittent spells, in order to keep pressure on the scars. Due to the scarring on his right arm, the arm drew up and could not be straightened out. This will leave Dial with a permanent limitation of the arm. When asked about future skin grafts the doctor testified that there were no good donor sites on Joe Dial due to his keloidal scar tendency but that risks would have to be taken.

Dr. Aronoff's opinion is that Joe Dial has a normal life expectancy, but will experience a great deal of pain and suffering in the future as he has in the past. There is no doubt that Dial will suffer for the rest of his life as a result of the accident.

He will need at least six future surgical procedures and possibly many more. The procedures will necessitate hospitalization. In addition to the gross deforming scars and changed structures of his face, Dial has problem areas on his back, arms and legs. Even if these areas improved with time, they have the tendency to be more easily injured than normal tissue, since these tissues do not have the natural defense mechanisms of normal skin. Scar tissue, particularly, does not have the ability to secrete subcutaneous material, normal sweat material. On Joe Dial all these glands and glandular structures have been destroyed by fire. These tissues are susceptible to infection or trauma or injury and do not have their normal elasticity . . . The danger of this skin cancer is a very significant feature in Joe Dial's future. Dr. Aronoff has advised Dial to stay out of the sun and to protect his skin with oils and lubricants. This will have to be done for the rest of his life. Dr. Aronoff also told him to leave this part of the country for the northwest where he will not experience extremes of cold or heat.

Dr. Aronoff plans to reconstruct one eyebrow and hopes to give Dial a little better skin coverage so that with time some of the scarring process will subside. But no matter what Dr. Aronoff does his opinion is that Joe Dial is going to be permanently deformed and grotesque. Oils and greases must be continually applied to his skin to prevent drying. Dial must avoid all injury to the scarred areas from stimuli such as excessive heat, excessive cold, chemical irritants, irritant oils or irritant detergents. The scarred area on his face has diminished sensation and he has a severe lack of motion in the face itself. . . . Dial's mouth is much smaller than it was previously, and will not return to its normal size. Most of the hair follicles on his face are permanently destroyed and he will not be able to grow a beard or mustache in order to cover up his scar tissues. He also has a high statistical risk of having epileptic seizures because of the scar tissue that has formed in his brain. As a result of the accident Joe Dial has suffered permanent brain damage. He is 'frontal lobish.' As opposed to his former quiet demeanor he is now facetious, garrulous, gives inappropriate responses and has mood-swaying periods. At one moment he might be joking and the next be bellicose.

His actions are now childlike, characterized by great bursts of enthusiasm and great bursts of anger. Small things bother him and he is unable to control his emotions. When he gets depressed he cries. When Dial first talked to Dr. Aronoff about his injuries he would not admit that he was badly injured. When he finally realized the extent of his injuries he became depressed. He feels that children make fun of him and that he is an object 'to be looked at.' During the last few months he had not been taking the strain well and his condition was 'literally getting to him.' Dial is clumsy. He falls over backwards while tying his shoes in a crouched position. That he does not have the control over his body that he used to makes him very unhappy. Prior to the accident Joe Dial had been offered a job in the department of neurophysiology at the University of Arizona. Since the accident Dial stays at home most of the time and everything seems to upset him. He is unhappy a lot of the time, but especially at night when his skin itches and he is unable to sleep. He is also unhappy because he cannot open his mouth very wide and cannot eat normally as he did before the accident.

Dr. Aronoff has noticed that Dial's responses are inappropriate. For instance he smiles at the wrong time and cries at the wrong time. While the face mask was being made, which is not a painful procedure, Dial broke out crying in the middle of the procedure. Since the accident Joe Dial's reading ability has been impaired. He cannot read as fast as he used to because he has trouble organizing ideas and remembering what he just read. Dial was an attractive man before the accident. He now spends a lot of time in front of the mirror looking at himself. Lately he has been going to the cafeteria at the University of Arizona at an hour when it is not crowded because he does not want to be there with other people. Recreational activities in which Joe Dial engaged prior to the accident have been impaired. He has had to change his mode of dress and must now wear soft, light-weight clothing. He must apply creams and greases to his body continually. He has trouble with infections in his grafts which have to be drained. Whereas prior to the accident he was full of energy, he now tires easily.

Dial's ability to think creatively and to apply knowledge to problems has been impaired, as well as his ability to be tactful and considerate in social relationships. He faces a probability of skin cancer and is aware of this. He faces a certainty of future surgery and the possibility of additional surgery depending on the outcome.

His appearance is very different from what he looked like before and he knows that people are repulsed by him. He is afraid to show his face in public places because he has experienced being pointed, stared and laughed at by children and adults. He feels that he looks grotesque and his self-concept, based on his appearance, has been extremely changed. His life is completely different now. His former plans are in essence ruined and he is beginning to realize this . . . He is tense, and has lost confidence in himself. In spite of all this, however, Dial was struggling to keep going. He needs psychiatric care now and will probably need this for a few more years. It is possible that he could break down and require hospitalization. Dr. Aronoff believes that at this point Dial is 'walking on very thin ice emotionally.' He is coping with the situation as best he can, but part of this ability to cope requires that he not think of the full implications of his injury . . .

Some of Dial's problems are strictly emotional. Not only does he have difficulty in the thinking process, but he has accompanying feelings about this difficulty. He has to cope with the fact that all of his former plans are now impossible. He has to cope with the fact that he looks grotesque. His appearance embarrasses him and he wishes his face was not visible when he is with people. He wonders how his family feels towards him. He cannot play with his daughter as he used to for fear of injury to the skin grafts. At the time of the trial he was using the defense mechanism of denial in order to cope with his problems. His sexual relationship with his wife has changed greatly, as he is afraid that he is repulsive to her. If he follows Dr. Aronoff's advice and moves to a new community, he will have great difficulty in establishing social contracts due to his appearance. Prior to the accident David Hudnall and Joe Dial ate lunch with their associates, but Dial has told Hudnall on several occasions that he does not want to eat lunch with them now because he does not want to spoil anyone's appetite. He is quite conscious of the way he looks and his appearance seems to be the center of his world now.

Dr. Johnson has noticed that Dial's personality has changed since his accident. Specifically, Dial cannot carry on a conversation without forgetting the train of thought. He cannot concentrate and forgets what was being discussed. He sometimes forgets the names of people he knows and forgets the names of common objects such as a note pad. In the middle of a conversation he discusses the subject of his disfigurement. Whereas prior to the accident he was a very easy person to get along with, easy to talk to and a very likeable person, he now appears to Dr. Johnson to be very strange, unable to relax and very conscious of the way people look at him. . . .

Dr. Stewart testified that since the accident Joe Dial has changed and he would not employ him today. Dial cannot be trusted with laboratory machinery because of his inability to remember. He cannot continue in his chosen field of electrical engineering. On August 6, 1971, the date of the accident, David Hudnall and his wife Patricia, had been married approximately eight years and had a three year-old son. Hudnall received a master of science degree in electrical engineering from the University of Florida. He worked with Joe Dial providing electronic support for the chairman of the department of physiology. As did Joe Dial, he helped design and make instruments for Dr. Johnson in the field of microcirculation. . . .

When rescued from the burning vehicle, Hudnall was conscious but incoherent and kept repeating, 'Get me out of here.' He was brought to the emergency room with Joe Dial. He had extreme burns on his neck and had second and third degree burns on his shoulder, arm, hand, left thigh, right upper thigh, right chest and right loin area. He was taken to the Burn Unit, treated for shock and was given intravenous morphine and fluids. A catheter was placed in his bladder to monitor his output and determine whether his kidneys were functioning. He was in the hospital for 58 days and went through the same tanking and debriding procedure as Joe Dial. Hudnall's pain threshold was lower than Joe Dial's and he suffered extreme pain and agony. He could hardly be moved because of the pain. He was conscious of his injuries and was aware of everything that had happened to him. He understood the severity of his injuries and was afraid his life was ruined. He thought that he was going to lose his right arm, despite the doctor's reassurance that this was not so. The tanking and debriding procedure was especially painful to Hudnall. He shivered and shook uncontrollably when lifted out of the water until he warmed up. The use of morphine was necessary to relieve his pain. . . . Furthermore, he is unable to play with his son as he did in the past since he is afraid to injure the grafts. His backpacking activities and his outings with the Southern Arizona Rescue Association are now at an end since the doctor has warned him that he cannot receive any kind of trauma to the grafts. The grafted areas of his skin have some of the same infirmities as Joe Dial's in that they do not have the inherent defense mechanisms of normal skin and there is a tendency to infection and irritation. Although he has had three graft operations to date, Hudnall will probably need ten more operations during the remainder of his life. It is necessary for him to be seen by the doctor at least every three months to assure that there is no irritation of the scars which might lead to skin cancer.

It was stipulated at trial that Hudnall's life expectancy is 41 years and the life expectancy of Joe Dial was stipulated to be 39 years. At trial both Dial and Hudnall exhibited the burned areas of their body to the jury while wearing bathing suits. The defense called no witnesses. Appellants claim that appellees' counsel was guilty of misconduct in his summation to the jury. . . . The main thrust of appellants' appeal concerns itself with the size of the verdicts. Appellants assert that the economic loss and pecuniary loss to Joe Dial could not have been and will not be more than $1,000,000, and the pecuniary loss, past and future, for Hudnall will not amount to more than $45,000. Therefore, appellants conclude that awarding the sum of $2,500,000 to Dial for past and future pain and suffering and $350,000 for past and future pain and suffering to Hudnall is shocking, extravagant and indicative of a verdict motivated by passion and prejudice and not by the evidence. . . . [A]ppellants maintain that in order to judge the outrageousness of the verdict the true value of the sum is to be determined by its power to obtain the necessaries of life. In this regard appellants point out that if Joe Dial put his 2.5 million dollars for pain and suffering into tax-free municipal bonds paying 6% interest, his annual yield would be $150,000 or $12,500 per month for noneconomic loss.

This, appellants maintain, is socially unacceptable because (1) it creates a personal fortune at the expense of another individual, (2) there must be a reasonable limit as to what can be expected, (3) society is not compensating war casualties who have sustained equal or worse injuries, and (4) if Dial had been injured on the job he would not have received any award for pain and suffering under the Workmen's Compensation laws of this state. . . .

Appellants state that 'it behooves us to pause and make a thoughtful inquiry into the magnitude of a burden that we ask society to shoulder. It seems apparent that we would never have permitted our tort law to reach a point where a single individual would have the burden of paying in excess of $2.5 million for non-economic losses claimed as a result of one auto accident.' As we understand appellants' argument, when a wrongdoer injures an innocent party, the focus should be on the ability of the wrongdoer to pay rather than on the injuries of the innocent. We do not agree with this contention. . . . [T]his court noted that the jury and the trial judge have a much better opportunity than do appellate judges to measure the actual damage suffered by plaintiffs and the amount which would compensate for their injuries.

The trial judge not only has the opportunity to hear and observe the evidence in the case but is also singularly able to observe the jurors in considering whether or not they were motivated by passion or prejudice in their verdict. Where the trial court has refused to interfere with the jury's determination of damages, this court cannot interpose its own judgment on the issue unless convinced that the verdict is so outrageously excessive as to suggest, at first blush, passion or prejudice. . . . . After a reading of the transcript and a review of the evidence, our conscience is not so shocked. [AFFIRMED].

NOTES

1. *A Long-History.* In *Ransom v. New York & Erie Railroad Co.,* 15 N.Y. 415, 424 (1857), the New York Appeals Court held that the plaintiff, injured by railroad negligence, was entitled to recovery for noneconomic damages for "bodily pain and suffering, without reference to the time when endured." The California Supreme Court upheld pain and suffering damages in a case where the plaintiff endured pain and suffering from a severe foot injury. *Aldrich v. Palmer,* 24 Cal. 513, 516–18 (1864). *See also Morse v. Auburn & Syracuse R.R. Co.,* 10 Barb. 621, 623 (N.Y. Sup. Ct. 1851) (holding that the general rule for pain and suffering is triggered where one person has received personal injury and mutilation by the careless or negligent act of another. "The bodily pain and suffering is part and parcel of the actual injury, for which the injured party is as much entitled to compensation in damages, as for loss of time or the outlay of money.").

Courts have long permitted factfinders to award damages for intangible injuries even though many categories of injury have no objective standard:

> There is no direct correspondence between money and harm to the body, feelings or reputation. There is no market price for a scar or for loss of hearing since the damages are not measured by the amount for which one would be willing to suffer the harm. The discretion of the judge or jury determines the amount of recovery, the only standard being such an amount as a reasonable person would estimate as fair compensation.

REST. 2D TORTS § 912, cmt. *d*.

2. *Quantifying Pain and Suffering.* Noneconomic damages are less quantifiable than pecuniary damages. Ellen Pryor contends that juries receive far more guidance about special damages (medical expenses and lost earnings) than the vague standards they receive when determining non-economic damages: "For impairment, mental anguish, and pain and suffering, juries inevitably are given vaguer standards, such as to 'fairly and reasonably compensate' the plaintiff, or to use 'good discretion' or 'enlightened conscience.' Ellen Pryor, *Rehabilitating Tort Compensation*, 91 GEO. L.J. 659, 660 (2003). What is a "fair" award for the pain and suffering caused by Joe Dial in *Dial v. Wry* above? $100,000? $1,000,000? $10,000,000? Suppose he suffered only disfiguring burns or scars but had full functionality. Can you fashion an objective standard to guide the factfinder? Should the jury be instructed to award the amount of money it would pay to avoid the pain and suffering? The amount it would accept to endure the same pain and suffering? Are either of these alternatives an objective standard? The "Golden Rule," asking the jury to put themselves into the position of the plaintiff in order to determine what would be fair compensation is not permitted. *See* DAN B. DOBBS, LAW OF REMEDIES § 8.1(4) (1993). See note 1 following the next principal case, *Walters v. Hitchcock, infra.* Should the lack of an objective standard operate to deny the plaintiff any recovery for his pain and suffering? Are you really compensating the plaintiff for something he has lost because of the tort? Given the lack of an objective standard for determining such damages, why should we impose this burden of adducing objective measures of the loss upon the tortfeasor? According to Judge Posner:

> We disagree with those students of tort law who believe that pain and suffering are not real costs and should not be allowable items of damages in a tort suit. No one likes pain and suffering and most people would pay a good deal of money to be free from them. If they were not recoverable in damages, the cost of negligence would be less to the tortfeasor and there would be more negligence, more accidents, more pain and suffering, and hence higher social costs.

Kwasny v. United States, 823 F.2d 194, 197 (7th Cir. 1987).

The Reporters of the Second Restatement summarize the traditional techniques of counsel in proving noneconomic damages:

> Efforts to provide suggestions or formulas for measuring with more certainty the amount of damages for pain and suffering have met with varying degrees of success. It is consistently held to be improper to suggest to the jury that they place themselves in the position of the injured person and determine the sum of money that they would require to incur his injuries. Substantial disagreement has developed among the courts, however, on the so-called "per-diem argument" — asking the jury to estimate the value of the pain and suffering for a day (or some other short period of time) and then to multiply that figure by the length of time that the pain may be expected to continue. Three views are taken: (1) some courts forbid the practice on the ground of its potential prejudice in giving the jury an illusion of precision in calculation and in substituting a formula for evidence; (2) other courts find the practice not unfair or unjust in providing a mathematical formula to aid the jury in making a reasonable award since the parties should have the opportunity to explain the components of the lump sum; and (3) still other courts treat the matter as in the sound discretion of the trial judge so long as he gives appropriate cautionary instructions that the formula is not proof and should be treated merely as suggestive. There is also a division of authority on whether counsel may state to the jury the amount of damages claimed or expected by the plaintiff, but a substantial majority of the courts do not treat this as improper.

REST. 2D TORTS §912, cmt. *b*.

3. *What Is Fair?* The victim who sustains personal injury is entitled to an award to fairly compensate him for his pain and suffering. As one court observed,

> [t]here is no exact yardstick by which pain and suffering can be measured and the various factors involved are not capable of proof in dollars. For this reason, the only standard for evaluation is such amount as twelve reasonable persons estimate to be fair compensation when that amount appears to be in harmony with the evidence and arrived at without passion or prejudice.

Tucker v. Lower, 434 P.2d 320, 327 (Kan. 1967).

Counsel for the plaintiff may argue on the basis of a per diem formula for pain and suffering damages as well as for loss of consortium. Such an argument asks the jury to consider what would be fair compensation for the plaintiff's proven level of pain and suffering on a daily basis; that amount should then be multiplied by the number of days remaining in the plaintiff's life expectancy. This approach has been upheld.

> Theoretically, the same argument could be used by the defense, as a means of demonstrating that the plaintiff's damage demand is unreasonable. By dividing the demand into time segments, defense counsel may be able to powerfully illustrate how exaggerated or ludicrous the plaintiff's claim is. However, as a practical matter, the defense usually avoids this type of argument, because it is prone to backfire, and because it places the debate in terms favorable to the plaintiff. Most

defendants thus prefer to cast their presentation in other terms for tactical reasons.

CLIFFORD W. TAYLOR, MICHIGAN PRACTICE: GUIDE §10.99 (2006).

WALTERS v. HITCHCOCK
697 P.2d 847 (Kan. 1985).

MCFARLAND, JUSTICE.

This is a medical malpractice action wherein plaintiff Lillian K. Walters received a $2,000,000 damage award against defendant C. Thomas Hitchcock, M.D. The defendant physician appeals from the jury's verdict and certain pretrial and post-trial rulings of the district court.

The facts may be summarized as follows. In December 1979, a lump on the neck of Lillian Walters was discovered by her family physician. Mrs. Walters was, at the time, approximately 32 years of age, married, with four minor children. She was not employed outside the home. The family physician conducted a number of tests and advised her to consult with a surgeon. Mrs. Walters was seen by defendant Hitchcock, a surgeon, on January 7, 1980. As a result of the prior testing and his physical examination of her, Dr. Hitchcock recommended surgical removal of diseased areas of the thyroid gland. There were indications of a possibly malignant condition. Surgery was scheduled for January 22, 1980. Mrs. Walters was advised the operation was a relatively low risk procedure with an anticipated three-day hospital stay and a small residual scar.

The operation proceeded in what appeared at the time to be a routine manner. Specimens were sent to the pathology laboratory and no malignancy was detected. The patient was sutured and sent to the recovery room. One day later Mrs. Walters' condition rapidly deteriorated. Her head ballooned in size, she became blind and suffered extreme respiratory distress. She was taken to the intensive care unit where a breathing tube was inserted. Shortly thereafter, Dr. Hitchcock was advised by the hospital pathology department that a one inch by one and one-half inch piece of esophagus tissue was connected to the thyroid specimen sent to the laboratory during surgery. Mrs. Walters' wound was now badly infected. She was taken to surgery. Dr. Hitchcock reopened the wound and observed a significant hole in the left front portion of her esophagus. He concluded that repair was not possible and sewed the esophagus shut — thereby closing it permanently.

At this point feeding was possible only through a tube inserted directly into Mrs. Walters' stomach. She regained her vision. Numerous hospitalizations and surgical procedures followed. Ultimately, colon interposition surgery was performed which involved making a sort of bypass esophagus from a portion of Mrs. Walters' colon. Additional facts relative to Mrs. Walters' condition and the quality of her life will be set forth in the discussion of the issue relative to the amount of damages awarded herein.

Mrs. Walters brought this action against Dr. Hitchcock based upon negligence in cutting into the esophagus and in failing to make prompt repair thereof. She sought $4,000,000 in damages. Dr. Hitchcock denied negligence and blamed the injury to the esophagus on the abnormal physiology of

Mrs. Walters. The jury awarded Mrs. Walters $2,000,000 in damages and Dr. Hitchcock appeals therefrom.

The first issue on appeal concerns alleged misconduct of plaintiff's counsel during closing argument. In his closing argument plaintiff's counsel stated: "Who would sell their esophagus for $4 million? I would not sell mine." Defendant contends this constitutes a prohibited "golden rule" argument. This term relates to arguments of counsel that jurors should place themselves in the position of the plaintiff. Such arguments are usually improper and may constitute reversible error.

Plaintiff argues the remarks were not asking the jurors to place themselves in plaintiff's shoes, and were merely hypothetical in nature.

The remarks actually span two categories. The comment commencing "Who would sell . . . " is, we believe, a fair argument relative to claimed damages and is not a "golden rule" argument. The comment that counsel would not sell his esophagus for that sum is testimonial in nature as it is a statement of counsel's personal opinion. This is an improper argument. Does this improper comment constitute reversible error? We believe not. To constitute reversible error there must be a likelihood that the improper remarks changed the result of the trial. We have examined the record and conclude that, in the totality of the circumstances, the improper comment constituted only harmless error.

Additionally, we note that counsel made a timely objection to the remarks and the objection was sustained. Counsel did not request a jury admonition and none was given. Further, the jury had been instructed:

> The evidence you should consider consists only of the testimony of the witnesses and the exhibits which the Court has received.
>
> Opening statements are made by the attorneys to acquaint you with the facts they expect to prove. Closing arguments, which you are about to hear, are made by the attorneys to discuss the facts and circumstances in this case, and should be confined to the evidence and to reasonable inferences to be drawn therefrom. Neither opening statements nor closing arguments are evidence, and any statement or argument made by the attorneys which is not based on the evidence should be disregarded."

We conclude this issue is without merit.

. . . For his final issue, defendant challenges the size of the verdict. In his brief defendant states:

> In advancing this argument, the defendant is definitely aware of the long line of Kansas cases on the subject and the guidelines that have evolved in those cases. The defendant realizes that the trial court will not be reversed in an order denying new trial *unless* the amount of the verdict, in light of the evidence, shocks the conscience of the appellate court.

Defendant, in support of his argument that the verdict was excessive, directs our attention to the following:

> 1. Plaintiff's medical bills by the time of trial were approximately $59,000.

2. There was no claim nor was the jury instructed with regard to lost wages or diminished future earning capacity as Mrs. Walters was not employed during the course of her 19-year marriage.

3. The repair surgery and reconstruction by colon interposition were working properly at the time of trial, and no further surgery, with respect to the surgical complication that occurred during the thyroidectomy, was contemplated. . . . . No further evidence was presented regarding future medical expenses.

The evidence herein bears out that medical science has done all that it can do to alleviate plaintiff's condition and no further surgery is contemplated, although the same is not ruled out. This does not mean the damage done to Mrs. Walters has been undone and that she has been restored to her previous condition. It simply means her condition cannot be helped by further surgery or treatment. The substitute esophagus fashioned from a part of Mrs. Walters' colon is, apparently, functioning as well as can be expected but that level of function is a source of permanent problems for Mrs. Walters. When she swallows, food does not automatically go to her stomach. It piles up in grotesque bulges in her throat and upper chest. It is necessary for her to manually massage the bulges downward to force the food to her stomach. The process is physically painful. As there is no valve to keep the contents of her stomach from traveling back up the makeshift esophagus, she cannot lie flat and must remain in a position where gravity will keep the contents of her stomach in place. Her condition is embarrassing, distasteful to persons around her, and a major obstacle to leading a normal life. She has serious ongoing digestive problems. At the time of trial her life expectancy was 41.9 years. The years between Mrs. Walters' injury and attainment of her present level of functioning were a nightmare of pain, disability, hospitalizations and surgical procedures. She has severe disfiguring scars on her neck and torso. Many activities, such as eating and sitting, continue to be painful.

After having reviewed the record, we conclude our collective consciences are not shocked by the size of the verdict herein. [AFFIRMED].

NOTES

1. *Exclusion of Golden Rule Arguments.* "The reason golden rule arguments are not permitted is because they encourage the jury to depart from neutrality and to decide the case on the improper basis of personal interest and bias." *State v. McHenry*, 78 P.3d 403 (Kan. 2003). Is it realistic to expect a juror to assess a plaintiff's injury without thinking about how he would feel if he were the victim? If not, what harm is done by allowing the juror to mentally place himself in the plaintiff's position when making a general damage award non pecuniary losses?

2. *Loss of Earning Capacity but an Absence of Employment.* Because this award is for loss of earning capacity, the victim need not be employed at the time of the accident. Thus, a child victim may be entitled to recover loss earning capacity on the basis of the minimum wage. Greater recovery may be too speculative, although the jury may be given wide discretion. Should evidence of a child victim's intelligence, or skill, or future plans, be relevant? *See Lesniak v. County of Bergen,* 117 N.J. 12 (1989). Should the gender or race of the child be taken into account?

The civil justice system undervalues women's work. Some courts may permit an award for loss of earning capacity. *Nelson v. Patrick*, 73 N.C. App. 1 (1985). If not, an award for value of the homemaker's household services would be appropriate. *See, e.g., De Long v. County of Erie,* 457 N.E.2d 717 (N.Y. 1983). *See generally* Martha Chamallas, *Civil Rights in Ordinary Torts Cases: Race, Gender and the Calculation of Economic Loss*, 38 LOY. L.A. L. REV. 1435 (2005); Frank M. McClellan, *The Dark Side of Tort Reform: Searching for Racial Justice*, 48 RUTGERS L. REV. 761 (1996). Comment, *Tort Damages for the Injured Homemaker*, 50 U. COLO. L. REV. 59 (1978).

3. *Marginality of Pain & Suffering Damages?* Non-pecuniary damages are often difficult to obtain because jurors have trouble understanding the concept of intangible damages. David Ball, a jury consultant notes: "Intangible damages are hard to get partly because jurors do not always see what purpose the money can serve, and also because jurors do not know how to figure out how much to give. Jurors have less trouble calculating tangible damages. Jurors see worthwhile purpose in paying medical expenses and lost wages and the amounts can be easily determined. NATIONAL INSTITUTE OF TRIAL ADVOCACY (NITA), DAVID BALL ON DAMAGES: A PLAINTIFF'S ATTORNEY'S GUIDE FOR PERSONAL INJURY AND WRONGFUL DEATH CASES 27 (2001). In the *Walters* case above, what arguments would the plaintiff's counsel and defense counsel use regarding intangible damages? How would the plaintiff's counsel counter the argument that the plaintiff will get along fine without intangible or pain and suffering damages? What would be the defense counsel's arguments to convince a jury not to give noneconomic damages? What do you think is the right amount of noneconomic damages (if any) in *Walters*?

4. *Contingent Fees.* Some states limit the amount of contingent fees that attorneys can be charged, depending on the amount collected. *See, e.g.,* FLA. STAT. §766.109(7)(a):

> The Legislature recognizes that the contingent attorney's fee system provides a method by which the citizens of this state are able to seek access to the courts as guaranteed by Art. I, §21 of the State Constitution. Additionally, the Legislature recognizes that the Supreme Court of this state has the jurisdiction and authority to adopt rules for the practice of law before all Florida courts, including the regulation of attorney's fees. Until such time as the Supreme Court adopts guidelines, the following schedule shall be presumed reasonable and not excessive. For recovery of damages up to $2 million:
>
> 1. Fifteen percent of the recovery if the claim is resolved through the acceptance of an offer of settlement . . . ;
>
> 2. Twenty percent of the recovery if the claim is resolved after initiating . . . arbitration . . . ;
>
> 3. Twenty-five percent of the recovery if the claim is settled within 90 days of suit being filed;

4. Thirty percent of the recovery if the claim is settled more than 90 days after suit is filed and prior to or during the course of mandatory settlement conference . . . or where all defendants admit liability and request trial on the issue of damages;

5. Thirty-five percent of the recovery if the claim is settled prior to the completion of the swearing of the jury;

6. Forty percent of the recovery if the claim is settled or judgment is satisfied prior to filing of the notice of appeal;

7. Forty-five percent of the recovery after notice of appeal is filed or post-judgment relief or action is required for recovery on the judgment.

For those amounts of a recovery in excess of $2 million, a contingency fee of 15 percent shall be presumed reasonable and not excessive.

Is such a schedule fair? Should the percentage be the same for settlement as for recovery in excess of $2 million? Should such a schedule be applied to a punitive award? *See Swafford v. Harris*, 967 S.W.2d 319 (Tenn. 1998), concerning a contingency fee agreement between a personal injury plaintiff and a physician for expert testimony and other services associated with that plaintiff's claims. After the claim was settled, the physician sued to collect his fee. The court concluded:

> [T]he medical and legal communities share the ethical prohibition against the use of contingency fees for expert witnesses which is contained in the respective professional codes for each profession and adopted by the State as the public policy of Tennessee. This public policy is re-enforced by the actions of the Tennessee Bar Association and the Tennessee Medical Association in adopting the Interprofessional Code of Cooperation, which provides in part that "under no circumstances may a physician charge or accept compensation for any service which is contingent upon the outcome of a lawsuit." Article VI, § 2.

> . . . Given this overwhelming weight of authority, we disagree with Dr. Swafford's contention that no controlling public policy existed or that the public policy was not applicable simply because he is not a member of the American or Tennessee Medical Associations. On the contrary, it is our view that sound public policy in this jurisdiction, as in others, is crystal clear: a contingency fee contract for the services of a physician acting in a medico-legal expert capacity is void as against public policy and therefore unenforceable. *Id* at 322–323.

Why is this type of agreement viewed differently from the attorney's fee based on the same contingency? Will tort reform efforts to reduce the share paid a lawyer help plaintiffs or will this reform make it more difficult for them to find representation? If a cap is placed on the plaintiff's legal fees should a cap also be placed on defendant's legal fees? Consider your responses to these questions from the perspectives of law and economics, critical race theory, social justice, and feminism.

McDOUGALD v. GARBER
536 N.E.2d 372 (N.Y. 1989)

WACHTLER, CHIEF JUDGE.

This appeal raises fundamental questions about the nature and role of non-pecuniary damages in personal injury litigation. By nonpecuniary damages, we mean those damages awarded to compensate an injured person for the physical and emotional consequences of the injury, such as pain and suffering and the loss of the ability to engage in certain activities. Pecuniary damages, on the other hand, compensate the victim for the economic consequences of the injury, such as medical expenses, lost earnings and the cost of custodial care.

The specific questions raised here deal with the assessment of nonpecuniary damages and are (1) whether some degree of cognitive awareness is a prerequisite to recovery for loss of enjoyment of life and (2) whether a jury should be instructed to consider and award damages for loss of enjoyment of life separately from damages for pain and suffering. We answer the first question in the affirmative and the second question in the negative.

On September 7, 1978, plaintiff Emma McDougald, then 31 years old, underwent a Caesarian section and tubal ligation at New York Infirmary. Defendant Garber performed the surgery; defendants Armengol and Kulkarni provided anesthesia. During the surgery, Mrs. McDougald suffered oxygen deprivation which resulted in severe brain damage and left her in a permanent comatose condition. This action was brought by Mrs. McDougald and her husband, suing derivatively, alleging that the injuries were caused by the defendants' acts of malpractice.

. . . At trial, defendants sought to show that Mrs. McDougald's injuries were so severe that she was incapable of either experiencing pain or appreciating her condition. Plaintiffs, on the other hand, introduced proof that Mrs. McDougald responded to certain stimuli to a sufficient extent to indicate that she was aware of her circumstances. Thus, the extent of Mrs. McDougald's cognitive abilities, if any, was sharply disputed.

The parties and the trial court agreed that Mrs. McDougald could not recover for pain and suffering unless she were conscious of the pain. Defendants maintained that such consciousness was also required to support an award for loss of enjoyment of life. The court, however, accepted plaintiffs' view that loss of enjoyment of life was compensable without regard to whether the plaintiff was aware of the loss. Accordingly, because the level of Mrs. McDougald's cognitive abilities was in dispute, the court instructed the jury to consider loss of enjoyment of life as an element of nonpecuniary damages separate from pain and suffering.

. . . We conclude that the court erred, both in instructing the jury that Mrs. McDougald's awareness was irrelevant to their consideration of damages for loss of enjoyment of life and in directing the jury to consider that aspect of damages separately from pain and suffering.

We begin with the familiar proposition that an award of damages to a person injured by the negligence of another is to compensate the victim, not to punish the wrongdoer. To be sure, placing the burden of compensation on the negligent party also serves as a deterrent, but purely punitive damages — that is, those which have no compensatory purpose — are prohibited unless the harmful conduct is intentional, malicious, outrageous, or otherwise aggravated beyond mere negligence.

Damages for nonpecuniary losses are, of course, among those that can be awarded as compensation to the victim. This aspect of damages, however, stands on less certain ground than does an award for pecuniary damages. An economic loss can be compensated in kind by an economic gain; but recovery for noneconomic losses such as pain and suffering and loss of enjoyment of life rests on "the legal fiction that money damages can compensate for a victim's injury" (*Howard v. Lecher*, 42 N.Y.2d 109, 111 (1977)). We accept this fiction, knowing that although money will neither ease the pain nor restore the victim's abilities, this device is as close as the law can come in its effort to right the wrong. We have no hope of evaluating what has been lost, but a monetary award may provide a measure of solace for the condition created.

Our willingness to indulge this fiction comes to an end, however, when it ceases to serve the compensatory goals of tort recovery. When that limit is met, further indulgence can only result in assessing damages that are punitive. The question posed by this case, then, is whether an award of damages for loss of enjoyment of life to a person whose injuries preclude any awareness of the loss serves a compensatory purpose. We conclude that it does not.

Simply put, an award of money damages in such circumstances has no meaning or utility to the injured person. An award for the loss of enjoyment of life "cannot provide [such a victim] with any consolation or ease any burden resting on him. . . . He cannot spend it upon necessities or pleasures. He cannot experience the pleasure of giving it away" (*Flannery v. United States*, 718 F.2d 108, 111 (1983)).

We recognize that, as the trial court noted, requiring some cognitive awareness as a prerequisite to recovery for loss of enjoyment of life will result in some cases "in the paradoxical situation that the greater the degree of brain injury inflicted by a negligent defendant, the smaller the award the plaintiff can recover in general damages" (*McDougald v. Garber*, 504 N.Y.S.2d 383 (1986)). The force of this argument, however — the temptation to achieve a balance between injury and damages — has nothing to do with meaningful compensation for the victim. Instead, the temptation is rooted in a desire to punish the defendant in proportion to the harm inflicted. However relevant such retributive symmetry may be in the criminal law, it has no place in the law of civil damages, at least in the absence of culpability beyond mere negligence.

Accordingly, we conclude that cognitive awareness is a prerequisite to recovery for loss of enjoyment of life. We do not go so far, however, as to require the fact finder to sort out varying degrees of cognition and determine at what level a particular deprivation can be fully appreciated. With respect to pain and suffering, the trial court charged simply that there must be "some level of awareness" in order for plaintiff to recover. We think that this is an appropriate standard for all aspects of nonpecuniary loss. No doubt the standard ignores analytically relevant levels of cognition, but we resist the desire for analytical purity in favor of simplicity. A more complex instruction might give the appearance of greater precision but, given the limits of our understanding of the human mind, it would in reality lead only to greater speculation.

We turn next to the question whether loss of enjoyment of life should be considered a category of damages separate from pain and suffering.

There is no dispute here that the fact finder may, in assessing nonpecuniary damages, consider the effect of the injuries on the plaintiff's capacity to lead a normal life. Traditionally, in this State and elsewhere, this aspect of suffering has not been treated as a separate category of damages; instead, the plaintiff's inability to enjoy life to its fullest has been considered one type of suffering to be factored into a general award for nonpecuniary damages, commonly known as pain and suffering.

Recently, however, there has been an attempt to segregate the suffering associated with physical pain from the mental anguish that stems from the inability to engage in certain activities, and to have juries provide a separate award for each.

Some courts have resisted the effort, primarily on the ground that duplicative and therefore excessive awards would result. Other courts have allowed separate awards, noting that the types of suffering involved are analytically distinguishable. Still other courts have questioned the propriety of the practice but held that, in the particular case, separate awards did not constitute reversible error.

. . . We do not dispute that distinctions can be found or created between the concepts of pain and suffering and loss of enjoyment of life. If the term "suffering" is limited to the emotional response to the sensation of pain, then the emotional response caused by the limitation of life's activities may be considered qualitatively different. But suffering need not be so limited — it can easily encompass the frustration and anguish caused by the inability to participate in activities that once brought pleasure. Traditionally, by treating loss of enjoyment of life as a permissible factor in assessing pain and suffering, courts have given the term this broad meaning. If we are to depart from this traditional approach and approve a separate award for loss of enjoyment of life, it must be on the basis that such an approach will yield a more accurate evaluation of the compensation due to the plaintiff. We have no doubt that, in general, the total award for nonpecuniary damages would increase if we adopted the rule. That separate awards are advocated by plaintiffs and resisted by defendants is sufficient evidence that larger awards are at stake here. But a larger award does not by itself indicate that the goal of compensation has been better served.

The advocates of separate awards contend that because pain and suffering and loss of enjoyment of life can be distinguished, they must be treated separately if the plaintiff is to be compensated fully for each distinct injury suffered. We disagree. Such an analytical approach may have its place when the subject is pecuniary damages, which can be calculated with some precision. But the estimation of nonpecuniary damages is not amenable to such analytical precision and may, in fact, suffer from its application. Translating human suffering into dollars and cents involves no mathematical formula; it rests, as we have said, on a legal fiction. The figure that emerges is unavoidably distorted by the translation. Application of this murky process to the component parts of nonpecuniary injuries (however analytically distinguishable they may be) cannot make it more accurate. If anything, the distortion will be amplified by repetition.

Thus, we are not persuaded that any salutary purpose would be served by having the jury make separate awards for pain and suffering and loss of enjoyment of life. We are confident, furthermore, that the trial advocate's art is a sufficient guarantee that none of the plaintiff's losses will be ignored by the jury.

The errors in the instructions given to the jury require a new trial on the issue of nonpecuniary damages to be awarded to plaintiff Emma McDougald. Defendants' remaining contentions are either without merit, beyond the scope of our review or are rendered academic by our disposition of the case.

Accordingly, the order of the Appellate Division, insofar as appealed from, should be modified, with costs to defendants, by granting a new trial on the issue of nonpecuniary damages of plaintiff Emma McDougald, and as so modified, [AFFIRMED].

TITONE, JUDGE, Dissenting.

The majority's holding represents a compromise position that neither comports with the fundamental principles of tort compensation nor furnishes a satisfactory, logically consistent framework for compensating nonpecuniary loss. Because I conclude that loss of enjoyment of life is an objective damage item, conceptually distinct from conscious pain and suffering, I can find no fault with the trial court's instruction authorizing separate awards and permitting an award for "loss of enjoyment of life" even in the absence of any awareness of that loss on the part of the injured plaintiff. Accordingly, I dissent.

. . . Having concluded that the injured plaintiff's awareness should not be necessary precondition to recovery for loss of enjoyment of life, I also have no difficulty going on to conclude that loss of enjoyment of life is a distinct damage item which is recoverable separate and apart from the award for conscious pain and suffering. The majority has rejected separate recovery, in part because it apparently perceives some overlap between the two damage categories and in part because it believes that the goal of enhancing the precision of jury awards for nonpecuniary loss would not be advanced. However, the overlap the majority perceives exists only if one assumes, as the majority evidently has, that the "loss of enjoyment" category of damages is designed to compensate only for "*the emotional response* caused by the limitation of life's activities" and "*the frustration and anguish caused by* the inability to participate in activities that once brought pleasure" (emphasis added), both of which are highly *subjective* concepts.

In fact, while "pain and suffering compensates the victim for the physical and mental discomfort caused by the injury; . . . loss of enjoyment of life compensates the victim for the limitations on the person's life created by the injury," a distinctly objective loss (*Thompson v. National R.R. Passenger*

Corp., 621 F.2d 814, 824 (6th Cir.), *cert. denied*, 449 U.S. 1035 (1980)). In other words, while the victim's "emotional response" and "frustration and anguish" are elements of the award for pain and suffering, the "limitation of life's activities" and the "inability to participate in activities" that the majority identifies are recoverable under the "loss of enjoyment of life" rubric. Thus, there is no real overlap, and no real basis for concern about potentially duplicative awards where, as here, there is a properly instructed jury.

NOTES

1. *Conscious Pain and Suffering.* Proof of "conscious pain and suffering" is required before noneconomic damages are recoverable. *See Swift v. State Farm Mut. Auto. Ins. Co.*, 796 F.2d 120, 123 (5th Cir. 1986). The plaintiff bears the burden of proving, by substantial evidence, that a decedent who is the subject of a wrongful death action survived and was conscious after the accident which resulted in the decedent's demise in order to recover damages for pain and suffering. *Bridges v. Enter. Prods. Co.*, 2007 U.S. Dist. LEXIS 8593 (S.D. Miss. 2007).

2. *Hedonic Damages.* Hedonic damages are for the lost ability of the plaintiff "to engage in and experience the ordinary value of life that he was experiencing prior to the injury." *Mercado v. Ahmed*, 974 F.2d 863, 869 (7th Cir. 1992). Hawaii's tort damages statute, for example, includes "damages for pain and suffering, mental anguish, disfigurement, *loss of enjoyment of life,* loss of consortium, and all other nonpecuniary losses or claims (emphasis added)." HAW. REV. STAT. § 663-8.5. The Hawaii Supreme Court defined hedonic damages as "damages 'for the loss of enjoyment of life, or for the value of life itself, as measured separately from the economic productive value that an injured or deceased person would have had.'" *Ozaki v. Ass'n of Apt. Owners*, 954 P.2d 652, 669 (Haw. 1998) (citation omitted). *See Smith v. Ingersoll-Rand Co.*, 214 F.3d 1235, 1245–46 (10th Cir. 2000) (affirming admission of expert testimony on issue of plaintiff's hedonic damages, stating that New Mexico law allows recovery of such damages). Montana is one of a number of states that has not taken a position on the recoverability of hedonic damages. *Dorn v. Burlington N. Santa Fe R.R. Co.*, 397 F.3d 1183, 1195 (9th Cir. 2005) (applying Montana law). *See Ramos v. Kuzas,* 600 N.E.2d 241, 242–43 (Ohio 1992) (newborn cannot suffer "hedonic" damages because she cannot be cognizant of the loss of enjoyment of life). *See also* Andrew Jay McClurg, *It's a Wonderful Life: The Case for Hedonic Damages in Wrongful Death Cases*, 66 NOTRE DAME L. REV. 57 (1990) (arguing that wrongful death statutes should be amended to include the recovery of loss of enjoyment of life damages).

Professor McClurg surveyed the states and found:

> Courts in twenty-one states and the District of Columbia have now interpreted their wrongful death statutes to allow for the recovery of loss of society and companionship-type damages, although the statutes do not expressly provide for such recovery . . . Contrarily, while nearly all states allow society and companionship-type damages, only a minority of states allow recovery for grief or mental anguish. . . .

Twenty-eight states and the District of Columbia appear to have rejected grief damages in wrongful death cases.

Andrew J. McClurg, *Dead Sorrow: A Story About Loss and a New Theory of Wrongful Death Damages*, 85 B.U. L. REV. 1, 24–28 (2005).

3. *Wrongful Death and Hedonic Damages.* Wrongful death statutes may include "the present net cash value of the life expectancy of the decedent; the loss of society and companionship of the decedent; the pain and suffering experienced by the deceased between the time of the injury and the subsequent demise and punitive damages." MISS. CODE ANN. §11-17-13 (2007). There is a division of authority regarding whether hedonic damages (loss of enjoyment of life) are recoverable in a wrongful death action. *Compare Romero v. Byers*, 872 P.2d 840 (N.M. 1994) (allowing such damages), *with Spencer v. A-I Crane Serv.* 880 S.W.2d 938 (Tenn. 1994) (denying such damages). There is also a division of authority as to whether the victim must be aware of his condition in order to recover for loss of enjoyment of life. *Compare Flannery v. United States*, 297 S.E.2d 433 (W. Va. 1983) (holding that "a plaintiff in a personal injury action who has been rendered permanently semi-comatose is entitled to recover for impairment of his capacity to enjoy life as a measure of the permanency of his injuries even though he may not be able to sense his loss of enjoyment of life"), *with Flannery v. United States*, 718 F.2d 108 (4th Cir. 1983) (damages for loss of enjoyment of life are not recoverable under the FTCA by a plaintiff who "is unaware of his loss," since he cannot use the money, he "cannot spend it upon necessities and pleasures," and "cannot experience the pleasure of giving it away"). Reconsider *McDougald v. Garber, supra*, in light of this note.

The damages scheme provided by Michigan's wrongful death statute allows hedonic damages "to be assessed at the moment before death occurred and not by considering death as the ultimate loss of enjoyment of life." *Frontier Ins. Co. v. Blaty*, 454 F.3d 590, 599 (6th Cir. 2006 applying Michigan law). As of 2002, only four states permit the awarding of hedonic damages in their "wrongful death statute where the decedent was killed instantly: Connecticut, Hawaii, New Hampshire, and New Mexico." *Choctaw Maid Farms v. Hailey,* 822 So.2d 911, 929 (Miss. 2002).

Some courts reject expert evidence regarding hedonic damages that are based on economic studies of what the average person would be willing to pay for the satisfaction or pleasure of living. *Montalvo v. Lapez*, 884 P.2d 345 (Haw. 1994). As the court said in *Ayers v. Robinson*, 887 F. Supp. 1049, 1061 (N.D. Ill. 1995), in rejecting such evidence, "the willingness-to-pay model estimates the value of a statistical life — a nameless, faceless member of society," while the jury's task is to "value the life of a specific individual." The economists' views concerning the accuracy of such studies, moreover, vary widely. Are these objections unique to hedonic damages evidence?

Hedonic damages compensate an individual for the loss of life and loss of the pleasures of living: "Hedonic damages encompass the "larger value of life including [the] economic moral [and] philosophical value with which you might hold life." Other elements of the hedonic value of life may include an individual's expectations for the future as well as enjoyment of past activities. In contrast to damages for pecuniary loss, these damages involve a more subjective analysis of the pleasure that the particular individual derived from living." *Mister v. Illinois* C.G.R. Co., 790 F. Supp. 1411, 1421 (S.D. Ill. 1992) (quoting Tina M. Tabacchi, *Note, Hedonic Damages: A New Trend in Compensation?*, 52 OHIO ST. L.J. 331, 331 (1991) (footnotes omitted) Many states, however, do not permit juries to award hedonic damages for the loss of the pleasures of life as a separate item of damages. *See Moore v. Kroger Co.*, 800 F. Supp. 429, 436 (N.D. Miss. 1992). A number of courts have ruled that hedonic damages duplicate pain and suffering awards. *See, e.g., Huff. v. Tracy*, 129 Cal. Rptr. 551 (Ct. App. 1976). *Cf. Thompson v. Nat'l R.R. Passenger Corp.*, 621 F.2d 814, 824 (6th Cir. 1980) (distinguishing hedonic damages from other types of damages because they compensate for loss of enjoyment of life).

Thomas F. Lambert Jr. advocated for full recovery for loss of enjoyment of life in this way:

> Holmes once wrote, 'Life is like an artichoke, You pull out a leaf; only the tip is edible.' We have 24 hours a day, and only in a few fleeting moments do we really live — embezzled heaven, it has been called. And those cherished intervals or episodes usually involve our doing the thing which we most love. . . . Even if these hobbies, avocations, diversions, recreations should be held to have no material value, they are the things that give sweetness to life, soften the endless labor of life and keep it from being full of quiet desperation or an endless succession of grey days. A traumatic personal injury which slams the door on the possibility of your client's engaging in the very activities which make life worth living — recreation, social family activities — has inflicted what may well amount to devastating harm on your client, loss of life.

Thomas F. Lambert Jr., *Tom on Torts*, 26 ATLA L. REP. 8 (1983).

4. *Pain and Suffering Caps.* Twenty-five states have capped noneconomic damages in medical malpractice actions. Michael L. Rustad, *Neglecting the Neglected: The Impact of Noneconomic Damage Caps on Meritorious Nursing Home Lawsuits*, 14 ELDER L.J. 331, 334 (2006). Efforts have been under foot at the federal level as well. President George W. Bush has proposed a hard cap of $250,000 on all noneconomic damages awarded in medical malpractice lawsuit awards and the "Senate is considering capping noneconomic damages awards against all health care providers, including those who treat nursing home patients, also at $250,000." *Id.* at 333.

States are enacting caps on noneconomic damages in the absence of reliable empirical data on the actual growth, size, ratio, plaintiff-defendant characteristics, factual foundation, and proportions of awards allocated to noneconomic damages. For this and other reasons, some, though certainly not all state caps on noneconomic damages have been struck down on constitutional grounds. *Compare Murphy v. Edmonds*, 601 A.2d 102 (Md. 1992) ($350,000 cap on noneconomic damages in personal injury action does not violate equal protection clause of Maryland constitution), *with Morris v. Savoy*, 576 N.E.2d 765 (Ohio 1991) ($200,000 cap on noneconomic damages violates due process clause of state constitution under rational basis test). *See* F. HARPER, F. JAMES & O. GRAY, THE LAW OF TORTS § 25.10 n.5, at 564 (1992 Cum. Supp. No. 2).

Florida's cap on noneconomic damages provides for exceptions:

> If the negligence resulted in a permanent vegetative state or death, the total noneconomic damages recoverable from all practitioners, regardless of the number of claimants, under this paragraph shall not exceed $1 million. In cases that do not involve death or permanent vegetative state, the patient injured by medical negligence may recover noneconomic damages not to exceed $1 million if: (1) The trial court determines that a manifest injustice would occur unless increased noneconomic damages are awarded, based on a finding that because of the special circumstances of the case, the noneconomic harm sustained by the injured patient was particularly severe; and (2) The trier of fact determines that the defendant's negligence caused a catastrophic injury to the patient.

FLA. STAT. § 766.118(2) (b).

A discussion of noneconomic damage caps is included in the chapter on tort reform, Chapter 16, *infra*.

5. *Gender Injustice & Caps on Noneconomic Damages.* Social justice and critical feminists have observed that caps on noneconomic damages disproportionately affect women. "Women tort victims, the elderly, particularly elderly women, as well as children who suffer the ultimate injury of death, are all disproportionately disadvantaged by a cap on noneconomic loss damages." Lucinda M. Finley, *The Hidden Victims of Tort Reform: Women, Children, and the Elderly*, 53 EMORY L.J. 1263, 1280 (2004). Because plaintiffs in nursing home cases have no lost wages or lost earning capacity, their recovery is based almost entirely on non-economic damages. An empirical study of nursing home negligence verdicts awarded from 1990 to 2004 in California, Florida and Texas concluded that "[n]oneconomic damages comprised either all of the compensatory damages awards or most of the total recovery in most cases." Michael L. Rustad, *Neglecting the Neglected: The Impact of Noneconomic Damage Caps on Meritorious Nursing Home Lawsuits*, 14 ELDER L.J. 331, 364 (2006). As a consequence, unqualified caps on noneconomic damages will have a disparate impact on recovery for elderly nursing home patients of both sexes.

Tort reform-driven caps limiting the amount of recovery can profoundly affect not only individual recovery but also the opportunity to challenge improper care of the elderly through tort actions. *See, e.g., Fuqua v. Horizon / CMS Healthcare Corp.*, No. 98-00-CV-1087-4, 2001 WL 267650 (N.D. Tex. Feb. 14, 2001) (awarding $2,710,000 in noneconomic damages and $310,000,000 for abject neglect that caused the resident to develop late-stage decubitus ulcers); *Marsalese v. Park Imperial Convalescent Ctr.*, No. 4C 027366, 1997 WL 372874 (Cal. Super. Ct. 1997) (awarding $45,000 in noneconomic damages to an eighty-one-year-old nursing home resident who developed bacterial pneumonia, "influenza, dehydration, hypoxia and decubitus ulcers surrounding his genitals and buttocks" while in the care of the defendant nursing home); *Estate of Dixon v. S. Park Rehab. & Nursing Ctr.*, 2000 WL 33231753 (Tex.

Dist. Ct. 2003) (awarding $6,970,000 in noneconomic damages to a nursing home resident whose injuries included severe dehydration and malnutrition as well as multiple pressure sores). The effect of tort reform in one state has been dramatic in the context of nursing homes:

> [T]ort reform has all but eliminated Texas nursing home cases, and a number of long-term care facilities have either stopped carrying insurance or have switched to $250,000 policies because they can settle most claims for $15,000 or less. Because the expenses for suing a nursing home often exceed the potential recovery, nursing home cases are no longer being filed in large numbers in Texas. Plaintiffs counsel representing nursing home residents are 'cherry-picking cases with well-off clients who can show economic damages,' leaving most elderly nursing home victims without the possibility of legal representation.

Michael L. Rustad, *Neglecting the Neglected: The Impact of Noneconomic Damage Caps on Meritorious Nursing Home Lawsuits*, at 334.

Caps on noneconomic damages also make it difficult for women to recover for reproductive injuries such as infertility, miscarriage, and stillbirths. Reproductive injuries tend to be purely a noneconomic injury, disproportionately suffered by women. In addition, caps on damages impact women in their caretaker roles. For example, "[c]aps on damages for birth injuries fall disproportionately on women who face a lifetime of caring for their severely brain-damaged infants. Tort reformers have convinced state legislatures to limit or cap noneconomic damages that compensate women for the pain and suffering resulting from loss of fertility or reproductive function." Thomas H. Koenig & Michael L. Rustad, In Defense of Tort Law 111 (2001). Notably, juries are not instructed on caps for noneconomic damages. *See Kodiak Island Borough v. Roe*, 63 P.3d 1009 (2003).

D. DAMAGE TO RELATIONS; WRONGFUL DEATH, SURVIVAL ACTIONS, AND LOSS OF CONSORTIUM

WEHNER v. WEINSTEIN
444 S.E.2d 27 (W. Va. 1994)

Miller, Justice.

These appeals are brought by the defendants in three civil actions that were consolidated for trial in the Circuit Court of Monongalia County. The plaintiffs are the administrator of the estate of Jennifer Wehner, who was killed when she was struck on a public sidewalk by a runaway pizza delivery car, and Nicole Fisher and Jessica Landau, who were injured in the same accident. The decedent and the two individual plaintiffs were students at West Virginia University. The jury returned verdicts against all the defendants and awarded $1,978,623 to the Wehner estate; $132,090.25 to Nicole Fisher; and $87,158.85 to Jessica Landau.

Brett Barry Weinstein, a defendant below and a member of the Sigma Phi Epsilon Fraternity (Fraternity), does not appeal the adverse jury verdict which found him to be 75 percent at fault. Shortly before the accident, Mr. Weinstein was at the Fraternity and was attempting to leave in his car, but was blocked by a pizza delivery car. In order to move the delivery car, Mr. Weinstein opened the car's door, released its hand brake, and placed the gear shift in neutral. He was assisted by the defendant Matthew Kiser, who was a pledge of the Fraternity. The jury found Mr. Kiser to be 5 percent at fault.

The delivery car was owned by Bossio Enterprises, Inc., dba Mario's Pizza, and was being driven by David Turner, who was delivering an order to an individual at the Fraternity. The jury found Mr. Turner was negligent in the manner he parked the vehicle, and it found Mario's Pizza, as the employer, to be 10 percent at fault.

The Fraternity was sued on the theory that it failed to supervise and control the actions of Mr. Weinstein and Mr. Kiser. The jury found Mr. Kiser to be negligent and also found him to be an agent of the Fraternity, thus making it vicariously liable. The Fraternity was found to be 5 percent at fault.

The Sigma Phi Epsilon Building Association, Inc. (Association), another defendant below, owns the real estate on which the Fraternity is located. The Association was sued on the basis that the premises were dangerous because of its location on a steep hill, that it failed to provide proper warnings for traffic entering and leaving the property, and that it did not supervise and control the actions of Mr. Weinstein and Mr. Kiser. The Association was found to be 5 percent at fault.

The defendants, except for Mr. Weinstein, each claim that as a matter of law, they should be found not liable. Each claim a common error as to the damages awarded in the wrongful death action. They assert that the damages should have been reduced by the reasonable value of the anticipated personal consumption expenses of the decedent throughout her normal life expectancy. We begin by discussing the liability of each defendant.

Mario's Pizza argues it was not reasonably foreseeable that after the car was parked with the brake on and the ignition key removed, that someone would enter the car, disengage the brake, put the car in neutral, and cause it to roll . . .

We believe there was sufficient evidence of proximate cause. The delivery car driver, Mr. Turner, had delivered pizza to the fraternity house on other occasions, and was familiar with the topography. He was aware that there was a parking lot adjacent to the house and used it on other occasions. However, this time, rather than park in the lot, he parked his vehicle against the normal traffic flow and blocked the driveway to the house.

Mr. Turner also knew the area where he parked was immediately adjacent to the steep sloping driveway. The area below the driveway contained many student-housing facilities. If the car moved from where Mr. Turner parked it, it would roll down the hill injuring any one of the students who frequently used the streets and adjacent sidewalks below the fraternity.

Mr. Turner also acknowledged that a number of students lived in the fraternity house and used the driveway that he blocked. He also was aware that parked vehicles had been tampered with in this area. He knew that he would be going inside the house to deliver the order and that the car doors were not locked and access could be gained to the interior of the car. Moreover, he was aware that the car had a standard transmission which could be shifted by the clutch pedal without a key in the ignition.

With these facts in mind, we believe it was for the jury to determine whether it was reasonably foreseeable under the circumstances that some person would attempt to move the vehicle to gain access to the driveway. The jurors could realize from their common knowledge the impetuous nature of college students and their tendency to act without mature consideration. This situation is no more extreme than the employer we found to be liable under proximate cause principles in *Robertson v. LeMaster*, 171 W. Va. 607, 301 S.E.2d 563 (1983). There, an employee who made several requests to leave finally was permitted to do so after he had worked some twenty-seven hours. While driving home, he fell asleep and ran into another vehicle injuring the plaintiffs. Suit was brought against the employer. We held it was reasonably foreseeable that such an event could occur under all the circumstances. . . .

What Mario's Pizza actually is arguing is not so much a foreseeability issue, but a claim that the actions of Mr. Weinstein and Mr. Kiser in releasing the hand brake, placing the car in neutral, and attempting to move it were independent or intervening causes of the accident. Mario's Pizza does not assert it was without any negligence, and, indeed, on this record, it could not. By utilizing what amounts to an intervening cause argument, it seeks to escape liability.

However, an intervening cause must operate independently of any other act. We do not believe in this case that this test can be met. The location of the delivery car blocking ingress and egress coupled with its close proximity to the steep driveway and the car's accessibility are all circumstances resulting from Mr. Turner's actions that contributed to cause the ultimate accident. It is the combination of negligent acts that is the hallmark of concurrent negligence.

[The court found the fraternity and the Association were not negligent. Failure to post signs "designating visitor, tenant and no parking areas" was "but a passive or static condition of the premises" and had nothing to do with the intervening acts of the other defendants." It also found that Mr. Kizer was not acting as an agent of the fraternity at the time of the accident.]

The defendants urge us to adopt a rule that in a wrongful death action where future loss of earnings is claimed, there be an offset for the decedent's personal living expenses. In this case, the trial court refused to accept this principle although urged to do so by the defendants. The parties recognize that in note 6 of *Harris v. Matherly Machinery, Inc.*, 187 W. Va. 234, 417 S.E.2d 925 (1992), we declined to address the issue. Consequently, this issue is a matter of first impression.

The Washington Supreme Court in *Hinzman v. Palmanteer*, 81 Wash. 2d 327, 332–33, 501 P.2d 1228, 1232 (1972), made this general summary of the law:

> Three theories have been developed for measuring the lost earning capacity of a decedent. . . . (1) The probable worth of the decedent's future net earnings had he lived to his normal life expectancy. Personal expenses are deducted from gross earnings to reach the net. . . . (2) The

present worth of decedent's probable future savings had he lived to a normal life expectancy. Probable personal and family expenditures are both subtracted from probable gross earnings. . . . (3) The present worth of decedent's future gross earnings. No expenses are deducted from the award computed.

The Washington court adopted the first theory by deducting the decedent's personal living expenses.

We recognize the defendants' claim that a majority of state courts that have considered the question allow a deduction for the decedent's personal consumption expenses. However, in reviewing these cases, we find that in most instances, the discussion in the cases of this issue is quite cursory. Often there is nothing more than a brief restatement of the rule without any analysis of its rationale or citation to other jurisdictions. In some jurisdictions the wrongful death statute relating to damages expressly provides a deduction for personal expenses, *see, e.g.*, *Air Florida, Inc. v. Hobbs*, 477 So. 2d 40 (Fla. Dist. Ct. App. 1985); *Romano v. Duke*, 111 R.I. 459 (1973), or in the case of North Carolina use the term "[n]et income." In most jurisdictions, the wrongful death statute as to the amount of damages to be awarded is quite general often utilizing only a standard of fair and just compensation for the pecuniary loss. There is no statutory language that speaks to recovery of lost earnings in many of these statutes. As a consequence, the courts in those jurisdictions are accorded considerable flexibility in determining the elements of damages that may be recovered and any limitations by way of deductions.

On the other hand, our wrongful death statute is quite detailed as to the various categories of damages that may be awarded. *See* W. VA. CODE, 55-7-6(c) (1992). In particular, it allows for "compensation for reasonably expected loss of (i) income of the decedent[.]" W. VA. CODE, 55-7-6(c)(1)(B)(i). We traditionally have stated that the elements of damages in a wrongful death action and their manner of distribution are governed by our statute. *See Arnold v. Turek*, 185 W. Va. 400 (1991); *Bond v. City of Huntington*, 166 W. Va. 581 (1981). In *Bond, supra*, we discussed our earlier cases that had added various damage components to our wrongful death statute. We determined that punitive damages could be recovered even though the statute did not specifically authorize them and came to this conclusion in Syllabus Point 1 of *Bond*:

Not only has the Legislature liberalized the wrongful death recovery statute through the years, but this Court has adopted a liberal construction of the statute from our earliest cases.

In the absence of any clear legislative language, we refuse to construe the phrase "reasonably expected loss of . . . income of the decedent," W. VA. CODE, 55-7-6(c)(1)(B)(i), to mean "net income." We, therefore, hold that the language of W. VA. CODE, 55-7-6(c)(1)(B)(i), that allows as part of the elements of damages in a wrongful death action compensation for reasonably expected loss of income of the decedent, does not require a deduction for estimated personal living expenses.

For the foregoing reasons, we affirm the judgment of the Circuit Court of Monongalia County against Matthew Kiser and Bossio Enterprises, Inc., dba Mario's Pizza, but we reverse the judgment against Sigma Phi Epsilon, a national fraternal organization and association, and Sigma Phi Epsilon Building Association, Inc., a corporation.

NOTES

1. *Wrongful Death Statutes.* Early English and American common law denied recovery when the victim or the tortfeasor died. Every state has abolished this harsh common law rule. Massachusetts also has recognized a limited right of recovery at common law. *See Gaudette v. Webb,* 284 N.E.2d 222 (Mass. 1972). However, recovery for wrongful death generally is governed by the language and judicial interpretation of the statute in the particular jurisdiction. The courts have been reluctant to create a common law cause of action for wrongful death. But the Supreme Court did just that in *Moragne v. State Marine Lines,* 398 U.S. 375 (1970), where neither federal nor state law provided a statutory cause of action for the death of a longshoreman killed while working aboard a vessel in navigable waters within the State of Florida. Overruling precedent, the Supreme Court recognized a federal common law maritime cause of action on behalf of the deceased. Where there is an applicable wrongful death statute, the courts usually consider themselves reduced to interpreting the statute.

Wrongful death damages were not recoverable at common law but today every jurisdiction has a wrongful death statute permitting compensation for "survivors for the pecuniary losses they suffer because of the tortious conduct of others." *Alexander v. Whitman,* 114 F.3d 1392, 1398 (3d Cir. 1996). New Jersey's wrongful death statute bases monetary damages on the amount that the "the decedent might reasonably have been expected to make to his or her survivors." *Id.* New Jersey restricts recovery "for pecuniary loss only, and not for injury to feelings, mental suffering, or loss of society or companionship." *Id.* New Jersey does permit minor children to recover for "the pecuniary value of the loss of care, guidance, and advice of a parent during their minority." *Id.* States vary significantly in what damages are recovered under their wrongful death statute, however, most wrongful death statutes permit the recovery of hospital, medical and funeral expenses.

2. *Wrongful Death Benefits or Survival.* There are two general types of benefits available under the statutes — wrongful death benefits and survival benefits. A statute may be denominated by one name or both, *i.e.,* it may be titled a "Wrongful Death Statute," a "Survival Statute," or a "Wrongful Death/Survival Statute." The terminology usually is not important. The major issues are what benefits are recoverable by which beneficiaries, and the effect of the victim's misconduct upon recovery. The wrongful death claim, properly speaking (as contrasted to the survival claim), establishes a new cause of action in favor of a designated beneficiary for the loss that beneficiary sustained as a result of the death of the victim. The elements of damage may include loss of support, loss of services, loss of society, and in the appropriate case, loss of other consortium with the victim. The survival statute traditionally allows recovery for the victim's conscious pain and suffering from injury to death, loss of earnings from injury to death, and medical expenses. Funeral expenses do not fit comfortably under either statute, and are variously recoverable under one or the other of these statutes. McClurg summarizes five components of recovery in a tortious wrongful death case:

> (1) the decedent's life itself; (2) the trauma and bereavement suffered by the decedent's survivors, collectively referred to in this article as "grief;" (3) the pecuniary value of financial and service contributions that the decedent could have been expected to make to his or her dependents; (4) the loss of the decedent's society and companionship, which in some states is considered a type of pecuniary loss under the fiction that society and companionship are lost "services" of the decedent with an ascertainable monetary value (placing them in category 3), but which in other states is viewed as an intangible or noneconomic loss; and (5) the direct costs associated with the death, such as funeral expenses.

Andrew J. McClurg, *Dead Sorrow*, *supra*, 85 B.U. L. REV., at 7.

Survival and wrongful death claims have different categories of recovery: "In most states the recourse of creditors [of the deceased] is limited to proceeds of a survival action and does not extend to the proceeds of a wrongful death action (which is for the exclusive benefit of the designated survivors)." F. HARPER, F. JAMES & O. GRAY, THE LAW OF TORTS § 24.6 n.12 (2d ed. 1986). New Jersey's Survivor's Act, in contrast to its Wrongful Death Act, contains no express limitation on the types of damages recoverable under the statute. The survival statute permits the "decedent's representatives the right to bring an action for trespass to person or property in the same manner as if the decedent had been living. Unlike a wrongful death action, which is a derivative action arising in favor of beneficiaries named under that act, the Survivor's Act preserves to the decedent's estate any personal cause of action that decedent would have had if he or she had survived." *In re Jacoby Airplane Crash Litig.*, 2006 U.S. Dist. LEXIS 87816 (D.N.J. 2006). New Jersey's survival statute states:

> In those actions based upon the wrongful act, neglect, or default of another, where death resulted from injuries for which the deceased would have had a cause of action if he had lived, the executor or administrator may recover all reasonable funeral and burial expenses in addition to damages accrued during the lifetime of the deceased.

N.J.S.A. § 2A:15-3.

3. *Non-Pecuniary Damages.* The first wrongful death/survival statutes, patterned after the Lord Campbell's Act described in *Moragne v. State Marine Lines*, 398 U.S. 375 (1970), restricted plaintiff's recovery to pecuniary damages — loss of support and services. One motivation may have been to avoid the use of the loss of life as the measure of damages because that measurement was deemed both impossible and repugnant. No jury verdict could be excessive because "[t]he death of a family member, particularly a child, involves inconsolable grief for which no amount of money can compensate." *Roberts v. Stevens Clinic Hosp.*, 345 S.E.2d 791 (W. Va. 1986). Some states still limit recovery to pecuniary damages, although a majority will permit recovery of non-pecuniary damages. Some courts have been creative in defining pecuniary damages. *See, e.g., Haumersen v. Ford Motor Co.,* 257 N.W.2d 7 (Iowa 1977) (award of present value of estate which seven-year-old decedent would reasonably be expected to have accumulated as a result of his own efforts from the date of majority through normal term of his life).

4. *Loss of Support.* The award for loss of support usually is determined by calculating the victim's loss of earnings (or earning capacity) during his projected lifetime and reducing that by the amount of those earnings that the victim would have spent on himself, *i.e.*, his personal consumption. Some courts also may reduce the award by the amount that the victim would have saved. In that case, the beneficiary may be entitled to an award for loss of his increased inheritance. *See, e.g., O'Toole v. United States,* 242 F.2d 308 (3d Cir. 1957).

5. *Wrongful Death of a Minor Child.* If the wrongful death statute limits recovery to pecuniary benefits only, and the victim is a child, what is the measure of the parents' recovery? If the cost of rearing the child is offset against the support the parents probably would have received from the child, there arguably is no pecuniary loss. As a consequence, early decisions sometimes denied the parents' recovery. Later cases permit recovery for loss of companionship and society. *See generally Siciliano v. Capitol City Shows, Inc.,* 475 A.2d 19 (N.H. 1984); *Davis v. Elizabeth Gen. Med. Ctr.,* 548 A.2d 528 (N.J. Super Ct. Law. Div. 1988).

6. *Loss of Consortium.* When an accident victim dies, her close relatives will no doubt suffer mental anguish and grief and a loss of support, services and society. Some or all of these elements are compensable under the wrongful death and/or survival statutes. Close relatives may experience the same kinds of suffering and loss if the victim is injured, particularly if the injury is catastrophic. Courts have been hesitant to award damages for mental anguish caused by injury to another, basing denial of recovery upon the concepts of limited duty or proximate or legal cause. The common law's treatment of the remaining elements — loss of support, services and society — has been more liberal. At early common law, the master whose servant was injured by tortious conduct could recover damages from the tortfeasor for the loss of the servant's services. Because the husband was entitled to his wife's services, he also was permitted to recover for loss of those services from the tortfeasor who injured the wife. Recovery was expanded to include loss of society with the injured wife. However, if the husband was injured, the wife could not recover for loss of society, because she was not entitled to the husband's services. Constitutional considerations of equal protection condemned this dual standard, and nearly every state has opted for permitting either spouse to recover for loss of consortium with the other injured spouse. In *Clark v. Hauck Mfg. Co.*, 910 S.W.2d 247 (Ky. 1995), the court said that a wife's loss of consortium claim for tortious injury to her husband lasted only to date of death and did not extend beyond her husband's death from the tort, since such an extension would result in a double recovery for the surviving spouse beyond that which the wrongful death statute affords.

In *Hibpshman v. Prudhoe Bay Supply, Inc.*, 734 P.2d 991, 994–95 (Alaska 1987), the Alaska Supreme Court recognized an independent cause of action for minor children for loss of parental consortium resulting from injuries tortiously inflicted on their parents by third persons. The court cited *Schreiner v. Fruit*, 519 P.2d 462, 465–66 (Alaska 1974) which recognized that a spouse had a right to sue for loss of consortium caused by negligent injury. Moreover, the *Hibpschman* court noted that Alaska's wrongful death statute recognizes recovery for loss of consortium when either a parent or child dies. *Id.* at 993–94. The *Hibpshman* court found no justification for distinguishing the loss of parental consortium from spousal consortium claims in either injury or death cases.

A famous Wisconsin case permitted recovery by the parent for loss of consortium with the injured child. *Shockley v. Prier*, 225 N.W.2d 495 (Wis. 1975). It has been followed in several other states. *See, e.g., Howard Frank, M.D., P.C. v. Superior Ct. of Ariz.*, 722 P.2d 955 (Ariz. 1986). Compare *Baxter v. Superior Ct.*, 563 P.2d 871 (Cal. 1977), denying recovery. Is there any reason for treating loss of child consortium differently from loss of parental consortium? If you were a legislator, would you vote for such a measure? Why? There now is substantial authority for recovery by a child for loss of consortium of an injured parent. *See, e.g., Berger v. Weber*, 411 Mich. 1 (1981), although the majority of courts still deny recovery. *See, e.g., Norwest v. Presbyterian Intercommunity Hosp.*, 293 Or. 543 (1982).

7. *Consortium Claims by Parents and Others.* In *Fernandez v. Walgreen Hastings Co.*, 968 P.2d 774 (N.M. 1998), the plaintiff claimed loss of consortium damages asserting that she was her granddaughter's guardian, caretaker, and provider of parental affection. Plaintiff had observed her twenty-two-month-old granddaughter suffocate and die after defendants negligently misfiled Margarita's prescription. The court concluded:

> In New Mexico, grandparents enjoy a special legal status in relation to their grandchildren. In our state, it is not uncommon for several generations of a family to live in the same home, as in this case. We hold that such foreseeability can exist where: (1) the victim was a minor; (2) the plaintiff was a familial care-taker, such as a parent or grandparent, who lived with and cared for the child for a significant period of time prior to the injury or death; (3) the child was seriously physically injured or killed; and (4) the plaintiff suffered emotional injury as a result of the loss of the child's companionship, society, comfort, aid, and protection. . . . It is foreseeable that a negligent actor may cause harm or injury to a minor child's caretaker and provider of parental affection, as well as to the child. It is not unreasonable to compensate such a family caregiver for loss of consortium. . . .

Id. at 784.

8. *Perspectives on Gender Injustice & Damages.* Feminist torts scholars have contended that torts damages do not fully take into account women's role as primary care taker. To what degree is the expansion of consortium claims a women's issue? *See* Lucinda Finley, *Feminist Jurisprudence — The 1990 Myra*

Bradwell Day Panel, 1 COLUM. J. GENDER & L. 5, 22 (1991). *See also,* Lucinda M. Finley, *A Break in the Silence: Including Women's Issues in a Torts Course,* 1 YALE J.L. & FEMINISM 41, 52 (1989) (arguing that torts casebooks fail to address women's household and childrearing roles because these losses are not easily commodified). Should legislators consider monetizing women's household or child rearing roles in consortium awards under wrongful death statutes? Should courts instruct juries to monetize household work in assessing damages in tort litigation? What are the problems in adjusting damages for gender issues? How would a pragmatist assess the tort system's refusal to monetize the loss of life because we "consider life priceless?" Andrew J. McClurg, *Dead Sorrow: A Story About Loss and a New Theory of Wrongful Death Damages,* 85 B.U. L. REV. 1, 7 (2005). How would a law and economics scholar respond to Professor McClurg's argument that the tort system undervalues the loss of life?

Tort law traditionally has undervalued damages of women in their caretaking and other familial roles:

> At common law, women were classified as personal property of the male head of household. Tort law provided remedies for theft of property, including a cause of action for abduction. Abduction was the taking of a man's wife by fraud, persuasion, or open violence — a tort that reflected the status of women as chattels. Husbands could recover damages from another man who "persuade[d] or entice[d his] wife to live separate from him without a sufficient cause." A husband could receive damages for the defendant having taken his wife, but could not repossess his spouse without her consent . . . Adultery was considered a crime against the public order as well as a civil injury to the husband. The cuckold had an action of *trespass vi et armis* against the adulterer, 'wherein the damages recovered were usually very large and exemplary.' Seduction was an action that considered the wife's social standing and her "previous behavior and character.' . . . The writ of ravishment provided remedies for heirs who married without their father's consent. Family torts addressed family property rights, not the rights of the child."

Michael L. Rustad & Thomas H. Koenig, *Taming the Tort Monster: The American Civil Justice System as a Battleground of Social Theory,* 68 BROOK. L. REV. 1, 21 (2002).

For additional reading by feminist scholars who argue that tort law must evolve further to protect women's rights see Leslie Bender, *From Gender Difference to Feminist Solidarity: Using Carol Gilligan and an Ethic of Care in Law,* 15 VT. L. REV. 1 (1990); Mary Kate Kearney, *Breaking the Silence: Tort Liability for Failing to Protect Children from Abuse,* 42 BUFF. L. REV. 404 (1994). *See also* Margo Schlanger, *Injured Women Before Common Law Courts: 1860–1930,* 21 HARV. WOMEN'S L.J. 79, 105–06 (1998); Martha Chamallas, *The Architecture of Bias: Deep Structures in Tort Law,* 146 U. PA. L. REV. 463 (1998).

E. PROPERTY DAMAGES

Chapter 2 explored personal property torts such as trespass to chattels and conversion as well as trespass to land. The general principle is that a defendant is liable for all property damages traceable to his wrongful act. Many jurisdictions limit property damages (trespass to chattels) or destroyed property (conversion) to market value. DAMAGES IN TORT ACTIONS, §1.02 at 1-10.1 (Matthew Bender 2006). Assume that Paula is involved in a car accident caused by the defendant's negligence. If Paula's luxury automobile had a $125,000 "blue book" value at the time of the accident but was worth only $60,000 after the accident, the difference would be recoverable. If Darla's boat sank because of faulty repairs, she could recover for the market value of the ship prior to its destruction. Similarly, if a cattle breeder brings an action for negligent inoculation of his herd, he can recover for the value of the animals slaughtered because they developed a disease such as Brucellosis. *Greieves v. Greenwood*, 550 N.E.2d 334 (Ind. Ct. App. 1990). Damages in personal property or real property tort cases are based upon the loss of market value caused by the defendant:

> One who converts or destroys a chattel is liable for its value, which normally is the exchange value. . . . If there is no evidence of the value of the chattel, damages to a substantial amount can not be granted. . . . Even in the matter of value there may be serious elements of uncertainty, as when there have been no recent sales of similar things in the vicinity. When the value to the user is the measure of recovery, especially when the subject matter cannot be replaced, the measure of recovery is left very largely to the discretion of the trier of fact. . . .

> When there has been harm to land or structures on land from a past invasion, the damages for permanent harm are normally the difference between the market value of the land before and after the harm. . . . The value thus ascribed to the land is ordinarily determined by the opinion of experts, which may vary widely, so that the application of the standard is often far from certain. In cases in which the plaintiff is living upon land affected by a nuisance and hence is allowed to recover for inconvenience or discomfort. . . . the jury is as unrestrained in its estimate of this element of damages as in other cases of damages for personal harm.

REST. 2D TORTS §912 cmt. *c*.

In cases where there is no established market value, the damages are calculated based on the diminution in value of the property to its owner. DAMAGES IN TORT ACTIONS, §1.02 at 1-10.1 (Matthew Bender 2006). The standard measure of recovery for property damages is repair or replacement "unless that amount is greater than the value or unless repair is impossible." *Id.* If property has been damaged or destroyed negligently, the owner can recover the money to restore the property to the state it was prior to the tortious injury. *Id.* at 1–24. If repairs are not feasible, the measure of damages "is the cost of repair if repairs are possible or, if repairs are not possible, the difference in the pre- and post-accident value of the property or replacement cost." *Id.* The plaintiff may also recover for loss of use or lost profits.

Courts draw a sharp distinction between recoverable property damages and pure economic losses. The U.S. Supreme Court in *East River S.S. Corp. v. Transamerica Delaval, Inc.*, 476 U.S. 878 (1986) held that in an admiralty action, one may not recover for injury to the product itself under strict liability or negligence. In *East River*, the plaintiff's losses were only damages to the turbine, which was the subject of the contract. The economic loss rule (ELR) precludes tort law recovery when economic loss is unaccompanied by personal injury or property damage. For example, a plaintiff may not recover in a products liability lawsuit where the only thing that failed was the product and there was no personal injury or other property damages. "Economic losses include not only diminution in value and consequential losses like lost profits, but also, as the term's name implies, the loss of electronic funds and failed investments." *Pavlovich v. Nat'l City Bank*, 435 F.3d 560 (6th Cir. 2006). *See* Anita Bernstein, *Keep It Simple: An Explanation Of The Rule Of No Recovery For Economic Loss*, 48 ARIZ. L. REV. 773 (2006); Jane Stapleton, *Comparative Economic Loss: Lessons From Case-Law-Focused 'Middle Theory,'* 50 U.C.L.A. L. REV. 531 (2002).

If the plaintiff can prove a tort independent of the breach of contract, she is not precluded from a tort recovery by the ELR. A claim of fraud in the inducement of the contract, for example, is outside the purview of the ELR. As you read the *Dave Matthews Band* case, consider what damages are awarded for the harm sustained? What were the problems of measuring property damages in the case? Courts distinguish between property damages compensated by the tort system and the economic loss rule that limits the plaintiff to a contract remedy. How did the plaintiffs bypass the ELR?

MERCURY SKYLINE YACHT CHARTERS v. DAVE MATTHEWS BAND
2005 U.S. Dist. LEXIS 29663 (N.D. Ill. Nov. 22, 2005)

In the summer of 2004, Wohl was an employee of the Dave Matthews Band (DMB) whose duties included driving one of the Four Seasons motor coaches leased by DMB for its summer concert tour. . . . The Four Seasons motor coach is equipped with, among other things, an 80 to 100 gallon collection tank for human waste . . . The tank is emptied by pushing a toggle switch located behind the driver's seat . . . The contents of the coach's tank empty through a drain located underneath the motor coach, and a full tank can be emptied in 90 seconds to 2 minutes. Wohl's responsibilities relating to the operation of the leased Four Seasons motor coaches included the disposal of the contents of the coach collection tank.

According to the Complaint, on August 7 and 8, 2004, DMB performed two concerts in East Troy, Wisconsin, at the Alpine Valley Music Theater. DMB's concert tour schedule causes the band to regularly travel through the state of Illinois, and DMB stayed at the Peninsula Hotel in downtown Chicago, Illinois, for its Wisconsin concert dates. On August 7 and 8, Four Seasons motor coaches were used to transport DMB, its crew, and equipment between the Peninsula Hotel and the Wisconsin concert site. On Sunday, August 8, at around 1 p.m., Wohl started driving a Four Seasons motor coach from a City of

Chicago coach staging area located on Kinzie Street, west of the Chicago River, and traveled east on Kinzie Street. . . . Wohl was driving the motor coach to the Peninsula Hotel where he was to provide transportation to a member of DMB . . . Wohl's route took him over the Chicago River via the Kinzie Street Bridge . . . The Kinzie Street Bridge has a large, open grated area at its center.

On summer weekend days, the downtown section of the Chicago River is used and traveled by a substantial number of commercial and recreational watercraft; this river traffic is readily visible from adjacent Chicago roadways and bridges. On Sunday, August 8, the motor vessel *Chicago's Little Lady* ("*Chicago's Little Lady*"), U.S. Coast Guard No. 1079694, was traveling northbound on the Chicago River. *Chicago's Little Lady*, which was operated by MSYC, was carrying approximately 117 passengers, 3 crew members, and a volunteer docent from the Chicago Architectural Foundation. At 1:18 p.m., the same time as Wohl was driving over the Kinzie Street Bridge, *Chicago's Little Lady* passed below the Kinzie Street Bridge . . . As Wohl drove the motor coach over the grated portion of the Kinzie Street Bridge, he slowed the vehicle. Wohl then intentionally discharged the contents of the motor coach's human waste collection tank through the drain underneath the coach. (*Id.*) The contents of the tank fell from the bottom of the motor coach, through the grates of the Kinzie Street Bridge, into the Chicago River and onto *Chicago's Little Lady*. The discharged contents of the tank — a foul-smelling, brownish-yellow liquid — drenched the vessel and dozens of its passengers, getting into passengers' eyes, mouths, and hair and soaking their clothing and personal belongings. Many passengers experienced nausea and vomiting from their exposure or proximity to the human waste. The waste spill onto *Chicago's Little Lady* and its passengers and crew prompted the ship's captain to turn the vessel around and return the ship to its landing. The Complaint further alleges that in the weeks following the dumping incident, MSYC personnel spent considerable time, energy, and money cleaning up *Chicago's Little Lady*. MSYC also addressed passenger refund requests and other passenger needs. In addition, MSYC responded to the local, national, and international media, and cooperated with law enforcement officials.

Plaintiff alleges that Defendants' tortious actions "proximately caused MSYC to suffer damages, including but not limited to lost profits from its architectural tour and charter business. . . ." For each count, Plaintiff seeks compensatory damages in excess of $50,000 and punitive damages in the amount of $5,000,000 and such other relief as the Court deems just and proper . . .

Wohl's motion seeks dismissal. . . . for failure to state a cause of action because plaintiff's recovery is barred by the application of the economic loss doctrine of Illinois law. . . . At common law [in Illinois], solely economic losses are generally not recoverable in tort actions;" this well-established proposition of Illinois law has come to be known as the economic loss rule. *See In re Chicago Flood Litig.*, 176 Ill. 2d 179, 680 N.E.2d 265, 274, 223 Ill. Dec. 532 (Ill. 1997) the Illinois Supreme Court adopted the economic loss rule and held that a products liability plaintiff cannot recover solely economic losses under the tort theories of strict liability, negligence, and innocent misrepresentation. . . . *Moorman* defined economic loss as "damages for inadequate value, costs of repair and replacement of the defective product, or consequent loss of profits-without any claim of personal injury or damage to other property as well as the diminution in the value of the product because it is inferior in quality and does not work for the general purposes for which it was manufactured and sold." *Id.* at 449. . . . The court reasoned that "tort theory is appropriately suited for personal injury or property damage resulting from a sudden or dangerous occurrence . . . The remedy for economic loss, loss relating to a purchaser's disappointed expectations due to deterioration, internal breakdown or nonaccidental cause, on the other hand, lies in contract." *Id.*

Plaintiff's claims for lost profits are not barred by the economic loss doctrine because Plaintiff's allegations satisfy the first exception to the economic loss rule, as articulated in *In re Chicago Flood Litig.* (stating that the first exception to the economic loss rule "is composed of a sudden, dangerous, or calamitous event coupled with personal injury or property damage."); *accord, e.g., Trans States Airlines v. Pratt & Whitney Canada, Inc.*, 177 Ill. 2d 21 (1997) ("'The event, by itself, does not constitute an exception to the economic loss rule. Rather, the exception is composed of a sudden, dangerous, or calamitous event coupled with personal injury or property damage.'") (quoting *In re Chicago Flood Litig.*, 680 N.E.2d at 275).

The Court will consider in turn the two elements of the first exception to the economic loss rule. *See, e.g., Mars, Inc. v. Heritage Builders of Effingham*, 763 N.E.2d 428, 435 (Ill. App. Ct. 2002) (describing the inquiry into the first exception to economic loss rule as "necessarily bipartite"). Courts have, somewhat circularly, defined a sudden and dangerous occurrence as "when the sudden occurrence is highly dangerous and presents the likelihood of personal injury or injury to other property.'" *Mars, Inc.*, 763 N.E.2d at 435 (quoting *Stepan Co. v. Winter Panel Corp.*, 948 F. Supp. 802, 808 (N.D. Ill. 1996)). Because Plaintiff's allegations suggest that the dumping of the human waste from the motor coach in the present matter happened quickly (*see, e.g.*, D.E. 1 P 29, 30 (the "spill" of waste "hit" and "drenched" ship and passengers)), and presented a material risk of personal injury or injury to property . . . ("noxious" waste "soaked the vessel and passenger's clothing and personal belongings")), the incident resembles events that courts applying Illinois law have found to be "sudden, dangerous, or calamitous." *See In re Chicago Flood Litig.*, 680 N.E.2d at 275–76 (underground flood); *MCI Worldcom Network Servs., Inc. v. Big John's Sewer Contractors, Inc.*, 2003 U.S. Dist. LEXIS 20103 (N.D. Ill. Nov. 7, 2003) (Castillo, J.) (excavation in violation of statutes); *Mars, Inc.*, 763 N.E.2d at 436 (thunderstorm. . . . (roof collapse). Precedent teaches that to satisfy the first exception to the economic loss rule, "the time period between the calamitous event (the collapsing roof, brake failure, or flood) and the damage to other property (the inventory and equipment, the vehicle, or water damage to a store) is short and sudden, almost contemporaneous." *Nabisco, Inc. v. American United Logistics, Inc.*, 2000 U.S. Dist. LEXIS 7873 (N.D. Ill., June 1, 2000) (Ashman, M.J.). . . . The contemporaneousness of the dumping and the damage to *Chicago's Little Lady* distinguishes the case at hand from cases where courts have not found a sudden or calamitous event . . .

Turning to the element of property damage, Plaintiff alleges that *Chicago's Little Lady* was "contaminated" and that cleaning up the ship required "considerable time, energy and expense. . . ." The allegations relating to the ship's condition after the spill are incorporated by reference in all the subsequent count. . . . The Court views Plaintiff's property damage allegations as falling within the range of property damage that courts have found sufficient, when coupled with a sudden or calamitous event, to apply the first exception to the economic loss rule. . . .

Wohl contends that *Palatine Nat'l Bank v. Charles Greengard Assocs. Inc.*, 456 N.E.2d 635 (Ill. App. Ct. 1983), is on point and establishes the proposition that clean up costs are to be treated as separate from property damage . . . The Court respectfully disagrees. In *Palatine Nat'l Bank*, property developers brought a tort action against an engineering firm, alleging that the firm had designed an inadequate storm and surface water drainage system . . . The court found that "the only possible allegation of property damage . . . the clean up and restoration of the premises due to the flood" was insufficient to meet the standard for the first exception to the economic loss doctrine, because "the damage relates to the natural accumulation of water on the premises and not to the type of sudden and dangerous occurrence best served by the policy of tort law.'" . . . Plaintiff's allegations of "human waste dumping" . . . differ significantly from the "natural accumulation of water" in *Palatine Nat'l Bank* . . . and was discussed previously, fall into the category of a sudden or dangerous occurrence. In addition, because the damages in *Palatine Nat'l Bank* sprang from the allegedly negligent performance of contracted-for services, the damages could also have been categorized as disappointed commercial expectations . . . which precedent teaches are barred by the economic loss rule . . . DMB requested that the Court dismiss or strike Plaintiff's prayer for relief for public nuisance to the extent that Plaintiff seeks recovery of "prospective or future damages," or damages other than for its "personal inconvenience, annoyance and discomfort." . . . To the extent that Plaintiff requests damages based on Defendants' future conduct, the Court agrees with DMB that future or prospective damages are unavailable for Plaintiff's public nuisance action . . . As an initial matter, recent Illinois Supreme Court precedent dealing with private nuisance instructs "[a] plaintiff in a private nuisance action may recover *all consequential damages* flowing from the injury to the use and enjoyment of his or her person or property. However, recovery of damages for solely economic loss is not permitted." *In re Chicago Flood Litig.*, 680 N.E.2d at 278 . . . For public nuisance actions, a private individual may recover damages only if he has "suffered harm of a kind different from that suffered by other members of the public exercising the right common to the public that was the subject of interference." *Young*, 821 N.E.2d at 1083 (internal quotation marks and citation omitted). The types of special damage that private plaintiffs bringing public nuisance actions may allege include, for example, "physical harm to chattels." . . . In the instant case, Plaintiff alleges physical harm to chattels, by stating, for example, that *Chicago's Little Lady* was "contaminated." . . . Plaintiff's allegations of harm are of a different type than the harm allegedly done to the public's rights of health and comfort. Therefore, Plaintiff has alleged sufficient special harm to state a claim for private damages and should be able to recover for those damages. *See In re Starlink Corn Prods. Liab.*

Litig., 212 F. Supp. 2d at 848 (farmers were able to state a claim for private action for public nuisance by alleging both contamination of the public's food supply (public harm) and damages to their fields, grain supply, and their crop sales (private harm)).

DMB suggests in passing that Plaintiff's damages for Count I, its claim of trespass, should be "similarly limited," because "the same rules of damages apply whether the action be in trespass or for a nuisance." . . . Assuming that DMB states a still-correct proposition of law, the Court's analysis permitting recovery of consequential damages for the public nuisance claim should apply for the trespass claim. Thus, the Court concludes that Plaintiff's recovery for Count I is not limited to damages for personal inconvenience, annoyance and discomfort. Accordingly, the Court grants DMB's motion to strike Plaintiff's claims for damages for Counts I and II to the extent that Plaintiff seeks future or prospective damages . . .

In summary, Plaintiff's allegations of a "sudden, dangerous or calamitous event," *i.e.*, the alleged dumping, coupled with the allegations of the contamination *of Chicago's Little Lady*, are sufficient to permit Plaintiff to state a claim for recovering lost profits under the first exception to the economic loss rule. Accordingly, the Court finds that Plaintiff's claims are not barred by the economic loss doctrine and denies Wohl's motion to dismiss . . . [Court also ruled that the plaintiff adequate stated cause of action for private nuisance but granted defense motions to strike gross negligence, tortious interference and punitive damages claims as well as plaintiff's claim for future or prospective damages].

NOTES

1. *Property Damages as Elements of Damages.* The standard measure of damages for personal property is the value of the property before and after the tort. If property is lost or destroyed, the measure of damages is reasonable market value before loss or destruction minus any salvage value. DAMAGES IN TORT ACTIONS, §1.02 at 1-23 (Matthew Bender 2006). If personal property has no established market value, an award is based upon the diminished value to the owner. *Id.* "In a typical case, a plaintiff may recover the diminution in value of real property only where the property cannot be repaired or the cost of repair exceeds the market value of the property." *Proctor v. 7-Eleven*, 180 Fed. App. 453 (4th Cir. May 18, 2006) (applying rule in action arising out of a gasoline leak from an underground storage tank at gas station).

2. *Property Damages for Temporary Nuisances.* Illinois, like many states, distinguishes between two kinds of damages for private nuisance — damages caused by permanent nuisances and those caused by temporary nuisances. The *Dave Matthews Band* court noted that the measure of damages for a permanent nuisance was the market value of the land while the proper measure of damages for temporary nuisance was discomfort, deprivation, and loss of enjoyment. The court applied a reasonable certainty rule in denying the plaintiff lost profits. How would a court measure lost future damages? Would

tourists stay away from the Chicago River tour boats because of the risk of similar incidents?

F. PUNITIVE DAMAGES

Punitive damages are awarded to punish and deter the defendant and others from repeating conduct harmful to the society. To award punitive damages, a jury must find that the conduct from which the claim arose constituted reckless indifference for the rights or safety of another. Jurisdictions vary in their punitive damages liability standards. In Iowa, for example, punitive damages are recoverable for conduct that is "willful or wanton when the actor has intentionally done an act of an unreasonable character in disregard of a known or obvious risk that was so great as to make it highly probable that harm would follow." IOWA CODE § 668A(1)(a). Punitive damages are not recoverable unless the plaintiff is awarded some compensatory damages. "And it is fundamental that a plaintiff who does not even allege a legally cognizable injury cannot obtain a tort judgment." *Jones v. Reagan*, 696 F.2d 551, 555 (7th Cir. 1983).

Punitive damages seek to punish the defendant for egregious conduct and deter him and others from engaging in such conduct in the future. In recent years, the U.S. Supreme Court has intervened in the state tort law governing awards of punitive damages, ruling that the due process clause of the 14th Amendment to the U.S. Constitution mandates that states use certain guidelines to control the size of jury awards for punitive damages. As you read the materials in this section consider the Supreme Court's mandates regarding the relationship of the size of the punitive damage award and the compensatory damage awards in light of the competing goals of tort law and punitive damages. Critically assess the current state of the law from perspectives of deterrence, corrective justice, and social justice.

Dramatic verdicts to punish systematic corporate misbehavior capture the public's imagination, leading to the popular misperception that punitive damages are commonly awarded. However, a 2001 survey of state tort cases found that tort plaintiffs received punitive damages in only 6% of the successful cases. The median punitive damages award was only $23,000 in tort trials and $15,000 in bench trials. Perhaps surprisingly, punitive damages were more likely to be awarded by judges (11%) than juries (5%). CIVIL JUSTICE SURVEY OF STATE COURTS, TORT TRIALS AND VERDICTS IN LARGE COUNTIES (2001) (Nov. 2004, NCJ 206240) at 5. Juries awarded punitive damages in 60% of libel cases as compared to only 5% of products liability cases. *Id.* at 5.

Further, the empirical reality is that tort judgments are subject to a number of judicial controls such as remittitur. A nationwide study of punitive damages in products liability litigation found, for example, that judges reversed or remitted over half of all punitive damages awards rendered in products liability actions for the period 1965–1990. Michael Rustad, *In Defense of Punitive Damages in Product Liability: Testing Tort Anecdotes with Empirical Data*, 78 IOWA L. REV. 1, 30 (1992). It is indisputable that judicial tort reform by the Supreme Court and many state courts over the past decade has made it more difficult for plaintiffs to recover punitive damages. See Chapter 16 *infra,* discussing legislative tort reform and other retrenchment efforts.

MATHIAS v. ACCOR ECONOMY LODGING, INC.
347 F.3d 672 (7th Cir. 2003)

POSNER, CIRCUIT JUDGE.

The plaintiffs brought this diversity suit governed by Illinois law against affiliated entities (which the parties treat as a single entity, as shall we) that own and operate the "Motel 6" chain of hotels and motels. One of these hotels (now a "Red Roof Inn," though still owned by the defendant) is in downtown Chicago. The plaintiffs, a brother and sister, were guests there and were bitten by bedbugs, which are making a comeback in the U.S. as a consequence of more conservative use of pesticides.

The plaintiffs claim that in allowing guests to be attacked by bedbugs in a motel that charges upwards of $100 a day for a room and would not like to be mistaken for a flophouse, the defendant was guilty of "willful and wanton conduct" and thus under Illinois law is liable for punitive as well as compensatory damages . . . The jury agreed and awarded each plaintiff $186,000 in punitive damages though only $5000 in compensatory damages. The defendant appeals, complaining primarily about the punitive-damages award. It also complains about some of the judge's evidentiary rulings, but these complaints are frivolous and require no discussion. The plaintiffs cross-appeal, complaining about the dismissal of a count of the complaint in which they alleged a violation of an Illinois consumer protection law. But they do not seek any additional damages, and so, provided we sustain the jury's verdict, we need not address the cross-appeal.

The defendant argues that at worst it is guilty of simple negligence, and if this is right the plaintiffs were not entitled by Illinois law to any award of punitive damages. It also complains that the award was excessive — indeed that any award in excess of $20,000 to each plaintiff would deprive the defendant of its property without due process of law. The first complaint has no possible merit, as the evidence of gross negligence, indeed of recklessness in the strong sense of an unjustifiable failure to avoid a *known* risk . . . In 1998, EcoLab, the extermination service that the motel used, discovered bedbugs in several rooms in the motel and recommended that it be hired to spray every room, for which it would charge the motel only $500; the motel refused.

The next year, bedbugs were again discovered in a room but EcoLab was asked to spray just that room. The motel tried to negotiate "a building sweep [by EcoLab] free of charge," but, not surprisingly, the negotiation failed. By the spring of 2000, the motel's manager "started noticing that there were refunds being given by my desk clerks and reports coming back from the guests that there were ticks in the rooms and bugs in the rooms that were biting.". . .

Further incidents of guests being bitten by insects and demanding and receiving refunds led the manager to recommend to her superior in the company that the motel be closed while every room was sprayed, but this was refused. This superior, a district manager, was a management-level employee of the defendant, and his knowledge of the risk and failure to take effective steps either to eliminate it or to warn the motel's guests are imputed to his employer for purposes of determining whether the employer should be liable for punitive damages . . . The employer's liability for compensatory damages is of course automatic on the basis of the principle of respondeat superior, since the district manager was acting within the scope of his employment.

The infestation continued and began to reach farcical proportions, as when a guest, after complaining of having been bitten repeatedly by insects while asleep in his room in the hotel was moved to another room only to discover insects there; and within 18 minutes of being moved to a third room he discovered insects in that room as well and had to be moved still again. (Odd that at that point he didn't flee the motel.) By July, the motel's management was acknowledging to EcoLab that there was a "major problem with bed bugs" and that all that was being done about it was "chasing them from room to room."

Desk clerks were instructed to call the "bedbugs" "ticks," apparently on the theory that customers would be less alarmed, though in fact ticks are more dangerous than bedbugs because they spread Lyme Disease and Rocky Mountain Spotted Fever. Rooms that the motel had placed on "Do not rent, bugs in room" status nevertheless were rented. It was in November that the plaintiffs checked into the motel. They were given Room 504, even though the motel had classified the room as "DO NOT RENT UNTIL TREATED," and it had not been treated. Indeed, that night 190 of the hotel's 191 rooms were occupied, even though a number of them had been placed on the same don't-rent status as Room 504.

One of the defendant's motions *in limine* that the judge denied was to exclude evidence concerning all other rooms — a good example of the frivolous character of the motions and of the defendant's pertinacious defense of them on appeal. Although bedbug bites are not as serious as the bites of some other insects, they are painful and unsightly. Motel 6 could not have rented any rooms at the prices it charged had it informed guests that the risk of being bitten by bedbugs was appreciable. Its failure either to warn guests or to take effective measures to eliminate the bedbugs amounted to fraud and probably to battery as well . . . . [A]s in the famous case of *Garratt v. Dailey*, 279 P.2d 1091, 1093–94 (Wash. 1955) which held that the five year old child would be liable for battery if he knew with substantial certainty that when he moved a chair the plaintiff would try to sit down where the chair had been and would land on the floor instead. . . .

But in what amount [the punitive damages]? In arguing that $20,000 was the maximum amount of punitive damages that a jury could constitutionally have awarded each plaintiff, the defendant points to the U.S. Supreme Court's recent statement that "few awards [of punitive damages] exceeding a single-digit ratio between punitive and compensatory damages, to a significant degree, will satisfy due process." *State Farm Mutual Automobile Ins. Co. v. Campbell*, 538 U.S. 408, 155 L. Ed. 2d 585, 123 S. Ct. 1513, 1524 (2003). The

Court considers the defendant's reprehensibility to be the emblem of punitive damages stating:

> We have instructed courts to determine the reprehensibility of a defendant by considering whether the harm caused was physical as opposed to economic; the tortuous conduct evinced an indifference to or a reckless disregard of the health or safety of others; the target of the conduct had financial vulnerability; the conduct involved repeated actions or was an isolated incident; and the harm was the result of intentional malice, trickery, or deceit , or more accident.

Id. at 420.

The Court went on to suggest that "four times the amount of compensatory damages might be close to the line of constitutional impropriety." *Id.* . . . Hence the defendant's proposed ceiling in this case of $20,000, four times the compensatory damages awarded to each plaintiff. The ratio of punitive to compensatory damages determined by the jury was, in contrast, 37.2 to 1. The Supreme Court did not, however, lay down a 4-to-1 or single-digit-ratio rule — it said merely that "there is a presumption against an award that has a 145-to-1 ratio," *State Farm Mutual Automobile Ins. Co. v. Campbell, supra,* 123 S. Ct. at 1524 — and it would be unreasonable to do so. We must consider why punitive damages are awarded and why the Court has decided that due process requires that such awards be limited. The second question is easier to answer than the first.

The term "punitive damages" implies punishment, and a standard principle of penal theory is that "the punishment should fit the crime" in the sense of being proportional to the wrongfulness of the defendant's action, though the principle is modified when the probability of detection is very low (a familiar example is the heavy fines for littering) or the crime is potentially lucrative (as in the case of trafficking in illegal drugs). Hence, with these qualifications, which in fact will figure in our analysis of this case, punitive damages should be proportional to the wrongfulness of the defendant's actions.

Another penal precept is that a defendant should have reasonable notice of the sanction for unlawful acts, so that he can make a rational determination of how to act; and so there have to be reasonably clear standards for determining the amount of punitive damages for particular wrongs. And a third precept, the core of the Aristotelian notion of corrective justice, and more broadly of the principle of the rule of law, is that sanctions should be based on the wrong done rather than on the status of the defendant; a person is punished for what he does, not for who he is, even if the who is a huge corporation.

What follows from these principles, however, is that punitive damages should be admeasured by standards or rules rather than in a completely ad hoc manner, and this does not tell us what the maximum ratio of punitive to compensatory damages should be in a particular case . . . England's common law courts first confirmed their authority to award punitive damages in the eighteenth century, see Dorsey D. Ellis, Jr., *Fairness and Efficiency in the Law of Punitive Damages,* 56 S. Cal. L. Rev. 1, 12–20 (1982), at a time when the institutional structure of criminal law enforcement was primitive and it made sense to leave certain minor crimes to be dealt with by the civil law. And still today one function of punitive-damages awards is to relieve the pressures on an overloaded system of criminal justice by providing a civil alternative to criminal prosecution of minor crimes. An example is deliberately spitting in a person's face, a criminal assault but because minor readily deterrable by the levying of what amounts to a civil fine through a suit for damages for the tort of battery.

Compensatory damages would not do the trick in such a case, and this for three reasons: because they are difficult to determine in the case of acts that inflict largely dignitary harms; because in the spitting case they would be too slight to give the victim an incentive to sue, and he might decide instead to respond with violence — and an age-old purpose of the law of torts is to provide a substitute for violent retaliation against wrongful injury — and because to limit the plaintiff to compensatory damages would enable the defendant to commit the offensive act with impunity provided that he was willing to pay, and again there would be a danger that his act would incite a breach of the peace by his victim.

When punitive damages are sought for billion-dollar oil spills and other huge economic injuries, the considerations that we have just canvassed fade. As the Court emphasized in *Campbell*, the fact that the plaintiffs in that case had been awarded very substantial compensatory damages — $1 million for a dispute over insurance coverage — greatly reduced the need for giving them a huge award of punitive damages ($145 million) as well in order to provide an effective remedy. Our case is closer to the spitting case. The defendant's behavior was outrageous but the compensable harm done was slight and at the same time difficult to quantify because a large element of it was emotional. And the defendant may well have profited from its misconduct because by concealing the infestation it was able to keep renting rooms. Refunds were frequent but may have cost less than the cost of closing the hotel for a thorough fumigation.

The hotel's attempt to pass off the bedbugs as ticks, which some guests might ignorantly have thought less unhealthful, may have postponed the instituting of litigation to rectify the hotel's misconduct. The award of punitive damages in this case thus serves the additional purpose of limiting the defendant's ability to profit from its fraud by escaping detection and (private) prosecution. If a tortfeasor is "caught" only half the time he commits torts, then when he is caught he should be punished twice as heavily in order to make up for the times he gets away.

Finally, if the total stakes in the case were capped at $50,000 (2 × [$5000 + $20,000]), the plaintiffs might well have had difficulty financing this lawsuit. It is here that the defendant's aggregate net worth of $1.6 billion becomes relevant. A defendant's wealth is not a sufficient basis for awarding punitive damages. *State Farm Mutual Automobile Ins. Co. v. Campbell, supra*, 123 S. Ct. at 1525; *BMW of North America, Inc. v. Gore, supra*, 517 U.S. at 591 (concurring opinion); *Zazu Designs v. L'Oreal, S.A.*, 979 F.2d 499, 508–09 (7th Cir. 1992). That would be discriminatory and would violate the rule of law, as we explained earlier, by making punishment depend on status rather than conduct.

Where wealth in the sense of resources enters is in enabling the defendant to mount an extremely aggressive defense against suits such as this and by doing so to make litigating against it very costly, which in turn may make it difficult for the plaintiffs to find a lawyer willing to handle their case, involving as it does only modest stakes, for the usual 33–40 percent contingent fee. In other words, the defendant is investing in developing a reputation intended to deter plaintiffs. It is difficult otherwise to explain the great stubbornness with which it has defended this case, making a host of frivolous evidentiary arguments despite the very modest stakes even when the punitive damages awarded by the jury are included.

As a detail (the parties having made nothing of the point), we note that "net worth" is not the correct measure of a corporation's resources. It is an accounting artifact that reflects the allocation of ownership between equity and debt claimants. A firm financed largely by equity investors has a large "net worth" (= the value of the equity claims), while the identical firm financed largely by debt may have only a small net worth because accountants treat debt as a liability. All things considered, we cannot say that the award of punitive damages was excessive, albeit the precise number chosen by the jury was arbitrary. It is probably not a coincidence that $5000 + $186,000 = $191,000/191 = $1,000: i.e., $1000 per room in the hotel.

But as there are no punitive-damages guidelines, corresponding to the federal and state sentencing guidelines, it is inevitable that the specific amount of punitive damages awarded whether by a judge or by a jury will be arbitrary. (Which is perhaps why the plaintiffs' lawyer did not suggest a number to the jury.) The judicial function is to police a range, not a point. See *BMW of North America, Inc. v. Gore, supra,* 517 U.S. at 582–83; *TXO Production Corp. v. Alliance Resources Corp.,* 509 U.S. 443, 458 (1993) (plurality opinion).

But it would have been helpful had the parties presented evidence concerning the regulatory or criminal penalties to which the defendant exposed itself by deliberately exposing its customers to a substantial risk of being bitten by bedbugs. That is an inquiry recommended by the Supreme Court. See *State Farm Mutual Automobile Ins. Co. v. Campbell, supra,* 123 S. Ct. at 1520, 1526; *BMW of North America, Inc. v. Gore, supra,* 517 U.S. at 583–85. But we do not think its omission invalidates the award. We can take judicial notice that deliberate exposure of hotel guests to the health risks created by insect infestations exposes the hotel's owner to sanctions under Illinois and Chicago law that in the aggregate are comparable in severity to that of the punitive damage award in this case.

"A person who causes bodily harm to or endangers the bodily safety of an individual by any means, commits reckless conduct if he performs recklessly the acts which cause the harm or endanger safety, whether they otherwise are lawful or unlawful." 720 ILCS 5/12-5(a). This is a misdemeanor, punishable by up to a year's imprisonment or a fine of $2500, or both. 720 ILCS 5/12-5(b); 730 ILCS 5/5-8-3(a)(1), 5/5-9-1(a)(2). (For the application of the reckless-conduct criminal statute to corporate officials, see *Illinois v. Chicago Magnet Wire Corp.,* 126 Ill. 2d 356 (1989).) Of course a corporation cannot be sent to prison, and $2500 is obviously much less than the $186,000 awarded to each plaintiff in this case as punitive damages. But this is just the beginning.

For, what is much more important, a Chicago hotel that permits unsanitary conditions to exist is subject to revocation of its license, without which it cannot operate. CHI. MUNIC. CODE §§ 4-4-280, 4-208-020, 050, 060, 110.

We are sure that the defendant would prefer to pay the punitive damages assessed in this case than to lose its license. [AFFIRMED].

NOTES

1. *Constitutionalizing Punitive Damages:* The United States. Supreme Court has taken an unusual interest in the tort remedy of punitive damages, having accepted writs of certiorari in eight recent cases: (1) *Browning-Ferris Indus. of Vt. v. Kelco Disposal, Inc.,* 492 U.S. 257 (1989) (ruling that large punitive damages award did not violate the Eighth Amendment against excessive fines); (2) *Pac. Mut. Life Ins., Co. v. Haslip,* 499 U.S. 1 (1991) (ruling that a large punitive damages award did not violate the defendant's substantive due process rights). (3) *TXO Prod. Corp. v. Alliance Res. Corp.,* 509 U.S. 443 (1993) (same); (4) *Honda Motor Co. v. Oberg*, 512 U.S. 415 (1994) (vacating a multi-million dollar punitive damages award against a Japanese manufacturer on the grounds that Oregon did not provide for a mandated post-verdict review of the award for excessiveness); (5) *BMW of N. Am., Inc. v. Gore,* 517 U.S. 559 (1996) (reversing multi-million dollar award against U.S. subsidiary of German automobile company on grounds that the award was so excessive as to violate substantive due process); (6) *Cooper Indus., Inc. v. Leatherman Tool Group, Inc.*, 532 U.S. 424 (2001) (vacating large punitive damages award in trade dress case because federal appellate court applied the wrong standard of review); (7) *State Farm Mut. Auto. Ins. Co. v. Campbell*, 538 U.S. 408 (2003) (reversing an award of $145 million in punitive damages, where full compensatory damages were $1 million, as excessive and in violation of the Due Process Clause of the Fourteenth Amendment); and (8) *Philip Morris USA v. Williams,* 127 S. Ct. 1057 (2007) (holding that punitive damages award based in part on jury's desire to punish defendant for harming nonparties amounted to a taking of property from defendant without due process).

In *Williams, supra*, 126 S. Ct. at 1068 Justice Ginsburg, joined by Justices Scalia and Thomas dissented:

> The purpose of punitive damages, it can hardly be denied, is not to compensate, but to punish. Punish for what? Not for harm actually caused "strangers to the litigation," . . . . the Court states, but for the *reprehensibility* of defendant's conduct. . . . "[C]onduct that risks harm to many," the Court observes, "is likely more reprehensible than conduct that risks harm to only a few." . . . The Court thus conveys that, when punitive damages are at issue, a jury is properly instructed to consider the extent of harm suffered by others as a measure of reprehensibility, but not to mete out punishment for injuries in fact sustained by nonparties . . .

> The right question regarding reprehensibility, the Court acknowledges . . . would train on "the harm that Philip Morris was prepared to inflict on the smoking public at large." . . . The Court identifies no evidence introduced and no charge delivered inconsistent with that inquiry.

Id. at 1068.

Is it possible to determine general deterrence if the jury does not consider what harm the tobacco company did to all smokers? The majority states that nonparties may be considered for purposes of determining reprehensibility and punishment. Why is it unconstitutional to consider nonparties for purpose of punishment but not to determine reprehensibility? Is this a distinction easily understood by a jury?

2. *The Size of the Award: Constitutional Questions.* In *Browning-Ferris, Indus. v. Kelco Disposal, Inc.*, 492 U.S. 257 (1989), the Court held that the excessive fines clause of the Eighth Amendment to the United States Constitution did not prohibit an award of punitive damages where the government neither prosecuted the claim nor shared in the punitive award. In *TXO Prod. Corp. v. Alliance Resources Corp.*, 509 U.S. 443 (1993) the Court found that due process was not violated by the imposition of a punitive damage award of $10 million against an oil and gas company, even though the award was 526 times greater than the actual damages. Although the Court recognized that due process places substantive limits on the amount of punitive damages, it found that there was no mathematical bright line with which to distinguish constitutionally acceptable awards from constitutionally unacceptable awards. Rather, the Court emphasized the reasonableness of the award and the existence of procedural safeguards as key factors in its constitutional calculus. In *BMW of N. Am., Inc. v. Gore,* 517 U.S. 559 (1996), the United States Supreme Court, in a 5-4 decision, found an award of $4 million punitive damages, reduced to $2 million by the state supreme court, to be nonetheless unconstitutional where the plaintiff was awarded compensatory damages of $4000 against the defendant who fraudulently sold plaintiff a repainted car (damaged by acid rain) as new. Has the Court clarified what is and is not an acceptable punitive damage award — or its basis for intervention? *See generally* Thomas C. Galligan, Jr., U.S. *Supreme Court Tort Reform: Limiting State Power to Articulate and Develop Tort Law — Defamation, Preemption, and Punitive Damages,* 74 U. CIN. L. REV. 1189 (2006) (questioning constitutionalization of punitive damages); Cass R. Sunstein et al., *Assessing Punitive Damages (With Notes on Cognition and Valuation in Law,* 107 YALE L. J. 2071, 2087 (1998) (Court imposing constraints on jury discretion that will provide fair notice to potential defendants and limit the role of arbitrary or irrelevant factors).

3. *Law and Economics of Damages.* Law and economics scholars view tort damages as legal sanctions used to internalize the external costs of beneficial activities. David D. Haddock, *An Ordinary Economic Rationale for Extraordinary Legal Sanctions,* 78 CAL. L. REV. 1, 6 (1990). *See also* Keith N. Hylton, *Punitive Damages and the Economic Theory of Penalties,* 87 GEO. L.J. 421 (1998); Keith N. Hylton & Thomas J. Miceli, *Should Tort Damages Be Multiplied?* 21 J.L. LAW, ECON. & ORG. 388 (2005).When is it necessary to impose a punitive sanction beyond making the plaintiff whole again? Are punitive damage necessary as a means of requiring the defendant to disgorge illicit gains? A. Mitchell Polinsky & Steven Shavell, *Punitive Damages: An Economic Analysis,* 111 HARV. L. REV. 869 (1998). Is illicit disgorgement of illicit gains underlying the punitive damages award in *Grimshaw*?

GRIMSHAW v. FORD MOTOR CO.
174 Cal. Rptr. 348 (Cal. Ct. App. 1981)

TAMURA, ACTING PRESIDING JUSTICE.

A 1972 Ford Pinto hatchback automobile unexpectedly stalled on a freeway, erupting into flames when it was rear-ended by a car proceeding in the same direction. Mrs. Lilly Gray, the driver of the Pinto, suffered fatal burns and 13-year-old Richard Grimshaw, a passenger in the Pinto, suffered severe and permanently disfiguring burns on his face and entire body. Grimshaw and the heirs of Mrs. Gray (Grays) sued Ford Motor Company and others. Following a six-month jury trial, verdicts were returned in favor of plaintiffs against Ford Motor Company. Grimshaw was awarded $2,516,000 compensatory damages and $125 million punitive damages; the Grays were awarded $559,680 in compensatory damages. On Ford's motion for a new trial, Grimshaw was required to remit all but $3½ million of the punitive award as a condition of denial of the motion.

Ford appeals from the judgment and from an order denying its motion for a judgment notwithstanding the verdict as to punitive damages. Grimshaw appeals from the order granting a conditional new trial and from the amended judgment entered pursuant to the order. The Grays have cross-appealed from the judgment and from an order denying leave to amend their complaint to seek punitive damages.

In November 1971, the Grays purchased a new 1972 Pinto hatchback manufactured by Ford in October 1971. The Grays had trouble with the car from the outset. During the first few months of ownership, they had to return the car to the dealer for repairs a number of times. Their car problems included excessive gas and oil consumption, down shifting of the automatic transmission, lack of power, and occasional stalling. It was later learned that the stalling and excessive fuel consumption were caused by a heavy carburetor float.

On May 28, 1972, Mrs. Gray, accompanied by 13-year-old Richard Grimshaw, set out in the Pinto from Anaheim for Barstow to meet Mr. Gray. The Pinto was then 6 months old and had been driven approximately 3000 miles. Mrs. Gray stopped in San Bernardino for gasoline, got back onto the freeway (Interstate 15) and proceeded toward her destination at 60–65 miles per hour. As she approached the Route 30 off-ramp where traffic was congested, she moved from the outer fast lane to the middle lane of the freeway. Shortly after this lane change, the Pinto suddenly stalled and coasted to a halt in the middle lane. It was later established that the carburetor float had become so saturated with gasoline that it suddenly sank, opening the float chamber and causing the engine to flood and stall. A car traveling immediately behind the Pinto was able to swerve and pass it but the driver of a 1962 Ford Galaxie was unable to avoid colliding with the Pinto. The Galaxie had been traveling from 50 to 55 miles per hour but before the impact had been braked to a speed of from 28 to 37 miles per hour.

At the moment of impact, the Pinto caught fire and its interior was engulfed in flames. According to plaintiffs' expert, the impact of the Galaxie had driven the Pinto's gas tank forward and caused it to be punctured by the flange or one of the bolts on the differential housing so that fuel sprayed from the punctured tank and entered the passenger compartment through gaps resulting from the separation of the rear wheel well sections from the floor pan. By the time the Pinto came to rest after the collision, both occupants had sustained serious burns. When they emerged from the vehicle, their clothing was almost completely burned off. Mrs. Gray died a few days later of congestive heart failure as a result of the burns. Grimshaw managed to survive but only through heroic medical measures. He had undergone numerous and extensive surgeries and skin grafts and must undergo additional surgeries over the next 10 years. He lost portions of several fingers on his left hand and portions of his left ear, while his face required many skin grafts from various portions of his body. Because Ford does not contest the amount of compensatory damages awarded to Grimshaw and the Grays, no purpose would be served by further description of the injuries suffered by Grimshaw or the damages sustained by the Grays.

In 1968, Ford began designing a new subcompact automobile, which ultimately became the Pinto. Mr. Iacocca, then a Ford vice president, conceived the project and was its moving force. Ford's objective was to build a carat or below 2000 pounds to sell for no more than $2000.

Ordinarily marketing surveys and preliminary engineering studies precede the styling of a new automobile line. Pinto, however, was a rush project, so that styling preceded engineering and dictated engineering design to a greater degree than usual. Among the engineering decisions dictated by styling was the placement of the fuel tank. It was then the preferred practice in Europe and Japan to locate the gas tank over the rear axle in subcompacts because a small vehicle has less "crush space" between the rear axle and the bumper than larger cars. The Pinto's styling, however, required the tank to be placed behind the rear axle leaving only 9 or 10 inches of "crush space" — far less than in any other American automobile or Ford overseas subcompact. In addition, the Pinto was designed so that its bumper was little more than a chrome strip, less substantial than the bumper of any other American car produced then or later. The Pinto's rear structure also lacked reinforcing members known as "hat sections" (two longitudinal side members) and horizontal cross-members running between them such as were found in cars of larger unitized construction and in all automobiles produced by Ford's overseas operations. The absence of the reinforcing members rendered the Pinto less crush resistant than other vehicles. Finally, the differential housing selected for the Pinto had an exposed flange and a line of exposed bolt heads. These protrusions were sufficient to puncture a gas tank driven forward against the differential upon rear impact.

During the development of the Pinto, prototypes were built and tested. Some were "mechanical prototypes" which duplicated mechanical features of the design but not its appearance while others, referred to as "engineering prototypes," were true duplicates of the design car. These prototypes as well as two production Pintos were crash-tested by Ford to determine, among other things, the integrity of the fuel system in rear-end accidents. Ford also conducted the tests to see if the Pinto as designed would meet a proposed federal regulation requiring all automobiles manufactured in 1972 to be able to withstand a 20-mile-per-hour fixed barrier impact without significant fuel spillage and all automobiles manufactured after January 1, 1973, to withstand a 30-mile-per-hour fixed barrier impact without significant fuel spillage.

The crash tests revealed that the Pinto's fuel system as designed could not meet the 20-mile-per-hour proposed standard. Mechanical prototypes struck from the rear with a moving barrier at 21 miles per hour caused the fuel tank to be driven forward and to be punctured, causing fuel leakage in excess of the standard prescribed by the proposed regulation. A production Pinto crash-tested at 21 miles per hour into a fixed barrier caused the fuel neck to be torn from the gas tank and the tank to be punctured by a bolt head on the differential housing. In at least one test, spilled fuel entered the driver's compartment through gaps resulting from the separation of the seams joining the rear wheel wells to the floor pan. The seam separation was occasioned by the lack of reinforcement in the rear structure and insufficient welds of the wheel wells to the floor pan.

Tests conducted by Ford on other vehicles, including modified or reinforced mechanical Pinto prototypes, proved safe at speeds at which the Pinto failed. Where rubber bladders had been installed in the tank, crash tests into fixed barriers at 21 miles per hour withstood leakage from punctures in the gas tank. Vehicles with fuel tanks installed above rather than behind the rear axle passed the fuel system integrity test at 31-miles-per-hour fixed barrier. A Pinto with two longitudinal hat sections added to firm up the rear structure passed a 20-mile per hour rear impact fixed barrier test with no fuel leakage.

When a prototype failed the fuel system integrity test, the standard of care for engineers in the industry was to redesign and retest it. The vulnerability of the production Pinto's fuel tank at speeds of 20- and 30-miles-per-hour fixed barrier tests could have been remedied by inexpensive "fixes," but Ford produced and sold the Pinto to the public without doing anything to remedy the defects. Design changes that would have enhanced the integrity of the fuel tank system at relatively little cost per car included the following: Longitudinal side members and cross members at $2.40 and $1.80, respectively; a single shock absorbent "flak suit" to protect the tank at $4; a tank within a tank and placement of the tank over the axle at $5.08 to $5.79; a nylon bladder within the tank at $5.25 to $8; placement of the tank over the axle surrounded with a protective barrier at a cost of $9.95 per car; substitution of a rear axle with a smooth differential housing at a cost of $2.10; imposition of a protective shield between the differential housing and the tank at $2.35; improvement and reinforcement of the bumper at $2.60; addition of eight inches of crush space a cost of $6.40. Equipping the car with a reinforced rear structure, smooth axle, improved bumper and additional crush space at a total cost of $15.30 would have made the fuel tank safe in a 34- to 38-mile-per-hour rear-end collision by a vehicle the size of the Ford Galaxie. If, in addition to the foregoing, a bladder or tank within a tank were used or if the tank were protected with a shield, it would have been safe in a 40- to 45-mile-per-hour rear impact. If the tank had been located over the rear axle, it would have been safe in a rear impact at 50 miles per hour or more.

The idea for the Pinto, as has been noted, was conceived by Mr. Iacocca, then executive vice-president of Ford. As the project approached actual production, the engineers responsible for the components of the project "signed off" to their immediate supervisors who in turn "signed off" to their superiors and so on up the chain of command until the entire project was approved for public release by Vice Presidents Alexander and MacDonald and ultimately by Mr. Iacocca. The Pinto crash tests results had been forwarded up the chain of command to the ultimate decision-makers and were known to the Ford officials who decided to go forward with production.

Harley Copp, a former Ford engineer and executive in charge of the crash testing program, testified that the highest level of Ford's management made the decision to go forward with the production of the Pinto, knowing that the gas tank was vulnerable to puncture and rupture at low rear impact speeds, creating a significant risk of death or injury from fire, and knowing that "fixes" were feasible at nominal cost. He testified that management's decision was based on the cost savings which would inure from omitting or delaying the "fixes."

Mr. Copp's testimony concerning management's awareness of the crash tests results and the vulnerability of the Pinto fuel system was corroborated by other evidence.

Ford contends that it was entitled to a judgment notwithstanding the verdict on the issue of punitive damages on two grounds: First, punitive damages are statutorily and constitutionally impermissible in a design defect case; second, there was no evidentiary support for a finding of malice or of corporate responsibility for malice. In any event, Ford maintains that the punitive damage award must be reversed because of erroneous instructions and excessiveness of the award.

The concept of punitive damages is rooted in the English common law and is a settled principle of the common law of this country. The doctrine was a part of the common law of this long before the Civil Code was adopted. When our laws were codified in 1872, the doctrine was incorporated in Civil Code section 3294, which at the time of trial read: "In an action for the breach of an obligation not arising from contract, where the defendant has been guilty of oppression, fraud, or malice, express or implied, the plaintiff, in addition to the actual damages, may recover damages for the sake of example and by way of punishing the defendant."

Ford argues that "malice" as used in section 3294 and as interpreted by our Supreme Court requires *animus malus* or evil motive — an intention to injure the person harmed — and that the term is therefore conceptually incompatible with an unintentional tort such as the manufacture and marketing of a defectively designed product. This contention runs counter to our decisional law. As this court recently noted, numerous California cases have interpreted the term "malice" as used in section 3294 to include not only a malicious intention to injure the specific person harmed, but conduct evincing "a conscious disregard of the probability that the actor's conduct will result in injury to others."

In *Taylor v. Superior Court of Los Angeles County*, 24 Cal. 3d 890 (1979), our high court's most recent pronouncement on the subject of punitive damages, the court observed that the availability of punitive damages has not been limited to cases in which there is an actual intent to harm plaintiff or others. (*Id.,* at p. 895.) The court concurred with the *Searle* (*G.D. Searle & Co. v. Superior Court of Sacramento County*, 49 Cal. App. 3d 22 (1975)) court's suggestion that conscious disregard of the safety of others is an appropriate description of the *animus malus* required by Civil Code section 3294, adding: "In order to justify an award of punitive damages on this basis, the plaintiff must establish that the defendant was aware of the probable dangerous consequences of his conduct, and that he wilfully and deliberately failed to avoid those consequences." (*Id.*, at pp. 895–896.)

The interpretation of the word "malice" as used in section 3294 to encompass conduct evincing callous and conscious disregard of public safety by those who manufacture and market mass produced articles is consonant with, and furthers the objectives of, punitive damages. The primary purposes of punitive damages are punishment and deterrence of like conduct by the wrongdoer and others. In the traditional noncommercial intentional tort, compensatory damages alone may serve as an effective deterrent against future wrongful conduct but in commerce-related torts, the manufacturer may find it more profitable to treat compensatory damages as a part of the cost of doing business rather than to remedy the defect. Deterrence of such "objectionable corporate policies" serves one of the principal purposes of Civil Code Section 3294. Governmental safety standards and the criminal law have failed to provide adequate consumer protection against the manufacture and distribution of defective products. Punitive damages thus remain as the most effective remedy for consumer protection against defectively designed mass produced articles. They provide a motive for private individuals to enforce rules of law and enable them to recoup the expenses of doing so which can be considerable and not otherwise recoverable.

Ford's contention that the statute is unconstitutional has been repeatedly rejected. Ford's argument that its due process rights were violated because it did not have "fair warning" that its conduct would render it liable for punitive damages under Civil Code Section 3294 ignores the long line of decisions in this state beginning with *Donnelly v. Southern Pacific Co.*, 18 Cal. 2d 863, 869–870 (1941), holding that punitive damages are recoverable in a nondeliberate or unintentional tort where the defendant's conduct constitutes a conscious disregard of the probability of injury to others. The related contention that application of Civil Code Section 3294 to the instant case would violate the ex post facto prohibition of the federal Constitution because at the time it designed the 1972 Pinto Ford had no warning that its conduct could be punished under Civil Code Section 3294 is equally without merit. This constitutional prohibition extends to criminal statutes and penalties, not to civil statutes. Moreover, at the very least since *Toole v. Richardson-Merrell, Inc.*, 251 Cal. App. 2d 689 (1967), it should have been clear that a manufacturer of a dangerous, defective product might be liable for punitive damages if it knowingly exposed others to the hazard.

Equally without merit is the argument that the statute permits an unlawful delegation of legislative power because it fails to provide sufficient guidance to the judge and jury. As we have explained, the doctrine of punitive damages and its application are governed by common law principles. Judicial development of common law legal principles does not constitute an unlawful usurpation of legislative power; it is a proper exercise of a power traditionally exercised by the judiciary. The precise contention now advanced has been previously rejected.

The related contention that the potential liability for punitive damages in other cases for the same design defect renders the imposition of such damages violative of Ford's due process rights also lacks merit. Followed to its logical conclusion, it would mean that punitive damages could never be assessed against a manufacturer of a mass produced article. No authorities are cited for such a proposition; indeed, as we have seen, the cases are to the contrary. We recognize the fact that multiplicity of awards may present a problem, but the mere possibility of a future award in a different case is not a ground for setting aside the award in this case, particularly as reduced by the trial judge. If Ford should be confronted with the possibility of an award in another case for the same conduct, it may raise the issue in that case. We add, moreover, that there is no necessary unfairness should the plaintiff in this case be rewarded to a greater extent than later plaintiffs. As Professor Owen has said in response to such a charge of unfairness: "This conception ignores the enormous diligence, imagination, and financial outlay required of initial plaintiffs to uncover and to prove the flagrant misconduct of a product manufacturer. In fact, subsequent plaintiffs will often ride to favorable verdicts and settlements on the coattails of the first comers." (Owen, *Punitive Damages in Products Liability Litigation*, 74 MICH. L. REV. 1258, 1325 (1976), fn. omitted.) That observation fits the instant case.

Ford contends that its motion for judgment notwithstanding the verdict should have been granted because the evidence was insufficient to support a finding of malice or corporate responsibility for such malice. The record fails to support the contention.

Through the results of the crash tests Ford knew that the Pinto's fuel tank and rear structure would expose consumers to serious injury or death in a 20- to 30-miles-per-hour collision. There was evidence that Ford could have corrected the hazardous design defects at minimal cost but decided to defer correction of the shortcomings by engaging in a cost-benefit analysis balancing human lives and limbs against corporate profits. Ford's institutional mentality was shown to be one of callous indifference to public safety. There was substantial evidence that Ford's conduct constituted "conscious disregard" of the probability of injury to members of the consuming public.

Ford's argument that there can be no liability for punitive damages because there was no evidence of corporate ratification of malicious misconduct is equally without merit.

California follows the Restatement rule that punitive damages can be awarded against a principal because of an action of an agent if, but only if, "(a) the principal authorized the doing and the manner of the act, or (b) the agent was unfit and the principal was reckless in employing him, or (c) the agent was employed in a managerial capacity and was acting in the scope of employment, or (d) the principal or a managerial agent of the principal ratified or approved the act." (RESTATEMENT (SECOND) OF TORTS (Tent. Draft No. 19,

1973) § 909.) . . . The present case comes within one or both of the categories described in subdivisions (c) and (d).

There is substantial evidence that management was aware of the crash tests showing the vulnerability of the Pinto's fuel tank to rupture at low speed rear impacts with consequent significant risk of injury or death of the occupants by fire. There was testimony from several sources that the test results were forwarded up the chain of command; Vice President Robert Alexander admitted to Mr. Copp that he was aware of the test results; Vice President Harold MacDonald, who chaired the product review meetings, was present at one of those meetings at which a report on the crash tests was considered and a decision was made to defer corrective action; and it may be inferred that Mr. Alexander, a regular attender of the product review meetings, was also present at that meeting. McDonald and Alexander were manifestly managerial employees possessing the discretion to make "decisions that will ultimately determine corporate policy." (*Egan v. Mutual of Omaha Ins. Co., supra*, 24 Cal. 3d 809, 823.) There was also evidence that Harold Johnson, an assistant chief engineer of research, and Mr. Max Jurosek, chief chassis engineer, were aware of the results of the crash tests and the defects in the Pinto's fuel tank system. Ford contends those two individuals did not occupy managerial positions because Mr. Copp testified that they admitted awareness of the defects but told him they were powerless to change the rear-end design of the Pinto. It may be inferred from the testimony, however, that the two engineers had approached management about redesigning the Pinto or that, being aware of management's attitude, they decided to do nothing. In either case the decision not to take corrective action was made by persons exercising managerial authority. Whether an employee acts in a "managerial capacity" does not necessarily depend on his "level" in the corporate hierarchy. (*Id.*, at p. 822.) As the *Egan* court said: ""Defendant should not be allowed to insulate itself from liability by giving an employee a nonmanagerial title and relegating to him crucial policy decisions."" (*Id.*, at p. 823, quoting concurring and dissenting opinion in *Merlo v. Standard Life & Acc. Ins. Co., supra*, 59 Cal. App. 3d at 25).

Ford argues that the jury should have been instructed that plaintiff had the burden of proving "malice" by "clear and convincing evidence." Ford's request for such an instruction was denied. Ford relies on cases involving the personal liberty of an individual. A similar contention was rejected in *Toole v. Richardson-Merrell, Inc.*, 251 Cal. App. 2d 689, 716 (1967), where the court refused to give an instruction that a defendant against whom punitive damages are sought is entitled to the presumption of innocence. Furthermore, the Supreme Court has recently rejected the clear and convincing test in a punitive damage case based upon fraud. (*Liodas v. Sahadi*, 19 Cal. 3d 278, 286–293 (1977)). The requested instruction on the burden of proof was properly denied.

Ford's final contention is that the amount of punitive damages awarded, even as reduced by the trial court, was so excessive that a new trial on that issue must be granted. Ford argues that its conduct was less reprehensible than those for which punitive damages have been awarded in California in the past; that the $312 million award is many times over the highest award for such damages ever upheld in California; and that the award exceeds maximum civil penalties that may be enforced under federal or state statutes against a manufacturer for marketing a defective automobile. We are unpersuaded.

In determining whether an award of punitive damages is excessive, comparison of the amount awarded with other awards in other cases is not a valid consideration. Nor does "[t]he fact that an award may set a precedent by its size" in and of itself render it suspect; whether the award was excessive must be assessed by examining the circumstances of the particular case. In deciding whether an award is excessive as a matter of law or was so grossly disproportionate as to raise the presumption that it was the product of passion or prejudice, the following factors should be weighed: the degree of reprehensibility of defendant's conduct, the wealth of the defendant, the amount of compensatory damages, and an amount which would serve as a deterrent effect on like conduct by defendant and others who may be so inclined. Applying the foregoing criteria to the instant case, the punitive damages award as reduced by the trial court was well within reason.

In assessing the propriety of a punitive damage award, as in assessing the propriety of any other judicial ruling based upon factual determinations, the evidence must be viewed in the light most favorable to the judgment.

Viewing the record thusly in the instant case, the conduct of Ford's management was reprehensible in the extreme. It exhibited a conscious and callous disregard of public safety in order to maximize corporate profits. Ford's self-evaluation of its conduct is based on a review of the evidence most favorable to it instead of on the basis of the evidence most favorable to the judgment. Unlike malicious conduct directed toward a single specific individual, Ford's tortious conduct endangered the lives of thousands of Pinto purchasers. Weighed against the factor of reprehensibility, the punitive damage award as reduced by the trial judge was not excessive.

Nor was the reduced award excessive taking into account defendant's wealth and the size of the compensatory award. Ford's net worth was $7.7 billion and its income after taxes for 1976 was over $983 million. The punitive award was approximately. 005 percent of Ford's net worth and approximately. 03 percent of its 1976 net income. The ratio of the punitive damages to compensatory damages was approximately 1.4 to 1. Significantly, Ford does not quarrel with the amount of the compensatory award to Grimshaw. Nor was the size of the award excessive in light of its deterrent purpose. An award which is so small that it can be simply written off as a part of the cost of doing business would have no deterrent effect. An award which affects the company's pricing of its product and thereby affects its competitive advantage would serve as a deterrent. The award in question was far from excessive as a deterrent against future wrongful conduct by Ford and others.

Ford complains that the punitive award is far greater than the maximum penalty that may be imposed under California or federal law prohibiting the sale of defective automobiles or other products. For example, Ford notes that California statutes provide a maximum fine of only $50 for the first offense and $100 for a second offense for a dealer who sells an automobile that fails to confirm to federal safety laws or is not equipped with required lights or brakes that a manufacturer who sells brake fluid in this state failing to meet statutory standards is subject to a maximum of only $50 and that the maximum penalty that may be imposed under federal law for violation of automobile safety standards is $1000 per vehicle up to a maximum of $800,000 for any related series of offenses. It is precisely because monetary penalties under government regulations prescribing business standards or the criminal law are so inadequate and ineffective as deterrents against a manufacturer and distributor of mass produced defective products that punitive damages must be of sufficient amount to discourage such practices. Instead of showing that the punitive damages award was excessive, the comparison between the award and the maximum penalties under state and federal statutes and regulations governing automotive safety demonstrates the propriety of the amount of punitive damages awarded.

[The court found that the remittitur was "fair and reasonable;" and that punitive damages are not recoverable under California law in a wrongful death (the *Gray*) action.]

NOTES

1. *The Punitive Damage Rationale. See* State Farm Mut. Auto. Ins. Co. v. Campbell, 538 U.S. 408, 417 (2003) (punitive damages "serve the same purposes as criminal penalties"). The functions of punitive damages generally are to punish and deter. Michigan's remedy of punitive damages is also to compensate for injured feelings. All but five states recognize the common law doctrine of punitive damages: Louisiana, Massachusetts, Nebraska, New Hampshire, and Washington. Louisiana is a civil code jurisdiction that refused to recognize punitive damages, except as statutorily authorized. Massachusetts does not recognize punitive damages except as may be available under specific statutory authorization such as the Commonwealth's wrongful death statute that is penal in form, but compensatory in effect. Washington, like Massachusetts, permits punitive damages only if specifically authorized by statute. Nebraska also refused to adopt the remedy of punitive damages.

The most common arguments for limiting or eliminating punitive damages are: (a) there is no empirical data confirming that punitive damages do in fact deter others; (b) punitive damages result in a "windfall" to the plaintiff which should be shared by the public generally; (c) it is unfair to permit the jury to impose a crippling remedy on a business or enterprise, particularly without rational guidelines; (d) the threat of punitive damages stifles industry creativity and reduces the number of new products available to the public. Some arguments supporting punitive damages are: (a) the tort victim is not fully compensated by compensatory damages, because he usually is unable to recover his attorney's fees and some of his other costs; (b) punitive damages provide supplemental compensation where the defendant's conduct is egregious. (c) punitive damages induce "private attorneys general" to provide the valuable service of suing wrongdoers and deterring highly undesirable conduct; (d) punitive damages help provide a safer society by deterring the creation of unsafe products and conduct. *See generally* Michael L. Rustad, *The Closing of Punitive Damages Iron Cage*, 38 Loy. L.A. L. Rev. 1297 (2005). *Cf.* Theodore B. Olson and Theodore J. Boutrous, The Constitutionality of

PUNITIVE DAMAGES (Washington Legal Foundation 1989) (contending that excessive punitive damages harm society by encumbering businesses and creating a competitive disadvantage). Should judges determine punitive damages rather than juries to resolve the problem of constitutionally excessive awards? If punitive damages serve larger societal purposes, why should the plaintiff receive the award? For example, should the plaintiff be required to remit a portion of punitive damages to the state for a public purpose?

2. *Tort Reforms Limiting Punitive Damages*: All but a few states that recognize the remedy of punitive damages have enacted limitations and restrictions on the availability of this remedy. A majority of states cap the amount of punitive damages or do not recognize the remedy. Michael L. Rustad, *The Closing of Iron Cage, supra*, 38 LOY. L.A. L. REV. at 1339. Capping punitive damages undermines the unpredictability of punitive damages that makes the defendant think twice before engaging in wrongful conduct that may be profitable, which violates community norms or disregards the public welfare. In contrast, a law and economics view is that caps on punitive damages are necessary to curb jury discretion. *Id.* Corporate defendants are critical of the standardless nature of punitive damages.

3. *Degrees of Negligence — Replayed.* Conduct which rises to the level of an intentional tort will justify an award of punitive damages. In most jurisdictions, something less will suffice. This level of conduct — something worse than negligence but less than intentional — has escaped precise definition. It is described by various terms, such as willful, wanton, conscious indifference, recklessness, reckless disregard for safety, flagrant indifference, or conscious disregard for the risk of harm to the victim. *See, e.g., Moran v. Johns-Manville Sales Corp.,* 691 F.2d 811 (6th Cir. 1982); *Taylor v. Super. Ct.,* 598 P.2d 854 (Cal. 1979). While jurisdictions employ different terminology in describing this "middle level" between negligence and intent, there are two common elements: (a) the conduct exposed the victim to a high probability of risk, and (b) the defendant took little or no care to avoid the harm.

A large number of states have enacted statutes that specify the state of mind required for punitive damages. In general, the culpability leading to punitive damages varies from gross negligence in some states, to actual malice in others. A recent survey concluded that twelve states now require proof that a defendant was acting maliciously in order to recover punitive damages. Another twenty-six states require the plaintiff to prove that the defendant's culpability is greater than gross negligence. Thus, the trend in the law is toward ratcheting up the standard of conduct required for punitive damages and a majority of states follow the REST. 2D TORTS standard for punitive damages, which requires "conduct that is outrageous, because of the defendant's evil motive or . . . reckless indifference to the rights of others." REST. 2D TORTS § 908.

Do these reforms address the question of whether defendants receive fair notice of the conduct that subjects them to punitive damages? What reforms could be instituted to give defendants fair notice of the conduct that leads to punitive damages? Should the Supreme Court be the institution that reforms punitive damages or state legislatures?

4. *The Burden of Proof.* Because punitive damages are "penal" in nature, the vast majority of jurisdictions require that the plaintiff prove the defendant's egregious conduct by "clear and convincing" evidence. Colorado is the only jurisdiction that requires plaintiffs to prove punitive damages "beyond a reasonable doubt." The reform of "clear and convincing" evidence is doctrinally symmetrical with the function of punitive damages as patrolling the conduct on the borderline between crime and tort. No empirical study has been done on the question of whether raising the standard of proof actually makes it more difficult to recover punitive damages.

5. *Multiple Perspectives on Punitive Damages?* Wealth-based punitive damages are optimally used to punish and deter wrongdoers where the probability of detection is very low and the probability of harm is very high. Most states permit the admissibility of the financial condition or wealth of the defendant to set punishment. The purpose of introducing evidence of wealth is to calibrate the amount of punitive damages to achieve the most efficient level of deterrence.

Law and economics scholars contend that the price of wrongdoing must be proportional to potential gain in order to have a deterrent effect. *See* WILLIAM M. LANDES & RICHARD A. POSNER, THE ECONOMIC STRUCTURE OF TORT LAW 160–63 (1987). However, these scholars are concerned with the possibility of over-deterrence despite the fact that a study by two law and economics scholars found that punitive damages were rarely awarded. *See* WILLIAM M. LANDES & RICHARD A. POSNER, THE ECONOMIC STRUCTURE OF TORT LAW, 304–07 (1987).

Should corporate defendants receive credits for prior punitive damages awards for the same conduct? Assuming that a defendant has been assessed prior punitive damages award for the same conduct, should there be a cap on the number and size of punitive damages awards? Should it matter if the defendant has continued the wrongdoing after earlier awards were handed down? What are the advantages and disadvantages of caps on the number of punitive damages awards for the same conduct?

PROBLEMS

15.1

Plaintiff ate seafood at defendant's restaurant and, as a result, became sick and vomited. After this experience, she would no longer eat any kind of seafood, which had previously been her favorite type of food. What damages, if any, can she and her husband recover from the restaurant?

15.2

"Heather Lewinski, a seventeen-year-old teenager, courageously testified about her psychological pain as a result of egregious medical malpractice when she was eight-years-old that left her face permanently and horribly disfigured. Among other side effects, she constantly drools. She described how other children made fun of her as she advanced through her teenage years. She had one self-initiated date, and it was a disaster. She told about her belief that she will never marry, will never have children, and will have to concentrate on raising and training dogs because they do not discriminate on the basis of human appearances. Unfortunately, despite her apparent intelligence, warm personality, and the unfairness of her condition, Heather is probably right — I saw her face, as did others who tearfully heard her testimony." Neil Vidmar, *Medical Malpractice Lawsuits: An Essay On Patient Interests, The Contingency Fee System, Juries, And Social Policy*, 38 LOY. L.A. L. REV. 1217, 1225 (2005). Assuming that this 18-year-old will live to age 78, what noneconomic damages would compensate her for her general damages? If you were representing Heather, what methodology would you use to determine non-economic or general damages? What objections would the defense likely pose to your methodology?

15.3

Plaintiff heard a car crash at a point where she had seen her child playing moments before. Thinking that her child had been hit, she rushed to the scene of the crash where she found her child covered with pieces of bloody broken glass from the car. The blood was from the car driver, who was seriously injured. In removing the glass from the child's body, plaintiff accidentally cut herself with one of the bloody pieces. It turned out that her child was unharmed from the crash, except for a few minor scratches. On being hospitalized, the driver of the car was diagnosed as HIV positive. Discuss Plaintiff's possible claims for emotional distress against the car driver.

15.4

Ann was involved in a one-car accident when she lost control of her car coming out of her ice-covered driveway, causing the car to run into a retaining wall. Her insurance company appraised the value of the automobile before the accident at $600. Because the lowest repair estimate Ann was able to obtain was $1000, the company declared the automobile a total loss, paid her $500 and allowed her to keep the car, which had a salvage value of $100. Although the body of the car was severely damaged, it was still drivable. The day after Ann received payment from her insurance company, Jones ran into Ann's car from the rear as she was stopped at a red light. Cost of repairing the damage done by Jones is $2000, making the total cost of repairing the car $3000. Assuming that Jones is negligent, what does he owe Ann?

15.5

Plaintiff and her husband enter defendant's supermarket and begin shopping, moving up and down the aisles. Plaintiff intends to purchase sugar, and turns into the aisle where the sugar is stocked. Her husband precedes her. In the aisle, ahead of them, lies a broken glass jar of cooking oil; the oil has spread across the aisle. Husband observes the oil, but manages to step across it. He says nothing to the plaintiff, who is looking at items on the shelves as she approaches the oil. She steps into the oil, and slips and falls. As a result Plaintiff (who is now 42-year-olds old) suffers back and knee injuries, must undergo a back operation, is in constant pain during the year between the accident and the surgery, and after the surgery is left with a 15% disability of the knee and a 25% disability of the back. She is no longer able to do housework, to work in the family's bookstore, or to engage in most of her former hobbies and pastimes. Although she was working full-time in the family store, she did not draw a salary, and no one was hired to replace her. The injury affected the wife's personality and her relations with her husband, her 18-year-old college daughter, her six-year-old son, and her mother. Husband has performed most of the housework since the wife's injury. Who may recover damages? For what losses?

15.6

Dan Defendant owns and operates the office building where Peter McNabb was employed. On December 24, 2007, Mr. McNabb, while leaving work, sustained a fractured left leg because of falling on the stairs in defendant's building. Mr. McNabb testified at trial that his fall occurred when his right foot slipped on the main landing and his left leg was pulled beneath him when he fell. The landing was made of marble and was slippery due to an accumulation of water. McNabb and other witnesses stated that a mat covered part of the landing but that it was saturated with water and was positioned so that an individual descending the stairs would first step on the bare, then wet, marble before reaching the mat. Witnesses attributed the slippery state of the landing to an accumulation of slush, water, and melted snow tracked in from outside the building. The following July McNabb fell while attempting to move a chair at home and fractured the same leg, but in a different place than had been broken in the earlier fall. A few months later McNabb suffered a stroke, which affected his right arm and leg. He was forced to have three toes on his left leg amputated because of the onset of gangrene in them. Assuming that Defendant was liable for negligent maintenance of the main landing of the office building and McNabb was not contributorily negligent, what damages are recoverable? What role does the "eggshell doctrine" play in the assessment of damages? Should damages be apportioned? On what basis?

15.7

Lucy Mercado traveled to Chicago, Illinois, from her home in Hammond, Indiana, with her four sons — including six-year-old Brian — to visit the Museum of Science and Industry. While walking in the museum parking lot, Brian slipped away from his mother, stepped out onto a crosswalk between two aisles of parked cars, and was struck on the crosswalk by a taxi driven by defendant Ahmed. The impact of the blow threw Brian four or five feet into the air and a distance of about one and one half car lengths. Brian was taken by ambulance to the University of Chicago, Wyler's Children's Hospital. The boy was examined for an extended period of time, about three to four hours, by a team of doctors and other hospital personnel and then released that same day. An examination of Brian's skull, eyes, and ears revealed no signs of head injury. The boy's reflexes, blood pressure, heart rate, and pulse were all normal. Trial testimony established that Brian, 11 years old, suffered from a wide range of problems prior to the accident. His ability to process visual and auditory information is substantially impaired, making reading, writing, and arithmetic very difficult for him. The boy has been diagnosed as suffering from severe emotional problems and as suicidal. He is unable to perform such rudimentary tasks as dressing properly or managing his personal hygiene. Both the plaintiff's and defendants' witnesses testified that Brian will require some form of institutionalization or structured environment for the remainder of his life. His employment prospects are limited to those positions, which require the performance of only the most menial tasks. Brian's mother has retained you to represent Brian. Your expert confirms that Brian suffered a closed head injury when the taxi in the museum parking lot struck him. Assume for this question that the taxi driver was negligently driven and there is no contributory negligence. What damages would you seek? What problems do you anticipate in seeking hedonic damages, future medical expenses, and future lost earnings?

15.8

Andrea suffered a catastrophic brain injury in a serious automobile accident when she was only eighteen years old. As the result of the accident, Andrea was bedridden and unable to eat, speak, or control her bowels or bladder. Her mother placed her in Caring Convalescent Hospital a licensed skilled nursing facility. She was fed intravenously through a stomach tube. She was partially paralyzed on the left side of her body, and was unable to turn herself over or summon help. Her right arm was in a restraint to prevent her from disturbing her feeding tube. She would smile when her grandmother stroked her hair or spoke to her, and she was aware of pain and discomfort and hunger and would communicate that awareness by yelling. She also was aware of regular feeding times, and would yell if her food was late. Although she did not recognize her mother, she was aware of her presence and seemed to know her from her repeated visits. Andrea's mother testified that appellant was "quite aware of anything other than the routine treatment," although she also testified that most of the time Nancy was unaware of her surroundings. Six months later Andrea's mother discovered that Andrea was raped and impregnated while under the care of the convalescent hospital. During this period, Andrea manifested a new restlessness and she whimpered a lot and cried more. Her pregnancy was discovered when she missed two consecutive menstrual periods The two other patients in Andrea's room were not very alert elderly women. Also against Andrea's mother's expressed wishes, male attendants were assigned to appellant. Several male employees abruptly quit their job at the Convalescent Hospital after Andrea's pregnancy was discovered. Further discovery revealed that Andrea had no male visitors and that Andrea was heavily sedated during the period in which she was raped. Andrea's mother has retained you to file a claim against the convalescent hospital. If you represent Andrea, what damages will you seek? What difficulties do you anticipate in recovering these items of damages?

15.9

Paula Plaintiff purchased Prada shoes from Big Store on a number of occasions during late 2006 and early 2007, using a debit card associated with her checking account. Sometime during this same period, personal financial information maintained on a computer network — including customers' credit card and debit card numbers, along with the corresponding names to those cards, and checking account numbers and drivers' license numbers provided by check writers — was stolen by a cyberthief. This included information from Big Store where plaintiff had purchased shoes using her debit card. The information "compromised" included the numbers and names associated with approximately 1,438,281 credit and debit cards and 96,385 checking account numbers and drivers' license numbers. Big Store became aware of the compromise of this information in March, 2007. In June, 2007, plaintiff received a letter from Big Store informing her that she was one of the customers whose personal information had been "stolen." Paula was given a new debit card "as protection," presumably from potential fraudulent charges on the card. After she received the new debit card, Paula purchased a "credit monitoring product" in order to "protect herself from identity theft." Although Paula proved that fraudulent charges have been made on *some* of the credit card and debit card accounts that were obtained from Big Store by the cyberthief, she has no evidence that her personal information has been misused. What elements of damages may Paula seek? What problems will Paula likely encounter in seeking compensation for the monitoring software and other damages?

15.10

Dan Defendant a forty-year-old truck driver picked up Peter Plaintiff, a 22-year-old hitchhiker around 7 pm. Around midnight that night, Defendant was 100 miles from his destination, but running late. Defendant was exhausted because he had been driving for 24 straight hours. He did not slow his truck down, intending to pass a pick-up on the left. As Defendant approached the truck, he became aware that it was sitting still in the road, and he saw another vehicle. It was approaching in the southbound lane in which Defendant was attempting to pass the pick-up truck. Unable to stop, and, in an effort to avoid hitting the pick-up truck in the rear, Defendant drove the "18-wheeler" truck off the road and into a ditch where it struck a tree. In the crash that resulted, Dan Defendant was thrown free from the wrecked truck, but Peter Plaintiff, a passenger, was pinned inside he cab. Soon afterwards, the cab of the "18-wheeler" truck was engulfed in flames. Willard Witness testified that he was sitting on his porch and observed the accident. He ran down to the wrecked truck and, while standing at the rear of the truck, heard someone say, "Somebody get me out of here." Fred Farr, another witness, ran down to the wrecked truck when he heard it impact the tree and, while standing on the truck with his head in the window of the cab, Fred heard someone say, "Somebody help me. Get me out of here." He was sure that the voice came from inside the truck. He tried to get to the person inside the truck but jumped off it as the truck began to tremble and the truck exploded into flames just as he got a few steps away. Peter Plaintiffs' body was burned and charred beyond recognition. He was unmarried and without children, dependents, or living parents and was survived by siblings. The representative of Plaintiff's estate filed a wrongful death suit against Defendant? What categories of damages are recoverable? How would pain and suffering and anguish be compensated on these facts? Are hedonic damages recoverable?

Chapter 16

TORT RETRENCHMENTS AND TORT ALTERNATIVES

A. INTRODUCTION

One of the most highly contested domestic issues is whether the tort liability system is in trouble. The tort system has been blamed for excessive litigation, unreasonably high verdicts, and the lack of available or affordable liability insurance, although, as this chapter will more fully describe, studies and reports both at the federal and state levels do not support these indictments. What is not disputable is that the question of the need for tort reform is highly contentious and politicized. Proponents of tort reform raise concerns about slowness, unpredictability, and cost of litigation. They characterize substantive tort law as creating opportunities for windfalls for plaintiffs who act irresponsibly and seek recompense without proof of fault or causation on the part of defendants. In their view, tort law enables greedy counsel to target actors with deep pockets who are exposed to liability because of consumer-focused plaintiffs who seek to and burden business and professionals with all costs of accidents. They characterize the tort liability system as in crisis, crippling competition and the economy.[1]

Defenders of the current tort system paint a strikingly different picture,[2] and hotly deny that there is a crisis or that the liability system is the root

---

[1] A sense of some of the political clashes and perspectives on the tort system can be gleaned from Chapter 1. A number of scholars and commentators call for radical surgery of the tort system. *See, e.g.*, PETER W. HUBER, LIABILITY: THE LEGAL REVOLUTION AND ITS CONSEQUENCES (1988) (characterizing expert testimony as "junk science" and calling for restrictions on admissibility); Amanda Lang, *A New Approach to Tort Reform: An Argument for the Establishment of Specialized Medical Courts*, 39 GA. L. REV. 293 (2004) (arguing for formation of specialized medical courts like the federal circuit court for patent cases to resolve medical malpractice); George Priest, *Punitive Damages Reform: The Case of Alabama*, 56 LA. L. REV. 825, 838 (1996) (calling for punitive damages reform in Alabama); Victor E. Schwartz & Mark A. Behrens, *A Proposal for Federal Product Liability Reform in the New Millennium*, 4 TEX. REV. L. & POL. 261 (2000) (developing case for federalizing products liability law); Victor E. Schwartz, Mark A. Behrens & Joseph P. Mastrosimone, *Reining in Punitive Damages "Run Wild": Proposals for Reform by Courts and Legislatures*, 65 BROOKLYN L. REV. 1003 (2000) (advocating judicial deference to legislative tort reform); Victor E. Schwartz & Mark A. Behrens, *Punitive Damages Reform — State Legislatures Can and Should Meet the Challenge Issued by the Supreme Court of the United States in* Haslip, 42 AM. U. L. REV. 1365 (1993) (arguing for statutory tort reforms limiting punitive damages).

[2] For a sampling of the work of critics of tort reform, see for example, Richard Abel, *The Real Torts Crisis — Too Few Claims*, 48 OHIO ST. L.J. 443 (1987) (contending that tort law does not adequately perform its compensatory function); Jay M. Feinman, *Unmaking and Remaking Tort Law*, 5 J. HIGH TECH. L. 61 (2005) (documenting tort reformers' organized campaign to roll back plaintiffs' rights in favor of corporate interests); Thomas C. Galligan, Jr., *U.S. Supreme Court Tort Reform: Limiting State Power to Articulate and Develop Tort Law — Defamation, Preemption, and Punitive Damages*, 74 U. CIN. L. REV. 1189 (2006) (explaining how the U.S. Supreme Court's judicial tort reform is interfering with the states' ability and authority to articulate, apply, and

cause for many of the problems identified by proponents of "tort reform." They question whether there is or has been a crisis attributable to systemic problems of torts. Many of the opponents of reform condemn well-financed and organized efforts by business and the insurance industry to ignore what empirical research findings reveal, and to cast compensatory and punitive damage awards as excessive and jurors biased in favor of plaintiffs. *See, e.g.,* Richard L. Abel, *Judges Write the Darndest Things: Judicial Mystification of Limitations on Tort Liability,* 80 TEX. L. REV. 1547, 1548 (2002) (describing tort reform as a "costly and expensive" campaign to disseminate myth that Americans file large numbers of frivolous cases and juries are excessively generous to victims). Defenders of the tort system point out that even the label "tort reform" clashes with its historical meaning which identified *reform* as a restructuring of the law to provide greater protection to accident victims. In contrast to tort reforms aimed toward providing greater protection for tort victims, tort reforms in the last few decades have been limiting plaintiffs' recovery and are concerned with retrenchment.

In the early 1900s state legislatures sought to provide a more efficient and fair compensation system by enacting worker's compensation statutes that provided injured workers with a right to compensation for accidents without having to prove fault on the part of their employers. *See, e.g., Ives v. South Buffalo Ry. Co.,* 94 N.E.431 (1911) (holding that worker's compensation statute deprived employers of due process in violation of state constitution because it required payment for accidents without proof of fault); *New York Central Ry. v. White,* 243 U.S. 188 (1917) (holding that worker's compensation statute did not violate Due Process Clause of U.S. Constitution).

After World War II, legislatures and courts around the country enacted progressive reforms aimed at providing greater protection and compensation to accident victims and more effective deterrence to risky or intentionally harmful conduct. THOMAS H. KOENIG & MICHAEL RUSTAD, IN DEFENSE OF TORT LAW 46 (2001). Tort reforms in the post-war period enabled the victims of medical malpractice, products liability, premises liability, and other substantive fields to redress injuries caused by excessive, preventable risks. The early common law insulated government and charities from liability. By 1985, every jurisdiction had abolished or scaled back charitable and other immunities. *Id.* at 54. In the 1940s and 1950s, states began to waive sovereign immunity, permitting recovery for property damage and personal injury caused by government

---

develop their own tort law); Thomas Koenig & Michael L. Rustad, *His and Her Tort Reform: Gender Injustice in Disguise,* 70 U. WASH. L. REV. 1 (1995) (documenting how caps on punitive damages, non-economic damages, and other restrictions negatively impact women plaintiffs); Frank McClellan, *The Dark Side of Tort Reform: Searching for Racial Justice,* 48 RUTGERS L. REV. 761, 784 (1996) (arguing "the only institutions in America where people of color have the power to make immediate wealth redistribution decisions are urban governments and juries"); Deborah Jones Merritt & Kathryn Ann Barry, *Is the Tort System in Crisis? New Empirical Evidence,* 60 OHIO ST. L.J. 315 (1999) (reviewing empirical evidence and finding no evidence of a tort crisis); Joseph A. Page, *Reforming Tort Reform,* 78 GEO. L.J. 649, 651, n.10 (1990) (contending that tort reform is a movement financed by habitual corporate defendants); Michael J. Saks, *Medical Malpractice: Facing Real Problems and Finding Real Solutions,* 35 WM. & MARY L. REV. 693, 703 (1994) (contending that there are too few medical malpractice claims leaving many patients without compensation); Michael L. Rustad, *The Closing of Punitive Damages' Iron Cage,* 38 LOY. L.A. L. REV. 1297 (2005) (contending that tort reforms enacted since 1979 excessively restrict punitive damages).

negligence. *See* Chapter 12, *supra*. Judicial tort reform in the latter half of the twentieth century resulted in the evolution of the doctrine of informed consent in medical malpractice, mass tort and products liability, premises liability, and recovery for prenatal injuries as described in Chapters 7, 9, 10, and 11 *supra*. Reflecting increased interest in the protection of civil liberties and equality, federal courts breathed new life into a Reconstruction-era federal civil rights statute, 42 U.S.C. § 1983, by recognizing a remedy for constitutional torts in a case about a black couple brutalized by police action in *Monroe v. Pape*, 365 U.S. 167 (1961). Principally by legislative efforts, jurisdictions replaced the regressive contributory negligence rule with comparative negligence regimes, described in Chapter 12. By 2000 all but one jurisdiction had moved to comparative negligence, rejecting the contributory negligence bar that was the rule at the turn of the last century.

The late twentieth-century and early twenty-first-century political and legal terrain, however, has been very different. Between 1980 and 2000 "thirty-two states have passed limits on the recovery of punitive damages, thirty-five states have imposed joint and several liability limitations, and eleven have limited potential recoveries for pain and suffering." THOMAS H. KOENIG & MICHAEL L. RUSTAD, IN DEFENSE OF TORT LAW 67 (2001).

This chapter examines some of the relevant commentaries considering this new "reform" movement, examining whether there is or has been a torts crisis which necessitates or supports radical change. The chapter identifies some of the pertinent issues that have been raised, and highlights typical laws proposed or passed in response to the perceived "crisis." The chapter begins with a consideration of the reports underlying calls for retrenchment of tort law in the states during the eighties and nineties. An analysis of the nature, purpose, and effects identified by these reports and their findings provides some guidance and offers perspective in evaluating recent tort retrenchment efforts. After taking a look at some of the principal tort-reform efforts, including judicial responses, the chapter will also explore some alternatives to the traditional adversarial system, including informal summary adjudication and settlement proceedings, the substitution of administrative remedies, and alternative dispute mechanisms such as mediation and arbitration that became popular beginning in the eighties. The chapter will also briefly explore the creation of funds in response to the extraordinary terrorist attack on 9/11 and in response to the peculiar problem of exposure to asbestos.

While reading the materials in this chapter, the student should consider whether these alternative approaches to our traditional process are better or worse than the civil litigation process as we know it. If these alternatives are useful, should tort remedies be retained in addition to these other measures? The reading is designed to raise questions about the civil jury system that require further critical assessment of the retrenchment effort. The jury system operates at the heart of the American civil as well as criminal system and represents a significant aspect of the commitment to democratic government. Are the values promoted by the jury system too great a price to pay in light of the efficiency demands of our current economic system? For an insightful social science perspective on the actual performance of juries in the context of medical malpractice cases, see NEIL VIDMAR, MEDICAL MALPRACTICE AND THE

AMERICAN JURY: CONFRONTING THE MYTHS ABOUT JURY INCOMPETENCE, DEEP POCKETS, AND OUTRAGEOUS DAMAGE AWARDS (1995). Do some of the recent tort reform measures and alternatives that are currently proposed suggest distrust of jurors as decision makers? Has this distrust increased as juries have become more representative in terms of race, ethnicity, and gender, particularly in urban settings? *See, e.g.,* Phoebe A. Haddon, *Rethinking the Jury,* 3 WM. & MARY BILL OF RIGHTS L. REV. 9 (1994); Frank McClellan, *The Dark Side of Tort Reform: Searching for Racial Justice,* 48 RUTGERS L. REV. 761 (1996); Jennifer Wriggins, *Torts, Race and the Value of Injury, 1900-1949,* 49 HOW. L.J. 99 (2005); Eric Helland & Alexander Tabarrok, *Race, Poverty, and American Tort Awards: Evidence from Three Data Sets,* 32 J. LEGAL STUD. 27 (2003*).* One can argue that elimination or substantial curtailment of the tort litigation system in American law would have a dramatic effect on the culture and appearance of justice, notwithstanding the fact that the vast majority of torts cases never reach the courthouse, much less the jury room. But there is no reason why alternative systems of dispute resolution cannot co-exist. Moreover, through experimentation, we can learn more about the successes and failures of tort litigation and the alternative contenders for the resolution of disputes.[3]

B. THE IMPETUS FOR REFORM IN THE EIGHTIES AND NINETIES

In October of 1985, the Attorney General of the United States established the "Tort Policy Working Group," an inter-agency working group consisting of representatives of ten agencies and the White House. One of the primary tasks of the group was to examine what they described as "the rapidly expanding crisis in liability insurance availability and affordability." In its February, 1986 report, the Working Group concluded that a crisis in liability insurance availability and affordability did exist. It attributed the crisis in part to large underwriting losses for 1984 and 1985, and sharp increases in liability premiums. It observed that these losses "appear to be largely a result of coverage written in the late 1970s and early 1980s which may have been underpriced because of the industry's desire to obtain premium income to invest at the then prevailing high interest rates." RICHARD K. WILLARD & ROBERT L. WILLMORE, U.S. DEPT OF JUSTICE, REPORT OF THE TORT POLICY WORKING GROUP ON THE

---

[3] Tort reform literature which considers these and other important questions about the system and decision-making structure abounds. In addition to the readings already mentioned in this chapter above, see Thomas Campbell, Daniel Kessler & George Shepherd, *The Causes and Effects of Liability Reform: Some Empirical Evidence* (National Bureau of Economic Research Working Paper No. 4989); Lucinda M. Finley, *The Hidden Victims of Tort Reform: Women, Children, and the Elderly,* 53 EMORY L.J. 1263 (2004); Marc Galanter, *The Day After the Litigation Explosion,* 46 MD. L. REV. 3 (1986); Samuel Gross & Kent Syverud, *Don't Try: Civil Jury Verdicts in a System Geared to Settlement,* 44 U.C.L.A. L. REV. 1 (1996); James Henderson & Theodore Eisenberg, *The Quiet Revolution in Products Liability: An Empirical Study of Legal Change,* 37 U.C.L.A. L. REV. 479 (1990); J. Clark Kelso, *One Lesson from the Six Monsanto Lectures on Tort Law Reform and Jurisprudence: Recognizing the Limits of Judicial Competence,* 26 VAL. U. L. REV. 765 (1992); George Priest, *The Current Insurance Crisis and Modern Tort Law,* 96 YALE L.J. 1521 (1987).

CAUSES, EXTENT, AND POLICY IMPLICATIONS OF THE CURRENT CRISIS IN INSURANCE AVAILABILITY AND AFFORDABILITY (Feb. 1986).

The Working Group also concluded "developments in tort law are a major cause for the sharp premium increases." It identified four specific problem areas: 1) the "movement toward no-fault liability"; 2) the "undermining of causation"; 3) the "explosive growth" in damage awards, "particularly with regard to noneconomic awards such as pain and suffering or punitive damages"; and 4) "excessive transaction costs of the tort system" where "virtually two-thirds of every dollar paid out through the tort system is lost to attorneys' fees and litigation expenses." *Id.* The Working Group found that there was a large increase in litigation, particularly for products liability and professional malpractice, during the decade preceding 1985. It also found that "the tremendous uncertainty . . . generated by rapidly changing standards of liability and causation" was an important factor in contributing to the lack of availability and affordability of liability insurance. The Working Group recommended eight reforms to tort law that should "significantly alleviate the crisis in insurance availability and affordability." *Id.* They included:

- Return to a fault-based standard for liability.

- Base causation findings on credible scientific and medical evidence and opinions.

- Eliminate joint and several liability where defendants have not acted in concert.

- Limit noneconomic damages (such as pain and suffering, mental anguish, or punitive damages) to a "fair and reasonable" maximum dollar amount.

- Provide for periodic (not lump-sum) payments for future medical care or lost income.

- Reduce awards where a plaintiff can be compensated by certain collateral sources to prevent a windfall double recovery.

- Limit attorneys' contingency fees to reasonable amounts on a "sliding scale."

- Encourage use of alternative dispute resolution mechanisms to resolve cases out of court.

Most states enacted some of these measures during the eighties and nineties. *See* Martha Middleton, *A Changing Landscape*, 81 A.B.A.J. at 56 (Summer 1995). States, moreover, have continued to enact additional tort reforms in the twenty-first century. For example, in 2003, Texas enacted a tort reform statute that capped noneconomic damages to $250,000 per defendant with an absolute limit of $750,000 against all defendants.

In March of 1987, the Tort Policy Working Group issued an "Update" on its 1986 report. The Group found that insurance "availability problems have substantially ameliorated since a year ago," but continued to exist "in certain lines of coverage, where they remain serious." UNITED STATES DEP'T OF JUSTICE, TORT POLICY WORKING GROUP, AN UPDATE ON LIABILITY (March 1987). The

Working Group took issue with the methodology of another study undertaken by the National Center for State Courts, which had disputed the Working Group's position on a crisis, concluding that "there had been only a nine percent increase in tort filings between 1978 and 1984, and . . . this increase roughly mirrored population growth (eight percent) during the same period." *Id.* The Working Group faulted this study among other reasons because it was based on data from only thirteen states, because it aggregated all tort filings, and because it failed "to account for the significant decrease in automobile accident lawsuits which has taken place in recent years." *Id.*

In 1988, the United States General Accounting Office (GAO) issued a report stating: "A variety of considerations enters into insurers' decisions as to whether to offer insurance and, if so, at what rates." U.S. General Accounting Office, Products Liability: Extent of "Litigation Explosion" in the Federal Courts Questioned, GAO/HRD-88-36BR (Jan. 1988). One of the factors cited by insurers for the rapid escalation in liability rates and the withdrawal of some types of insurance during the mid-1980s was a "litigation explosion" as evidenced by the increase in products liability cases filed in federal courts. The report concluded, however, that only one product, asbestos, constituted a significant part of the growth and it also did not find that the growth related to products in general was either rapidly accelerating or explosive. *Id.* Similarly, another pair of commentators observed:

> Total claims . . . increased dramatically during the period from 1975 through 1986. These increased costs, however, were not significantly attributable to an increased number of claims against insured parties during that period. When the number of claims against insureds is adjusted for changes in the risk assumed by insurers because of variations in both the number of insureds and the level of the insureds' activities, the number of incurred claims in Other Liability insurance coverages actually declined during the period from 1975 through 1984.

David Nye & Donald Gifford, *The Myth of the Liability Insurance Claims Explosion: An Empirical Rebuttal*, 41 VAND. L. REV. 909, 922 (1988).

In response to a request from the chairman of the Subcommittee on Commerce, Consumer Protection, and Competitiveness of the United States House of Representatives, the GAO in 1989 issued a report on a study of products liability verdicts and case resolutions in five states for the period 1983-1985. *See* GAO/HRD-89-99 (Sept. 1989). The GAO selected the following states to study: Arizona, Massachusetts, Missouri, North Dakota, and South Carolina. The GAO chose these states based on the amount of information available for products liability litigation, and the relative costs associated with obtaining the information. Although the study did not include large industrial states, the report said that the states represented "a mix in terms of region of the country, degrees of urbanization, numbers of manufacturers and manufacturing employees, and tort laws." *Id.* The GAO found that "in general, damage awards were not erratic or excessive," and that the size of compensatory awards "is strongly associated with injury severity and the amount of the underlying economic loss." Indeed, it found previous studies had shown that "the total amount awarded is frequently insufficient to cover just the economic losses when these losses are large." *Id.*

Some states had already enacted "caps" (discussed below) on punitive damages by the time of the study but the GAO study found few punitive awards in the cases it studied would have exceeded these caps, had the caps applied. The GAO study concluded that appeals and post-trial settlement negotiations "serve to reduce the size of most extremely large awards and eliminate many of the unjustified punitive awards." *Id.* It also stated that defendant's negligence "was a basis for liability in about two-thirds of verdicts for plaintiffs, a higher rate than had been assumed previously." *Id.* The GAO opined that a proposed federal products liability statute would enhance uniformity across states, but "would have affected only a minority of cases studied." *Id.* Two proposals, the adoption of comparative fault and the allowance of a credit against judgment for amounts "previously paid or to be paid by workers' compensation" in connection with an injury, would have potentially affected more awards than other proposed reforms, the GAO concluded. As a consequence, the Report made no recommendations for change. *Id.*

Other nongovernmental studies during the relevant time period also suggest lack of clarity about whether a crisis exists and question whether the tort system is a likely cause of that crisis, if there is one. Studying federal court civil filings from 1978 to 1984, Professor Marc Galanter concluded that while overall civil filings increased by 89% during that period, tort filings increased by only 42%. During the period from 1960 to 1986, because of increases attributable to other categories "tort filings fell to 16.5% of total civil filings — less than half the portion in 1960." Marc Galanter, *The Life and Times of the Big Six, or, the Federal Courts Since the Good Old Days*, 1988 WIS. L. REV. 921, 936. Areas where there were substantial increases included recovery cases brought by the federal government (mainly for overpayment of veterans' benefits and for defaulted student loans), civil rights claims, prisoner petitions, and social security cases. Professor Galanter noted, however, that only a "small fraction of all litigation in the United States takes place in the federal courts," and "patterns in the federal courts are sufficiently distinctive to limit our ability to draw from trends in federal courts conclusions about patterns of litigation elsewhere." *Id.* at 923-24.

A 1987 study by the Rand Corporation found that the total amount awarded by juries as well as the mean verdict increased greatly in San Francisco, California and Cook County, Illinois, in the period between 1960 and 1979. The Rand researchers found little change in traditional tort litigation such as routine automobile accident cases and slip and fall cases. However, it found increases in jury verdicts occurred in what it described as "high stakes" litigation such as medical malpractice and products liability. MARK PETERSON, CIVIL JURIES IN THE 1980S: TRENDS IN JURY TRIALS AND VERDICTS IN CALIFORNIA AND COOK COUNTY, ILLINOIS (THE RAND CORPORATION INSTITUTE FOR CIVIL JUSTICE, 1987) at v. The Rand study found that the median jury verdict decreased in Cook County, Illinois during the 1980s. In contrast, California saw a "substantial increase in the size of awards during the 1980s." *Id.* at vi. The Rand researchers describe "a more complicated picture of jury verdicts during the 1980s because the number and types of trials changed." *Id.* at v.

Some commentators have characterized the tort liability crisis as one generated by the insurance industry trying to explain rising insurance rates. *See* Henry Reske, *Was There a Liability Crisis?* 75 A.B.A. J. 46 (Jan. 1989). The author reported that:

> [l]awsuits filed by 19 states in state courts and in federal court in California are forcing a re-examination of the "liability crisis" and the accusing finger is pointed directly at the insurance industry, which has been in the vanguard of the tort reform movement. The antitrust suits charge that four major insurance companies and some 28 other defendants illegally conspired to limit the availability of commercial general liability insurance, including pollution coverage, and to cut their share of other costs, such as legal expenses to defend against claims. . . . The insurance industry has two sources of income: it makes money from selling policies and from investments. When interest rates are high, as they were in the late 1970s and early 1980s, the insurance industry reaps the benefits. Prices were cut as companies competed to sell more policies to generate more money to invest. The *Wall Street Journal,* quoting the General Accounting Office, said that in 1983 industry profits on general-liability insurance dropped to $118 million from $847 million in 1979. To make up for the low profits, insurance rates began to rise . . . .

Id. at 50.

In Nicolas Terry, *The Malpractice Crisis in the United States: A Dispatch from the Trenches,* 2(5) PROF. NEGLIGENCE 145 (1986), Professor Terry offers a perspective on the relationship between the insurance industry's pricing and increases in medical malpractice premiums that were said by others to be linked to litigation costs and burgeoning claims:

> During the late 1970s interest rates were high. Therefore, the insurance industry was able to record very high investment returns on its premiums prior to paying out any claims. High profits generated increased interest in writing policies by insurers to acquire investment income, and hence increased competition between insurers. . . .

> As the market went "soft" some panic-stricken insurers pulled out of markets or looked for quick ways to recoup their previous discounts. Insurers increased medical malpractice premiums and orchestrated a "crisis" which "focus[ed] the public's, the health industry's and the legislatures' anger upon the lawyers."

Id. at 148.

An article by Donald C. Dilworth, in TRIAL, summarizes the 1994 findings of the National Center for State Courts concerning litigation increases and excessive verdicts in its report, *Examining the Work of State Courts*:

> Between 1984 and 1994, civil caseloads rose only 24 percent, while criminal caseloads rose 35 percent, juvenile caseloads 59 percent, and domestic relations caseloads 65 percent. Most tort cases filed in state courts are automobile cases (60 percent) or premises cases (17 percent). Medical negligence and products liability cases together account

for less than 10 percent of tort claims. Only 3 percent of tort cases are resolved by jury trial. At those trials, plaintiffs in 1994 won 49 percent of the time.

The median award to plaintiffs who won at jury trials was $51,000. Million-dollar awards, cited frequently as an indicator that the tort system is "out of control," were awarded in only 8 percent of jury trials won by plaintiffs (one-tenth of 1 percent of tort cases). Juries awarded punitive damages in only 4 percent of tort cases in which the defendant was found liable. The median punitive damages award was $38,000.

Donald C. Dilworth, *Court Statistics Confirm No Litigation Explosion*, TRIAL (May 1996) at 19. Dilworth concludes: "Although torts are currently center stage in the civil litigation debate, there is no evidence that the number of tort cases is increasing. In fact, litigation declined steadily since 1990." *Id. See also* Marc Galanter, *The Day After the Litigation Explosion*, 46 MD. L. REV. 3 (1986) (challenging the perception that litigiousness prompted insurance rate increases.)

C. IS THERE A TORT CRISIS? THE DEBATE CONTINUES

There continues to be significant controversy in the research and conclusions of proponents and opponents of tort reform as to whether there is or ever was adequate substantiation of a problem or set of problems in need of being addressed through statutory or other reform. *See, e.g.,* Jordyn McAfree, *Medical Malpractice Crisis Factional or Fictional?: An Overview of the GAO Report as Interpreted by the Proponents and Opponents of Tort Reform*, 9 MICH. ST. J. MED. & LAW 161 (2005). Despite scholarly debate, much of the public (including students) have come to believe that frivolous law suits and escalating, unfair verdicts won by greedy plaintiffs and their attorneys have hurt business and the economy. Reconsider the discussion in Chapter 1, *supra*, on the McDonald's coffee case. *See, e.g.*, Stephen Daniels & Joanne Martin, *The Impact That It Has Had Is Between People's Ears: Tort Reform, Mass Culture, and the Plaintiffs' Lawyers*, 50 DE PAUL L. REV. 453 (2000). Regardless of the weight of the evidence suggesting that reform was necessary in the eighties and nineties, has the need for additional measures of reform ended? Noting the American public's "love-hate relationship with tort," Professor John C.P. Goldberg observes:

We tend to froth over accounts — often distorted — of hundreds of thousands or even millions of dollars changing hands over repainted BMWs and spilled coffee. On the other hand, many of us are apparently anxious to retain the right to sue HMOs for negligent coverage decisions. More fundamentally, we cannot really accept that, when it is one of "us" — instead of one of "those" whiners who is the victim of a wrongdoing — the state need not provide a means of individualized redress.

John C.P. Goldberg, *Unloved: Tort in the Modern Legal Academy*, 55 VAND. L. REV. 1501, 1503 (2002). Despite this ambivalence, Professor Goldberg observes that notions of responsibility and recourse that undergird tort law remain an unusually prominent feature of political culture, affecting the impetus for "reform."

In his 2007 State of the Union Address, President George W. Bush asked Congress for federal tort reform (as he has frequently done during his years of administration). Congress has, in fact, enacted a number of federal tort reform measures. The General Aviation Revitalization Act of 1994, Pub. L. No. 103-298, 108 Stat. 1552 (codified in 49 U.S.C. §40101 (2007), was the first federal tort reform statute. This federal statute imposed an eighteen-year statute of repose for claims involving small aircraft. Two years later, Congress enacted the Small Business Protection Act of 1996, Pub. L. No. 104-188 §1(a), 110 Stat. 1755 (codified in scattered sections of 26 U.S.C. (2007)), which gave small businesses a tax deduction for punitive damages and noneconomic damages. The Amtrak Reform and Accountability Act of 1997, Pub. L. No. 105-134 §2, 111 Stat. 2571 (reprinted in notes for 49 U.S.C. §24101 (2007)), imposed a $200 million cap on total damages for Amtrak accidents. In 1998, Congress enacted the Biomaterial Access Assurance Act of 1998, Pub. L. No. 105-23, §1, 112 Stat. 1519 (codified at 21 U.S.C. §§1601-1606 (2007)) which gave the suppliers of raw material or components of medical implants immunity from products liability lawsuits. THOMAS H. KOENIG & MICHAEL L. RUSTAD, IN DEFENSE OF TORT LAW 65 (2002). The Class Action Fairness Act, Pub. L. No. 109-1, 119 Stat. 4 (codified at 28 U.S.C. §1332(d) (2007), conferred federal diversity jurisdiction over class actions where the plaintiffs' aggregate amount in controversy is greater than $5 million. 28 U.S.C. §1332(d)(2) (2007). The federal class action statute also changes rules for aggregating claims and caps punitive damages. *Id.* §1332(d)(3) (2007). Congress has also recently enacted immunity provisions for gun manufacturers. *See* Protection of Lawful Commerce in Arms Act, Pub. L. No. 109-92, §2, 119 Stat. 2095, codified at 15 U.S.C. §§7901-03 (2007).

Notwithstanding the narrowly defined national tort reform statutes identified above, broad-scale federal legislative reform efforts have for the most part been unsuccessful. Congress has considered:

- The establishment of a national no-fault auto insurance system which eliminates the concept of fault (by not having to prove it) but reduces recovery for injuries

- Changes to the rights of plaintiffs to bring class action lawsuits

- Caps on noneconomic damages at $250,000

- Limits on attorneys' fees, either as part of settlement or in judgments

- Legal immunity for certain industries like drug companies, nursing homes, medical device manufacturers, and HMOs

- Restrictions on punitive damage awards

- Caps or changes in the standard of care or burden of proof in medical malpractice, products, and other liability claims.

As discussed more fully below, many of these provisions have been enacted into state law. What does the congressional willingness to support discrete, industry-focused retrenchment efforts (rather than broad-based change) suggest? Is there a need for further reform — statewide or at the federal level? Is this continued push for reform symbolic of a movement away from an earlier focus on social equality reflected in the Civil Rights movement to one concerned with individual responsibility as a way of thinking about justice? Consider your response in light of the perspectives found in Chapter 1.

NOTES

1. *Disparities in Findings about the Tort Crisis.* How does one explain the widely differing findings and conclusions of the Tort Policy Working Group and GAO Reports? Notice that federal government agencies prepared the dueling studies of the tort system, although the GAO was likely more independent of federal executive positions than the Tort Policy Working Group. The Galanter study raises questions about the existence of a tort crisis, if one can assume the federal picture approximates that in the state courts. *See also* Marc Galanter, *Real World Torts: An Antidote to Anecdote*, 55 MD. L. REV. 1093 (1996). What considerations led to the assumption that a crisis (or several) crises existed — or continues?

Advocates of "tort reform" also assert that punitive damage awards have made substantial contributions to the "tort crisis." Contradicting this assertion, Professor Landes and Judge Posner found no evidence of skyrocketing punitive damages awards, in either size or number. WILLIAM M. LANDES & RICHARD A. POSNER, THE ECONOMIC STRUCTURE OF TORT LAW, 304-07 (1987) (insignificance of punitive damages in sample is evidence that they are not being routinely awarded). *See also* Michael Rustad & Thomas Koenig, *Reconceptualizing Punitive Damages in Medical Malpractice: Targeting Amoral Corporations, Not "Moral Monsters,"* 47 RUTGERS L. REV. 975, 981–92 (1995) (concluding that medical malpractice cases decided in state and federal courts over three decades rarely awarded punitive damages); Deborah Jones Merritt & Kathryn Ann Barry, *Is the Tort System in Crisis? New Empirical Evidence*, 60 OHIO ST. L.J. 315, 388 (1999) (uncovering no punitive awards in medical malpractice or products liability cases in a twelve-year period in Franklin County, Ohio).

2. *Is There a Torts Crisis?* Given the controversy as to what caused the shortage and high cost of insurance in the eighties and conflicting views about whether there were alarming increases in tort-related filings and awards (aside from asbestos), was tort "reform" justified? How should courts respond to the legislative efforts to meet a perceived crisis in light of these uncertainties? Are there constitutional constraints on what the legislatures can do in response to these perceived crises?

Some commentators have suggested that we need more empirical research to shed light on the civil litigation process in order to properly address the sources of problems. *See* Michael Saks, *If There Be a Crisis, How Shall We*

Know It?, 46 MD. L. REV. 63 (1986). Others offer evidence that perceptions about systematic problems are misplaced. *See, e.g.,* Merritt & Barry, *supra,* 60 OHIO ST. L.J. 315. *But see, e.g.,* Gerald Walpin, *America's Failing Civil Justice System: Can We Learn from Other Countries?*, 41 N.Y.L. SCH. L. REV. 647 (1997) (presenting anecdotal evidence of tort crisis because of costs, delays and mechanisms unique to American system such as class actions and civil jury rights). If the assumptions about a crisis are unfounded or questionable at best, is it troublesome that tort reform measures often adversely affect members of groups that are least able to protect themselves with insurance or other provisions for "safety-nets"? *See* Frank M. McClellan, *The Dark Side of Tort Reform: Searching for Racial Justice*, 48 RUTGERS L. REV. 761 (1996); Lucinda Finley, *Female Trouble: The Implications of Tort Reform for Women*, 64 TENN. L. REV. 847 (1997). *See also Ferdon v. Wisconsin Patients Compensation Fund*, 701 N.W.2d 440 (2005), discussed *infra.* Recent technological advancements in courthouses across the country can facilitate data collection about suits, permitting scholars to address questions about the litigation process and to learn more about the effects of particular reform alternatives.

3. *Continuing Crisis?* It is notable that the Working Groups' recommendations included return to fault-based liability and causation rules. Have courts promoted meaningful tort "reform"? For example, does the approach of the Restatement (Third) of Torts in products liability (discussed in Chapter 10, *supra*) and apportionment (discussed in Chapter 15, *supra*) suggest that retrenchment by judicial decision making is successful? *See* Thomas C. Galligan, Jr., *U.S. Supreme Court Tort Reform: Limiting State Power to Articulate and Develop Tort Law Defamation, Preemption, and Punitive Damages*, 74 U. CIN. L. REV. 1189 (2006) (documenting Supreme Court reformist strategies).

4. *Strict Liability, Fault-Based Liability, and Social Justice: Ideological Flip-Flop.* According to Stephen Sugarman, tort reform in recent years has witnessed an ideological shift. Conservatives once defended the tort system and liberals sought to reform it. Now, the "left" embraces the tort system and the "right" pushes for tort reform. In addition to taking an "ideological somersault, American tort law has become much more politically prominent." Stephen D. Sugarman, Ideological Flip-Flop: American Liberals Are Now the Primary Supporters of Tort Law 1 (U.C. Berkeley Public Law Research Paper No. 925244, available at http://papers.ssrn.com/sol3/papers.cfm?abstract_id =925244. Sugarman explains that in the past, conservatives supported tort law because it resonated with conservative values such as individual responsibility for his/her/its harm. In contrast, the ideological left divided on tort law values. For example, many on the left shy away from blaming individuals for social woes resulting from structural factors while liberal populists are eager to blame "business and political leaders for abusing power at the expense of the ordinary citizen." *Id.* at 2. Also, many on the left have been skeptical about whether technological progress is "progress"; as a consequence, the left has been pushing for strict liability to ensure "progress" pays its way.

Today, the support for tort law has witnessed an "ideological somersault"; the left supports the fault-based system and the right calls for reform. Sugarman observes that these changes in the ideological landscape accompanied the erosion of many of the defense-side structural advantages, previously enjoyed by enterprise defendants and insurers of defendants. Now, on the left are the "main supporters of the fault-based tort system — calling it a crucial weapon in support of progressive causes." *Id.* at 14. The victims are winning in court: "Liberal supporters today seem uninterested in converting tort law itself into an efficient compensation machine. They are not generally pushing to turn tort law from a fault system into a strict liability system . . . [because] they want to be able to prove fault . . . as a way of achieving larger verdicts." *Id.* at 14.

Faced with ever increasing tort liability exposure, conservatives confront the ideological paradox of "reduc[ing] and stabiliz[ing] the exposure faced by their business and insurer allies, while remaining committed to the basic idea of private law as society's core mechanism for accident regulation and victim compensation." *Id.* at 16. The conservatives have taken their tort reform fight to the legislature, seeking to put caps on damages or restrict other access to the courts.

D.   LIMITATIONS ON RECOVERY

1.   Caps on Damages

The tort reform movement of the 1970s and 1980s spawned legislation designed to reduce the amount of recovery by an injured victim as a means of stemming rising insurance costs and, as a consequence, manufacturing, healthcare, and other industry costs. One common type of legislation places an upper limit, or "cap," on the amount of damages that a personal injury plaintiff can recover. The cap frequently applies only to noneconomic damages, i.e., damages other than medical expenses and loss of earnings. *See, e.g.,* ALASKA STAT. § 09.17.010 (2007) (limiting noneconomic damages for personal injuries to $1 million, or the injured party's life expectancy multiplied by $25,000, whichever is greater); CAL. CIV. CODE § 3333.2 (2007) (the most frequently cited model for caps on medical malpractice awards, this thirty-year-old statute limits recovery of noneconomic damages in medical malpractice claims to $250,000); COLO. REV. STAT. 13-21-102.5 (2006) (capping most noneconomic damages for tort claims other than medical malpractice at $250,000, with an outer limit of $500,000); MISS. CODE ANN. § 11-1-60 (2007) (limiting noneconomic damages to $500,000 for medical malpractice claims, and $1 million for all other claims); OHIO REV. CODE ANN. 2315.18 (2007) (limiting noneconomic damages to the greater of $250,000 or three times the amount of economic damages, with exceptions made for certain long-term injuries). The perceived medical malpractice "crisis" in the seventies also led legislators to limit damages recoverable in medical malpractice actions and to similarly insulate other industries from claims discussed below.

Legal scholars who have studied the effects of reform such as caps have tended to be skeptical as to whether the reforms have achieved the objectives of containing costs of suits or alleviating the problem of availability and price of insurance. *See* Alexee Deep Conroy, *Lessons Learned from the "Laboratories of Democracy": A Critique of Federal Medical Liability Reform*, 91 CORNELL L.

REV. 1159, 1202 (2006); Ryan T. Emery, *Unwise and Unnecessary: Statutory Caps on Non-Economic Damages in Medical Malpractice Cases and the Appellate Review Alternative,* 69 ALB. L. REV. 913 (2006); Adam D. Glassman, *The Imposition of Federal Caps in Medical Malpractice Liability Actions: Will They Cure the Current Crisis in Health Care?,* 37 AKRON L. REV. 417 (2004); Elizabeth Stewart Poisson, *Addressing the Impropriety of Statutory Caps on Pain and Suffering Awards in the Medical Liability System,* 82 N.C. L. REV. 759 (2004); Catherine M. Sharkey, *Unintended Consequences of Medical Malpractice Damage Caps,* 80 N.Y.U. L. REV. 391 (2005).

The principal case which follows identifies some of the earlier bases for challenging damage caps. Are these arguments against imposition of legislative caps persuasive? What is the strongest argument in favor of finding such a cap unlawful? Do such arguments have applicability in other, more recent retrenchment contexts?

SOFIE v. FIBREBOARD CORP.
771 P.2d 711 (Wash. 1989)

UTTER, JUSTICE.

Austin and Marcia Sofie challenge the constitutionality of RCW 4.56.250. This statute, part of the 1986 tort reform act, places a limit on the noneconomic damages recoverable by a personal injury or wrongful death plaintiff. The Sofies brought a direct appeal to this court after the trial judge in their tort action, under the direction of the statute, reduced the jury's award of noneconomic damages. . . .

The Sofies argue that RCW 4.56.250 violates their constitutional rights to trial by jury, equal protection, and due process. We find that the statute's damages limit interferes with the jury's traditional function to determine damages. Therefore, RCW 4.56.250 violates article 1, section 21 of the Washington Constitution, which protects as inviolate the right to a jury. . . .

The Washington Legislature passed RCW 4.56.250 in 1986 partly as a response to rising insurance premiums for liability coverage. The damages limit that the statute creates operates on a formula based upon the age of the plaintiff.[1]

---

[1] RCW 4.56.250 states:

"(1) As used in this section, the following terms have the meanings indicated unless the context clearly requires otherwise.

"(a) 'Economic damages' means objectively verifiable monetary losses, including medical expenses, loss of earnings, burial costs, loss of use of property, cost of replacement or repair, cost of obtaining substitute domestic services, loss of employment, and loss of business or employment opportunities.

"(b) 'Noneconomic damages' means subjective, nonmonetary losses, including, but not limited to pain, suffering, inconvenience, mental anguish, disability or disfigurement incurred by the injured party, emotional distress, loss of society and companionship, loss of consortium, injury to reputation and humiliation, and destruction of the parent-child relationship.

. . .

As a result, the older a plaintiff is, the less he or she will be able to recover in noneconomic damages. The trial judge applies the limit to the damages found by the trier of fact. If the case is tried before a jury, the jury determines the amount of noneconomic damages without knowledge of the limit. The jury goes about its normal business and the judge reduces, according to the statute's formula and without notifying the jury, any damage verdicts that exceed the limit.

In September 1987, the Sofies sued Fibreboard Corporation and other asbestos manufacturers for the harm caused to Mr. Sofie by their asbestos products. Mr. Sofie, then aged 67, was suffering from a form of lung cancer — mesothelioma — caused by exposure to asbestos during his career as a pipefitter. At trial, Mr. Sofie's attorneys presented evidence of the extreme pain he experienced as a result of the disease. The testimony indicated that Mr. Sofie spent what remained of his life waiting for the next "morphine cocktail," for the next hot bath, for anything that would lessen his consuming physical agony.

At the end of the trial, the jury found the defendants at fault for Mr. Sofie's disease. They returned a verdict of $1,345,833 in favor of the Sofies. Of this amount, $1,154,592 went to compensate noneconomic damages: $477,200 for Mr. Sofie's pain and suffering and $677,392 for Mrs. Sofie's loss of consortium. While the trial judge specifically found the jury's finding of damages reasonable, he indicated he was compelled under the damages limit to reduce the noneconomic portion of the verdict to $125,136.45, resulting in a total judgment of $316,377.45.

Appellants argue that RCW 4.56.250 violates their right to equal protection under the law as guaranteed by [Washington Constitution article 1, section 12]. This constitutional provision states:

No law shall be passed granting to any citizen, class of citizens, or corporation other than municipal, privileges or immunities which upon the same terms shall not equally belong to all citizens, or corporations.

[The court notes that varying levels of scrutiny have been applied by different courts reviewing laws under such a constitutional provision.]

Courts in some other states have struck down similar tort damage limits on equal protection grounds. *See, e.g., Carson v. Maurer,* 424 A.2d 825, 830 (N.H. 1980) (striking limit on noneconomic damages after finding right to

---

"(2) In no action seeking damages for personal injury or death may a claimant recover a judgment for noneconomic damages exceeding an amount determined by multiplying 0.43 by the average annual wage and by the life expectancy of the person incurring noneconomic damages, as the life expectancy is determined by the life expectancy tables adopted by the insurance commissioner. For purposes of determining the maximum amount allowable for noneconomic damages, a claimant's life expectancy shall not be less than fifteen years. The limitation contained in this subsection applies to all claims for noneconomic damages made by a claimant who incurred bodily injury. Claims for loss of consortium, loss of society and companionship, destruction of the parent-child relationship, and all other derivative claims asserted by persons who did not sustain bodily injury are to be included within the limitation on claims for noneconomic damages arising from the same bodily injury.

"(3) If a case is tried to a jury, the jury shall not be informed of the limitation contained in subsection (2) of this section."

recover for personal injuries an "important substantive right").... Other courts, however, have upheld limits, analyzing the legislation under the rational basis test. *See, e.g., Fein v. Permanente Medical Group,* 695 P.2d 665 (Cal. 1985), *appeal dismissed,* 474 U.S. 892 (1985); *see also Boyd v. Bulala,* 647 F. Supp. 781 (W.D. Va. 1986) (finding that damages limit passes the rational basis test under equal protection analysis but violates the right to a jury trial)....

The dispositive issue of this case is the right to a jury trial.

This court has long approached the review of legislative enactments with great care. The wisdom of legislation is not justiciable; our only power is to determine the legislation's constitutional validity. In matters of economic legislation, we follow the rule giving every reasonable presumption in favor of the constitutionality of the law or ordinance. We employ this caution to avoid substituting our judgment for the judgment of the Legislature....

[Concluding that the Federal Constitution's Seventh Amendment jury guarantees do not apply to state civil trials under the Fourteenth Amendment, the Court looked to the state constitution].

Article 1, section 21 states:

> The right of trial by jury shall remain inviolate, but the legislature may provide for a jury of any number less than twelve in courts not of record, and for a verdict by nine or more jurors in civil cases in any court of record, and for waiving of the jury in civil cases where the consent of the parties interested is given thereto.

Our basic rule in interpreting article 1, section 21 is to look to the right as it existed at the time of the constitution's adoption in 1889....

State ex rel. Mullen v. Doherty, [16 Wash. 382, 47 P. 958 (1897)], being close in time to 1889, provides some contemporary insight.... In *Mullen,* we cited section 248 of the Code of 1881, in force at the time of the constitution's passage, to determine the jury's role in the constitutional scheme: "either party shall have the right in an action at law, upon an issue of fact, to demand a trial by jury." *Mullen,* 16 Wash. at 385. Subsequent cases underscore the jury's fact finding province as the essence of the right's scope.

At issue in the present case is whether the measure of damages is a question of fact within the jury's province. Our past decisions show that it is indeed....

The jury's role in determining noneconomic damages is perhaps even more essential. In *Bingaman v. Grays Harbor Community Hosp.,* 699 P.2d 1230 (Wash. 1985), the husband of a woman who died painfully 35 hours after giving birth, the result of medical malpractice, brought a wrongful death and survival action. The only issue before this court was whether the trial judge had properly reduced the jury's damage verdict of $412,000 for the woman's pain and suffering. In resolving the issue in the plaintiff's favor, we stated: "The determination of the amount of damages, *particularly in actions of this nature,* is primarily and peculiarly within the province of the jury, ..." (Italics ours.)....

... The weight of authority from other states, both numerically and persuasively, supports the conclusion that Washington's damages limit violates the right to trial by jury....

NOTES

1. *Constitutionality of Caps.* More than half the states have now adopted some form of statutory caps on awards for noneconomic harm. The cases continue to divide on whether damage caps like that challenged in *Sofie* are constitutional. *Compare English v. New England Med. Ctr., Inc.*, 541 N.E.2d 329 (Mass. 1989) (statutory cap on tort liability of charitable institutions held constitutional) *with Best v. Taylor Mach. Works, Inc.*, 689 N.E.2d 1057 (Ill. 1997) (cap offends special legislation prohibition and violates separation of powers). *See also Trovato v. DeVeau*, 736 A.2d 1212 (N.H. 1999) ($50,000 cap on wrongful death claims where no dependent relative survives violates right to remedy and equal protection); *Brannigan v. Usitalo*, 587 A.2d 1232 (N.H. 1991) (limitation of noneconomic damages to $875,000 violates equal protection). Some courts have found the limitation on noneconomic damages — particularly if the ceiling amount is low — offends fundamental notions of fairness and therefore is in violation of the state's due process clause. *See Morris v. Savoy*, 576 N.E.2d 765 (Ohio 1991) (finding that absent any evidence that medical malpractice claims exceeding $200,000 were responsible for higher insurance rates, a cap designed to promote the general welfare at the expense of the most injured plaintiffs was arbitrary and unreasonable). Do you agree with the reasoning and the conclusion that such caps are fundamentally unfair? In *Judd ex rel. Montgomery v. Drezga*, 103 P.3d 135 (Utah 2004), the court concluded that a statutory cap on quality of life damages was not arbitrary or unreasonable. It stated that

> [a]lthough malpractice insurance rates may not be entirely controlled by [damage awards], they are undoubtedly subject to some measure of fluctuation based on paid claims. . . . While it is recognized that such a cap heavily punishes those most severely injured, it . . . has no impact on a victim's recovery of damages for actual expenses, loss of earning capacity, or other economic measures of injury. Rather, it is limited to the one area where caps have proven effective — quality of life damages, which are difficult to predict but nevertheless must be accounted for by insurers.

Id. at 142. Contrary to the reasoning in *Sofie*, above, the court concluded that the statutory reform measure did not violate the right to a jury trial because the jury had fulfilled its role when it determined the amount of diminishment of the child's quality of life even though the amount arrived at exceeded the cap. *Id.* at 144. The court reasoned that the cap represented the law to be applied, not an improper usurpation of jury prerogatives. For a discussion of the positions taken by courts in response to caps, see Robert S. Peck, *Violating the Inviolate: Caps on Damages and the Right to Trial by Jury*, 31 DAYTON L. REV. 307 (2006).

2. *Effects of Caps on Women, Minorities, and the Elderly.* Is a more persuasive basis for challenging these caps that they unfairly limit recovery for claims that are purely emotional and therefore more profoundly affect some plaintiffs, like women, the elderly, and the poor, groups who are less likely to have amassed economic damages? *See* Lucinda M. Finley, *The Hidden Victims of Tort Reform: Women, Children, and the Elderly*, 53 EMORY L.J. 1263, 1265 (2004) (arguing, based on empirical data, that "[w]hile damages caps are not likely to alter the hard market/soft market cycles that affect premium rates and insurance availability, they do make it less likely that certain types of injuries will be redressed through the courts. . . . Moreover, the effects of this changed legal landscape do not fall equally on all members of U.S. society. . . . [Rather they] have a significant adverse impact on women and the elderly."). *See also* Frank M. McClellan, *The Dark Side of Tort Reform: Searching for Racial Justice,* 48 RUTGERS L. REV. 761 (1996) (examining the effects of caps and other reform on people of color).

3. *Other Effects of Caps?* What other implications of caps should be considered in evaluating the caps' efficacy and fairness? *See* Robert D. Cooter & Ariel Porat, *Liability Externalities and Mandatory Choices: Should Doctors Pay Less?* http:// www.bepress.com/jtl/vol1/iss1/art2; Mary J. Davis, *Mass Tort Litigation: Congress' Silent But Deadly Reform Effort,* 64 TENN. L. REV. 913 (1997) (criticizing proposed tort reform measures that reduce protection of public by reducing deterrence of tortfeasors); Linda Babcock & Greg Pogarsky, *Damage Caps and Settlement: A Behavioral Approach,* 28 J. LEG. STUD. 341 (1999) (caps affect settlement propensity). *See also* Catherine M. Sharkey, *Unintended Consequences of Medical Malpractice Damages Caps,* 80 N.Y.U. L. REV. 391, 493 (2005) (empirical evidence uncovers "cross-over" effect, resulting in total damage amounts staying stable despite caps on noneconomic damages).

2. Structured Payments

Another device designed to reduce tort recovery is the "structured judgment," in which the victim receives periodic payment of future accruing installments of loss of earnings and medical expenses rather than a lump sum payment based on a projected life (and income-earning) span. The installments terminate when the victim dies. Thus, if the victim does not live through her projected life span, there is a reduction of the tortfeasor's liability. *See, e.g., American Bank & Trust Co. v. Community Hosp. of Los Gatos-Saratoga,* 683 P.2d 670 (Cal. 1984). *But see Desiderio v. Ochs,* 791 N.E.2d 941 (N.Y. 2003). The structured judgment is an outgrowth of the structured settlement, in which the parties agree that the victim will receive stipulated sums periodically for a fixed period of time, usually the victim's lifetime. The structured settlement provides the victim with financial security throughout the person's lifetime, while effecting a saving to the tortfeasor, and has developed into a useful settlement negotiation tool that may be attractive to plaintiffs and defendants.

> Structured settlements are a type of settlement designed to provide certain tax advantages. In a structured settlement the claimant receives periodic payments rather than a lump sum, and all of these payments are considered damages received on account of personal injuries or sickness and are thus excludable from income. Accordingly, a structured settlement effectively shelters from taxation the returns from the investment of the lump-sum payment.

Arneson v. Arneson, 670 N.W.2d 904, 914-15 (S.D. 2003).

A court cannot issue a structured judgment without agreement of the parties or statutory authorization. *Gretchen v. United States,* 618 F.2d 177 (2d Cir.

1980). A structured judgment entered over the objection of plaintiff raises significant issues regarding freedom of choice and self-determination. Some states have required or permitted "structured judgments" in medical malpractice cases and in suits against public entities. *See, e.g.,* CAL. CIV. PROC. CODE § 667.7 (2007); LA. REV. STAT. § 40:1299.42 (2007). *See generally* Thomas Elligett, *Periodic Payment of Judgments,* 46 INS. COUN. J. 130 (1979); Philip Corboy, *Structured Injustice: Compulsory Periodic Payment of Judgments,* 66 A.B.A. J. 1524 (1980); Charles Krause, *Structured Settlements for Tort Victims,* 66 A.B.A. J. 1527 (1980).

NOTES

1. *Structured Settlements vs. Structured Judgments.* What concerns are raised by requiring structured judgments as contrasted with a negotiated structured settlement? The Ohio Supreme Court in *Galayda v. Lake Hospital Systems,* 644 N.E.2d 298 (Ohio 1994), held that the state's medical negligence periodic-payment statute violated state constitutional rights of trial by jury and due process because the statute prohibited plaintiffs from receiving their whole jury award. The court further found insufficient evidence of any relation between the statute and the availability or affordability of medical negligence insurance. Notably, a structured settlement or structured judgment is subject to uncertainties regarding the financial solvency of the long-term payer.

2. *Law and Economics of Periodic Payments.* Commentators agree that the proper way to analyze a structured settlement as a matter of economics is as a cash settlement from the tortfeasor to the victim of the discounted present value of the structured settlement, followed by a loan of the present value from the victim to the tortfeasor in return for the structured payments.

Gregory L. Germain, *Avoiding Phantom Income in Bankruptcy: A Proposal for Reform,* 5 FLA. TAX L. REV. 249, 251 (2001). Which payment mechanism is more consistent with the goal of deterrence, the lump sump or periodic payment method of paying damages? What kinds of concerns will a social justice proponent raise in response to a proposal to structure a settlement discounted to present value?

3. *Medical Surveillance Expenses Conceptualized as Periodic Payment.* A court may award a plaintiff the remedy of medical monitoring in a toxic torts case. Periodic medical examinations may be required where a plaintiff has been exposed to pollutants but has not yet manifested a disease. *See* Amy B. Blumenberg, *Medical Monitoring Funds: The Periodic Payment of Future Medical Surveillance Expenses in Toxic Exposure Litigation,* 43 HAST. L.J. 661, 661 (1992) (comparing medical surveillance expenses to periodic payment awards).

3. Punitive Damages

Much of the tort reform controversy has centered on punitive damages. Over half of the states have enacted some limitation on punitive damages by statute. For example, Georgia caps punitive damage awards at $250,000 for all claims except ones based on products liability or cases where the tortfeasor was willfully impaired at the time when he/she harmed the plaintiff. GA. CODE ANN. § 51-12-5.1 (2007). Idaho also sets the punitive damages cap at $250,000 or three times the actual damages, whichever is greater. IDAHO CODE ANN. § 6-1604 (2007). Virginia has a $350,000 limit, VA. CODE ANN. § 8.01-38.1 (2006), while Kansas limits punitive damages to the lesser of the defendant's annual gross income, or $5 million, or one-and-one-half times the profit the defendant gained from the misconduct. KAN. STAT. ANN. § 60-3702 (2006). In order to recover punitive damages, some states require proof that conduct was "outrageous" or "evidenced reckless indifference" by "clear and convincing" evidence. *See, e.g.,* ALASKA STAT. § 09.17.020 (2007); KY. REV. STAT. ANN. § 411.184 (2006).

Empirical studies have not borne out the contentions that punitive damages are awarded frequently, are often excessive, or are burgeoning. *See* Neil Vidmar & Mary Rose, *Punitive Damages by Juries in Florida: In Terrorem and In Reality*, 38 HARV. J. ON LEGIS. 487, 507-511 (2001). Notwithstanding the lack of empirical support for the view that punitive damage awards are out of control, many state legislatures have passed statutes to restrict the award of punitive damages. Forty-five out of the fifty-one state jurisdictions and the District of Columbia either do not recognize punitive damages or have enacted one or more limitations on this remedy since 1979. Michael L. Rustad, *The Closing of Punitive Damages' Iron Cage,* 38 LOY. L.A. L. REV. 1297, 1360 (2005) (documenting tort reforms in fifty-one jurisdiction survey). The vast majority of states have enacted reforms such as raising the burden of proof from preponderance of the evidence to "clear and convincing" evidence. Colorado is the only state to require proof of punitive damages beyond a reasonable doubt. *Id.* at 1324.

Twenty-two states have strengthened jury instructions in punitive damages litigation. *Id.* at 1360. A growing number of states are requiring the plaintiff to remit a portion of the award to the state treasury. Ten states require the plaintiff to share a portion of the award with the state treasury or a designated public entity. Alaska requires half of every award be deposited into that state's general fund. ALASKA STAT. § 09.17.020(j) (2007). Georgia's state-sharing requires payment of 75% of punitive damages to the state. GA. CODE ANN. § 51-12-5.1(e)(2) (2007). A number of states restrict the pleading of punitive damages, prohibit ad damnum clauses (i.e., mentioning the amount of money sought), and restrict evidence on punitive damages, including limiting admissibility of corporate wealth, delay discovery of financial evidence, and bifurcate trials into the compensatory and punitive damages phases. For additional discussion of punitive damage formulations see Chapter 15.

The United States Supreme Court also has expressed concern about unlimited damage awards. The Court in *TXO Production Corp. v. Alliance Resources Corp.*, 509 U.S. 443, 458 (1993), observed that there is no "mathematical bright line" for determining whether punitive damages are so grossly excessive they violate the defendant's constitutional guarantees. In a number of recent cases, however, the Court has indicated that juries are limited in their ability to confer punitive damages that lack proportionality to compensable harm and suggested that something more than a single-digit ratio of compensable to punitive damages might prove troublesome. The Court has also concluded that states lack authority to punish defendants using punitive damages in response to conduct outside of the state or for conduct bearing no relation to harm targeted in the victim's claims. For a more detailed discussion of the Supreme Court's disposition of cases related to punitive damages, see Chapter 15.

STATE FARM MUTUAL AUTOMOBILE INS. CO. v. CAMPBELL
538 U.S. 408 (2003)

KENNEDY, JUSTICE.

We address once again the measure of punishment, by means of punitive damages, a State may impose upon a defendant in a civil case. The question is whether, in the circumstances we shall recount, an award of $145 million in punitive damages, where full compensatory damages are $1 million, is excessive and in violation of the Due Process Clause of the Fourteenth Amendment to the Constitution of the United States . . .

In 1981, Curtis Campbell (Campbell) was driving with his wife, Inez Preece Campbell, in Cache County, Utah. He decided to pass six vans traveling ahead of them on a two-lane highway. Todd Ospital was driving a small car approaching from the opposite direction. To avoid a head-on collision with Campbell, who by then was driving on the wrong side of the highway and toward oncoming traffic, Ospital swerved onto the shoulder, lost control of his automobile, and collided with a vehicle driven by Robert G. Slusher. Ospital was killed, and Slusher was rendered permanently disabled. The Campbells escaped unscathed.

In the ensuing wrongful death and tort action, Campbell insisted he was not at fault. Early investigations did support differing conclusions . . . but "a consensus was reached early on by the investigators and witnesses that Mr. Campbell's unsafe pass had indeed caused the crash." Campbell's insurance company, petitioner State Farm Mutual Automobile Insurance Company (State Farm), nonetheless decided to contest liability and declined offers by Slusher and Ospital's estate (Ospital) to settle the claims for the policy limit of $50,000 ($25,000 per claimant). State Farm also ignored the advice of one of its own investigators and took the case to trial, assuring the Campbells that . . . "they had no liability for the accident . . . and that they did not need to procure separate counsel." To the contrary, a jury determined that Campbell was 100 percent at fault, and a judgment was returned for $185,849, far more than the amount offered in settlement.

At first State Farm refused to cover the $135,849 in excess liability. Its counsel made this clear to the Campbells: "You may want to put for sale signs on your property to get things moving." . . . Nor was State Farm willing to post a supersedeas bond to allow Campbell to appeal the judgment against him. Campbell obtained his own counsel to appeal the verdict. During the pendency of the appeal, in late 1984, Slusher, Ospital, and the Campbells reached an agreement whereby Slusher and Ospital agreed not to seek satisfaction of their claims against the Campbells. In exchange the Campbells agreed to pursue a bad faith action against State Farm and to be represented by

Slusher's and Ospital's attorneys. The Campbells also agreed that Slusher and Ospital would have a right to play a part in all major decisions concerning the bad faith action. No settlement could be concluded without Slusher's and Ospital's approval, and Slusher and Ospital would receive 90 percent of any verdict against State Farm.

In 1989, the Utah Supreme Court denied Campbell's appeal in the wrongful death and tort actions. State Farm then paid the entire judgment, including the amounts in excess of the policy limits. The Campbells nonetheless filed a complaint against State Farm alleging bad faith, fraud, and intentional infliction of emotional distress. The trial court initially granted State Farm's motion for summary judgment because State Farm had paid the excess verdict, but that ruling was reversed on appeal. At State Farm's request the trial court bifurcated the trial into two phases conducted before different juries. In the first phase the jury determined that State Farm's decision not to settle was unreasonable because there was a substantial likelihood of an excess verdict.

Before the second phase of the action against State Farm we decided *BMW of North America, Inc. v. Gore*, 517 U.S. 559 (1996), and refused to sustain a $2 million punitive damages award which accompanied a verdict of only $4,000 in compensatory damages. Based on that decision, State Farm again moved for the exclusion of evidence of dissimilar out-of-state conduct. The trial court denied State Farm's motion.

The second phase addressed State Farm's liability for fraud and intentional infliction of emotional distress, as well as compensatory and punitive damages. The Utah Supreme Court aptly characterized this phase of the trial:

> State Farm argued during phase II that its decision to take the case to trial was an 'honest mistake' that did not warrant punitive damages. In contrast, the Campbells introduced evidence that State Farm's decision to take the case to trial was a result of a national scheme to meet corporate fiscal goals by capping payouts on claims company wide. This scheme was referred to as State Farm's 'Performance, Planning and Review,' or PP & R, policy. To prove the existence of this scheme, the trial court allowed the Campbells to introduce extensive expert testimony regarding fraudulent practices by State Farm in its nation-wide operations. Although State Farm moved prior to phase II of the trial for the exclusion of such evidence and continued to object to it at trial, the trial court ruled that such evidence was admissible to determine whether State Farm's conduct in the Campbell case was indeed intentional and sufficiently egregious to warrant punitive damages. . . .

Evidence pertaining to the PP&R policy concerned State Farm's business practices for over 20 years in numerous States. Most of these practices bore no relation to third-party automobile insurance claims, the type of claim underlying the Campbells' complaint against the company. The jury awarded the Campbells $2.6 million in compensatory damages and $145 million in punitive damages, which the trial court reduced to $1 million and $25 million respectively. Both parties appealed.

The Utah Supreme Court sought to apply the three guideposts we identified in *Gore supra,* at 574-75, and it reinstated the $145 million punitive damages award. Relying in large part on the extensive evidence concerning the PP&R policy, the court concluded State Farm's conduct was reprehensible. The court also relied upon State Farm's "massive wealth" and on testimony indicating that "State Farm's actions, because of their clandestine nature, will be punished at most in one out of every 50,000 cases as a matter of statistical probability," and concluded that the ratio between punitive and compensatory damages was not unwarranted. Finally, the court noted that the punitive damages award was not excessive when compared to various civil and criminal penalties State Farm could have faced, including $10,000 for each act of fraud, the suspension of its license to conduct business in Utah, the disgorgement of profits, and imprisonment. We granted certiorari.

We recognized in *Cooper Industries, Inc. v. Leatherman Tool Group, Inc.,* 532 U.S. 424 (2001), that in our judicial system compensatory and punitive damages, although usually awarded at the same time by the same decisionmaker, serve different purposes. *Id.* at 432. Compensatory damages "are intended to redress the concrete loss that the plaintiff has suffered by reason of the defendant's wrongful conduct." By contrast, punitive damages serve a broader function; they are aimed at deterrence and retribution. . . .

While States possess discretion over the imposition of punitive damages, it is well established that there are procedural and substantive constitutional limitations on these awards. *Cooper Industries, supra; Gore,* 517 U.S., at 559. . . . The Due Process Clause of the Fourteenth Amendment prohibits the imposition of grossly excessive or arbitrary punishments on a tortfeasor. . . .

"This constitutional concern, itself harkening back to the Magna Carta, arises out of the basic unfairness of depriving citizens of life, liberty, or property, through the application, not of law and legal processes, but of arbitrary coercion." . . . The reason is that "elementary notions of fairness enshrined in our constitutional jurisprudence dictate that a person receive fair notice not only of the conduct that will subject him to punishment, but also of the severity of the penalty that a State may impose." *Id.,* at 574; *Cooper Industries, supra,* at 433. . . . To the extent an award is grossly excessive, it furthers no legitimate purpose and constitutes an arbitrary deprivation of property. . . .

Although these awards serve the same purposes as criminal penalties, defendants subjected to punitive damages in civil cases have not been accorded the protections applicable in a criminal proceeding. This increases our concerns over the imprecise manner in which punitive damages systems are administered. We have admonished that "punitive damages pose an acute danger of arbitrary deprivation of property. Jury instructions typically leave the jury with wide discretion in choosing amounts, and the presentation of evidence of a defendant's net worth creates the potential that juries will use their verdicts to express biases against big businesses . . . " *Honda Motor,* [*Co. v. Oberg,* 512 U.S. 415, 432 (1994)] . . . *supra,* at 432. Our concerns are heightened when the decisionmaker is presented, as we shall discuss, with evidence that has little bearing as to the amount of punitive damages that should be awarded. Vague instructions, or those that merely inform the jury to avoid "passion or prejudice" do little to aid the decisionmaker in its task of assigning appropriate weight to evidence that is relevant. . . .

[I]n *Gore supra,* 517 U.S. 559, we instructed courts reviewing punitive damages to consider three guideposts: (1) the degree of reprehensibility of the defendant's misconduct; (2) the disparity between the actual or potential harm suffered by the plaintiff and the punitive damages award; and (3) the difference between the punitive damages awarded by the jury and the civil penalties authorized or imposed in comparable cases. *Id.,* at 575. . . . Exacting appellate review ensures that an award of punitive damages is based upon an "application of law, rather than a decision maker's caprice."

Under the principles outlined in *BMW of North America, Inc. v. Gore,* this case is neither close nor difficult. It was error to reinstate the jury's $145 million punitive damages award. . . .

"The most important indicium of the reasonableness of a punitive damages award is the degree of reprehensibility of the defendant's conduct." *Gore, supra,* at 575. We have instructed courts to determine the reprehensibility of a defendant by considering whether: the harm caused was physical as opposed to economic; the tortious conduct evinced an indifference to or a reckless disregard of the health or safety of others; the target of the conduct had financial vulnerability; the conduct involved repeated actions or was an isolated incident; and the harm was the result of intentional malice, trickery, or deceit, or mere accident. 517 U.S., at 576-577. The existence of any one of these factors weighing in favor of a plaintiff may not be sufficient to sustain a punitive damages award; and the absence of all of them renders any award suspect. It should be presumed a plaintiff has been made whole for his injuries by compensatory damages, so punitive damages should only be awarded if the defendant's culpability, after having paid compensatory damages, is so reprehensible as to warrant the imposition of further sanctions to achieve punishment or deterrence. *Id.,* at 575.

Applying these factors in the instant case, we must acknowledge that State Farm's handling of the claims against the Campbells merits no praise. The trial court found that State Farm's employees altered the company's records to make Campbell appear less culpable. State Farm disregarded the overwhelming likelihood of liability and the near-certain probability that, by taking the case to trial, a judgment in excess of the policy limits would be awarded. State Farm amplified the harm by at first assuring the Campbells their assets would be safe from any verdict and by later telling them, postjudgment, to put a for-sale sign on their house. While we do not suggest there was error in awarding punitive damages based upon State Farm's conduct toward the Campbells, a more modest punishment for this reprehensible conduct could have satisfied the State's legitimate objectives, and the Utah courts should have gone no further.

This case, instead, was used as a platform to expose, and punish, the perceived deficiencies of State Farm's operations throughout the country. This was, as well, an explicit rationale of the trial court's decision in approving the award, though reduced from $145 million to $25 million. . . .

From their opening statements onward the Campbells framed this case as a chance to rebuke State Farm for its nationwide activities. . . . This was a position maintained throughout the litigation. In opposing State Farm's motion to exclude such evidence under *Gore*, the Campbells' counsel convinced the trial court that there was no limitation on the scope of evidence that could be considered under our precedents. . . .

A State cannot punish a defendant for conduct that may have been lawful where it occurred. *Gore, supra*, at 572. . . . Nor, as a general rule, does a State have a legitimate concern in imposing punitive damages to punish a defendant for unlawful acts committed outside of the State's jurisdiction. Any proper adjudication of conduct that occurred outside Utah to other persons would require their inclusion, and, to those parties, the Utah courts, in the usual case, would need to apply the laws of their relevant jurisdiction. . . .

Lawful out-of-state conduct may be probative when it demonstrates the deliberateness and culpability of the defendant's action in the State where it is tortious, but that conduct must have a nexus to the specific harm suffered by the plaintiff. A jury must be instructed, furthermore, that it may not use evidence of out-of-state conduct to punish a defendant for action that was lawful in the jurisdiction where it occurred. *Gore*, 517 U.S., at 572-573. . . . A basic principle of federalism is that each State may make its own reasoned judgment about what conduct is permitted or proscribed within its borders, and each State alone can determine what measure of punishment, if any, to impose on a defendant who acts within its jurisdiction. *Id.*, at 569. . . .

The courts awarded punitive damages to punish and deter conduct that bore no relation to the Campbells' harm. A defendant's dissimilar acts, independent from the acts upon which liability was premised, may not serve as the basis for punitive damages. A defendant should be punished for the conduct that harmed the plaintiff, not for being an unsavory individual or business. Due process does not permit courts, in the calculation of punitive damages, to adjudicate the merits of other parties' hypothetical claims against a defendant under the guise of the reprehensibility analysis, but we have no doubt the Utah Supreme Court did that here. . . . Punishment on these bases creates the possibility of multiple punitive damages awards for the same conduct; for in the usual case nonparties are not bound by the judgment some other plaintiff obtains. . . .

The same reasons lead us to conclude the Utah Supreme Court's decision cannot be justified on the grounds that State Farm was a recidivist. Although "our holdings that a recidivist may be punished more severely than a first offender recognize that repeated misconduct is more reprehensible than an individual instance of malfeasance," *Gore, supra*, at 577, in the context of civil actions courts must ensure the conduct in question replicates the prior transgressions. . . .

Turning to the second *Gore* guidepost we . . . decline again to impose a bright-line ratio which a punitive damages award cannot exceed. Our jurisprudence and the principles it has now established demonstrate, however, that, in practice, few awards exceeding a single-digit ratio between punitive and compensatory damages, to a significant degree, will satisfy due process. . . .

Nonetheless, because there are no rigid benchmarks that a punitive damages award may not surpass, ratios greater than those we have previously upheld may comport with due process where "a particularly egregious act has resulted in only a small amount of economic damages." . . . The converse is also true, however. When compensatory damages are substantial, then a lesser ratio, perhaps only equal to compensatory damages, can reach the outermost limit of the due process guarantee. The precise award in any case, of course, must be based upon the facts and circumstances of the defendant's conduct and the harm to the plaintiff.

In sum, courts must ensure that the measure of punishment is both reasonable and proportionate to the amount of harm to the plaintiff and to the general damages recovered. . . . The compensatory damages for the injury suffered here, moreover, likely were based on a component which was duplicated in the punitive award. Much of the distress was caused by the outrage and humiliation the Campbells suffered at the actions of their insurer; and it is a major role of punitive damages to condemn such conduct. Compensatory damages, however, already contain this punitive element. See Restatement (Second) of Torts § 908, Comment c, p. 466 (1977) ("In many cases in which compensatory damages include an amount for emotional distress, such as humiliation or indignation aroused by the defendant's act, there is no clear line of demarcation between punishment and compensation and a verdict for a specified amount frequently includes elements of both.") . . .

The third guidepost in *Gore* is the disparity between the punitive damages award and the "civil penalties authorized or imposed in comparable cases." *Id.,* at 575. We note that, in the past, we have also looked to criminal penalties that could be imposed. *Id.,* at 583; *Haslip,* 499 U.S., at 23. The existence of a criminal penalty does have bearing on the seriousness with which a State views the wrongful action. When used to determine the dollar amount of the award, however, the criminal penalty has less utility. Great care must be taken to avoid use of the civil process to assess criminal penalties that can be imposed only after the heightened protections of a criminal trial have been observed, including, of course, its higher standards of proof. Punitive damages are not a substitute for the criminal process, and the remote possibility of a criminal sanction does not automatically sustain a punitive damages award. . . .

. . . The most relevant civil sanction under Utah state law for the wrong done to the Campbells appears to be a $10,000 fine for an act of fraud, [*Campbell v. State Farm*], 2001 UT 89, 2001 Utah LEXIS 170, 2001 WL 1246676, at *17, an amount dwarfed by the $145 million punitive damages award. . . .

An application of the *Gore* guideposts to the facts of this case, especially in light of the substantial compensatory damages awarded (a portion of which contained a punitive element), likely would justify a punitive damages award at or near the amount of compensatory damages. The punitive award of $145 million, therefore, was neither reasonable nor proportionate to the wrong committed, and it was an irrational and arbitrary deprivation of the property of the defendant. The proper calculation of punitive damages under the principles we have discussed should be resolved, in the first instance, by the Utah courts.

The judgment of the Utah Supreme Court is reversed, and the case is remanded for proceedings not inconsistent with this opinion.

JUSTICE GINSBURG, dissenting.

. . . In *Gore*, I stated why I resisted the Court's foray into punitive damages "territory traditionally within the States' domain." 517 U.S., at 612 (dissenting opinion). I adhere to those views, and note again that, unlike federal habeas corpus review of state-court convictions under 28 U.S.C. §2254, the Court "works at this business [of checking state courts] alone," unaided by the participation of federal district courts and courts of appeals. 517 U.S., at 613. It was once recognized that "the laws of the particular State must suffice [to superintend punitive damages awards] until judges or legislators authorized to do so initiate system-wide change." *Haslip*, 499 U.S., at 42 (Kennedy, J., concurring in judgment). I would adhere to that traditional view . . . that this Court has no warrant to reform state law governing awards of punitive damages. *Gore*, 517 U.S., at 607 (Ginsburg, J., dissenting). Even if I were prepared to accept the flexible guides prescribed in *Gore*, I would not join the Court's swift conversion of those guides into instructions that begin to resemble marching orders. For the reasons stated, I would leave the judgment of the Utah Supreme Court undisturbed.

NOTES

1. *Constitutional Guideposts.* In *State Farm* the Court relied on three guideposts developed in *BMW of North America, Inc v. Gore*, 517 U.S. 559 (1996) to determine whether a punitive damage award was excessive: (1) the defendant's reprehensibility; (2) the ratio between punitive and compensatory damages; and (3) a comparison of existing criminal and civil penalties for similar misconduct. Applying these guidelines, for the first time in *Gore,* the Court found the punitive award (which had been $4 million but reduced by the state supreme court to $2 million as compared with $4,000 in compensatory damages awarded by the jury) to be offensive to fundamental fairness to which defendants are entitled. Notably the guideposts for determining whether an award is excessive are similar to what common-law state courts use in reviewing punitive damage awards. *See* Thomas C. Galligan, Jr., *U.S. Supreme Court Tort Reform: Limiting State Power to Articulate and Develop Tort Law — Defamation, Preemption, and Punitive Damages*, 74 U. CIN. L. REV. 1189, 1248 (2006). In a later case, *Cooper Industries, Inc. v. Leatherman Tool Group*, 532 U.S. 424 (2001), the Court determined that the consideration of whether a punitive damages award was excessive should be given de novo review. Is it troublesome that the Court has transformed the common-law factors for evaluating punitive damages into a constitutionalized basis for Supreme Court oversight? *See* Galligan, *supra,* 74 U. CIN. L. REV. at 1248: "[J]ury mistrust sits at the core of this transformation [of a common-law standard to a constitutional limitation on punitive awards]." Is the Court usurping the role of the jury? Is it intruding in the province of a state court to "define articulate, and apply its own tort law"? *See* Paul Mogin, *Why Judges, Not Juries, Should Set Punitive Damages*, 65 U. CHI. L. REV. 179 (1998).

2. *Societal Damages.* As mentioned in the text preceding the principal case, some state statutes require that a portion of the punitive damages awarded in particular claims must be shared with the state or placed in a special fund. *See, e.g.,* GA. CODE ANN. §51-12-5.1 (2006) (requiring 75% of any punitive damage award to be paid into the State treasury); MO. STAT. ANN. §537.675 (2007) (channeling 50% of all punitive damage awards into a general tort victims' compensation fund). Based on what reasoning is such a sharing provision justified? *See* Catherine M. Sharkey, *Punitive Damages as Societal Damages,* 113 YALE L.J. 347, 453 (2003) (arguing that punitive damages perform not only a retributive function but can be understood as "societal damages"). Is such a requirement for paying part of the damages award into the public fisc problematic? *See* Galligan, *supra,* 74 U. CIN. L. REV. at 1244, n.212 (arguing Eighth Amendment prohibition on cruel and unusual punishment might be basis for challenging such a requirement). *See also Browning-Ferris Indus. v. Kelco Disposal,* 492 U.S. 257 (1989) (Eighth Amendment claim challenging punitive damages). Consider state efforts to allocate punitive damages in this way by applying social justice and law and economics perspectives found in Chapter 1, *supra.*

3. *Single-Digit Ratio.* On what basis does the *State Farm* Court — while still maintaining that no "bright-line" certainty exists for determining an appropriate ratio of punitive and compensatory damages — conclude that "single-digit multipliers are more likely to comport with due process?" The Court notes that some cases justify higher awards, for example, where the injury is hard to detect or where the monetary value of noneconomic harm is difficult to determine. Similarly, if the compensatory damages are extremely high, the Court suggests that a lesser ratio is justified. Does the Court's punitive damages treatment lead to the conclusion that every large punitive damage award is at risk of constitutional challenge? *See* Galligan, *supra,* 74 U. CIN. L. REV. at 1257 ("The exception to the 'every case a constitutional case' statement may be in states where punitive damages are capped by statute.") Aren't statutory caps of punitive damages also troublesome? If the purpose of punitive damages is to make the punishment fit the offense, how is a one-size-fits-all, approach justifiable?

4. *Harm to Persons Other Than the Plaintiff.* It can be argued that the Supreme Court's jurisprudence in this area is confusing, creates rather than eliminates certainty, and and offends the deference normally accorded states. *See* Galligan, *supra,* 74 U. CIN. L. REV. at 1257. In *Phillip Morris USA v. Williamson,* 549 U.S. ___, No. 05-1256 (Feb. 20, 2007), in a 5-4 majority decision authored by Justice Breyer, the Supreme Court held that a state violates a defendant's right to due process when it allows a jury to consider harm to strangers to the litigation in determining the amount of punitive damages that should be awarded in a tort case. The state supreme court had determined that the jury verdict justified the $79.5 million in punitive damages. The attorney for the defendant argued that the Oregon courts had permitted the jury to punish the cigarette manufacturing company for harm to Oregon smokers who had not filed suit. The plaintiff's lawyer responded that the award was consistent with Supreme Court precedent — based on the reprehensibility of the cigarette manufacturer's behavior in engaging in a market-directed fraud and driven by their deliberate decisions at the highest levels of the company to deceive customers and endanger their health. Upholding the award, the Oregon Supreme Court had characterized the conduct as "extraordinarily reprehensible." The majority of the U.S. Supreme Court found the defendant's argument persuasive: The majority argued that

> [e]vidence of actual harm to nonparties can help to show that the conduct that harmed the plaintiff also posed a substantial risk of harm to the general public, and so was particularly reprehensible. . . . Yet . . . a jury may not go further than this and use a punitive damages verdict to punish a defendant directly on account of harms it is alleged to have visited on nonparties.

Does the Court's "reprehensibility" standard provide courts with sufficient clarity in the future as to how much in punitive damages is permissible in a mass tort case of this nature? Consider the difficulties facing lawyers in instructing the jury about how to arrive at an appropriate determination that the case is eligible for punitive damages and how much it is appropriate to award.

4. The Collateral Source Rule

The collateral source rule provides that the defendant receives no credit for sums received by the plaintiff from non-tortfeasor sources as a result of the defendant's tort. Proponents of "reform" have attacked this rule as economically wasteful, permitting double recovery by plaintiffs. The counterargument is that the tortfeasor should not receive a windfall as a result of the plaintiff's thrift or others' largesse. As in the other contexts of retrenchment, courts disagree about whether to eliminate the collateral source rule. *Compare Carson v. Mauer,* 424 A.2d 825 (N.H. 1991) (abrogation of collateral source rule and $250,000 noneconomic damage cap to medical malpractice action violates equal protection) *and Boucher v. Sayeed,* 459 A.2d 87 (R.I. 1983) (admitting evidence of collateral source payments in medical malpractice cases violates equal protection), *with Marsh v. Green,* 782 So. 2d 223 (Ala. 2000) (overruling past precedent and upholding the legislature's repeal of the collateral source rule). The *Marsh* court concluded that its concerns about transferring such funds were policy matters upon which the court had no right to second guess the legislature.

In *Moorhead v. Crozer Chester Medical Center,* 765 A.2d 786, 791 (Pa. 2001), the Pennsylvania Supreme Court held that the plaintiff is not entitled to recover damages from a tortfeasor in an amount greater than was actually paid and that the collateral source rule is inapplicable to charges never paid or incurred from the collateral source.

NOTES

1. *Constitutional Challenge.* Part of the legislature's tort reform, TENN. CODE ANN. § 29-26-119 (2007) provides that "insurance provided by an employer . . . , by social security benefits, service benefits, programs, unemployment benefits, or any other source," shall reduce medical malpractice claims, except that no deduction shall be made for "the assets of the claimants or of the members of the claimant's immediate family and insurance purchased in whole or in part, privately and individually." How should a litigant challenge this kind of retrenchment? In *Sorrell v. Thevenir*, 633 N.E.2d 504 (Ohio 1994), the court held the state's statutory elimination of the collateral source rule was unconstitutional. Ruling that the purported basis for eliminating the rule lacked rationality, the court concluded that no empirical evidence demonstrated that an insurance crisis exists, or that the statute would affect any such crisis. Other courts have upheld collateral source provisions, as noted above.

2. *Windfall or Insurance?* What are the advantages and disadvantages of maintaining the collateral source rule? Some jurisdictions have limited their collateral source rules in settings involving governmental aid such as Medicaid or Medicare, on the basis that allowing a person to "pocket the windfall" would be unjust to taxpayers. *See Bates v. Hogg*, 921 P.2d 249, 253 (Kan. Ct. App. 1996). Do you agree? Compare *Ellsworth v. Schelbrock*, 611 N.W.2d 764, 768 (Wis. 2000) (Medicare is a form of insurance paid for by taxes collected for society in general; the program is social legislation and is equivalent to health insurance for the needy and, just as any insurance form, it is an acceptable collateral source).

3. *Impeachment Evidence.* Should evidence of collateral sources be admissible to prove plaintiff's alleged malingering? Noting mixed results in other jurisdictions, the court in *Proctor v. Castelletti*, 911 P.2d 853, 854 (Nev. 1996), held that evidence of collateral sources was not admissible, concluding that the "excessive prejudicial nature of the evidence mandates its exclusion."

5. State Referenda

Reform efforts have taken the form of referenda or voter initiatives in recent years. Fearing litigation challenging their legislative efforts in courts, proponents of reform sometimes seek constitutional authority for their actions, through public referenda if such initiatives are available in the jurisdiction. For example, in 2003, lawmakers in Texas passed one of the toughest reform packages in the nation. After the legislation's passage proponents placed Proposition 12 (a constitutional amendment) before the voters of the state in a referendum. As a consequence of the successful referendum vote, there is constitutional protection from voters easily challenging the enactment. California's Proposition 64, a ballot initiative, attempted to limit recovery in consumer cases. The California proposition required plaintiffs to prove that an alleged violation of the state's consumer law actually injured them and imposed procedural burdens associated with class actions. *See, e.g.,* Sharon J. Arkin, *The Unfair Competition Law After Proposition 64: Changing the Consumer Landscape*, 32 West. St. U. L. Rev. 155 (2005). Ballot initiatives are not always successful. In November 2005, Washington state voters rejected Health Care Access Initiative 330, an initiative to reform medical liability laws. Ballot initiatives in Oregon and Wyoming also failed in 2004.

E.   SUBSTANTIVE LAW REFORM

Responding to perceptions of crises, many states passed reform provisions that purport to reduce excessive recoveries and frivolous suits and address the problem of overburdened courts. Although there have also been efforts to address these concerns on a uniform basis at the federal level, these federal efforts have not been as successful.

1. Products Liability

By the mid-nineties, more than half of the states had enacted legislation intended to limit products liability claims and amounts of recovery. The Tennessee Products Liability Act of 1978, codified at TENN. CODE ANN. §§ 29-28-101 to 29-28-108 (2007), is fairly typical of comprehensive legislative efforts. The statute restricts products claims to those resulting in personal injury from the manufacture, business sale, or lease of unreasonably dangerous or unsafe products. It provides a statute of repose that bars claims filed more than six years from the date of injury or ten years after the product is first purchased for use or consumption, whichever occurs first. It provides a rebuttable presumption that a product is *not* unreasonably dangerous as to any aspect of the product that complies with any federal or state statute or administrative regulation existing at the time the product was manufactured.

A product is also not defective or unreasonably dangerous if it complies with the state of scientific and technical knowledge available to the manufacturer or seller when the product is placed on the market. In making the determination of defectiveness and unreasonable danger, evidence of customary designs, methods, standards, and techniques of manufacturing, inspecting, and testing by other manufacturers or sellers of similar products are relevant. The legislation also provides that a non-manufacturing seller (*e.g.*, a retailer or wholesaler) cannot be held liable in strict tort unless the manufacturer of the product is not subject to service of process in the state or has been judicially declared insolvent.

Efforts to produce a comprehensive federal response have not proven easy. As discussed earlier in the chapter, after more than a decade of attempts to pass substantive reform of products liability law, Congress in 1994 passed the General Aviation Revitalization Act, 49 USC § 40101, providing a statute of repose of 18 years for manufacturers of small aircraft and parts. Congress also enacted the Protection of Lawful Commerce in Arms Act in 2005, insulating gun manufacturers from municipal and other tort liability for shootings. 15 U.S.C. §§ 7901-03.

Congress has proposed legislation that would restrict or limit strict liability for product defects, provide a state of the art defense, eliminate or restrict joint liability, place a cap on recoverable damages, limit or restrict the recovery of punitive damages, establish a statute of repose, eliminate or restrict the collateral source rule, and limit product supplier contribution claims against plaintiffs' employers. In 1996, both houses passed legislation entitled The Common Sense Products Liability Legislative Reform Act, but President Clinton vetoed the legislation. Although the coalition of business groups and other proponents of reform have continued to support change, these groups have not agreed on how to proceed, reflecting the competing and somewhat conflicting-agenda of the "reform" proponents.

Congress has also passed legislation that restricts the state courts' ability to certify nationwide class actions and to stem the proliferation of "coupon settlements" that are of little benefit to class members but are lucrative in fees for class counsel. The Class Action Fairness Act broadens federal court jurisdiction over class actions; it amends the diversity statute to authorize federal jurisdiction over class actions that exceed $5 million in aggregate amount in controversy and in which any plaintiff is diverse with any defendant. 28 U.S.C. §1332(d)(2). The Act also requires courts presiding over class actions in which coupon settlements are proposed to calculate class counsel's attorney's fee based on either the value of the coupons actually redeemed by class members or by the hours reasonably spent by counsel on the case. *Id.* §1712.

Commentators are skeptical about the desirability of federal reform legislation. Proponents of a uniform products liability law argue that it will provide predictability and eliminate conflicting rulings of the states. Others doubt whether the proposed federal legislation would afford substantially greater predictability, and respond that uniformity would not be achieved because application of the proposed statute would likely be left to state courts. Moreover, some opponents of federal reform assert that there is substantial virtue in retaining the experimental-laboratory concept of state-based tort systems. *See, e.g.,* Harvey S. Perlman, *Products Liability Reform in Congress: An Issue of Federalism,* 48 OHIO ST. L.J. 503, 508-09 (1987). Professor Perlman sees a need to protect against what he calls the "spillover" effect, whereby the consumers of one state may be required to bear a significant part of the ultimate cost of products claims in other states, because of the patchwork pattern of statutory reform. As a solution to this problem, Professor Perlman suggests that the law of the place of product manufacture should apply to all claims against the manufacturer, so that the consumer can choose products with the controlling state law in mind. Additionally, he proposes that legislation might "facilitate competition in the insurance industry" so as to provide an impetus for the calculation of products liability insurance premiums on a state-by-state, rather than a national, basis. *Id.* at 509.

Scholars have also observed that judicial reform of products liability principles has already had significant impact in this substantive area, affecting the number of cases filed, success rates, and the size of verdicts. *See, e.g.,* James Henderson & Theodore Eisenberg, *The Quiet Revolution in Products Liability: An Empirical Study of Legal Change,* 37 U.C.L.A. L. REV. 479 (1990). In addition, in the products liability and medical malpractice arena, evidence shows that judges are more aggressively scrutinizing the substantive merits of claims and exercising their gate-keeping power, resulting in dismissals, summary judgments, reversals, and remittitur of damages. Notably, in addition to assuming an oversight role in determining whether punitive claims are excessive in *Pacific Mutual Life Ins. Co. v. Haslip,* 499 U.S. 1 (1991), *State Farm,* and *Williamson,* discussed *supra* in this chapter, the Supreme Court in *Daubert v. Merrell Dow Pharmaceuticals, Inc.,* 509 U.S. 579 (1993), has also emphasized a judicial gatekeeper's role in causation claims. *See, e.g.,* Lucinda Finley, *Guarding the Gate to the Courthouse: How Trial Judges Are Using Their*

Evidentiary Screening Role to Remake Tort Causation Rules, 49 DE PAUL L. REV. 335 (1999). D. Michael Risinger writes in *Navigating Expert Reliability: Are Criminal Standards of Certainty Being Left on the Dock?*, 64 ALB. L. REV. 99 (2000), that the effect of the *Daubert* gate-keeping function in the courts has been that defendants in civil cases win their *Daubert* challenges substantially more frequently than plaintiffs, and that the prosecution wins much more frequently than defendants in criminal cases. *See* JOHN C.P. GOLDBERG, TORT LAW: RESPONSIBILITIES AND REDRESS 959-1038 (2004).

2. Medical Malpractice

Perceptions of medical malpractice crises in the seventies and again in the mid-eighties also led to legislative restrictions on tort recoveries in this field in many states. The enactments often included statutes of repose, provisions insulating physicians who volunteer their services, for example, in school athletic events or low-cost medical clinics, and provisions requiring dismissal of the suit if an admissible expert opinion is not obtained soon after commencement of the suit.

Although credible scholars have presented empirical evidence refuting the contention that excessive or frivolous litigation and other deficiencies of the tort system have created a crisis in insurance, leading to escalating healthcare costs and driving doctors out of the profession, proponents of tort reform continue to claim the tort system is responsible for these consequences. *See* Neil Vidmar, Russell M. Robinson II, & Kara MacKillop, *"Judicial Hellholes:" Medical Malpractice Claims, Verdicts and the "Doctor Exodus" in Illinois*, 59 VAND. L. REV. 1309 (2006); Paul Weiler, *Reforming Medical Malpractice in a Radically Moderate — and Ethical — Fashion*, 54 DEPAUL L. REV. 205 (2005). As more than one writer has observed, these malpractice crises "have been first and foremost crises of insurance, and most of the impetus for tort reform comes from problems in the insurance markets." Randall R. Bovbjerg, *Legislation on Medical Malpractice*, 22 U.C. DAVIS L. REV. 499, 504 (1989). Bovbjerg and others who have explored why these crises have occurred lay blame on cycles in insurance pricing and availability. The reasons why the cycles occur, however, are unclear. "Continuing rises in claims and payments are the underlying cause, but the dynamics of the insurance market seems to be the precipitating factor, and no consensus exists on how much each is to blame." *Id.* at 506. *See also* Alexee Deep Conroy, *Lessons Learned from the "Laboratories of Democracy": A Critique of Federal Medical Liability Reform*, 91 CORNELL L. REV. 1159 (2006); Adam D. Glassman, *The Imposition of Federal Caps in Medical Malpractice Liability Actions: Will They Cure the Current Crisis in Health Care?*, 37 AKRON L. REV. 417 (2004).

There is no consensus on why medical claims and awards have risen. "Reasons commonly listed include an erosion in physician-patient relationships, higher patient expectations, more experts and numerous attorneys for malpractice plaintiffs, greater willingness of physicians to testify, a more compensation-oriented world view among judges and juries, and changes in legal doctrine favorable to malpractice plaintiffs. . . ." *Bovbjerg, supra*, 22 U.C. DAVIS L. REV. at 525 (1989). Empirical studies indicate that plaintiffs bring far fewer claims of avoidable, negligent maloccurence than actually occur. The claims not brought outnumber those brought by negligently injured patients by as high as ten to one, according to extrapolations from hospital chart reviews by doctors. *See, e.g.,* Paul C. Weiler, A MEASURE OF MALPRACTICE 62 (1993). A finding of a recent task force of the ABA was similar: only about two percent of victims of malpractice sue. John Gibeaut, *The Med-Mal Divide,* 91 A.BA. J. 39 (March 2005).

Bovbjerg found, however, that there were considerable downturns in the frequency of claims after publications of crises, although these downturns occurred too quickly to be the result of reform and "no one really understands why such large changes occur." Bovbjerg, 22 U.C. DAVIS L. REV. at 510–11. He opines that the "crisis-generated publicity about liability problems may subtly have altered the general attitudes of claims adjusters, judges, and jurors about liability cases and thus discouraged plaintiffs and their attorneys from bringing some claims." *Id.* at 551-52. Those claims that are filed are likely ones that involve potentially large awards.

The state legislative changes enacted in response to the perceived malpractice crises of the mid-seventies and mid-eighties were extensive but the responses were different in the two decades. More states enacted strong reforms in the 1980s (caps, collateral source offsets, structured awards, and changes in joint and several liability) while states earlier had enacted seemingly less consequential efforts (bars on dollar *ad damnums,* informed consent changes, statutes of frauds, and *res ipsa loquitur* modifications). Arbitration and pretrial screening almost disappeared as reforms, perhaps reflecting concerns that they do not cut system costs. In the case of caps on recoverable damages, there were two significant changes from the seventies to the eighties: a shift towards placing caps on noneconomic damages only (typically, damages for pain and suffering) as opposed to damages in general, and a shift towards generic tort caps as opposed to caps on medical malpractice recoveries alone, perhaps reflecting responses by the courts.

Although some commentators have argued that legislative enactments have helped to address the problem of availability of liability coverage, it appears that only reform (like caps) accompanied by more effective regulation of insurance premiums has been proven responsive. Crisis-driven legislation, moreover, may be bad legal strategy, since it may create a self-fulfilling prophecy. *See* Bovbjerg, *supra,* 22 U.C. DAVIS L. REV. at 553-54. It is very unclear whether tort reform can generally be demonstrated to avert shortrun crisis (a characteristic of insurance cycles). Early on Bovbjerg observed: "Conceptually, one would expect legal changes to change behavior over time, not suddenly, and other developments seem more plausibly to be related to the rapid shifts in insurance markets." *Id.* at 554. It is probably safe to say the question is open whether tort reform is an effective means of responding to insurance shortages and certainly doubtful whether reform in the long run will address the problem of the increasingly high cost of healthcare. Notably, medical malpractice litigation costs comprised less than 3% of healthcare costs, casting doubt on the ability of tort reform to make a significant impact on this troublesome social problem. CONG. BUDGET OFFICE, Limiting Tort Liability for Medical Malpractice (Jan. 8, 2004), available at http://www.cbo.gov/ftpdoc.cfm?index=4968&type=0, at 6, *cited in* Randolph I. Gordon & Brook Assefa, *A Tale of Two Initiatives: Where Propaganda Meets Fact in the Debate Over America's Healthcare,* 4 SEATTLE J. SOC. JUS. 693 (2006).

FERDON v. WISCONSIN PATIENTS COMPENSATION FUND
701 N.W.2d 440 (2005)

ABRAHAMSON, CHIEF JUSTICE.

FACTS

According to evidence produced at trial that the jury apparently accepted, as the doctor was delivering Matthew Ferdon, the doctor pulled on Matthew Ferdon's head. The manner in which the doctor pulled caused an injury called obstetric brachial plexus palsy. As a result of this injury, Matthew Ferdon's right arm is partially paralyzed and deformed. Matthew Ferdon underwent surgeries and occupational therapy; as a result of the injury, more surgery and more therapy will be required. Matthew Ferdon's right arm will never function normally.

Through his guardian ad litem, Vincent Petrucelli, Matthew Ferdon brought negligence claims against the doctor and the hospital. The Fund, as required, was named as a defendant. [In Wisconsin, "[m]alpractice claimants seeking damages in excess of $200,000 must name the fund as a defendant, and the fund may appear and defend against the action. *State ex rel. Strykowski v. Wilkie,* 261 N.W.2d 434 (Wis. 1978)]. Matthew Ferdon's parents, Cynthia and Dennis Ferdon, also brought a negligence claim, seeking to recover for loss of society and companionship. A jury found the delivery doctor negligent for the injuries Matthew Ferdon sustained during the birth.

The jury awarded the following damages to Matthew Ferdon: (1) Future medical and hospital expenses: $403,000; and (2) Past and future personal injuries (noneconomic damages): $700,000. The jury made no award to Matthew Ferdon for loss of future earning capacity. The jury awarded $87,600 to Cynthia and Dennis Ferdon as compensation for the personal care they will render for Matthew until the age of 18.

After the verdict, the Fund moved the circuit court to reduce the $700,000 personal injury award to $410,322, the amount of the $350,000 cap (adjusted for inflation) on noneconomic damages recoverable in a medical malpractice action under Wis. Stat. §§ 655.017 and 893.55(4)(d). Further, the Fund moved to have the award for future medical and hospital expenses exceeding $100,000 placed under the Fund's control pursuant to Wis. Stat. § 655.015.

The circuit court granted the Fund's motions, reducing the noneconomic damage award to the statutorily limited amount of $410,322 and ordering that $168,667.67 of the future medical and hospital expenses be paid into the reimbursement fund.[14] Matthew Ferdon appealed; the court of appeals summarily

---

[14] The amount of $168,667.67 reflects the portion of the award over $100,000 that is left after attorney fees are taken out of the jury's award for future medical expenses. The overall award of $403,000 is the amount the jury felt was necessary to pay Matthew Ferdon's future medical expenses, reduced to present value. The jury was asked to determine the present value of future medical expenses as required by Wis. Stat. § 893.55(4)(e). Awards are reduced to their present value because a lump sum received today may be worth more than the same amount spread out over a period of years. Section 893.55(4)(e) provides:

affirmed the circuit court based on its reading of *State ex rel. Strykowski v. Wilkie.* . . .

II. MEDICAL MALPRACTICE STATUTES

In Wisconsin, a claim for injury resulting from medical malpractice by a health care provider is subject to the provisions of chapter 655. Chapter 655 provides the exclusive procedures for the "prosecution of malpractice claims against a health care provider." Among the damages available to a claimant are noneconomic damages, including damages to compensate for pain and suffering, mental distress, loss of enjoyment of normal activity, and loss of society and companionship. [19]

The Fund was created to pay medical malpractice claims that exceed primary insurance thresholds established by statute. The primary malpractice coverage is $1,000,000 for each occurrence and $3,000,000 per policy year. Health care providers must participate in the Fund. Although noneconomic damages are capped, the Fund provides unlimited liability coverage for economic damages exceeding the primary limits.

Should a claimant recover noneconomic damages as a result of a medical malpractice injury, those damages are statutorily capped pursuant to Wis. Stat. §§ 655.017 and 893.55(4) at $350,000, a sum to be adjusted annually to reflect inflation.

Section 655.017 reads as follows:

> *Limitation on noneconomic damages.* The amount of noneconomic damages recoverable by a claimant or plaintiff under this chapter for acts or omissions of a health care provider if the act or omission occurs on or after May 25, 1995, and for acts or omissions of an employee of a health care provider, acting within the scope of his or her employment and

---

Economic damages recovered under ch. 655 for bodily injury or death, including any action or proceeding based on contribution or indemnification, shall be determined for the period during which the damages are expected to accrue, taking into account the estimated life expectancy of the person, then reduced to present value, taking into account the effects of inflation.

The jury was informed that Matthew Ferdon was six years old, that he had a life expectancy of 69 years, and that the award should take into account economic conditions and the effect of inflation. With respect to present value, the jury was instructed that their award should be reduced to present value "because a sum received today can be invested and earn money at current interest rates."

From the $403,000 award for future medical expenses, it appears that the amount of $134,333.33 (amounting to one-third) was earmarked as "an amount sufficient to pay the cost of collection, including attorney fees reduced to present value" as required by § 655.015, leaving a balance of $268,666.67. Section 655.015 requires that of the $268,666.67, $100,000 is to go to Matthew Ferdon, with the remainder deposited into an account with the Fund for payment of future medical expenses consistent with § 655.015 and Wis. Admin. Code § Ins 17.26.

[19] "Noneconomic" damages are defined in Wis. Stat. § 893.55(4)(a). That subsection reads:

(4)(a) In this subsection, "noneconomic damages" means moneys intended to compensate for pain and suffering; humiliation; embarrassment; worry; mental distress; noneconomic effects of disability including loss of enjoyment of the normal activities, benefits and pleasures of life and loss of mental or physical health, well-being or bodily functions; loss of consortium, society and companionship; or loss of love and affection.

providing health care services, for acts or omissions occurring on or after May 25, 1995, is subject to the limits under §893.55(4)(d) and (f).

The financial limits to which §655.017 refers are contained in Wis. Stat. §893.55(4)(d), which reads as follows:

> (d) The limit on total noneconomic damages for each occurrence under par. (b) on or after May 25, 1995, shall be $350,000 and shall be adjusted by the director of state courts to reflect changes in the consumer price index for all urban consumers, U.S. city average, as determined by the U.S. department of labor, at least annually thereafter, with the adjustment limit to apply to awards subsequent to such adjustments.

The parties do not dispute that in the instant case the inflation-adjusted cap authorized by Wis. Stat. §893.55(4)(d) was $410,322. . . .

[The court discusses principles of stare decisis and standards governing review of statutes challenged on the basis of the state's requirements of equal protection. The majority opinion employs a traditional "rational basis" standard to assess the validity of the statute.]

The rational basis test does not require the legislature to choose the best or wisest means to achieve its goals. Deference to the means chosen is due even if the court believes that the same goal could be achieved in a more effective manner.

Nevertheless, judicial deference to the legislature and the presumption of constitutionality of statutes do not require a court to acquiesce in the constitutionality of every statute. A court need not, and should not, blindly accept the claims of the legislature. For judicial review under rational basis to have any meaning, there must be a meaningful level of scrutiny, a thoughtful examination of not only the legislative purpose, but also the relationship between the legislation and the purpose. The court must "probe beneath the claims of the government to determine if the constitutional 'requirement of some rationality in the nature of the class singled out' has been met." . . .

The Classifications

The task of drawing lines, that is the task of creating classifications, is a legislative one in which perfection "is neither possible nor necessary." The court's goal is to determine whether the classification scheme rationally advances the legislative objective. In limiting noneconomic damages in medical malpractice actions, Wis. Stat. §§655.017 and 893.55(4)(d) together create a number of classifications and sub-classifications.[97] One main classification is relevant to the present case, and one sub-classification is implicated:

---

[97] There are two large classifications of plaintiffs and defendants created by the statutes whom we do not address here. (1) Two classes of tort plaintiffs are created by the $350,000 cap: those injured by the medical malpractice of health care providers covered by chapter 655 and therefore subject to the cap on noneconomic damages, and those injured by tortious conduct of non-health care providers who are not subject to the $350,000 cap on noneconomic damages. The court has held that medical malpractice actions are substantially distinct from other tort actions. *Czapinski v. St. Francis Hosp., Inc.,* . . . 613 N.W.2d 120 (2000). (2) Two classes of tortfeasors are created by the $350,000 cap: health care tortfeasors and non-health care tortfeasors. Health care tortfeasors whose conduct producing the most harm (in excess of the $350,000 cap) are partially shielded by the $350,000 cap on noneconomic damage awards, as compared with health care tortfeasors whose conduct produces less harm.

The main classification is the distinction between medical malpractice victims who suffer over $350,000 in noneconomic damages, and medical malpractice victims who suffer less than $350,000 in noneconomic damages. That is, the cap divides the universe of injured medical malpractice victims into a class of severely injured victims and less severely injured victims. Severely injured victims with more than $350,000 in noneconomic damages receive only part of their damages; less severely injured victims with $350,000 or less in noneconomic damages receive their full damages. In other words, the statutory cap creates a class of fully compensated victims and partially compensated victims. Thus, the cap's greatest impact falls on the most severely injured victims.

A main sub-classification is created as part of the $350,000 cap on noneconomic damages. A single cap applies to all victims of a medical malpractice occurrence regardless of the number of victims/claimants. Because the total noneconomic damages recoverable for bodily injury or death may not exceed the $350,000 limit for each occurrence, the total award for a patient's claim for noneconomic damages (such as pain, suffering and disability) and the claims of the patient's spouse, minor children, or parents for loss of society and companionship cannot exceed $350,000. Thus, classes of victims are created depending on whether the patient has a spouse, minor children, or a parent. An injured patient who is single may recover the entire $350,000, while a married injured patient shares the cap with his or her spouse; a non-married injured patient with children shares the $350,000 with the children; a married injured patient with children shares the cap with the spouse and children.

With these classifications in mind, we turn to the legislature's objectives for enacting a $350,000 cap on noneconomic damages in medical malpractice actions.

C. Legislative Objectives

Identifying the legislative objectives will allow us to determine whether the legislatively created classifications are rationally related to achieving appropriate legislative objectives.

Although the legislature did not explicitly state its objectives as such, it made a number of findings when it enacted chapter 655. These findings give a strong indication of the legislature's objectives. . . .

In sum, the legislature found that malpractice lawsuits raise the cost of medical malpractice insurance for providers. According to the legislature, higher medical malpractice insurance costs, in turn, harm the public because they result in increased medical costs for the public and because health care providers might leave Wisconsin. The legislature also found that health care providers were practicing defensive medicine because of the rising number of claims and that they might refuse to enter the Wisconsin health care market. These legislative findings are not binding on the court but carry great weight.

From the findings set forth when chapter 655 was enacted in 1975, we can deduce a primary, overall legislative objective and five interconnected legislative objectives that led to adoption of the $350,000 cap on noneconomic damage awards.

The primary, overall legislative objective is to ensure the quality of health care for the people of Wisconsin. The legislature obviously did not intend to reach this objective by shielding negligent health care providers from responsibility for their negligent actions. After all, "it is a major contradiction to legislate for quality health care on one hand, while on the other hand, in the same statute, to reward negligent health care providers." A cap on noneconomic damages diminishes tort liability for health care providers and diminishes the deterrent effect of tort law.

In sum, chapter 655 was designed by the legislature to help limit the increasing cost of health care and possible "diminishing . . . availability of health care in Wisconsin." The legislature's immediate objective in enacting the $350,000 cap was apparently to ensure the availability of sufficient liability insurance at a reasonable cost to cover claims of patients. "Taming the costs of medical malpractice and ensuring access to affordable health care are legitimate legislative objectives." The legislative cap and the classification of medical malpractice victims appear to express a legislative balancing of objectives: to ensure quality health care in the state; to compensate injured victims of medical malpractice; and to protect health care providers from excessive costs of medical malpractice insurance.

D. The Rational Basis

1

We now explore whether a rational relationship exists between the legislative objective of compensating victims fairly and the classification of medical malpractice victims into two groups — those who suffer noneconomic damages under $350,000 and those who suffer noneconomic damages over $350,000. With regard to the classification of victims, "the Equal Protection Clause 'imposes a requirement of some rationality in the nature of the class singled out.' "[citations omitted.]

No one disputes that the cap does not apply equally to all medical malpractice victims. Indeed, the burden of the cap falls entirely on the most seriously injured victims of medical malpractice. Those who suffer the most severe injuries will not be fully compensated for their noneconomic damages, while those who suffer relatively minor injuries with lower noneconomic damages will be fully compensated.[115] The greater the injury, the smaller the fraction of noneconomic damages the victim will receive.

According to a 1992 report by the Wisconsin Office of the Commissioner of Insurance, children from ages 0 to 2 with medical malpractice injuries comprise less than 10% of malpractice claims, yet their claims comprise a large portion of the paid claims and expenses of insurers and the Fund. That is, "plaintiffs with the most severe injuries appear to be at the highest risk for inadequate compensation. Hence, the worst-off may suffer a kind of 'double jeopardy' under caps."

---

[115] The lower the cap, the larger the number of people affected. The higher the cap, the smaller the number of people affected.

Young people are most affected by the $350,000 cap on noneconomic damages, not only because they suffer a disproportionate share of serious injuries from medical malpractice, but also because many can expect to be affected by their injuries over a 60- or 70-year life expectancy. This case is a perfect example. Matthew Ferdon has a life expectancy of 69 years; he was injured at birth. An older person with a similarly serious medical malpractice injury will have to live with the injury for a shorter period. Yet both the young and the old are subject to the $350,000 cap on noneconomic damages. Furthermore, because an injured patient shares the cap with family members, the cap has a disparate effect on patients with families.

The legislature enjoys wide latitude in economic regulation. But when the legislature shifts the economic burden of medical malpractice from insurance companies and negligent health care providers to a small group of vulnerable, injured patients, the legislative action does not appear rational. Limiting a patient's recovery on the basis of youth or how many family members he or she has does not appear to be germane to any objective of the law.

If the legislature's objective was to ensure that Wisconsin people injured as a result of medical malpractice are compensated fairly, no rational basis exists for treating the most seriously injured patients of medical malpractice less favorably than those less seriously injured. No rational basis exists for forcing the most severely injured patients to provide monetary relief to health care providers and their insurers.

At least as to the legislative objective of ensuring fair compensation, the legislative classification created by a $350,000 cap on noneconomic damages is arbitrary and creates an undue hardship on a small unfortunate group of plaintiffs. Limitations on noneconomic damages are regressive.

This court made these very same observations in 1995 in . . . a successful due process challenge to the retroactivity of the $1,000,000 cap on noneconomic damage awards. This court concluded that the cap unfairly sought to repair the tort system at the expense of those more seriously injured:

> There is yet one more measure of unfairness that the cap extracts, not just to the plaintiff's but to all people whose noneconomic damages exceed [the cap]. The underlying assertion of the defendants, and of all who seek to impose a cap, is that the tort system is "broke" or at least badly in need of repair. Assuming the truth of that assertion for the sake of argument, the cap imposed here seeks to fix that system at the sole expense of those most seriously injured. That strikes us as neither fair nor equitable. A person whose noneconomic damages is [at or below the cap] recovers 100 percent of his or her noneconomic loss. Those whose injuries exceed the cap receive but a fraction.

We therefore conclude that a rational relationship does not exist between the classifications of victims in the $350,000 cap on noneconomic damages and the legislative objective of compensating victims of medical malpractice fairly. . . . [The court goes on to find that there is no rational basis for the legislative finding that the limit on noneconomic damages will provide citizens with reasonably priced medical malpractice insurance.]

[Concurring and dissenting opinions omitted.]

NOTES

1. *Judicial Mixed Messages About the Validity of Caps.* Notably, at the time of the enactment of the cap provisions which were the focus of the challenge in *Ferdon*, Wisconsin was not considered a particularly troublesome state with respect to healthcare costs and liability insurance increases. The court's decision, however, spurred doctors to push the legislature to enact another cap. WIS. STAT. § 655.017. The amended provision, enacted in 2006, sets the noneconomic cap at $750,000 and specifies its reasoning for establishing the limit. Compare *Etheridge v. Medical Center Hospitals*, 376 S.E.2d 525 (Va. 1989) (upholding $750,000 damage cap imposed by legislature, concluding it did not violate due process, trial by jury or equal protection guarantees and did not compromise court's power under separation of powers doctrine). *See also Davis v. Parham*, 208 S.W.3d 162 (Ark. 2005) (statute of limitations imposed for medical malpractice claims not determined to be offensive "special legislation"). What explains the disparities in courts' views about the validity of noneconomic medical malpractice caps?

2. *Questionable Effects of Noneconomic Damages Caps: Jury Message?* A recent empirical study by Professor Catherine Sharkey challenges whether noneconomic caps actually are effective in stemming compensatory damages in litigated cases. She found a "cross-over effect" — that is, awards of economic damages increased when noneconomic damages are restricted, leaving total awards similar in size before and after the passage of caps. *See* Catherine M. Sharkey, *Unintended Consequences of Medical Malpractice Damages Caps*, 80 N.Y.U. L. REV. 391, 493 (2005). What does such a surprising finding say about the strategies of lawyers faced with caps in the jurisdiction in which they litigate? What policy considerations regarding reform do these findings raise? What message are jurors sending?

3. *Medical Liability Alternatives?* Some commentators argue that special panels or funds should be available to resolve disputes related to medical injuries, similar to workplace injuries. *See, e.g.*, Virginia's Birth-Related Injury Compensation Act, VA. CODE ANN. §§ 38.2-5000 to 38.2-5021 (Supp. 1988) (substituting a panel judgment for tort recovery and automatically compensating any newborn deemed to have incurred injury to the brain or spinal cord occurring in the course of labor or in the immediate post-delivery period). Is the creation of a fund to compensate for certain medical maloccurences a better way to address medical malpractice claims? See the discussion about the creation of compensation funds in response to 9/11 and asbestos-related claims set forth below.

Is the goal in medical malpractice and products liability to reduce the number or amount of claims? Is your answer affected by the reports discussed above, of the small number of filings as contrasted with avoidable medical error or by recent studies documenting that cyclical economic factors, not litigation, affect medical insurance rates? *See* Alexee Deep Conroy, *Lessons Learned from the "Laboratories of Democracy:" A Critique of Federal Medical Liability Reform*, 91 CORNEL L. REV. 1159 (2006).

As in other areas discussed in this chapter, there is an abundance of literature on tort reform and its effect on medical malpractice suits. In addition to other commentary already mentioned, see Claudia H. Williams & Michelle M. Mello, Medical Malpractice: Impact of the Crisis and Effect of State Tort Reforms, Robert Wood Johnson Research Synthesis Report No. 10 (May 2006); David M. Studdert et al., Claims, Errors, and Compensation Payments in Medical Malpractice Litigation, NEW. ENG. J. MED. 354 (19): 2024-33 (May 11, 2006). *See also* Nicolas P. Terry, *To HIPAA, a Son: Assessing the Technical, Conceptual, and Legal Frameworks for Patient Safety Information*, 12 WIDENER L. REV. 133 (2005).

3. Joint and Several Liability

During the mid-1980s about 35 states enacted legislation eliminating or restricting joint and several liability in various ways. *See* Richard W. Wright, *Allocating Liability Among Multiple Responsible Causes: A Principled Defense of Joint and Several Liability,* 21 U.C. DAVIS L. REV. 1141 (1988). A major impetus for these enactments again was a perceived tort crisis, coupled with a feeling that it is "unfair" to hold a defendant liable for an injury that was the fault of another wrongdoer. REST. 3D APPORT. OF LIAB. § 17 cmt. *a* (2000) confirms that joint and several liability "has been substantially modified in most jurisdictions both as a result of the adoption of comparative fault and tort reform during the 1980s and 1990s." *See* Chapter 13, *supra.*

Traditionally courts justified joint liability (in effect, holding a defendant liable for all the plaintiff's damages, even though another at-fault person may have contributed to the injury) on the grounds that, as between an innocent plaintiff and a guilty defendant, the risk of non-recovery against another potential tortfeasor should rest with the guilty defendant (through an action for contribution or indemnity), rather than with the innocent plaintiff (in an original suit). The fairness argument against joint liability may have the most appeal where both plaintiff and defendant are at fault and there is another tortfeasor who is judgment-proof or immune. With the widespread adoption of comparative fault, the justification for joint liability disappears in those situations in which the plaintiff also is at fault. But what if the plaintiff is innocent in a comparative fault jurisdiction? *See, e.g.,* Frank L. Marist & Thomas C. Galligan, Jr., *Burying Caesar: Civil Justice Reform and the Changing Face of Louisiana Tort Law*, 71 TUL. L. REV. 339 (1996). Even with statutory reform, joint liability is generally retained in the context of vicarious liability of an actor, and in those situations where defendants act in concert. For a more detailed discussion of joint and several liability, see *Piner v. Superior Court*, 962 P.2d 909, 914 (Ariz. 1998), discussed in Chapter 13, *supra.*

NOTES

1. *The Marginally Responsible Defendant.* One concern about joint and several liability is with the defendant who is only slightly at fault but who nevertheless may be responsible for all of the damages. Consider for example *Gehres v. Phoenix,* 753 P.2d 174 (Ariz. 1987). In *Gehres*, the defendant tavern served an allegedly intoxicated patron, who later killed plaintiff's deceased in a car collision while seeking to elude police officers during a high-speed car chase. The jury found the drunk driver 95% at fault, the tavern 3%, and the city 2%.

The drunk driver was killed in the crash, and his estate was insolvent. The court held that either the tavern or the city could be made to pay the entire damages for the wrongful death of plaintiff's deceased. After this suit, the Arizona legislature abolished joint liability in tort for concurrent tortfeasors. *See* ARIZ. REV. STAT. § 12-2506.

Suppose in *Gehres* the "fault" lay with the tavern and bad weather conditions? Fault would not be attributed to the weather conditions. Is an inanimate "faulty" cause different from an insolvent, immune, or unidentifiable, faulty human cause for purposes of determining the degree of fault fairly attributable to the tavern? Suppose the only party at fault was the tavern; how much fault would then be attributable to the tavern?

How sound are criticisms leveled at "marginal fault" cases? Is a fact-finder's determination that a concurrent tortfeasor is, say, 3% responsible a reflection on that defendant's degree of fault, the standard of care, or an assessment of the relative fault of all the actors? For a more detailed discussion of joint and several liability problems and "reform"-related efforts to apportion see Chapter 13, *supra*.

2. *Diversity of Views About Joint and Several Liability.* The states have taken a variety of positions on joint and several liability. For an effort to catalogue and analyze the principal approaches taken, see REST. 3D TORTS § 17, REPORTERS' NOTES.

3. *Uniform Contribution Among Tortfeasors Act.* The Uniform Contribution Among Tortfeasors Act, 12 U.L.A 87, directs the fact-finder to compare cause as well as fault in making a damage apportionment. Is this a fairer approach for determining whether and under what circumstances to eliminate joint liability and move to several liability?

F. PREEMPTION

State statutes may be direct and unambiguous in granting tort rights or immunities. However, many state and federal statutes have a more indirect or tangential effect. A statute can expressly preempt or restrict a statutory or common-law claim or remedy. For example, the Tennessee products liability statute, TENN. CODE ANNOT. § 29-28-104 (2006), provides that product compliance with a statutory or administrative regulation creates a rebuttable presumption of nondefectiveness. A statute may also be read as impliedly preempting, in whole or in part, a previously recognized statutory or common-law claim or remedy; in that case, a court must determine whether the preempting provision occupies the field, or conflicts substantially with the purpose of the previous statutory or common-law provision.

In this era of tort retrenchment, courts have faced difficult questions about the effect of federal statutes and regulations that explicitly or by implication preempt common-law tort rights and remedies. *See, e.g.,* Howard L. Dorfman, Vivian M. Quinn, & Elizabeth A. Brophy, *Presumption of Innocence: FDA's Authority to Regulate the Specifics of Prescription Drug Labeling and the Preemption Debate,* 61 FOOD DRUG L.J. 585, 594-604 (2006). The Supremacy Clause of the U.S. Constitution requires that state law must give way if it conflicts with federal law or where it can be inferred that Congress intended to displace state law. Thomas C. Galligan, Jr., *U.S. Supreme Court Tort Reform: Limiting State Power to Articulate and Develop Tort Law — Defamation, Preemption, and Punitive Damages*, 74 U. CIN. L. REV. 1189, 1223 (2006). Because preemption may be explicitly set forth or inferred by the court from the language or structure of legislation, courts potentially wield great power in construing reform-focused statutes.

Traditionally, courts recognized a presumption *against* implied preemption in the case of federal legislation operating to preempt state tort and regulatory law, provided the state law was not clearly incompatible with the federal regulation. This presumption is attributable in part to concerns about federalism and intrusion into the states' domain. In addition, it is widely recognized that regulatory legislation is frequently the result of political compromise. Thus some courts have asserted that preemption should not be easily inferred in settings where the state's regulation or common law reflects a decision to impose a higher threshold of safety, offering more protection to tort victims than the federal alternative. *See, e.g., Witczak v. Pfizer*, Inc., 377 F. Supp. 2d 726 (D. Minn. 2005).

There has been a recent spate of litigation concerning statutory preemption, particularly after the Supreme Court's ruling in *Cippollone v. Ligett Group, Inc.* 505 U.S. 504 (1992) (plurality treatment of a variety of smokers' liability claims contended to be preempted by the Cigarette Labeling and Advertising Act of 1965 and Public Health Cigarette Smoking Act of 1969). Notably, in *Aetna Health v. Davila*, 542 U.S. 200 (2004), the Court held ERISA (Employment Retirement Income Security Act of 1974, Pub. L. No. 93-406, 88 Stat. 829, codified at 29 U.S.C. § 1106) preempts tort actions against managed care organizations that provide healthcare benefits under an ERISA plan. Prior to *Davila*, the lower federal and state courts had struggled to distinguish the conduct of managed care companies that made them subject to state tort liability and the conduct that was immunized from state liability. The effect of *Davila* is that most individuals who obtain healthcare coverage as part of employee benefits are not able to pursue tort remedies against managed care companies while those who have non-ERISA healthcare coverage benefits will also have the protection of state tort law.

Plaintiffs' state common-law claims have sometimes prevailed even where a federal regulation expressly provides that no state may "establish or continue in effect . . . [a common-law statutory provision] which is different from, or in addition to, any requirement under this chapter." *See Medtronic, Inc. v. Lohr*, 518 U.S. 470, 484 (1996) (addressing the effect of 21 U.S.C. § 360k(a)(1)). Conversely, manufacturers have successfully challenged common-law damages claims in contexts where they have complied with federal regulatory standards. *See Geier v. American Honda Motor Co.*, 529 U.S. 861 (2000) (finding no express preemption, Court ruled that the federal law impliedly preempted common-law claims in order to avoid interfering with the federal scheme).

The federal courts have found preemption of state law expressly or by implication in some federal regulatory contexts, such as legislation dealing with airbag safety, and The Federal Insecticide, Fungicide, and Rodenticide Act (FIFRA) (Federal Insecticide, Fungicide, and Rodenticide Act, Pub. L. 109-279,

61 Stat. 163, codified at 7 U.S.C. § 136). Most recently, prescription drug manufacturers have raised highly controversial but often successful challenges to
state product liability claims, arguing that Food and Drug Administration
(FDA) regulations displace the state law. *See, e.g., Flynn v. Am. Home Prods.
Corp.*, 627 N.W.2d 342 (Minn. Ct. App. 2001) (holding that the state-law claims
of a woman harmed from taking the weight loss drug Phen-fen were preempted by FDA approval of the drug, regardless of whether its manufacturer
had failed to tell the FDA about harmful side effects of the drug that the
manufacturer may have learned about).

See generally Barbara L. Atwell, *Products Liability and Preemption: A
Judicial Framework*, 39 BUFF. L. REV. 181 (1990); Richard C. Ausness, *Federal
Preemption of State Products Liability Doctrines*, 44 S. CAROLINA L. REV. 187
(1993); Peter L. Kahn, *Regulation and Simple Arithmetic: Shifting the
Perspective on Tort Reform*, 72 N. CAROLINA L. REV. 1129 (1994); Ralph Nader
& Joseph A. Page, A*utomobile-Design Liability and Compliance with Federal
Standards*, 64 GEO.WASH. L. REV. 414 (1996). *See also* Richard A. Nagareda,
FDA Preemption: When Tort Law Meets the Administrative State, http://www.
bepres.com/jtl/vol1/iss1/art4; Richard A. Epstein, *Why the FDA Must Preempt
Tort Litigation: A Critique of Chevron Deference and a Response to Richard
Nagareda*, http://www.bepress.com/jtl/vol1/iss1/art5; Elissa Levy, Note, *The
Health Act's FDA Defense to Punitive Damages: A Gift to Drug Makers or to the
Public?*, 74 FORD. L. REV. 2425 (2006) (arguing that punitive awards should be
barred if pharmaceutical companies comply with FDA regulations because of
the special need for drugs and because of the comprehensive nature of FDA
regulations).

NOTES

1. *Statutory Interpretation.* Courts considering preemption challenges are
essentially engaged in statutory interpretation and "[t]his 'particular statute'-
based focus makes it hard to draw general conclusions and, in fact, contributes
to the overall confusion" in the recent doctrinal developments in this area.
Galligan, *supra*, 74 U. CIN. L. REV. at 1242. Is this an area where the Court
seems poised to promote retrenchment?

2. *Implied Preemption with the Aid of Agency Regulations.* In 2006, the FDA
promulgated Labeling Regulations that have persuaded some courts to rethink
their interpretation of implied preemption. Prior to the regulations, courts
appeared reluctant to find preemption of personal injury claims. After the
promulgation of the 2006 new prescription drug labeling rules, there are
mixed results in preemption challenges. Some courts have ruled that failure-
to-warn state claims are preempted by the labeling requirements, while others
disagree, taking a more traditional posture of leaning towards preserving common-law protection. *Compare, e.g., Colacicco v. Apotex, Inc.,* 432 F. Supp. 2d 514
(E.D. Pa. 2006) (notice of appeal filed June 19, 2006) (dismissing state-law
claim of failure to warn of risks associated with Paxil, an anti-depressant
drug), *with e.g., Jackson v. Pfizer, Inc.*, 432 F. Supp. 2d 964 (D. Neb. 2006) (giving no deference to the FDA, and dismissing FDA's regulatory preamble as
"not persuasive," court ruled federal regulation did not preempt Nebraska

failure to warn claims related to the drugs Zoloft and Effexor). In support of its ruling in *Jackson*, the court also quoted *Missouri Board of Examiners for Hearing Instrument Specialists v. Help Express, Inc.,* 447 F.3d 1033, 1035 (8th Cir. 2006) (noting that implied preemption is rarely found). *See also Perry v. Norvatis Pharm.* Corp., 2006 U.S. Dist. LEXIS 75319 (E.D. Pa. 2006). Distinguishing *Colacicco, supra,* the Eastern District for Pennsylvania in this case stated that in contrast with regulations related to antidepressants, the regulation of drug for the treatment of atopic dermatitis was not one where it is impossible to comply with federal and state law). Dorfman, *supra,* 61 FOOD & DRUG L.J. at 617. Is it surprising that the FDA would take the position that its labeling requirements have a preemptive effect? Notably, the FDA through the Department of Justice has filed amicus briefs contending that its regulation "is pervasive so as to ensure each drug's optimal use by requiring inclusion of only scientifically substantiated warnings" and that "[p]laintiff's failure to warn cases . . . stand as an obstacle to the FDA's accomplishment of its congressionally mandated purpose of ensuring the public health" and therefore courts ought to recognize preemption. Dorfman, *supra,* 61 FOOD & DRUG L.J. at 591. What are the arguments a plaintiff is likely to make in response to these assertions?

G.   ALTERNATIVE DISPUTE MECHANISMS: TRIAL-RELATED DEVICES

From the simplest assault and battery, to the devastating, negligently performed medical procedure, to the complex toxic tort or products liability case, the relationship between torts and the classic litigation model seems at first blush to be unquestionable. Indeed, the relationship between torts and traditional litigation techniques may seem almost paradigmatic. Whether used critically or not, phrases such as "hired gun" and "battle of experts" pervade any discussion of tort law and process.

A seasoned student of torts, however, will soon conclude that the classical litigation model is not without limitations. It becomes apparent, for example, that entire classes of cases go unresolved because they are too "small" to attract contingent-fee-based representation. Large numbers of plaintiffs effectively turn away from the courts because litigation, even if successful, fails to provide anything other than the rather clumsy remedy of monetary damages, not meeting the needs arising out of their controversies. Parties often settle meritorious tort claims too cheaply, compromised because they are faced with the costs and delays inherent in the traditional process. Moreover, the adversarial process seems particularly unsuited for some claims, leading to skepticism about whether it is able to accomplish justice.

Challenges to traditional litigation techniques have struck at the heart of mainstream tort law. Does litigation continue to represent the most efficient solution for complex products liability and environmental actions? Should an unsuccessful medical result inevitably lead to the rupture of the physician-patient relationship in open court? Is the jury an effective decision-making body in resolving most disputes? Commentators have proposed alternatives to the litigation process, drawing on the experiences of dispute resolutions in other contexts. For example, for years, labor arbitrators have handled grievances under collective bargaining agreements. Arbitration of automobile insurance claims is now widespread. Divorces and child-custody disputes are often mediated. And, pertinently, today the overwhelming majority of tort disputes are negotiated to settlement, a fact which may be easily overlooked or unduly minimized in part because of the traditional casebook focus upon decisions of the appellate courts. Lastly, administrative disposition of claims often eclipse the importance of courts in healthcare and civil rights.

In the torts area, alternative dispute resolution mechanisms are not limited to arbitration and negotiation. Forward-thinking judges have infused the traditional litigation process with innovative alternative devices and legislatures have been particularly active in tailoring particular dispute resolution devices to address discrete areas of tort law. In addition, many individuals and organizations have adopted existing consensual arrangements or created new mechanisms to address their disputes. As a consequence, it has become easy to challenge the assumptions about the resolution of controversies potentially arising as tort claims: (1) that disputants are adversaries — *i.e.,* if one wins, others must lose — and (2) that disputes may be resolved through application, by a third "disinterested" decision maker, of some general rule of law. These assumptions, plainly, are polar opposites of those which may underlie alternative dispute resolution processes: (1) that all parties can benefit from a creative solution to which each agrees; and (2) that the situation is unique and therefore not to be governed by any general principle except to the extent that the parties accept it. *See generally Symposium: Quality of Dispute Resolution*, 66 DENV. U. L. REV. 499 (1989); Harry T. Edwards, *Alternate Dispute Resolution: Panacea or Anathema?,* 99 HARV. L. REV. 668 (1986); Leonard Riskin, *Mediation and Lawyers,* 43 OHIO ST. L.J. 29, 43–48 (1982). The following sections briefly highlight some of the dispute resolution alternatives that are presently being employed.

1. Summary Jury Trial

One of the alternative mechanisms utilized within the traditional litigation structure is the summary jury trial (SJT). A pre-trial procedure often used in cases where settlement seems unlikely and negotiations seem at an impasse, SJT can add appreciably to the settlement of trial-bound cases. If settlement is not achieved, the case can go to trial. In a summary jury proceeding, counsel present abbreviated arguments to jurors who render an informal verdict that guides the settlement of the case. Normally, six mock jurors are chosen after a brief voir dire conducted by the court. Following short opening statements, all evidence is presented in the form of a descriptive summary to the mock jury through the parties' attorneys. Live witnesses do not testify. Because evidentiary objections are discouraged, some of the evidence disclosed to the mock jury might not be admissible at a real trial.

Following counsels' presentations, the jury is given an abbreviated charge and then retires to deliberate. The jury then returns a "verdict." To emphasize the settlement function of the exercise, counsel often asks the mock jury to assess damages even if it finds no liability. Also, the court and jurors join the attorneys and parties after the "verdict" is returned in an informal discussion of the strength and weaknesses of each side's case. Thomas Lambros, *The Summary Jury Trial — An Alternative Method of Resolving Disputes,* 69 JUDICATURE 286, 289 (Feb.-Mar. 1986); Thomas Lambros, *The Summary Jury Trial and Other Alternative Methods of Dispute Resolution:* A Report to the Judicial Conference of the United States Committee on the Operation of the Jury System, 103 F.R.D. 461, 483-84 (1984); S. Arthur Spiegel, *Summary Jury Trials,* 54 U. CIN. L. REV. 829 (1986).

SJT is attractive because it uses the input of a jury of lay persons as fact-finders. The decision from the SJT inevitably results in both sides reexamining and reevaluating their positions and demands. SJT can permit clarification of the issues, and even if it does not promote settlement, it can effectuate more careful preparation for trial. In *Federal Reserve Bank of Minneapolis v. Carey-Canada, Inc.,* 123 F.R.D. 603, 604-05 (D. Minn. 1988), the court observed:

> The SJT represents one alternative . . . to secure to civil litigants just, speedy, and inexpensive determination of their claims of which litigants may be otherwise deprived because of the overwhelming and overburdening caseloads in many federal courts.

In contrast, then-Professor, now Judge, Richard Posner expressed skepticism about the advantages brought by this mechanism. He poses these questions: "What is it about summary jury trial which stimulates settlement? Is it the result of the SJU or, notwithstanding the SJT verdict, the realization that trial verdicts essentially are unpredictable? Or the psychological shift of the parties' attention from pre-resolution to resolution matters?" Richard Posner, *The Summary Jury Trial and Other Methods of Alternative Dispute Resolution: Some Cautionary Observations,* 53 U. CHI. L. REV. 366 (1980).

The prevailing authority is that SJT participation cannot be compelled. *Strandell v. Jackson County,* 838 F.2d 884 (7th Cir. 1987) (Rule 16(c) of the Federal Rules of Civil Procedure does not authorize a mandatory SJT since rule "was not intended to require that an unwilling litigant be sidetracked from the normal course of litigation"). *But see Federal Reserve Bank of Minneapolis v. Carey-Canada, Inc.,* 123 F.R.D. 603 (D. Minn. 1988) (federal magistrate ruled that the right to compel participation in a SJT is within inherent jurisdiction of the court).

2. Mini-Trials

Mini-trials have much in common with the process used in court-ordered or encouraged SJTs. The principal distinction is that the mini-trial operates independently from any official proceeding. The mini-trial and other related mechanisms such as "rent-a-judge," raise difficult issues about our commitment to the public process of dispute resolution. What is the impact on the civil system of permitting these private arrangements? For example, attorneys often rely on retired judges to preside and they are paid well and have great flexibility in such opportunities. Will judges consider these "private judging" options attractive enough to opt out of the public process? *See* Comment,

Whose Dispute Is This Anyway?: The Propriety of the Mini-Trial in Promoting Corporate Dispute Resolution, 1987 MO. J. DISP. RES. 133.

The so-called "rent-a-judge" mechanism is not inevitably private. Notably, CAL. CIV. PROC. CODE § 638 (2007) provides:

> A referee may be appointed upon the agreement of the parties filed with the clerk, or judge, or entered in the minutes or upon the motion of a party to a written contract or lease that provides that any controversy arising therefrom shall be heard by a referee if the court finds a reference agreement exists between the parties:

> (a) To hear and determine any or all of the issues in an action or proceeding, wheather of fact or of law, and to report a statement decision.

> (b) To ascertain a fact necessary to enable the court to determine an action or proceeding.

> CAL. CIV. PROC. CODE § 644 (2007) states:

> (a) In the case of a consensual general reference pursuant to Section 638, the decision of the referee or commissioner upon the whole issue must stand as the decision of the court, and upon filing of the statement of decision with the clerk of the court, or with the judge where there is no clerk, judgment may be entered thereon in the same manner as if the action had been tried by the court.

> (b) In the case of all other references, the decision of the referee or commissioner is only advisory. The court may adopt the referee's recommendations in whole or in part after independently considering the referee's findings and any objections and responses thereto filed with the court.

3. Court-Induced and Other Settlement Techniques

Drawing on their inherent authority to manage and to preserve the efficiency and integrity of the judicial process, some federal courts have engaged in aggressive settlement tactics such as ordering represented parties to appear at pretrial settlement conferences. How far can these aggressive tactics go? For example, the United States Court of Appeals for the Seventh Circuit sustained a federal magistrate's sanctions against the defendant who had been ordered to send a corporate representative with authority to settle to a pretrial conference and failed to comply. *G. Heileman Brewing Co. v. Joseph Oat Corp.,* 871 F.2d 648 (7th Cir. 1989).

States have undertaken other steps to require settlement consideration. For example, FLA. STAT. § 766.108 (2007) provides:

> (2)(a) In any action for damages based on personal injury or wrongful death arising out of medical malpractice, whether in tort or contract, the court shall require a settlement conference at least 3 weeks before the date set for trial.

(b) Attorneys who will conduct the trial, parties, and persons with authority to settle shall attend the settlement conference held before the court unless excused by the court for good cause.

Scholars have questioned whether such a provision interferes with the client's representation decision. *See generally* Judith Resnik, *Managerial Judges,* 96 HARV. L. REV. 376 (1982); Carrie Menkel-Meadow, *For and Against Settlement: Uses and Abuses of the Mandatory Settlement Conference,* 33 U.C.L.A. L. REV. 485 (1985); Marc Galanter, *The Quality of Settlements,* 1988 J. DISP. RES. 55.

Another useful settlement device is computer modeling of settlement values in complex, multi-party litigation. One example of the use of this device occurred in asbestos litigation. Judge Lambros of the Northern District Court of Ohio utilized computer modeling to suggest settlement values in the cases. By bifurcating discovery and first seeking only information necessary to assess settlement value, special masters appointed by the judge could match data, expressed in terms of 380 variables, related to cases already completed in that geographical area. The computer model was adjusted for inflation and provided a suggested settlement value for the case in point. The historical matches were presented to the parties at a settlement conference in an attempt to narrow the range of the negotiations. *See* Steve Nelson, Asbestos Case Plan Submitted, 6 LEGAL TIMES No. 21 (Oct. 24, 1983) at 6; Rich Arthurs, Counsel Debate Computer Value in Settlement Talks, 7 LEGAL TIMES No. 10 (Aug. 6, 1984) at 1; John Riley, Asbestos: New Approaches, Lawyers, Judges Strive to Break Gridlock, 6 NAT'L L.J. No. 35 (May 7, 1984) at 1; Ken Myers, Routine? No, It Was a Slugfest, 11 NATIONAL L. J. No. 6 (Oct. 17, 1988) at 8. Attorneys for 1,200 Dalkon Shield claimants reportedly developed computer modeling software to prepare settlement positions for their clients. Karen Dillon, Software to Speed Dalkon Claims, 10 AM. Law. No. 6 (Jul./Aug. 1988) at 17.

Massive or complex cases may be assigned to special masters for settlement scheduling. Faced with a docket of over 4,000 asbestos cases, a Maryland district court judge appointed Kenneth R. Feinberg as special master. Feinberg had helped negotiate settlements in the Agent Orange and Dalkon Shield cases. Most of the plaintiffs were represented by one attorney, but there were 85 defendants. Feinberg concentrated on negotiating a scheduled approach to settlement (based on age and type of injury) between the plaintiffs' attorney and individual defendants rather than the defendants as a group. Stephen Labaton, *Business and the Law: A Plan to Speed Asbestos Cases,* N.Y. TIMES, Oct. 23, 1989, at 22, col. 1. Feinberg and another special master, David I. Shapiro, became instrumental players in settlement negotiations in the Agent Orange litigation upon appointment by Federal Judge Jack B. Weinstein. Sixteen Vietnam Was veterans and seven chemical companies reached a settlement totaling $180 million. *See* W. John Moore, *Long Road Ends in Agent Orange Pact,* 6 LEGAL TIMES NO. 49 (May 14, 1984) at 2. It is notable that the special masters usually met with one side and then the other, rather than conduct face-to-face meetings with both sides.

4. Settlement Funds

Several recent massive tort events have posed new challenges for the torts litigation system in sharp relief; administrative funds have become a useful vehicle for securing compensation and addressing the problem of massive claims that would tax the resources of the courts. This administrative proceeding alternative is not new, but its significance lies in the parties' ability to respond to both private claims and social concerns related to the controversy.

a. Post-911 Victims Compensation Fund

The Victims Compensation Act enacted by Congress in 2001, 49 U.S.C. § 40101, provided a quick response to compensation claims of victims of the terrorist attacks on 9/11 and their families, entitling families who lost members to recover and compensating survivors for injuries related to the attacks. All claimants who agree to accept compensation through the fund waive all civil remedies in connection with the attacks and therefore are precluded from suing New York City, the World Trade Center, and airlines involved in the attacks. Fund administrators processed claims for over 2800 deaths. Each family received $250,000 for pain and suffering related to the events and each surviving spouse (including domestic partners) and dependent child received $100,000 for loss of companionship. Total awards ranged from $250,000 to $7.1 million and the average award was a little over $2 million. More than 2600 personal injury claims were filed and these awards ranged from $500 to $8.6 million. Robert M. Ackerman, *The September 11th Victim Compensation Fund: An Effective Administrative Response to a National Tragedy,* 10 HARV. NEGOT. L. REV. 135, 181 (2005*).* Under the provisions of the law, collateral sources would reduce compensation paid, excluding $1.5 billion raised by charities for the victims. Diana Henriques, Victims Get a Break on Early Charity, N. Y. TIMES, Dec. 20, 2001, at B7. Was this provision added in response to reform proponents' interest in changing the collateral source rule?

Some commentators have criticized the manner of distribution of compensation. *See* Martha Chamallas, *Civil Rights in Ordinary Tort Cases: Race, Gender, and the Calculation of Economic Loss,* 38 LOY. LA. L. REV. 1435 (2005) (noting possible gender-related disparities in awards). Kenneth Feinberg, well known for his work as Special Master in other complex massive tort settings, served as Administrator of the Fund. In his view, part of the success of the Fund can be attributed to the Fund's efforts to reach every victim, let them tell their stories, and respond to their noneconomic as well as economic injuries. Feinberg argues that this Fund, and investigative process was a response to a unique social event in our history and should not be repeated (regardless of the likelihood of reoccurrence of a similar tragedy or other extraordinary event). Kenneth Feinberg, Remarks at the Annual Meeting of the Association of American Law Schools (Wash. D.C. Jan. 4, 2007). For a detailed report reviewing the compensation for loss and other matters published by the Rand Corp., see http://www.rand.org/pubs/monographs/2004/rand_MG264.pdf.

b. Asbestos Litigation Settlement Techniques

Because of its complexities and the sheer volume of cases, the asbestos litigation led courts to adopt innovative dispute resolution techniques that have sometimes challenged the traditional litigation model and tested the capacity of the civil liability system to handle such problems. As a consequence of this product's broad and significant harm-producing exposure, asbestos litigation burgeoned over decades and single-handedly ruptured the torts (and insurance) systems, exacerbating the perception of a crisis in torts. *See generally* Comment, *Alternatives to Litigation: Toxic Torts and Alternate Dispute Resolution — A Proposed Solution to the Mass Tort Case,* 20 RUTGERS L.J. 779 (1989).

Early focus was on the appropriate response of substantive products liability law to the manufacturers of a product with dangerous properties that manufacturers claimed not to have known at the time of production. *See, e.g., Borel v. Fibreboard Paper Prods. Corp.,* 493 F.2d 1076, 1089 (5th Cir. 1973), cert. denied, 419 U.S. 869 (1974); *Beshada v. Johns-Manville Prods. Corp.,* 447 A.2d 539, 545-46 (1982). Then workers and their families made ever-mounting filings, including, initially, some 40,000 shipyard workers and installers of insulation materials, followed by a host of other affected workers. The extraordinary volume of work-related filings nearly paralyzed some courts. Later, in a second wave, school districts and end-users of the product brought more than 15,000 suits for property damage. A third wave of cases involved thousands of tire and rubber workers and others from service industries with somewhat more incidental contact with asbestos in their workplaces. These waves of suits paralleled claims by the 50 or so asbestos manufacturers against their 75 coverage-disputing insurers, and many manufacturers sought to limit their exposure to liability in Chapter 11 reorganizations. *See, e.g., Keene Corp. v. Insurance Co. of N. Am.,* 667 F.2d 1034 (D.C. Cir. 1981), *cert. denied,* 455 U.S. 1007 (1982).

The astronomical number of plaintiffs, the unusually large number of co-defendants, and the complex causation issues stimulated the development and use of several innovative approaches to dispute resolution such as summary jury trials and computer modeling discussed *supra.* One noteworthy alternative was the establishment of the Asbestos Claims Facility, a product of the so-called "Wellington Agreement," named after Harry H. Wellington, a former dean of Yale Law School. *See generally* Harry H. Wellington, *Asbestos: The Private Management of a Public Problem,* 33 CLEV. ST. L. REV. 375 (1984) (from which much of the description which follows comes); Comment, *The Asbestos Claims Facility — An Alternative to Litigation,* 24 DUQ. L. REV. 833 (1986). The 1985 agreement followed mediation and negotiation using novel dispute resolution techniques which promised to settle outstanding cases between 34 major asbestos producers and their 16 insurers. The objective was to make a single settlement offer of compensatory but not punitive damages to claimants. Under the terms of the agreement, each claimant could refuse the offer, mediate or arbitrate the offer, or go to trial against a presumably unified group of defendants. The Claims Facility members shared costs of the Claim Facility, a not-for-profit corporation, in proportion to their pre-Wellington payments. Significantly, one defendant, the heavily exposed Johns-Manville Corporation, was not a member of the Claims Facility. Although the Claims Facility's original workload consisted of cases transferred from about a thousand law firms which had been defending claims, the Claims Facility intended to permit unrepresented claimants to register directly with it.

Plaintiffs' attorneys were wary, alleging that the Claims Facility was primarily a coordinator of the defense's litigation tactics and a vehicle designed to delay the processing of claims. Indeed, an antitrust suit was filed against the producers and insurers for their participation in the Claims Facility. However, in its first two-and-a-half years, the Claims Facility apparently settled some 20,000 cases. The Claims Facility collapsed in 1988 because of the third wave of filings involving workers outside of the installation trades. Many of the larger producers complained that the financing of the Claims Facility's operations and settlements had been based on the case profile of the first wave of filings, and was inappropriate for the later claims. A new Facility — the Center for Claims Resolution — was established, in which a much smaller number of producers and insurers participated. Asbestos claims continue to challenge the capacity of the system.

After thirty years of litigation, continuing concerns about effectively and fairly resolving the myriad asbestos suits led to the Fairness in Asbestos Injury Resolution Act of 2005, a federal proposal for handling remaining cases, which would establish a $140 billion privately financed asbestos trust fund. The fund proposal has languished in Congress. Martha Neil, *Backing Away from the Abyss*, 92 A.B.A. J. 26 (Sept. 2006). *See generally* Kenneth Feinberg, *The Toxic Tort Litigation Crisis: Conceptual Problems and Proposed Solutions*, 24 Hous. L. Rev. 155 (1987); Peter Schuck, *The Role of Judges in Settling Complex Cases: The Agent Orange Example*, 53 U. Chi. L. Rev. 337 (1980).

NOTES

1. *Philosophical Underpinnings of ADR.* What should be the "philosophical map" that lawyers draw upon in modern dispute resolution? What risks and benefits are presented by a shift away from the classical litigation model? ADR can promote satisfactory resolution of controversies but what are the risks parties should assess in using ADR? Do such risks unfairly limit some plaintiffs' access to courts and to juries? Consider how law and economics, social justice, and critical race theories affect your answers to these questions. How would a pragmatist or feminist theorist respond? *See generally* Frank Sandler, *Alternative Methods of Dispute Resolution: An Overview*, 37 U. Fla. L. Rev. 1 (1985). *But see* Trina Grillo, *The Mediation Alternative: Process Dangers for Women*, 100 Yale L.J. 1545 (1991) (questioning whether mediation adequately protects women and people of color from bias typically associated with formal procedures).

2. *Risks of Privatization?* Should the mini-trial or rent-a judge mechanism be subjected to any closer scrutiny than other private forms of settlement negotiation? How do these alternatives differ from private arbitration, or judicially-annexed arbitration? *See generally* Note, *The California Rent-A-Judge Experiment: Constitutional and Policy Considerations of Pay-As-You-Go*

Courts, 94 HARV. L. REV. 1592 (1981). Do these mechanisms suggest that we might see evolving total privatization of the legal system? How successful are the most sophisticated negotiation techniques in the absence of the pressure from an imminent, lengthy and expensive trial?

3. *Prediction or Resolution?* What is it about a summary jury trial that stimulates settlement? Is it the result of the SJT or, notwithstanding the SJT verdict, the realization that trial verdicts essentially are unpredictable? Is it significant that there is a psychological shift of the parties' attention from pre-resolution to resolution matters? For a look at other mechanisms that have been developed *within* the traditional litigation structure, see the survey by A. Leo Levin & Deirdre Golash, *Alternative Dispute Resolution in Federal District Courts,* 37 U. FLA. L. REV. 29 (1985). *See generally* Deborah Hensler, *Resolving Mass Toxic Torts: Myths and Realities,* 1989 U. ILL. L. REV. 89.

4. *ADR — Well Suited for Business?* In what ways are the informal dispute mechanisms particularly well tailored to the resolution of business disputes? For an exposition of the choice of ADR mechanisms for such conflicts, see Steven Goldberg, Eric Green & Frank Sander, *Litigation, Arbitration or Mediation: A Dialogue,* 75 A.B.A.J. 70 (June 1989). Consider the strategy, often used in settlement, of meeting with one party and then the other rather than together. What advantages are offered by this approach?

5. *ADR-in-the-Books vs. ADR in Action.* The level of satisfaction that the litigants experience is, of course, critical to an assessment of the success of the various alternatives to the traditional dispute resolution system. In one study of tort litigants' views of trials, court-annexed arbitration, and judicial settlement conferences, the results show that participants are able to distinguish the competing values and features of the alternatives. In particular, the litigants cared strongly about whether their cases received dignified, careful, and unbiased hearings. They also wanted to exercise some control over the handling and ultimate outcome of their cases. Overall, they wanted procedures with which they could feel "comfortable" — but their specifications for comfort did not necessarily match the expectations of practitioners. Although one might have thought that the trial, with its formality and impersonality, would prove more troubling to litigants than other more informal, participatory procedures such as settlement conferences, for many respondents, trials engendered a desirable sense of control and participation in the process. The study suggests that the litigants felt that trials increased, not decreased, their involvement in the legal process. The litigants often preferred trial to settlement — they found the trial fair as well as more satisfactory.

Respondents seemed favorably disposed to some less formal alternative procedures than trials like the court-annexed arbitration. However, respondents also seemed to favor arbitration but not because it was relatively informal. They liked it because, like a trial, arbitration struck them as dignified and careful. While a sense of dignity and carefulness in the process seemed important, the actual costs, outcome, and duration of the cases had surprisingly little impact on levels of satisfaction. Litigation costs bore no substantial relationship to perceived fairness or satisfaction. Winners tended to be happier than losers, but this factor accounted for only a small portion of the variation in litigants' responses. And delay correlated even less closely with litigant satisfaction and perceived fairness than did case outcome. R-3708-ICJ, *The Instit. For Civil Justice Ann. Rep.* Apr. 1, 1990-March 31, 1991, at 18.

H. MANDATORY ARBITRATION AS AN ALTERNATIVE TO TORT LITIGATION

1. Pretrial Review and the Right of Access to the Courts

State statutes providing for pretrial arbitration are controversial. In *Firelock, Inc. v. District Court*, 776 P.2d 1090 (Colo. 1989), the court upheld the constitutionality of Colorado's mandatory, but nonbinding, pretrial arbitration procedure, a procedure intended to provide access to a vehicle for resolving disputes quickly and without the costs of trial. According to Justice Erickson, concurring:

> While I acknowledge that the right of access to the courts is an important one, the burgeoning case load in our courts has itself caused delay and increased costs. Access to the courts for all litigants may be improved by different alternatives for dispute resolution, such as arbitration and mediation.

Id. at 1100. In contrast, Justice Lohr, dissenting, found the mandatory arbitration procedure an unconstitutional restriction on the right of access to the courts in two ways:

> First, the litigant may not present his claim to a court until he has undergone the delay and expense attendant to an arbitration proceeding. Second, in order to obtain access to a court after arbitration has been completed, the litigant must accept the consequence that he will be required to pay the costs of the arbitration proceeding, including arbitrator fees, up to a maximum of $1,000 should he fail to improve his position by more than ten percent. These burdens of time and expense are considerable and will likely have the practical effect of preventing litigants with smaller claims from ever obtaining access to the courts to assert them. . . . The majority does not explain why these obviously important limitations on a litigant's fundamental right of access to the courts are permissible except to analogize them to the collection of docket fees, the award of costs to a prevailing party, and the imposition of certain other incidental costs of litigation applicable in special situations. The majority simply offers the conclusion that the burdens are reasonable. I cannot agree. . . .

Id. at 1101-02. *See also Rothstein v. Kuosen Fung*, 2004 U.S. Dist. LEXIS 18409 (S.D.N.Y. 2004) (arbitration can only be compelled with agreement of the parties and not through fraud). In contrast, in *Mattos v. Thompson*, 421 A.2d 190, 191 (Pa. 1980), the court concluded that Pennsylvania's pretrial review system "failed in its goal to render expeditious resolution to medical malpractice claims and consequently imposes an oppressive burden upon the right to jury trial guaranteed by our state constitution." It concluded that the delays in litigation caused by the procedure "are unconscionable and irreparably rip the fabric of public confidence in the efficiency and effectiveness of our judicial system." *Id.* at 195.

2. Medical Malpractice Arbitration Provisions

In an effort to address escalating costs and respond to the perceived malpractice crisis, some "reform" advocates have supported the use of arbitration panels comprised of attorneys and doctors who can evaluate the case before a trial takes place. Statutory provisions to arbitrate medical malpractice disputes before trial have proliferated. Frequently, the state's general arbitration statute, often an adoption of the Uniform Arbitration Act of 1955 (7 U.L.A. 1 (1978 & Supp. 2005)), or the Uniform Arbitration Act of 2000, governs disputes. However, some legislatures have passed specific medical malpractice arbitration provisions.

Enacting a specific medical malpractice arbitration provision has certain advantages. First, it can tailor the process to the particular nature of a medical claim. Second, it can provide a degree of protection for the patient. Third, enactment of such a statute should determine whether a medical malpractice claim is arbitrable in that state. The typical malpractice arbitration act will identify the parties who may execute a malpractice arbitration agreement, regulate certain substantive provisions in the agreement, and address the content of pre-execution disclosure.

Courts have generally rejected challenges to these statutes. In *Morris v. Metriyakool*, 344 N.W.2d 736 (Mich. 1984), the plaintiff challenged the constitutionality of the Michigan statute. The challenge focused on the provision that one of the arbitrators must be a physician or a hospital administrator. Mich. Comp. Laws § 600.5044(2) (1989). The court, however, denied the plaintiffs' procedural due process claim of decision-making bias. Justice Ryan, concurring, added:

> Here, the State of Michigan has not compelled the parties to arbitrate their disputes concerning medical malpractice, but has merely announced the circumstances under which its courts will not interfere with a private agreement to arbitrate medical malpractice disputes. Indeed, the crux of plaintiffs' complaint is not that the state has acted, but that the state has refused to act to prohibit private agreements to arbitrate before a three-person panel, one of whom is a doctor or a hospital administrator.

Id. at 753. However, even if the state had compelled the arbitration, the majority of the Michigan court would have upheld the procedure. The majority stated:

> [I]t has not been demonstrated that the medical members of these panels have a direct pecuniary interest or that their decision may have any substantial effect on the availability of insurance or insurance premiums. We have been shown no grounds sufficient for us to conclude that these decisionmakers will not act with honesty and integrity.

Id. at 740.

3. Concerns About Mandatory Arbitration as a Substitute for Litigation

In *Gilmer v. InterstateJohnson Lane Corp.*, 500 U.S. 20 (1991), defendant, plaintiff's employer, required plaintiff, a financial services representative, to sign an arbitration agreement whereby plaintiff agreed to arbitrate all employment disputes and all termination-of-employment disputes. Defendant terminated plaintiff's employment when plaintiff reached 62 years of age, and plaintiff then filed a suit against defendant under the Age Discrimination in Employment Act of 1967 (ADEA), 29 U.S.C. §621 *et seq.* Defendant moved to compel arbitration. Affirming the Court of Appeals, the U.S. Supreme Court upheld defendant's motion. The Court rejected plaintiff's claim that he could not obtain effective judicial review of an arbitration decision. It also rejected his claim of inequality of bargaining power, saying that such inequality "is not a sufficient reason to hold that arbitration agreements are never enforceable in the employment context." 500 U.S. at 33.

There is growing concern, particularly among members of the plaintiffs' bar, over the widespread, growing use of arbitration agreements to preclude litigation of numerous types of consumer claims. Fraud, interest, and similar concerns form the only bases for judicial review of these arbitration decisions. The Ninth Circuit held in *Circuit City Stores, Inc. v. Adams*, 194 F.3d 1070 (9th Cir. 1999), that an arbitration agreement, signed by an employee at the time of job application, was an "employment contract" and thus the Federal Arbitration Act, 9 U.S.C. §1 *et seq.* did not apply. Therefore, the court said, the plaintiff could bring a lawsuit against his employer under a state fair employment statute. The Supreme Court reversed, 532 U.S. 105 (2001), holding that the employment contract exception applied only to transportation workers. Significantly, on remand, the Ninth Circuit found that the arbitration agreement was unconscionable and thus unenforceable because it was one-sided. *Circuit City Stores, Inc. v. Adams*, 279 F.3d 889 (9th Cir. 2002). *See also Green Tree Financial Corp. v. Randolph*, 531 U.S. 79 (2000) (upholding consumer contract arbitration clause requiring mobile home purchaser to arbitrate her truth-in-lending claim against the defendant which financed her purchase of the home).

4. Mediation

Mediation is the intervention in a dispute by an acceptable third party with no binding decision-making authority who assists the disputants in negotiating a settlement of issues. The mediator facilitates the process by establishing ground rules and guiding the disputants through the resolution process to reach a mutually acceptable solution. In managing the discussion, the mediator may work in the presence of all the parties to the dispute or with each party separately. Like arbitration, mediation has become a well-established, often statutorily recognized alternative to the trial process. Virginia's mediation provision is exemplary.

VIRGINIA MEDIATION ACT
VA. CODE ANN. §§ 8.01-581.21 to 8.01-581.23 (2002)

§ 8.01-581.21. Definitions.

As used in this chapter:

"Mediation" means a process in which a mediator facilitates communication between the parties and, without deciding the issues or imposing a solution on the parties, enables them to understand and to reach a mutually agreeable resolution to their dispute.

"Mediation program" means a program through which mediators or mediation is made available and includes the director, agents and employees of the program.

"Mediator" means an impartial third party selected by agreement of the parties to a controversy to assist them in mediation.

§ 8.01-581.22. Confidentiality; exceptions.

All memoranda, work products and other materials contained in the case files of a mediator or mediation program are confidential. Any communication made in or in connection with the mediation, which relates to the controversy being mediated, including screening, intake, and scheduling a mediation, whether made to the mediator, mediation program staff, to a party, or to any other person, is confidential. However, a written mediated agreement signed by the parties shall not be confidential, unless the parties otherwise agree in writing.

Confidential materials and communications are not subject to disclosure in discovery or in any judicial or administrative proceeding except (i) where all parties to the mediation agree, in writing, to waive the confidentiality, (ii) in a subsequent action between the mediator or mediation program and a party to the mediation for damages arising out of the mediation, (iii) statements, memoranda, materials and other tangible evidence, otherwise subject to discovery, which were not prepared specifically for use in and actually used in the mediation, (iv) where a threat to inflict bodily injury is made, (v) where communications are intentionally used to plan, attempt to commit, or commit a crime or conceal an ongoing crime, (vi) where an ethics complaint is made against the mediator by a party to the mediation to the extent necessary for the complainant to prove misconduct and the mediator to defend against such complaint, (vii) where communications are sought or offered to prove or disprove a claim or complaint of misconduct or malpractice filed against a party's legal representative based on conduct occurring during a mediation, (viii) where communications are sought or offered to prove or disprove any of the grounds listed in § 8.01-581.26 in a proceeding to vacate a mediated agreement, or (ix) as provided by law or rule. The use of attorney work product in a mediation shall not result in a waiver of the attorney work product privilege.

Notwithstanding the provisions of this section, in any case where the dispute involves support of the minor children of the parties, financial information, including information contained in the child support guidelines worksheet, and written reasons for any deviation from the guidelines shall be disclosed to each party and the court for the purpose of computing a basic child support amount pursuant to § 20-108.2.

§ 8.01-581.23. Civil immunity.

When a mediation is provided by a mediator who is certified pursuant to guidelines promulgated by the Judicial Council of Virginia, or who is trained and serves as a mediator through the statewide mediation program established pursuant to § 2.2-1001(2), then that mediator, mediation programs for which that mediator is providing services, and a mediator co-mediating with that mediator shall be immune from civil liability for, or resulting from, any act or omission done or made while engaged in efforts to assist or conduct a mediation, unless the act or omission was made or done in bad faith, with malicious intent or in a manner exhibiting a willful, wanton disregard of the rights, safety or property of another. This language is not intended to abrogate any other immunity that may be applicable to a mediator.

NOTES

1. *Pretrial Arbitration Procedures.* Are pretrial review (or nonbinding arbitration) panels designed to deter frivolous claims or reduce insurer exposure? Do they encourage settlement or merely chill meritorious claims?

2. *Medical Professional Panel Participation.* What arguments would you make to counter the view that in the absence of actual bias, the requirement of medical members on the panel is not troublesome? Is the absence of pecuniary interest or of evidence of bias sufficient protection? Consider your answer from the Perspectives discussed in Chapter 1.

3. *Equal Bargaining Participants.* Arbitration between relatively equal bargainers such as labor unions and employers may be fair. But is it clear that a fair bargaining relationship exists in the context of consumer claims? Where, for example, Title VII civil rights claims are involved, won't such arbitration clauses undermine the civil rights damage provisions (such as pain and suffering, punitive damages) and the right to trial by jury?

4. *Arbitration vs. Mediation.* What distinguishes mediation from mechanisms such as arbitration? What does a mediator seek to achieve? Issue resolution? Issue definition? Dialogue? What kinds of tort disputes is mediation best able to resolve? Are there any kinds of tort disputes that you would rule out for mediation? Do you think it is appropriate to make choices to mediate on the basis of the general kinds of tort dispute at issue, or is an individualized assessment of the claim or set of claims preferable? For a primer on mediation, see Leonard Riskin, *The Special Place of Mediation in Alternative Dispute Resolution,* 37 U. FLA. L. REV. 19 (1985).

5. *The Mediator's Role.* How important is mediation's lack of formality? Should a mediator have a "laid-back" style? Should a mediator move discussion to settlement or merely facilitate party initiatives and discussion? To what extent is a lawyer suited for the role of mediator? *See generally* Jeffrey W. Stempel, *The Need for Institutionalizing a Flexible Concept of the Mediator's Role*, 24 FLA. ST. U. L. REV. 949 (1997); Robert Bush, *Efficiency and Protection, or Empowerment and Recognition?: The Mediator's Role and Ethical Standards in Mediation*, 41 U. FLA. L. REV. 253 (1989); Leonard Riskin, *Toward New Standards for the Neutral Lawyer in Mediation*, 26 ARIZ. L. REV. 329, 359-60 (1984). Does the lawyer-mediator have any special malpractice exposure? *See* VA. CODE ANN. §8.01-581.23, *supra.*

In the now-classic book, GETTING TO YES, the authors state the primary goals of good mediation: (1) do not bargain about positions, but bargain instead about interests; (2) separate the people (the personalities) from the problem; (3) invent options for mutual gain; and (4) insist on objective criteria. ROGER FISHER, WILLIAM URY & BRUCE PATTON, GETTING TO YES (2d ed. 1991). The thrust of their book is that the good mediator should objectify and develop the parties' interests in terms of mutual gain. But suppose the interests at stake are intensely subjective? Suppose what is involved is a personality, or a symbolic disagreement which has much deeper underlying significance?

6. *Mediation as an Alternative to Malpractice?* When, and to what extent, is mediation a suitable mechanism in resolving a physician-patient dispute? *See generally* Jennifer K. Robbennolt, *What We Know and Don't Know About the Role of Apologies in Resolving Health Care Disputes*, 21 GA. ST. U.L. REV. 1009 (2005); Comment, *Healing Angry Wounds: The Roles of Apology and Mediation in Disputes Between Physicians and Patients*, 1987 MO. J. DISP. RES. 111. Would mediation be more suitable to some kinds of physician "wrongdoing" than others? Who decides? Is there any particular public benefit in having complex "business v. business" disputes litigated, or is arbitration or mediation of such disputes preferable? *See generally* Kenneth Ehrman, *Why Business Lawyers Should Use Mediation*, 75 A.B.A. J. 73 (June 1989).

7. *Inequities in ADR?* Much of the focus of the alternative dispute resolution movement has been on the removal of disputes from the traditional public litigation model and "privatizing" either the mechanism (e.g., through mediation and arbitration) or the resolution (e.g., settlement rather than trial) of disputes. Professor Owen Fiss has provided a critique of ADR with this in mind:

> I do not believe that settlement as a generic practice is preferable to judgment or should be institutionalized on a wholesale and indiscriminate basis. It should be treated instead as a highly problematic technique for streamlining dockets. Settlement is for me the civil analogue of plea bargaining: Consent is often coerced; the bargain may be struck by someone without authority; the absence of a trial and judgment renders subsequent judicial involvement troublesome; and although dockets are trimmed, justice may not be done. Like plea bargaining, settlement is a capitulation to the conditions of mass society and should be neither encouraged nor praised.

Owen Fiss, *Against Settlement*, 93 YALE L.J. 1073, 1075 (1984). *See also* the colloquy between Professors Andrew McThenia & Thomas L. Shaffer, *For Reconciliation*, 94 YALE L.J. 1660 (1985). *See also* Owen Fiss, *Out of Eden*, 94 YALE L.J. 1669 (1985). Do you agree with Professor Fiss's assessment?

Professor Fiss also raises the question of the appropriateness of private dispute resolution mechanisms when the parties have disparate litigation resources. Fiss, *Against Settlement, supra,* 93 YALE L.J. at 1076-78; *cf.* Marc Galanter, *Why the "Haves" Come Out Ahead: Speculations on the Limits of Legal Change*, 9 LAW & SOC'Y REV. 95, 97 (1974). Although he is not focusing on ADR, Professor Galanter makes a useful distinction between litigation's "one-shotters" and its "repeat players" in the process. *See also* Joel B. Grossman, Herbert M. Kritzer & Stewart Macaulay, *Do the "Haves" Still Come Out Ahead?*, 33 Law & Soc'y Rev. 803 (1999). A related issue concerns the extent to which nontraditional mechanisms are race and gender neutral. *See, e.g.,* Michael Z. Green, *Tackling Employment Discrimination with ADR: Does Mediation Offer a Shield for the Haves or Real Opportunity for the Have-Nots?*, 26 BERKELE J. EMP. & LAB. L. 321 (2005); Trina Grillo, *The Mediation Alternative: Process Dangers for Women,* 100 YALE L.J. 1545 (1991); Richard Delgado, Chris Dunn, Pamela Brown, Hellena Lee & David Hubert, *Fairness and Formality: Minimizing the Risk of Prejudice in Alternative Dispute Resolution,* 1985 WIS. L. REV. 1359; Janet Rifkin, *Mediation From a Feminist Perspective: Promise and Problems*, 2 LAW & INEQ. J 21 (1984). Couldn't similar questions be raised with respect to judges and juries?

8. *"Gag" Agreements.* One concern is that settlement agreements frequently contain "gag" clauses prohibiting parties from discuss the terms. Should these agreements be prohibited as against public policy? Consider the effect of the following provision: "A settlement agreement involving a claim for medical malpractice shall not prohibit any party to the agreement from discussing with or reporting to the Division of Medical Quality Assurance the events giving rise to the claim." FLA. STAT. ANN. §766.113 (2007).

Former Chief Judge Wachtler of the New York Court of Appeals has observed:

> I think that when you have the courts being used for redressing a wrong, it is the public that is providing and paying for the court procedure and making it available for private litigants. These litigants should not then say to the public, "It's none of your business." . . . [With a sealed record] no one knows whether we can really eat the fish out of the Hudson or buy G.E. toasters.

Elizabeth Kolbert, *Chief Judge of New York Urges Less Secrecy in Civil Settlements*, N. Y. TIMES, Jun. 20, 1990, at A1.

I. ALTERNATIVES TO THE TORT SYSTEM

Even before the torts "crises" of the seventies and eighties, the torts system in this country was the brunt of widespread criticism. Critics have argued that the system is too cumbersome, too expensive, too slow and too unpredictable in outcome. They point out that among those who receive compensation, the relatively smaller claims are overcompensated and the larger ones under compensated. Moreover, commentators contend that the deterrent and compensatory goals of tort law are hopelessly at odds, resulting in the process serving neither satisfactorily.

Some academicians have been vociferous in their criticism. For example, Fleming James is perhaps best known for his persistent indictment of a fault-based torts process in earlier times. *See, e.g.,* Fleming James, *Contribution Among Tortfeasors: A Pragmatic Criticism,* 54 HARV. L. REV, 1156 (1941). Challengers to the system also include Professor John G. Fleming, author of THE AMERICAN TORT PROCESS 18-19 (1988), who made the following observations about the tort system:

> The most negative feature of the tort system is its staggering overhead cost. Compared with other accident compensation systems, even those administered by private insurance like American workers' compensation (30 per cent) and health insurance (15 per cent), let alone with state insurance funds like New Zealand's accident compensation plan (8 per cent), its cost inefficiency is difficult to justify by any competing advantages over its competitors. . . . Studies in the United States raise operating costs to $1.07 for automobile and $1.25 for product liability. In the protracted asbestos litigation it has cost $1.59 in combined litigation expenses to deliver $1 to the average plaintiff. As a result, in combination with the high component of damages for non-pecuniary injury, only about 15 per cent of the cost of the tort system accounts for out-of-pocket losses.

In *Doing Away With Tort Law*, 73 CAL. L. REV. 555, 587 (1985), Professor Sugarman is skeptical whether tort law significantly deters socially undesirable, dangerous conduct. "Self-preservation instincts, market forces, personal morality and governmental regulation" combine to adequately control such conduct independently of tort law. *Id.* at 561. Cataloging all the inefficiencies and unpredictable aspects of the tort system, Professor Sugarman proposes that the system be replaced with a no-fault scheme "as part of the function of our regular social insurance and employee-benefit system." Employers would pay "for short-term benefits using enterprise revenues. An expanded social security system, funded by payroll and income taxes, would provide long-term benefits." Regulatory agencies "bolstered by new citizen participation roles" would provide the primary deterrent force. Tort actions "might remain for cases of intentional wrongdoing, and private injunction remedies would still be available to stop unreasonably dangerous conduct." *Id.* at 664.

Professor Jeffrey O'Connell, one of the foremost proponents of a no-fault scheme as a substitute for tort remedies, conceded that the adoption of a system of national insurance for all accidental injuries is politically infeasible because of the great expense involved and because there are competing demands (such as mass-transit systems, pollution control, law enforcement and education) for limited tax dollar resources that will take precedence over any accident insurance program. JEFFREY O'CONNELL, ENDING INSULT TO INJURY 75 (1975). He proposed instead to permit businesses to elect a no-fault plan covering specified risks and amounts of liability of their choosing. This would be a one-sided voluntary program (i.e., potential victims would not have a choice of whether or not to adopt the plan). *See generally* Jeffrey O'Connell, *A "Neo No-Fault Contract" in Lieu of Tort: Preaccident Guarantees of Postaccident Settlement Offers,* 73 CAL. L. REV. 898 (1985).

The preceding sections of this chapter suggested that one approach to the perceived problem of excessive costs related to recovery under the tort system is to retrench on tort law remedies; another, intended to meet concerns of tort inefficiency as well as cost, is to adopt voluntary, alternative dispute resolution mechanisms such as arbitration and negotiation. An alternative response, often urged by reform-minded academicians, is to abolish part or all of the tort system and to substitute for it an administrative no-fault compensation scheme, financed by some form of taxation. The no-fault compensation scheme for redress of injuries has been accepted in this country through workers' compensation for workplace injury and disease, and less widely, through no-fault automobile insurance. Indeed, there are other public and private health and unemployment insurance schemes (e.g., social security, Medicare, Medicaid) that supplement, but generally do not supplant, the tort system.

NOTES

1. *Does Tort Law Really Deter?* Professor Sugarman contends that no convincing empirical evidence exists to support the conclusion that tort law is an effective deterrent. But does convincing empirical evidence exist to support the conclusion that it is not an effective deterrent? Where should the burden of proof lie?

2. *Regulatory Alternatives?* There is also ongoing debate regarding whether the tort system's deterrent function might be better served by other means, such as governmental safety regulation. Are agency regulators better equipped than courts to set standards of safety? Although some administrative agencies have been successful in regulating safety, in the products liability area administrative agencies, such as the Consumer Product Safety Commission, have promulgated few effective design safety standards. For example, the Food and Drug Administration has come under attack in the wake of charges that drug manufacturers have compromised (knowingly and unknowingly) the reporting process for alerting doctors to dangerous side effects of drugs. For a thorough discussion of the issues related to deferring to the FDA for safety, see Allison M. Zieve & Brian Wolfman, *The FDA's Argument for Eradicating State Law: Why It Is Wrong and Warrants No Deference,* 34 PROD. SAFETY & LIAB. REPTR (BNA 2006) No. 12, at 308-316. Should society devote more resources to accident prevention through product or drug safety regulations or are there other barriers to regulation that cannot be addressed merely by deploying resources?

3. *Is Tort Law a Failed System?* In PATRICK ATIYAH, WRONGS AND REMEDIES IN THE TWENTY-FIRST CENTURY (Peter Birks ed., Oxford U. Press 1996), the author criticizes personal injury tort law as a failed system, observing that the guilty party "hardly ever pays a single penny," but rather it is the guilty party's insurer or employer who pays; recovery is unpredictable, depending on a "forensic lottery;" and deterrence arguments are weakened or demolished by the widespread availability of liability insurance. How do you think a proponent of law and economics, corrective justice, or social justice would respond to this argument?

4. *Compensation of Victims.* Notwithstanding "reformists'" efforts to limit recovery, compensation remains a principal goal of tort law. Professor Mark Rahdert has observed:

> [I]t seems unrealistic to cast aside the goal of compensation through cost spreading, as an important element in the mix of values that support imposing liability. Compensating victims of one kind or another is one of the major undertakings of government in our society. We devote considerable energy to that undertaking. We spend a great deal of money for it. We pay taxes to support it. And in so doing so we either wittingly or unwittingly embrace the validity of cost spreading as a mechanism for combatting the undesirable effects of personal loss or disadvantage. It would seem strange for a society that finds the value of compensation through cost spreading so appealing in other domains to deny its significance in a legal system that deals explicitly and almost exclusively with injury. If the victims of tortious injury were grouped together as victims of some single disaster, we should surely recognize the legitimacy of their claims for compensation. . . . That the victims in the tort system usually suffer their injuries in small groups or alone, or that their injury comes from an act of enterprise rather than an act of God, should not materially alter our collective judgment concerning the social value of compensating loss.

MARK C. RAHDERT, COVERING ACCIDENT COSTS: INSURANCE, LIABILITY, AND TORT REFORM 180 (1995). Do you agree with Professor Rahdert's reasoning? Has the tort system been successful in providing compensation for loss? Does it continue to be? And what about justice? In what ways does the compensation goal respond to notions of social justice?

PROBLEMS

16.1

Samuel Son was an economics major at Lowgrade College of Business and Administration in Anystate. Samuel spent his days watching "soaps" on television and his evenings listening to "classic rock" radio stations. At the end of his junior year the economics department finally gave up any hope that Samuel would achieve a graduating GPA and dismissed him for academic reasons. Samuel filed suit against Lowgrade, his professors, and all the students in the top ten percent of his matriculation class, alleging intentional infliction of emotional harm, civil RICO, and educational malpractice. Following a dramatic, albeit temporary, increase in medical malpractice insurance rates, Anystate recently had added the following provision to its civil procedure code:

(a) In any action for damages due to personal injury, property damage or death based upon the provision of professional services, the court shall appoint a three-person expert review panel within 40 days after filing of an answer to a summons and complaint.

(b) The review panel shall examine any evidence it thinks fit and, not more than 120 days after selection of the panel, it shall make a written report to the parties and to the court.

(c) The report of the review panel is admissible in evidence at a subsequent trial de novo. Any finding by the panel as to the compliance or noncompliance of the defendant with any professional standard of care shall create a rebuttable presumption as to said compliance or noncompliance in subsequent proceedings.

Samuel Son files a motion for a protective order, seeking to avoid presentation of his case to a review panel, on the basis that Anystate's review panel procedure is constitutionally defective.

As Son's attorney, what arguments will you make? Is it likely your arguments will prevail?

16.2

Dr. Onco successfully removed a cyst from Patrick Patient. At that time Patrick signed an agreement to arbitrate any medical malpractice claims. Two years later, Dr. Cology, Dr. Onco's partner, treated Patrick by removing a facial mole. Dr. Cology removed the mole, but according to Patrick's complaint, Dr. Cology negligently caused severe facial discoloration around the site of the mole. Dr. Cology's insurer settled Patrick's medical malpractice claim.

Anne, Patrick's wife, now files suit against Dr. Cology for loss of consortium and negligent infliction of emotional harm. The emotional harm claim was premised on Anne's allegation that Dr. Cology knew that she was waiting for Patrick in the medical suite following the operation, and that Dr. Cology had failed to tell her how Patrick would appear following the surgery.

Can Dr. Cology compel Anne to arbitrate her claims?

Suppose that two years before Patrick's first visit, the same partnership treated Anne Patient for a mild skin cancer and had her sign an identical arbitration agreement as the one currently in question. Would she be bound to arbitrate her claims?

16.3

Bill and Ruth Major and their 14-year-old daughter, Natalie, live in West Anytown in a quiet subdivision with stagnant property values. Natalie is something of a "problem" child. However, she is at her best when in the company of Colin, the 15-year-old son of Jane and Clarence Harris, the Majors' neighbors. Recently, the Majors granted Natalie her birthday wish and gave her a B-B gun — one exactly like the gun that Colin Harris received from Jane and Clarence for his birthday. During the two-week period which followed her birthday, Natalie terrified the occupants of the subdivision by taking random shots at passing automobiles, pedestrians, and pets. She was unsuccessful in her marksmanship until she turned her B-B gun on the Harris' greenhouse. Several shots later Natalie had severely damaged the greenhouse, and Mrs. Harris' prize-winning giant squash was fatally exposed to adverse weather conditions. Mr. and Mrs. Harris are understandably upset by this turn of events.

In part because they were distressed that Natalie might represent a considerable negative influence upon Colin, Mr. and Mrs. Harris filed suit against Natalie for trespass to their greenhouse, and against the Majors for negligent entrustment and negligent supervision, claiming $5,000 in compensatory damages and $50,000 in punitive damages. They also informed their property insurer, First Indemnity (FI), of their loss. Bill, Ruth, and Natalie Major have notified Unexpected Loss Mutual (ULM), their homeowner liability carrier, of the suits and requested defense and indemnification. Their insurer has undertaken the defense under a "reservation of rights."

The property insurer for Mr. and Mrs. Harris wishes to bring this matter to a speedy conclusion so as to release some of its adjusters for work on some earthquake claims on the West Coast. Both FI and ULM have been experimenting with mediation with regard to claims valued at below $5,000. Jointly, they approach you and ask you to mediate the claims detailed above.

Do you consider this to be an appropriate case for mediation? Are any other alternative mechanisms suitable for resolution of this dispute? In this case, what might you as a mediator be able to do which a trial judge could not or would not do? How do you think this case should be resolved? If you were mediating this dispute, would you tell the parties what you thought were the correct legal solutions to the issues presented?

16.4

How would you devise a suitable legislative rule to guide courts in assessing punitive damages?

16.5

Granny Hall, eighty-eight, died at the Over the Hill Nursing Home of sepsis, which is an overwhelming bacterial infection that poisons the blood, often found in nursing home patients experiencing neglect. A doctor who specializes in geriatric medicine evaluated Granny Hall's medical records and concluded that her death was caused or exacerbated by malnutrition and multiple decubitus ulcers that created infection in her bones. In fact Granny Hall's malnutrition and infection were so severe that her weight dropped from one hundred forty to seventy-five pounds in the five weeks before her death. Granny Hall's daughter, Annie, consults you about taking her case. The applicable jurisdiction has enacted a cap on noneconomic damages of $250,000. How will the cap impact your decision to take Granny Hall's case?

16.6

Assume that same facts as in 16.5. You have made the decision to take Granny's case but learn that her daughter agreed to mandatory arbitration as a precondition to her admission to Over the Hill. What are the advantages and disadvantages of mandatory arbitration versus litigation in this case? What arguments would you use to challenge the enforceability of the mandatory arbitration agreement?   '

INDEX

[References are to pages.]

[References are to pages.]

[References are to pages.]

[References are to pages.]

[References are to pages.]

[References are to pages.]